GCSE Mathematics

Foundation Level

Q: What's the best way to get through GCSE Maths?
A: By taking the square route.

That was a joke, obviously. The real answer is: by using this CGP book. It's packed with study notes, examples and indispensable tips for every topic, plus enough practice questions to keep you happy throughout the course.

It even includes a free Online Edition to read on your PC, Mac or tablet!

How to get your free Online Edition

Go to **cgpbooks.co.uk/extras** and enter this code...

3529 3651 5145 9160

This code will only work once. If someone has used this book before you, they may have already claimed the Online Edition.

Published by CGP

Editors:
Adam Bartlett, Michael Bushell, Sarah George, Tom Miles, Ali Palin, Rosa Roberts, David Ryan, Caley Simpson, Michael Weynberg, Ruth Wilbourne.

Contributors:
Katharine Brown, Pamela Chatley, Eva Cowlishaw, Alastair Duncombe, Paul Garrett, Geoff Gibb, Stephen Green, Philip Hale, Phil Harvey, Judy Hornigold, Claire Jackson, Mark Moody, Charlotte O'Brien, Philip Potten, Rosemary Rogers, Manpreet Sambi, Neil Saunders, Jan Walker, Kieran Wardell, Jeanette Whiteman.

With thanks to Liam Dyer, Helen Kennedy, Sam Mann, Lauren McNaughten, Deanne Morris, Glenn Rogers and Emma Stubbs for the proofreading.

With thanks to Ana Pungartnik for the copyright research.

Cover design concept by emc design ltd.

Clipart from Corel®
Printed by Elanders Ltd, Newcastle upon Tyne.

Contents

Section 19 — Pythagoras and Trigonometry

Section 20 — Vectors

Section 21 — Constructions

Section 22 — Area and Perimeter

Section 23 — 3D Shapes

Section 24 — Transformations

Section 25 — Collecting Data

Section 26 — Analysing Data

Section 27 — Probability

About this Book

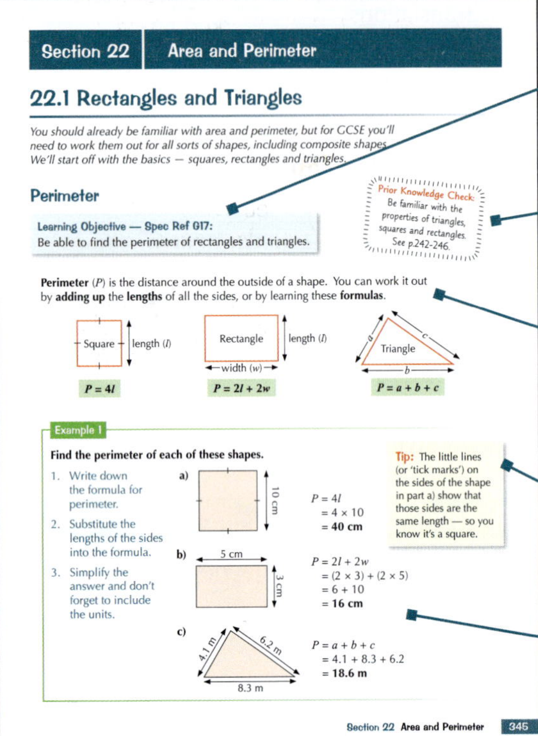

Section 22 Area and Perimeter

22.1 Rectangles and Triangles

You should already be familiar with area and perimeter, but for GCSE you'll need to work them out for all sorts of shapes, including composite shapes. We'll start off with the basics — squares, rectangles and triangles.

Perimeter

Learning Objective — Spec Ref G17:
Be able to find the perimeter of rectangles and triangles.

Prior Knowledge Check: Be familiar with the properties of triangles, squares and rectangles. See p.242-246.

Perimeter (P) is the distance around the outside of a shape. You can work it out by **adding up** the **lengths** of all the sides, or by learning these **formulas**.

$P = 4l$ $P = 2l + 2w$ $P = a + b + c$

Example 1

Find the perimeter of each of these shapes.

1. Write down the formula for perimeter.
2. Substitute the lengths of the sides into the formula.
3. Simplify the answer and don't forget to include the units.

a) $P = 4l$
$= 4 \times 10$
$= \mathbf{40\ cm}$

b) $P = 2l + 2w$
$= (2 \times 3) + (2 \times 5)$
$= 6 + 10$
$= \mathbf{16\ cm}$

c) $P = a + b + c$
$= 4.1 + 8.3 + 6.2$
$= \mathbf{18.6\ m}$

Tip: The little lines (or 'tick marks') on the sides of the shape in part a) show that those sides are the same length — so you know it's a square.

Section 22 Area and Perimeter 345

Learning Objectives

Showing which bits of the specification are covered in each section.

Prior Knowledge Checks

Pointing you to the parts of the book that you should be familiar with before moving on to this topic.

Explanations

Clear explanations of every topic.

Tips

Lots of useful tips to help you get your head around the tricky bits.

Examples

Plenty of step-by-step worked examples.

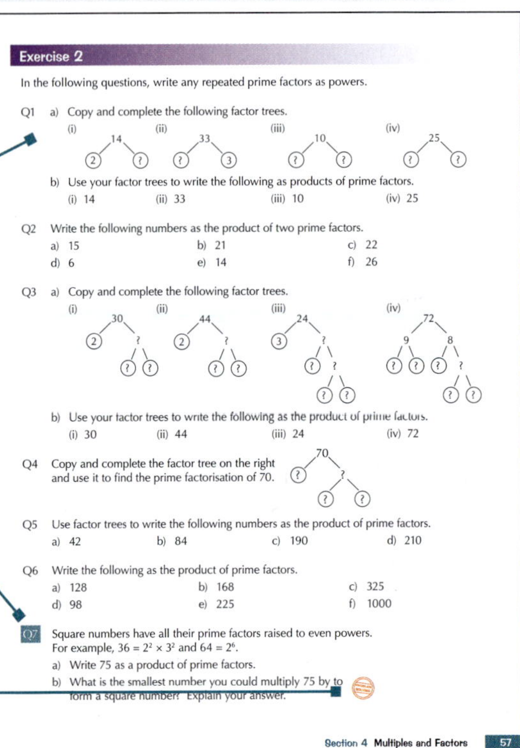

Exercise 2

In the following questions, write any repeated prime factors as powers.

Q1 a) Copy and complete the following factor trees.
(i) 14 (ii) 33 (iii) 10 (iv) 25

b) Use your factor trees to write the following as products of prime factors.
(i) 14 (ii) 33 (iii) 10 (iv) 25

Q2 Write the following numbers as the product of two prime factors.
a) 15 b) 21 c) 22
d) 6 e) 14 f) 26

Q3 a) Copy and complete the following factor trees.
(i) 30 (ii) 44 (iii) 24 (iv) 72

b) Use your factor trees to write the following as the product of prime factors.
(i) 30 (ii) 44 (iii) 24 (iv) 72

Q4 Copy and complete the factor tree on the right and use it to find the prime factorisation of 70.

Q5 Use factor trees to write the following numbers as the product of prime factors.
a) 42 b) 84 c) 190 d) 210

Q6 Write the following as the product of prime factors.
a) 128 b) 168 c) 325
d) 98 e) 225 f) 1000

Q7 Square numbers have all their prime factors raised to even powers.
For example, $36 = 2^2 \times 3^2$ and $64 = 2^6$.
a) Write 75 as a product of prime factors.
b) What is the smallest number you could multiply 75 by to form a square number? Explain your answer.

Section 4 Multiples and Factors 57

Exercises (with worked answers)

- Lots of practice for every topic, with fully worked answers at the back of the book.
- The more challenging questions are marked like this: Q1

Problem Solving

Problem solving questions involve skills such as combining different areas of maths or interpreting given information to identify what's being asked for. Questions that involve problem solving are marked with stamps.

PROBLEM SOLVING

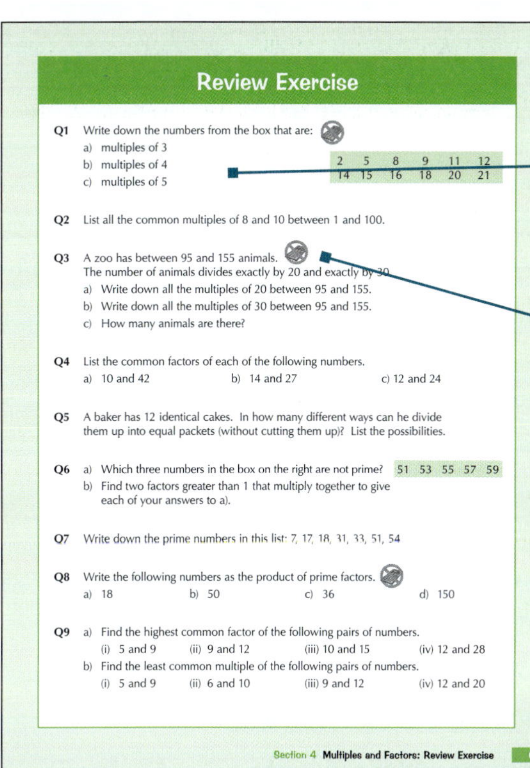

Review Exercise
Q1 Write down the numbers from the box that are:
a) multiples of 3
b) multiples of 4
c) multiples of 5
2 5 8 9 11 12
14 15 16 18 20 21
Q2 List all the common multiples of 8 and 10 between 1 and 100.
Q3 A zoo has between 95 and 155 animals.
The number of animals divides exactly by 20 and exactly by 30.
a) Write down all the multiples of 20 between 95 and 155.
b) Write down all the multiples of 30 between 95 and 155.
c) How many animals are there?
Q4 List the common factors of each of the following numbers.
a) 10 and 42 b) 14 and 27 c) 12 and 24
Q5 A baker has 12 identical cakes. In how many different ways can he divide them up into equal packets (without cutting them up)? List the possibilities.
Q6 a) Which three numbers in the box on the right are not prime? 51 53 55 57 59
b) Find two factors greater than 1 that multiply together to give each of your answers to a).
Q7 Write down the prime numbers in this list: 7, 17, 18, 31, 33, 51, 54
Q8 Write the following numbers as the product of prime factors.
a) 18 b) 50 c) 36 d) 150
Q9 a) Find the highest common factor of the following pairs of numbers.
(i) 5 and 9 (ii) 9 and 12 (iii) 10 and 15 (iv) 12 and 28
b) Find the least common multiple of the following pairs of numbers.
(i) 5 and 9 (ii) 6 and 10 (iii) 9 and 12 (iv) 12 and 20
Section 4 Multiples and Factors: Review Exercise 61

Review Exercises

Mixed questions covering the whole section, with fully worked answers.

Non-Calculator Questions

There are some methods you'll have to be able to do without a calculator. Stamps on certain questions let you know that you can't use a calculator for them.

Exam-Style Questions

Questions in the same style as the ones you'll get in the exam, with worked solutions and mark schemes.

Mixed Exam-Style Questions

At the end of the book is a set of exam questions covering a mixture of different topics from across the GCSE 9-1 course.

Glossary

All the definitions you need to know for the exam, plus other useful words.

Formula Page

Contains all the formulas that you need to know for your GCSE exams. You'll find it inside the back cover.

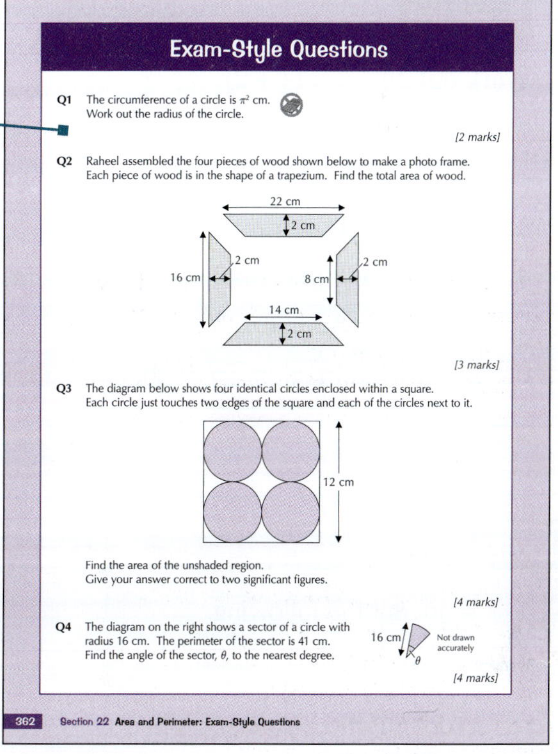

Exam-Style Questions
Q1 The circumference of a circle is π² cm.
Work out the radius of the circle.
[2 marks]
Q2 Raheel assembled the four pieces of wood shown below to make a photo frame.
Each piece of wood is in the shape of a trapezium. Find the total area of wood.
22 cm
2 cm
16 cm
8 cm
14 cm
[3 marks]
Q3 The diagram below shows four identical circles enclosed within a square.
Each circle just touches two edges of the square and each of the circles next to it.
12 cm
Find the area of the unshaded region.
Give your answer correct to two significant figures.
[4 marks]
Q4 The diagram on the right shows a sector of a circle with radius 16 cm. The perimeter of the sector is 41 cm.
Find the angle of the sector, θ, to the nearest degree.
Not drawn accurately
[4 marks]
362 Section 22 Area and Perimeter: Exam-Style Questions

1.1 Orders of Operations

What a nice, fun start to the book — no calculators allowed. It's all about adding, subtracting, multiplying and dividing, but the trick is knowing how to do it all in the right order.

Learning Objective — Spec Ref N3:
Know the correct order in which to apply operations, including dealing with brackets.

Operations in mathematics are things like addition, subtraction, multiplication and division. The **order** in which each of these is carried out within a calculation is **very important**.

BODMAS tells you the correct order to carry out these operations.

Tip: The 'Other' operations are things like powers or roots — see Section 3.

Brackets, **O**ther, **D**ivision, **M**ultiplication, **A**ddition, **S**ubtraction

If there are two or more **consecutive** divisions and/or multiplications (e.g. $3 \times 6 \div 9 \times 5$), they should be done in order, **from left to right**. The same goes for **addition and subtraction**.

Example 1

Work out 20 – 3 × (4 + 2).

1. There are **B**rackets, so do that operation first. ⟶ $20 - 3 \times (4 + 2) = 20 - 3 \times 6$
2. There are no '**O**ther' operations.
3. There is no **D**ivision.
4. There is **M**ultiplication, so do that operation next. ⟶ $20 - 3 \times 6 = 20 - 18$
5. There is no **A**ddition.
6. There is **S**ubtraction, so do that operation next. ⟶ $20 - 18 = \mathbf{2}$

Exercise 1

Q1 Work out the following.

a) $5 + 1 \times 3$ b) $11 - 2 \times 5$ c) $24 \div 4 + 2$ d) $18 - 10 \div 5$

Q2 Work out the following.

a) $6 \times (4 + 3)$ b) $11 - (2 + 3)$ c) $(8 - 7) \times (6 + 5)$ d) $56 \div (2 \times 4)$

Q3 Work out the following.

a) $2 \times (8 + 4) - 7$ b) $18 \div (9 - 12 \div 4)$ c) $100 \div (8 + 3 \times 4)$

d) $20 - (5 \times 3 + 2)$ e) $48 \div 3 - 7 \times 2$ f) $36 - (7 + 4 \times 4)$

Q4 Copy each of the following and insert brackets to make the calculation correct.

a) $9 \times 7 - 5 = 18$ b) $18 - 6 \div 3 = 4$ c) $5 + 2 \times 6 - 2 = 28$

d) $21 \div 4 + 3 = 3$ e) $13 - 5 \times 13 - 1 = 96$ f) $6 + 8 - 7 \times 5 = 35$

Q5 Copy each of the following and: (i) fill in the blanks with either +, –, × or ÷ ,
(ii) add any brackets needed to complete the calculation.

a) 16 □ 6 ÷ 3 = 14 b) 11 □ 3 + 5 = 38 c) 3 □ 6 □ 9 = 9

d) 8 □ 2 □ 6 = 10 e) 3 □ 7 □ 4 = 40 f) 14 □ 6 □ 8 = 1

Example 2

Work out $\frac{2 \times 4 + 12}{9 - 5}$.

1. You need to divide the top line by the bottom line.
2. Work out what's on the top and the bottom separately.

Top line: $2 \times 4 + 12$

1. No **B**rackets, '**O**ther' operations or **D**ivision
2. There is **M**ultiplication, so do that operation first. ⟶ $2 \times 4 = 8$
3. Then do the **A**ddition. ⟶ $8 + 12 = \mathbf{20}$

Bottom line: $9 - 5$

There is only **S**ubtraction here. ⟶ $9 - 5 = \mathbf{4}$

3. After putting the values for the top and bottom line back into the fraction, you get this expression. ⟶ $\frac{20}{4}$
4. It only has **D**ivision. ⟶ $20 \div 4 = \mathbf{5}$

Exercise 2

Q1 Work out the following.

a) $\frac{4 - 1 + 5}{2 \times 2}$ b) $\frac{6 + (11 - 8)}{7 - 5}$ c) $\frac{16}{4 \times (5 - 3)}$ d) $\frac{4 \times (7 + 5)}{6 + 3 \times 2}$

e) $\frac{12 \div (9 - 5)}{25 \div 5}$ f) $\frac{8 \times 2 \div 4}{5 - 6 + 7}$ g) $\frac{3 \times 3}{21 \div (12 - 5)}$ h) $\frac{36 \div (11 - 2)}{8 - 8 \div 2}$

1.2 Negative Numbers

You can add, subtract, multiply and divide with negative numbers too, but there are few things that might catch you out if you're not careful. Be sure to keep track of all those minus signs...

Adding and Subtracting Negative Numbers

Learning Objective — Spec Ref N2:
Add and subtract negative numbers.

Negative numbers are numbers which are **less than zero**.

You can count places on a **number line** to help with calculations involving negative numbers.

Example 1

Work out: a) –1 + 4 b) –2 – 3 + 1

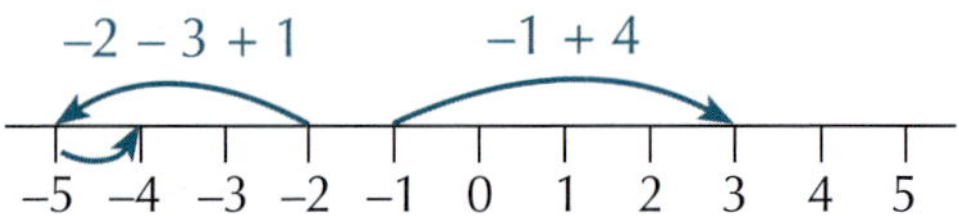

Tip: If you find it useful, draw your own number line when answering negative number questions.

a) Start at –1 and count 4 places to the right. ⟶ –1 + 4 = **3**

b) Start at –2, count 3 places to the left, and then 1 place to the right. ⟶ –2 – 3 + 1 = **–4**

Exercise 1

Q1 Work out the following.

a) –4 + 3 b) –1 + 5 c) –2 + 1
d) 6 – 17 e) –13 + 18 f) 11 – 19

Q2 Work out the following.

a) –3 + 2 – 1 b) –2 + 8 – 5 c) 8 – 5 – 3
d) –1 – 7 – 4 e) –9 + 13 + 11 f) 7 – 18 + 11

Q3 Copy the following calculations and fill in the blanks to make the equations correct.

a) –3 + □ = –1 b) 5 – □ = –10 c) □ + 7 = 4 d) □ – 2 = –6

The thermometer on the right shows temperature. Use it to answer **Questions 4-7**.

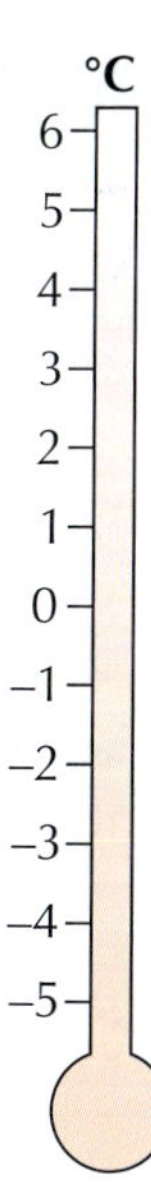

Q4 a) Find the temperature that is 3 °C lower than –1 °C.
b) Find the temperature that is 8 °C higher than –5 °C.

Q5 Find the difference between the following temperatures.
a) –4 °C and 3 °C
b) –2 °C and –5 °C

Q6 At midday the temperature was 6 °C. By midnight, the temperature had decreased by 7 °C. What was the temperature at midnight?

Q7 At 5 am, the temperature was –5 °C. At 11 pm, the temperature was –1 °C. What was the difference in temperature between these two times?

Rules for Adding and Subtracting Negative Numbers

When adding and subtracting negative numbers, there are two rules you need to know:

1. Adding a negative number is the same as subtracting a positive number. → **'+' next to '–' means subtract**
2. Subtracting a negative number is the same as adding a positive number. → **'–' next to '–' means add**

Example 2

Work out:

a) 1 – (–4) '–' next to '–' means add. 1 – (–4) = 1 + 4 = **5**

b) –5 + (–2) '+' next to '–' means subtract. –5 + (–2) = –5 – 2 = **–7**

Exercise 2

Q1 Work out the following.

a) 4 – (–2) b) –3 – (–5) c) –7 + (–2) d) –5 + (–5)
e) 9 + (– 2) f) –13 – (–3) g) –6 + (–3) h) 1 – (–12)

Q2 Work out the following.

a) –1 + (–4) – 1 b) 6 – (–2) + (–3) c) 7 + (–6) – (–8)
d) –8 + (–8) – (–12) e) 9 – (–13) + (–2) f) –3 + (–11) + (–6)

Q3 Find the difference between the following numbers by subtracting one from the other.

a) 6 and –5 b) –10 and –6 c) –8 and 4 d) –5 and –12

Multiplying and Dividing Negative Numbers

Learning Objective — Spec Ref N2:
Multiply and divide negative numbers.

When you multiply or divide two numbers which have the **same** sign, the answer is **positive** — e.g. (–6) × (–7) = 42 and (–40) ÷ (–10) = 4.

When you multiply or divide two numbers with **opposite** signs, the answer is **negative** — e.g. (–4) × 6 = –24 and 35 ÷ (–7) = –5.

Tip: You can think of two minus signs cancelling each other out. If there's only one minus, it stays.

Example 3

Work out:

a) 24 ÷ (–6)

The signs are opposite (one positive, one negative), so the answer is negative. ⟶ 24 ÷ –6 = **–4**

b) –5 × (–8)

The signs are the same (both negative), so the answer is positive. ⟶ –5 × –8 = **40**

c) –3 × 7

The signs are different (one negative, one positive), so the answer is negative. ⟶ –3 × 7 = **–21**

Exercise 3

Q1 Work out the following.

a) 3 × (–4) b) 2 × (–8) c) (–9) × 6
d) (–15) ÷ 3 e) (–15) ÷ (–3) f) 12 ÷ (–4)

Q2 Copy the following calculations and fill in the blanks.

a) –3 × □ = –6 b) –14 ÷ □ = –2 c) □ × 4 = –16 d) □ ÷ (–2) = –5
e) –8 × □ = –24 f) –18 ÷ □ = 3 g) □ × (–3) = 36 h) □ ÷ 11 = –7

Q3 Work out the following.

a) 2 × 4 ÷ (–2) b) (–5) × (–6) ÷ 3 c) (–3) × (–5) × (–6)
d) (–63) × (–2) ÷ (–9) e) [55 ÷ (–11)] × (–9) f) [(–24) ÷ 8)] ÷ 3

1.3 Whole Number Arithmetic

There's no getting around it — you need to be able to handle big numbers without a calculator.

Addition and Subtraction

Learning Objective — Spec Ref N2:
Add and subtract large numbers without using a calculator.

When adding or subtracting **large numbers**, write one number **above the other**, then add or subtract **one column at a time**.

It's important to make sure that the digits are lined up correctly, or you'll get the wrong answer.

Tip: The units in each number should be lined up, as should the tens, and the hundreds, etc.

Example 1

Work out 145 + 28.

1. Write one number above the other and make sure each column lines up, from right to left.
2. Add together the digits in each column, starting with the furthest right.
3. If the digits in a column add up to 10 or more, you'll need to 'carry' a 1. In the first column here 5 + 8 = 13, so you write 3 in the column you're working with, and carry 1 to the next — add that on when you add the next column (4 + 2 + 1 here).

```
  1 4 5      1 4 5      1 4 5
+   2 8    +   2 8    +   2 8
  -----      -----      -----
      3        7 3      1 7 3
    1          1          1
```

Example 2

Work out 364 – 128.

1. Write the bigger number above the smaller one.
2. Subtract the digits in each column, starting with the furthest right.
3. If the top digit is smaller than the bottom digit, borrow 10 from the next column. To do this, subtract 1 from the top digit in that column, and write 1 in front of the digit in your current column. Doing this to the 1st column here gives 14 – 8 = 6.
4. Don't forget you've borrowed when you subtract the next column. In the 2nd column here, you get 5 – 2 = 3.

```
  3 ⁵6̸ ¹4     3 ⁵6̸ ¹4     3 ⁵6̸ ¹4
– 1  2  8   – 1  2  8   – 1  2  8
  -------     -------     -------
        6        3  6     2  3  6
```

Example 3

Tasmin has £305 in her bank account. She uses £146 to buy a television. How much money is left in her account?

1. You need to subtract 146 from 305, so set out the subtraction as usual.
2. In the column furthest to the right, 5 is less than 6 so you need to borrow from the middle column. But there's a 0 there, so you have to borrow from the column furthest to the left first.

$$\begin{array}{r} 3\,0\,5 \\ -\ 1\,4\,6 \\ \hline \end{array} \longrightarrow \begin{array}{r} {}^{2}\not{3}\,{}^{1}0\,5 \\ -\ 1\,4\,6 \\ \hline \end{array} \longrightarrow \begin{array}{r} {}^{2}\not{3}\,\overset{9}{\not{1}\!\!\not{0}}\,{}^{1}5 \\ -\ 1\,4\,6 \\ \hline \end{array}$$

3. Once the borrowing is sorted, subtract each column as usual.

$$\begin{array}{r} {}^{2}\not{3}\,\overset{9}{\not{1}\!\!\not{0}}\,{}^{1}5 \\ -\ 1\,4\,6 \\ \hline 9 \end{array} \longrightarrow \begin{array}{r} {}^{2}\not{3}\,\overset{9}{\not{1}\!\!\not{0}}\,{}^{1}5 \\ -\ 1\,4\,6 \\ \hline 5\,9 \end{array} \longrightarrow \begin{array}{r} {}^{2}\not{3}\,\overset{9}{\not{1}\!\!\not{0}}\,{}^{1}5 \\ -\ 1\,4\,6 \\ \hline 1\,5\,9 \end{array}$$

So she has **£159** left.

Exercise 1

Q1 Copy and work out the following.

a) $\begin{array}{r} 2\,3 \\ +\ 5\,6 \\ \hline \end{array}$ b) $\begin{array}{r} 1\,2\,2 \\ +\ 9\,7 \\ \hline \end{array}$ c) $\begin{array}{r} 2\,4\,3 \\ +\ 1\,7\,8 \\ \hline \end{array}$

d) $\begin{array}{r} 7\,3 \\ -\ 2\,7 \\ \hline \end{array}$ e) $\begin{array}{r} 1\,8\,1 \\ -\ 3\,5 \\ \hline \end{array}$ f) $\begin{array}{r} 2\,3\,3 \\ -\ 1\,8\,7 \\ \hline \end{array}$

Q2 Work out the following.

a) 342 + 679 b) 604 + 288 c) 506 – 278
d) 2513 + 241 e) 2942 – 324 f) 4003 – 1235

Q3 Work out the following.

a) 41 + 112 + 213 b) 764 + 138 – 345 c) 123 + 478 + 215
d) 221 + 126 – 98 e) (498 – 137) + 556 f) (987 – 451) + 221

Q4 Lisa has 38 marbles, John has 52 marbles and Bina has 65 marbles. How many marbles do they have altogether?

Q5 An art club has £2146 in the bank. It spends £224 on art supplies. How much money does it have left?

Q6 The village of Great Missingham has a population of 1845. The neighbouring village of Fentley has a population of 1257. How many more people live in Great Missingham than Fentley?

Multiplication

Learning Objective — Spec Ref N2:
Multiply large numbers without using a calculator.

There are two methods for multiplying large numbers. Example 4 uses **long multiplication**, while Example 5 uses a **grid method.**

For both methods it's **very important** that the digits are **lined up** properly, starting on the right hand side.

Tip: If you're multiplying in an exam, just pick your favourite method.

Example 4

Work out 254 × 26.

1. Write one number above the other, making sure the columns line up.
2. Multiply each digit of 254 by 6, working from right to left. If the answer is 10 or more, carry the ten's digit. This is 254 × 6.
3. Now put a 0 in the right-hand column and multiply each digit of 254 by 2, carrying digits where necessary. This is 254 × 20.
4. Add the two rows together to find the final answer.

$$\begin{array}{r} 2\,5\,4 \\ \times\;\;2\,6 \\ \hline {}_{2}4 \end{array} \qquad \begin{array}{r} 2\,5\,4 \\ \times\;\;2\,6 \\ \hline {}_{3}2{}_{2}4 \end{array} \qquad \begin{array}{r} 2\,5\,4 \\ \times\;\;2\,6 \\ \hline 1\,5{}_{3}2{}_{2}4 \end{array}$$

$$\begin{array}{r} 2\,5\,4 \\ \times\;\;2\,6 \\ \hline 1\,5{}_{3}2{}_{2}4 \\ 0 \end{array} \qquad \begin{array}{r} 2\,5\,4 \\ \times\;\;2\,6 \\ \hline 1\,5{}_{3}2{}_{2}4 \\ 8\,0 \end{array} \qquad \begin{array}{r} 2\,5\,4 \\ \times\;\;2\,6 \\ \hline 1\,5{}_{3}2{}_{2}4 \\ {}_{1}0\,8\,0 \end{array} \qquad \begin{array}{r} 2\,5\,4 \\ \times\;\;2\,6 \\ \hline 1\,5{}_{3}2{}_{2}4 \\ 5{}_{1}0\,8\,0 \end{array}$$

$$\begin{array}{r} 1\,5\,4 \\ \times\;\;2\,6 \\ \hline 1\,5{}_{3}2{}_{2}4 \\ 5{}_{1}0\,8\,0 \\ \hline 6\,6{}_{1}0\,4 \end{array}$$

So 254 × 26 = **6604**

Exercise 2

Use **long multiplication** to answer these questions.

Q1 Work out:

a) 66 × 72 b) 79 × 86 c) 83 × 81

d) 100 × 26 e) 114 × 30 f) 216 × 54

Q2 Jilly tells her friend that there are 46 days until Christmas. How many hours is this?

Q3 Dom's monthly electricity bill is £33. How much does he spend on electricity each year?

Q4 Work out the following.

a) 1347 × 20 b) 3669 × 21 c) 2623 × 42 d) 2578 × 36

Example 5

Work out 254 × 26.

1. Split each number up into units, tens, hundreds etc.
2. Put these around the outside of a grid.
3. Multiply the numbers at the edge of each box. To multiply by 200, multiply by 2, then by 100. To multiply by 50, multiply by 5, then by 10.
4. Add the numbers from the boxes to find the final answer.

	200	50	4
20	20 × 200 = 4000	20 × 50 = 1000	20 × 4 = 80
6	6 × 200 = 1200	6 × 50 = 300	6 × 4 = 24

```
  4000
  1000
    80
  1200
   300
+   24
------
  6604
   1
```

Tip: When adding, line up all the numbers on top of each other, from right to left.

So 254 × 26 = **6604**

Exercise 3

Q1 Work out the following using the grid method.

a) 13 × 12 b) 11 × 17 c) 52 × 10 d) 16 × 24

e) 367 × 62 f) 498 × 69 g) 511 × 55 h) 568 × 74

Q2 Sheila earns £243 per week. How much does she earn in 52 weeks?

Q3 The weight of a storage container is 14 tonnes. A cargo ship can carry 230 of these containers. How many tonnes can the cargo ship carry?

Q4 A box of matches contains 85 matches. There are 160 boxes in a carton. How many matches are there in a carton?

Q5 Hamza is making biscuits. Each biscuit uses 22 g of flour. Can he make 27 biscuits from a 500 g bag of flour?

Q6 Work out the following.

a) 2271 × 25 b) 5624 × 42 c) 1211 × 34 d) 4526 × 19

Division

Learning Objective — Spec Ref N2:
Divide numbers without using a calculator.

There are different ways to divide numbers without using a calculator. Example 6 shows '**short division**' and Example 7 shows '**long division**'.

Example 6

Work out 6148 ÷ 4.

Write the division with the number you want to divide inside and the number you're dividing by to the left.

1. Look at the first digit, 6. 4 goes into 6 once with 2 left over, so write 1 above 6, keeping the columns in line. Then carry the remainder, 2, over to the next column.

$$\begin{array}{r} 1 \\ 4\overline{)6\,^{2}1\,4\,8} \end{array}$$

2. Move to the next column — 2 was carried over, so find the number of times 4 goes into 21, **not** 1. 4 goes into 21 five times with 1 left over, so write 5 above the line and carry the 1 over to the next column.

$$\begin{array}{r} 1\,5 \\ 4\overline{)6\,^{2}1\,^{1}4\,8} \end{array}$$

3. In the next column, 4 goes into 14 three times with 2 left over, so write 3 above the line and carry the 2 to the next column.

$$\begin{array}{r} 1\,5\,3 \\ 4\overline{)6\,^{2}1\,^{1}4\,^{2}8} \end{array}$$

4. Finally, 4 goes into 28 seven times with nothing left over, so write 7 above the line.

$$\begin{array}{r} \mathbf{1\,5\,3\,7} \\ 4\overline{)6\,^{2}1\,^{1}4\,^{2}8} \end{array}$$

So 6148 ÷ 4 = **1537**

Long division is similar to short division, but uses **written subtraction** to find **remainders** (the "left over" numbers) instead of carrying digits across.

Example 7

Work out 385 ÷ 16.

1. 16 does not go into 3, so write 0 above the line and look at the first **two** digits instead, 38.
2. 16 × 2 = 32 but 16 × 3 = 48, so 16 goes into 38 twice. Write 2 above the line at the top, then write 32 underneath 38 and subtract. This gives a difference of 6.

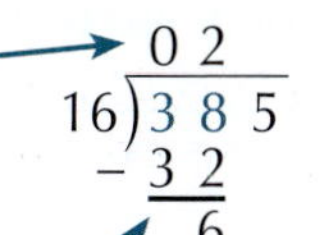

3. Instead of carrying the remainder over to the next column, bring the digit in the next column down.

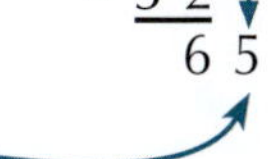

4. Look at how many 16's go into 65. 16 × 4 = 64, so write 4 above the line at the top, and write 64 underneath 65 and subtract.
5. When there are no more digits to bring down, the number on top gives you the whole part of the answer, and any number at the bottom is the remainder. To get an exact answer for the division, write the remainder as a fraction of the number you divided by.

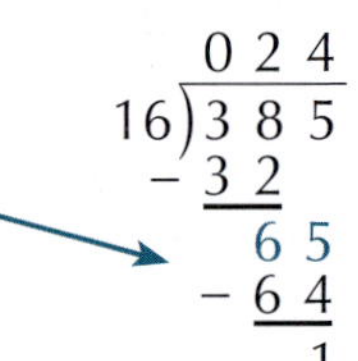

$385 \div 16 =$ **24 remainder 1**

$= \mathbf{24\frac{1}{16}}$

Exercise 4

Q1 Use short division to work out the following.

a) $7\overline{)357}$ b) $7\overline{)238}$ c) $9\overline{)603}$

d) $8\overline{)3616}$ e) $4\overline{)2240}$ f) $6\overline{)3732}$

Q2 Use short division to work out the following, giving the remainder as a fraction.

a) $361 \div 5$ b) $5213 \div 3$ c) $4198 \div 5$

d) $671 \div 9$ e) $2545 \div 6$ f) $2674 \div 8$

Q3 Use long division to work out the following.

a) $23\overline{)644}$ b) $19\overline{)608}$ c) $18\overline{)738}$

d) $17\overline{)816}$ e) $28\overline{)8680}$ f) $26\overline{)9152}$

Q4 Use long division to work out the following. Give any remainders as fractions.

a) $846 \div 32$ b) $945 \div 45$ c) $711 \div 21$

d) $6718 \div 25$ e) $8323 \div 31$ f) $8539 \div 44$

Q5 A postage stamp costs 41p. How many stamps could you buy for £5.00, and how much change would you receive?

Q6 672 people are divided into 24 equal groups. How many people are in each group?

Q7 An egg box can hold 6 eggs. How many egg boxes are needed to hold 1350 eggs?

Q8 22 washing machines cost £7634 in total. How much does each washing machine cost?

Q9 a) Mike earns £22 464 per year. How much does he earn per week? (Assume 1 year = 52 weeks.)

b) Andrea earns £24 636 per year. How much does she earn per month?

1.4 Decimals

Decimals are a way to show numbers that aren't whole numbers. They will come up a lot in maths, so make sure you understand what they mean and how they work before moving on.

Decimals

Learning Objective — Spec Ref N2:
Understand place values in decimals.

The digits that come after a **decimal point** show the **part** of a number that is **less than 1**. You can work out the **value** of each digit by looking at its **position** after the decimal point.

6	2	7	.	3	8	1
Hundreds	Tens	Units		Tenths	Hundredths	Thousandths

Example 1

What is the value of each of the digits in 0.692?

1. The 6 is in the tenths column. Six tenths = $\frac{6}{10}$
2. The 9 is in the hundredths column. Nine hundredths = $\frac{9}{100}$
3. The 2 is in the thousandths column. Two thousandths = $\frac{2}{1000}$

Tip: You don't need to simplify these fractions any further.

Exercise 1

Q1 Write down the value of the 7 in 4.271.

Q2 Write down the value of the 3 in 6.382.

Q3 Write down the value of the 8 in 0.718.

Q4 Write down the value of the 1 in 9.0361.

Q5 Write down the value of the 2 in 2.37.

Q6 Write down the following as decimal numbers.

a) seven tenths b) two hundredths c) five thousandths

d) $\frac{7}{100}$ e) $\frac{1}{1000}$ f) $\frac{8}{10}$

Ordering Decimals

Learning Objective — Spec Ref N1:
Order and compare decimals.

You can order decimals by comparing the digits at each **place value**.

If you have a few numbers, it can help to arrange them **on top of each other**, lining up their decimal points. Then **compare** the digits in each column, working from **left to right**.

Tip: Be careful with negative numbers — remember they're always smaller than positive ones.

Example 2

Put the decimals 8.092, 8.2, 8.09 and 8.9 in order of size, from smallest to largest.

1. Write the numbers on top of each other and fill in any gaps with 0's. Then compare the digits in each column of the list.

8.092	8.092	8.090
8.200	8.090	8.092
8.090	8.200	8.200
8.900	8.900	8.900

2. The 1st column doesn't help. In the 2nd, 9 is bigger than 2, and 2 is bigger than 0. So make a new list with 8.9 at the bottom (as it's biggest), and 8.2 next up.
3. Then look at the 3rd column in the new list. The two 9's don't help, so move onto the 4th column. 2 is bigger than 0, so swap 8.092 and 8.09 to get the final order.

The correct order is **8.09, 8.092, 8.2, 8.9**

Example 3

Put the decimals –1.02, 2.1, 0.12 and –1.2 in order, from lowest to highest.

Compare the negative and positive numbers separately, then combine. With negatives, a larger digit means that number comes lower in the list.

Comparing the tenths shows –1.2 is less than –1.02

Comparing the units shows 0.12 is less than 2.1

The correct order is: **–1.2, –1.02, 0.12, 2.1**

Exercise 2

Q1 Write down the larger number in each of the following pairs.

a) 0.3, 0.31 b) 0.09, 0.009 c) 0.427, 0.472 d) 18.07, 17.08

Q2 Put each of the following lists of decimals in order of size, from lowest to highest.

a) 0.02, 0.2, 0.15 b) 0.6, 6.1, –0.6, –6 c) 4.05, 5.04, 5.4, 4.5

d) 1.05, 1.5, –1.5, 1.55 e) 0.61, 0.51, 0.16, 0.15 f) 0.9, –0.05, –0.09, –0.095

1.5 Adding and Subtracting Decimals

Performing operations with decimals is very similar to the methods you know for whole numbers. The main difference is that it's really important that the decimal point is kept in the right place.

Learning Objective — Spec Ref N2:
Add and subtract decimals without using a calculator.

To add and subtract **decimals**, arrange them in columns like you would for whole numbers — just make sure you line up the **decimal points**. You might have to **add in 0's** to fill in any gaps.

Example 1

Work out 4.53 + 1.6

1. Write one number above the other, lining up the decimal points.
2. Fill in any gaps with 0's.
3. Add the digits one column at a time.
4. Carry digits just like when adding whole numbers.

$$\begin{array}{r} 4.53 \\ +\,1.60 \\ \hline .\ \ 3 \end{array} \qquad \begin{array}{r} 4.53 \\ +\,1.60 \\ \hline {}_{1}.13 \end{array} \qquad \begin{array}{r} 4.53 \\ +\,1.60 \\ \hline 6_{1}.13 \end{array}$$

So 4.53 + 1.6 = **6.13**

Example 2

Work out 8.5 – 3.07

1. Write one number above the other, lining up the decimal points.
2. Fill in any gaps with 0's.
3. Subtract the digits one column at a time.
4. Borrow digits just like when subtracting whole numbers.

$$\begin{array}{r} 8.\overset{4}{\cancel{5}}{}^{1}0 \\ -\,3.07 \\ \hline .\ \ 3 \end{array} \qquad \begin{array}{r} 8.\overset{4}{\cancel{5}}{}^{1}0 \\ -\,3.07 \\ \hline .43 \end{array} \qquad \begin{array}{r} 8.\overset{4}{\cancel{5}}{}^{1}0 \\ -\,3.07 \\ \hline 5.43 \end{array}$$

So 8.5 – 3.07 = **5.43**

Exercise 1

Q1 Copy and work out the following.

a) $\begin{array}{r} 5.1 \\ +\,1.8 \\ \hline \end{array}$ b) $\begin{array}{r} 6.3 \\ +\,5.4 \\ \hline \end{array}$ c) $\begin{array}{r} 5.7 \\ +\,12.6 \\ \hline \end{array}$ d) $\begin{array}{r} 4.8 \\ +\,5.3 \\ \hline \end{array}$

Q2 Copy and work out the following.

a) $\begin{array}{r} 5.6 \\ -\ 0.3 \\ \hline \end{array}$ b) $\begin{array}{r} 9.9 \\ -\ 4.2 \\ \hline \end{array}$ c) $\begin{array}{r} 5.3 \\ -\ 2.8 \\ \hline \end{array}$ d) $\begin{array}{r} 8.5 \\ -\ 1.9 \\ \hline \end{array}$

Q3 Work out the following.

a) 10.83 + 7.4 b) 0.029 + 1.8 c) 91.7 + 0.492 d) 6.474 + 0.92
e) 7.89 + 4.789 f) 0.888 + 1.02 g) 0.02 + 0.991 h) 3.41 + 22.169

Q4 Work out the following.

a) 24.63 – 7.5 b) 6.78 – 5.6 c) 73.46 – 8.5 d) 9.915 – 3.7
e) 3.52 – 0.126 f) 9.1 – 7.02 g) 11.2 – 1.89 h) 1.1 – 0.839

Q5 Work out the following.

a) 3.81 + 9.54 b) 2.81 – 0.16 c) 2.75 + 9.45 d) 8.67 + 0.95
e) 3.8 – 0.59 f) 15.1 – 0.08 g) 6.25 + 5.6 h) 1.97 + 21.7

Example 3

Work out 4 – 0.91

1. Write any whole numbers as decimals by adding 0's after the decimal point, then line up the decimal points.

$\begin{array}{r} 4.00 \\ -\ 0.91 \\ \hline . \end{array}$

2. Subtract the digits one column at a time. As you can't borrow from 0, borrow from the 4 instead.

$\begin{array}{r} \overset{3}{\cancel{4}}.\overset{9}{\cancel{0}}\,{}^{1}0 \\ -\ 0.91 \\ \hline .9 \end{array}$ $\begin{array}{r} \overset{3}{\cancel{4}}.\overset{9}{\cancel{0}}\,{}^{1}0 \\ -\ 0.91 \\ \hline 3.09 \end{array}$

So 4 – 0.91 = **3.09**

Tip: Put the decimal point in the answer straight away, directly below the others.

Exercise 2

Q1 Work out the following.

a) 6 – 5.1 b) 23 – 18.51 c) 12 – 5.028 d) 13 – 6.453

Q2 Work out the following.

a) 2 + 1.8 b) 3.7 + 6 c) 12.7 + 7.34 d) 9.49 + 13
e) 38 + 6.92 f) 5 – 0.8 g) 9 – 4.2 h) 24 – 5.7

Q3 Work out the following.

a) 6.474 + 0.92 + 3 b) 2.39 + 8 + 0.26 c) 12.24 + 4 + 1.2
d) 2 + 4.123 + 1.86 e) 16.8 + 4.17 + 2 f) 2.64 + 13 + 1.012

Example 4

A rope is 8 m long. 6.46 m of the rope is cut off. How much of the original rope is left?

1. Turn the question into a calculation. You want to find 8 – 6.46, so write the 8 as a decimal by adding 0's, then line up the decimal points.

$$\begin{array}{r} 8.00 \\ -\ 6.46 \\ \hline . \end{array}$$

2. Subtract the digits one column at a time. As you can't borrow from 0, borrow from the 8 instead.

$$\begin{array}{r} 8.00 \\ -\ 6.46 \\ \hline . \end{array} \quad \begin{array}{r} \overset{7}{\cancel{8}}.\overset{9}{\cancel{0}}{}^{1}0 \\ -\ 6.46 \\ \hline .\ \ 4 \end{array} \quad \begin{array}{r} \overset{7}{\cancel{8}}.\overset{9}{\cancel{0}}{}^{1}0 \\ -\ 6.46 \\ \hline .54 \end{array} \quad \begin{array}{r} \overset{7}{\cancel{8}}.\overset{9}{\cancel{0}}{}^{1}0 \\ -\ 6.46 \\ \hline 1.54 \end{array}$$

3. Remember to make sure you are answering the question. You are looking for a length in metres.

8 – 6.46 = 1.54, so **1.54 m** of rope is left.

Tip: Always read the question carefully to check whether it's asking you to perform addition or subtraction.

Exercise 3

Q1 Malcolm travels 2.3 km to the shops, then a further 4.6 km to his aunt's house. How far does he travel in total?

Q2 Sunita buys a hat for £18.50 and a bag for £31. How much does she spend altogether?

Q3 A plank of wood is 4 m long. A 2.75 m long piece is cut from the plank. What length of wood is left?

Q4 Joan goes out for a meal. The bill for the meal comes to £66.50. She uses a voucher which entitles her to £15 off her meal. How much does she have left to pay?

Q5 Ashkan spends £71.42 at the supermarket. His receipt says that he has saved £11.79 on special offers. How much would he have spent if there had been no special offers?

Q6 On his first run, Ted sprints 100 m in 15.32 seconds. On his second run, he is 0.47 seconds quicker. How long did he take on his second run?

1.6 Multiplying and Dividing Decimals

Multiplying or dividing decimals is a little trickier than addition or subtraction. Rather than keeping the decimal point in the same place, it can move depending on the numbers being used.

Multiplying and Dividing by 10, 100, 1000

Learning Objective — Spec Ref N2:
Multiply and divide decimals by 10, 100, 1000.

When multiplying a number by 10, 100 or 1000, each digit in the number moves to the **left**.

× 10 — each digit moves **one place** to the left.
× 100 — each digit moves **two places** to the left.
× 1000 — each digit moves **three places** to the left.

Tip: The rule continues for bigger powers of 10 — e.g. × 10 000 means each digit moves 4 places to the left, etc.

Example 1

Work out: a) 0.478 × 100 b) 1.35 × 1000

a) Move each digit two places to the left. 0.478 × 100 = **47.8**

b) Move each digit three places to the left.
Fill in any gaps with 0's. 1.35 × 1000 = **1350**

When dividing a number by 10, 100 or 1000, each digit in the number moves to the **right**.

÷ 10 — each digit moves **one place** to the right.
÷ 100 — each digit moves **two places** to the right.
÷ 1000 — each digit moves **three places** to the right.

Tip: You can use the same idea for other powers of 10 — e.g. ÷ 10 000 means each digit moves 4 places to the right, etc.

Example 2

Work out: a) 923.1 ÷ 100 b) 51.4 ÷ 1000

a) Move each digit two places to the right. 923.1 ÷ 100 = **9.231**

b) Move each digit three places to the right.
Fill in any gaps after the decimal point with 0's. 51.4 ÷ 1000 = **0.0514**

Exercise 1

Q1 Work out the following.

a) 0.92×10 b) 1.41×100 c) 0.23×1000

d) 14.6×100 e) 0.019×1000 f) 13.04×10

Q2 Work out the following.

a) $861.5 \div 100$ b) $381.7 \div 10$ c) $549.1 \div 1000$

d) $6.3 \div 10$ e) $5.1 \div 1000$ f) $0.94 \div 100$

Multiplying Decimals

Learning Objectives — Spec Ref N2:

- Multiplying two decimals without using a calculator.
- Multiply a decimal and a whole number without using a calculator.

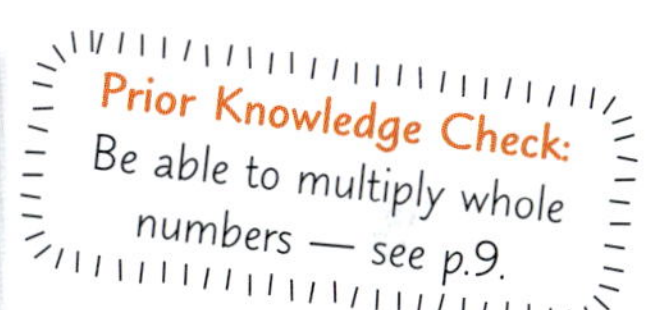

Prior Knowledge Check:
Be able to multiply whole numbers — see p.9.

If you know the result of a multiplication involving **whole numbers**, you can use it to find the result of related **decimal** multiplications.

You do this by considering how to turn the whole numbers into the decimals you're interested in, by **multiplying or dividing** by 10, 100 or 1000.

Example 3

Given that 167 × 486 = 81 162, work out 1.67 × 0.486

1. Work out how to turn 167 into 1.67. $167 \div 100 = 1.67$
2. Work out how to turn 486 into 0.486. $486 \div 1000 = 0.486$
3. Apply both operations to the answer of the original calculation. So $1.67 \times 0.486 = 81\ 162 \div 100 \div 1000$ $= \mathbf{0.81162}$

Exercise 2

Q1 You are given that $132 \times 238 = 31\ 416$.
Use this information to work out the following.

a) 13.2×238 b) 1.32×23.8 c) 1.32×0.238 d) 0.132×0.238

Q2 You are given that $401 \times 119 = 47\ 719$.
Use this information to work out the following.

a) 40.1×11.9 b) 4.01×1.19 c) 0.401×1.19 d) 0.401×0.119

When multiplying two decimals from scratch:

- **Ignore** the decimal point and multiply them as **whole numbers**.
- Then add in the decimal point in the **right place** at the end.

To work out where the decimal point should go, **add** together the number of digits **after the decimal points** in the two numbers you're multiplying — this will tell you the number of digits after the decimal point in your answer.

Tip: What you're actually doing here is multiplying by powers of 10 and then dividing by them again.

Example 4

Work out 0.32 × 0.6

1. Ignore the decimal points and treat it as a whole number multiplication.

$$\begin{array}{r} 3\ 2 \\ \times\quad 6 \\ \hline {}_{1}2 \end{array} \qquad \begin{array}{r} 3\ 2 \\ \times\quad 6 \\ \hline 1\ 9\ {}_{1}2 \end{array}$$

2. There are three digits in total after the decimal points in the question (two in 0.32 and one in 0.6), so the answer should have three digits after the decimal point.

So 0.32 × 0.6 = **0.192**

Example 5

Work out 0.57 × 2.4

1. Ignore the decimal points and treat it as a whole number multiplication.

$$\begin{array}{r} 5\ 7 \\ \times\ 2\ 4 \\ \hline {}_{2}8 \end{array} \qquad \begin{array}{r} 5\ 7 \\ \times\ 2\ 4 \\ \hline 2\ 2\ {}_{2}8 \end{array}$$

2. There are three digits in total after the decimal points in the question (two in 0.57, one in 2.4), so the answer should have three digits after the decimal point.

$$\begin{array}{r} 5\ 7 \\ \times\ 2\ 4 \\ \hline 2\ 2\ {}_{2}8 \\ 0 \end{array} \qquad \begin{array}{r} 5\ 7 \\ \times\ 2\ 4 \\ \hline 2\ 2\ {}_{2}8 \\ {}_{1}4\ 0 \end{array} \qquad \begin{array}{r} 5\ 7 \\ \times\ 2\ 4 \\ \hline 2\ 2\ {}_{2}8 \\ 1\ 1\ {}_{1}4\ 0 \end{array} \qquad \begin{array}{r} 5\ 7 \\ \times\ 2\ 4 \\ \hline 2\ 2\ {}_{2}8 \\ 1\ 1\ {}_{1}4\ 0 \\ \hline 1\ 3\ 6\ 8 \end{array}$$

So 0.57 × 2.4 = **1.368**

Exercise 3

Q1 Work out the following.

a) 6.7 × 8 b) 0.65 × 9 c) 0.9 × 0.8 d) 0.6 × 0.3

e) 0.01 × 0.6 f) 0.61 × 0.7 g) 0.33 × 0.02 h) 0.007 × 0.006

Q2 Work out the following.

a) 6.3 × 2.1 b) 1.4 × 2.3 c) 2.4 × 1.8

d) 8.6 × 6.9 e) 0.16 × 3.3 f) 5.1 × 0.23

Example 6

Work out 1.36 × 200

1. 1.36 × 200 = 1.36 × 2 × 100, so break the multiplication down into two stages.
2. First calculate 1.36 × 2 by ignoring the decimal point and adding it in at the end.
3. There are two digits after the decimal point in the question (1.36), so the answer will have two digits after the decimal place.
4. Then multiply by 100 by moving each digit two places to the left.

$$\begin{array}{r} 136 \\ \times\quad 2 \\ \hline {}_1 2 \end{array} \qquad \begin{array}{r} 136 \\ \times\quad 2 \\ \hline 7{}_1 2 \end{array} \qquad \begin{array}{r} 136 \\ \times\quad 2 \\ \hline 27{}_1 2 \end{array}$$

136 × 2 = 272
so 1.36 × 2 = 2.72

1.36 × 200 = 2.72 × 100
= **272**

Exercise 4

Q1 Work out the following.

a) 3.1 × 40 b) 0.7 × 600 c) 0.061 × 2000 d) 11.06 × 80

e) 12.1 × 30 f) 1.007 × 400 g) 101.8 × 60 h) 0.903 × 5000

Dividing Decimals

Learning Objective — Spec Ref N2:
Divide decimals without using a calculator.

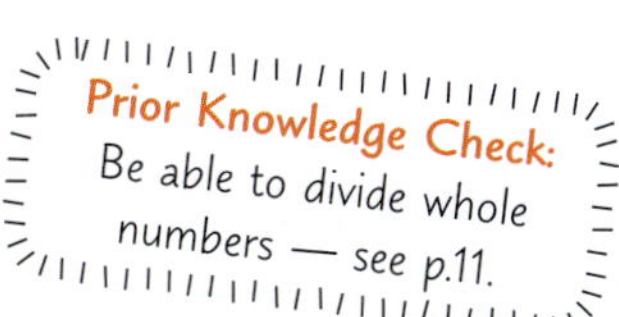

Prior Knowledge Check:
Be able to divide whole numbers — see p.11.

When dividing decimals, it's important that you **set up** the division properly — make sure the **decimal point** in the answer is **directly above** the decimal point inside the division.

Example 7

Work out 5.16 ÷ 8

1. Position the decimal point in the answer directly above the one inside the division.
2. Divide as you would with whole numbers.
3. You may need to add zeros to the decimal you're dividing.

$$8\overline{)5.{}^516}\ \text{ with } 0.\text{ above}$$

$$\begin{array}{r} 0.6 \\ 8\overline{)5.{}^51{}^36} \end{array} \qquad \begin{array}{r} 0.64 \\ 8\overline{)5.{}^51{}^36{}^40} \end{array} \qquad \begin{array}{r} 0.645 \\ 8\overline{)5.{}^51{}^36{}^40} \end{array}$$

So 5.16 ÷ 8 = **0.645**

Tip: You could also use long division.

Exercise 5

Q1 Copy and work out the following.

a) $2\overline{)5.4}$ b) $3\overline{)9.6}$ c) $6\overline{)9.24}$ d) $5\overline{)2.65}$

e) $7\overline{)7.21}$ f) $9\overline{)4.05}$ g) $7\overline{)98.7}$ h) $4\overline{)0.924}$

Q2 Work out the following.

a) $8.52 \div 4$ b) $112.8 \div 4$ c) $1.02 \div 3$ d) $5.62 \div 8$

e) $0.052 \div 5$ f) $12.06 \div 8$ g) $3.061 \div 5$ h) $0.0612 \div 6$

When the number you're **dividing by** is a decimal, convert the calculation into a division by a whole number by **multiplying** both numbers by a **power of 10**. Then divide as usual.

Example 8

Work out 8.16 ÷ 0.2

1. Multiply both numbers by 10, so you are dividing by a whole number.
2. Divide as usual.

$\times 10$ ($8.16 \div 0.2$) $\times 10$

$= 81.6 \div 2$

$\begin{array}{r} 4\ .\ \\ 2\overline{)81.6} \end{array}$ $\begin{array}{r} 40.\ \\ 2\overline{)81.^{1}6} \end{array}$ $\begin{array}{r} 40.8 \\ 2\overline{)81.^{1}6} \end{array}$

So $8.16 \div 0.2 =$ **40.8**

Tip: Only the number that you're dividing by needs to be a whole number.

Exercise 6

Q1 Consider the calculation $6.4 \div 0.4$.

a) Multiply both numbers by 10 to form an equivalent calculation which involves dividing by a whole number.

b) Use your answer to work out $6.4 \div 0.4$.

Q2 Consider the calculation $0.384 \div 0.12$.

a) Multiply both numbers by 100 to form an equivalent calculation which involves dividing by a whole number.

b) Use your answer to work out $0.384 \div 0.12$.

Q3 Consider the calculation $3.8 \div 0.008$.

a) Write down an equivalent calculation which involves dividing by a whole number.

b) Use your answer to work out $3.8 \div 0.008$.

Q4 Work out the following.

a) $6.4 \div 0.2$ b) $3.54 \div 0.4$ c) $0.624 \div 0.3$

Q5 Work out the following.

a) $22.56 \div 0.03$ b) $0.257 \div 0.05$ c) $0.039 \div 0.06$

Q6 Work out the following.

a) $0.081 \div 0.009$ b) $0.008 \div 0.4$ c) $1.44 \div 1.2$

When you are dividing by a whole number that's a **multiple** of a **power of 10**, start by **splitting** up that number. E.g. if you were dividing by 4000, you'd write this as 4×1000. Then you can start **dividing**:

- First divide by the **smaller** number — so in the example above you'd divide by 4 first.
- Then divide by the correct **power of 10** to get the final answer — so you'd divide by 1000 in the example.

Tip: Always split the number using the biggest power of 10 that you can. E.g. $4000 = 4 \times 1000$ instead of using $4000 = 40 \times 100$.

Example 9

Work out 96.6 ÷ 300.

1. Write 300 as something multiplied by a power of 10. — $300 = 3 \times 100$
2. First work out 96.6 ÷ 3. — $96.6 \div 3 = 3\overset{\;3\;2.2}{\overline{)9\;6.6}}$
3. Then divide by 100 to get the final answer. — $32.2 \div 100 =$ **0.322**

Exercise 7

Q1 Consider the calculation $7.3 \div 50$.

a) Work out $7.3 \div 5$.

b) Use your answer to work out $7.3 \div 50$.

Q2 Consider the calculation $2.41 \div 400$.

a) Work out $2.41 \div 4$.

b) Use your answer to work out $2.41 \div 400$.

Q3 Work out the following.

a) $6.08 \div 40$ b) $5.74 \div 700$ c) $25.47 \div 900$ d) $13.722 \div 3000$

Review Exercise

Q1 Work out the following.

a) $6 + 4 \times 2$ b) $48 \div (4 + 2)$ c) $(13 - 5) \times 12$

Q2 Work out the following.

a) $-5 + 8$ b) $6 - (-2)$ c) $-8 \times (-5)$ d) $54 \div (-9)$

Q3 Work out the following.

a) $256 + 312$ b) $841 - 346$ c) $1632 + 421$ d) $2830 - 394$

Q4 Laura receives £14 pocket money each week.
How much money does she get in 52 weeks?

Q5 462 pupils are going on a school trip. A coach can seat 54 children.
How many coaches will be needed for the trip?

Q6 Write down the value of the 6 in 0.956.

Q7 Put each of the following lists of decimals in order of size, from lowest to highest.

a) −0.01, 0.1, −0.09, −0.1 b) −0.5, −0.45, −0.55, −5 c) −7, −7.1, −7.07, 0.007

Q8 Work out the following.

a) $6.78 - 5.6$ b) $1.6 + 4.35$ c) $0.78 + 1.3$ d) $4.32 - 2.17$

Q9 Work out the following.

a) 7.8×1000 b) 0.006×100 c) $25.9 \div 10$ d) $901.5 \div 100$

Q10 You are given that $221 \times 168 = 37\ 128$. Work out the following.

a) 2.21×1.68 b) 0.221×1.68 c) 221×0.168

Q11 1 litre is equal to 1.76 pints. How many pints are there in 5 litres?

Q12 A 2.72 m ribbon is cut into pieces of length 0.08 m. How many pieces will there be?

Exam-Style Questions

Q1 In New York, the evening temperature was –4 °C.
During the night, the temperature dropped by 7 °C.
What was the lowest temperature that night?

[1 mark]

Q2 Work out the following calculation.
$12 + 1.3 + 0.25$

[1 mark]

Q3 You are given that $539 \times 28 = 15092$.
Use the above result to work out the value of:

a) 539×14

[1 mark]

b) 5390×0.28

[1 mark]

c) $1\ 509\ 200 \div 53.9$

[2 marks]

Q4 Rani has to work out $5 + 3 \times 4$. She gives the answer 32.
Explain what she has done wrong and give the correct answer.

[2 marks]

Q5 It costs £35.55 to buy nine identical books.
How much would it cost to buy seven of these books?

[2 marks]

Q6 Put one pair of brackets into each of these calculations so that the answer is correct.

a) $3 \times 2 - 4 \div 2 = -3$

[1 mark]

b) $8 + 6 \div 5 \times 10 = 92$

[1 mark]

2.1 Rounding — Whole Numbers

Numbers can be approximated by (or rounded to) whole numbers. As you'll see later, these approximations can be used to find estimates and to check answers to difficult calculations.

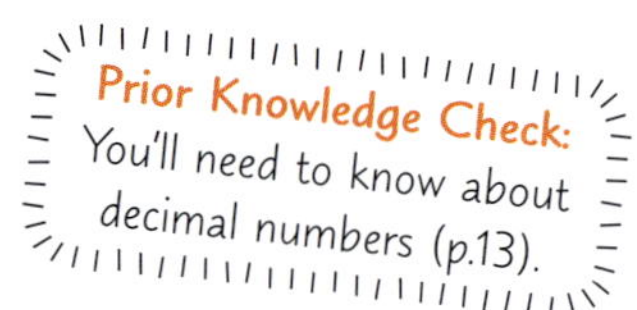

Prior Knowledge Check:
You'll need to know about decimal numbers (p.13).

Learning Objective — Spec Ref N15:
Round numbers to the nearest whole number, ten, hundred etc.

Numbers can be **rounded** to make them easier to work with.
For example, a number like 5468.9 could be rounded to:

- the nearest **whole number** (= 5469)
- the nearest **ten** (= 5470)
- the nearest **hundred** (= 5500)
- the nearest **thousand** (= 5000)

To round any number to a **whole number** use the following method:

1. **Identify** the position of the '**last digit**' that you want to keep.
   E.g. if you're rounding to the nearest ten, then this last digit is in the tens place.
2. Look at the next digit to the **right** — called **the decider**.
3. If the decider is **5 or more**, then **round up** the last digit.
   If the decider is **4 or less**, then **leave** the last digit as it is.
4. All digits to the right of the last digit should be **zero**, and there should be **no digits** after the decimal point.

Tip: When you're rounding up a digit, just add 1 to it.

Example 1

Round 18.6 to the nearest ten.

1. The 'last digit' is in the tens place. — (1)8.6 — the 'last digit' is 1.
2. The decider is the next digit to the right. — 1(8).6 — the decider is 8.
3. The decider is more than 5, so round up.
4. All digits after the 'last digit' should be zero. — 18.6 rounds up to **20**

Things are a little trickier if you need to **round up** and the last digit is 9.
You need to replace the 9 with a 0 and **carry 1 to the left** (by adding a 1 to the digit to its left).

This is easier to understand by looking at an example:

Example 2

Round 39 742 to the nearest thousand.

1. The 'last digit' is in the thousands place. The decider is the next digit to the right. — 3(9)742 — the 'last digit' is 9.
   39(7)42 — the decider is 7.
2. The decider is more than 5, so round up. The last digit is a 9, so replace with 0 and carry the 1. → $\overset{4}{\cancel{3}}$0 000
3. Replace the decider and all the digits to its right with 0s. — 39 742 rounds up to **40 000**

Exercise 1

Q1 Write down all the numbers from the box that round to 14 to the nearest whole number.

14.1	14.9	14.02	15.499	14.5	15.01
13.7	14.09	13.3	13.4999	14.4999	13.901

Q2 Round the following to the nearest whole number.
a) 9.7 b) 8.4 c) 12.2 d) 39.8

Q3 Round the following to the nearest hundred.
a) 158 b) 596 c) 650 d) 4714

Q4 Round the following to the nearest thousand.
a) 2536 b) 8516 c) 7218 d) 9500

Q5 Round the numbers on these calculator displays to the nearest: (i) whole number (ii) ten
a) 18.2 b) 16.479 c) 20.15000 1 d) 14.999999

Q6 Matilda says Italy has an area of 301 225 km². Round this figure to the nearest thousand.

Q7 At its closest, Jupiter is about 390 682 810 miles from Earth.
Write this distance to the nearest million miles.

2.2 Rounding — Decimal Places

Decimal places are the digits that come after a decimal point. They show parts of numbers — tenths, hundredths, thousandths etc. You can round to decimal places, just like with whole numbers.

Learning Objective — Spec Ref N15:
Round numbers to a given number of decimal places.

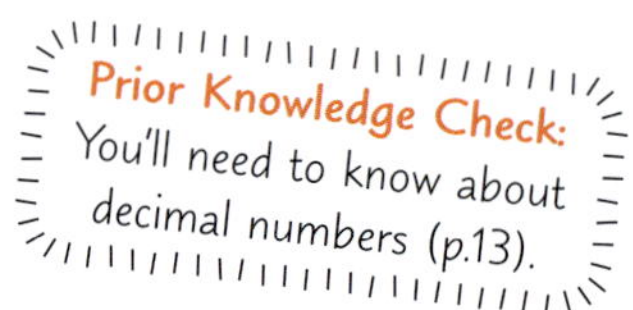

Prior Knowledge Check:
You'll need to know about decimal numbers (p.13).

You can round to different numbers of **decimal places** (**d.p.**).

For example, a number like 8.9471 could be rounded:

- to **one** decimal place (= 8.9)
- to **two** decimal places (= 8.95)
- to **three** decimal places (= 8.947)

Tip: 1 decimal place is the same as 'the nearest tenth', 2 decimal places is the same as 'the nearest hundredth' and so on.

The method for rounding to a given number of **decimal places** is basically the same as the method on page 26:

1. **Identify** the position of the '**last digit**' that you want to keep. E.g. when rounding to 2 d.p., it's the digit in the hundredths place.
2. Look at the next digit to the **right** (**the decider**).
3. If the decider is **5 or more**, then **round up** the last digit. If the decider is **4 or less**, then **leave** the last digit as it is.
4. There must be **no more digits** after the last digit (not even zeros).

Example 1

a) Round 4.7623 to one decimal place.

1. The 'last digit' is in the first d.p. (the tenths place). — 4.7623 — the 'last digit' is 7.
2. The decider is the next digit to the right. — 4.7623 — the decider is 6.
3. The decider is more than 5, so round up the last digit and remove all other digits. — 4.7623 rounds up to **4.8**

b) Round 4.7623 to three decimal places.

1. The 'last digit' is in the third d.p. (the thousandths place). — 4.7623 — the 'last digit' is 2.
2. The decider is the next digit to the right. — 4.7623 — the decider is 3.
3. The decider is less than 5, so leave the last digit as it is and remove all the other digits. — 4.7623 rounds down to **4.762**

Just like with whole numbers, things get a little tricky when you need to round up and the **last digit is a 9**. Just like on page 27, you need to **carry a 1** to the left.

After rounding up, your last digit will be a **zero**. You still need to **remove** all other digits after the last digit (even if they are more zeros).

Example 2

Round 3.896 to two decimal places.

1. The 'last digit' is in the second d.p. (the hundredths place). — 3.896 — the 'last digit' is 9.
   The decider is the next digit to the right. — 3.896 — the decider is 6.
2. The decider is more than 5, so round up.
   The last digit is 9, so replace with 0 and carry the 1. → 3.$\overset{9}{\not{8}}$0
3. Remove all the other digits after the last digit. — 3.896 rounds up to **3.90**

Exercise 1

Q1 Write down all the numbers from the box that round to 0.4 to one decimal place.

0.41	0.45	0.347	0.47204	0.335	0.405
0.35	0.4295	0.5216	0.4124	0.4671	0.307

Q2 Round the following numbers to one decimal place.
a) 0.23 b) 0.678 c) 2.6893 d) 0.9324

Q3 Round the following numbers to two decimal places.
a) 4.567 b) 0.0424 c) 6.2971 d) 0.35273

Q4 Round the following numbers to three decimal places.
a) 0.96734 b) 0.25471 c) 2.43658 d) 6.532561

Q5 Round these numbers to the number of decimal places (d.p.) specified.
a) 0.19745 — to 2 d.p. b) 0.68361 — to 1 d.p.
c) 5.73174 — to 3 d.p. d) 0.000635 — to 3 d.p.

Not shown actual size.

Q6 The mass of the field vole on the right is 0.0384 kg.
Round this mass to two decimal places.

Q7 Usain measures his height to be 1.7 m to the nearest 10 cm.
Is it possible for Usain's exact height to be 1.76 m? Explain your answer.

2.3 Rounding — Significant Figures

One more type of rounding now. It's a biggie, but not too tough. Once you know how to identify significant figures, you can round just like rounding to whole numbers or decimal places.

Learning Objective — Spec Ref N15:
Round whole numbers and decimals to a given number of significant figures.

The **first significant figure** in a number is the first digit that **isn't 0**.

All the digits that follow the first significant figure are also **significant figures**, regardless of whether or not they're **zeros**. So, 307 has **three** significant figures — 3, 0 and 7.

You can round to different numbers of **significant figures** (s.f.).
For example, 217 304 could be rounded:

- to **one** significant figure (= 200 000)
- to **two** significant figures (= 220 000)
- to **three** significant figures (= 217 000)

The method for significant figures is **identical** to the one for decimal places — except it can be a bit harder to locate the **last digit**. There are a few key things to note:

- The '**last digit**' is the significant figure you're **rounding to**. E.g. rounding to 2 s.f. means the 'last digit' is the **second** s.f.
- After rounding, fill in all the places up to the decimal point with 0s. (You may need to include a 0 after the decimal point to make up the correct number of significant figures — e.g. 32.0)

Tip: If the last s.f. is **after** the decimal point, don't add any extra zeros to the end.

Example 1

a) Round 56 291 to two significant figures.

1. The 'last digit' is the second s.f. and the decider is the next digit to the right.

   56291 — the 'last digit' is 6.
   56291 — the decider is 2.

2. The decider is less than 5, so leave the last digit as it is and fill in all the places up to the decimal point with zeros.

   56 291 rounds down to **56 000**

b) Round 6.597 to three significant figures.

1. The decider is more than 5, so round up. The last digit is a 9, so you'll need to carry the 1.

   6.597 — the 'last digit' is 9.
   6.597 — the decider is 7.

2. Keep the zero so you've got the correct number of significant figures.

   6.60

3. The last significant figure is after the decimal point, so don't add any more zeros.

   6.597 rounds up to **6.60**

Exercise 1

Q1 Round the following numbers to: (i) 1 s.f. (ii) 2 s.f. (iii) 3 s.f.

a) 7036 b) 6551 c) 7067 d) 2649

Q2 Round the following numbers to the number of significant figures (s.f.) indicated.

a) 45.89 — to 1 s.f. b) 5689.6 — to 3 s.f. c) 6.497 — to 3 s.f.

d) 360.8 — to 2 s.f. e) 6527 — to 2 s.f. f) 756 557 — to 3 s.f.

g) 46.745 — to 3 s.f. h) 376.25 — to 2 s.f. i) 79 477 — to 2 s.f.

Q3 The speed of sound is approximately 1236 km/h.
Round this speed to two significant figures.

Rounding Decimals to Significant Figures

Zeros at the start of a decimal do **not** count as significant figures. The first significant figure is the first **non-zero digit**.

For example, 0.001520 has **four** significant figures — 1, 5, 2 and 0.

You can round decimals to significant figures using the **same method** as on the previous page.

Tip: Remember — **all** the digits following the first s.f. are also significant figures, regardless of whether or not they're zeros.

Example 2

Round 0.06826 to one significant figure.

1. The 'last digit' is the first significant figure and the decider is the next digit to the right.
   0.06826 — the 'last digit' is 6.
   0.06826 — the decider is 8.
2. The decider is more than 5, so round up.
   0.06826 rounds up to **0.07**
3. Remove any digits to the right, and do not add any more zeros.

Exercise 2

Q1 Round the following numbers to: (i) 1 s.f. (ii) 2 s.f. (iii) 3 s.f.

a) 0.003753 b) 0.02644 c) 0.0001792

d) 0.03970 e) 0.5635 f) 0.0007049

Q2 Round the following numbers to the number of significant figures (s.f.) indicated.

a) 0.004567 — to 1 s.f. b) 0.1962 — to 2 s.f. c) 0.0043862 — to 3 s.f.

d) 0.006204 — to 1 s.f. e) 0.009557 — to 2 s.f. f) 0.00060384 — to 3 s.f.

Q3 The density of the hydrogen gas in a balloon is 0.0899 kg/m^3.
Round this density to one significant figure.

2.4 Estimating Answers

Rounded numbers can be used in calculations to estimate answers.
By comparing an exact calculation with an estimate, you can see if it looks 'about right'.

Learning Objectives — Spec Ref N14:
- Find estimates using approximate values.
- Check answers to calculations using estimates.

Using rounded numbers in a **calculation** gives an **estimate** of the actual answer. By **simplifying** in this way, you get an **approximate value**. To find an estimate of a calculation:

- Round every number to one significant figure.
- Work out the answer using the rounded values.

Tip: The symbol '≈' is used when estimating. It means 'is approximately equal to'.

Example 1

By rounding each number to one significant figure, estimate $\frac{78.43 \times 6.24}{19.76}$.

1. Round each number to 1 s.f. — 78.43 = 80 (1 s.f.), 6.24 = 6 (1 s.f.), 19.76 = 20 (1 s.f.)
2. Replace the numbers in the calculation with the rounded values. — $\frac{78.43 \times 6.24}{19.76} \approx \frac{80 \times 6}{20}$
3. Work out the estimate. — $\frac{80 \times 6}{20} = \frac{480}{20} = \mathbf{24}$

An estimate to a calculation will probably be **different** to the actual answer. You can usually figure out if your answer will be an **overestimate** or an **underestimate**:

- **Addition** or **multiplication** — if both numbers are rounded **up** you'll get an **overestimate** and if both numbers are rounded **down** you'll get an **underestimate**.
- **Subtraction** or **division** — you'll get an **overestimate** if you rounded the **1st number up** and the **2nd number down**, and an **underestimate** if you rounded the **1st number down** and the **2nd number up**.

Example 2

By rounding each number to 1 s.f., estimate 42.6 ÷ 7.8.
Is your answer an overestimate or an underestimate?

1. Round each number to 1 s.f. to find an estimate. — 42.6 ÷ 7.8 ≈ 40 ÷ 8 = **5**
2. The calculation is a division — the 1st number was rounded down and the 2nd number was rounded up. — **underestimate**.

Exercise 1

Q1 By rounding each number to one significant figure, estimate the following.

a) 437 + 175 b) 310 + 876 c) 784 – 279

d) 0.516 – 0.322 e) 184 + 722 f) 838 – 121

Q2 By rounding each number to one significant figure:
(i) estimate the calculation (ii) say whether this is an overestimate or an underestimate.

a) 23 + 43 b) 59×5.7 c) 40.4 + 5.1

d) 18×79 e) 276 + 19 f) 587×8.81

Q3 Use rounding to choose the correct answer (A, B or C) for each of the following calculations.

a) 1.76×6.3 A: 1.328 B: 5.788 C: 11.088

b) 582×2.1 A: 119.52 B: 1222.2 C: 4545.2

c) $\frac{57.5 \times 3.78}{16.1}$ A: 1.65 B: 6.3 C: 13.5

Q4 By rounding each number to one significant figure:
(i) estimate the calculation (ii) say whether this is an overestimate or an underestimate.

a) $\frac{8.9}{3.1}$ b) 33 – 17 c) $\frac{43}{18}$

d) 37.3 – 5.2 e) 112 – 68 f) $\frac{9.98}{2.14}$

Q5 By rounding each number to one significant figure, estimate the following.

a) $\frac{68.8 + 27.3}{23.7}$ b) $\frac{5.6 \times 9.68}{5.14}$ c) $\frac{\sqrt{38.6 + 56.3}}{1.678}$

Q6 The decimal points have been missed out from each of the answers to these calculations. Use rounding to find an approximate answer in each case, and then decide where the decimal point should be.

a) $18.5 \times 3.2 = 592$ b) $\frac{325.26}{5.2} = 6255$

c) $\frac{19.8 \times 27.4}{3.3} = 1644$ d) $\frac{\sqrt{48.4 \times 8.1}}{4.8} = 4125$

Q7 It costs £4.70 to buy the toys needed for one 'Child's Party Bag'. If 21 children attend a party, estimate how much it would cost to buy all the toys for the party bags.

Q8 A smoothie factory operates for 62 hours per week.
It makes 324 litres of smoothie per hour.
Each litre of smoothie contains 14 strawberries.

a) Estimate the number of strawberries used each week.

b) Is your answer to a) an overestimate or an underestimate?
Give a reason for your answer.

Use Estimates to Check Answers

Even though an **estimated** answer **isn't exact**, it can still be useful. You can use an estimate to **check** your calculations — in other words, to see if your actual answer looks 'about right'.

Example 3

Hiromi uses a calculator to work out $\frac{27\,891 \times 628}{18}$ and gets the answer 973 086.

Use approximations to decide whether Hiromi's answer is sensible.

1. Round each number to 1 s.f.

   27 891 = 30 000 (1 s.f.), 628 = 600 (1 s.f.) and 18 = 20 (1 s.f.)

2. Replace the numbers in the calculation with the rounded values and work out the estimate.

   $$\frac{27\,891 \times 628}{18} \approx \frac{30\,000 \times 600}{20}$$
   $$= \frac{18\,000\,000}{20} = 900\,000$$

3. Compare the estimate to the calculated answer given in the question. Decide if the numbers seem close to each other.

   The approximate answer is close to the calculated answer, so **Hiromi's answer is sensible.**

Exercise 2

Q1 For each of the following:

(i) Use your calculator to work out the value of the calculation and write down your full calculator display.

(ii) Use approximations to check if your answer to part (i) is sensible.

a) 112.62×268.9

b) $\frac{52.668 \times \sqrt{104.04}}{3.78}$

c) $5.39^2 \times \sqrt[3]{1012} \div 2.36$

Q2 Sam has done the calculation 56.2 × 34.7 on his calculator. The calculator display is shown on the right. Alex says Sam must have pressed a wrong button at some point.

a) By rounding each number in the calculation to 1 s.f., estimate 56.2 × 34.7.

b) Do you think Sam pressed a wrong button at some point? Explain your answer.

Q3 A company posts an update saying "We had a great day today, selling 987 items at a price of £27.85 each, so we made over £32 000 in total." Use approximations to show that the company is wrong.

Q4 Karen earns £6.85 per hour. One week she works for 42 hours and is paid £287.70. Use approximations to see if it looks like Karen has been paid correctly or not.

2.5 Rounding Errors

Rounding leaves some uncertainty between the actual number and the rounded number. Error intervals show you the range of values that a rounded number could actually be.

Error Intervals for Rounded Numbers

Learning Objectives — Spec Ref N15/N16:
- Interpret rounded numbers.
- Use inequality notation to describe error intervals.

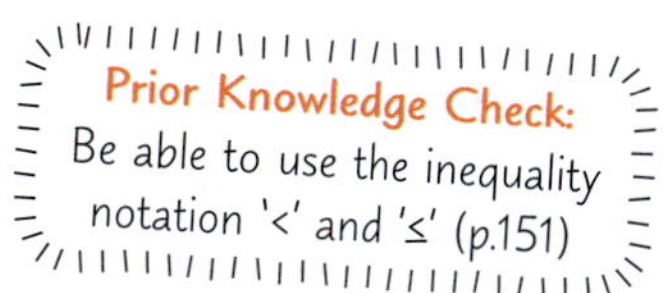
Prior Knowledge Check:
Be able to use the inequality notation '<' and '≤' (p.151)

When a number has been rounded to a given **rounding unit**, the actual number could be up to **half a unit** bigger or smaller than the rounded number. For example, if a number has been rounded to 1 d.p., the **rounding unit** is **0.1** so the actual value is anything up to **0.05 either side**.

Once you know these **maximum** and **minimum values** of a rounded number, you can show the **error interval** using **inequalities**:

- The actual value is **greater than or equal to** the **minimum**.
- The actual value is **strictly less than** the **maximum**.
  (If it was exactly equal to the maximum value, it would round up to the next unit.)

The error interval is the interval of **possible values** the actual number can be, from the **smallest possible number** that rounds **up** to the given number to the **largest possible number** that rounds **down** to the given number.

Example 1

m = 20 when rounded to 1 s.f. Find the error interval for m.

1. The first significant figure of 20 lies in the tens column. So the rounding unit is 10. Half the rounding unit is $10 \div 2 = 5$.

   Minimum value of m is $20 - 5 = 15$.
   Maximum value of m is $20 + 5 = 25$.

2. The actual value of m can be greater than or equal to 15 but is strictly less than 25.

   The error interval is $\mathbf{15 \leq m < 25}$.

Exercise 1

Q1 Find the minimum and maximum values of the following rounded values.

a) 80 rounded to the nearest whole number

b) 400 rounded to 1 significant figure.

Q2 Each of the following values have been rounded as shown.
Write down the error interval for each value.

a) $a = 60$ to the nearest ten
b) $b = 9$ to the nearest whole number
c) $c = 500$ to the nearest hundred
d) $d = 15\ 000$ to the nearest thousand

Q3 Write down the error interval for each of the following values, which have been rounded as shown.

a) $a = 7.6$ to 1 d.p.
b) $b = 0.3$ to 1 s.f.
c) $c = 2.55$ to 2 d.p.
d) $d = 50$ to 1 s.f.
e) $e = 109.9$ to 1 d.p.
f) $f = 540$ to 2 s.f.

Q4 The length, l cm, of a piece of rope is 76 cm correct to the nearest centimetre.
Write down the error interval for l.

Q5 Alasdair is canoeing down a river and has travelled 10 km to the nearest 100 m.
Write down the error interval for d, the actual distance in km he has travelled.

Q6 The number of sweets in a jar is 670, to the nearest 10.
What is the maximum possible number of sweets in the jar?

Error Intervals for Truncated Numbers

Learning Objectives — Spec Ref N15:

- Be able to truncate numbers.
- Use inequality notation to describe error intervals.

You **truncate** a number by chopping off decimal places — e.g. 77.889 truncated to 1 d.p. is 77.8.
The **actual value** of a truncated number can be up to a **whole rounding unit bigger but no smaller**.

Example 2

$x = 62.1$ truncated to 1 decimal place.
Find the error interval for x.

The rounding unit is 0.1. x has been truncated, so it can be up to 0.1 bigger, but no smaller.

$\mathbf{62.1 \le x < 62.2}$

Tip: Just like before, it's a strict inequality (<) on the right.

Exercise 2

Q1 Truncate the following values to the given number of decimal places.

a) 1.354 to 1 d.p.
b) 19.133 to 2 d.p.
c) 103.67183 to 3 d.p.

Q2 Find the error interval for the following numbers, which have been truncated as shown.

a) $x = 1.3$ to 1 d.p.
b) $y = 5.13$ to 2 d.p.
c) $z = 7.731$ to 3 d.p.

Review Exercise

Q1 Round the following to: (i) the nearest ten
(ii) the nearest hundred
(iii) the nearest thousand

a) 6724 b) 25 361 c) 8499.3 d) 3822.8

Q2 Round the following to: (i) 1 d.p. (ii) 2 d.p. (iii) 3 d.p.

a) 2.6893 b) 0.3249 c) 5.6023 d) 0.0525

Q3 Round the following numbers to the number of significant figures (s.f.) indicated.

a) 4589 — to 1 s.f. b) 56 986 — to 3 s.f. c) 6.792 — to 2 s.f.
d) 360.8 — to 1 s.f. e) 6527 — to 2 s.f. f) 756 557 — to 3 s.f.

Q4 Jade buys four items costing £1.35, £8.52, £14.09 and £17.93.
Estimate how much she spent by rounding each price to the nearest pound.

Q5 By rounding each number to 1 s.f., estimate each of the following calculations.

a) $\frac{64.4 \times 5.6}{17 \times 9.5}$ b) $\frac{310.33 \times 2.68}{316.39 \times 0.82}$ c) $\frac{13.7 \times 5.2}{12.3 \div 3.9}$

Q6 a) Pens cost 32 pence each. Estimate the cost of 14 pens.
Give your answer in pounds.

b) Is your answer to a) an underestimate or an overestimate?
Give a reason for your answer.

Q7 a) Work out the value of $24.37 \div \sqrt{3.9}$.
Write down all the numbers on our calculator.

b) Use an estimate to decide whether your answer to part a) is sensible.

Q8 Write down the error interval for the following rounded numbers.

a) $a = 50$ to 1 s.f. b) $b = 5690$ to 3 s.f. c) $c = 7$ to 1 s.f.
d) $d = 360$ to 2 s.f. e) $e = 6500$ to 2 s.f. f) $f = 757\ 000$ to 3 s.f.

Q9 Given that the following values have been truncated to 2 d.p.,
find the error interval for each value.

a) $s = 6.57$ b) $t = 25.71$ c) $w = 13.29$

Exam-Style Questions

Q1 Write the number 45.768 to 1 decimal place.

[1 mark]

Q2 a) Work out $\frac{3.5^4}{\sqrt{0.007}}$. Write down your entire calculator display.

[2 marks]

b) Write your answer to part a):

(i) to 3 decimal places

[1 mark]

(ii) to 3 significant figures

[1 mark]

Q3 $x = \frac{628}{\sqrt{97} + 9.6}$

a) By rounding each number to 1 significant figure, estimate the value of x.

[2 marks]

b) Explain why your answer in part a) is an underestimate of the actual value of x.

[1 mark]

Q4 The audience at a rock concert, r, was 7300, correct to the nearest hundred.
Write down the error interval for r.

[2 marks]

Q5 The weight of a dog, w is 8 kg, rounded to the nearest kg.

a) Write down the error interval for w.

[2 marks]

b) Another dog weighs 6 kg, rounded to the nearest kg.
Kayla says "the total weight of the two dogs must be at least 14 kg."
Give an example to show that Kayla is wrong.

[2 marks]

3.1 Squares, Cubes and Roots

Section 3 is all about powers — where numbers are multiplied by themselves a number of times. Squares and cubes are important types of powers, so make sure you get your head around them.

Squares and Cubes

Learning Objectives — Spec Ref N6:
- Recognise square numbers and cube numbers.
- Evaluate square numbers and cube numbers.

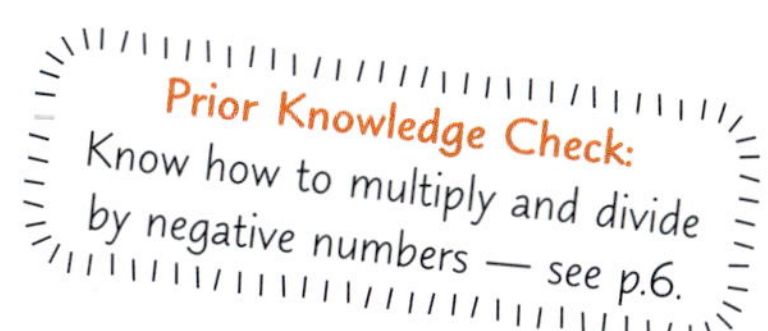

Prior Knowledge Check:
Know how to multiply and divide by negative numbers — see p.6.

Squares show that a number is multiplied by itself.
For example, $4 \times 4 = 4^2 = 16$ is the **square** of 4, and 16 is called a **square number**.

If you square a number, you always get a **positive** answer because you're multiplying the **same signs** together.

The first 10 square numbers are shown in this table.

1^2	2^2	3^2	4^2	5^2	6^2	7^2	8^2	9^2	10^2
1	4	9	16	25	36	49	64	81	100

Cubes show that a number is multiplied by itself and then by itself again.
For example $4 \times 4 \times 4 = 4^3 = 64$ is the **cube** of 4, and 64 is called a **cube number**.

Cubing a number can give a **positive or negative** answer since there are **three multiples** of the same sign — the answer will be the same sign as whatever the **original** number was.

The first 5 cube numbers are shown in this table.

1^3	2^3	3^3	4^3	5^3
1	8	27	64	125

Example 1

Find: a) 5^2 — $5^2 = 5 \times 5 = \mathbf{25}$

b) $(-5)^2$ — $(-5)^2 = -5 \times -5 = \mathbf{25}$

c) 5^3 — $5^3 = 5 \times 5 \times 5 = \mathbf{125}$

d) $(-5)^3$ — $(-5)^3 = -5 \times -5 \times -5 = \mathbf{-125}$

Exercise 1

Q1 Evaluate the following. Use a calculator where necessary.

a) 6^2 b) 12^2 c) 15^2 d) 20^2

e) $(-4)^2$ f) 0.3^2 g) 0.6^2 h) $(-0.2)^2$

Q2 Evaluate the following. Use a calculator where necessary.

a) 3^3 b) 6^3 c) 11^3 d) 20^3

e) $(-3)^3$ f) $(-10)^3$ g) 0.4^3 h) $(-0.5)^3$

Square Roots

Learning Objective — Spec Ref N6/N7:
Evaluate square roots.

Finding a **square root** is the **opposite** of squaring.
A square root of x is a number that **multiplies with itself** to give x.

Every **positive** number has **two** square roots — one **positive** ($\sqrt{x}$) and one **negative** ($-\sqrt{x}$).

For example, the positive square root of 2 is $\sqrt{2}$.
And the negative square root of 2 is $-\sqrt{2}$.

Negative numbers **don't have** square roots.

$$\sqrt{x} \times \sqrt{x} = (\sqrt{x})^2 = x$$
$$(-\sqrt{x}) \times (-\sqrt{x}) = (-\sqrt{x})^2 = x$$

Example 2

Find both square roots of 16.

1. $4^2 = 16$, so the positive square root is 4. $\sqrt{16} = \mathbf{4}$
2. There's also the negative square root. Remember, $(-4) \times (-4) = 16$ too. $-\sqrt{16} = \mathbf{-4}$

Tip: Make sure you know your square numbers — then it'll be easy to write down their square roots.

Exercise 2

Q1 Find the positive and negative square roots of each of these numbers. 

a) 1 b) 4 c) 9 d) 16

e) 25 f) 36 g) 64 h) 100

Q2 Calculate the following.

a) $\sqrt{49}$ b) $-\sqrt{49}$ c) $\sqrt{81}$ d) $-\sqrt{81}$

e) $\sqrt{121}$ f) $\sqrt{169}$ g) $-\sqrt{144}$ h) $\sqrt{400}$

Q3 Find both square roots of the following numbers. Use a calculator where necessary.

a) 64 b) 121 c) 10 000 d) 196

Q4 Calculate the following.

a) $\sqrt{9}+\sqrt{16}$ b) $\sqrt{25}-\sqrt{4}$ c) $\sqrt{100}-\sqrt{49}$

Cube Roots

Learning Objective — Spec Ref N6/N7:
Evaluate cube roots.

The **cube root** of a number x is the number that when **multiplied by itself** and then **by itself again** gives x. Finding a cube root is the **opposite of cubing**.

Every number has **exactly one** cube root.
The symbol $\sqrt[3]{\ }$ is used for cube roots.

$$\sqrt[3]{x}\times\sqrt[3]{x}\times\sqrt[3]{x}=(\sqrt[3]{x})^3=x$$

Example 3

Find the cube root of: a) 64 b) –64

a) $4^3 = 64$, so the cube root of 64 is 4. $\sqrt[3]{64} = \mathbf{4}$

b) $(-4)^3 = -64$, so the cube root of –64 is –4. $\sqrt[3]{-64} = \mathbf{-4}$

Tip: Just like square numbers, knowing your cube numbers makes finding cube roots much easier.

Exercise 3

Q1 Copy and complete the table.

x	1	8	27	1000	–1	–8	–27	–1000
$\sqrt[3]{x}$				10				

Q2 Find the following cube roots. Use a calculator where necessary.

a) $\sqrt[3]{64}$ b) $\sqrt[3]{125}$ c) $\sqrt[3]{1331}$ d) $\sqrt[3]{-64}$

e) $\sqrt[3]{-125}$ f) $\sqrt[3]{512}$ g) $\sqrt[3]{216}$ h) $\sqrt[3]{-729}$

Q3 Calculate:

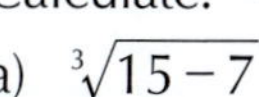

a) $\sqrt[3]{15-7}$ b) $\sqrt[3]{39+5^2}$ c) $\sqrt[3]{4^2-43}$

3.2 Indices

Indices (or powers) are a useful shorthand that allow you to write repeated multiplications with just two symbols — a base and an index. Squares and cubes are two simple examples of indices.

Indices

Tip: Indices is the plural of index.

Learning Objective — Spec Ref A1/A4:
Work with numbers in index notation.

Powers show something that is being multiplied by itself. Powers are usually written using '**index notation**' — involving a **base** and an **index**.

base → 2^3 ← index

For example, $2 \times 2 \times 2 \times 2 = 2^4$ — this is four 2's multiplied together, and is read as "**2 to the power 4**".
And $5 \times 5 \times 5 \times 5 \times 5 \times 5 = 5^6$ — this is six 5's multiplied together, and is read as "**5 to the power 6**".

Example 1

a) Rewrite $3 \times 3 \times 3 \times 3 \times 3$ using index notation.

There are five 3's multiplied together. $3 \times 3 \times 3 \times 3 \times 3 = \mathbf{3^5}$

b) Rewrite 100 000 using powers of 10.

Multiply 10 by 10 until you reach 100 000. $100\,000 = 10 \times 10 \times 10 \times 10 \times 10 = \mathbf{10^5}$

c) Evaluate 5^4.

There are four 5's multiplied together. $5^4 = 5 \times 5 \times 5 \times 5 = \mathbf{625}$

Exercise 1

Q1 Write the following using index notation.

a) 3×3 b) $2 \times 2 \times 2$ c) $7 \times 7 \times 7 \times 7 \times 7$
d) $9 \times 9 \times 9 \times 9 \times 9 \times 9$ e) $12 \times 12 \times 12 \times 12$ f) $17 \times 17 \times 17$

Q2 a) Use a calculator to evaluate these powers of 10.

(i) 10^5 (ii) 10^7 (iii) 10^8 (iv) 10^9

b) Copy and complete the following sentences. (Here, n is a positive whole number.)

(i) *"10^{15} can be written as a '1' followed by ________ zeros."*

(ii) *"10^n can be written as a '1' followed by ________ zeros."*

Q3 Rewrite the following as powers of 10.

a) 100 b) 1000 c) 10 000 d) 1 million

Q4 Use a calculator to evaluate these powers.

a) 2^4 b) 2^5 c) 3^4 d) 4^6
e) 6^4 f) 17^3 g) 5^5 h) 3^5

Q5 Evaluate the following using a calculator.
(Remember to work out powers **before** carrying out any addition or subtraction.)

a) $3^4 + 2^3$ b) $2^6 + 3^5$ c) $3^7 - 4^2$ d) $10^3 - 6^4$

Q6 Evaluate the following using a calculator.

a) $8^7 \div 4^6$ b) $10^4 \times 10^3$ c) $2^4 \times 2^2$ d) $3^4 \div 5^4$

Q7 Evaluate the following using a calculator.

a) $(5 - 2)^3$ b) $(2^2)^2$ c) $(3^2)^2$ d) $(8 - 5)^4$
e) $(7 + 3)^5$ f) $6^4 - 7^2$ g) $2 + 10^4$ h) $(150 - 50)^6$

Example 2

a) Rewrite $a \times a \times a \times a \times a \times a$ using index notation.

There are 6 a's multiplied together. $a \times a \times a \times a \times a \times a = \boldsymbol{a^6}$

b) Rewrite $b \times b \times b \times b \times c \times c$ using index notation.

There are 4 b's multiplied together, and 2 c's. $b \times b \times b \times b \times c \times c = b^4 \times c^2 = \boldsymbol{b^4c^2}$

Tip: Indices work in exactly the same way for letters as they do for numbers.

Exercise 2

Q1 Rewrite the following using index notation.

a) $h \times h \times h \times h$ b) $t \times t \times t \times t \times t$ c) $s \times s \times s \times s \times s \times s \times s$

Q2 Rewrite the following using index notation.

a) $a \times a \times b \times b \times b$ b) $k \times k \times k \times k \times f \times f \times f$ c) $m \times m \times m \times m \times n \times n$
d) $s \times s \times s \times s \times t$ e) $w \times w \times w \times v \times v \times v$ f) $p \times p \times q \times q \times q \times q \times q$

Q3 Evaluate these powers using a calculator, given that $x = 2$ and $y = 5$.

a) x^2y^2 b) x^3y^2 c) x^2y^3
d) x^5y^2 e) x^4y^3 f) x^4y^4

3.3 Laws of Indices

The laws of indices are important rules that help you work with expressions involving powers.

Working with Indices

Learning Objective — Spec Ref N7/A4:
Use the laws of indices to simplify expressions.

You can use the laws of indices to multiply and divide powers with the same base.

1) To **multiply** two powers with the same base, **add** the indices: $a^m \times a^n = a^{m+n}$
2) To **divide** two powers with the same base, **subtract** the indices: $a^m \div a^n = a^{m-n}$
3) To **raise** one power to another power, **multiply** the indices: $(a^m)^n = a^{m \times n}$
4) To raise a **fraction** to a power, apply the power to the **numerator** and **denominator** (see p.63): $\left(\frac{a}{b}\right)^n = \frac{a^n}{b^n}$

There are two other important index facts you need to know.

1) Anything to the **power 1** is **itself**: $a^1 = a$
2) Anything to the **power 0** is **1**: $a^0 = 1$

Example 1

Simplify the following, leaving the answers in index form.

a) $3^8 \times 3^5$ — This is multiplication, so add the indices. $3^8 \times 3^5 = 3^{8+5} = \mathbf{3^{13}}$

b) $\frac{10^8}{10^5}$ — This is division ($\frac{10^8}{10^5} = 10^8 \div 10^5$), so subtract the indices. $10^8 \div 10^5 = 10^{8-5} = \mathbf{10^3}$

c) $(2^7)^2$ — For one power raised to another power, multiply the indices. $(2^7)^2 = 2^{7\times 2} = \mathbf{2^{14}}$

d) $a^7 \times a^3$ — The laws of indices work in exactly the same way with variables. $a^7 \times a^3 = a^{7+3} = \mathbf{a^{10}}$

Exercise 1

Q1 Simplify these expressions. Leave your answers in index form.

a) $3^2 \times 3^6$ b) $10^7 \times 10^3$ c) $4^7 \times 4^4$ d) 7×7^6

Q2 Simplify these expressions. Leave your answers in index form.

a) $6^7 \div 6^4$ b) $8^6 \div 8^3$ c) $5^7 \div 5^2$ d) $6^8 \div 6^6$

Q3 Simplify these expressions. Leave your answers in index form.

a) $(4^3)^3$ b) $(11^2)^5$ c) $(100^3)^{23}$

d) $\frac{2^8}{2^5}$ e) $\left(\frac{2^7}{5}\right)^3$ f) $\left(\frac{4^6}{4^3}\right)^2$

Q4 Simplify these expressions. Leave your answers in index form.

a) $4^5 \times 4^{11}$ b) $12^7 \div 12^3$ c) $8^2 \times 8^9$ d) $(6^8)^4$

e) $(3^{12})^4$ f) $7^{11} \div 7^6$ g) $4^{15} \div 4^7$ h) $(11^0)^9$

Q5 For each of the following, find the number that should replace the square.

a) $s^9 \times s^{■} = s^{14}$ b) $t^5 \div t^{■} = t^3$ c) $r^7 \times r^{■} = r^{13}$ d) $(p^7)^{■} = p^{49}$

e) $k^{■} \div k^5 = 1$ f) $a^{■} \times a^7 = a^{15}$ g) $m^5 \div m^{-4} = m^{■}$ h) $(q^5)^{■} = q^{25}$

Negative Indices

Prior Knowledge Check:
Know how to find the reciprocal of a number — see p.80.

You can evaluate powers that have a **negative index** by taking the **reciprocal** of the base and making the index **positive**.

The reciprocal is found by turning the base **upside down**.

E.g. the reciprocal of a is $\frac{1}{a}$ and the reciprocal of $\frac{a}{b}$ is $\frac{b}{a}$

$$\boldsymbol{a^{-n} = \frac{1}{a^n}}$$

$$\boldsymbol{\left(\frac{a}{b}\right)^{-m} = \left(\frac{b}{a}\right)^m = \frac{b^m}{a^m}}$$

The **laws of indices** work in exactly the **same way** for negative indices.
It's often easier to leave the index negative when simplifying expressions.

Example 2

Evaluate 5^{-3}

1. Take the reciprocal of the base and make the index positive.
2. Evaluate the denominator.

$$5^{-3} = \frac{1}{5^3} = \frac{1}{5 \times 5 \times 5} = \mathbf{\frac{1}{125}}$$

Exercise 2

Q1 Evaluate the following. Give fractions in their simplest form.

a) 8^{-2} b) 2^{-3} c) 5^{-2} d) 3^{-3}

e) 2^{-4} f) $\left(\frac{1}{9}\right)^{-2}$ g) $\left(\frac{4}{5}\right)^{-2}$ h) $\left(\frac{2}{6}\right)^{-3}$

Q2 Simplify these expressions. Leave your answers in index form.

a) $j^{-13} \div j^7$ b) $(n^7)^{-3}$ c) $p^{-8} \times p^{-6}$ d) $y^8 \div y^{-2}$

e) $(k^{-3})^6$ f) $\frac{b^5}{b^9}$ g) $d^{-7} \times d^2$ h) $\frac{x^{60}}{x^{-8}}$

Q3 For each of the following, find the number that should replace the square.

a) $l^{■} \times l^{-8} = l^3$ b) $b^{■} \div b^7 = b^{-10}$ c) $c^{-15} \times c^{■} = c^8$ d) $(y^{-4})^{■} = y^{16}$

Calculating with Indices

Learning Objective — Spec Ref N7/A4:
Use the laws of indices to work with complex expressions.

Prior Knowledge Check:
Be able to use the laws of indices — see page 44.

Complicated expressions, made up of many terms with indices, can often be **simplified** to a single term by using the **laws of indices**.

Example 3

Simplify each expression without using a calculator. Leave your answers in index form.

a) $2^6 \times 2^8 \div 2^2$

Apply the index laws to each step. $2^6 \times 2^8 \div 2^2 = 2^{6+8-2} = \mathbf{2^{12}}$

b) $\dfrac{2^3 \times 2^5}{2^8 \div 2^6}$

1. Work out the top and bottom lines of the fraction separately.
2. Then you can do the final division.

$$\frac{2^3 \times 2^5}{2^8 \div 2^6} = \frac{2^{3+5}}{2^{8-6}} = \frac{2^8}{2^2} = 2^{8-2} = \mathbf{2^6}$$

Tip: These questions can look scary at first, but once you break them into steps they really aren't that bad.

Exercise 3

In Questions 1 and 2, simplify each expression, leaving your answers in index form.

Q1 a) $3^2 \times 3^5 \times 3^7$ b) $(8^6)^2 \times 8^5$ c) $(12^8 \div 12^4)^3$ d) $(4^3)^6 \div 4^{16}$

Q2 a) $\dfrac{3^4 \times 3^5}{3^6}$ b) $\dfrac{8^{25} \div 8^2}{8^6 \times 8^{10}}$ c) $\dfrac{(7^5)^7 \div 7^{12}}{7^5 \times 7^9}$ d) $\dfrac{(5^{10} \div 5^8)^4}{5^4 \div 5^2}$

Q3 Which of the expressions in the box below are equal to 1?

$\dfrac{4^4 \div 4^3}{4}$ $\dfrac{7^{16}}{7^8 \times 7^2}$ $\dfrac{3^8 - 3^7}{3}$ $\dfrac{5^5 \times 5^9}{(5^2)^7}$ $\dfrac{(9^2)^2 - 9^0}{9^3}$

Q4 Simplify these expressions. Leave your answers in index form.

a) $\left(\dfrac{2^{-5} \times 2^7}{2^3}\right)^5$ b) $\left(\dfrac{7^3}{7}\right)^3 \times 7^{-2}$ c) $\dfrac{9^{-3} \times 9^{15}}{(9^{-3})^{-2}}$ d) $\left(\dfrac{3^{-8} \times 3^{12}}{3^2}\right)^{-6}$

Q5 Simplify each of the following expressions.

a) $a^6 \times a^5 \div a^4$ b) $(p^5 \div p^3)^6$ c) $\dfrac{(t^6 \div t^3)^4}{t^9 \div t^4}$ d) $\dfrac{(c^{-4})^3}{c^{-8} \div c^4}$

3.4 Standard Form

Standard form allows you to write very large or very small numbers without having to write lots of zeros. E.g. 12 000 000 000 can be written as 1.2×10^{10} and 0.000 000 345 as 3.45×10^{-7}.

Standard Form

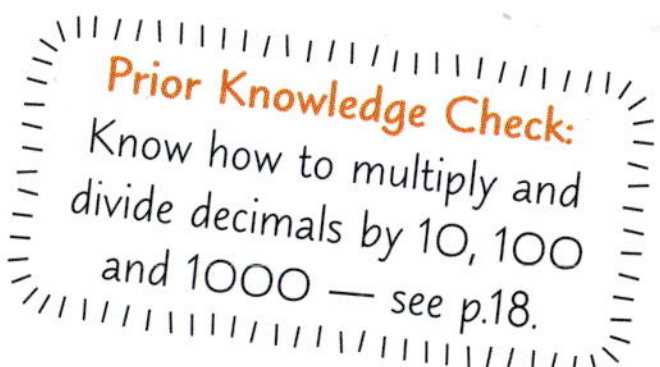

Prior Knowledge Check:
Know how to multiply and divide decimals by 10, 100 and 1000 — see p.18.

Learning Objective — Spec Ref N9:
Write and interpret numbers in standard form.

In **standard form** (or standard index form), numbers are written like this:

$$A \times 10^n$$

A can be **any number** between 1 and 10 (but not 10 itself)

n can be **any integer** (whole number).

There are three vital things you need to know about standard form:

- The **front number**, A, must always be **between 1 and 10** (i.e. $1 \le A < 10$).
- The power of 10, n, is how far the **decimal point moves**.
- n is **positive** for **BIG** numbers and **negative** for **SMALL** numbers.

Tip: It's handy to think of the decimal point moving, but it's actually the digits that shift around it.

Example 1

Write these numbers in standard form: a) 360 000 b) 0.000036

a) 1. Move the decimal point until 360 000 becomes 3.6. The decimal point has moved 5 places.

2. The number is big so n must be +5.

$3\,6\,0\,0\,0\,0.0 = \mathbf{3.6 \times 10^5}$

b) 1. As in part a), the decimal point moves 5 places to make the number 3.6.

2. The number is small so n must be –5.

$0.0\,0\,0\,0\,3\,6 = \mathbf{3.6 \times 10^{-5}}$

Tip: Once you have an answer, check that it satisfies the three vital things described above.

Exercise 1

Q1 Write the following numbers in standard form.

a) 250 b) 7340 c) 48 000 d) 5 900 000

Q2 Write the following numbers in standard form.

a) 0.375 b) 0.0067 c) 0.000078 d) 0.07070

Example 2

Write the following standard form numbers as ordinary numbers.

a) $\mathbf{3.5 \times 10^3}$

1. The power is positive so the number will be big.
2. The decimal point moves 3 places. $3.5 \times 10^3 = \mathbf{3\,5\,0\,0.0}$

b) $\mathbf{4.67 \times 10^{-5}}$

1. The power is negative so the number will be small.
2. The decimal point moves 5 places. $4.67 \times 10^{-5} = \mathbf{0.0\,0\,0\,0\,4\,6\,7}$

Exercise 2

Q1 Write the following out as ordinary numbers.

a) 3×10^6 b) 9.4×10^4 c) 1.989×10^8 d) 7.20×10^0

e) 3.56×10^{-6} f) 4.23×10^{-2} g) 8.88×10^{-5} h) 1.9×10^{-8}

Calculations in Standard Form

Learning Objectives — Spec Ref N9:

- Multiply and divide numbers in standard form.
- Add and subtract numbers in standard form.

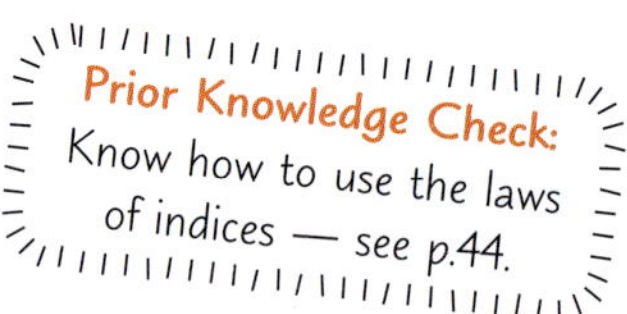

Prior Knowledge Check:
Know how to use the laws of indices — see p.44.

To **multiply** or **divide** numbers in standard form:

- **Rearrange** the calculations so that the **front numbers** are **together**.
E.g. rewrite $(4 \times 10^6) \times (8 \times 10^2)$ as $(4 \times 8) \times (10^6 \times 10^2)$.
- **Multiply or divide** the front numbers and use the **laws of indices** (p.44) to multiply or divide the powers of 10.
- Make sure your answer is still in **standard form** — if not, use the method from p.47.

Example 3

Calculate $(2.4 \times 10^7) \times (5.2 \times 10^3)$. Give your answer in standard form.

1. Rearrange to put the front numbers and powers of 10 together. $(2.4 \times 5.2) \times (10^7 \times 10^3)$
2. Multiply the front numbers and use the laws of indices. $= 12.48 \times 10^{7+3}$
3. 12.48 isn't between 1 and 10 so this isn't in standard form. $= 12.48 \times 10^{10}$
Convert 12.48 to standard form. $= 1.248 \times 10 \times 10^{10}$
4. Add the indices again to get the answer in standard form. $= \mathbf{1.248 \times 10^{11}}$

Example 4

Calculate $(9.6 \times 10^7) \div (1.2 \times 10^4)$. Give your answer in standard form.

1. Rewrite as a fraction.
2. Separate the front numbers and powers of 10.
3. Simplify the two fractions.

$$\frac{9.6 \times 10^7}{1.2 \times 10^4} = \frac{9.6}{1.2} \times \frac{10^7}{10^4}$$

$$= 8 \times 10^{7-4} = \mathbf{8 \times 10^3}$$

Exercise 3

Give your answers to these questions in standard form.

Q1 a) $(3 \times 10^7) \times (2 \times 10^4)$ b) $(4 \times 10^9) \times (2 \times 10^{-4})$ c) $(6 \times 10^5) \times (1.4 \times 10^2)$

Q2 a) $(9 \times 10^6) \div (3 \times 10^4)$ b) $(1.8 \times 10^{-4}) \div (0.9 \times 10^8)$ c) $(8.1 \times 10^{-1}) \div (9 \times 10^{-3})$

To **add** or **subtract** numbers in standard form:

- Check the **powers of 10** are the **same** in both terms.
- **Add or subtract** the front numbers.
- Make sure your answer is still in **standard form** at the end.

Example 5

Calculate $(3.7 \times 10^3) + (8.2 \times 10^3)$ without using a calculator.
Give your answer in standard form.

1. The powers of 10 match so add the numbers.
2. The answer isn't in standard form (because 11.9 is bigger than 10), so convert it to standard form.

$(3.7 + 8.2) \times 10^3$

$= 11.9 \times 10^3$

$= 1.19 \times 10 \times 10^3$

$= \mathbf{1.19 \times 10^4}$

Tip: For subtraction questions, use the same method, but subtract the front numbers instead.

Exercise 4

Give your answers to these questions in standard form.

Q1 a) $(5 \times 10^3) + (3 \times 10^3)$ b) $(6.4 \times 10^2) + (3.2 \times 10^2)$ c) $(6.9 \times 10^{-4}) + (3.8 \times 10^{-4})$

Q2 a) $(4.5 \times 10^{-2}) - (3.3 \times 10^{-2})$ b) $(1.8 \times 10^4) - (1.2 \times 10^4)$ c) $(6.4 \times 10^2) - (6.3 \times 10^2)$

Review Exercise

Q1 Evaluate the following. Use a calculator where necessary.

a) $(-5)^3$ b) 0.5^3 c) $(-0.3)^3$ d) $(-12)^3$

e) 0.1^2 f) $(-0.4)^2$ g) $((-2)^2)^3$ h) $((-2)^3)^2$

Q2 Evaluate the following using a calculator.

a) $3^2 - 2^3$ b) $5^2 - 6^2$ c) 3×2^8 d) 8×5^4

Q3 Evaluate the following. Use a calculator where necessary.

a) $-\sqrt{36}$ b) $\sqrt{361}$ c) $\sqrt[3]{-343}$ d) $-\sqrt{10^2 - 19}$

Q4 Rewrite the following using index notation.

a) $k \times k \times l \times l \times k \times k$ b) $z \times y \times y \times y$ c) $m \times n \times m \times n \times m$

Q5 Simplify these expressions. Leave your answers in index form. 

a) $a^6 \times a^4$ b) $15^{12} \div 15^{-14}$ c) $(45^2)^{-9}$ d) $\dfrac{20^{222}}{20^{210}}$

Q6 Evaluate the following. Give any fractions in their simplest forms. 

a) 8^{-1} b) 4^{-2} c) $\left(\dfrac{1}{3}\right)^{-3}$ d) $\left(\dfrac{4}{6}\right)^{-2}$

Q7 Simplify the following. Leave your answer in index form.

a) $\dfrac{4^4 \times 4^6}{4^8 \times 4}$ b) $\dfrac{(5^5 \times 5^5)^2}{5^8 \div 5^3}$ c) $\left(\dfrac{2^5 \times 2^5}{2^3}\right)^4$

Q8 Write the following numbers in standard form.

a) 330 b) 2 750 000 c) 0.0025 d) 0.0005002

Q9 Write the following out as ordinary numbers.

a) 4×10^2 b) 8.8×10^5 c) 6.69×10^{-1} d) 7.05×10^{-6}

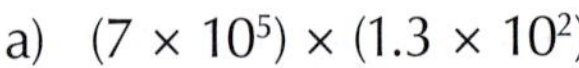

Q10 Do these questions. Give your answers in standard form.

a) $(7 \times 10^5) \times (1.3 \times 10^2)$ b) $(8.8 \times 10^3) \div (4 \times 10^8)$

c) $(1.9 \times 10^6) + (9.1 \times 10^6)$ d) $(5.9 \times 10^{-8}) - (3.4 \times 10^{-8})$

Exam-Style Questions

Q1 Find the value of $(4.2 - 0.81)^2 + \sqrt{289}$

[1 mark]

Q2 Simplify the following expressions:

a) $2x^3 \times 4x^4$

[1 mark]

b) $(3y^2)^4$

[2 marks]

c) $5z^0$

[1 mark]

Q3 a) Find the value of n when $4^n = 64$

[1 mark]

b) Find the value of k when $2^2 \times 3^k \times 5 = 540$.

[3 marks]

Q4 Mustafa has attempted to write the numbers 650 million and 0.000234 in standard form. His working is shown below.
For each attempt, explain a mistake that Mustafa has made.

a) 650 million = 650 000 000 = 0.65×10^9

[1 mark]

b) $0.000234 = 2.34 \times 10^4$

[1 mark]

Q5 Here is some information about Mercury and Venus. 

Mercury	
Number of Earth days to orbit Sun	88
Distance travelled in orbit of Sun	3.6×10^8 km

Venus	
Number of Earth days to orbit Sun	225
Distance travelled in orbit of Sun	6.8×10^8 km

Calculate which planet travels further in one Earth day, and state by how much.
Give your answer in standard form to a suitable degree of accuracy.

[5 marks]

4.1 Finding Multiples and Factors

To tackle multiples and factors, you need to know your times tables — that's all there is to it.

Multiples

Learning Objective — Spec Ref N4:
Identify and find multiples and common multiples.

A **multiple** of a number is one that is in its **times table**.
E.g. the multiples of 2 are 2, 4, 6, 8, 10... and the multiples of 5 are 5, 10, 15, 20, 25...

A **common multiple** of two (or more) numbers is a multiple of both (or all) of those numbers.
10 is in both lists above, so 10 is a common multiple of 2 and 5.
Both 2 and 5 divide into 10 exactly.

Example 1

a) List the multiples of 5 between 23 and 43.

Starting at 20, the times table of 5 is: 20, 25, 30, 35, 40, 45...
So the multiples between 23 and 43 are: **25, 30, 35, 40**

b) Which of the numbers in the box below are:

24	7	28	35	39

(i) multiples of 3?

3 divides into 24 and 39 exactly — so 24 and 39 are multiples of 3. But 3 doesn't divide exactly into 7, 28 or 35 — these aren't multiples of 3.

(i) **24 and 39**

(ii) multiples of 5?

The only number in the box that 5 divides into exactly is 35.

(ii) **35**

(iii) common multiples of 4 and 7?

The multiples of 4 are 24 and 28, while the multiples of 7 are 7, 28 and 35. So the only common multiple is 28.

(iii) **28**

Exercise 1

Q1 List the first five multiples of: a) 4 b) 10 c) 3 d) 6 e) 7

Q2 a) List the multiples of 8 between 10 and 20.
b) List the multiples of 9 between 20 and 50.

Q3 Write down the numbers from the box that are:
a) multiples of 10
b) multiples of 15
c) common multiples of 10 and 15

5	10	15	20	25	30	35
40	45	50	55	60	65	70
75	80	85	90	95	100	105

Q4 List all the common multiples of 5 and 6 between 1 and 40.

Q5 List the common multiples of 3 and 4 between 19 and 35.

Factors

Learning Objective — Spec Ref N4:
Identify and find factors and common factors.

The **factors** of a number are the numbers that divide into it exactly. E.g. the factors of 8 are 1, 2, 4 and 8 — all these numbers divide into 8 exactly.

A **common factor** of two (or more) numbers is a factor of both (or all) those numbers. E.g. the factors of 12 are 1, 2, 3, 4, 6 and 12, so the common factors of 8 and 12 are 1, 2 and 4.

Tip: Any two factors that multiply to give the number are called a **factor pair.** For example, 3 and 6 are a factor pair of 18.

Example 2

Write down all the factors of 18.

1. Check if 1, 2, 3, 4... divide into the number. Write down each number that divides in exactly, and also its 'factor partner' in a multiplication.

$1 \times 18 = 18$ — so 1 and 18 are factors
$2 \times 9 = 18$ — so 2 and 9 are factors
$3 \times 6 = 18$ — so 3 and 6 are factors
$4 \times - = 18$ — so 4 is not a factor
$5 \times - = 18$ — so 5 is not a factor
$6 \times 3 = 18$ — 6 and 3 are repeated so stop.

2. Stop checking when you reach a number already in an earlier multiplication, or when a factor is repeated in a multiplication.

3. List all the numbers in your multiplications.

So the factors of 18 are **1, 2, 3, 6, 9, 18.**

Example 3

Find the common factors of 6 and 20.

1. Find the factors of 6 and 20.

$1 \times 6 = 6$ — so 1 and 6 are factors
$2 \times 3 = 6$ — so 2 and 3 are factors
$3 \times 2 = 6$ — 3 and 2 are repeated so stop.

So the factors of 6 are: **1, 2, 3, 6**

$1 \times 20 = 20$ — so 1 and 20 are factors
$2 \times 10 = 20$ — so 2 and 10 are factors
$3 \times - = 20$ — so 3 is not a factor
$4 \times 5 = 20$ — so 4 and 5 are factors
$5 \times 4 = 20$ — 5 and 4 are repeated so stop.

So the factors of 20 are: **1, 2, 4, 5, 10, 20**

2. The common factors are the numbers that appear in both lists.

So the common factors of 6 and 20 are **1 and 2**.

Exercise 2

Q1 List the numbers from the box on the right that are factors of: 2 3 5 6 12 15

a) 6 b) 24 c) 30
d) 36 e) 20 f) 45

Q2 List all the factors of the following numbers.

a) 10 b) 4 c) 13
d) 25 e) 24 f) 35

Q3 a) List all the factors of 15.
b) List all the factors of 21.
c) List the common factors of 15 and 21.

Q4 List the common factors of the following pairs of numbers.

a) 15, 20 b) 12, 15 c) 30, 45
d) 50, 90 e) 25, 50 f) 21, 22

Q5 a) Which number is a factor of all other numbers?
b) Which two numbers are factors of all even numbers?
c) Which two numbers must be factors of all numbers whose last digit is 5?

Q6 List the common factors of the following sets of numbers.

a) 15, 20, 25 b) 12, 18, 20
c) 30, 45, 50 d) 15, 16, 17

4.2 Prime Numbers

There's a key definition coming up — prime numbers. Once you know what they are (and how to find them), you can move on to writing numbers as products of prime factors.

Prime Numbers

Learning Objective — Spec Ref N4:
Identify and find prime numbers.

A **prime number** is a number that has no other factors except **itself** and **1**.

In other words, the only numbers that **divide exactly** into a prime number are itself and 1.

Here are a few things to note about prime numbers:

- 1 is **not** classed as a prime number — this is a common mistake.
- 2 is the only **even** prime number — so any other even number is **not** prime.
- Prime numbers end in **1**, **3**, **7** or **9** (2 and 5 are the only exceptions to this rule). But **not all** numbers ending in 1, 3, 7 or 9 are prime (e.g. $27 = 3 \times 9$, so it isn't prime).

Example 1

Which of the numbers in the box on the right are prime?

16 17 18 19 20

1. Look for factors of each of the numbers.
2. If you can find factors other than 1 and the number itself, then the number isn't prime.
3. If there are no factors other than 1 and the number itself, then the number is prime.

$16 = 2 \times 8$, and so 16 isn't prime
$18 = 3 \times 6$, and so 18 isn't prime
$20 = 4 \times 5$, and so 20 isn't prime

17 has no factors other than 1 and 17.
19 has no factors other than 1 and 19.

So the prime numbers are **17 and 19**.

Exercise 1

Q1 a) Which three numbers in the box on the right are not prime? 31 33 35 37 39

b) Find two factors greater than 1 that multiply together to give each of your answers to a).

Q2 Write down the prime numbers in this list: 5, 15, 22, 34, 47, 51, 59

Q3 Find all the prime numbers between 20 and 30.

Q4 a) For each of the following, find a factor greater than 1 but less than the number itself:
(i) 4 (ii) 14 (iii) 34 (iv) 74

b) Explain why any number with last digit 4 <u>cannot</u> be prime.

Q5 Without doing any calculations, explain how you can tell that none of the following numbers in the list below are prime.

20	30	40	50	70	90	110	130

Writing a Number as a Product of Primes

Learning Objectives — Spec Ref N4:
- Understand the unique factorisation theorem.
- Find the prime factorisation of a number.
- Write a prime factorisation using product notation.

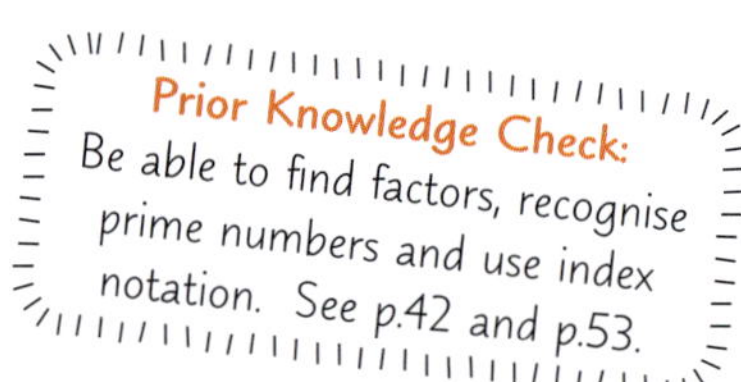

Prior Knowledge Check:
Be able to find factors, recognise prime numbers and use index notation. See p.42 and p.53.

Whole numbers which are **not** prime can be broken down into **prime factors**. The product of these prime factors is the original number — the group of prime factors is known as the **prime factorisation** of the number. For example, the prime factorisation of 28 is $2 \times 2 \times 7$.

The prime factorisation of every number is **unique** — each number only has **one** prime factorisation, and no two numbers can have the **same one**.

To find a prime factorisation, you can use a **factor tree**. A factor tree breaks a number into factors then breaks these factors into smaller factors, and keeps going until all of the factors are prime.

If the prime factorisation has **repeated factors**, you can write it using **index notation** (i.e. as a product of powers). So the prime factorisation of 28 can be written as $2^2 \times 7$.

Example 2

Write 12 as the product of prime factors.

Make a factor tree.

1. First find any two factors whose product is 12. $12 = 2 \times 6$, so create two branches with these factors and circle any factors that are prime.
2. Repeat step 1 for any factors you didn't circle ($6 = 2 \times 3$).
3. Stop when all the branches end in a circle. The product of all the circled primes is the number you started with.

12 → (2), 6
6 → (2), (3)

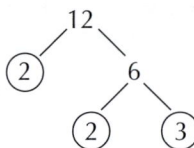

$12 = 2 \times 2 \times 3$, or $\mathbf{12 = 2^2 \times 3}$

Tip: You could have started with any two factors of 12 on the first branches — e.g. 3 and 4. The rest of the tree would look a bit different, but the prime factorisation would be exactly the same.

Exercise 2

In the following questions, write any repeated prime factors as powers.

Q1 a) Copy and complete the following factor trees.

(i)

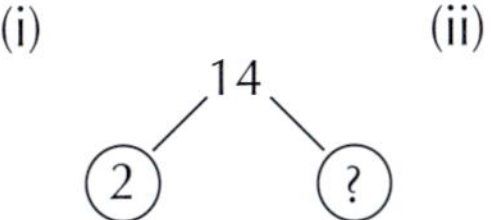

(ii)

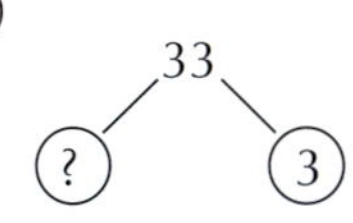

(iii)

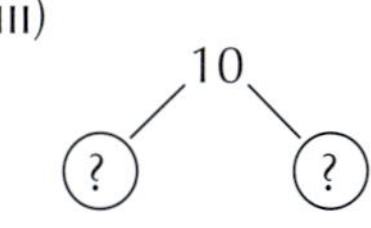

(iv)

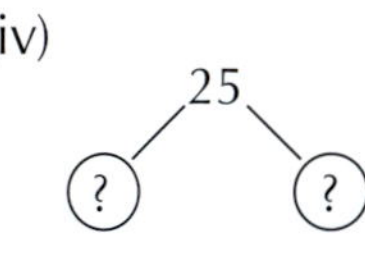

b) Use your factor trees to write the following as products of prime factors.

(i) 14 (ii) 33 (iii) 10 (iv) 25

Q2 Write the following numbers as the product of two prime factors.

a) 15 b) 21 c) 22

d) 6 e) 14 f) 26

Q3 a) Copy and complete the following factor trees.

(i)

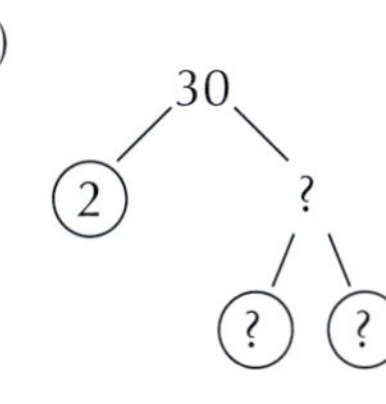

(ii)

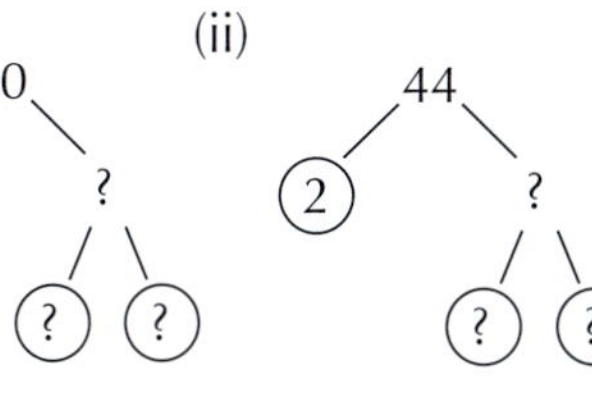

(iii)

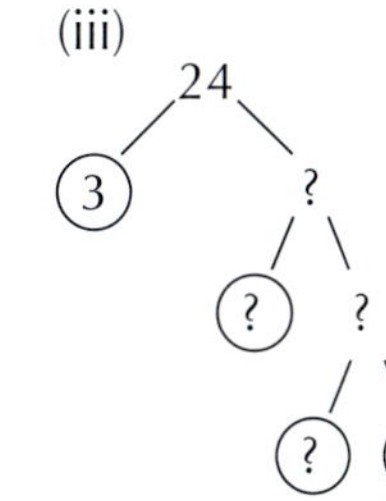

(iv)

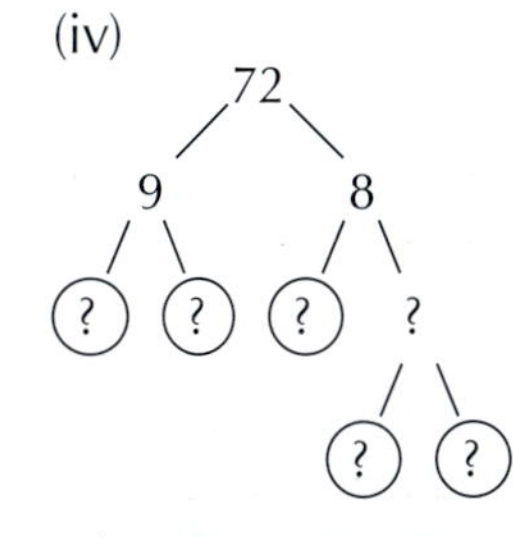

b) Use your factor trees to write the following as the product of prime factors.

(i) 30 (ii) 44 (iii) 24 (iv) 72

Q4 Copy and complete the factor tree on the right and use it to find the prime factorisation of 70.

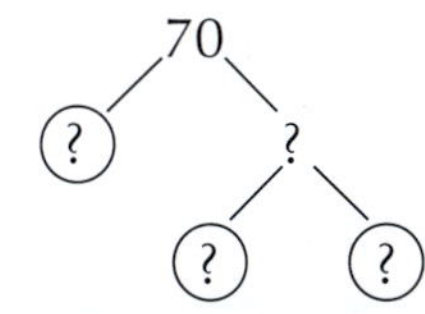

Q5 Use factor trees to write the following numbers as the product of prime factors.

a) 42 b) 84 c) 190 d) 210

Q6 Write the following as the product of prime factors.

a) 128 b) 168 c) 325

d) 98 e) 225 f) 1000

Q7 Square numbers have all their prime factors raised to even powers. For example, $36 = 2^2 \times 3^2$ and $64 = 2^6$.

a) Write 75 as a product of prime factors.

b) What is the smallest number you could multiply 75 by to form a square number? Explain your answer.

4.3 LCM and HCF

Now that you've got your head around multiples and factors, it's time to start looking at the 'lowest common multiple' and 'highest common factor' — or LCM and HCF for short.

Lowest Common Multiple (LCM)

Learning Objectives — Spec Ref N4:
- Understand the term 'lowest common multiple'.
- Be able to find the lowest common multiple of a set of numbers.

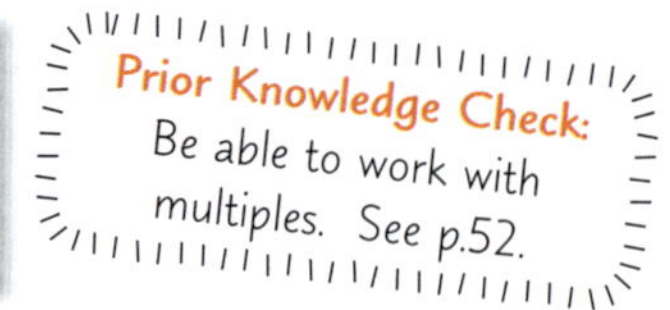

Prior Knowledge Check:
Be able to work with multiples. See p.52.

If you're given two (or more) numbers, then you can find their **lowest common multiple** (LCM).

As the name suggests, the LCM is basically the smallest number that is a multiple of both (or all) of the numbers. In other words:

The LCM is the **smallest** number that will **divide** by **all** the numbers in a list.

Tip: The LCM is the smallest number in the times table of all the numbers in the list.

If you're given a set of numbers, you can find their LCM by **listing multiples** of each number, then identifying the **first one** that appears in **every list**.

Example 1

Find the lowest common multiple (LCM) of 4, 6 and 8.

1. Find the multiples of 4, 6 and 8.
2. The LCM is the smallest number that appears in all three lists.

Multiples of 4 are: 4, 8, 12, 16, 20, 24, 28...
Multiples of 6 are: 6, 12, 18, 24, 30, 36...
Multiples of 8 are: 8, 16, 24, 32, 40, 48...

So the LCM of 4, 6 and 8 is **24**.

Exercise 1

Q1 a) Find the first 5 multiples of 9 and the first 5 multiples of 12.
b) Hence find the LCM of 9 and 12.

Q2 a) Find the first 10 multiples of 5 and the first 10 multiples of 7.
b) Hence find the LCM of 5 and 7.

Q3 Find the LCM of each of the following pairs of numbers.

a) 3 and 4 b) 6 and 8 c) 2 and 10

d) 6 and 7 e) 10 and 15 f) 15 and 20

Q4 Find the LCM of each of the sets of numbers below.

a) 3, 6, 8 b) 3, 5, 6 c) 4, 9, 12

Example 2

Jane and Alec are running around a small circular track.
It takes Jane 10 seconds to run one lap and Alec 12 seconds.

If they both start from the same point on the track at exactly the same time, how long will it be before they next cross the start line together?

1. Find the number of seconds after which Jane will cross the start line.

Jane crosses the start line after the following numbers of seconds: 10, 20, 30, 40, 50, (60), 70...

2. Find the number of seconds after which Alec will cross the start line.

Alec crosses the start line after the following numbers of seconds: 12, 24, 36, 48, (60) 72...

3. Find the smallest number that is in both lists

So they will next cross the start line together after **60 seconds**.

Exercise 2

Q1 Laurence and Naima are cycling around a course. They leave the start-line at the same time and each do 10 laps. It takes Laurence 8 minutes to do one lap and Naima 12 minutes.

a) After how many minutes does Laurence pass the start-line? Write down all possible answers.

b) After how many minutes does Naima pass the start-line? Write down all possible answers.

c) When will they first pass the start-line together?

Q2 Mike visits Oscar every 4 days, while Narinda visits Oscar every 5 days. If they both visited today, how many days will it be before they visit on the same day again?

Q3 Jill divides a pile of sweets into 5 equal piles. Kay then divides the same sweets into 7 equal piles. What is the smallest number of sweets there could be?

Q4 A garden centre has between 95 and 205 potted plants.
They can be arranged exactly in rows of 25 and exactly in rows of 30.
How many plants are there?

Highest Common Factor (HCF)

Learning Objectives — Spec Ref N4:
- Understand the term 'highest common factor'.
- Be able to find the highest common factor of a set of numbers.

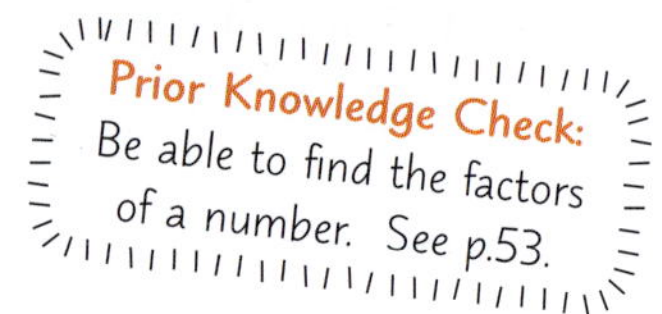
Prior Knowledge Check:
Be able to find the factors of a number. See p.53.

You may also be asked to find the **highest common factor** (HCF) of a list of numbers. The HCF is just the largest value that is a factor of all the numbers in the list. In other words:

HCF is the **largest** number that will **divide into all** the numbers in your list.

To find the HCF of a set of numbers, list the factors of each number, then pick the biggest one that's in every list.

Example 3

Find the highest common factor of 12 and 15.

1. Find the factors of both numbers. The common factors are the numbers in both lists.

   The factors of 12 are: (1) 2, (3) 4, 6, 12

   The factors of 15 are: (1) (3) 5, 15

2. The HCF is the biggest number that appears in both lists.

   So the highest common factor of 12 and 15 is **3**.

Exercise 3

Q1 a) Find the common factors of 12 and 20.
b) Hence find the highest common factor (HCF) of 12 and 20.

Q2 a) List the common factors of 20 and 30.
b) Use your list to find the HCF of 20 and 30.

Q3 Find the HCF of the following pairs of numbers.
a) 8 and 12 b) 24 and 32 c) 18 and 24
d) 36 and 60 e) 14 and 15 f) 12 and 36

Q4 Write down the following:
a) the HCF of 11 and 12 b) the HCF of 21 and 22

Q5 Find the HCF of the following sets of numbers.
a) 6, 8, 16 b) 12, 15, 18 c) 24, 30, 36 d) 18, 36, 72

Review Exercise

Q1 Write down the numbers from the box that are:

a) multiples of 3

b) multiples of 4

c) multiples of 5

2	5	8	9	11	12
14	15	16	18	20	21

Q2 List all the common multiples of 8 and 10 between 1 and 100.

Q3 A zoo has between 95 and 155 animals.
The number of animals divides exactly by 20 and exactly by 30.

a) Write down all the multiples of 20 between 95 and 155.

b) Write down all the multiples of 30 between 95 and 155.

c) How many animals are there?

Q4 List the common factors of each of the following numbers.

a) 10 and 42 b) 14 and 27 c) 12 and 24

Q5 A baker has 12 identical cakes. In how many different ways can he divide them up into equal packets (without cutting them up)? List the possibilities.

Q6 a) Which three numbers in the box on the right are not prime?

51	53	55	57	59

b) Find two factors greater than 1 that multiply together to give each of your answers to a).

Q7 Write down the prime numbers in this list: 7, 17, 18, 31, 33, 51, 54

Q8 Write the following numbers as the product of prime factors.

a) 18 b) 50 c) 36 d) 150

Q9 a) Find the highest common factor of the following pairs of numbers.

(i) 5 and 9 (ii) 9 and 12 (iii) 10 and 15 (iv) 12 and 28

b) Find the least common multiple of the following pairs of numbers.

(i) 5 and 9 (ii) 6 and 10 (iii) 9 and 12 (iv) 12 and 20

Exam-Style Questions

Q1 Here is a list of numbers.

8 11 15 17 21 28

From the list, write down a number that is:

a) a multiple of both 2 and 7

[1 mark]

b) a factor of 32

[1 mark]

c) 1 more than a prime number.

[1 mark]

Q2 a) Write down all the factors of 50, giving your answer in ascending order.

[1 mark]

b) Find the smallest prime number that is bigger than 50.

[1 mark]

Q3 Find the HCF of 48 and 60. 

[2 marks]

Q4 Write 380 as a product of its prime factors.

[2 marks]

Q5 The lowest common multiple of two numbers is 60.
The highest common factor of the same two numbers is 4.
Neither of the numbers is 4 or 60. What are the numbers?

[2 marks]

Q6 For this question, you are given that $525 = \sqrt{275\,625}$. 

a) Express 525 as a product of prime factors.

[2 marks]

b) Use your answer to part a) to write 275 625 as a product of prime factors.

[1 mark]

5.1 Equivalent Fractions

Fractions are a way of writing one number divided by another. As different divisions can give the same answer (e.g 1 ÷ 3 is the same as 2 ÷ 6), different fractions can have the same value.

Learning Objective — Spec Ref N3:
Be able to find equivalent fractions.

The **fraction** $\frac{a}{b}$ is another way of writing the **division** $a \div b$.

- The number **above the line** (a) is called the **numerator**.
- The number **below the line** (b) is called the **denominator**.

There are lots of **different ways** to write the **same amount** using fractions — these are known as **equivalent fractions**.

For example, one half is the same as two quarters, three sixths, etc. You can see this on the diagrams below:

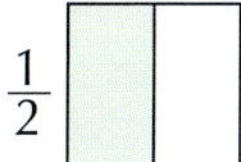

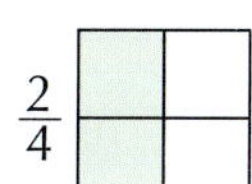

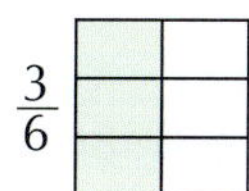

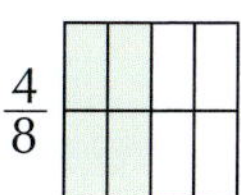

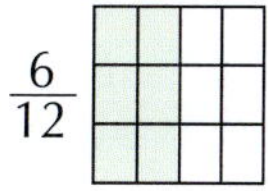

Tip: Notice that the same proportion of the shape is shaded in each diagram.

To find an equivalent fraction, **multiply** or **divide** both the numerator and the denominator by the **same thing** — for example:

- $\frac{3}{9}$ and $\frac{1}{3}$ are equivalent fractions because $\frac{3}{9} = \frac{3 \div 3}{9 \div 3} = \frac{1}{3}$.
- $\frac{1}{4}$ and $\frac{2}{8}$ are equivalent fractions because $\frac{1}{4} = \frac{1 \times 2}{4 \times 2} = \frac{2}{8}$.

Example 1

Find the value that needs to replace the square: $\frac{1}{5} = \frac{\square}{20}$

1. Find what you need to multiply by to get from one denominator to the other.

$$\frac{1}{5} = \frac{\square}{20} \quad (5 \xrightarrow{\times 4} 20)$$

2. Multiply the numerator by the same number.

$$\frac{1}{5} = \frac{\mathbf{4}}{20} \quad (1 \xrightarrow{\times 4} 4)$$

Example 2

Find the value of b if $\frac{12}{30} = \frac{4}{b}$.

1. Find what you need to divide by to get from one numerator to the other.

$$\frac{12}{30} = \frac{4}{b} \quad (\div 3)$$

2. Divide the denominator by the same number.

$$\frac{12}{30} = \frac{4}{10} \quad (\div 3)$$

So b = **10**.

Exercise 1

Q1 Replace the stars to make fractions equivalent to $\frac{1}{3}$. Use the circles to help.

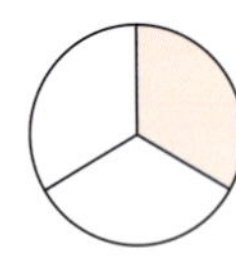 a) 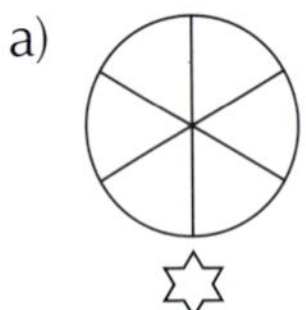 b) 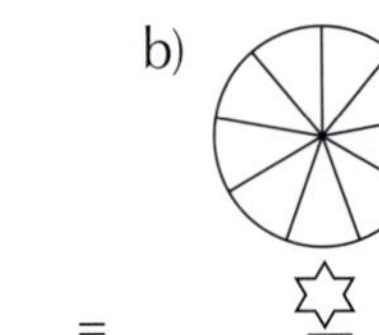 c) 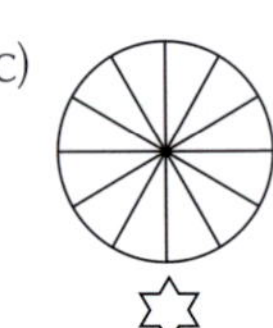

$\frac{1}{3} = \frac{☆}{6} = \frac{☆}{9} = \frac{☆}{12}$

Q2 Find the values of the letters in the following fractions.

a) $\frac{1}{5} = \frac{a}{10}$ b) $\frac{1}{4} = \frac{b}{12}$ c) $\frac{1}{5} = \frac{5}{c}$ d) $\frac{1}{6} = \frac{3}{d}$

e) $\frac{e}{9} = \frac{15}{27}$ f) $\frac{f}{51} = \frac{9}{17}$ g) $\frac{11}{g} = \frac{55}{80}$ h) $\frac{1}{h} = \frac{11}{121}$

Simplifying Fractions

Learning Objectives — Spec Ref N3/R3:
- Be able to write fractions in their simplest form.
- Be able to write one quantity as a fraction of another.

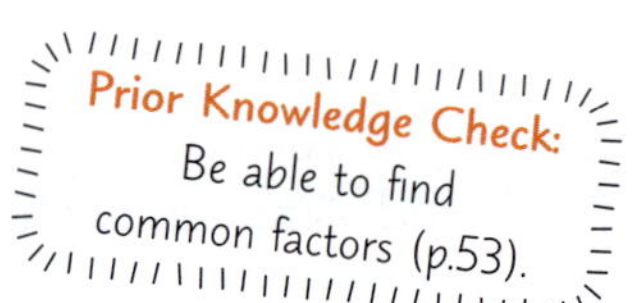

Simplifying a fraction means finding an equivalent fraction with the **smallest** possible whole numbers. This is also known as 'expressing a fraction in its **lowest terms**'.

To simplify a fraction:

- Look for a **common factor** of the numerator and denominator.
- **Divide both** the numerator and denominator by this factor.
- **Repeat** this process with the new fraction. When you can find no common factor (except 1) the fraction is in its **simplest form**.

Tip: You can get to the simplest form in one step if you spot the **highest common factor** right away.

Example 3

Express $\frac{24}{30}$ as a fraction in its lowest terms.

1. Divide the numerator and denominator by any common factor. Here, 3 is a common factor of 24 and 30.
2. Repeat this until the numerator and denominator have no more common factors. Here, 2 is a common factor of 8 and 10.
3. 4 and 5 have no common factors, so this fraction is in its lowest terms.

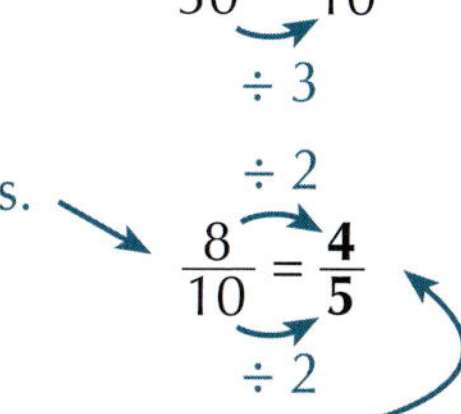

$$\frac{24}{30} = \frac{8}{10} \quad (\div 3)$$

$$\frac{8}{10} = \frac{\mathbf{4}}{\mathbf{5}} \quad (\div 2)$$

Tip: Dividing 24 and 30 by their highest common factor (= 6) will get the answer in a single step.

To express one number **as a fraction** of another:

- Write the **first number** as the **numerator**
- Write the **second number** as the **denominator**.
- **Simplify** and put the fraction in its **lowest terms**.

Example 4

At a restaurant, 24 out of 36 customers said they liked their food. Write this as a fraction in its simplest form.

1. Write the 24 as the numerator and 36 as the denominator.
2. Simplify by dividing 24 and 36 by a common factor — here it's 12.
3. 2 and 3 have no common factor, so this fraction is in its lowest terms.

$$\frac{24}{36} = \frac{\mathbf{2}}{\mathbf{3}} \quad (\div 12)$$

Exercise 2

Q1 Write the following fractions in their lowest terms.

a) $\frac{3}{9}$ b) $\frac{5}{20}$ c) $\frac{8}{16}$ d) $\frac{4}{32}$

e) $\frac{9}{45}$ f) $\frac{15}{36}$ g) $\frac{24}{64}$ h) $\frac{30}{40}$

Q2 Simplify these fractions. Then state which fraction is not equivalent to the other two.

a) $\frac{6}{18}, \frac{4}{20}, \frac{9}{27}$ b) $\frac{6}{8}, \frac{9}{15}, \frac{15}{25}$ c) $\frac{4}{18}, \frac{6}{33}, \frac{10}{45}$

Q3 There are 300 animals on a farm. 50 of them are cows, 70 are pigs and the rest are sheep. What is each type of animal as a fraction of the total number of animals? Write each of your answers in its simplest form.

5.2 Mixed Numbers

All fractions you've seen so far have been smaller than 1. You can write numbers bigger than 1 as fractions in two different ways — either as mixed numbers or as improper fractions.

Learning Objective — Spec Ref N2:
Be able to convert between mixed numbers and improper fractions.

Mixed numbers and improper fractions are two ways of writing numbers greater than 1 that **aren't whole numbers**.

- A **mixed number** is a quantity that has a **whole part** and a **fraction part**. For example, $2\frac{1}{2}$ (two-and-a-half) is a mixed number.
- An **improper fraction** is a fraction where the numerator is **bigger** than the denominator. For example, $\frac{5}{2}$ is an improper fraction.

Converting from Mixed Numbers to Improper Fractions

To **convert** a mixed number to an **improper fraction**:

- Find a **fraction** that is **equivalent** to the **whole part** and has the **same denominator** as the **fraction part**.
- Then **add** this to the **fraction part** of the mixed number.

Example 1

Write the mixed number $4\frac{3}{5}$ as an improper fraction.

1. Find the fraction which is equivalent to 4 and has 5 as the denominator.

$$4 = \frac{4}{1} = \frac{20}{5} \quad (\times 5 \text{ top and bottom})$$

2. Combine the two fractions into one improper fraction by adding the numerators.

$$\text{So } 4\frac{3}{5} = \frac{20}{5} + \frac{3}{5} = \frac{20+3}{5} = \mathbf{\frac{23}{5}}$$

Exercise 1

Q1 Use the diagrams to form improper fractions equivalent to the whole numbers.

a) $2 = \frac{☆}{3}$  

Clue: *How many thirds are there in 2?*

b) $3 = \frac{☆}{4}$ 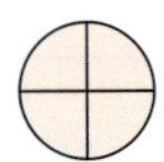 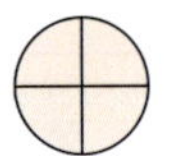 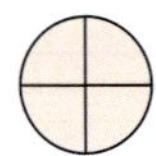

Clue: *How many quarters are there in 3?*

Q2 a) Find the value of a if $4 = \frac{a}{3}$.

b) Use your answer to write the mixed number $4\frac{1}{3}$ as an improper fraction.

Q3 Find the values of the letters to write the following mixed numbers as improper fractions.

a) $1\frac{1}{3} = \frac{a}{3}$ b) $1\frac{2}{7} = \frac{b}{7}$ c) $2\frac{1}{2} = \frac{c}{2}$

Q4 Write the following mixed numbers as improper fractions.

a) $1\frac{4}{5}$ b) $1\frac{5}{12}$ c) $2\frac{9}{10}$

d) $5\frac{3}{10}$ e) $4\frac{3}{4}$ f) $9\frac{5}{6}$

Converting from Improper Fractions to Mixed Numbers

To **convert** an improper fraction to a **mixed number**:

- **Divide** the numerator by the denominator — the answer gives you the **whole part**.
- The **remainder** gives the **numerator** of the **fraction part** — the **denominator** stays the same.

Example 2

Write the improper fraction $\frac{13}{5}$ as a mixed number.

1. Divide the numerator by the denominator.

$13 \div 5 = 2$ remainder 3

2. The whole part of the result (2) is the whole part of your mixed number. The remainder (3) tells you the fraction part.

So $\frac{13}{5} = 2 + \frac{3}{5} = \mathbf{2\frac{3}{5}}$

Exercise 2

Q1 a) Work out $11 \div 7$, giving your answer as a whole number and a remainder.

b) Use your answer to write $\frac{11}{7}$ as a mixed number in its simplest terms.

Q2 Write the following improper fractions as mixed numbers.

a) $\frac{5}{3}$ b) $\frac{9}{5}$ c) $\frac{13}{11}$

d) $\frac{9}{4}$ e) $\frac{20}{9}$ f) $\frac{11}{3}$

Q3 a) Write '12 out of 5' as an improper fraction.

b) Convert the improper fraction into a mixed number.

5.3 Ordering Fractions

It can be difficult to figure out whether one fraction is bigger or smaller than another just by looking at them. The trick is to find equivalent fractions that have the same denominator.

Finding a Common Denominator

Learning Objective — Spec Ref N4:
Be able to write fractions over a common denominator.

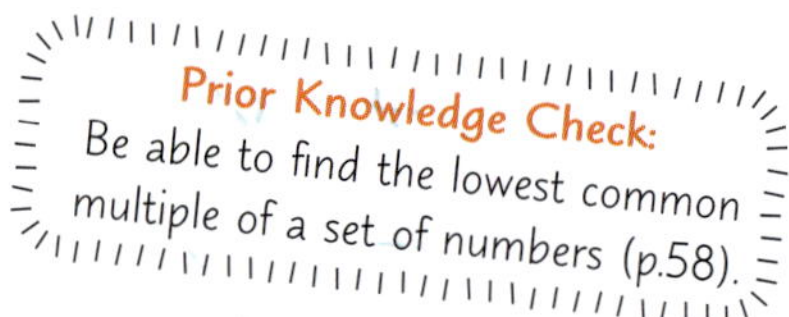

Prior Knowledge Check:
Be able to find the lowest common multiple of a set of numbers (p.58).

To put two fractions over a **common denominator**:

- Find the **lowest common multiple** (LCM) of the denominators of the fractions.
- Write each fraction as an **equivalent fraction** with this number as its denominator.

Example 1

Rewrite the following pairs of fractions so they have a common denominator.

a) $\frac{1}{2}$ **and** $\frac{1}{8}$

Use 8 as the common denominator, since 8 is a multiple of 2 and 8.

So find a fraction equivalent to $\frac{1}{2}$ with 8 as the denominator.

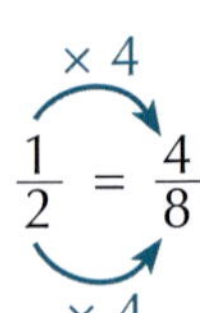

$$\frac{1}{2} = \frac{4}{8} \quad (\times 4)$$

So the fractions are equivalent to $\frac{4}{8}$ **and** $\frac{1}{8}$.

b) $\frac{5}{6}$ **and** $\frac{3}{8}$

24 is a multiple of both 6 and 8, so use this as the common denominator.

Rewrite the two fractions so that they have 24 as the denominator.

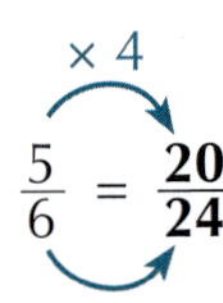

$$\frac{5}{6} = \frac{20}{24} \quad (\times 4) \qquad \frac{3}{8} = \frac{9}{24} \quad (\times 3)$$

Exercise 1

Q1 Rewrite the following pairs of fractions so that they have a common denominator.

a) $\frac{1}{3}, \frac{1}{6}$ b) $\frac{1}{5}, \frac{3}{10}$ c) $\frac{1}{4}, \frac{5}{16}$ d) $\frac{2}{5}, \frac{7}{20}$

e) $\frac{2}{9}, \frac{1}{3}$ f) $\frac{2}{3}, \frac{3}{4}$ g) $\frac{5}{6}, \frac{1}{7}$ h) $\frac{2}{9}, \frac{1}{2}$

Q2 Rewrite the following groups of fractions so that they have a common denominator.

a) $\frac{3}{4}, \frac{5}{8}, \frac{7}{12}$ b) $\frac{1}{5}, \frac{7}{10}, \frac{9}{20}$ c) $\frac{1}{7}, \frac{4}{21}, \frac{5}{14}$

d) $\frac{1}{2}, \frac{3}{8}, \frac{2}{3}$ e) $\frac{2}{5}, \frac{5}{12}, \frac{11}{30}$ f) $\frac{1}{8}, \frac{7}{20}, \frac{3}{5}$

Ordering Fractions

Learning Objective — Spec Ref N1:
Be able to order and compare positive and negative fractions.

To put fractions in **order**:

- Put all the fractions over a **common denominator**.
- **Order** the fractions by ordering their **numerators**. The **smaller** the numerator, the **smaller** the fraction.

Tip: You can use the '<' (less than) and '>' (more than) symbols to show how two fractions compare.

Example 2

Rewrite $\frac{5}{6}$ and $\frac{7}{8}$ so that they have a common denominator and say which is larger.

1. The lowest common multiple of 6 and 8 is 24, so find equivalent fractions that have a denominator of 24.

$\frac{5}{6} \xrightarrow{\times 4} \frac{20}{24}$ $\frac{7}{8} \xrightarrow{\times 3} \frac{21}{24}$

2. Compare the numerators: 20 < 21.

$\frac{20}{24} < \frac{21}{24}$, so $\frac{21}{24} = \frac{7}{8}$ **is larger.**

Example 3

Put the fractions $\frac{1}{2}$, $\frac{3}{8}$ and $\frac{3}{4}$ in order from smallest to largest.

1. The LCM of 2, 8 and 4 is 8, so find equivalent fractions that have a denominator of 8.

$\frac{1}{2} \xrightarrow{\times 4} \frac{4}{8}$ $\frac{3}{4} \xrightarrow{\times 2} \frac{6}{8}$

So the fractions are equivalent to $\frac{4}{8}$, $\frac{3}{8}$ and $\frac{6}{8}$.

2. Use the numerators to put the fractions in order.

From smallest to largest, these are: $\frac{3}{8}, \frac{4}{8}, \frac{6}{8}$.

So in order, the original fractions are $\mathbf{\frac{3}{8}, \frac{1}{2}, \frac{3}{4}}$.

Exercise 2

Q1 Find the larger fraction in each pair below.

a) $\frac{1}{4}, \frac{5}{8}$ b) $\frac{3}{5}, \frac{7}{10}$ c) $\frac{4}{7}, \frac{9}{14}$ d) $\frac{11}{18}, \frac{2}{3}$

e) $\frac{5}{6}, \frac{3}{4}$ f) $\frac{2}{3}, \frac{3}{5}$ g) $\frac{2}{3}, \frac{3}{4}$ h) $\frac{7}{10}, \frac{3}{4}$

In **Questions 2 and 3**, put each of the sets of fractions in order, from smallest to largest.

Q2 a) $\frac{1}{2}, \frac{5}{8}, \frac{7}{16}$ b) $\frac{2}{5}, \frac{3}{10}, \frac{7}{20}$ c) $\frac{3}{4}, \frac{7}{12}, \frac{5}{8}$

Q3 a) $\frac{7}{8}, \frac{5}{6}, \frac{13}{16}$ b) $\frac{4}{15}, \frac{7}{27}, \frac{13}{45}$ c) $\frac{5}{16}, \frac{7}{20}, \frac{9}{25}$

Negative Fractions

Just like whole numbers and decimals, fractions can be **negative**.

- The **minus sign** is placed **in front** of a negative fraction.
- **Negative fractions** can be **ordered** with other fractions (both positive and negative). Put all fractions over a common denominator, as before, and treat the **numerator** of a negative fraction as a **negative number**.
  For example, $-\frac{2}{3}$ is **less than** $\frac{1}{3}$ because –2 is **less than** 1.

Tip: Mixed numbers can also be negative. To order these, first convert them to improper fractions.

Example 4

Put the fractions $-\frac{5}{6}, \frac{1}{2}$ and $-\frac{2}{3}$ in order from smallest to largest.

1. The lowest common multiple of 6, 2 and 3 is 6. Find equivalent fractions with a denominator of 6.

$\frac{1}{2} = \frac{3}{6}$ (×3) $\quad -\frac{2}{3} = -\frac{4}{6}$ (×2)

2. Compare the numerators: –5 < –4 < 3.

$-\frac{5}{6} < -\frac{4}{6} < \frac{3}{6}$, so $\mathbf{-\frac{5}{6} < -\frac{2}{3} < \frac{1}{2}}$

Exercise 3

Q1 a) Rewrite the fractions $-\frac{4}{15}, \frac{2}{9}$ and $-\frac{1}{3}$ so that they have a common denominator.

b) Use your answer to write the fractions $-\frac{4}{15}, \frac{2}{9}$ and $-\frac{1}{3}$ in order (smallest to largest).

Q2 Write down the smallest fraction in each list below:

a) $-\frac{4}{9}, -\frac{5}{12}$ b) $-\frac{9}{10}, \frac{4}{5}$ c) $-\frac{1}{4}, \frac{5}{2}$ $-\frac{3}{11}$

5.4 Adding and Subtracting Fractions

You can add and subtract fractions just like whole and decimal numbers. The result is often an improper fraction, so you might be asked to convert it to a mixed number. You can also add and subtract mixed numbers, as well as combinations of mixed numbers and fractions.

Learning Objective — Spec Ref N2:
Be able to add and subtract fractions.

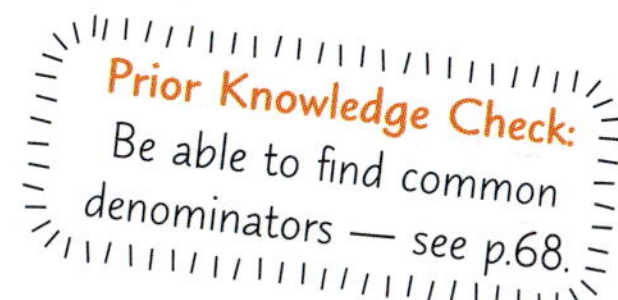

Prior Knowledge Check:
Be able to find common denominators — see p.68.

To **add or subtract** fractions:

- Put the fractions over a **common denominator**.
- Then add or subtract the **numerators**.
- **Simplify** the resulting fraction if necessary.

Tip: If your answer has a negative numerator, move the minus sign in front of the fraction.

Example 1

Work out $\frac{2}{5} + \frac{2}{3}$. Give you answer as a mixed number.

1. Rewrite the fractions with a common denominator of 15. → $\frac{2}{5} \overset{\times 3}{=} \frac{6}{15}$ $\quad \frac{2}{3} \overset{\times 5}{=} \frac{10}{15}$
2. Rewrite the addition using your new fractions. Then add or subtract the numerators. → So $\frac{2}{5} + \frac{2}{3} = \frac{6}{15} + \frac{10}{15}$ $= \frac{6+10}{15}$
3. Convert the improper fraction to a mixed number. → $= \frac{16}{15} = \mathbf{1\frac{1}{15}}$

Exercise 1

Q1 Work out the following. Give your answers in their simplest form.

a) $\frac{1}{3} + \frac{1}{3}$ b) $\frac{4}{5} - \frac{2}{5}$ c) $\frac{5}{11} - \frac{3}{11}$ d) $\frac{1}{10} + \frac{3}{10}$

Q2 Work out the following. Give your answers as mixed numbers in their simplest form.

a) $\frac{5}{8} + \frac{7}{8}$ b) $\frac{3}{4} + \frac{3}{4}$ c) $\frac{8}{15} + \frac{13}{15} - \frac{2}{15}$ d) $\frac{17}{20} + \frac{19}{20} - \frac{7}{20}$

Q3 a) Rewrite the fractions $\frac{1}{2}$ and $\frac{1}{4}$ with a common denominator.

b) Work out $\frac{1}{2} + \frac{1}{4}$.

Q4 Work out the following:

a) $\frac{3}{5}+\frac{1}{10}$ b) $\frac{1}{4}+\frac{3}{8}$ c) $\frac{4}{9}-\frac{1}{3}$ d) $\frac{3}{4}-\frac{3}{8}$

Q5 Work out the following.
Give any answer that is greater than 1 as a mixed number in its simplest form.

a) $\frac{1}{9}+\frac{5}{9}+\frac{11}{18}$ b) $\frac{3}{4}+\frac{1}{8}-\frac{7}{16}$ c) $\frac{6}{7}+\frac{1}{14}-\frac{1}{2}$ d) $\frac{1}{4}+\frac{2}{3}+\frac{5}{6}$

If you're given a **wordy question** then you'll have to figure out what to do with the **fractions**.

Example 2

In a maths exam $\frac{1}{2}$ of the questions are on number topics, $\frac{1}{3}$ of the questions are on algebra, and the rest are on geometry. What fraction of the questions are geometry questions?

1. The fractions of number questions, algebra questions and geometry questions must add up to 1.

   Fraction of geometry questions $= 1 - \frac{1}{2} - \frac{1}{3}$

2. Put the fractions over a common denominator. (Remember, anything divided by itself is 1, so you can write $1 = \frac{6}{6}$.)

   $1 = \frac{6}{6}$ $\frac{1}{2} = \frac{3}{6}$ (× 3) $\frac{1}{3} = \frac{2}{6}$ (× 2)

3. Subtract to find the fraction of geometry questions.

   Fraction of geometry questions $= \frac{6}{6} - \frac{3}{6} - \frac{2}{6}$
   $= \frac{6-3-2}{6} = \mathbf{\frac{1}{6}}$

Exercise 2

Q1 $\frac{4}{9}$ of the pupils in one class are boys. What fraction of the class are girls?

Q2 Jake, Amar and Olga are sharing a cake. Jake eats $\frac{2}{7}$ of the cake, Amar eats $\frac{3}{7}$ and Olga eats the rest. What fraction of the cake does Olga eat?

Q3 $\frac{1}{5}$ of the flowers in a garden are roses. $\frac{3}{10}$ of the flowers are tulips. What fraction of the flowers are neither roses nor tulips?

Q4 A bag contains a mixture of sweets. $\frac{2}{5}$ of the sweets are chocolates, $\frac{1}{4}$ are toffees and the rest are mints. What fraction of the sweets are mints?

Q5 In a school survey, $\frac{1}{2}$ of the pupils said they walk to school. $\frac{1}{5}$ said they catch the bus. The rest arrive by car. What fraction come to school by car?

Adding and Subtracting Mixed Numbers

Learning Objective — Spec Ref N2:
Be able to add and subtract mixed numbers.

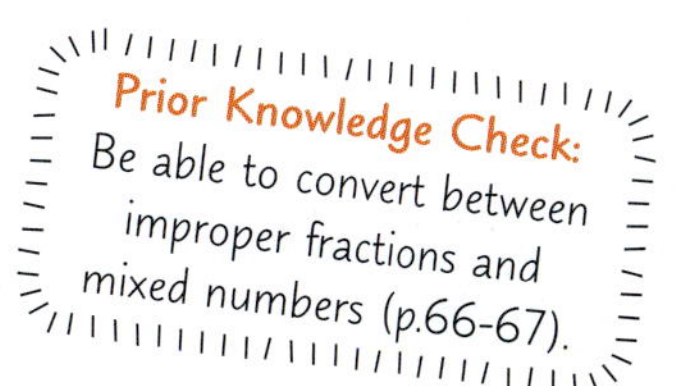

Prior Knowledge Check:
Be able to convert between improper fractions and mixed numbers (p.66-67).

There are two methods for adding and subtracting **mixed numbers**.

Method 1 — Use Improper Fractions

Change the mixed numbers into **improper fractions** (see p.66), then add and subtract by getting them over a **common denominator** — like you did on page 71.

Example 3

Work out $1\frac{1}{3} + 2\frac{5}{6}$ by converting each term to an improper fraction.

1. Write the mixed numbers as improper fractions. $1\frac{1}{3} = \frac{3}{3} + \frac{1}{3} = \frac{4}{3}$ and $2\frac{5}{6} = \frac{12}{6} + \frac{5}{6} = \frac{17}{6}$
2. Rewrite the improper fractions with a common denominator of 6. $\frac{4}{3} \overset{\times 2}{=} \frac{8}{6}$ and $\frac{17}{6}$
3. Add the numerators. $1\frac{1}{3} + 2\frac{5}{6} = \frac{8}{6} + \frac{17}{6} = \frac{25}{6}$
4. Give your answer as a mixed number in its simplest form. $25 \div 6 = 4$ remainder 1, so $\frac{25}{6} = \mathbf{4\frac{1}{6}}$

Tip: If one denominator is a multiple of the other, you only need to rewrite one fraction.

Exercise 3

Q1 a) Write the mixed number $1\frac{4}{5}$ as an improper fraction.

b) Use part a) to work out $1\frac{4}{5} + \frac{3}{5}$, giving your answer as a mixed number.

Q2 a) Write the following as improper fractions: (i) $2\frac{1}{5}$ (ii) $1\frac{3}{5}$

b) Use your answers to work out $2\frac{1}{5} - 1\frac{3}{5}$.

Q3 By writing each term as a proper or improper fraction, work out the following. Give your answers as mixed numbers in their simplest form, where appropriate.

a) $1\frac{2}{3} + \frac{1}{3}$ b) $2\frac{3}{8} + \frac{7}{8}$ c) $1\frac{5}{6} + 1\frac{1}{6}$

d) $4\frac{5}{12} - 2\frac{11}{12}$ e) $5\frac{7}{11} + \frac{5}{11}$ f) $3\frac{2}{5} - \frac{4}{5}$

Method 2 — Separate the Whole and Fraction Parts

Add/subtract the whole parts and the fraction parts **separately**, and then **add** the results. This method is particularly useful when the **whole** parts or the **denominators** are **big**.

Example 4

Work out $5\frac{1}{4} + 3\frac{1}{2}$ by adding whole parts and fraction parts separately.

1. Add the whole parts. $5 + 3 = 8$
2. Add the fraction parts in the usual way. $\frac{1}{4} + \frac{1}{2} = \frac{1}{4} + \frac{2}{4} = \frac{3}{4}$
3. Add the results. $8 + \frac{3}{4} = \mathbf{8\frac{3}{4}}$

In a **subtraction**, you **subtract** the whole and fraction parts **separately**, but you still **add** the results at the end. Note: subtracting the fractions might give you a **negative** fraction — e.g. subtracting rather than adding in Example 4 would give:
$5\frac{1}{4} - 3\frac{1}{2} = (5 - 3) + \left(\frac{1}{4} - \frac{1}{2}\right) = 2 + \left(-\frac{1}{4}\right) = 2 - \frac{1}{4} = 1\frac{3}{4}$.

In an **addition**, adding the fraction parts might result in an **improper fraction**.

Example 5

Work out $6\frac{2}{3} + 1\frac{3}{4}$ by adding whole parts and fraction parts separately.

1. Add the whole parts. $6 + 1 = 7$
2. Add the fraction parts in the usual way. The result is an improper fraction, so convert it to a mixed number. $\frac{2}{3} + \frac{3}{4} = \frac{8}{12} + \frac{9}{12} = \frac{17}{12} = 1\frac{5}{12}$
3. Add the results. $7 + 1\frac{5}{12} = \mathbf{8\frac{5}{12}}$

Exercise 4

Q1 By separating into whole and fraction parts, work out the following.

a) $4\frac{1}{9} + 3\frac{4}{9}$ b) $3\frac{1}{5} + 2\frac{3}{7}$ c) $2\frac{5}{8} + 6\frac{2}{3}$

Q2 a) Work out $\frac{2}{5} - \frac{4}{5}$.

b) Use your answer to work out $2\frac{2}{5} - 1\frac{4}{5}$.

Q3 By separating into whole and fraction parts, work out the following.

a) $3\frac{3}{4} - \frac{5}{7}$ b) $2\frac{1}{4} - 1\frac{6}{7}$ c) $5\frac{2}{5} - 3\frac{7}{9}$

5.5 Multiplying and Dividing Fractions

Being able to multiply by fractions is really useful — it lets you find fractions of amounts. Once you've got multiplying sorted, you'll find dividing by fractions to be no harder —to divide, all you need to do is flip the fraction upside-down and multiply instead.

Multiplying by Unit Fractions

Learning Objective — Spec Ref N2/N12:
Be able to multiply whole numbers by unit fractions.

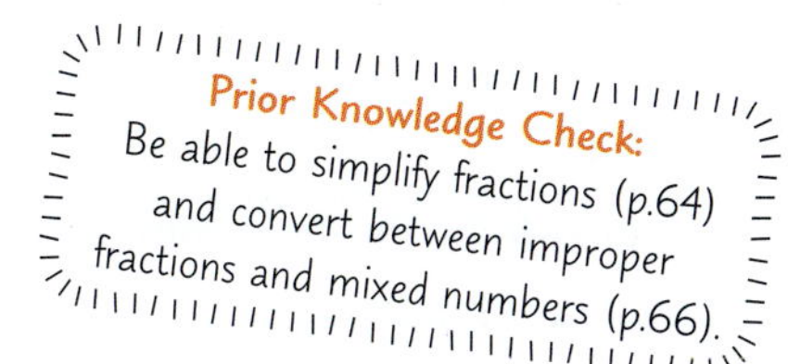

Prior Knowledge Check:
Be able to simplify fractions (p.64) and convert between improper fractions and mixed numbers (p.66).

A **unit fraction** has 1 as its numerator — for example, these are all unit fractions: $\frac{1}{2}, \frac{1}{3}, \frac{1}{5}, \frac{1}{10}$.
Multiplying by a **unit fraction** is the same as **dividing** by a **whole number**.

For example, multiplying by $\frac{1}{2}$ is the same as dividing by 2.

Example 1

Work out: a) $12 \times \frac{1}{3}$ b) $10 \times -\frac{1}{4}$

a) Multiplying by $\frac{1}{3}$ is the same as dividing by 3. Remember $12 \div 3$ can be written as $\frac{12}{3}$.

$12 \times \frac{1}{3} = \frac{12}{3} = \mathbf{4}$

b) Multiplying by $-\frac{1}{4}$ is the same as dividing by –4. $10 \div (-4)$ can be written as $-\frac{10}{4}$.

$10 \times -\frac{1}{4} = -\frac{10}{4} = -2\frac{2}{4} = \mathbf{-2\frac{1}{2}}$

Tip: Have a look back to page 6 to remind yourself how to multiply and divide with negatives.

Exercise 1

Q1 Work out the following.

a) $8 \times \frac{1}{4}$ b) $10 \times \frac{1}{5}$ c) $15 \times \frac{1}{5}$ d) $45 \times \frac{1}{3}$

Q2 Work out the following. Write your answers as mixed numbers.

a) $18 \times \frac{1}{4}$ b) $15 \times \frac{1}{6}$ c) $17 \times \frac{1}{2}$ d) $25 \times \frac{1}{10}$

Q3 Work out the following. Write your answers as mixed numbers.

a) $48 \times -\frac{1}{6}$ b) $80 \times -\frac{1}{10}$ c) $25 \times -\frac{1}{6}$ d) $40 \times -\frac{1}{3}$

Multiplying Whole Numbers by Fractions

Learning Objectives — Spec Ref N2/N12:

- Be able to multiply whole numbers by fractions.
- Be able to find fractions of amounts.

Prior Knowledge Check: Be able to identify common factors (p.53).

To multiply a **whole number** by a fraction:

- **Multiply** by the **numerator**.
- **Divide** by the **denominator**.

You can do these steps in either order. If **multiplying** first is going to give you a **big** number, and the **denominator** is a **factor** of the **whole** number, **dividing** first might be better.

Example 2

Work out these multiplications:

a) $15 \times \frac{2}{5}$

You need to multiply 15 by 2, and then divide by 5. (Or you can divide by 5, and then multiply by 2 — you'll get the same answer.)

$$15 \times \frac{2}{5} = \frac{15 \times 2}{5} = \frac{30}{5} = \mathbf{6}$$

b) $5 \times \frac{3}{4}$

You need to multiply 5 by 3, and then divide by 4. (Or you can divide by 4, and then multiply by 3.)

$$5 \times \frac{3}{4} = \frac{5 \times 3}{4} = \frac{15}{4} = \mathbf{3\frac{3}{4}}$$

If the whole number and the fraction's denominator have a **common factor**, then you can **cancel** it before carrying out the rest of the calculation.

Example 3

Work out $35 \times \frac{7}{25}$. Give your answer as a mixed number in its simplest form.

1. 25 and 35 are both multiples of 5. 25 = 5 × 5 and 35 = 7 × 5.
2. Cancel the 5s...
3. ... then multiply and divide as usual.

$$35 \times \frac{7}{25} = \frac{35 \times 7}{25}$$

$$= \frac{7 \times 5 \times 7}{5 \times 5}$$

$$= \frac{7 \times \cancel{5} \times 7}{\cancel{5} \times 5}$$

$$= \frac{7 \times 7}{5} = \frac{49}{5} = \mathbf{9\frac{4}{5}}$$

Tip: If you didn't cancel first, you'd get $\frac{245}{25}$, which then simplifies to $9\frac{4}{5}$.

Exercise 2

Q1 Work out the following. Write your answers as simply as possible.

a) $12 \times \frac{2}{3}$ b) $28 \times \frac{3}{4}$ c) $15 \times \frac{4}{5}$ d) $48 \times \frac{3}{8}$

e) $60 \times \frac{5}{12}$ f) $32 \times \frac{7}{16}$ g) $100 \times -\frac{7}{25}$ h) $-96 \times -\frac{7}{12}$

Q2 Work out the following. Give your answers as mixed numbers in their simplest form.

a) $15 \times \frac{3}{4}$ b) $22 \times \frac{2}{5}$ c) $7 \times -\frac{3}{11}$ d) $6 \times -\frac{5}{8}$

Q3 Calculate $45 \times \frac{5}{18}$. Give your answer as a mixed number in its simplest form.

You can find **fractions of amounts** by **multiplying** the amount by the fraction in question.

Example 4

Find $\frac{3}{4}$ of 18. Give your answer as a mixed number in its simplest form.

1. You can replace 'of' with a multiplication sign. $\frac{3}{4}$ of $18 = \frac{3}{4} \times 18$
2. Since 18 isn't a multiple of 4, do 3 × 18 and write this on the top of the fraction. $\frac{3}{4} \times 18 = \frac{3 \times 18}{4} = \frac{54}{4}$
3. Simplify the fraction and convert to a mixed number. $\frac{54}{4} = \frac{27}{2} = \frac{26+1}{2} = \mathbf{13\frac{1}{2}}$

Exercise 3

Q1 Find the following.

a) $\frac{3}{4}$ of 36 b) $\frac{2}{3}$ of 33 c) $\frac{3}{8}$ of 64 d) $\frac{5}{12}$ of 72

e) $\frac{5}{6}$ of 18 f) $\frac{3}{5}$ of 15 g) $\frac{5}{6}$ of 33 h) $\frac{7}{12}$ of 45

Q2 Find the following.

a) $\frac{3}{2}$ of 18 b) $\frac{5}{3}$ of 21 c) $\frac{11}{9}$ of 72

Q3 Out of a class of 27 students, $\frac{2}{3}$ prefer rounders to cricket.
How many students prefer rounders?

Multiplying Fractions and Mixed Numbers

Learning Objectives — Spec Ref N2/N12:
- Be able to multiply fractions together.
- Be able to multiply mixed numbers together.

To multiply two or more **fractions**, multiply their numerators and denominators **separately**.

Example 5

Work out: a) $\frac{2}{3} \times \frac{4}{5}$ b) $\frac{3}{4} \times \frac{2}{9}$

1. Multiply the numerators together to get the new numerator, and the denominators together to get the new denominator.
2. Simplify your answer as much as possible.

a) $\frac{2}{3} \times \frac{4}{5} = \frac{2 \times 4}{4 \times 5} = \mathbf{\frac{8}{15}}$

b) $\frac{3}{4} \times \frac{2}{9} = \frac{3 \times 2}{4 \times 9} = \frac{6}{36} = \mathbf{\frac{1}{6}}$

To make calculations easier, you can **cancel** any **factors** that appear in the numerator and denominator of **either** fraction. It helps to cancel all **common factors** as early as possible.

Example 6

Work out $\frac{7}{25} \times \frac{15}{16}$.

1. 25 and 15 share a common factor (5), so cancel that first.
2. Multiply the numerators together and the denominators together.

$$\frac{7}{25} \times \frac{15}{16} = \frac{7}{5 \times \cancel{5}} \times \frac{3 \times \cancel{5}}{16}$$
$$= \frac{7}{5} \times \frac{3}{16}$$
$$= \frac{7 \times 3}{5 \times 16} = \mathbf{\frac{21}{80}}$$

Tip: If you didn't cancel the 5, you'd get $\frac{7 \times 15}{25 \times 16} = \frac{105}{400}$. This still simplifies to $\frac{21}{80}$, but it's much harder to work with.

Exercise 4

Q1 Work out the following.

a) $\frac{1}{6} \times \frac{1}{3}$ b) $\frac{2}{5} \times \frac{1}{3}$ c) $\frac{3}{4} \times \frac{1}{7}$ d) $\frac{1}{5} \times \frac{3}{5}$

e) $\frac{5}{6} \times \frac{1}{4}$ f) $\frac{4}{5} \times \frac{2}{7}$ g) $-\frac{2}{7} \times \frac{5}{7}$ h) $-\frac{3}{8} \times -\frac{7}{10}$

Q2 Work out the following. Give your answers in their lowest terms.

a) $\frac{1}{4} \times \frac{2}{3}$ b) $\frac{3}{5} \times \frac{1}{6}$ c) $\frac{5}{6} \times \frac{2}{15}$ d) $\frac{5}{12} \times \frac{3}{4}$

e) $\frac{4}{42} \times \frac{18}{8}$ f) $\frac{22}{5} \times \frac{15}{77}$ g) $-\frac{6}{7} \times \frac{7}{8}$ h) $\frac{7}{10} \times -\frac{5}{14}$

Q3 Calculate $\frac{3}{5}$ of $\frac{15}{8}$. Give your answer as a mixed number in its simplest form.

To multiply by **mixed numbers**, change them into **improper fractions** first.

Example 7

Work out $4\frac{1}{2} \times 3\frac{3}{5}$.

1. Write the mixed numbers as improper fractions. $4\frac{1}{2} = \frac{8}{2} + \frac{1}{2} = \frac{9}{2}$ and $3\frac{3}{5} = \frac{15}{5} + \frac{3}{5} = \frac{18}{5}$
2. Multiply the two fractions. So $4\frac{1}{2} \times 3\frac{3}{5} = \frac{9}{2} \times \frac{18}{5} = \frac{9 \times 18}{2 \times 5}$
3. Write your answer as a mixed number in its simplest form. $= \frac{162}{10} = 16\frac{2}{10} = \mathbf{16\frac{1}{5}}$.

(or $\frac{162}{10} = \frac{81 \times \cancel{2}}{5 \times \cancel{2}} = \frac{81}{5} = \mathbf{16\frac{1}{5}}$)

Exercise 5

Q1 Work out the following. 

a) $1\frac{1}{2} \times \frac{1}{3}$ b) $2\frac{1}{5} \times \frac{3}{4}$ c) $1\frac{5}{6} \times \frac{2}{3}$

d) $3\frac{3}{4} \times \frac{2}{5}$ e) $2\frac{1}{7} \times \frac{2}{9}$ f) $2\frac{4}{9} \times \frac{3}{8}$

Q2 a) Write the mixed number $3\frac{2}{5}$ as an improper fraction. 

b) Write the mixed number $1\frac{1}{2}$ as an improper fraction.

c) Use your answer to work out $3\frac{2}{5} \times 1\frac{1}{2}$.

Q3 Work out the following.

a) $1\frac{1}{5} \times 1\frac{1}{4}$ b) $2\frac{2}{5} \times 1\frac{2}{3}$ c) $1\frac{3}{5} \times 1\frac{3}{4}$

d) $2\frac{3}{7} \times 3\frac{1}{6}$ e) $3\frac{4}{9} \times 1\frac{7}{8}$ f) $2\frac{6}{7} \times 2\frac{1}{9}$

Dividing by Fractions

Learning Objectives — Spec Ref N2/N12:
- Be able to find the reciprocal of a number or fraction.
- Be able to divide by fractions and mixed numbers.

- The **reciprocal** of a number is just **1 ÷ that number.** The reciprocal of a **whole number** is always a **unit fraction**. For example, the reciprocal of 4 is $\frac{1}{4}$.

Tip: The reciprocal of a negative number is also negative.

- To find the reciprocal of a **fraction**, just **swap** its numerator and denominator (in other words, **flip it upside-down**). For example, the reciprocal of $\frac{3}{5}$ is $\frac{5}{3}$.
- To find the reciprocal of a **mixed number**, convert it to an **improper fraction** first.

Example 8

Find the reciprocal of each number, giving your answer as a fraction in its lowest terms.

a) **3** **b)** $\mathbf{\frac{4}{5}}$ **c)** $\mathbf{2\frac{5}{6}}$

a) The reciprocal of 3 is 1 ÷ 3. So write this as a fraction.

The reciprocal of 3 is $\mathbf{\frac{1}{3}}$.

b) To find the reciprocal, just swap the numerator and the denominator.

The reciprocal of $\frac{4}{5}$ is $\mathbf{\frac{5}{4}}$.

c) 1. Convert to an improper fraction.

$2\frac{5}{6} = \frac{12}{6} + \frac{5}{6} = \frac{17}{6}$

2. Flip the fraction upside-down.

The reciprocal of $2\frac{5}{6}$ is $\mathbf{\frac{6}{17}}$.

Exercise 6

Q1 Find the reciprocal of each of the following.

a) 5 b) 12 c) 9 d) 27

Q2 Find the reciprocal of each of the following.

a) $\frac{1}{3}$ b) $-\frac{1}{7}$ c) $\frac{4}{5}$ d) $-\frac{5}{8}$

Q3 Find the reciprocal of each of the following. Start by writing each as an improper fraction.

a) $1\frac{3}{5}$ b) $2\frac{1}{7}$ c) $1\frac{4}{9}$ d) $-2\frac{3}{4}$

Dividing by Fractions

Dividing by a number is the same as **multiplying** by its **reciprocal**.

So, to divide a number by a **fraction**:

- Calculate the **reciprocal** of the fraction.
- **Multiply** the number by this reciprocal.

Tip: Once you've got a multiplication, the method is exactly the same as on p.78.

Example 9

Work out: a) $\frac{1}{2} \div \frac{2}{3}$ b) $\frac{4}{7} \div 2$

a) Multiply $\frac{1}{2}$ by the reciprocal of $\frac{2}{3}$. $\frac{1}{2} \div \frac{2}{3} = \frac{1}{2} \times \frac{3}{2} = \frac{1 \times 3}{2 \times 2} = \mathbf{\frac{3}{4}}$

b) Multiply $\frac{4}{7}$ by the reciprocal of 2. $\frac{4}{7} \div 2 = \frac{4}{7} \times \frac{1}{2} = \frac{4 \times 1}{7 \times 2} = \frac{4}{14} = \mathbf{\frac{2}{7}}$

Example 10

Find $2\frac{2}{3} \div 1\frac{1}{5}$ as a mixed number in its lowest terms.

1. Write both numbers as improper fractions. $2\frac{2}{3} = \frac{6}{3} + \frac{2}{3} = \frac{8}{3}$ and $1\frac{1}{5} = \frac{5}{5} + \frac{1}{5} = \frac{6}{5}$
2. Flip the $\frac{6}{5}$ upside down and change the ÷ into a ×. $2\frac{2}{3} \div 1\frac{1}{5} = \frac{8}{3} \div \frac{6}{5}$ $= \frac{8}{3} \times \frac{5}{6} = \frac{2 \times 4}{3} \times \frac{5}{2 \times 3} = \frac{4 \times 5}{3 \times 3}$
3. Convert the improper fraction into a mixed number. $= \frac{20}{9} = \mathbf{2\frac{2}{9}}$

Exercise 7

Q1 Work out the following.

a) $\frac{1}{5} \div \frac{2}{3}$ b) $\frac{1}{6} \div \frac{2}{5}$ c) $2 \div \frac{2}{3}$ d) $\frac{2}{3} \div 4$

e) $\frac{5}{12} \div \frac{4}{5}$ f) $\frac{15}{7} \div 6$ g) $-\frac{3}{8} \div \frac{2}{5}$ h) $-\frac{7}{10} \div \frac{5}{7}$

Q2 By first rewriting any mixed numbers as improper fractions, work out the following.

a) $1\frac{1}{2} \div 4$ b) $3\frac{1}{3} \div 6$ c) $5 \div 1\frac{3}{5}$ d) $2 \div 1\frac{7}{8}$

Q3 By first rewriting any mixed numbers as improper fractions, work out the following.

a) $1\frac{1}{3} \div \frac{2}{5}$ b) $2\frac{1}{2} \div \frac{1}{3}$ c) $\frac{3}{4} \div 2\frac{1}{3}$ d) $\frac{4}{7} \div 3\frac{1}{2}$

e) $1\frac{1}{4} \div 1\frac{1}{5}$ f) $2\frac{2}{3} \div 1\frac{1}{4}$ g) $4\frac{5}{6} \div 2\frac{1}{3}$ h) $3\frac{2}{3} \div \left(-2\frac{1}{10}\right)$

5.6 Fractions and Decimals

Fractions and decimals are different ways of writing numbers. You'll need to know how to write fractions as decimals, with and without the help of a calculator.

Converting Fractions to Decimals using a Calculator

Learning Objective — Spec Ref N10:
Be able to convert fractions to decimals using a calculator.

You can use a **calculator** to convert a fraction to a decimal — just **divide** the numerator by the denominator. Make sure you write down **all the digits** that you see on your calculator display.

Example 1

Use a calculator to convert the following fractions to decimals.

a) $\mathbf{\frac{5}{16}}$ Divide the numerator by the denominator. $\frac{5}{16} = 5 \div 16 = \mathbf{0.3125}$

b) $\mathbf{1\frac{2}{5}}$ You can convert to an improper fraction. $1\frac{2}{5} = \frac{7}{5} = 7 \div 5 = \mathbf{1.4}$

Or, you can work out the fraction part, then add on the whole part. $\frac{2}{5} = 2 \div 5 = 0.4$, so $1\frac{2}{5} = 1 + 0.4 = \mathbf{1.4}$

Tip: Your calculator might have a button to go between fractions and decimals, but you should still learn these methods.

Exercise 1

Q1 Use a calculator to convert the following fractions to decimals.

a) $\frac{5}{8}$ b) $\frac{7}{20}$ c) $\frac{7}{16}$ d) $\frac{5}{32}$

e) $\frac{7}{40}$ f) $\frac{23}{50}$ g) $\frac{176}{200}$ h) $\frac{329}{500}$

Q2 Use a calculator to convert the following mixed numbers to decimals.

a) $1\frac{3}{8}$ b) $2\frac{1}{8}$ c) $6\frac{7}{20}$ d) $2\frac{37}{100}$

e) $4\frac{719}{1000}$ f) $5\frac{19}{25}$ g) $7\frac{11}{32}$ h) $8\frac{7}{16}$

Converting Fractions to Decimals Without Using a Calculator

Learning Objective — Spec Ref N10:
Convert fractions to decimals without using a calculator.

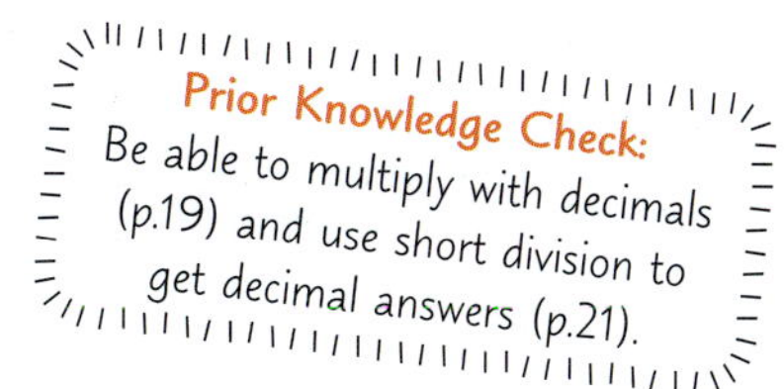

There are a couple of ways to **convert** fractions to **decimals** if you don't have a calculator.

Method 1 — Find an Equivalent Fraction

You can find an **equivalent fraction** with a **denominator** of **10, 100** or **1000** and then use one of the following conversions:

$$\frac{1}{10} = 0.1, \quad \frac{1}{100} = 0.01, \quad \frac{1}{1000} = 0.001$$

Tip: These conversions are just dividing 1 by 10, 100 and 1000 (see p.18).

Example 2

Write $\frac{7}{10}$ as a decimal.

1. Write the fraction as a multiple of $\frac{1}{10}$. $\quad \frac{7}{10} = 7 \times \frac{1}{10}$
2. Use the conversion $\frac{1}{10} = 0.1$ $\quad = 7 \times 0.1 = \mathbf{0.7}$

Example 3

Write the following fractions as decimals.

a) $\frac{4}{5}$

1. Multiply top and bottom to find an equivalent fraction with a denominator of 10. $\quad \frac{4}{5} \overset{\times 2}{=} \frac{8}{10}$ (× 2 top and bottom)
2. Then rewrite as a decimal. $\quad \frac{8}{10} = 8 \times \frac{1}{10} = 8 \times 0.1 = \mathbf{0.8}$

b) $\frac{123}{300}$

1. Divide top and bottom to find an equivalent fraction with a denominator of 100. $\quad \frac{123}{300} \overset{\div 3}{=} \frac{41}{100}$ (÷ 3 top and bottom)
2. Then rewrite as a decimal. $\quad \frac{41}{100} = 41 \times \frac{1}{100} = 41 \times 0.01 = \mathbf{0.41}$

Exercise 2

Q1 Write the following fractions as decimals.

a) $\frac{9}{10}$ b) $\frac{2}{10}$ c) $\frac{3}{10}$ d) $\frac{8}{10}$

e) $\frac{91}{100}$ f) $\frac{42}{100}$ g) $\frac{99}{100}$ h) $\frac{8}{100}$

i) $\frac{7}{1000}$ j) $\frac{201}{1000}$ k) $\frac{41}{1000}$ l) $\frac{27}{1000}$

Q2 a) Find a fraction which is equivalent to $\frac{8}{25}$ and which has a denominator of 100.

b) Use your answer to write $\frac{8}{25}$ as a decimal.

Q3 Write the following fractions as decimals.

a) $\frac{3}{5}$ b) $\frac{9}{30}$ c) $\frac{45}{50}$ d) $\frac{22}{25}$

e) $\frac{96}{300}$ f) $\frac{33}{250}$ g) $\frac{103}{200}$ h) $\frac{306}{3000}$

Q4 Write the following numbers as decimals.

a) $\frac{11}{10}$ b) $\frac{14}{5}$ c) $5\frac{7}{25}$ d) $3\frac{11}{200}$

Method 2 — Using Short Division

You can divide the numerator by the denominator using **short division**.
You'll have to keep putting **zeros** after the decimal point until the division is completed.

Example 4

Write $\frac{1}{8}$ as a decimal.

You need to work out 1 ÷ 8.

1. 8 doesn't go into 1, so the answer will begin with "0.". Write the decimal point in the answer directly above the decimal point in 1.0. → $8\overline{)1.{}^{1}0}$ with answer 0.
2. 8 goes into 10 once, with remainder 2. → $8\overline{)1.{}^{1}0{}^{2}0}$ with answer 0.1
3. 8 goes into 20 twice, with remainder 4. → $8\overline{)1.{}^{1}0{}^{2}0{}^{4}0}$ with answer 0.12
4. 8 goes into 40 exactly 5 times. → $8\overline{)1.{}^{1}0{}^{2}0{}^{4}0}$ with answer 0.125

So $\frac{1}{8}$ = **0.125**

Tip: Write the 1 as 1.0 to start with, then add zeros as needed.

Exercise 3

Q1 a) Write $\frac{3}{8}$ as a decimal by finding $3 \div 8$.

b) Write $\frac{5}{16}$ as a decimal by finding $5 \div 16$.

Q2 Write the following fractions as decimals by using short division.

a) $\frac{1}{4}$ b) $\frac{3}{4}$ c) $\frac{1}{20}$ d) $\frac{1}{40}$

e) $\frac{1}{16}$ f) $\frac{7}{8}$ g) $\frac{7}{40}$ h) $\frac{13}{80}$

Converting Decimals to Fractions

Learning Objective — Spec Ref N10:
Convert decimals to fractions without using a calculator.

Prior Knowledge Check:
Be able to simplify fractions (p.64).

You can quickly convert a decimal to a fraction by using a **denominator** of **10, 100, 1000** or another **power of 10**.

Converting Decimals that are Smaller Than 1

To convert a decimal that is **smaller than 1** to a fraction:

- Write the bit after the decimal point as the **numerator**.
- Use a power of 10 as the **denominator** with the same **number of zeros** as the number of decimal places.

Tip: A decimal smaller than 1 has only a 0 before the decimal point.

Example 5

Write the following decimals as fractions in their simplest form.

a) 0.24 There are two decimal places, so the denominator should have two zeros — it's 100. Remember to simplify your answer.

$$0.24 = \frac{24}{100} = \mathbf{\frac{6}{25}} \quad (\div 4 \text{ top and bottom})$$

b) 0.025 There are three decimal places, so the denominator should have three zeros — it's 1000. Remember to simplify your answer.

$$0.025 = \frac{25}{1000} = \mathbf{\frac{1}{40}} \quad (\div 25 \text{ top and bottom})$$

Exercise 4

Q1 Convert the following decimals to fractions. Give your answers in their simplest form.
a) 0.7 b) 0.9 c) 0.1 d) 0.4

Q2 Convert the following decimals to fractions.
a) 0.93 b) 0.07 c) 0.23 d) 0.47

Q3 Convert the following decimals to fractions. Give your answers in their simplest form.
a) 0.004 b) 0.801 c) 0.983 d) 0.098

Q4 Convert 0.1002 to a fraction, giving your answer in its simplest form.

Converting Decimals that are Bigger Than 1

To convert a decimal that is **bigger than 1** to a fraction:

- Write the number as the **numerator**, removing the decimal point.
- Use a power of 10 as the **denominator** with the same **number of zeros** as the number of decimal places.

Tip: A decimal bigger than 1 has a non-zero digit before the decimal point.

Example 6

Write the following decimals as improper fractions in their simplest form.

a) 3.5 There's just 1 decimal place, so the denominator should have one zero — it's 10. Remember to simplify your answer.

$$3.5 = \frac{35}{10} = \frac{\mathbf{7}}{\mathbf{2}} \quad (\div 5)$$

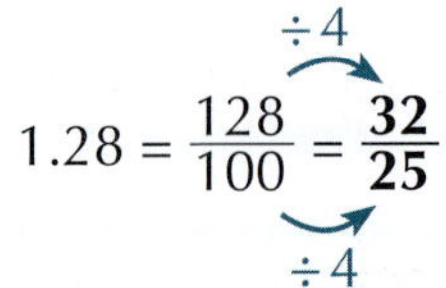

b) 1.28 There are two decimal places, so the denominator should have two zeros — it's 100. Remember to simplify your answer.

$$1.28 = \frac{128}{100} = \frac{\mathbf{32}}{\mathbf{25}} \quad (\div 4)$$

Exercise 5

Q1 Convert the following decimals to fractions. Give your answers in their simplest form.
a) 1.2 b) 3.4 c) 4.7 d) 8.4

Q2 Convert the following decimals to fractions. Give your answers in their simplest form.
a) 3.02 b) 1.55 c) 2.05 d) 18.2

Review Exercise

Q1 Find the values of the letters in the following equivalent fractions. 

a) $\frac{3}{4} = \frac{a}{16}$ b) $\frac{7}{12} = \frac{35}{b}$ c) $\frac{c}{3} = \frac{10}{15}$

Q2 a) Which of the following is a common factor of 45 and 75? 9 25 2 5 

b) Write $\frac{45}{75}$ in its lowest terms.

Q3 Express each of the following as a fraction in its simplest terms. 

a) 4 as a fraction of 24 b) 12 as a fraction of 66

Q4 a) Write $7\frac{2}{3}$ as an improper fraction. 

b) Write $\frac{26}{4}$ as a mixed number in its simplest form.

Q5 Rewrite the following pairs of fractions so they have a common denominator, and say which of each pair is the smaller of the two fractions. 

a) $\frac{2}{7}, \frac{5}{28}$ b) $\frac{1}{8}, \frac{1}{6}$ c) $\frac{2}{5}, \frac{4}{9}$

Q6 Work out the following. Giving your answers in their simplest form. 

a) $\frac{1}{5} + \frac{1}{3}$ b) $\frac{9}{10} - \frac{5}{6}$ c) $6\frac{3}{8} - \frac{7}{8}$

Q7 a) Write the mixed number $1\frac{3}{7}$ as an improper fraction. 

b) Use your answer from a) to work out $1\frac{3}{7} \times \frac{2}{3}$.

Q8 a) What is the reciprocal of $\frac{3}{8}$? 

b) Calculate $\frac{1}{6} \div \frac{3}{8}$. Give your answer in its simplest form.

Q9 Use a calculator to express $\frac{23}{40}$ as a decimal.

Q10 a) Convert $\frac{12}{25}$ to a decimal. 

b) Convert 0.35 to a fraction. Give your answer in its simplest form.

Exam-Style Questions

Q1 Work out:

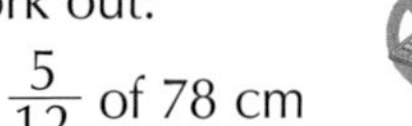

a) $\frac{5}{12}$ of 78 cm

[2 marks]

b) $15 \div 2\frac{1}{2}$

[2 marks]

Q2 Write 3.125 as a mixed number in its simplest form.

[2 marks]

Q3 Ruby buys some meat and uses $\frac{3}{4}$ of it to make a cottage pie.

She then uses $\frac{3}{5}$ of the remaining meat to make ravioli.
Work out the fraction of the meat Ruby has left over.
Give your answer in its lowest terms.

[3 marks]

Q4 Sam makes some dumplings. Each dumpling uses $5\frac{1}{3}$ g of butter.

Sam has 120 g of butter. Work out the number of dumplings Sam can make.

[3 marks]

Q5 A supermarket has boxes of peppers which are either green, red or yellow.

In one box, $\frac{2}{5}$ of the peppers are green, there are 24 red peppers,
and there are four times as many red as there are yellow peppers.

a) Work out the total number of peppers in the box.

[3 marks]

b) Write the fraction of red peppers in the box as a decimal.

[2 marks]

Section 6 Ratios

6.1 Ratios

Like fractions and percentages, ratios are a way of showing proportion. They tell you how the size of one thing relates to the size of another thing, or sometimes to several other things. They crop up in lots of real-life situations, such as on map scales and in recipes.

Simplifying Ratios

Learning Objective — Spec Ref R4:
Write ratios in their simplest form.

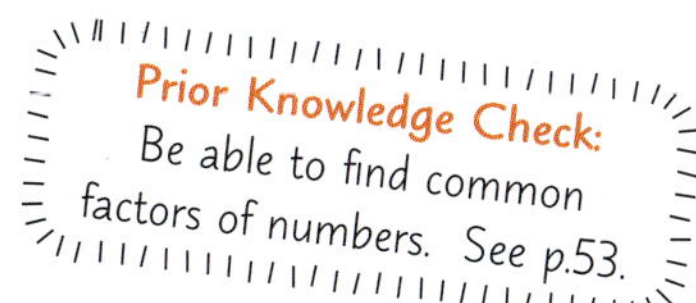

Prior Knowledge Check:
Be able to find common factors of numbers. See p.53.

Ratios are used to compare quantities. If you have an amount a of one thing and an amount b of another thing, then the **ratio of a to b** is written $a:b$.

- For example, here the ratio of circles to squares is **6:4**.

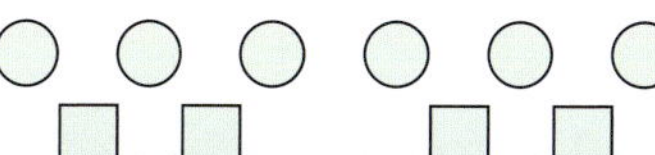

You can **simplify** ratios by dividing each number by a **common factor**, just like you do with fractions.

- The ratio 6:4 simplifies to **3:2** by dividing both sides by 2.

A ratio is in its **simplest form** when all parts are whole numbers, but they have no common factor that is greater than 1.

Tip: A ratio $a:b:c$, with three quantities, can be simplified by dividing all parts by a common factor.

Example 1

There are 15 fiction books and 10 non-fiction books on a shelf.

a) Write down the ratio of fiction books to non-fiction books.

Write down the ratio with the quantities in the order that you're asked to give them.

fiction : non-fiction
15 : 10

b) Write this ratio in its simplest form.

1. Divide both sides by the same number — a common factor of the two sides.
2. Stop when you can't divide any further and leave whole numbers on each side.

5 is a common factor.

15 : 10 → (÷5, ÷5) → 3 : 2

The simplest form is **3:2**.

Tip: You can get to the simplest form of a ratio in one step by dividing both sides by their highest common factor.

Exercise 1

Q1 Write down the ratio of stars to triangles.

Q2 On a farm there are 15 pigs and 23 cows. Write down the ratio of cows to pigs.

Q3 Write down each of the following ratios in its simplest form.

a) 2 : 8 b) 5 : 15 c) 40 : 10 d) 4 : 6

Q4 Write down each of the following ratios in its simplest form.

a) 6 : 2 : 4 b) 15 : 12 : 3 c) 14 : 10 : 2 d) 24 : 12 : 20

Q5 A floor is made up of 24 black tiles and 8 white tiles.
Find the ratio of black tiles to white tiles in its simplest form.

Q6 At a party there are 36 girls and 27 boys. What is the ratio of girls to boys?
Give your answer in its simplest form.

Q7 A school has 595 pupils and 170 computers.
Write down the ratio of computers to pupils in its simplest form.

Q8 Paul and Soraya share a bag of 42 sweets. Paul has 16 sweets and Soraya has the rest.
Find the ratio of Soraya's sweets to Paul's sweets, giving your answer in its simplest form.

Ratios with Different Units

When you have a ratio involving **different units**, you must **convert** all quantities to the **same unit** before simplifying.

You don't need to include the units in the ratio after **simplifying**.

Tip: You'll need to know your unit conversions — see p.263 for these.

Example 2

Write the ratio 1 m : 40 cm in its simplest form.

1. Rewrite the ratio so that the units are the same.
   1 m = 100 cm, so 1 m : 40 cm is the same as 100 cm : 40 cm.
2. Remove the units altogether.
   100 : 40
3. Simplify as usual by dividing each side by the highest common factor, 20.
   ÷20 ÷20
   5 : 2

The simplest form is **5 : 2**.

Exercise 2

Q1 Write these ratios in their simplest form.

a) 10p : £1 b) 20 mm : 4 cm c) 10 g : 1 kg

d) 2 weeks : 7 days e) 40p : £1 f) 30 cm : 2 m

Q2 Give the following ratios in their simplest form.

a) 1 m : 150 mm b) 8 cm : 1.1 m c) 9 g : 0.3 kg

d) 2.5 hours : 20 mins e) £1.25 : 75p f) 65 m : 1.3 km

Q3 A jug of orange squash is made using 50 ml of orange concentrate and 1 litre of water. Find the ratio of concentrate to water in its simplest form.

Q4 Alexsy runs in two cross-country races. He runs the first in 45 minutes and the second in 3½ hours. Find the ratio of his first race time to his second race time in its simplest form.

Q5 The icing for some cupcakes is made by mixing 1.6 kg of icing sugar with 640 g of butter. Find the ratio of butter to icing sugar. Give your answer in its simplest form.

Writing Ratios in the Form 1 : n

Learning Objective — Spec Ref R4:
Convert ratios to the form $1:n$.

Practical problems can often involve finding 'how much of b is needed for **every one** of a'.

In these situations, it's useful to have the ratio in the form **1 : *n***. To write a ratio $a:b$ in this form, just **divide both sides** by ***a***.

$$a:b \longrightarrow 1:\frac{b}{a}$$

Tip: b doesn't have to be a factor of a. You can leave $\frac{b}{a}$ as a fraction or as a decimal.

Example 3

Nigel makes his favourite smoothie by mixing half a litre of blueberry juice with 100 millilitres of plain yoghurt. How much yoghurt does he use for every millilitre of juice?

1. Write down the ratio of juice to yoghurt and remove the units.

   1 litre = 1000 ml, so 0.5 litres : 100 ml is the same as 500 ml : 100 ml.

2. You want the juice side (the left-hand side) to equal 1, so divide both sides by 500.

   500 : 100 → (÷500, ÷500) → 1 : 0.2

3. Use the simplified ratio to answer the question.

   So he uses **0.2 ml** of yoghurt for every 1 ml of juice.

Exercise 3

Q1 Write down the following ratios in the form $1:n$.

a) 2:6 b) 7:35 c) 6:24 d) 30:120

e) 2:7 f) 4:26 g) 8:26 h) 2:1

Q2 Write down each of these ratios in the form $1:n$.

a) 10 mm:5 cm b) 12p:£6 c) 30 mins:2 hours d) 500 g:20 kg

Q3 In a pond there are 7 frogs and 56 fish. Find the ratio of frogs to fish in the form $1:n$.

Q4 On a garage forecourt there are 15 red cars and 45 silver cars. Find the ratio of red cars to silver cars in the form $1:n$.

Q5 A recipe uses 125 ml of chocolate syrup and 2.5 litres of milk. Write the ratio of chocolate syrup to milk in the form $1:n$.

Q6 Two towns 4.8 km apart are shown on a map 12 cm apart. Find the ratio of the map distance to the true distance in the form $1:n$.

Ratios and Fractions

Learning Objectives — Spec Ref N11/R8:

- Use ratios to find fractions.
- Use fractions to find ratios.

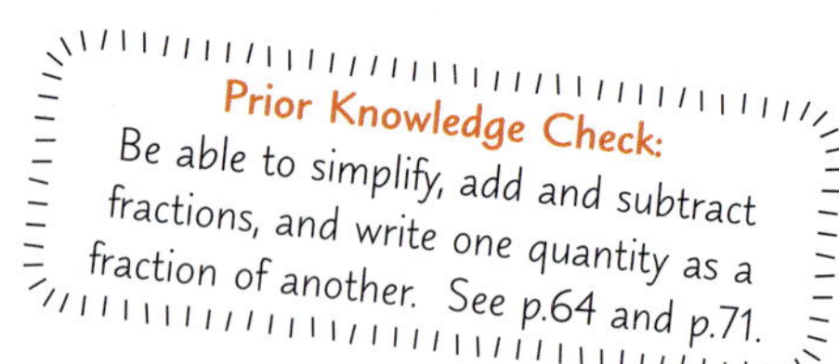

Prior Knowledge Check:
Be able to simplify, add and subtract fractions, and write one quantity as a fraction of another. See p.64 and p.71.

If you have a ratio $a:b$ (or $a:b:c$), you can find the **fraction** of one part out of the total:

- First find the **total** number of **parts** in the ratio, i.e. $a + b$ (or $a + b + c$).
- Make a **fraction** with the **part** you're interested in as the fraction's **numerator**, and the **total** number of parts as the fraction's **denominator** — then **simplify** if necessary.

Example 4

A box of doughnuts contains jam doughnuts and chocolate doughnuts in the ratio 3:5. What fraction of the doughnuts are chocolate flavoured?

1. Add the numbers to find the total number of parts. — $3 + 5 = 8$ parts altogether.
2. Write a fraction with the number of parts that are chocolate as the numerator and the total number of parts as the denominator. — $\frac{5}{8}$ of the doughnuts are chocolate flavoured.

Exercise 4

Q1 A tiled floor has blue and white tiles in the ratio 1 : 3. What fraction of the tiles are blue?

Q2 A necklace has yellow beads and red beads in the ratio 3 : 2.
What fraction of the beads are red?

Q3 A bag contains 21 balls. The balls are blue, green and red in the ratio 1 : 2 : 4. PROBLEM SOLVING
Decide whether each of these statements is true or false.

a) $\frac{1}{7}$ of the balls are blue.

b) 3 of the balls are blue.

c) $\frac{2}{4}$ of the balls are red or green.

d) The ratio of blue to red balls is 1 : 4.

e) There are more red balls than green balls.

When quantities are given as fractions, you can put them into ratio form.

- Express each quantity as a fraction with a **common denominator**.
- Then the **numerators** of each fraction go into the ratio.

Example 5

All of Ishan's DVDs are either horror films or comedies.
If $\frac{2}{7}$ of his DVDs are horror films, find the ratio of comedies to horror films.

1. Write each part as a fraction over a common denominator.
2. Write the numerators in ratio form in the order you were asked for.

$\frac{2}{7}$ are horror films,
so $1 - \frac{2}{7} = \frac{5}{7}$ are comedies.

Ratio of comedies to horror is **5 : 2**.

Exercise 5

Q1 Aiden has a bag of red and green Jelly Babies. $\frac{1}{3}$ of the Jelly Babies are red.
Write down the ratio of red to green Jelly Babies.

Q2 $\frac{3}{19}$ of the members of a chess club are left-handed.
Write down the ratio of right-handed club members to left-handed club members.

Q3 During one day at a pizza restaurant, $\frac{3}{8}$ of the pizzas ordered were pepperoni, $\frac{1}{2}$ were goat's cheese and the rest were spicy chicken.
Write down the ratio of pepperoni to goat's cheese to spicy chicken.

6.2 Using Ratios

Now that you're familiar with ratios, it's time to see how they can be used to solve different types of problems. These aren't too tricky as long as you understand what the ratio tells you, so look back at the previous few pages if you need a little reminder.

Part : Part Ratios

Learning Objective — Spec Ref R5:
Be able to use ratios to find unknown amounts.

A **part:part** ratio $a:b$ describes the **relationship** between two **quantities** — for every ***a*** lots of the first quantity, there are ***b*** lots of the second quantity.

If you know the **ratio** of one quantity to another, and you know **how big one** of them is, you can use this information to find the size of the **other**.

Example 1

The ratio of men to women in an office is 3:4.
If there are 9 men in the office, how many women are there?

1. Write down what you know and what you need to find out. $3:4 = 9:?$
2. Work out what you have to multiply the left-hand side of the ratio by to get from 3 to 9. Then multiply the right-hand side by the same number.

$$\times 3 \quad 3:4 \quad \times 3$$
$$9:12$$

So there are **12 women**.

Exercise 1

Q1 For a class of pupils, the ratio of blue eyes to brown eyes is 2 : 3.
If 8 pupils have blue eyes, how many pupils have brown eyes?

Q2 The ages of a father and son are in the ratio 8 : 3. If the father is 48, how old is the son?

Q3 The ratio of red to yellow sweets in a bag is 3 : 4.
If the bag contains 12 yellow sweets, how many red sweets are there?

Q4 In a wood there are oak trees and beech trees in the ratio 2 : 9.
If there are 42 oak trees, how many beech trees are there?

Q5 In a supermarket the ratio of apples to bananas is 5 : 3.
If there are 450 bananas, how many apples are there?

Q6 A recipe uses sugar and butter in the ratio 2 : 1.
How much butter would be needed with 100 g of sugar?

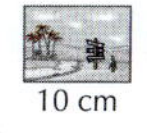

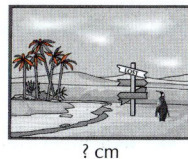

Q7 A photo with a width of 10 cm is enlarged so that the ratio of the original and enlarged photos' widths is 2 : 7. How wide is the enlarged photo?

Q8 The ratio of children to adults in a swimming pool must be 5 : 1 or less. If there are 32 children, how many adults must there be?

Q9 A TV-show producer is selecting a studio audience. He wants the ratio of under 30s to those aged 30 or over to be at least 8 : 1. If 100 under 30s are selected, find the maximum number of people aged 30 or over.

A **part : part : part** ratio $a : b : c$ can be used in the same way.

- It contains three **part : part** ratios — these are $a : b$, $b : c$ and $a : c$.
- Given a part : part : part ratio and **one quantity**, you can work out the **other two** quantities.

Tip: You won't always need every bit of the ratio, as in the example below.

Example 2

A cereal contains raisins, nuts and oats in the ratio 2 : 3 : 5. If a box of the cereal contains 200 g of raisins and 300 g of nuts, find how many grams of oats it contains.

1. Write the ratio of one of the quantities you know to the one you want to find.
2. Find the number that both sides of the ratio have to be multiplied by. Remember to give the mass in grams.

The ratio of nuts to oats is 3 : 5.

3 : 5
= 300 : ? → × 100 (3 : 5 → 300 : 500) × 100

So it contains **500 g oats.**

Exercise 2

Q1 A fruit punch is made by mixing pineapple juice, orange juice, and lemonade in the ratio 1 : 3 : 6. If 500 ml of pineapple juice is used, how much orange juice is needed?

Q2 Mai, Lizzy and Dave have heights in the ratio 31 : 33 : 37.
Mai is 155 cm tall. How tall are Lizzy and Dave?

Q3 Max, Molly and Hasan are at a bus stop. The number of minutes they have waited can be represented by the ratio 3 : 7 : 2. Molly has been waiting for 1 hour and 10 minutes. Calculate how long Max and Hasan have been waiting for.

Part : Whole Ratios

Learning Objective — Spec Ref R5:
Be able to change between part : part and part : whole ratios.

A **part : whole** ratio describes how **one** quantity relates to the **whole** (or **total**).

- To convert a **part : part** ratio $a:b$ into a **part : whole** ratio, choose which part you want to keep (a or b) and find the **total** $a + b$. Then the part : whole ratio is $\boldsymbol{a:a+b}$ (or $\boldsymbol{b:a+b}$).
- To convert a **part : whole** ratio $a:w$ into a **part : part** ratio, you subtract the **known part**, a, from the **whole**, w, to find the **unknown** part $\boldsymbol{w-a}$. Then the part : part ratio is $\boldsymbol{a:w-a}$.

Example 3

A recipe uses white flour and brown flour in a ratio of 2 : 1.
What is the ratio of white flour used to the total amount of flour used?

1. Find the total number of parts. — There are 2 + 1 = 3 parts altogether.
2. So 2 parts of white flour is used for every 3 parts in total. — So white flour : total flour is **2 : 3**.

Example 4

A shop sells only green and brown garden sheds. The ratio of green sheds sold to the total number of sheds sold is 5 : 7. What is the ratio of green sheds sold to brown sheds sold?

Subtract to find the number of brown sheds sold for every 5 green sheds, then write as a ratio. — 7 – 5 = 2 brown sheds per 5 green sheds. So green : brown is **5 : 2**.

Exercise 3

Q1 A biscuit tin only contains digestives and bourbons. The ratio of digestives to the total number of biscuits is 4 : 7. What is the ratio of digestives to bourbons?

Q2 When Dan makes a cup of tea, the ratio of water to milk is 15 : 2. What is the ratio of water to the total amount of liquid in the cup?

Q3 A rock album is sold as a digital download and on a CD. The ratio of digital downloads to total albums sold is 53 : 99. What is the ratio of digital downloads to CDs sold?

Q4 A bouquet of flowers contains only roses, tulips and daisies in the ratio 3 : 5 : 9. What is the ratio of roses to the total number of flowers?

6.3 Dividing in a Given Ratio

Ratios can be used to share things out unequally. The ratio tells you how many shares there are and what the size of each share should be. You can use both part : part and part : whole ratios for sharing, but you might have to come up with the ratio yourself from information in the question.

Learning Objectives — Spec Ref R5/R6:
- Divide quantities in a given part : part or part : whole ratio.
- Be able to write a ratio given a multiplicative relationship between two quantities.

Part : part ratios can be used to divide an amount into two or more **shares**. The numbers in the ratio show how many parts of the whole each share gets. To share an amount in a given ratio:

- **Add up** all the quantities to get the **total** number of parts, i.e. $a + b$ or $a + b + c$.
- **Divide** the amount to be shared by the total number of parts. This tells you the amount that **one part** is worth.
- **Multiply** the amount for one part by each quantity in the ratio. This gives you the amount in **each share**.

Tip: After you've calculated the shares, check they add up to the total amount.

Example 1

Divide £54 in the ratio 4 : 5.

1. Add the numbers to find the total number of parts.
   4 + 5 = 9 parts altogether
2. Work out the amount for one part.
   9 parts = £54
   So 1 part = £54 ÷ 9 = £6
3. Then multiply the amount for one part by each quantity in the ratio.
   £6 × 4 = £24
   £6 × 5 = £30
   So the shares are **£24** and **£30**.
   (Check: £24 + £30 = £54 ✔)

Example 2

A drink is made using apple juice, blackcurrant juice and lemonade in the ratio 3 : 2 : 5. How much lemonade is needed to make 5 litres of the drink?

1. Add the numbers to find the total number of parts.
   3 + 2 + 5 = 10 parts altogether
2. Work out the amount for one part.
   10 parts = 5 litres
   So 1 part = 0.5 litres
3. Then multiply the amount for one part by the quantity for lemonade in the ratio.
   0.5 litres × 5
   = **2.5 litres of lemonade**

Exercise 1

Q1 Divide £48 in the following ratios.

a) 2 : 1 b) 1 : 3 c) 5 : 1 d) 7 : 5

Q2 Share 90 kg in these ratios.

a) 4 : 1 b) 7 : 2 c) 8 : 7 d) 12 : 18

Q3 Divide 72 cm in the following ratios.

a) 2 : 3 : 1 b) 2 : 2 : 5 c) 5 : 3 : 4 d) 7 : 6 : 5

Q4 Kat and Lincoln share 30 cupcakes in the ratio 3 : 2. How many do they each get?

Q5 Three friends win £6000 between them. They decide to share the money in the ratio 3 : 5 : 4. Calculate the amounts they each receive.

Q6 The length and width of a rectangle are in the ratio 5 : 1. If the perimeter of the rectangle is 72 cm, calculate the length and the width of the rectangle.

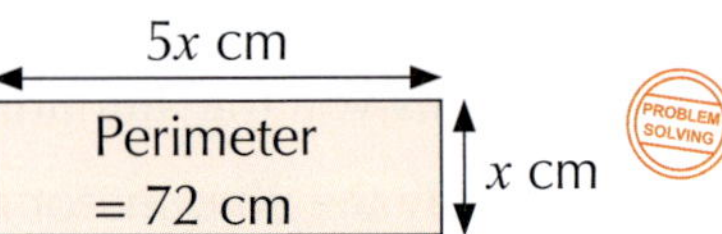

If you're given a **part : whole** ratio, you can just **divide** the amount by the total number of parts (the whole). You may need to work out the **unknown part** of the ratio, as you did on p.96.

Example 3

A box of 45 chocolates contains dark and milk chocolates. The ratio of milk chocolates to the total number of chocolates is 7 : 9. How many of each chocolate are in the box?

1. Work out the unknown part.

   There are 9 – 7 = 2 parts dark chocolate.

2. Work out the amount for one part. The ratio 2 : 9 is part : whole, so there are 9 parts in total.

   9 parts = 45 chocolates, so
   1 part = 45 ÷ 9 = 5 chocolates

3. Multiply the amount for one part by the number of parts for each share.

   5 × 7 = **35 milk chocolates**
   5 × 2 = **10 dark chocolates**

Exercise 2

Q1 A farmer has a flock of 60 sheep that he splits into two parts. Write down the size of each part when the flock is divided according to the following part : whole ratios.

a) 1 : 2 b) 2 : 3 c) 4 : 5 d) 7 : 12

Q2 Orange paint is made by mixing yellow and red paint.
The ratio of yellow paint to the total volume of paint is 4 : 7.
How much of each colour is needed to make 42 litres of orange paint?

Q3 In a school of 600 pupils, the ratio of right-handed pupils to the total number of students is 7 : 8. How many left-handed pupils are there?

Multiplicative Relationships

Instead of a ratio, you might be given a **multiplicative relationship** between two or more quantities. To divide an amount into shares, you will first need to turn this relationship into a **ratio**.

For example, if you're told there are five times as many sparrows as pigeons, first write down the ratio of sparrows to pigeons — it's 5 : 1.

Tip: These can be wordy questions. But once you've picked out the numbers, you'll find they're the usual ratio problems.

Example 4

A reptile house contains only snakes and lizards, with twice as many snakes as lizards. If there's a total of 24 reptiles, how many snakes and how many lizards are there?

1. Work out the ratio from the information you're given. — There are 2 snakes for every lizard, so the ratio of snakes to lizards is 2 : 1.
2. Work out the amount for one part. — There are 2 + 1 = 3 parts in total, so 1 part = 24 ÷ 3 = 8 reptiles.
3. Multiply the amount for one part by each quantity in the ratio. — 8 × 2 = **16 snakes**, 8 × 1 = **8 lizards**

Exercise 3

Q1 A piggy bank contains only 5p and 20p coins. There are three times as many 5p coins as 20p coins, and 32 coins in total. How many 20p coins does the piggy bank contain?

Q2 There are 30 passengers on a bus. There are four times as many passengers not on the phone as there are on the phone. How many passengers are not on their phones?

Q3 Daniel gets one-and-a-half times as much profit from a business as his partner Elsa. How much of a £5700 profit does Daniel get?

Q4 For a fruit salad, Celia uses twice the weight of raspberries as grapes, and three times the weight of strawberries as grapes. How much of each fruit did Celia use in a 450 g fruit salad?

Q5 Nicky, Jacinta and Samir share a bag of 35 sweets so that Nicky gets half as much as Jacinta, and Samir gets half as much as Nicky. How many sweets do each of them get?

Review Exercise

Q1 There are 17 boys and 14 girls in a class. Write down the ratio of girls to boys.

Q2 Write down each of the following ratios in its simplest form.

a) 24 : 6 b) 2 cm : 8 mm c) 6 : 3 : 15 d) 0.03 kg : 10 g : 25 g

Q3 An animal sanctuary has 120 animals, 40 of which are donkeys.
Write the ratio of donkeys to other animals in the form $1 : n$.

Q4 In Amy's sock drawer there are spotty, stripy and plain socks in the ratio 5 : 1 : 4.
What fraction of Amy's socks are stripy?

Q5 $\frac{5}{12}$ of the children at a school eat school dinners and the rest bring a packed lunch.
What is the ratio of children with a packed lunch to those who eat school dinners?

Q6 The ratio of green to red peppers in a risotto is 2 : 5. A restaurant uses 20 red peppers to make some risotto. How many green peppers does it use?

Q7 Meera and Sabrina share a holiday job. They split the money they make in the ratio 7 : 6 (Meera : Sabrina). If Sabrina gets £48, how much does Meera get?

Q8 Share 56 m in these ratios.

a) 1 : 7 b) 4 : 4 c) 10 : 4 d) 22 : 6

Q9 Gemma, Alisha and Omar have a combined height of 496 cm.
If their heights are in the ratio 19 : 20 : 23, how tall are they?

Q10 Lauren and Cara receive £1200 in total from their Grandad. The ratio of the money given to Lauren to the total amount is 2 : 3. How much money did Cara get?

Q11 A patch of garden contains daisy, dandelion and thistle plants. There are twice as many dandelions as daisies, and three times as many thistles as dandelions.

PROBLEM SOLVING

a) What is the ratio of daisies to dandelions to thistles?
b) If there are 54 plants in total, how many thistles are there?

Exam-Style Questions

Q1 a) Explain why the ratio 30 : 48 can be written as 5 : 8.

[1 mark]

b) Use part a) to write the ratio 30 : 48 in the form 1 : n, where n is a decimal.

[2 marks]

Q2 A football squad of 24 players has three times as many right-footed players as it does left-footed players.

a) Write down the ratio of right-footed players to left-footed players.

[1 mark]

b) How many players are right-footed?

[2 marks]

c) What fraction of players are left-footed?

[2 marks]

Q3 A badminton club has 330 members. 240 are adults and the rest are children. Two thirds of the children are boys and the rest are girls.

a) Show that the ratio of adults : boys : girls is 8 : 2 : 1

[2 marks]

A year ago, the club had 200 adult members but the ratio adults : boys : girls was the same as it is now.

b) Work out the number of boys in the club a year ago.

[2 marks]

Q4 The weight of flour in two bags is in the ratio 4 : 5.

a) Write this ratio in the form 1 : n.

[1 mark]

Alan says "If I add the same amount of flour to each bag, then the two bags will still be in the same ratio."

b) Show that Alan is incorrect.

[2 marks]

c) Explain what Alan could have done to the amount of flour in each bag to keep the ratio the same.

[1 mark]

7.1 Percentages

'Per cent' means 'out of 100'. Writing an amount as a percentage means writing it as a number out of 100. Percentages are written using the % symbol and are useful for showing proportions.

Writing One Number as a Percentage of Another

Learning Objectives — Spec Ref R9:
- Be able to write one number as a percentage of another without a calculator.
- Be able to write one number as a percentage of another using a calculator.

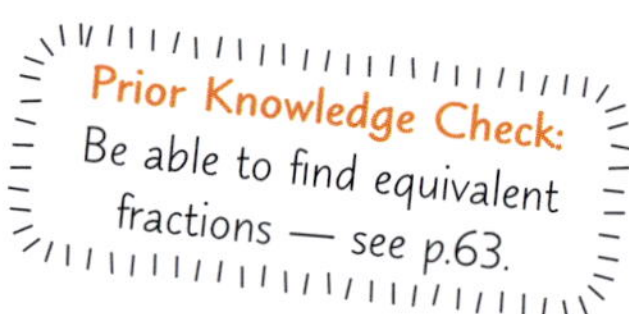

Prior Knowledge Check:
Be able to find equivalent fractions — see p.63.

Here's how to write one number as a **percentage** of another number without a calculator.

- Make a **fraction** by writing the first number over the second number.
- Change that fraction into an **equivalent fraction** that has a denominator of 100.
- The **numerator** of the equivalent fraction will then tell you the percentage.

Example 1

Out of 100 cars in a car park, 38 are red. What percentage of the cars are red?

1. Write the amount as a fraction. $\frac{38}{100}$
2. The amount is already written 'out of 100'.
3. Write the amount as a percentage. So **38%** of the cars are red.

Example 2

Express 15 as a percentage of 50.

1. Write the amount as a fraction. $\frac{15}{50}$
2. Write an equivalent fraction which is 'out of 100' by multiplying the top and bottom by the same number. $\frac{15}{50} = \frac{30}{100}$ (× 2 top and bottom)
3. The percentage is the numerator of the equivalent fraction. So 15 is **30%** of 50.

Exercise 1

Q1 Each grid below is made up of 100 small squares.
Find the percentage of each grid that is shaded.

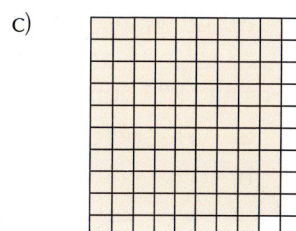

a) 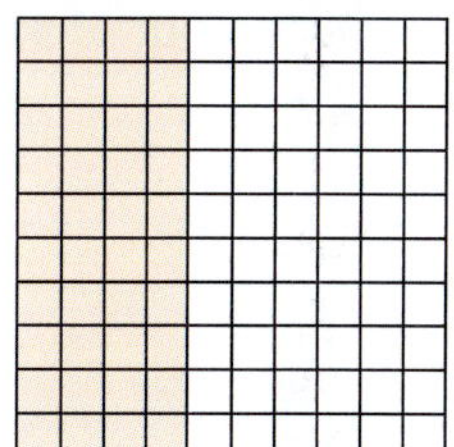

b) 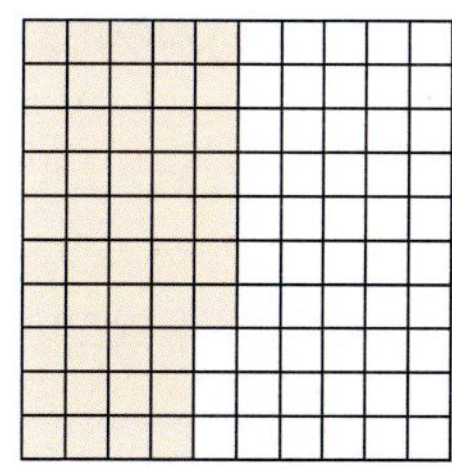

c) 

Q2 Write each of the following amounts as a percentage.

a) 13 out of 100 b) 27 out of 100 c) 76 out of 100 d) 243 out of 100

Q3 A football team scored 100 goals in one season.
13 of these goals were penalties.
What percentage of the goals scored were **not** penalties?

Q4 There are 300 coloured counters in a bag. 45 of these counters are green.

a) Write the number of green counters as a fraction of the total number of counters.

b) Find the fraction equivalent to your answer to part a) which has 100 as the denominator.

c) Hence express the amount of green counters as a percentage.

Q5 Write each of the following amounts as a percentage.

a) 11 out of 25 b) 33 out of 50 c) 3 out of 20 d) 21 out of 10

e) 12 out of 200 f) 99 out of 300 g) 600 out of 400 h) 890 out of 1000

You might need to use **more than one step** to find the equivalent fraction.

Example 3

Express 45 as a percentage of 180.

1. Write the amount as a fraction.
2. It may take more than one step to write the fraction out of 100.
3. Write the amount as a percentage.

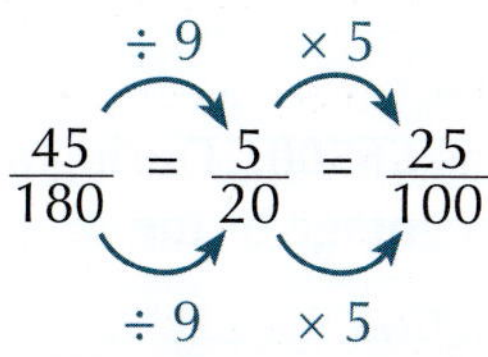

$$\frac{45}{180} = \frac{5}{20} = \frac{25}{100}$$

So 45 is **25%** of 180.

Tip: When finding percentages that require more than one step, try to first get the denominator equal to a factor of 100. E.g. 4, 5, 10, 20, etc.

Exercise 2

Q1 Write each of the following amounts as a percentage.

a) 8 out of 32 b) 36 out of 60 c) 24 out of 40

d) 48 out of 120 e) 34 out of 170 f) 42 out of 35

Q2 Out of 24 pupils in a class, 18 walk to school.

a) What percentage of the class walk to school?

b) What percentage of the class do not walk to school?

Q3 There are 55 chocolates in a tin. 33 of the chocolates are milk chocolate. The rest are dark chocolate. What percentage are dark chocolate?

Q4 39 out of 65 people in a book club have blonde hair. What percentage do not have blonde hair?

Sometimes it's **hard** to find an equivalent fraction that has a denominator of 100. When this happens, it is easier to **divide** the top number by the bottom number and then **multiply** the result **by 100**. You can **use a calculator** if the division is tricky.

Example 4

Express 333 as a percentage of 360.

1. Write the amount as a fraction. $\frac{333}{360}$
2. It's not easy to rewrite this as a fraction out of 100. So divide using a calculator instead. $333 \div 360 = 0.925$
3. Multiply by 100% to write as a percentage. $0.925 \times 100\% =$ **92.5%**

Tip: Here we're converting from a fraction to a decimal, then to a percentage — see p.108.

Example 5

The original price of a car was £6500. During a sale, Jennifer bought the car for £4550. What percentage of the original price did she pay?

1. Write the amount as a fraction. $\frac{£4550}{£6500}$
2. Divide using a calculator. $4550 \div 6500 = 0.7$
3. Multiply by 100% to write as a percentage. $0.7 \times 100\% =$ **70%**

Exercise 3

Q1 Write each of the following amounts as a percentage.

a) 15 out of 24 b) 77 out of 275 c) 61 out of 500 d) 1512 out of 375

Q2 A school has 875 pupils. 525 are boys. What is this as a percentage?

Q3 Express £252 as a percentage of £560.

Q4 171 out of 180 raffle tickets were sold for a summer fete.
What percentage of the tickets were sold?

Q5 a) Express 31.36 as a percentage of 32.

b) Express £117.30 as a percentage of £782.

Q6 The jackpot for a lottery was £10 250. Caitlin won £1896.25.
What percentage of the total jackpot did she win?

Q7 Curtis receives £5.60 pocket money per week from his parents,
and £2.40 pocket money per week from his grandparents.
What percentage of his total pocket money comes from his grandparents?

Finding a Percentage without a Calculator

Learning Objective — Spec Ref N12:
Be able to find a percentage of an amount without a calculator.

You can find some percentages without a calculator using the following rules.

- **50%** $= \frac{1}{2}$, so find 50% of something by **dividing by 2** (or multiplying by $\frac{1}{2}$).
- **25%** $= \frac{1}{4}$, so find 25% of something by **dividing by 4** (or multiplying by $\frac{1}{4}$).
- **10%** $= \frac{1}{10}$, so find 10% of something by **dividing by 10** (or multiplying by $\frac{1}{10}$).
- **5%** $= \frac{1}{20}$, so find 5% of something by **dividing by 20** (or by dividing 10% of something by 2).
- **1%** $= \frac{1}{100}$, so find 1% of something by **dividing by 100** (or multiplying by $\frac{1}{100}$).

To find other percentages, add up combinations of the percentages above,
e.g. 65% = 50% + 10% + 5%.

Example 6

Find 75% of 44.

1. First find 25% by dividing by 4. 25% of 44 = 44 ÷ 4 = 11
2. 75% = 3 × 25%, so multiply by 3. So 75% of 44 = 3 × 11 = **33**

Tip: You could also find 75% by adding together 50%, 20% and 5%.

Example 7

Find 35% of 70.

1. First find 10% of 70 by dividing by 10. 10% of 70 = 70 ÷ 10 = 7
2. 30% = 3 × 10%, so multiply 7 by 3 to find 30%. 30% of 70 = 3 × 7 = 21
3. 5% = 10% ÷ 2, so divide 7 by 2 to find 5%. 5% of 70 = 7 ÷ 2 = 3.5
4. 35% = 30% + 5%, so add the two amounts to find 35%. So 35% of 70 = 21 + 3.5 = **24.5**

Exercise 4

Q1 Find each of the following.

a) 50% of 24 b) 50% of 15 c) 25% of 36
d) 25% of 120 e) 10% of 90 f) 10% of 270

Q2 a) Find 25% of 48.
b) Use your answer to find 75% of 48.

Q3 a) Find 10% of 120.
b) Use your answer to find the following.
(i) 5% of 120 (ii) 20% of 120 (iii) 25% of 120

Q4 Find each of the following.

a) 75% of 12 b) 125% of 20 c) 5% of 260
d) 31% of 200 e) 110% of 70 f) 46% of 500

Q5 What is 83% of £30?

Q6 A wooden plank is 9 m long. 55% of the plank is cut off.
What length of wood has been cut off?

Q7 Shima has £1400 in her savings account. She gives 95% of her savings to charity.
How much does she give to charity?

Finding a Percentage with a Calculator

Learning Objective — Spec Ref N12:
Be able to find a percentage of an amount using a calculator.

To find a percentage of an amount, first **divide** the percentage by **100%** to change the percentage into a **decimal**. Then multiply the amount by the decimal.

Example 8

Find 67% of 138.

1. Divide by 100% to turn 67% into a decimal. $67\% \div 100\% = 0.67$
2. Multiply 138 by the decimal. $0.67 \times 138 = \mathbf{92.46}$

Exercise 5

Q1 Find each of the following.

a) 17% of 200 b) 9% of 11 c) 3% of 210

d) 158% of 615 e) 59% of 713 f) 282% of 823

Q2 What is 12% of 68 kg?

Q3 Jeff is on a journey of 385 km.
So far, he has completed 31% of his journey.
How far has he travelled?

Q4 125 people work in an office. 52% of the office workers are men.
How many workers is this?

Q5 The cost of an adult's ticket for a theme park is £42.
A child's ticket is 68% of the price of an adult's ticket.
How much does a child's ticket cost?

Q6 Which is larger, 22% of £57 or 46% of £28? By how much?

Q7 A jug can hold 2.4 litres of water. It is 34% full.
How much more water will fit in the jug?

7.2 Percentages, Fractions and Decimals

Percentages, fractions and decimals are three different ways of showing a proportion of something. It's really important that you are able to convert between all three of them.

Converting between Percentages, Fractions and Decimals

Learning Objective — Spec Ref R9:
Be able to convert between percentages, fractions and decimals.

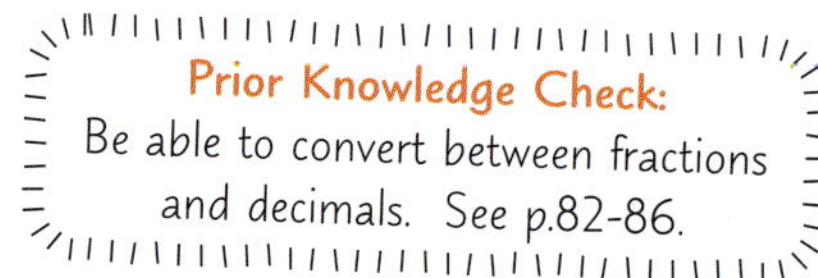

Prior Knowledge Check:
Be able to convert between fractions and decimals. See p.82-86.

You can switch between percentages, fractions and decimals in the following ways.

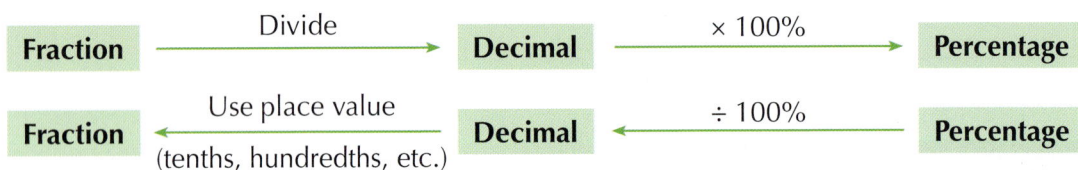

Fraction —Divide→ **Decimal** —× 100%→ **Percentage**

Fraction ←Use place value (tenths, hundredths, etc.)— **Decimal** ←÷ 100%— **Percentage**

You can convert directly from a fraction to a percentage by finding an **equivalent fraction** with a **denominator of 100** — then the **numerator** gives the percentage.

You can also convert directly from a percentage to a fraction by writing the **percentage as the numerator** and **100 as the denominator** — then **simplify** the fraction.

Example 1

Write 24% as: a) a decimal b) a fraction in its simplest terms.

a) Divide by 100% to write as a decimal. 24% ÷ 100% = **0.24**

b) The final digit of 0.24 (the '4') is in the hundredths column, so write 0.24 as 24 hundredths. Then simplify by dividing the top and bottom by 4.

$$0.24 = \frac{24}{100} = \mathbf{\frac{6}{25}} \quad (\div 4 \text{ top and bottom})$$

Tip: For a reminder about simplifying fractions, have a look at page 64.

Example 2

Write $\frac{3}{8}$ as: a) a decimal b) a percentage.

a) Calculate 3 ÷ 8 using short division. The answer will be a decimal.

$$8\overline{)3.{}^{3}0{}^{6}0{}^{4}0} = 0.375 \qquad \text{So } \frac{3}{8} = \mathbf{0.375}$$

b) Multiply the decimal by 100% to find the percentage. 0.375 × 100% = **37.5%**

Exercise 1

Q1 Each grid below is made up of 100 small squares.
Find the proportion of each grid that is shaded as:
(i) a percentage, (ii) a decimal, and (iii) a fraction in its simplest terms.

a) 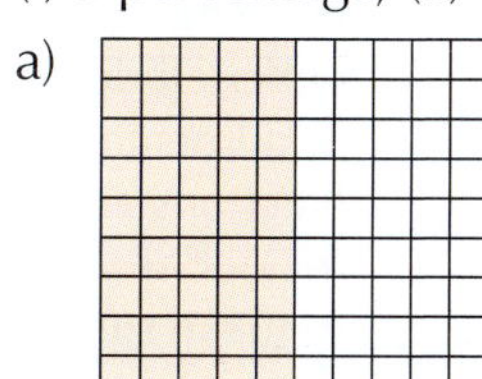

b) 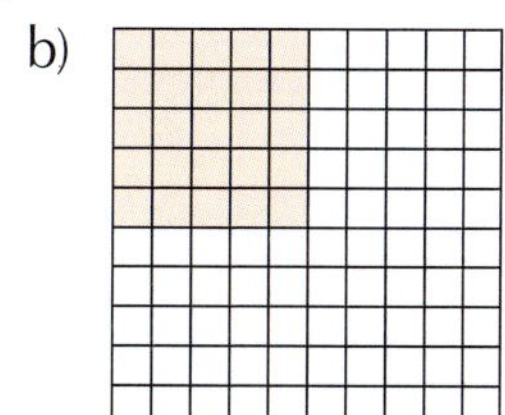

c) 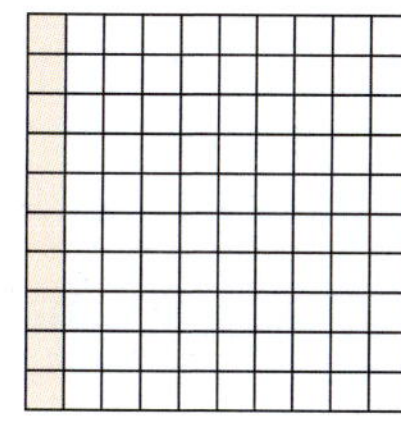

Q2 a) Find the fraction equivalent to $\frac{3}{20}$ which has 100 as the denominator.

b) Write $\frac{3}{20}$ as (i) a percentage, and (ii) a decimal.

Q3 Write each of the following percentages as
(i) a decimal, and (ii) a fraction in its simplest terms.

a) 30% b) 5% c) 13% d) 96%

Q4 Write each of the following fractions as (i) a decimal, and (ii) a percentage.

a) $\frac{79}{100}$ b) $\frac{2}{5}$ c) $\frac{4}{25}$ d) $\frac{7}{8}$

Q5 Write each of the following decimals as
(i) a percentage, and (ii) a fraction in its simplest terms.

a) 0.35 b) 0.86 c) 1.2 d) 0.125

Q6 Raj answers 76% of the questions in a test correctly.
Write this as a decimal.

Q7 $\frac{3}{5}$ of the pupils in a class are right-handed.
What percentage of the class are right-handed?

Comparing Percentages, Fractions and Decimals

Learning Objective — Spec Ref R9:
Be able to compare and order percentages, fractions and decimals.

As percentages, fractions and decimals are all used to represent proportions, it's useful to be able to **compare** them — you'll have to **convert** them all into the **same form** first.

Example 3

Put $\frac{1}{4}$, 24% and 0.244 in order, from smallest to largest.

Write the amounts in the same form.
In this example, they'll all be written as decimals.

1. Calculate 1 ÷ 4 to write $\frac{1}{4}$ as a decimal. — $\frac{1}{4} = 0.25$
2. Calculate 24% ÷ 100% to write 24% as a decimal. — 24% ÷ 100% = 0.24
3. Put the decimals in order, from smallest to largest. — 0.24, 0.244, 0.25
4. Rewrite in their original forms. — **24%, 0.244, $\frac{1}{4}$**

Tip: It's best to write the amounts as either all decimals or all percentages. Fractions are a bit trickier as you need to make sure the denominators are the same before comparing them.

Exercise 2

Q1 For each of the following pairs, write down which is larger.

a) 0.35, 32% b) 0.4, 4% c) 0.09, 90%

d) 0.2, $\frac{21}{100}$ e) 0.6, $\frac{7}{10}$ f) 0.55, $\frac{3}{5}$

Q2 Put the numbers in each of the following lists in order, from smallest to largest.

a) 0.42, 25%, $\frac{2}{5}$ b) 0.505, 45%, $\frac{1}{2}$ c) 0.37, 38%, $\frac{4}{10}$

d) 22%, 0.2, $\frac{6}{25}$ e) 0.13, 12.5%, $\frac{3}{20}$ f) 0.25, 23%, $\frac{9}{40}$

Q3 Two shops are having a sale. PROBLEM SOLVING
Shop A is offering $\frac{1}{25}$ off all items, while Shop B is offering 5% off all items.
Which shop is reducing its prices by the greater percentage?

Q4 Margaret is buying a car. She needs to pay $\frac{2}{5}$ of the total cost as a deposit.

Her parents give her 35% of the cost of the car to help her buy it.
Is this enough to pay the deposit?

Q5 In a season, Team X won 14 out of the 20 matches they played. PROBLEM SOLVING
Team Y won 60% of their matches.
Which team had the highest proportion of wins?

Q6 Oliver and Jen each try flicking a set of counters into a box. PROBLEM SOLVING
Oliver gets 65% of the counters into the box. Jen gets $\frac{11}{20}$ of the counters into the box.
Who got more counters into the box?

Percentage, Fraction and Decimal Problems

Learning Objective — Spec Ref R9:
Be able to solve problems involving percentages, fractions and decimals.

You might need to convert between percentages, fractions and decimals before you're able to solve a problem. The first step will usually be **converting** them to the **same form**. Once you've converted them there's still work to do — don't forget to answer the question.

Example 4

$\frac{1}{4}$ of pupils in a school bring a packed lunch, 65% have school dinners, and the rest go home for lunch. What percentage of pupils go home for lunch?

1. Write $\frac{1}{4}$ as a percentage by writing it as a fraction out of 100.

   $\frac{1}{4} = \frac{25}{100}$ (× 25 top and bottom) So $\frac{1}{4} = 25\%$

2. Find the percentage that don't go home for lunch by adding the percentages for 'packed lunches' and 'school dinners'.

   25% + 65% = 90%

3. Subtract this from 100% to find the percentage who do go home for lunch.

   100% – 90% = **10%**

Tip: Think about your final answer when deciding how to convert. If you need to find a percentage, it's usually best to convert everything to percentages.

Exercise 3

Q1 $\frac{3}{4}$ of the people at a concert arrived by train, 0.05 walked, and the rest came by car. What percentage came by car?

Q2 $\frac{3}{5}$ of the footballs in a bag are white, 20% are black, and the rest are blue. What percentage of footballs are blue?

Q3 Beverley eats 0.3 of a pie, Victoria eats $\frac{1}{10}$, Patrick eats 20%, and Gus eats the rest. What percentage of the pie does Gus eat?

Q4 Ainslie is keeping a record of the birds in his garden.
Of the birds he has seen this month, $\frac{3}{8}$ were sparrows,
41.5% were blackbirds, and the rest were robins.
What percentage were robins?

7.3 Percentage Increase and Decrease

Percentages are often used to describe a change in an amount. The change could be an increase or a decrease, so make sure you know which one you're trying to find before tackling a question.

Calculating Amounts After a Percentage Increase or Decrease

Learning Objective — Spec Ref R9/N12:
Be able to find new amounts after a percentage increase or decrease.

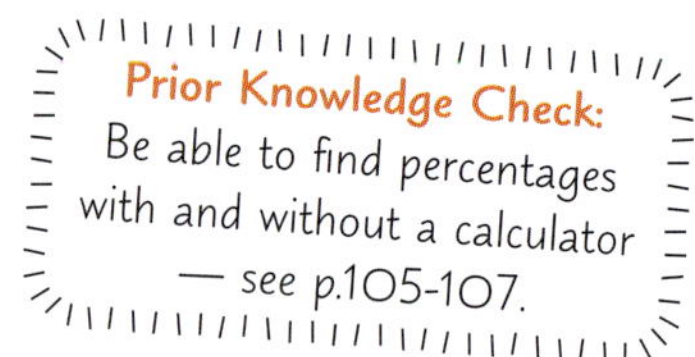

Prior Knowledge Check:
Be able to find percentages with and without a calculator
— see p.105-107.

To **increase** an amount by a percentage without using a calculator:

- Calculate the percentage.
- **Add it** to the original amount.

To **decrease** an amount by a percentage, **subtract** the percentage from the original amount.

Example 1

Increase 450 by 15% without using your calculator.

1. Find 10% and 5% of 450. — 10% of 450 = 450 ÷ 10 = 45
   5% of 450 = 45 ÷ 2 = 22.5
2. Add these to find 15% of 450. — So 15% of 450 = 45 + 22.5 = 67.5
3. Add this to the original amount. — 450 + 67.5 = **517.5**

Exercise 1

Q1 a) Find 50% of 360.
b) Increase 360 by 50%.

Q2 a) Find 30% of 120.
b) Increase 120 by 30%.

Q3 a) Find 10% of 160.
b) Decrease 160 by 10%.

Q4 a) Find 20% of 84.
b) Decrease 84 by 20%.

Q5 Increase each of the following amounts by the percentage given.
a) 90 by 10% b) 11 by 80% c) 140 by 45%

Q6 Decrease each of the following amounts by the percentage given.
a) 24 by 25% b) 55 by 70% c) 150 by 55%

Using a Multiplier

If you're using a calculator, you can find a percentage increase or decrease in one go using a **multiplier**. To find the multiplier:

- **Convert** the percentage to a decimal
- **Add it to 1** for a percentage increase, **or subtract it from 1** for a percentage decrease.

Then **multiply the amount** in the question by the multiplier to find the answer.

Tip: The method on the previous page also works with a calculator — use the method you prefer.

Example 2

Increase 425 by 18%.

1. Convert the percentage to a decimal. — $18\% \div 100\% = 0.18$
2. It's a percentage increase, so add to 1 to find the multiplier. — Multiplier $= 1 + 0.18$ $= 1.18$
3. Multiply 425 by the multiplier. — $425 \times 1.18 =$ **501.5**

Tip: A percentage increase has a multiplier greater than 1. A percentage decease has a multiplier less than 1.

Example 3

Decrease 326 by 12%.

1. Convert the percentage to a decimal. — $12\% \div 100\% = 0.12$
2. It's a percentage decrease, so subtract from 1 to find the multiplier. — Multiplier $= 1 - 0.12 = 0.88$
3. Multiply 326 by the multiplier. — $326 \times 0.88 =$ **286.88**

Exercise 2

Q1 Increase each of the following amounts by the percentage given.

a) 490 by 11% b) 101 by 16% c) 55 by 37%

d) 2523 by 67% e) 1036 by 23% f) 36 500 by 32%

Q2 Decrease each of the following amounts by the percentage given.

a) 77 by 8% b) 36 by 21% c) 101 by 43%

d) 8612 by 39% e) 75 250 by 4% f) 116 000 by 18%

Q3 a) Increase £89.50 by 62%. b) Decrease 58 kg by 19%.

Simple Interest

Learning Objective — Spec Ref R9:
Be able to solve problems involving simple interest.

Interest is a percentage of money that is added on to an amount over a period of time. **Simple interest** is when a certain percentage of the **original amount** is paid at regular intervals (usually once per year). Since simple interest is always based on the original amount, and the original amount **never changes**, the interest paid is the **same** every time.

Example 4

Fabian deposits £150 into an account which pays 5% simple interest per year. Without using a calculator, work out how much will be in the account after one year.

1. Find 5% of £150. — 10% of £150 = £15, so 5% of £150 = £15 ÷ 2 = £7.50
2. Add this to £150. — £150 + £7.50 = **£157.50**

Exercise 3

Q1 Leroy deposits £230 into an account which pays 5% simple interest per year. How much will be in the account after one year?

Q2 Kimberley deposits £890 into an account which pays 3% simple interest per year. How much will be in the account after three years?

Percentage Increase and Decrease Problems

Learning Objective — Spec Ref R9:
Be able to solve problems involving percentage increase and decrease.

You might come across **wordy problems** that involve percentage increase or decrease.

- Read the question **carefully** and work out if it's an **increase** or **decrease** problem (or both).
- Calculate the result of the increase or decrease using the **methods** you've learnt.

Tip: Check that you've answered the question fully — some problems have more than one step.

Example 5

Shop A sells a type of oven for £300 and then increases its prices by 5%.
Shop B sells the same type of oven for £290 and increases its prices by 10%.
Without using a calculator, work out which shop now has the cheaper price.

1. Calculate the new price for each shop.

Shop A	Shop B
10% of 300 = 30 So 5% of 300 = 15	10% of 290 = 29
£300 + £15 = £315	£290 + £29 = £319

2. Compare the new prices to see which is cheaper.

£315 < £319 ⇒ **Shop A** is cheaper

Exercise 4

Q1 Damelza's salary of £24 500 is increased by 15%.
What is her new salary?

Q2 A kettle originally costing £42 is reduced by 75% in a sale.
What is the sale price of the kettle?

Q3 20% VAT is added to the basic price of a TV to give the selling price.
The basic price of the TV is £485. What is the selling price?

Q4 A couple go out for a meal in a restaurant.
The total cost of the meal is £63, but the couple have a voucher for 13% off the bill.
How much do the couple pay?

Q5 David's height increased by 20% between the ages of 6 and 10.
He was 50 inches tall when he was 6. How tall was he when he was 10?

Q6 At the start of a journey, Natalie's car had 8 gallons of fuel, and Jason's car had 12 gallons of fuel.
During the journey, Natalie used 25% of her fuel, and Jason used 40% of his fuel.
Who had more fuel left at the end of the journey? By how much?

PROBLEM SOLVING

Q7 Last year, Elsie's gas bill was £480 and her electricity bill was £612.
This year, her gas bill has increased by 2% and her electricity bill has decreased by 4%.
Which is now the more expensive bill? By how much?

PROBLEM SOLVING

Q8 Alison earns £31 000 per year. One year, she gets a pay rise of 3%.
The following year, she gets a pay cut of 2%. How much does she now earn?

Finding a Change as a Percentage

Learning Objective — Spec Ref R9:
Be able to express the change in an amount as a percentage.

To find a percentage increase or decrease:

- Calculate the **difference** between the new amount and the original amount.
- Find this as a percentage of the **original amount**.

Example 6

In a sale, the cost of a CD is reduced from £15 to £9. Find the percentage decrease.

1. Find the difference between the new cost and the original cost.

£15 – £9 = £6

2. Write the difference as a fraction of the original cost...
3. ...then write the fraction out of 100 to find the percentage decrease.

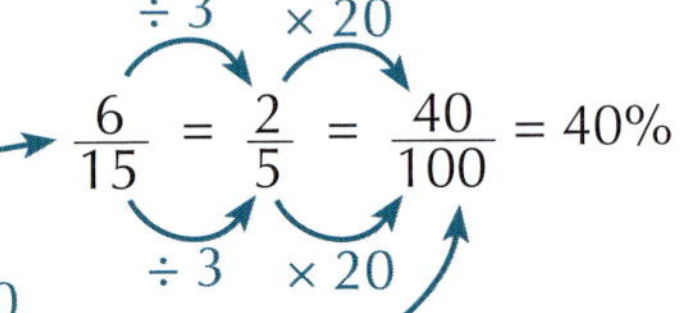

$$\frac{6}{15} = \frac{2}{5} = \frac{40}{100} = 40\%$$

(÷ 3, × 20)

So it is a **40%** decrease.

Tip: Remember to always divide by the original cost.

Exercise 5

Q1 Find the percentage increase when:

a) a price of £10 is increased to £12.
b) a price of £20 is increased to £22.
c) a price of £140 is increased to £161.
d) a price of £120 is increased to £174.

Q2 Find the percentage decrease when:

a) a price of £10 is decreased to £8.
b) a price of £25 is decreased to £22.
c) a price of £80 is decreased to £64.
d) a price of £150 is decreased to £138

Q3 The number of people working for a company increases from 50 to 72.

a) Find the difference in the number of people working for the company.
b) Write your answer to part a) as a fraction of the original amount.
c) Find the percentage increase in the number of people working for the company.

Q4 The price of a local newspaper increases from 80p to £1.
Find the percentage increase.

Q5 In a sale, the price of a toaster is reduced from £50 to £30.
Find the percentage reduction.

Q6 Percy is on a healthy eating plan.
His weight drops from 90 kg to 72 kg.

a) Find the amount of weight Percy has lost.
b) Find the percentage decrease in Percy's weight.

When you are allowed to **use a calculator** to find a change as a percentage, use the same method but find the percentage using the calculator technique shown on page 104.

Example 7

The price of a holiday increases from £320 to £364.80.
Find the percentage increase.

1. Find the difference between the new cost and the original cost. — £364.80 – £320 = £44.80
2. Divide the difference by the original amount using a calculator. — $\frac{44.80}{320} = 44.80 \div 320 = 0.14$
3. Multiply by 100 to find the percentage increase. — $0.14 \times 100 = 14$
So it is a **14%** increase.

Exercise 6

Q1 A shop owner buys a pair of trainers for £52 and sells them for £70.20.
What is her percentage profit?

Q2 The height of a sunflower increases from 1.3 m to 2.08 m over the course of summer.
What is the percentage increase in its height?

Q3 During a season, the average attendance for a local sports team's matches was 11 350.
The following season, the average attendance was 11 123.
Find the percentage decrease.

Q4 A car is bought for £12 950.
Three years later, it is sold for £8806.
After another three years, it is sold again for £4403.

a) Find the percentage decrease in the car's price over the first three years.
b) Find the percentage decrease in the car's price over the next three years.
c) Find the percentage decrease in the car's price over the whole six years.

Finding the Original Value

Learning Objective — Spec Ref R9:
Be able to find the original amount after a percentage increase or decrease.

If you know the **new amount** after a percentage increase or decrease, you can find the **original value** using the following steps:

- Write the new amount as a **percentage** of the original value.
- **Divide** the new amount by the percentage to find **1%** of the original value.
- **Multiply by 100** to find the original value (100%).

Example 8

The value of a painting increases by 12% to £1680.
What was the painting worth before it increased in value?

1. A 12% increase means the new amount is 112% of the original value.
2. Divide by 112 to find 1% of the original value.
3. Multiply by 100 to get the original value.

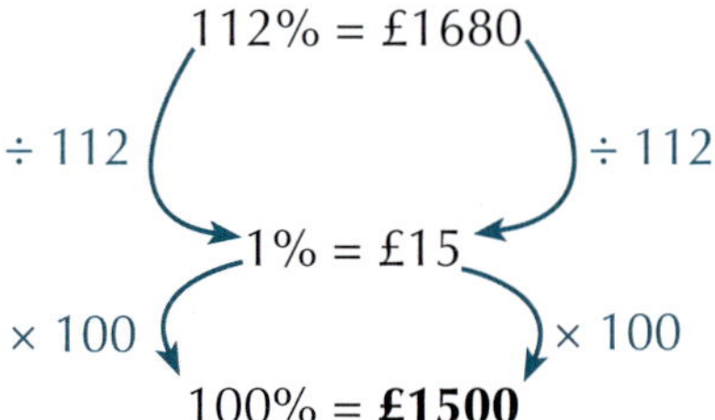

Tip: If it's a percentage increase, add the percentage to 100% to get the percentage of the original amount. For a percentage decrease, subtract from 100%.

Exercise 7

Q1 A fridge costs £200 after a 50% reduction.
Calculate the original price of the fridge.

Q2 Andy buys a top hat that has been reduced in a sale by 35%.
If the sale price is £13.00, find the original price.

Q3 The owner of a furniture shop increased the price of a bookcase by 26%.
If the bookcase is now priced at £819, what was the price before the increase?

Q4 An estate agent reduced the price of a house by 4%.
If the house is now for sale at £192 000, what was its original price?

Q5 In the past year, the number of frogs living in a pond has increased by 10% to 528, and the number of newts living there has increased by 15% to 621.
How many frogs and how many newts lived in the pond a year ago?

7.4 Compound Growth and Decay

Compound percentage changes involve repeating a percentage increase or decrease. At each step, the percentage change is applied to the current amount, rather than the original amount.

Compound Growth

Learning Objective — Spec Ref R16:
Be able to solve compound growth problems.

Compound growth is when a **percentage increase** is **repeatedly** applied to a quantity. The percentage increase is applied to the **current value** at each step. Compound growth applied to money is known as **compound interest**. E.g. if £1000 is increased by 10% each year:

- After 1 year: £1000 × 1.1 = £1100
- After 2 years: £1100 × 1.1 = £1210
- After 3 years: £1210 × 1.1 = £1331

Example 1

**Mr Zupnik invests £600 in a bank account at 5% per annum compound interest.
How much money will he have in the bank after two years?**

1. Find the multiplier for the percentage increase.
   5% ÷ 100% = 0.05
   So the multiplier = 1 + 0.05 = 1.05
2. 'Per annum' means 'per year'.
   Multiply to find the amount after one year.
   £600 × 1.05 = £630
3. Multiply again to find the amount after two years.
   £630 × 1.05 = **£661.50**

Exercise 1

Q1 A bank pays 3% per annum compound interest.
Calculate how much interest these accounts will earn.
Give your answer to the nearest penny.

a) £250 invested for 1 year.

b) £45 invested for 3 years.

c) £1500 invested for 2 years.

Q2 Josephine invests £3500 in a bank account that pays annual compound interest of 4.5%.
How much money (to the nearest penny) will she have in the bank after:

a) 2 years, b) 3 years?

Compound Decay

Learning Objective — Spec Ref R16:
Be able to solve compound decay problems.

Compound decay is the opposite of compound growth — it's when a **percentage decrease** is **repeatedly** applied to a quantity, and acts on the **current amount** each time.

When applied to money, compound decay is known as **depreciation**.

Example 2

Mrs Jones buys a laptop for £360. It depreciates at a rate of 35% per annum. How much will the laptop be worth after three years? Give your answer to 2 d.p.

1. Find the multiplier for the percentage decrease.
   35% ÷ 100% = 0.35
   So the multiplier = 1 – 0.35
   = 0.65
2. Multiply to find the amount after one year.
   £360 × 0.65 = £234
3. Multiply again to find the amount after two years.
   £234 × 0.65 = £152.10
4. Multiply one last time to find the amount after three years.
   £152.10 × 0.65 = £98.865
   = **£98.87 (2 d.p.)**

Tip: After the first step, remember to multiply the **current** amount not the original amount.

Exercise 2

Q1 Mr Quasar buys a television for £320.
Its value depreciates at a rate of 15% per year.
What is its value after: a) 2 years? b) 3 years?

Q2 Alan is visiting Las Vegas and has taken $1000 spending money.
He spends his money at a rate of 5% a day.
How much money will Alan have after 2 days?

Q3 A painting is bought for £12 000.
The value of the painting depreciates at a rate of 6% per year for the first two years, and then by 17% in the third year. What is the value of the painting three years after it was bought? Give your answer to the nearest penny.

The Formula

Learning Objective — Spec Ref R16:
Use the formula for compound growth and decay.

The **formula** for compound growth and decay is: $\boldsymbol{P_n = P_0 \times (\text{multiplier})^n}$

where P_n = amount after n hours/days/years,
P_0 = initial amount,
n = number of hours/days/years

Example 3

Calculate the total compound interest paid on £500 over 6 years if it's paid at a rate of 4% per year.

1. Use the formula for compound growth: $P_n = P_0 \times (\text{multiplier})^n$
2. Plug in the numbers... $P_0 = £500$, multiplier $= 1.04$, $n = 6$
   $P_6 = £500 \times (1.04)^6 = £632.6595...$
3. Subtract the initial figure from the final value to find the interest paid. Interest $= P_6 - P_0$
   $= £632.6595... - £500$
   $= £132.6595... =$ **£132.66**

Tip: Always check the context before giving your final answer. Here it makes sense to round to 2 d.p. as it's money, but sometimes only a whole number fits the context.

Exercise 3

Q1 Calculate the amount of money (to the nearest penny) you would have if you invested:
a) £1000 at an annual rate of 4% for 8 years.
b) £600 at an annual rate of 5.2% for 7 years.

Q2 Calculate the value (to the nearest £100) of a house after six years if it was bought for £650 000 and house prices are falling at a rate of 2% per annum.

Q3 A colony of ants has set up home in Mr Murphy's shed. PROBLEM SOLVING
At 9 am on Monday there were 250 ants.
If the colony of ants grows at a rate of 6% per day, how many ants will there be at 9 am on Saturday?

Q4 Mr Butterworth is on a diet and is losing weight at a rate of 2% of his total body weight every week. PROBLEM SOLVING
If he weighs 110 kg when he starts his diet, what will his body weight be at the end of 8 weeks? Give your answer to one decimal place.

Review Exercise

Q1 A chess club has 25 members. 12 of these members are female.
Express the number of female members of the club as a percentage.

Q2 A coat normally costs £160. In a sale, the coat's price was reduced by 35%.
How much cheaper is the sale price than the normal price?

Q3 Each grid on the right is made up of 25 small squares.
Find the proportion of each grid that is shaded as
(i) a fraction in its simplest terms,
(ii) a percentage,
(iii) a decimal.

a) 

b) 

Q4 Write $\frac{31}{500}$, 0.061 and 6% in order, from smallest to largest.

Q5 A pot of yoghurt normally contains 450 g.
A special offer pot contains 55% extra free.
How many grams of yoghurt does the special offer pot contain?

Q6 Two shops had a sale on a suit that had previously cost £92.
Shop A had 70% off the original price, while Shop B had $\frac{7}{8}$ off.
Which shop had the lower price, and by how much?

PROBLEM SOLVING

Q7 Tony deposits £3250 into a savings account that earns 8.5% simple interest per year.
How much will he have at the end of the year?

Q8 In an experiment, the mass of a chemical drops from 75 g to 69 g.
Find the percentage decrease.

Q9 Dave loves a bargain and buys a feather boa which has been reduced in price by 70%.
If the sale price is £2.85, what was the original price of the boa?

Q10 The population of an island is 12 500. Each year, the population increases by 8%.
What is the population of the island after 5 years?

Exam-Style Questions

Q1 Gemma's phone contract gives her 750 MB of data each month. 
One month, she buys 15% more data.
How much data does she have this month?

[2 marks]

Q2 Increase 3.7 metres by 24%.
Give your answer correct to the nearest centimetre.

[3 marks]

Q3 In 2016 a football club was worth £375 million.
In 2017 the football club was worth £450 million.
Show that the percentage increase in the value of the football club from 2016 to 2017 was 20%.

[2 marks]

Q4 A large box in a school gym's equipment cupboard contains 20 basketballs and 12 footballs.
The school receives eight new basketballs which are added to the box.
Work out the percentage of balls in the box which are now basketballs.

[2 marks]

Q5 Claire buys a sports car for £68 000.
It will depreciate at 20% per annum for the first two years and at 15% per annum for the next three years.
What is the value of the sports car after 5 years?

[4 marks]

Q6 30% of the animals in a wildlife park are lemurs.
40% of the lemurs are ring-tailed lemurs.
What percentage of the animals in the wildlife park are ring-tailed lemurs?

[2 marks]

8.1 Simplifying Expressions

Algebraic expressions involve variables (letters that represent numbers) and don't contain an equals sign — e.g. x, $3a + b$, $y^2 + z^2$. You can simplify them to avoid writing the same thing over and over.

Collecting Like Terms

Learning Objective — Spec Ref A1/A3/A4:
Be able to simplify algebraic expressions by collecting like terms.

These are all algebraic expressions:

a $6b$ xyz $a + b$ $x^2 + y^2 + z^2$

Tip: a is the same as $1a$, and $6b$ is the same as $6 \times b$.

Terms are the individual parts of an expression and **include** the plus or minus signs.
E.g. in the expression $2x + 6 - 3xy$, the terms are $2x$, 6 and $-3xy$.

Expressions can sometimes be **simplified** by collecting **like terms**.
'Like terms' are terms that contain **exactly the same** combination of letters.
For example xy, $-3xy$ and $2yx$ are all like terms, since the only letters are xy.

Example 1

Simplify this expression by collecting like terms: $4a + 3b - a - 7b$

1. First write the like terms next to each other. Take the sign with the term when you move it.
2. $4a$ and $-a$ are like terms as they just contain a. Together these give $4a - a = 3a$.
3. $3b$ and $-7b$ are like terms as they just contain b. Together these give $3b - 7b = -4b$.

$$4a + 3b - a - 7b = 4a - a + 3b - 7b$$
$$= 3a + 3b - 7b$$
$$= \mathbf{3a - 4b}$$

Example 2

Simplify the expression $x + 4y + 4 - 2x - y - 3$ by collecting like terms.

1. Terms involving no letters at all are like terms.
2. Collect them together in the same way as terms containing letters.

$$x + 4y + 4 - 2x - y - 3$$
$$= x - 2x + 4y - y + 4 - 3$$
$$= \mathbf{-x + 3y + 1}$$

Exercise 1

Q1 Simplify these expressions by collecting like terms.

a) $2x + 3x + x$ b) $7p - 2p + 3p - 4p$ c) $c + c + c + d + d$

d) $a + b + a - a + b$ e) $5a - 2a + 5b + 2b$ f) $4b + 8c - b - 5c$

Q2 Simplify these expressions by collecting like terms.

a) $2c + 4 + c + 7$ b) $3x + 6 - 6x - 4$ c) $5y + 12 - 9y - 7$

d) $-m + 5 - 8m + 16$ e) $-4x - 2 + 7x + 12$ f) $13a + 8 + 8a + 2$

Q3 Simplify these expressions.

a) $x + 7 + 4x + y + 5$ b) $a + 2b + b - 8 - 5a$

c) $13a - 5b + 8a + 12b + 7$ d) $8p + 6q + 14 - 6r - 4p - 14r - 2q - 23$

Example 3

Simplify the expression $x + 3x^2 + yx + 7 + 4x^2 + 2xy - 3$ by collecting like terms.

There are four sets of like terms:
(i) terms involving just x
(ii) terms involving x^2
(iii) terms involving xy (or yx, which means the same)
(iv) terms involving just numbers

$x + 3x^2 + yx + 7 + 4x^2 + 2xy - 3$
$= x$
$+ (3x^2 + 4x^2)$
$+ (yx + 2xy)$
$+ (7 - 3)$

Collect the different sets together separately.

$= \mathbf{x + 7x^2 + 3xy + 4}$

Exercise 2

Q1 Simplify the following expressions by collecting like terms.

a) $x^2 + 3x + 2 + 2x + 3$ b) $x^2 + 4x + 1 + 3x - 3$ c) $x^2 + 4x + x^2 + 2x + 4$

d) $x^2 + 2x^2 + 4x - 3x$ e) $p^2 - 5p + 2p^2 + 3p$ f) $3p^2 + 6q + p^2 - 4q + 3p^2$

g) $8 + 6p^2 - 5 + pq + p^2$ h) $4p + 5q - pq + p^2 - 7q$ i) $a^2 + 7b + 2a^2 + 5ab - 3b$

Q2 Simplify the following expressions by collecting like terms.

a) $ab + cd - xy + 3ab - 2cd + 3yx + 2x^2$ b) $pq + 3pq + p^2 - 2qp + q^2$

Q3 By collecting number terms and root terms, simplify the following.

a) $7 + 3\sqrt{3} + 6 - 2\sqrt{3}$ b) $-2 - 13\sqrt{7} - 7 + 3\sqrt{7}$ c) $11 - 7\sqrt{5} - 11 - 8\sqrt{5}$

Multiplying and Dividing Letters

Learning Objectives — Spec Ref A1/A4:
- Use and interpret algebraic notation.
- Use the laws of indices when multiplying and dividing variables.

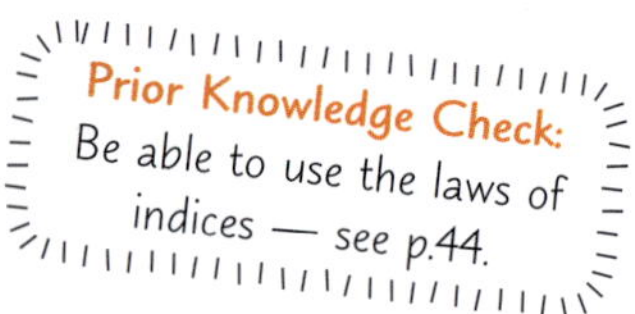

Prior Knowledge Check:
Be able to use the laws of indices — see p.44.

When you've got numbers and variables **multiplied** or **divided** by each other, you should deal with the numbers and each letter **separately**.
You can use the **laws of indices** to write each term as **simply** as possible.

The most useful laws of indices are: $a^m \times a^n = a^{m+n}$ $a^m \div a^n = a^{m-n}$ $(a^m)^n = a^{m \times n}$

There are some more rules that might help you with these questions:

- abc means $a \times b \times c$ — the × symbols are left out to make it clearer.
- $ab^2 = a \times b \times b$ — only the b is squared.
- $(ab)^2 = ab \times ab = a \times a \times b \times b = a^2b^2$ — the whole bracket is squared.
- $(-a)^2 = (-a) \times (-a) = (-1) \times (-1) \times a \times a = a^2$ — squaring a negative makes it positive.
- $2ab \times 3a = 2 \times 3 \times a \times a \times b = 6a^2b$ — multiply the numbers and variables separately.
- $\frac{a}{b} = a \div b$ — use the power rules from p.44 if dividing by powers of the same letter.
- $6a^5 \div 3a^3 = (6 \div 3)(a^5 \div a^3) = 2a^2$ — divide the numbers and variables separately.

Example 4

Simplify these expressions: a) $b \times b \times b \times b$ b) $4a \times 5b$ c) $6a^2 \div 3a$

1. If the same letter is multiplied by itself, write it as a power.
2. Multiply numbers and letters separately.

a) $b \times b \times b \times b = \mathbf{b^4}$

b) $4a \times 5b = 4 \times 5 \times a \times b = \mathbf{20ab}$

c) $6a^2 \div 3a = (6 \div 3) \times (a^2 \div a) = \mathbf{2a}$

Exercise 3

Q1 Simplify the following expressions.

a) $a \times a \times a$ b) $2a \times 3a$ c) $-8p \times 2q$ d) $3a \times 7a$

e) $5x \times 3y$ f) $m \times m \times -m \times m$ g) $12a \times 4b$ h) $6p \times 8p$

Q2 Simplify the following expressions.

a) $a \times ab$ b) $4m^3 \div m$ c) $(r^2)^3$ d) $3(st)^2$

e) $4a^2 \times 5a$ f) $-9s^4 \div -3s^3$ g) $4a^4b^3 \times 2ab^2$ h) $\frac{6y^2}{3y}$

8.2 Expanding Brackets

When brackets show up, you'll often want to expand them to get rid of them. Single brackets are pretty straightforward, but with two sets of brackets there's a lot to keep track of.

a(b + c)

Learning Objective — Spec Ref A4:
Be able to expand a single term multiplied by a bracket.

You can **expand** (or remove) brackets by multiplying everything **inside** the brackets by the letter or number **in front**.
Remember that $a(b + c) = a \times (b + c) = (a \times b) + (a \times c)$.

$$a(b + c) = ab + ac$$
$$a(b - c) = ab - ac$$

Example 1

Expand the brackets in these expressions: a) $3(a + 2)$ b) $8(2n - 3)$

a) Multiply both a and 2 by 3. $3(a + 2) = (3 \times a) + (3 \times 2) = \mathbf{3a + 6}$

b) Multiply both $2n$ and 3 by 8. $8(2n - 3) = (8 \times 2n) - (8 \times 3) = \mathbf{16n - 24}$

Example 2

Expand the brackets in these expressions: a) $m(n + 7)$ b) $a(a - 4)$

a) Multiply both n and 7 by m. $m(n + 7) = (m \times n) + (m \times 7) = \mathbf{mn + 7m}$

b) Multiply both a and 4 by a. $a(a - 4) = (a \times a) - (a \times 4) = \mathbf{a^2 - 4a}$

Exercise 1

Q1 Expand the brackets in these expressions.

a) $2(a + 5)$ b) $4(b + 3)$ c) $5(d + 7)$ d) $3(p + 4)$
e) $3(5 + p)$ f) $7(6 + g)$ g) $5(3 - y)$ h) $8(a - b)$

Q2 Expand the brackets in these expressions.

a) $x(y + 5)$ b) $p(q + 2)$ c) $x(8 - x)$ d) $a(b - 12)$
e) $3(2p + 4)$ f) $5(4t - 8)$ g) $3(u + 8v)$ h) $7(5n - 6m)$

Example 3

Expand the brackets in this expression: $-b(4 - 2b)$

1. Multiply 4 and $2b$ by $-b$.
2. Be careful with the signs — multiplying by a negative will change the signs of the terms inside the brackets.

$$-b(4 - 2b) = (-b \times 4) - (-b \times 2b)$$
$$= (-4b) - (-2b^2)$$
$$= \mathbf{-4b + 2b^2}$$

Exercise 2

Q1 Expand the brackets in the following expressions.

a) $-(q + 2)$ b) $-(x + 7)$ c) $-8(7 - w)$ d) $-5(5 - x)$
e) $-v(v + 4)$ f) $-v(v - 5)$ g) $-x(12 - x)$ h) $-y(4 + y)$

Q2 Expand the brackets in the following expressions.

a) $-6(5g - 3)$ b) $-7(4v + 8)$ c) $-2(5 + 4m)$ d) $-5(10 - 8v)$
e) $-5(2 + 3n)$ f) $-4z(8 - 2z)$ g) $-2(6b - 3)$ h) $-4y(2y + 6)$

When doing **calculations** involving brackets, expand all brackets **first**.

Example 4

Simplify the following expressions: a) $2(a + 5) + 3(a + 2)$ b) $3(x + 2) - 5(2x + 1)$

a) Multiply out both brackets. Then collect like terms.

$$2(a + 5) + 3(a + 2) = (2a + 10) + (3a + 6)$$
$$= 2a + 10 + 3a + 6$$
$$= \mathbf{5a + 16}$$

b) Multiply out the individual brackets. The minus sign before the second set of brackets reverses the sign of each term inside those brackets.

$$3(x + 2) - 5(2x + 1) = (3x + 6) - (10x + 5)$$
$$= 3x + 6 - 10x - 5$$
$$= \mathbf{-7x + 1}$$

Exercise 3

Q1 Simplify the following expressions.

a) $2(z + 3) + 4(z + 2)$ b) $3(c + 1) + 5(c + 7)$ c) $4(u + 6) + 8(u + 5)$
d) $7(t - 3) + 2(t + 12)$ e) $8(m - 2) + 9(m + 5)$ f) $5(p - 3) - (p + 6)$
g) $2(j - 5) - (j - 3)$ h) $5(y - 4) - (y - 2)$ i) $5(3c - 6) - (c - 3)$

Q2 Simplify the following expressions.

a) $5(2q + 5) - 2(q - 2)$ b) $2(3c - 8) - 8(c + 4)$ c) $5(q - 2) - 3(q - 4)$

Q3 Simplify the following expressions.

a) $2(-z + 2) + 3z(3z + 6)$ b) $4p(3p + 5) - 3(p + 1)$ c) $9b(2b + 5) + 4b(6b + 6)$

(a + b)(c + d)

Learning Objective — Spec Ref A4:
Be able to expand two brackets multiplied together.

When expanding **pairs** of brackets, multiply each term in the left bracket by each term in the right bracket. If each bracket contains two terms (brackets like this are called **binomials**), you can use **FOIL** to keep track of which terms you need to multiply:

F IRST — multiply the first term from each bracket
O UTSIDE — multiply the terms on the outside
I NSIDE — multiply the terms on the inside
L AST — multiply the last term from each bracket

$$(a + b)(c + d) = ac + ad + bc + bd$$

You'll always get four terms after multiplying binomials together this way.
Sometimes you can then **simplify** by collecting like terms — see p.124.

Example 5

Expand the brackets in the following expression: $(q + 4)(p + 3)$

1. Multiply each term in the left bracket by each term in the right bracket using FOIL.

$(q + 4)(p + 3) = qp + 3q + 4p + 12$

2. It's a good idea to write the letters in each term of the answer in alphabetical order.

$= \mathbf{pq + 3q + 4p + 12}$

Example 6

Expand the following expression: $(2x + 1)(3x - 2)$

1. Expand the brackets using FOIL — be careful when multiplying terms with coefficients.

$(2x + 1)(3x - 2) = 6x^2 - 4x + 3x - 2$

2. Simplify by collecting like terms.

$= \mathbf{6x^2 - x - 2}$

Exercise 4

Q1 Expand the brackets in the following expressions.

a) $(a + 2)(b + 3)$ b) $(j + 4)(k - 5)$ c) $(x - 4)(y - 1)$ d) $(x + 6)(y + 2)$

e) $(9 - a)(b - 3)$ f) $(t - 5)(s + 3)$ g) $(5x + 4)(3 - y)$ h) $(3a - 1)(2b + 2)$

Q2 Expand the brackets in the following expressions.

a) $(x + 8)(x + 3)$ b) $(b + 2)(b - 4)$ c) $(a - 1)(a + 2)$ d) $(d + 7)(d + 6)$

e) $(z - 12)(z + 9)$ f) $(c + 5)(3 - c)$ g) $(3y - 8)(6 - y)$ h) $(2x + 2)(2x + 3)$

(a + b)²

Learning Objective — Spec Ref A4:
Be able to expand the square of a bracket.

Tip: Remember that you cannot just square each term inside the brackets to expand them. E.g. $(a + b)^2 \neq a^2 + b^2$.

If you have to expand **squared brackets** write them out as **two sets** of brackets — e.g. $(a + b)^2 = (a + b)(a + b)$
Then you can expand using **FOIL** — like on p.129.

Example 7

Expand the brackets in the following expression: $3(x - 2)^2$

1. Write out $(x - 2)^2$ as two sets of brackets.
2. Use FOIL to expand the brackets — leave the '3 ×' alone for now.
3. Collect like terms, then multiply each term in the brackets by 3.

$3(x - 2)^2 = 3 \times (x - 2)(x - 2)$

$= 3 \times (x^2 - 2x - 2x + 4)$

$= 3 \times (x^2 - 4x + 4)$

$= \mathbf{3x^2 - 12x + 12}$

Exercise 5

Q1 Expand the brackets in the following expressions.

a) $(x + 1)^2$ b) $(x + 4)^2$ c) $(x + 5)^2$ d) $(x - 2)^2$

e) $(x - 3)^2$ f) $(x - 7)^2$ g) $3(x + 3)^2$ h) $2(x - 6)^2$

Q2 Expand the brackets in the following expressions.

a) $(5x + 2)^2$ b) $(2x + 6)^2$ c) $(3x - 1)^2$

8.3 Factorising

Factorising an expression means adding brackets in where there weren't any before.
It's called factorising because you need to look for common factors of all the different terms.

Taking Out Common Factors

Learning Objective — Spec Ref A4:
Be able to factorise expressions by taking out common factors.

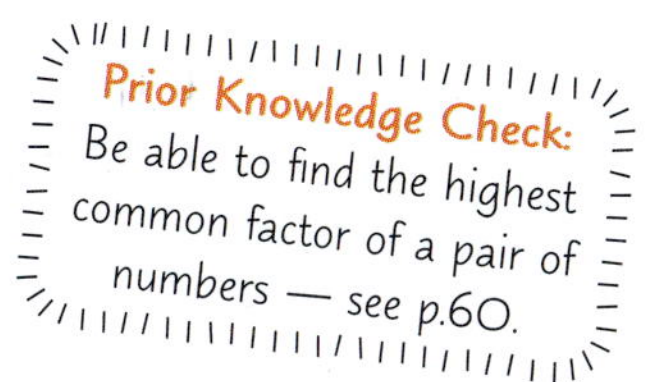

Prior Knowledge Check:
Be able to find the highest common factor of a pair of numbers — see p.60.

Factorising is the opposite of expanding brackets.
You look for a **common factor** of all the terms in an expression and 'take it outside' the brackets.
These common factors could be **numbers**, **variables** or **both**.

To factorise an expression **fully**, you need to find the **highest common factor** of all the terms.

Tip: You can check you have factorised correctly by expanding the brackets again.

Example 1

Factorise the expression $12x - 18y$.

1. 6 is the highest common factor of $12x$ and $18y$. So 6 goes outside the brackets. — $12x - 18y = 6(\quad - \quad)$
2. Divide each term by the common factor, and write the results inside the brackets. — $12x \div 6 = 2x$ and $18y \div 6 = 3y$. So $12x - 18y = \mathbf{6(2x - 3y)}$

Tip: If you used 2 or 3 as the factor instead of 6, you would get an expression that wasn't fully factorised, e.g. $2(6x - 9y)$.

When factorising **variables**, the highest common factor is the **highest power** of the variable that will go into every term.

You'll need to remember how to **divide** two powers: $a^m \div a^n = \frac{a^m}{a^n} = a^{m-n}$

Example 2

Factorise $3x^2 + 2x$.

1. x is the only common factor of $3x^2$ and $3x$. So x goes outside the brackets. — $3x^2 + 2x = x(\quad + \quad)$
2. Divide each term by the common factor, and write the results inside the brackets. — $3x^2 \div x = 3x$ and $2x \div x = 2$. So $3x^2 + 2x = \mathbf{x(3x + 2)}$

Exercise 1

Q1 Factorise the following expressions.

a) $2a + 10$ b) $3b + 12$ c) $20c + 15$ d) $18 + 12x$

e) $8c + 12f$ f) $25d + 35e$ g) $12x + 16y$ h) $3x + 9y$

Q2 Factorise the following expressions.

a) $3a^2 + 7a$ b) $4b^2 + 19b$ c) $2x^2 + 9x$ d) $7y + 15y^2$

e) $4x^2 - 9x$ f) $21q^2 - 16q$ g) $15y - 7y^2$ h) $27z^2 + 11z$

Sometimes the highest common factor of all the terms might have both **numbers and variables** in it.

It's usually best to work out the highest common factor for the numbers and for the letters **separately**.

Tip: You have factorised fully when the terms left inside the brackets have no common factors.

Example 3

Factorise the expression $15x^2 - 10xy$.

1. The HCF of 15 and 10 is 5, and the HCF of x^2 and xy is x.
2. The HCF of $15x^2$ and $10xy$ is $5x$. So $5x$ goes outside the brackets — $15x^2 - 10xy = 5x(\quad - \quad)$
3. Divide each term by the common factor. — $15x^2 \div 5x = 3x$ and $10xy \div 5x = 2y$
4. Write the results inside the brackets. — $15x^2 - 10xy = \mathbf{5x(3x - 2y)}$

Tip: $15x^2$ doesn't have a y in it, so neither will the HCF.

Exercise 2

Q1 The expression $4xy^2 + 8x^2y$ contains two terms.

a) What is the highest numerical common factor of both terms?

b) What is the highest power of x that is common to both terms?

c) What is the highest power of y that is common to both terms?

d) Factorise the expression.

Q2 Factorise these expressions.

a) $5a^2 + 5a$ b) $4b + 8b^2$ c) $6c^2 - 9c$ d) $12d - 16d^2$

Q3 Factorise these expressions.

a) $10c^2 - 5cd$ b) $20x^2 - 10xy$ c) $9x^2 + 6xy$ d) $12x^2 + 8xy$

e) $6a^2 + 9ab$ f) $12pq - 8p^2$ g) $8a^2 + 6ab^2$ h) $24x^2y - 16xy^2$

Factorising Quadratics

Learning Objective — Spec Ref A4:
Be able to factorise a quadratic expression.

A **quadratic expression** is an expression where the highest power of the variable (e.g. x) is **2**.
They have the form $\boldsymbol{x^2 + bx + c}$ where b and c are numbers.

You can **factorise** some quadratics into the form $\boldsymbol{(x + d)(x + e)}$, but it's usually **not clear** what the values of d and e are.

Tip: If a quadratic can be factorised, only one combination of d and e will work.

Here's the method to find them:

- Write out the brackets as $(x \quad)(x \quad)$ — don't put the signs or numbers in yet.
- Find pairs of numbers that **multiply to give** $\boldsymbol{c}$ — this is just like finding **factors** (see p.53). You can **ignore the sign** of c for now.
- Choose the pair of numbers that also **add** or **subtract** to give $\boldsymbol{b}$ (ignoring signs here too).
- Write one number in each bracket, then fill in the + or – signs so that b and c work out with the **correct signs**. Check they're right by expanding the brackets to get back to the original expression.

If c is **positive**, then the two brackets will have the same sign (both + or both –), and if c is **negative** then the signs will be different (one + and one –).

Example 4

Factorise: a) $x^2 + 7x + 10$ b) $x^2 + 2x - 15$

a)
1. Find all the pairs of numbers that multiply to give 10 .
   1×10 or 2×5
2. Find the pair that add/subtract to give 7.
   $1 + 10 = 11$, $10 - 1 = 9$
   $2 + 5 = 7$ (circled), $5 - 2 = 3$
3. You need +2 and +5 to give +7, so both brackets should have + signs.
   So $x^2 + 7x + 10 = \boldsymbol{(x + 2)(x + 5)}$
4. Check your answer by expanding the brackets.
   $(x + 2)(x + 5) = x^2 + 2x + 5x + 10$
   $= x^2 + 7x + 10$

b)
1. Find all the pairs of numbers that multiply to give 15.
   1×15 or 3×5
2. Find the pair that add/subtract to give 2.
   $1 + 15 = 16$, $15 - 1 = 14$
   $3 + 5 = 8$, $5 - 3 = 2$ (circled)
3. You need +5 and –3 to give +2, so put a + with the 5 and a – with the 3.
   So $x^2 + 2x - 15 = \boldsymbol{(x + 5)(x - 3)}$
4. Check your answer by expanding the brackets.
   $(x + 5)(x - 3) = x^2 - 3x + 5x - 15$
   $= x^2 + 2x - 15$

Exercise 3

Q1 Factorise each of the following expressions.

a) $x^2 + 7x + 6$ b) $x^2 + 7x + 12$ c) $x^2 + 8x + 7$ d) $x^2 + 6x + 9$

e) $x^2 + 6x + 8$ f) $y^2 + 8y + 15$ g) $z^2 + 9z + 14$ h) $v^2 + 11v + 24$

Q2 Factorise each of the following expressions.

a) $x^2 + 2x - 3$ b) $x^2 - 6x + 8$ c) $x^2 - 2x - 8$ d) $x^2 - 5x + 4$

e) $x^2 - 3x - 10$ f) $x^2 + 2x - 8$ g) $r^2 + 6r - 27$ h) $u^2 - 15u + 54$

Difference of Two Squares

Learning Objective — Spec Ref A4:
Be able to factorise a difference of two squares.

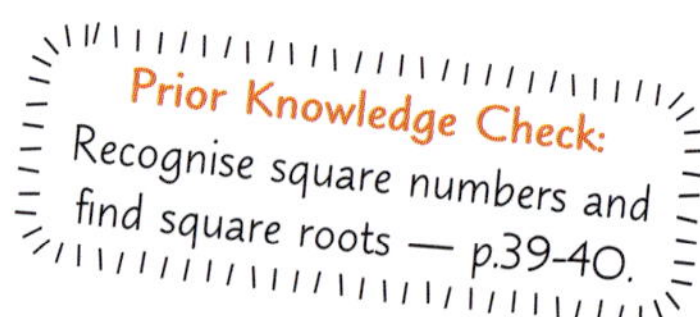

Prior Knowledge Check:
Recognise square numbers and find square roots — p.39-40.

Some quadratic expressions have **no middle term** e.g. $x^2 - 49$.
They're of the form 'one thing squared' take away 'another thing squared'.

When you **factorise** these, you get two brackets that are **the same**, except that one has a **+ sign** and one has a **– sign**. For example, $x^2 - 49$ factorises to $(x + 7)(x - 7)$.

The general rule is $a^2 - b^2 = (a + b)(a - b)$ — this is known as the **difference of two squares**.

Example 5

Factorise: a) $x^2 - 16$ b) $x^2 - 7$

a) Write the expression in the form $a^2 - b^2$, then use the rule given above.

$x^2 - 16 = x^2 - 4^2 = \mathbf{(x + 4)(x - 4)}$

b) 7 isn't a square number, but you can write 7 as $(\sqrt{7})^2$ so that you can use the formula.

$x^2 - 7 = x^2 - (\sqrt{7})^2$
$= \mathbf{(x + \sqrt{7})(x - \sqrt{7})}$

Exercise 4

Q1 Factorise each of the following expressions.

a) $x^2 - 25$ b) $x^2 - 9$ c) $x^2 - 4$ d) $x^2 - 36$

e) $x^2 - 81$ f) $x^2 - 64$ g) $b^2 - 121$ h) $t^2 - 144$

Q2 Factorise each of the following expressions.

a) $x^2 - 5$ b) $x^2 - 3$ c) $x^2 - 11$ d) $x^2 - y^2$

Review Exercise

Q1 Simplify these expressions by collecting like terms.

a) $4s + s + 2s + 7s$
b) $5m - 2m + 8m - 6m$
c) $x + y + x + y + x - y$
d) $16p + 4q + 4 - 2p + 3q - 8$
e) $5s + 7t^2 - 3s^2 + 2s + 2t^2 - s$
f) $6b^2 + 7b + 9 - 4b^2 + 5b - 2$

Q2 Simplify the following expressions.

a) $a \times ab$
b) $4a^2 \div 2a$
c) $2p \times 7q^2$
d) $12e^3 \div 4e$
e) $-3i^2 \times 8i^3$
f) $15d^4 \div 5d^2$

Q3 Expand the brackets in these expressions.

a) $4(x + 8)$
b) $6(5 - r)$
c) $-2(7 + y)$
d) $8(h - 2)$
e) $h(h + 3)$
f) $-4n(n + 2)$
g) $4w(u - 7)$
h) $-2x(12 - v)$

Q4 Simplify the following expressions.

a) $4(c + 3) + 6(c + 2)$
b) $5(u + 4) + 3(u + 8)$
c) $5(b - 6) + 7(b + 4)$
d) $2(c - 6) - (c + 5)$
e) $5(q - 3) - (q + 1)$
f) $2(j - 5) - (j - 3)$

Q5 Expand and simplify the brackets in the following expressions.

a) $(2 + x)(8 + y)$
b) $(x - 3)(x - 5)$
c) $3(j - 2)(k + 4)$
d) $(n + 5)(m - 4)$
e) $(3 + r)(s + 4)$
f) $(z - 8)^2$

Q6 Factorise these expressions.

a) $2x + 4y$
b) $8x + 24$
c) $4y - 6y^2$
d) $20y + 12xy$
e) $15ab - 10a^2$
f) $60x + 144y$
g) $28r + 40r^2s$
h) $4ab - 8a^2b$
i) $14m^2n - 35mn^2$

Q7 Factorise each of the following expressions.

a) $y^2 + 10y + 21$
b) $x^2 - 4x - 5$
c) $t^2 - 8t + 16$
d) $x^2 - x - 12$
e) $x^2 + 5x - 6$
f) $x^2 - 4x - 45$

Q8 Factorise each of the following expressions.

a) $x^2 - 100$
b) $y^2 - 36$
c) $y^2 - 121$

Exam-Style Questions

Q1 Complete this table.

Expression	Simplified expression
$a + a + a$	
$3a^2 + 2a^2$	
$4a^2 + 6a - a^2$	

[3 marks]

Q2 Fully simplify the following expressions:

a) $v + v + w - w - w - w - w$

[1 mark]

b) $5 \times 7 \times x \times x$

[1 mark]

c) $6y - 3yz - 8y + 10yz$

[1 mark]

Q3 Expand and simplify:

a) $x(x^2 - 4y) + 9xy$

[2 marks]

b) $(2x - 7)^2$

[2 marks]

Q4 Factorise the following expressions:

a) $7c + 56$

[1 mark]

b) $d^2 + 5d - 2de$

[2 marks]

Q5 a) Factorise $y^2 + 12y + 32$

[2 marks]

b) Factorise $x^2 - 169$

[2 marks]

9.1 Solving Equations

Solving an equation means finding the value of an unknown letter that makes both sides equal. For example, the solution to $2x + 3 = 11$ is $x = 4$ — because if $x = 4$, both sides equal 11.

Basic Equations

Learning Objective — Spec Ref A17:
Be able to solve algebraic equations.

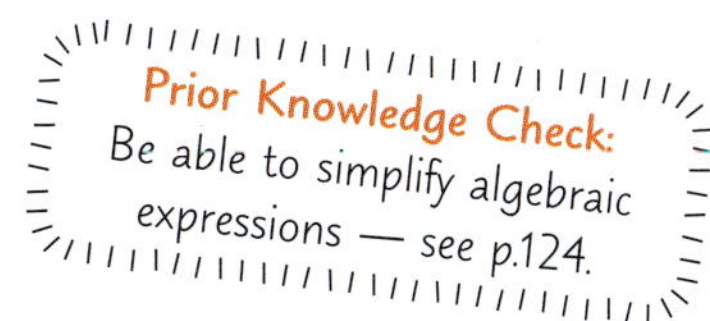

Prior Knowledge Check:
Be able to simplify algebraic expressions — see p.124.

You can solve some simpler equations using the '**common sense**' approach.

E.g. Start with the equation: $9 + x = 12$
This means: $9 + \text{something} = 12$
And you know that: $9 + 3 = 12$
So the 'something' must equal 3, which means $\boldsymbol{x = 3}$.

For harder equations, the 'common sense' approach isn't very useful. Instead, you'll need to solve most equations by **rearranging** them, until you end up with '$x =$ ' on one side.

When you're rearranging, remember these rules:

- Whatever you do to **one side** of the equation you **must** do to the **other side**.
- To get rid of something, do the **opposite**:
  + and – are opposites.
  × and ÷ are opposites.
- Keep rearranging the equation until x is **on its own**.

Tip: Remember, $2x$ means $2 \times x$. So to rearrange something like $2x = 12$, you do the opposite of × which is ÷. So ÷ both sides by 2 to get $x = 6$.

Example 1

Solve the equation $x + 8 = 15$.

1. You need to get rid of the '+ 8' to get x on its own.

$x + 8 = 15$

2. The opposite of + is –, so subtract 8 from both sides.

$x + 8 - 8 = 15 - 8$
$x = 15 - 8$
$\boldsymbol{x = 7}$

3. Check your answer by putting it in the original equation and checking both sides are the same.

$x + 8 = 7 + 8 = 15$ ✔

Tip: It's really important to check your answer at the end. It's very easy to make a silly mistake when rearranging.

When there is a **minus sign** in front of the x, get rid of it by **adding x** to both sides.

Example 2

Solve the equation $15 - x = 7$.

1. Add x to both sides of the equation
2. Now that x is positive, you can solve the equation as usual.

$15 - x = 7$
$15 = x + 7$
$15 - 7 = x$
$8 = x \Rightarrow \mathbf{x = 8}$

Tip: It doesn't matter which side the x ends up on, as long as it's on its own.

Exercise 1

Q1 Get x alone on one side of the equation to solve these equations.

a) $x + 9 = 12$ b) $x + 5 = 16$ c) $x - 2 = 14$

d) $x - 7 = -19$ e) $-2 = 7 + x$ f) $32 = x - 17$

Q2 Solve these equations. Start by adding x to both sides.

a) $12 - x = 9$ b) $4 - x = 2$ c) $2 - x = 7$

d) $19 = 14 - x$ e) $14 = 8 - x$ f) $7 = 5 - x$

Q3 Solve the following equations.

a) $x + 7 = 12$ b) $5 - x = 21$ c) $16 = x + 10$

d) $x - 8 = 14$ e) $12 - x = 23$ f) $35 = 31 - x$

Q4 Solve the following equations.

a) $x - 7.3 = 1.6$ b) $6.03 - x = 0.58$ c) $3.47 = 7.18 + x$ d) $5.2 = 2.8 - x$

If one side of the equation has something like $5x$ or $-4x$, you **divide** to get x on its own.
If it's something like $\frac{x}{7}$ or $-\frac{x}{3}$, you **multiply**.

Example 3

Solve the equation $\frac{x}{5} = 3$.

1. Multiply both sides by 5.
2. Remember: $\frac{x}{5} \times 5 = x$

$\frac{x}{5} = 3 \longrightarrow \frac{x}{5} \times 5 = 3 \times 5$

$\mathbf{x = 15}$

Sometimes you'll need to multiply or divide by a **negative** number — make sure you use the rules for negative numbers given on p.6.

Example 4

Solve the equation $-6x = 9$.

1. Divide both sides by –6. $-6x = 9 \longrightarrow -6x \div (-6) = 9 \div (-6)$
2. Remember: $-6x \div (-6) = x$ $\mathbf{x = -1.5}$

Exercise 2

Q1 Solve the following equations.

a) $\frac{x}{3} = 2$ b) $\frac{x}{6} = -3$ c) $\frac{x}{3} = 0.4$ d) $\frac{x}{11} = -0.5$

e) $8x = 24$ f) $4.5x = 81$ g) $5x = -20$ h) $3.5x = -7$

Q2 Solve these equations by multiplying or dividing both sides by a negative number.

a) $-7x = -56$ b) $-9x = 108$ c) $-4.5x = -2.7$

d) $-\frac{x}{4} = 3$ e) $-\frac{x}{5} = 6$ f) $-\frac{x}{10} = 1.1$

Sometimes the x term is being **both** multiplied and divided.
Treat the multiplication and division **separately**, and rearrange the equation one step at a time.

Example 5

Solve the equation $\frac{3x}{4} = 6$.

1. Multiply both sides by 4. $\frac{3x}{4} = 6 \Rightarrow 3x = 6 \times 4 = 24$
2. Then divide both sides by 3. $\Rightarrow x = 24 \div 3 \Rightarrow \mathbf{x = 8}$

Tip: You could have divided by 3 first and then multiplied by 4.

Exercise 3

Q1 Solve the following equations.

a) $\frac{4x}{3} = 12$ b) $\frac{2x}{5} = 6$ c) $\frac{6x}{7} = 12$ d) $\frac{5x}{6} = 3$

e) $\frac{7x}{5} = 1.4$ f) $\frac{2x}{1.5} = -0.2$ g) $\frac{3x}{0.1} = -0.6$ h) $\frac{11x}{2.2} = 6.3$

Two-Step Equations

Learning Objective — Spec Ref A17:
Be able to solve equations that involve more than one step.

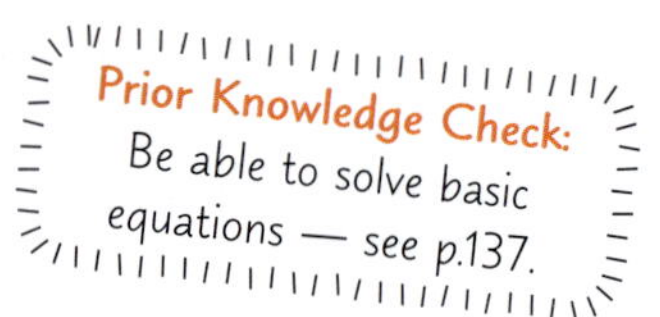

Prior Knowledge Check:
Be able to solve basic equations — see p.137.

'Two-step equations' are equations that look something like $3x - 2 = 10$ or $15 - 4x = 3$. They need to be solved in **two stages**, which you need to do in the **right order**:

- Addition or subtraction **first**
- Multiplication or division **second**.

Following these rules avoids dealing with too many **fractions** and makes solving much **easier**.

Example 6

Solve the equation $2x + 3 = 11$.

1. $2x + 3$ means:
   (i) multiply your value of x by 2, (ii) add 3 to it.
   To get x on its own, 'undo' these steps, but in the opposite order. $2x + 3 = 11$
2. First, subtract 3. $2x = 11 - 3 = 8$
3. Then divide by 2 to find the answer. $x = 8 \div 2 \Rightarrow \boldsymbol{x = 4}$
4. Check your answer. $2 \times 4 + 3 = 8 + 3 = 11$ ✔

Exercise 4

Q1 Solve the following two-step equations.

a) $8x + 10 = 66$ b) $10x + 15 = 115$ c) $12x + 9 = 105$

d) $1.5x + 3 = 93$ e) $4x + 12 = -8$ f) $2x + 9 = -2$

Q2 Solve the following equations.

a) $16x - 6 = 10$ b) $15x - 8 = 22$ c) $14x - 17 = 25$

d) $2.6x - 7 = -59$ e) $18x - 6 = -60$ f) $20x - 12 = -132$

Q3 The expression $\frac{x}{2} - 1$ means 'divide x by 2, then subtract 1'.

'Undo' these two steps in the opposite order to solve this equation: $\frac{x}{2} - 1 = 3$

Q4 Solve the following equations.

a) $\frac{x}{2} + 1 = 7$ b) $\frac{x}{6} + 4 = 16$ c) $\frac{x}{10} - 3 = -1$

d) $\frac{x}{4} - 5 = -9$ e) $\frac{x}{2} - 1 = 3.5$ f) $\frac{x}{7} - 8 = -11$

Q5 a) Write down the equation you get if you add $5x$ to both sides of the equation $20 - 5x = 10$.
b) Solve your equation to find x.

Q6 Solve the following equations.
a) $12 - 4x = 8$ b) $47 - 9x = 11$ c) $8 - 7x = 22$ d) $17 - 10x = 107$

Harder Equations

Learning Objectives — Spec Ref A17:
- Be able to solve equations involving brackets.
- Be able to solve equations where the unknown appears twice.

Some equations involve **brackets** — you need to **get rid** of the brackets before you can solve the equation. There are **two ways** to do this:

- **expand** the brackets
- **divide** both sides by the number in front of the brackets.

Tip: See p.127-130 for how to expand brackets.

You can use whichever method you find **easier** as both will give you the same answer. Both methods are shown in the example below.

Example 7

Solve the equation $8(x + 2) = 36$.

Either:

1. Multiply out the brackets. $8x + 16 = 36$
2. Subtract 16. $8x = 36 - 16 = 20$
3. And then divide by 8. $x = 20 \div 8 = 2.5$

$\mathbf{x = 2.5}$

Or:

1. $8(x + 2)$ means: "add 2 to x, then multiply by 8". $8(x + 2) = 36$
2. So to find x, first divide by 8. $x + 2 = 36 \div 8 = 4.5$
3. And then subtract 2. $x = 4.5 - 2 = 2.5$

$\mathbf{x = 2.5}$

Exercise 5

Q1 Solve the following equations.

a) $7(x + 4) = 63$ b) $8(x + 4) = 88$ c) $11(x + 3) = 132$

d) $16(x - 3) = -80$ e) $13(x - 4) = -91$ f) $14(x - 2) = -98$

Q2 Solve the following equations.

a) $315 = 21(6 - x)$ b) $12.5(x - 4) = 75$ c) $36 = 7.2(2 - x)$

Some equations will have an x term on **both sides** of the equation.
To tackle these, first rearrange the equation so you have all the ***x*-terms** on **one side** and all the **numbers** on the **other side**. You can then solve them in the usual way.

Example 8

Solve the equation $5x + 6 = 2x + 18$.

1. First subtract $2x$ from both sides, which leaves x terms on only one side of the equation.
2. Now you can solve the equation. Subtract 6 from both sides... ...and then divide by 3.
3. Plug your answer back into the equation to check — you should get the same number on both sides.

$$5x + 6 = 2x + 18$$
$$5x + 6 - 2x = 2x + 18 - 2x$$
$$3x + 6 = 18$$
$$3x = 18 - 6 = 12$$
$$x = 12 \div 3 \Rightarrow \mathbf{x = 4}$$

Check: $(5 \times 4) + 6 = 26$
$(2 \times 4) + 18 = 26$ ✔

Exercise 6

Q1 Solve these equations.

a) $6x - 4 = 2x + 16$ b) $17x + 2 = 7x - 8$ c) $9x - 26 = 5x - 14$

d) $8x + 4 = 2x + 40$ e) $15x - 8 = 4x + 47$ f) $21x - 5 = 5x + 11$

Q2 Solve the following equations.

a) $13x - 35 = 45 - 3x$ b) $20x + 18 = 54 - 16x$ c) $17x - 9 = 57 - 5x$

d) $82 - 8x = 10 - 6x$ e) $33 - 7x = -12 - 2x$ f) $4x - 15 = 147 - 14x$

Q3 Solve the following equations.

a) $4x - 3 = 0.5 - 3x$ b) $10x - 18 = 10.2 + 4x$

c) $4x - 8.6 = 48.1 - 5x$ d) $-x + 1 = 28 + 2x$

You might get brackets on **both sides** of the equation.
Expand both brackets before doing any other rearranging.

Example 9

Solve the equation $4(x + 2) = 2(x + 6)$.

1. Multiply out both of the brackets.
2. Now you can solve the equation in the usual way.
3. Remember to check your answer.

$4(x + 2) = 2(x + 6)$

$4x + 8 = 2x + 12$

$2x + 8 = 12$

$2x = 4 \Rightarrow \mathbf{x = 2}$

$4 \times (2 + 2) = 16$ and $2 \times (2 + 6) = 16$ ✔

Exercise 7

Q1 Solve the following equations by first multiplying out the brackets.

a) $3(x + 2) = x + 14$ b) $9(x - 1) = x + 15$ c) $6(x + 2) = 3x + 48$

d) $8(x - 8) = 2(x - 2)$ e) $4(4 - x) = 2(x - 1)$ f) $20(x - 2) = 5(x + 1)$

Q2 Solve the following equations.

a) $5(x - 5) = 2(x - 14)$ b) $2(x - 2) = 5(x - 8)$ c) $4(x - 2) = 6(x + 3)$

d) $6(x - 1.5) = 2(x - 3.5)$ e) $9(x - 3.3) = -6(x + 1.7)$ f) $-4(x - 3) = 8(0.7 - x)$

Q3 Solve the following equations.

a) $7(3x + 2) = 5(9x - 0.08)$ b) $7(2x + \frac{1}{7}) = 14(3x - 0.5)$

c) $10(x - 2) = -2(\frac{4}{3} + 7x)$ d) $4(3x - 3) = -2(\frac{76}{9} + 5x)$

Most of the time it's better to get rid of a **fraction** before starting to rearrange anything else.
You do this by multiplying **both sides** of the equation by the **denominator** of the fraction.

Example 10

Solve the equation $\frac{x}{3} = 7 - 2x$.

1. Multiply both sides by 3.
2. Then solve in the normal way.

$\frac{x}{3} = 7 - 2x \Rightarrow x = 3(7 - 2x)$

$x = 21 - 6x$

$7x = 21 \Rightarrow \mathbf{x = 3}$

Tip: If you tried to rearrange by adding $2x$ first you would have $2x + \frac{x}{3}$, which makes things messier.

Exercise 8

Q1 Solve the following equations. Start by multiplying both sides by a number.

a) $\frac{x}{4} = 1 - x$ b) $\frac{x}{3} = 8 - x$ c) $\frac{x}{5} = 11 - 2x$

d) $\frac{x}{4} = 10 - x$ e) $\frac{x}{5} = x + 4$ f) $\frac{x}{5} = -22 - 2x$

Q2 Solve the following equations.

a) $\frac{x}{3} = 2(x - 5)$ b) $\frac{x}{2} = 4(x - 7)$ c) $\frac{x}{5} = 2(x + 9)$

d) $\frac{x}{2} = 2(x + 5)$ e) $\frac{x}{4} = -2(x + 18)$ f) $\frac{x}{4} = 3(x - 55)$

If there's a **fraction** on **both sides** of the equation, there's a trick known as **cross-multiplying** to get rid of both fractions at the **same time**.

You need to multiply the **numerator** of each fraction by the **denominator** of the other.

$\frac{a}{b} = \frac{c}{d}$ becomes $a \times d = c \times b$

Example 11

Solve the equation $\frac{x-2}{2} = \frac{6-x}{6}$.

1. Cross-multiply — multiply the top of each fraction by the bottom of the other.
2. Then solve in the normal way. Expand the brackets...
   ... get x terms on one side...
   ... and divide by 8.

$\frac{x-2}{2} = \frac{6-x}{6}$

$6(x - 2) = 2(6 - x)$

$6x - 12 = 12 - 2x$

$8x = 24$

$\boldsymbol{x = 3}$

Tip: Step 1 is the same as multiplying both sides by 2 and then multiplying both sides by 6.

Exercise 9

Q1 Solve the following equations.

a) $\frac{x+4}{2} = \frac{x+10}{3}$ b) $\frac{x+2}{2} = \frac{x+4}{6}$ c) $\frac{x+3}{4} = \frac{x+9}{7}$

d) $\frac{x-2}{3} = \frac{x+4}{5}$ e) $\frac{x-3}{4} = \frac{x+2}{8}$ f) $\frac{x-6}{5} = \frac{x+3}{8}$

Q2 Solve the following equations.

a) $\frac{x-6}{2} = \frac{8-2x}{4}$ b) $\frac{x-9}{2} = \frac{2-3x}{4}$ c) $\frac{x-12}{6} = \frac{4-2x}{3}$

9.2 Forming Your Own Equations

Some problems in the real world can be solved by forming an equation and then solving it. You'll need to be able to write an equation using the information from a wordy problem.

Word Problems

Learning Objectives — Spec Ref A21:
- Be able to set up an algebraic equation for a given situation.
- Know how to interpret the solution of an algebraic equation in context.

Sometimes you'll need to **write** your own equation based on a **description** of a situation.

- Read the question **very carefully** so you don't **miss** any information.
- Call the **unknown** quantity in the situation 'x'.
- Make an equation in **terms of x** by using the information in the **question**. For example, if someone has **3 more** than the unknown, this would be $x + 3$, if there is **twice as much**, this would be $2x$, etc.
- **Simplify** your equation as much as possible, then **solve** it using the usual methods.

Example 1

I think of a number, double it, and add 3. The result equals 17. What is the number I thought of?

1. You don't know what the number is yet. — Call the number x.
2. Doubling x gives $2x$. Then adding 3 gives $2x + 3$. The result is 17. → Then: $2x + 3 = 17$
3. Solve the equation in the normal way. → $2x = 17 - 3 = 14$ $\Rightarrow$ $x = 7$

Tip: Remember to check your answer.

Exercise 1

Q1 Which number did I think of in each situation below?
"I think of a number, and then..."

a) ...I add 5 to it. The result equals 12.

b) ...I multiply it by 2, and then subtract 5. The result equals 15.

c) ...I divide it by 4, and then add 10. The result equals 14.

Example 2

One day a furniture store sells 3 times as many leather sofas as it does fabric sofas. On this day it sells a total of 28 sofas. How many leather sofas were sold?

1. Call the number of fabric sofas sold x.
   Then the number of leather sofas sold is $3x$.
2. 28 sofas are sold in total, so use this to write an equation.

$$x + 3x = 28$$
$$4x = 28$$

3. Solve the equation to find x.

$$x = 28 \div 4 = 7$$

4. Multiply by 3 to find the number of leather sofas sold.

$$3x = 3 \times 7 = 21$$

21 leather sofas were sold.

Exercise 2

Q1 A bride and groom each invite an equal number of guests to their wedding. All of the groom's guests are able to come, but 8 of the bride's guests can't come. If a total of 60 guests can attend, how many guests did the groom invite?

Q2 One day a bed shop sells a total of 54 beds. 10 fewer king-size beds were sold than single beds, and 16 more double beds were sold than single beds. How many single beds were sold?

Q3 Rufina makes and sells 20 fruit scones and 10 cheese scones. The ingredients cost £y in total. She sells each fruit scone for £x and each cheese scone for 10p more than a fruit scone.

a) Write an expression in terms of x and y for the profit, in £, that she makes.

b) If she spent £6 on ingredients and made a profit of £10, what was the selling price of a fruit scone?

Shape Problems

Learning Objective — Spec Ref A21:
Be able to form and solve equations using known properties of shapes.

You might have to use the **properties of shapes** to form an equation, which you can then use to find side lengths or angles. You'll need to use your knowledge of:

- **Angle rules** of shapes, e.g. sum of angles in a triangle = 180°.
- The formulas for **areas** of different shapes.
- Finding the **perimeter** of different shapes.

Tip: These are covered in Section 15 and Section 22.

Example 3

The perimeter of this rectangle is 78 cm. Write an equation involving x to show this. Then solve your equation to find x.

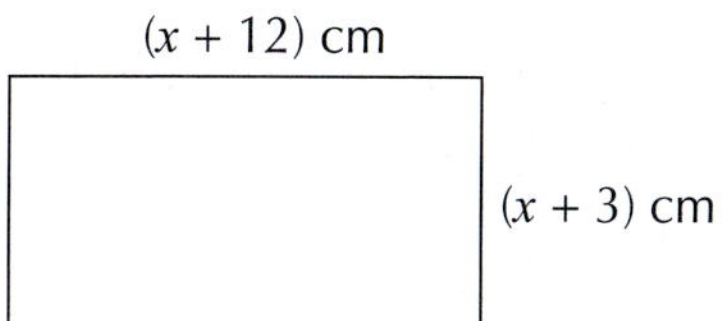

1. Find the perimeter by adding together the lengths of all the sides. This must equal 78.

   Perimeter $= (x + 12) + (x + 3) + (x + 12) + (x + 3)$
   $= 4x + 30$

   So $4x + 30 = 78$.

2. Solve the equation in the normal way.

   $4x = 78 - 30 = 48$
   $x = 48 \div 4$
   $\mathbf{x = 12}$

Tip: Check your answer works in the context — e.g. length must be positive.

Example 4

Use the triangle to write an equation involving x. Solve your equation to find x.

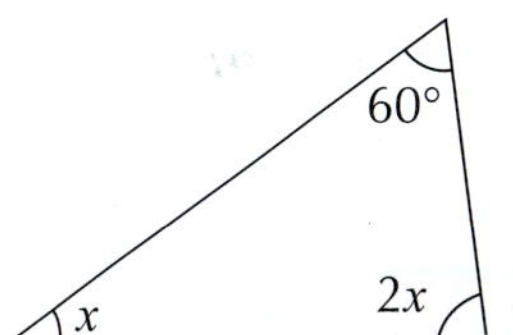

1. The angles in a triangle always add up to 180°. $x + 2x + 60° = 180°$
2. Simplify your equation. $3x + 60° = 180°$
3. Solve the equation in the normal way.

   $3x = 180° - 60° = 120°$
   $x = 120° \div 3$
   $\mathbf{x = 40°}$

Exercise 3

Q1 For the triangle on the right:

a) Write an equation involving x. (All the angles are measured in degrees.)

b) Solve your equation to find x.

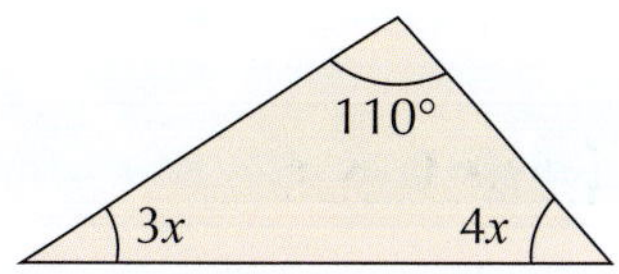

Q2 For each shape below:

(i) Write an equation involving x.

(ii) Solve your equation to find x.

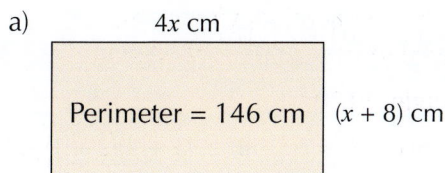

a) 4x cm, Perimeter = 146 cm, (x + 8) cm

b)

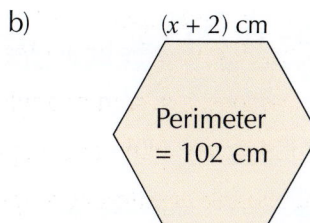

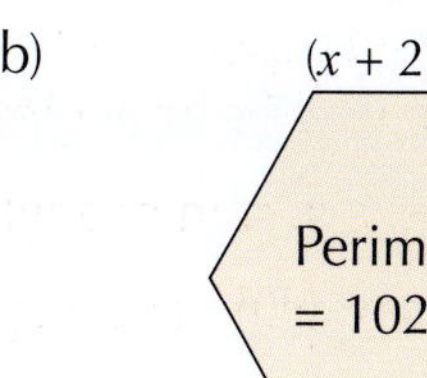

9.3 Identities

Identities look like equations with an extra line, but there's an important difference — equations are only true for a particular value (or values) of x, but identities are always true, no matter what.

Learning Objective — Spec Ref A3/A6:
Understand the difference between equations and identities.

An **equation** is a way of showing that two expressions are equal for some particular values of an unknown.

Identities are like equations, but are **always true**, for **any value** of the unknown. Identities have the symbol '$\equiv$' instead of '='.

E.g. $x - 1 = 2$ is an equation — it's only true when $x = 3$.
$x + 1 \equiv 1 + x$ is an identity — it's always true, whatever the value of x.

In identity questions, you should **rearrange** the expressions on either side **separately** to see if they're the **same**.

You **don't** need to take things to the other side, like you would if you were solving an equation.

Example 1

Show that $(x + 6)(x - 3) \equiv x(x + 3) - 18$

1. Expand and simplify both sides of the identity separately.

   LHS: $(x + 6)(x - 3) = x^2 - 3x + 6x - 18$
   $= x^2 + 3x - 18$

   RHS: $x(x + 3) - 18 = x^2 + 3x - 18$

2. Both sides give the same expression.

   So $(x + 6)(x - 3) \equiv x(x + 3) - 18$

Tip: LHS means "left-hand side" and RHS is "right-hand side".

Exercise 1

Q1 For each of the following, state whether or not you could replace the box with the symbol '$\equiv$'.

a) $4x \square 10$

b) $x^2 + 2x + 1 \square 0$

c) $-x^2 + 3 \square 3 - x^2$

d) $2(x + 1) \square x - 1$

e) $3(x + 2) - x \square 2(x + 3)$

f) $3(2 - 3x) + 2 \square 8x$

Q2 Show that:

a) $(x + 4)^2 - 4 \equiv (x + 6)(x + 2)$

b) $5(x + 2) + (x^2 - 4) \equiv (x + 4)(x + 1) + 2$

9.4 Proof

Proof questions can be confusing — it's not always obvious where to start and where you want to end up. Don't worry though, there are some handy tricks you can use to help you to get started.

Learning Objective — Spec Ref A6:
Be able to show that mathematical statements are true or false.

Proof is all about showing that something is **true or false**.

You can use these **facts** to make proof questions much easier:

- Any **even number** can be written as $\mathbf{2n}$ — i.e. as "2 × an integer".
- Any **odd number** can be written as $\mathbf{2n + 1}$ — i.e. as "(2 × an integer) + 1".
- **Consecutive numbers** can be written as $\mathbf{n}$, $\mathbf{(n + 1)}$, $\mathbf{(n + 2)}$, etc.
- **Consecutive even** numbers are written as $\mathbf{2n}$, $\mathbf{(2n + 2)}$, $\mathbf{(2n + 4)}$, etc. and **consecutive odd** numbers as $\mathbf{(2n + 1)}$, $\mathbf{(2n + 3)}$, $\mathbf{(2n + 5)}$, etc. **Nonconsecutive numbers** need different letters, such as $\mathbf{a}$, $\mathbf{b}$, $\mathbf{c}$ etc.
- The **sum**, **difference** and **product** of integers is **always** an integer.

Tip: n is a common letter used for integers (whole numbers), but you can use any letter you like.

Example 1

Show that the product of two odd numbers is odd.

1. Take two odd numbers.

$2a + 1$ and $2b + 1$, where a and b are integers.

2. Multiply them together and rearrange into the form $2n + 1$ (where n is an integer).

$$(2a + 1)(2b + 1) = 4ab + 2a + 2b + 1 = 2(2ab + a + b) + 1 = 2n + 1$$

where $n = (2ab + a + b)$ is an integer

So the **product of two odd numbers is odd**.

Exercise 1

Q1 Show that the product of an even number and an odd number is always even.

Q2 Show that the sum of two consecutive square numbers is always odd.

To show that a statement is **false**, you can just find an **example** where it **doesn't work**. This is called a **counter example**.

There are usually lots of counter examples you could give, but you only need to find **one**. Make sure you show clearly **why** the statement doesn't work for your example.

Example 2

Show that the following statement is false by finding a counter example:
"The difference between two consecutive square numbers is always prime."

Try consecutive square numbers until you find a pair that doesn't work:

1 and 4 — difference = 3 (prime)
4 and 9 — difference = 5 (prime)
9 and 16 — difference = 7 (prime)
16 and 25 — difference = 9 (NOT prime), so the **statement is false.**

Tip: You don't have to go through loads of examples if you can spot one that's wrong straightaway.

Exercise 2

Show that the statements in Q1 and Q2 are false by finding a suitable counter example for each.

Q1 "The sum of three consecutive integers is always bigger than each individual number."

Q2 "The difference between any two prime numbers is always an even number."

To show that something is a **multiple** of a particular number, you need to write it as that number multiplied by an integer. You'll often need to **factorise** to show this.

E.g. if you wanted to show that something was a multiple of 4, you'd need to be able to write it as $\mathbf{4n}$, where n is some integer. If you **can't** write it in this form then it is **not** a multiple of 4.

Example 3

Show that the sum of three consecutive integers is a multiple of 3.

1. Take three consecutive integers.

   n, $n + 1$ and $n + 2$, where n is an integer.

2. Add them together and factorise into the form $3 \times$ integer.

   $n + n + 1 + n + 2 = 3n + 3 = 3(n + 1)$
   where $n + 1$ is an integer

   So the sum of three consecutive numbers is a **multiple of 3.**

Exercise 3

Q1 Show that the sum of two consecutive odd integers is a multiple of 4.

Q2 Let $x = 2(y + 5) + 4(y + 1) - 2$, where y is an integer. Show that x is a multiple of 6.

9.5 Inequalities

Inequality symbols can be used to compare numbers or to compare algebraic expressions. They can also be used to describe the range of values that a variable can take (e.g. $x < 4$).

Inequalities

Learning Objectives — Spec Ref A3/A22:

- Understand and be able to use the four inequality symbols.
- Know how to represent inequalities on a number line.

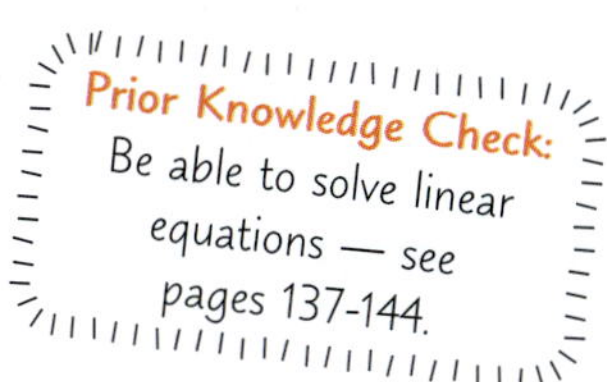

Prior Knowledge Check:
Be able to solve linear equations — see pages 137-144.

You write inequalities using these symbols:

$>$ greater than	$<$ less than	$\geq$ greater than or equal to	$\leq$ less than or equal to

Greater than ($>$) and less than ($<$) are called **strict inequalities**.

You can show inequalities **visually** on a **number line**, using a **circle** to show the **boundary value** and an **arrow** to show which values are part of the solution.

Example 1

Show the following inequalities on a number line: a) $x > 1$ b) $x \leq 1$

a) The empty circle shows 1 is not included, as $x = 1$ does not make $x > 1$ true.

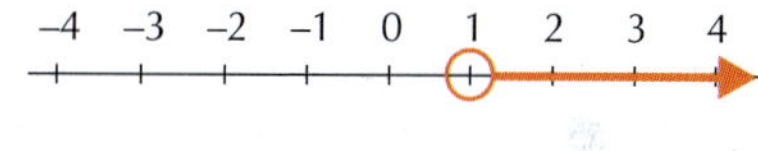

b) The solid circle shows 1 is included, as $x = 1$ does make $x \leq 1$ true.

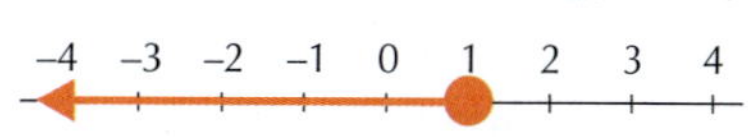

Exercise 1

Q1 Insert $>$ or $<$ in each of the boxes to complete the following inequalities.

a) $6 \square 1$ b) $2 \square 8$ c) $-1 \square -3$ d) $-7 \square 1$

Q2 Describe in words what is meant by the following inequalities.

a) $x \geq 1$ b) $x < 7$ c) $x > -4$ d) $x \leq 9$

Q3 Write each of the following as an inequality.

a) x is greater than 4 b) x is less than or equal to 12 c) x is less than 3

Q4 Show the following inequalities on a number line.

a) $x \geq 12$ b) $x < 22$ c) $x > -6$ d) $x \leq -3$

Algebra with Inequalities

Learning Objective — Spec Ref A3/A22:
Be able to solve inequalities using algebra.

The rules for solving inequalities are **very similar** to the rules for solving equations. The **solution** to an inequality will usually be an inequality with x on one side and a **number** on the other.

Tip: You have to be careful if you need to multiply or divide by a negative number — see next page.

Example 2

Solve the inequalities: a) $x + 4 < 8$ b) $2 \leq x - 7$
Show your solutions on a number line.

1. You need to get x on its own on one side. But you must always do the same to both sides of an inequality.

a) $x + 4 < 8$

$x + 4 - 4 < 8 - 4$

$\boldsymbol{x < 4}$

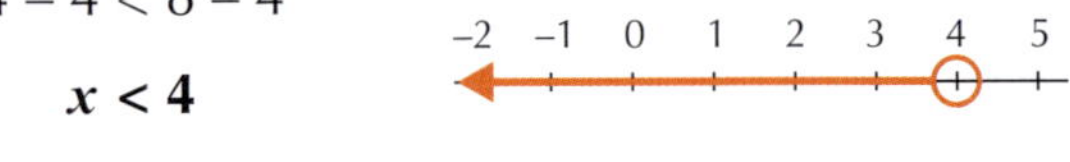

2. If the question uses < or >, so will your answer. If the question uses ≤ or ≥, so will your answer.

b) $2 \leq x - 7$

$2 + 7 \leq x - 7 + 7$

$9 \leq x \Rightarrow \boldsymbol{x \geq 9}$

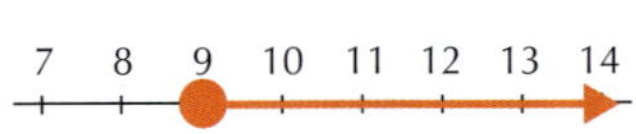

Exercise 2

Q1 Solve the following inequalities. Show each of your solutions on a number line.

a) $x + 9 > 14$ b) $x + 3 \leq 12$ c) $x - 5 < -3$ d) $x + 1 \leq -1$

Q2 Solve the following inequalities.

a) $x - 9 > 8$ b) $x + 7 < 17$ c) $x + 12 < -18$ d) $x - 8 \leq -3$

Q3 This question is about the inequality $6 > x$.

a) Describe in words what is meant by this inequality.

b) Rewrite the inequality by completing the following: $x \square 6$

c) Show the solution to this inequality on a number line.

Q4 Rewrite each of these inequalities with x on the left-hand side.

a) $12 \geq x$ b) $4 < x$ c) $15 \leq x$ d) $14 > x$

Q5 Solve the following inequalities. Show each of your solutions on a number line.

a) $18 < x + 2$ b) $12 \leq x - 4$ c) $1 > x - 17$ d) $31 \geq x + 30$

If you need to **multiply or divide** to solve an inequality, you can solve it the same way as you would an equation — as long as you are multiplying or dividing by a **positive** number.

Example 3

Solve the following inequalities: a) $4x < 12$ b) $\frac{x}{3} \geq 5$

1. Do the same to both sides of an inequality.
2. You are only multiplying or dividing by positive numbers so you can just solve as usual.

a)
$$4x < 12$$
$$4x \div 4 < 12 \div 4$$
$$\boldsymbol{x < 3}$$

b)
$$\frac{x}{3} \geq 5$$
$$\frac{x}{3} \times 3 \geq 5 \times 3$$
$$\boldsymbol{x \geq 15}$$

If you're **multiplying** or **dividing** by a **negative number** then the inequality sign '**flips over**'.

- '<' turns into '>' and '>' turns into '<'.
- '≤' turns into '≥' and '≥' turns into '≤'.

Tip: This is the most important rule to remember when it comes to inequalities.

Example 4

Solve the following inequalities: a) $-3x < 9$ b) $-\frac{x}{4} \geq 8$

1. Do the same to both sides of an inequality.
2. Multiplying or dividing by a negative number changes the direction of the inequality sign.

a)
$$-3x < 9$$
$$-3x \div -3 > 9 \div -3$$
$$\boldsymbol{x > -3}$$

b)
$$-\frac{x}{4} \geq 8$$
$$-\frac{x}{4} \times -4 \leq 8 \times -4$$
$$\boldsymbol{x \leq -32}$$

Exercise 3

Q1 Solve the following inequalities.

a) $3x \geq 9$ b) $5x < -25$ c) $2x > 8$ d) $7x \leq 21$

Q2 Solve the following inequalities.

a) $\frac{x}{2} \geq 3$ b) $\frac{x}{5} < 2$ c) $\frac{x}{5.5} < 1.2$ d) $\frac{x}{2.5} > -3.2$

Q3 Solve the following inequalities.

a) $-4x < -16$ b) $-9x > -72$ c) $-11x \leq 33$ d) $-2x < 45$

Q4 Solve the following inequalities.

a) $-\frac{x}{3} < 8$ b) $-\frac{x}{5} \leq -4$ c) $-\frac{x}{1.1} \geq 10$ d) $-\frac{x}{0.2} > -2.1$

You can solve harder inequalities in the **same way** as you solved harder equations on page 141.

Example 5

Solve the following inequality: $-\frac{x+4}{2} \leq 3$

1. First multiply by –2 and switch the inequality sign.
2. Then subtract 4.

$$-\frac{x+4}{2} \leq 3$$
$$x + 4 \geq 3 \times -2$$
$$x + 4 \geq -6$$
$$x \geq -6 - 4$$
$$\mathbf{x \geq -10}$$

Tip: Remember to switch the inequality sign if you multiply or divide by a negative number.

Exercise 4

Solve each of the inequalities in Questions 1-3.

Q1 a) $7x - 12 > 65$ b) $2x + 16 \geq -8$ c) $-8x - 4.2 < 12.6$ d) $4x + 2.6 \leq 28.6$

Q2 a) $\frac{x+2}{3} < 1$ b) $\frac{x-8}{2} > 7$ c) $\frac{x+4}{5} \geq 2$ d) $-\frac{x-6}{4} \leq 0.5$

Q3 a) $\frac{x}{4} - 2.5 \geq 1$ b) $\frac{x}{2} + 5.5 > 7$ c) $-\frac{x}{8} - 3.1 < -1$ d) $\frac{x}{3.2} + 1.3 \leq 5$

Compound Inequalities

Learning Objectives — Spec Ref A3/A22:
- Be able to solve compound inequalities.
- Know how to represent compound inequalities on a number line.

A **compound inequality** combines multiple inequalities into one. For example, $3 < x \leq 9$ means that $x > 3$ **and** $x \leq 9$ — so if x is an integer (whole number), the solutions are 4, 5, 6, 7, 8 and 9.

To solve a compound inequality, you can just **split it up** into two **simple inequalities** and solve each one separately. Then **combine** your solutions back into one inequality at the **end**.

Just like for simple inequalities, you can give a solution using a **number line** The only difference is that this time the solution will be shown by **two circles** with a line between them.
E.g. If the solution is $-2 < x \leq 1$, then on a number line it would be:

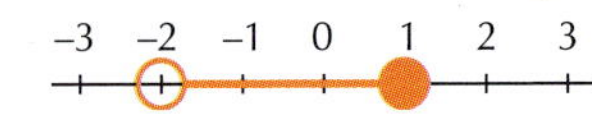

Example 6

Show the inequality $2 \leq x < 4$ on a number line.

1. Write down the two separate inequalities. — $2 \leq x < 4$ means $2 \leq x$ and $x < 4$.
2. Find the number x is greater than... ...and the number x is less than. — $2 \leq x$ is the same as $x \geq 2$, so $x \geq 2$ and $x < 4$.
3. Draw the number line. Here, x is between 2 and 4 (including 2, but not including 4).

Example 7

Solve the inequality $-1 < 2x + 2 < 4$. Show your solution on a number line.

1. Write down the two separate inequalities.

$-1 < 2x + 2$ and $2x + 2 < 4$

2. Solve the inequalities separately, then write the solution as a compound inequality.

① $-1 < 2x + 2$
$-3 < 2x$
$-1.5 < x$

② $2x + 2 < 4$
$2x < 2$
$x < 1$

So $\mathbf{-1.5 < x < 1}$.

3. Draw the number line.

−2 −1.5 −1 −0.5 0 0.5 1 1.5

Exercise 5

Q1 List the **integers** which satisfy the following inequalities.

a) $2 < x \leq 4$ b) $-5 \leq x < 1$ c) $6 \leq x \leq 13$

Q2 Show the following inequalities on a number line.

a) $1 < x \leq 6$ b) $-1 \leq x < 8$ c) $-2.4 \leq x < 1.6$

Q3 Solve the following inequalities. Show each of your solutions on a number line.

a) $7 < x + 3 \leq 15$ b) $2 \leq x - 4 \leq 12$ c) $-5.6 < x - 6.8 < 12.9$

Q4 Solve the following inequalities.

a) $32 < 2x \leq 42$ b) $-24 < 8x \leq 40$ c) $27 < 4.5x \leq 72$

Q5 Solve the following inequalities.

a) $17 < 6x + 5 < 29$ b) $8 < 3x - 4 \leq 26$

c) $-42 \leq 7x + 7 < 91$ d) $9 \leq 1.5x + 3 \leq 9.9$

9.6 Simultaneous Equations

Simultaneous equations are a pair of equations, which contain two unknowns (e.g. x and y). The solution to these equations will be a pair of values for x and y, that make both equations true.

Solving Simultaneous Equations

Learning Objective — Spec Ref A19:
Be able to solve two equations simultaneously.

You can solve simultaneous equations using the **elimination method**, where you **add** the two equations together (or **subtract** one from the other) so that **one variable** is eliminated.

This works if either x or y has the **same coefficient** in **both equations** — you **eliminate** the variable with **matching** coefficients:

- If the matching coefficients have the **same sign** (both + or both –), **subtract** one equation from the other.
- If the coefficients have **opposite signs** (one + and one –), **add** the two equations.

Tip: A coefficient is just the number in front of a variable.

Example 1

Solve the simultaneous equations: **(1)** $\mathbf{x + y = 11}$
(2) $\mathbf{x - 3y = 7}$

1. Subtract equation (2) from equation (1) to eliminate x.

$$\begin{aligned} x + y &= 11 \\ -(x - 3y &= 7) \\ \hline 4y &= 4 \end{aligned}$$

2. Solve the equation for y.

$$y = 1$$

3. Put $y = 1$ into one of the original equations and solve for x.

Plug into (1): $x + 1 = 11 \Rightarrow x = 10$

4. Use the other equation to check the answer.

Check in (2): $x - 3y = 10 - 3 \times 1 = 7$ ✔
So $\mathbf{x = 10, y = 1}$

Tip: Start off by looking for matching coefficients — here the coefficient of x is 1 in both equations, so you eliminate x.

Exercise 1

Solve each of the following pairs of simultaneous equations.

Q1 a) $x + 3y = 10$
$x + y = 6$

b) [illegible]$x + 3y = 13$
[illegible]$x - y = 5$

c) $x + 2y = 6$
$x + y = 2$

d) $2x - y = 7$
$4x + y = 23$

e) $3x - 2y = 16$
$2x + 2y = 14$

f) $2x + 4y = 16$
$3x + 4y = 24$

If **neither** variable has the same coefficient, you'll have to **multiply** one or both equations to make one set of **coefficients match**.
For example, if you had the equations $2x + y = 4$ and $3x + 2y = 7$, you'd multiply the first equation by 2 to make the y-coefficients match.

You then add or subtract using the **elimination method** to find the solutions.

Example 2

Solve the simultaneous equations: **(1)** $\mathbf{5x - 4y = 13}$
(2) $\mathbf{2x + 6y = -10}$

1. Multiply equation (1) by 3 and equation (2) by 2 to get $-12y$ in one and $+12y$ in the other.
2. Add the resulting equations to eliminate y.
3. Solve the equation for x.
4. Put $x = 1$ into one of the equations and solve for y.
5. Use the other equation to check.

$$\begin{aligned} 3 \times (1)&: \quad 15x - 12y = 39 \\ 2 \times (2)&: \; + \; 4x + 12y = -20 \\ &\quad 19x = 19 \\ &\quad x = 1 \end{aligned}$$

Plug into (1): $5(1) - 4y = 13$
$-4y = 8 \Rightarrow y = -2$

Check in (2): $2x + 6y = 2(1) + 6(-2) = -10$ ✔
So $\mathbf{x = 1,\ y = -2}$

Exercise 2

Q1 a) $3x + 2y = 16$
$2x + y = 9$

b) $4x + 3y = 16$
$5x - y = 1$

c) $5x - 3y = 12$
$2x - y = 5$

d) $2e + 5f = 16$
$3e - 2f = 5$

e) $3d - 2e = 8$
$5d - 3e = 14$

f) $5k + 3l = 4$
$3k + 2l = 3$

Forming Simultaneous Equations

Learning Objective — Spec Ref A21:
Be able to form a set of simultaneous equations using real-life information.

Prior Knowledge Check:
Be able to form equations from word problems — see page 145.

Some **word problems** contain **two unknowns**. You'll need to use the **information** in the question to work out what the unknowns are (they could be the number of two different items, or the cost of the items, etc.). Then **form** your own **simultaneous equations** from the information given to you.

Tip: Read the question carefully to make sure you are forming both of the equations correctly.

Follow these rules to form your own simultaneous equations:

- **Assign** a letter to each of your unknowns.
- Form the two simultaneous equations using the **information in the question**.
- **Simplify** both equations as much as possible (this will make **solving** them easier).
- You may need to **rearrange** one (or both) of the equations into the form $\boldsymbol{ax + by = c}$.

Example 3

Sue buys 4 dining chairs and 1 table for £142. Ken buys 6 of the same chairs and 2 of the same tables for £254. What is the price of one chair? What is the price of one table?

1. Choose some variables.

   Let the cost of one chair be £c and the cost of one table be £t.

2. Write the question as two simultaneous equations — one equation about what Sue bought and one about what Ken bought.

   $$(1)\quad 4c + t = 142$$
   $$(2)\quad 6c + 2t = 254$$

3. Multiply equation (1) by 2 to give the same coefficients of t and label it (3). Subtract equation (2) from (3)

   $$\begin{aligned} 2\times(1)=(3):&\quad 8c + 2t = 284 \\ (2):&\quad -(6c + 2t = 254) \\ &\quad \overline{2c \qquad\;\; = 30} \end{aligned}$$

4. Solve the resulting equation for c.

   $$c = 15$$

5. Put $c = 15$ into equation (1) and solve for t.

   $4 \times 15 + t = 142$
   $60 + t = 142 \Rightarrow t = 82$

6. Use equation (2) to check the answer.

   $6c + 2t = 6 \times 15 + 2 \times 82 = 254$ ✔

7. Write the answer in terms of the original question.

   The chairs cost £15 each.
   The tables cost £82 each.

Tip: Always give your answer in the context of the question.

Exercise 3

Q1 The sum of two numbers, x and y, is 58. The difference between x and y is 22. Given that x is greater than y, use simultaneous equations to find both numbers.

Q2 Mountain bikes and road bikes are sold in a shop.
One day the shop sells 1 mountain bike and 2 road bikes, for a total of £350.
The price of a mountain bike is £50 more than the price of a road bike.
Calculate the price of each bike.

Q3 A grandfather with 7 grandchildren bought 6 sherbet dips and 1 Supa-Choc bar for £1.70 last week.
He bought 3 sherbet dips and 4 Supa-Choc bars for £2.60 the week before.
Calculate the price of each item.

9.7 Solving Quadratic Equations

You've already seen quadratic expressions of the form $x^2 + bx + c$.
When such an expression is set equal to zero, this forms a quadratic equation.

Learning Objective — Spec Ref A18:
Be able to solve quadratic equations using factorisation.

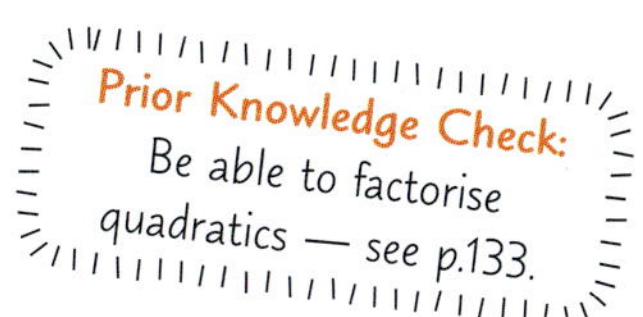

Prior Knowledge Check:
Be able to factorise
quadratics — see p.133.

Quadratic equations are equations of the form $\mathbf{x^2 + bx + c = 0}$, where b and c are constants.
The way you **solve** them depends on the **values** of $\mathbf{b}$ and $\mathbf{c}$.
If $\mathbf{b = 0}$, there is no x term, so you can just **rearrange** and take the **square root**.

Example 1

Solve the equation $x^2 - 16 = 0$.

1. Rearrange the equation to get x^2 on its own. $x^2 = 16$
2. Square root both sides. $x = \pm 4$
3. Write down the positive and negative values for x. $\mathbf{x = 4}$ or $\mathbf{x = -4}$

Tip: Remember to take the positive and negative square roots.

Exercise 1

Q1 Solve the following equations, giving exact solutions.

a) $x^2 - 4 = 0$ b) $x^2 - 1 = 0$ c) $x^2 - 25 = 0$ d) $x^2 - 64 = 0$
e) $x^2 - 121 = 0$ f) $x^2 - 100 = 0$ g) $x^2 - 2 = 0$ h) $x^2 - 7 = 0$

When $\mathbf{c = 0}$ the quadratic has the form $\mathbf{x^2 + bx = 0}$, which can be factorised to give: $\mathbf{x(x + b) = 0}$.
If two numbers multiply to make 0, then one of them must be 0.
So $\mathbf{x = 0}$ **or** $\mathbf{x + b = 0}$, which means $\mathbf{x = 0}$ and $\mathbf{x = -b}$ are the solutions of the quadratic.

Example 2

Solve the equation $x^2 - 7x = 0$.

1. Factorise the left-hand side. $x(x - 7) = 0$
2. Set each factor equal to zero. $x = 0$ or $x - 7 = 0$
3. Solve to find the two possible values for x. $\mathbf{x = 0}$ or $\mathbf{x = 7}$

Tip: If you get an x on its own outside the brackets, then you know one of the solutions is $x = 0$.

Exercise 2

Q1 Find the possible values of x for each of the following.

a) $x(x + 8) = 0$ b) $x(x - 5) = 0$ c) $x(x + 6) = 0$

d) $x(3 - x) = 0$ e) $x(4 - x) = 0$ f) $x(-2 - x) = 0$

Q2 Solve the following equations.

a) $x^2 + 6x = 0$ b) $x^2 - 6x = 0$ c) $x^2 - 24x = 0$

d) $x^2 + 5x = 0$ e) $x - x^2 = 0$ f) $12x - x^2 = 0$

If b and c are **non-zero**, then the quadratic equation has the standard form $\boldsymbol{x^2 + bx + c = 0}$. You'll need to **factorise** the quadratic into **two brackets** to get an equation in the form $\boldsymbol{(x + m)(x + n) = 0}$ (where m and n are integers that can be positive or negative). Then either $x + m = 0$ or $x + n = 0$, which you can **solve** to find the two possible **x-values**.

Example 3

Solve the equation $x^2 - 3x + 2 = 0$.

1. Factorise the left-hand side. $(x - 1)(x - 2) = 0$
2. Put each factor equal to zero. $x - 1 = 0$ or $x - 2 = 0$
3. Solve to find the two possible values for x. $\boldsymbol{x = 1}$ or $\boldsymbol{x = 2}$

Exercise 3

Q1 Find the possible values of x for each of the following.

a) $(x - 5)(x - 1) = 0$ b) $(x + 2)(x + 6) = 0$ c) $(x - 9)(x + 7) = 0$

Q2 a) Factorise the following expressions.

(i) $x^2 + 7x + 10$ (ii) $x^2 + 9x + 20$

(iii) $x^2 + 13x + 36$ (iv) $x^2 + 2x - 24$

b) Use your answers to part (a) to solve the following equations.

(i) $x^2 + 7x + 10 = 0$ (ii) $x^2 + 9x + 20 = 0$

(iii) $x^2 + 13x + 36 = 0$ (iv) $x^2 + 2x - 24 = 0$

Q3 Solve the following equations by factorising.

a) $x^2 + 2x + 1 = 0$ b) $x^2 - 7x + 12 = 0$ c) $x^2 + 4x + 4 = 0$

d) $x^2 - 4x + 4 = 0$ e) $x^2 + 2x - 15 = 0$ f) $x^2 - 4x - 21 = 0$

Review Exercise

Q1 Solve the following equations.

a) $\frac{x+8}{3} = 4$

b) $9 + 5x = 54$

c) $72 = 4.5(8 + 2x)$

d) $7(x - 3) = 3(x - 6)$

Q2 An electrician charges £x for each hour worked plus a £35 call-out charge. She does a job lasting 4 hours for which her total bill is £170. How much does the electrician charge per hour?

Q3 a) Use the triangle on the right to write an equation involving x.

b) Use your equation to find the sizes of the triangle's angles.

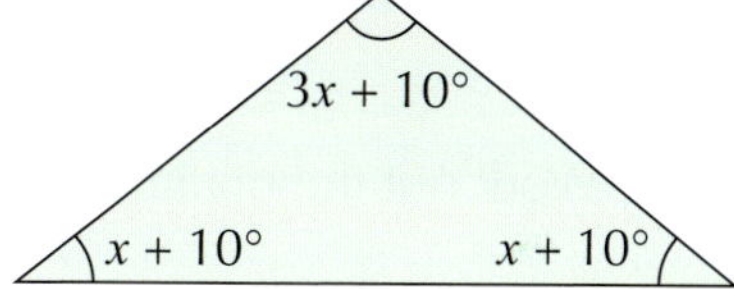

Q4 Show that: $x(x - 1) + 2(x - 3) \equiv (x + 3)(x - 2)$

Q5 Use a counter example to show that the following statement is false:
"The sum of two square numbers is never a square number."

Q6 Show that the sum of an even number and an odd number is always odd.

Q7 Solve the following inequalities. Show each of your solutions on a number line.

a) $x + 2.7 \geq 6.2$

b) $-\frac{x}{9} < 7$

c) $-5 \leq 12x + 7 < 43$

Q8 Solve the following simultaneous equations.

a) $m - 3n = 7$
$5m + 4n = -3$

b) $4u + 7v = 15$
$5u - 2v = 8$

Q9 Solve the following equations.

a) $x^2 - 36 = 0$

b) $x^2 - 81 = 0$

c) $x^2 - 3 = 0$

Q10 Solve the following equations.

a) $x^2 - 4x = 0$

b) $x^2 + 9x + 18 = 0$

c) $x^2 + 9x - 22 = 0$

Exam-Style Questions

Q1 Solve:

a) $2x + 5 = 19$

[1 mark]

b) $3(2x - 1) = 2(x + 4)$

[3 marks]

Q2 $7 \leq x < 15$ is a compound inequality, where x is an integer

a) Write down the maximum value of x.

[1 mark]

b) Work out the minimum value of x^2.

[1 mark]

Q3 Anish is x years old. Bethany is three times as old as Anish. PROBLEM SOLVING
Cate is two years younger than Anish. The sum of all their ages is 58 years.
By forming and solving an equation, find the value of x.

[3 marks]

Q4 Bill buys 2 chews and 3 lollies and pays 84p. PROBLEM SOLVING
Aisha buys 3 chews and 1 lolly and pays 63p.
How much will Rita pay when she buys 7 chews and 5 lollies?

[4 marks]

Q5 The diagram shows a rectangle with area 10 cm². PROBLEM SOLVING
The length is 3 cm more than the width.

$x + 3$ cm

x cm

Not to scale

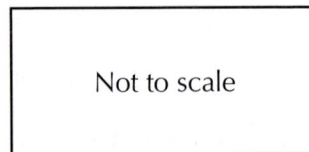

a) Show that $x^2 + 3x - 10 = 0$.

[2 marks]

b) Solve $x^2 + 3x - 10 = 0$ and write down the length and width of the rectangle.

[4 marks]

Section 10	Formulas and Functions

10.1 Formulas

A formula is a mathematical set of instructions for working something out. For example, $s = 4t + 3$ is a formula for working out the value of s — it tells you how to find s, assuming you know the value of t. You can use formulas to help solve real-life problems mathematically.

Writing Formulas

Learning Objective — Spec Ref A3/A5:
Use given information to write a formula.

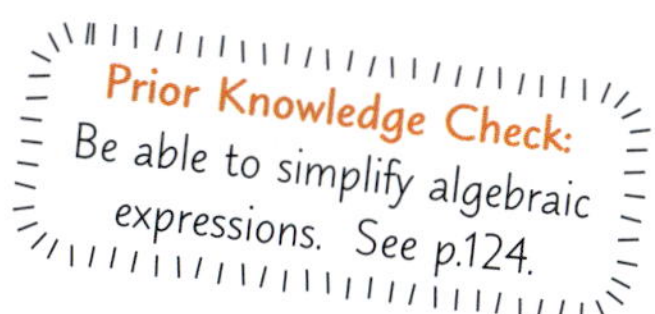

Prior Knowledge Check:
Be able to simplify algebraic expressions. See p.124.

Formulas show **relationships** between different **quantities**, which are represented by **letters**.

For example, the formula for the area of a rectangle, $A = l \times w$, shows how the area (A) is connected to the length (l) and the width (w).

There are **two parts** to every formula:

- The **letter** before the equals sign is called the **subject** of the formula.
- The part after the equals sign is an **algebraic expression** which tells you the **value** of the subject.

So to **write** a formula, you need to be able to write an **expression** to go on the **right-hand side**. That means picking out the **key bits** of maths from the given **information**. These questions can be quite wordy, so take note of the important stuff as you read along.

Example 1

Write an expression for the number of marbles I have in each case below.

a) I have a bag containing m marbles. I then lose 8 marbles.

1. "I have a bag containing m marbles" — so use the letter m to represent the number of marbles in the bag. m
2. "I then lose 8 marbles" — so you need to subtract 8. $\boldsymbol{m - 8}$

b) My brother has 12 marbles, which is m more marbles than I own.

1. "My brother has 12 marbles..." — jot this down. 12
2. "...which is m more marbles than I own" — this means I have m fewer marbles than my brother, so subtract m. $\boldsymbol{12 - m}$

Example 2

My friend has m marbles. I had twice as many marbles as my friend, but then I lost 6 of them. Write an expression for how many marbles I have now.

1. "My friend has m marbles" — use the letter m. m
2. "I had twice as many marbles" — so multiply m by 2. $2m$
3. "...then I lost 6 of them" — so subtract 6. $\mathbf{2m - 6}$

Tip: '$2m$' is a short way of writing '$2 \times m$' — you don't need to write the × sign.

Exercise 1

Q1 Write an algebraic expression for each of the quantities asked for below.

a) I have c carrots. Su has 6 more carrots than me. How many carrots does Su have?

b) Daisy has p plants. Iris has 8 fewer plants. How many plants does Iris have?

Q2 Claudia owns f films. Barry owns twice as many films as Claudia.

a) How many films does Barry own?

b) How many films do Claudia and Barry own in total?

c) How many films would they own in total if they each gave away 3 of their films?

Q3 I have b flower bulbs. To find the number of flowers that should grow from them, multiply the number of bulbs by 3 and then add 5. How many flowers should I expect to grow?

Q4 Alf has £18. He then works in a shop for h hours. For each hour he works, he is paid £8. How much money (in pounds) does Alf have now?

Q5 I'm thinking of a number, x, and a smaller number, y. Write an expression for:

a) The square of the smaller number minus the cube of the larger number.

b) The square root of the sum of both numbers.

All that practice at writing expressions will help you out with **writing formulas**.

To write a **formula** from given information you need to:

- **Identify** the **subject** of the formula — for example, if you're asked to write a formula for the cost (C) of..., then $\boldsymbol{C}$ is the subject.
- Use the **information** to write an **expression** that will give you the **value** of the **subject**.
- Write out the formula by putting the subject **equal to** the expression.

Example 3

The cost (C) of hiring a bike is £5 per hour plus a fixed cost of £25.
Write a formula for the cost in pounds of hiring a bike for h hours.

1. Identify the subject of the formula.

   The subject is C, the total cost of hiring a bike.

2. You need an expression for the total cost. Multiply the number of hours (h) by the cost per hour (£5). Then add on the fixed cost of £25.

   Cost (in £) for h hours = $h \times 5 = 5h$
   Total cost (in £) is $5h + 25$

3. A formula for C must start with '$C = ...$'.

   So $\mathbf{C = 5h + 25}$

Exercise 2

Q1 It costs £3 per hour to park a car.
Write a formula for the cost in pounds (C) to park for h hours.

Q2 It takes 2 minutes to drive 1 km.
Write a formula for the time taken in minutes (T) to drive k km.

Q3 Tom gets paid w pounds for each hour he works in his local shop.
Write a formula for the total amount he gets paid in pounds (P) if he works for 8 hours.

Q4 Kojo runs r km, but Ellie runs 5 km less.
Write a formula for the distance in km (d) that Ellie runs.

Q5 Write a formula for the cost in pounds (C) of hiring a minibus for n hours if it costs £5.50 for each hour plus a fixed charge of £F.

Q6 The instructions for cooking a goose are to cook for 50 minutes per kg, plus 25 minutes.
Write a formula to find the time taken (t minutes) to cook a goose weighing n kg.

Q7 Write a formula for the cost in pounds (C) of having t trees cut down if it costs p pounds per tree plus a fixed amount of £25.

Q8 To hire a boat costs a £10 fixed fee plus 22 pence per mile for each mile covered.
Write a formula for finding the cost in pounds (C) of hiring a boat and covering m miles.

Q9 To hire a bouncy castle costs a £125 fixed fee plus 80 pence per minute it is used.
Write a formula for the cost in pounds (C) of hiring a bouncy castle for h hours.

Substituting into Formulas

Learning Objective — Spec Ref A2:
Substitute values into a given formula.

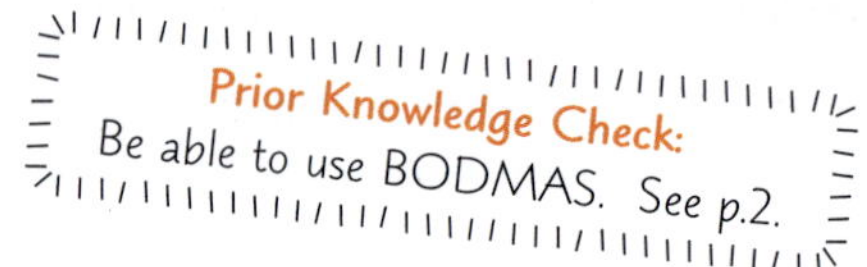

Prior Knowledge Check:
Be able to use BODMAS. See p.2.

You can **evaluate** a formula by replacing the **letters** in the formula with actual **values**. This is called **substitution**. Here's the method to follow:

- Write out the formula.
- Write it out again, substituting numbers for letters.
- Work out the calculation — using the correct order of operations (BODMAS).

Example 4

Use the formula $v = u + 5a$ to find v if $u = 3$ and $a = -18$.

1. Write out the formula. $v = u + 5a$
2. Replace each letter with its value. $v = 3 + 5 \times (-18)$
3. Work out the calculation step by step — you do multiplication before addition. $v = 3 + (-90)$
   $v = \mathbf{-87}$

Tip: Be careful substituting in negative numbers. You can use brackets so the minus sign doesn't get lost.

A formula can include all sorts of operations, such as **powers** and **brackets**, which can make things a bit trickier. Stick to the **method** above and you'll be able to evaluate these too.

Example 5

The sum of the first n square numbers is $1^2 + 2^2 + 3^2 + 4^2 + ... + n^2$.
This sum (S) is given by the formula $S = \frac{n}{6}(2n^2 + 3n + 1)$.
Use the formula to find S when $n = 10$.

1. Write out the formula. $S = \frac{n}{6}(2n^2 + 3n + 1)$
2. Replace n with 10. $= \frac{10}{6}(2 \times 10^2 + 3 \times 10 + 1)$
3. Work out the calculation using BODMAS:
   Evaluate the brackets first.
   Inside the brackets: (i) Find 10^2 first. $= \frac{10}{6}(2 \times 100 + 3 \times 10 + 1)$
   (ii) Then do the multiplications. $= \frac{10}{6}(200 + 30 + 1)$
   (iii) Then do the additions. $= \frac{10}{6} \times 231$

   Now evaluate the rest. $= \mathbf{385}$

Exercise 3

Q1 Find the value of y in each of the following given that $x = 7$.

a) $y = x + 4$ b) $y = x - 3$ c) $y = 12 - x$ d) $y = 6x$

Q2 Find the value of y in each of the following given that $m = -3$.

a) $y = m - 8$ b) $y = 3m^2$ c) $y = -4 + m$ d) $y = \frac{12}{m}$

Q3 If $m = 4$ and $n = 3$, then find the value of p in each of the following.

a) $p = mn$ b) $p = m^2$ c) $p = m - n^2$ d) $p = \frac{3m}{n}$

Q4 If $x = -4$ and $y = -3$, then find the value of z in each of the following.

a) $z = x + 2$ b) $z = y - 1$ c) $z = -x + 2y$ d) $z = 6x - y$

Q5 Use the formula $S = \frac{1}{2}n(n + 1)$ to find S when:

a) $n = 10$ b) $n = 100$ c) $n = 1000$ d) $n = 5000$

Q6 Use the formula $s = ut + \frac{1}{2}at^2$ to find s if:

a) $u = 7$, $a = 2$ and $t = 4$ b) $u = 24$, $a = 11$ and $t = 13$

c) $u = -11$, $a = -9.81$ and $t = 12.2$ d) $u = 66.6$, $a = -1.64$ and $t = 14.2$

Wordy problems work in the same way — you write out the formula and substitute in the values. If a question involves **units**, don't forgot to include them in your **answer**.

Example 6

The temperature in degrees Fahrenheit (f) is given by the formula $f = 1.8c + 32$, where c is the temperature in degrees Celsius. Convert the following temperatures to degrees Fahrenheit: a) –17 °C b) 37.4 °C

	a)	b)
1. Write out the formula.	**a)** $f = 1.8c + 32$	**b)** $f = 1.8c + 32$
2. Identify the number to substitute for c.	$c = -17$	$c = 37.4$
3. Replace c with its value, and do the calculation.	$f = 1.8 \times (-17) + 32$ $= -30.6 + 32 = 1.4$	$f = 1.8 \times 37.4 + 32$ $= 67.32 + 32 = 99.32$
4. Give your answer with units.	So –17 °C = **1.4 °F**	So 37.4 °C = **99.32 °F**

Example 7

The taxi fare, £T, for a journey is calculated using the formula $T = 0.8m + 2.5$, where m is the distance of the journey in miles. How much is the fare for a 5 mile journey?

1. Write out the formula. $T = 0.8m + 2.5$
2. The journey is 5 miles so $m = 5$. $T = 0.8 \times 5 + 2.5$ $= 6.5$
3. Give your answer in the context of the question. So the fare is **£6.50**

Exercise 4

Q1 Use the formula $A = \frac{1}{2}bh$ to find the area (A, in m^2) of a triangle with base b and height h, if:

a) $b = 4$ m, $h = 6$ m b) $b = 2$ m, $h = 3$ m c) $b = 0.4$ m, $h = 1.8$ m

Q2 The formula for working out the speed (s, in metres per second) of a moving object is $s = \frac{d}{t}$, where d is the distance travelled (in metres) and t is the time taken (in seconds). Find the speed (in metres per second) of each of the following. Give your answers to 3 significant figures.

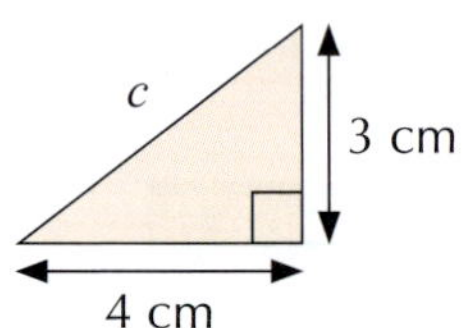

a) a runner who travels 800 metres in 110 seconds

b) a cheetah that travels 400 metres in 14 seconds

Q3 The length, c, of the longest side of a right-angled triangle is given by the formula $c = \sqrt{a^2 + b^2}$, where a and b are the lengths of the other two sides. Use the formula to work out the length of the longest side of the triangle drawn on the right.

c

3 cm

4 cm

Q4 The area (A, in cm^2) of this circle is given by the formula $A = \pi r^2$. Find A for the values of r below. Give your answers to 1 decimal place.

a) $r = 5$ cm b) $r = 3.5$ cm

c) $r = 11.1$ cm d) $r = 6.4$ cm

r

Q5 The number of seconds (T) taken for a pendulum to swing forwards and then backwards once is given by the formula $T = 2\pi\sqrt{\frac{l}{10}}$, where l is the length of the pendulum in metres. Calculate (to 1 decimal place) how long it will take a pendulum to swing backwards and forwards once if:

a) $l = 1$ metre b) $l = 0.5$ metres c) $l = 16$ metres

Rearranging Formulas

Learning Objective — Spec Ref A5:
Rearrange formulas to change the subject.

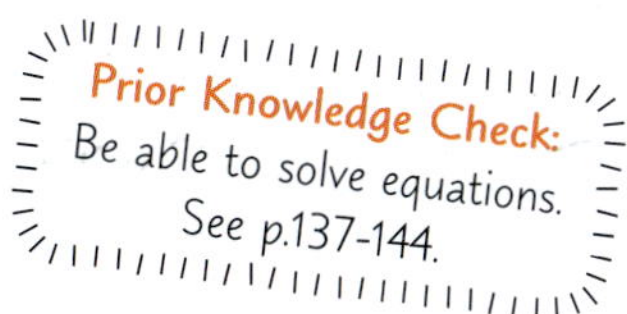
Prior Knowledge Check:
Be able to solve equations.
See p.137-144.

Rearranging formulas means making a different letter the **subject**.
For example, getting a formula beginning '$y = ...$' from '$x = 3y + 2$'.

You're aiming to get the new subject **on its own** on one side of the '=' sign. The method is just like solving an equation — you carry out **opposite operations** until you get the letter on its own, making sure to always do the **same thing** on **both sides**.

Tip: – is the opposite of +, and ÷ is the opposite of ×.

Example 8

Make x the subject of the following formulas.

a) $y = x + 4$

1. Write down the original formula. You want to get x on its own. $\quad y = x + 4$
2. The opposite of + 4 is – 4, so subtract 4 from both sides. $\quad y - 4 = x + 4 - 4$, $\quad y - 4 = x$
3. x is on its own, but you need to write the formula with x on the left-hand side. $\quad \mathbf{x = y - 4}$

b) $y = 6x$

1. Write down the original formula. You want to get x on its own. $\quad y = 6x$
2. The opposite of × 6 is ÷ 6, so divide both sides by 6. $\quad \frac{y}{6} = \frac{6x}{6} = x$
3. Write the formula with x on the left-hand side. $\quad \mathbf{x = \frac{y}{6}}$

If the subject is **squared**, you'll need to take **square roots** — remember, there's a **negative root** as well as a positive root, so you'll need a **± sign**.

Example 9

Make z the subject of the formula $w = z^2$.

1. Write down the original formula. You want to get z on its own. $\quad w = z^2$
2. z is squared, so take the square root of each side. $\quad \pm\sqrt{w} = z$
3. Write the formula with z on the left-hand side. $\quad \mathbf{z = \pm\sqrt{w}}$

Exercise 5

Q1 Make x the subject of the following formulas. All your answers should begin 'x ='.

a) $y = x + 2$ b) $b = x - 5$ c) $z = 7 + x$

Q2 Make x the subject of the following formulas.

a) $z = 4x$ b) $p = 17x$ c) $r = 4.2x$

Q3 Make x the subject of the following formulas.

a) $y = \frac{x}{8}$ b) $z = \frac{x}{17}$ c) $t = \frac{x}{8.6}$

Q4 Make x the subject of the following formulas.

a) $abc = 2x$ b) $t = xy$ c) $uv + y = 4.2x$

Q5 Make s the subject of the following formulas.

a) $m = \frac{4}{5}s$ b) $r = -16s$ c) $p = -14.2s$

d) $a = \frac{5}{4}s$ e) $b = \sqrt{s}$ f) $c = s^2$

Two-Step Rearrangements

For trickier formulas you need to carry out **two steps** to change the **subject**. For example, you might need to **add** a number to both sides in the **first step**, then **multiply** both sides by a number in the **second step**.

You'll need to decide which order to do the steps — do what makes the maths easier.

Example 10

Rearrange $a = 3b + 4$ to make b the subject of the formula.

$3b + 4$ means 'take your value of b and then (i) multiply by 3 and (ii) add 4'. To get b on its own, you need to undo these steps, but in the opposite order.

1. Write down the original formula. $a = 3b + 4$
2. The opposite of + 4 is – 4, so subtract 4 from both sides. $a - 4 = 3b + 4 - 4$; $a - 4 = 3b$
3. The opposite of × 3 is ÷ 3, so divide both sides by 3. $\frac{a-4}{3} = \frac{3b}{3} = b$
4. Write the formula with b on the left-hand side. $\mathbf{b = \frac{a-4}{3}}$

Tip: Be careful when dividing the left-hand side here — make sure you divide everything by 3.

Example 11

Make r the subject of $s = \frac{r-1}{2}$

$\frac{r-1}{2}$ means 'take your value of r and then (i) subtract 1 and (ii) divide by 2'.
To get r on its own, you need to undo these steps, but in the opposite order.

1. Write down the original formula. $s = \frac{r-1}{2}$
2. The opposite of ÷ 2 is × 2, so multiply both sides by 2. $2s = r - 1$
3. The opposite of – 1 is + 1, so add 1 to both sides. $2s + 1 = r$
4. Write the formula with r on the left-hand side. $\boldsymbol{r = 2s + 1}$

Exercise 6

Q1 Make x the subject of the following formulas.

a) $y = 5x + 3$ b) $z = 8x - 2$ c) $p = 15x + 18$

Q2 Make y the subject of the following formulas.

a) $z = \frac{y+4}{3}$ b) $x = \frac{7+y}{4}$ c) $s = \frac{y-2}{9}$

Q3 Make x the subject of the following formulas.

a) $u = 4(x - 2)$ b) $v = 8(x + 4)$ c) $w = 3(x - 4)$

Q4 Make y the subject of the following formulas.

a) $p + 3 = 4y - 2$ b) $q + 7 = 9y + 11$ c) $r - 5 = 21y - 9$

Q5 The surface area (A) of the shape on the right is given approximately by the formula $A = 21.5d^2$.

a) Rearrange the formula to make d the subject.

b) Find d if:

(i) $A = 344$ cm^2 (ii) $A = 134.375$ cm^2

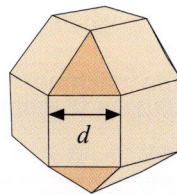

Q6 The perimeter (P) of the shape on the right is given by the formula $P = 2(2x + y)$.

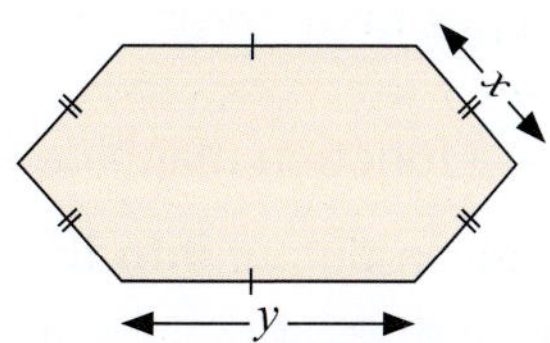

a) Rearrange the formula to make x the subject.

b) Find x if:

(i) $P = 14$ and $y = 3$ (ii) $P = 32$ and $y = 4$

Q7 Make x the subject of these formulas:

a) $x + y = 6x$ b) $y = \sqrt{x} + 2$ c) $\frac{3 + xy + x}{x + 1} = y$

10.2 Functions

A function is a mathematical instruction that turns one number into a new number. Diagrams called 'function machines' are used to show how a function works, step-by-step.

Learning Objective — Spec Ref A7:
Be able to use functions to find inputs and outputs.

A **function** takes a number (the **input**), does a calculation with it, then gives back a new number (the **output**). For example, the calculation could be 'multiply by 4 then add 5', or 'subtract 3 then divide by 8'.

A **function machine** is a **diagram** that breaks a function down into **steps**. To find the **output** from a given **input**, just follow the steps and see what comes out.

For example, this **function machine** represents the function 'multiply by 4 then add 5':

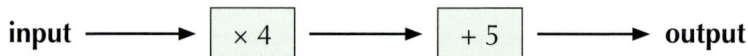

input ⟶ [× 4] ⟶ [+ 5] ⟶ **output**

There are two steps to this machine: the first is '**multiply** the **input** by **4**' and the second is '**add 5** to the **number** you get **from step 1** to give the **output**'.

Example 1

This function machine represents the function 'multiply by 3 then add 4'.

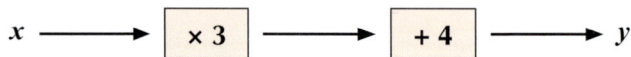

x ⟶ [**× 3**] ⟶ [**+ 4**] ⟶ y

Find the value of y when x = 3.

Put $x = 3$ into the machine and work forwards through the steps.

$3 \xrightarrow{\times 3} 9 \xrightarrow{+4} 13$ So y = **13**.

You can use a function machine **in reverse** to **find the input** from a **given output**:

- Put the given output **into the end** of the function machine.
- Work backwards by doing the **opposite operations** in **reverse order**.

Example 2

Here is a function machine:

$x \longrightarrow \boxed{\times 3} \longrightarrow \boxed{+4} \longrightarrow y$

Find the value of x when $y = 37$.

Put $y = 37$ into the end of the machine and work backwards using opposite operations.

1. The opposite of $+ 4$ is $- 4$.
2. The opposite of $\times 3$ is $\div 3$.

$37 \xrightarrow{-4} 33 \xrightarrow{\div 3} 11$

So x = **11**

Tip: Check your answer by putting it back into the machine:
11 $\times 3 = 33$
$33 + 4 =$ **37** ✓

Exercise 1

Q1 The function machine below represents the function 'divide by 5 then add 7'.

$x \longrightarrow \boxed{\div 5} \longrightarrow \boxed{+7} \longrightarrow y$

Find the value of y for the following values of x.

a) $x = 20$ b) $x = 35$ c) $x = 45$ d) $x = -10$

Q2 The function machine below represents the function 'subtract 3 then multiply by 6'.

$x \longrightarrow \boxed{-3} \longrightarrow \boxed{\times 6} \longrightarrow y$

a) What is the value of y when $x = 11$? b) Given that $y = 72$, find the value of x.

Q3 The equation $y = 7x - 2$ is represented by the function machine below.

$x \longrightarrow \boxed{\times 7} \longrightarrow \boxed{-2} \longrightarrow y$

a) Given that $x = -1$, find the value of y. b) When $y = 19$, find the value of x.

Q4 Jared wants to write the equation $y = 4x + 1$ as a function machine.

a) Copy and complete this function machine to show Jared's equation.

$x \longrightarrow \boxed{} \longrightarrow \boxed{} \longrightarrow y$

b) Use the function machine to find the value of x when $y = 17$.

Q5 For the function machine below, show there's a value where the input is equal to the output.

$x \longrightarrow \boxed{\times 6} \longrightarrow \boxed{-10} \longrightarrow y$

Review Exercise

Q1 Chloe gets 45 fewer free minutes on her mobile phone each month than Wassim.

a) If Wassim gets w free minutes, write a formula for the number of free minutes (c) Chloe gets.

b) Find c when $w = 125$.

Q2 The number of matchsticks (m) needed to make h hexagons as shown is given by the formula $m = 5h + 1$.

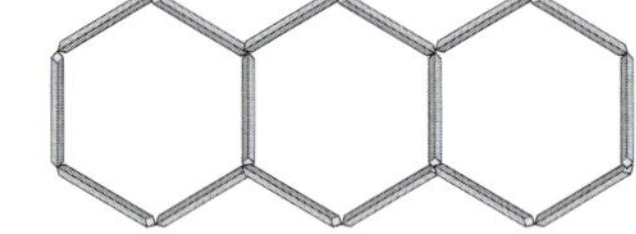

a) Rearrange this formula to make h the subject.

b) Use your formula to find h when $m = 36$.

Q3 An isosceles triangle has one angle of size x and two angles of size y. The formula for y in terms of x is $y = \frac{180° - x}{2}$.

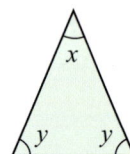

a) Find y when $x = 30°$.

b) Rearrange the formula to make x the subject.

Q4 The formula for calculating the cost (C, in £) of gas is represented by the following function machine, where n is the number of units used.

a) Find the cost if 275 units of gas were used.

b) How many units of gas were used if the gas bill is £40.50?

Q5 Debi is decorating her bathroom walls with black tiles and white tiles. She uses 3 white tiles for every black tile, plus an extra 50 white tiles.

a) Copy and complete the function machine below to represent the number of white tiles used, w, given the number of black tiles used, b.

b) If Debi uses 200 black tiles, how many white tiles does she use?

c) The function machine below shows the total number of tiles used, t, given the number of black tiles used, b.

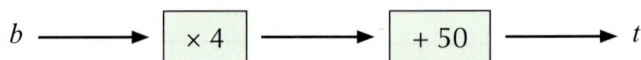

If Debi uses 530 tiles in total, how many black tiles does she use?

Exam-Style Questions

Q1 Make b the subject of the formula $y = a + \frac{b}{x}$. 

[2 marks]

Q2 Look at the function machine below.

input ⟶ -4 ⟶ $\div 25$ ⟶ output

a) Work out the output when the input is 17, giving your answer as a decimal.

[1 mark]

b) Work out the input when the output is 5.

[2 marks]

c) Find an expression in terms of x for the input when the output is $3x$, giving your answer in its simplest form.

[1 mark]

Q3 To book a swimming pool for a party, there is a fixed charge of £30, plus a fee of £1.25 for each person who attends.

a) Write a formula to calculate the hire cost (C, in £) for n people.

[1 mark]

b) Calculate the hire cost when 32 people attend.

[1 mark]

c) Rearrange your formula to make n the subject.

[2 marks]

d) If the total cost of hiring the pool was £80, how many people attended the party?

[1 mark]

Q4 Fill in the missing operation to complete the function machine below. 

[2 marks]

11.1 Term to Term Rules

A sequence is a list of numbers or shapes which follows a particular rule. Each number or shape in the sequence is called a term. Term to term rules tell you how to go from one term to the next.

Number Sequences

Learning Objectives — Spec Ref A23:
- Find rules for simple number sequences.
- Use the rule for a sequence to find terms in the sequence.

There are different types of **number sequences** that follow different rules to get from one term to the next. The first ones you should know about are **arithmetic** and **geometric** sequences.

Arithmetic Sequences

Arithmetic sequences are sequences where you **add** (or **subtract)** the **same number** each time to get from one term to the next. The number you add is called the **common difference**.

2, 5, 8, 11, 14
+3 +3 +3 +3

The rule is 'add 3 to the previous term'.

27, 21, 15, 9, 3
−6 −6 −6 −6

The rule is 'subtract 6 from the previous term'.

Geometric Sequences

Geometric sequences are sequences where you find the next term by **multiplying** (or **dividing)** by the **same number** each time. The number you multiply by is called the **common ratio**.

2, 10, 50, 250, 1250
×5 ×5 ×5 ×5

The rule is 'multiply the previous term by 5'.

48, 24, 12, 6, 3
÷2 ÷2 ÷2 ÷2

The rule is 'divide the previous term by 2'.

Example 1

The first term of a sequence is 3. The rule for finding the next term in the sequence is 'add 4 to the previous term'. Write down the first 5 terms of the sequence.

1. The first term is 3, so write this down.
2. Add 4 each time to find the terms.

3, 7, 11, 15, 19
+4 +4 +4 +4

Example 2

Consider the sequence 2, 6, 18, 54...
a) Explain the rule for finding the next term in the sequence.
b) Write down the next three terms in the sequence.

1. This time the rule for finding the next term involves multiplication.

a) Multiply the previous term by 3.

2. Multiply each term by 3 to get the next term.

b) 54, **162, 486, 1458.**

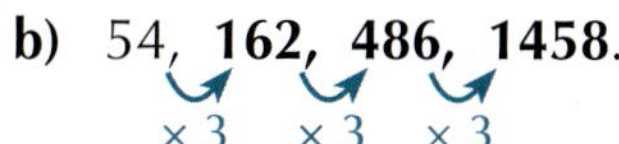

Exercise 1

Q1 The first term of a sequence is 5. The rule for finding the next term in the sequence is 'add 4 to the previous term'. Write down the first 5 terms of the sequence.

Q2 The first term of a sequence is 2. The rule for finding the next term in the sequence is 'multiply the previous term by 2'. Write down the first 5 terms of the sequence.

Q3 Write down the first 5 terms of the sequence with:

a) first term = 100; further terms generated by the rule 'subtract 6 from the previous term'.

b) first term = 40; further terms generated by the rule 'divide the previous term by 2'.

c) first term = 11; further terms generated by the rule 'multiply the previous term by –2'.

Q4 The first four terms of a sequence are 3, 6, 9, 12.

a) Write down what you add to each term in the sequence to find the next term.

b) Write down the next three terms in the sequence.

Q5 For the following sequences: (i) explain the rule for finding the next term in the sequence.
(ii) find the next three terms in the sequence.

a) 3, 5, 7, 9... b) 4, 12, 36, 108... c) 16, 8, 4, 2... d) 5, 3, 1, –1...
e) 1, 1.5, 2, 2.5... f) –1, –3, –9, –27... g) 1000, 100, 10, 1... h) 1, –2, 4, –8...

Q6 The first four terms of a sequence are 4, 10, 16, 22.

a) Explain the rule for finding the next term in this sequence.

b) Use your rule to find: (i) the 5th term (ii) the 6th term (iii) the 8th term

Q7 Copy the following sequences and fill in the blanks.

a) 9, 5, □, –3, –7, –11
b) –72, □, –18, –9, □, –2.25
c) □, 0.8, 3.2, 12.8, □, 204.8
d) –63, –55, □, □, □, –23

Special Number Sequences

Learning Objective — Spec Ref A24:
Recognise and use sequences of square, cube and triangular numbers, and quadratic and Fibonacci-type sequences.

Quadratic Sequences

In a **quadratic** sequence, the **difference** between terms **changes** by the **same amount** each time.

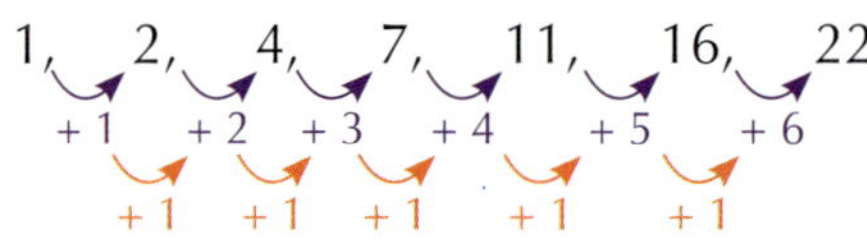

Fibonacci-Type Sequences

The **Fibonacci sequence** is a special sequence that starts 1, 1, 2, 3, 5... and follows the rule '**add together** the **previous two terms**'. A **Fibonacci-type sequence** is a sequence that follows the same rule, but starts with a different number.

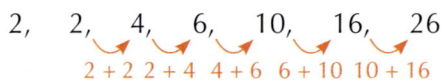

2, 2, 4, 6, 10, 16, 26

2 + 2 2 + 4 4 + 6 6 + 10 10 + 16

Sequences of Triangular, Square and Cube Numbers

Some sequences are harder to spot by their term to term rules. Common ones to watch out for are the **square numbers**: 1, 4, 9... (i.e. 1^2, 2^2, 3^2...), the **cube** numbers: 1, 8, 27 (i.e. 1^3, 2^3, 3^3...), and **triangular numbers** (shown below):

To make the sequence of triangular numbers, **start at 1** and then **add 2**, then **3**, then **4**, then **5** etc. to each new term.

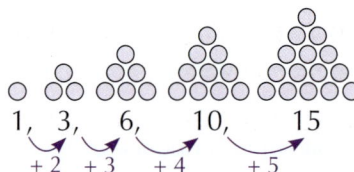

1, 3, 6, 10, 15

+ 2 + 3 + 4 + 5

Example 3

Find the next three terms in the sequence 4, 5, 7, 10...

1. Try finding the difference between neighbouring terms.
2. Here, the difference is increasing by 1 each time.
3. Use this to find the next three terms in the sequence. Start with 10. Then add 4. Then add 5. Then add 6.

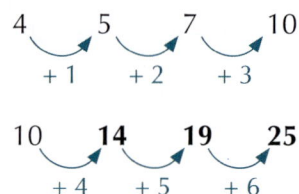

4, 5, 7, 10 (+ 1, + 2, + 3)

10, **14**, **19**, **25** (+ 4, + 5, + 6)

Exercise 2

Q1 Consider the sequence 7, 8, 10, 13, 17...

a) Find the difference between each term and the next for the first five terms.

b) Find the next three terms in the sequence.

Q2 For each sequence below, find:

(i) the difference between each term and the next for the first five terms,

(ii) the next three terms in the sequence.

a) 5, 7, 11, 17, 25...

b) 20, 18, 15, 11, 6...

c) 3, 4, 6, 9, 13...

d) 1, 2, 0, 3, –1...

Q3 The sequence 1, 1, 2, 3, 5... is known as the Fibonacci sequence. Each term in the sequence is found by adding together the previous two terms. Find the next three terms in the sequence.

Shape Sequences

Learning Objective — Spec Ref A23:
Find rules for patterns of shapes and use them to find patterns in a sequence.

Patterns of **shapes** can form **sequences**. Just like number sequences, you need to find the **rule** to get from one pattern to the next — then use that rule to find more patterns in the sequence.

Example 4

The matchstick shapes on the right form the first three patterns in a sequence.

Draw the fourth and fifth patterns in the sequence.

1. First work out how to get from one pattern to the next. You have to add 3 matchsticks to add an extra square to the previous pattern.

2. The fourth pattern is the next one in the sequence, so add 3 matchsticks to the third pattern to get the fourth...

3. Add another 3 matchsticks to that to get the fifth.

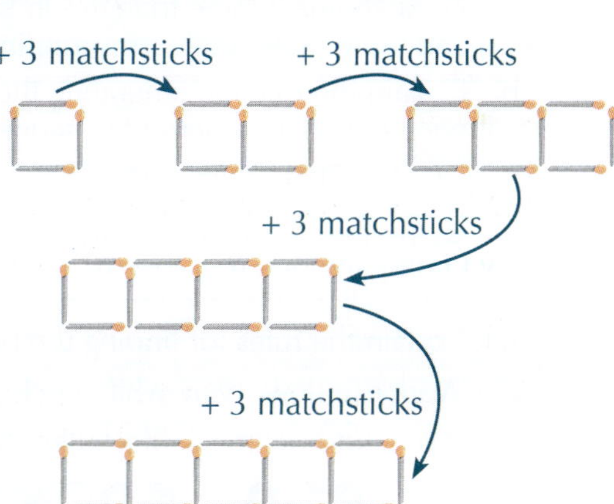

Example 5

The black and white circles on the right form the first 3 patterns in a sequence. Find the number of black circles and the number of white circles in the 9th pattern.

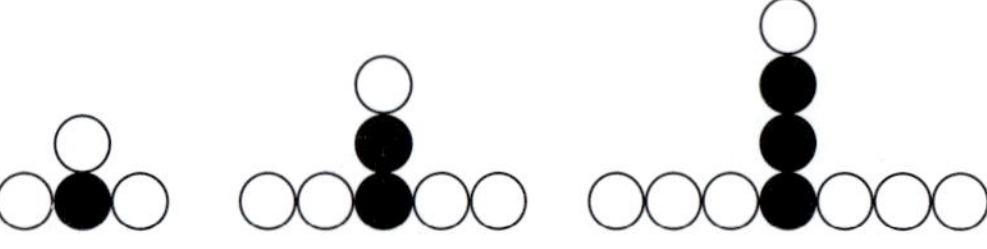

1. Write the numbers of each colour of circle in each pattern as two number sequences.

   Black circles: 1, 2, 3
   White circles: 3, 5, 7

2. Find the term to term rules for each sequence.

   Rule for black circles: +1 each time.
   Rule for white circles: +2 each time.

3. Starting at the 3rd term, apply these rules 6 times to get the 9th term.
   Black: add on 6 lots of 1 to the 3rd term.
   White: add on 6 lots of 2 to the 3rd term.

   $3 + (6 \times 1) =$ **9 black circles**
   $7 + (6 \times 2) =$ **19 white circles**

Exercise 3

Q1 The first three patterns of several sequences are shown below.
For each of the sequences: (i) explain the rule for making the next pattern,
(ii) draw the fourth and fifth patterns in the sequence,
(iii) find the number of matches needed for the sixth pattern.

a)

b)

c)

Q2 Below is a sequence of triangles made up of different numbers of circles.
The numbers of circles in each triangle form a sequence called the 'triangle numbers'.
For example, the first three triangle numbers are 1, 3 and 6.

a) Draw the next three triangles in the sequence, and write down the corresponding triangle numbers.

b) Explain the rule for generating the next triangle number in the sequence.

c) Find the 7th triangle number.

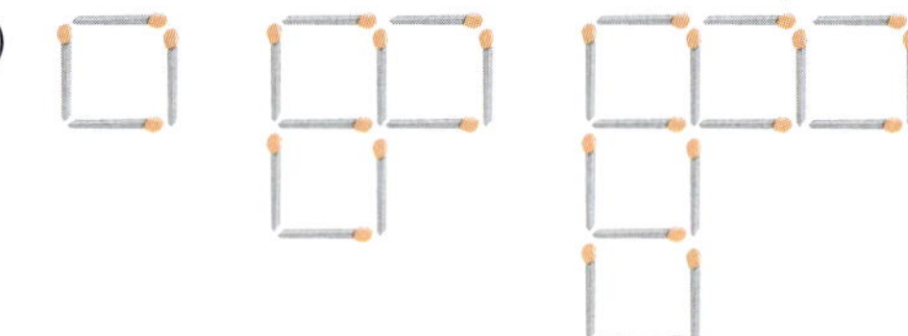

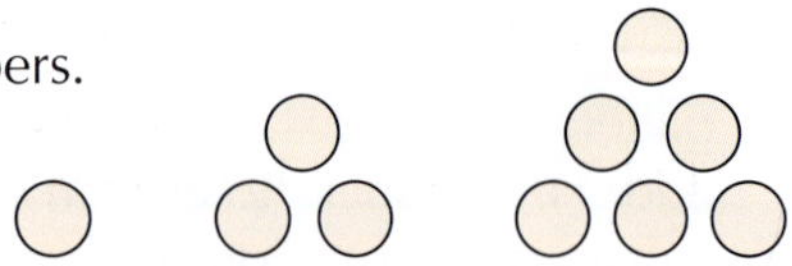

Q3 For each of the sequences below:

(i) Draw the next three patterns in the sequence.

(ii) Explain the rules for finding the number of circles of each colour in the next pattern.

(iii) Work out how many white circles there are in the 7th pattern.

(iv) Work out how many black circles there are in the 10th pattern.

a) ○  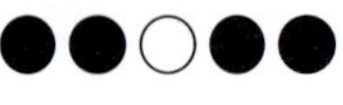

b)   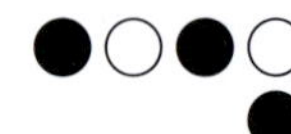  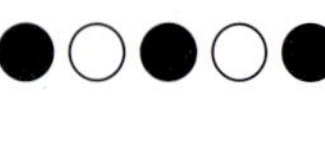 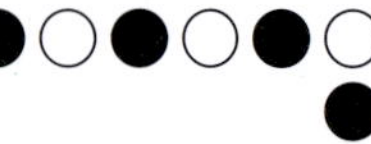

11.2 Position to Term Rules

Using a term to term rule is fine for the first few terms, but it can be a chore if you want the hundredth term. That's where using a position to term rule is helpful — instead of defining a term by the terms that come before, you define it by its position in the sequence.

Learning Objective — Spec Ref A23:
Use the nth term to find terms in a sequence.

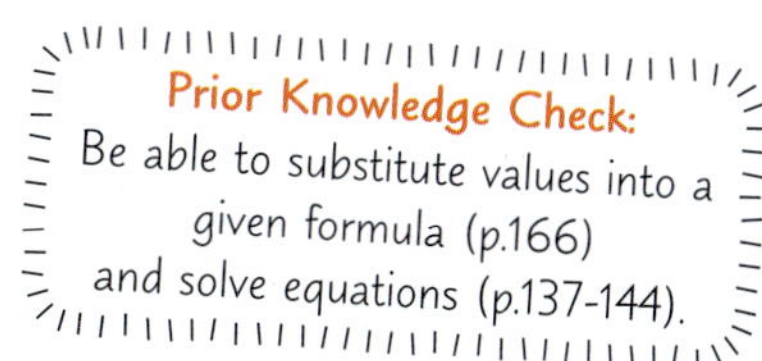

You can work out the **value** of a term in a sequence by using its **position** (n) in the sequence — the 1st term has $n = 1$, the 2nd term has $n = 2$, the 10th term has $n = 10$, and so on.

The ***n*th term formula** tells you what to do to n to get the value of that term.
So if the nth term was $5n + 2$, you'd **multiply** n by 5 then **add** 2 to get the term.

Example 1

The nth term of a sequence is $2n - 1$. Find the first four terms of the sequence.

1. To find the 1st, 2nd, 3rd and 4th terms of the sequence, substitute the values $n = 1$, $n = 2$, $n = 3$ and $n = 4$ into the formula.

   $(2 \times 1) - 1 = 1$

   $(2 \times 2) - 1 = 3$

   $(2 \times 3) - 1 = 5$

   $(2 \times 4) - 1 = 7$

2. Write the terms in order to form the sequence.

   So the first four terms are **1, 3, 5, 7**.

Exercise 1

Q1 The nth term of a sequence is $20 - 2n$. Find the value of:

a) the 1st term b) the 2nd term c) the 3rd term d) the 4th term

Q2 Find the first four terms of a sequence if the nth term is given by:

a) $n + 5$ b) $3n + 2$ c) $10n - 8$ d) $12 - n$

e) $-7 - 3n$ f) $3 - 4n$ g) $2n^2$ h) $2n^2 + 3$

Q3 The nth term of a sequence is $2n + 20$. Find the value of:

a) the 5th term b) the 10th term c) the 20th term d) the 100th term

Q4 The nth term of a sequence is $100 - 3n$. Find the value of:

a) the 3rd term b) the 10th term c) the 30th term d) the 40th term

If you know the value of a term in a sequence, but not its position, set up and solve an **equation** using the nth term rule to find the position, n.

Example 2

The nth term of a sequence is $4n + 5$. Which term has the value 41?

1. Make the nth term equal to 41. $4n + 5 = 41$
2. Solve the equation to find n. $4n = 36$

$n = 9$

So the **9th term** is 41.

Example 3

The nth term of a sequence is $2n - 7$.
Which is the first term in this sequence to have a value greater than 50?

1. Find the value of n which would give a value of 50. As before, set up and solve an equation for n.

$2n - 7 = 50$

$2n = 57$

$n = 28.5$

2. The sequence is increasing, so the first term that will give a value over 50 will be the next whole number value of n.

So the first term with a value greater than 50 is the **29th term**.

3. Check your answer by working out some terms in the sequence.

Check:
28th term = $(2 \times 28) - 7 = 49$ (<50)
29th term = $(2 \times 29) - 7 = 51$ (>50) ✔

Exercise 2

Q1 The nth term of a sequence is $2n + 6$. Which term has the value 20?

Q2 The nth term of a sequence is $17 - 2n$. Find which terms have the following values.
a) 3 b) 9 c) –7

Q3 The nth term of a sequence is $n^2 + 1$. Find which terms have the following values.
a) 5 b) 50 c) 82

Q4 The nth term of a sequence is $4n - 10$.
Which term in the sequence is the last to have a value less than 75?

Q5 The nth term of a sequence is $6n + 2$.
Which term in the sequence is the first to have a value greater than 40?

Q6 The formulas for the number of matches in the nth pattern of the following 'matchstick sequences' are shown below. For each of the sequences:
(i) find the number of matches needed to make the 6th pattern,
(ii) find the value of n for the last pattern you could make with 100 matches.

a)   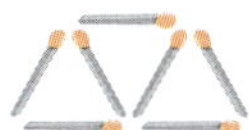

Number of matches in nth pattern = $2n + 1$

b)  

Number of matches in nth pattern = $4n - 1$

You can use the nth term to **check** if a given value is a term in that sequence. As before, set up and solve an equation to find the value of n for a given (suspected) term. The term is **only** part of the sequence if n is a **whole number**. If not, you know the value is **not** part of the sequence.

Example 4

A sequence has nth term $3n + 2$. Is 37 a term in the sequence?

1. Make an equation by setting the formula for the nth term equal to 37.
2. Then solve your equation to find n.
3. Since n is not a whole number, 37 is not a term in the sequence.

$3n + 2 = 37$

$3n = 35$

$n = 11.666...$

So 37 **is not** a term in the sequence.

Exercise 3

Q1 A sequence has nth term $2n + 1$. Show that 54 is not a term in this sequence.

Q2 Show that 80 is a term in the sequence with nth term equal to $3n - 1$.

Q3 A sequence has nth term $21 - 2n$. Show that -1 is a term in this sequence, and write down the corresponding value of n to show its position.

Q4 A sequence has nth term equal to $17 + 3n$.
Determine whether each of the following is a term in this sequence.
a) 52 b) 98 c) 248 d) 996

Q5 A sequence has nth term equal to $4n - 9$. Determine whether each of the following is a term in this sequence. For those that are, state the corresponding value of n.
a) 43 b) 71 c) 138 d) 879

11.3 Finding a Position to Term Rule

You know how to find the terms in a sequence from the nth term rule, but you also need to be able to do it in reverse — working out the rule yourself from some terms in a sequence.

Learning Objective — Spec Ref A25:
Be able to write formulas for the nth term in a sequence.

Prior Knowledge Check:
Be able to substitute values into a given formula (p.166) and solve equations (p.137-144).

You can find the nth term of an arithmetic sequence by looking at its terms:

- Find the **coefficient** of n by finding the **common difference** — the bit you add or subtract to get from one term to the next.
- For example, if the common difference was 2, the **nth term rule** would be '$2n$ + something'.
- Find the 'something' by comparing **multiples** of the common difference with the terms in the sequence, and seeing what you need to **add** and **subtract**.

Tip: The coefficient is just the number next to n — so the coefficient of $3n$ is 3, and of $-4n$ is -4.

This might be easier to understand by looking at an example:

Example 1

a) Find the nth term of the sequence 5, 7, 9, 11...

1. Find the difference between each term and the next.
2. Here, the terms increase by 2 each time, so the coefficient of n is 2.

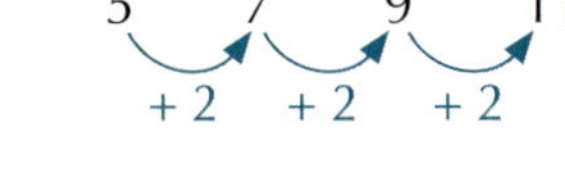

3. Work out what you need to add or subtract to get from $2n$ to the term in the sequence.
4. To get to each term from $2n$, you need to add 3. This tells you that '+ 3' is in the nth term rule.

$2n$: 2 4 6 8
↓+ 3 ↓+ 3 ↓+ 3 ↓+ 3
Term: 5 7 9 11

5. Combine the two parts to find the nth term rule.

So the nth term is $\mathbf{2n + 3}$

6. Check your formula by using it to find a term you know.

Check: 2nd term ($n = 2$) is $(2 \times 2) + 3 = 7$ ✔

b) Find the 50th term in the sequence.

1. You worked out the nth rule formula in part a), so now you can use it to find the 50th term.

The nth term is $\mathbf{2n + 3}$

2. Substitute $n = 50$ into $2n + 3$.

$(2 \times 50) + 3 = 100 + 3 = \mathbf{103}$

Example 2

Find the nth term of the sequence 45, 42, 39, 36...

1. Find the difference between each term and the next.

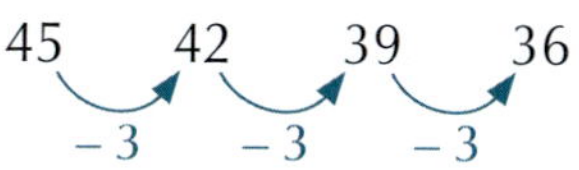

2. Here, the terms decrease by 3 each time, so the coefficient of n is –3.
3. Work out what you need to add or subtract to get from $-3n$ to the term in the sequence.

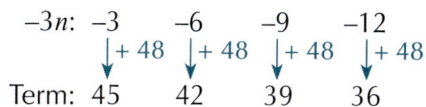

$-3n$:	–3	–6	–9	–12
	↓+ 48	↓+ 48	↓+ 48	↓+ 48
Term:	45	42	39	36

4. To get to each term from $-3n$, you need to add 48. This tells you that '+ 48' is in the nth term rule.
5. Combine the two parts to find the nth term rule. So the nth term is $\mathbf{-3n + 48}$
6. Check your formula by using it to find a term you know. Check: 2nd term ($n = 2$) is $(-3 \times 2) + 48 = 42$ ✔

Exercise 1

Q1 The first 4 terms of a sequence are: 9, 13, 17, 21

a) Find the difference between each term and the next.

b) Find the formula for the nth term of the sequence, and use a term to check it.

Q2 Find the formula for the nth term of each of the following sequences.

a) 7, 13, 19, 25... b) 6, 16, 26, 36... c) 41, 81, 121, 161...

d) –1, 1, 3, 5... e) –9, –5, –1, 3... f) –45, –26, –7, 12...

Q3 Find the formula for the nth term of each of the following sequences.

a) 10, 8, 6, 4... b) 40, 37, 34, 31... c) 78, 69, 60, 51...

d) 4, –1, –6, –11... e) –10, –25, –40, –55... f) –39, –51, –63, –75...

Q4 Find the number of matchsticks in the nth pattern of the following sequences.

a) b)

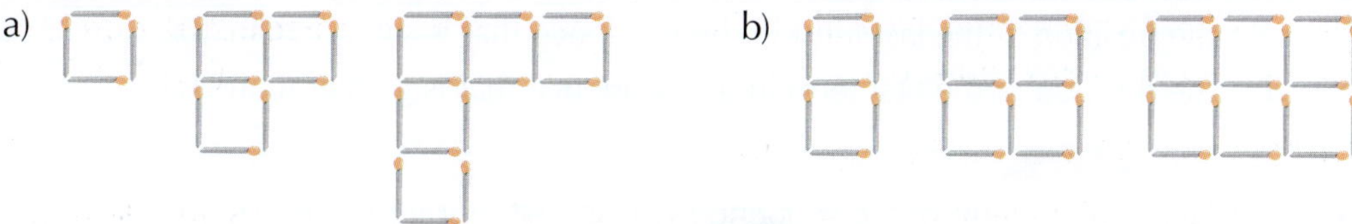

Q5 a) Find the nth term of the sequence 8, 11, 14, 17...

PROBLEM SOLVING

b) Use your answer to part a) to write down the nth term of the sequence 9, 12, 15, 18...

Review Exercise

Q1 For the following sequences: (i) explain the rule for finding the next term,
(ii) write down the next three terms in the sequence.

a) 4, 7, 10, 13... b) 192, 96, 48, 24... c) 0, –4, –8, –12...

d) –4, –2, 0, 2... e) 11, 8, 5, 2... f) 2, –6, 18, –54...

Q2 A sequence begins 7, 9, 13, 19, 27...

a) Find the difference between the neighbouring terms for the first five terms.

b) Find the next three terms in the sequence.

Q3 For the following sequence of circles:

a) Draw the next three patterns in the sequence.

b) Explain the rule for generating the number of circles in the next pattern.

c) Work out how many circles there are in the 8th pattern.

Q4 A sequence has the nth term $-3 - 2n$. Write down the first four terms of the sequence.

Q5 Each of the following gives the nth term for a different sequence.
For each sequence, find: (i) the 5th term (ii) the 10th term (iii) the 100th term

a) $4n + 12$ b) $30 - 3n$ c) $100n - 8$ d) $n(n - 1)$

Q6 The nth term of a sequence is $50 - 6n$. Find which terms have the following values.

a) 2 b) 8 c) 14 d) 26

Q7 An expression for the nth term of a sequence is $7n - 3$. Find:

a) the position of the last term in the sequence that is smaller than 100,

b) the position of the first term in the sequence that is greater than 205.

Q8 a) Find the nth term of the sequence whose first four terms are 12, 18, 24, 30...

b) Is 86 a term in this sequence?

Q9 Find an expression in terms of n for the number of dots in the nth term of the sequence on the right.

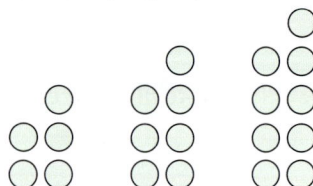

Exam-Style Questions

Q1 A quadratic sequence starts 3, 5, 9, 15... Find the next term in the sequence. 

[2 marks]

Q2 In a chemistry lesson, Yuki uses a set of balls and rods to make models of molecules. His first model uses 5 balls and 4 rods, and the models form the following sequence:

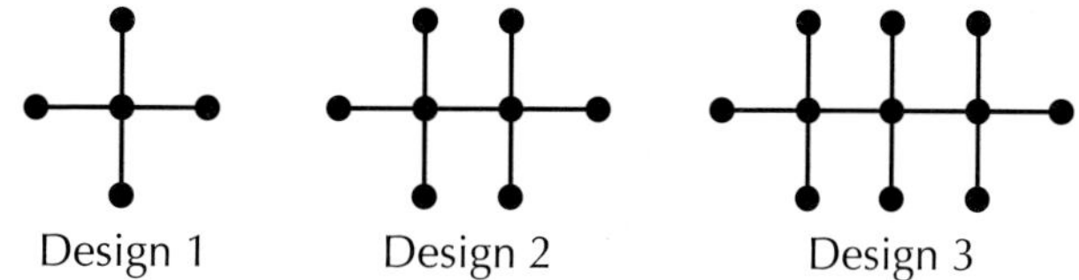

a) Draw design number 4.

[1 mark]

b) How many rods will be needed to make design number 8?

[2 marks]

c) Design n will require $3n + 2$ balls. Write down a simplified expression in terms of n for the number of rods needed for design n.

[1 mark]

Q3 a) Write down the next term in this sequence: 2, 6, 10, 14...

[1 mark]

b) The nth term of this sequence is $4n - 2$. Work out the 210th term.

[2 marks]

c) Jane says that 74 is a term in this sequence. Is Jane correct? Show how you decide.

[2 marks]

Q4 Find the nth term of this sequence: –11, –2, 7, 16...

[2 marks]

Section 12 Graphs and Equations

12.1 Coordinates

Axes, coordinates and quadrants are used to help pin-point a location. Just remember that in a pair of coordinates, the horizontal (x) one comes first, followed by the vertical (y) one. And make sure you don't get tripped up by the negative numbers in the different quadrants.

Coordinates and Quadrants

Learning Objective — Spec Ref A8:
Be able to identify, specify and plot points using their coordinates in all four quadrants.

A grid can be split into **four** different **quadrants** (regions) using a line going **left-to-right** (the ***x*-axis**) and a line going **top-to-bottom** (the ***y*-axis**).

Coordinates describe the **position** of a point. They are written in **pairs** inside brackets with:

- The ***x*-coordinate** (left or right) **first**.
- The ***y*-coordinate** (up or down) **second**.

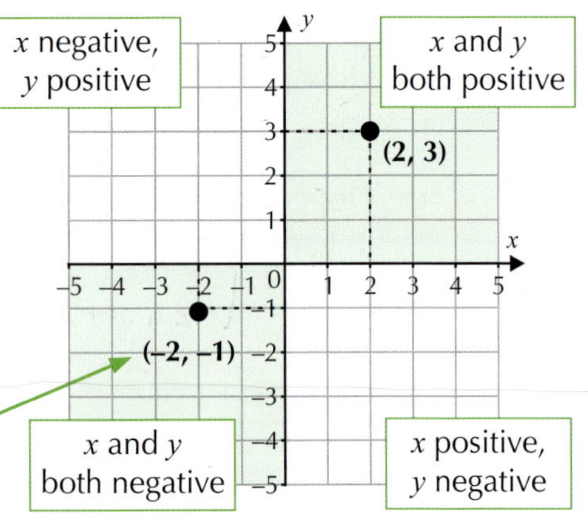

The **origin** is the point **(0, 0)** — this is where the x- and y-axis intersect. If you go **left** from the origin the ***x*-coordinate** becomes **negative**, and if you **down** from the origin the ***y*-coordinate** becomes **negative**.

For example, the point **(–2, –1)** is positioned **2 to the left** on the ***x*-axis** and **1 down** on the ***y*-axis**, but the point **(2, 3)** is positioned **2 to the right** on the ***x*-axis** and **3 up** on the ***y*-axis**.

Example 1

Write down the coordinates of the vertices of the triangle *ABC* shown below.

1. Follow the grid line up or down from each point and read off the x-coordinate.
2. Follow the grid line left or right from each point and read off the y-coordinate.
3. Write the coordinates in brackets with the x-coordinate first.

   The coordinates are ***A*(–4, –3)**, ***B*(–2, 4)**, ***C*(3, –2)**.

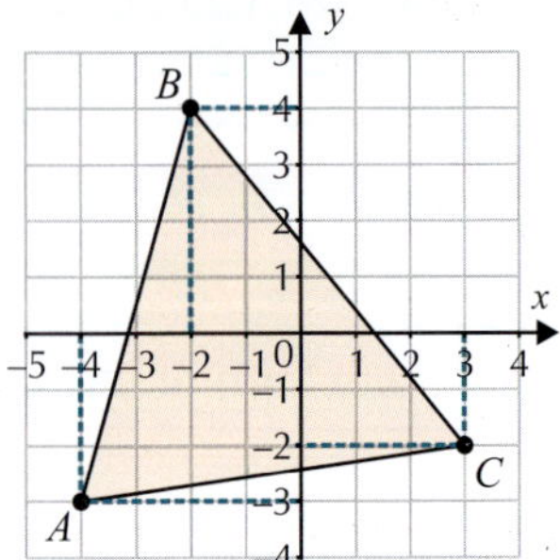

Exercise 1

Q1 The four quadrants are labelled on the grid on the right.
Write down which quadrants each of the following points lies in.

a) (2, 2) b) (1, –1) c) (–2, –1) d) (–1, 1)

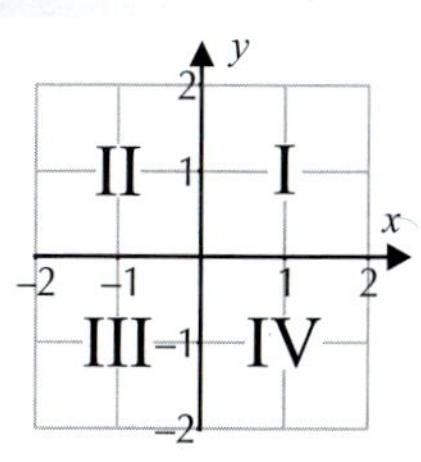

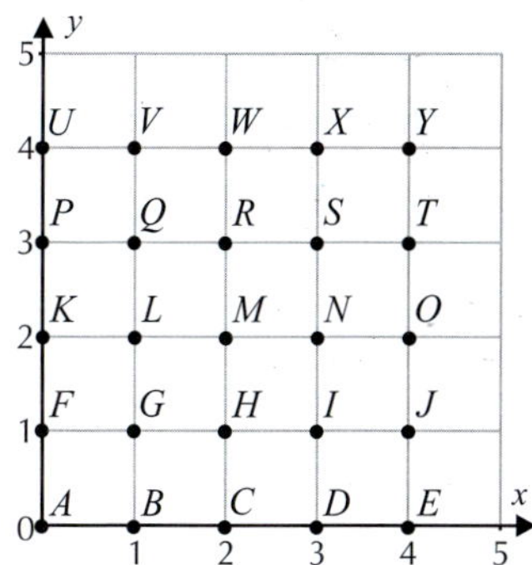

Q2 Use the grid on the left to answer this question.

a) Write down the coordinates of the following points.
(i) A (ii) M (iii) Q (iv) U (v) Y

b) Write down the sentence given by the letters with the following coordinates.

(3, 4) - (2, 0) (4, 2) (4, 2) (2, 3) (3, 0) (3, 1) (3, 2) (0, 0) (4, 3) (4, 0)
(2, 0) (4, 2) (2, 2) (4, 0) (3, 3) (0, 1) (3, 1) (2, 3) (3, 3) (4, 3)

Q3 Use the grid on the right for this question.

a) The following sets of coordinates spell out the names of shapes. Write down the name of each shape.
(i) (2, –4) (–4, –4) (–5, –6) (–4, 5) (–2, –4) (–5, 3)
(ii) (2, 5) (–4, 1) (–2, –4) (2, 5) (4, 1) (–5, 3)
(iii) (2, 5) (–5, –6) (–2, 5) (3, –2) (–4, 1) (4, 5)

b) Write down the sets of coordinates which spell out the names of the following shapes.
(i) kite (ii) sphere (iii) triangle

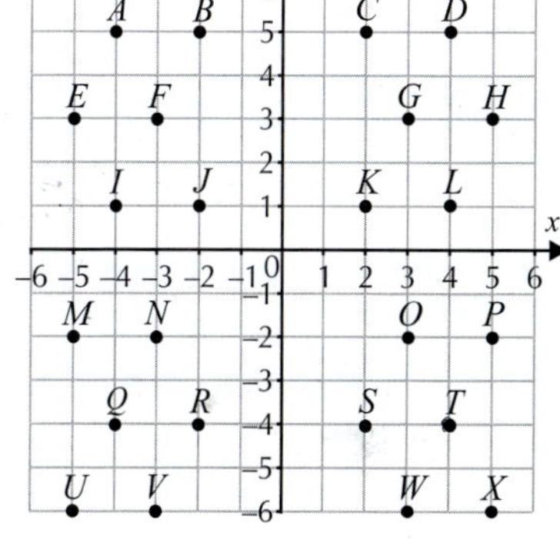

Plotting a point means **marking** its **position** on a grid. To plot a point, find its ***x*-coordinate** and then read up or down to the correct ***y*-coordinate** — draw a **dot** to mark this position.

Example 2

Draw the shape *WXYZ* with vertices *W*(–4, 5), *X*(3, 2), *Y*(4, –3) and *Z*(–5, –2).

1. Some of the coordinates are negative, so your axes need to go below zero.
2. Read across the horizontal axis for the x-coordinates.
3. Read up and down the vertical axis for the y-coordinates.
4. Plot the points and connect them to draw the shape. In a shape like $WXYZ$, connect adjacent letters (WX, XY and YZ) and also the first and last (WZ).

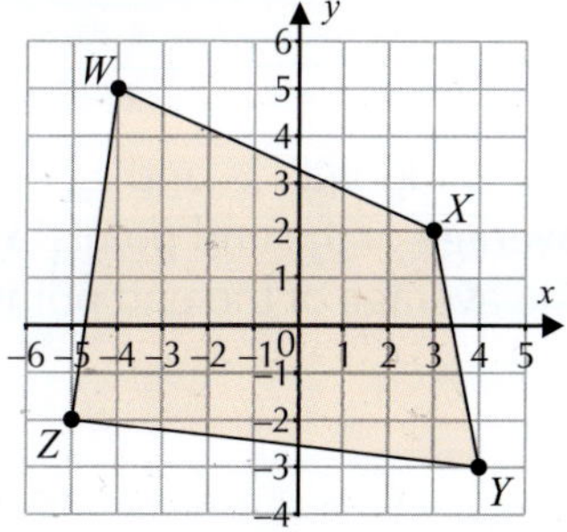

Exercise 2

Q1 On separate copies of the grid on the right, draw the shapes whose vertices are given by the following sets of coordinates.

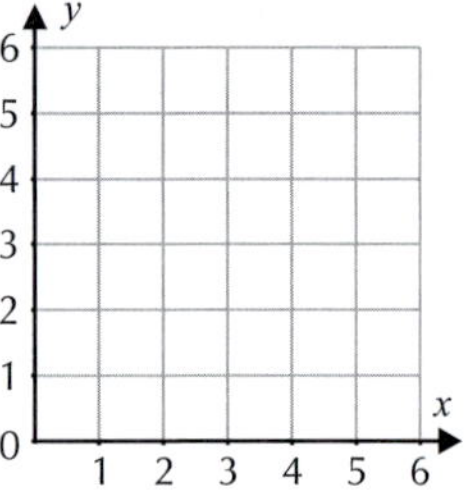

a) $A(2, 1)$, $B(2, 4)$, $C(5, 4)$, $D(5, 1)$

b) $E(1, 1)$, $F(6, 3)$, $G(3, 5)$

c) $H(1, 3)$, $I(3, 5)$, $J(6, 3)$, $K(3, 1)$

d) $L(2, 6)$, $M(5, 5)$, $N(5, 3)$, $O(2, 1)$

Q2 Draw a coordinate grid ranging from –4 to 4 on the x-axis and y-axis. Plot the following points on your grid. Join the points you have plotted.

$A(4, 3)$ $B(1, -3)$ $C(-3, -3)$ $D(-2, 1)$

Q3 Draw a coordinate grid ranging from –5 to 5 on the x-axis and y-axis. Plot the following points on your grid. Join the points you have plotted.

$A(0, 5)$ $B(1, 1)$ $C(5, 1)$ $D(2, -1)$ $E(3, -4)$

$F(0, -2)$ $G(-3, -4)$ $H(-2, -1)$ $I(-5, 1)$ $J(-1, 1)$

Midpoints of Line Segments

Learning Objective — Spec Ref A8:
Be able to find the coordinates of the midpoint of a line segment.

A **line segment** is part of a line, lying between two **end points**.

The **midpoint** of a line segment is **halfway** between the end points. If (x_1, y_1) and (x_2, y_2) are the coordinates of the **end points**, you can use the following **formula** to find the coordinates of the **midpoint**.

Tip: Line segments have end points, unlike lines which go on forever in both directions.

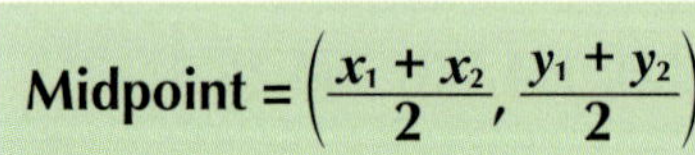

$$\text{Midpoint} = \left(\frac{x_1 + x_2}{2}, \frac{y_1 + y_2}{2}\right)$$

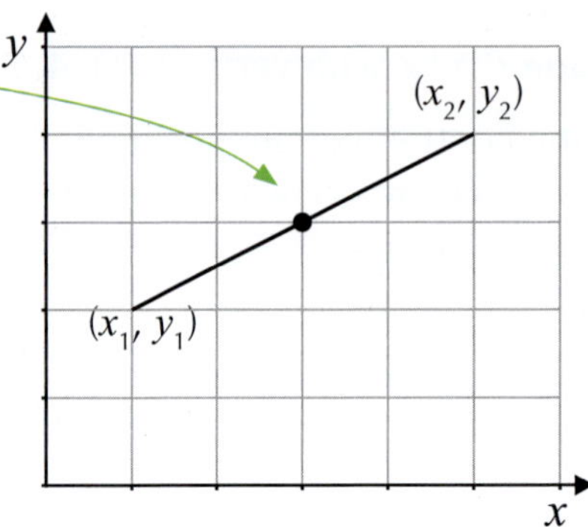

The midpoint's x- and y-coordinates equal the **average** of the end points' **x-coordinates** and the average of the end points' **y-coordinates**.

Example 3

Find the midpoint of the line segment AB, shown on the right.

1. Write down the coordinates of the end points A and B.
2. Write down the formula for the midpoint.
3. Put in the x- and y-coordinates of A and B.

$A(-3, 4)$ and $B(5, 2)$

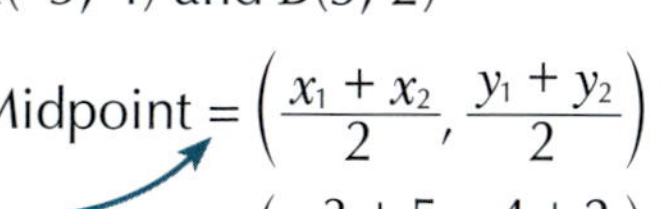

$$\text{Midpoint} = \left(\frac{x_1 + x_2}{2}, \frac{y_1 + y_2}{2}\right)$$

$$= \left(\frac{-3 + 5}{2}, \frac{4 + 2}{2}\right)$$

$$= \mathbf{(1, 3)}$$

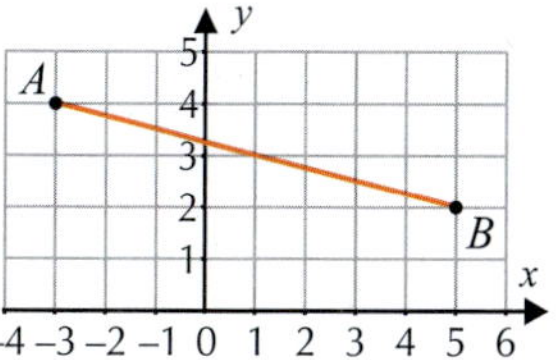

Exercise 3

Q1 A line segment XY is shown on the grid on the right.

a) Write down the coordinates of the points X and Y.

b) Use the coordinates of X and Y to calculate the coordinates of M, the midpoint of XY.

c) Plot the point M on a copy of the diagram. Use a ruler to check that the distances XM and MY are equal.

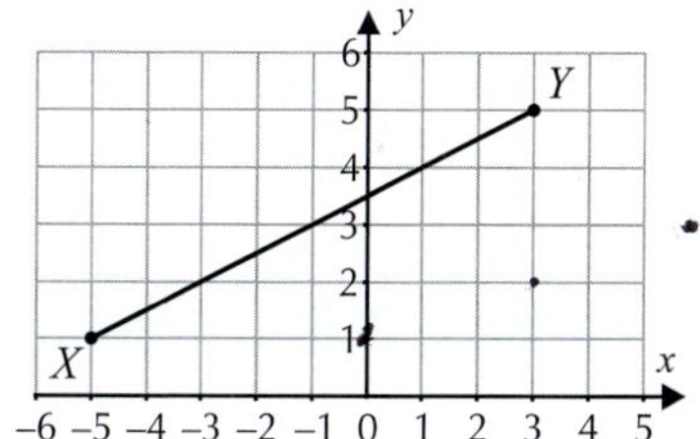

Q2 The points P and Q have coordinates $P(1, 0)$ and $Q(3, 5)$.

a) Find the coordinates of M, the midpoint of PQ.

b) Check your answer:

(i) Plot P and Q on a square grid.
Join the points to form the line segment PQ.

(ii) Plot the point M. Check that M is the midpoint of PQ.

Q3 Find the coordinates of the midpoint of the line segment AB, where A and B have coordinates:

a) $A(1, 1)$, $B(3, 5)$ b) $A(0, 1)$, $B(6, 3)$

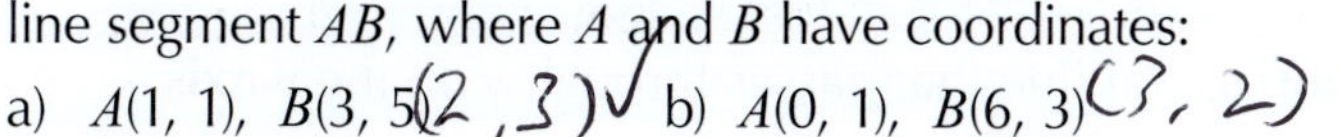

c) $A(0, -4)$, $B(-5, 1)$ d) $A(-2, 0)$, $B(1, -8)$

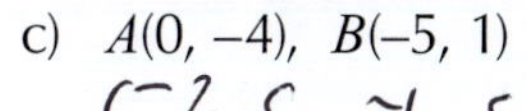

Q4 Use the diagram on the right to find the midpoints of the following line segments.

a) AF b) AC c) DF

d) BE e) BF f) CE

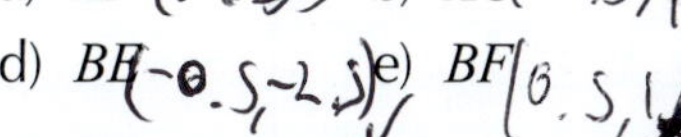

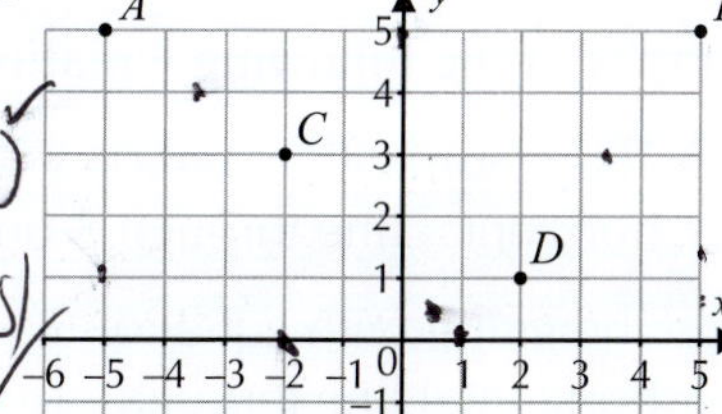

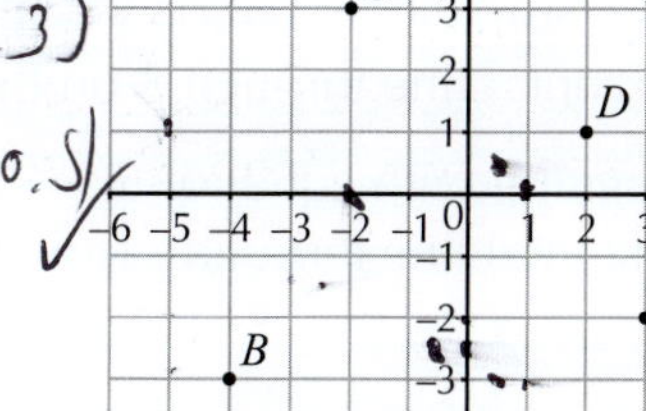

12.2 Horizontal and Vertical Graphs

This is a gentle introduction to straight-line graphs — horizontal lines are parallel to the x-axis (they go across the page) and vertical lines are parallel to the y-axis (they go down the page).

Learning Objective — Spec Ref A9:
Recognise and draw horizontal and vertical lines on a set of axes.

All **horizontal** lines have the equation $\mathbf{y = a}$ (where a is a number), as every point on the same horizontal line has the same y-coordinate.

All **vertical** lines have the equation $\mathbf{x = b}$ (where b is a number), as every point on the same vertical line has the same x-coordinate.

Tip: $y = a$ intersects the y-axis at $(0, a)$. $x = b$ intersects the x-axis at $(b, 0)$.

The equation of the $\mathbf{x}$**-axis** is $\mathbf{y = 0}$ and the equation of the $\mathbf{y}$**-axis** is $\mathbf{x = 0}$.

Example 1

Write down the equations of the lines marked A-D.

1. Every point on the line marked A has y-coordinate 1. A is the line $\mathbf{y = 1}$
2. Every point on the line marked B has x-coordinate 2. B is the line $\mathbf{x = 2}$
3. Every point on the line marked C has y-coordinate –4. C is the line $\mathbf{y = -4}$
4. Every point on the line marked D has x-coordinate –2. D is the line $\mathbf{x = -2}$

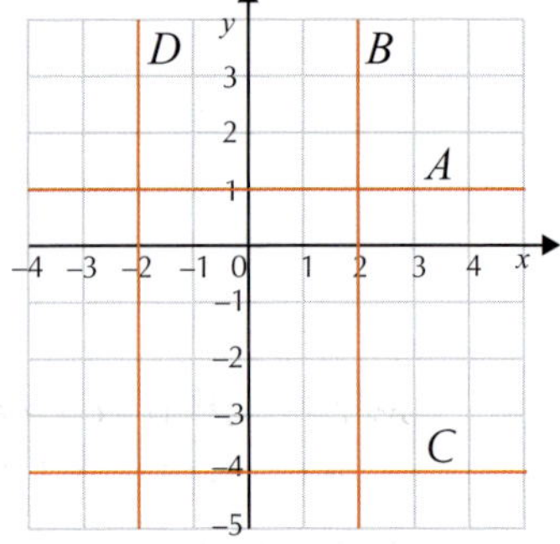

To **draw** the line $y = a$, draw a **horizontal** line that passes through a on the $\mathbf{y}$**-axis**.

Example 2

Plot the graphs of the following equations.

a) $\mathbf{y = 3}$ The graph with equation $y = 3$ is a horizontal line through 3 on the y-axis.

b) $\mathbf{y = -1}$ The graph with equation $y = -1$ is a horizontal line through –1 on the y-axis.

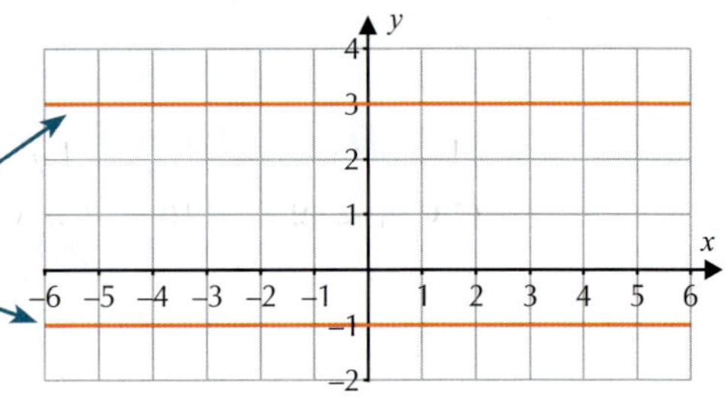

To **draw** the line $x = b$, draw a **vertical** line that passes through b on the ***x*-axis**.

Example 3

Plot the graphs of the following equations.

a) $x = -4$ The graph with equation $x = -4$ is a vertical line through –4 on the x-axis.

b) $x = 2$ The graph with equation $x = 2$ is a vertical line through 2 on the x-axis.

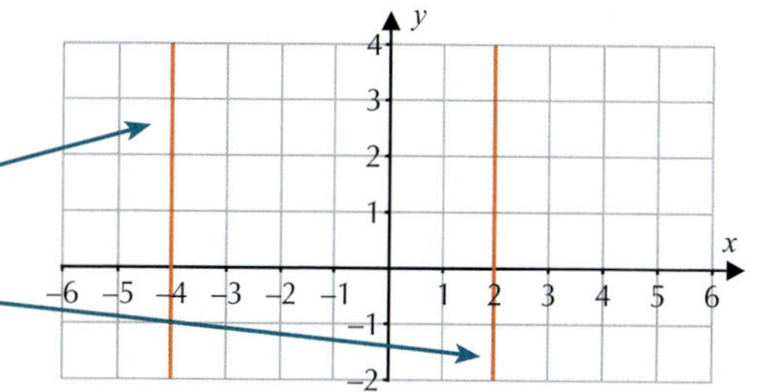

Exercise 1

Q1 Write down the equations of each of the lines labelled A to E on this diagram.

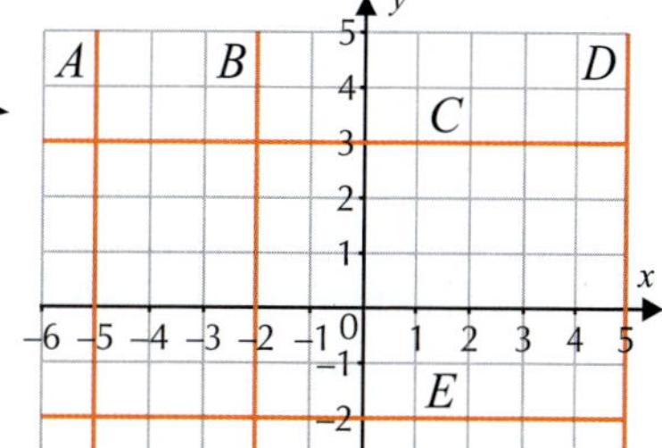

Q2 Draw a set of coordinate axes and plot the graphs with the following equations.

a) $y = 3$ b) $y = -6$ c) $y = -1$

d) $x = 2$ e) $x = 4$ f) $x = -4$

Q3 a) What is the y-coordinate of every point on the x-axis?

b) Write down the equation of the x-axis.

Q4 Draw a set of coordinate axes.

a) Plot the horizontal line which passes through the point (2, –2).

b) What is the equation of this line?

Q5 Draw a set of coordinate axes.

a) Plot the vertical line which passes through the point (1, –3).

b) What is the equation of this line?

Q6 Write down the equation of the line which is parallel to the x-axis, and which passes through the point (4, 8).

Q7 Write down the equation of the line which is parallel to the y-axis, and which passes through the point (–2, –6).

Q8 Draw a set of coordinate axes.

a) Plot the points P(3, –1) and Q(–1, –1).

b) What is the equation of the line that contains points P and Q?

12.3 Other Straight-Line Graphs

Horizontal and vertical lines are certainly nice, but life isn't always so straightforward. You need to do a bit more preparation work when you're plotting other straight lines.

Drawing Straight-Line Graphs

Learning Objective — Spec Ref A9/A12:
Be able to draw straight-line graphs on a set of axes.

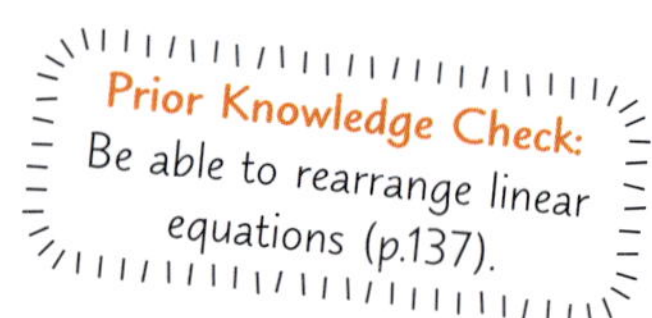

Prior Knowledge Check:
Be able to rearrange linear equations (p.137).

The equation of a straight line which **isn't** horizontal or vertical contains **both x and y** (e.g. $y = 2x + 4$). If an equation **only** contains x and y terms (e.g. $y = 5x$), then the line passes through the **origin (0, 0)**.

There are a couple of different methods you can use to draw these straight-line graphs:

- Make a **table of values** — find the values of y for different values of x, plot the points and join with a straight line. You only have to plot two points to be able to sketch the graph, but it's often useful to plot more than two, in case one of the points you plot is incorrect.
- Find the **value of x** when **$y = 0$** and the **value of y** when **$x = 0$**.
  Plot these two points and join with a straight line. Both points should lie on the axes.
  Extend your line to cover the range of x-values required (usually specified in the question).

Example 1

a) Complete the table to show the value of $y = 2x + 1$ for values of x from 0 to 5.

x	0	1	2	3	4	5
y						

Use the equation $y = 2x + 1$ to find the y-value corresponding to each value of x.

x	0	1	2	3	4	5
y	$2 \times 0 + 1 =$ **1**	$2 \times 1 + 1 =$ **3**	$2 \times 2 + 1 =$ **5**	$2 \times 3 + 1 =$ **7**	$2 \times 4 + 1 =$ **9**	$2 \times 5 + 1 =$ **11**

b) Plot the points from the table, and hence draw the graph of $y = 2x + 1$ for x from 0 to 5.

1. Use your table to find the coordinates to plot — just read off the x- and y-values from each column.

   The points to plot are (0, 1), (1, 3), (2, 5), (3, 7), (4, 9) and (5, 11).

2. Plot each point on the grid, then join them up with a straight line.

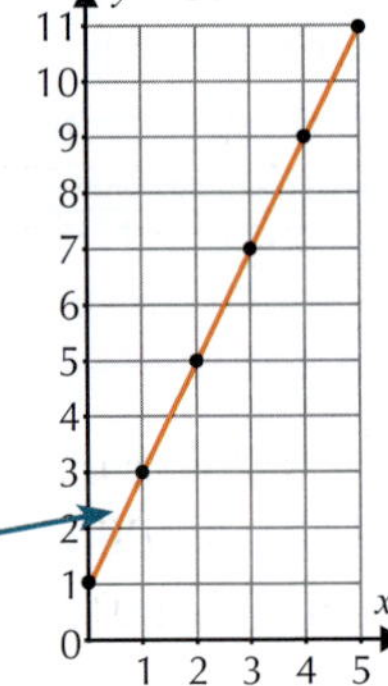

Tip: Choose sensible values for x, e.g. whole numbers are usually easier to plot.

Example 2

Draw the graph of $y + 2x = 4$ for $-1 \leq x \leq 3$.

1. Put $x = 0$ into the equation to find the value of y — this is where it crosses the y-axis.

   When $x = 0$, $y + 2(0) = 4$, so $y = 4$.

2. Put $y = 0$ into the equation to find the value of x — this is where it crosses the x-axis.

   When $y = 0$, $0 + 2x = 4$, so $2x = 4 \Rightarrow x = 2$.
   So the graph crosses the axes at (0, 4) and (2, 0).

3. Mark the points (0, 4) and (2, 0) on your graph and draw a straight line passing through them. Make sure you extend it to cover the whole range of x-values asked for in the question.

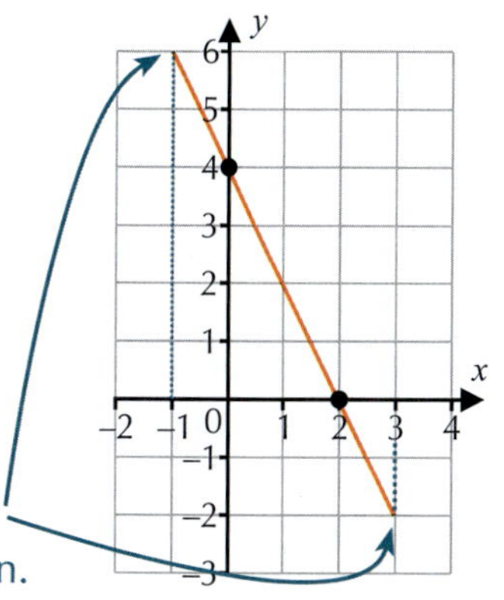

Exercise 1

Q1 a) Copy and complete the table below to show the value of $y = x + 2$ for values of x from 0 to 5.

x	0	1	2	3	4	5
y	2	3				
Coordinates	(0, 2)					

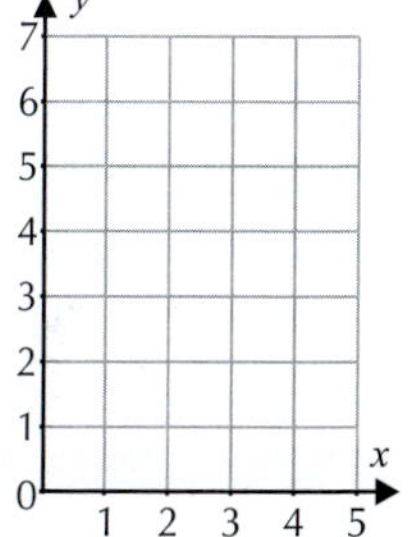

b) Copy the grid on the right and plot the coordinates from your table.

c) Join up the points to draw the graph of $y = x + 2$ for values of x from 0 to 5.

Q2 a) Make y the subject of the equation $2y - 2x = -8$ (so it's in the form '$y = ...$').

b) Copy and complete the table below to show the value of y for values of x from 0 to 5.

x	0	1	2	3	4	5
y	–4					
Coordinates						

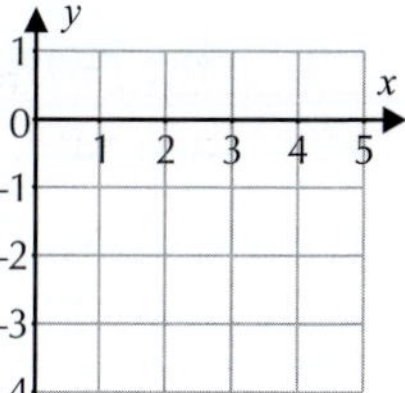

c) Copy the grid on the right and plot the coordinates from your table.

d) Join up the points to draw the graph for values of x from 0 to 5.

Q3 Draw the graphs of the following equations by first finding the value of y when $x = 0$, and the value of x when $y = 0$.

a) $y = x + 7$ for x from –7 to 0

b) $y = 3x - 6$ for x from 0 to 4

c) $y + 2x = 8$ for x from 0 to 5

d) $y + 5x = 7.5$ for x from 0 to 2

Solving Equations Graphically

Learning Objective — Spec Ref A17:
Be able to solve linear equations graphically.

You can use the graph of $y = ax + b$ to **solve** the equation $ax + b = 0$.

- Find where this graph **crosses** the ***x*-axis** — this is the point where $y = ax + b = 0$.
- Read off the ***x*-coordinate** of this point — this is the **solution** to the linear equation.

Tip: Check your answer by substituting the value of x back into the equation.

Example 3

Use the graph on the right to solve the equation $2x - 1 = 0$.

1. Find where the graph crosses the x-axis. — The graph crosses the x-axis at $(\frac{1}{2}, 0)$.
2. Read off the x-coordinate. — So the solution is $x = \frac{1}{2}$.
3. Check your answer. — Check: $2 \times \frac{1}{2} - 1 = 1 - 1 = 0$ ✔

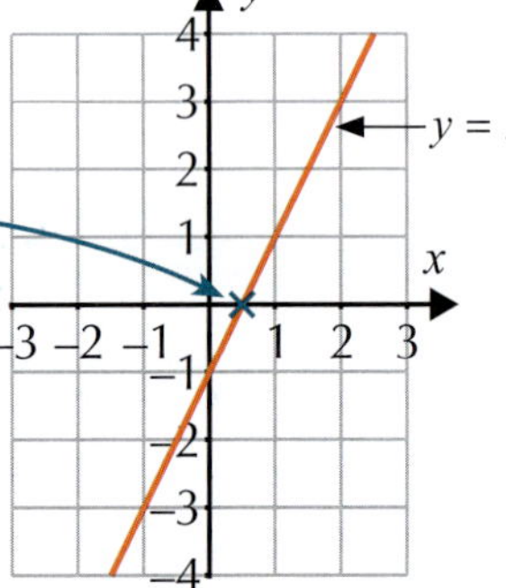

Exercise 2

Q1 The graph of $y = 2x - 4$ is shown below.

a) Write down the coordinates of the point where the graph crosses the x-axis.

b) Hence, solve the equation $2x - 4 = 0$.

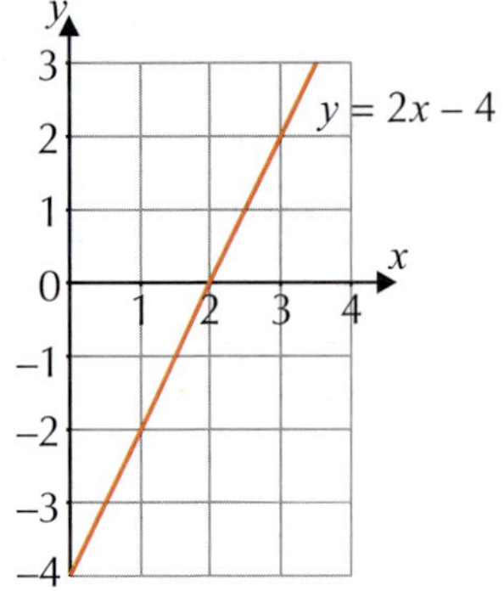

Q2 Use the graphs on the grid below to solve the following equations:

a) $0.5x - 2 = 0$

b) $-2x + 1 = 0$

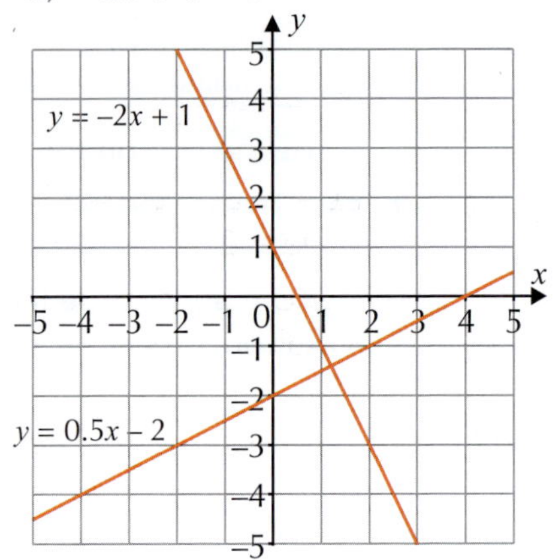

If you're given the graph of $y = ax + b$, you can actually **solve** the equation $ax + b = c$ for **any number** c. On the same axes, draw the graph of $y = c$. Now find the **point** where the two lines **intersect** — the **x-coordinate** of this point is the **solution**.

You can solve any equation that can be **rearranged** into the form '$ax + b = c$' in this way.

Example 4

The graph of $y = 2x - 1$ is shown below.

a) Use the graph to solve the equation $2x - 1 = 4$.

1. Draw the graph of $y = 4$. — $y = 4$ crosses $y = 2x - 1$ at $(2\frac{1}{2}, 4)$.
2. Find the point where the two lines cross, and read off the x-coordinate. — So the solution is $x = 2\frac{1}{2}$.
3. Check your answer. — $2 \times 2\frac{1}{2} - 1 = 5 - 1 = 4$ ✔

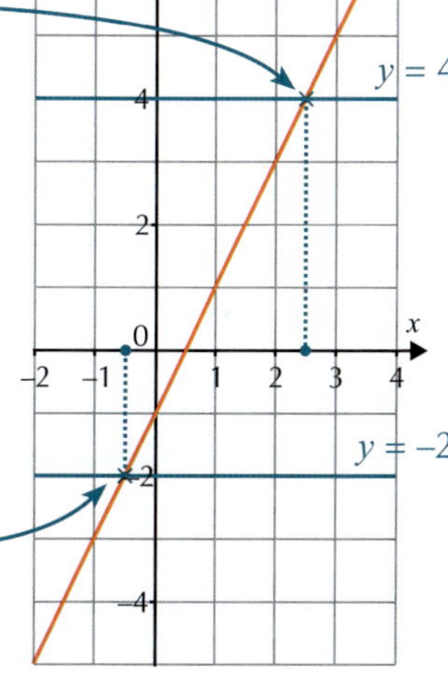

b) Use the graph to solve the equation $2x + 1 = 0$.

1. Subtract 2 from both sides to get '$2x - 1$' on the left. — $2x + 1 - 2 = 0 - 2$, $2x - 1 = -2$
2. Draw the graph of $y = -2$. — $y = -2$ crosses $y = 2x - 1$ at $(-\frac{1}{2}, -2)$.
3. Find the point where the two lines cross, and read off the x-coordinate. — So the solution is $x = -\frac{1}{2}$.
4. Check your answer. — $2 \times \left(-\frac{1}{2}\right) + 1 = -1 + 1 = 0$ ✔

Exercise 3

Use the diagram on the right for Questions 1-3.

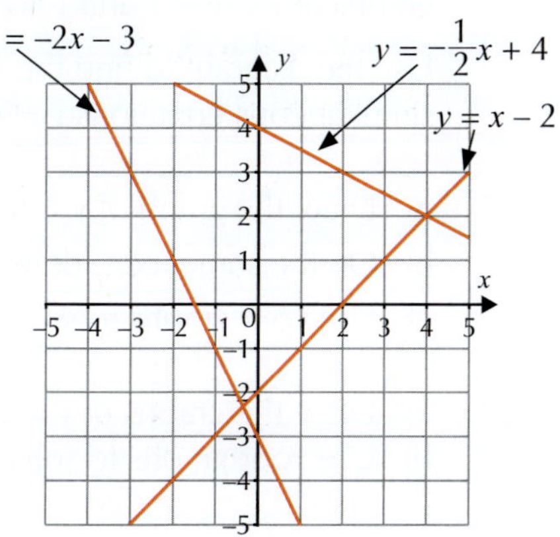

Q1 Use the graphs to solve the following equations.

a) $-2x - 3 = 1$

b) $x - 2 = -4$

c) $-2x - 3 = -5$

d) $-\frac{1}{2}x + 4 = 2\frac{1}{2}$

Q2 a) Rearrange the equation $-2x + 2 = 1$ to get '$-2x - 3$' on the left-hand side.

b) Hence, use the graph of $y = -2x - 3$ to solve the equation $-2x + 2 = 1$.

Q3 Use the graphs to solve the following equations.

a) $x - 1 = 2$

b) $-2x - 5 = 0$

c) $-\frac{1}{2}x - 1 = -2$

Solving Simultaneous Equations Graphically

Learning Objective — Spec Ref A19:
Be able to solve simultaneous equations graphically.

You can solve **simultaneous equations** by plotting the graphs of both equations and finding the point where they **intersect**.

Tip: You plot straight lines like before, with two on the same grid.

Example 5

Solve the following simultaneous equations graphically: $y = 8 - x$ and $y = 2x + 2$.

1. Both equations are straight lines. Make a table of x- and y-values and plot them.

$y = 8 - x$

x	0	4	8
y	8	4	0

2. Draw a straight line through each set of points.

$y = 2x + 2$

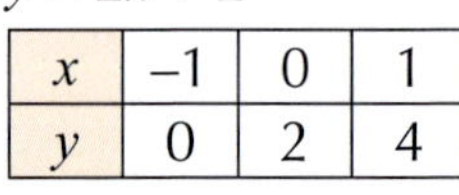

x	–1	0	1
y	0	2	4

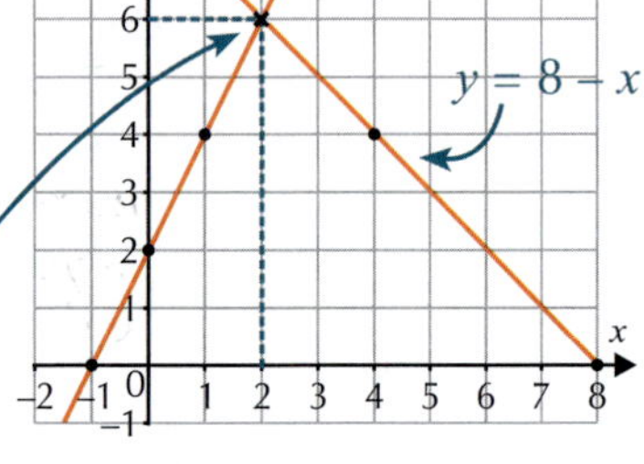

3. Find the x- and y-values of the point where the graphs intersect.

The graphs cross at (2, 6). So the solution is $x = 2$ and $y = 6$.

4. Check your answer.

$8 - 2 = 6$ ✔ and $2 \times 2 + 2 = 4 + 2 = 6$ ✔

Exercise 4

Q1 The diagram on the right shows the graphs of $y = x + 3$ and $y = -x + 7$.

Use the diagram to find the solution to the simultaneous equations $y = x + 3$ and $y = -x + 7$.

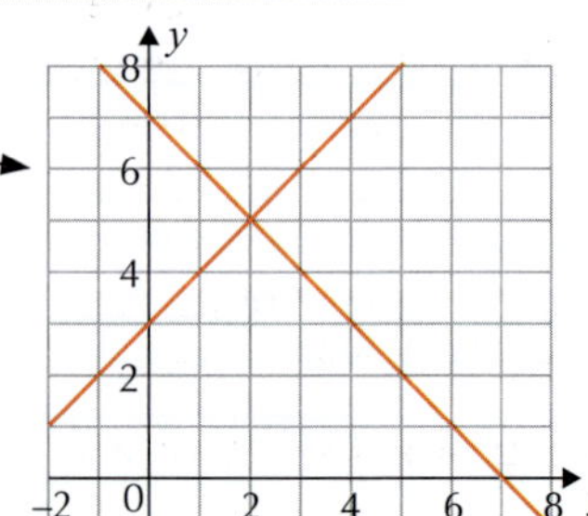

Q2 a) Draw the graph of $y = 5 - x$.

b) On the same axes, draw the graph of $y = x - 3$.

c) Use your graphs to solve the simultaneous equations $y = 5 - x$ and $y = x - 3$.

Q3 a) Draw the graphs of $y = 2 - 2x$ and $y = x + 5$ on the same axes.

b) Use your graphs to solve the equation $2 - 2x = x + 5$.

Q4 a) Draw the graphs of $y = x + 3$ and $y = x - 2$.

b) Explain how this shows that the simultaneous equations $y = x + 3$ and $y = x - 2$ have no solutions.

12.4 Gradients

The gradient of a straight-line tells you how steep it is — the bigger the number, the steeper the line. Gradients come in handy for lots of things — for example, in real life, you'll see gradients on road signs to describe the steepness of hills and slopes.

Learning Objective — Spec Ref A10:
Be able to find the gradient of a straight line.

To find the **gradient** of a line, divide the '**vertical distance**' (the change in the y-coordinates) between **two points** on the line by the '**horizontal distance**' (the change in the x-coordinates) between those points.

$$\text{Gradient} = \frac{\text{Vertical distance}}{\text{Horizontal distance}} = \frac{\text{Change in } y}{\text{Change in } x} = \frac{y_2 - y_1}{x_2 - x_1}$$

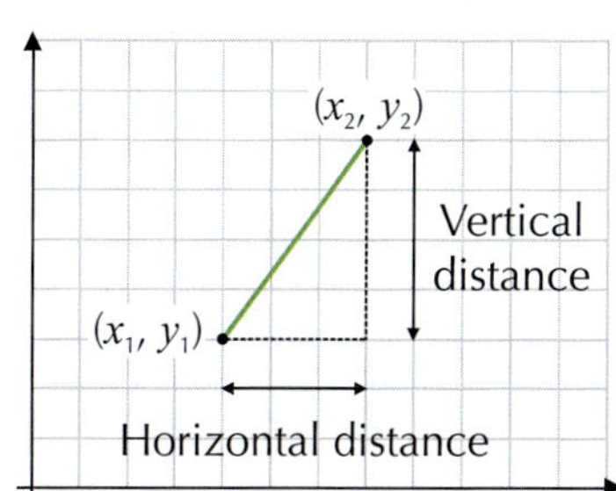

Make sure you subtract the x-coordinates and y-coordinates in the **same order** — i.e. if you do $y_2 - y_1$ on the numerator, you must do $x_2 - x_1$ on the denominator.

The **sign** of the gradient is important:

- A line sloping **upwards** from left to right has a **positive gradient**.
- A line sloping **downwards** from left to right has a **negative gradient**.

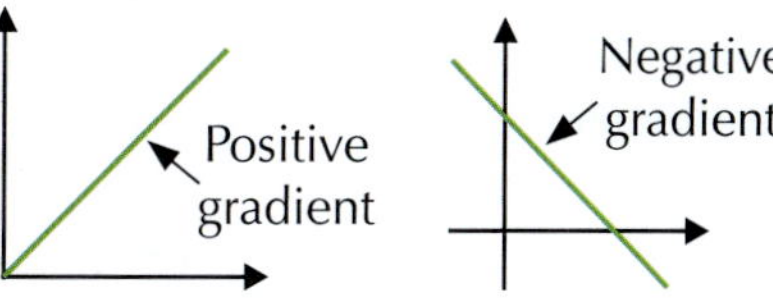

Gradients can be given in different ways — e.g. if the gradient is $\frac{1}{4}$, it has a **ratio** of **1 : 4**, a **percentage** of **25%** and you can say that the **slope** is **"1 in 4"**. Generally, your answer should be a **fraction**.

Road signs use %

Example 1

Find the gradient of the line containing the points $P(-3, 1)$ and $Q(4, 5)$.

1. Call the coordinates of P (x_1, y_1). Call the coordinates of Q (x_2, y_2).
2. Use the formula to calculate the gradient.
3. The line slopes upwards from left to right, so you should get a positive answer.

$$\text{Gradient} = \frac{y_2 - y_1}{x_2 - x_1} = \frac{5 - 1}{4 - (-3)} = \frac{4}{7}$$

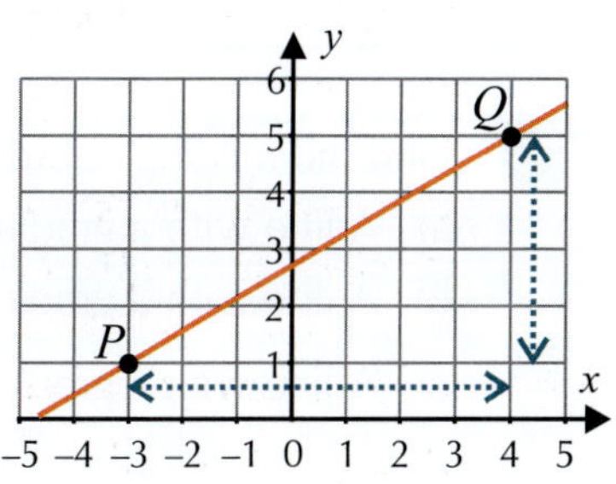

Exercise 1

Q1 The grid spacing in this question is 1 unit.

a) Write down the vertical distance between the points X and Y.

b) Write down the horizontal distance between X and Y.

c) State whether the gradient is positive or negative.

d) Calculate the gradient of the line segment XY.

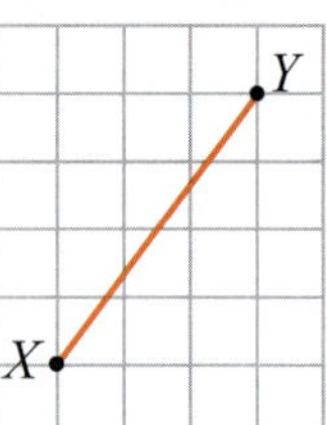

Q2 Find the gradient of each of the following line segments. The grid spacing is 1 unit.

a) 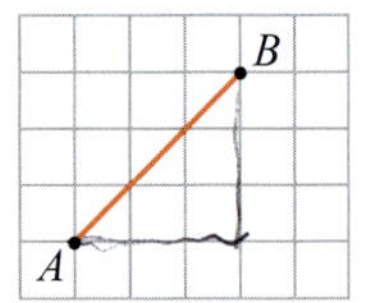

b) 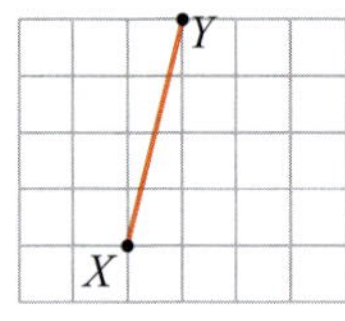

c) 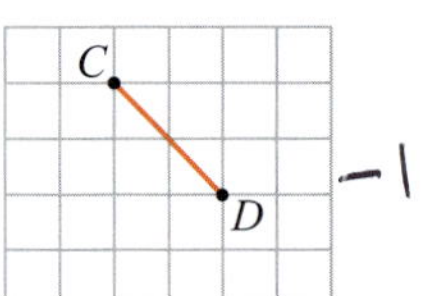

d) 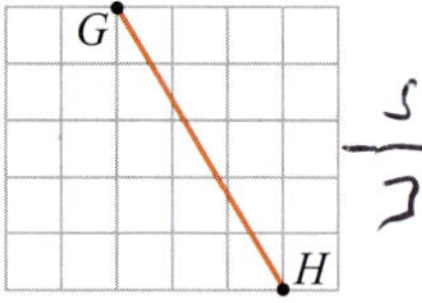

Q3 Use the points shown to find the gradient of each of the following lines.

a) 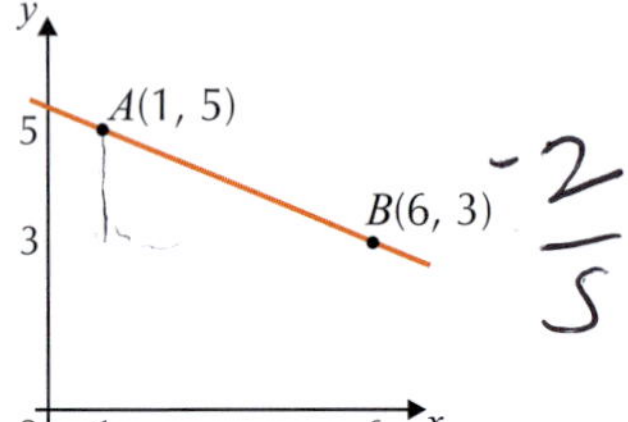

b) 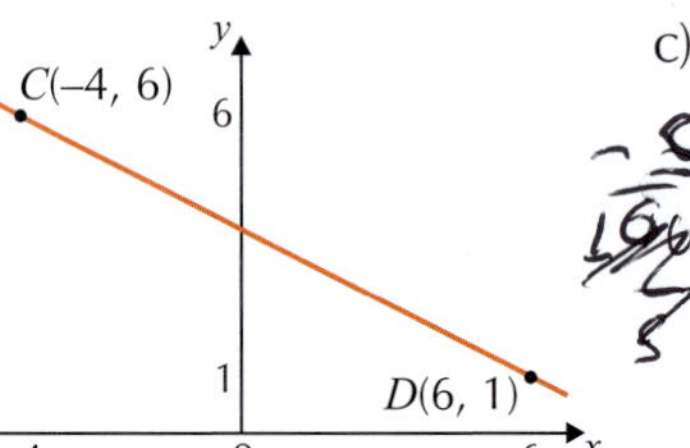

c) 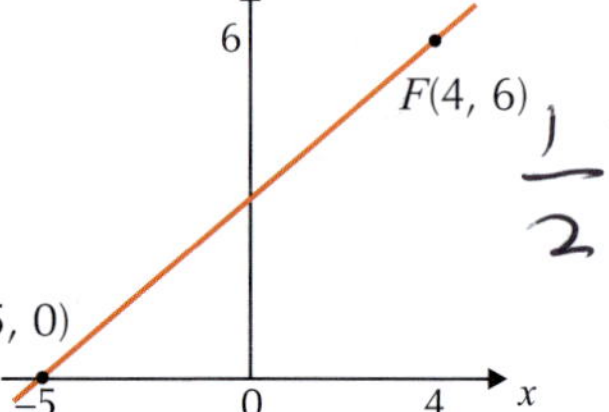

Q4 For each line shown below:

(i) Use the axes to find the coordinates of each of the marked points.

(ii) Find the gradient of each of the lines.

a) 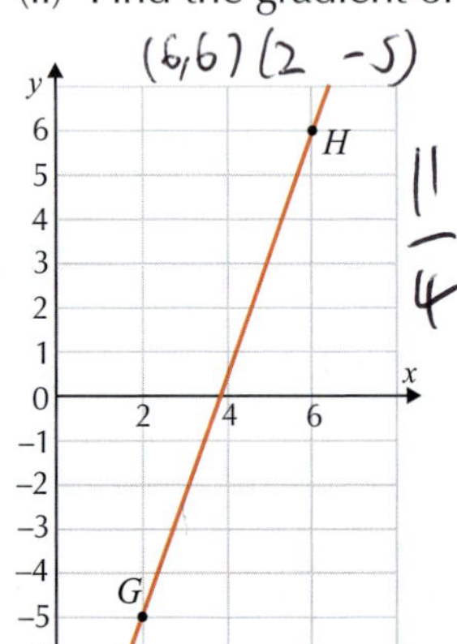

b) 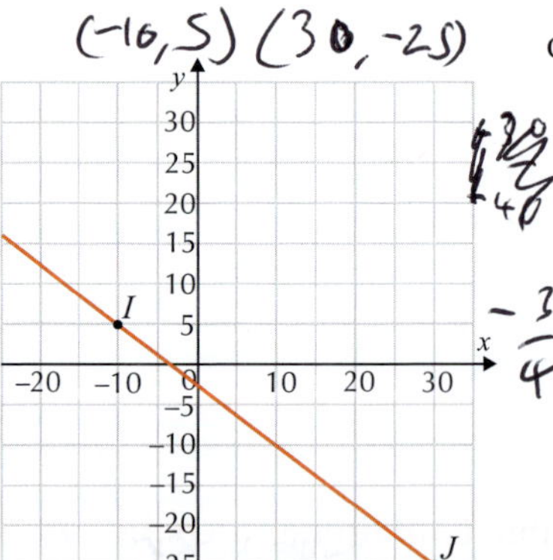

c) 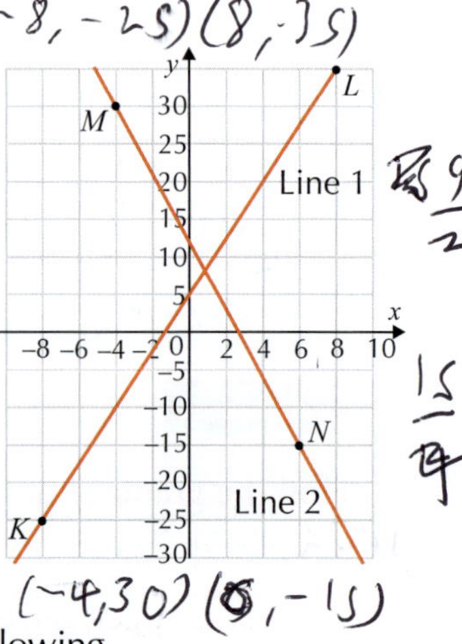

Q5 Find the missing coordinates, marked by letters, in each of the following.

a) A line with a gradient of 1 that goes through points (3, 5) and (7, a).

b) A line with a gradient of 2 that goes through points (1, 1) and (b, 5).

c) A line with a gradient of $\frac{1}{2}$ that goes through points (0, 0) and (8, c).

12.5 Equations of Straight-Line Graphs

The equation of a straight line depends on two things — the gradient of the line, and the point where it crosses the y-axis (the y-intercept). If you know these you can write down the equation.

y = mx + c

Learning Objective — Spec Ref A10:
Identify and interpret gradients and the y-intercept in equations of straight lines.

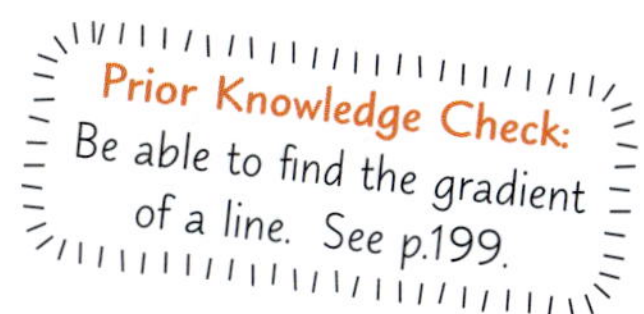

Prior Knowledge Check:
Be able to find the gradient of a line. See p.199.

The **equation** of a **straight line** can be written in the form $\boldsymbol{y = mx + c}$,
where m and c are numbers — for example, $y = 3x + 5$ ($m = 3$, $c = 5$).

When written in this form:

- $\boldsymbol{m}$ is the **gradient** of the line,
- $\boldsymbol{c}$ tells you the $\boldsymbol{y}$**-intercept** — the point where the line crosses the y-axis.

Make sure you don't mix up m and c when you get something like $y = 5 + 2x$.
Remember, m is the number in front of the x and c is the number on its own.

Watch out for **minus signs** too — both m and c can be negative (e.g. $y = -2x - 5$).

Example 1

Write down the gradient and the coordinates of the y-intercept of $y = 2x + 1$.

The equation is in the form $y = mx + c$, so you just need to read the values for the gradient and y-intercept from the equation.

$y = \textcircled{2}x + \textcircled{1}$ (m = 2, c = 1)

The question asks for the coordinates of the y-intercept, so don't forget the x-coordinate.

gradient = **2**
y-intercept = **(0, 1)**

Tip: The x-coordinate of the y-intercept will always be 0.

Exercise 1

Q1 Write down the equation of the straight line with gradient = 2 and y-intercept = (0, 3).

Q2 Find the gradient and the coordinates of the y-intercept for each of the following graphs.

a) $y = 3x + 2$ b) $y = 2x - 4$ c) $y = 5x - 11$

d) $y = -3x + 7$ e) $y = 4x$ f) $y = \frac{1}{2}x - 1$

g) $y = x - 6$ h) $y = -x + 5$ i) $y = 3 - 6x$

Q3 Match the graphs to the correct equation from the box.

$y = x + 2$	$y = \frac{7}{3}x - 1$	$y = -x + 6$	$y = 3x$	$y = -\frac{1}{3}x + 4$	$y = \frac{1}{3}x + 2$

A

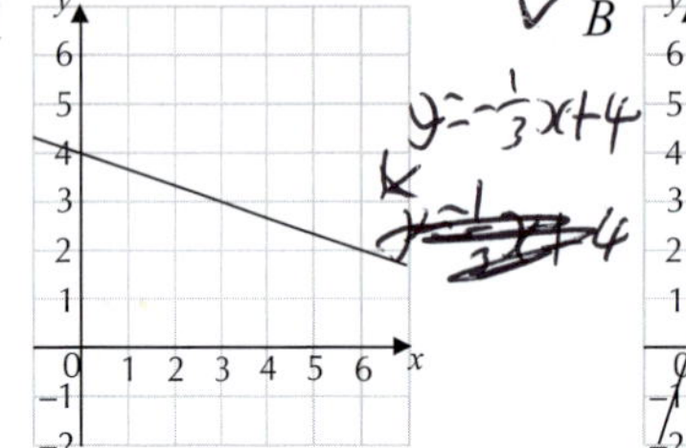

B

C

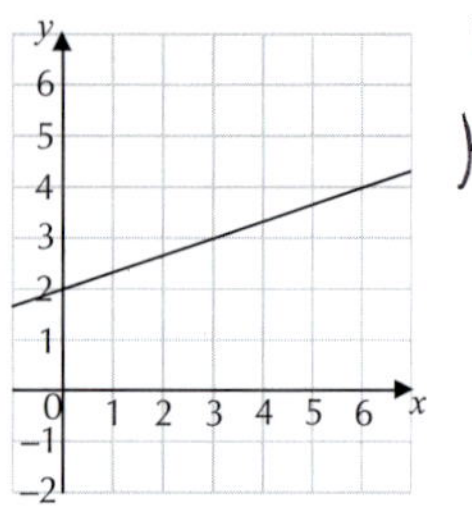

D

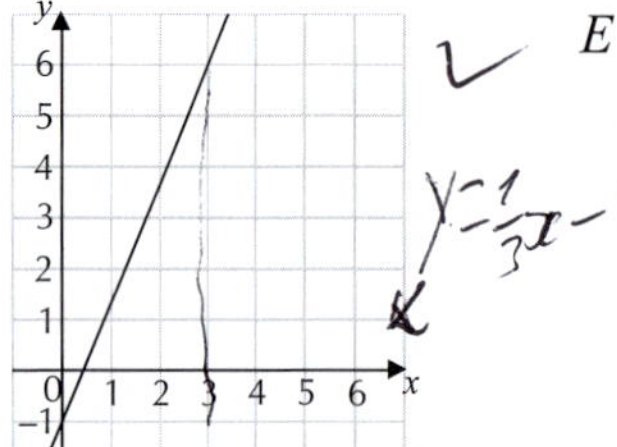

E

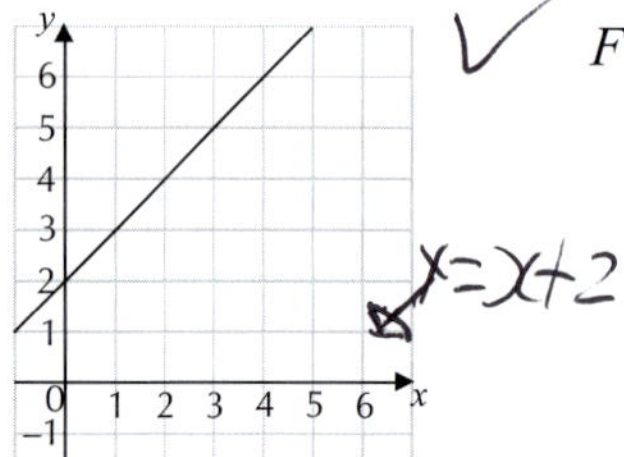

F

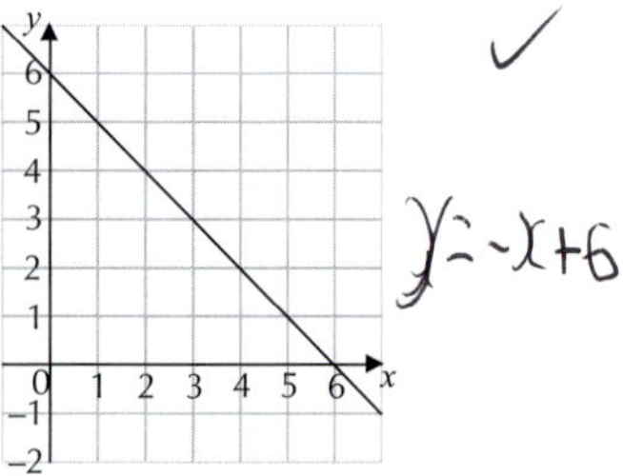

If you're given an equation that isn't in $y = mx + c$ form, **rearrange** it into this form.
For example, $y - 3x = 2$ can be rearranged to $y = 3x + 2$ (with $m = 3$ and $c = 2$).

Example 2

Find the gradient and the coordinates of the *y*-intercept of 2*x* + 3*y* = 12.

1. Rearrange the equation into the form $y = mx + c$.

$$2x + 3y = 12 \quad (-\,2x)$$
$$3y = -2x + 12 \quad (\div 3)$$
$$y = -\frac{2}{3}x + 4$$

($m = -\frac{2}{3}$, $c = 4$)

2. Write down the values for the gradient and *y*-intercept.

gradient = $\mathbf{-\frac{2}{3}}$
y-intercept = **(0, 4)**

Tip: To check your answer, substitute the *x*- and *y*-values of the *y*-intercept into the original equation:
$2 \times 0 + 3 \times 4 = 12$ ✔

Exercise 2

Q1 Find the gradient and the coordinates of the *y*-intercept for each of the following graphs.

a) $3y = 9 - 3x$ b) $y - 5 = 7x$ c) $3x + y = 1$

d) $3y - 6x = 15$ e) $4y - 6x + 8 = 0$ f) $6x - 3y + 1 = 0$

Parallel Lines

Learning Objective — Spec Ref A9:
Know that parallel lines have the same gradient.

Lines that are **parallel** have the **same gradient** — so their equations (in $y = mx + c$ form) all have the same value of $\boldsymbol{m}$.

For example, the lines $y = \mathbf{3}x$, $y = \mathbf{3}x - 2$ and $y = \mathbf{3}x + 4$ are all parallel.

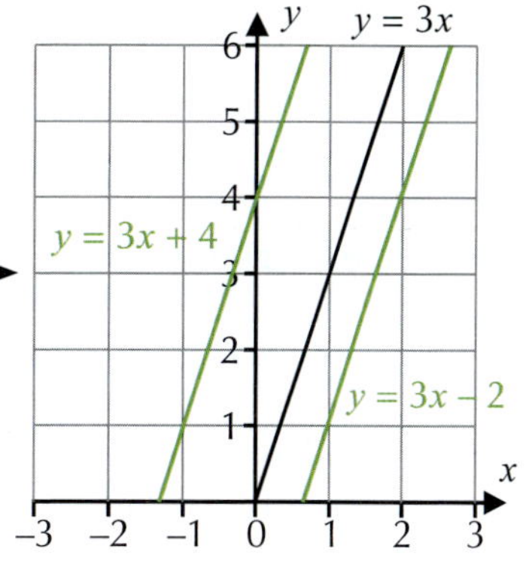

To **check** if two lines are parallel, **rearrange** their equations so that they're both in $y = mx + c$ form, then **compare** the values of m.

Example 3

Which of the following lines is parallel to the line $2x + y = 5$?
***A*: $y = 3 - 2x$ *B*: $x + y = 5$ *C*: $y - 2x = 6$**

1. Rearrange the equation into the form $y = mx + c$ to find its gradient.

   $2x + y = 5$
   $y = 5 - 2x$
   $y = -2x + 5$, so the gradient $(m) = -2$.

2. Rearrange the other equations in the same way. Any that have $m = -2$ will be parallel to $2x + y = 5$.

A: $y = 3 - 2x$	*B*: $x + y = 5$	*C*: $y - 2x = 6$
$y = -2x + 3$	$y = -x + 5$	$y = 2x + 6$
$m = -2$	$m = -1$	$m = 2$

So **line *A*** is parallel to $2x + y = 5$.

Exercise 3

Q1 Write down the equations of three lines that are parallel to:

a) $y = 5x - 1$ b) $x + y = 7$

Q2 Which of the following are the equations of lines parallel to: a) $y = 2x - 1$ b) $2x - 3y = 0$

A: $y - 2x = 4$ *B*: $2y = 2x + 5$ *C*: $2x - y = 2$

D: $2x + y + 7 = 0$ *E*: $3y + 2x = 2$ *F*: $6x - 9y = -2$

Q3 Which of the lines listed below are parallel to the line shown in the diagram?

A: $y + 3x = 2$ *B*: $3y = 7 - x$ *C*: $y = 4 - 3x$

D: $x - 3y = 8$ *E*: $y = 3 - \frac{1}{3}x$ *F*: $6y = -2x$

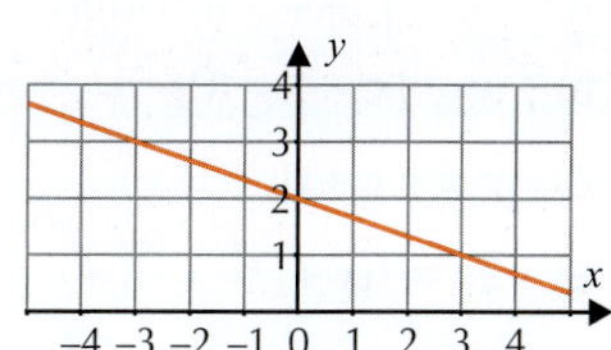

Finding the Equation of a Line

Learning Objectives — Spec Ref A9:
- Find the equation of a straight line given its gradient and a point on the line.
- Find the equation of a straight line given the coordinates of two points on the line.

You can find the equation of a line using its **gradient** and **one point** on the line.

- First, substitute the values of the **gradient** (m) and the **coordinates** of the known point (x, y) into $y = mx + c$. You'll be left with an equation where c is the only unknown.
- **Solve** this equation to find the value of c.
- Finally, put your values of m and c into $y = mx + c$ to give the **equation of the line**.

Tip: You might need to find the gradient from the equation of a parallel line — look back at p.203 for this.

Example 4

Find the equation of the line which passes through the point (5, 8) and has a gradient of 3.

1. Write down the equation $y = mx + c$, then substitute the values of the gradient m and the known point (x, y).
   $y = mx + c$
   $8 = 3 \times 5 + c$
   $8 = 15 + c$
2. Solve the equation to find the value of c.
   $8 - 15 = 15 + c - 15$
   $-7 = c$
3. Put your values of m and c into $y = mx + c$.
   So the equation of the line is $\boldsymbol{y = 3x - 7}$.

Tip: It's a good idea to check the known point works in your equation:
$3 \times 5 - 7 = 15 - 7 = 8$ ✔

Exercise 4

Q1 Find the equations of the following lines based on the information given.

a) gradient = 8, passes through (0, 2)
b) gradient = –1, passes through (0, 7)
c) gradient = 3, passes through (1, 10)
d) gradient = $\frac{1}{2}$, passes through (4, –5)
e) gradient = –7, passes through (2, –4)
f) gradient = 5, passes through (–3, –7)

Q2 For each of the following, find the equation of the line which is parallel to the given line and passes through the given point. Give your answers in the form $y = mx + c$.

a) $y = 3x + 2$, (0, 5)
b) $y = 5x - 3$, (1, –4)
c) $y = 2x + 1$, (1, 6)
d) $y = \frac{1}{2}x + 3$, (6, –7)
e) $2y = 6x + 3$, (–3, 4)
f) $x + y = 4$, (8, 8)

If you only know **two points** on the line, you can calculate the **gradient** of the line using the method on p.199. Then follow the method from the previous page (using either of the two points) to find the **equation of the line**.

Example 5

Find the equation of the straight line that passes through the points $A(-3, -4)$ and $B(-1, 2)$.

1. Write down the equation for a straight line. $y = mx + c$
2. Find the gradient (m) of the line. $m = \frac{y_2 - y_1}{x_2 - x_1} = \frac{2-(-4)}{-1-(-3)} = \frac{6}{2} = 3$
3. Substitute the value for the gradient and the x and y values for one of the points into $y = mx + c$, then solve to find c.
   At point B, $x = -1$ and $y = 2$.
   $2 = 3 \times (-1) + c$
   $2 = -3 + c$
   $c = 5$
4. Put your values of m and c into $y = mx + c$. So the equation of the line is $\mathbf{y = 3x + 5}$.

Exercise 5

Q1 Find the equations of the lines passing through the following points.

a) (3, 7) and (5, 11)　　b) (5, 1) and (2, –5)　　c) (4, 1) and (–3, –6)

d) (–2, 1) and (1, 7)　　e) (2, 8) and (–1, –1)　　f) (–3, 2) and (–2, 5)

Q2 Find the equations of the lines A to H shown below.
Write all your answers in the form $y = mx + c$.

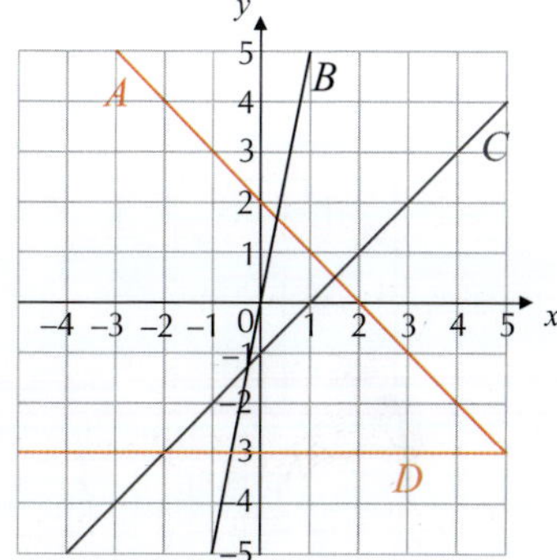

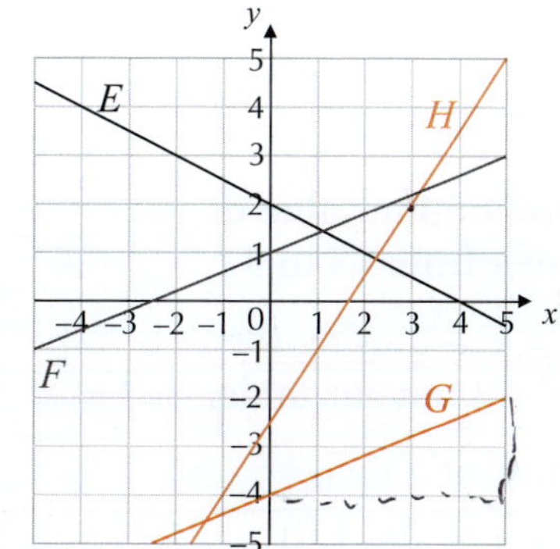

Q3 Find the equation of the line shown in the diagram on the right.

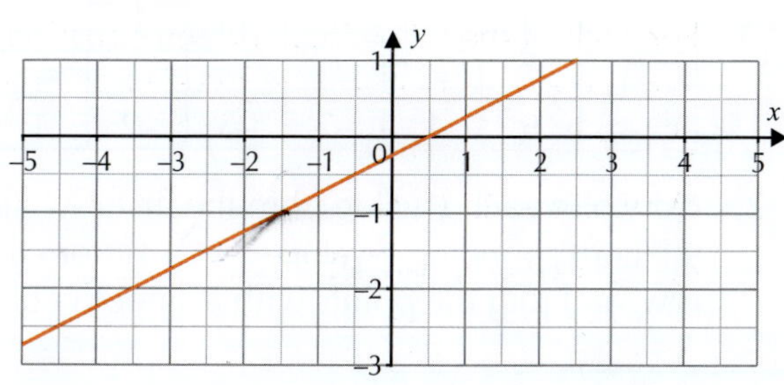

12.6 Quadratic Graphs

Quadratic expressions and equations were covered in Section 8 and Section 9. In a quadratic function $y = ax^2 + bx + c$, values of x and y are connected using a quadratic expression. You can plot graphs of such functions using a table of values like you did for straight lines.

Drawing Quadratic Graphs

Learning Objective — Spec Ref A12:
Be able to draw the graphs of quadratic functions.

Quadratic functions always involve an x^2 **term** (but no higher powers of x, such as x^3, x^4...). The graph of a quadratic function is always a **curve** called a **parabola**.

- If the coefficient of x^2 is **positive** (e.g. $3x^2 + x - 2$), the parabola is **u-shaped**.
- If the coefficient of x^2 is **negative** (e.g. $-3x^2 - x + 2$), the parabola is **n-shaped**.

Making a **table** can help with **drawing** quadratic graphs:

- In the **first row** write the **x-values** that you're going to plot.
- Make a **row** for each **term** in the quadratic and find the value of that term for each x-value.
- The **last row** in the table is the **quadratic itself** — because you have calculated each term, you can just **add** the values in that column.
- Now you can **plot** the graph using the values in the **first and last row** of each column. Join the points with a **smooth curve** — if it's not smooth, then you've got a point wrong.

Tip: The range of x-values will be given in the question.

Example 1

a) Complete the table to find the value of $y = x^2 - 3$ for values of x from –3 to 3.

b) Draw the graph of $y = x^2 - 3$ using the values of x and $y = x^2 - 3$ in your table.

x	–3	–2	–1	0	1	2	3
x^2							
–3							
$x^2 - 3$							

1. Fill in the table one row at a time.

x	–3	–2	–1	0	1	2	3
x^2	9	4	1	0	1	4	9
–3	–3	–3	–3	–3	–3	–3	–3
$x^2 - 3$	6	1	–2	–3	–2	1	6

2. Now plot each x-value from the first row against the corresponding y-value ($= x^2 - 3$) from the third row, and join the points with a smooth curve.

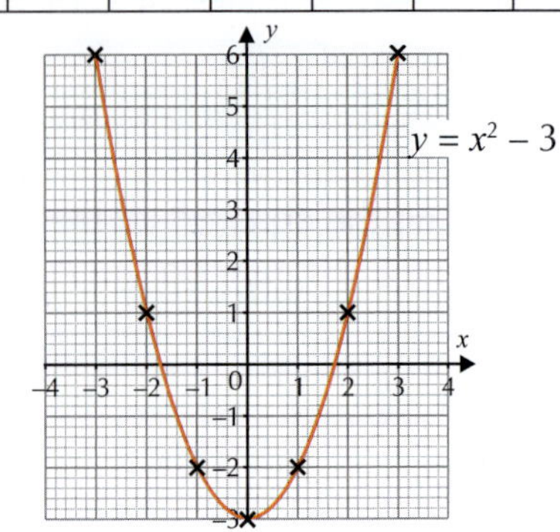

Exercise 1

Q1 a) Copy and complete the table below to find the value of $y = x^2 + 2$ for values of x from –3 to 3.

x	–3	–2	–1	0	1	2	3
x^2	9		1			4	
2	2		2			2	
$x^2 + 2$	11		3			6	

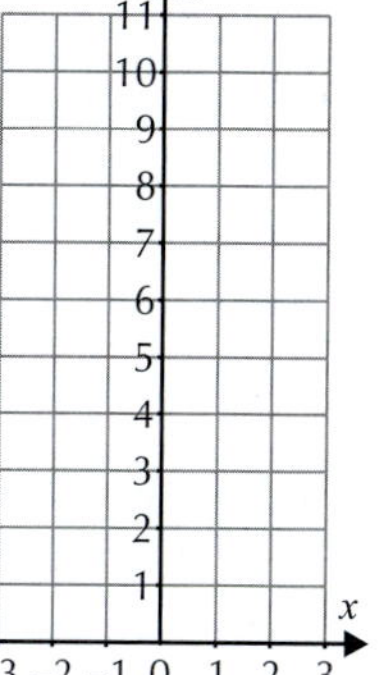

b) Copy the grid on the right and plot the points from your table.

c) Join up the points to draw the graph of $y = x^2 + 2$.

Q2 a) Copy and complete the table to show the value of $y = x^2 - 1$ for values of x from –3 to 3.

b) Draw a set of axes with x-values from –3 to 3 and y-values from –1 to 8. Draw the graph of $y = x^2 - 1$ on your axes.

x	–3	–2	–1	0	1	2	3
x^2		4					9
–1		–1					–1
$x^2 - 1$		3					8

Q3 For each of the following equations:

(i) Complete a table to show the value of y for values of x from –3 to 3.

(ii) Draw a graph of the equation on suitable axes.

a) $y = x^2 + 3$

b) $y = 5 - x^2$

Example 2

a) Complete the table to find the value of $y = x^2 - x$ for values of x from –3 to 3.

b) Draw the graph of $y = x^2 - x$ for values of x from –3 to 3.

x	–3	–2	–1	0	1	2	3
x^2		4			1		
$-x$		2			–1		
$x^2 - x$		6			0		

1. Fill in the table one row at a time. Find the entry for the '$x^2 - x$' row by adding the entries in the 'x^2' and '$-x$' rows.

x	–3	–2	–1	0	1	2	3
x^2	9	4	1	0	1	4	9
$-x$	3	2	1	0	–1	–2	–3
$x^2 - x$	12	6	2	0	0	2	6

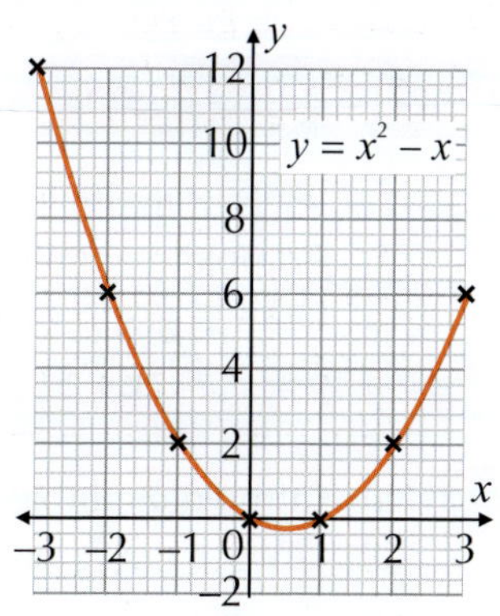

2. Now plot each x-value from the first row against the corresponding y-value ($= x^2 - x$) from the fourth row. Join the points with a smooth curve.

Exercise 2

Q1 a) Copy and complete the table to show the value of $y = x^2 - 2x$ for values of x from –3 to 3.

x	–3	–2	–1	0	1	2	3
x^2		4					9
$-2x$		4					–6
$x^2 - 2x$		8					3

b) Draw a set of axes with x-values from –3 to 3 and y-values from –1 to 15. Draw the graph of $y = x^2 - 2x$ on your axes.

Q2 For each of the following quadratic equations:

(i) Complete a table to show the value of y for values of x from –3 to 3.

(ii) Draw a graph of the equation on suitable axes.

a) $y = x^2 + 3x$ b) $y = x^2 - 4x$

Example 3

Draw the graph of $y = x^2 + 3x - 2$ for values of x from –3 to 3.

1. Make a table — include separate rows for x^2, $3x$ and –2. The last row should add the three entries above.

x	–3	–2	–1	0	1	2	3
x^2	9	4	1	0	1	4	9
$3x$	–9	–6	–3	0	3	6	9
–2	–2	–2	–2	–2	–2	–2	–2
$x^2 + 3x - 2$	–2	–4	–4	–2	2	8	16

2. Now plot each x-value from the first row against the corresponding y-value ($= x^2 + 3x - 2$) from the final row. Join the points with a smooth curve.

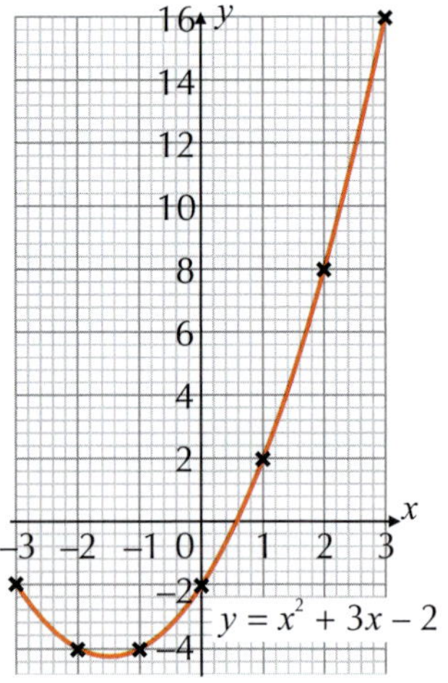

Exercise 3

Q1 For each of the following quadratic equations:

(i) Complete a table to show the value of y for values of x from –3 to 3.

(ii) Draw a graph of the equation on suitable axes.

a) $y = x^2 + 2x + 5$ b) $y = -x^2 - x - 1$

Q2 a) Complete a table to show the value of $y = 2x^2 + 3x - 7$ for values of x from –4 to 4.

b) Draw a graph of $y = 2x^2 + 3x - 7$ on suitable axes.

Solving Quadratic Equations Graphically

Learning Objective — Spec Ref A11/A18:
Be able to solve quadratic equations graphically.

You can use the **graph** of $y = ax^2 + bx + c$ to estimate solutions to the **quadratic equation** $ax^2 + bx + c = 0$ — the method is:

- Find the **points** where the x-axis **intersects** the quadratic graph — this is where $y = 0$. It can happen **once**, **twice** or **not at all**.
- **Read off** the **x-coordinates** of these points — they will be **approximate solutions** to the quadratic equation.

Tip: Often, you can only estimate because it's hard to read off the exact value — read the scale carefully and just be as accurate as you can.

Example 4

This graph shows the curve $y = x^2 - 2x - 1$. Use the graph to estimate both solutions (or roots) to the equation $x^2 - 2x - 1 = 0$. Give your answers to 1 decimal place.

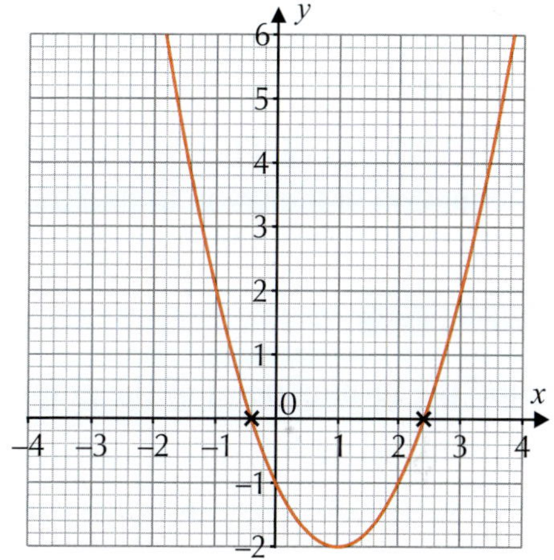

1. The left hand side of the equation $x^2 - 2x - 1 = 0$ is represented by the curve $y = x^2 - 2x - 1$ and the right-hand side is represented by the line $y = 0$ (the x-axis).
2. So, the estimated solutions are found where the curve crosses the x-axis. Read off the x-values:

$\mathbf{x = -0.4}$ and $\mathbf{x = 2.4}$

Exercise 4

Q1 Using the graphs shown below, find the solutions to the following equations.

a) $x^2 + 4x = 0$

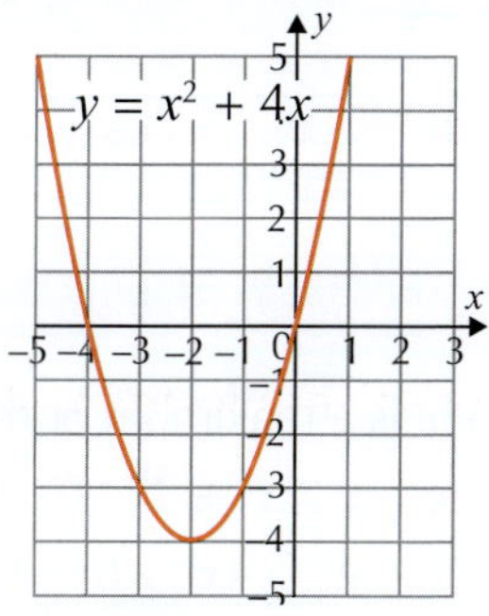

b) $x^2 - 2x - 3 = 0$

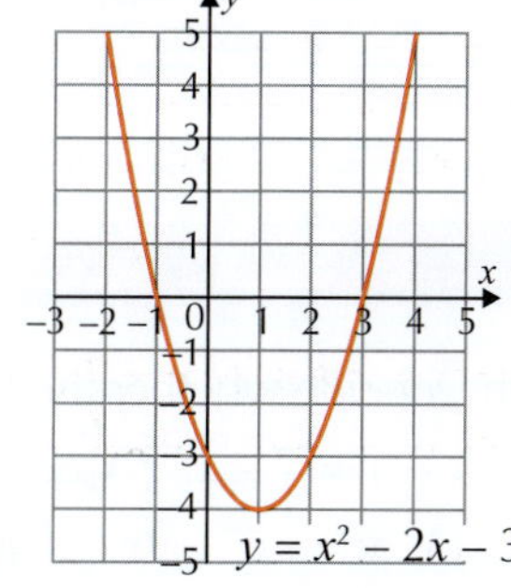

c) $-x^2 + 4 = 0$

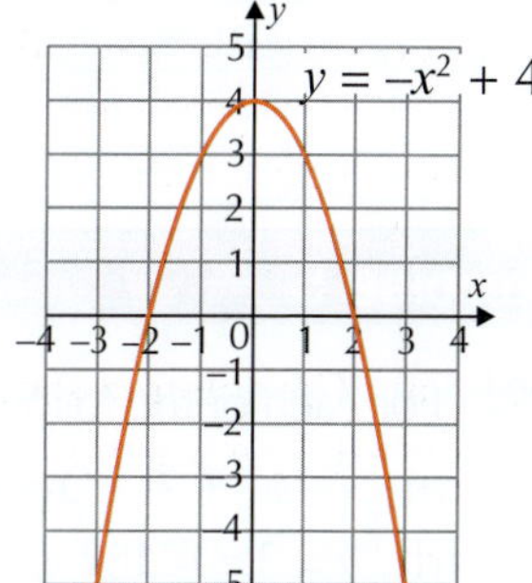

Q2 a) Draw the graph of $y = x^2 - 5x + 3$ for values of x from 0 to 5.

b) Use your graph to estimate the solutions to the equation $x^2 - 5x + 3 = 0$. Give your answers to 1 decimal place.

Turning Points of Quadratics

Learning Objective — Spec Ref A11:
Be able to identify the turning points of quadratic curves.

The **turning point** of a quadratic graph is at the **minimum** y-value if the curve is **u-shaped** or at the **maximum** y-value if the curve is **n-shaped**.

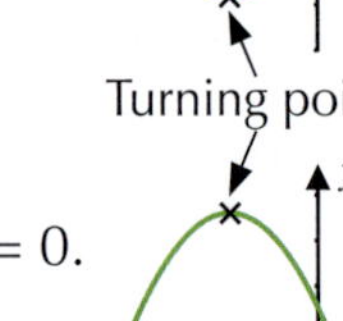

The **coordinates** of the turning point can be found as follows.

- The **x-coordinate** of the turning point is always **halfway** between any two points on the curve with the **same y-value**: (x_1, y) and (x_2, y). The points where the curve **intersects the x-axis** are often used, as they both have $y = 0$.
- The turning point has x-coordinate $\frac{x_1 + x_2}{2}$. Put this value of x into the **equation** of the graph to find the **y-coordinate** of the turning point.

Example 5

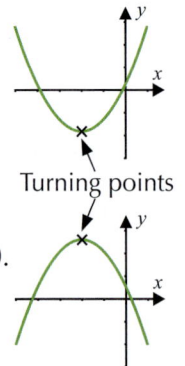

Find the turning point of the graph of $y = x^2 + x - 6$.

1. Find two points on the curve with the same y-value.

   The curve crosses the x-axis at (–3, 0) and (2, 0).

2. The x-coordinate of the turning point is halfway between these two x-values.

   x-coordinate = (–3 + 2) ÷ 2 = –0.5

3. Put the x-coordinate back into the equation to find the y-coordinate.

   y-coordinate = $(-0.5)^2 + (-0.5) - 6 = -6.25$
   So the turning point has coordinates **(–0.5, –6.25)**.

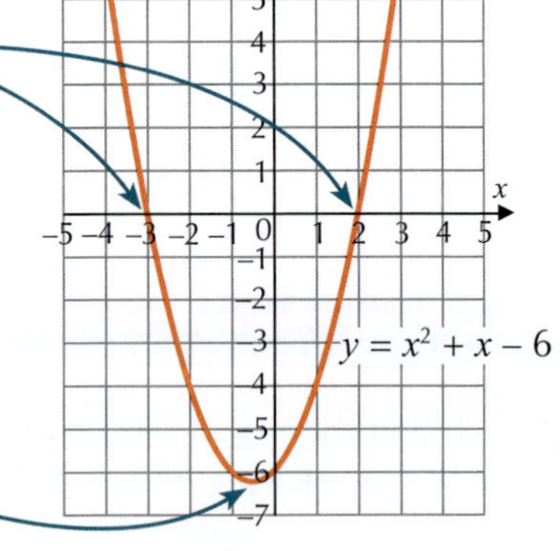

Exercise 5

Q1 For each of the following graphs, decide whether the turning point is a maximum or minimum.

a) $y = x^2 + 2$ min b) $y = 7 - x^2$ max c) $y = x^2 + 2x$ min

d) $y = 3x^2 - 10x + 7$ min e) $y = -x^2 + 9x - 5$ max f) $y = -4x^2 + 6x + 7$ max

Q2 Find the coordinates of the turning points of these graphs.

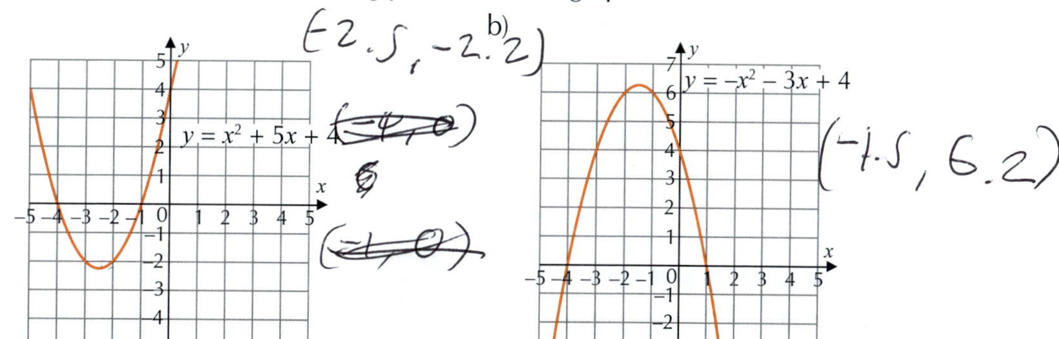

Q3 Find the turning points of these equations given the two points on the curve.

a) $y = x^2 - 6x$ goes through points (–1, 7) and (7, 7).

b) $y = x^2 - 2x + 3$ goes through points (0, 3) and (2, 3).

c) $y = 8x - x^2$ goes through points (2, 12) and (6, 12).

You can also find the **turning point** if you only have the **equation** of the quadratic. Make a **table** as if you were going to plot the graph and look for **two** x-values that give the **same** y-value. Once you have these x-values, you can follow the method from the previous page.

Tip: You don't need to draw the graph — the table is just to make spotting the x-values easier.

Example 6

Find the turning point of the graph of $y = x^2 - 3x + 7$.

1. Draw a table of values and look for two x-values that give the same y-value.

x	–2	–1	0	1	2
y	17	11	7	5	5

2. The x-coordinate of the turning point is halfway between these two x-values.

$x = 1$ and $x = 2$ both give $y = 5$

x-coordinate = $(1 + 2) \div 2 = 1.5$

3. Put the x-coordinate back into the equation to find the y-coordinate.

y-coordinate = $1.5^2 - (3 \times 1.5) + 7 = 4.75$

So the turning point = **(1.5, 4.75)**.

Exercise 6

Q1 By drawing tables for x values in the range $-3 \leq x \leq 3$, find the turning points of each of these curves.

a) $y = x^2 - 2x$

b) $y = x^2 + 3x + 11$

c) $y = x^2 + 5x - 9$

d) $y = 3x^2 + 12x - 8$

e) $y = -2x^2 - 2x + 9$

f) $y = -6x^2 + 18x - 3$

12.7 Harder Graphs

In this topic you'll learn about cubic and reciprocal functions — cubics have an x^3 term and reciprocals involve dividing by x. The graphs of these functions have their own distinctive shape.

Cubic Graphs

Learning Objective — Spec Ref A12:
Recognise and be able to sketch the graphs of cubic functions.

Cubic functions have x^3 as the **highest power** of x.
Cubic graphs all have the same basic shape — a curve with a '**wiggle**' in the middle.

- If the coefficient of x^3 is **positive**, the curve goes **up** from the **bottom left**.

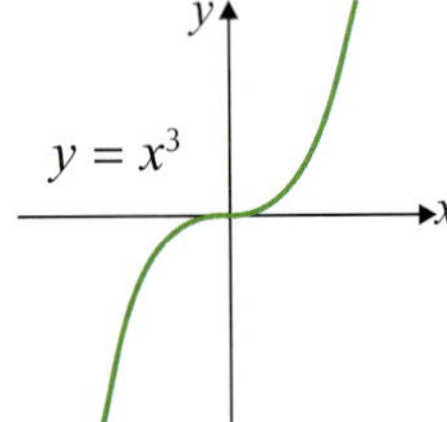

- If the coefficient of x^3 is **negative**, the curve goes **down** from the **top left**.

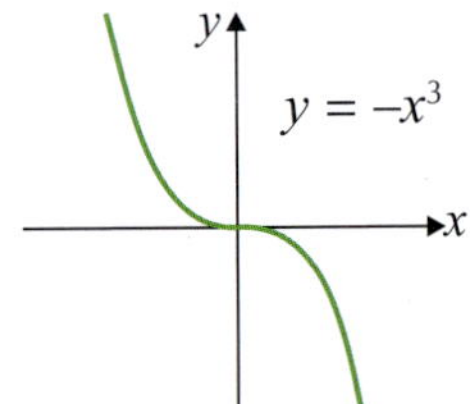

To **draw the graph** of a cubic function $y = ax^3 + bx^2 + cx + d$, find y-values using x-values in a **table**, then **plot** the coordinates and draw a **smooth curve** through the points.

Tip: This is like the method for plotting quadratics on p.206.

Example 1

Draw the graph of $y = x^3 + 1$.

1. Draw a table with rows for each term to help you work out the y-value for each value of x.

x	–3	–2	–1	0	1	2
x^3	–27	–8	–1	0	1	8
+1	1	1	1	1	1	1
$x^3 + 1$	–26	–7	0	1	2	9

2. Plot the coordinates and join the points with a smooth curve — use a pencil, as it may take a few tries to get right.

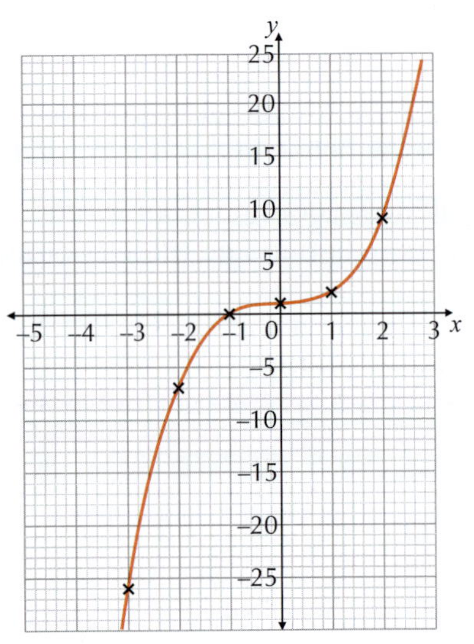

Exercise 1

Q1 Copy and complete each table and draw graphs for the following cubic equations.

a) $y = x^3 + 5$

x	–3	–2	–1	0	1	2	3
x^3	–27					8	
$x^3 + 5$	–22					13	

b) $y = 5 - x^3$

x	–3	–2	–1	0	1	2	3
5		5					5
$-x^3$		8					–27
$5 - x^3$		13					–22

c) $y = -4 - x^3$

x	–3	–2	–1	0	1	2	3
–4	–4				–4		
$-x^3$	27				–1		
$-4 - x^3$	23				–5		

Q2 Draw the graph of $y = x^3 + 3$ for values of x between –3 and 3.

Q3 Draw the graph of $y = x^3 - 3x + 7$ for values of x between –4 and 4.

Reciprocal Graphs

Learning Objective — Spec Ref A12:
Recognise and be able to sketch the graphs of reciprocal functions.

The equations of basic **reciprocal** graphs have the form: $y = \frac{A}{x}$ where A is constant

A reciprocal graph appears as **two curves**,
which are **symmetrical** about the lines $y = x$ and $y = -x$ and don't touch either the x- or y-axis.

When A is **positive** the curves are in the **top-right** and **bottom-left** quadrants.

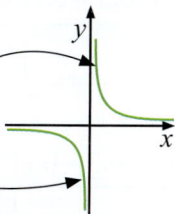

When A is **negative** the curves are in the **top-left** and **bottom-right** quadrants.

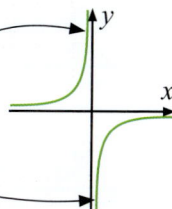

To **draw the graph** of a reciprocal function, make a table of x- and y-values — use both **positive** and **negative** values of x, and include **decimal values** between **–1** and **1**. **Plot** the coordinates from the table and draw **two smooth curves** through the points.

Example 2

Draw the graph of $y = \frac{1}{x}$ for values of x between –5 and 5.

1. Draw a table of values for the equation.

x	–5	–4	–2	–1	–0.5	–0.2
$\frac{1}{x}$	–0.2	–0.25	–0.5	–1	–2	–5

x	0.2	0.5	1	2	4	5
$\frac{1}{x}$	5	2	1	0.5	0.25	0.2

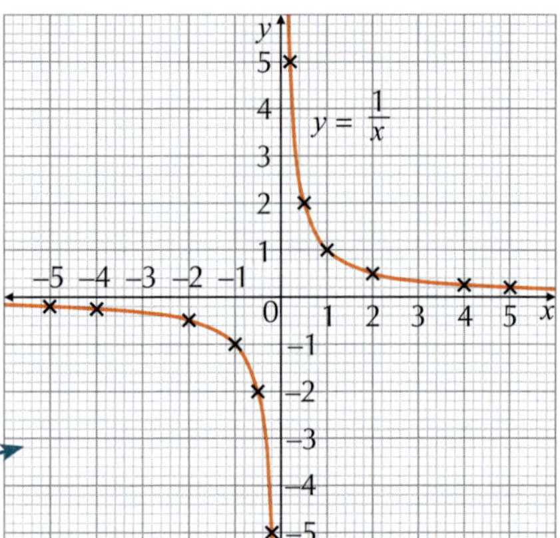

2. Plot the coordinates and join the points to make two smooth curves.

Exercise 2

Q1 Which of these equations would produce a reciprocal graph?

A: $y = \frac{x}{3}$	B: $y = \frac{9}{x}$	C: $y = \frac{6}{-x}$	D: $9 = \frac{y}{x}$
E: $xy = 5$	F: $3 = \frac{x}{y}$	G: $y = \frac{8}{2x}$	H: $y = \frac{2}{x} + x$

Q2 Copy and complete each table and draw graphs for the following reciprocal functions.

a) $y = \frac{2}{x}$

x	–5	–4	–2	–1	–0.5	–0.1	0.1	0.5	1	2	4	5
$\frac{2}{x}$		–0.5		–2						1		

b) $y = -\frac{1}{x}$

x	–5	–4	–2	–1	–0.5	–0.1	0.1	0.5	1	2	4	5
$-\frac{1}{x}$		0.25		1								

c) $y = \frac{3}{x}$

x	–5	–4	–2	–1	–0.5	–0.1	0.1	0.5	1	2	4	5
$\frac{3}{x}$		–0.75		–3								

Review Exercise

Q1 a) Plot the points $A(0, 4)$, $B(2, 6)$, $C(4, 4)$ and $D(2, 0)$ on a set of axes.

b) Join the points. What kind of shape have you made?

Q2 The points A and B have coordinates $A(2, 5)$ and $B(-4, 1)$.
Find the coordinates of the midpoint of the line segment AB.

Q3 a) Write down the coordinates of each of the points A to E.

b) Find the coordinates of the midpoint of AB.

c) Find the coordinates of the midpoint of BC.

d) Write down the equation of the line that passes through points A and E.

e) Find the gradient of the line BC.

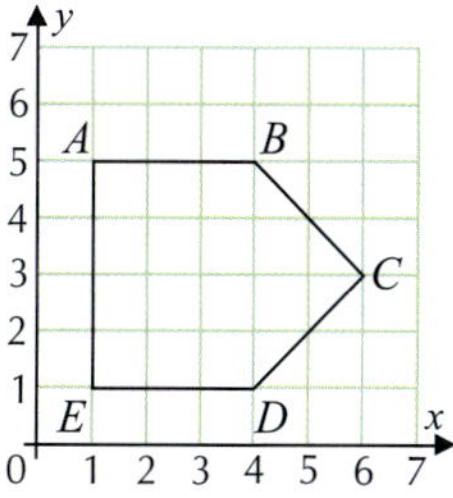

Q4 Draw each of the following lines on a set of axes.

a) $x = 1$ b) $y = -3$ c) $x = -1$ d) $y = 5$

Q5 Find the gradient of each of the line segments shown below.

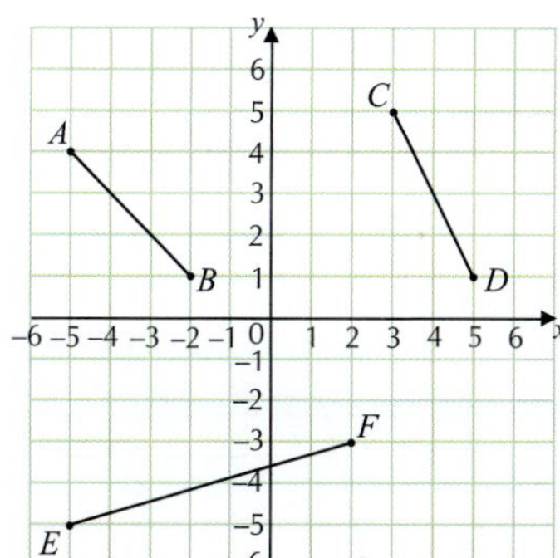

Q6 Match the graphs shown below with the correct equation from the list:

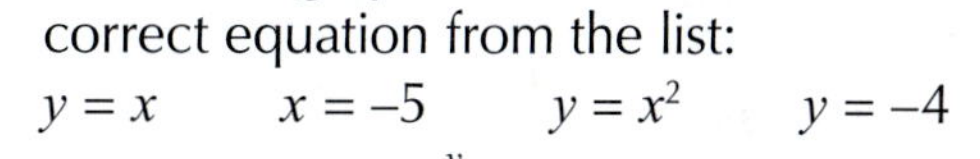
$y = x$ $x = -5$ $y = x^2$ $y = -4$

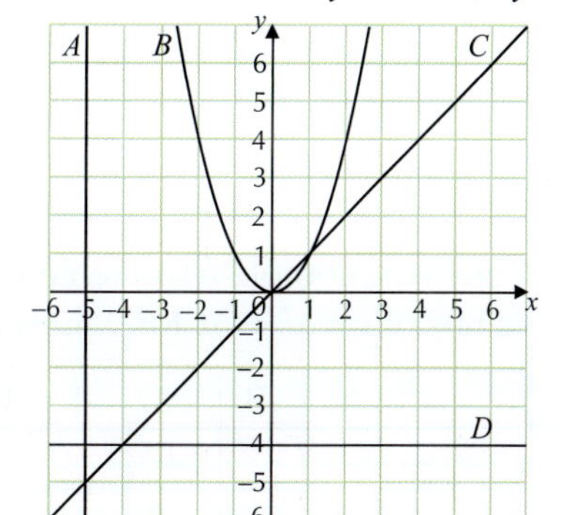

Q7 a) Copy and complete the table to show the value of $y = 2x + 2$ for values of x from –3 to 3.

b) Plot the graph of $y = 2x + 2$.

c) Use your graph solve the equation $2x + 2 = 5$.

x	–3	–2	–1	0	1	2	3
y							
Coordinates							

Q8 a) On the same axes, draw the graphs of $y = 2x + 3$ and $y = 4x + 2$.
b) Use your graphs to solve the simultaneous equations $y = 2x + 3$ and $y = 4x + 2$.

Q9 Find the gradient of the line passing through the following points.
a) (0, 0) and (3, 15)
b) (–4, –5) and (–1, 4)
c) (–7, 2) and (–4, –1)
d) (5, –2) and (2, 10)

Q10 For each of the following equations, write down:
(i) the gradient of the line
(ii) the coordinates of the line's y-intercept
a) $y = 2x + 3$
b) $y = 3 - x$
c) $y = -\frac{2}{3}x - 1$

Q11 a) Draw the line $y = 6 - 3x$ for values of x from –1 to 3.
b) Find the equation of the line parallel to this one that passes through (2, –4).

Q12 Sketch the general shape of the following:
a) A quadratic graph where the number in front of the x^2 term is positive.
b) A cubic graph where the number in front of the x^3 term is negative.
c) A reciprocal graph of the form $y = \frac{A}{x}$ where A is positive.

Q13 The graph on the right shows the curve $y = 3 - x - x^2$. Use the graph to estimate the solutions to the equation $3 - x - x^2 = 0$. Give your answers to 1 decimal place.

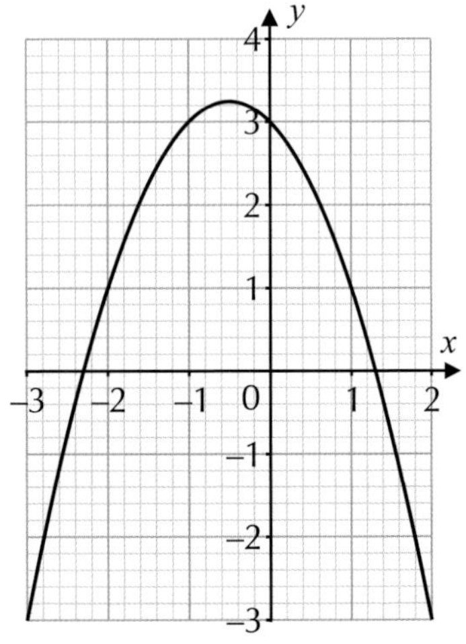

Q14 a) Copy and complete the table below to show the values of $y = x^2 + 5x$ for values of x from –4 to 2.

x	–4	–3	–2	–1	0	1	2
x^2			4				
$5x$			–10				
$x^2 + 5x$			–6				

b) Draw the graph of $y = x^2 + 5x$ for values of x from –4 to 2.
c) Find the coordinates of the turning point of your graph.

Exam-Style Questions

Q1 The diagram on the right shows a 1 cm² grid.
Point B has coordinates that are whole numbers and point B is 5 cm from point A.
On the grid, mark two points where point B could be.

[2 marks]

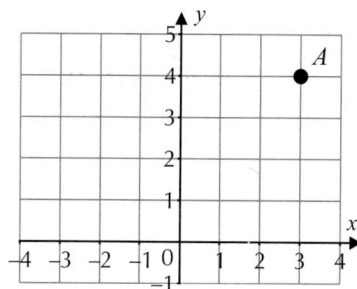

Q2 Point A has coordinates (–2, 1). Point B has coordinates (3, k).
The gradient of the line AB is –1.5.
Work out the value of k.

[3 marks]

Q3 The diagram on the right shows a line drawn on a pair of axes.

a) Write down the coordinates of the two points A and B.

[2 marks]

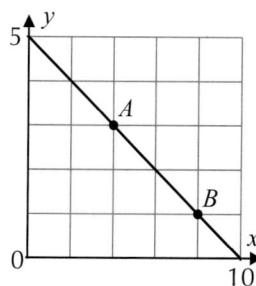

b) Complete the equation for this line:
$y = 5$..................

[2 marks]

Q4 The line BC is shown on the grid below.

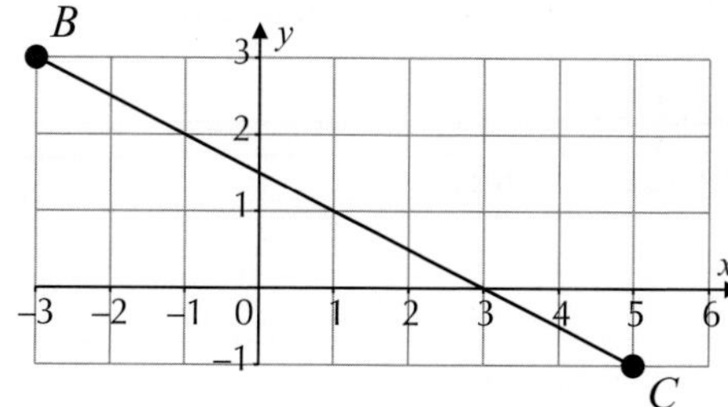

a) Write down the coordinates of where the line segment BC intersects the y-axis.

[1 mark]

b) Work out the coordinates of the midpoint of the line segment BC.

[1 mark]

Q5 The graph of a quadratic $y = ax^2 + bx + c$ is shown on the right for values of x from –3 to 5.

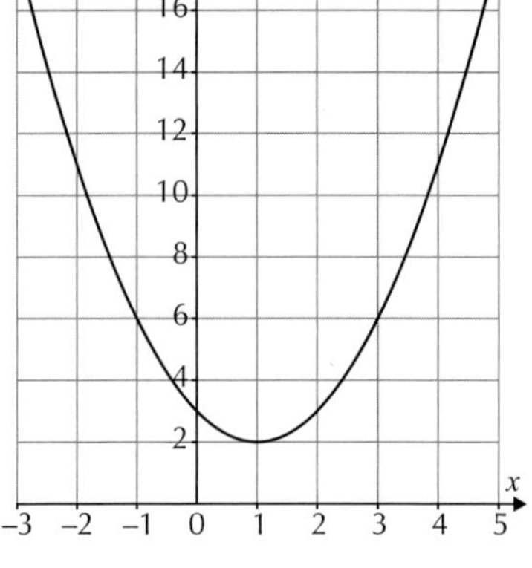

a) Write down the coordinates of the turning point of the graph.

[1 mark]

b) Use the graph to write down the value of y for $x = 3$.

[1 mark]

c) Use the graph to find the negative value of x for which $y = 6$.

[1 mark]

Q6 This is part of the graph of $y = 2x^2 - 4x - 5$.

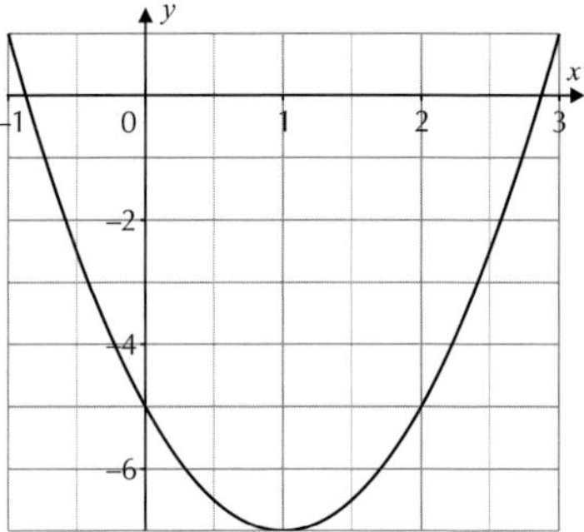

a) Write down the equation of the line of symmetry of the graph.

[1 mark]

b) Use the graph to estimate the solutions of $2x^2 - 4x - 5 = 0$ to 1 d.p.

[2 marks]

Q7 Mike has sketched the graph of $y = \frac{1}{x}$. Write down two things that are wrong with his sketch.

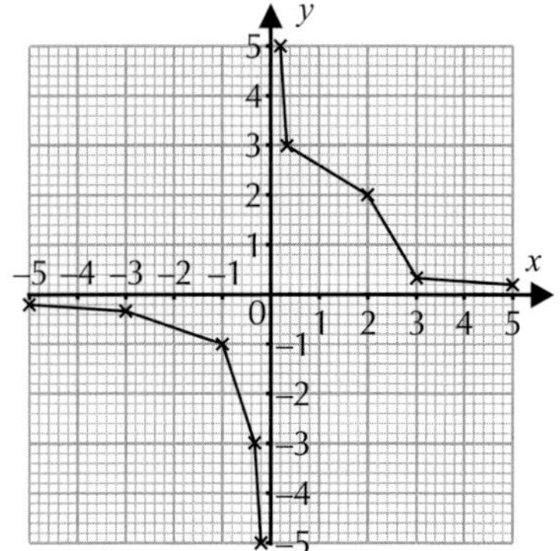

[2 marks]

13.1 Interpreting Real-Life Graphs

Sometimes, graphs show something more interesting than just how y changes with x. They can be used to illustrate motion (such as in distance-time graphs), unit conversions (such as changing between temperatures in °C and °F), and many other connections between real-life quantities.

Linear Graphs

Learning Objective — Spec Ref A14:
Understand and interpret straight-line graphs that represent real-life situations.

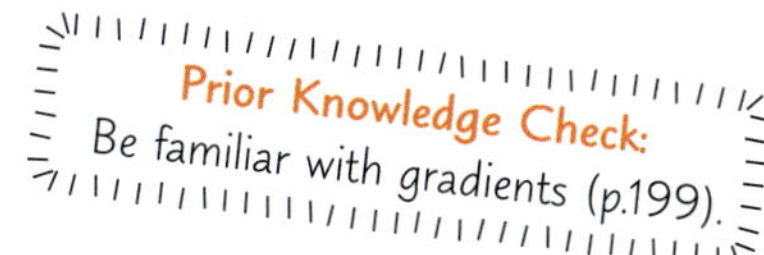

Straight-line graphs can be used to show how one thing **changes** in relation to another when the **rate of change** is **fixed** — for example, when **converting** between different **units**.

To **read off** values from a graph:

- Draw a **straight line** from **one axis** to the **graph**.
- Draw **another** straight line at a **right angle** to the first from the **graph** to the **other axis**.
- **Read off** the **value** from this axis, including any **units**.

Tip: To convert units, start from the axis that shows the units you're converting from, and finish on the axis showing those you're converting to.

Example 1

The graph shown can be used to convert between temperatures in degrees Celsius (°C) and degrees Fahrenheit (°F).

a) **Convert 10 °C to °F.**

Draw a line up from 10 °C until you reach the graph. Then draw a line across to find the amount in °F.

10 °C = **50 °F**

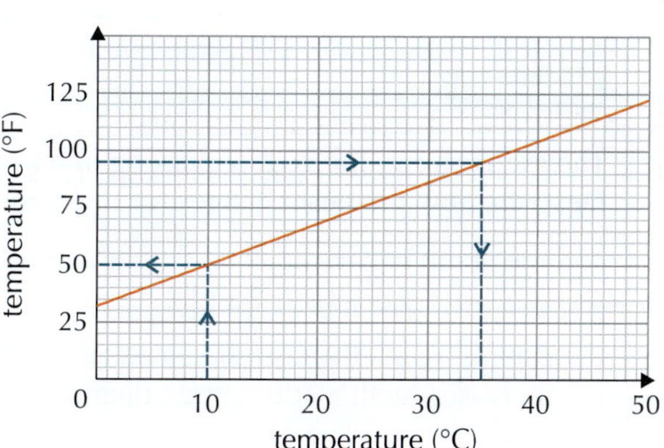

b) **Convert 95 °F to °C.**

Draw a line across from 95 °F until you reach the graph. Then draw a line down to find the amount in °C.

95 °F = **35 °C**

Exercise 1

The graph on the right can be used to convert between pounds (£) and euros (€). Use the graph to answer these questions.

Q1 Use the graph to convert the following amounts from pounds to euros.

a) £50 b) £250 c) £110

Q2 Use the graph to convert the following amounts from euros to pounds.

a) €50 b) €200 c) €360

Q3 A dress costs €130. How much is this in pounds?

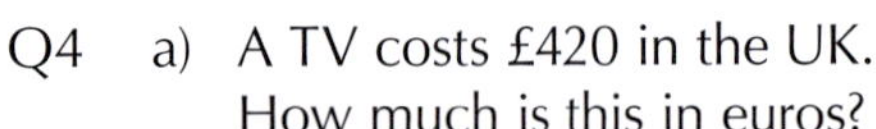

Q4 a) A TV costs £420 in the UK. How much is this in euros?

b) The price of the TV in France is €470. How much is this in pounds?

c) In which country is the TV cheaper?

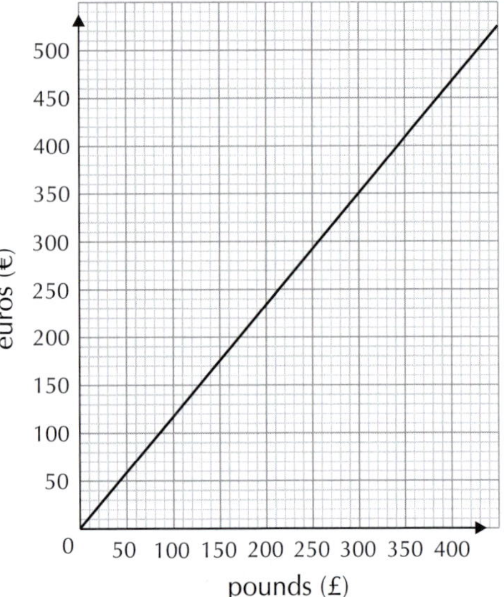

When **describing** straight-line graphs, look at the following **features** and **interpret** them in the **context** of the graph:

- The **direction** of the graph — i.e. is the variable on the vertical axis **increasing** or **decreasing** as the other increases?
- The **gradient** (steepness) — this shows the **rate of change** of one variable with the other. The **steeper** the line, the **faster** the quantity on the **vertical axis** is changing compared to the quantity on the **horizontal axis**.

Tip: Graphs are sometimes made up of a few straight lines with different gradients — you'll need to work out what's happening in each section.

Example 2

The graph shows the cost of parking in a multistorey car park. Describe how the cost changes for different parking durations.

1. The graph is flat initially — it has a constant value of £5 between 0 and 2 hours.
2. After 2 hours, the cost increases as the duration increases, with a constant gradient.

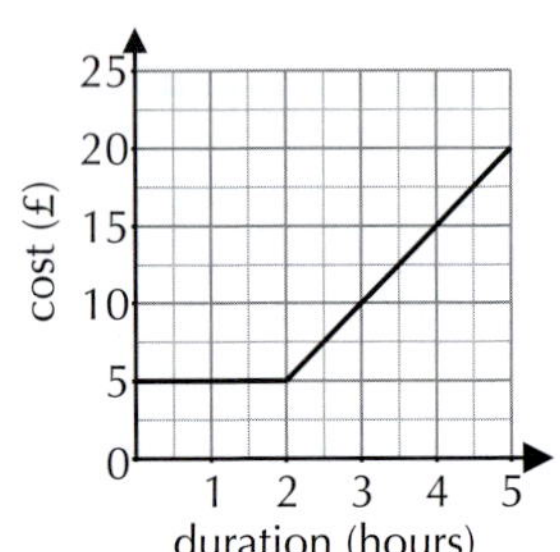

The cost of parking is **fixed** at £5 for up to 2 hours. From 2 hours onwards, the cost **increases at a constant rate** of £5 per hour.

Exercise 2

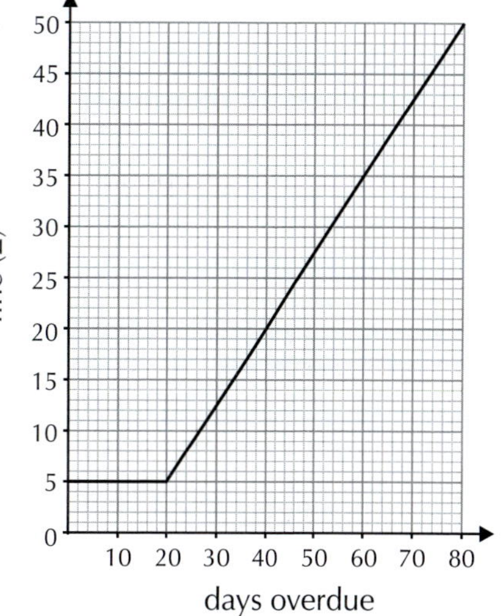

The graph on the right shows the cost of a fine for returning a library book late. Use the graph to answer **Questions 1-3**.

Q1 There is a basic fine, which is fixed up to a certain number of days.

a) What is the cost of this basic fine?

b) What is the longest time a book can be overdue and still receive the basic fine?

Q2 Estimate the fine for a book that is 50 days overdue.

Q3 Tamar receives a fine of £38. How many days was her book overdue?

Q4 Katherine (K), Lemar (L) and Morag (M) climbed a mountain with a summit that is 1 km above sea level. The graphs below show their progress over 4 hours.

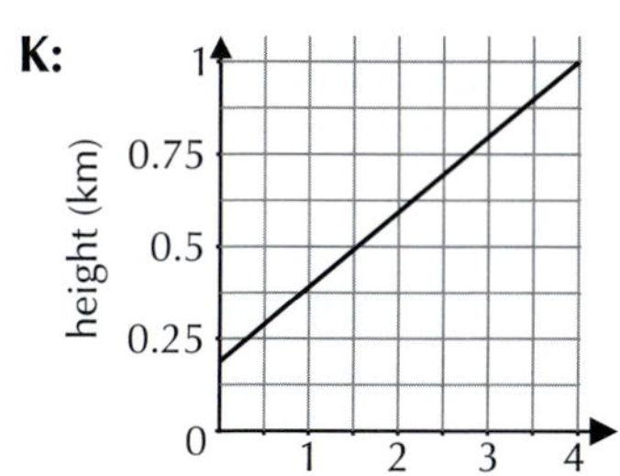

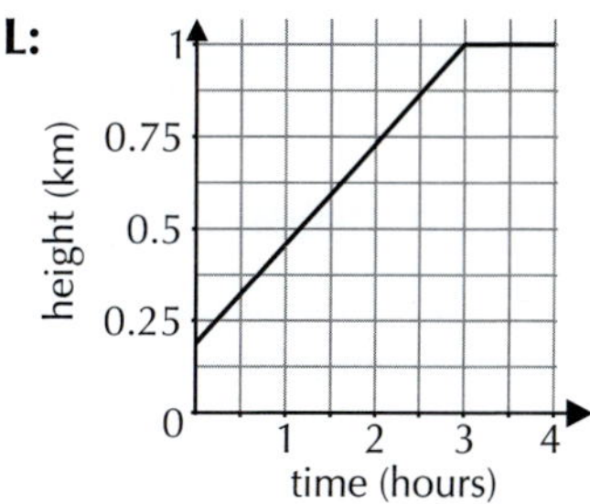

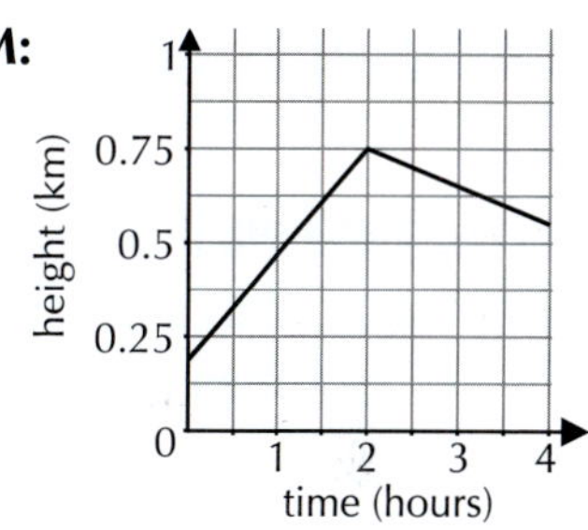

a) Which climbers reached the summit? Explain your answer.

b) Which climber reached the summit first?

Non-linear Graphs

Learning Objective — Spec Ref A14:
Understand and interpret curves that represent real-life situations.

Tip: A non-linear graph is a graph that isn't a straight line.

Graphs describing **real-life situations** can be almost **any shape**. Whatever the shape, the gradient (steepness of the graph) still shows the **rate of change** — how fast the y-axis quantity is changing compared to the x-axis quantity.

When describing a **non-linear graph**, look at the **direction** and **gradient** like you did for linear graphs on p.220 — and look out for any **change** in **direction** or **gradient**.

Use the **method** you saw on p.219 to **read off** values from a non-linear graph.

Example 3

The graph shows the temperature of an oven as it heats up.

a) Describe how the temperature of the oven changes during the first 10 minutes shown on the graph.

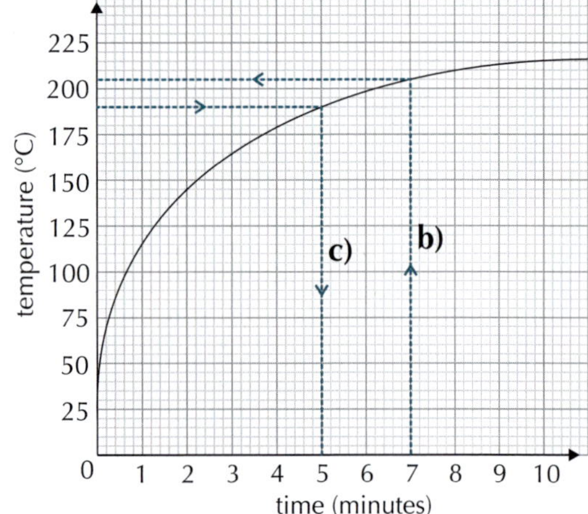

1. Look at the direction of the graph — temperature is increasing with time.
2. The gradient of the graph is steep initially and quite flat towards the end.
3. The graph doesn't change direction (it keeps increasing), but the gradient decreases over time.
4. Relate these features to the context:

The temperature of the oven **rises** for the entire 10 minutes. This rise is **rapid at first** but then **becomes slower** as the oven heats up.

b) What is the temperature of the oven after 7 minutes?

Follow the grid upwards from 7 minutes until you reach the curve, then read across to find the temperature.

After 7 minutes the oven is at **205 °C**.

c) How long does it take for the temperature to reach 190 °C?

Follow the grid across from 190 °C until you reach the curve, then read down to find the number of minutes.

It takes **5 minutes** for the oven to reach 190 °C.

Exercise 3

Q1 Each statement below describes one of the graphs to the right. Match each statement with the correct graph.

a) The temperature rose quickly, and then fell again gradually.

b) The number of people who needed hospital treatment stayed at the same level all year.

c) The cost of gold went up more and more quickly.

d) The temperature fell overnight, but then climbed quickly again the next morning.

K:

L:

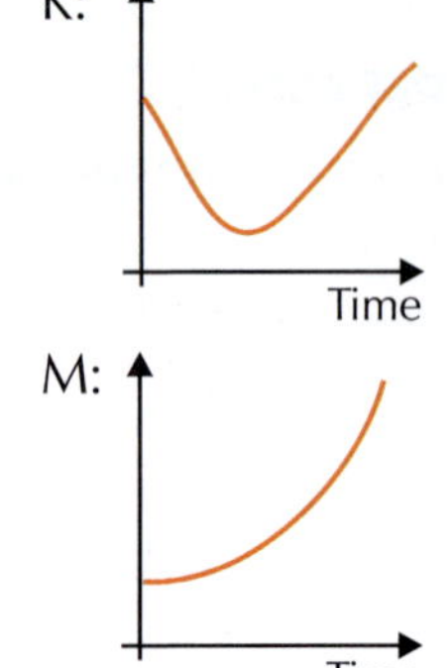

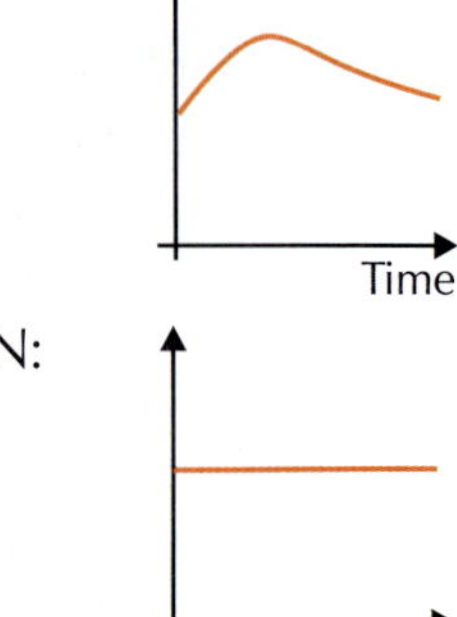

M:

Time

N:

Time

Q2 The graph shows the depth of water in a harbour one day between the times of 08:00 and 20:00.

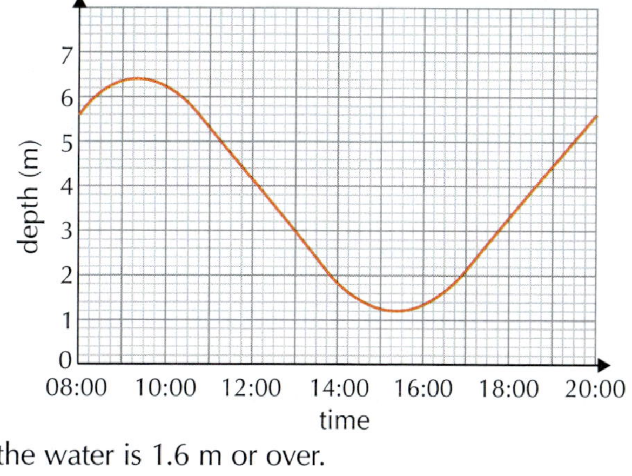

a) Describe how the depth of water changed over this time period.

b) At approximately what time was the depth of water the greatest?

c) What was the minimum depth of water during this period?

d) At approximately what times was the water 3 m deep?

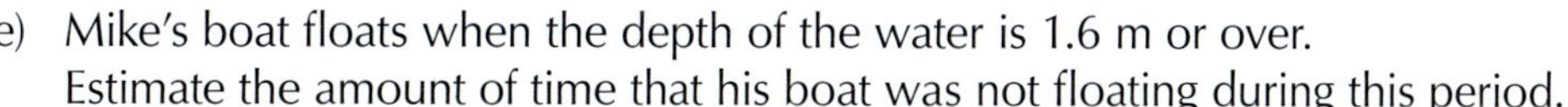

e) Mike's boat floats when the depth of the water is 1.6 m or over. Estimate the amount of time that his boat was not floating during this period.

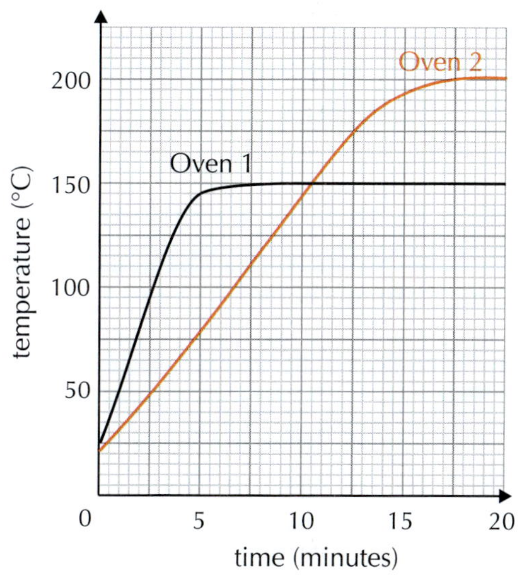

Q3 The graph on the left shows the temperature in two ovens as they warm up.

a) Which oven reaches 100 °C more quickly?

b) Which oven reaches a higher maximum temperature?

c) Estimate how long it takes Oven 2 to reach its maximum temperature.

d) (i) After how long are the two ovens at the same temperature?

(ii) What temperature do they both reach at this time?

e) What do the gradients of the lines represent?

Q4 a) Vase P is 30 cm tall. The depth of water in Vase P as it is filled up is shown on the graph below. By how much does the depth of water in P increase:

(i) between 0 and 5 seconds?

(ii) between 10 and 15 seconds?

(iii) between 25 and 30 seconds?

b) Vase Q is also 30 cm tall. The depth of water in Vase Q is also shown on the graph. By how much does the depth of water in Q increase:

(i) between 0 and 5 seconds?

(ii) between 10 and 15 seconds?

(iii) between 25 and 30 seconds?

c) Describe the difference between how the depth of water increases in Vase P and Vase Q.

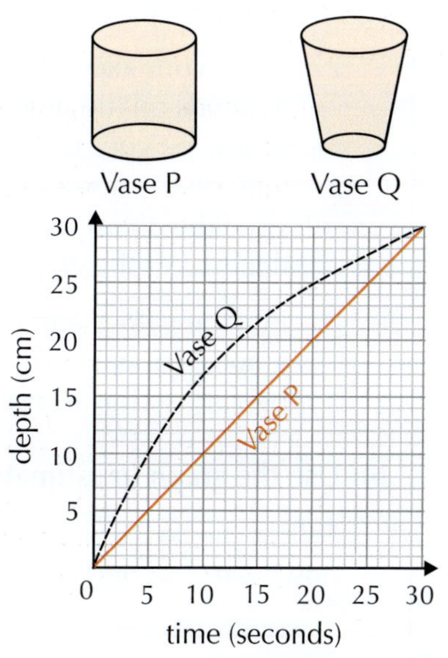

13.2 Drawing Real-Life Graphs

Now you know how to interpret real-life graphs, it's time to have a go at drawing them. You'll need a ruler to draw straight lines and a steady hand to draw smooth curves.

Learning Objective — Spec Ref A14:
Draw graphs that represent real-life situations.

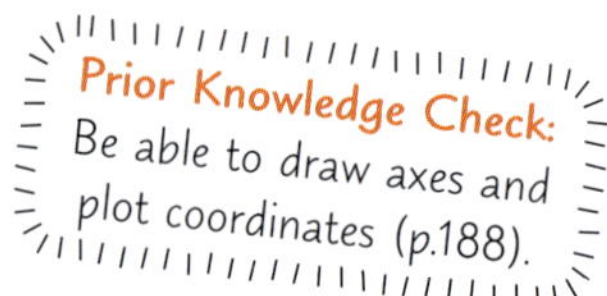

Prior Knowledge Check:
Be able to draw axes and plot coordinates (p.188).

To **draw** a graph representing a **real-life situation** you need to:

- Fill a **table of values** of points to plot. For a **straight line**, you'll need at least **three** points. But if the graph is a **curve**, you'll need **more than three** points.
- Draw and label your **axes** — the variable that **depends** on the other usually goes on the **vertical axis**.
- Then **plot** the points from the table as **coordinates** and join them by drawing a **straight line** or a **smooth curve** through them.

Tip: Make sure your axes are long enough to fit on all the points from your table.

Example 1

A plumber charges customers a standard fee of £40, plus £30 per hour for all work carried out.

a) Draw a graph to show how the plumber's fee varies with the amount of time the job takes.

1. Make a table showing the fee for different numbers of hours.
   A 1-hour job costs £40 + £30 = £70.
   A 2-hour job costs £40 + (2 × £30) = £100.
   A 3-hour job costs £40 + (3 × £30) = £130, etc.

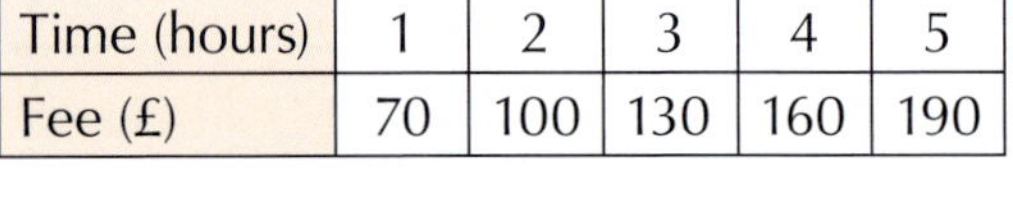

Time (hours)	1	2	3	4	5
Fee (£)	70	100	130	160	190

2. Draw your axes. The cost of the job depends on the time it takes to complete, so the fee goes on the vertical axis and time on the horizontal axis. Make sure you label them and choose a scale that makes the graph easy to read.
3. Plot the values and join the points to draw the graph. For each extra hour, the fee increases by £30, so this is a straight-line graph.

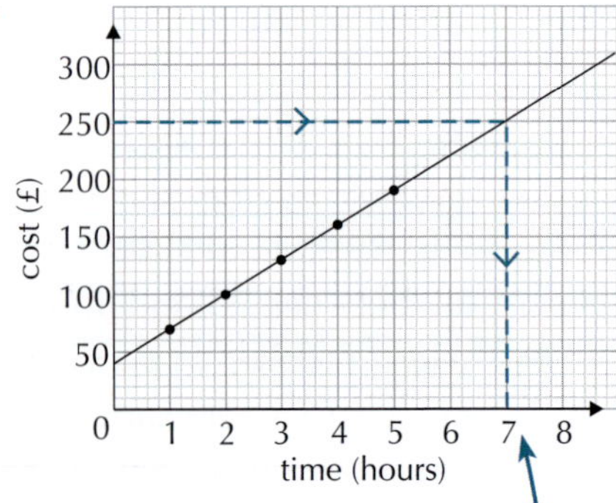

b) Use the graph to estimate the amount of time taken to do a job costing £250.

Follow the grid across from £250, then read downwards to find the correct time.

The job would have taken **7 hours**.

Example 2

The temperature of a cup of tea was measured at regular intervals as it cooled down. Draw a graph to illustrate how the temperature of the tea changes over time.

Time (minutes)	1	2	3	4	5	6
Temperature (°C)	80	78	73	62	50	43

1. Draw the axes — the temperature goes on the vertical axis and time on the horizontal axis. The temperature values are between 43 °C and 80 °C, so you can cut some of the vertical axis from the bottom of the scale.
2. Plot the values in the table as coordinates.
3. Draw a smooth curve through the points. There shouldn't be any sudden changes of direction or sharp kinks.

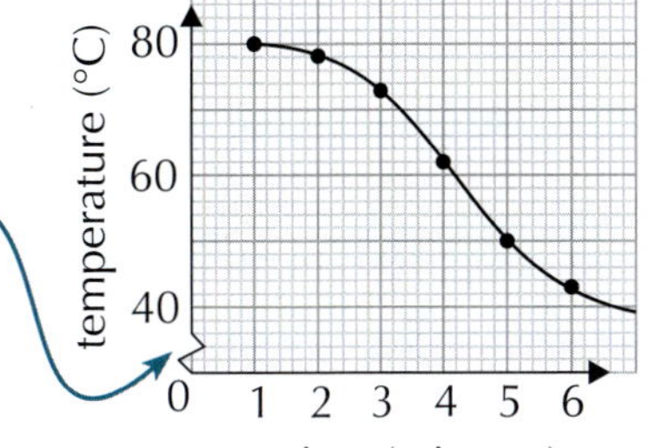

Exercise 1

Q1 The instructions for cooking different weights of chicken are as follows:

'Cook for 35 mins per kg, plus an extra 25 minutes.'

a) Copy and complete the table to show the cooking times for chickens of different weights.

Weight (kg)	1	2	3	4	5
Time (minutes)					

b) Draw a set of axes on a sheet of graph paper. Plot the time on the vertical axis and the weight on the horizontal axis. Then plot the values from your table to draw a graph showing the cooking times for different weights of chicken.

c) A chicken cooks in 110 minutes. What is the weight of the chicken?

Q2 This table shows how the fuel efficiency of a car in miles per gallon (mpg) varies with the speed of the car in miles per hour (mph).

Speed (mph)	55	60	65	70	75	80
Fuel Efficiency (mpg)	32.3	30.7	28.9	27.0	24.9	22.7

a) Plot the points from the table on a pair of axes and join them with a smooth curve.

b) Use your graph to predict the fuel efficiency of the car when it is travelling at 73 mph.

Review Exercise

Q1 The graph on the right can be used to convert between kilometres per hour (km/h) and miles per hour (mph).

a) Convert 38 km/h into miles per hour.

b) Convert 27 mph into km/h.

c) The speed limit on a particular road is 30 mph. A driver travels at 52 km/h. By how many miles per hour is the driver breaking the speed limit?

d) The maximum speed limit in the UK is 70 mph. The maximum speed limit in Spain is 120 km/h. Which country has the higher speed limit, and by how much?

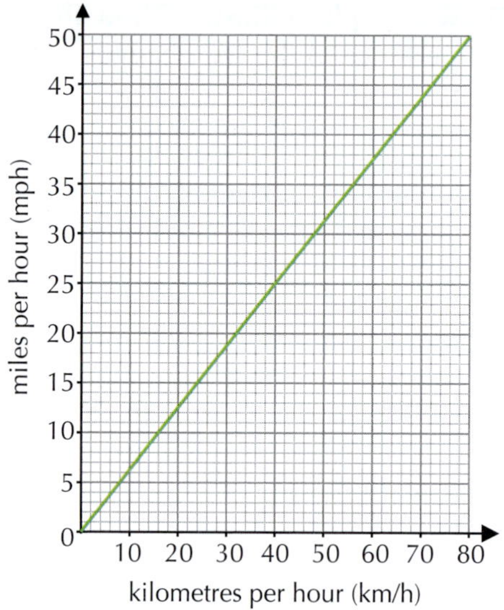

Q2 A scientist is conducting an experiment. The graph on the right shows the temperature of the experiment after t seconds.

a) Give a brief description of how the temperature changes in the first 8 seconds of the experiment.

b) State the maximum temperature that it reaches.

c) A temperature of 8 °C was recorded twice. At what times was the temperature 8 °C?

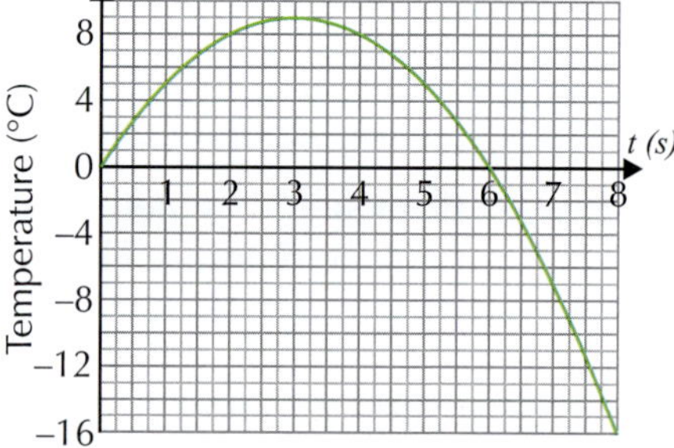

Q3 Helena is a baby girl. A health visitor records the weight of Helena every two months. The measurements are shown in the table below.

Age (months)	0	2	4	6	8	10	12	14	16
Weight (kg)	3.2	4.6	5.9	7.0	7.9	8.7	9.3	9.8	10.2

a) Draw a graph to show this information.
Plot age on the horizontal axis and weight on the vertical axis.
Join your points with a smooth curve.

b) Keira is 9 months old and has a weight of 9.1 kg.
Use your graph to estimate how much heavier Keira is than Helena was at 9 months old.

Exam-Style Questions

Q1 The graph below shows how the depth of a lake varies, measured between a point on beach A and a point on beach B on the opposite side of the lake.

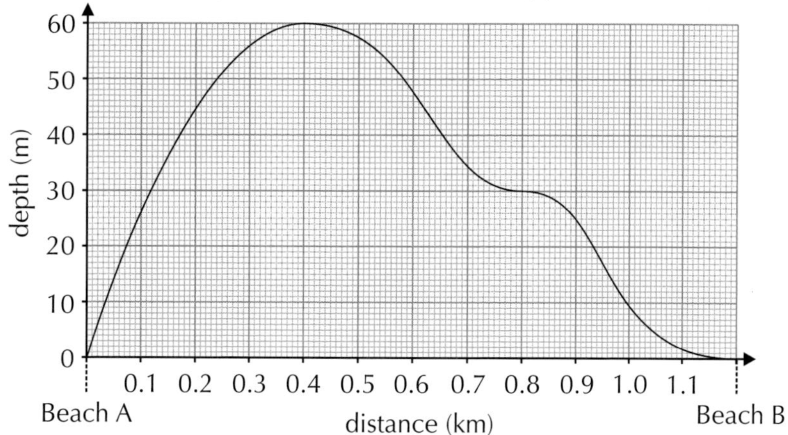

a) What is the maximum depth of the lake between the two beaches?

[1 mark]

b) Herons are long-legged birds that fish in shallow water. On which beach would you most likely find herons? Explain your answer.

[2 marks]

Q2 A cafe buys coffee beans from suppliers in Kenya and Peru.
The Kenyan supplier charges a rate of £2.50 per kilogram.
The Peruvian supplier charges a rate of £1 per kilogram, plus a fixed fee of £25.

a) Complete the following table of values.

Weight (kg)	10	20	30	40	50
Cost (£) of Kenyan coffee	25	50			
Cost (£) of Peruvian coffee	35				

[2 marks]

b) Using your table, draw a graph showing how the cost of Kenyan coffee beans varies with the weight of the beans purchased.

[2 marks]

c) On the same axes as part a), draw the graph for Peruvian coffee beans.

[2 marks]

d) Estimate the weight at which the two suppliers charge the same amount.

[1 mark]

14.1 Direct Proportion

Proportion is about how things change in relation to each other.
If two things are in direct proportion, they increase and decrease together.

Learning Objective — Spec Ref R7/R10:
Understand and use direct proportion.

Saying two things are in **direct proportion** means the **ratio** between them is always the **same**. For example, if one item costs £2, two items will cost £4, three items will cost £6, etc. — the ratio is always 1 item : £2. Quantities that are in direct proportion **increase** or **decrease** by the same **scale factor** — e.g. if you double the number of items, the cost doubles as well.

You can solve direct proportion problems using this method:

- **Divide** to find out how much of one thing you get for every **one** of the other — e.g. the price per item.
- Then **multiply** to find the **scaled** amount — e.g. the cost of 8 items.

Just remember: **DIVIDE FOR ONE, THEN MULTIPLY FOR ALL**

Example 1

If 8 chocolate bars cost £6, calculate the cost of 10 chocolate bars.

1. Divide the cost of 8 bars by 8 to find the cost of 1 bar.
2. Then multiply by 10 to find the cost of 10 chocolate bars.

8 bars cost £6
1 bar costs £6 ÷ 8 = £0.75
10 bars cost £0.75 × 10 = **£7.50**

Example 2

Oliver has 30 euros (€) left over from a holiday in France. If the exchange rate is £1 = €1.14, how many pounds can he exchange his euros for?

1. Divide both sides of the equation "£1 = €1.14" by 1.14 to find the number of pounds per euro.

€1.14 = £1
€1 = £1 ÷ 1.14 = £0.877...

2. Then multiply this by the number of euros Oliver has.

€30 = 30 × £0.877...
= **£26.32**
(to the nearest penny)

Tip: You're given the ratio of euros to pounds, but you need to find the ratio of pounds to euros.

Exercise 1

Q1 If 1 pair of jeans costs £35, find the cost of the following:
a) 2 pairs of jeans b) 5 pairs of jeans c) 20 pairs of jeans

Q2 The cost of 8 identical books is £36. What is the cost of 12 of these books?

Q3 If 1 DVD costs £7.50, work out how many DVDs you can buy for: a) £22.50 b) £60

Q4 A car uses 35 litres of petrol to travel 250 km.
a) How far, to the nearest km, can the car travel on 50 litres of petrol?
b) How many litres of petrol would the car use to travel 400 km?

Q5 Grace buys 11 pens for £12.32 and 6 note pads for £5.88.
How much would she pay altogether for 8 pens and 5 note pads?

You can use the proportion method to work out which of a set of options is the **best value for money**. Just use the 'divide for one' part to get the **cost per item** (or amount of the item per penny), and then **compare** them.

Example 3

A supermarket sells bread buns in packs of 6, 12 and 24.
The pack of 6 costs 78p, the pack of 12 costs £1.44 and the pack of 24 costs £3.00.
Which pack size represents the best value for money?

1. For each pack divide the cost by the pack size to get the price per bread bun.
2. The pack with the best value for money is the one with the lowest cost per bread bun.

6 pack: 78p ÷ 6 = 13p per bread bun
12 pack: £1.44 ÷ 12 = 12p per bread bun
24 pack: £3.00 ÷ 24 = 12.5p per bread bun

The **12 pack** is the best value for money.

Exercise 2

Q1 A greengrocer's sells apples individually, in packs of 6, or in bags of 10. They cost 30p each individually, the pack of 6 costs £1.50, and the bag of 10 costs £2.40.
Which of these options represents the best value for money?

Q2 A coffee shop sells coffee in small, medium and large cups. A small coffee is 240 ml and costs £2, a medium coffee is 350 ml and costs £3, and a large coffee is 470 ml and costs £4. Which size of cup represents the best value for money?

Q3 Sausages are sold in packs of 6, 8 or 10. The pack of 6 costs £2.18, the pack of 8 costs £2.80, and the pack of 10 costs £3.46. Which pack represents the best value for money?

Graphs of Direct Proportion

Learning Objective — Spec Ref R10:

Recognise, interpret and be able to draw the graphs of two directly proportional quantities.

Prior Knowledge Check:

Be able to draw and interpret straight lines on a graph. See p.194, p.219-220.

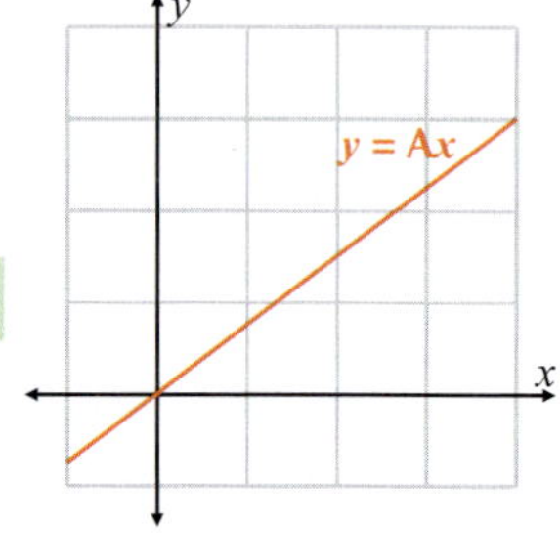

Two quantities are **directly proportional** if, when you plot them on a graph, you get a **straight line** through the **origin**.

The **general equation** for two quantities in direct proportion is $\mathbf{y = Ax}$ where y is directly proportional to x and A is just a number.

Example 4

y is directly proportional to x. When $x = 10$, $y = 25$.

Sketch the graph of this direct proportion.

1. A sketch only requires the rough shape of the graph with the important points labelled.
2. As x and y are directly proportional, the graph is a straight line through the origin. You also know that it goes through the point (10, 25), so mark these two points and draw a straight line through them.

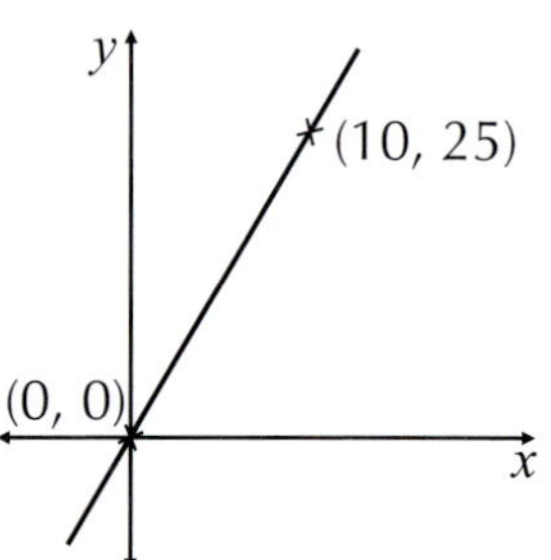

Example 5

y is directly proportional to x. Fill in the gaps in the table below.

x	3	5	10	12	
y		25			100

1. From the table you can see that when $x = 5$, $y = 25$. You can use the 'divide for one, multiply for all' method to find the missing values.
2. Divide x and y by 5 to find the value of y when $x = 1$. When $x = 1$, $y = 25 \div 5 = 5$.
3. Now multiply each value of x in the table by 5 to get the missing values of y, and divide the value of y by 5 to get the missing value of x.

x	3	5	10	12	$100 \div 5 =$ **20**
y	$3 \times 5 =$ **15**	25	$10 \times 5 =$ **50**	$12 \times 5 =$ **60**	100

Exercise 3

Q1 Which of these graphs shows that y is directly proportional to x? Explain your answer.

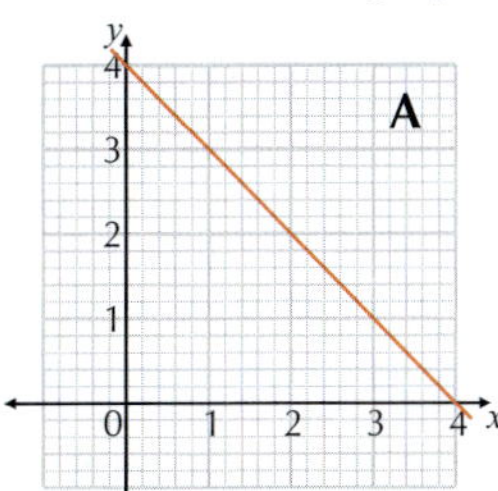

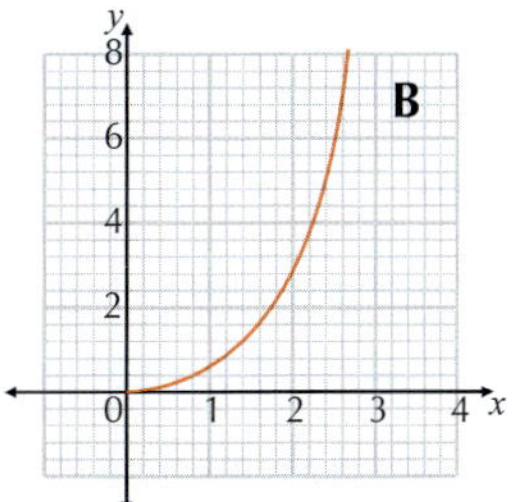

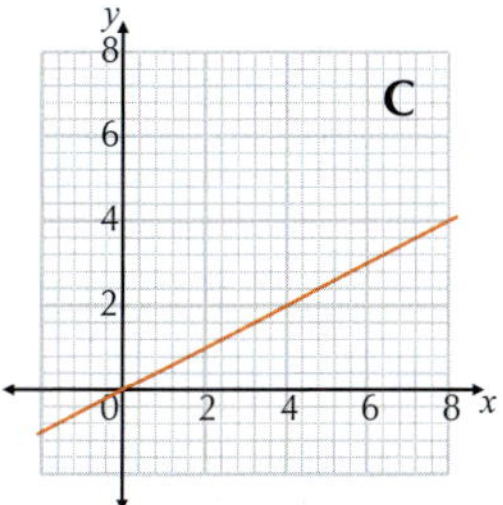

Q2 Sketch the graphs of the following proportions:

a) y is directly proportional to x. When $x = 20$, $y = 8$.

b) s is directly proportional to t. When $t = 80$, $s = 15$.

Q3 In each of the following tables, y is directly proportional to x.

(i) Copy and complete each table. (ii) Draw the graph of each direct proportion.

a)

x	8	12
y	2	

b)

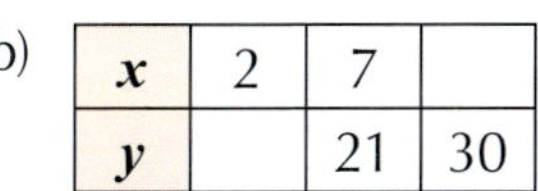

x	2	7	
y		21	30

c)

x	–2	0	3	
y	–10			30

Example 6

y is directly proportional to x. When $y = 42$, $x = 6$.

a) Write an equation in the form $y = Ax$ to represent this direct proportion.

1. Put the values of x and y into the equation $y = Ax$ and rearrange it to find A.

$y = Ax$
$42 = A \times 6$
$A = 42 \div 6 = 7$

2. Put your value of A into the equation $y = Ax$.

$\mathbf{y = 7x}$

b) Calculate the value of y when $x = 51$.

Substitute $x = 51$ into your equation from part a).

$y = 7 \times 51 = \mathbf{357}$

Exercise 4

Q1 j is directly proportional to h. When $j = 15$, $h = 5$.

a) Write an equation to represent this direct proportion.

b) Work out the value of j when $h = 40$.

c) Sketch the graph of this direct proportion.

Q2 p is directly proportional to q. When $p = 14$, $q = 4$.

a) Accurately draw the graph of this direct proportion.

b) Use your graph to find the value of p when $q = 8$.

14.2 Inverse Proportion

If two things are inversely proportional, one thing gets smaller as the other gets bigger.

Learning Objective — Spec Ref R7/R10:
Understand and use inverse proportion.

If the two quantities are **inversely proportional**, then one quantity decreases as another increases. For example, **speed** and **time** are inversely proportional, so if you run faster (speed **increases**), it will take less time to finish a race (time **decreases**).

Solving inverse proportion problems is the **opposite** of solving direct proportion problems, so you need to switch the method from p.228 around.

For inverse proportion problems:

MULTIPLY FOR ONE, THEN DIVIDE FOR ALL

Example 1

Four people take five hours to dig a hole.
How long would it take ten people to dig the same sized hole at the same rate?

1. Multiply the time by 4 (the number of people) to find the time it would take one person.

   4 people take 5 hours
   1 person will take
   $5 \times 4 = 20$ hours

2. Divide by 10 (the new number of people) to find the time for 10 people.

   10 people will take
   $20 \div 10 =$ **2 hours.**

Tip: Check your answer makes sense — there are more people digging, so it should take less time.

Exercise 1

Q1 It takes three people two hours to paint a wall.
How long would it take six people to paint the same wall at the same rate?

Q2 A journey takes two hours when travelling at an average speed of 30 mph.
How long would the same journey take when travelling at an average speed of 45 mph?

Q3 Four chefs can prepare a meal in 20 minutes. They hire an extra chef. How long will it take five chefs to prepare the same meal, working at the same rate as the original four?

Q4 It will take five builders 62 days to complete a particular project.

a) At this rate, how long would the project take if there were only two builders?

b) If the project needed completing in under 40 days, what is the minimum number of builders that would be required?

When **two quantities change**, split the calculation up into **stages** and change one quantity at a time. Decide if the amount should go **up** or **down** at each stage of the calculation.

Example 2

It takes 5 examiners 4 hours to mark 125 exam papers.
How long would it take 8 examiners to mark 200 papers at the same rate?

1. Split the calculation up into stages — first change the number of examiners, then the number of papers.
2. Find how long it would take 1 examiner to mark 125 papers (multiply by 5), then find how long it would take 8 examiners (divide by 8).

To mark 125 papers:
5 examiners take 4 hours
1 examiner takes $4 \times 5 = 20$ hours
8 examiners take $20 \div 8 = 2.5$ hours

3. Find how long it would take 8 examiners to mark 1 paper (divide by 125), then how long it would take them to mark 200 papers (multiply by 200).

For 8 examiners:
1 paper takes $2.5 \div 125 = 0.02$ hours
200 papers take $0.02 \times 200 =$ **4 hours**.

Exercise 2

Q1 It takes 3 hours for two people to clean six identical rooms.
How long would it take five people to clean 20 of the same rooms at the same rate?

Q2 It takes 144 minutes for two bakers to bake 72 identical buns. How long would it take for five bakers to bake 90 of these buns if they each work at the same rate?

Q3 Fourteen people can paint 35 identical plates in two hours.
At this rate, how long would it take 20 people to paint 60 identical plates?

Graphs of Inverse Proportion

Prior Knowledge Check: Recognising and sketching reciprocal graphs. See p.213.

Learning Objective — Spec Ref R10/R13:
Recognise, interpret and be able to draw the graphs of two inversely proportional quantities.

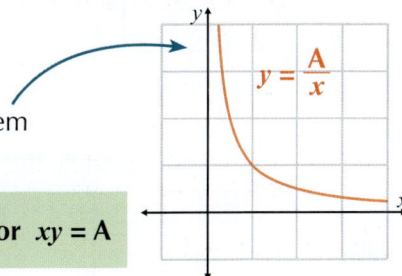

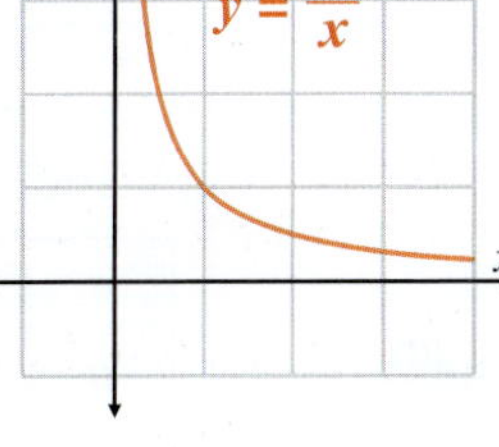

When two quantities are **inversely proportional**, plotting them on a graph looks like this. This is a **reciprocal** graph.

The **general equation** for an inverse proportion is: $y = \frac{A}{x}$ or $xy = A$

Saying 'y is **inversely proportional** to x' is the same as saying 'y is **proportional** to $\frac{1}{x}$' — the two statements are **equivalent**.

Example 3

y is inversely proportional to x. Fill in the gaps in the table below.

x	1		5	10
y		100		20

1. From the table you can see that when $x = 10$, $y = 20$. Using this you can work out A using the equation $xy = A$.
2. Once you know A, you can substitute in either x or y to find the other. E.g. when $x = 5$, $5y = 200$ so $y = 40$

When $x = 10$ and $y = 20$
$A = 10 \times 20 = 200$

x	1	$x \times 100 = 200$ $x = 200 \div 100 = \mathbf{2}$	5	10
y	$y = \mathbf{200}$	100	$5 \times y = 200$ $y = 200 \div 5 = \mathbf{40}$	20

Exercise 3

Q1 Which of these graphs shows that y is inversely proportional to x? Explain your answer.

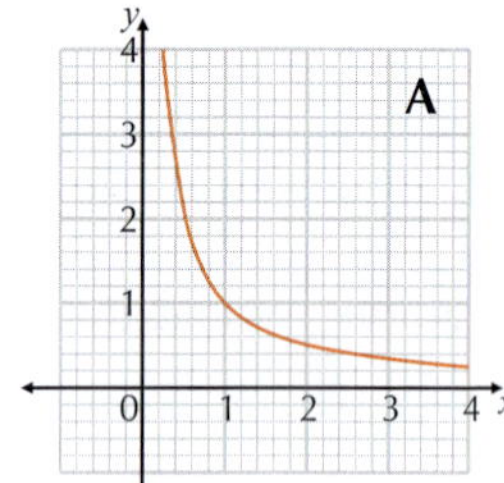

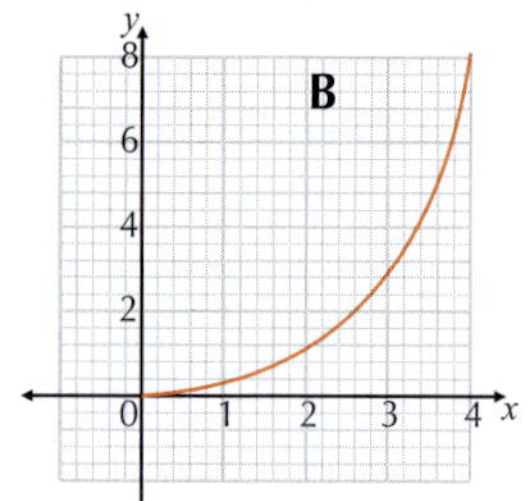

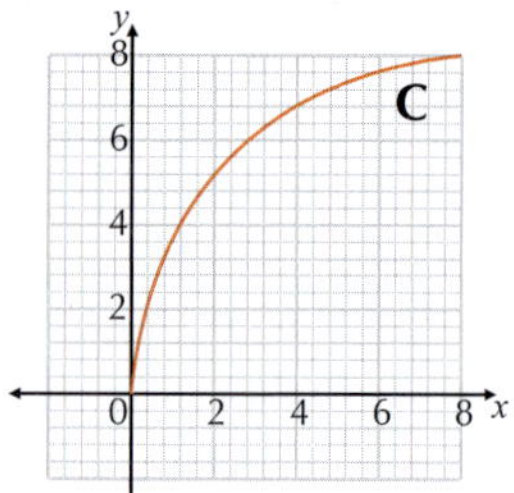

Q2 Which of the equations below show that y is inversely proportional to x?

$y = \frac{4}{x}$ $\quad$ $y = \frac{7}{x} + 3$ $\quad$ $\frac{y}{x} = 8$ $\quad$ $yx = 9$ $\quad$ $y = 3 - \frac{1}{x}$

Q3 In each of the following tables, y is inversely proportional to x. Use this information to copy and complete each table.

a)

x	12	6
y	15	

b)

x	2	4	8	10
y			20	

c)

x		4	20	100
y	320		4	

Q4 p is inversely proportional to q.

a) Copy and complete the following table:

q	0.2	0.4	0.5	1	2	4	5	10
p					1			

b) Use the table to draw the graph of this inverse proportion.

Review Exercise

Q1 It costs £20 to put 12.5 litres of petrol in a car.
How much will it cost for a full tank of petrol, if the tank holds 60 litres?

Q2 Emma changed £500 into rand (R) before going on holiday to South Africa.
The exchange rate at the time was £1 = R 17.5.

a) How many rand did she get for her £500?

On holiday Emma spent R 6200. When she got home, she changed the rand she had left over back into pounds. The exchange rate had changed to £1 = R 16.9.

b) How much money, in pounds, did she get back? 

Q3 It takes a runner 8 minutes to run 5 laps of a 400 m track. How many minutes will it take the runner, running at the same speed, to complete 9 laps of a 200 m track?

PROBLEM SOLVING

Q4 A shop sells chocolates in different sized boxes. A box of 8 chocolates costs £3.50, a box of 12 chocolates costs £4.70, and a box of 20 chocolates costs £8.15.
Which of these represents the best value for money?

Q5 b is directly proportional to a.

a	2	4	7	10
b	6			

a) Copy and complete the table.

b) Use the table to draw an accurate graph of this direct proportion.

Q6 y is directly proportional to x and when $y = 32$, $x = 4$. 

a) Find y when $x = 8$.

b) Find x when $y = 48$.

c) Find an equation in the form $y = Ax$ to represent this direct proportion.

Q7 8 chickens will lay 20 eggs in 3 days. The chickens always lay eggs at the same rate.

a) How many days will it take 12 chickens to lay 20 eggs?

b) How many chickens would be required if a farmer needed 30 eggs each day?

Q8 In each of the following tables, y is inversely proportional to x.
Use this information to copy and complete the following tables.

a)

x		7
y	25.2	9

b)

x		3	6	30
y	180		15	

Exam-Style Questions

Q1 Kitchen rolls each have 100 sheets per roll and cost £1.20. The manufacturer reduces the number of sheets on a roll to 90 and the price to £1.10.

Is the new roll better value for money than the original? Show your working.

[2 marks]

Q2 Hermain uses this recipe to make muffins. 

Makes 12 muffins:	
360 g	self-raising flour
200 g	caster sugar
250 ml	milk
125 ml	vegetable oil
4	medium eggs

a) Work out how much self-raising flour she will need to make 20 muffins.

[2 marks]

b) Sketch a graph to represent the relationship between the number of muffins Hermain makes and the amount of caster sugar she needs.

[2 marks]

Q3 Niall is cleaning the carpets in a hotel. The foyer area has 258 m^2 of carpet which takes him 24 minutes to clean. The bar area has 68.8 m^2 of carpet.

Work out how long it will take Niall to clean the carpet in the bar area if he works at the same rate, giving your answer in minutes and seconds.

[3 marks]

Q4 At an election, a council employed 840 staff, who counted 45 802 votes in 96 minutes. A second council employed 560 staff to count half as many votes.

a) Estimate how long it took the staff of the second council to count their votes.

[3 marks]

b) What assumption have you made in calculating your answer to part a)?

[1 mark]

15.1 Basic Angle Properties

Angles along a straight line or around a single point always add up to a particular number. You can use these facts to find the size of an unknown angle by forming and solving an equation.

Learning Objectives — Spec Ref G3:
- Find angles that lie on a straight line.
- Find angles that form a right angle.
- Find angles around a point.

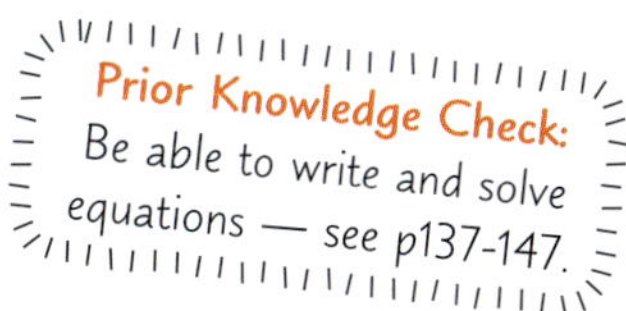

Prior Knowledge Check:
Be able to write and solve equations — see p137-147.

Angles at a point **on a straight line** add up to **180°**.

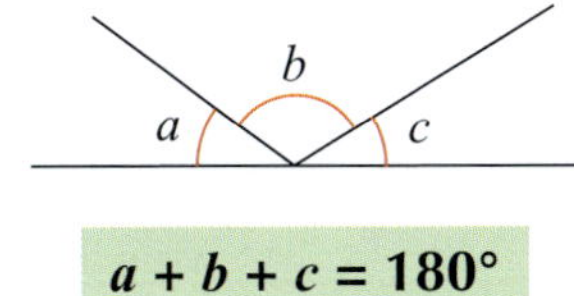

$a + b + c = 180°$

Perpendicular lines meet at 90° to form a **right angle** (shown by the little **square**).

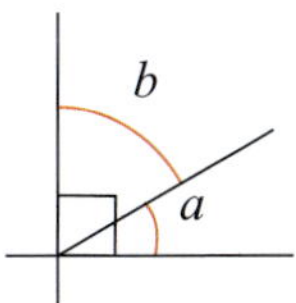

Angles within a **right angle** add up to **90°**.

$a + b = 90°$

Example 1

Find the size of angle *a* in the diagram on the right.

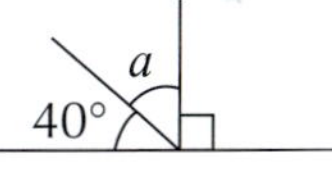

1. Angles on a straight line add up to 180°. Use this to form an equation in terms of a. — $40° + a + 90° = 180°$
2. Simplify the equation. — $a + 130° = 180°$
3. Solve the equation to find a. — $a = 180° - 130°$

$\mathbf{a = 50°}$

Tip: Most of the time angles aren't drawn accurately, so you can't measure them with a protractor.

Exercise 1

Q1 Find the value of each letter in the diagrams below. None of the angles are drawn accurately.

a) 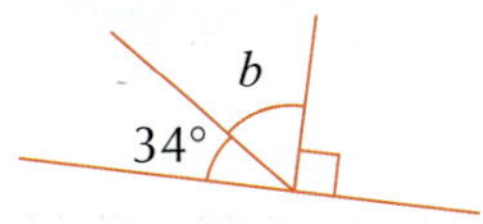

b) 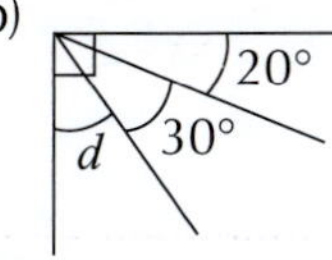

c) 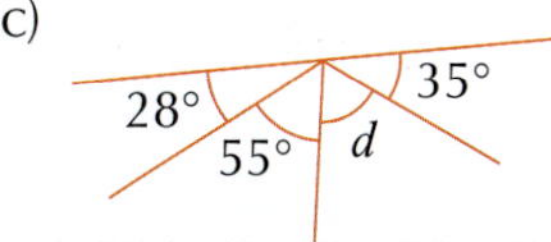

Q2 Find the value of each letter in the diagrams below.
None of the angles are drawn accurately.

a)

b) 110° a a

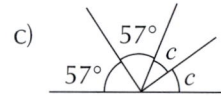

c) 57° 57° c c

Angles around a **point** add up to **360°**.

You can use this fact to find **unknown** angles by writing and **solving** equations, like in the example shown below.

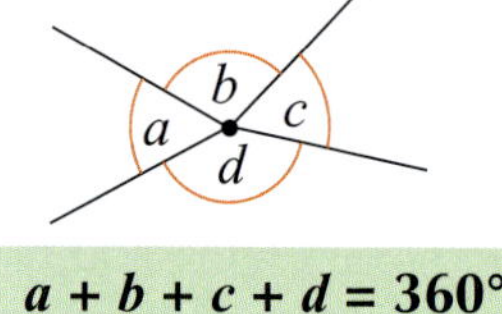

$\boldsymbol{a + b + c + d = 360°}$

Example 2

Find the value of a in the diagram on the right.

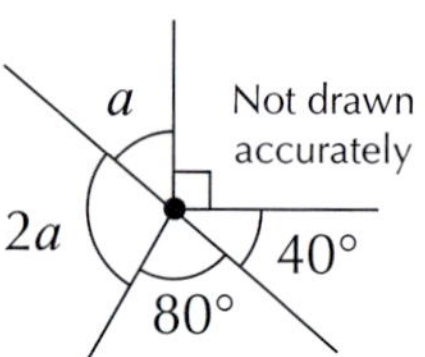

1. The angles are around a point so they must add up to 360°. Use this to form an equation. $a + 2a + 80° + 40° + 90° = 360°$
2. Simplify the equation. $3a + 210° = 360°$
   $3a = 150°$
3. Then solve the equation to find a. $a = 150° \div 3$
   $\boldsymbol{a = 50°}$

Tip: Remember to write the degree symbol in your answer.

Exercise 2

Q1 Find the value of each letter in the diagrams below. None of the angles are drawn accurately.

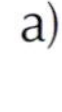

a)

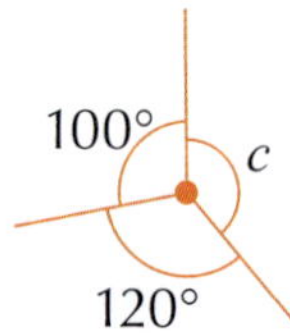

b)

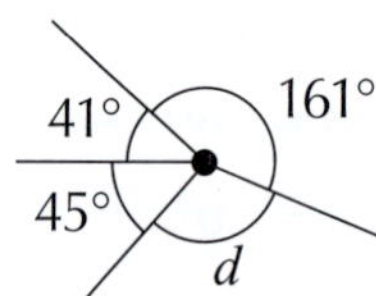

c)

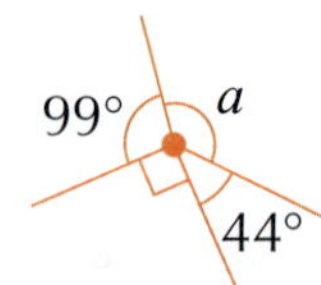

Q2 Find the value of each letter in the diagrams below. None of the angles are drawn accurately.

a)

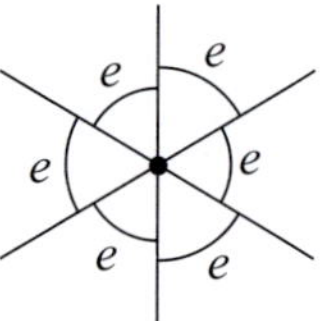

b)

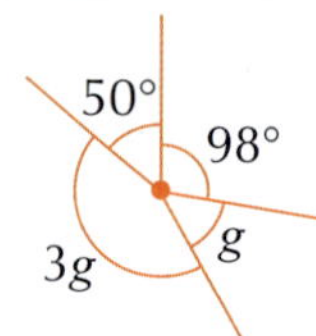

c)

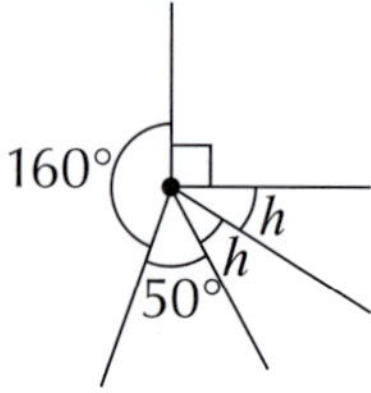

15.2 Parallel and Intersecting Lines

There are a few different rules which connect the angles created where two lines intersect, and where a line crosses two parallel lines. Let's start with the one where just two lines cross...

Vertically Opposite Angles

Learning Objective — Spec Ref G3:
Find vertically opposite angles.

When any **two lines intersect**, it produces **two pairs** of angles.
The angles opposite one another are known as **vertically opposite angles**, and vertically opposite angles are always **equal**.

In the diagram on the right, the two angles **labelled** $\boldsymbol{a}$ are **vertically opposite**, so they are **equal**. Similarly, the two angles **labelled** $\boldsymbol{b}$ are vertically opposite, so they are equal as well.

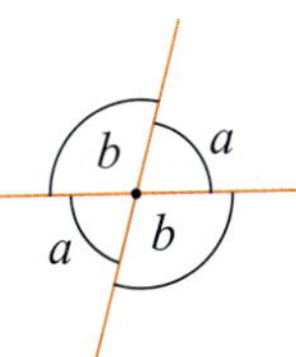

Also, because the two **distinct** angles (i.e. a and b) form a straight line, they add up to **180°** — so $a + b = 180°$.

$$a + b = 180°$$

Example 1

Find the values of a, b and c shown in the diagram below.

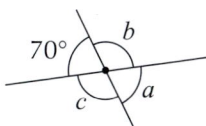

1. a and 70° are vertically opposite angles, so they are equal. — $\boldsymbol{a = 70°}$
2. b and the angle marked 70° lie on a straight line, so they add up to 180°. — $70° + b = 180°$, $b = 180° - 70°$, $\boldsymbol{b = 110°}$
3. c and b are vertically opposite angles, so they are equal. — $c = b = \boldsymbol{110°}$

Exercise 1

Q1 Find the missing angles marked by letters. The angles aren't drawn accurately.

a)

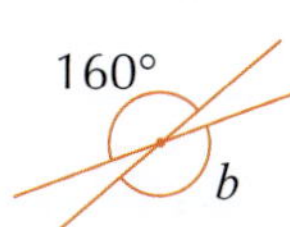

b)

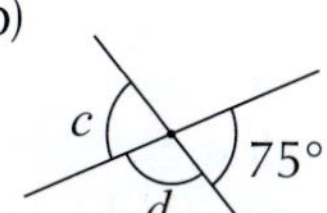

c)

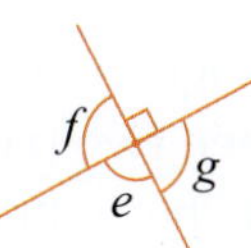

Q2 Find the value of a in the diagram shown on the right.

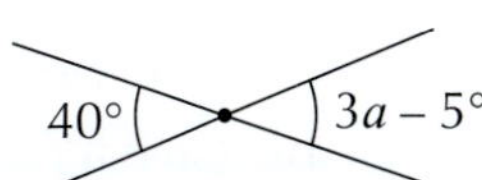

Alternate Angles

Learning Objective — Spec Ref G3:
Find alternate angles.

When a straight line crosses two **parallel** lines, it forms two pairs of **alternate angles** in a sort of **Z-shape** — as shown in the diagrams below. Alternate angles are always **equal**.

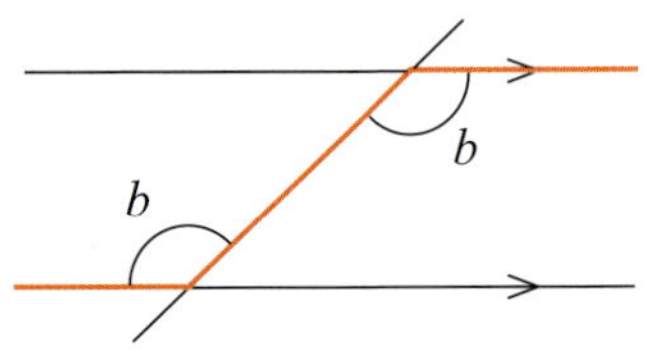

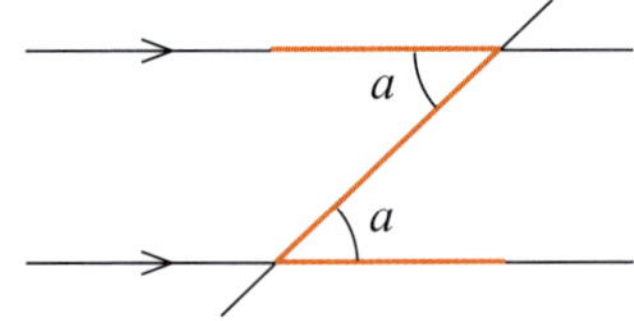

Tip: The small arrows in the diagram show that those two lines are parallel.

Example 2

Find the values of *a*, *b* and *c* in the diagram below.

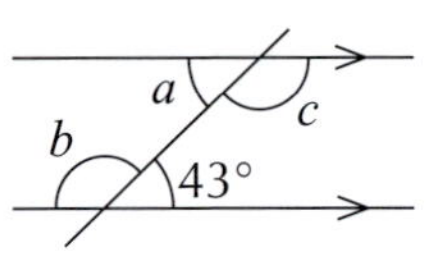

1. *a* and 43° are alternate angles, so they are equal. — $\boldsymbol{a = 43°}$
2. *b* and the angle marked 43° lie on a straight line, so they add up to 180°. — $43° + b = 180°$, $b = 180° - 43°$, $\boldsymbol{b = 137°}$
3. *c* and *b* are alternate angles, so they are equal. — $c = b = \mathbf{137°}$

Exercise 2

Q1 Find the missing angles marked by letters.

a)

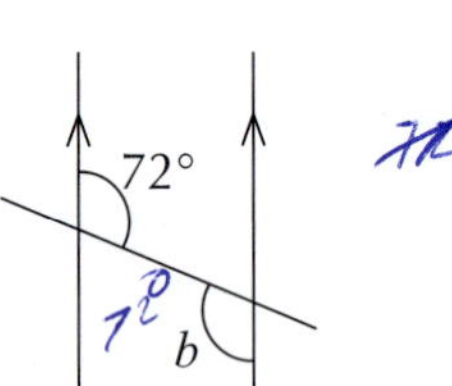

b)

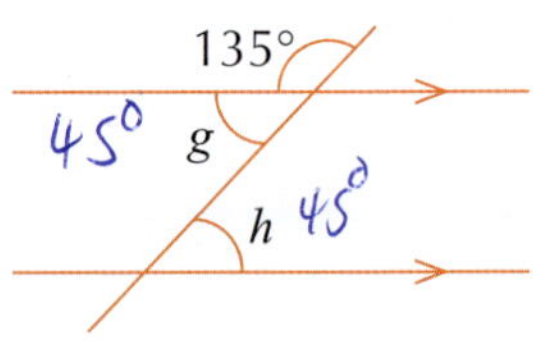

c)

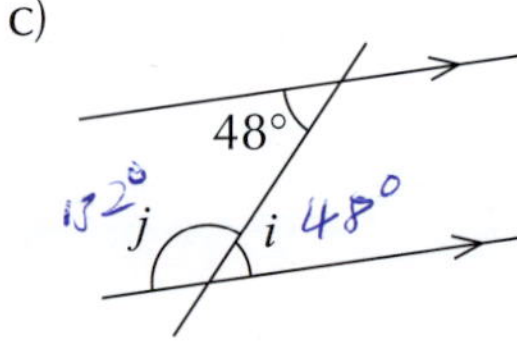

Q2 The diagram on the right shows a staircase between two parallel floors of a building. The staircase makes an angle of 42° with the lower floor.

a) Write down the angle that the staircase makes with the upper floor, marked *x* on the diagram.

b) Give a reason for your answer.

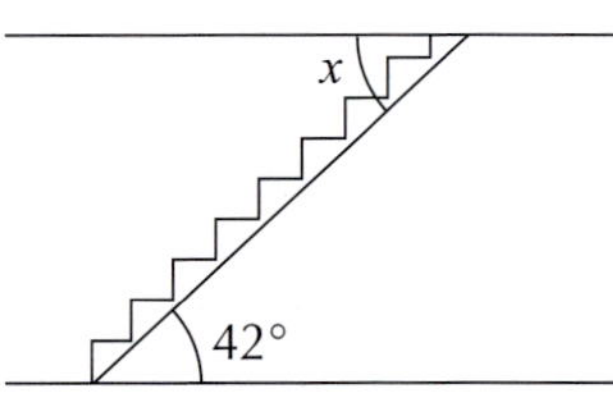

Corresponding Angles and Allied Angles

Learning Objective — Spec Ref G3:
Find corresponding and allied angles.

Corresponding angles form an **F-shape**. Corresponding angles are always **equal**.

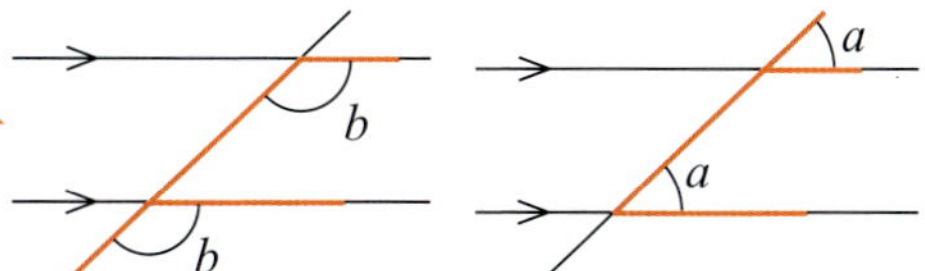

Allied angles form a **C-** or **U-shape**. They always **add up to 180°**.

$a + b = 180°$

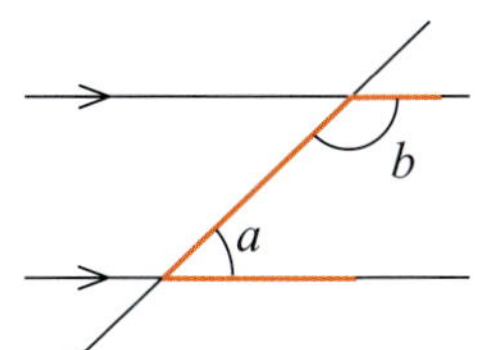

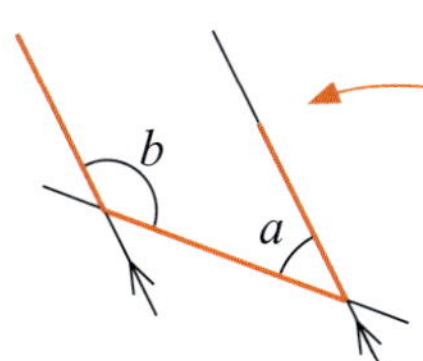

Tip: State which rules you're using when solving geometry problems — e.g. say "because these are allied angles" or "as the angles all lie on a straight line". Make sure you use the proper terms — don't describe them as "angles in a Z-shape".

Example 3

Find the values of *a*, *b* and *c* shown in the diagram below.

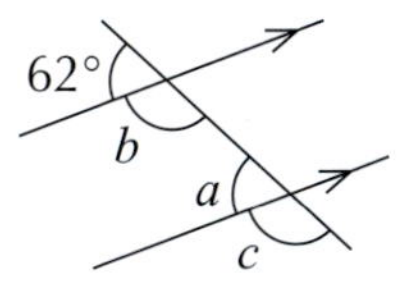

1. *a* and 62° are corresponding angles, so they are equal. **$a = 62°$**
2. *b* and the angle marked 62° lie on a straight line, so they add up to 180°. (Or you could say *a* and *b* are allied angles, so they add up to 180°.) $62° + b = 180°$; $b = 180° - 62°$; **$b = 118°$**
3. *c* and *b* are corresponding angles, so they're equal. **$c = b = 118°$**

Exercise 3

Q1 Find the missing angles marked by letters.

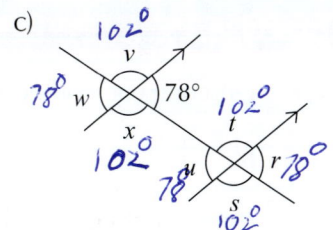

a)

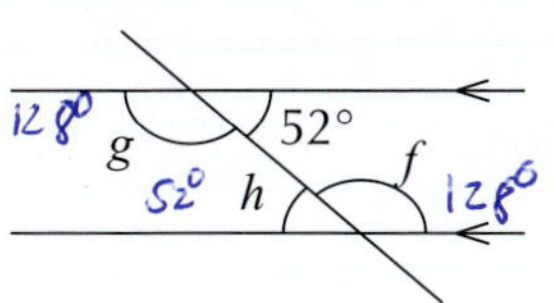

b)

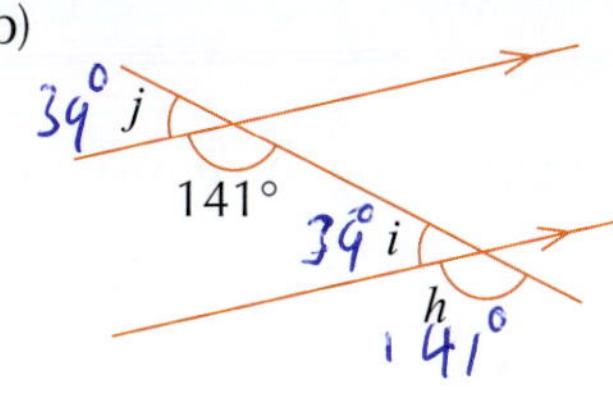

c)

v
w
78°
x
t
u
r
s

Q2 Two wooden posts stand vertically on sloped ground. The first post makes an angle of 99° with the downward slope, as shown. Find the angle that the second post makes with the upward slope, labelled *y* on the diagram.

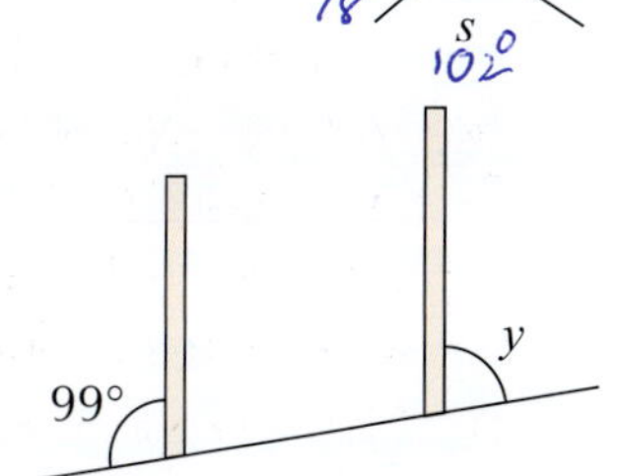

15.3 Triangles

Triangles are perhaps the simplest of the 2D shapes because they only have three sides. But there are different types depending on the lengths of their sides and the sizes of their angles.

Learning Objectives — Spec Ref G3/G4:
- Know the properties of different types of triangles.
- Know and be able to prove that the angles in a triangle sum to 180°.
- Be able to find missing angles in triangles.

There are **different** types of triangles that you need to know about. Make sure you know the defining features of each type.

Tip: 'Tick marks' are used to show sides are the same length.

An **equilateral** triangle has 3 equal sides and 3 equal angles (each of 60°).

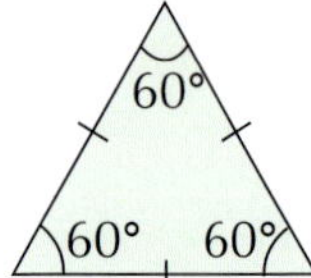

An **isosceles** triangle has 2 equal sides and 2 equal angles.

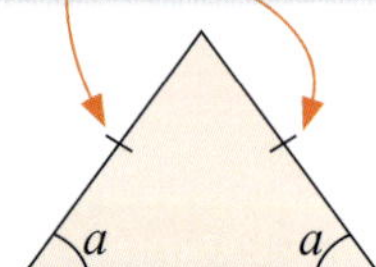

The sides and angles of a **scalene** triangle are all different.

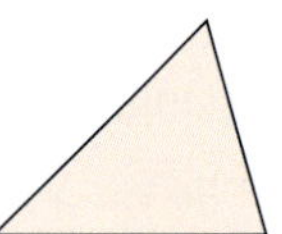

A **right-angled** triangle has 1 right angle (90°).

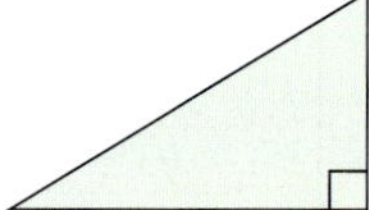

You might occasionally see triangles described by the size of their angles:

An **acute-angled** triangle has 3 acute angles (less than 90°).

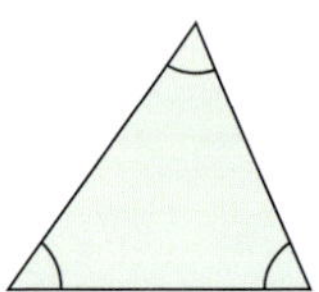

An **obtuse-angled** triangle has 1 obtuse angle (between 90° and 180°).

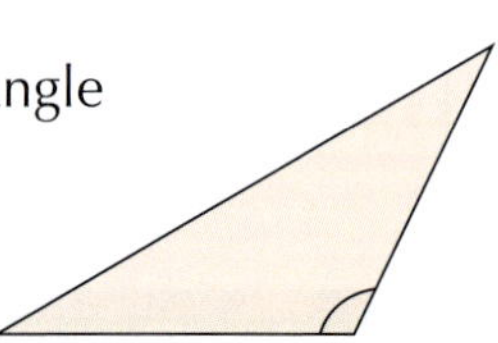

Exercise 1

Q1 Describe each of these triangles using the above definitions.

a) 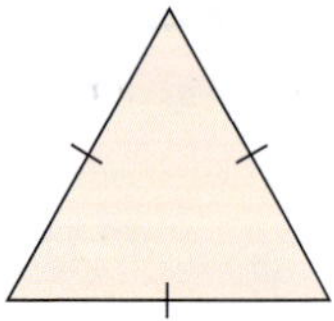

b) 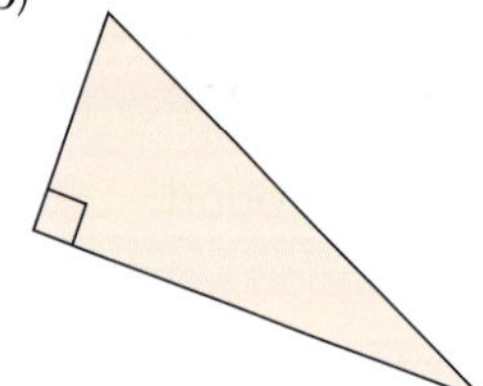

c) 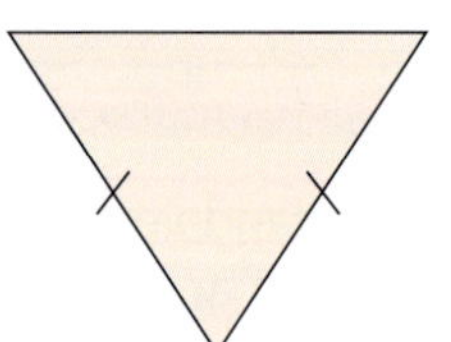

d) 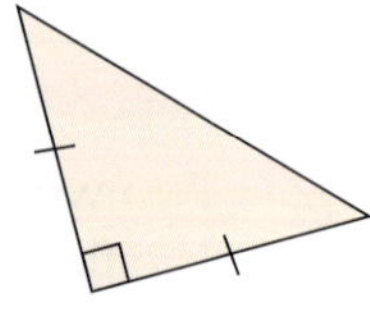

For **any** triangle, the angles inside (a, b and c) **add up to 180°**. You can use this to set up an **equation** that you can **solve** to find missing angles.

$$a + b + c = 180°$$

To **prove** this rule:

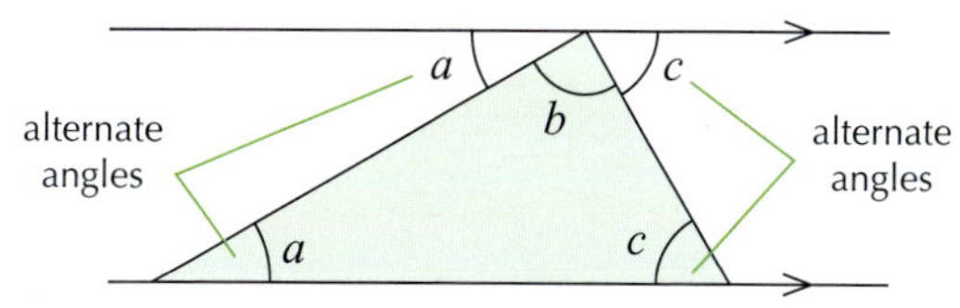

- Draw **parallel lines** at the top and base of the triangle, as shown on the right.
- Then use the fact that **alternate** angles are equal (see page 240) to work out the angles that lie on a **straight line with** b.
- **Angles on a straight line** add up to **180°** (see p.237) — so $a + b + c = 180°$.

Example 1

Find the value of x in the triangle shown below.

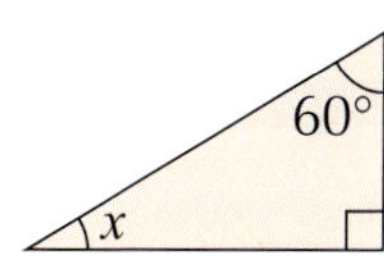

1. The angles in a triangle add up to 180°. Use this to form an equation in terms of x.
   $x + 60° + 90° = 180°$
   $x + 150° = 180°$
2. Solve your equation to find x.
   $x = 180° - 150° = \mathbf{30°}$

Exercise 2

Q1 Find the missing angles marked with letters. Diagrams have not been drawn accurately.

a)

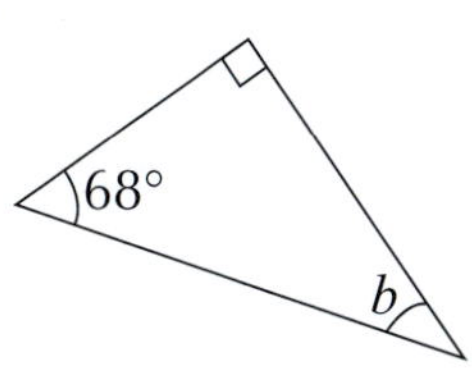

b)

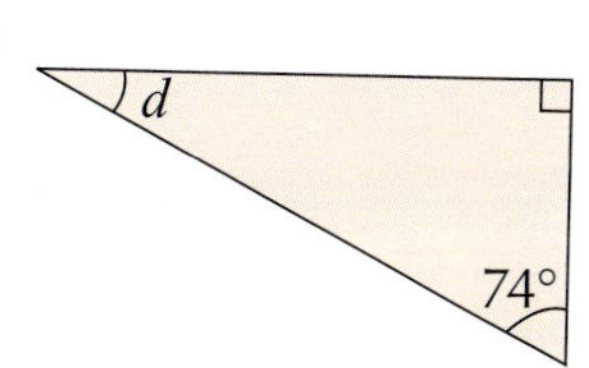

c)

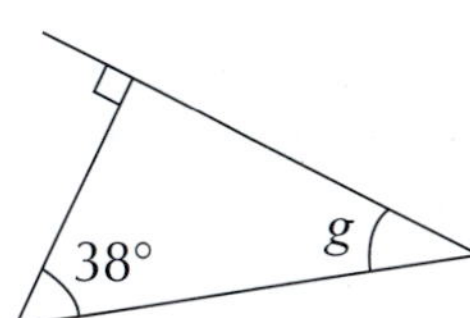

Q2 Look at the diagram on the right. Explain why a triangle with the angles shown in the diagram **cannot** exist.

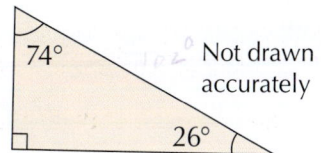

74°
26°
Not drawn accurately

Q3 Find the missing angles marked with letters. Diagrams have not been drawn accurately.

a)

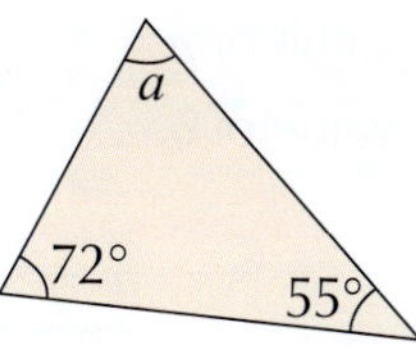

b)

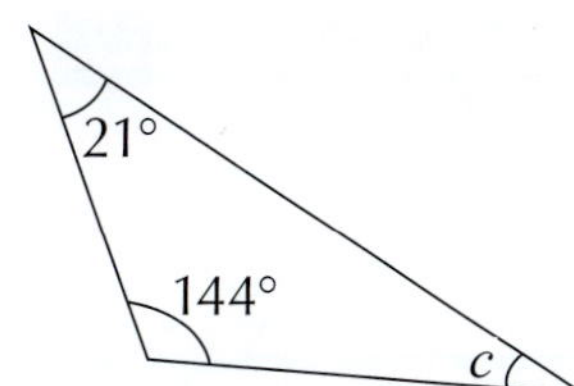

c)

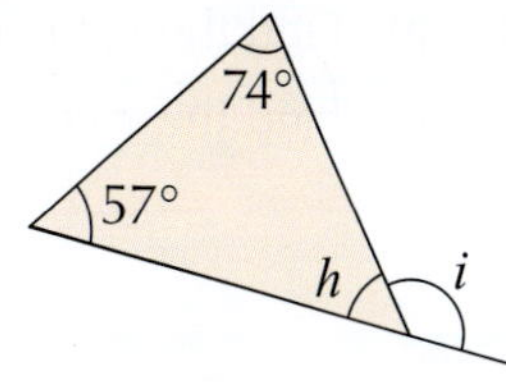

Example 2

a) Find the value of x in the triangle below.

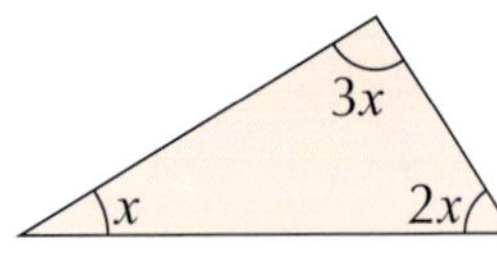

1. The angles in the triangle must add up to 180°, so set up an equation in x.
2. Solve your equation to find x.

$x + 2x + 3x = 180°$
$6x = 180°$
$\boldsymbol{x} = 180° \div 6 = \mathbf{30°}$

b) Find the value of y in the isosceles triangle below.

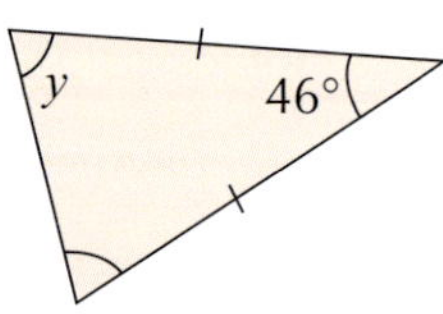

1. The triangle is isosceles so the unmarked angle must be equal to y.
2. All three angles must sum to 180°, so form an equation in y.
3. Solve your equation to find y.

$y + y + 46° = 180°$
$2y = 134°$
$\boldsymbol{y} = 134° \div 2 = \mathbf{67°}$

Exercise 3

The angles in this exercise have not been drawn accurately, so don't try to measure them.

Q1 Find the values of the letters shown in the following diagrams.

a)
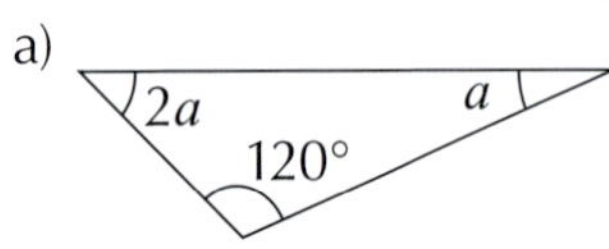

b)
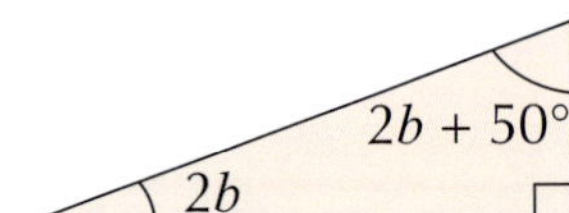

c)
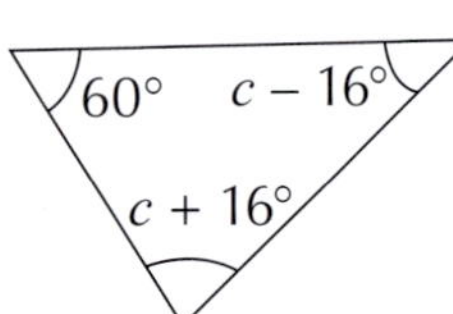

Q2 Find the values of the letters in each of these diagrams.

a)
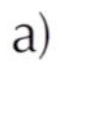
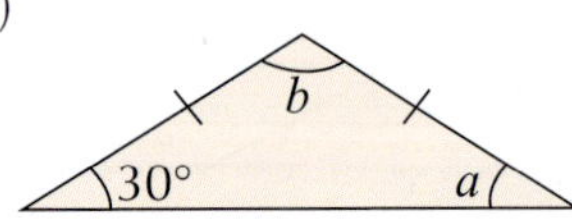

b)
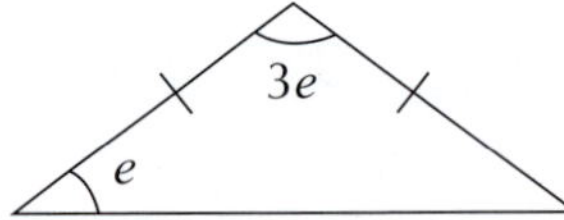

c)
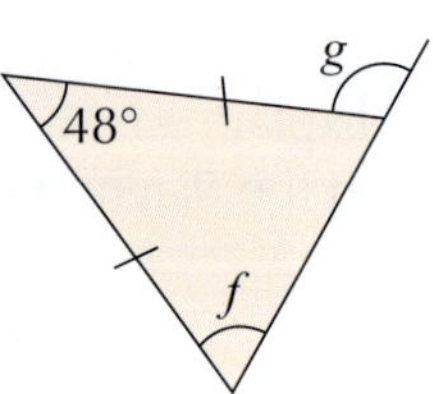

Q3 a) Find the value of x.
b) Find the value of y.

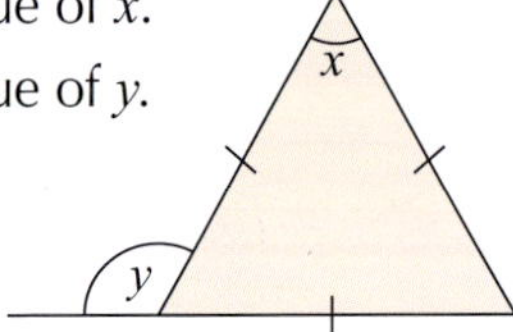

Q4 a) Find the value of p.
b) Find the value of q.

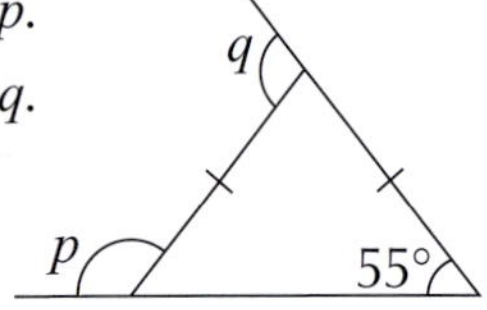

15.4 Quadrilaterals

Quadrilaterals are shapes with four sides. You're probably familiar with squares and rectangles, two of the simplest quadrilaterals, but the next few pages will introduce you to lots of other types.

Quadrilaterals

Learning Objectives — Spec Ref G3:

- Know that the angles in a quadrilateral add up to 360°.
- Be able to find missing angles in quadrilaterals.

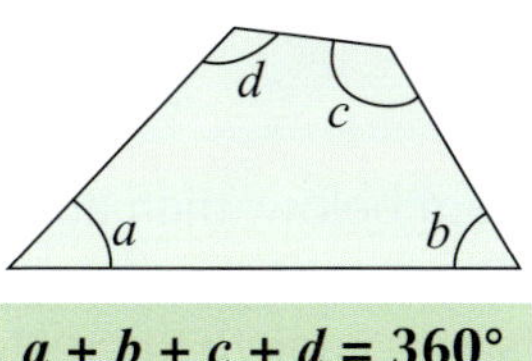

$$a + b + c + d = 360°$$

The **angles** in a quadrilateral always **add up to 360°**.

You can find **unknown** angles by forming an equation and then **rearranging**.

Tip: There's a method on page 250 which you can use to show that the angles add up to 360°.

Example 1

Find the missing angle x in this quadrilateral.

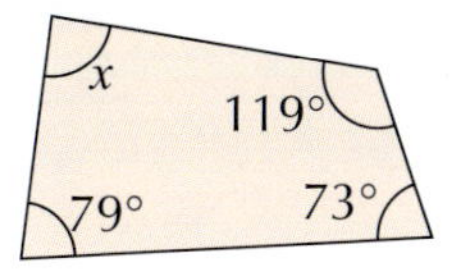

1. The angles in a quadrilateral add up to 360°, so write an equation involving x.
2. Then solve your equation to find the value of x.

$79° + 73° + 119° + x = 360°$

$271° + x = 360°$

$x = 360° - 271° = $ **89°**

Exercise 1

Q1 Find the size of the angles marked by letters in the following quadrilaterals. (They're not drawn accurately, so don't try to measure them.)

a)

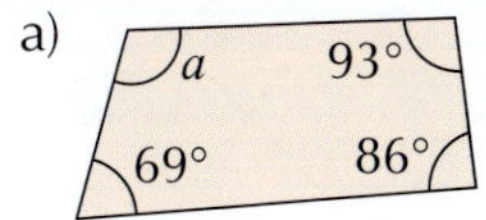

b)

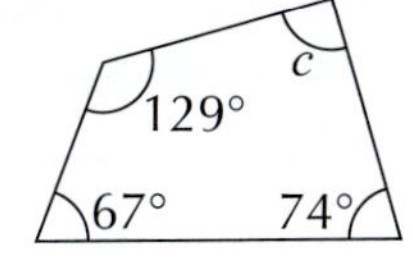

c)

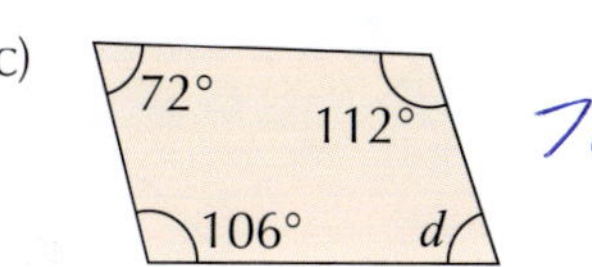

Q2 Find the values of the letters in the quadrilaterals below.

a)

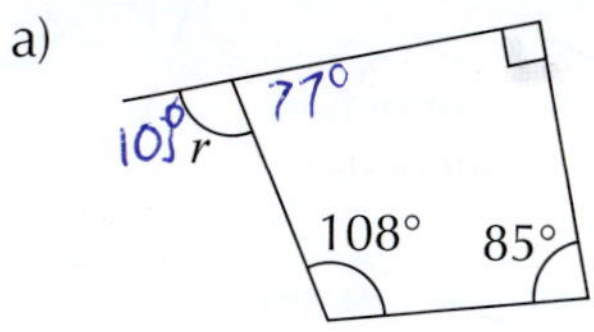

b)

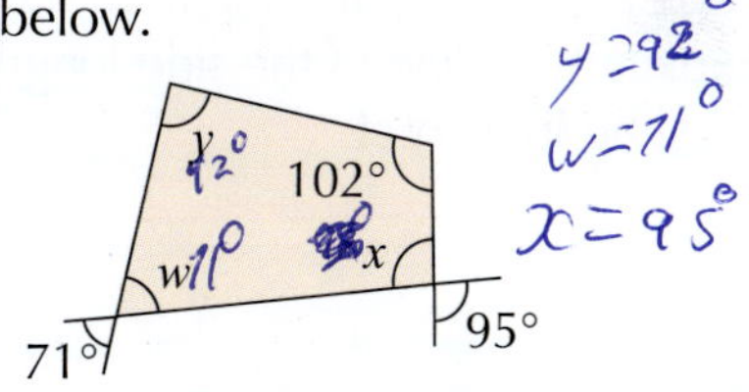

Squares and Rectangles

Learning Objective — Spec Ref G4:
Know the properties of squares and rectangles.

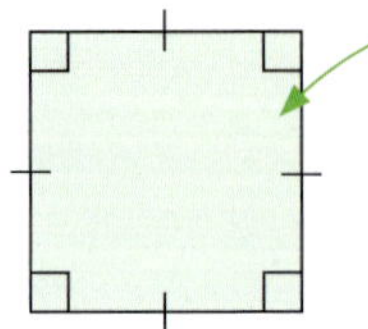

A **square** is a quadrilateral with 4 equal sides and 4 angles of 90°.

A **rectangle** is a quadrilateral with 4 angles of 90° and opposite sides of the same length.

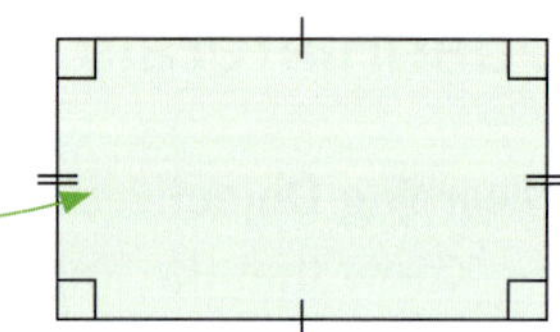

Exercise 2

Q1 Copy the diagram below, then add two more points to form a square. Join the points to complete the square.

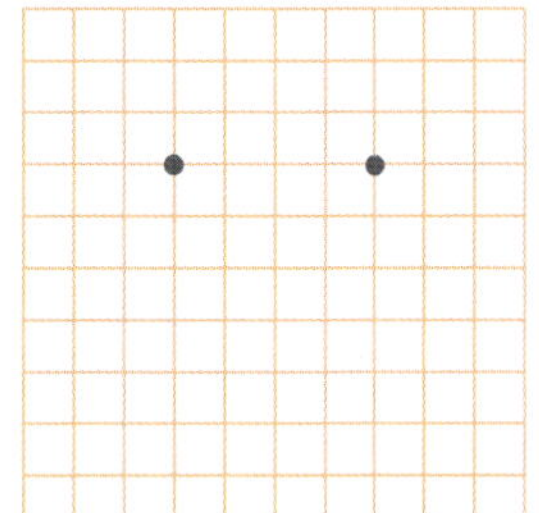

Q2 Copy the diagram below, then add two more points to form a rectangle. Join the points to complete the rectangle.

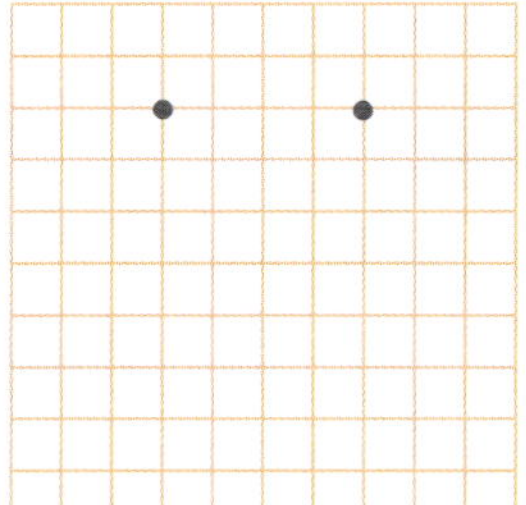

Q3 a) Measure the length of the diagonals on the square on the right. What do you notice?

b) At what angle do the two diagonals cross?

c) By measuring diagonals, determine which of the following are squares.

(i)

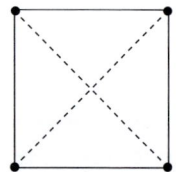

(ii)

(iii)

Q4 Look at this diagram of a rectangle. Explain why one of the side lengths must be **incorrect**.

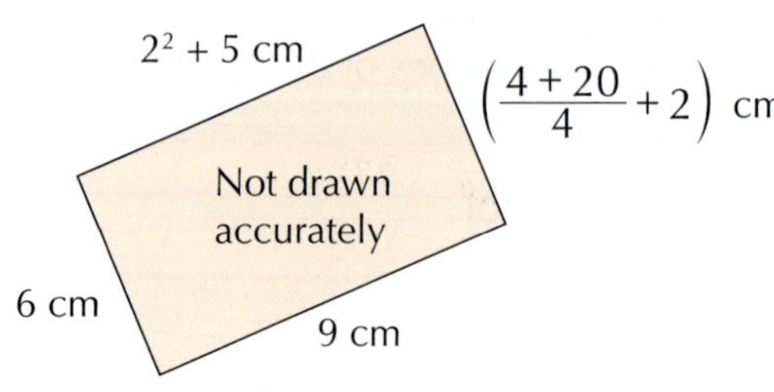

Parallelograms and Rhombuses

Learning Objective — Spec Ref G4:
Know the properties of parallelograms and rhombuses.

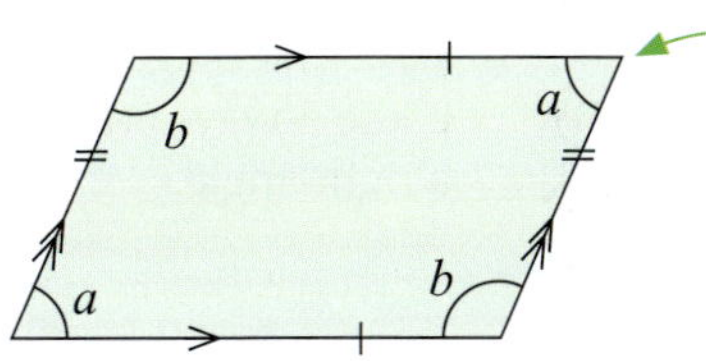

A **parallelogram** is a quadrilateral with 2 pairs of equal, parallel sides.

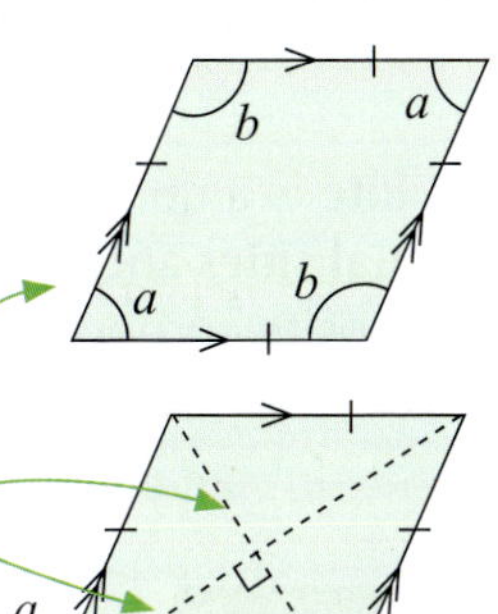

A **rhombus** is a parallelogram where all the sides are the same length. The **diagonals** of a rhombus **bisect** the angles (i.e. cut them in half) and cross at a **right angle**.

Opposite angles in parallelograms and rhombuses are **equal**, and **neighbouring angles** always add up to **180°**: $\boldsymbol{a + b = 180°}$
This is because the **parallel lines** that make up the sides of these shapes mean a and b are **allied angles** (page 241).

Example 2

Find the size of the angles marked with letters in this rhombus.

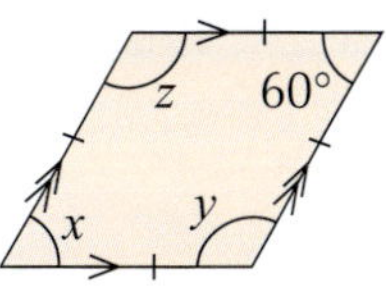

1. Opposite angles in a rhombus are equal. Use this fact to find angle x. $\quad \boldsymbol{x = 60°}$
2. Neighbouring angles in a rhombus add up to 180°. Use this fact to find angle y. $\quad 60° + y = 180°$
   $y = 180° - 60°$
   $\boldsymbol{y = 120°}$
3. Opposite angles in a rhombus are equal, so z is the same size as y. $\quad \boldsymbol{z = 120°}$

Tip: You could have found z first, using the fact that z and 60° are neighbouring angles.

Exercise 3

Q1 a) Copy the diagram on the right. Add one more point and join the points to form a rhombus.

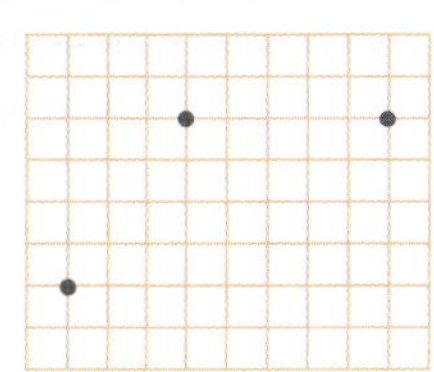

b) On a new grid, plot four points to form a parallelogram.

Q2 Calculate the size of the angles marked by letters in these quadrilaterals. (They're not drawn accurately, so don't try to measure them.)

a)

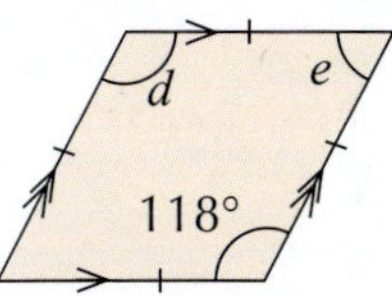

b)

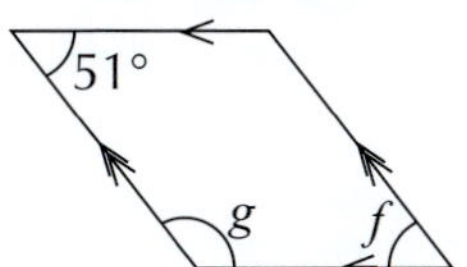

c)

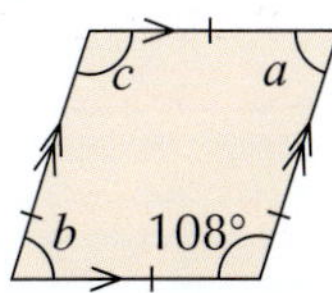

Kites

Learning Objective — Spec Ref G4:
Know the properties of kites.

A **kite** is a quadrilateral with **2 pairs** of **equal sides** and **1 pair** of **equal angles** in opposite corners, as shown on the diagram. (The other pair of angles aren't generally equal.)

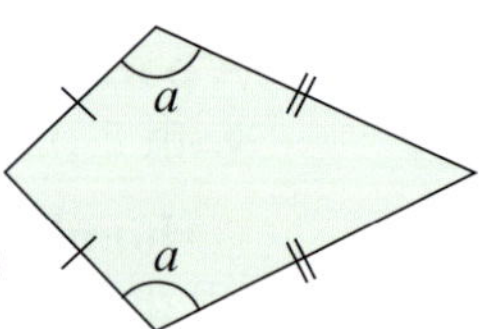

Tip: The diagonals of a kite always cross at a right angle.

Example 3

Find the size of the angles marked with letters in the kite below.

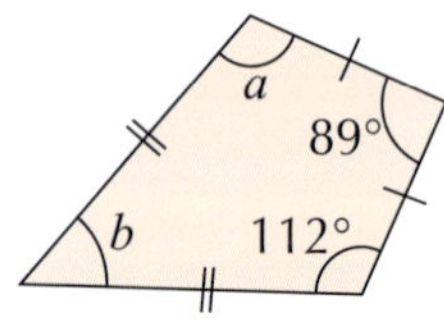

1. a and the 112° angle must be equal. $\quad$ $\boldsymbol{a = 112°}$
2. A kite is a quadrilateral, so its angles add up to 360°. Use this to write an equation in terms of b.
   $112° + 89° + 112° + b = 360°$
   $313° + b = 360°$
   $b = 360° - 313° = \mathbf{47°}$

Exercise 4

Q1 Which letter goes in each box to complete the sentences about this kite?

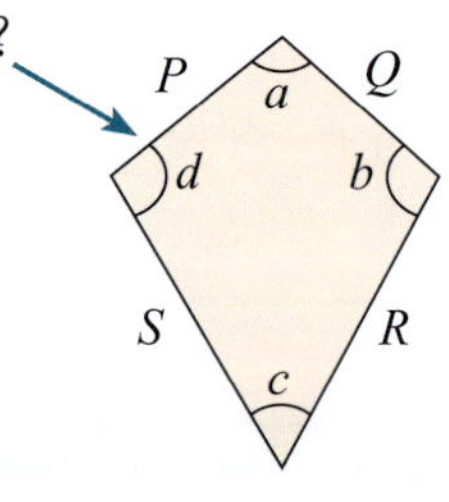

a) Angle b is the same size as angle ☐

b) The length of side P is the same as the length of side ☐

c) The length of side R is the same as the length of side ☐

Q2 Find the size of the angles marked by letters in these kites. (They're not drawn accurately, so don't try to measure them.)

a)

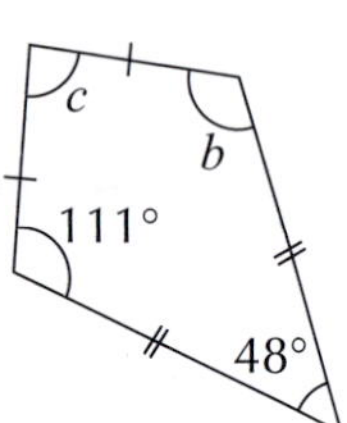

b)

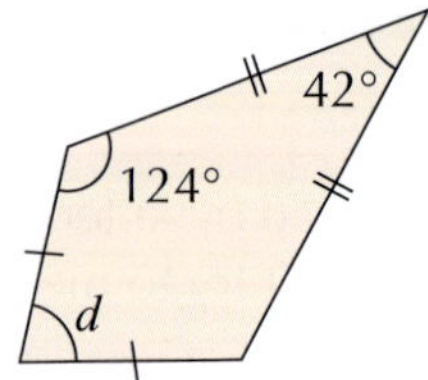

c)

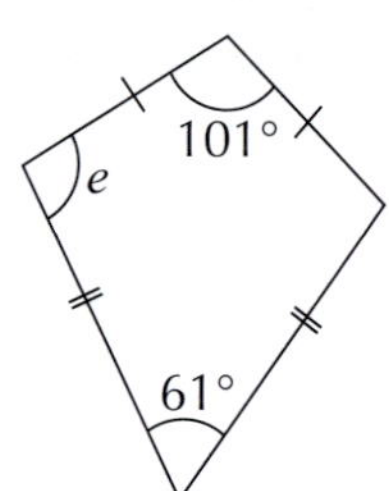

Trapeziums

Learning Objective — Spec Ref G4:
Know the properties of trapeziums and isosceles trapeziums.

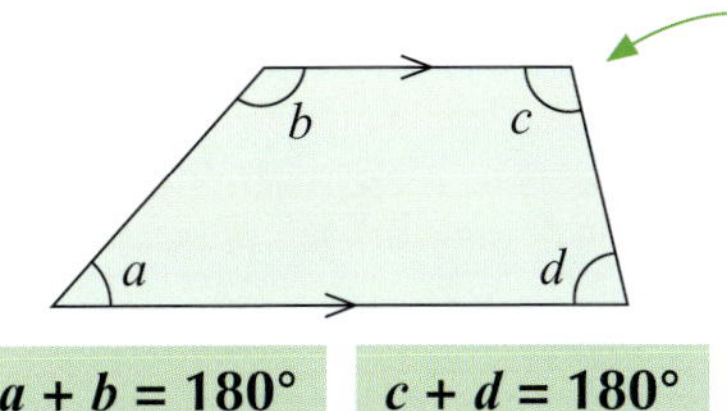

$a + b = 180°$ $c + d = 180°$

A **trapezium** is a quadrilateral with 1 pair of parallel sides.

An **isosceles trapezium** is a trapezium with 2 pairs of equal angles and 2 sides of the same length.

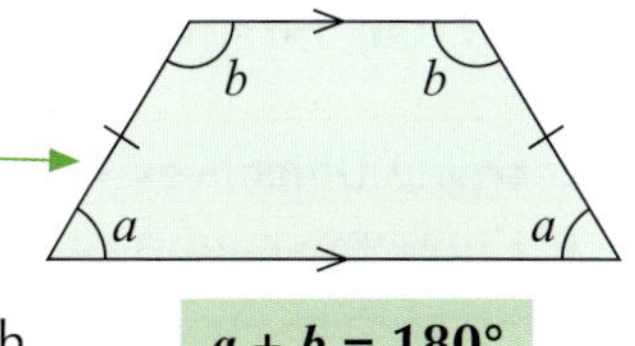

$a + b = 180°$

Because of the **allied angles** created by the parallel sides, pairs of angles **add up to 180°** as shown.

Example 4

Find the size of the angles marked with letters in the trapezium below.

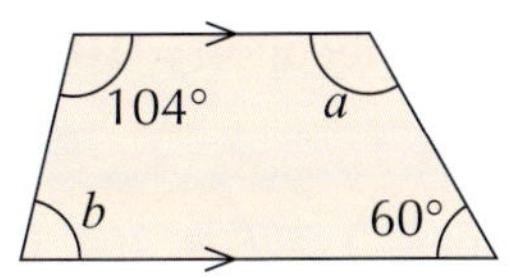

1. a and the 60° angle must add up to 180°. $a + 60° = 180°$
   $\boldsymbol{a} = 180° - 60° = \mathbf{120°}$
2. Similarly, b and the 104° angle must add up to 180°. $b + 104° = 180°$
   $\boldsymbol{b} = 180° - 104° = \mathbf{76°}$

Exercise 5

Q1 Choose the correct word from each pair to complete the following sentences.

a) A trapezium is a quadrilateral with one pair of (**parallel / equal**) sides.

b) An isosceles trapezium has (**one pair / two pairs**) of equal angles.

c) An isosceles trapezium has (**one pair / two pairs**) of parallel sides.

d) An isosceles trapezium has (**one pair / two pairs**) of equal sides.

e) The angles in a trapezium add up to (**180° / 360°**).

Q2 Find the size of the angles marked by letters in these trapeziums.
(They're not drawn accurately, so don't try to measure them.)

a)

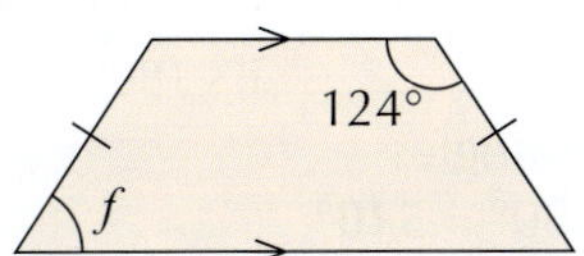

b)

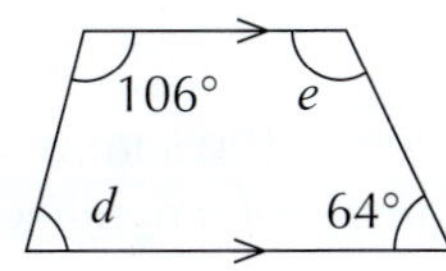

c)

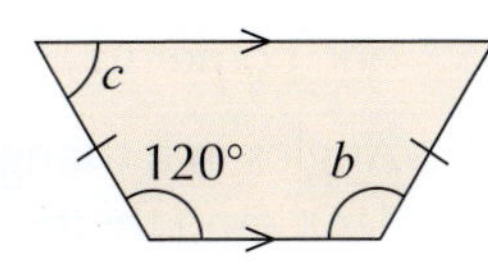

15.5 Interior and Exterior Angles

You've met lots of polygons before — they're just 2D shapes with straight sides. These pages will show you how to work out the number of sides and the sizes of angles in polygon problems.

Interior Angles

Learning Objectives — Spec Ref G1/G3:
- Know the names of different types of polygons.
- Be able to find the sum of the interior angles in a polygon by splitting it into triangles.

A polygon is a **2D shape** whose sides are all **straight**.

The **triangles** and **quadrilaterals** on the previous pages were three- and four-sided polygons. The box on the right shows the names of some other polygons — their names depend on the **number of sides** they have.

pentagon = **5** sides	**oct**agon = **8** sides
hexagon = **6** sides	**non**agon = **9** sides
heptagon = **7** sides	**dec**agon = **10** sides

A **regular** polygon has sides of **equal length** and angles that are all **equal**.
An **equilateral triangle** is a regular triangle and a **square** is a regular quadrilateral.

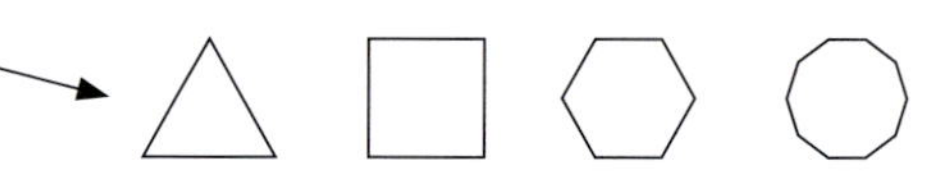

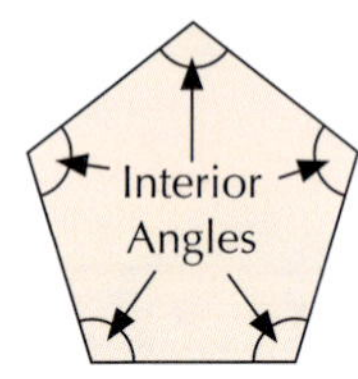

The **interior angles** of a polygon are the angles inside each vertex (corner). The interior angles of a regular pentagon are shown on the left.

You can find the **sum of the interior angles** by splitting the polygon into **triangles** and then using the rule that angles in a triangle add up to **180°** — you'll see how this works in the example below.

Example 1

Find the sum of the interior angles of a pentagon.

1. First draw any pentagon — it doesn't have to be regular.
2. Split the pentagon into triangles by drawing lines from one corner to all the others.
3. Angles in a triangle add up to 180°, and there are 3 triangles.

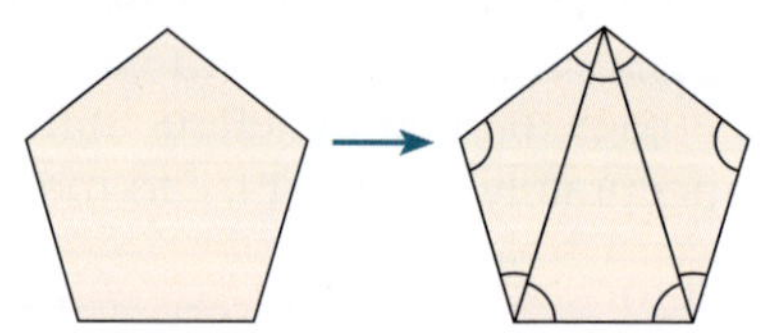

The sum of the interior angles of a pentagon is 3 × 180° = **540°**

Tip: Quadrilaterals can be split into two triangles. This explains why the sum of their angles is 360° (see page 245) — it's 180° × 2.

Example 2

A pentagon has four interior angles of 100°. Find the size of the fifth angle.

1. The interior angles of a pentagon add up to 540°. Use this fact to write an equation for the size of the missing angle, x.

   $100° + 100° + 100° + 100° + x = 540°$
   $400° + x = 540°$

2. Solve your equation to find x.

   $x = 540° - 400° = \mathbf{140°}$

Exercise 1

Q1 By dividing each shape into triangles, find the sum of the interior angles of the shapes on the right.

a) 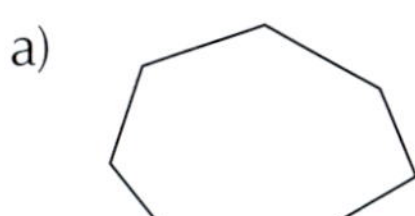

b)

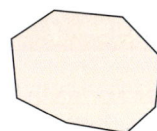

Q2 Sketch the polygon shown on the right.

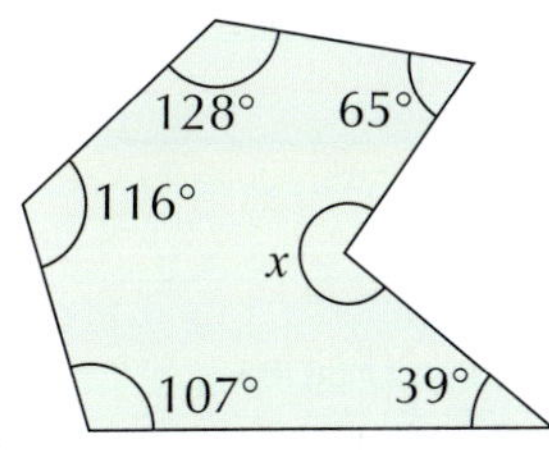

a) What happens when you try to divide the polygon into triangles by drawing a line from the 65° angle to each of the other corners?

b) Join the corner marked x to each of the other corners to split the shape into triangles.

c) Find the sum of the interior angles of the shape.

d) Find the size of the angle marked x.

The Formula for the Sum of the Interior Angles

Learning Objective — Spec Ref G3:
Know and be able to use the formula for the sum of the interior angles in a polygon.

You can always divide a polygon of n sides into $\boldsymbol{n - 2}$ **triangles**. Using this and the fact that the sum of the angles in a triangle is **180°**, you can create a **formula** for the sum of the interior angles:

$$S = (n - 2) \times 180°$$

where S is the **sum** of a polygon's **interior angles** and n is the **number of sides**.

This formula works for both **regular** and **irregular** polygons. Once you've found the value of the **sum of the interior angles**, you can use it to find the size of **individual angles** in the shape — as shown in the example on the next page.

Example 3

Find the size of each of the interior angles of a regular hexagon.

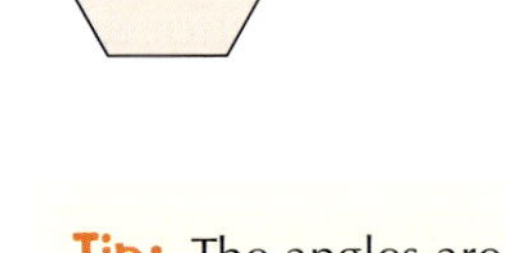

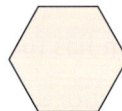

1. Use the formula to find the sum of the interior angles of a hexagon. A hexagon has 6 sides so $n = 6$.

   $S = (6 - 2) \times 180°$
   $= 4 \times 180° = 720°$

2. All the angles in the hexagon are equal, so divide the sum by the number of angles.

   So each interior angle of a regular hexagon is $720° \div 6 =$ **120°**

Tip: The angles are equal because the polygon is **regular**.

Exercise 2

Q1 For each of the shapes below, determine whether or not it is a polygon, and give reasons why.

a) 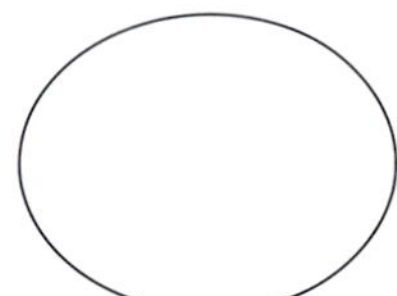

b) 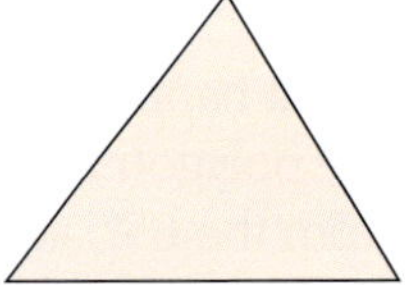

c) 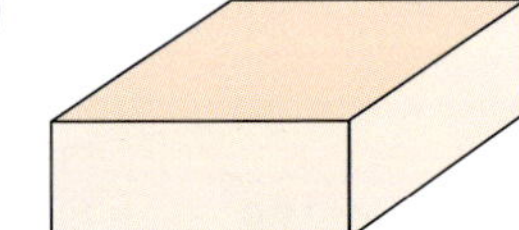

Q2 Find the sum of the interior angles of a polygon with:

a) 10 sides b) 12 sides c) 20 sides

Q3 A regular heptagon is shown on the right.

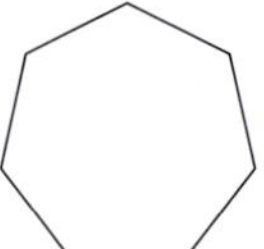

a) Find the sum of the interior angles of a heptagon.

b) Find the size of each of the interior angles of a regular heptagon to 2 d.p.

Q4 Find the size of each of the interior angles in the following shapes.

a) Regular octagon (8 sides)

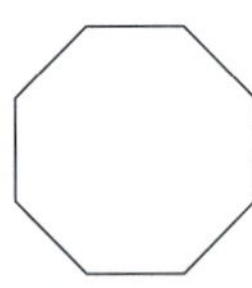

b) Regular nonagon (9 sides)

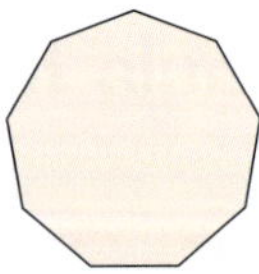

Q5 The shapes below are not drawn accurately. For each of the shapes:

(i) Find the sum of the interior angles (ii) Find the size of the missing angle.

a) 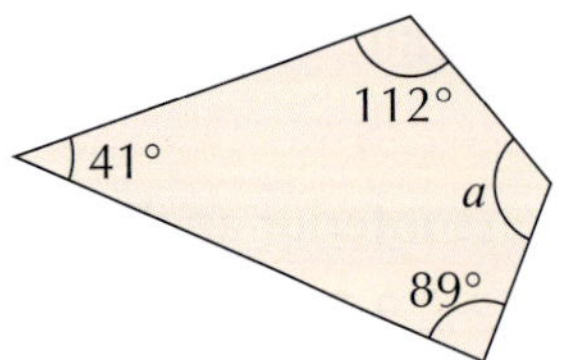

b) 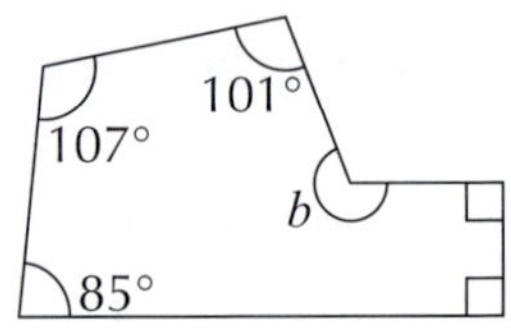

c) 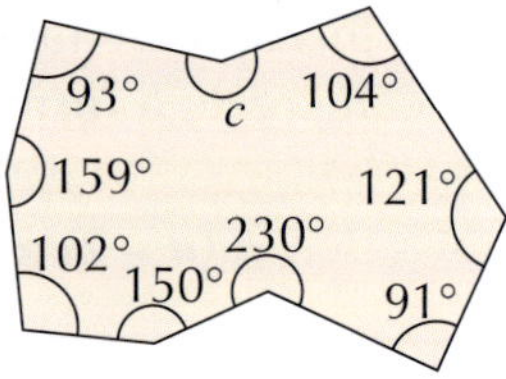

Exterior Angles

Learning Objective — Spec Ref G3:
Find interior and exterior angles of regular and irregular polygons.

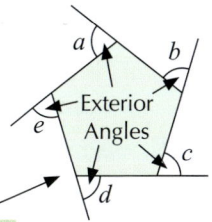

An **exterior angle** of a polygon is an angle between a **side** and a **line** that extends out from one of the **neighbouring sides**. For example, the exterior angles of a regular pentagon are shown on the right.

For any polygon, the exterior angles always **add up to 360°**. In the case of the pentagon, this is: $\boldsymbol{a + b + c + d + e = 360°}$

Since the exterior angle and the neighbouring interior angle lie on a straight line, they must **add up to 180°** (see page 237). So you can use this formula to find an **interior angle** given the exterior angle:

Interior angle = 180° – Exterior angle

For a **regular** polygon, the interior angles are all equal, and this means the **exterior angles are all equal** too. Then the formula for the size of an exterior angle for a regular n-sided polygon is:

$$\textbf{Exterior angle} = \frac{360°}{n}$$

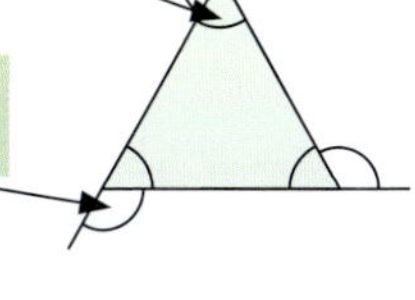

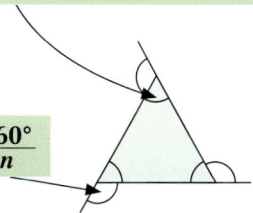

Example 4

Find the size of each of the exterior angles of a regular hexagon.

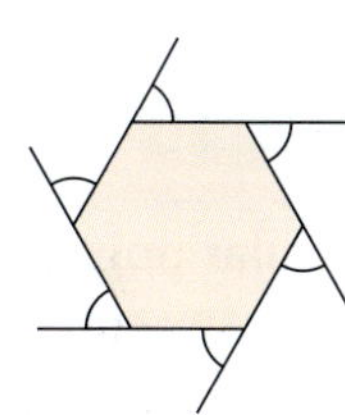

A hexagon has 6 sides.
The hexagon is regular so put $n = 6$ into the exterior angle formula.

$360° \div 6 = 60°$

So each exterior angle is **60°**.

Example 5

Prove that the exterior angle of a triangle is equal to the sum of the two non-adjacent interior angles.

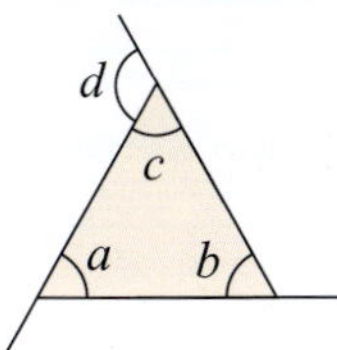

1. You need to show that $a + b = d$.
2. The exterior angle and neighbouring interior angle add up to 180°. $\quad d + c = 180° \Rightarrow c = 180° - d$
3. The angles in the triangle also add up to 180°. $\quad a + b + c = 180°$
4. Substitute in the expression for c, then rearrange to get the result. $\quad a + b + (180° - d) = 180°$
   $\boldsymbol{a + b = d}$

Tip: Writing what you are trying to show is useful, as it tells you what to aim for.

Exercise 3

Q1 The diagram on the right shows a regular pentagon with the exterior angles marked on.

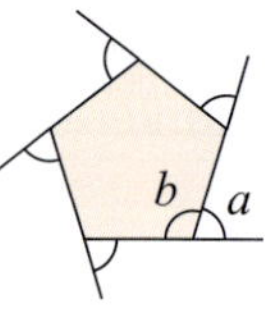

a) Find a, the size of each of the exterior angles of the pentagon.

b) Hence find b, the size of each of the interior angles of the pentagon.

Q2 a) Find the size of each of the exterior angles (to 2 d.p.) of the following polygons.

(i) regular heptagon (ii) regular octagon (iii) regular nonagon

b) Use your answers to part a) to find the size of each of the interior angles of these polygons.

Q3 Find the size of the angles marked by letters in these diagrams.

a)

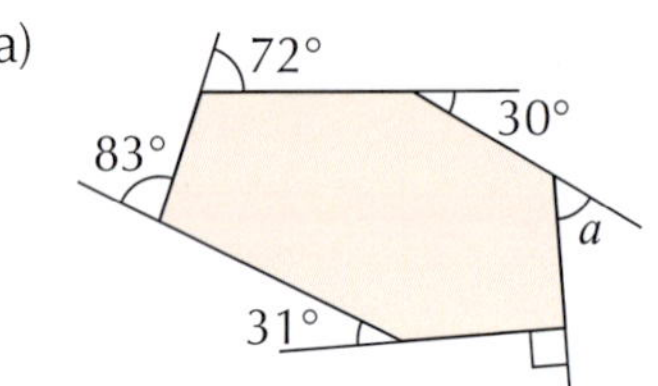

Diagrams not drawn accurately.

b)

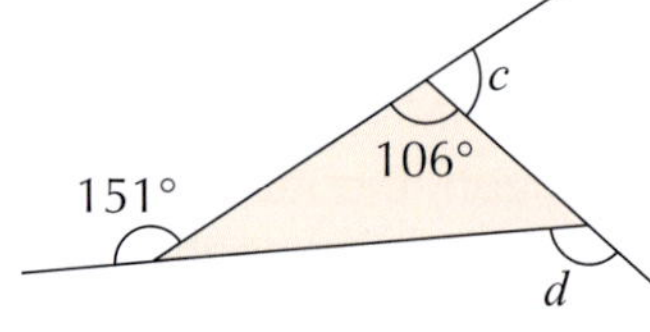

Q4 Find the size of the unknown exterior angle in a shape whose other exterior angles are:

a) 100°, 68°, 84° and 55° b) 30°, 68°, 45°, 52°, 75° and 50°

Example 6

A regular polygon has exterior angles of 30°. How many sides does the polygon have?

1. It's a regular polygon so put 30° into the exterior angle formula. $30° = \frac{360°}{n}$
2. Solve the equation for n. $n = 360° \div 30° = 12$
So the regular polygon has **12 sides**.

Tip: A 12-sided polygon is called a dodecagon.

Exercise 4

Q1 The exterior angles of some regular polygons are given below.
For each exterior angle, find:
(i) the number of sides the polygon has,
(ii) the size of each of the polygon's interior angles,
(iii) the sum of the polygon's interior angles.

a) 90° b) 40° c) 6° d) 4°

15.6 Symmetry

Symmetry is when a shape can be reflected or rotated and still look exactly the same afterwards. E.g. rotating a square by 90° puts each vertex in a different place but the square looks the same.

Learning Objectives — Spec Ref G1:
- Recognise lines of symmetry and rotational symmetry of 2D shapes.
- Be able to find the sum of the interior angles in a polygon by splitting it into triangles.

A line of **symmetry** on a shape is a **mirror line**, where you can fold the shape so that both halves match up **exactly**. Each side of the line of symmetry is a **reflection** of the other.

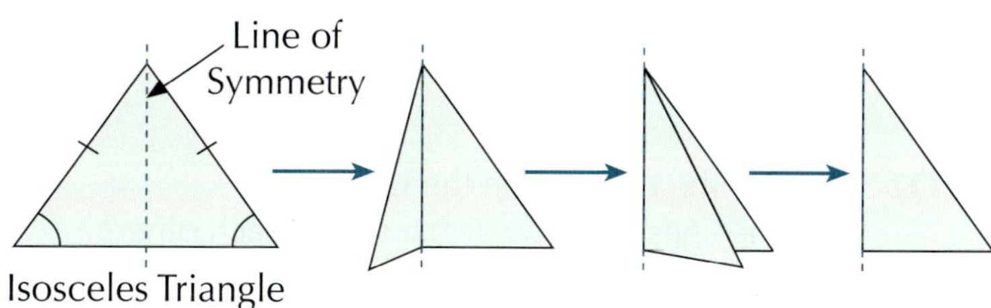

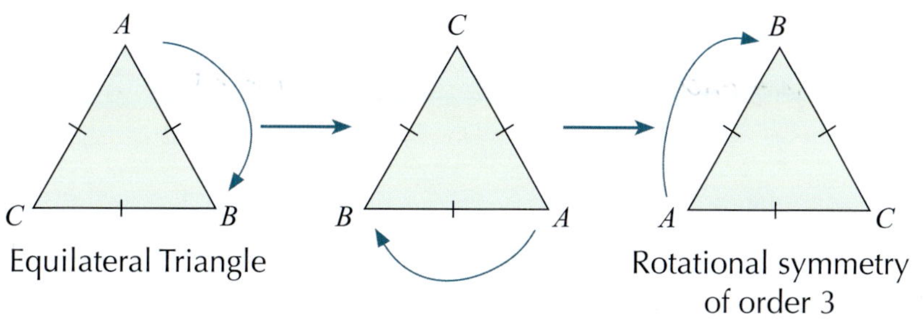

The order of **rotational symmetry** of a shape is the number of positions you can **rotate** (turn) the shape into so that it looks **exactly** the same.

A shape that only looks the same **once** every complete turn has rotational symmetry of **order 1** (or no rotational symmetry).

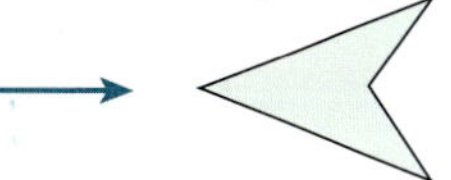

Exercise 1

Q1 Sketch each of the shapes below, then draw on any lines of symmetry. State the number of lines of symmetry you have drawn for each shape.

a) rectangle b) rhombus c) isosceles trapezium

d) regular pentagon e) regular hexagon f) regular heptagon

Q2 Find the order of rotational symmetry of each of the following shapes.

a) 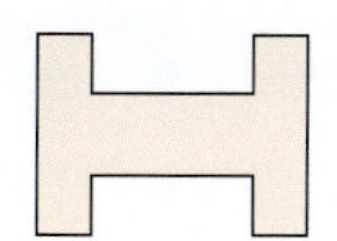 b) 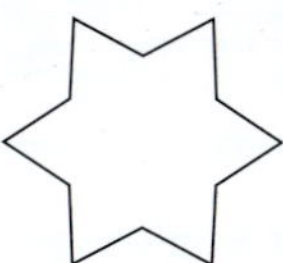 c) 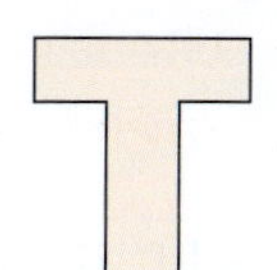 d) 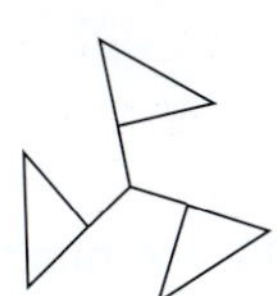

Review Exercise

The angles in this exercise have not been drawn accurately, so don't try to measure them.

Q1 Find the value of each letter.

a)

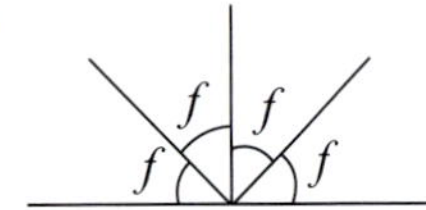

b)

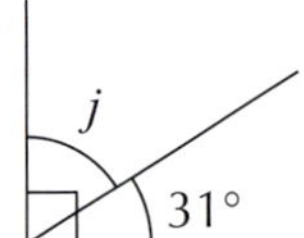

c)

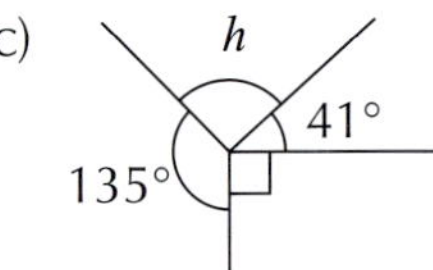

Q2 Look at the diagram on the right.
Are the lines AB and CD parallel to each other?
Explain your answer.

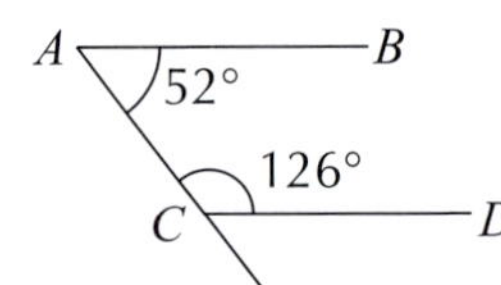

Q3 Find the value of each letter.

a)

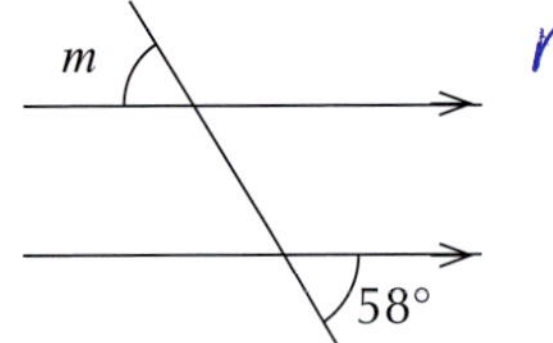

b)

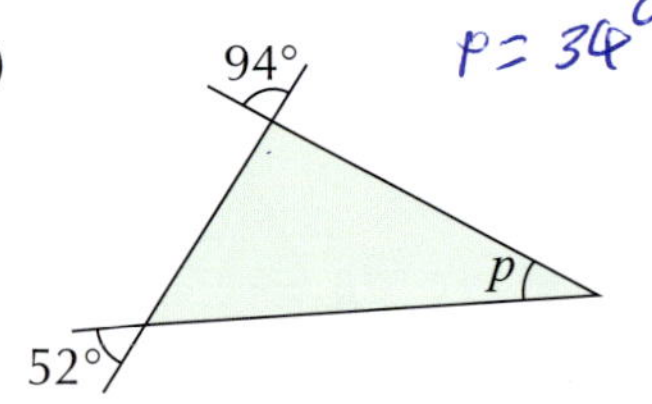

c)

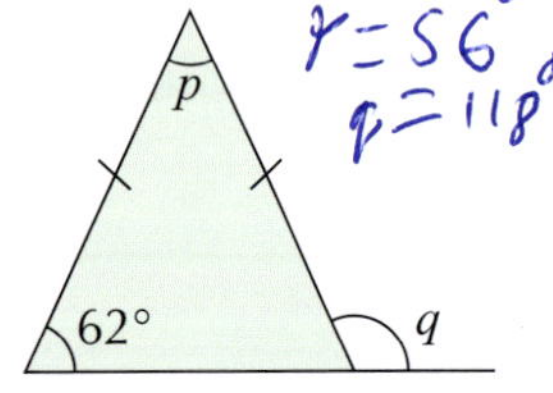

d)

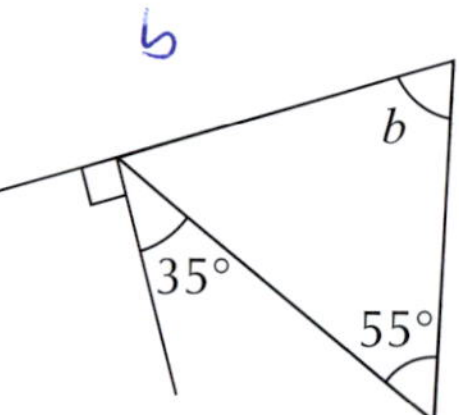

e)

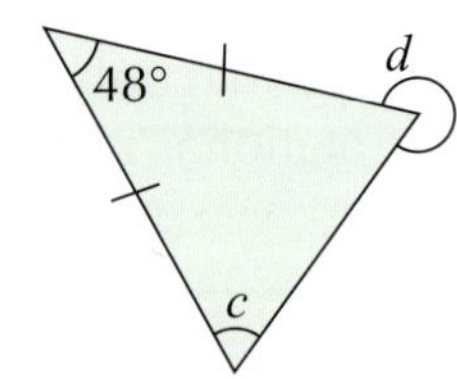

Q4 Match one name from the box to each of the quadrilaterals below.

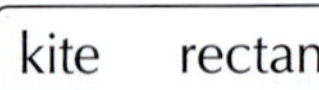

kite	rectangle	trapezium	parallelogram

a)

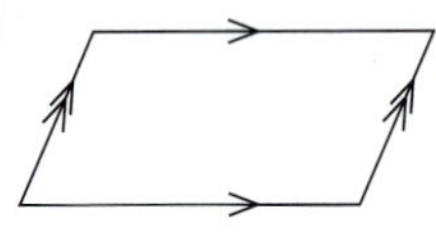

b)

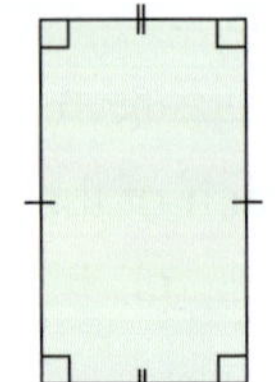

c)

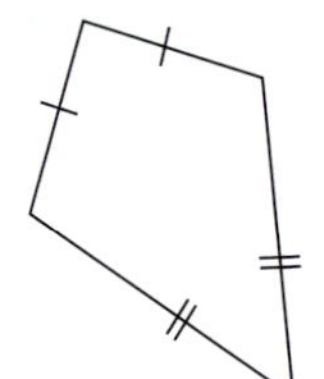

d)

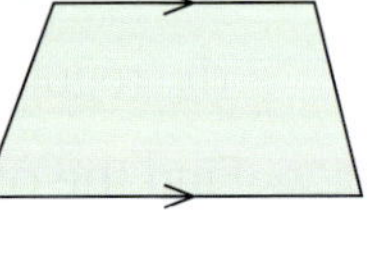

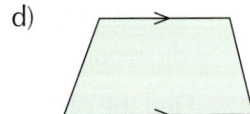

Q5 A quadrilateral has 40°, 83° and 99° interior angles.
Find the size of the fourth angle.

Q6 Find the value of each letter.

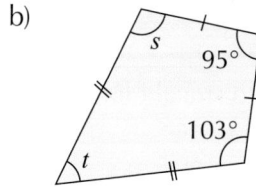

a) 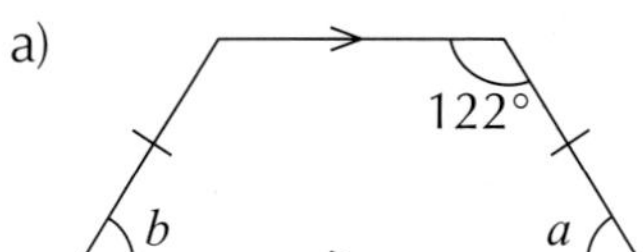

b) s 95° 103° t

c) 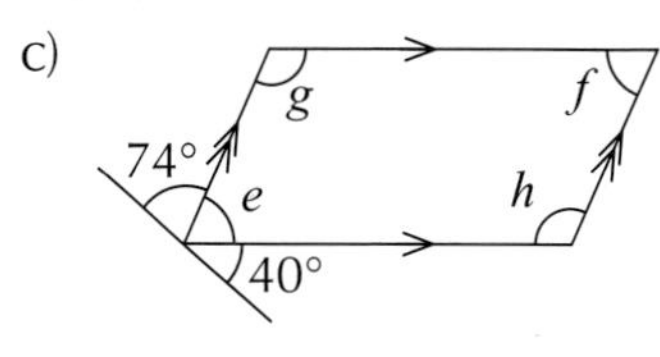

Q7 The diagram on the right shows a kite and a square.

a) Write down the value of a.

b) Use your answer to find the size of angles b and c.

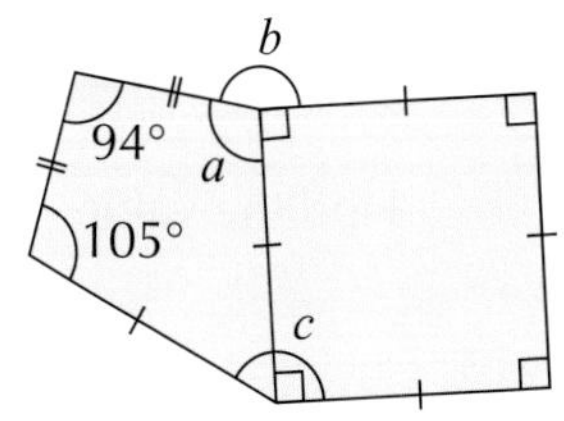

Q8

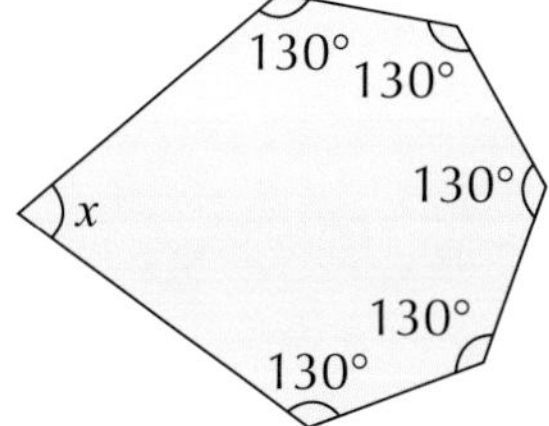

The shape shown on the left has 6 sides.

a) Calculate the sum of the interior angles of a hexagon.

b) Use your answer to find angle x.

Q9 A regular polygon has exterior angles of 45°.

a) How many sides does the polygon have?
What is the name of this kind of polygon?

b) Sketch the polygon.

c) What is the size of each of the polygon's interior angles?

d) What is the sum of the polygon's interior angles?

Q10 Decide which of the shapes below matches each of the descriptions.

A 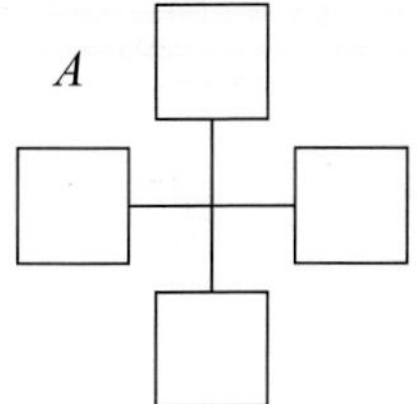

B 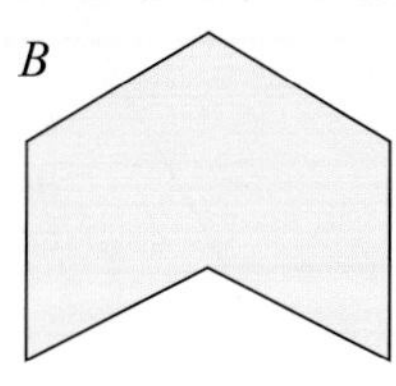

C 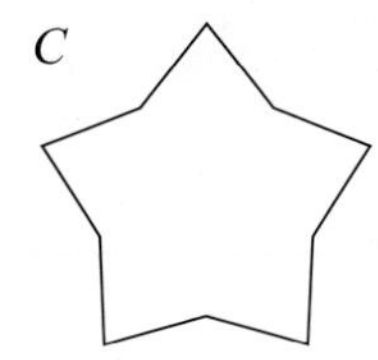

D 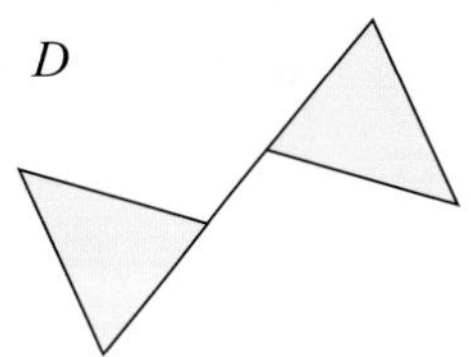

a) 1 line of symmetry, no rotational symmetry.

b) 4 lines of symmetry, rotational symmetry of order 4.

c) No lines of symmetry, rotational symmetry of order 2.

d) 5 lines of symmetry, rotational symmetry of order 5.

Exam-Style Questions

Q1 The diagram below shows two straight lines meeting at a point.

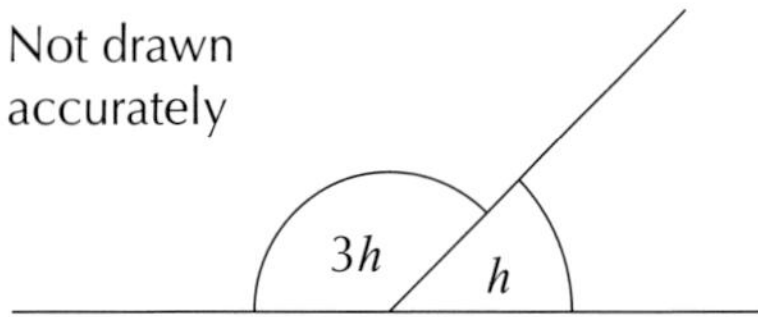

Find the value of h.

[2 marks]

Q2 The diagram below shows a quadrilateral.

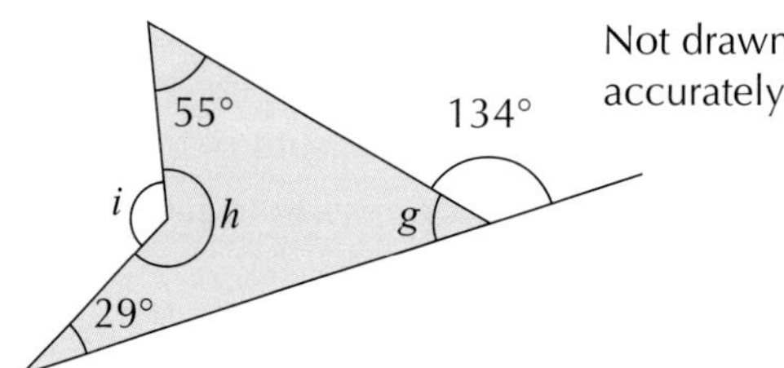

Find the values of the letters.

[3 marks]

Q3 The diagram shows a parallelogram.
$ABCD$ is a straight line. EBF is a straight line.
Angle BFG is 56°.

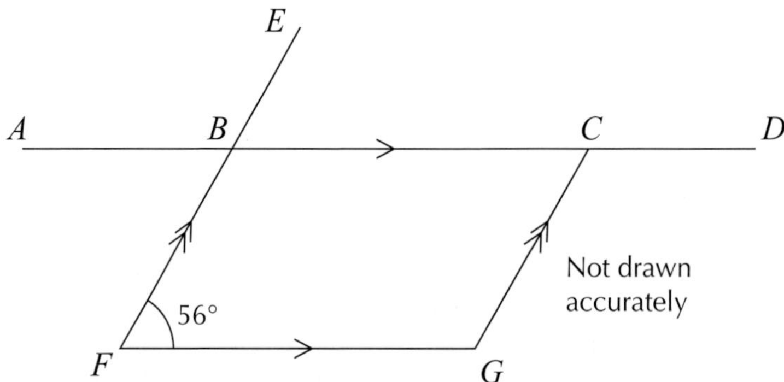

a) Write down the size of angle EBC.

[1 mark]

b) Find the size of angle DCG. Give a reason for each step of your working.

[2 marks]

Q4 The diagram below shows a seven-sided shape.

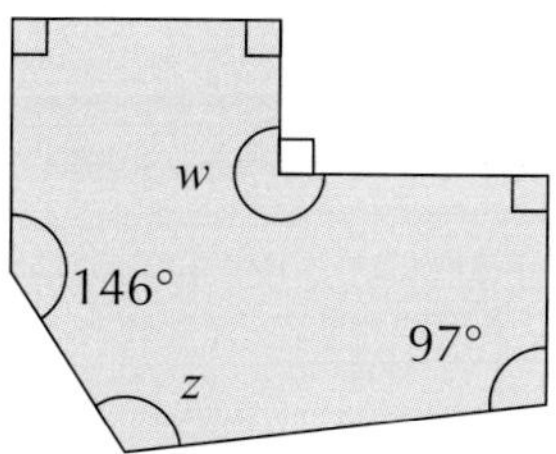

Not drawn accurately

Find the value of angles w and z.

[3 marks]

Q5 The diagram below shows a quadrilateral.

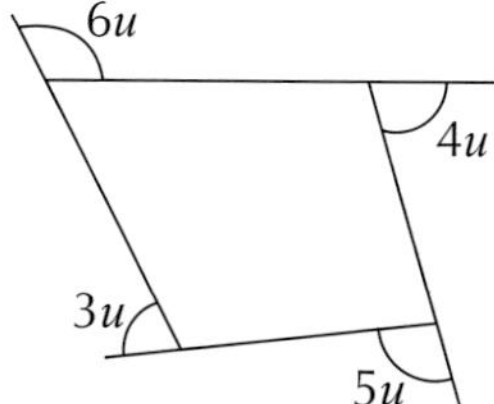

Find the value of u.

[2 marks]

Q6 The diagram below shows an equilateral triangle ABC and an isosceles triangle ACE where $AC = EC$. The triangles have a common side, AC, and EAD is a straight line. Angle $ECB = 38°$.

Not drawn accurately

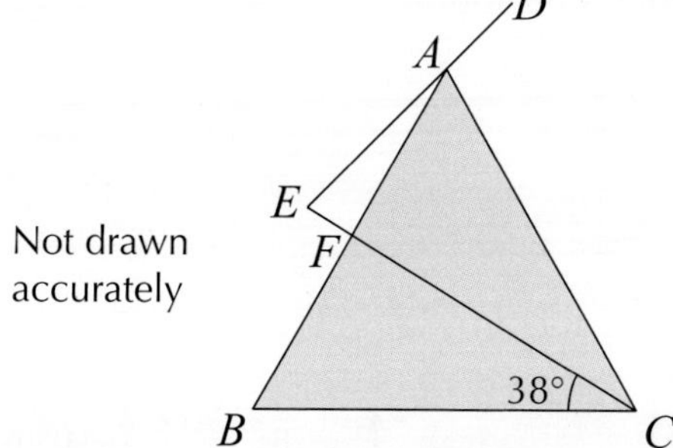

Prove that angle $DAC = 101°$.

[3 marks]

16.1 Reading Scales

You always use the same method to read scales — even when they use different units.

Reading Scales

Learning Objective — Spec Ref G14:
Be able to read values off scales.

The **main values** on a scale are **labelled**, but the smaller values are not. To find the **smaller values**, you need to work out what each **gap** between the smaller marks represents.

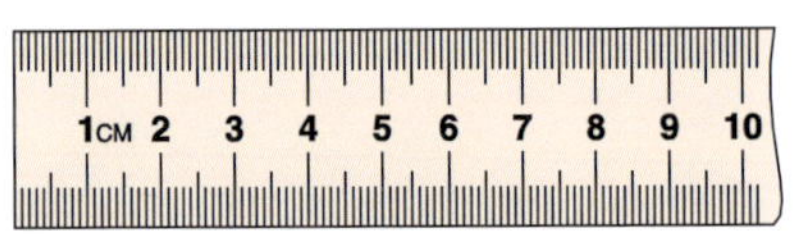

The **gap** between each pair of labelled marks on a scale is always the **same amount** — on the ruler above, the gap between each big mark is 1 cm. To work out what each small gap represents, **divide** the distance between two big marks by the **number of small gaps**. There are 10 gaps between each big mark, so each small gap is 1 cm ÷ 10 = 0.1 cm, or **1 mm**.

Example 1

Write down the volume of liquid in the beaker on the right.

1. Find the interval between the numbered marks. — 40 – 30 = 10 ml
2. Divide this interval by the number of smaller divisions between each number to find what each division represents. Here, there are 2 divisions between each number. — 10 ÷ 2 = 5 ml
3. The amount in the beaker is 20 ml, plus the amount represented by one small division. — 20 + 5 = **25 ml**

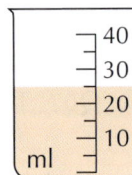

Exercise 1

Q1 Write down the lengths shown by the arrows on the ruler, giving your answers in cm.

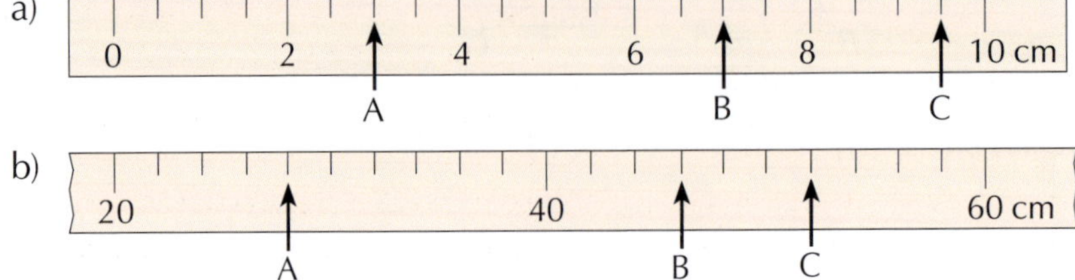

Q2 Use the fact that 1 cm = 10 mm to write down the length of each of the bugs in mm.

a)

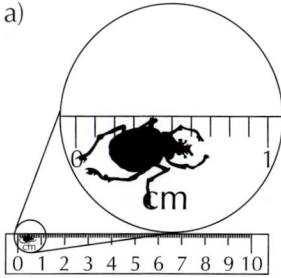

b)

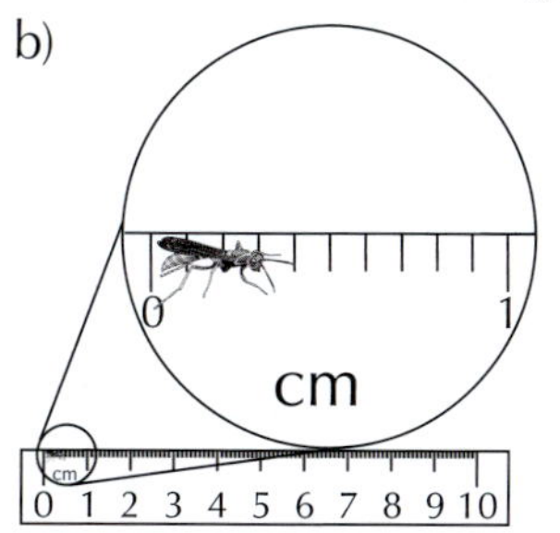

c)

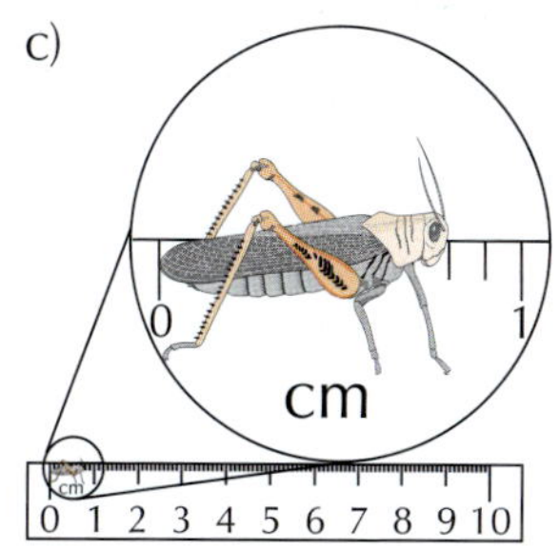

Q3 Write down the mass shown by the arrow on each scale.

a)

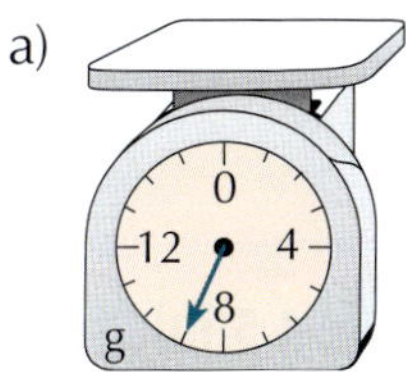

b)

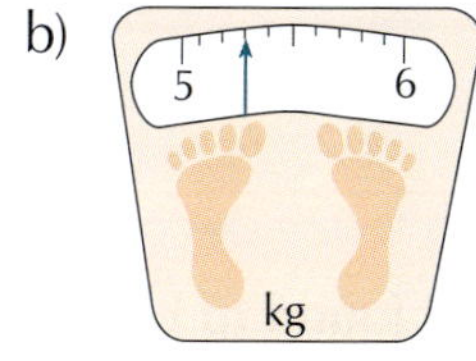

c)

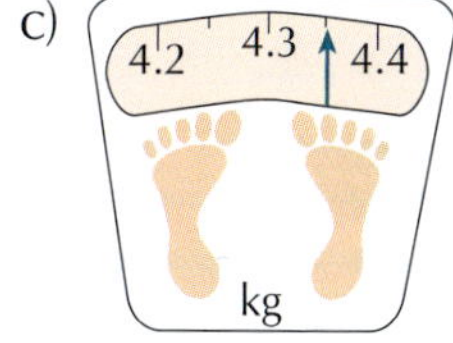

Q4 Write down:

a) the weight of the bananas,

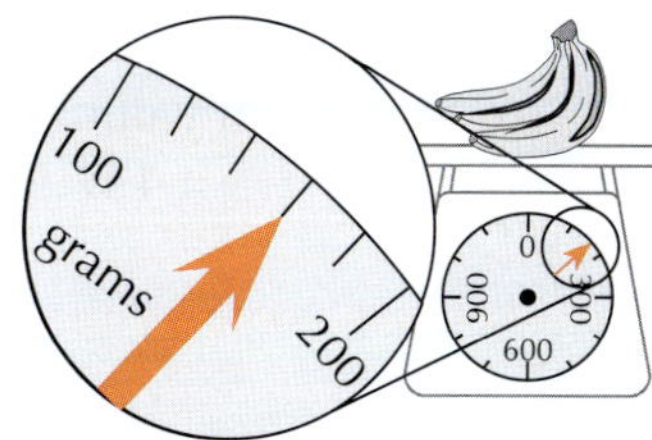

b) the volume of liquid in the bottle.

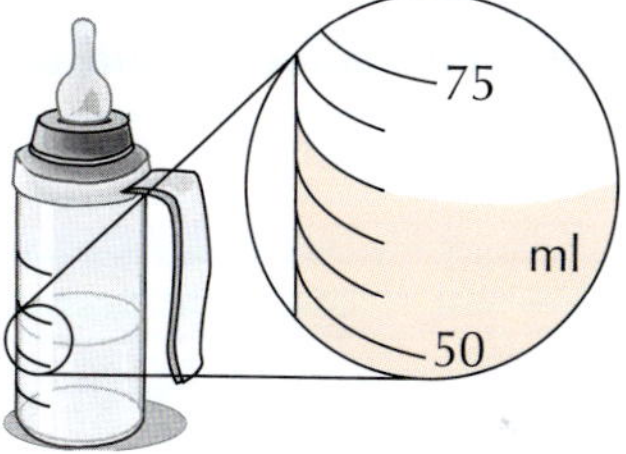

Inaccuracy of Measurements

Learning Objectives — Spec Ref N15/N16:

- Understand that measurements may be inaccurate due to rounding errors.
- Find the maximum and minimum possible values of a measurement.

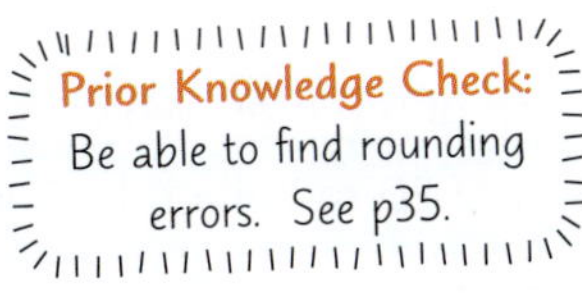

Prior Knowledge Check:
Be able to find rounding errors. See p35.

The **accuracy** of a measurement depends on the device being used to make that measurement.

For example, this ruler measures to the nearest millimetre — so both these bugs seem to be 9 mm long. But using a more **precise** piece of equipment, you can see the first bug is actually slightly shorter than the second.

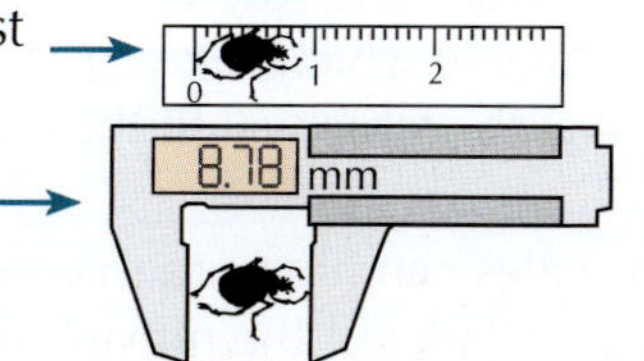

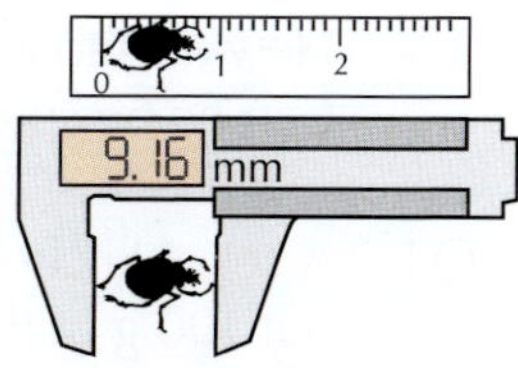

When you measure to the nearest millimetre, anything from 8.5 mm up to 9.5 mm would round to 9 mm. We say that 8.5 mm is the **minimum value** and 9.5 mm is the **maximum value**. In general, the max. and min. values for measurements are '**+ half a unit**' and '**– half a unit**'.

Example 2

The length of a pen is measured and found to be 15 cm, to the nearest 1 cm. Write down the maximum and minimum length the pen could be.

1. The length has been rounded to the nearest cm. So half a unit is 1 cm ÷ 2 = 0.5 cm.
2. Find the minimum value by subtracting half a unit. — Minimum value: 15 – 0.5 = **14.5 cm**
3. Find the maximum value by adding half a unit. — Maximum value: 15 + 0.5 = **15.5 cm**

Tip: The biggest value that would round down to 15 cm is 15.4999..., but we call 15.5 cm the maximum because it's easier to write.

Example 3

The volume of a teacup is measured and found to be 135 ml, to the nearest 5 ml. Write down the maximum and minimum possible volume of the teacup.

1. The volume has been rounded to the nearest 5 ml. So half a unit is 5 ml ÷ 2 = 2.5 ml.
2. Find the minimum value by subtracting half a unit.
3. Find the maximum value by adding half a unit.

Minimum value: 135 – 2.5 = **132.5 ml**

Maximum value: 135 + 2.5 = **137.5 ml**

Exercise 2

Q1 Find the maximum and minimum values for each of these measurements.

a) A length of 10 cm, which has been measured to the nearest 1 cm.

b) A volume of 18 litres, which has been measured to the nearest 1 litre.

c) A volume of 65 litres, which has been measured to the nearest 5 litres.

d) A length of 20 m, which has been measured to the nearest 2 m.

Q2 A pipette contains 5.7 cm^3 of liquid, measured to the nearest 0.1 cm^3. What is the greatest amount of liquid that could be in the pipette?

Q3 Elliot's house has a front door frame which is 96.5 cm wide. He wants to buy a table which is given as 95 cm wide, to the nearest 2 cm. Can he be sure that the table will fit through his door frame? PROBLEM SOLVING

Q4 A set of kitchen scales can measure masses correct to the nearest 10 g. Janek weighs out 100 g of flour. Work out the maximum and minimum possible mass of the flour.

Q5 Will and Kyle measure their heights. They are both 170 cm tall to the nearest 10 cm. What is the maximum possible difference between their heights?

16.2 Converting Units — Length, Mass and Volume

Metric units are a system of units based on powers of 10. E.g., a centimetre is 10 millimetres, a metre is 100 centimetres etc. This topic covers the metric units for length, mass and volume.

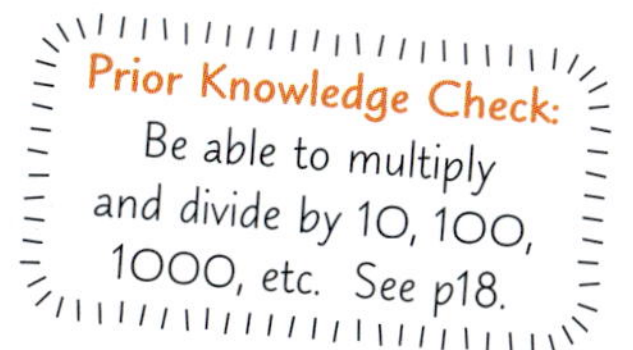

Prior Knowledge Check:
Be able to multiply
and divide by 10, 100,
1000, etc. See p18.

Learning Objective — Spec Ref N13/R1/G14:
Convert between different metric units for length, mass and volume.

The **metric units** for length, mass and volume are as follows.

- **Length** is measured in **millimetres** (mm), **centimetres** (cm), **metres** (m) and **kilometres** (km).
- **Mass** is measured in **milligrams** (mg), **grams** (g), **kilograms** (kg) and **tonnes**.
- **Volume** is measured in **millilitres** (ml), **litres** (l) and **cubic centimetres** (cm^3).

To **convert** between different units of length, mass or volume, you **multiply** or **divide** by a **conversion factor**. The most commonly used conversion factors are shown below.

Length
1 cm = 10 mm
1 m = 100 cm
1 km = 1000 m

Mass
1 g = 1000 mg
1 kg = 1000 g
1 tonne = 1000 kg

Volume
1 litre (l) = 1000 ml
1 ml = 1 cm^3

When converting from small units to **bigger units** (e.g. cm to m), you **divide** by the conversion factor. When converting from big units to **smaller units**, you **multiply** by the conversion factor.

Always **check** your answers to make sure they seem **reasonable** — e.g. if you converted an elephant's height from m to cm and got 0.025 cm, you'd know you'd gone wrong. You'd expect **more** small units than big units — there are 100 cm in 1 m, so you'd expect there to be more centimetres than metres.

Example 1

a) Convert 2.5 m into cm.

1. There are 100 cm in 1 m, so the conversion factor is 100. — 1 m = 100 cm
2. cm are smaller than m, so you need to multiply by the conversion factor to change m into cm. — So 2.5 m = 2.5 × 100 = **250 cm**

b) Convert 2500 m into km.

1. There are 1000 m in 1 km, so the conversion factor is 1000. — 1 km = 1000 m
2. km are bigger than m, so you need to divide by the conversion factor to change m into km. — 2500 m = 2500 ÷ 1000 = **2.5 km**

Exercise 1

For Questions 1-3, convert each measurement into the units given.

Q1 a) 2 cm into mm b) 15 ml into cm^3 c) 2.3 tonnes into kg

Q2 a) 3400 m into km b) 50 cm into m c) 246 kg into tonnes

Q3 a) 3 kg into g b) 379 mm into cm c) 22.3 mg into g

Q4 a) Convert 1.2 kg to grams.
b) Use your answer to find how many 30 g servings there are in a 1.2 kg box of cereal.

Q5 Convert each measurement into the units given.
a) 0.6 tonnes into g b) 62 m into mm c) 302 300 mg into kg

To **compare** measurements, or to add or subtract them, they need to be in the **same units**.

Example 2

Find the total of 0.2 tonnes, 31.8 kg and 1700 g. Give your answer in kg.

1. Convert tonnes to kg. kg are smaller than tonnes, so multiply by the conversion factor. 0.2 tonnes = 0.2 × 1000 = 200 kg
2. Convert g to kg. kg are bigger than g, so divide by the conversion factor. 1700 g = 1700 ÷ 1000 = 1.7 kg
3. The masses are all now in kg, so they can be added together. 200 kg + 31.8 kg + 1.7 kg = **233.5 kg**

Exercise 2

Q1 Complete each calculation.
a) 3200 ml + 75.3 litres = ☐ litres b) 681 cm + 51.2 m = ☐ cm
c) 3 kg + 375 g + 0.2 kg = ☐ kg d) 100 cm + 0.35 m + 12.6 m = ☐ cm
e) 4000 g + 200 kg + 1 tonne = ☐ kg f) 300 cm^3 + 0.7 litres + 250 ml = ☐ ml

Q2 How many metres further is a journey of 3.4 km than a journey of 1800 m?

Q3 A recycling van collects 3200 g of paper, 15 kg of aluminium, 0.72 tonnes of glass and 3.2 kg of cardboard. What is the mass of all the recycling in kg?

Q4 Amirah, Trevor and Elsie get into a cable car while skiing. Amirah weighs 55.2 kg, Trevor weighs 78.1 kg and Elsie weighs 65.9 kg. Each person's equipment weighs 9000 g. The cable car is unsafe when carrying a mass of over a quarter of a tonne. Will Amirah, Trevor and Elsie be safe?

Example 3

Seo-yun is making orange squash. She uses 240 ml of cordial and 3.5 litres of water.
a) How much orange squash does she make? Give your answer in cm³.

1. Convert litres to ml. ml are smaller than litres, so you need to multiply by the conversion factor.

   1 litre = 1000 ml
   3.5 litres = 3.5 × 1000
   = 3500 ml

2. Add 240 ml to 3500 ml.

   3500 ml + 240 ml = 3740 ml

3. 1 cm³ = 1 ml, so swap ml for cm³.

   3740 ml = **3740 cm³**

b) She pours the orange squash into glasses that each hold 0.25 litres. What is the minimum number of glasses needed to hold all the squash?

1. Convert ml to litres. Litres are bigger than ml, so you need to divide by the conversion factor.

   1000 ml = 1 litre
   3740 ml = 3740 ÷ 1000
   = 3.74 litres

2. Divide 3.74 by 0.25 to find how many glasses she will need.

   3.74 ÷ 0.25 = 14.96

3. You need to round up to a whole number.

   Seo-yun will need **15 glasses.**

Exercise 3

Q1 Callum buys 2 tonnes of topsoil for his gardening business. If he uses 250 kg each day, how long will his supply last?

Q2 Milly runs a 1500 m fun run, a 100 m sprint and a 13.2 km race. How many km has she run in total?

Q3 A café puts two slices of ham into every ham sandwich. A slice of ham weighs 10 g. If the café expects to sell 500 ham sandwiches, how many 1.5 kg packs of ham do they need to order?

Q4 A reservoir contains 600 000 litres of water. A stream flowing into it adds 750 000 ml of water a day.

a) If no water was removed from the reservoir, how many litres would the volume of water increase by each day?

b) The reservoir can only hold 800 000 litres of water. How many days will it take for the reservoir to start overflowing?

Q5 A recipe for lasagne needs 0.7 kg of minced beef, 400 g of tomato sauce, 300 g of cheese sauce, 0.2 kg of pasta sheets and 2500 mg of herbs and spices.

a) How many kg do these ingredients weigh?

b) If 0.2 kg of ingredients will feed one person, how many people does this recipe feed?

16.3 Converting Units — Area and Volume

Converting between units for area and volume is similar to what you've already seen with length and mass, but now you've got more dimensions to deal with...

Area

Learning Objective — Spec Ref R1/G14:
Convert between different metric units for area.

Prior Knowledge Check: Be able to find areas of rectangles. See page 346.

The area of a shape is found by multiplying **two lengths** — so area is measured in **units squared** (e.g. m^2, cm^2, mm^2).

$1 \text{ cm}^2 = 10 \times 10 = 100 \text{ mm}^2$

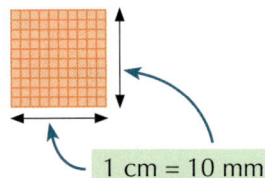

To convert between different units of area, **multiply** or **divide** by the **square** of the 'length' conversion factor. For example, the **conversion factor** between cm and mm is 10. This means the conversion factor between cm^2 and mm^2 is $10^2 = 10 \times 10 = 100$.

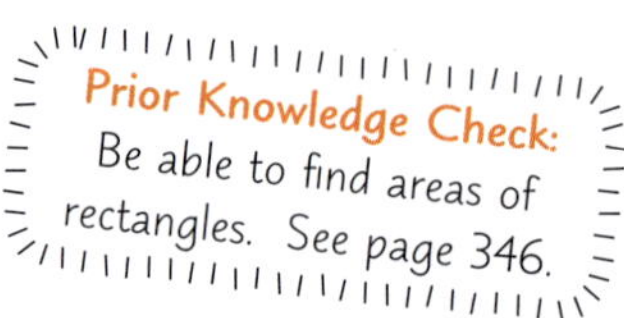

1 cm = 10 mm

Here are some commonly used conversion factors for area.

Area

$1 \text{ cm}^2 = 10^2 \text{ mm}^2 = 100 \text{ mm}^2$

$1 \text{ m}^2 = 100^2 \text{ cm}^2 = 10\,000 \text{ cm}^2$

$1 \text{ km}^2 = 1000^2 \text{ m}^2 = 1\,000\,000 \text{ m}^2$

Tip: You're dividing or multiplying by the conversion factor twice — once for each dimension.

As on p.263, **divide** by the conversion factor when converting from small units to **bigger units** and **multiply** by the conversion factor when converting from big units to **smaller units**.

Example 1

Find the area of the rectangle on the right in mm^2 by:

a) first converting its length and width to mm

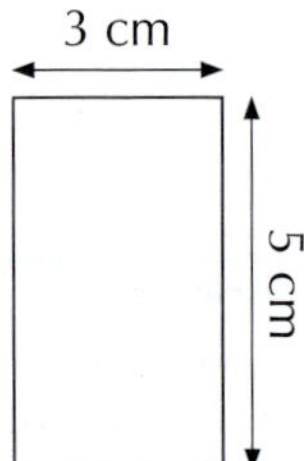

1. Convert the sides to mm. mm are smaller than cm, so multiply by the conversion factor. $5 \text{ cm} = 5 \times 10 = 50 \text{ mm}$, $3 \text{ cm} = 3 \times 10 = 30 \text{ mm}$
2. Multiply to get the area. $50 \times 30 = $ **1500 mm^2**

b) first finding the area in cm^2 and then using the appropriate conversion factor.

1. Find the area in cm^2. $5 \times 3 = 15 \text{ cm}^2$
2. Find the conversion factor from cm^2 to mm^2. 1 cm = 10 mm, so $1 \text{ cm}^2 = 10 \times 10 = 100 \text{ mm}^2$
3. Use the conversion factor to convert 15 cm^2 to mm^2. $15 \text{ cm}^2 = 15 \times 100 = $ **1500 mm^2**

Tip: mm are smaller than cm, so multiply by the conversion factor for the area.

Example 2

Convert an area of 600 cm² to m².

1. Work out the conversion factor from cm² to m².
   1 m = 100 cm,
   so 1 m² = 100 × 100 = 10 000 cm²

2. m are bigger than cm, so divide by the conversion factor.
   600 cm² = 600 ÷ 10 000 = **0.06 m²**

Exercise 1

Q1 Work out the area (in m²) of a rectangular farm measuring 2 km by 3 km by:
   a) first converting its length and width to m
   b) first finding the area in km² and then using the appropriate conversion factor.

Q2 Convert each of the following areas into the units given.
   a) 26 cm² into mm²   b) 1.05 m² into cm²   c) 1.2 m² into cm²
   d) 1750 cm² into m²   e) 8500 mm² into cm²   f) 27 cm² into m²

Q3 One bottle of weedkiller can treat an area of 16 m². How many bottles of this weedkiller should Ali buy to treat her lawn measuring 990 cm by 430 cm?

Q4 Sandeesh wants to carpet two rectangular rooms. One of the rooms measures 1.7 m by 3 m, the other is 670 cm by 420 cm. How many square metres of carpet will she need?

Volume

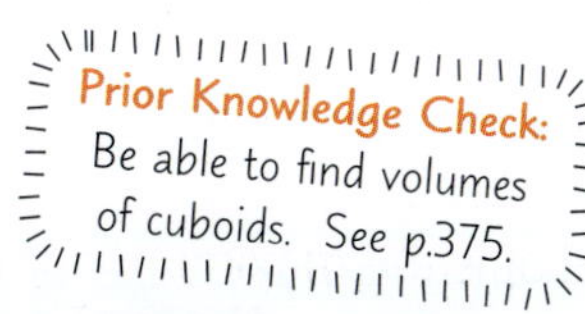

Prior Knowledge Check:
Be able to find volumes of cuboids. See p.375.

Learning Objective — Spec Ref R1/G14:
Convert between different metric units for volume.

1 cm³ = 10 × 10 × 10 = 1000 mm³

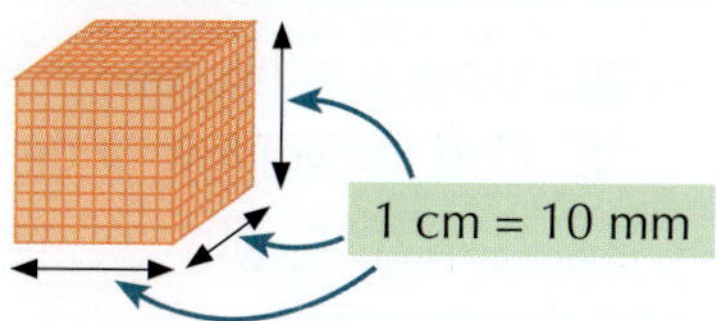

The volume of a shape is found by multiplying **three lengths**, so it is measured in **units cubed** (e.g. m³, cm³, mm³).

To convert between different units of volume, **multiply** or **divide** by the cube of the 'length' conversion factor.

For example, the **conversion factor** between cm and mm is 10. This means the conversion factor between cm³ and mm³ is $10^3 = 10 \times 10 \times 10 = 1000$.

The table on the right shows some commonly used conversion factors for volume.

Volume
1 cm³ = 10^3 mm³ = 1000 mm³
1 m³ = 100^3 cm³ = 1 000 000 cm³
1 km³ = 1000^3 m³ = 1×10^9 m³

Example 3

Convert a volume of 382 000 cm³ to m³.

1. Work out the conversion factor from cm³ to m³.

   1 m = 100 cm, so
   $1 \text{ m}^3 = 100^3 = 100 \times 100 \times 100$
   $= 1\ 000\ 000 \text{ cm}^3$

2. m are bigger than cm, so divide by the conversion factor.

   So $382\ 000 \text{ cm}^3 = 382\ 000 \div 1\ 000\ 000 =$ **0.382 m³**

Exercise 2

Q1 Work out the volume (in m³) of the swimming pool shown by:

a) first converting its length, width and depth to m

b) first finding the volume in cm³ and then using the appropriate conversion factor.

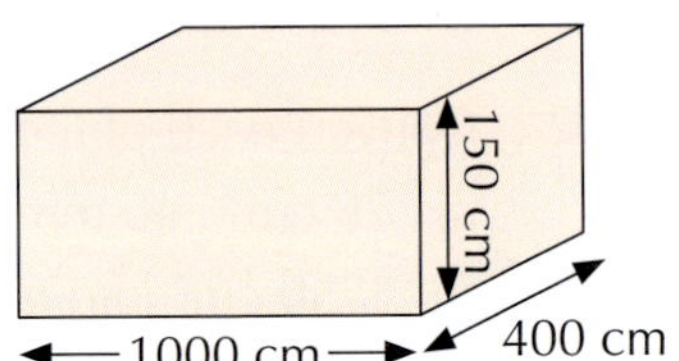

Q2 Convert each of these volumes into the units given.

a) 0.001 km³ into m³

b) 17.6 m³ into cm³

c) 1.2 km³ into m³

d) 16 000 mm³ into cm³

e) 150 m³ into km³

f) 35.9 cm³ into m³

Q3 A brand of coffee powder is sold in cuboid packets with dimensions 20 cm by 25 cm by 10 cm. A volume of 0.003 m³ of coffee powder has already been used from one packet. What volume (in m³) of coffee powder is left, assuming the packet was initially full?

Q4 A box is 10.5 cm long by 5.3 cm wide by 8.67 cm tall. Find the volume of the box in mm³.

Q5 What is the maximum number of these solid plastic bricks that can be made out of 1 m³ of plastic?

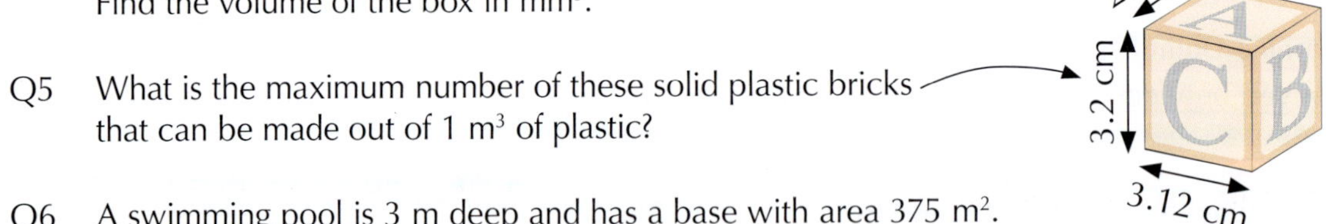

Q6 A swimming pool is 3 m deep and has a base with area 375 m².

a) Work out the volume of the swimming pool in m³.

b) Find the volume of the pool in cm³.

c) How many litres of water can the pool hold?

Q7 a) Convert 0.56 m³ to cm³.

b) Use your answer to a) to convert 0.56 m³ into mm³.

16.4 Metric and Imperial Units

The conversion factors for imperial units aren't as nice as the metric ones, but you can still use the same method to switch to different imperial units or between metric and imperial units.

Learning Objective — Spec Ref N13/R1/G14:
Convert between metric and imperial units.

The **imperial units** for length, mass and volume are as follows:

- **Length** is measured in **inches** (in), **feet**, **yards** and **miles**. There are **12 inches** in 1 foot, **3 feet** in 1 yard and **1760 yards** in 1 mile.
- **Mass** is measured in **ounces** (oz), **pounds** (lb) and **stones**. There are **16 ounces** in 1 pound and **14 pounds** in a stone.
- **Volume** is measured in **pints** and **gallons**. There are **8 pints** in 1 gallon.

Tip: As 1 foot = 12 inches, the conversion factor from feet to inches is 12.

There are **approximate conversion factors** to switch between metric and imperial units — e.g. there are approximately 2.5 cm in 1 inch. The symbol '≈' means 'approximately equal to'.

To **convert** between metric and imperial units, just **multiply** or **divide** by the conversion factors below.

Length	Mass	Volume
1 inch ≈ 2.5 cm	1 ounce ≈ 28 g	1 litre ≈ 1.76 pints
1 foot ≈ 30 cm	1 pound ≈ 450 g	1 gallon ≈ 4.5 litres
1 yard ≈ 90 cm	1 stone ≈ 6400 g	
1 mile ≈ 1.6 km	1 kg ≈ 2.2 pounds	

Tip: You'll be given metric to imperial conversion factors in an exam if they're needed. But don't be surprised if the numbers are slightly different to these.

Example 1

a) Convert 15 miles into km.

1. 1 mile ≈ 1.6 km so the conversion factor is 1.6. — 1 mile ≈ 1.6 km
2. A km is smaller than a mile, so multiply by the conversion factor. — So 15 miles ≈ 15 × 1.6 = **24 km**

b) Convert 10 km into miles.

1. Again, the conversion factor is 1.6. — 1 mile ≈ 1.6 km
2. A mile is bigger than a km, so divide by the conversion factor. — So 10 km ≈ 10 ÷ 1.6 = **6.25 miles**

Exercise 1

In these questions, use the conversion factors given on the previous page.

Q1 Convert these measurements into different imperial units:

a) 2 feet into inches b) 0.5 gallons into pints c) 9 gallons into pints
d) 56 pounds into stone e) 60 inches into feet f) 32 pints into gallons

Q2 Convert these measurements from imperial units to metric units.

a) 4 inches into cm b) 3 ounces into g c) 10 stone into g
d) 5 yards into cm e) 25 miles into km f) 6 feet into cm

Q3 Convert these measurements from metric units to imperial units.

a) 8 km into miles b) 100 pints into litres c) 12 800 g into stone
d) 25 cm into inches e) 56 g into ounces f) 16.5 pounds into kg

Q4 A running track is 400 m long. How many laps of the track make one mile? 

Q5 a) Convert 18 yards into cm.
b) Use your answer to part a) to convert 18 yards into metres.

Q6 Convert each measurement into the units given.

a) 11 feet into m b) 1 stone into kg c) 16 pints into ml

Often when you're converting between metric and imperial units, you'll need to convert the imperial units **to** and **from** a **mixture of big and small units** (e.g. feet and inches):

- To write small imperial units as a **mixture of big and small units** (e.g. inches to feet and inches), you **divide** by the conversion factor and keep the **remainder** in the smaller units.
- To write a **mixture** of big and small units in **smaller units** (e.g. feet and inches to inches), you **multiply** the big unit by the conversion factor and **add** the remaining small units.

Example 2

Convert 6 pounds and 4 ounces into kilograms.

1. Write the whole mass in the same unit. Ounces are smaller than pounds, so multiply by the conversion factor.

1 pound = 16 ounces,
6 pounds = 6 × 16 = 96 ounces

So 6 pounds and 4 ounces = 96 + 4
= 100 ounces

2. Convert this from ounces into grams. Grams are smaller than ounces, so multiply by the conversion factor.

1 ounce ≈ 28 grams,
100 ounces ≈ 100 × 28 = 2800 g

3. Then convert the result from grams to kilograms.

2800 g = 2800 ÷ 1000 = **2.8 kg**

Example 3

Convert 160 cm into feet and inches.

1. First, convert 160 cm into inches. Inches are bigger than cm, so divide by the conversion factor.

   1 inch ≈ 2.5 cm,
   160 cm ≈ 160 ÷ 2.5 = 64 inches

2. Convert 64 inches into feet and inches. Feet are bigger than inches, so divide by the conversion factor.

   1 foot = 12 inches,
   64 ÷ 12 = 5 remainder 4

3. Keep the remainder in inches.

   So 160 cm ≈ **5 feet 4 inches**

Exercise 2

In these questions, use the conversion factors given on page 269.

Q1 Convert each of the following measurements into the units given.

a) 3 ft 7 in to inches b) 12 ft 5 in to inches c) 5 lb 2 oz to ounces
d) 280 in to feet and inches e) 72 oz to lb and oz f) 200 oz to lb and oz

Q2 For each of the following:

(i) Convert the mass into ounces. (ii) Write this in pounds and ounces.

a) 1904 g b) 840 g c) 4.9 kg d) 0.98 kg

Q3 Convert each of the following into feet and inches.

a) 50 cm b) 105 cm c) 2 m d) 3.4 m

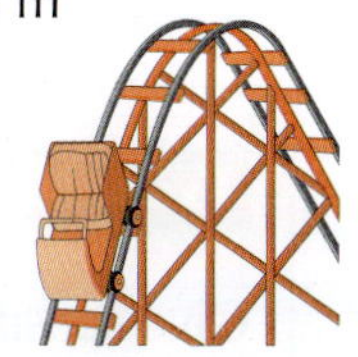

Q4 A ride at a theme park states you must be 140 cm or over to ride.
Maddie is 4 foot 5 inches and Lily is 4 foot 9 inches.
Can they both go on the ride?

Q5 Jamie and Oliver are cooking. They need 1 pound and 12 ounces of tofu for their recipe. They see a 750 g packet of tofu in the supermarket. Will this be enough?

Q6 The weights of 8 people getting into a lift are shown below.

7 stone 2 pounds	11 stone 4 pounds	16 stone	15 stone 4 pounds
10 stone 3 pounds	12 stone	8 stone 9 pounds	13 stone 1 pound

The lift has a weight limit of 0.8 tonnes.
Will the total weight of the 8 people exceed the limit?

16.5 Estimating in Real Life

When something is tricky to measure properly, you can look at how big it is compared to something else, and use that to estimate its size.

Learning Objective — Spec Ref N14:
Estimate the size of real-life objects by comparison.

You can **estimate** how big something is by comparing it with something you already know the size of. For example, the average height of a man is approximately 1.8 m, so something half as tall as an average-height man would be just under a metre tall.

An estimate does not have to be completely accurate, but make sure your answer seems **realistic** and is given in **suitable units**.

Example 1

Estimate the height of this lamp post.

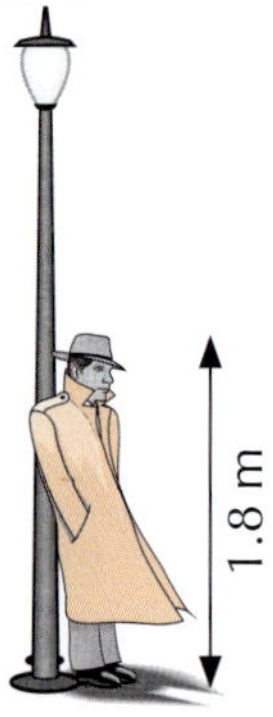

1. Estimate the height of the man. — Average height of a man ≈ 1.8 m.
2. Compare the height of the lamp post and the man. — The lamp post is roughly twice the height of the man.
3. Estimate the height of the lamp post by multiplying the height of the man by 2. — Height of the lamp post ≈ 2 × 1.8 m = **3.6 m**

Example 2

Give sensible units for measuring the height of a room.

When you give a measurement, use units that mean the value isn't too big or too small.

Most rooms are taller than an average person, but not that much taller — roughly 2 to 3 metres. So it makes sense to measure the height of a room in metres (or possibly cm).

A sensible unit is **metres**.

You wouldn't use km or mm to measure the height of a room — the number in km would be very small (0.002 km), and the number in mm would be very big (2000 mm).

Tip: It's usually easier to estimate in real life using metric units, but feet (or feet and inches) would be an acceptable answer in imperial units.

Exercise 1

Q1 For each of the following, suggest a sensible unit of measurement, using:

(i) metric units (ii) imperial units

a) the length of a pencil
b) the mass of a tomato
c) the height of a house
d) the length of an ant
e) the mass of a bus
f) the weight of a baby
g) the distance from Birmingham to Manchester

Q2 Estimate each of the following, using sensible metric units.

a) the height of your bedroom
b) the height of a football goal
c) the arm span of an average man
d) the volume of a mug

For Questions 3-5 give your answer in sensible units.

Q3 Estimate:

a) the height of this house,
b) the height of this elephant.

Q4 Estimate the length and height of the bus.

Q5 Estimate:

a) the height and length of this dinosaur by comparing it with a chicken,
b) the height of this rhino by comparing it with a domestic cat.

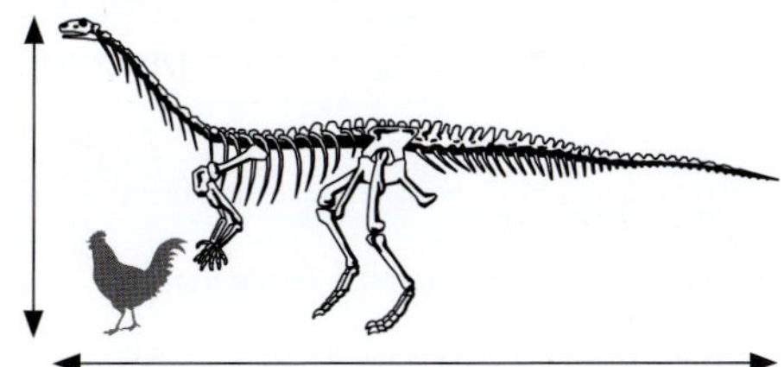

Review Exercise

Q1 Write down the volume of liquid shown in each of these containers.

a) 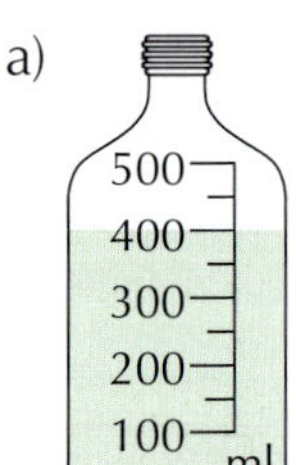

b) 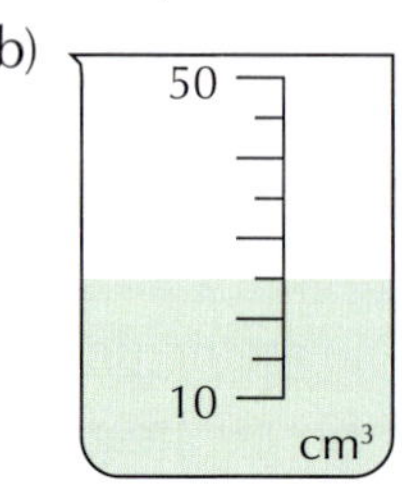

c) 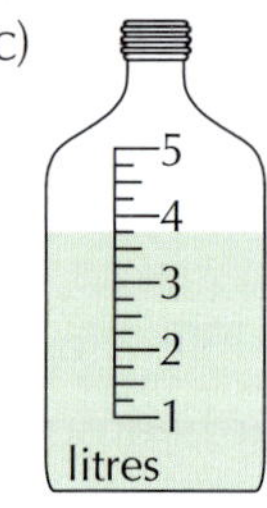

d) 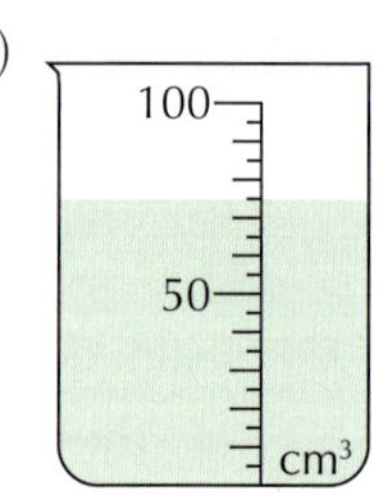

Q2 A snake is measured to be 10.6 m long to the nearest 0.2 m.
Write down the maximum and minimum possible length of the snake.

Q3 Jane is having a party for 30 guests. Her glasses have a capacity of 400 ml each.
If she wants everyone to have a full glass of juice, how many 2 litre bottles of juice should she buy?

Q4 A recipe uses 450 g of flour, 0.2 kg of margarine, 300 g of fruit and 0.1 kg of sugar.
How much more than 1 kg is the total mass of these ingredients? Give your answer in kg.

Q5 a) Calculate the area (in mm^2) of a sticker measuring 20 mm by 40 mm.

b) Convert this area to cm^2 by using the appropriate conversion factor.

Q6 A carton of apple juice measures 7 cm by 50 mm by 0.17 m, and is completely full.

a) Find the volume of the carton in cm^3.

b) Hati fills 7 glasses, each of which has a volume of 20 cm^3, with juice.
How much juice (in cm^3) does she use?

c) How much juice (in mm^3) will she have left in the carton?

Q7 Convert these measurements from imperial units to metric.

a) 3 ounces into g
b) 2 gallons into litres
c) 10 stone into g
d) 5 yards into cm
e) 2.7 inches into cm
f) 4.5 pints into litres

Q8 Estimate each of the following, using sensible units:

a) the length of a family car
b) the diameter of a football
c) the height of a doorway
d) the volume of a lunch box carton of juice

Exam-Style Questions

Q1 a) Change 625 cm into metres. 

[1 mark]

b) Change 3.94 kg into grams. 

[1 mark]

Q2 The diagram on the right shows an adult of average height stood on level ground next to a double-decker bus. Use the diagram to estimate the height of the bus, giving your answer in an appropriate metric unit.

[2 marks]

Q3 Jack buys 1.2 kg of flour. How many pizzas can he make if each pizza needs 300 g of flour? 

[1 mark]

Q4 Grace has made 7.35 litres of fruit punch to serve at a party. She serves it by filling glasses which hold exactly 250 ml.

a) How many full glasses will she be able to serve?

[2 marks]

b) How much punch will she have left over once she has filled as many glasses as possible? Write your answer in litres.

[1 mark]

Q5 1 stone ≈ 6400 g, 1 pound ≈ 450 g, 1 ounce ≈ 28 g.
An airline allows each passenger to travel with 18 kg of luggage.
Iona has one bag that weighs 10 pounds 2 ounces, and a second bag that weighs 2 stone. Can she take both bags with her on the flight?

[3 marks]

Q6 Lotte's car travels 55 miles per gallon of petrol. Her car contains 45 litres of petrol.

a) How many miles can she travel?
Use the approximation 1 gallon ≈ 4.5 litres.

[2 marks]

b) If petrol costs £5 per gallon, how much did the petrol in her car cost?

[1 mark]

17.1 Speed, Distance and Time

The speed of an object is the distance it travels divided by the time it takes to travel the distance. Speed is an example of a compound measure. Compound measures are a combination of two or more other measurements — in this case, distance and time.

Finding an Object's Speed

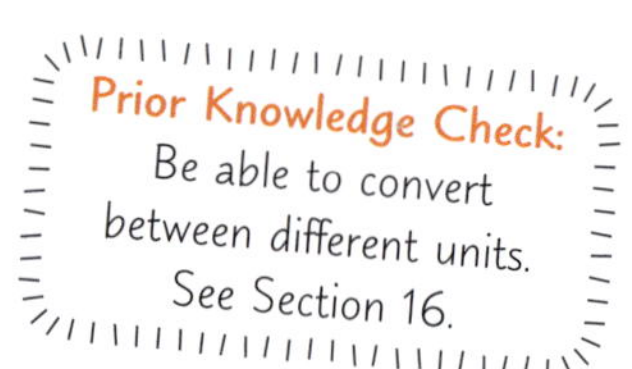

Prior Knowledge Check:
Be able to convert between different units.
See Section 16.

Learning Objective — Spec Ref N13/R1/R11:
Be able to calculate an object's speed given distance and time.

Distance, time and (average) speed are connected by the **formula**:

$$\textbf{Speed} = \frac{\textbf{Distance}}{\textbf{Time}}$$

The formula gives the **average speed** of the journey — the actual speed is likely to change throughout. The units for speed are **distance per unit time**, e.g. **km per hour** or **metres per second**.

Tip: Other examples of compound measures include rates of pay (e.g. £ per hour) and prices per unit mass/volume (e.g. £ per kg or pence per ml).

Example 1

A car travels 150 km in 3 hours. What is the average speed of the car?

1. Substitute the distance and time into the formula for speed.
2. The units of speed are a combination of the units of distance (here, km) and time (here, hours).

$$\text{Speed} = \frac{\text{Distance}}{\text{Time}} = \frac{150\text{ km}}{3\text{ hours}} = \mathbf{50\text{ km/h}}.$$

Example 2

A car travels 81 km in 45 minutes. What is the average speed of the car in km/h?

1. Convert the time to hours.

$$45\text{ minutes} = 45 \div 60 = 0.75\text{ hours}$$

2. Substitute the distance and time into the formula. The units of speed are a combination of the units of distance (km) and time (hours).

$$\text{Speed} = \frac{\text{Distance}}{\text{Time}} = \frac{81\text{ km}}{0.75\text{ hours}} = \mathbf{108\text{ km/h}}$$

Exercise 1

Q1 Calculate the average speed of each of the following journeys.

a) distance = 30 km, time = 2 hours

b) distance = 60 km, time = 3 hours

c) distance = 150 miles, time = 5 hours

d) distance = 140 miles, time = 4 hours

Q2 Find the average speed of the following.

a) a car travelling 80 km in 2 hours

b) a snail crawling 50 cm in 500 seconds

c) a plane flying 1800 miles in 3 hours

d) a lift travelling 100 m in 80 seconds

Q3 Find the average speed of the following in km/h.

a) a tractor moving 10 km in 30 minutes

b) a train travelling 30 000 m in 2.5 hours

c) a river flowing 2.25 km in 45 minutes

d) a balloon rising 700 m in 3 minutes

Tip: Convert the units to kilometres and hours first.

Finding Distance or Time

Learning Objective — Spec Ref N13/R1/R11:
Know and be able to use the formula linking speed, distance and time to find the distance of a journey or the time a journey took.

You can **rearrange** the speed formula to give formulas for **distance** and **time**:

Distance = Speed × Time

Time = $\frac{\textbf{Distance}}{\textbf{Speed}}$

You can use the **formula triangle** given below to help you remember all three of the formulas. To use the formula triangle, **cover up** the measurement that you want to find and **write down** the two measurements that are left.

- To find **speed**, cover up **S** to leave $\frac{\mathbf{D}}{\mathbf{T}}$
- To find **distance**, cover up **D** to leave **S × T**
- To find **time**, cover up **T** to leave $\frac{\mathbf{D}}{\mathbf{S}}$

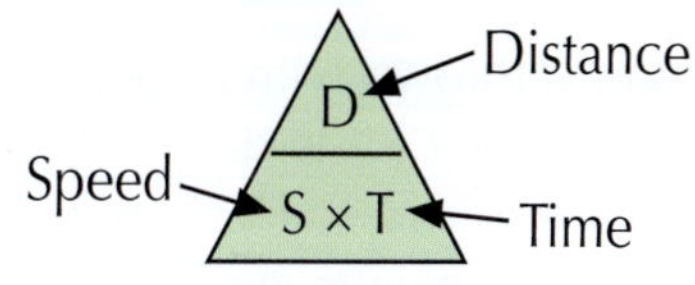

Remember to always **check the units** before doing a calculation. If you have **speed** in **mph** and **time** in **minutes**, then doing speed × time won't give you the correct answer.

Example 3

A man runs for 30 minutes with an average speed of 12 km/h. How far does he run?

1. The speed is in km/h, so convert the time into hours. — 30 minutes = 0.5 hours
2. Write down the formula for distance. — Distance = Speed × Time
3. Substitute the speed and time into the formula. — 12 km/h × 0.5 hours = **6 km**.
4. The speed is in km/h, so the distance will be in km.

Example 4

A train travels 60 miles at a speed of 100 mph. How many minutes will the journey take?

1. Write down the formula for time. — $\text{Time} = \frac{\text{Distance}}{\text{Speed}}$
2. Substitute the distance and speed into the formula. — $\frac{60\text{ miles}}{100\text{ mph}} = 0.6\text{ hours}$
3. Convert your answer into minutes. — 0.6 hours = 0.6 × 60 minutes = **36 minutes**

Exercise 2

Q1 For each of the following, use the speed and time given to calculate the distance travelled.

a) speed = 20 km/h, time = 2 hours
b) speed = 10 m/s, time = 50 seconds
c) speed = 3 km/h, time = 24 hours
d) speed = 70 mph, time = 2.5 hours

Q2 For each of the following, use the speed and distance given to calculate the time taken.

a) speed = 2 km/h, distance = 4 km
b) speed = 15 m/s, distance = 45 m
c) speed = 60 mph, distance = 150 miles
d) speed = 24 km/h, distance = 6 km

Q3 Find the distance travelled by a bus moving at 30 mph for 4 hours.

Q4 A dart is thrown with a speed of 15 m/s. It hits a dartboard 2.4 m away.
For how long is the dart in the air?

Q5 A flight to Spain takes 2 hours. The plane travels at an average speed of 490 mph.
How far does the plane travel?

Q6 A train travels at 56 km/h for 5.6 km. How many minutes does the journey take?

Q7 A girl skates at an average speed of 7.5 mph. How far does she skate in 15 minutes?

Converting Between Units of Speed

Learning Objective — Spec Ref N13/R1/R11:
Be able to convert between units of speed.

To **convert** between units of speed, you can convert the **individual units** that make it up. For example, to convert **km/h to m/s** you would need to do **two separate conversions:**

- First convert **km** to **metres** (to give m per hour),
- Then convert **hours** to **seconds** (to give m/s).

Tip: It doesn't matter which unit you convert first, but always check your conversions to make sure your answers are sensible.

Example 5

A swallow is flying at a speed of 9 m/s. What is its speed in km/h?

1. Work out the conversion factor for m to km. There'll be fewer km/s than m/s, so divide.

   1 km = 1000 m
   9 m/s = (9 ÷ 1000) km/s = 0.009 km/s

2. Work out the conversion factor for s to h. There'll be more km/h than km/s, so multiply.

   1 hour = 60 min = (60 × 60) s
   0.009 km/s = (0.009 × 60 × 60) km/h
   = **32.4 km/h**

Example 6

Using the conversion 1 mile ≈ 1.6 km, what is 8 km/h in mph?

Use the conversion factor for km to miles. There'll be fewer miles per hour than km/h, so divide.

1 mile ≈ 1.6 km

8 km/h ≈ $\frac{8}{1.6}$ = **5 mph**

Exercise 3

Q1 Convert each of the speeds below into the given units.
a) 50 m/s into km/h b) 72 km/h into m/s c) 26.5 m/s into km/h

Q2 James is cycling at 18 km/h. What is his speed in m/s?

Q3 Using the conversion 1 mile ≈ 1.6 km, convert each of these speeds into the given units.
a) 54 km/h to mph b) 25 mph to km/h c) 94.4 km/h to mph

Q4 A slug is moving at 0.5 cm/s. What is its speed in metres per minute (m/min)?

Q5 A train travels at 40 m/s. What is the train's speed in mph?

17.2 Density, Mass and Volume

Density is another compound measure — it's a combination of mass and volume.

Learning Objective — Spec Ref N13/R1/R11:
Know and be able to use the formula linking density, mass and volume.

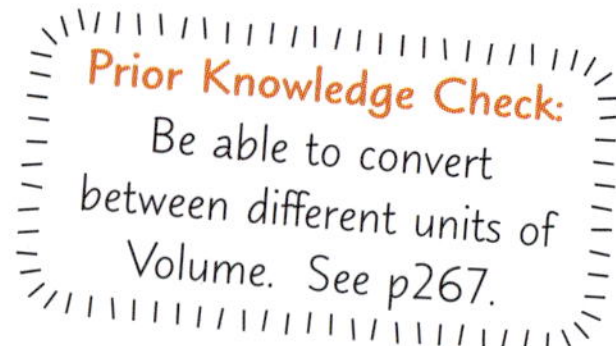

Prior Knowledge Check:
Be able to convert between different units of volume. See p267.

Density is the **mass per unit volume** of a substance and is usually measured in kg/m³ or g/cm³. Different substances have **different densities** — for example, gold has a **higher density** than ice. The **formula** that connects density, mass and volume is:

$$\textbf{Density} = \frac{\textbf{Mass}}{\textbf{Volume}}$$

You can rearrange the formula to find mass and volume.

$$\textbf{Volume} = \frac{\textbf{Mass}}{\textbf{Density}} \qquad \textbf{Mass = Density × Volume}$$

The **formula triangle** on the right gives a summary of all the formulas. Remember to **check the units** of the measurements that you're putting into a formula — that way you'll know the units of the measurement that comes out.

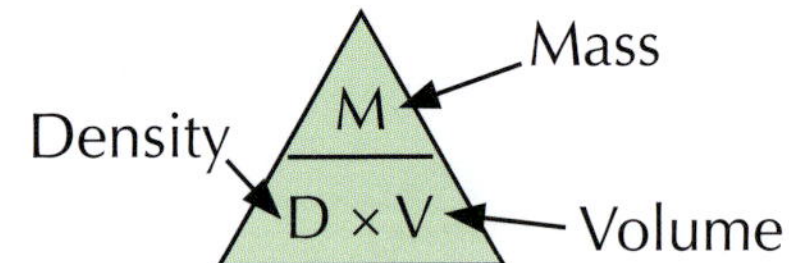

Example 1

A 20 g block of wood has a volume of 50 cm³.

a) Calculate the density of the wooden block in g/cm³.

1. Substitute the mass and volume into the formula for density.
2. The units of density are a combination of the units of mass (g) and volume (cm³).

$$\text{Density} = \frac{\text{Mass}}{\text{Volume}} = \frac{20\text{ g}}{50\text{ cm}^3} = \mathbf{0.4\ g/cm^3}$$

b) What is its density in kg/m³?

1. Work out the conversion factor for g to kg. There'll be fewer kg/cm³ than g/cm³, so divide.

$1\text{ kg} = 1000\text{ g}$

$0.4\text{ g/cm}^3 = (0.4 \div 1000)\text{ kg/cm}^3 = 0.0004\text{ kg/cm}^3$

2. Work out the conversion factor for cm³ to m³. There'll be more kg/m³ than kg/cm³, so multiply.

$1\text{ m}^3 = (100 \times 100 \times 100)\text{ cm}^3 = 1\,000\,000\text{ cm}^3$

$0.0004\text{ kg/cm}^3 = (0.0004 \times 1\,000\,000)\text{ kg/m}^3 = \mathbf{400\ kg/m^3}$

Example 2

The mass of water in a bathtub is 180 kg. Water has a density of 1000 kg/m³. What is the volume of water in the bathtub?

1. Write down the formula for volume.
   $$\text{Volume} = \frac{\text{Mass}}{\text{Density}}$$
2. Check units — the mass is in kg and the density is in kg/m³, so your answer will be in m³.
   Mass = 180 kg, Density = 1000 kg/m³
3. Substitute the numbers into the formula.
   $$\text{Volume} = \frac{180 \text{ kg}}{1000 \text{ kg/m}^3} = \mathbf{0.18 \text{ m}^3}$$

Exercise 1

Q1 For each of the following, use the mass and volume to calculate the density in kg/m³.

a) mass = 20 kg, volume = 5 m³
b) mass = 300 kg, volume = 5 m³
c) mass = 1000 kg, volume = 4 m³
d) mass = 63 000 kg, volume = 700 m³

Q2 A 1840 kg concrete block has a volume of 0.8 m³.
Calculate the density of the concrete block.

Q3 a) Write down the formula to calculate volume from density and mass.

b) Use your answer to calculate the volume for each of the following.

(i) density = 8 kg/m³, mass = 40 kg
(ii) density = 15 kg/m³, mass = 750 kg
(iii) density = 240 kg/m³, mass = 4800 kg

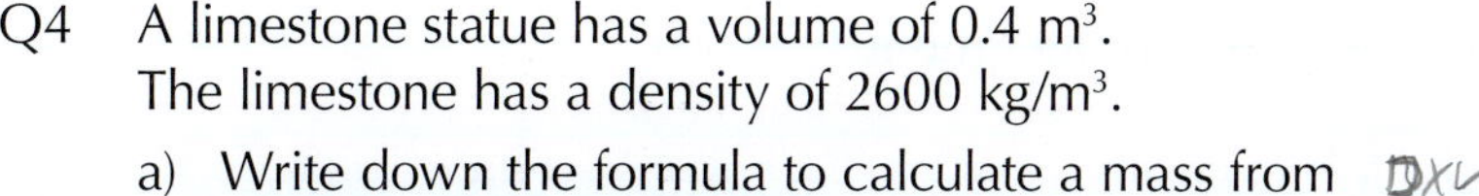

Q4 A limestone statue has a volume of 0.4 m³.
The limestone has a density of 2600 kg/m³.

a) Write down the formula to calculate a mass from a volume and a density.

b) Calculate the mass of the statue.

Q5 A cricket ball has a mass of 0.15 kg and a volume of 200 cm³.
Calculate the density of the cricket ball in kg/m³.

Q6 A paperweight has a volume of 8 cm³ and a density of 11 500 kg/m³.
Calculate the mass of the paperweight.

Q7 A roll of aluminium foil has a density of 2.7 g/cm³.
What is the density of aluminium in kg/m³?

17.3 Pressure, Force and Area

Like speed and density, pressure is a compound measure — it's a combination of force and area.

Learning Objective — Spec Ref N13/R1/R11:
Know and be able to use the formula linking pressure, force and area.

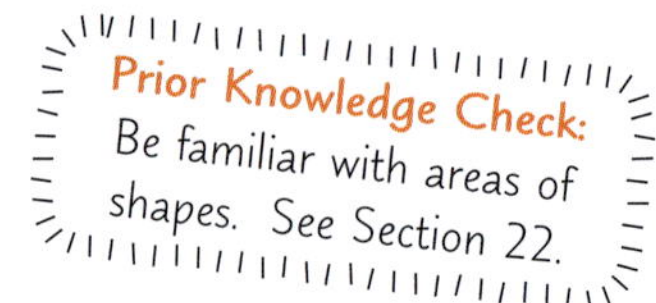

Prior Knowledge Check:
Be familiar with areas of shapes. See Section 22.

Pressure is the **force** exerted by an object **per unit area**. Pressure is usually measured in **N/m²** (also known as pascals, **Pa**), or **N/cm²**, where **N** is **newtons**, the unit of force.

The **formula** that connects pressure, force and area is:

$$\textbf{Pressure} = \frac{\textbf{Force}}{\textbf{Area}}$$

You can rearrange the formula to find **force** and **area**:

$$\textbf{Force} = \textbf{Pressure} \times \textbf{Area} \qquad \textbf{Area} = \frac{\textbf{Force}}{\textbf{Pressure}}$$

The **formula triangle** on the right gives a summary of these formulas. Don't forget to **check your units** throughout so that you know the units of your final measurement.

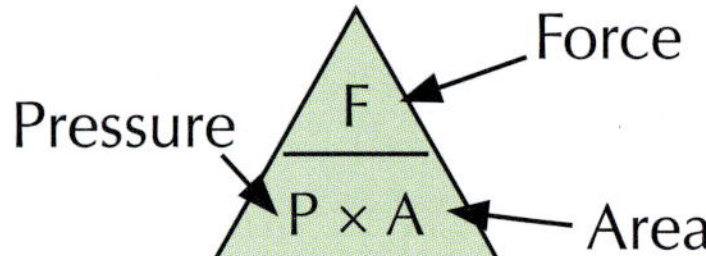

Example 1

An object is resting with its base on horizontal ground. The area of the object's base is 20 cm² and the object weighs 60 N.

a) What pressure is the object exerting on the ground?

1. Write down the formula for pressure. — $\text{Pressure} = \frac{\text{Force}}{\text{Area}}$
2. Check units — you have force in N and area in cm², so your answer will be in N/cm². — Force = 60 N, Area = 20 cm²
3. Substitute the numbers into the formula. — $\text{Pressure} = \frac{60\text{ N}}{20\text{ cm}^2} = \mathbf{3\ N/cm^2}$

b) What is the pressure in N/m²?

1. Work out the conversion factor for N/cm² to N/m². — $1\text{ m}^2 = (100 \times 100)\text{ cm}^2 = 10\,000\text{ cm}^2$
2. There will be more N/m² than N/cm², so multiply. — $3\text{ N/cm}^2 = 3 \times 10\,000 = \mathbf{30\,000\ N/m^2}$

Example 2

A laptop with a base of 0.07 m² is resting on a desk and exerting a pressure of 330 N/m². What is the weight of the laptop?

1. Write down the formula for force. — Force = Pressure × Area
2. Check units — you have area in m^2 and pressure in N/m^2, so your answer will be in N. — Pressure = 330 N/m^2, Area = 0.07 m^2
3. Substitute the numbers into the formula. — Force = 330 N/m^2 × 0.07 m^2 = **23.1 N**

Tip: Weight is the force of an object on a surface due to gravity.

Exercise 1

Q1 For each of the following, use the area and force to calculate the pressure.

a) Area = 3 cm^2, Force = 27 N
b) Area = 5 m^2, Force = 125 N
c) Area = 4 m^2, Force = 4800 N
d) Area = 80 cm^2, Force = 640 N

Q2 Calculate the area in each of the following situations.

a) Pressure = 6 N/cm^2, Force = 36 N
b) Pressure = 120 N/m^2, Force = 840 N
c) Pressure = 2.5 N/cm^2, Force = 10 N
d) Pressure = 180 N/m^2, Force = 540 N

Q3 Calculate the force in each of the following situations.

a) Pressure = 300 N/m^2, Area = 5 m
b) Pressure = 36 N/cm^2, Area = 30 cm^2

Q4 A cube has edges of length 10 cm. When it rests on horizontal ground it exerts a pressure of 0.02 N/cm^2. What is its weight?

Q5 A cube of metal with a volume of 512 cm^3 is resting with one of its faces on horizontal ground. The cube has a weight of 1792 N.

a) What is the area of each face of the cube?
b) What pressure is the cube exerting on the ground?

Q6 A square-based pyramid is resting with its square face on horizontal ground. The pyramid has a weight of 45 N and its square face has a side length of 3 cm. What pressure is the pyramid exerting on the ground?

Give your answer in: a) N/cm^2 b) N/m^2

17.4 Distance-Time Graphs

Distance-time graphs are used to show the journey of an object over a given period of time.

Representing a Journey on a Distance-Time Graph

Learning Objective — Spec Ref A14:
Draw and interpret distance-time graphs.

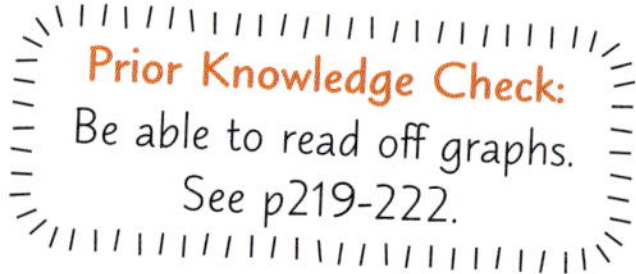

Prior Knowledge Check:
Be able to read off graphs.
See p219-222.

A **distance-time** graph shows how far an object has travelled in a particular period of time.

- When the graph is **going up**, the object is **moving away**.
- When the graph is **going down**, the object is **coming back**.
- A **straight** line shows the object is moving at a **constant speed**.
- A **horizontal** line means the object is **stationary**.

Tip: Be careful when reading distance-time graphs — they show distance from a point, not always total distance travelled.

Example 1

Danny cycles 5 miles in 20 minutes. He stops and rests for 10 minutes, then returns to his starting point in 30 minutes. Copy the axes on the right and use them to draw a graph of Danny's journey.

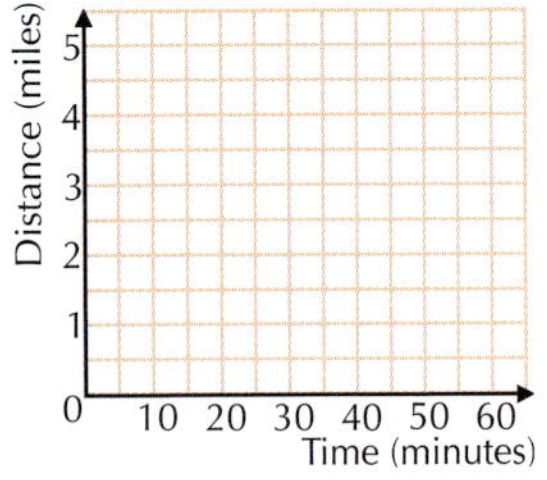

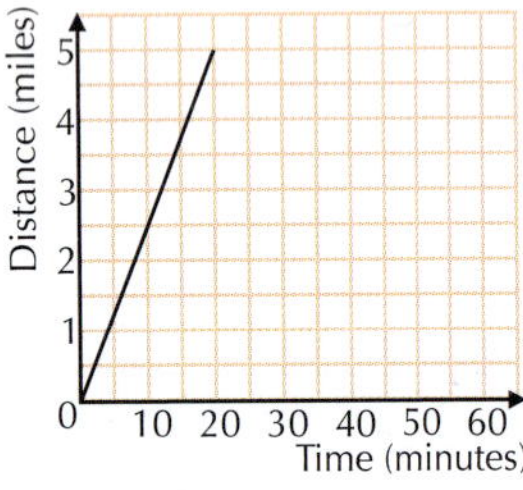

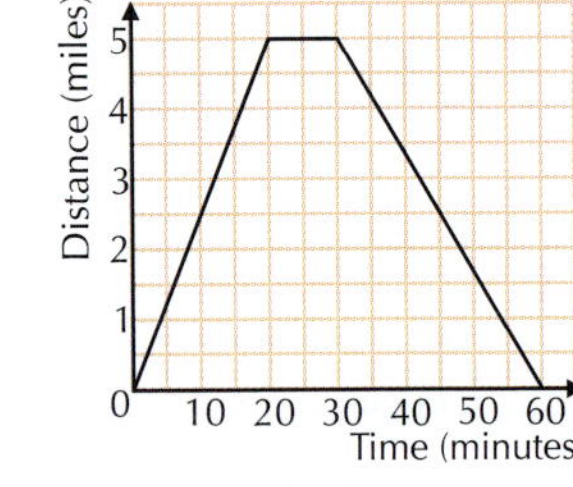

1. The first part of the graph shows 5 miles being covered in 20 minutes. It's a straight line from the origin to the point representing 20 minutes on the x-axis and 5 miles on the y-axis.
2. The second part of the graph shows no distance covered during the next 10 minutes. It's a horizontal line from 20 minutes to 30 minutes (on the x-axis).
3. The final part of the graph shows the 5-mile return journey taking 30 minutes. It's a straight line back to a distance of 0 miles (on the y-axis) and to a time of 60 minutes (on the x-axis).

Exercise 1

Q1 Adi is a keen cyclist. The following points describe the different stages of one of her bike rides.

- Adi cycles 30 km in 2 hours.
- She stops and rests for half an hour.
- She then cycles a further 40 km in 2.5 hours.

Copy the coordinate grid on the right.

a) Draw a straight line on the grid to represent the first stage of Adi's journey.

b) The second stage of her ride is represented by a horizontal line. Draw this part of the graph.

c) (i) After the third stage of her ride, how far is Adi from her original starting point?

(ii) Draw the straight line representing the third stage of Adi's ride.

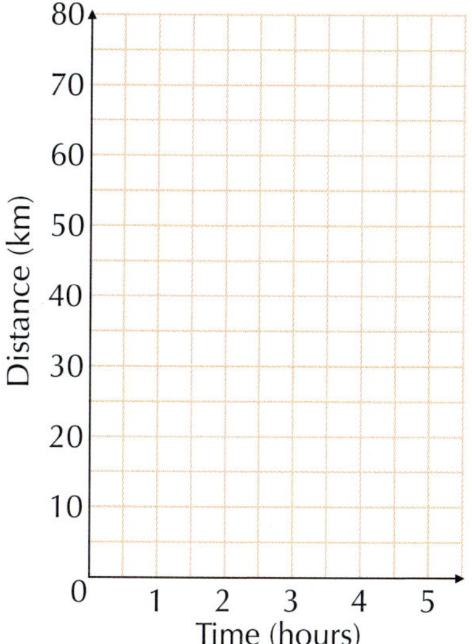

Draw a graph representing each of the journeys described in **Questions 2-3**.

Q2 Yemi drives 50 km in 1 hour, stops at a service station for half an hour, then drives a further 30 km in half an hour.

Q3 Sandy walks 2 km to the bus stop in 20 minutes. She waits for 10 minutes for a bus to arrive. She then travels a further 5 km on the bus in 15 minutes.

Q4 The graph on the right shows a family's car journey. The family left home at 8:00 am.

a) How far had the family travelled when they stopped?

b) How long did the family stay at their destination before setting off home?

c) (i) What time did they start the journey back home?

(ii) How long did the journey home take?

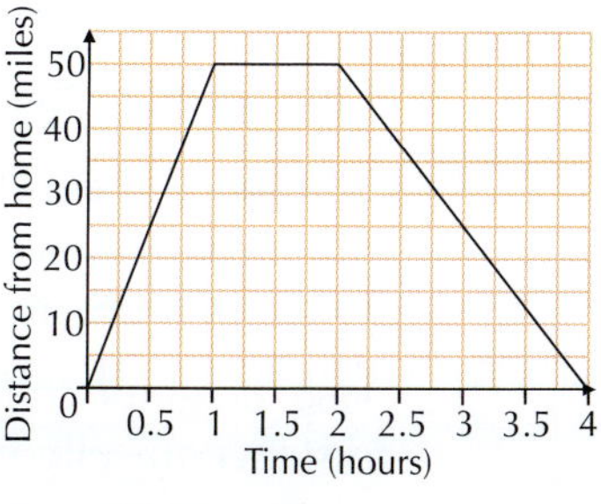

Q5 Describe the journey that is represented by each of these distance-time graphs.

a)

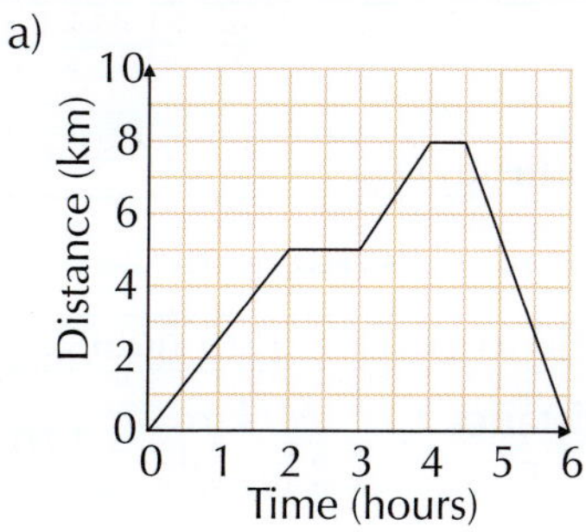

b)

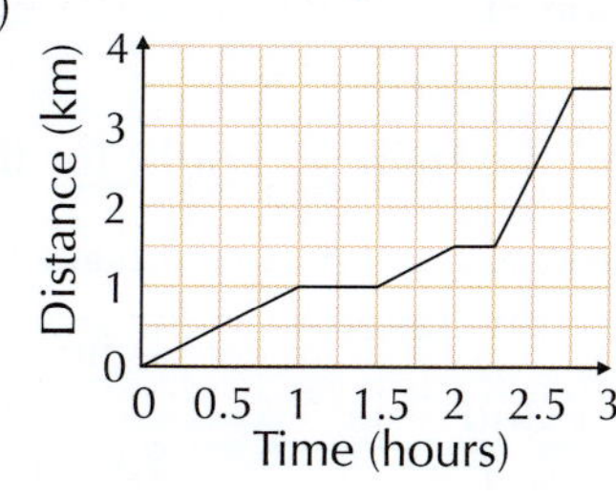

c)

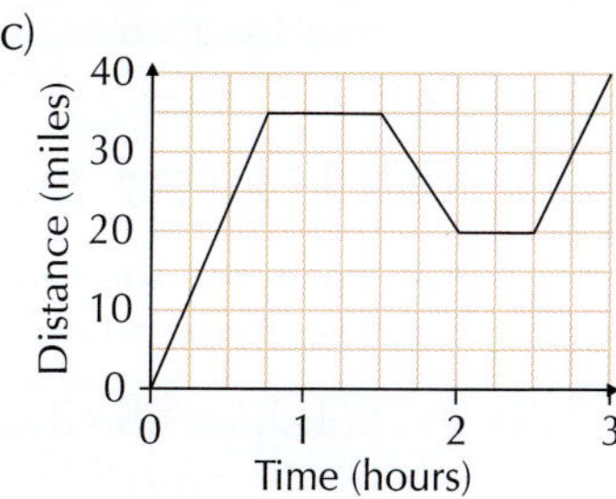

Finding Speed from a Distance-Time Graph

Learning Objective — Spec Ref A14/R14:
Be able to find speed from a distance-time graph.

The **gradient** of a distance-time graph shows the **speed** of the object.

- The steeper the graph, the faster the object is moving.
- Remember, a horizontal line means the object is stationary.

You can work out the speed at any stage of the journey by dividing the **distance travelled** by the **time taken**.

To calculate the **average speed** across the whole journey, divide the **total distance travelled** by the **total time taken**.

Tip: If the graph goes up and down, add up the distance travelled at each stage to find the total distance travelled.

Example 2

The graph below represents a train journey from Clumpton Station to Hillybrook Station.

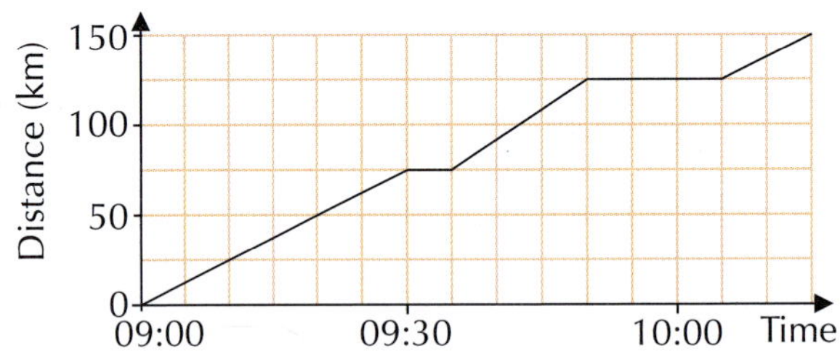

a) Find the speed of the train (in km/h) at 9:15.

1. The speed is constant from 9:00 until 9:30, so the speed at 9:15 is equal to the average speed over this time.
2. Use the graph to find the distance travelled in this time.
3. Substitute the distance and time into the formula for speed.

Distance = 75 km

Time = 30 mins = 0.5 hours

$$\text{Speed} = \frac{\text{Distance}}{\text{Time}} = \frac{75\text{ km}}{0.5\text{ hours}} = \mathbf{150\text{ km/h}}$$

b) Find the average speed of the train (in km/h) for this journey.

1. Work out the total distance travelled and the total time taken.
2. Substitute the distance and time into the formula for speed.

Distance = 150 – 0 = 150 km

Time = 09:00 to 10:15 = 1.25 hours

$$\text{Speed} = \frac{\text{Distance}}{\text{Time}} = \frac{150\text{ km}}{1.25\text{ hours}} = \mathbf{120\text{ km/h}}$$

Exercise 2

Q1 Find the speed of the object represented by each of the following distance-time graphs.

a) 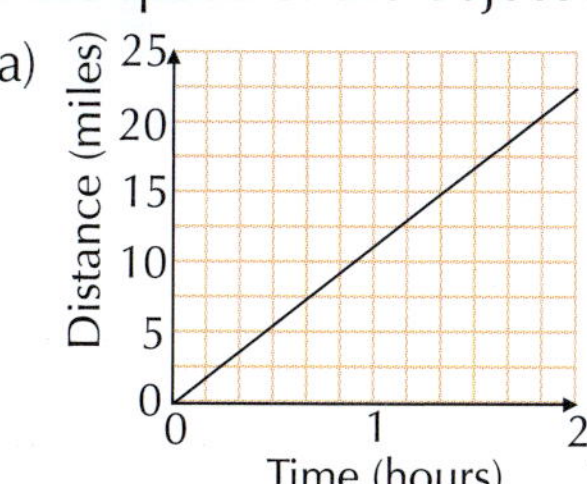

b) 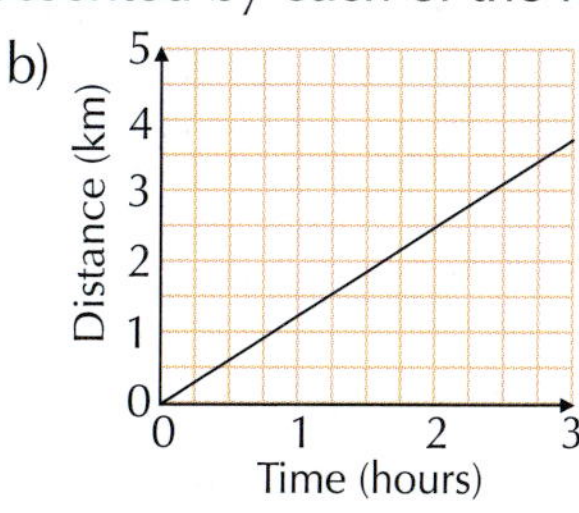

c) 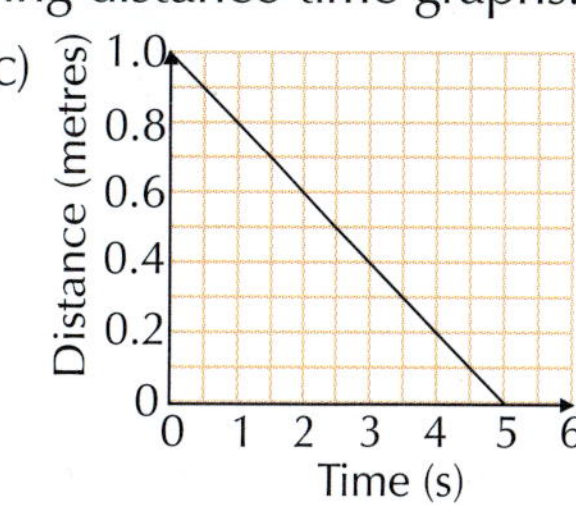

Q2 This graph shows Gil's journey to work. His journey consisted of two stages of travelling, separated by a break of 30 minutes.

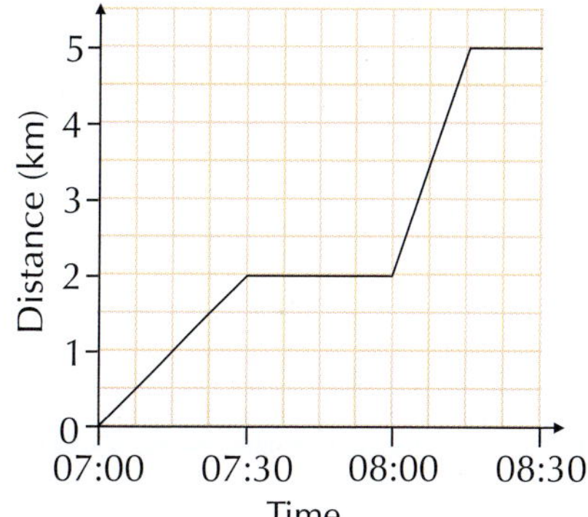

a) Without carrying out any calculations, state which of the journey's two stages was at a higher speed. Explain your answer.

b) (i) How far did he travel in stage 1 of his journey (the first 30 minutes)?

(ii) What was his speed (in km/h) for the first stage?

c) What was his speed (in km/h) during the second stage of his journey?

Q3 The graph shows Sophie's trek.
She stopped for a rest at 12:00 and for lunch at 13:00.

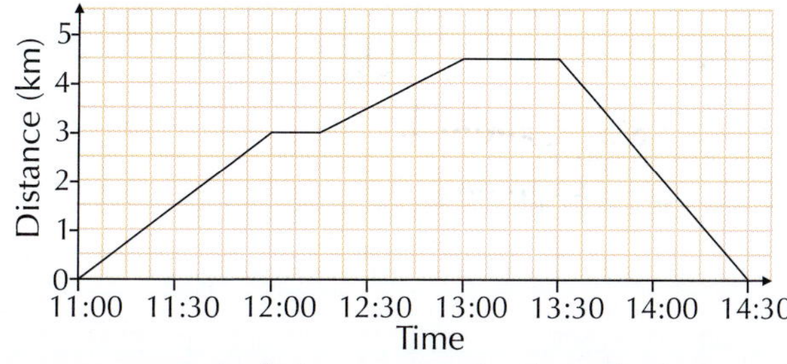

a) Without carrying out any calculations, state the times between which she was walking fastest. Explain your answer.

b) (i) For how long did she walk before she first stopped for a rest?

(ii) How far did she walk during this time?

(iii) What was her average speed during this first part of her walk?

c) What was Sophie's average speed after her rest but before she stopped for lunch?

d) What was her average speed after lunch?

Q4 Draw distance-time graphs to show the following journeys.

a) Ashna catches a train at 10:00, then travels 200 miles at an average speed of 100 mph.

b) Jasper sets off at 09:00 and drives 120 miles at an average speed of 40 mph.
After 1 hour at his destination, he drives back to his starting point at an average speed of 60 mph.

Review Exercise

Q1 A football is passed between two players 10 m apart. The ball travels for 2.5 seconds. Find the average speed of the ball in m/s.

Q2 A yacht travels 13.5 km in 15 minutes.

a) What is its average speed in km/h? b) What is this speed in m/s?

Q3 An object has a mass of 2500 kg and a volume of 50 m^3.

a) What is the object's density in kg/m^3?

b) What is its density in g/cm^3?

Q4 For each of the following, calculate the missing measure.

a) Pressure = ? N/m^2, Area = 4 m^2, Force = 4800 N

b) Pressure = 180 N/m^2, Area = ? m^2, Force = 540 N

c) Pressure = 28 N/cm^2, Area = 14 cm^2, Force = ? N

Q5 Helena is going on a journey. The following points describe her journey.

- Helena sets off from home and travels 40 km by bus, as shown on the graph.
- She gets off the bus and then waits half an hour for a train.
- She gets on the train and travels for a further 1 hour 30 minutes, as shown on the graph.
- She spends 30 minutes at her destination.
- She then returns home by taxi at an average speed of 60 km/h.

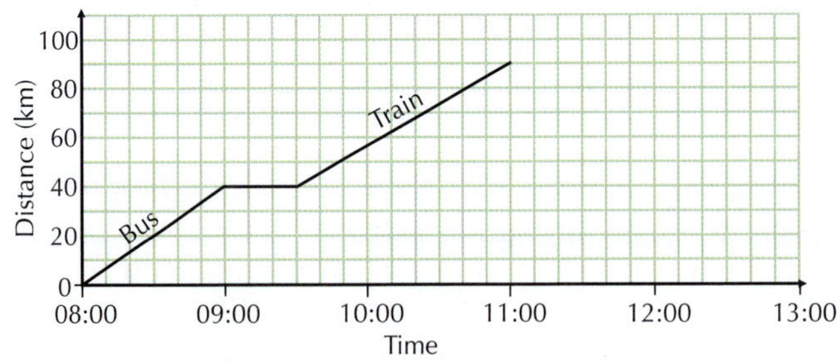

a) Find the average speed Helena travelled:

(i) by bus. (ii) by train.

b) Copy the above graph, and extend the line to show Helena's 30 minutes at her destination.

c) Find the time it took Helena to travel home by taxi.

d) Show Helena's taxi ride home on your graph.

Exam-Style Questions

Q1 Tash goes for a run. Her run is shown on the distance-time graph to the right.

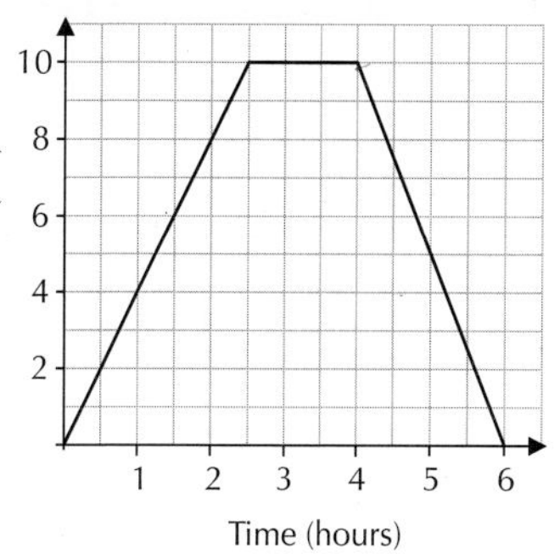

a) Describe the three stages of her run. *[3 marks]*

b) Explain what the gradient of the graph represents. *[1 mark]*

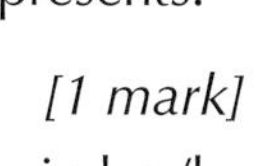

c) Calculate her speed on her return journey in km/h. *[2 marks]*

Q2 Will drives his vintage bus to a bus rally 60 miles away.
His average speed for the journey is 24 mph and he arrives at 11:10 am.
Work out what time he set off. *[2 marks]*

Q3 The density of steel is approximately 8 g/cm^3. A solid steel cube has a side length of 5 cm. Find the mass of the cube in kilograms. *[2 marks]*

Q4 A skip exerts a pressure of 625 N/m^2 over a ground area of 40 000 cm^2.
Calculate the force in N exerted by the skip on the ground. *[3 marks]*

Q5 Charlotte is a runner. She runs at a pace of 1 km in 4 minutes 45 seconds.
Calculate the time that Charlotte will take to run 800 m at this pace. *[3 marks]*

Q6 36 cm^3 of copper and 4 cm^3 of tin are melted down and mixed to make a bronze medal. The densities of copper and tin are 9 g/cm^3 and 7 g/cm^3 respectively.
Work out the mass of the medal. *[2 marks]*

18.1 Scale Drawings

It's important for things like maps to show distances accurately, but scaled to a useful size. Using scales is all about ratios and converting between different units of length.

Scales with Units

Learning Objective — Spec Ref R2/G15:
Interpret scale drawings and maps where the units are given.

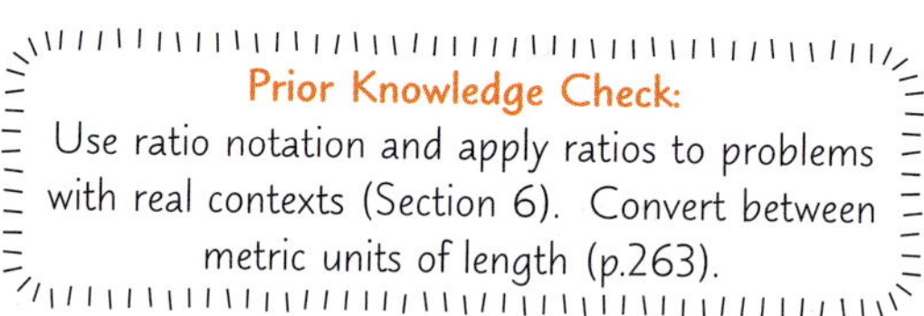

Prior Knowledge Check:
Use ratio notation and apply ratios to problems with real contexts (Section 6). Convert between metric units of length (p.263).

A **scale** tells you the **relationship** between distances on a **map** or **plan** and distances in **real life**. For example, a map scale of 1 cm : 10 m means that 1 cm on the **map** represents a **real-life** distance of 10 m.

- To work out what a distance on the map **represents in real life**, **multiply** the **map distance** by the number on the right-hand side of the **map scale** ratio. So for a map with a scale of 1 cm : 10 m, a map distance of 2.5 cm would be $2.5 \times 10 = 25$ m in real life.
- To convert **real-life distances** to **map distances**, you **divide** the real-life distance by the map scale number. So 500 m in real life would be represented by $500 \div 10 = 50$ cm on a map with scale 1 cm : 10 m.

Be careful with units — the units of **map distances** should match the **left-hand side** of the **scale** ratio, and **real-life distances** should have the same units as the **right-hand side**.

Tip: You might need to convert the units of a measurement before you start calculating.

Example 1

A plan of a garden is drawn to a scale of 1 cm : 5 m.

a) The distance between two trees is measured on the plan as 3 cm. What is the actual distance between the trees?

The scale is 1 cm : 5 m, so to convert from cm on the map to m in real life, multiply by 5.

1 cm represents 5 m, so
3 cm represents $3 \times 5 =$ **15 m**

b) The actual distance between the garden shed and the pond is measured as 250 cm. What would the distance between the shed and the pond be on the plan?

1. The RHS of the scale is in m, so convert 250 cm to m. — 250 cm = 2.5 m
2. Then divide by 5 to find the map distance. — 2.5 m is shown as $2.5 \div 5 =$ **0.5 cm**

Example 2

The distance between two villages is 12 km. This is represented on a map by a distance of 24 cm. Express the scale of the map in the form 1 cm : n km.

1. Write down the distances you are given as a scale. — 24 cm : 12 km
2. Divide both sides by 24 to find the scale in the form 1 cm : n km. — (24 ÷ 24) cm : (12 ÷ 24) km
   1 cm : 0.5 km

Exercise 1

Q1 A map scale is given as 1 cm : 2 km.

a) Convert the following distances on the map to actual distances.
(i) 4 cm (ii) 22 cm (iii) 0.5 cm (iv) 0.25 cm

b) Convert the following actual distances to distances on the map.
(i) 10 km (ii) 14 km (iii) 7 km (iv) 1.4 km

Q2 An atlas uses a scale of 1 cm : 100 km. Find the actual distances represented by:
a) 7 cm b) 1.5 cm c) 6.22 cm d) 43 mm

Q3 The scale on a map of Europe is 1 cm : 50 km. Find the distance used on the map to represent the following actual distances.
a) 150 km b) 600 km c) 1000 km d) 15 000 m

Q4 The distance from Madrid to Malaga is shown on a map as 11 cm.
The actual distance is 440 km. Express the scale of the map in the form 1 cm : n km.

Q5 The distance from Thenford to Syresham is 12 km. This is shown on a map as 4 cm.

a) Express the scale of the map in the form 1 cm : n km.

b) The same map shows the distance from Chacombe to Badby as 7 cm.
What is the actual distance between these two villages?

Q6 You are asked to draw up the plans for a building using the scale 1 cm : 0.5 m.
Find the lengths you should draw on the plan to represent the following actual distances.
a) 4 m b) 18 m c) 21 m d) 1180 cm

Q7 To the right is the plan for a kitchen surface.
Measure the appropriate lengths on the plan to find the actual dimensions of the following:
a) the sink area b) the hob area

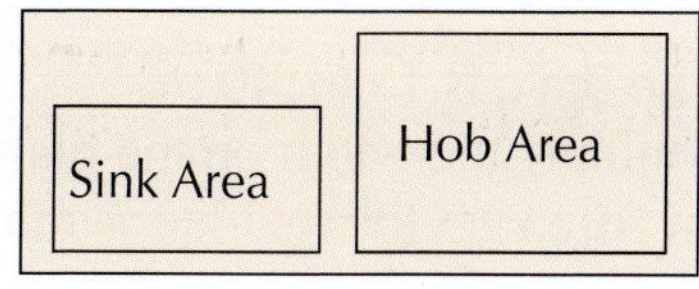

1 mm : 3 cm

Scales without Units

Learning Objective — Spec Ref R2/G15:
Interpret scale drawings and maps where no units are given.

A scale **without units** (e.g. 1 : 100) means you can use **any units** as long as they're the **same on both sides**. So 1 : 100 could be 1 cm : 100 cm, 1 mm : 100 mm, etc. It's often best to pick the units that **match** the measurement you're given in the problem.

Example 3

A map uses a scale of 1 : 200.
What is the actual distance between two points which appear 35 cm apart on the map?

1. Write the scale down using centimetres, to match the distance given in the question. — 1 cm : 200 cm
2. Multiply the map distance by the number on the right-hand side of the scale. — 35 cm represents 35 × 200 = 7000 cm.
3. Give your answer using sensible units. — 1 m = 100 cm, so the actual distance is: 7000 ÷ 100 = **70 m**.

Scales **without units** sometimes have a **big number** on the right-hand side. Once you've written such a scale **with units**, it often makes sense to **convert** one side to **different units**, so you end up with a smaller number in the ratio. E.g. you can write the ratio 1 : 100 as 1 cm : 100 cm, and then use the conversion 1 m = 100 cm to write this as 1 cm : 1 m.

Example 4

The plan of the grounds of a stately home has a scale of 1 : 4000.

a) Represent this scale in the form 1 cm : *n* m.

1. Write the scale down using centimetres, to match the left-hand side of 1 cm : *n* m. — 1 cm : 4000 cm
2. Convert the right-hand side to metres by dividing by 100. — 1 cm : (4000 ÷ 100) m

1 cm : 40 m

Tip: You could also do it starting with m:
1 m : 4000 m
100 cm : 4000 m
1 cm : 40 m

b) On the plan, one of the lakes is 11.5 cm wide. Calculate the actual width of the lake.

The scale is 1 cm : 40 m. Multiply the width on the plan by 40 to get the real-life width. — 1 cm represents 40 m, so 11.5 cm represents 11.5 × 40 = **460 m**

Exercise 2

Q1 A map scale is given as 1 : 350.

a) Convert the following distances on the map to actual distances in m.

(i) 2 cm (ii) 7 cm (iii) 9.9 cm (iv) 25.7 cm

b) Convert the following actual distances to distances on the map.

(i) 700 cm (ii) 875 cm (iii) 945 cm (iv) 1.47 m

Q2 A plan uses the scale 1 : 75. Find the actual distances, in m, represented by:

a) 4 cm b) 11 cm c) 7.9 cm d) 17.2 cm

Q3 Convert these actual distances to the lengths they will appear on a map with scale 1 : 1000. Give your answers in cm.

a) 300 m b) 1400 m c) 120 m d) 0.43 km

Q4 Toy furniture is made to a scale of 1 : 40. Find the dimensions of the actual furniture, in m, when the toys have the following measurements.

a) Width of bed: 3.5 cm b) Length of table: 3.2 cm c) Height of chair: 2.4 cm

Q5 A road of length 6.7 km is to be drawn on a map. The scale of the map is 1 : 250 000. How long will the road be on the map? Give your answer in cm.

Q6 A model railway uses a scale of 1 : 500. Use the actual measurements given below to find measurements for the model in cm.

a) Length of carriage: 20 m b) Height of coal tower: 30 m

c) Length of footbridge: 100 m d) Height of signal box: 6 m

Q7 On the plans for a house, 3 cm represents the length of a garden with actual length 18 m.

a) Find the map scale in the form 1 cm : d m.

b) On the plan, the width of the garden is 1.2 cm. What is its actual width in metres?

c) The lounge has a length of 4.5 m. What is the corresponding length on the plan?

Q8 A path of length 4.5 km is shown on a map as a line of length 3 cm.

a) Express the scale in the form 1 cm : n km.

b) Express the scale in the form 1 : k.

Q9 The plan to the right shows the main tourist attractions of a major city.
Find the actual distances, in km, between:

a) the museum and the cathedral

b) the art gallery and the theatre

c) the cathedral and the park

Constructing Scale Drawings

Learning Objective — Spec Ref R2/G15:
Construct accurate plans using a given scale.

If you know the **measurements** of something, you can draw an **accurate plan** using a given scale. **Convert** all the distances to lengths on the plan, then use your **ruler** to draw lines of the required lengths.

Tip: Use a sharp pencil to keep things nice and precise.

Example 5

The diagram shows a rough sketch of a garden.
Use the scale 1 : 400 to draw an accurate plan of the garden.

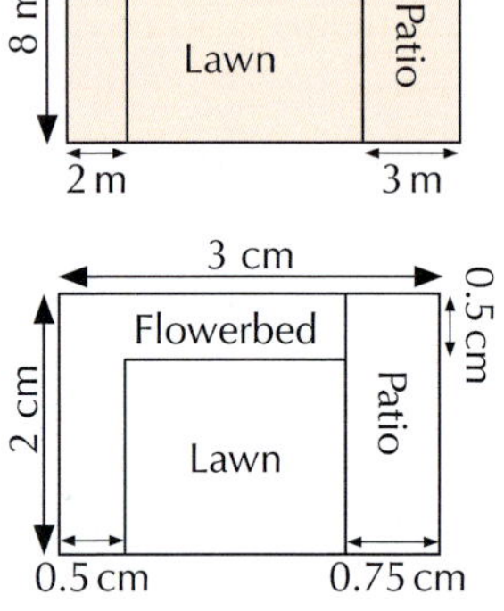

1. Write down the scale in cm. — 1 cm : 400 cm
2. Change the right-hand side to metres by dividing by 100. — 1 cm : 4 m
3. Use the scale to work out the lengths on the plan, then use these lengths to draw your plan. — 4 m is shown as 1 cm, so:
   12 m is shown as 12 ÷ 4 = 3 cm
   8 m is shown as 8 ÷ 4 = 2 cm
   2 m is shown as 2 ÷ 4 = 0.5 cm
   3 m is shown as 3 ÷ 4 = 0.75 cm

Exercise 3

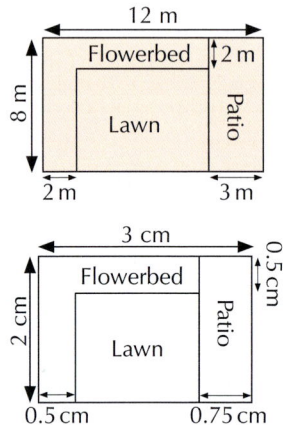

Q1 A sketch of the floor plan for a symmetrical squash court is shown below. Use the scale 1 : 50 to draw an accurate plan of the court.

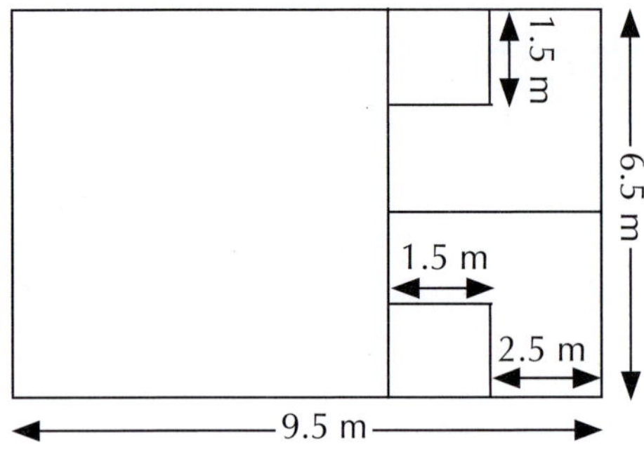

Q2 Below is a sketch of a park lake.

a) Draw an accurate plan of the lake using the scale 1 cm : 3 m.

b) There is a duck house at the intersection of AC and BD. Use your plan to find the actual distance from the duck house to point B.

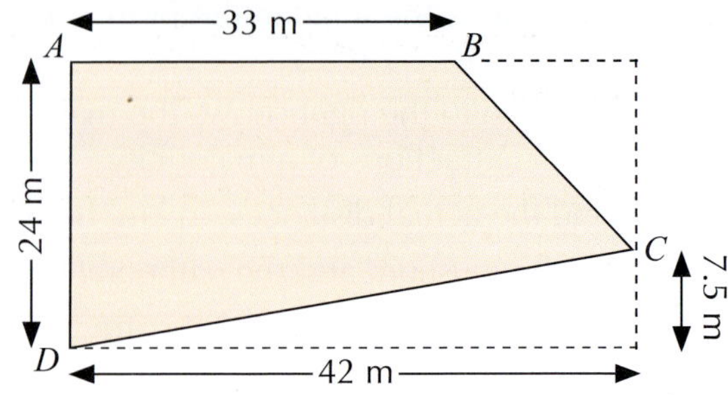

18.2 Bearings

Bearings are used in navigation to describe which direction something is in, relative to a north line.

Learning Objective — Spec Ref G15:
Understand and use bearings.

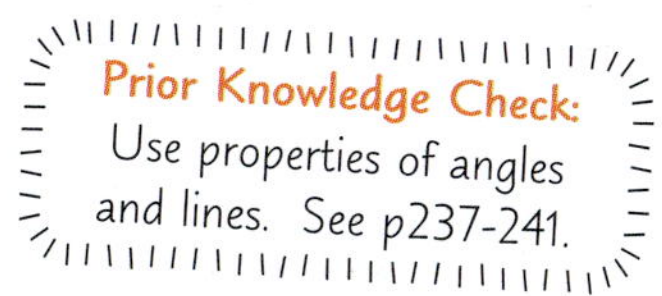

Prior Knowledge Check:
Use properties of angles and lines. See p237-241.

A **bearing** tells you the direction of one point from another. Bearings are given as **three-figure angles**, measured **clockwise** from the **north line**. For example, a bearing that's 60° clockwise from north will be written as 060°. To find a bearing:

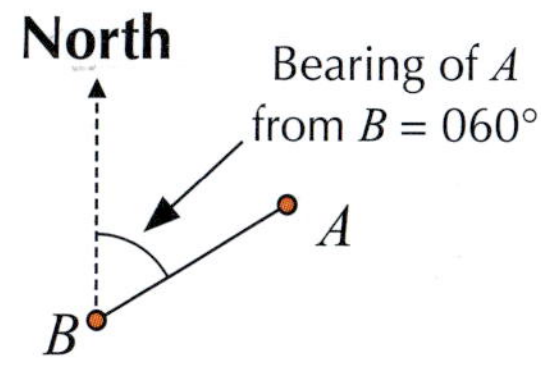

- Find the point you are going '**from**'.
- Draw the **north line** at this point.
- Then go **clockwise** to find the angle you want — this is the **bearing**.

As well as the information you're given, you might have to use the **properties of angles** (angles **around a point**, on a **straight line**, and on **parallel lines** — see Section 15) to find a bearing.

Example 1

a) Find the bearing of *B* from *A*.

b) Find the bearing of *C* from *A*.

1. Draw a north line at the point you're going 'from' — here it's A.
2. Find the clockwise angle from the north line.
3. Give the bearing as a three-figure number.

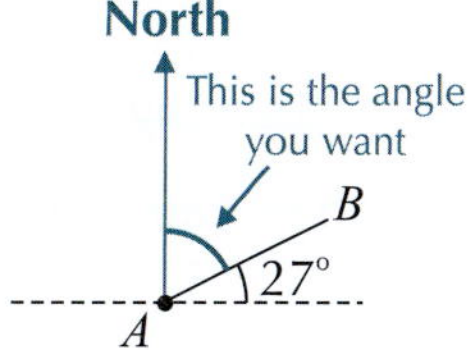

North
This is the angle you want
C
35°
A

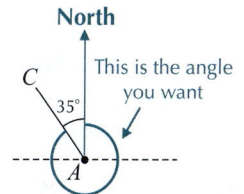

a) $90° - 27° = 63°$
So the bearing of B from A is **063°**.

b) $360° - 35° = 325°$
So the bearing of C from A is **325°**.

Exercise 1

Q1 Write these compass directions as bearings.

a) East b) Northeast c) South d) Northwest

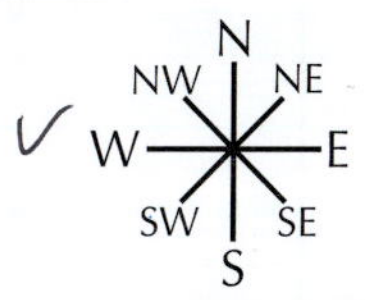

Q2 Find the bearing of B from A in the following.

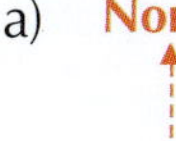

a) 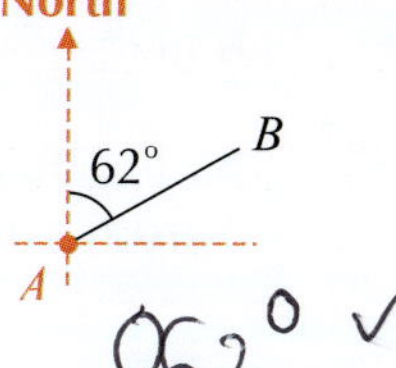

b) 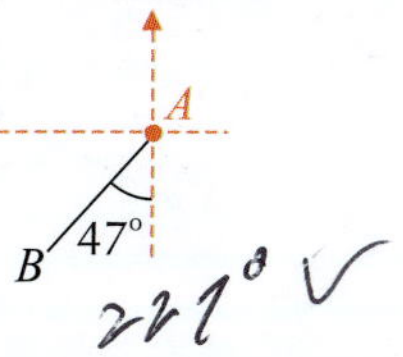

c) 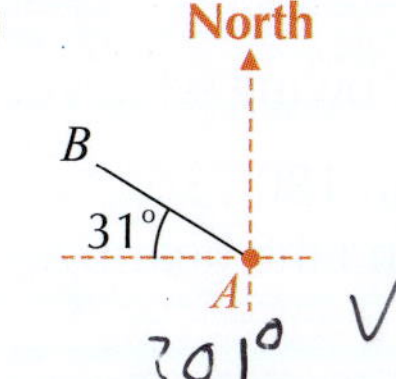

d) 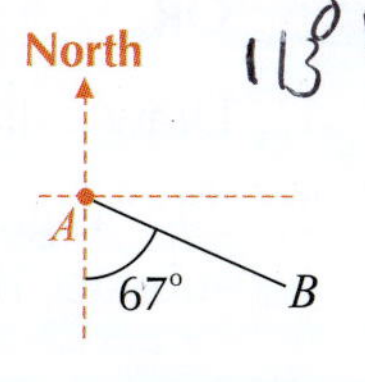

Q3 A ship travels in a direction which is 25° north of due east. Write this as a bearing.

Q4 Find the angle θ in each of the following using the information given.

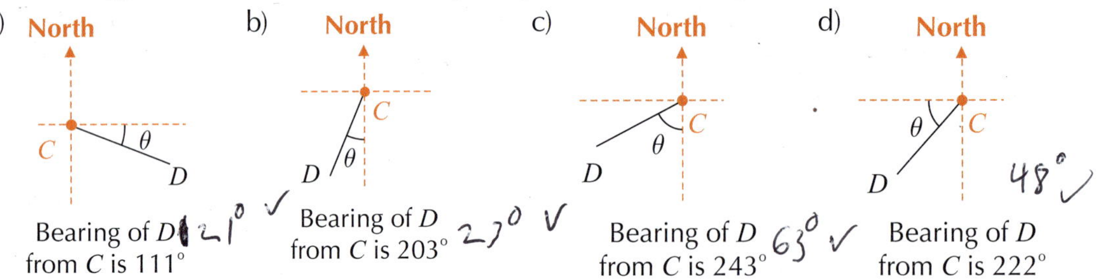

Q5 Mark a point O and draw in a north line. Use a protractor to help you draw the points a) to d) with the following bearings from O.

a) 040° b) 321° c) 163° d) 263°

Since **north lines** are always **parallel** to each other, you can use the properties of **alternate**, **allied** and **corresponding** angles (see p.239-241) to work out the bearing of A from B, when **given** the bearing of B from A.

Tip: If you're not given a diagram, always start by doing a sketch yourself.

You might notice that the bearing of A from B is always either **180° more** or **180° less** than the bearing of B from A.

- If the given bearing is **less than 180°**, then you can **add** 180° to get the other bearing.
- If the bearing is **more than 180°**, then **subtract** 180° to find the bearing you want.

Example 2

The bearing of *X* from *Y* is 244°. Find the bearing of *Y* from *X*.

1. Draw a diagram showing what you know. Label the angle you're trying to find.
2. Find the alternate angle to the one you're looking for. 244° – 180° = 64°
3. Alternate angles are equal, so these two are the same. Make sure you give your answer as a three-figure bearing.

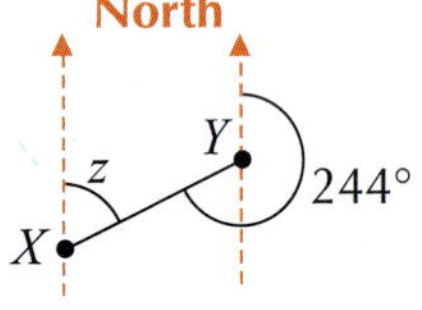

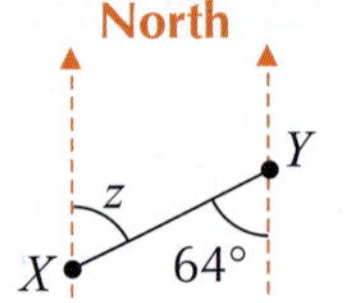

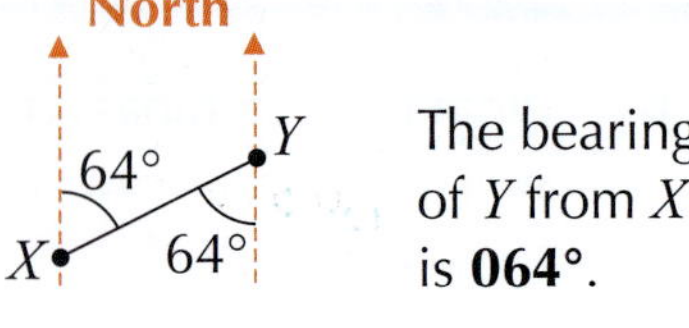

The bearing of Y from X is **064°**.

OR

1. Draw a diagram showing what you know.
2. 244° is greater than 180°, so subtract 180° to find the bearing.

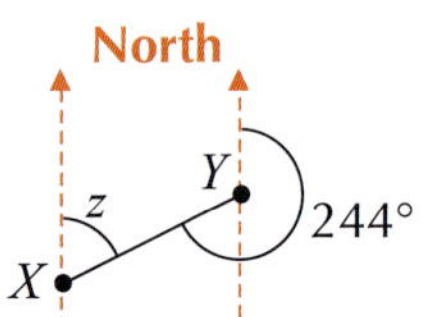

244° – 180° = 64°

So the bearing of Y from X is **064°**.

Exercise 2

Q1 a) The bearing of B from A is 218°. Find the bearing of A from B.

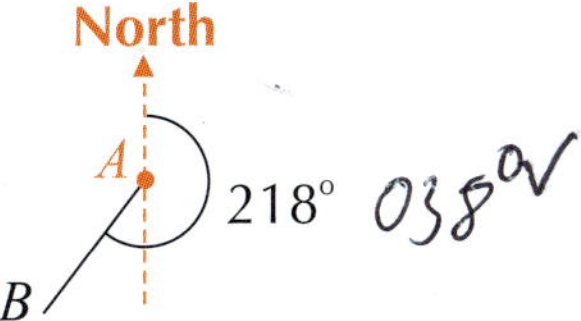

b) The bearing of D from C is 125°. Find the bearing of C from D.

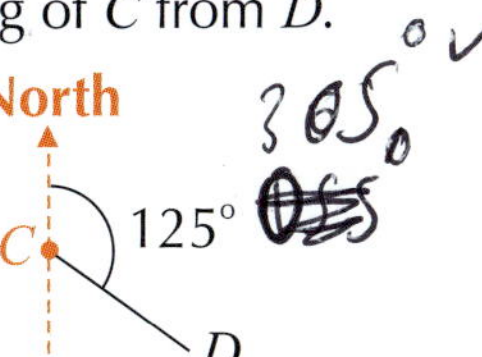

c) The bearing of F from E is 310°. Find the bearing of E from F.

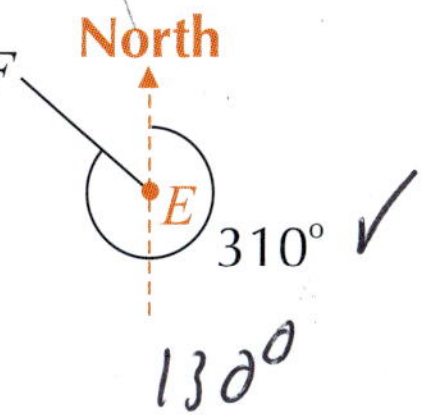

Q2 Find the bearing of N from M given that the bearing of M from N is:

a) 200° b) 330° c) 117° d) 015°

Q3 a) Measure the angle θ in the diagram.

b) Write down the bearing of R from S.

North
R
θ
S

Q4 The point Z lies southeast of the point Y.

a) Write down the bearing of Z from Y.

b) Find the bearing of Y from Z.

Q5 Find the bearing of:

a) B from A b) C from A c) E from A

d) A from B e) A from C f) A from D

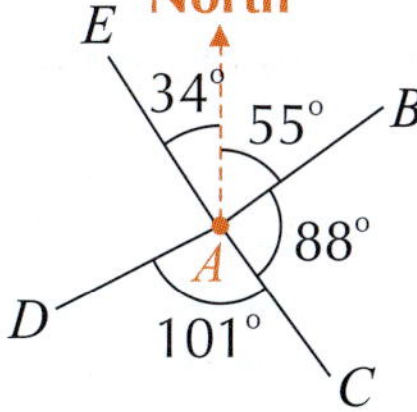

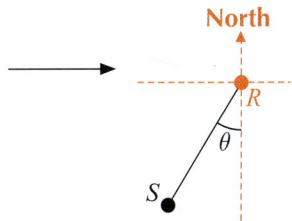

Bearings can also be used to draw **scale diagrams** (see method on p.294).
Use your **protractor** to draw any bearings and make sure any **north lines** are vertical.

Example 3

The points P and Q are a distance of 75 km apart. Q lies on a bearing of 055° from P. Use the scale 1 cm : 25 km to draw an accurate scale diagram of P and Q.

1. Draw P and a north line. Use your protractor to measure and draw the required angle clockwise from North.

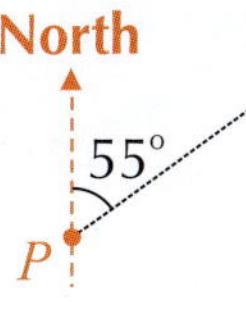

2. Use the scale to work out the distance between the two points.

25 km is shown by 1 cm, so 75 km is shown by 75 ÷ 25 = **3 cm**.

3. Draw Q the correct distance and direction from P.

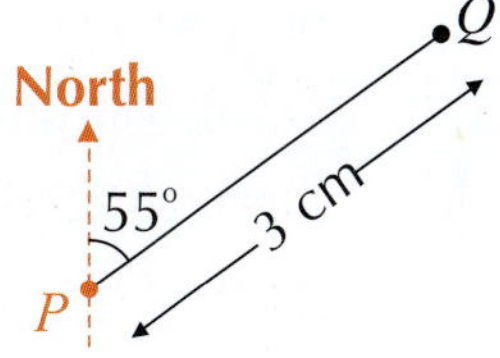

Exercise 3

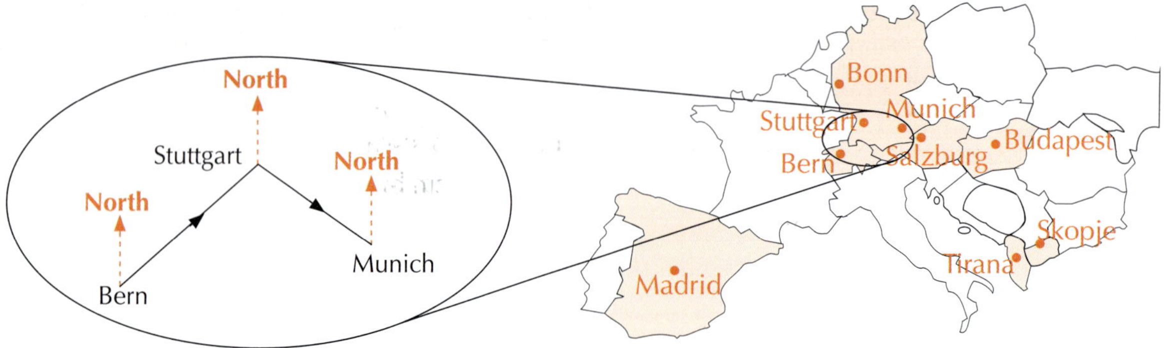

Q1 Above is a rough map of part of Europe.
A pilot flies from Bern to Stuttgart, then on to Munich.
This is shown on the enlarged part of the map, which uses a scale of 1 cm : 100 km.

a) Find the distance and bearings of the following stages of the journey.
   (i) Bern to Stuttgart (ii) Stuttgart to Munich

b) The pilot returns directly from Munich to Bern.
   Find the actual distance travelled in this stage.

Q2 Skopje is 150 km from Tirana, on a bearing of 048°.
Draw an accurate scale diagram of Skopje and Tirana using the scale 1 cm : 30 km.

Q3 Salzburg lies 540 km from Bonn, on a bearing of 125°.
Draw an accurate scale diagram of the two locations using the scale 1 cm : 90 km.

Q4 A pilot flies 2000 km from Budapest to Madrid, on a bearing of 242°.
Draw an accurate scale diagram of the journey using the scale 1 : 100 000 000.

Q5 Use the scale 1 : 22 000 000 to draw an accurate scale diagram of a 880 km journey from Budapest to Bern, on a bearing of 263°.

Q6 The scale drawing on the right shows three more European cities.
The scale of the diagram is 1 : 10 000 000.

a) Use the diagram to find the following distances.
   (i) PQ
   (ii) QR
   (iii) PR

b) Use a protractor to find the following bearings.
   (i) Q from P
   (ii) R from Q
   (iii) P from R

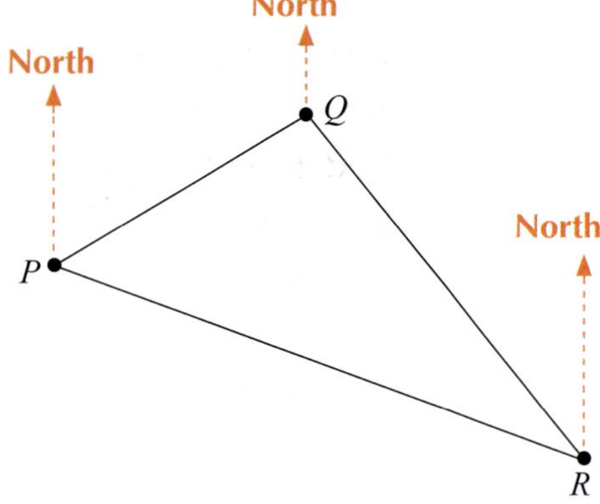

Review Exercise

Q1 The floor plan of a house is drawn to a scale of 1 cm : 2 m.
Find the actual dimensions of the rooms if they are shown on the plan as:

a) 2.7 cm by 1.5 cm b) 3.2 cm by 2.2 cm

c) 1.85 cm by 1.4 cm d) 0.9 cm by 1.35 cm

Q2 The plan to the right represents the distances between A, B and C.
The actual distance AB is 150 m.

a) Measure AB on the plan to find the scale in the form 1 cm : n m.

b) Use your scale to find:

(i) the distance AC (ii) the distance BC

Q3 Draw an accurate plan of the kitchen shown to the right using the scale 1 : 20.

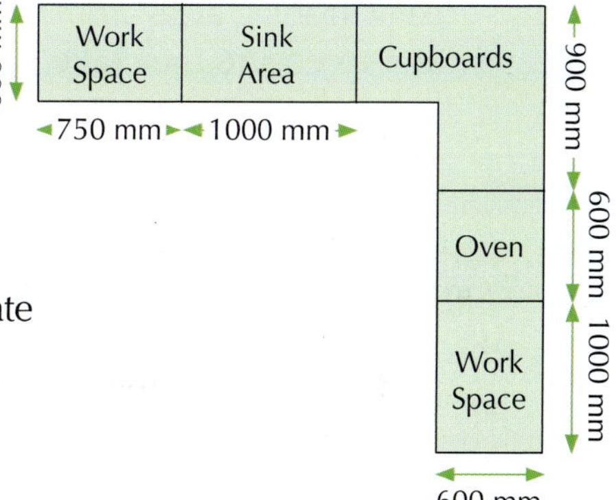

Q4 A jogger runs 230 m on a bearing of 020°, then 390 m on a bearing of 110°.

a) Use the scale 1 cm : 100 m to draw an accurate scale diagram of the two stages of his run.

b) Find the angle the jogger changes direction by after the first stage of his run.

Q5 Town A is 14 km north of Town B, which is 14 km east of Town C.
Find the following bearings.

a) Town B from Town A b) Town C from Town B c) Town C from Town A

Q6 Leicester is 100 km south of Doncaster. King's Lynn is 100 km east of Leicester.

a) Sketch the layout of the three locations.

b) Find the bearing of King's Lynn from Leicester.

c) Draw a north line through Doncaster. Find the bearings from Doncaster of:

(i) Leicester (ii) King's Lynn

d) Draw a north line through King's Lynn. Find the bearings from King's Lynn of:

(i) Leicester (ii) Doncaster

Exam-Style Questions

Q1 On a 1 : 25 000 scale map, the length of a reservoir is 3.8 cm. Work out the real life length of the reservoir, giving your answer in metres.

[2 marks]

Q2 The diagram on the right shows an accurate scale plan of a walk. The actual distance from The Knott to Hartsop Village is 12 km.

a) Find the scale of the plan in the form 1 cm : n km.

[2 marks]

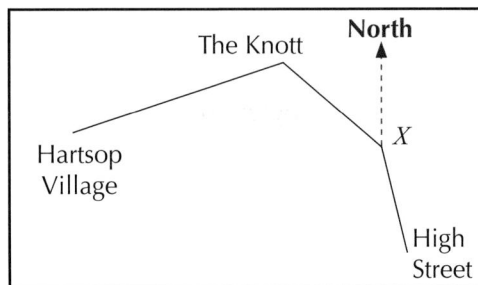

b) Point X lies between High Street and The Knott. There are two paths leading away from X. What bearing should a walker take at X to ensure they take the correct path to The Knott?

[1 mark]

Q3 Part of a city is laid out as a rectangle, divided into 12 identical squares, as shown on the diagram on the right. 3 locations in this city ware labelled as the points A, B and C.

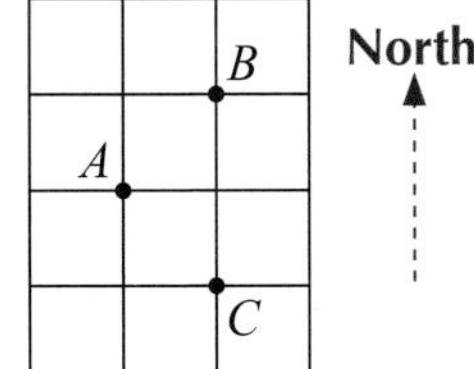

a) Write down the three figure bearing of B from A.

[1 mark]

b) Work out the three figure bearing of A from C.

[1 mark]

Q4 A boat sails on a bearing of 055° for 2000 m.
It then changes course and sails on a bearing of 100° for 1500 m.

a) Draw a scale diagram of the boat's journey. Use the scale 1 cm : 500 m.

[3 marks]

The boat returns directly to its starting point. Use your scale diagram to find:

b) the direct return distance,

[1 mark]

c) the bearing of the return journey.

[1 mark]

19.1 Pythagoras' Theorem

Pythagoras' theorem can be applied to all right-angled triangles. You use it to find the length of one side if you know the lengths of the other two sides.

Learning Objective — Spec Ref G6/G20:
Use Pythagoras' theorem to find missing lengths in right-angled triangles.

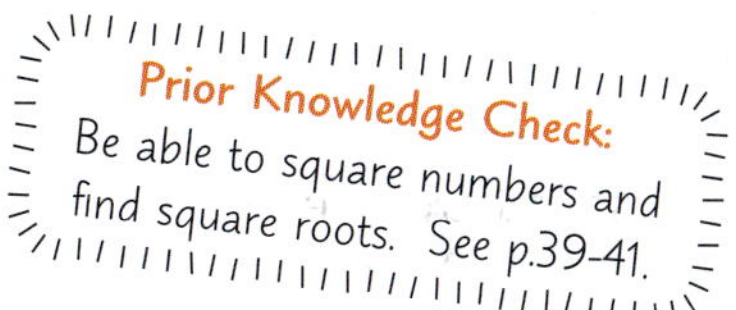

Prior Knowledge Check:
Be able to square numbers and find square roots. See p.39-41.

The lengths of the sides in a **right-angled triangle** always follow the rule:

$$h^2 = a^2 + b^2$$

h is the **hypotenuse** — this is the **longest** side, which is always **opposite** the right angle. a and b are the **shorter** sides.

This is **Pythagoras' theorem** and it is used to find lengths in right-angled triangles.

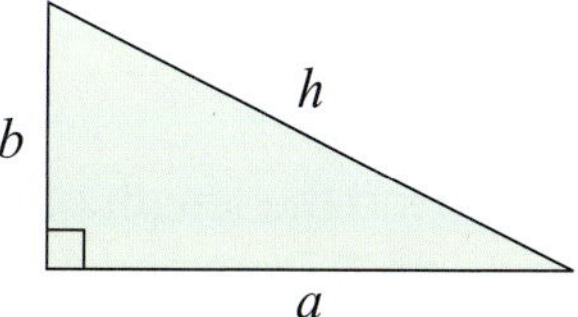

Finding the Hypotenuse

To find the length of the hypotenuse in a right-angled triangle:

- **Substitute** the values of a and b into the formula given above.
- **Add** together the squared lengths, a^2 and b^2, to get h^2.
- Take the **square root** of h^2 to find the hypotenuse, h.

Example 1

Find the length x on the triangle shown. Give your answer to 2 decimal places.

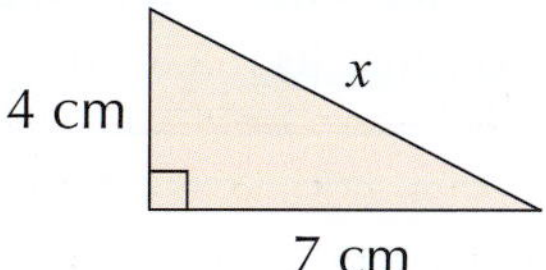

1. x is the hypotenuse, so substitute x for h in the formula and replace a and b with 7 and 4.
   $h^2 = a^2 + b^2$
   $x^2 = 7^2 + 4^2$
2. Add the squared lengths together to get x^2.
   $x^2 = 49 + 16 = 65$
3. Take the square root to find x. Don't forget to round your answer and use the correct units.
   $x = \sqrt{65} = 8.0622...$
   So $x =$ **8.06 cm** (2 d.p.)

Tip: If the question had asked for an exact length, you'd leave the square root in your answer — so the exact length of x is $\sqrt{65}$.

Exercise 1

Q1 Find the length of the hypotenuse in each of the triangles below.

a)

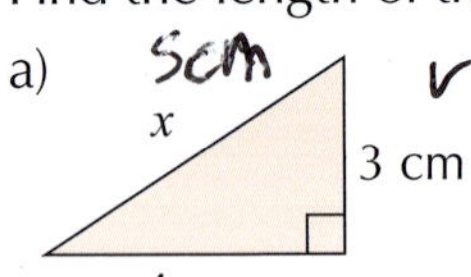

b)

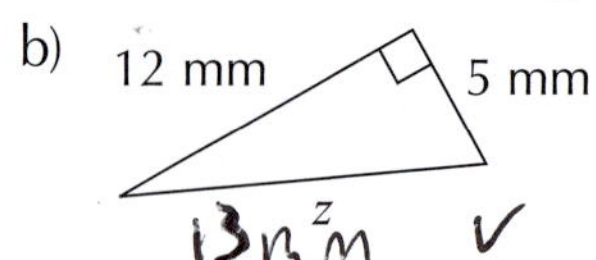

c)

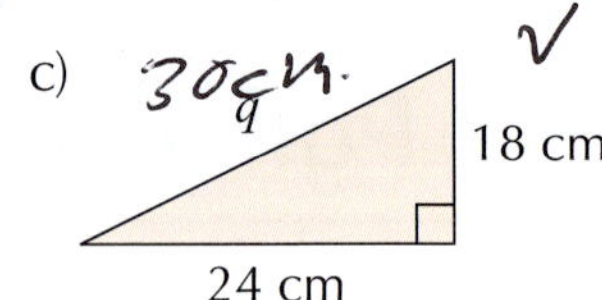

Q2 Find the length of the hypotenuse in each of the triangles below.
Give your answers to 2 decimal places.

a)

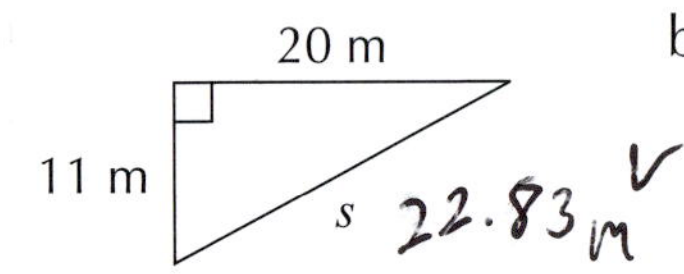

b)

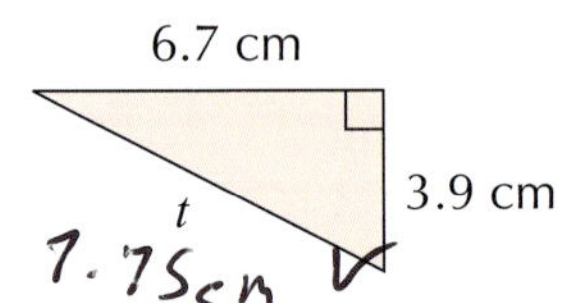

c)

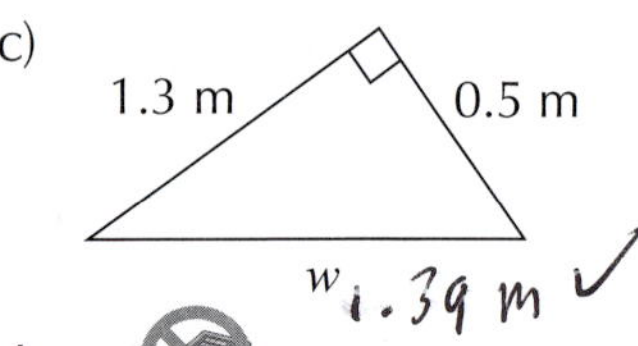

Q3 Find the exact length of the hypotenuse in each of the triangles below.

a)

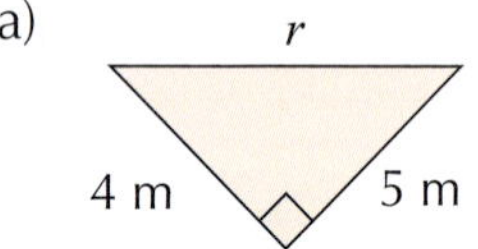

b)

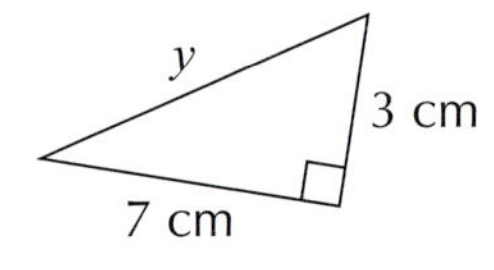

c)

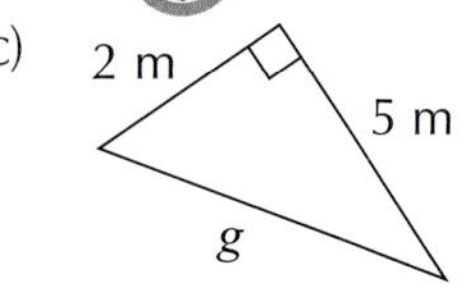

Q4 Find the length of the longest side of a right-angled triangle if the other sides are 8.7 cm and 6.1 cm in length. Give your answer to 2 decimal places.

Q5 Find the length of the hypotenuse of a right-angled triangle if the shorter sides have the following lengths. Give your answers to 2 decimal places.

a) $a = 5$ cm, $b = 7$ cm b) $a = 4$ cm, $b = 11$ cm c) $a = 6.3$ mm, $b = 1.9$ mm

Q6 In triangle XYZ, angle XYZ is 90°, XY is 21 cm and YZ is 32 cm. Find the exact length XZ.

Finding a Shorter Side

You can also use Pythagoras' theorem to find one of the **shorter sides** if you know the hypotenuse and the other side. To do this, **substitute** in the values and then **rearrange** the formula to make the unknown length the subject.

Example 2

Find the length *a* on the triangle shown. Give your answer to 2 decimal places.

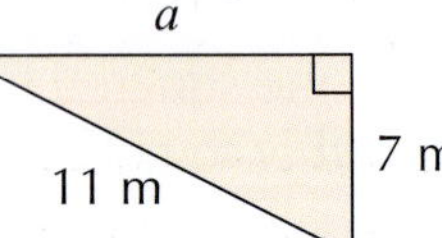

1. a is one of the shorter sides, so use Pythagoras' formula with $h = 11$ and $b = 7$.

$h^2 = a^2 + b^2$
$11^2 = a^2 + 7^2$

2. Rearrange to find a^2.

$a^2 = 11^2 - 7^2$
$a^2 = 121 - 49 = 72$

3. Take the square root, round your answer and use the correct units.

$a = \sqrt{72} = 8.4852...$
So $a =$ **8.49 m** (2 d.p.)

Exercise 2

Q1 Find the lengths of the missing sides in these triangles.

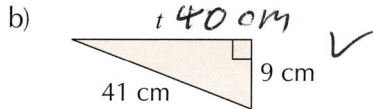

a)

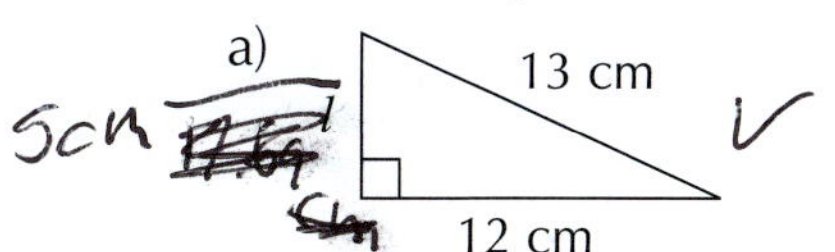

b)

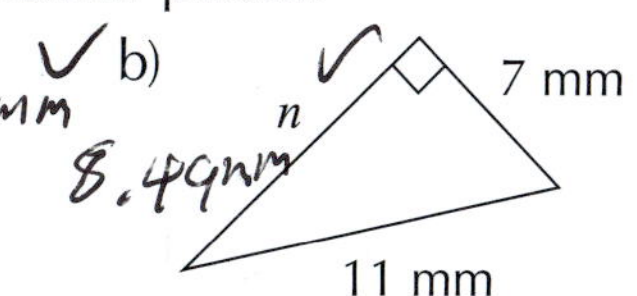

c)

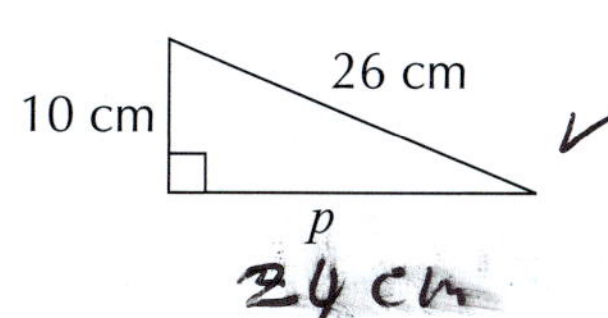

Q2 Find the length of the missing side in each of the triangles below. Give your answers to 2 decimal places.

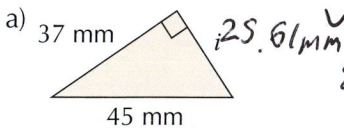

a)

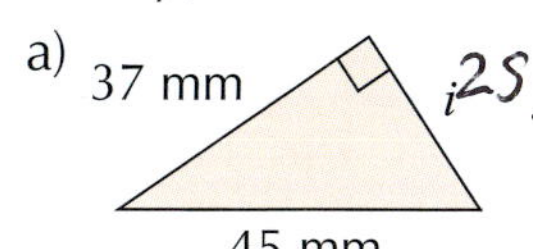

b)

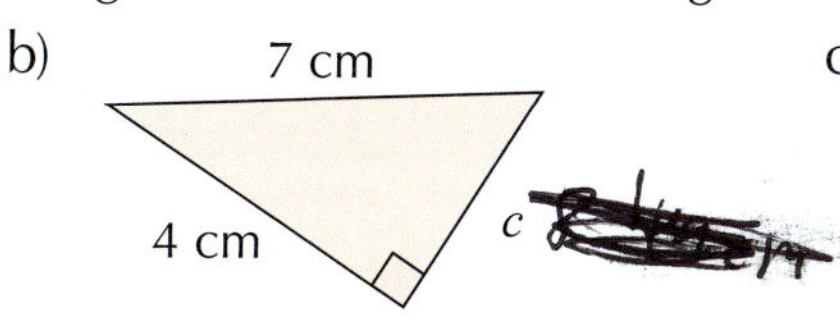

c)

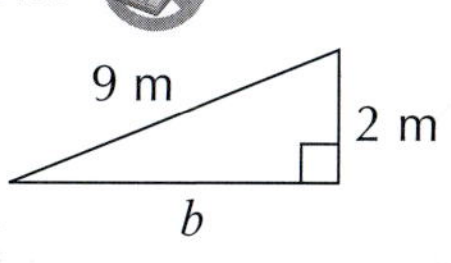

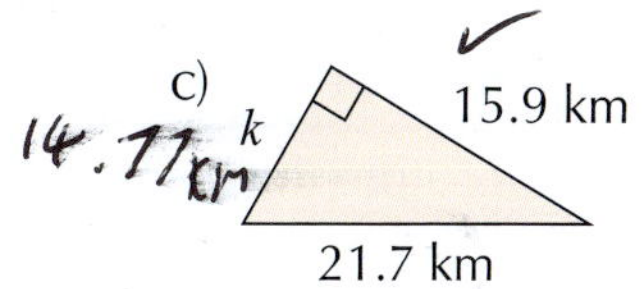

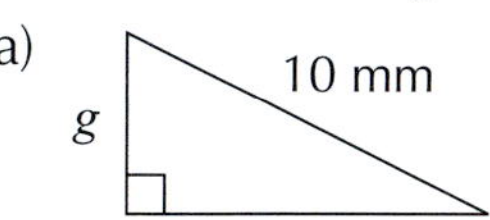

Q3 Find the exact length of the missing side in each of the triangles below.

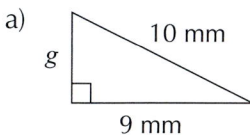

a) g, 10 mm, 9 mm

b) 7 cm, 4 cm, c

c) 9 m, 2 m, b

Q4 Find the length b in the right-angled triangle with the values of a and h given below. Give your answers to 2 decimal places.

a) $a = 1$ cm, $h = 8$ cm

b) $a = 6$ m, $h = 13$ m

c) $a = 4.1$ mm, $h = 11.3$ mm

d) $a = 17.7$ cm, $h = 22.9$ cm

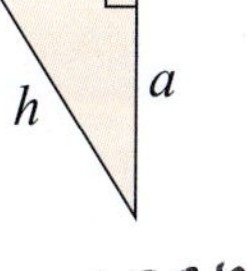

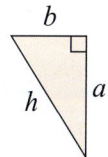

Q5 The lengths of the longest and shortest sides of a right-angled triangle are 17.3 cm and 6.6 cm. Find the length of the third side to 2 decimal places.

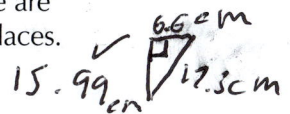

Using Pythagoras' Theorem

You can use Pythagoras' theorem to **say** whether a triangle is **right-angled** or **not**. Label the sides a, b and c, where c is the longest side. If the sides **satisfy** the rule $a^2 + b^2 = c^2$, then the triangle **is** right-angled. If they don't satisfy the rule, the triangle is not right-angled.

For example, consider a triangle with sides of length 3 cm, 6 cm and 7 cm. $3^2 + 6^2 = 9 + 36 = 45$, but $7^2 = 49$. $45 \neq 49$, so the triangle is **not right-angled**.

Tip: The symbol ≠ means 'is not equal to'.

Pythagoras' theorem can be used in lots of other situations too — you just have to look for ways to **create** a right-angled triangle. For example:

- **Splitting** an **equilateral** or **isosceles triangle** in half can create two identical right-angled triangles.
- The **straight line** between two pairs of **coordinates** forms the hypotenuse of a right-angled triangle with shorter sides equal to the difference in the x-coordinates and the difference in the y-coordinates (see Example 3 on the next page).

Example 3

Find the exact distance between points A and B on the grid.

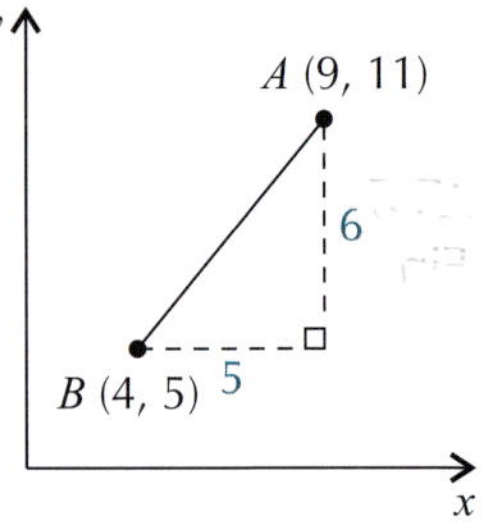

1. Create a right-angled triangle with hypotenuse AB.
2. Find the length of the horizontal side by working out the difference in the x-coordinates.
   Difference in x-coordinates: $9 - 4 = 5$
3. Find the length of the vertical side by working out the difference in the y-coordinates.
   Difference in y-coordinates: $11 - 5 = 6$
4. Substitute the values into the formula.
   $AB^2 = 5^2 + 6^2 = 25 + 36 = 61$
5. Take the square root to find the distance. Leave your answer as a square root.
   $AB = \sqrt{61}$

Tip: Remember — 'exact distance' means you don't work out the value of the square root.

Pythagoras' theorem can also be applied to **real life situations**. The formula is used in the **same way**, you just have to link your answer back to the **context** of the situation. If you're struggling to work out what's going on, **sketch a diagram** to help you picture it.

Example 4

A TV has a height of 40 cm and width of w cm.
Its diagonal measures 82 cm. Will the TV fit in a box 75 cm wide?

1. The height, width and diagonal form a right-angled triangle, so substitute these values into the formula.
   $h^2 = a^2 + b^2$
   $82^2 = 40^2 + w^2$
2. Rearrange to find w^2.
   $w^2 = 82^2 - 40^2 = 6724 - 1600 = 5124$
3. Take the square root to find w.
   $w = \sqrt{5124} = 71.58$ cm (2 d.p.)
4. Use your result to draw a conclusion — make sure you actually answer the question.
   $71.58 < 75$ so **yes, the TV will fit in the box.**

Exercise 3

Q1 Use Pythagoras' theorem to decide whether or not the following triangles are right-angled.

a) $a = 9$ cm, $b = 12$ cm, $h = 15$ cm

b) $a = 8$ mm, $b = 7$ mm, $h = 11$ mm

Q2 Find the distance PS in the rectangle on the right.
Give your answer to 2 decimal places.

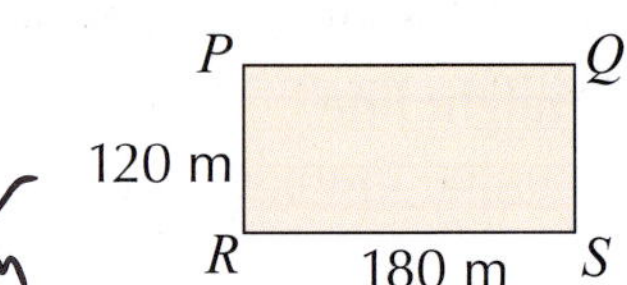

Q3 I run 540 m south and then 970 m east. What is my final distance from my starting point? Give your answer to the nearest metre.

In Questions 4-13, give your answers to 2 decimal places (unless told otherwise).

Q4 XYZ is an isosceles triangle. M is the mid-point of YZ. Find the length of XY.

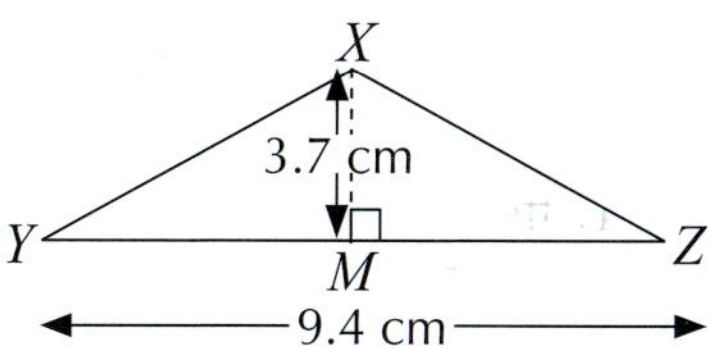

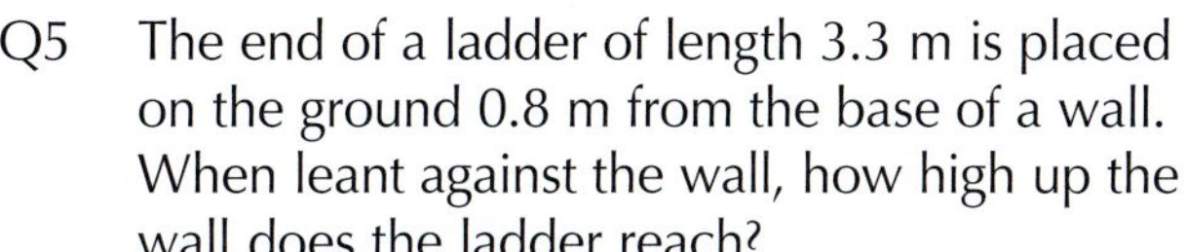

Q5 The end of a ladder of length 3.3 m is placed on the ground 0.8 m from the base of a wall. When leant against the wall, how high up the wall does the ladder reach?

Q6 A slice of toast is in the shape of a right-angled triangle. The hypotenuse of the triangle has length 14 cm, and a shorter side is of length 11 cm. Find the length of the third side.

Q7 The triangle JKL is drawn inside a circle centred on O, as shown. JK and KL have lengths 4.9 cm and 6.8 cm respectively.

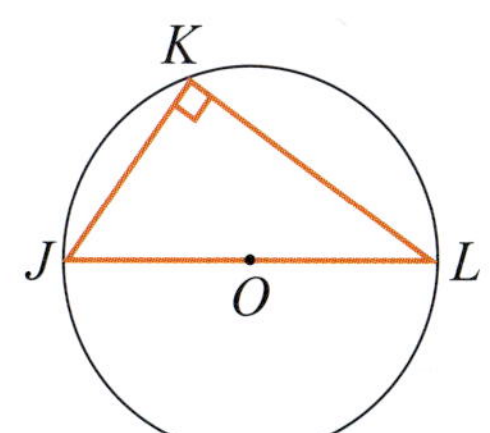

a) Find the length of JL.

b) Find the radius of the circle.

Q8 Find the exact length of each line segment AB.

a)

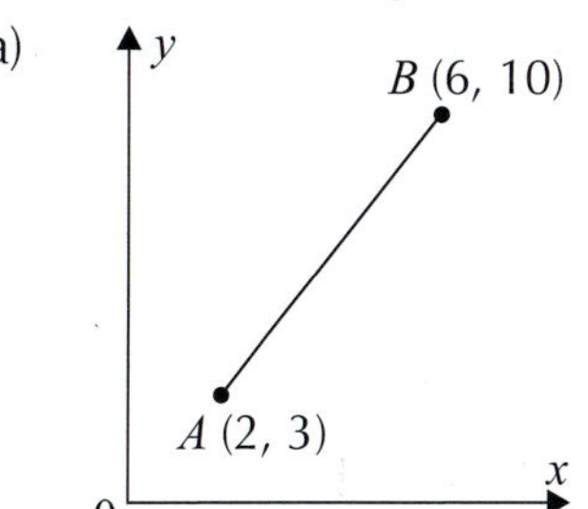

b)

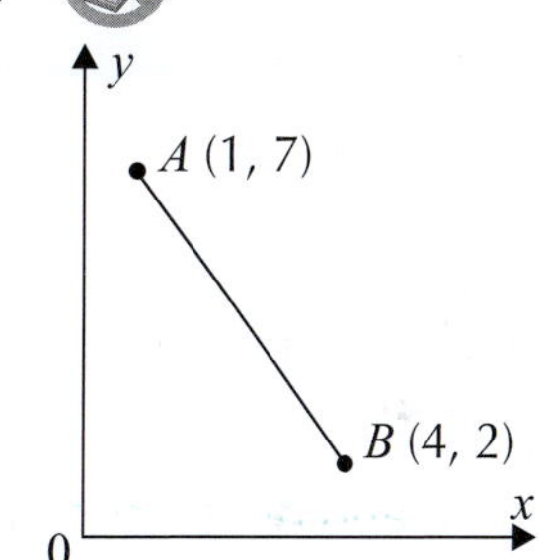

Q9 Find the radius of the base of the cone shown on the right.

29.2 cm

22.4 cm

Q10 A kite gets stuck at the top of a tree. The kite's 15 m string is taut, and its other end is held on the ground, 8.5 m from the base of the tree. Find the height of the tree.

Q11 Newtown is 88 km northwest of Oldtown. Bigton is 142 km from Newtown, and lies northeast of Oldtown. What is the distance from Bigton to Oldtown? Give your answer to the nearest kilometre.

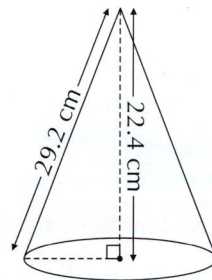

Q12 A spaghetti jar is in the shape of a cylinder. The jar has radius 6 cm and height 28 cm. What is the length of the longest stick of dried spaghetti that will fit inside the jar?

Q13 What is the height of the kite on the right?

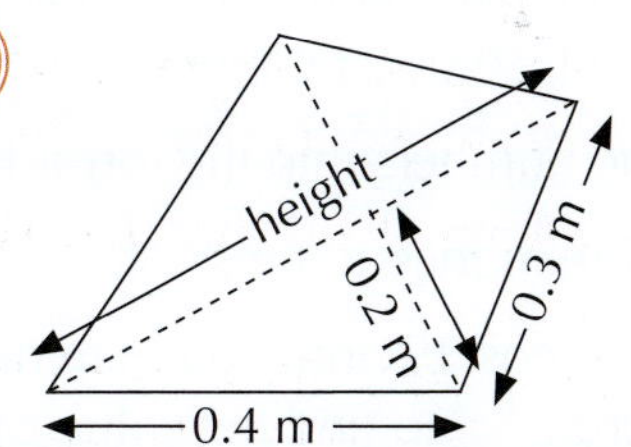

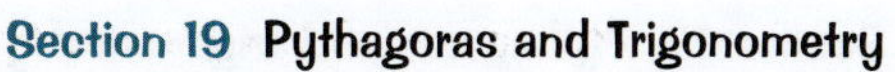

19.2 Trigonometry — Sin, Cos and Tan

Trigonometry allows you to find missing sides and angles in triangles. For right-angled triangles, you'll need to know the sine (sin), cosine (cos) and tangent (tan) formulas.

The Three Formulas

Learning Objective — Spec Ref G20:
Use trigonometry to find missing lengths and angles in right-angled triangles.

Trigonometry can be used to find lengths or angles in **right-angled triangles**. For a given angle x (as shown on the diagram on the right):

- The side opposite the right angle is the **hypotenuse**.
- The side opposite the given angle is the **opposite**.
- The side between the given angle and the right-angle is the **adjacent**.

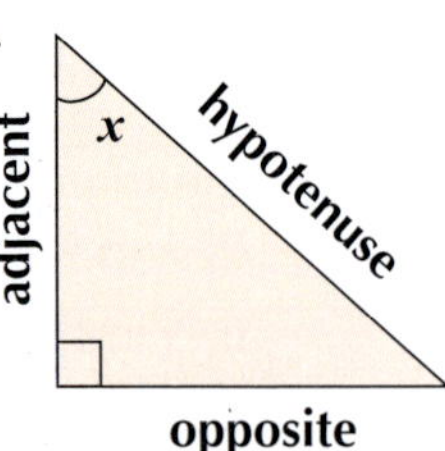

The three sides of a right-angled triangle are linked by the following formulas:

$$\sin x = \frac{\text{opp}}{\text{hyp}}, \quad \cos x = \frac{\text{adj}}{\text{hyp}}, \quad \tan x = \frac{\text{opp}}{\text{adj}}$$

Tip: Remember 'SOH CAH TOA' to help you decide which formula you need to use — and always label the sides of your triangle that you're interested in.

If you're given **one angle** and **one side**, you can use trigonometry to find an **unknown side length**.

Start by looking at the side you've been **given** and the side you **want to find** — this will tell you which formula to use. For example, if you had the **hypotenuse** and wanted to find the **adjacent**, you'd use the **cos** formula as it contains these two sides. **Substitute** the values you know into the formula and **rearrange** it to find the length you want.

Example 1

Find the length of side y. Give your answer correct to 3 significant figures.

1. Start by labelling the two sides.

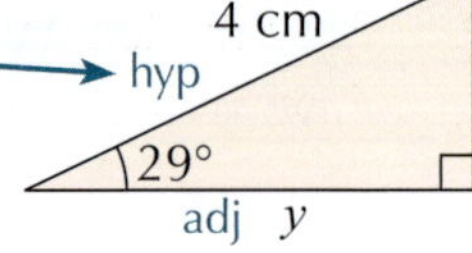

2. You can see from the labels that you're given the hypotenuse and asked to find the adjacent, so use the formula for cos x. $\cos x = \frac{\text{adj}}{\text{hyp}}$
3. Put the numbers into the formula... $\cos 29° = \frac{y}{4}$
4. ...and rearrange to find y. $4 \cos 29° = y$
5. Input '4 cos 29' into your calculator and press '=' to find the value of y. $y = 3.4984... =$ **3.50 cm** (3 s.f.)

Example 2

Find the length of side w. Give your answer correct to 3 significant figures.

1. Start by labelling the two sides.
2. You can see from the labels that you're given the opposite and asked to find the adjacent, so use the formula for tan x. $\tan x = \frac{\text{opp}}{\text{adj}}$
3. Put the numbers into the formula... $\tan 42° = \frac{11}{w}$
4. ...and rearrange to find w. $w \tan 42° = 11$
5. Input '11 ÷ tan 42' into your calculator and press '=' to find the value of w. $w = \frac{11}{\tan 42°} = 12.216...$ $= \mathbf{12.2\ cm}$ (3 s.f.)

42° adj w opp 11 cm

Tip: Be careful — w is on the bottom of the fraction, so the rearrangement is slightly different.

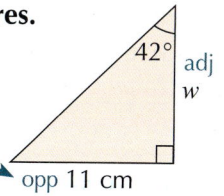

Exercise 1

Q1 Label each of the triangles below with letters to show the hypotenuse (H), opposite (O) and adjacent (A) sides, in relation to the labelled angle.

a) 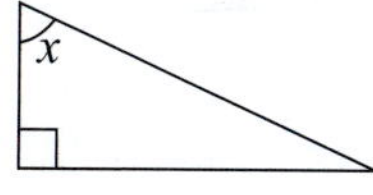

b) 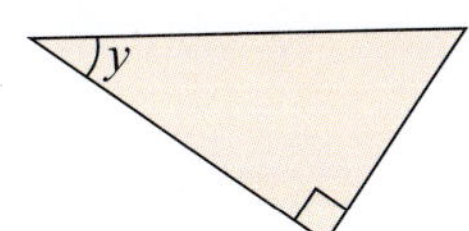

c) 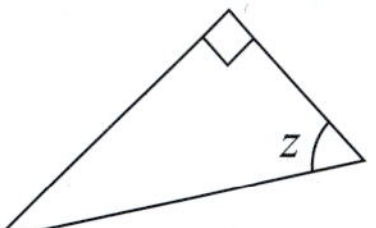

Q2 Find the lengths of the missing sides marked with letters. Give your answers to 3 significant figures.

a) 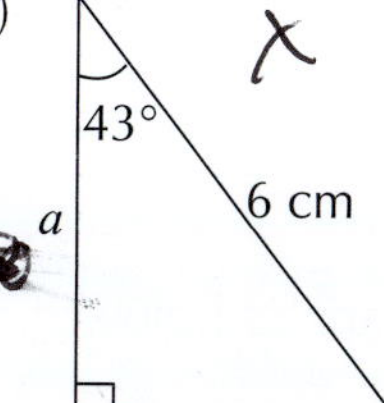

b) 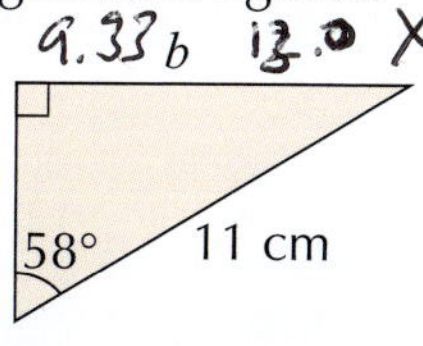

c) 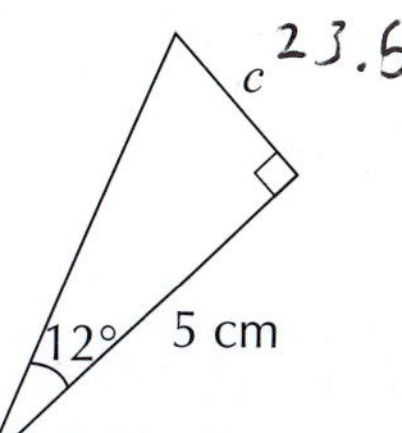

d) 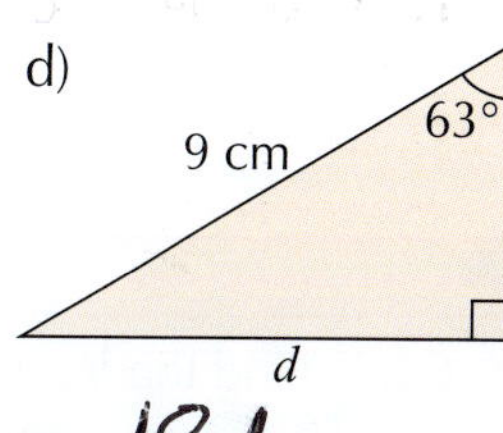

Q3 Find the lengths of the missing sides marked with letters. Give your answers to 3 significant figures.

a) 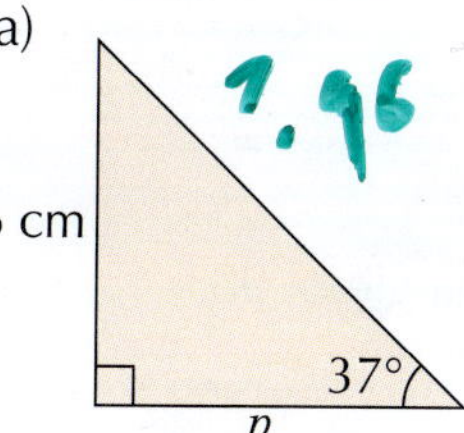

b) 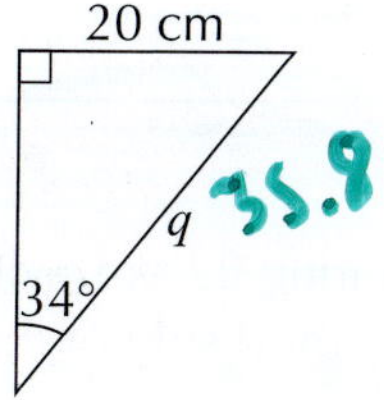

c) 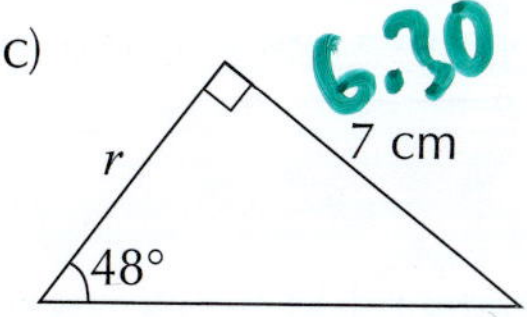

d) 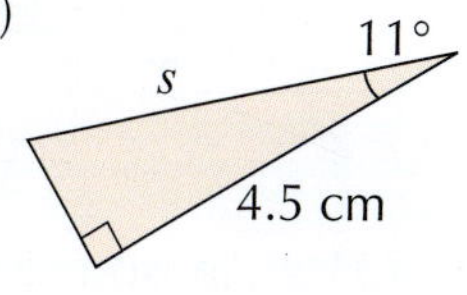

Example 3

Find the missing side length of the isosceles triangle shown. Give your answer correct to 3 significant figures.

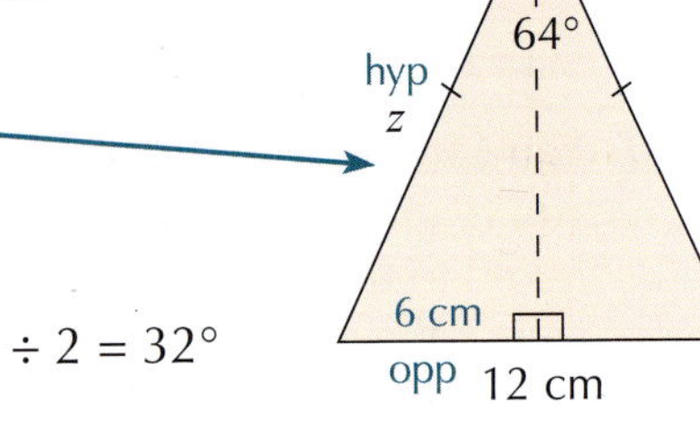

1. Create a right-angled triangle by splitting the triangle in half. Label the two sides of your new triangle.
2. Divide the angle by 2 to find the angle in your right-angled triangle. $64 \div 2 = 32°$
   Divide the length of the base by 2 to find the base length of your right-angled triangle. $12 \div 2 = 6$ cm
3. Now you have the opposite and you need to find the hypotenuse, so use the formula for sin x. $\sin x = \frac{\text{opp}}{\text{hyp}}$
4. Put the numbers into the formula... $\sin 32° = \frac{6}{z}$
5. ...and rearrange to find z. $z \sin 32° = 6$
6. Input '6 ÷ sin 32' into your calculator and press '=' to find the value of z. $z = \frac{6}{\sin 32°}$
   $= 11.322... =$ **11.3 cm** (3 s.f.)

Exercise 2

Q1 Find the length of the side labelled with a letter in each of the triangles below. Give your answers to 3 significant figures.

a)

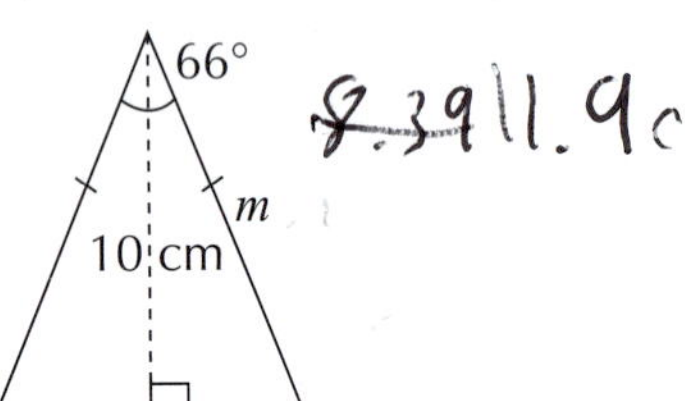

b)

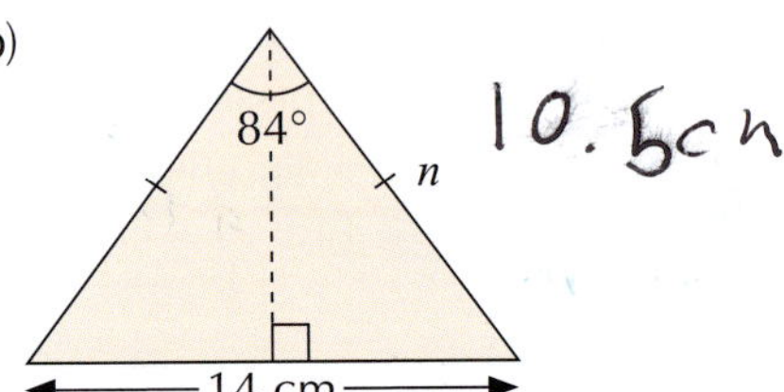

Q2 Find the length of the side labelled with a letter in each of the triangles below. Give your answers to 3 significant figures.

a)

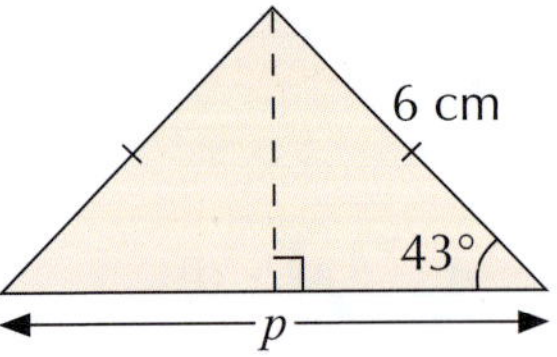

b)

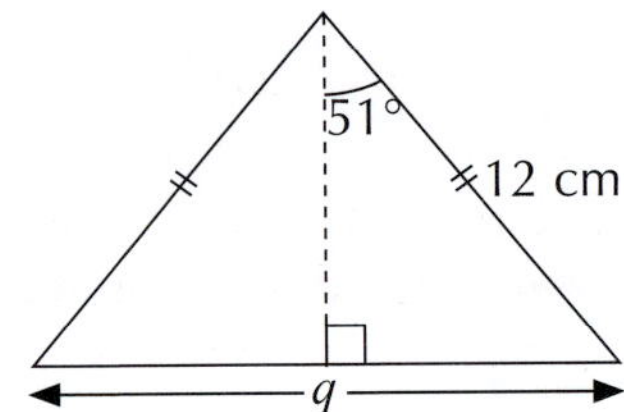

Q3 An isosceles triangle has two sides measuring 22 cm, with an angle of 98° between them. What is the length of the third side of the triangle? Give your answer to 3 significant figures.

You can also use the trig formulas to find an **angle** if you know two side lengths. You have to use the **inverse functions** of sin, cos and tan (written $\sin^{-1}$, $\cos^{-1}$ and $\tan^{-1}$), which return an **angle**.

To find an angle, work out which formula you need from the sides you're given as before, then **substitute** in the known values — this will give you a **fraction** on the right-hand side, e.g. $\sin x = \frac{1}{2}$. Take the **inverse trig function** of the fraction to get the angle — so here you'd do $x = \sin^{-1}\left(\frac{1}{2}\right) = 30°$.

Tip: Inverse trig functions are usually found on a calculator by pressing 'shift' or '2nd' before pressing sin, cos or tan.

Example 4

Find the size of angle x. Give your answer correct to 1 decimal place.

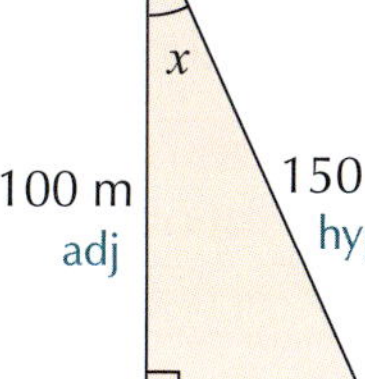

1. Start by labelling the sides of the triangle.
2. You're given the adjacent and the hypotenuse, so use the formula for cos x. $\cos x = \frac{\text{adj}}{\text{hyp}} = \frac{100}{150}$
3. Take the inverse of cos to find the angle. $x = \cos^{-1}\left(\frac{100}{150}\right)$
4. Input '$\cos^{-1}(100 \div 150)$' into your calculator and press '=' to find the value of x. $x = 48.189... =$ **48.2°** (1 d.p.)

Example 5

Find the size of angle x. Give your answer correct to 1 decimal place.

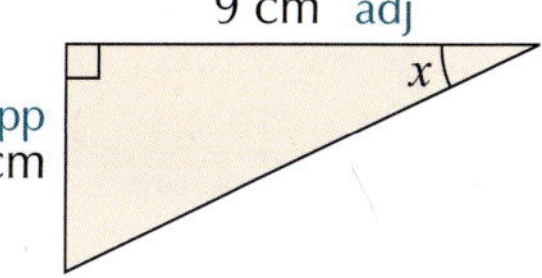

1. Start by labelling the sides of the triangle.
2. You're given the opposite and the adjacent, so use the formula for tan x. $\tan x = \frac{\text{opp}}{\text{adj}} = \frac{3}{9}$

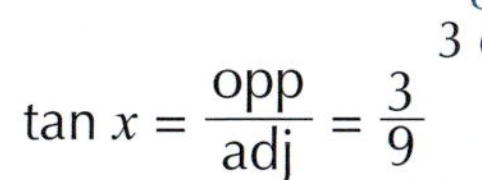

3. Take the inverse of tan to find the angle. $x = \tan^{-1}\left(\frac{3}{9}\right)$
4. Use your calculator to find the value of x. $x = 18.434... =$ **18.4°** (1 d.p.)

Trigonometry can be used to work out angles of **elevation** and **depression**.

The **angle of elevation** is the angle between a **horizontal line** and the **line of sight** of an observer at the same level **looking up**. E.g. the angle made when looking up at a hovering helicopter.

The **angle of depression** is the angle between a **horizontal line** and the **line of sight** of an observer at the same level **looking down**. E.g. the angle made when looking down from a window.

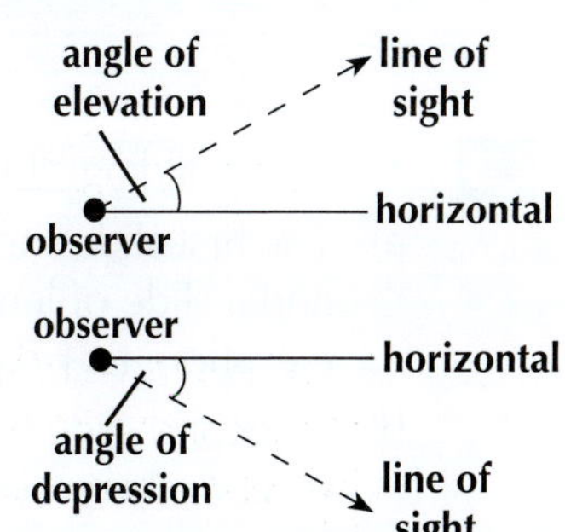

For problems that ask for an angle of elevation or depression, use the information given to **draw** a right-angled triangle and use the formulas in the **same way** as usual. Remember to relate your answer to the **original context** of the problem.

Example 6

Liz holds one end of a 7 m paper chain out of her window. Phil stands in the garden below holding the other end so it's taut. Phil's end of the paper chain is 6 m vertically below Liz's end. Find the size of the angle of depression from Liz to Phil. Give your answer to 1 decimal place.

1. Use the information to draw a right-angled triangle — the angle of depression is the angle below the horizontal. Label the sides of your triangle.

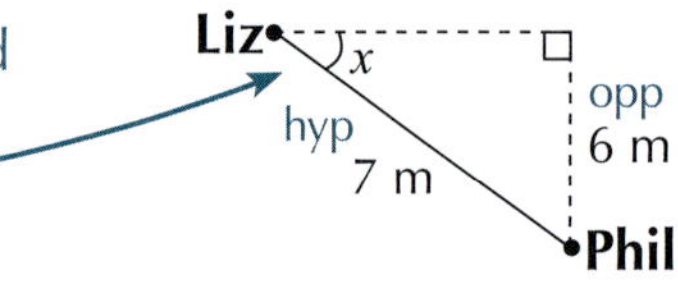

2. You're given the hypotenuse and the opposite, so use the formula for sin x. $\sin x = \frac{\text{opp}}{\text{hyp}} = \frac{6}{7}$
3. Take the inverse of sin to find the angle. $x = \sin^{-1}\left(\frac{6}{7}\right)$
4. Use your calculator to find the value of x. $x = 58.997... =$ **59.0°** (1 d.p.)

Exercise 3

Q1 Find the sizes of the missing angles marked with letters. Give your answers to 1 d.p.

a)

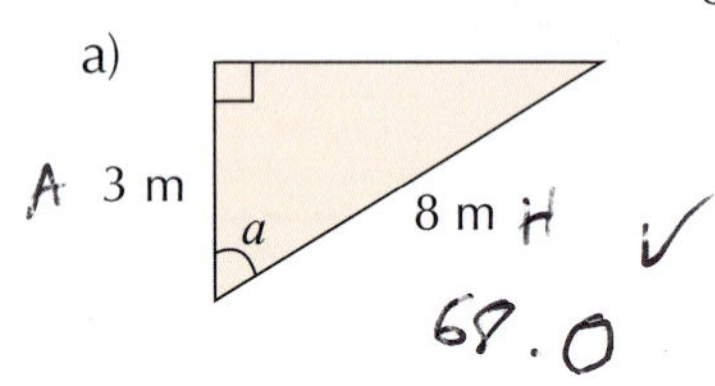

b)

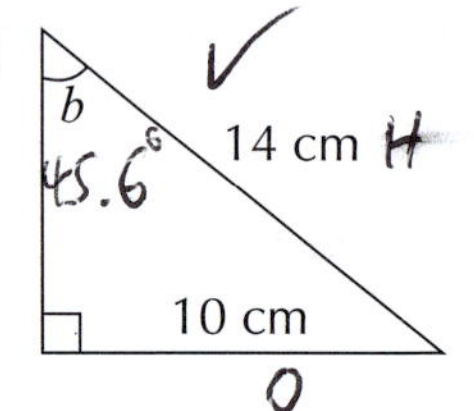

c)

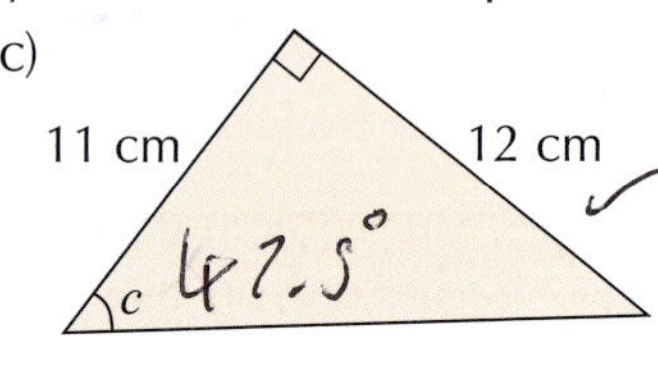

Q2 Find the sizes of the missing angles marked with letters, giving your answers to 1 d.p.

a)

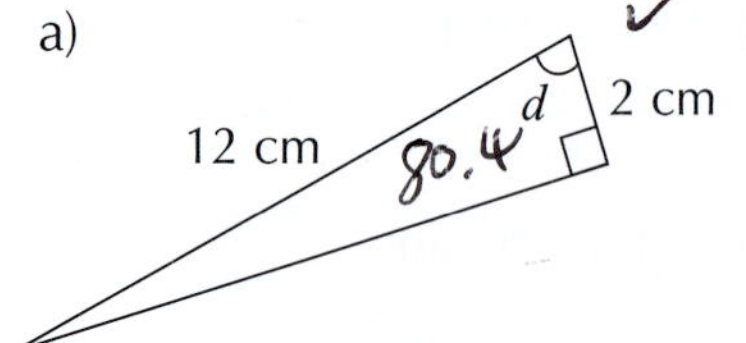

b)

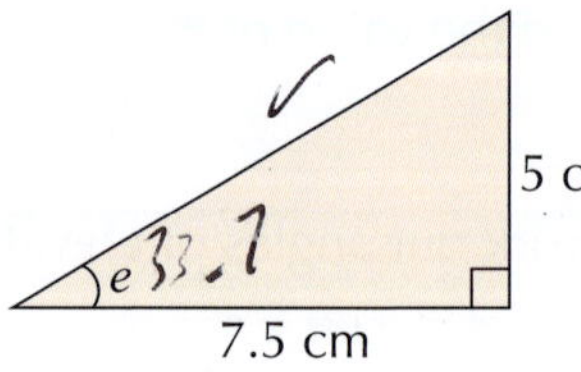

c)

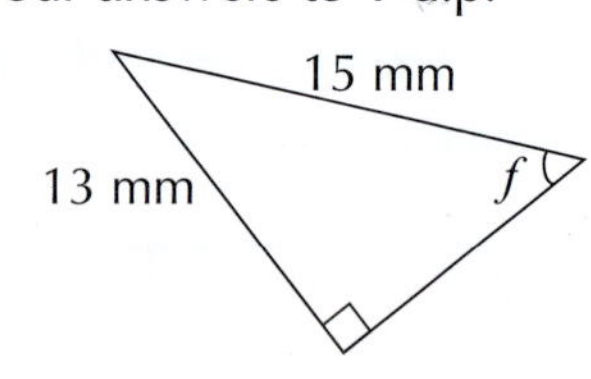

Q3 Maha is building slides for an adventure playground.

8 m 24 m m

a) The first slide she builds has an 8 m high vertical ladder and a slide of length 24 m. Find m, the slide's angle of elevation, to 1 d.p.

b) A second slide has a 4 m vertical ladder, and the base of the slide reaches the ground 5.5 m from the base of the ladder as shown. Find q, the angle of depression at the top of the this slide, to 1 d.p.

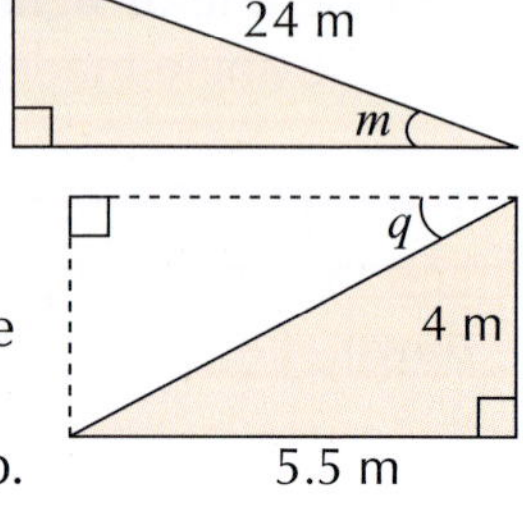

Common Trig Values

Learning Objective — Spec Ref G21:
Know and be able to find trig values for common angles.

The sin, cos and tan of some angles have **exact values** as shown below.
You need to know these for trigonometry questions where you're not allowed a calculator.

$\sin 0° = 0$	$\sin 30° = \frac{1}{2}$	$\sin 45° = \frac{\sqrt{2}}{2}$	$\sin 60° = \frac{\sqrt{3}}{2}$	$\sin 90° = 1$
$\cos 0° = 1$	$\cos 30° = \frac{\sqrt{3}}{2}$	$\cos 45° = \frac{\sqrt{2}}{2}$	$\cos 60° = \frac{1}{2}$	$\cos 90° = 0$
$\tan 0° = 0$	$\tan 30° = \frac{\sqrt{3}}{3}$	$\tan 45° = 1$	$\tan 60° = \sqrt{3}$	

Example 7

Without using a calculator, find the exact length of side y in the triangle below.

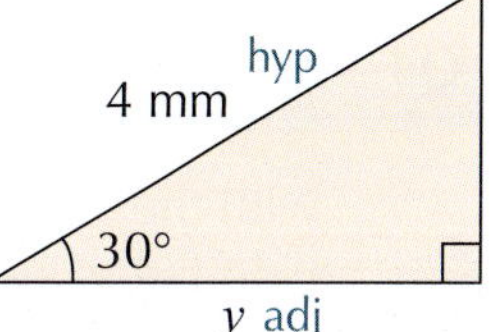

1. Label the triangle.
2. You're given the hypotenuse and want to find the adjacent, so use the formula for cos x. $\cos x = \frac{\text{adj}}{\text{hyp}}$
3. Substitute in the values you know and rearrange the formula to make y the subject. $\cos 30° = \frac{y}{4}$
4. Replace cos 30° with its exact value. $y = 4 \times \cos 30° = 4 \times \frac{\sqrt{3}}{2} = \mathbf{2\sqrt{3}}$ **mm**

Exercise 4

Q1 Find the size of the angles marked with letters.

a)

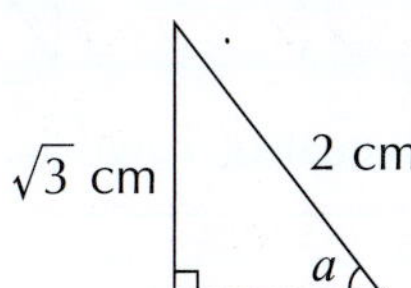

b)

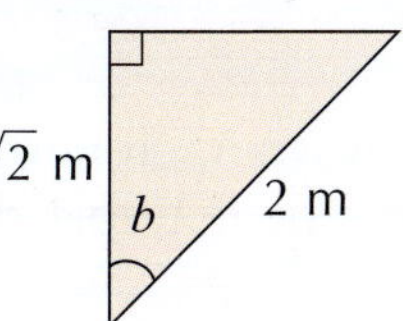

c)

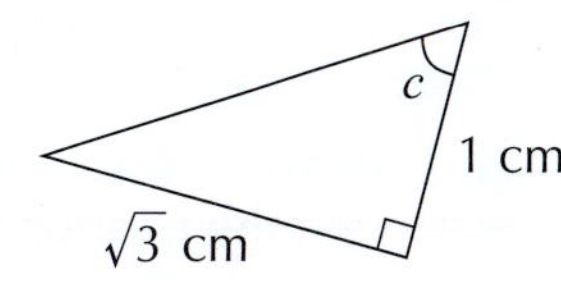

Q2 Find the exact length of the sides marked with letters.

a)

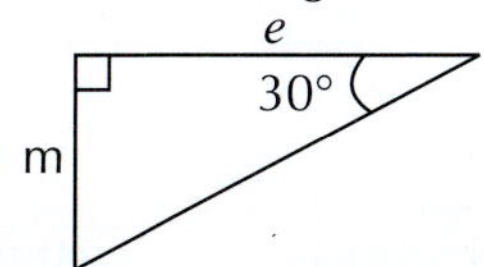

b)

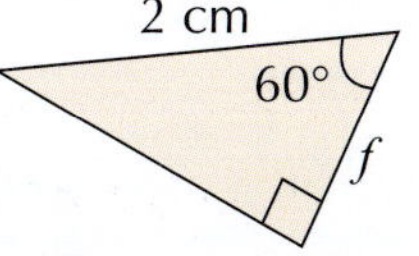

c)

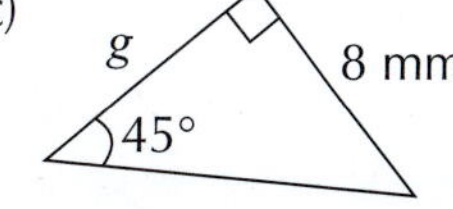

Q3 Show that: $\tan 45° + \sin 60° = \frac{2 + \sqrt{3}}{2}$

Q4 Triangle DEF is isosceles. $DF = 7\sqrt{2}$ cm and angle $DEF = 90°$.
What is the exact length of side DE?

Review Exercise

Q1 The points P and R have coordinates $P(1, 3)$ and $R(7, 8)$.
Find the length of the line segment PR, correct to 1 d.p.

Q2 A pilot flies 150 km on a bearing of 090°, then 270 km on a bearing of 180°.
Find the direct distance from his start point to his end point. Give your answer to the nearest kilometre.

Q3 Find the lengths of the sides marked with letters in each of the following.
Give your answers to 3 significant figures.

a) 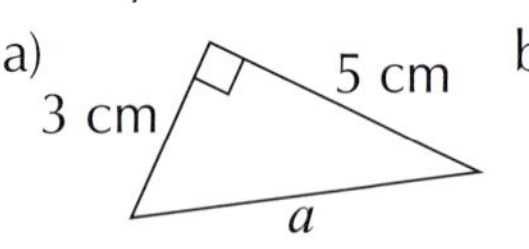

b) 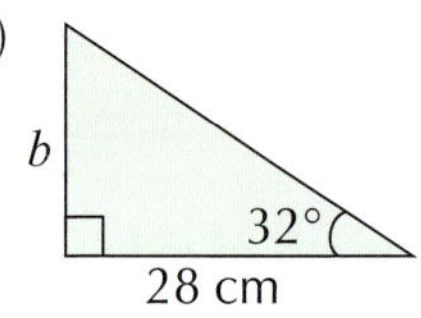

c) 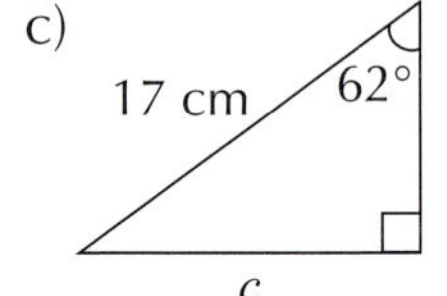

d) 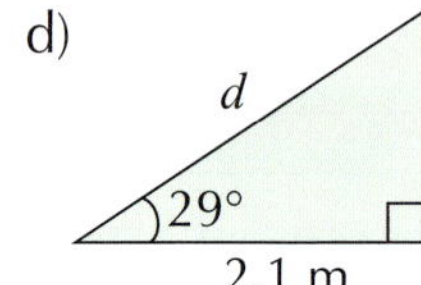

Q4 A ladder is leaning against the side of a tower. The base of the ladder is placed 8 m away from the bottom of the tower, making an angle of 68° with the ground. It reaches a window h m above the ground.
Find the value of h, giving your answer to 1 decimal place.

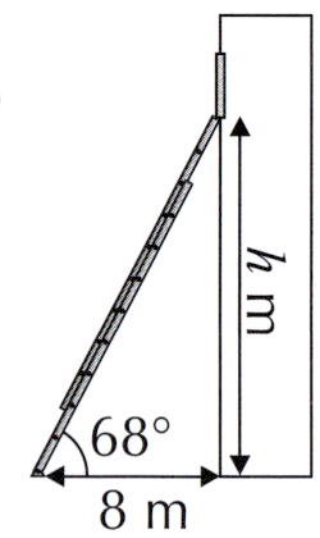

Q5 A kite with taut string of length 5.8 m is flying in the air.
The kite is 4.1 m vertically higher than the other end of the string.
Find the angle between the string and the horizontal, to 1 d.p.

Q6 The shape shown is made up of two right-angled triangles.
Find the value of x. Give your answer to 1 d.p.

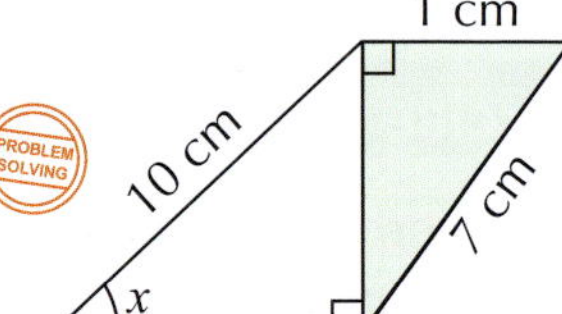

Q7 Town W is 25 km due south of Town X. Town Y is 42 km due east of Town W.
Find the bearing of Town Y from Town X, to 1 d.p.

Q8 Find the exact lengths of the sides marked with letters in each of the following.

a) 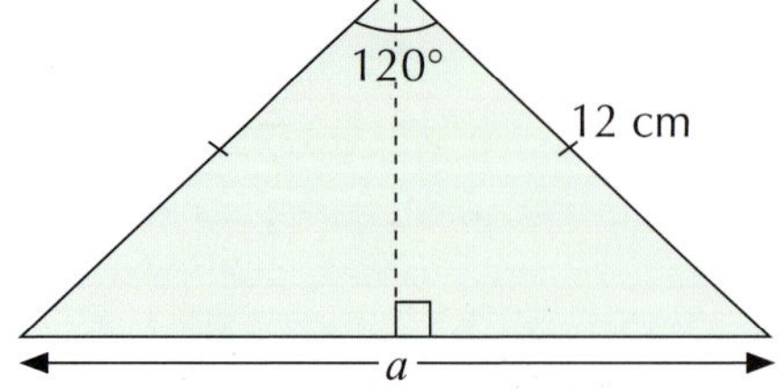

b) 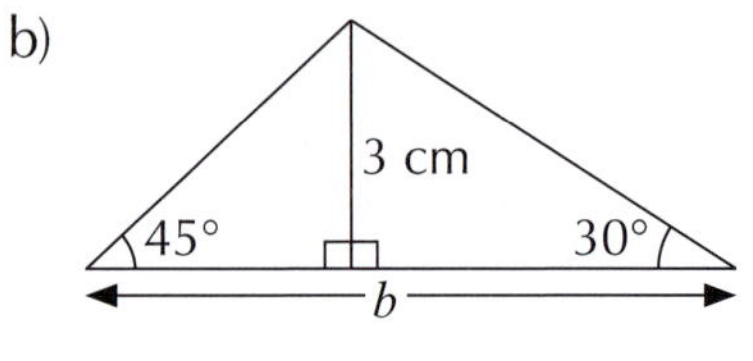

Exam-Style Questions

Q1 A pilot flies 860 km from Lyon to Prague. She then flies 426 km south to Ljubljana, which is directly east of Lyon. Find the distance from Ljubljana to Lyon to the nearest kilometre.

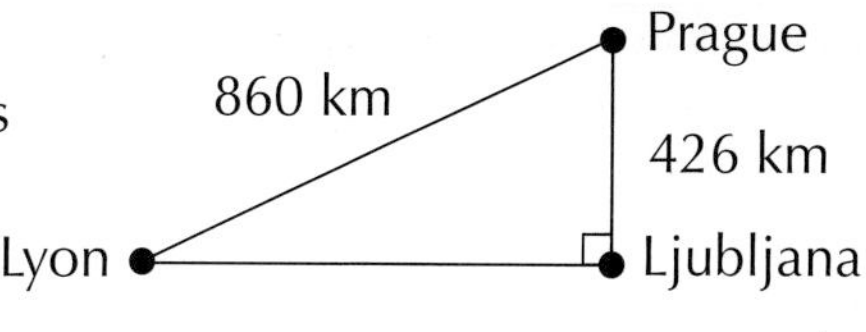

[2 marks]

Q2 Calculate the length of the shortest side of the rectangle below. Give your answer to 2 decimal places.

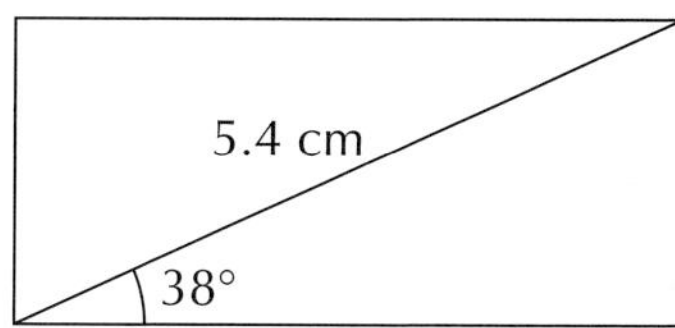

[2 marks]

Q3 *ABC* is a right-angled triangle. Find the value of sin *ACB*, giving your answer as a fraction.

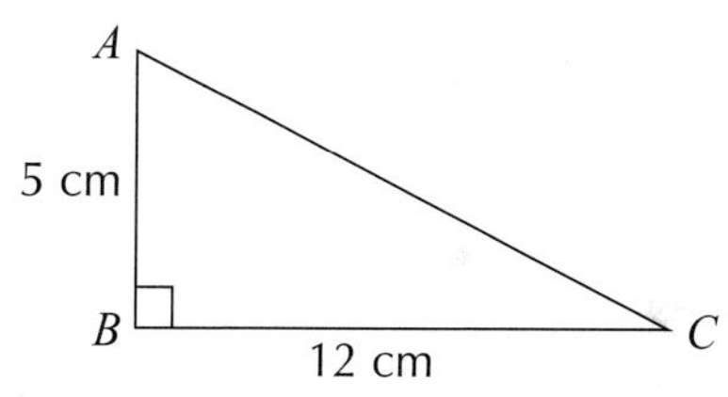

[3 marks]

Q4

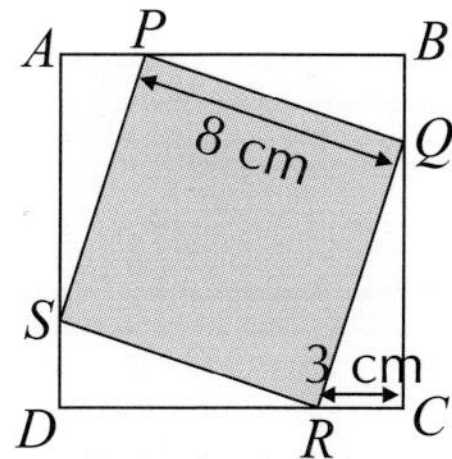

The square *PQRS* is drawn inside another square *ABCD*, as shown in the diagram on the left. Find the side length of *ABCD* to 1 decimal place.

[3 marks]

Q5 Find the exact length of diagonal *AC* of the rhombus on the right.

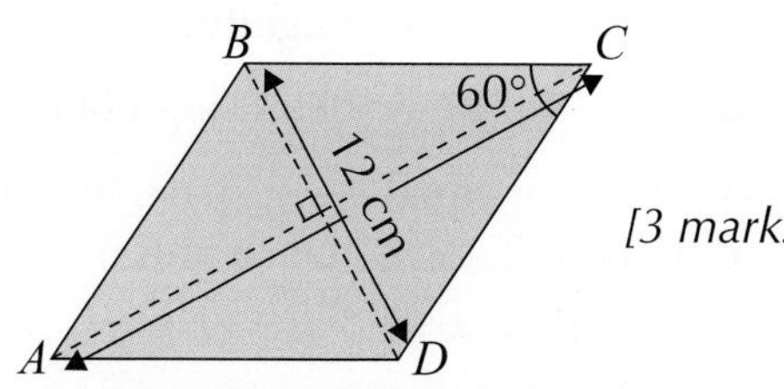

[3 marks]

20.1 Column Vectors

Time for something completely different now — vectors. You can think of them as straight lines from one point in space to another.

Vectors and Scalars

Learning Objectives — Spec Ref G25:
- Understand and use vector notation.
- Be able to multiply vectors by scalars.

A **vector** has **magnitude** (size or length) and **direction**.

There are various ways to represent a vector — it can be:

- written as a **column vector** (positive numbers mean right or up, negative numbers mean left or down).

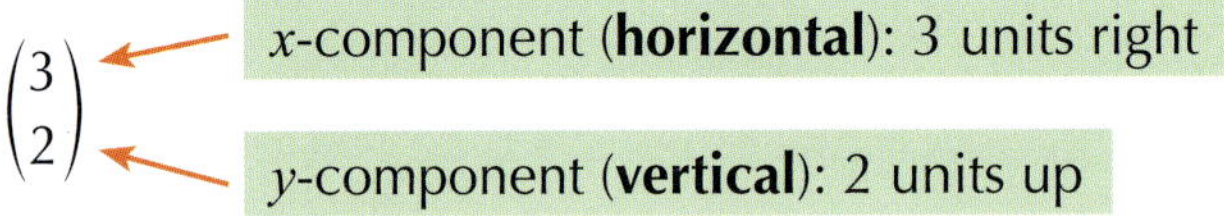

- shown on a diagram by an **arrow**.

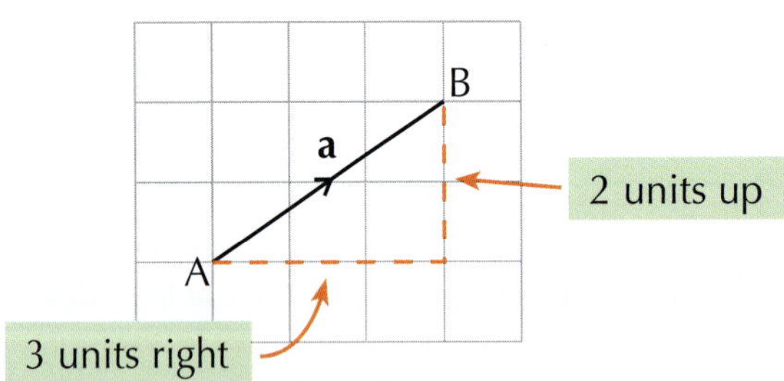

Tip: These two vectors are exactly the same — they're just shown in different ways.

Vectors can be written using their **end points**, so $\overrightarrow{AB}$ means the vector **from A to B** and $\overrightarrow{BA}$ means the vector **from B to A**. $\overrightarrow{AB}$ and $\overrightarrow{BA}$ are **different** vectors — they have the **same magnitude** but **different directions**.

Vectors can also be written using **bold** letters (**a**) or **underlined** letters ($\underline{a}$ or $\underset{\sim}{a}$).

Two vectors are **equal** if they have the **same magnitude** and **direction**. E.g. vectors **m** and **n** are equal vectors, even though they have different start and end points.

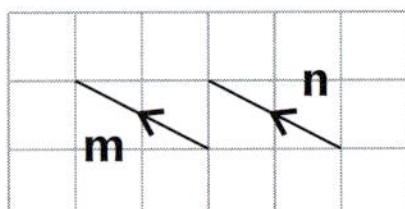

Example 1

a) Draw the vector m = $\begin{pmatrix} -3 \\ 2 \end{pmatrix}$.

1. The positive and negative directions in column vectors are the same as they are for coordinates.
2. So –3 in the x-component means '3 units left', and 2 in the y-component means '2 units up'.
3. Make sure that you label the vector **m**, and add an arrow to show its direction.

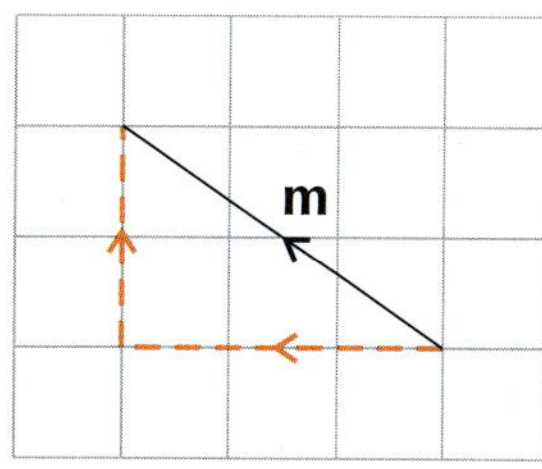

Tip: It doesn't matter where the vector is drawn on the grid. You can choose any starting point — as long as the end point is 3 units to the left and 2 units up.

b) The vector $\overrightarrow{PQ}$ is drawn on the right. Write $\overrightarrow{PQ}$ as a column vector.

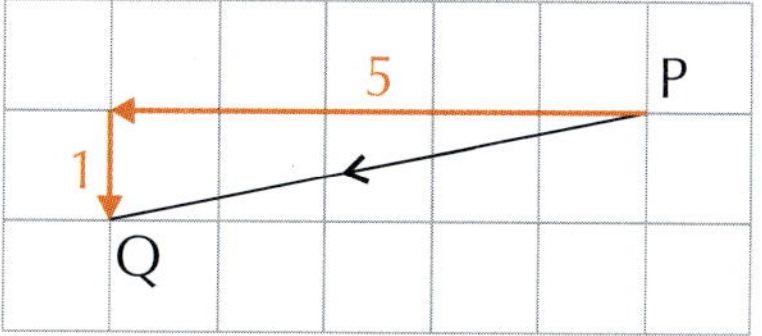

1. Start at P and count the number of units in the horizontal and vertical directions.
2. Write the number of horizontal units on the top and the number of vertical units on the bottom. Remember that if the direction is left or down, you write the negative.

$$\overrightarrow{PQ} = \begin{pmatrix} -5 \\ -1 \end{pmatrix}$$

Exercise 1

Q1 Draw arrows to represent the following vectors.

a) $\begin{pmatrix} 1 \\ 4 \end{pmatrix}$ b) $\begin{pmatrix} 3 \\ 5 \end{pmatrix}$ c) $\begin{pmatrix} -2 \\ 4 \end{pmatrix}$ d) $\begin{pmatrix} 0 \\ 5 \end{pmatrix}$

e) $\begin{pmatrix} -3 \\ -5 \end{pmatrix}$ f) $\begin{pmatrix} 3 \\ 0 \end{pmatrix}$ g) $\begin{pmatrix} -3 \\ -3 \end{pmatrix}$ h) $\begin{pmatrix} 0 \\ -3 \end{pmatrix}$

Q2 Write down the column vectors represented by these arrows:

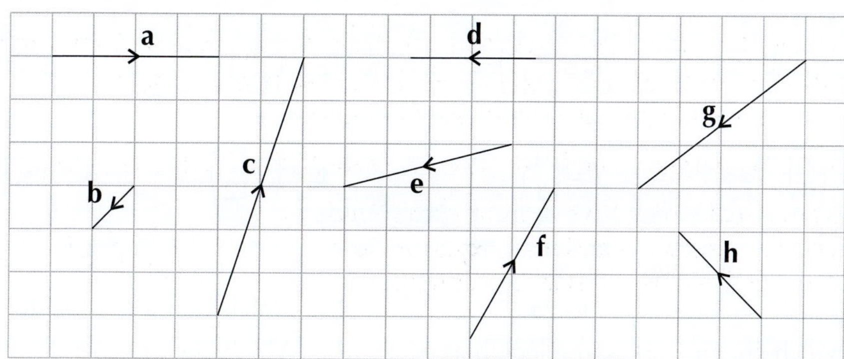

A **scalar** is just a number (like all the ones you're used to working with). Unlike vectors, scalars have magnitude (size) but **no direction**. A vector can be **multiplied** by a scalar to give another vector. To do the multiplication, you multiply each of the vector's **components** by the scalar.

The resulting vector is **parallel** to the original vector.
If the scalar is **negative**, the direction of the vector is **reversed**.

Example 2

If vector p = $\begin{pmatrix} 2 \\ -3 \end{pmatrix}$**, write the following as column vectors: a) 2p b)** $\frac{1}{2}$**p c) –p**

Multiply a vector by a scalar by multiplying the x-component and the y-component separately.

a) $2\mathbf{p} = \begin{pmatrix} 2 \times 2 \\ 2 \times -3 \end{pmatrix} = \begin{pmatrix} \mathbf{4} \\ \mathbf{-6} \end{pmatrix}$

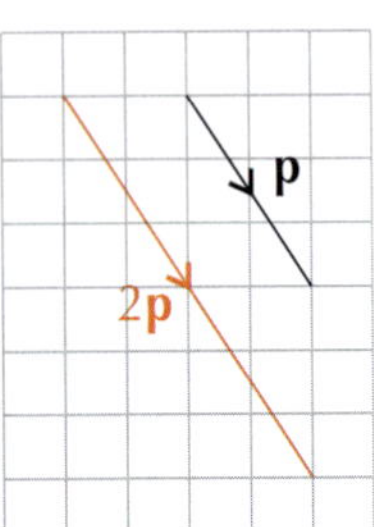

The direction has stayed the same but the magnitude has doubled.

b) $\frac{1}{2}\mathbf{p} = \begin{pmatrix} \frac{1}{2} \times 2 \\ \frac{1}{2} \times -3 \end{pmatrix} = \begin{pmatrix} \mathbf{1} \\ -\frac{\mathbf{3}}{\mathbf{2}} \end{pmatrix}$

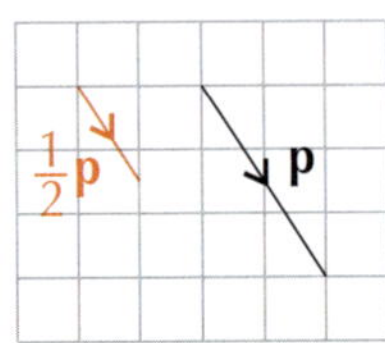

The direction has stayed the same but the magnitude has halved.

c) $-\mathbf{p} = \begin{pmatrix} -1 \times 2 \\ -1 \times -3 \end{pmatrix} = \begin{pmatrix} \mathbf{-2} \\ \mathbf{3} \end{pmatrix}$

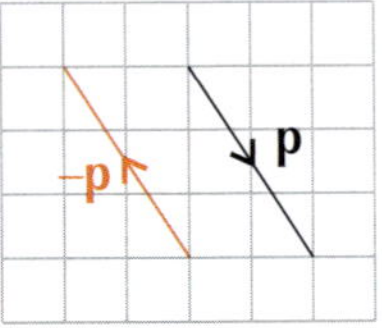

The direction has reversed but the magnitude has stayed the same.

Exercise 2

Q1 If **q** = $\begin{pmatrix} -1 \\ 3 \end{pmatrix}$, find and draw the following vectors.

a) 3**q** b) 5**q** c) $\frac{3}{2}$**q** d) –2**q**

Q2

$\mathbf{a} = \begin{pmatrix} 4 \\ -2 \end{pmatrix}$	$\mathbf{b} = \begin{pmatrix} -1 \\ 4 \end{pmatrix}$	$\mathbf{c} = \begin{pmatrix} 3 \\ 12 \end{pmatrix}$	$\mathbf{d} = \begin{pmatrix} 8 \\ -4 \end{pmatrix}$
$\mathbf{e} = \begin{pmatrix} 1 \\ 4 \end{pmatrix}$	$\mathbf{f} = \begin{pmatrix} 0 \\ 3 \end{pmatrix}$	$\mathbf{g} = \begin{pmatrix} 3 \\ -12 \end{pmatrix}$	$\mathbf{h} = \begin{pmatrix} 6 \\ 0 \end{pmatrix}$

From the list of vectors above:

a) Which vector is equal to 2**a**?

b) Which vector is equal to –3**b**?

c) Which vector is the same length as **e**?

d) Which vector is parallel to **c**?

Adding and Subtracting Vectors

Learning Objective — Spec Ref G25:
Be able to add and subtract vectors.

To **add** or **subtract** column vectors, you add or subtract the x-components and y-components separately. The sum of two or more vectors is called the **resultant vector**.

Vectors can also be added by drawing them in a chain, nose-to-tail. The resultant vector goes in a **straight line** from the **start** to the **end** of the chain of vectors.

When you add two vectors, it doesn't matter which comes first, i.e. $\mathbf{a} + \mathbf{b} = \mathbf{b} + \mathbf{a}$. Be careful when subtracting though — just like with ordinary numbers $\mathbf{a} - \mathbf{b} = -\mathbf{b} + \mathbf{a}$, not $\mathbf{b} - \mathbf{a}$.

Example 3

Look at these three vectors: $\mathbf{p} = \begin{pmatrix} 3 \\ 1 \end{pmatrix}$ $\mathbf{q} = \begin{pmatrix} -2 \\ 0 \end{pmatrix}$ $\mathbf{r} = \begin{pmatrix} 1 \\ -3 \end{pmatrix}$

Work out the following and draw the resultant vectors:

a) $\mathbf{p} + \mathbf{q}$ **b)** $\mathbf{r} - \mathbf{q}$ **c)** $2\mathbf{q} + \mathbf{p} - \mathbf{r}$

Add and subtract the x-components and the y-components separately.

a) $\begin{pmatrix} 3 \\ 1 \end{pmatrix} + \begin{pmatrix} -2 \\ 0 \end{pmatrix} = \begin{pmatrix} 3 + (-2) \\ 1 + 0 \end{pmatrix} = \begin{pmatrix} \mathbf{1} \\ \mathbf{1} \end{pmatrix}$ →

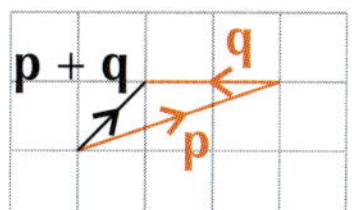

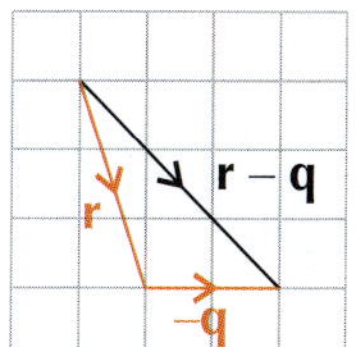

b) $\begin{pmatrix} 1 \\ -3 \end{pmatrix} - \begin{pmatrix} -2 \\ 0 \end{pmatrix} = \begin{pmatrix} 1 - (-2) \\ -3 - 0 \end{pmatrix} = \begin{pmatrix} \mathbf{3} \\ \mathbf{-3} \end{pmatrix}$ →

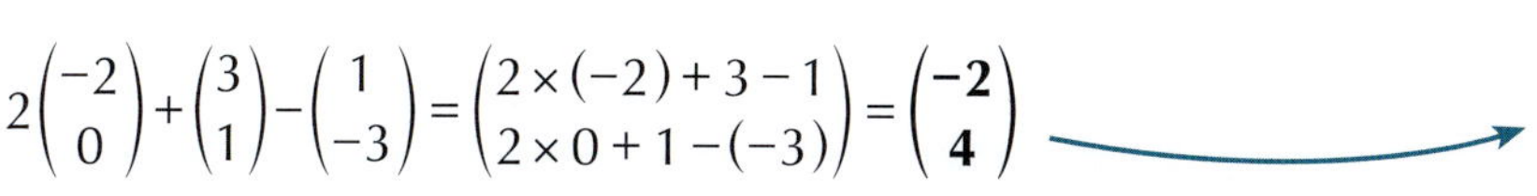

c) $2\begin{pmatrix} -2 \\ 0 \end{pmatrix} + \begin{pmatrix} 3 \\ 1 \end{pmatrix} - \begin{pmatrix} 1 \\ -3 \end{pmatrix} = \begin{pmatrix} 2 \times (-2) + 3 - 1 \\ 2 \times 0 + 1 - (-3) \end{pmatrix} = \begin{pmatrix} \mathbf{-2} \\ \mathbf{4} \end{pmatrix}$ →

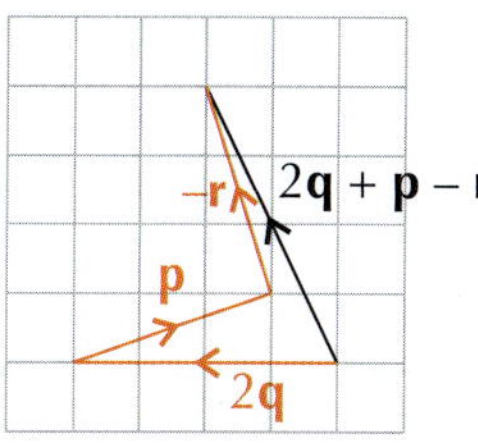

Exercise 3

Q1 Write the answers to the following calculations as column vectors. For each expression, draw arrows to represent the two given vectors and the resultant vector.

a) $\begin{pmatrix} 5 \\ 2 \end{pmatrix} + \begin{pmatrix} 3 \\ 4 \end{pmatrix}$ b) $\begin{pmatrix} 4 \\ -1 \end{pmatrix} + \begin{pmatrix} 1 \\ 6 \end{pmatrix}$ c) $\begin{pmatrix} 2 \\ -1 \end{pmatrix} - \begin{pmatrix} -2 \\ 2 \end{pmatrix}$ d) $\begin{pmatrix} -3 \\ 0 \end{pmatrix} - \begin{pmatrix} 6 \\ 2 \end{pmatrix}$

Q2 If $\mathbf{a} = \begin{pmatrix} 2 \\ 3 \end{pmatrix}$, $\mathbf{b} = \begin{pmatrix} 0 \\ -2 \end{pmatrix}$ and $\mathbf{c} = \begin{pmatrix} -1 \\ 4 \end{pmatrix}$, work out:

a) $\mathbf{b} + \mathbf{c}$ b) $\mathbf{c} - \mathbf{a}$ c) $2\mathbf{c} + \mathbf{a}$ d) $3\mathbf{a} + \mathbf{b}$

e) $\mathbf{a} - 2\mathbf{c}$ f) $\mathbf{a} + \mathbf{b} - \mathbf{c}$ g) $5\mathbf{b} + 4\mathbf{c}$ h) $4\mathbf{a} - \mathbf{b} + 3\mathbf{c}$

Q3 $\mathbf{u} = \begin{pmatrix} 6 \\ -2 \end{pmatrix}$, $\mathbf{v} = \begin{pmatrix} -2 \\ 3 \end{pmatrix}$ and $\mathbf{w} = \begin{pmatrix} 1 \\ 2 \end{pmatrix}$

a) Work out $\mathbf{u} + 2\mathbf{v}$.

b) Draw the vectors $\mathbf{u} + 2\mathbf{v}$ and $\mathbf{w}$.

c) What do you notice about the directions of the vectors $\mathbf{u} + 2\mathbf{v}$ and $\mathbf{w}$?

You can also write a vector as a **sum** of given vectors.

Example 4

Describe the following vectors in terms of a and b.

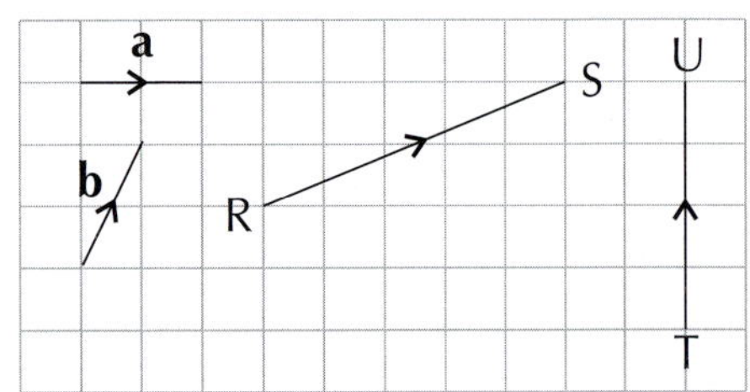

a) $\overrightarrow{RS}$

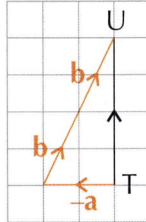

1. Find a route from R to S using just vectors **a** and **b**.

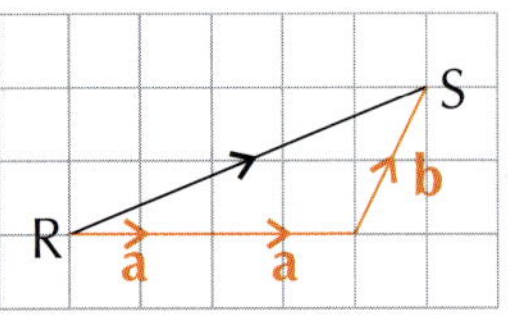

2. So two lots of vector **a** and then vector **b** takes you from R to S.

$\overrightarrow{RS} = \mathbf{2a + b}$

3. You can check the answer by doing the vector addition — from the diagram, $\overrightarrow{RS} = \begin{pmatrix} 5 \\ 2 \end{pmatrix}$, $\mathbf{a} = \begin{pmatrix} 2 \\ 0 \end{pmatrix}$ and $\mathbf{b} = \begin{pmatrix} 1 \\ 2 \end{pmatrix}$.

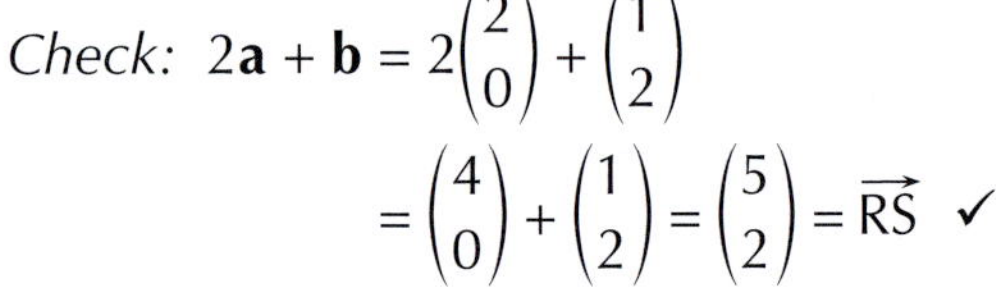

Check: $2\mathbf{a} + \mathbf{b} = 2\begin{pmatrix} 2 \\ 0 \end{pmatrix} + \begin{pmatrix} 1 \\ 2 \end{pmatrix}$

$= \begin{pmatrix} 4 \\ 0 \end{pmatrix} + \begin{pmatrix} 1 \\ 2 \end{pmatrix} = \begin{pmatrix} 5 \\ 2 \end{pmatrix} = \overrightarrow{RS}$ ✓

b) $\overrightarrow{TU}$

1. The reverse of **a** and then two lots of **b** takes you from T to U.

2. Remember to check the answer by doing the vector addition.

$\overrightarrow{TU} = \mathbf{-a + 2b}$

Check: $-\mathbf{a} + 2\mathbf{b} = -\begin{pmatrix} 2 \\ 0 \end{pmatrix} + 2\begin{pmatrix} 1 \\ 2 \end{pmatrix}$

$= \begin{pmatrix} -2 \\ 0 \end{pmatrix} + \begin{pmatrix} 2 \\ 4 \end{pmatrix} = \begin{pmatrix} 0 \\ 4 \end{pmatrix} = \overrightarrow{TU}$ ✓

Exercise 4

Q1

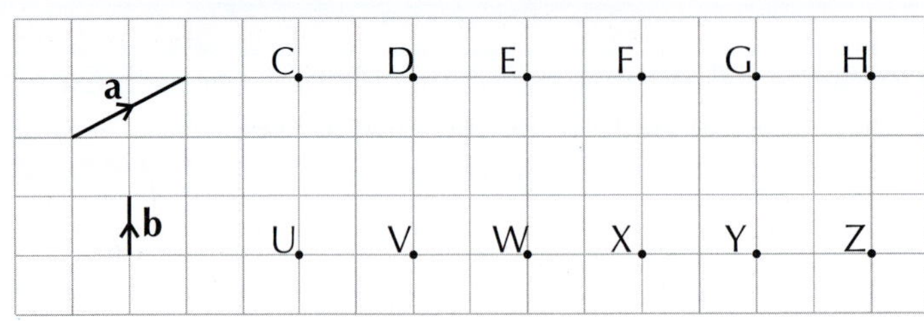

Write the following vectors in terms of **a** and **b**.

a) $\overrightarrow{WH}$

b) $\overrightarrow{ZH}$

c) $\overrightarrow{FX}$

d) $\overrightarrow{UD}$

e) $\overrightarrow{DU}$

f) $\overrightarrow{FZ}$

g) $\overrightarrow{CZ}$

h) $\overrightarrow{DW}$

20.2 Vector Geometry

Vectors can be used in geometry to describe the lines that make up shapes — you can then use the vectors along with properties of the shape to solve problems.

Learning Objective — Spec Ref G25:
Use vectors to solve geometry problems.

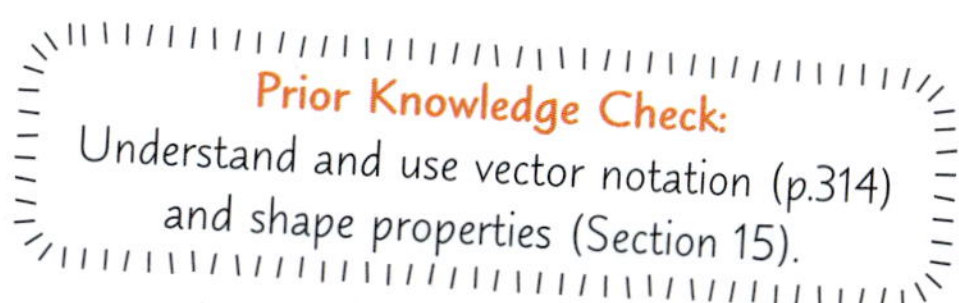

Prior Knowledge Check:
Understand and use vector notation (p.314) and shape properties (Section 15).

The first step to any vector geometry problem is working out what information you already **know** and what you need to **find**. Always work with a **diagram** — if you're not given one, **draw your own**. Then it'll be easier to see which vectors you need to add, subtract or multiply to get to the answer.

Example 1

In triangle OAB, $\overrightarrow{OA}$ = a and $\overrightarrow{OB}$ = b.
Write down, in terms of a and b: a) $\overrightarrow{AO}$ b) $\overrightarrow{AB}$ c) $\overrightarrow{BA}$

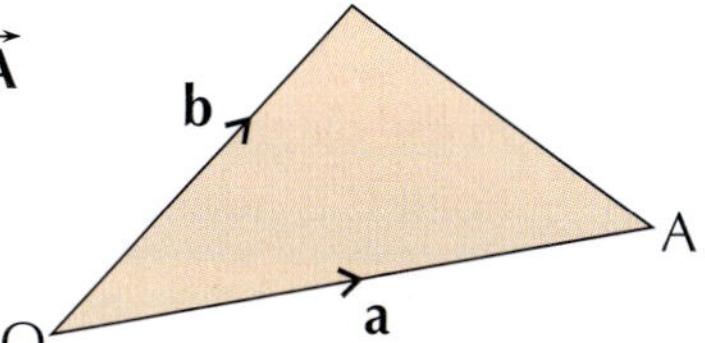

a) To get from A to O, you go backwards along the vector **a**, so you need the reverse vector of **a**. $\overrightarrow{AO} = -\mathbf{a}$

b) To get from A to B, you go backwards along **a** and then along **b**. $\overrightarrow{AB} = -\mathbf{a} + \mathbf{b}$

c) To get from B to A, you go backwards along **b** and then along **a**. $\overrightarrow{BA} = -\mathbf{b} + \mathbf{a}$

Example 2

WXYZ is a parallelogram. $\overrightarrow{WX}$ = u and $\overrightarrow{WZ}$ = v.
M is the midpoint of WY.
Write down, in terms of u and v: a) $\overrightarrow{WY}$ b) $\overrightarrow{WM}$

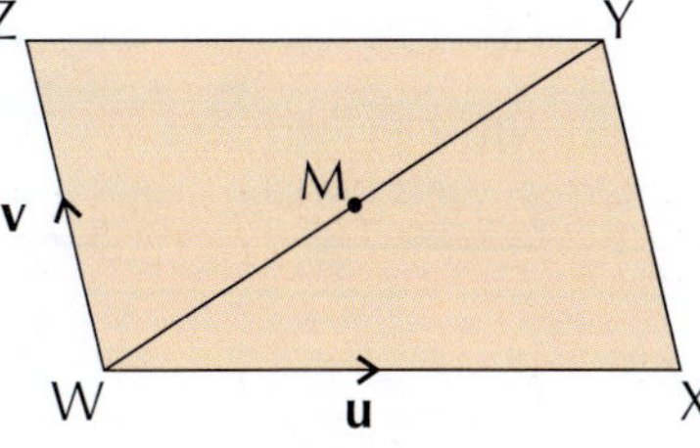

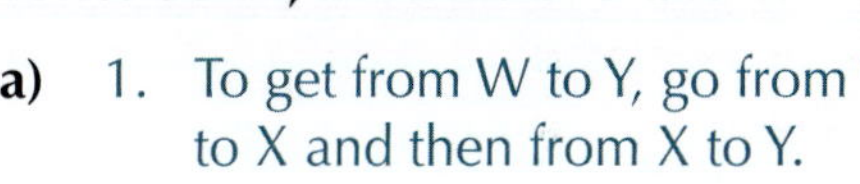

a) 1. To get from W to Y, go from W to X and then from X to Y. $\overrightarrow{WY} = \overrightarrow{WX} + \overrightarrow{XY}$

2. To get from W to X, you go along **u**. $\overrightarrow{WX} = \mathbf{u}$

3. The line XY isn't labelled with a vector — but the shape is a parallelogram, so XY and WZ are parallel and the same length. So the vectors between X and Y and between W and Z are the same. $\overrightarrow{XY} = \overrightarrow{WZ} = \mathbf{v}$

So $\overrightarrow{WY} = \overrightarrow{WX} + \overrightarrow{XY}$
$= \mathbf{u} + \mathbf{v}$

Tip: You could also go from W to Z and then from Z to Y. The vector $\overrightarrow{ZY} = \overrightarrow{WX}$, so you end up with the answer of **u** + **v**.

b) 1. W to M is the same direction as W to Y, but it's half the distance.

2. Halve the vector $\overrightarrow{WY}$ by multiplying the answer from part a) by $\frac{1}{2}$.

$$\overrightarrow{WM} = \frac{1}{2}\overrightarrow{WY}$$
$$= \frac{1}{2}(\mathbf{u} + \mathbf{v})$$
$$= \mathbf{\frac{1}{2}u + \frac{1}{2}v}$$

Exercise 1

Q1 ABCD is a trapezium. $\overrightarrow{AB} = 4\mathbf{p}$, $\overrightarrow{AD} = \mathbf{q}$ and $\overrightarrow{DC} = \mathbf{p}$.
Write the following vectors in terms of **p** and **q**:

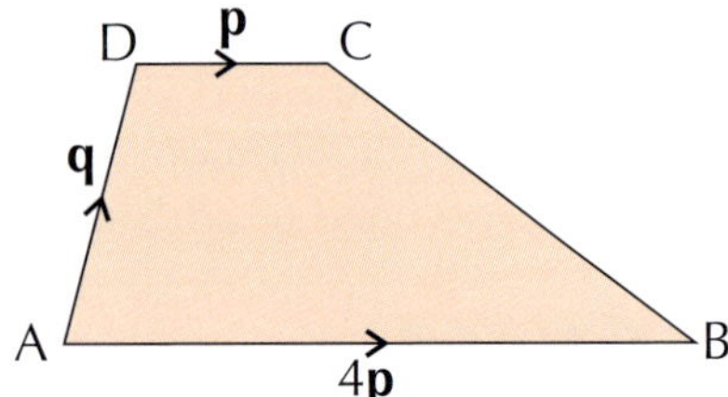

a) $\overrightarrow{BA}$
b) $\overrightarrow{CD}$
c) $\overrightarrow{AC}$
d) $\overrightarrow{CA}$
e) $\overrightarrow{CB}$
f) $\overrightarrow{BD}$

Q2 In the diagram on the right, $\overrightarrow{OA} = \mathbf{a}$ and $\overrightarrow{OB} = \mathbf{b}$.
Point C is added such that $\overrightarrow{OC} = \mathbf{a} + \mathbf{b}$.

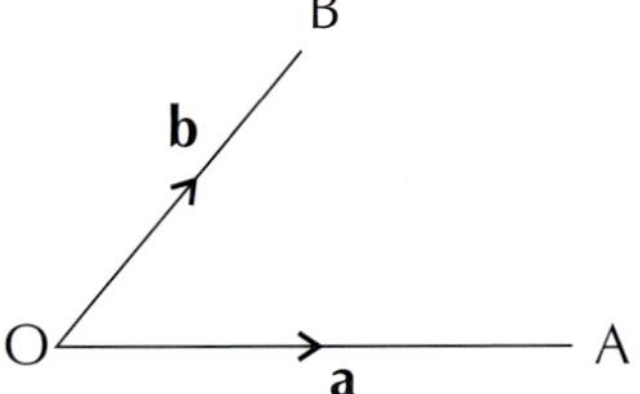

a) Write down, in terms of **a** and **b**:
(i) $\overrightarrow{CO}$ (ii) $\overrightarrow{AB}$

b) What type of shape is OACB?

Q3 In the triangle OBD, $\overrightarrow{OA} = \mathbf{a}$ is $\frac{1}{4}$ of the length of $\overrightarrow{OB}$ and $\overrightarrow{OC} = \mathbf{c}$ is $\frac{1}{3}$ of the length of $\overrightarrow{OD}$.

Write down, in terms of **a** and **c**:

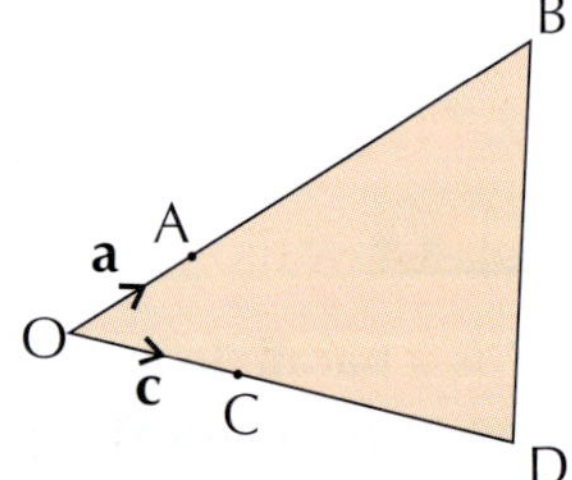

a) $\overrightarrow{OB}$
b) $\overrightarrow{OD}$
c) $\overrightarrow{AB}$
d) $\overrightarrow{CD}$
e) $\overrightarrow{DB}$
f) $\overrightarrow{BD}$

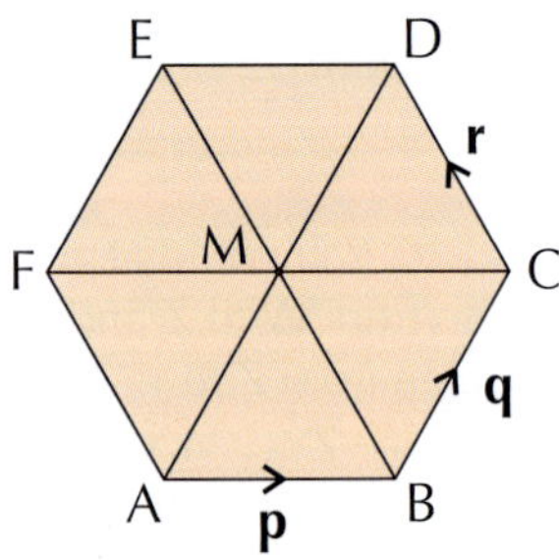

Q4 ABCDEF is a regular hexagon.
M is the centre of the hexagon.
$\overrightarrow{AB} = \mathbf{p}$ and $\overrightarrow{BC} = \mathbf{q}$ and $\overrightarrow{CD} = \mathbf{r}$.

The following vectors can all be written, in terms of **p**, **q** and **r**, in multiple different ways. For each vector, write down two ways.

a) $\overrightarrow{ED}$
b) $\overrightarrow{FE}$
c) $\overrightarrow{AF}$
d) $\overrightarrow{EF}$
e) $\overrightarrow{MF}$
f) $\overrightarrow{EM}$

Review Exercise

Q1 a) Match the following column vectors to the correct vectors in the diagram below.

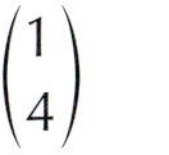 $\begin{pmatrix}-2\\-4\end{pmatrix}$

$\begin{pmatrix}-4\\-1\end{pmatrix}$ $\begin{pmatrix}4\\-2\end{pmatrix}$

$\begin{pmatrix}0\\-5\end{pmatrix}$ $\begin{pmatrix}3\\4\end{pmatrix}$

$\begin{pmatrix}4\\-1\end{pmatrix}$ 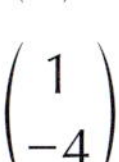

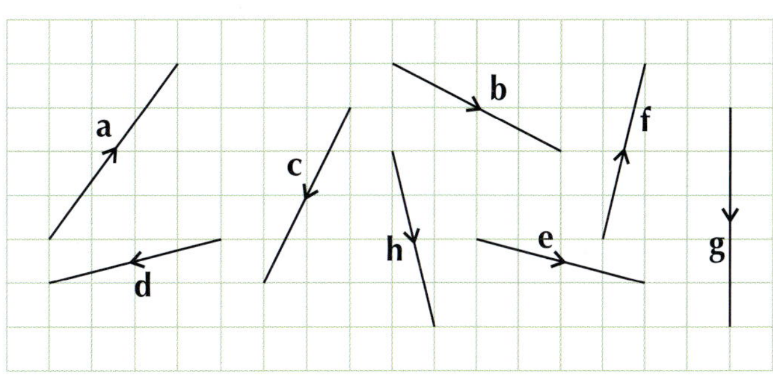

b) Which vector has the same length as **c**?

c) Four of the vectors have the same length. Which vectors are these?

Q2 If $\mathbf{p} = \begin{pmatrix}4\\-3\end{pmatrix}$, $\mathbf{q} = \begin{pmatrix}0\\2\end{pmatrix}$ and $\mathbf{r} = \begin{pmatrix}-1\\5\end{pmatrix}$, find:

a) $3\mathbf{p}$ b) $2\mathbf{q} + \mathbf{r}$ c) $\mathbf{r} - 2\mathbf{p}$ d) $\mathbf{p} + 5\mathbf{r} - 3\mathbf{q}$

Q3 $\mathbf{a} = \begin{pmatrix}6\\-4\end{pmatrix}$ $\mathbf{b} = \begin{pmatrix}-2\\3\end{pmatrix}$ $\mathbf{c} = \begin{pmatrix}1\\2\end{pmatrix}$ $\mathbf{d} = \begin{pmatrix}4\\-2\end{pmatrix}$ $\mathbf{e} = \begin{pmatrix}3\\6\end{pmatrix}$ $\mathbf{f} = \begin{pmatrix}4\\-6\end{pmatrix}$

a) Draw the vector **a** + **b** and write down the resultant vector as a column vector.

b) Draw the vector **e** – **d** and write down the resultant vector as a column vector.

c) Which two of the above vectors can be added to give the resultant vector $\begin{pmatrix}10\\-10\end{pmatrix}$?

d) Which two of the above vectors can be added to give the resultant vector $\begin{pmatrix}1\\9\end{pmatrix}$?

e) Which vector above is parallel to **c**?

f) Which vector above is parallel to **b**?

Q4 PQRS is a trapezium. $\overrightarrow{PQ} = \mathbf{m}$ and $\overrightarrow{SP} = \mathbf{n}$.
The side SR is five times as long as the side PQ.

a) Write down $\overrightarrow{SR}$ in terms of **m** and **n**.

b) Find $\overrightarrow{QR}$ in terms of **m** and **n**.

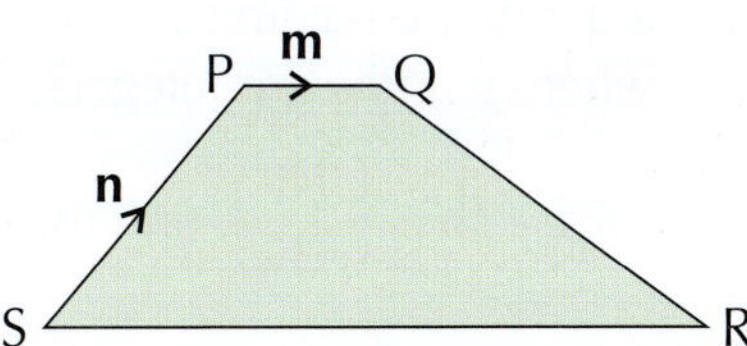

Exam-Style Questions

Q1 The triangle ABC is shown below. $\overrightarrow{AB} = \mathbf{u}$ and $\overrightarrow{CB} = \mathbf{v}$.
Write the vector $\overrightarrow{AC}$ in terms of $\mathbf{u}$ and $\mathbf{v}$.

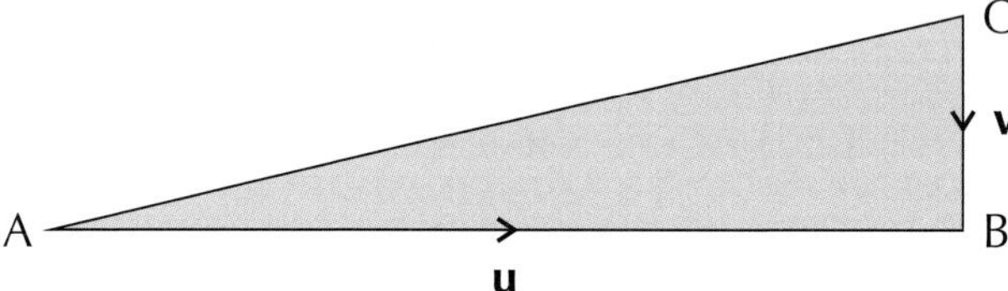

[2 marks]

Q2 $\mathbf{m} = \begin{pmatrix} 5 \\ 0 \end{pmatrix}$ $\mathbf{n} = \begin{pmatrix} -3 \\ -1 \end{pmatrix}$

Write $\mathbf{m} + 4\mathbf{n}$ as a column vector.

[2 marks]

Q3 The vectors **a**, **b**, **c** and **d** are drawn on the square grid below.
Write the vectors **c** and **d** each in terms of **a** and **b**.

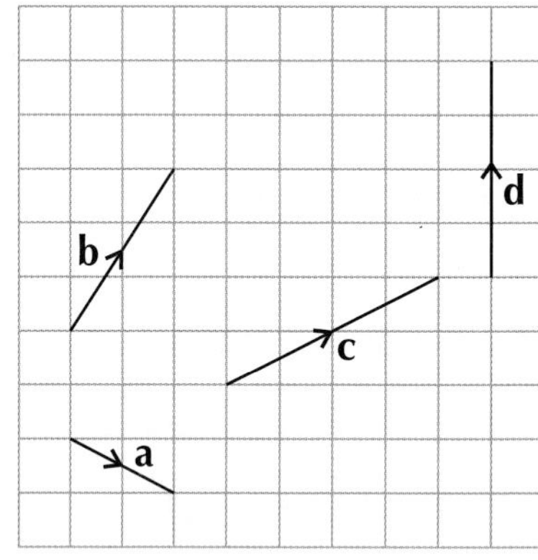

[2 marks]

Q4 **a** and **b** are column vectors such that $\mathbf{a} = \begin{pmatrix} 5p \\ 4q \end{pmatrix}$ and $\mathbf{b} = \begin{pmatrix} 4 \\ 0 \end{pmatrix}$,
where p and q are integers.

If $2\mathbf{a} - 3\mathbf{b} = \begin{pmatrix} 18 \\ -32 \end{pmatrix}$, find the values of p and q.

[4 marks]

Section 21 Constructions

21.1 Circles

Circles come up a lot in Maths... they'll crop up with loci later in this section, and with area and perimeter in Section 22 First, you need to know what the different parts of a circle are called.

Radius and Diameter

Learning Objective — Spec Ref G9:
Be familiar with the diameter and radius of a circle.

Radius (r): a line from the centre of a circle to the edge.
The circle's centre is the same distance from all points on the edge.

Diameter (d): a line from one side of a circle to the other through the centre.

The diameter is **twice** the radius: $\boldsymbol{d = 2r}$

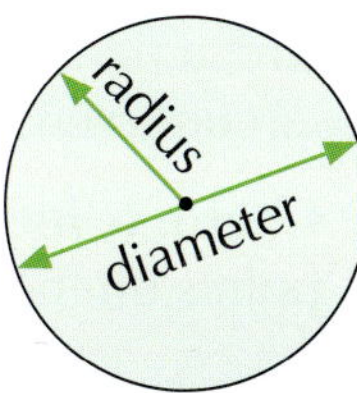

Example 1

a) A circle has radius 4 cm. What is its diameter?

1. Use the formula $d = 2r$. — $d = 2r$
2. Remember to use the correct units. — $d = 2 \times 4 =$ **8 cm**

b) A circle has diameter 7 m. What is its radius?

1. Rearrange the formula $d = 2r$. — $r = \frac{d}{2}$
2. Remember to use the correct units. — So $r = 7 \div 2 =$ **3.5 m**

Exercise 1

Q1 Find the diameter of a circle with radius:

a) 4 cm b) 6 cm c) 30 mm d) 4.2 mm

Q2 Find the radius of a circle with diameter:

a) 2 cm b) 12 cm c) 13 m d) 0.02 cm

Q3 Use compasses to draw a circle with:

a) a radius of 4 cm b) a diameter of 80 mm c) a diameter of 6 cm

More Parts of Circles

Learning Objective — Spec Ref G9:
Be able to identify the different parts of a circle.

There are a few more parts of a circle that you need to know.

Circumference: the distance around the outside of a circle.

Tip: Make sure you are completely happy with these terms — you will need to use them frequently.

Tangent: a straight line that just touches the circle.

Arc: a part of the circumference.

Chord: a line between two points on the edge of the circle.

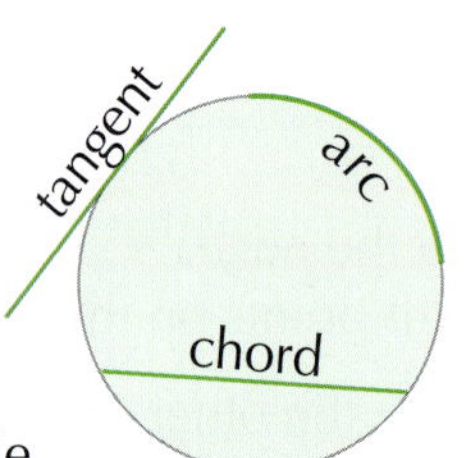

Sector: an area of a circle like a "slice of pie".

Segment: an area of a circle between an arc and a chord.

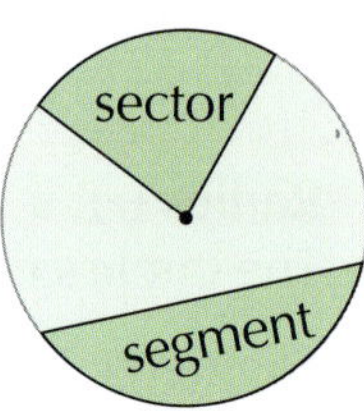

Exercise 2

Q1 Name the feature highlighted in each diagram below.

a)

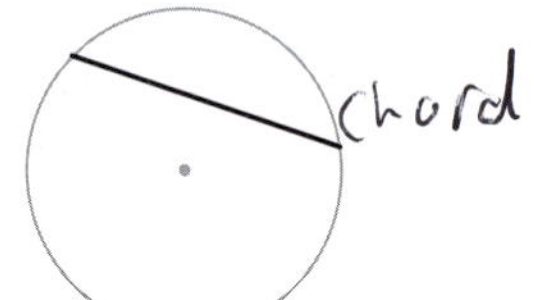

b)

c)

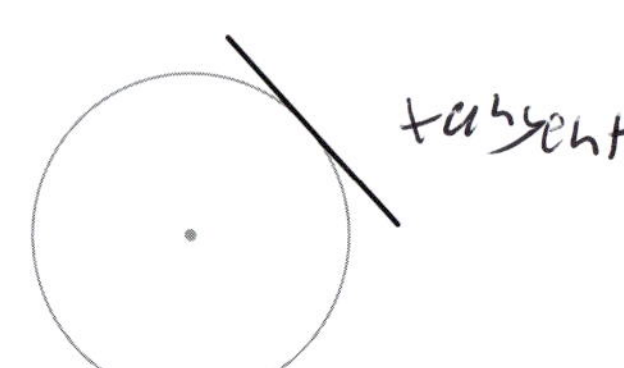

d)

e)

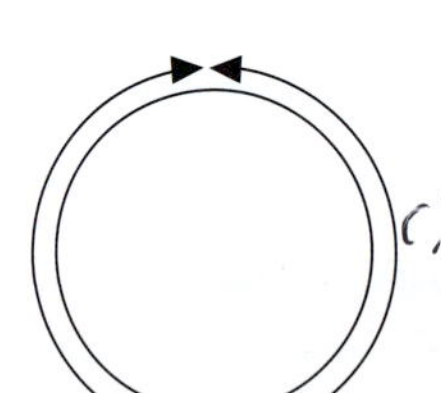

f)

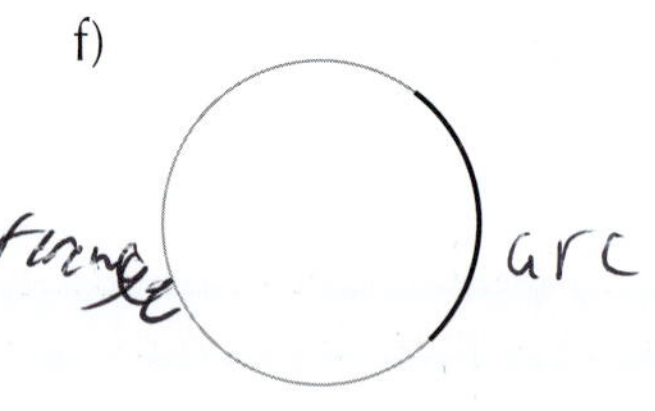

Q2 Draw a circle. Then draw and label the following features.

a) a chord b) an arc c) a tangent d) a diameter

Q3 Draw a circle. Then draw and label the following features.

a) a sector b) a segment c) a radius

21.2 Lines, Angles and Triangles

Over the next few pages you'll learn how to "construct" triangles — i.e. draw them accurately using just a pencil, a ruler, a pair of compasses and a protractor. Before you start constructing triangles, you need to make sure you can use a ruler, protractor and pair of compasses correctly.

Learning Objectives — Spec Ref G1/G15:
- Be able to measures lines and angles accurately.
- Be able to draw triangles accurately using a ruler and a protractor.

For this topic, you'll need to know how to use:

A **ruler** to measure **lengths**.

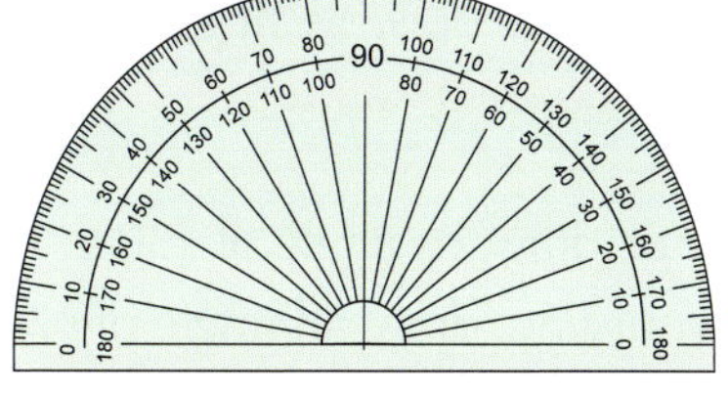

A **protractor** to measure **angles**.

Tip: A protractor has two scales. Always count up in steps of 10° from your start line (at 0°) to make sure you're using the correct scale.

Example 1

Measure the size of angle a.

1. Put the protractor's cross exactly where the two lines meet with the 0° line along one of the lines.
2. Count up in steps of 10°, then use the smaller lines on the scale to find the final answer.

a = 24°

3. The answer is 24°, not 156°, because you counted up to 24° from 0°.

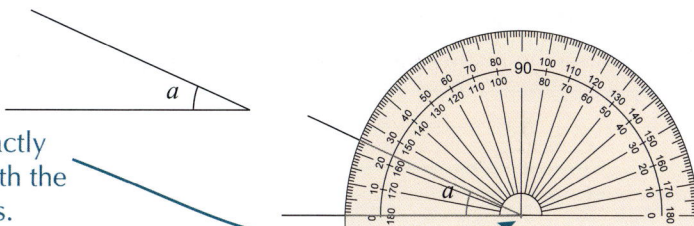

It can be **difficult** to describe which angle you are talking about if there is more than one angle at that point.

In a diagram whose vertices have been labelled with letters, each angle can be described using three letters.

E.g. In the diagram, angle ABD = 72°.

- The **middle** letter is where the angle is.
- The other two letters tell you which two lines enclose the angle.

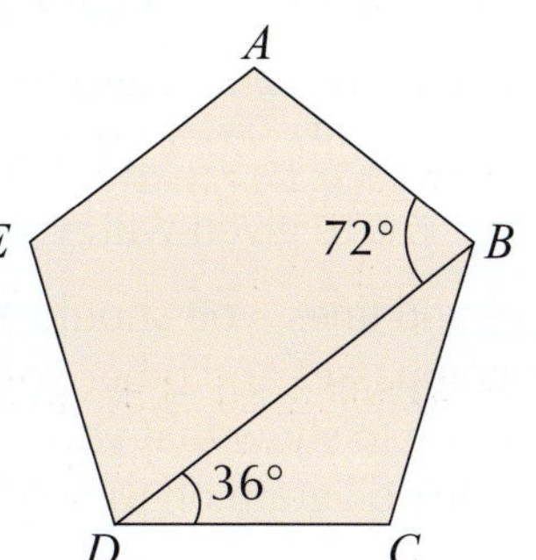

Tip: Always include the word **'angle'** before the three letters or you'll be talking about the **triangle** made from those three points, not the angle. E.g. angle BDC = 36°, but BDC is a triangle.

Exercise 1

Q1 In each diagram below, measure the size of the angle and the length of the lines.

a)

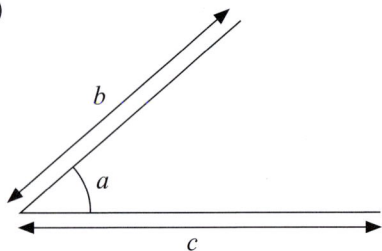

b)

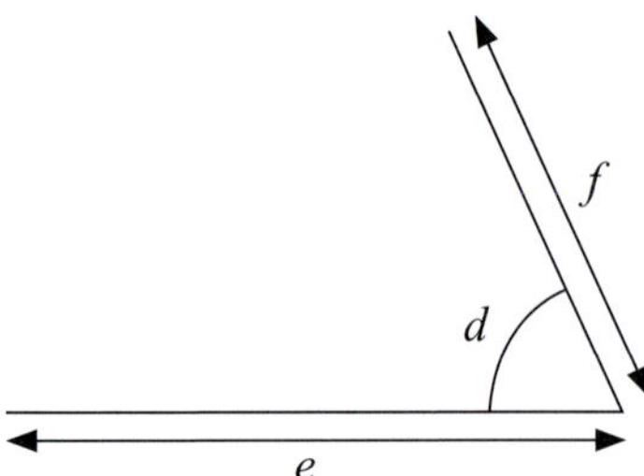

Q2 Draw a line 6 cm long.

a) On one end of your line, draw an angle of 70°.

b) On the other end of your line, draw an angle of 30°.

Q3 Draw a line 8.5 cm long.

a) On one end of your line, draw an angle of 130°.

b) On the other end of your line, draw an angle of 170°.

Q4 Measure all the angles in the triangles below.
Make sure your answers add up to 180°.

a)

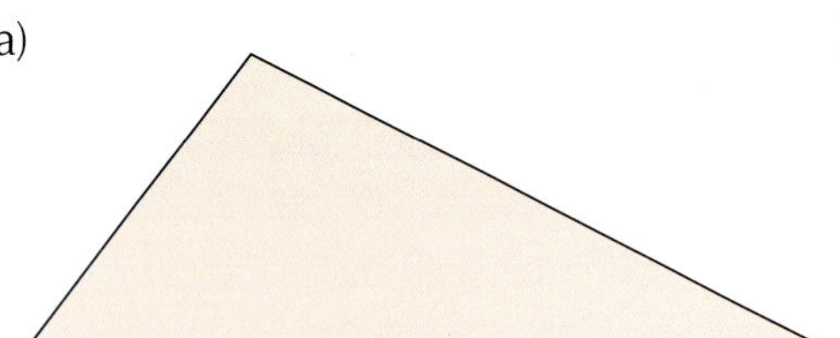

b)

Constructing a triangle

To construct a triangle, you need **three** pieces of information about it. These could be **lengths** of the sides or the **angles** between them.

- If you're given a **side length**, use your **ruler** to measure the length and draw an arc with your **compasses** if necessary.
- Measure any **angles** that you're given with your **protractor**.

When constructing shapes and lines, you should **always** leave the **arcs from your compasses** and other **construction lines** on your finished drawing to show that you've used the right method — like in the diagram on the right.

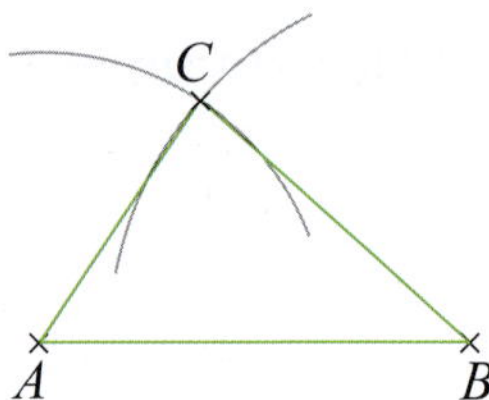

Example 2

Draw triangle *ABC*, where side *AB* is 4 cm, angle *BAC* is 55°, and angle *ABC* is 35°.

1. Draw and label the side you know the length of.

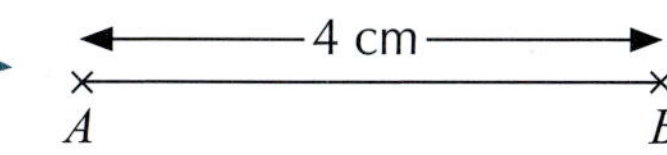

2. Measure an angle of 55° at *A* with a protractor. Mark the angle with a dot.

3. Draw a faint line from *A* through the dot.

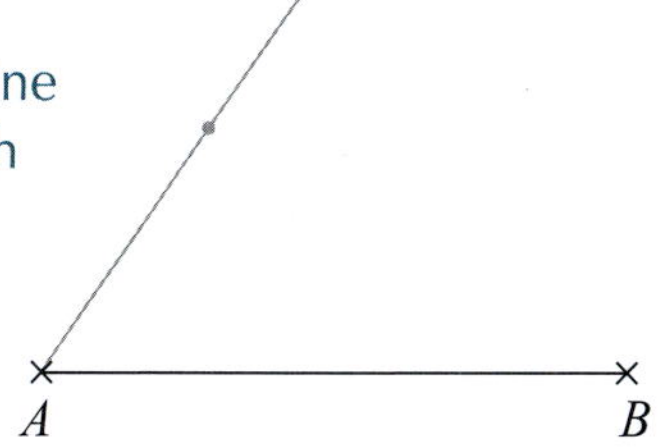

4. Draw the second angle in the same way, and complete the triangle.

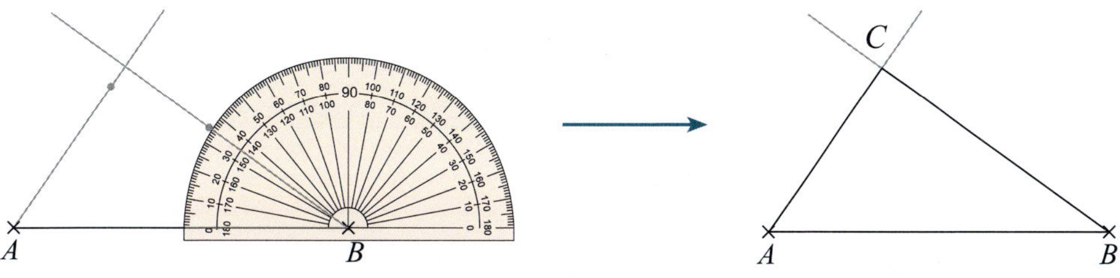

Exercise 2

Q1 Draw the following triangles accurately, then measure the lengths marked *l*.

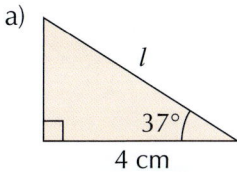

a)

l

37°

4 cm

b)

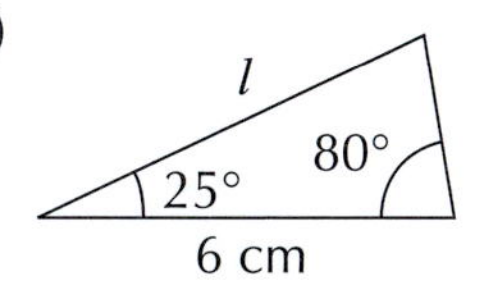

c)

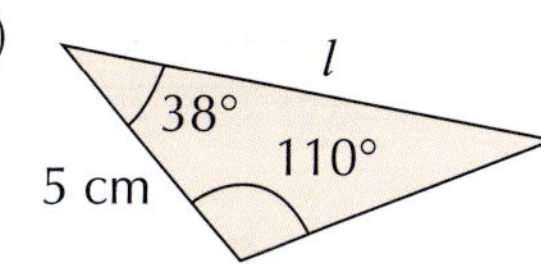

Q2 a) Draw each of the triangles *ABC* described below.

(i) $AB = 4$ cm, angle $BAC = 55°$, angle $CBA = 35°$.

(ii) $AB = 8$ cm, angle $BAC = 22°$, angle $CBA = 107°$.

(iii) $AB = 6.5$ cm, angle $BAC = 65°$, angle $CBA = 30°$.

b) Measure the length of side *BC* in each of your triangles in part a).

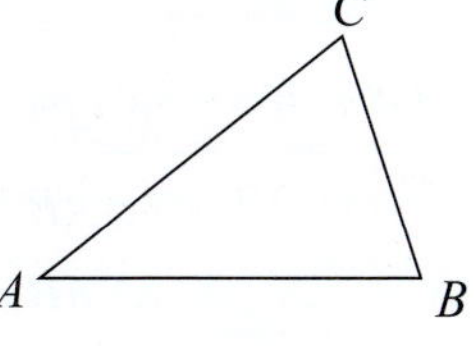

Q3 Alec is standing 5 km directly west of Brenda. At noon, Alec starts to walk northeast, while Brenda starts to walk at the same speed northwest.

By carefully drawing their paths on a scale drawing using 1 cm to represent 1 km, find how far from their starting points they eventually meet.

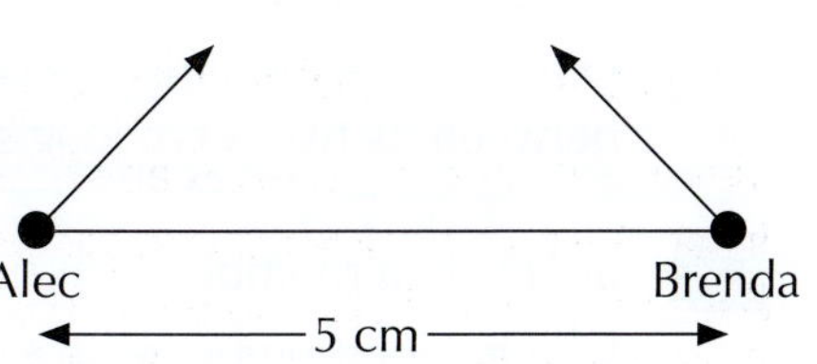

Example 3

Draw triangle *ABC*, where *AB* is 4 cm, *BC* is 4 cm, and angle *ABC* is 25°.

1. Draw and label a side you know the length of.

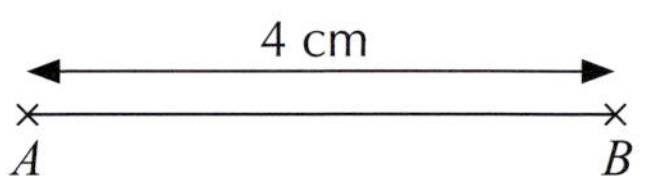

2. Measure an angle of 25° at *B* with a protractor. Mark the angle with a dot.

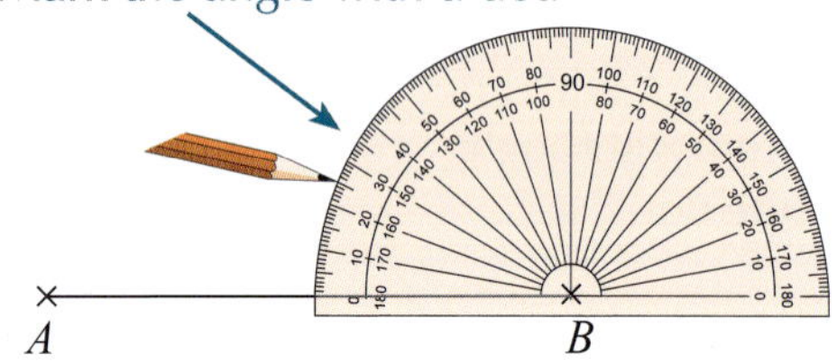

3. Draw a faint line from *B* through the dot.

A B

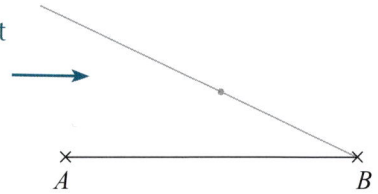

4. Point *C* is 4 cm along this line.
5. Complete the triangle by drawing the line *AC*.

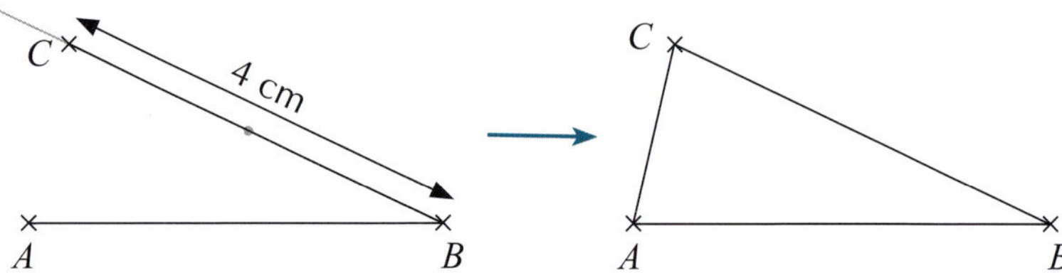

Exercise 3

Q1 Draw the following triangles accurately, then measure the lengths marked *l*.

a)

5 cm
l
12 cm

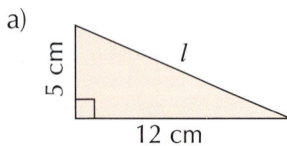

b)

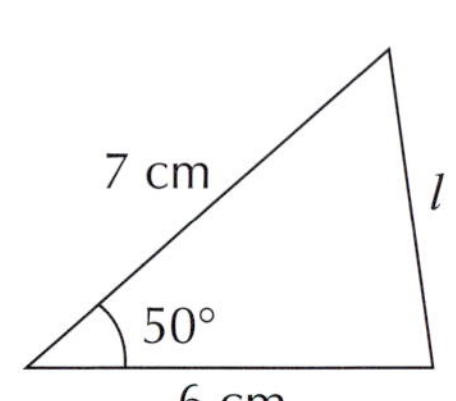

c)

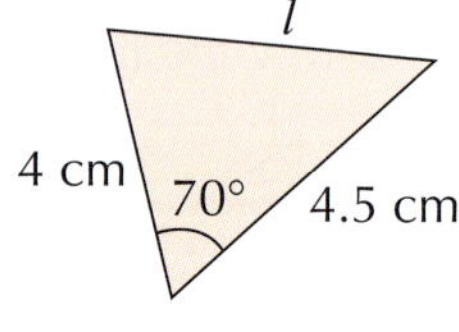

Q2 a) Draw each of the triangles *ABC* described below.

(i) *AB* = 6 cm, *BC* = 7 cm, angle *ABC* = 40°.

(ii) *AB* = 4 cm, *BC* = 3 cm, angle *ABC* = 110°.

(iii) *AB* = 65 mm, *BC* = 53 mm, angle *ABC* = 20°.

(iv) *AB* = 45 mm, *BC* = 45 mm, angle *ABC* = 45°.

b) Measure the length of side *AC* in each of your triangles in part a).

Q3 Draw an isosceles triangle with an angle of 50° between its two 5 cm long sides.

Q4 a) Draw a rhombus with sides measuring 6 cm and two angles of 40°.

b) Draw a rhombus with sides measuring 4.5 cm and two angles of 110°.

Example 4

Draw triangle *ABC*, where *AB* is 3 cm, *BC* is 2.5 cm, and *AC* is 2 cm.

1. Draw and label one of the sides.

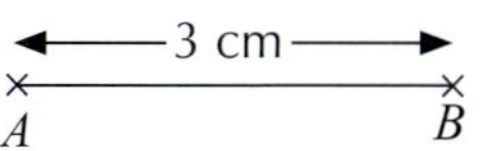

2. Set your compasses to 2.5 cm. Draw an arc 2.5 cm from *B*.

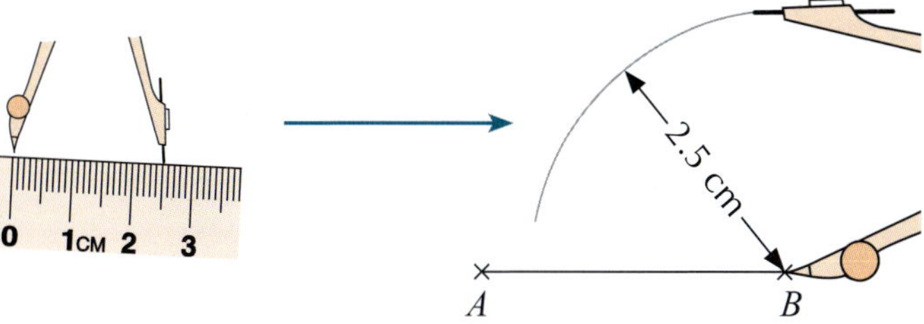

3. Now set your compasses to 2 cm. Draw an arc 2 cm from *A*.

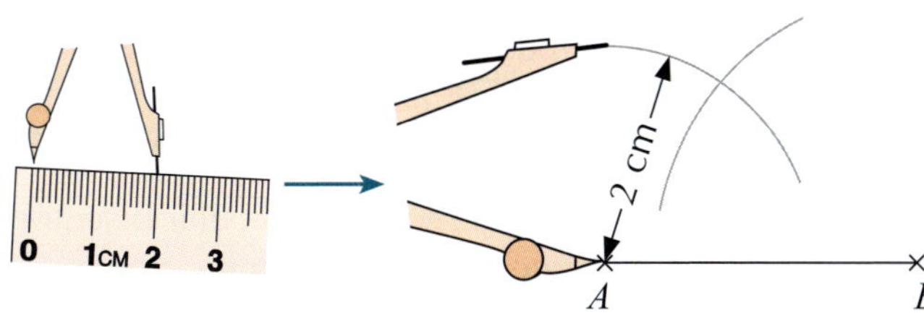

4. *C* is where your arcs cross.

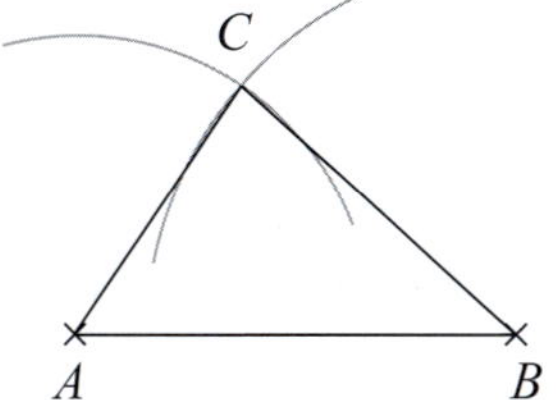

Tip: Make sure that your compasses don't change length while you are drawing — most have a screw that you can tighten.

Exercise 4

Q1 These triangles are not drawn accurately.
Draw them accurately using the measurements given.

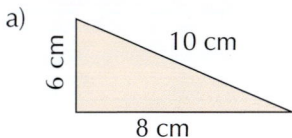

a) 6 cm, 10 cm, 8 cm

b)

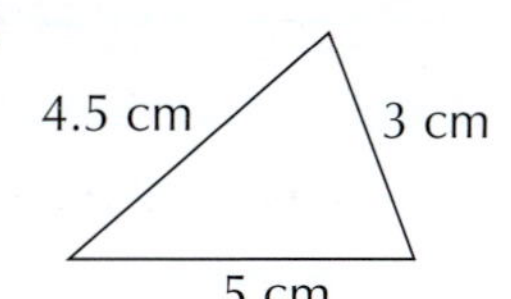

c)

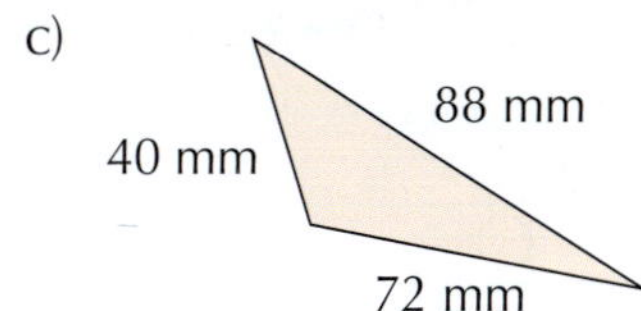

Q2 Draw each of the triangles *ABC* described below.

a) *AB* is 5 cm, *BC* is 6 cm, *AC* is 7 cm.

b) *AB* is 4 cm, *BC* is 7 cm, *AC* is 9 cm.

c) *AB* is 4.6 cm, *BC* is 5.4 cm, *AC* is 8.4 cm.

21.3 More Constructions

There are many other constructions that you can make using your pencil, ruler and compasses. In this topic you'll see them being used to draw perpendicular lines, split angles in half, and more.

Constructing a Perpendicular Bisector

Learning Objective — Spec Ref G1/G2:
Be able to construct a perpendicular bisector.

The **perpendicular bisector** of a line AB is at **right angles** to the line, and cuts it in **half**.

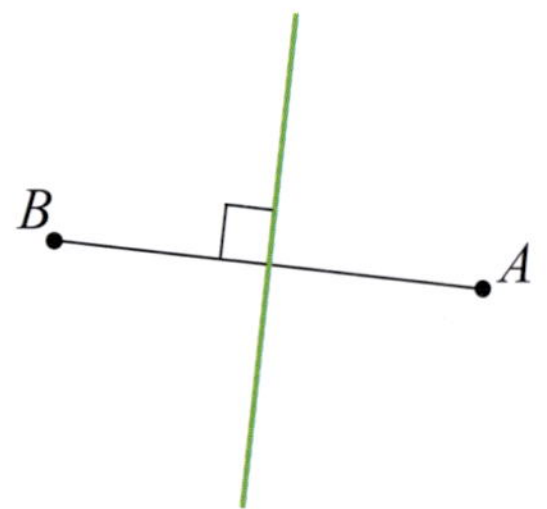

All points on the perpendicular bisector are **equally far** from both A and B (this is important when drawing loci — see page 339).

You can use this fact to draw perpendicular bisectors **without measuring** the distances — just use your compasses to find two points that are the **same distance** from A and B, then the perpendicular bisector will **pass through both** of these points.

Example 1

Draw a line AB which is 3 cm long and construct its perpendicular bisector.

1. Draw AB.

3 cm

A B

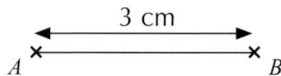

2. Place the compass point at A, with the radius set at more than half of the length AB. Draw two arcs as shown.

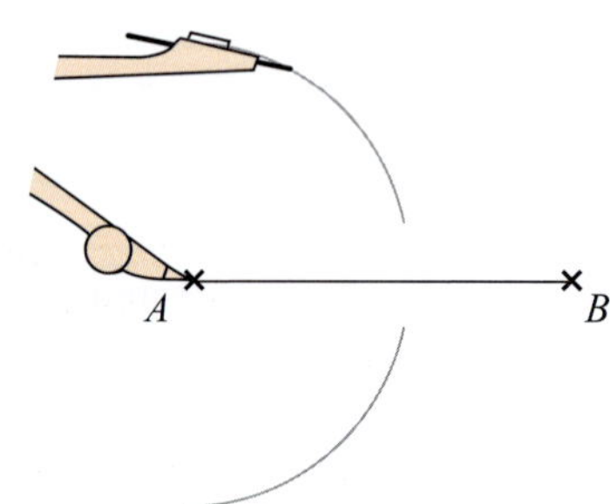

3. Keep the radius the same and put the compass point at B. Draw two more arcs.

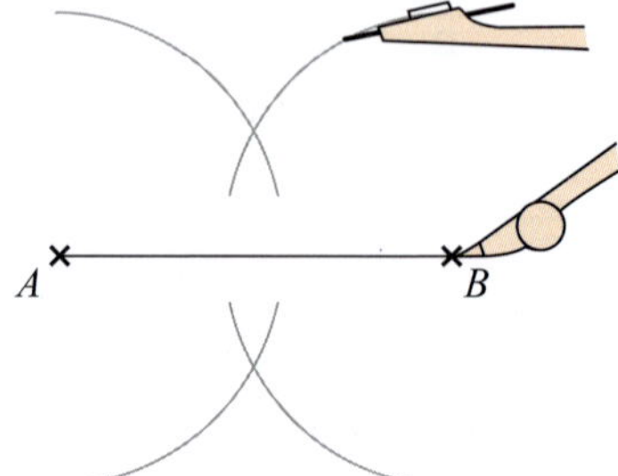

4. Use a ruler to draw a straight line through the points where the arcs meet. This is the perpendicular bisector.

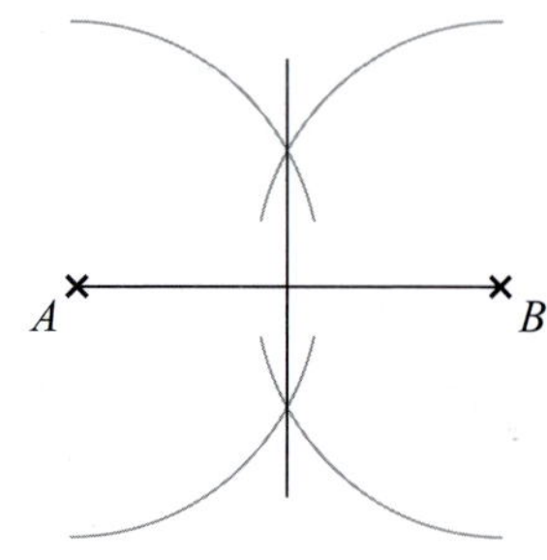

Exercise 1

Q1 Draw a horizontal line PQ 5 cm long.
Construct its perpendicular bisector using a ruler and compasses only.

Q2 Draw a vertical line XY 9 cm long.
Construct its perpendicular bisector using a ruler and compasses only.

Q3 Draw a line AB 7 cm long.
Construct its perpendicular bisector using a ruler and compasses only.

Q4 a) Draw a line AB 6 cm long.
Construct the perpendicular bisector of AB.
b) Draw the rhombus $ACBD$ with diagonals 6 cm and 8 cm.

a) Draw a circle with radius 5 cm, and draw any two chords.
Label your chords AB and CD.
b) Construct the perpendicular bisector of chord AB.
c) Construct the perpendicular bisector of chord CD.
d) Where do the two perpendicular bisectors meet?

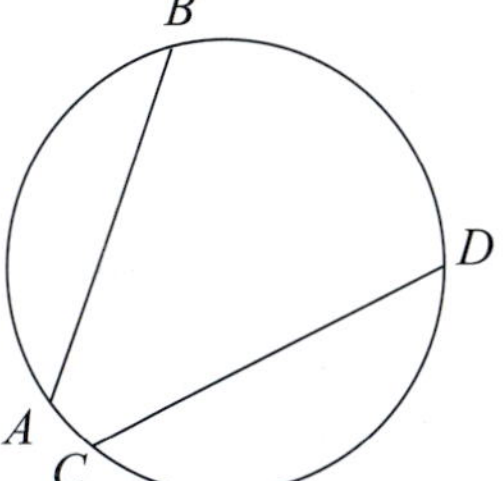

Constructing an Angle Bisector

Learning Objective — Spec Ref G1/G2:
Be able to construct an angle bisector.

An **angle bisector** is the line that cuts an angle in half.
All points on the angle bisector are the **same distance** from each of the two lines that enclose the angle (this is also useful for drawing loci — see page 339).

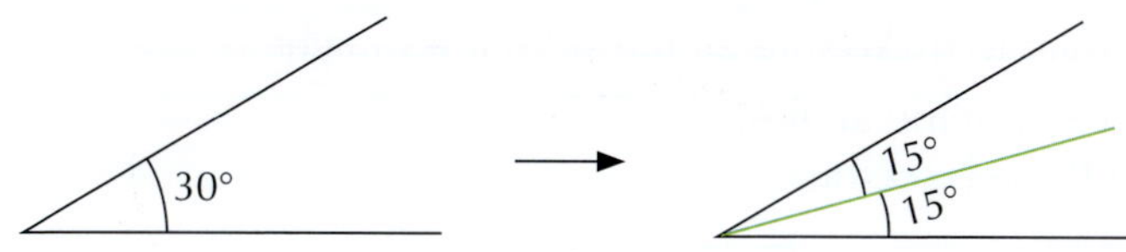

Just like the perpendicular bisector, you can use your ruler and compasses to construct an angle bisector **without measuring** the angles with a protractor. The **method** for constructing an angle bisector is shown in the next example.

Tip: After constructing an angle bisector you know the two new angles — they're both half the original angle.

Example 2

Draw an angle of 60° using a protractor, then construct the angle bisector using only a ruler and compasses.

1. Place the point of the compasses on the angle... ...and draw arcs crossing both lines... ...using the same radius.

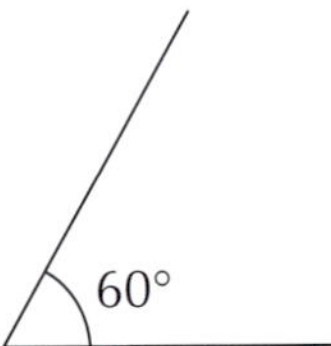

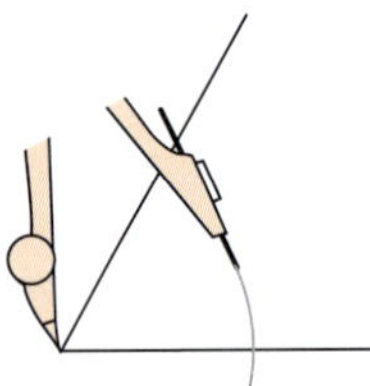

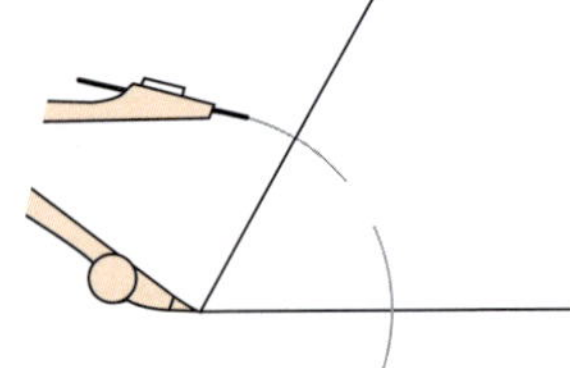

2. Now place the point of the compasses where your arcs cross the lines and, from each point, draw a new arc (using the same radius).

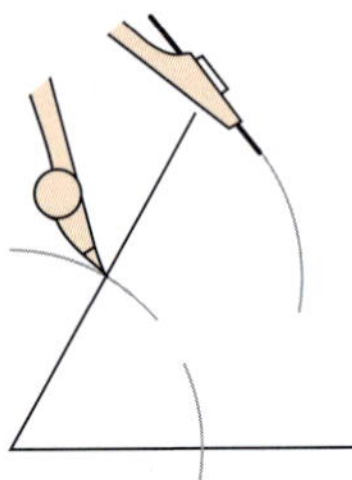

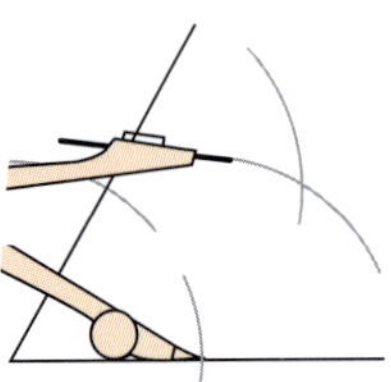

3. Draw the angle bisector through the point where the arcs cross.

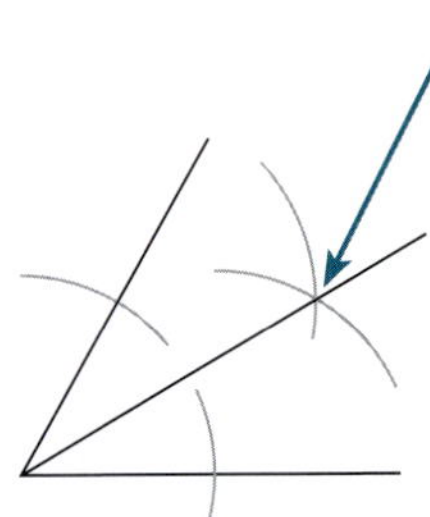

Tip: You can check your answer by measuring the angles with a protractor — they should both be 30°.

Exercise 2

Q1 Draw the following angles using a protractor.
For each angle, construct the angle bisector using a ruler and compasses.

a) 100° b) 44° c) 70° d) 65°

Check each of your angle bisectors with a protractor.

Q2 a) Draw any triangle. Use a ruler to make sure all the sides are straight.

b) Construct the bisectors of each of the angles.
What do you notice about these bisectors?

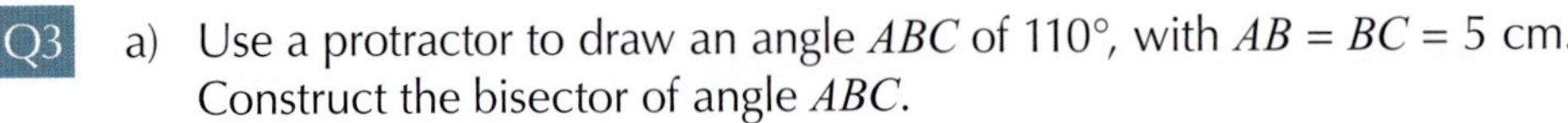

Q3 a) Use a protractor to draw an angle ABC of 110°, with $AB = BC = 5$ cm.
Construct the bisector of angle ABC.

b) Mark point D on your drawing, where D is the point on the angle bisector with $BD = 8$ cm. What kind of quadrilateral is $ABCD$?

Constructing a Perpendicular from a Point to a Line

Learning Objective — Spec Ref G1/G2:
Be able to construct a perpendicular from a point to a line.

The **perpendicular** from a point to a line is the **shortest path** between them.
It should **pass through** the point, and meet the line at **90°**.

Constructing one of these is similar to constructing a **perpendicular bisector**, except you need to work **backwards** — first, you find two points **on the line**, then you use them to find the perpendicular.

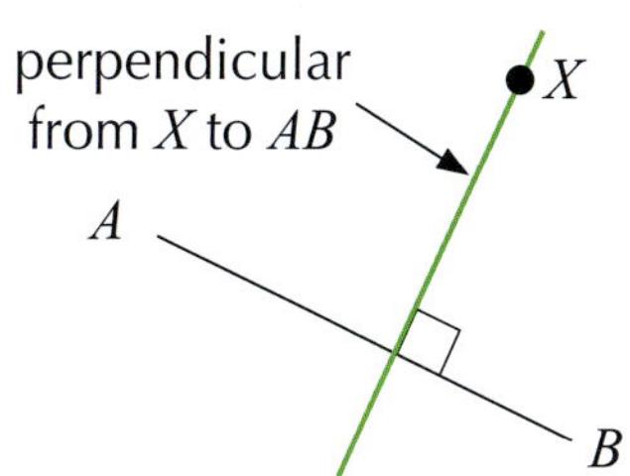

Example 3

Construct the perpendicular from the point X to the line AB using only a ruler and a pair of compasses.

X

A ——— B

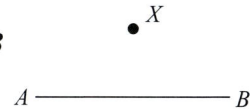

1. Draw an arc centred on X cutting the line twice.

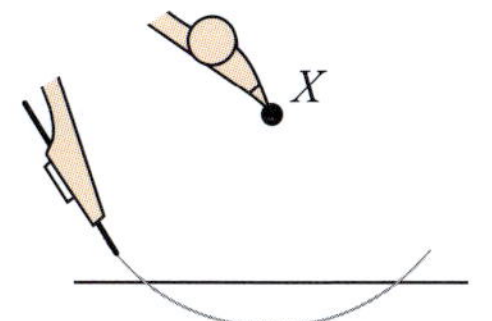

Tip: You may need to extend the line with a ruler to make the arc cut the line twice.

2. Draw an arc centred on one of the points where your arc meets the line.

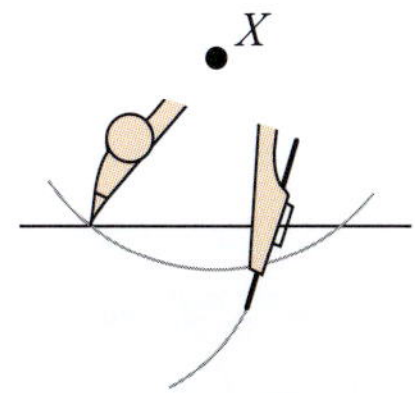

3. Do the same for the other point, keeping the radius the same.

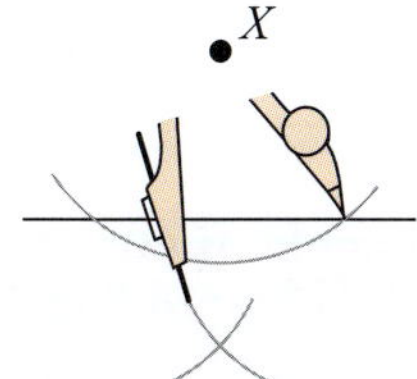

4. Draw the perpendicular to where the arcs cross.

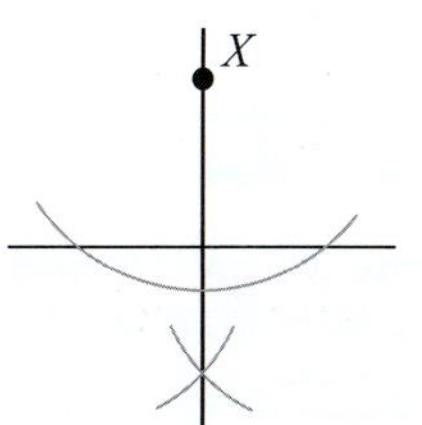

Exercise 3

Q1 Use a ruler to draw a triangle like the one on the right.
Construct the perpendicular from X to the line YZ.

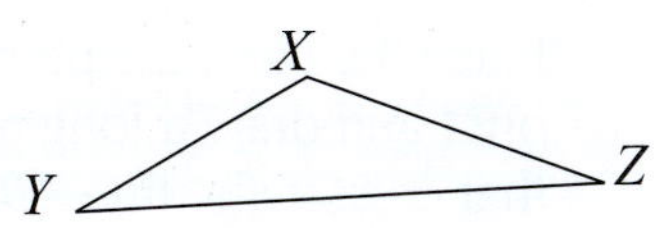

Q2 a) On squared paper draw axes with x-values from 0 to 10 and y-values from 0 to 10.
b) Plot the points $A(1, 2)$, $B(9, 1)$ and $C(6, 8)$.
c) Construct the perpendicular from point C to the line AB.

Q3 Draw three points not on a straight line.
Label your points P, Q and R.
Draw a long straight line passing through your points P and Q.
Construct the perpendicular from R to this line.

Q4 a) Draw any triangle. Use a ruler to make sure all the sides are straight.
b) Construct a perpendicular from each of the triangle's corners to the opposite side.
What do you notice about these lines?

Q5 a) Construct triangle DEF, where $DE = 5$ cm, $DF = 6$ cm and angle $FDE = 55°$.
b) Construct the perpendicular from F to DE.
Label the point where the perpendicular meets DE as point G.
c) Measure the length FG.
Use your result to work out the area of the triangle to 1 decimal place.

Constructing an Angle of 60°

Learning Objective — Spec Ref G1/G2:
Be able to construct an angle of 60°.

To construct a **60° angle** you can take advantage of the fact that all the interior angles of an **equilateral triangle** are 60°.

Start by drawing a line, then set your compasses to match its **length** and draw an arc from **each end** of the line. The point where the arcs cross will form an **equilateral triangle** with the **end points** of the line.

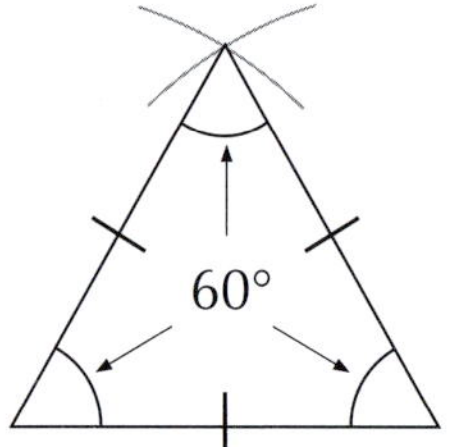

Example 4

Draw a line AB and construct an angle of 60° at A.

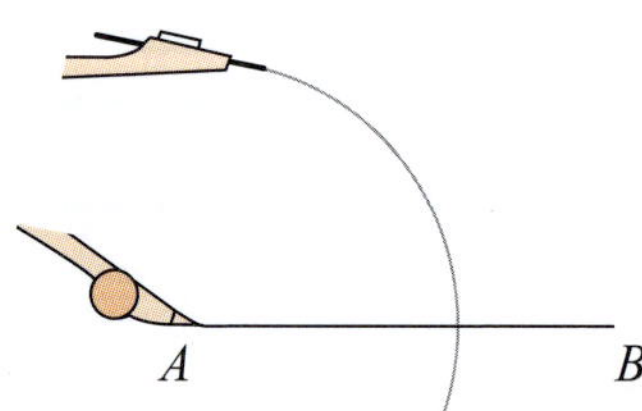

1. Place the compass point on A and draw a long arc that crosses the line AB.

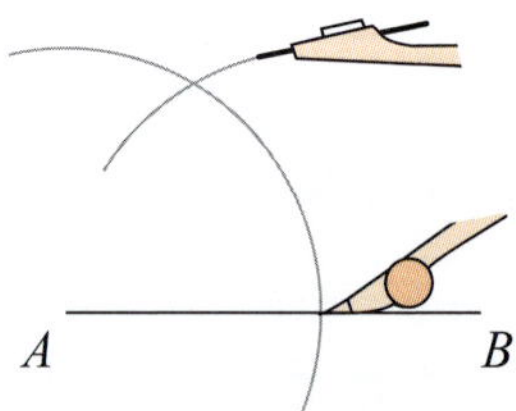

2. Place the compass point where the arc meets the line, and draw another arc of the same radius.

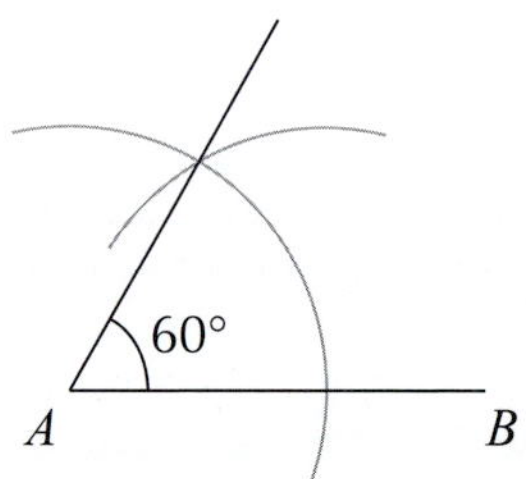

3. Draw a straight line through A and the point where your arcs cross. The angle will be 60°.

Exercise 4

Q1 Draw a line AB measuring 5 cm. Construct an angle of 60° at A.

Q2 a) Draw a line measuring 6 cm. Construct an angle of 60° at each end of the line. Join your lines to form a triangle.

b) By measuring the lengths of the sides, check that your triangle is equilateral.

Constructing an Angle of 30°

Learning Objective — Spec Ref G1/G2:
Be able to construct an angle of 30°.

To construct a **30° angle**, first construct a 60° angle.
You can then construct the **angle bisector** to get **two** angles of 30°.

Tip: You form the angle bisector in exactly the same way as usual — see p.331.

Example 5

Draw a line AB and construct an angle of 30° at A.

1. Construct an angle of 60° at A.

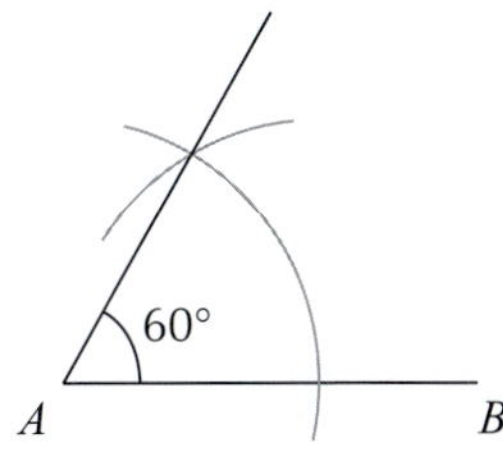

2. Now bisect this angle. You can use the arc from step 1 — place the point of the compasses where your arc crosses the lines and, from each point, draw a new arc (using the same radius).

3. Finally, draw a straight line through A and the point where your arcs cross to get a 30° angle.

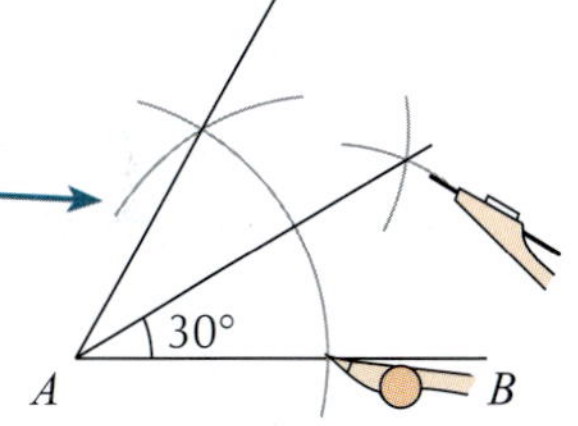

Exercise 5

Q1 Draw a line AB measuring 6 cm. Construct an angle of 30° at A.

Q2 a) Construct the triangle ABC where AB = 7 cm, angle CAB = 60° and angle CBA = 30°.

b) Check that angle ACB is a right angle using a protractor.

Q3 Construct an isosceles triangle PQR where PQ = 8 cm and the angles RPQ and RQP are both 30°.

Constructing an Angle of 90°

Learning Objective — Spec Ref G1/G2:
Be able to construct an angle of 90°.

Constructing a **90° angle** is a bit like constructing a **perpendicular from a point to a line** (see p.333) except now the point is **on the line**.

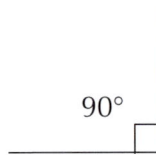

90°

Tip: Remember that a small square shows an angle is 90°.

Example 6

Construct an angle of 90°.

1. Draw a straight line, and mark the point where you want to form the right angle.

2. Draw arcs of the same radius on either side of your point.

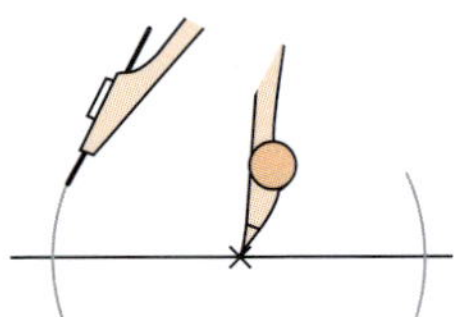

Tip: The size of the radius doesn't matter as long as it's the same for both arcs.

3. Increase the radius of your compasses, and draw two arcs of the same radius — one arc centred on each of the intersections.

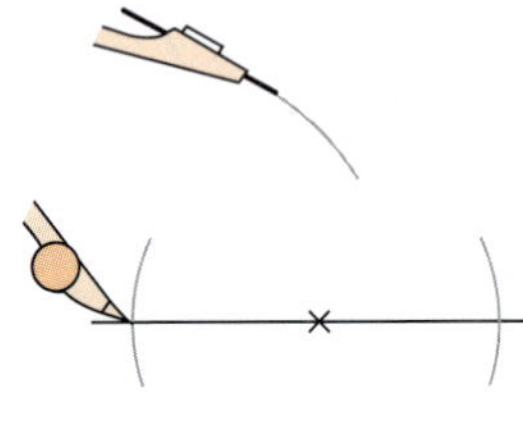

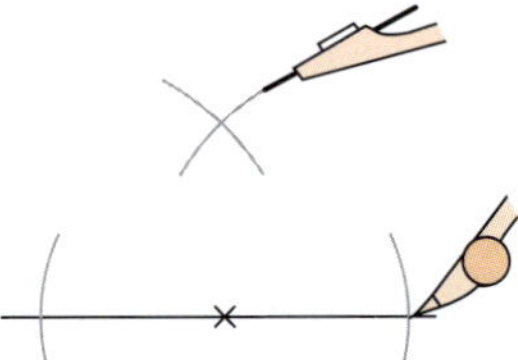

4. Draw a straight line to complete the right angle.

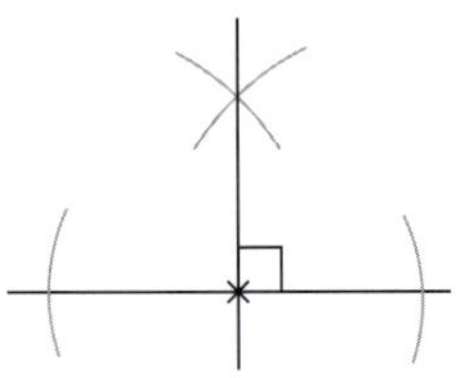

Exercise 6

Q1 a) Draw a straight line, and mark a point roughly halfway along it. Label the point X.
b) Construct a right angle at X using only a ruler and compasses.

Q2 Using a ruler and compasses only, construct a rectangle with sides of length 5 cm and 7 cm.

Q3 Using a ruler and compasses only, construct a square with sides of length 6 cm.

Constructing an Angle of 45°

Learning Objective — Spec Ref G1/G2:
Be able to construct an angle of 45°.

Tip: Using a sharp pencil will improve the accuracy of the angles in your constructions.

If you need to construct an angle of 45°, just construct the **angle bisector** (p.331) of the 90° angle.

Example 7

Construct an angle of 45°.

1. Construct an angle of 90° (see previous page).
2. Form the angle bisector to make an angle of 45° using the same method as on page 331.

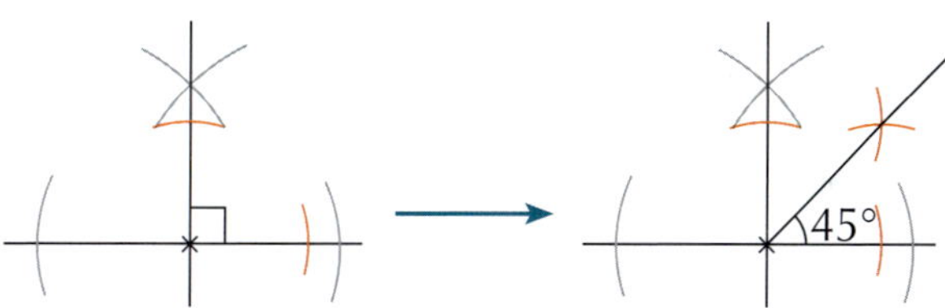

Exercise 7

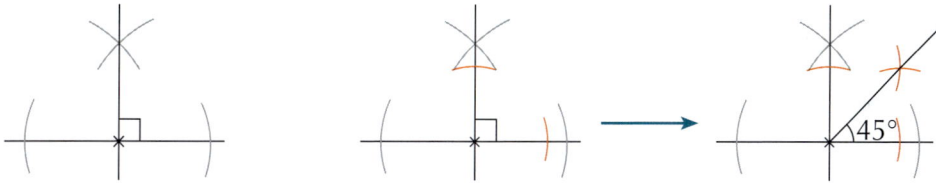

Q1 a) Draw a straight line, and mark a point roughly halfway along it. Label the point X.
b) Construct an angle of 45° at X using only a ruler and compasses.

Q2 Construct an isosceles triangle ABC where $AB = 8$ cm and the angles CAB and CBA are both 45°.

Constructing Parallel Lines

Learning Objective — Spec Ref G1/G2:
Be able to construct parallel lines.

To construct a line that is **parallel** to another, passing **through a given point**, the first step is to construct the **perpendicular from the point to the line** (see p.333).

Once you've done that, you just need to construct a **right angle** at the point using the method on the previous page.

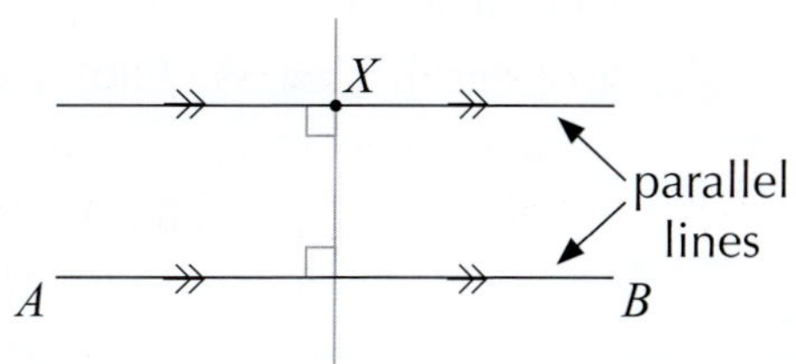

Example 8

Construct a line parallel to *AB* through the point *P*.

1. Construct the line perpendicular to *AB* passing through *P* (p.330).

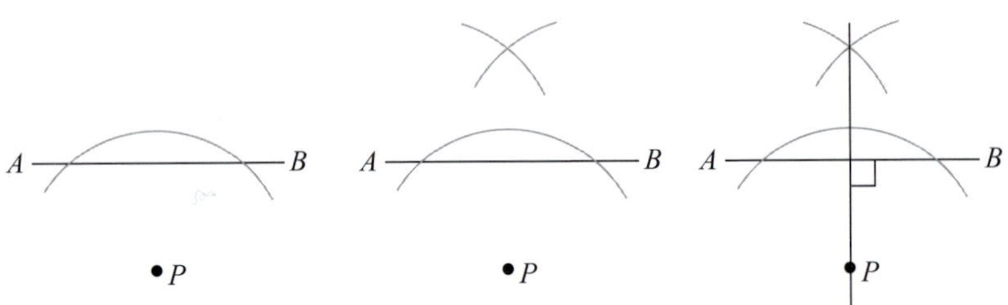

2. Construct a right angle (p.336) to this line at point *P*. This will be parallel to *AB*.

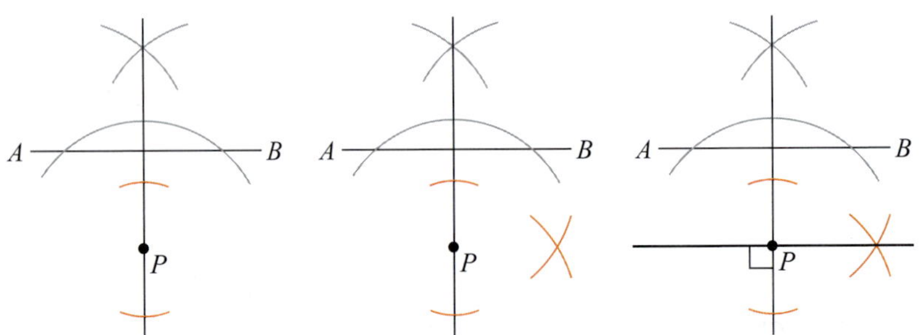

Tip: You could also construct the parallel line through *P* by constructing a right angle anywhere on line *AB*, then constructing the perpendicular from *P* to this new line.

Exercise 8

Q1 Draw a line *AB*, and mark a point *P* approximately 4 cm from your line. Construct a line parallel to *AB* through the point *P*.

Q2 a) On squared paper draw axes with *x*-values from 0 to 10 and *y*-values from 0 to 10.

b) Plot the points *A*(5, 2), *B*(10, 4) and *C*(1, 6).

c) Construct a line parallel to *BC* that passes through the point *A*.

Q3 Draw two straight lines that cross each other at a single point. By adding two parallel lines, construct a parallelogram.

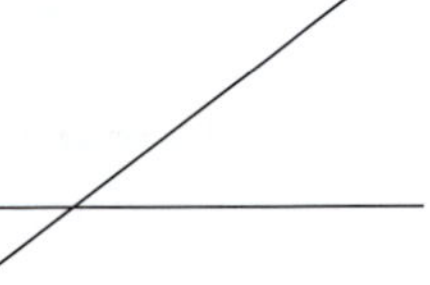

Q4 Draw a line *AB* 10 cm long.

a) Construct angles of 60° at points *A* and *B*, as shown.

b) Mark point *C* on the line 3 cm from *B*.

c) By drawing a line parallel to *AB*, complete the trapezium *ABCD*.

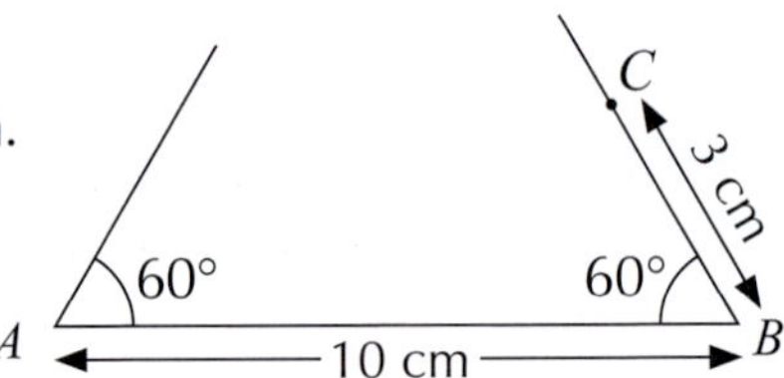

21.4 Loci

A common use for constructions is to find all the points that are a given distance from something or the same distance from two things. These sets of points are called loci (pronounced low-kai).

Learning Objectives — Spec Ref G2:
- Construct the locus of points that are a given distance from a point or a line.
- Construct the locus of points that are equidistant from two points or two lines.
- Solve problems involving loci.

A **locus** (plural **loci**) is a **set of points** which satisfy a particular condition.

The types of loci you need to know are:

- The set of points that are a **fixed distance away** from a point, a line or another kind of shape.
- The set of points that are **equidistant** (i.e. the **same distance**) from two points or two lines.

Tip: Make sure you're comfortable using your ruler and compasses before drawing loci.

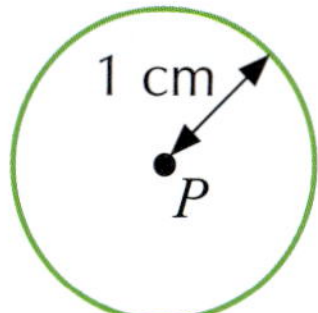

The locus of points that are a fixed distance, e.g. 1 cm, from a **point** P is a **circle** with radius 1 cm centred on P.

To construct this, set your **compasses** to the given distance and draw a circle around the point.

The locus of points that are a fixed distance from a **line** AB is a 'sausage shape'.

To construct this, use your compasses to draw the ends, which are **semicircles**, then join them up with your ruler.

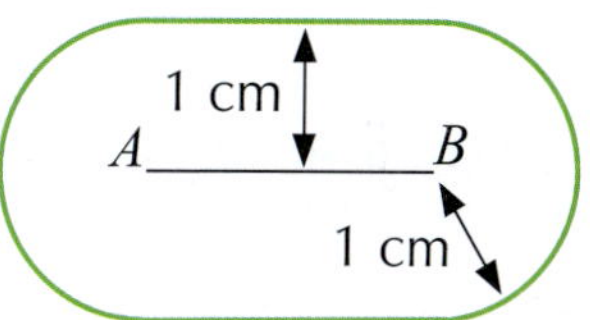

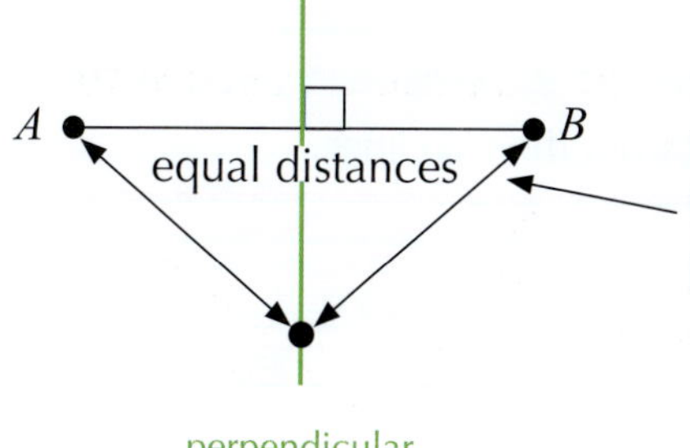

The locus of points equidistant from **two points** A and B is the **perpendicular bisector** of AB.

Tip: There's help with constructing perpendicular bisectors on page 330.

The locus of points equidistant from **two lines** is their **angle bisector** (see page 331).

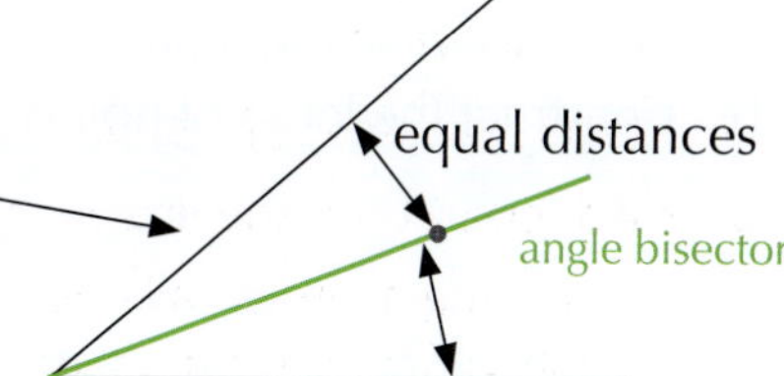

Example 1

The line AB is 2.6 cm long.
Construct the locus of points that are 5 mm from AB.

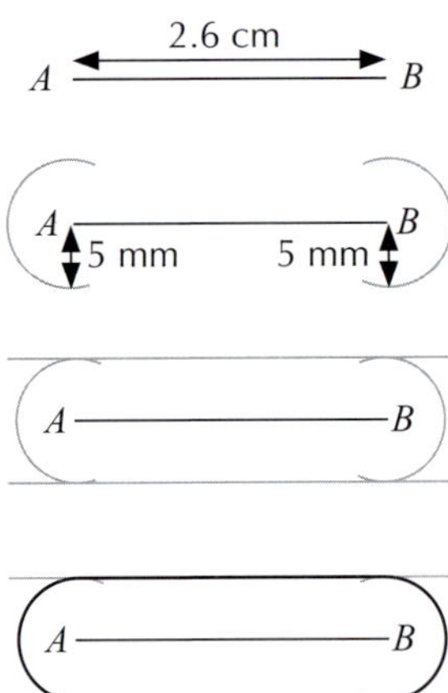

1. Draw the line AB using a ruler.
2. Set your compasses to 5 mm and draw arcs around each end of the line. Make sure each arc is slightly more than a semicircle.
3. Using your ruler, join the tops and bottoms of the arcs with straight lines.
4. Mark the locus of points, leaving your construction lines on the diagram. Remember to use your compasses again to draw an accurate diagram.

Exercise 1

Q1 Draw a 7 cm long line AB.
Construct the locus of all the points 2 cm from the line.

Q2 a) Mark a point X on your page.
Draw the locus of all points which are 3 cm from X.

b) Shade the locus of all points that are less than 3 cm from X.

Q3 Mark two points A and B on your page 6 cm apart.
Construct the locus of all points which are equidistant from A and B.

Q4 Draw two lines that meet at an angle of 50°.
Construct the locus of all points which are equidistant from the two lines.

Q5 Draw a line AB 6 cm long.
Draw the locus of all points which are 3 cm from AB.

Q6 a) Draw axes on squared paper with x- and y-values from 0 to 10.
Plot the points $P(2, 7)$ and $Q(10, 3)$.

b) Construct the locus of points which are equidistant from P and Q.

You might have to draw **more than one locus** to find the region that satisfies **multiple conditions**.

Example 2

Shade the locus of points inside rectangle *ABCD* that are:

- **more than 2 cm from point *A*,**
- **less than 1 cm from side *CD*.**

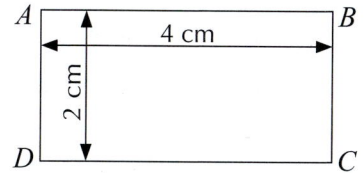

1. Use your compasses to construct an arc of radius 2 cm around *A*. The first condition means that points on or within this arc are excluded.

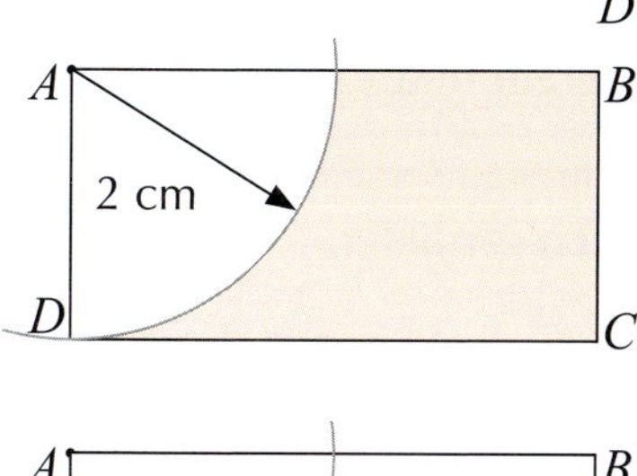

2. Using a ruler, draw a line 1 cm from *CD*. The second condition means that points that are on or above this line are also excluded.

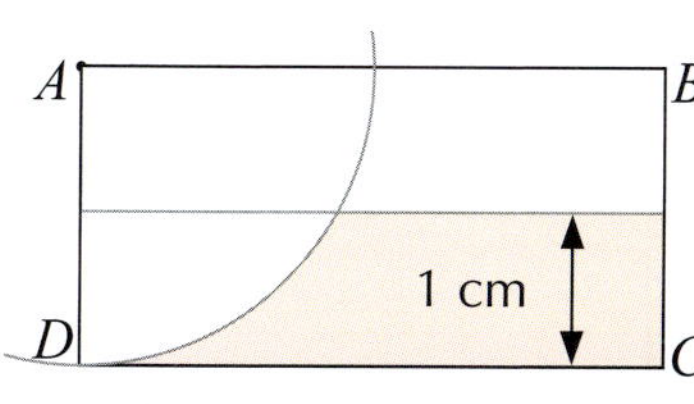

Tip: Read the question carefully to check whether it's asking for less than, more than, or equal to a distance.

Exercise 2

Q1 a) Mark points *P* and *Q* on your page 5 cm apart.

b) Draw the locus of points which are 3 cm from *P*.

c) Draw the locus of points which are 4 cm from *Q*.

d) Show clearly which points are both 3 cm from *P* and 4 cm from *Q*.

Q2 Draw the 5 cm square *ABCD* as shown on the right.
Shade the locus of points inside the square *ABCD* that are:

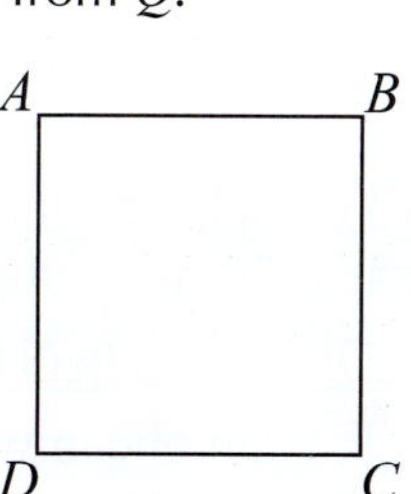

- less than 3 cm from point *B* and
- more than 4 cm from side *AD*

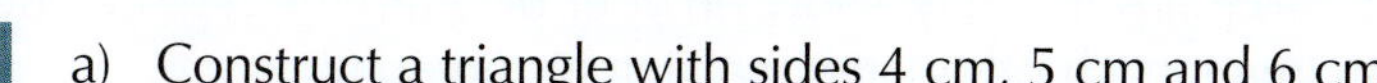

Q3 a) Construct a triangle with sides 4 cm, 5 cm and 6 cm.

b) Draw the locus of all points which are exactly 1 cm from any of the triangle's sides.

Q4 a) Construct an isosceles triangle *DEF* with $DE = EF = 5$ cm and $DF = 3$ cm.

b) Draw the locus of points which are equidistant from *D* and *F* and less than 2 cm from *E*.

Loci can also be used to solve **real-life problems**, particularly on **scale diagrams** (see p.290).

Example 3

The diagram shows a plan of a greenhouse, drawn at a scale of 1 cm to 4 m. The greenhouse has a path through the middle modelled by a straight line, and four sprinklers, shown as dots on the plan.

The sprinklers can water plants within a 4 m radius. The gardener can water anything up to 6 m away from the path using a hosepipe. Shade the area on the diagram that can be watered.

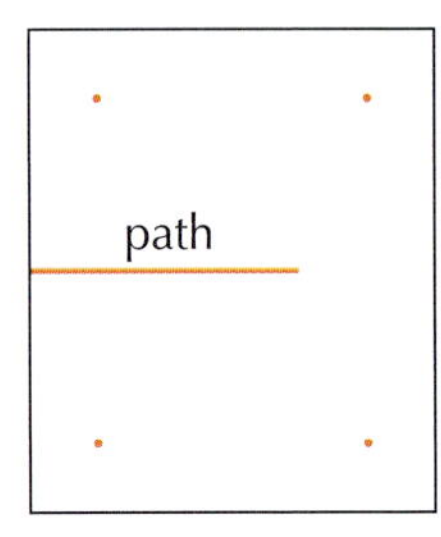

1. 1 cm = 4 m. So draw arcs of radius 1 cm around each sprinkler, and shade the region inside.

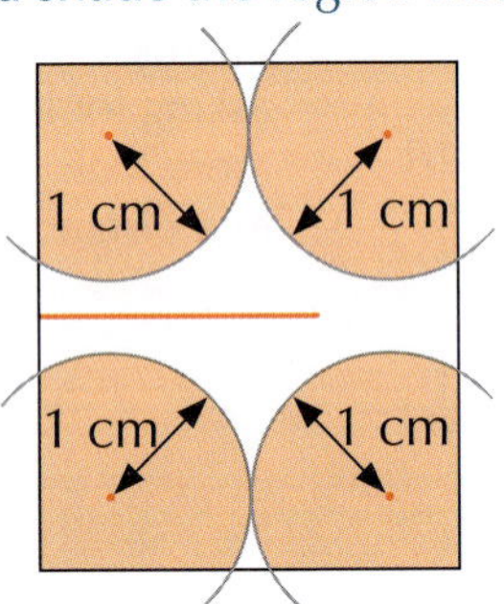

2. 6 m in real life is $6 \div 4 = 1.5$ cm on the diagram. Construct the locus of points that are 1.5 cm away from the path and shade the region inside.

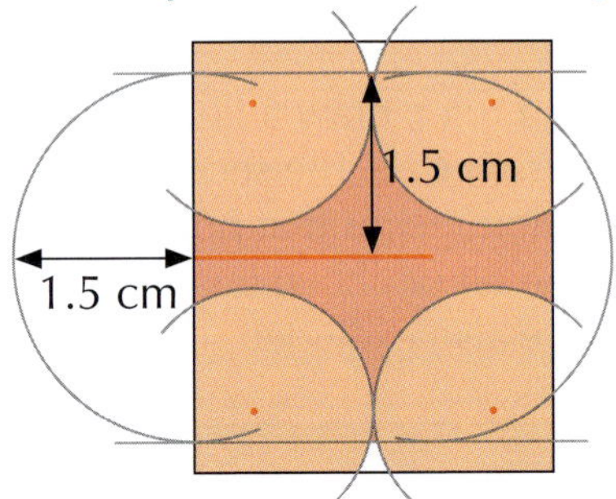

Exercise 3

Q1 A ship sails so that it is always the same distance from a port P and a lighthouse L. The lighthouse and the port are 3 km apart.

a) Draw a scale diagram showing the port and lighthouse. Use a scale of 1 cm:1 km.

b) Show the path of the ship on your diagram.

Q2 Two camels set off at the same time from towns A and B, located 50 miles apart in the desert.

a) Draw a scale diagram showing towns A and B. Use a scale of 1 cm : 10 miles.

b) If a camel can walk up to 40 miles in a day, show on your diagram the region where the camels could possibly meet each other after walking for one day.

Q3 A walled rectangular yard has length 4 m and width 2 m. A dog is secured by a lead of length 1 m to a post in the corner of the yard.

a) Show on an accurate scale drawing the area in which the dog can move. Use the scale 1 cm : 1 m.

b) The post is replaced with a 3 m rail mounted horizontally along one of the long walls, with one end in the corner. If the end of the lead attached to the rail is free to slide, show the area in which the dog can move.

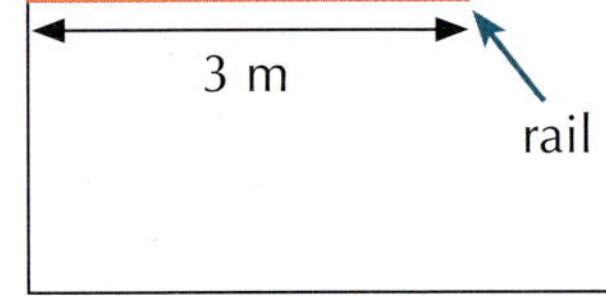

Review Exercise

Q1 What part of the circle does each label show in the diagrams below?

a)

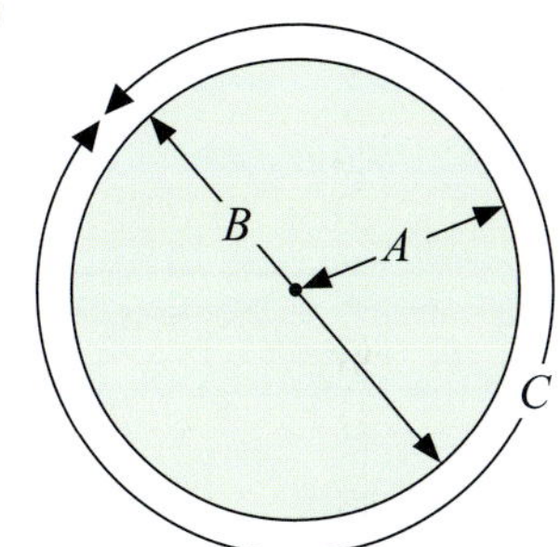

b)

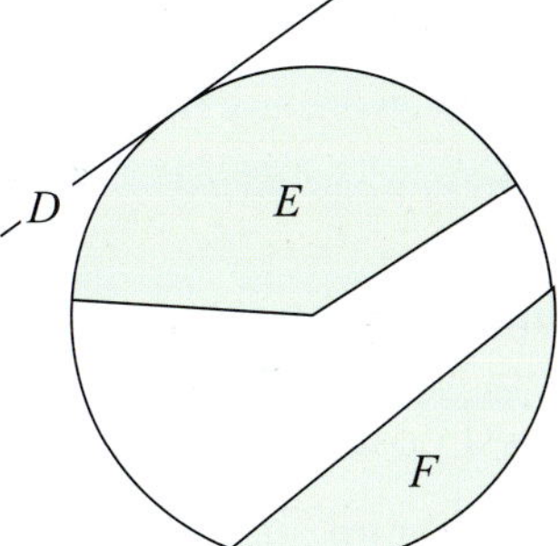

Q2 In the diagram to the right, measure the size of the angle and the length of the lines.

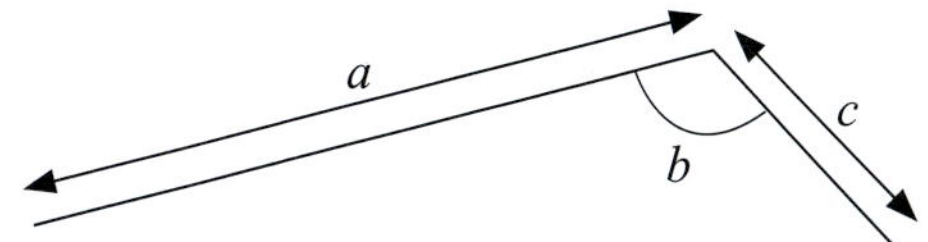

Q3 These triangles are not drawn accurately.
Draw them accurately using the measurements given.

a)

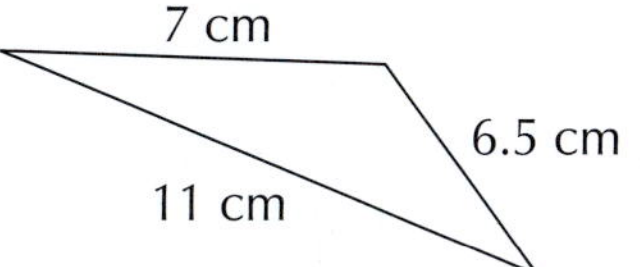

b)

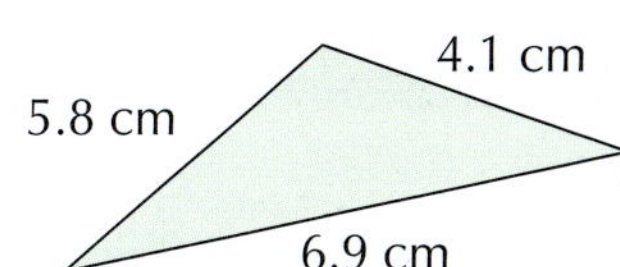

Q4 a) Construct an equilateral triangle *DEF* with sides of length 5.8 cm.

b) Construct a line that is parallel to side *DE* and passes through point *F*.

Q5 a) Using only a ruler and a pair of compasses, construct the triangle *ABC* with *AB* = 7.4 cm, angle *CAB* = 60° and angle *ABC* = 45°.

b) Calculate the size of angle *ACB*.
Check the angle in your drawing using a protractor.

Q6 Two walls of a field meet at an angle of 80°.
A bonfire has to be the same distance from each wall and 3 m from the corner. Copy the diagram on the right, then use a ruler and pair of compasses to show the position of the fire.

Scale
1 cm : 0.5 m

80°

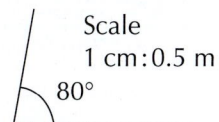

Exam-Style Questions

Q1 Construct an isosceles triangle with two sides of length 7.1 cm and an angle of 22° between them.

[3 marks]

Q2 A swimmer is in the sea at point S. They want to get to the beach by swimming the shortest possible distance.

Copy the diagram and construct a line from S to the beach to show the route they should take.

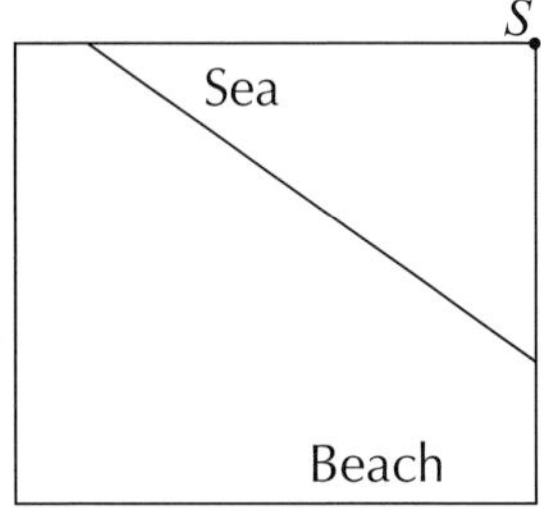

[3 marks]

Q3 Draw a line AB 8 cm long.

a) Construct an angle of 60° at A.

[2 marks]

b) Complete the construction of a rhombus $ABCD$ with sides of length 8 cm.

[3 marks]

Q4 The council is planning to build a new road to the north of a motorway. The road must be:

- parallel to the motorway
- 400 m from the motorway

By copying the diagram on the right and using a scale of 1 cm : 100 m, construct a diagram showing the path of the new road.

[3 marks]

Q5 Some students are doing a treasure hunt. They know the treasure is:

- located in a square region $ABCD$, which measures 10 m × 10 m
- the same distance from AB as from AD
- 7 m from corner C.

Draw a scale diagram to show the location of the treasure. Use a scale of 1 cm : 1 m.

[4 marks]

22.1 Rectangles and Triangles

You should already be familiar with area and perimeter, but for GCSE you'll need to work them out for all sorts of shapes, including composite shapes. We'll start off with the basics — squares, rectangles and triangles.

Perimeter

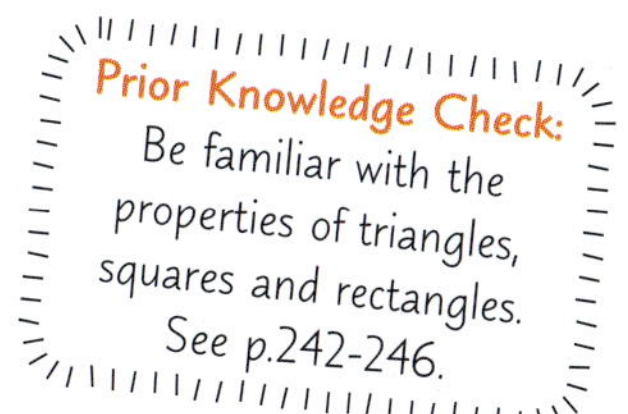

Prior Knowledge Check:
Be familiar with the properties of triangles, squares and rectangles.
See p.242-246.

Learning Objective — Spec Ref G17:
Be able to find the perimeter of rectangles and triangles.

Perimeter (P) is the distance around the outside of a shape. You can work it out by **adding up** the **lengths** of all the sides, or by learning these **formulas**.

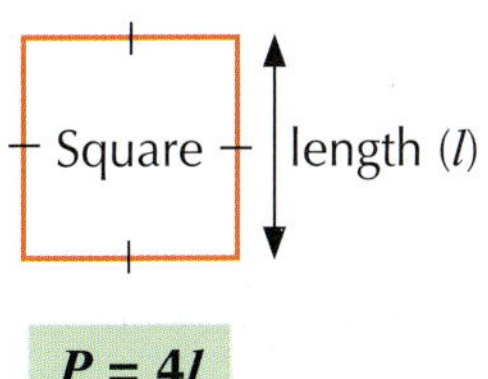

$P = 4l$

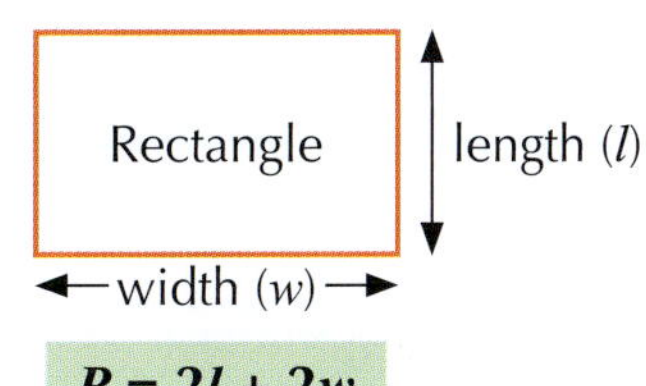

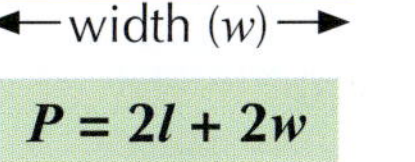

$P = 2l + 2w$

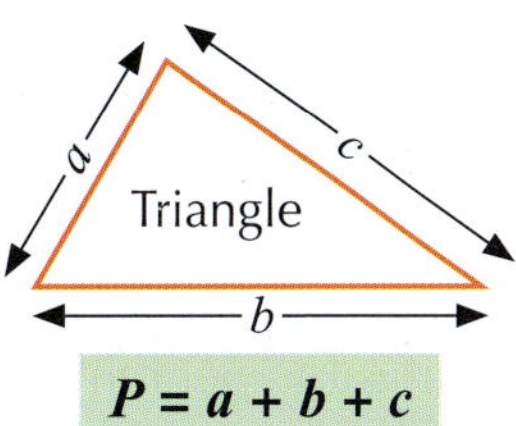

$P = a + b + c$

Example 1

Find the perimeter of each of these shapes.

1. Write down the formula for perimeter.
2. Substitute the lengths of the sides into the formula.
3. Simplify the answer and don't forget to include the units.

a)

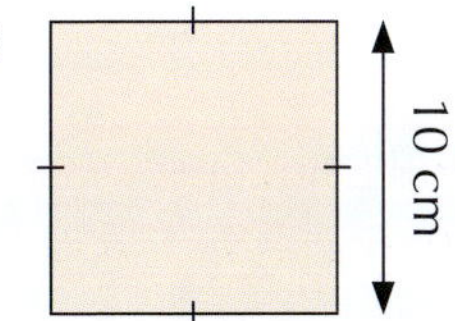

$P = 4l$
$= 4 \times 10$
$= \mathbf{40\ cm}$

Tip: The little lines (or 'tick marks') on the sides of the shape in part a) show that those sides are the same length — so you know it's a square.

b)

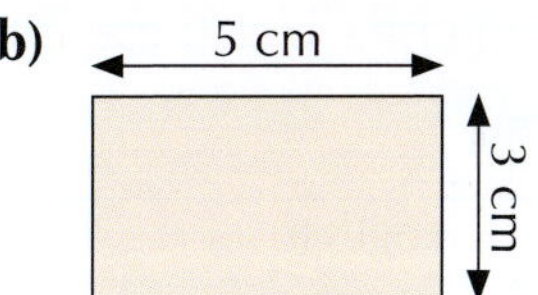

$P = 2l + 2w$
$= (2 \times 3) + (2 \times 5)$
$= 6 + 10$
$= \mathbf{16\ cm}$

c)

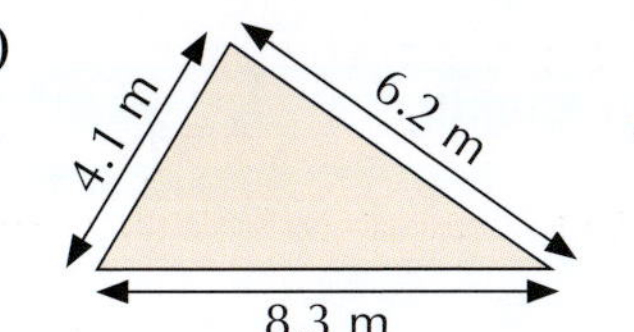

$P = a + b + c$
$= 4.1 + 8.3 + 6.2$
$= \mathbf{18.6\ m}$

Exercise 1

Q1 Find the perimeters of the shapes below.

a)

3 cm

5 cm

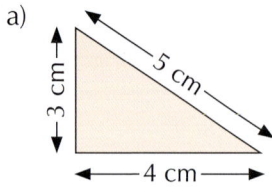

4 cm

b)

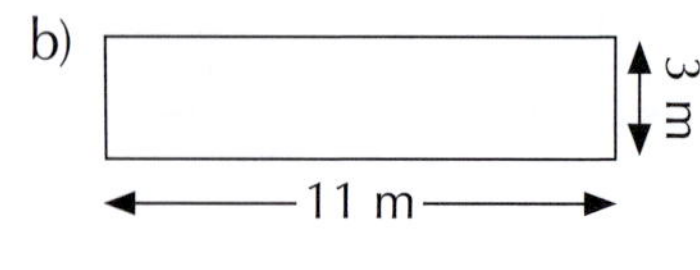

c)

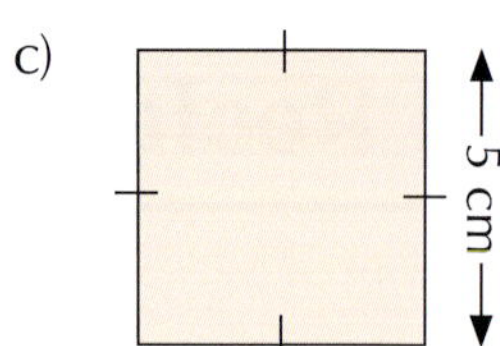

d)

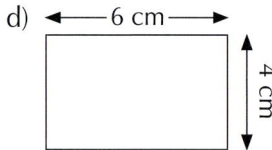

6 cm

4 cm

e)

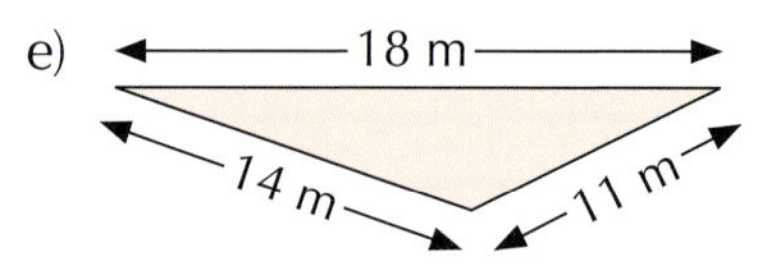

f)

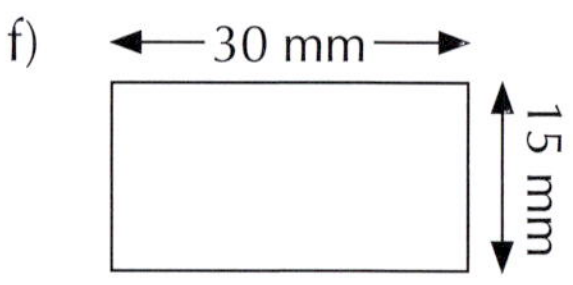

Q2 Find the perimeter of each shape described below.

a) A square with sides of length 4 cm

b) A triangle where two sides measure 5 cm and one side measures 7 cm

c) A rectangle of width 6 m and length 8 m

Q3 The police need to cordon off and then search a rectangular crime scene measuring 2.1 m by 2.8 m. What is the perimeter of the crime scene?

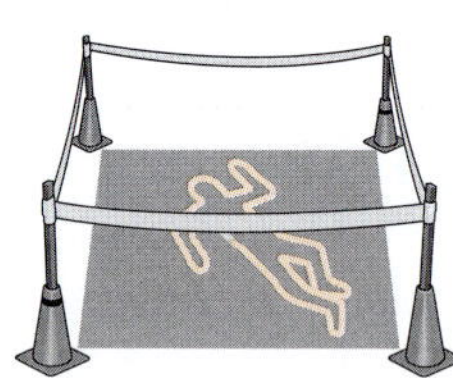

Area

Learning Objective — Spec Ref G16:
Be able to find the area of rectangles and triangles.

Area (A) is the amount of space inside a shape. It's measured in '**units squared**' — e.g. if the shape has sides in cm then the area will be in cm². Use these **formulas** to work it out:

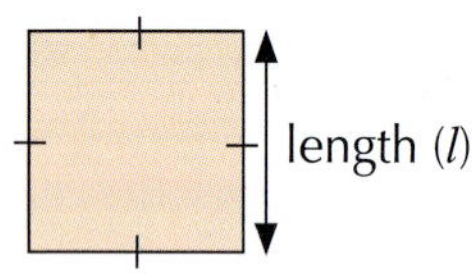

Area = (side length)²

$A = l^2$

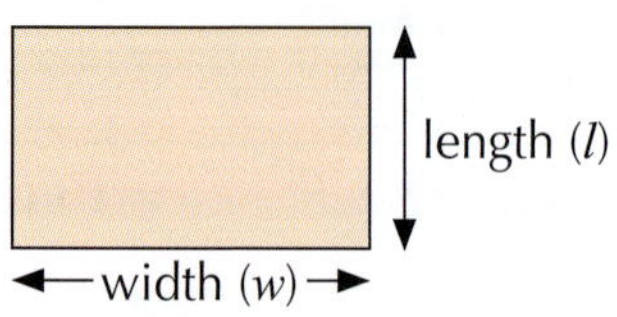

Area = length × width

$A = lw$

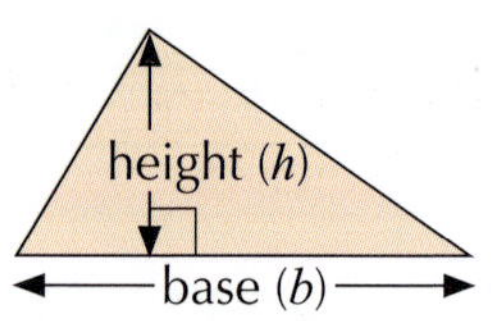

Area = $\frac{1}{2}$ × base × perpendicular height

$A = \frac{1}{2}bh$

Example 2

Find the area of each of these shapes.

a)

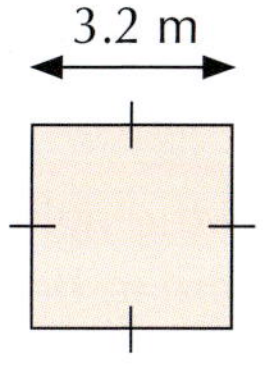

b)

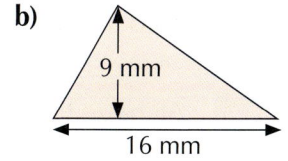

1. Write down the formula for area.
2. Substitute the lengths into the formula.
3. It's an area, so use 'squared' units.

a) $A = l^2$
$= 3.2^2$
$= \mathbf{10.24\ m^2}$

b) $A = \frac{1}{2}bh$
$= \frac{1}{2} \times 16 \times 9$
$= \mathbf{72\ mm^2}$

Exercise 2

Q1 Find the areas of the shapes below.

a)

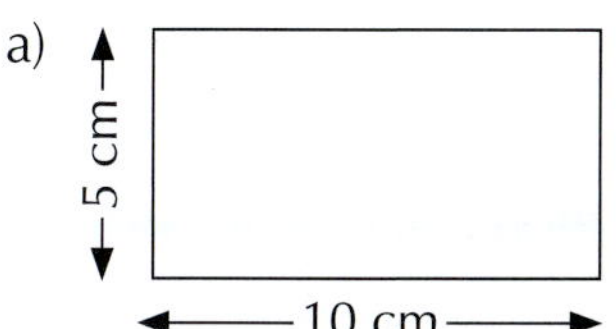

b)

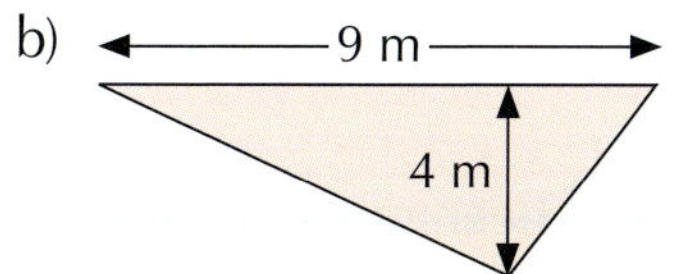

c)

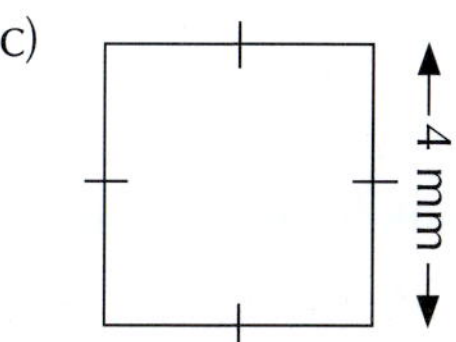

d)

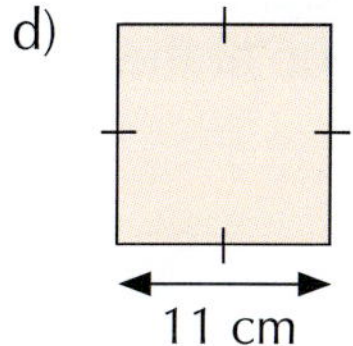

e)

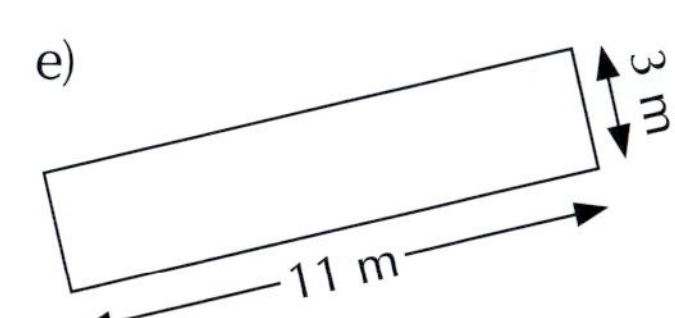

f)

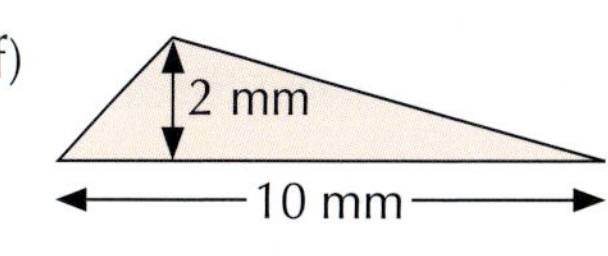

Q2 Find the area of each shape described below.

a) A rectangle 23 mm long and 15 mm wide

b) A square with 17 m sides

c) A triangle with a base of 4 cm and a height of 12.5 cm

Q3 Barb has a rectangular lawn 23.5 m long by 17.3 m wide. She is going to mow the lawn. What area will Barb have to mow (to the nearest m^2)?

Q4 A rectangular floor measures 9 m by 7.5 m.
It is to be tiled using square tiles with sides of length 0.5 m.

a) What is the area of the floor?

b) What is the area of one of the tiles?

c) How many tiles will be needed to cover the floor?

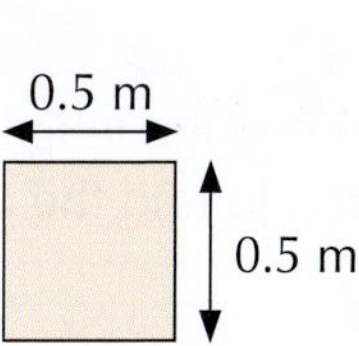

Q5 A rectangular garden 24 m long and 5.4 m wide is to be re-turfed.
Turf is bought in rolls that are 60 cm wide and 8 m long.
How many rolls of turf are needed to cover the garden? PROBLEM SOLVING

Q6 Ali bakes the cake shown on the right. PROBLEM SOLVING
If the top and the four sides are to be iced, what area of icing will be needed?

8 cm
22 cm
28 cm

Composite Shapes involving Rectangles and Triangles

Learning Objective — Spec Ref G16/G17:
Be able to find the perimeter and area of composite shapes made from rectangles and triangles.

A **composite shape** is one that has been made up from two or more basic shapes.

To find the **perimeter** of a composite shape, use the lengths you're given to find any that are **missing** and then **add up** the lengths of all of the sides.

To find the **area** of a composite shape, **split it up** into shapes that you recognise.
Then work out the area of each of these shapes separately and **add them** up at the end.

Example 3

Find the perimeter of the shape below.

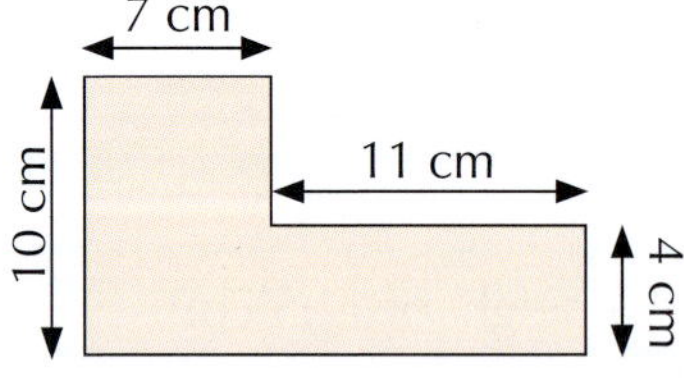

Tip: To find a missing side length, look at the lengths of the sides that are parallel to it.

1. Label the missing sides, and find their lengths.

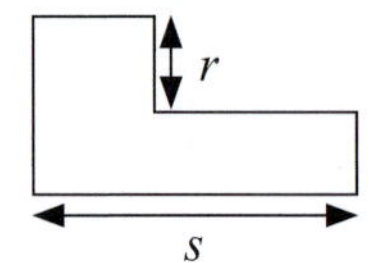

$r = 10 - 4 = 6$ cm
$s = 7 + 11 = 18$ cm

2. Add up the lengths of all the sides to find the perimeter.

Perimeter = 7 + 6 + 11 + 4 + 18 + 10
= **56 cm**

Example 4

Find the area of the shape from Example 3.

1. Split the shape into rectangles A and B, and find their areas.

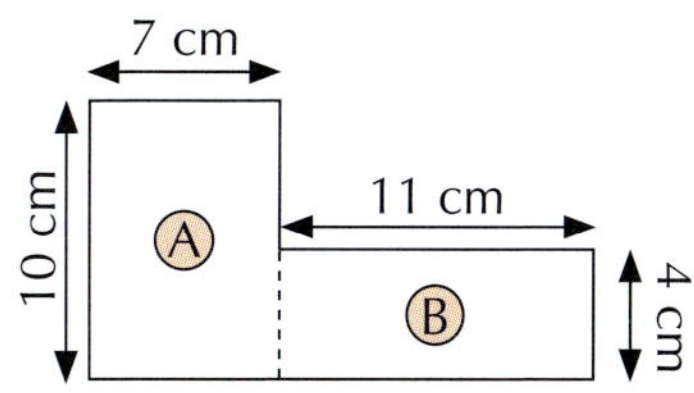

Area of rectangle A = length × width
= 10 × 7
= 70 cm²

Area of rectangle B = length × width
= 4 × 11
= 44 cm²

2. Add these up to find the total area.

Total area of shape = 70 + 44 = **114 cm²**

Exercise 3

Q1 Find the area of each shape below.

a)

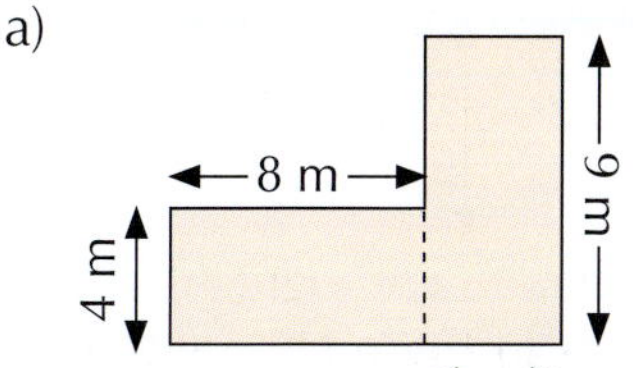

b)

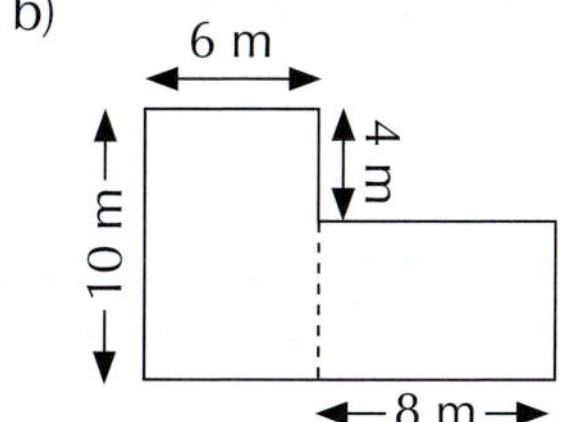

c)

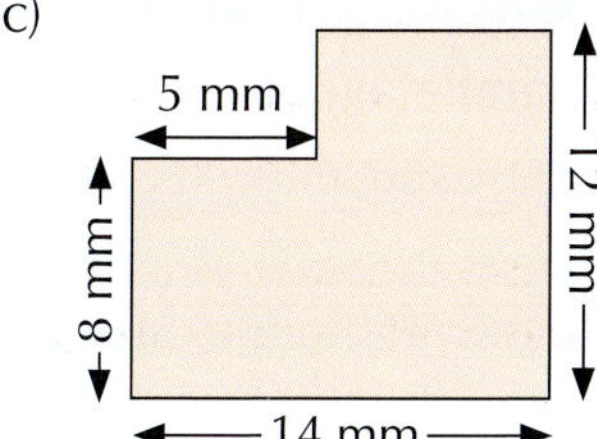

Q2 For each shape below, find: (i) its perimeter, (ii) its area.

a)

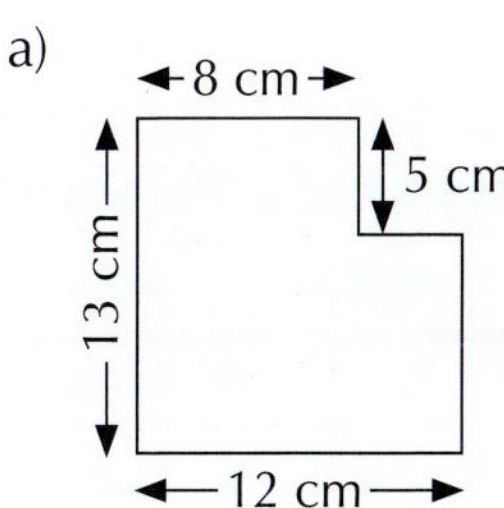

b)

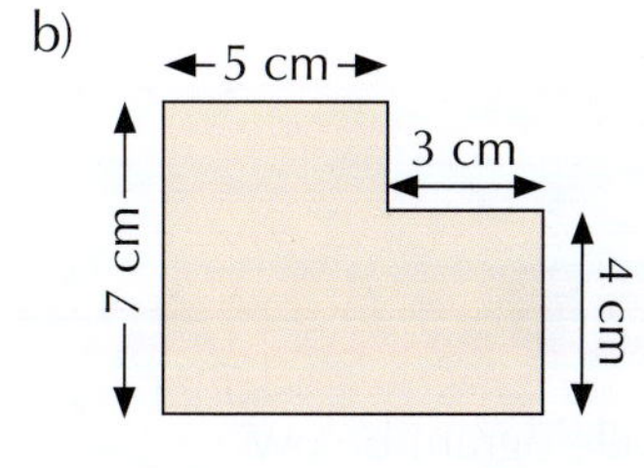

c)

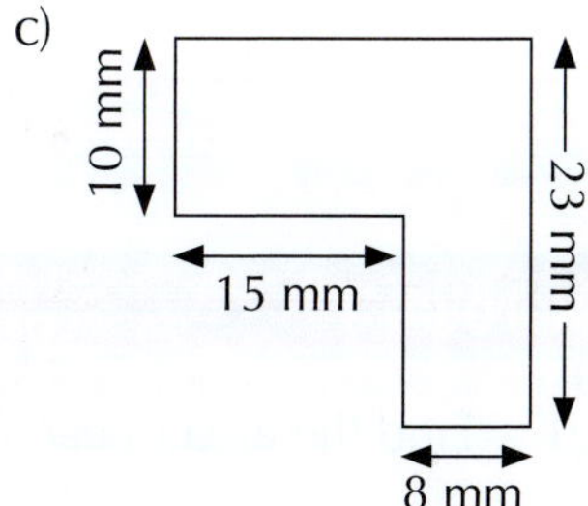

Q3 Find the area of the shapes below by splitting them into a rectangle and a triangle.

a)

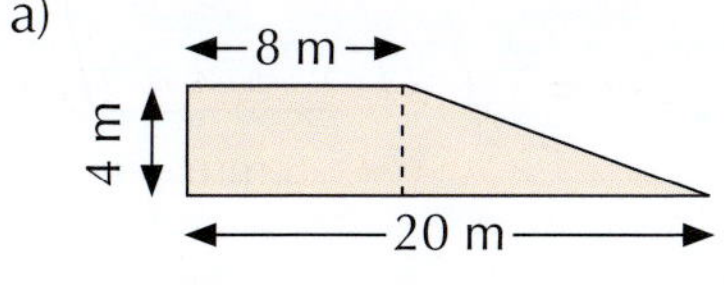

b)

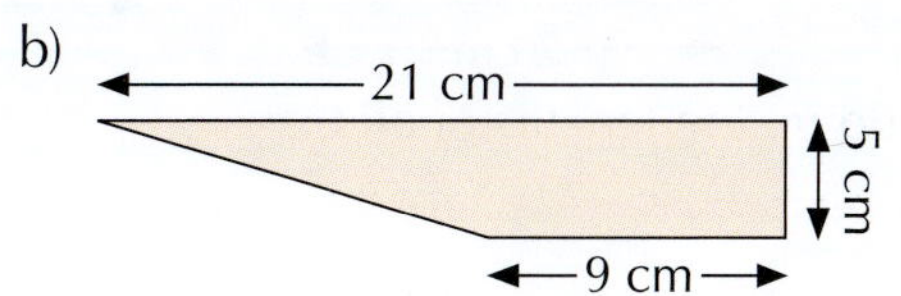

22.2 Other Quadrilaterals

Now that the simple shapes are out of the way, it's time to move on to the perimeter and area of some more complicated shapes — parallelograms and trapeziums.

Parallelograms

Learning Objective — Spec Ref G16/G17:
Be able to find the perimeter and area of parallelograms.

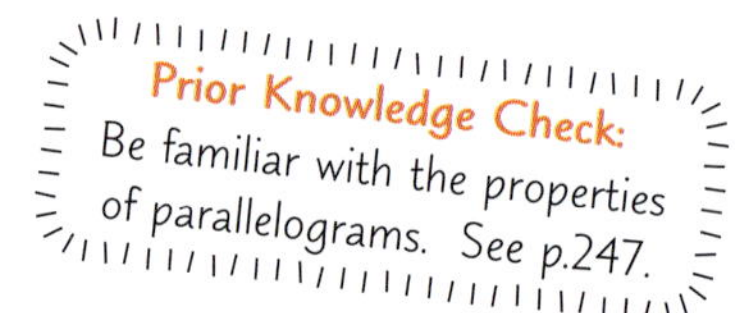

Prior Knowledge Check:
Be familiar with the properties of parallelograms. See p.247.

Parallelograms have **two pairs** of **parallel** sides, with opposite sides being the same length. Parallel sides are shown with **matching arrows**.

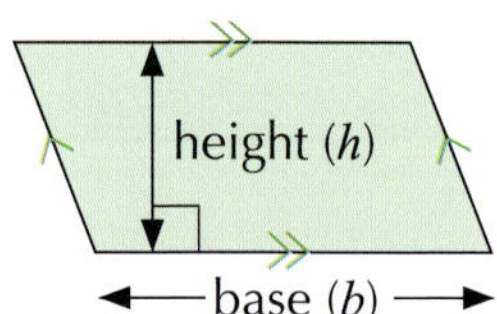

The **area** of a parallelogram is given by the formula: $\boldsymbol{A = bh}$

Here, h is the **perpendicular height** — it's measured at right angles to the base.

Example 1

Find the area of the parallelogram on the right.

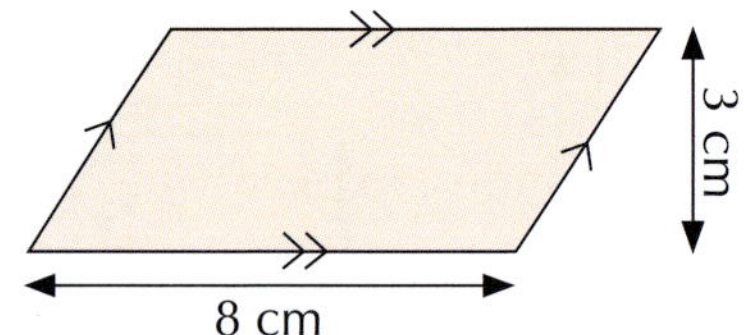

1. Write down the formula for the area of a parallelogram. $A = bh$
2. Substitute in the values for b and h. $= 8 \times 3$
3. Use 'squared' units — here, it's cm². $= \mathbf{24\ cm^2}$

Tip: Remember that h is the perpendicular height, not the length of the second set of parallel sides.

Exercise 1

Q1 Find the area of each parallelogram below.

a) 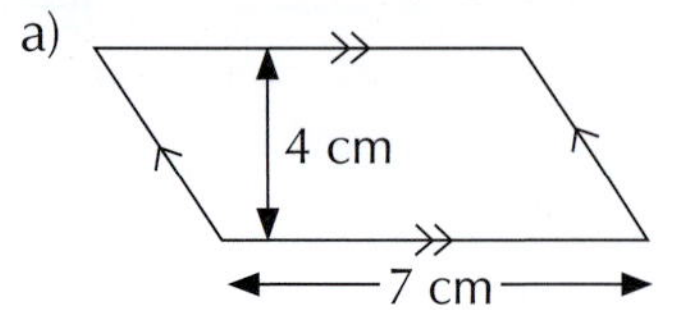

b) 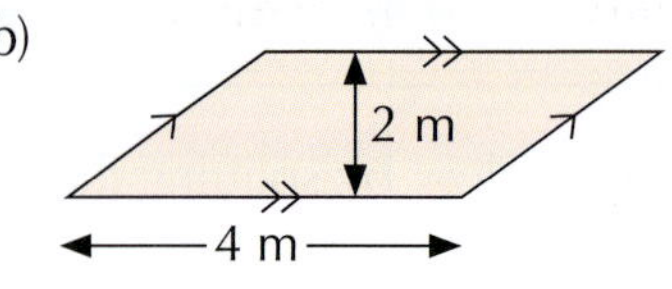

c) 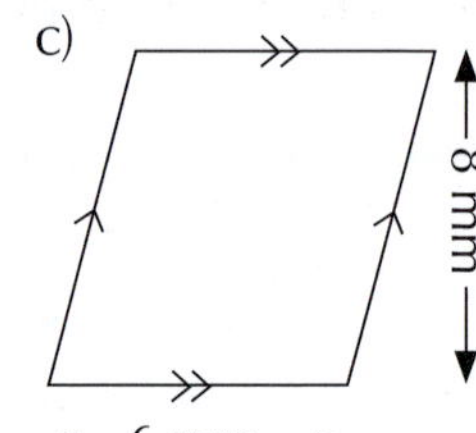

Q2 For each of these parallelograms, find: (i) the area, (ii) the perimeter.

a)

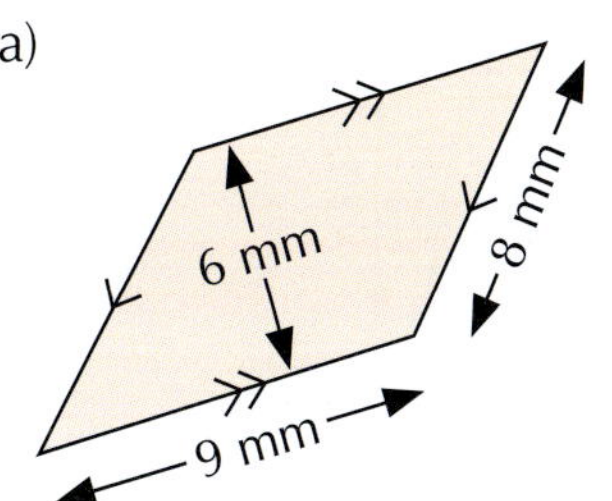

b)

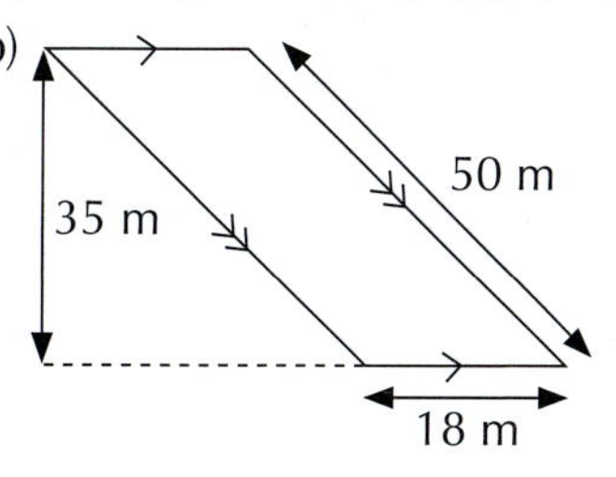

c)

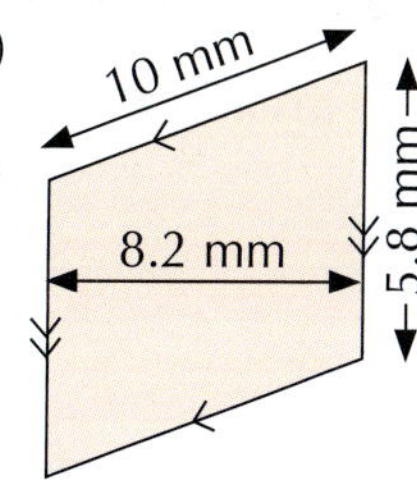

Q3 The logo of a company that designs rockets consists of two identical parallelograms, as shown on the right. Find the total area of the logo.

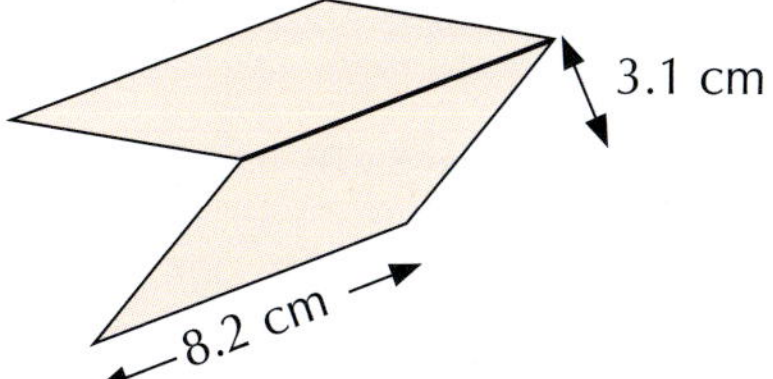

Q4 The picture on the right shows part of a tiled wall. All the tiles are identical parallelograms. Find the area of one tile.

PROBLEM SOLVING

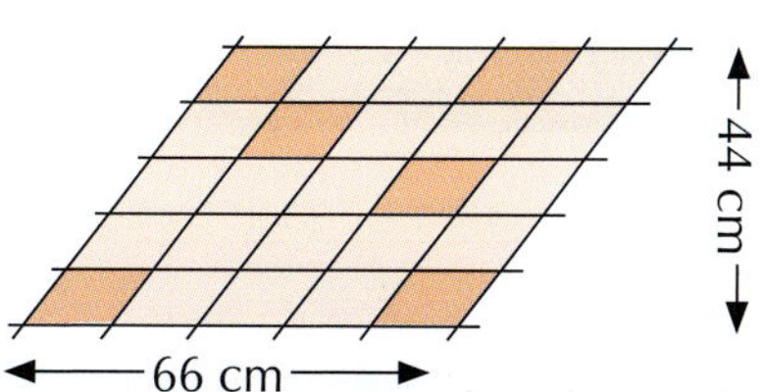

Q5 Without doing any calculations, explain which of the shapes below has the larger area.

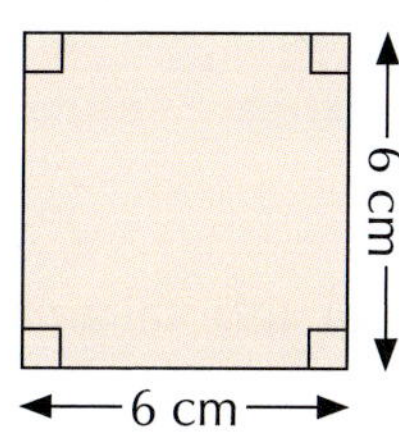

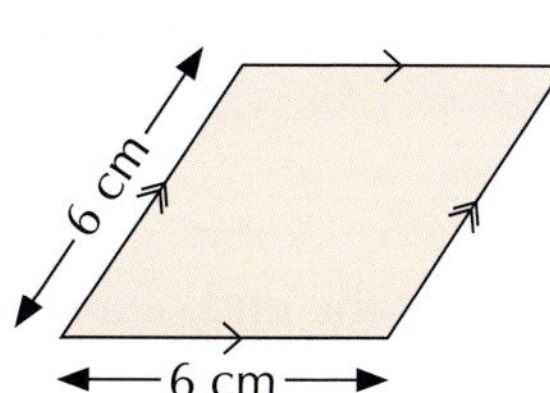

Trapeziums

Learning Objective — Spec Ref G16/G17:
Be able to find the perimeter and area of trapeziums.

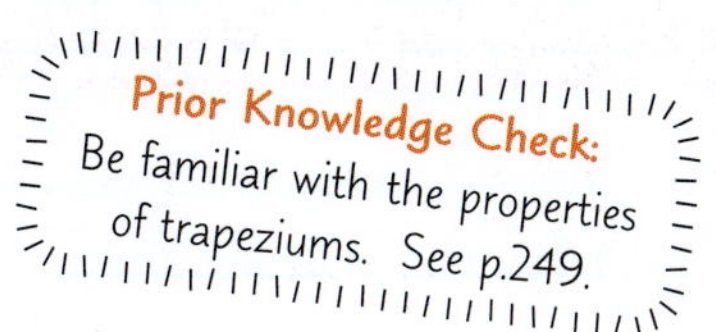

The shape on the right is a **trapezium**.
It has **one pair** of **parallel** sides.

The **area** of a trapezium is given by this formula: $A = \frac{1}{2}(a + b) \times h$

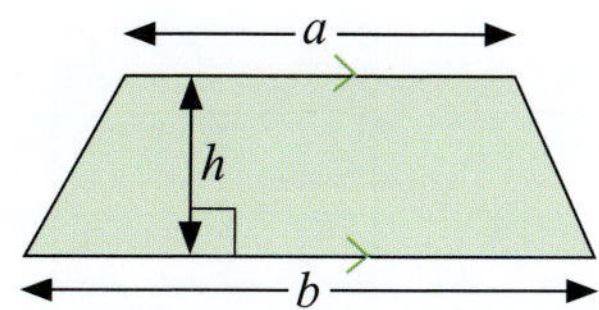

Remember, a and b are the parallel sides, and h is the **perpendicular** height.

Example 2

Find the area of the trapezium on the right.

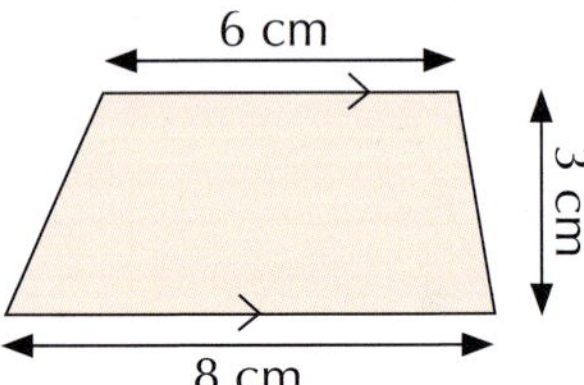

1. Write down the formula for the area of a trapezium. $A = \frac{1}{2}(a + b) \times h$
2. Substitute in the values for a, b and h. $= \frac{1}{2}(6 + 8) \times 3$

   $= \frac{1}{2} \times 14 \times 3$
3. Use 'squared' units — here, it's cm². $= 7 \times 3 =$ **21 cm²**

Exercise 2

Q1 Find the area of each trapezium below.

a)

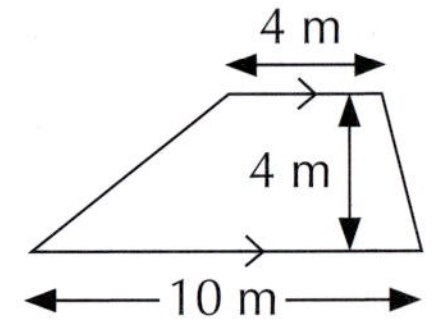

b)

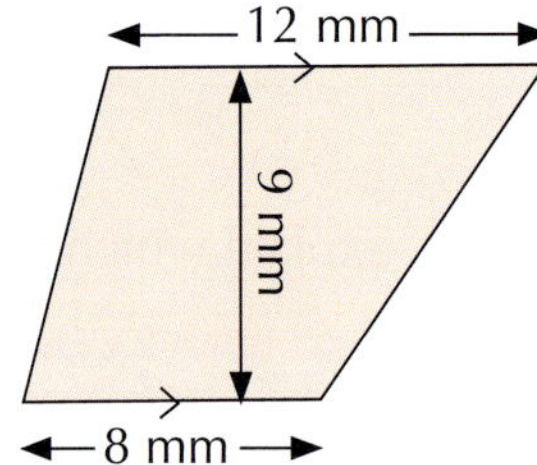

c)

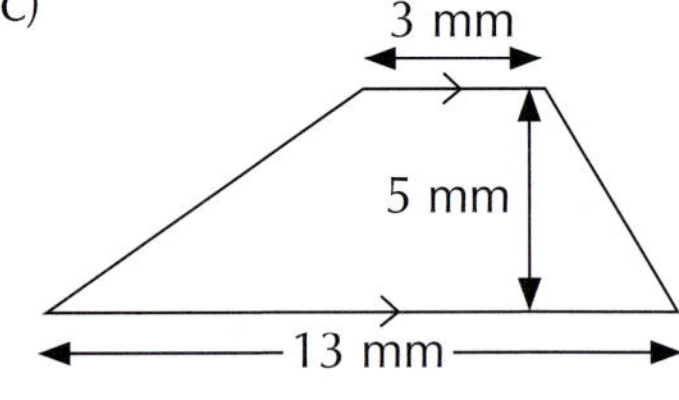

Q2 The picture below shows the end of a barn. Find: a) its total area, b) its perimeter.

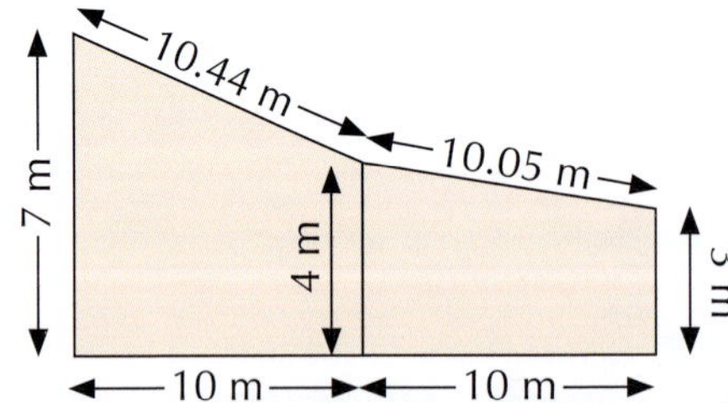

Q3 What can you say about the area of these two shapes? Explain your answer.

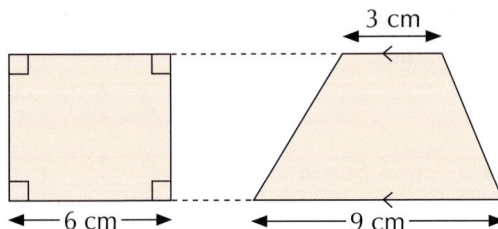

3 cm

6 cm

9 cm

Composite Shapes involving Parallelograms and Trapeziums

Learning Objective — Spec Ref G16/G17:
Be able to find the perimeter and area of composite shapes made from parallelograms and trapeziums.

Composite shapes made up of parallelograms and trapeziums can be treated in the same way as shapes made of rectangles and triangles. When finding perimeters, remember that **opposite sides** on a parallelogram are the **same length** — this can be helpful for finding missing lengths.

Sometimes, instead of two shapes being joined together to make a bigger shape, a **big shape** can have a smaller shape **cut out** of it. In this case, **subtract** the area of the **smaller** shape from the area of the bigger one.

Example 3

For the composite shape on the right, find:
a) its area, b) its perimeter.

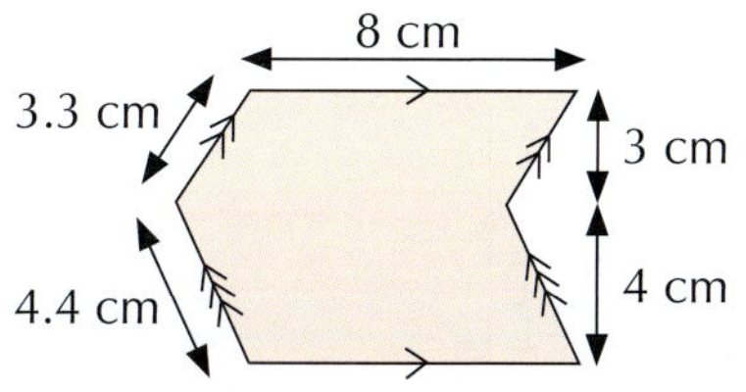

a) 1. Split the shape into two parallelograms, A and B, and find their areas.

2. Add these areas to find the total area.

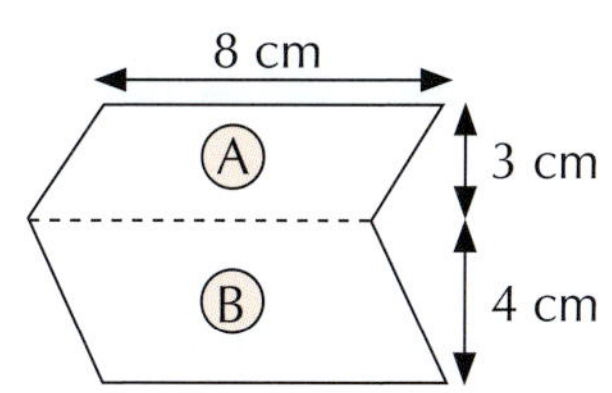

Area of A = $bh = 8 \times 3 = 24$ cm^2

Area of B = $bh = 8 \times 4 = 32$ cm^2

Total area = 24 + 32
= **56 cm^2**

b) The perimeter is the distance around the outside of the shape.

$P = 8 + 3.3 + 4.4 + 8 + 4.4 + 3.3$
= **31.4 cm**

Example 4

Find the area of the shape on the right.

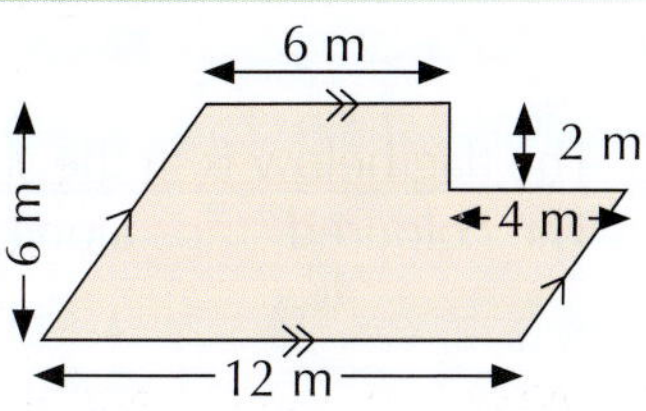

1. Form a parallelogram (A) by adding a trapezium (B) to the corner of the original shape.

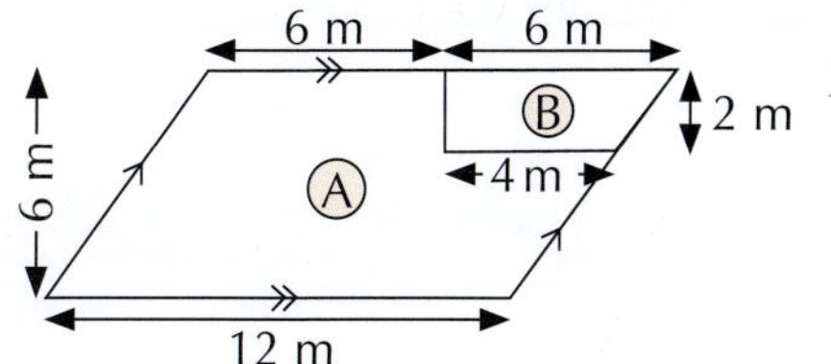

2. Find the areas of parallelogram A and trapezium B.

Area of A = bh
= $12 \times 6 = 72$ m^2

Area of B = $\frac{1}{2}(a + b) \times h$
= $\frac{1}{2}(6 + 4) \times 2 = 10$ m^2

3. Subtract B from A to find the original shape's area.

Area = 72 − 10
= **62 m^2**

Exercise 3

Q1 Find each shaded area below.

a)

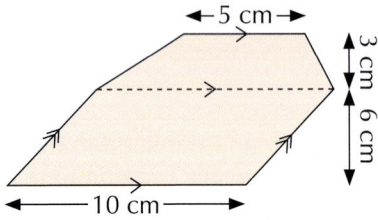

5 cm
3 cm
6 cm
10 cm

b)

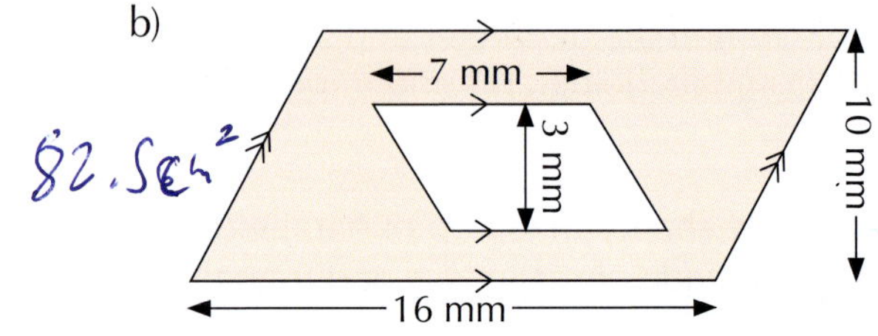

Q2 For each shape below, find: (i) the area, (ii) the perimeter.
The dotted lines show lines of symmetry.

a)

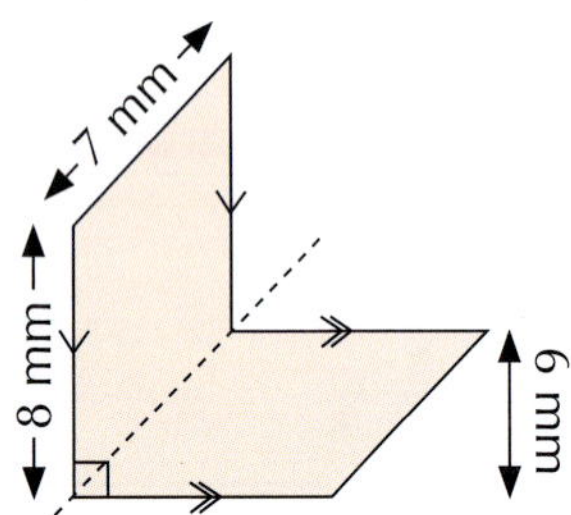

b)

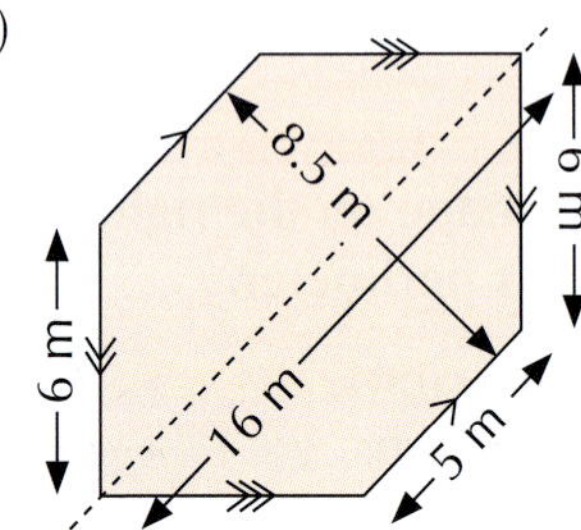

c)

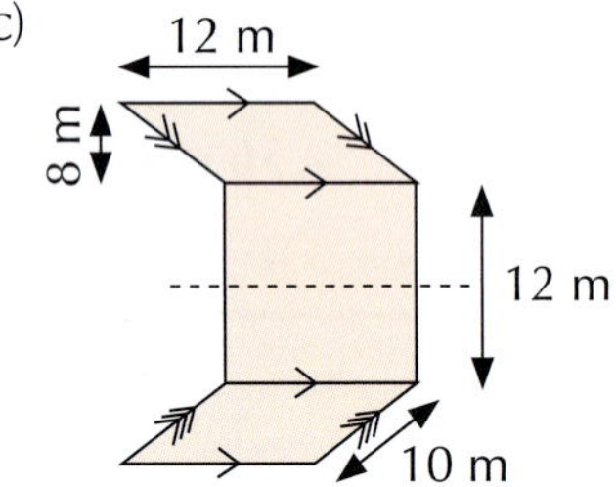

d)

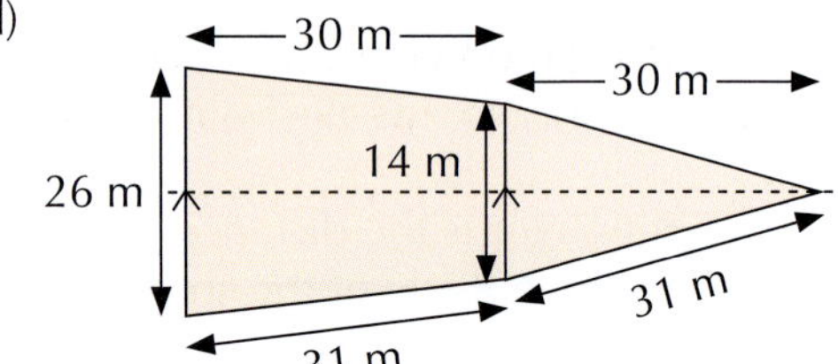

Q3 The flag below is in the shape of a trapezium.
The coloured strips along the top and bottom edges are parallelograms.

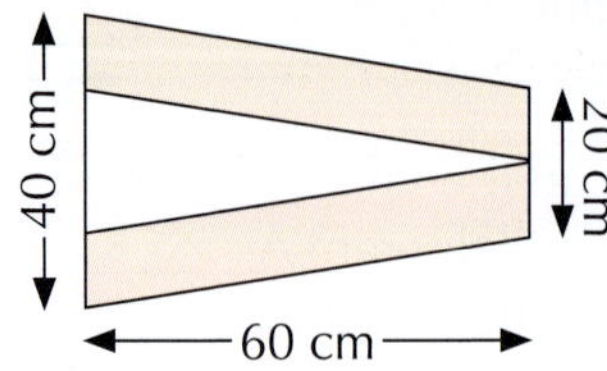

a) Find the total area of the flag.

b) Find the total area of the coloured strips.

22.3 Circumference of a Circle

There are more formulas you need to know on the next few pages, this time featuring your good friend π. Make sure you know where the π button lives on your calculator — you'll need it a lot for circle questions.

Learning Objective — Spec Ref G17:
Be able to find the circumference of a circle.

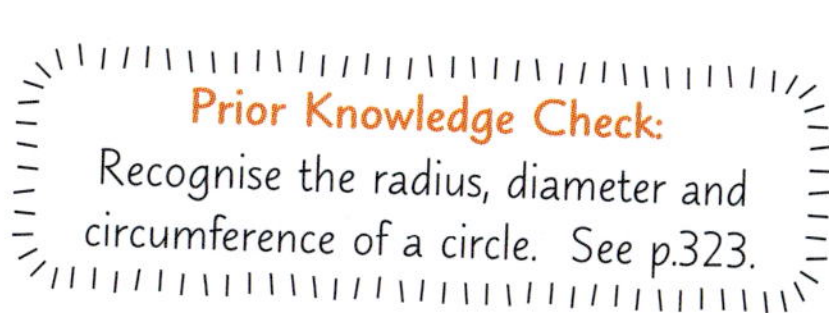

Prior Knowledge Check:
Recognise the radius, diameter and circumference of a circle. See p.323.

The **circumference** of a circle is the distance all the way around its edge. You can find the circumference (C) of a circle if you know its **diameter** (d) or its **radius** (r) using this formula: $C = \pi d = 2\pi r$

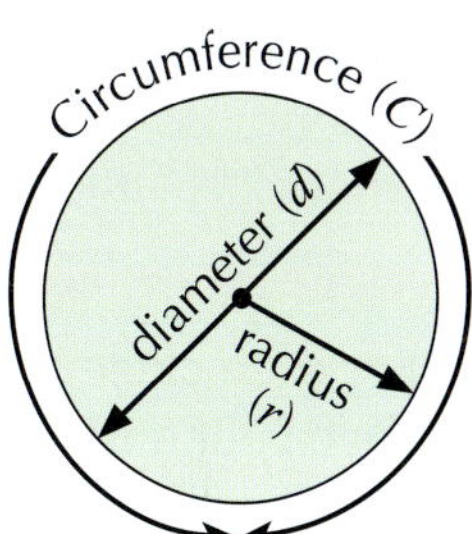

Remember that the diameter of a circle is always **twice as long** as the radius: $d = 2r$

You might be asked to give an **exact answer** or to give your answer **in terms of π**. This means that you **shouldn't** use your calculator to evaluate π — so instead of 31.415... you would write your answer as 10π.

Example 1

Find the circumference of the circle shown below. Give your answer to one decimal place.

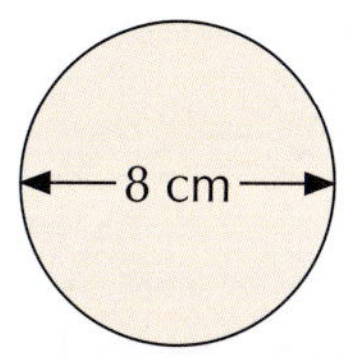

1. Write down the diameter. $d = 8$ cm
2. Use the formula $C = \pi d$. $C = \pi d$
3. Round your answer and use the correct units.

$= \pi \times 8$
$= 25.1327...$
$=$ **25.1 cm** (1 d.p.)

Tip: If your calculator doesn't have a π button, then use the value 3.142.

Example 2

Find the circumference of a circle which has radius 6 m. Give your answer in terms of π.

1. Write down the radius. $r = 6$ m
2. Use the formula $C = 2\pi r$. $C = 2\pi r$
3. Simplify your answer and use the correct units.

$= 2 \times \pi \times 6$
$=$ **12π m**

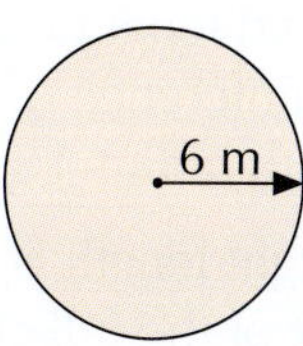

Exercise 1

Q1 Find the circumference of each circle. Give your answers to 1 decimal place.

a) 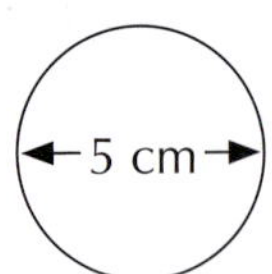

b) 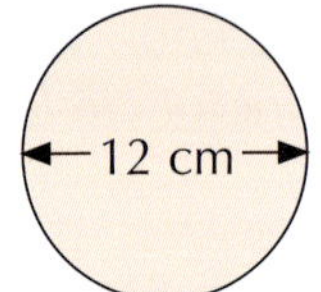

c) 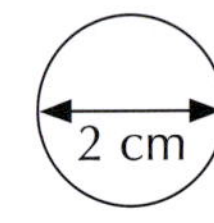

d) 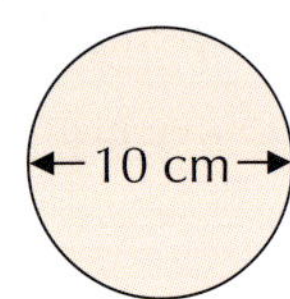

Q2 Find the exact circumference of each of these circles. 

a) 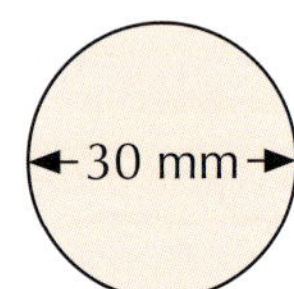

b) 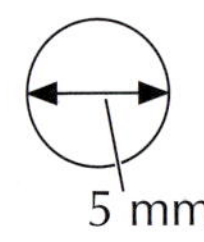

c) 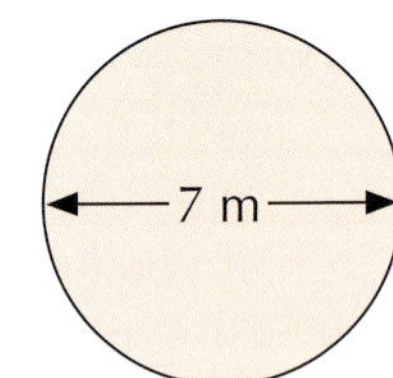

d) 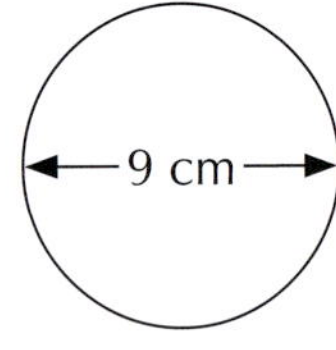

Q3 For each circle below: (i) write down the diameter, (ii) find its circumference. Give your answers to 1 decimal place.

a) 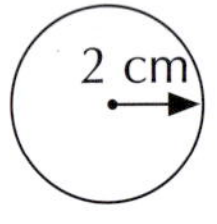

b) 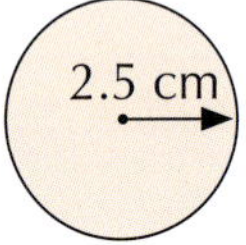

c) 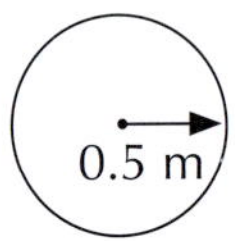

d) 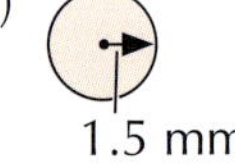

Q4 Find the exact circumference of the circles with the diameter (d) or radius (r) given below. 

a) $d = 4$ cm b) $d = 8$ mm c) $r = 14$ km d) $r = 0.1$ km

A **semicircle** is **half** of a circle. You might need to find the perimeter of semicircles or **composite shapes** which include parts of circles. You can make use of the formula for the **circumference** of a circle to find the length of any **curved sides** — e.g. the curved part of a semicircle has a length of $\frac{1}{2} \times C$, where C is the circumference of the **full circle**.

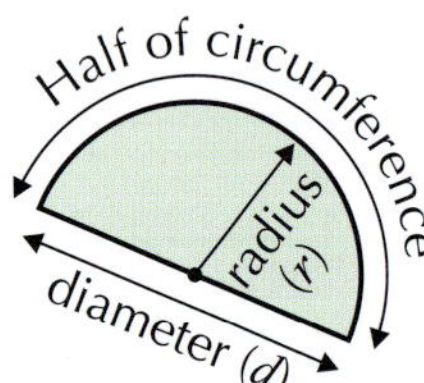

Example 3

Find the perimeter of the semicircle below, correct to one decimal place.

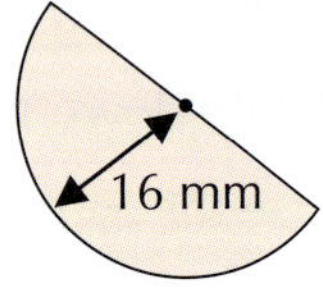

1. The curved length is half the circumference of a circle with radius 16 mm.

   Curved length $= 2\pi r \div 2$
   $= 2 \times \pi \times 16 \div 2$
   $= 50.265...$ mm

2. The straight length is the diameter of the full circle.

   Straight length $= d = 2r = 2 \times 16$
   $= 32$ mm

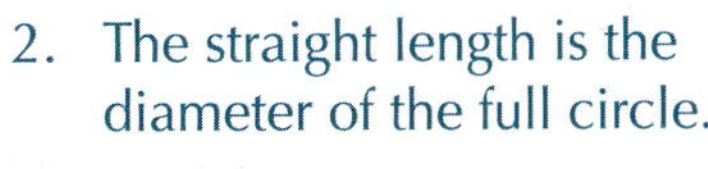

3. Add up the two lengths to find the perimeter.

   Total length = curved length + straight length
   $= 50.265... + 32 =$ **82.3 mm** (1 d.p.)

Example 4

The shape on the right consists of a semicircle on top of a rectangle. Find the perimeter of the shape to one decimal place.

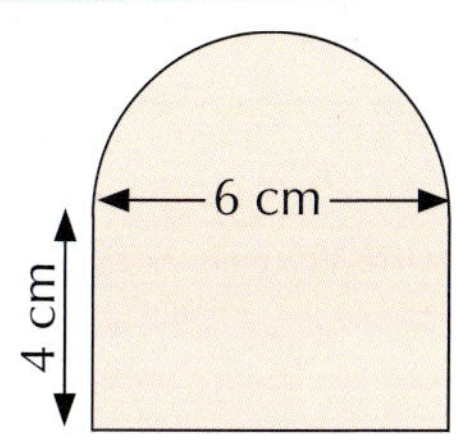

1. Find the curved length. This is half the circumference of a circle with diameter 6 cm.

   Curved length $= \pi d \div 2$
   $= \pi \times 6 \div 2$
   $= 9.424...$ cm

2. Find the total length of the straight sides.

   Total of straight sides $= 4 + 6 + 4$
   $= 14$ cm

3. Add the two parts.

   Total length = curved length + straight length
   $= 9.424... + 14$
   $=$ **23.4 cm** (1 d.p.)

Exercise 2

Q1 Find the perimeter of each shape below. Give your answers to 1 decimal place.

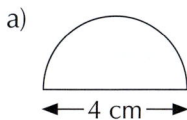

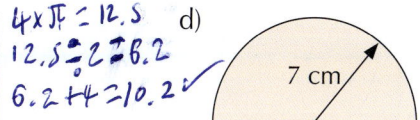

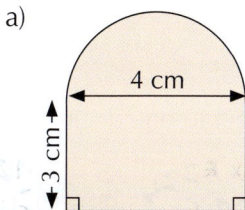

a) 4 cm

b) c)

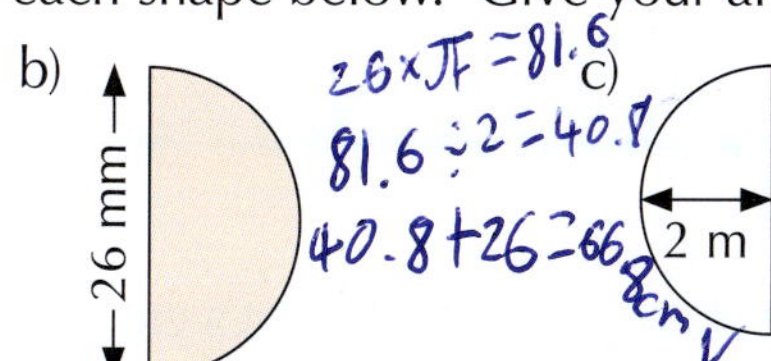

d)

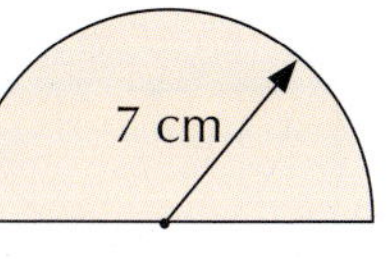

Q2 Find the perimeter of each shape below. Give your answers to 1 decimal place.

a) 4 cm, 3 cm

b)

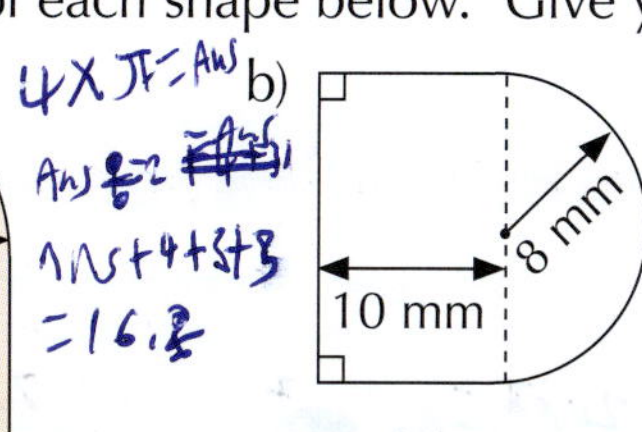

c)

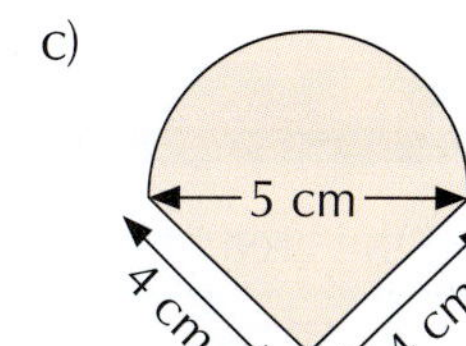

d)

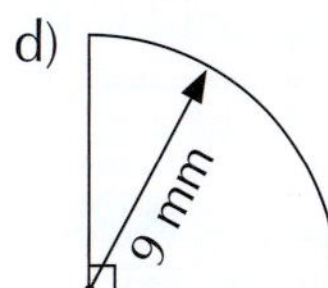

e)

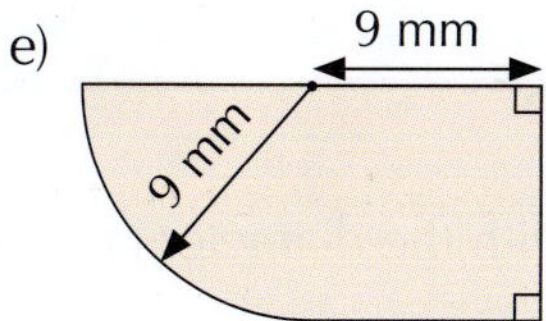

f)

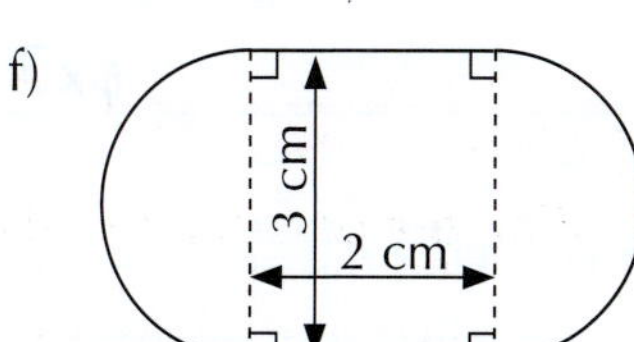

Q3 Alec used wooden fencing to build a semicircular sheep pen, with a wall forming the straight side. If the radius of the semicircle is 16 m, how many metres of fencing did Alec have to use (to 1 d.p.)?

Q4 A running track consists of two semicircles of radius 80 m, joined together by two straight sections, each with length 100 m. Calculate the length of the running track to the nearest metre.

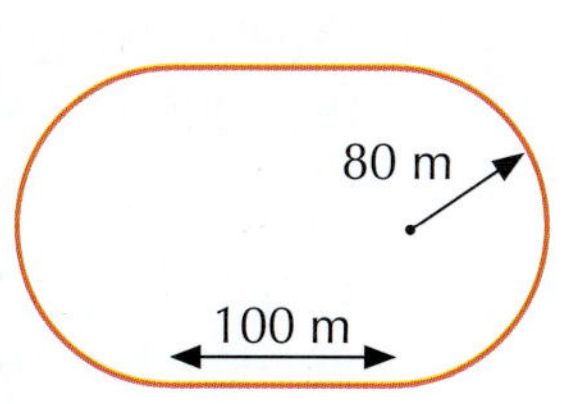

22.4 Area of a Circle

Another page, another formula. This one also involves circles and π, so make sure that you don't get it confused with the circumference formulas from earlier on.

Learning Objective — Spec Ref G17:
Be able to find the area of a circle.

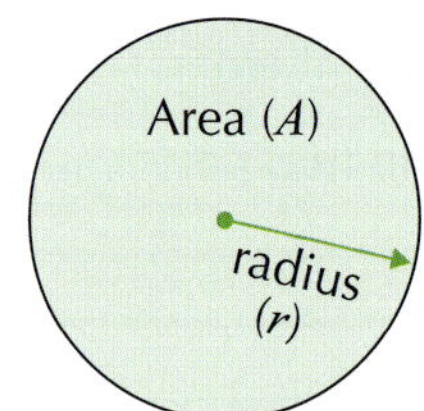

The **area** (A) of a circle is given by this formula: $A = \pi r^2$

If you're given the **diameter** of the circle, make sure you **divide by 2** to get the radius before you use the formula.

Example 1

Find the area of the circle below. Give your answer to one decimal place.

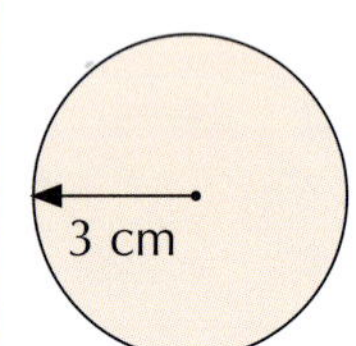

1. Write down the radius. — $r = 3$ cm
2. Use the formula $A = \pi r^2$. (Remember: $r^2 = r \times r$) — $A = \pi r^2 = \pi \times 3 \times 3 = 28.274...$
3. Round your answer. And use 'squared' units — here, it's cm². — $A =$ **28.3 cm²** (1 d.p.)

Exercise 1

Q1 Find the area of each of these circles. Give your answers correct to one decimal place.

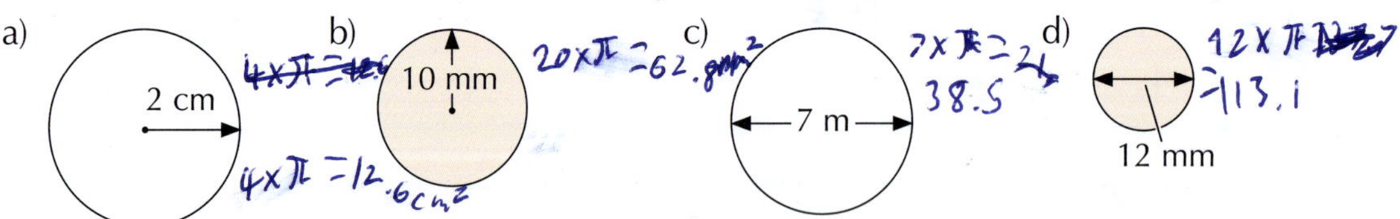

Q2 Find the areas of the circles with the diameter (d) or radius (r) given below. Give your answers in terms of π.

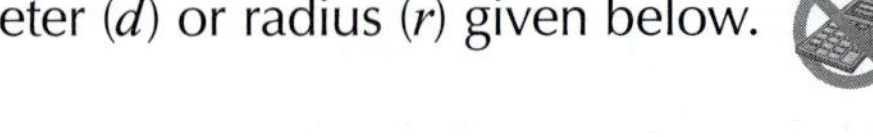

a) $r = 7$ mm b) $r = 5$ cm c) $d = 18$ km d) $d = 3$ m

Q3 What is the area of a circular reservoir of radius 0.82 km? Give your answer to two decimal places.

Q4 Which of the two shapes on the right has the greater area?

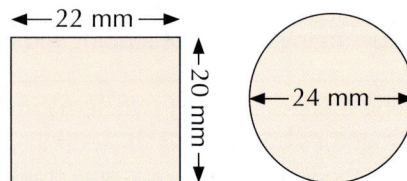

22 mm
20 mm
24 mm

Find the area of **composite shapes** involving parts of circles by **splitting** the shape into ones that you recognise. The area of a **semicircle** is just **half** the area of the full circle.

Example 2

Find the area of the shape on the right. Give your answer to one decimal place.

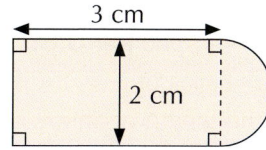

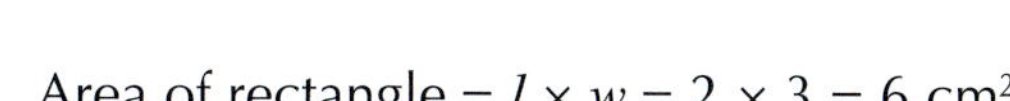

1. Divide the shape into a rectangle and a semicircle.
2. Find the area of the rectangle. — Area of rectangle = $l \times w = 2 \times 3 = 6$ cm^2
3. Find the area of the semicircle. The diameter is 2 cm, so the radius is $2 \div 2 = 1$ cm. — Area of semicircle = (area of circle of radius 1 cm) $\div$ 2
$= \pi r^2 \div 2 = \pi \times 1^2 \div 2$
$= 1.5707...$ cm^2
4. Add up the two areas. — Total area = area of rectangle + area of semicircle
$= 6 + 1.5707...$
$=$ **7.6 cm²** (1 d.p.)

Exercise 2

Q1 Find the area of each shape below. Give your answers to one decimal place.

a)

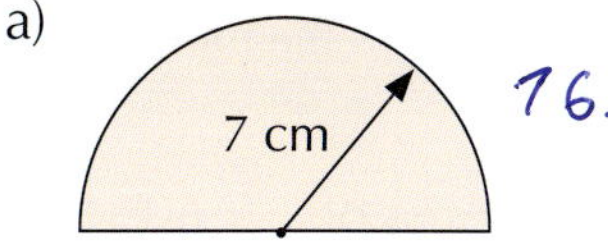

b) c)

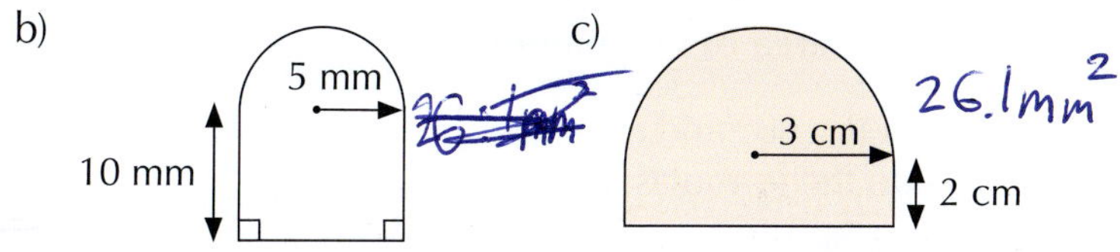

d)

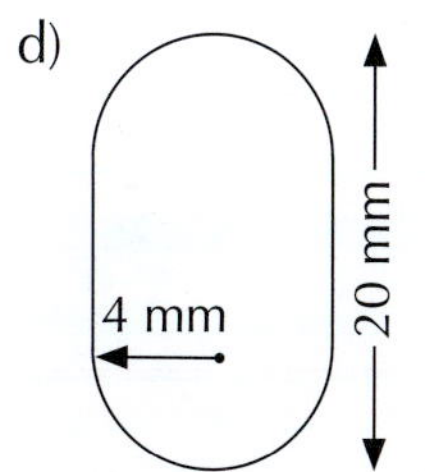

e)

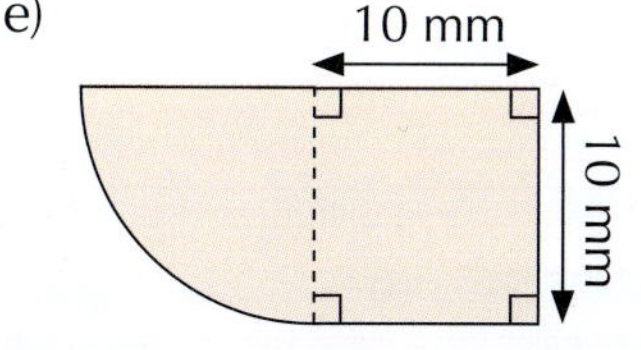

f)

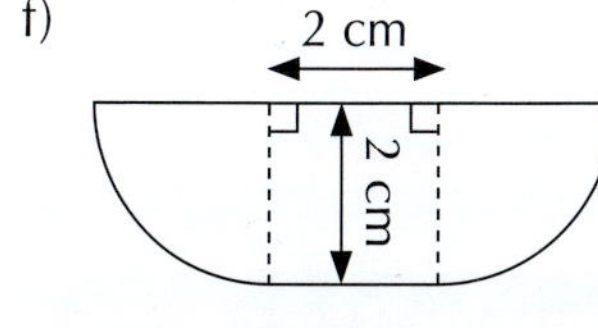

Q2 A church window is in the shape of a rectangle 1 m wide and 2 m high, with a semicircle on top, as shown on the right. What is its area to two decimal places?

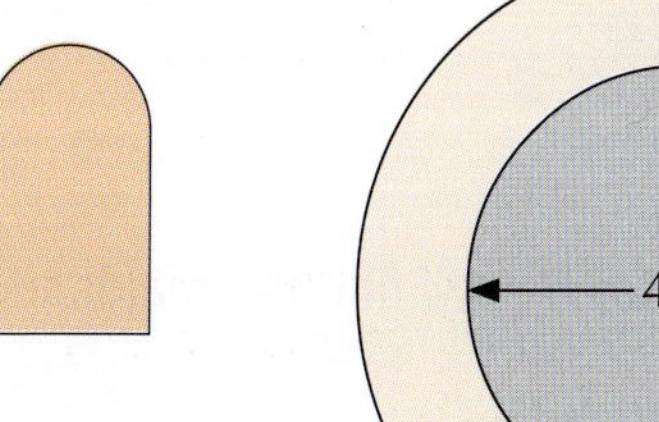

Q3 A circular pond of diameter 4 m is surrounded by a path 1 m wide, as shown in the diagram. What is the area of the path to the nearest square metre?

PROBLEM SOLVING

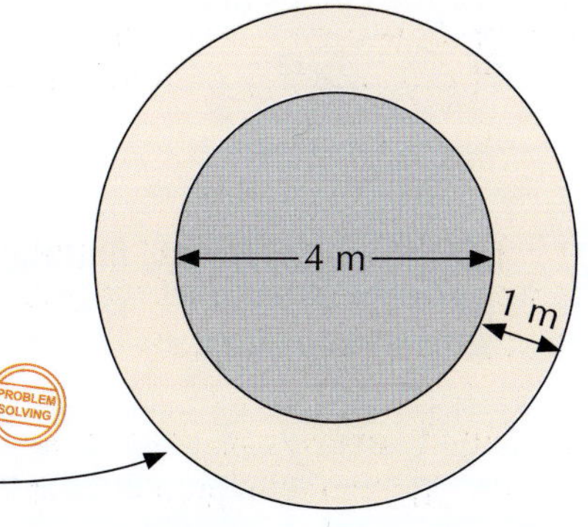

22.5 Arcs and Sectors of Circles

A couple more definitions and two more formulas to learn, and then that's circles all done.

Learning Objectives — Spec Ref G18:

- Be able to find the area of a sector of a circle.
- Be able to find the length of an arc of a circle.

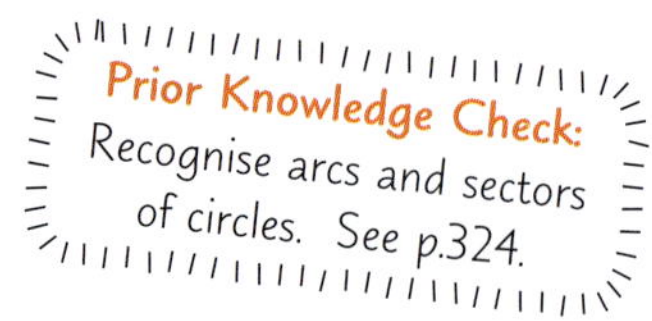

Prior Knowledge Check:
Recognise arcs and sectors of circles. See p.324.

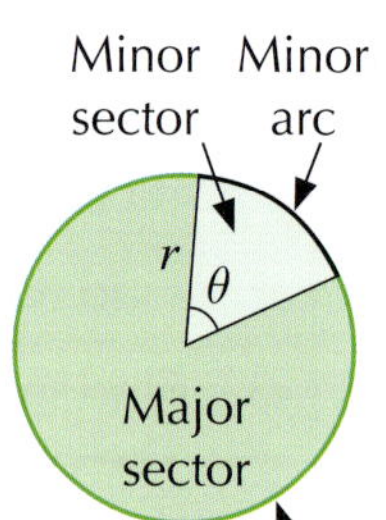

You saw on p.324 that a **sector** is a 'slice' of a circle and an **arc** is a part of the circumference. If the angle in a sector is **less than 180°** then it's called a **minor** sector, and if the angle is **more than 180°** then it's called a **major** sector.

You can use the following **formulas** to find an arc length and a sector area:

$$\text{Length of arc} = \frac{\theta}{360°} \times \text{circumference of circle} = \boldsymbol{\frac{\theta}{360°} \times 2\pi r}$$

$$\text{Area of sector} = \frac{\theta}{360°} \times \text{area of circle} = \boldsymbol{\frac{\theta}{360°} \times \pi r^2}$$

Example 1

For the circle on the right, calculate the exact length of the minor arc and the exact area of the minor sector.

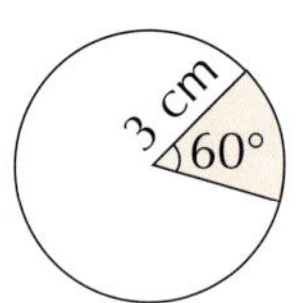

Tip: 60° < 180°, so the shaded region is the minor sector.

1. Put $\theta = 60°$ and $r = 3$ cm into the formulas.
2. For exact solutions, leave the answers in terms of π.

$$\text{Length of arc} = \frac{60°}{360°} \times (2 \times \pi \times 3) = \frac{1}{6} \times 6\pi = \boldsymbol{\pi \text{ cm}}$$

$$\text{Area of sector} = \frac{60°}{360°} \times \pi \times 3^2 = \frac{1}{6} \times 9\pi = \boldsymbol{\frac{3}{2}\pi \text{ cm}^2}$$

Exercise 1

Q1 For the circles below, find the exact minor arc length and exact minor sector area.

a) 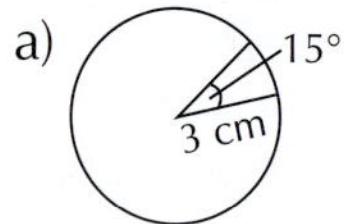

b) 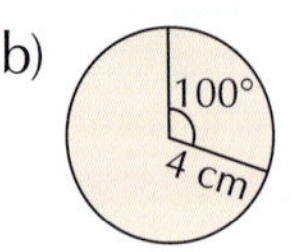

c) 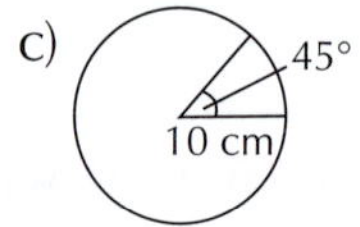

d) 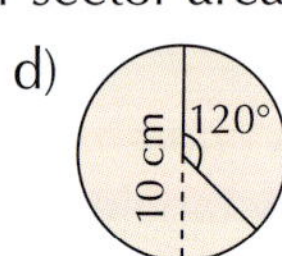

Q2 For the circles below, find the major sector area and major arc length to 2 decimal places.

a) 

b) 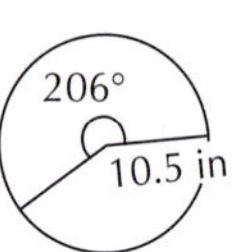

c) 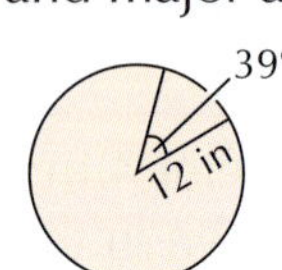

d) 

Review Exercise

Q1 For each shape below, find: (i) its perimeter, (ii) its area.

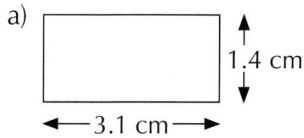

a)

1.4 cm

3.1 cm

b)

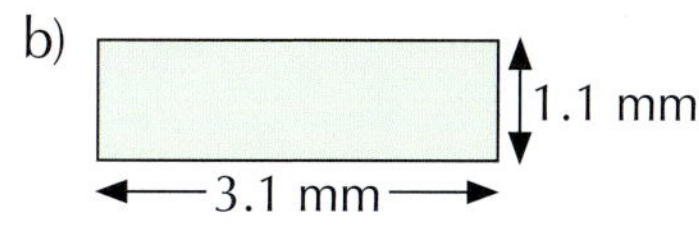

c)

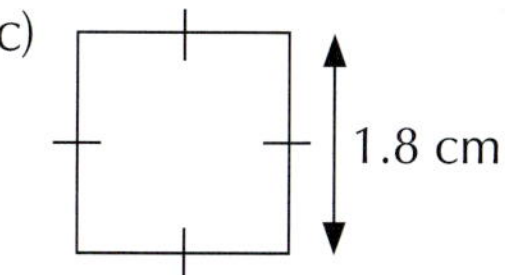

Q2 For each of the triangles below, find: (i) its perimeter, (ii) its area.

a)

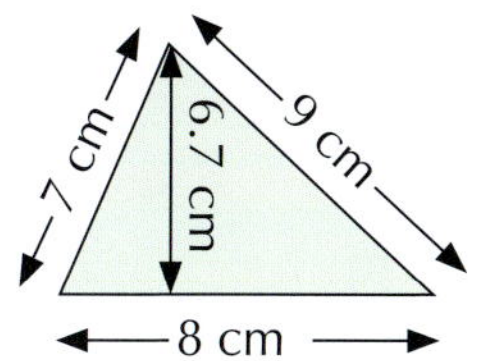

b)

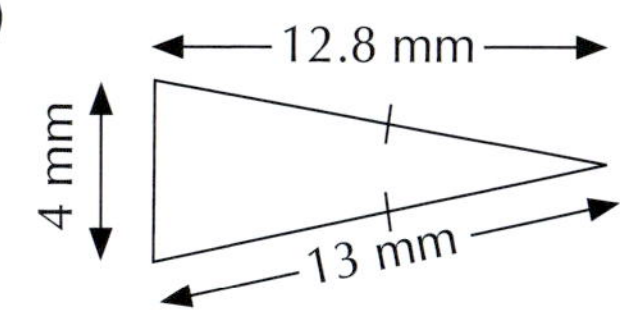

c)

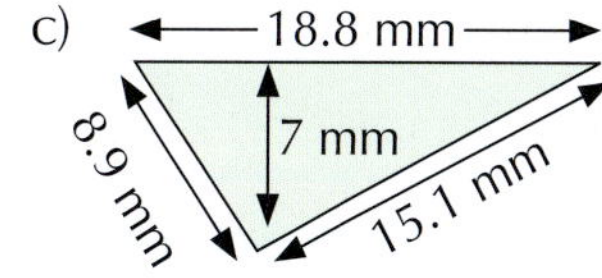

Q3 Find the area of each shape below.

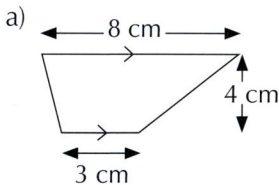

a)

8 cm

4 cm

3 cm

b)

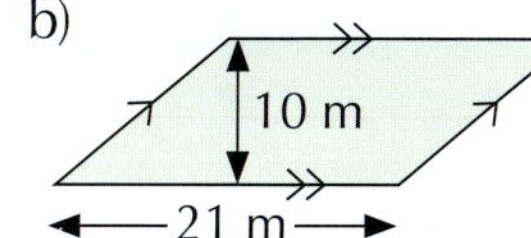

c)

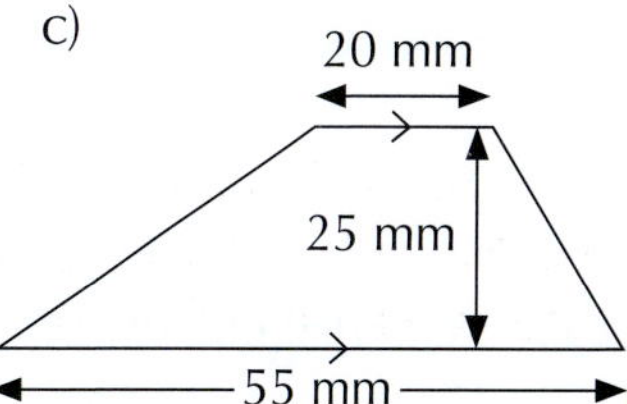

Q4 Find, to 1 decimal place, the shaded area in each of the following shapes.

a)

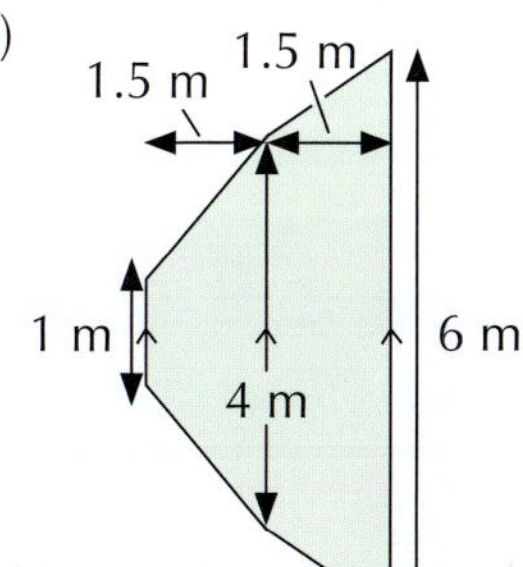

b)

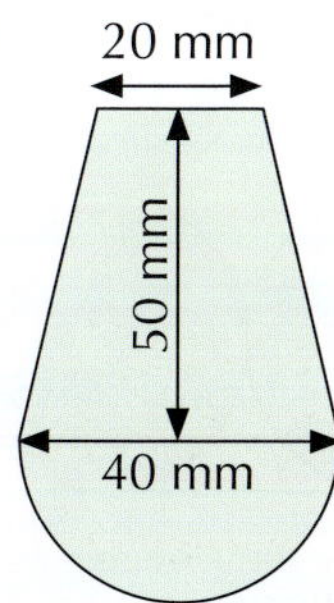

c)

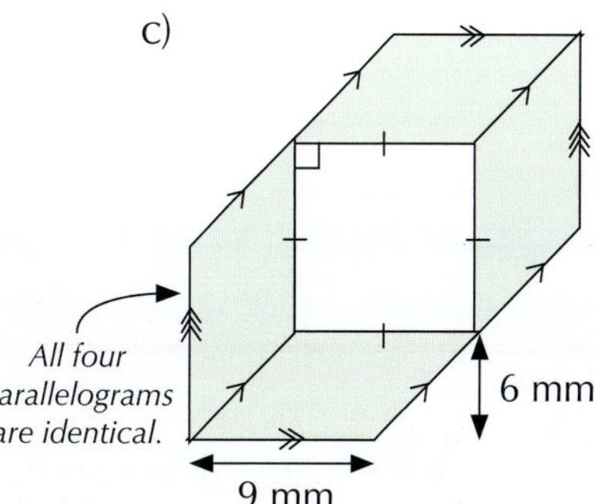

Q5 a) A 2p coin has a radius of 1.3 cm. What is its circumference to two decimal places?

b) A 5p coin has a diameter of 1.8 cm.
Which has the greater area: a 2p coin or two 5p coins?

Q6 Find the exact minor arc length and sector area for a circle with diameter 10 m and major sector angle 320°.

Exam-Style Questions

Q1 The circumference of a circle is π^2 cm.
Work out the radius of the circle.

[2 marks]

Q2 Raheel assembled the four pieces of wood shown below to make a photo frame.
Each piece of wood is in the shape of a trapezium. Find the total area of wood.

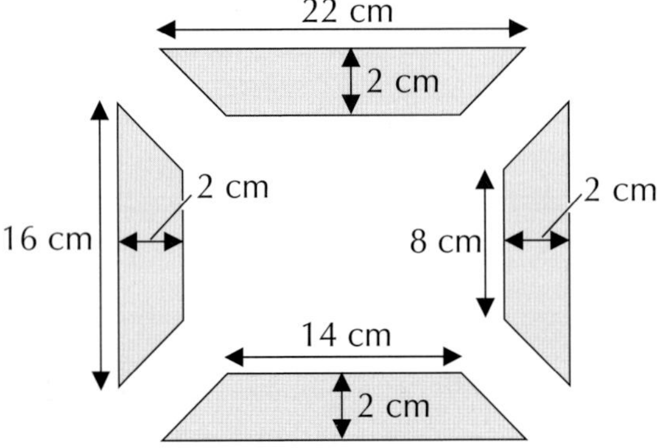

[3 marks]

Q3 The diagram below shows four identical circles enclosed within a square.
Each circle just touches two edges of the square and each of the circles next to it.

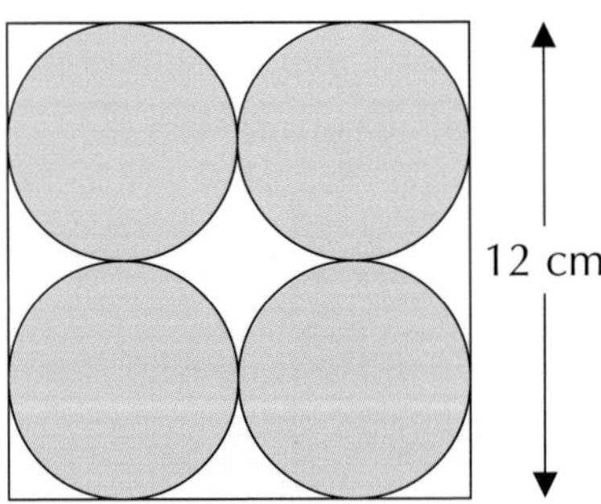

Find the area of the unshaded region.
Give your answer correct to two significant figures.

[4 marks]

Q4 The diagram on the right shows a sector of a circle with radius 16 cm. The perimeter of the sector is 41 cm.
Find the angle of the sector, θ, to the nearest degree.

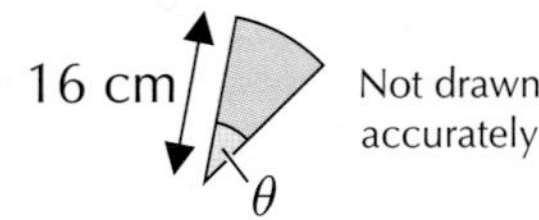

[4 marks]

Section 23 3D Shapes

23.1 Properties of 3D Shapes

3D (three-dimensional) shapes are objects that fill the real world. They have length, width and depth, unlike 2D shapes which are flat. They take all sorts of different forms, so let's start off by going through the ones you'll see most often in maths questions.

Different Solids

Learning Objective — Spec Ref G12:
Identify the faces, vertices and edges of 3D shapes.

Tip: 'Solids' is just another word for 3D shapes.

These are the most **common** solids that you need to be able to recognise.

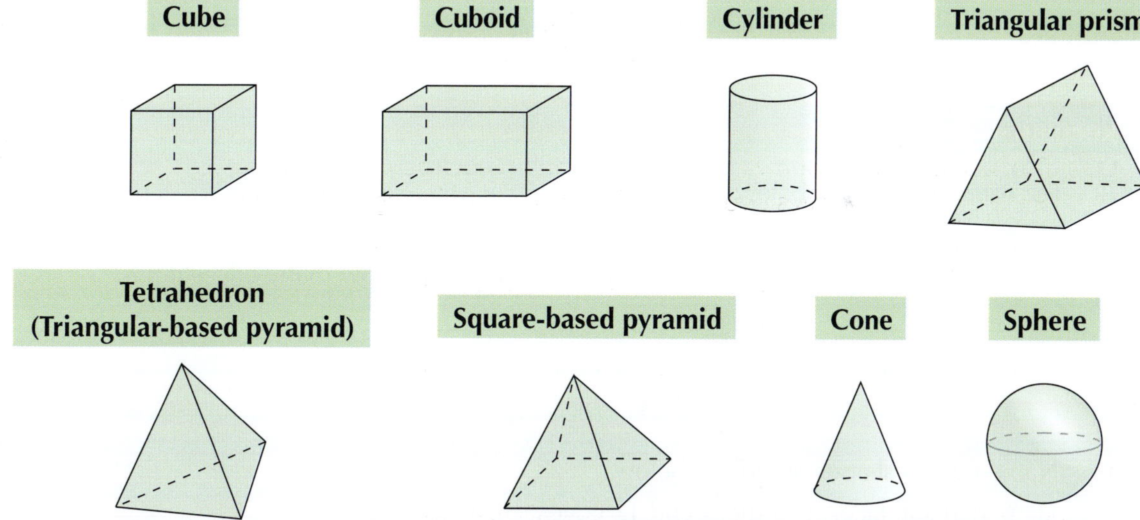

A **prism** is a 3D shape which has a **constant cross-section**.

This means that if you **slice** the shape anywhere along its length **parallel** to the faces at the end of the length, the new face you produce is **exactly the same** as those faces at the end.

For example, a **triangular prism** has a **triangle** as its constant cross-section and a **cylinder** has a **circle**.

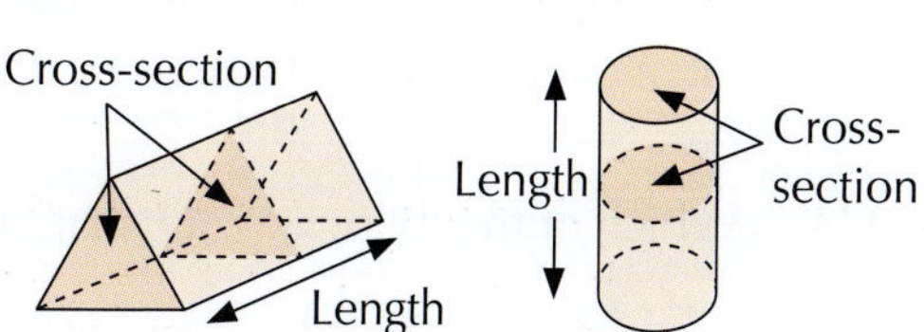

You need to know how to **describe** the different **parts** of a 3D shape.

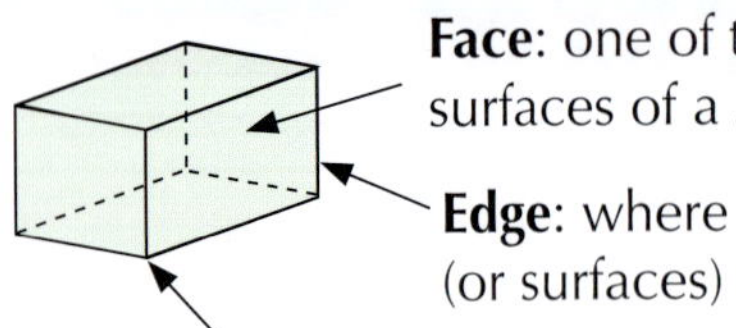
Face: one of the flat surfaces of a 3D shape.
Edge: where two faces (or surfaces) meet.
Vertex (plural = 'vertices'): a corner.

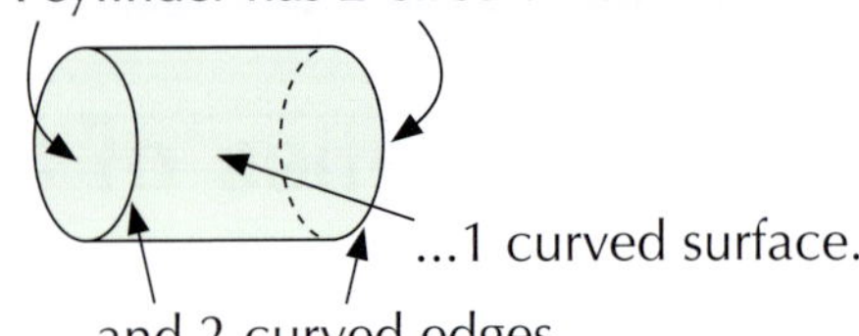
A cylinder has 2 circular faces...
...1 curved surface...
...and 2 curved edges.

Example 1

How many faces, vertices and edges does a cube have?

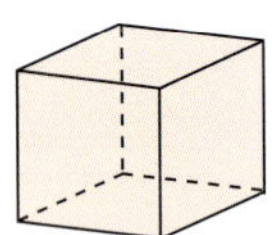

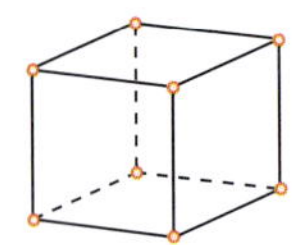

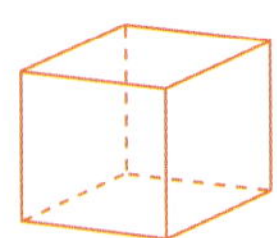

1. Count the number of flat surfaces.
2. Count the number of corners.
3. Count how many places two faces meet.

So a cube has **6 faces**, **8 vertices** and **12 edges**.

Exercise 1

Q1 For each of the solids below:

(i) give the name of the solid,

(ii) write down how many faces, how many vertices and how many edges it has.

a) 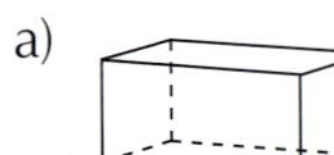

b) 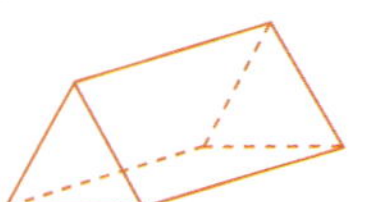

c) 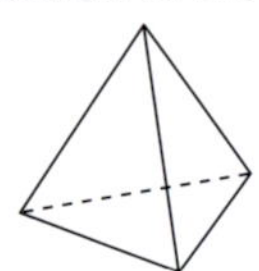

d) 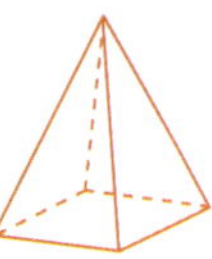

Q2 Name the 3D shapes described below.

a) 6 identical faces, 8 vertices and 12 edges

b) 2 parallel triangular faces, 3 rectangular faces

c) 4 triangular faces, 6 edges

d) 1 square face, 4 identical triangular faces

e) 2 circular faces, 1 curved surface and 2 curved edges

Q3 Which of the following 3D shapes are prisms?

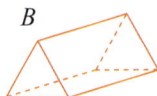

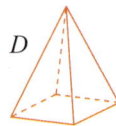

A 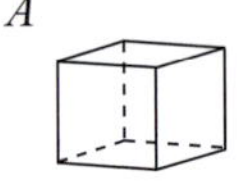

B 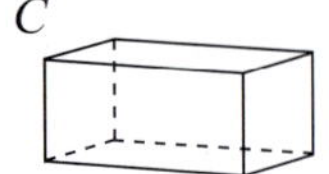

C

D 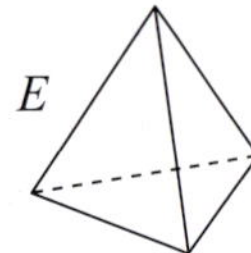

E

Nets

Learning Objective — Spec Ref G12:
Be able to use and draw nets of 3D shapes.

A **net** of a 3D shape is a **2D shape** (2D means two-dimensional, or '**flat**') that can be **folded** to make the 3D shape. For example, the nets of a cube and of a cylinder are shown below.

Net of a cube

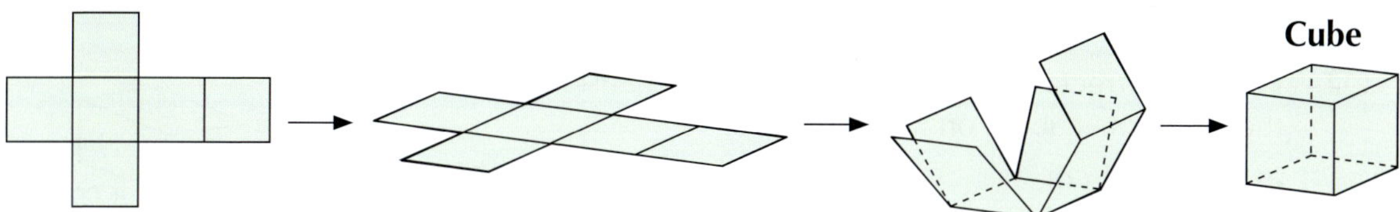

Net of a cylinder

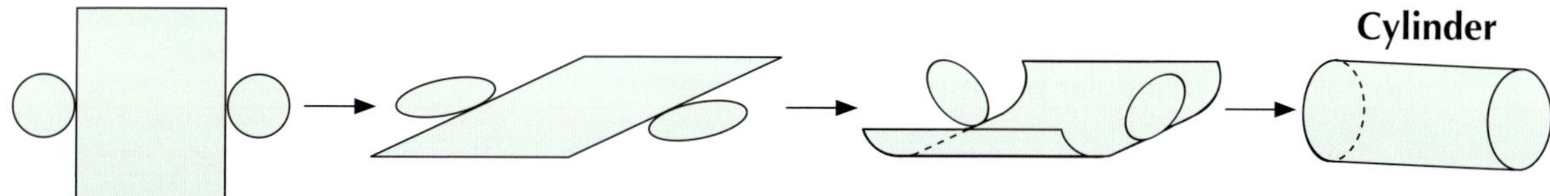

Example 2

How many triangles and how many rectangles are there in the net of a triangular prism?

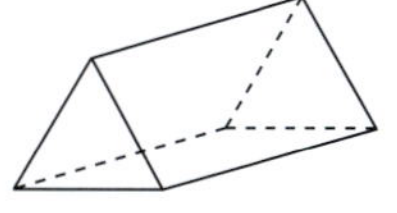

1. Sketch a triangular prism.

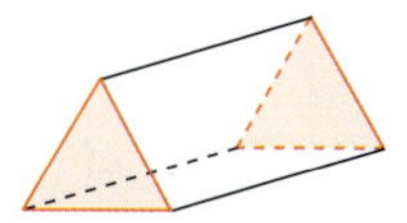

2. Count the triangular faces — this will be the number of triangles in the net.

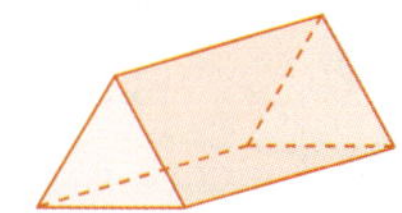

3. Count the rectangular faces — this will be the number of rectangles in the net.

So the net will have **2 triangles** and **3 rectangles**.

Exercise 2

Q1 State how many (i) squares and (ii) triangles there will be in the nets of the following.

a) tetrahedron b) cube c) square-based pyramid

Q2 How many faces will the 3D shape with this net have?

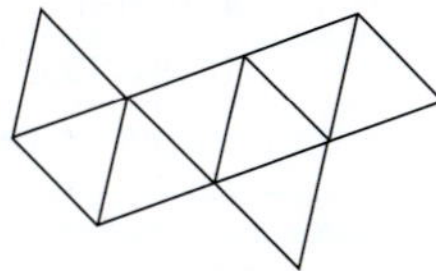

Q3 Name and sketch the 3D shapes with the following nets. Mark the edge lengths on your sketches.

a) 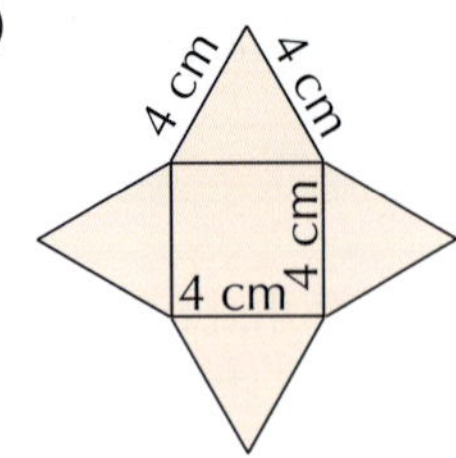

b) 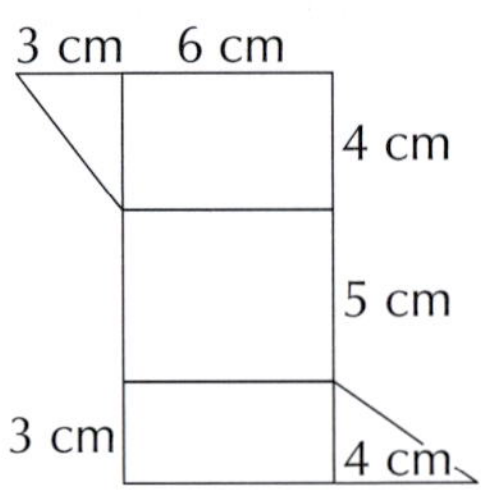

c) 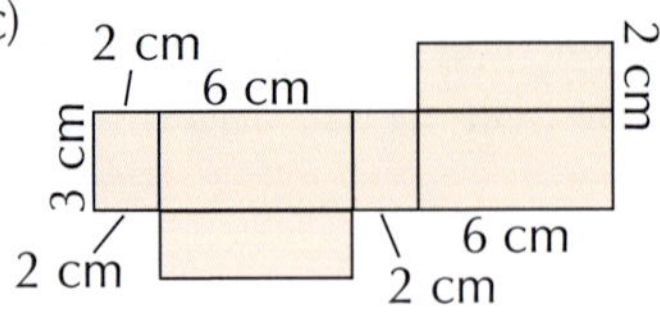

Q4 How many rectangles with the following dimensions will the net of the cuboid on the right have?

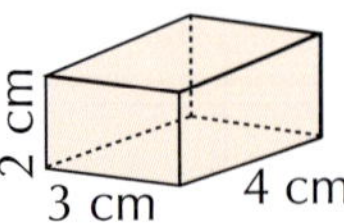

a) 2 cm × 3 cm b) 2 cm × 4 cm

c) 3 cm × 4 cm d) 2 cm × 2 cm

Q5 How many rectangles with the following dimensions will the net of the triangular prism on the right have?

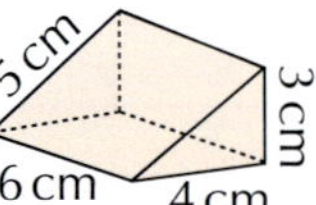

a) 4 cm × 6 cm b) 5 cm × 6 cm

c) 3 cm × 6 cm d) 3 cm × 4 cm

Q6 Which of the nets *A*, *B* or *C* is the net of the triangular prism shown below?

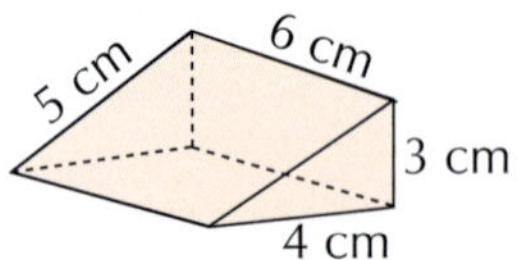

A 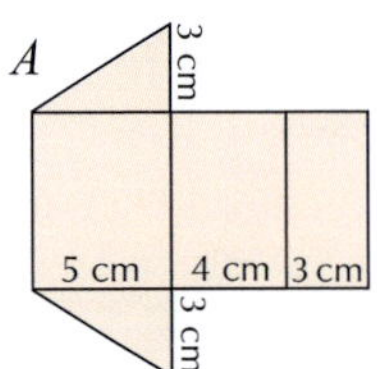

B 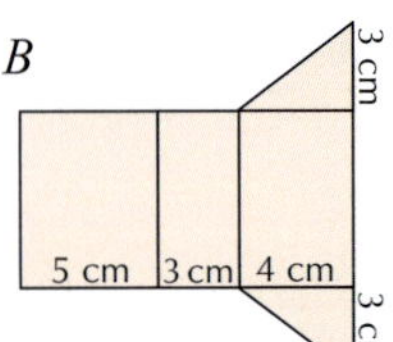

C 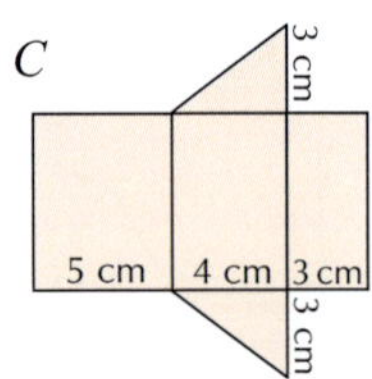

To draw the net of a 3D shape, imagine '**unfolding**' the shape so that **all its faces** are laid out **flat**. If you're not given a diagram of the 3D shape, it'll help if you make a quick **sketch** of it first.

Tip: Don't forget any hidden faces, such as the shape's base.

Example 3

Draw a net for a cuboid with dimensions 2 cm × 2 cm × 3 cm. Label the net with its dimensions.

1. Sketch the cuboid.

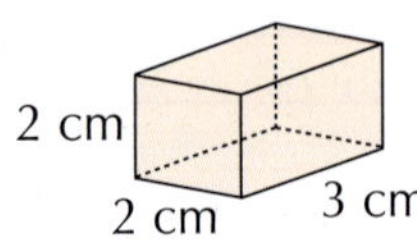

2. Draw it 'unfolded' — there could be several ways of doing this.

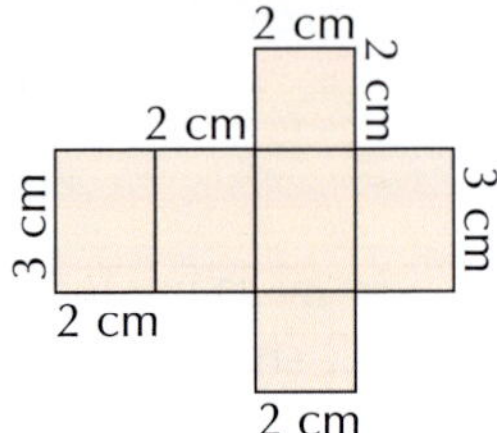

Example 4

Draw a net for the cylinder shown on the right. Label the net with its dimensions.

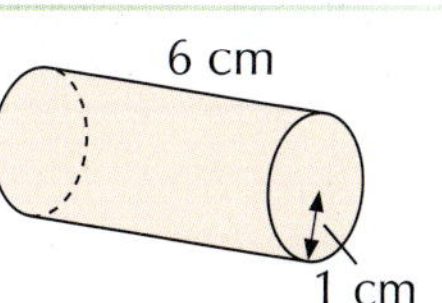

1. The tube can be 'unfolded' to give a rectangle. Its width will be 6 cm but you need to calculate its length, l.
2. The length is the same as the circumference of the circular ends of the cylinder, so use $C = 2\pi r$ (p.355).

$$l = 2\pi r$$
$$= 2 \times \pi \times 1$$
$$= 6.28 \text{ cm (2 d.p.)}$$

3. Draw and label the rectangle and add on the circular ends to the sides.

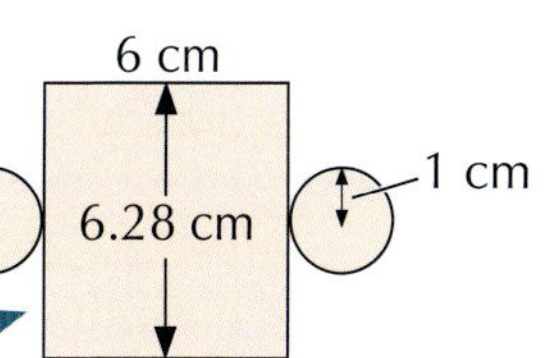

Exercise 3

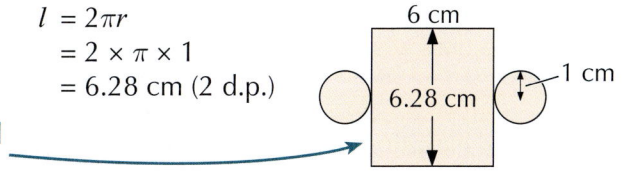

Q1 Copy and complete the unfinished nets of the objects shown below.

a)

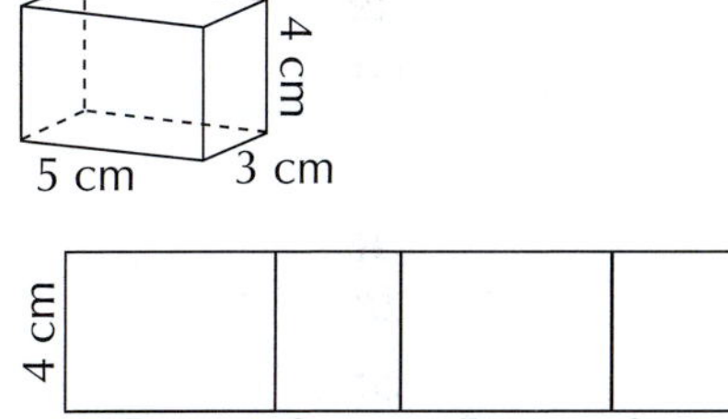

b)

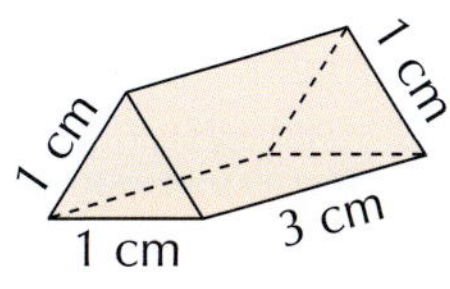

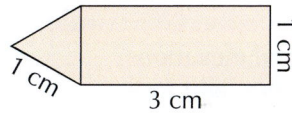

Q2 Draw a net of each of the following objects. Label each net with its dimensions.

a)

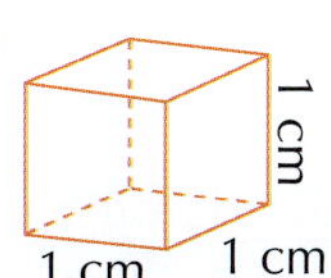

b)

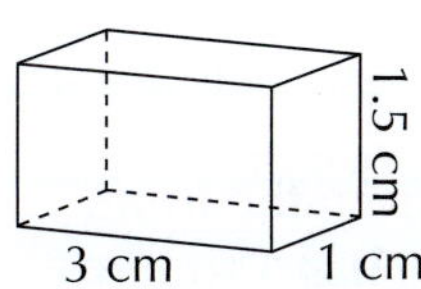

c)

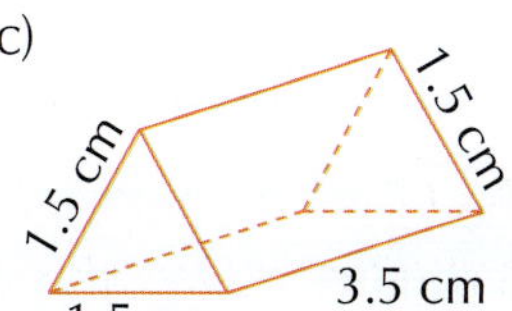

d)

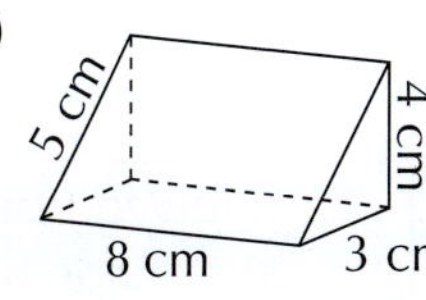

e)

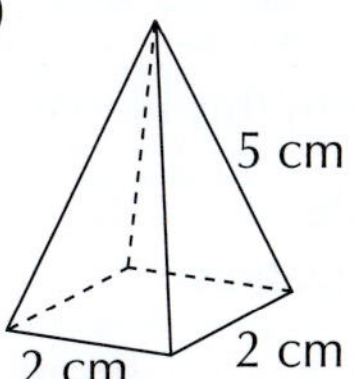

f)

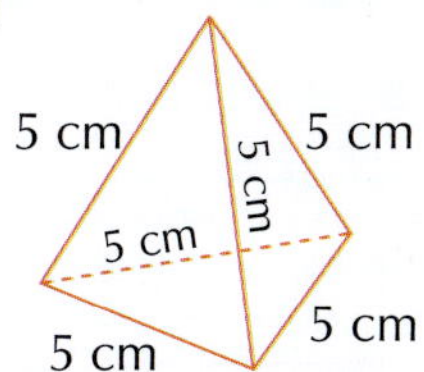

g)

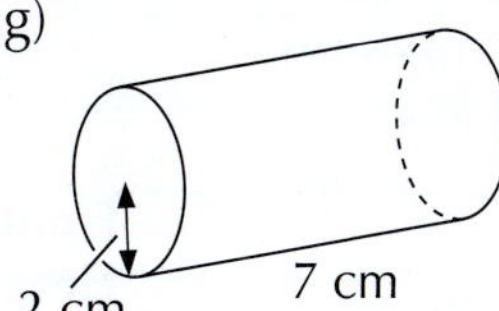

h)

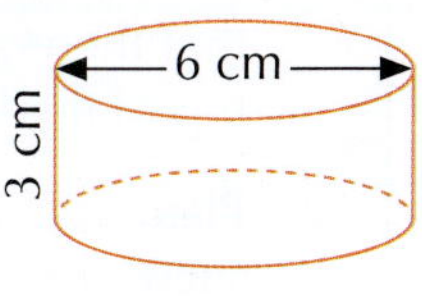

Q3 Draw a net of each of the following objects. Label each net with its dimensions.

a) a cube with 2 cm edges

b) a 1.5 cm × 2 cm × 2.5 cm cuboid

c) a tetrahedron with 3.5 cm edges

d) a cylinder of length 4 cm and radius 2.5 cm

23.2 Plans and Elevations

It can be difficult to draw 3D shapes accurately on paper — sometimes it's clearer to draw 2D plans and elevations of the 3D shape to show what it looks like from different sides.

Learning Objective — Spec Ref G13:
Be able to draw plans and elevations of 3D shapes.

Plans and **elevations**, also known as **projections**, are **2D representations** of **3D objects** viewed from particular directions. There are **three** different projections:

- **Plan** — the 2D view looking **vertically downwards** on the 3D object.
- **Front elevation** — the 2D view looking **horizontally** from the **front** of the 3D object.
- **Side elevation** — the 2D view looking **horizontally** from the **side** of the 3D object.

Tip: The directions for the front and side elevations are usually indicated by arrows.

Example 1

Draw the plan and elevations of the shape on the right from the directions indicated.

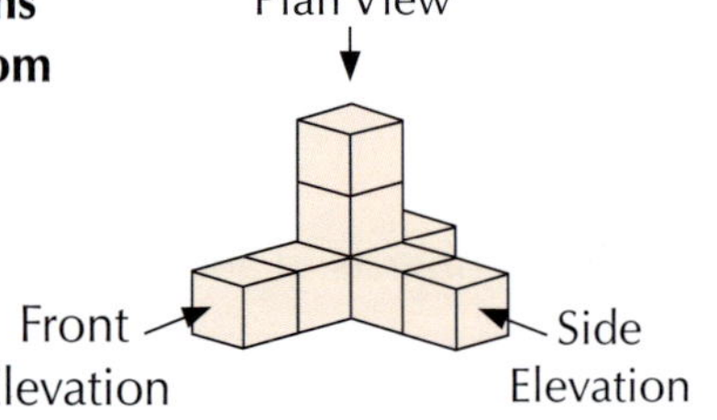

Tip: For the elevations, imagine you're standing in front and to the side of the shape.

1. Viewed from above, the shape has 6 squares arranged in a sideways T-shape. You can't tell that there are 2 cubes on top of the base layer.

Plan View

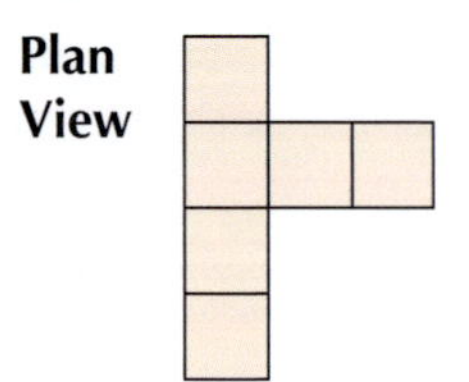

2. Viewed from the front, the shape has 5 squares in an L-shape. You can't see the change in depth.

Front Elevation

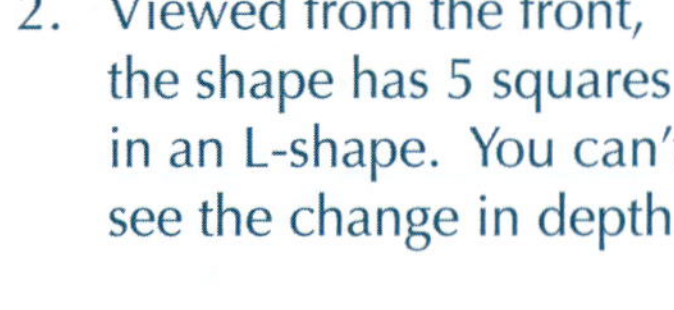

3. Viewed from the side, the shape has 6 squares in an upside-down T-shape. Again, you can't see a change in depth from this elevation.

Side Elevation

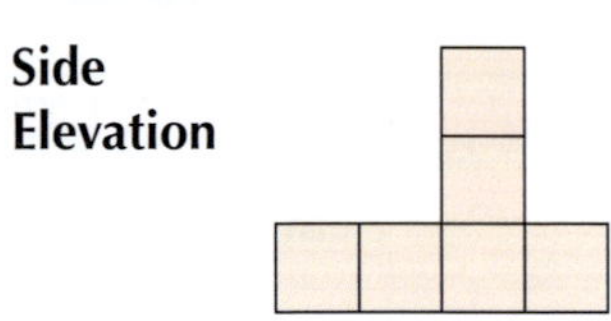

Exercise 1

Q1 Below are the front and side elevations of the given objects.
Draw the plan view for each.

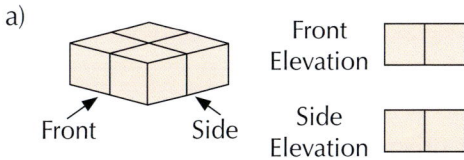

a)

Front Side

Front Elevation

Side Elevation

b)

Front Side

Front Elevation

Side Elevation

Q2 Below are the plan view and front elevation of the given objects.
Draw the side elevation for each.

a)

b)

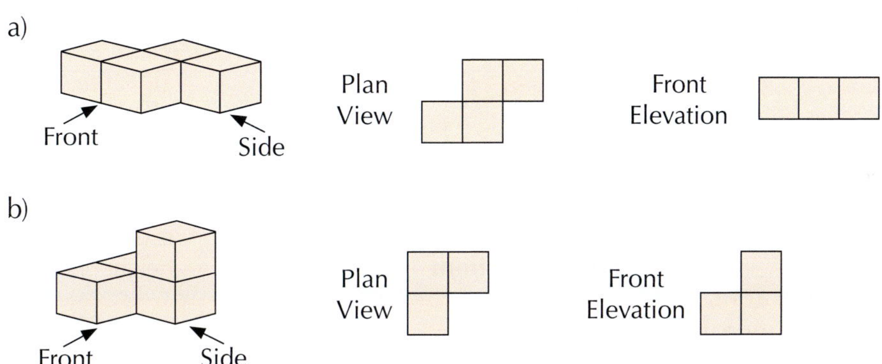

Q3 For each of the following, draw:

(i) the plan view,

(ii) the front and side elevations, using the directions shown in a).

a)

Front Side

b)

c)

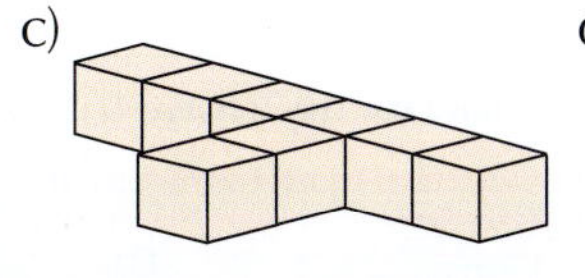

d)

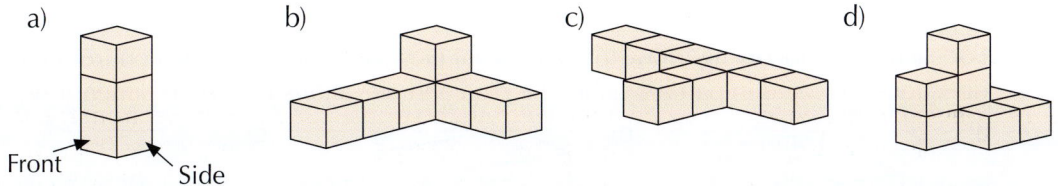

Q4 Which of the solid objects *A*, *B* or *C* below corresponds to the plan and elevations shown?

Plan View

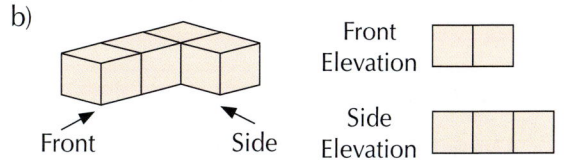

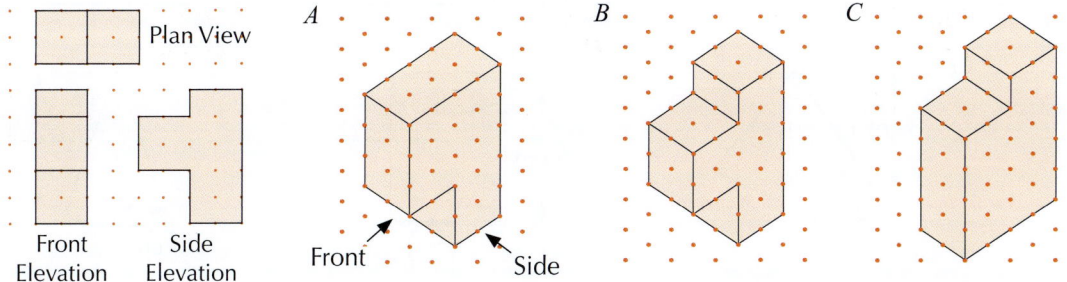

Front Elevation Side Elevation

A

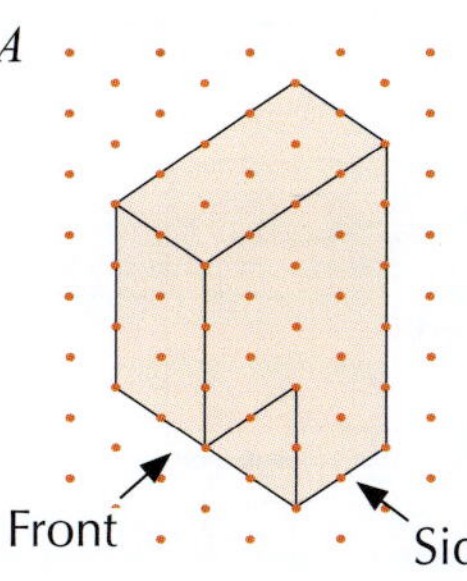

B

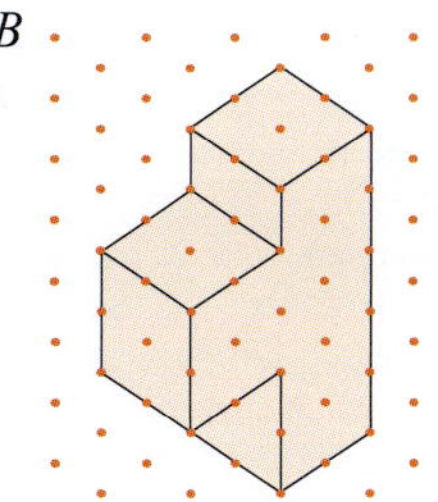

C

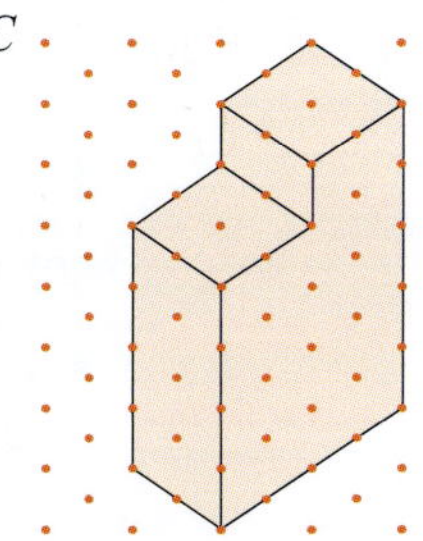

Projections are trickier when the 3D shape has **sloped** or **curved** faces, but it helps to think about how the shape would look if it was **squashed flat** from the direction you're given. A **sloping** face is always projected as the **same type** of shape (e.g. a sloping triangular face will be projected onto a triangle) — but its **dimensions** will be decided by the dimensions of **other faces** of the shape. The example below shows how this works.

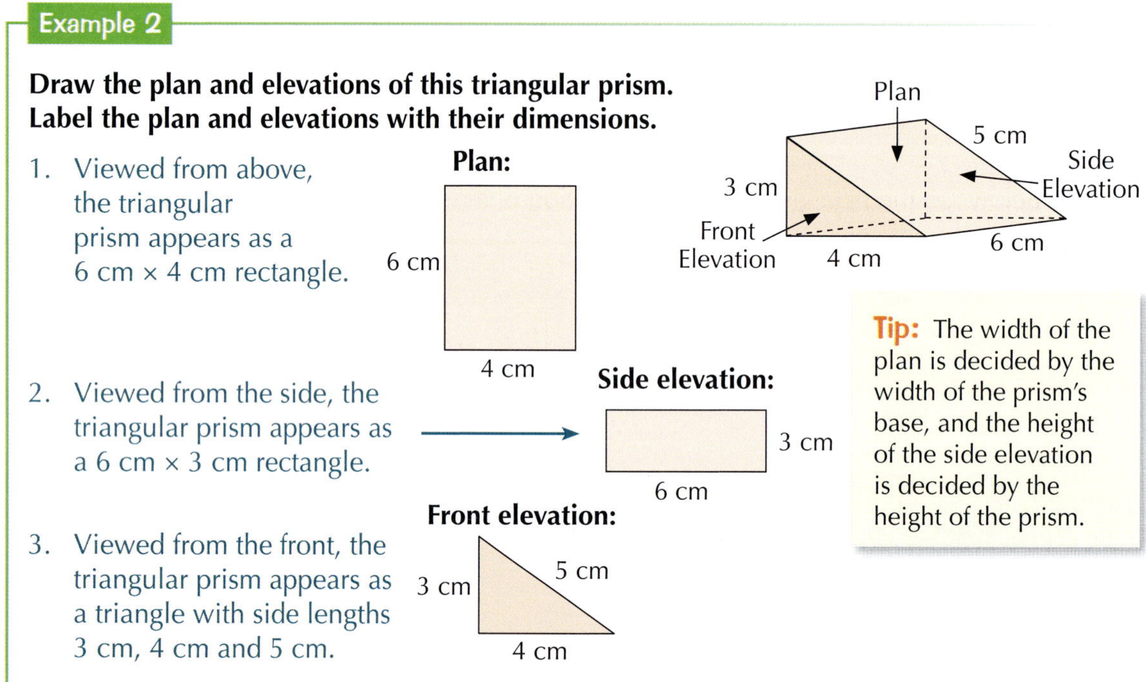

Example 2
Draw the plan and elevations of this triangular prism.
Label the plan and elevations with their dimensions.
Plan
5 cm
Side
Elevation
3 cm
Front
Elevation
4 cm
6 cm
1. Viewed from above, the triangular prism appears as a 6 cm × 4 cm rectangle.
Plan:
6 cm
4 cm
2. Viewed from the side, the triangular prism appears as a 6 cm × 3 cm rectangle.
Side elevation:
3 cm
6 cm
3. Viewed from the front, the triangular prism appears as a triangle with side lengths 3 cm, 4 cm and 5 cm.
Front elevation:
3 cm
5 cm
4 cm
Tip: The width of the plan is decided by the width of the prism's base, and the height of the side elevation is decided by the height of the prism.

Exercise 2

Q1 For each of the following, draw the plan, front elevation and side elevation from the directions indicated in part a). Label the plan and elevations with their dimensions.

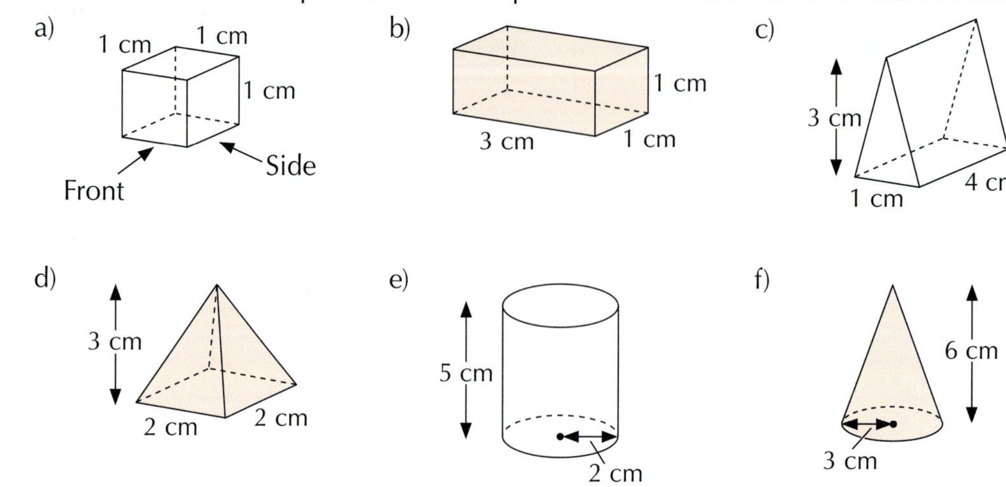

23.3 Isometric Drawings

Pictures of 3D shapes drawn on a grid of dots or lines arranged in a pattern of equilateral triangles are called isometric drawings.

Learning Objective — Spec Ref G13:
Be able to draw 3D shapes on isometric paper.

The grid of **dots** and grid of **lines** on the right are examples of **isometric paper**.

To draw a 3D shape on isometric paper, you have to use the following rules:

- **Vertical lines** on the shape are shown by **vertical lines** on the isometric paper.
- **Horizontal lines** on the shape are shown by **diagonal lines** on the isometric paper.

Each space between the dots in the vertical or diagonal directions represents **one unit of length** (e.g. 1 cm or 1 m).

Example 1

Draw the triangular prism shown on the right on isometric paper.

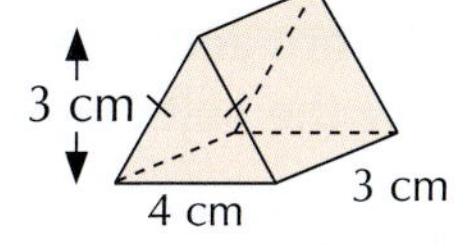

1. Join the dots with vertical lines for the vertical lines in the 3D shape and with diagonal lines for the horizontal lines.
2. Build up the drawing as shown below, using the dots to show the dimensions.
3. The triangle has a vertical height of 3 cm, so draw a vertical line 3 spaces long.
4. It has a horizontal width of 4 cm, so draw a diagonal line 4 spaces long.
5. The depth of the object is 3 cm so draw a diagonal line 3 spaces long.

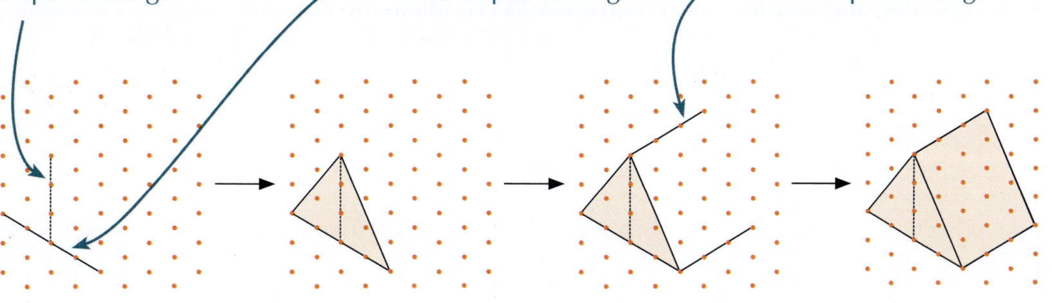

Exercise 1

Q1 Draw the following cuboids and prisms on isometric paper.

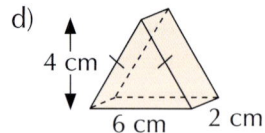

a) 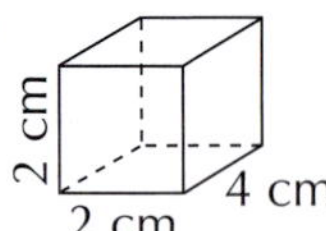

b) 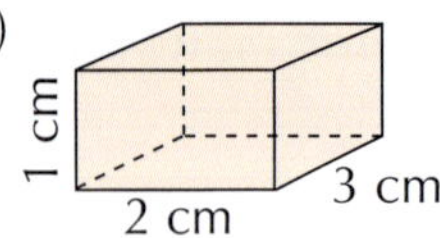

c) 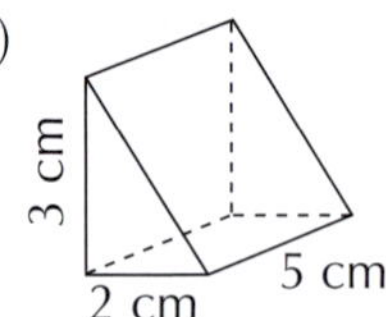

d) 4 cm 6 cm 2 cm

Q2 Draw the following prisms on isometric paper.

a) 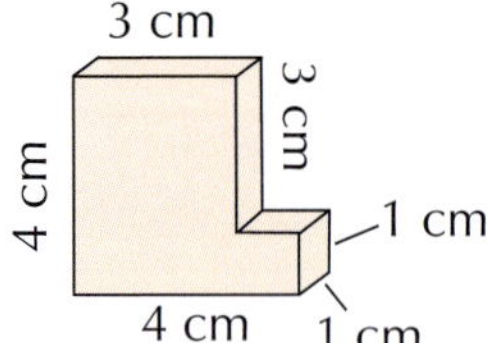

b) 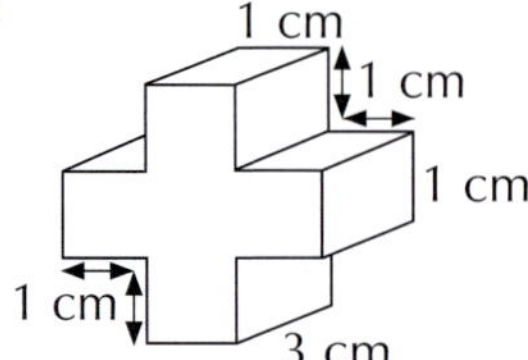

c) 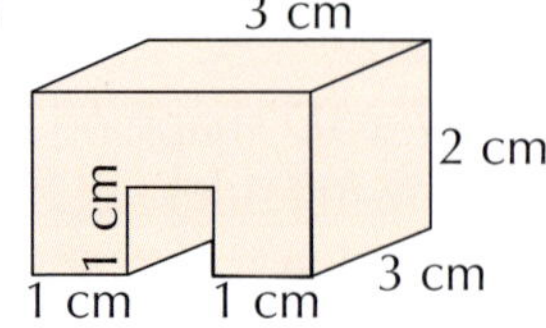

You can also use **projections** (see p.368) to draw 3D shapes on isometric paper. It's often helpful to **picture** or **sketch the shape** first, then use the dimensions to draw it **accurately**.

Example 2

The diagram on the right shows the plan, and front and side elevations of a 3D object. Draw the object on isometric paper.

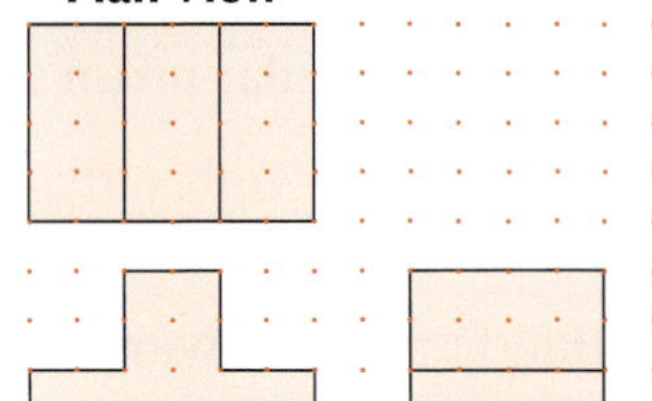

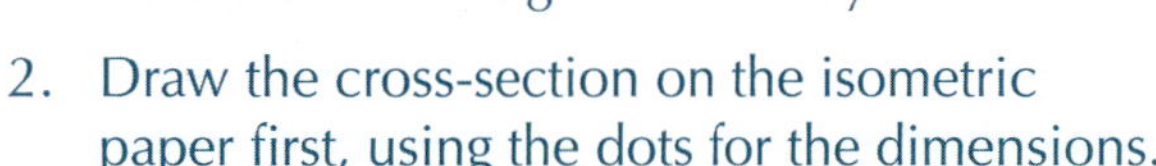

1. Try to picture the shape. It's a prism with the front elevation as its cross-section, which you can see since the plan view and side elevation have the same height all the way across.
2. Draw the cross-section on the isometric paper first, using the dots for the dimensions.
3. Use the side elevation and plan view to complete the drawing.

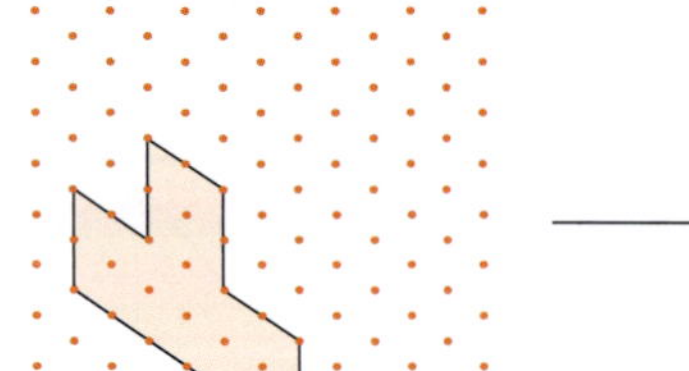
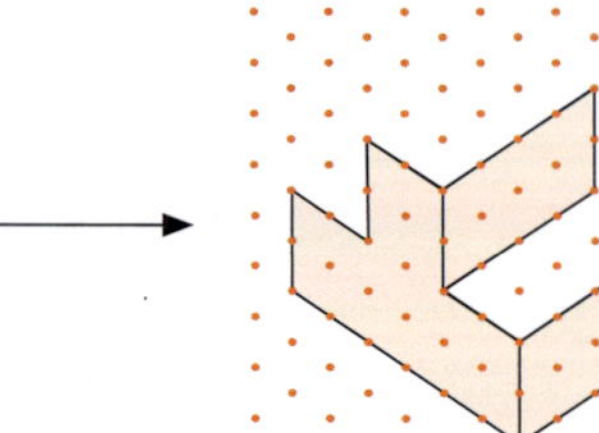
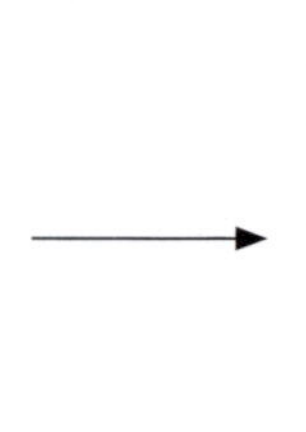
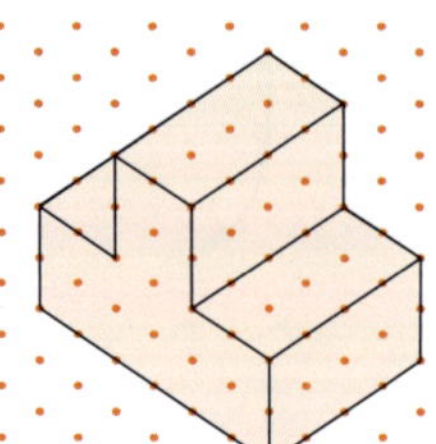

Exercise 2

Q1 The following diagrams show the constant cross-section of prisms of length 3 cm. Draw each prism on isometric paper.

a) 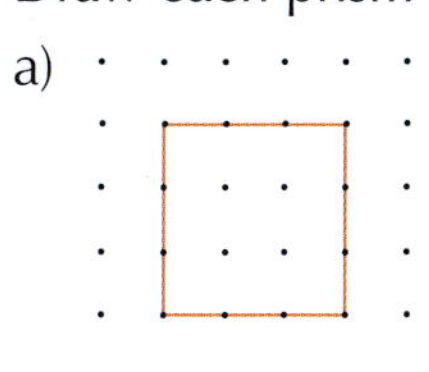

b) 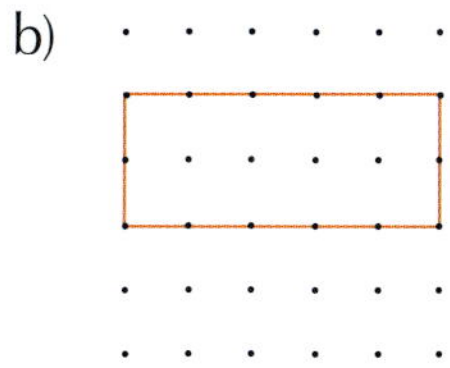

c) 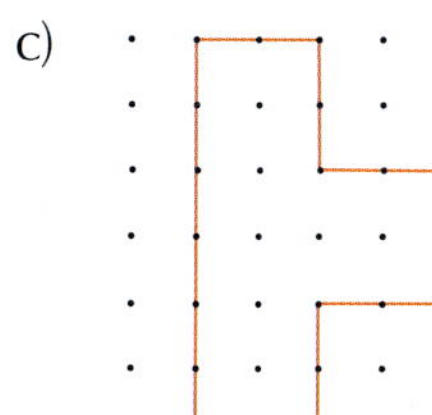

Q2 The following diagrams show the constant cross-section of prisms of length 2 cm. Draw each prism on isometric paper.

a) 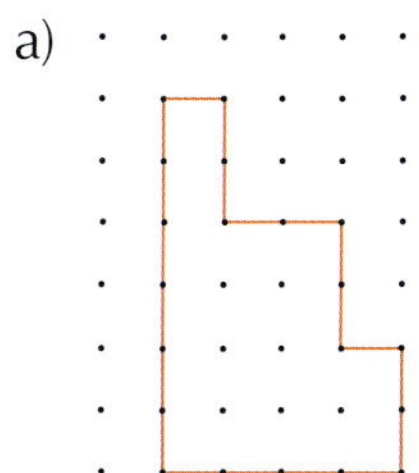

b) 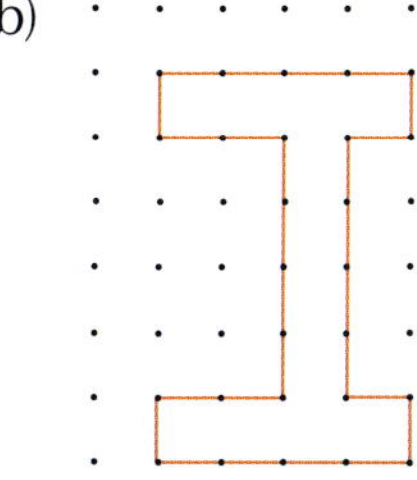

c) 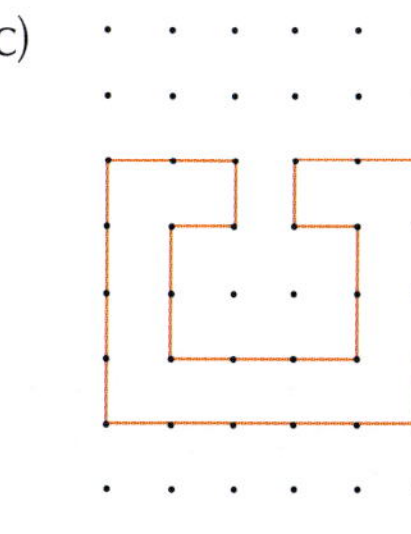

Q3 The following diagrams show the plan, and front and side elevations of different 3D objects. For each of the objects:

(i) use the projections to sketch the object and label the dimensions,

(ii) draw each object on isometric paper.

a) 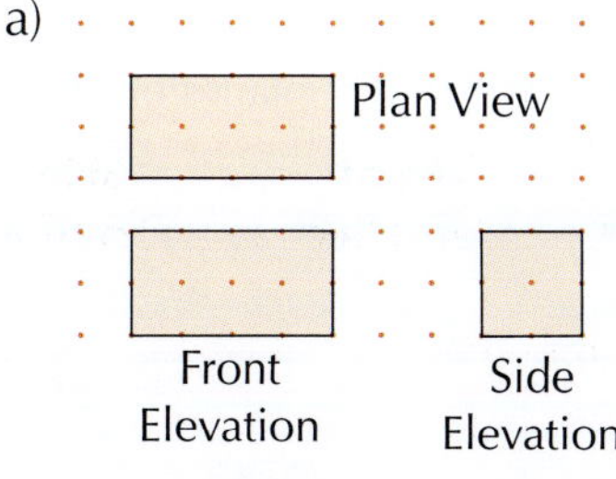

b) 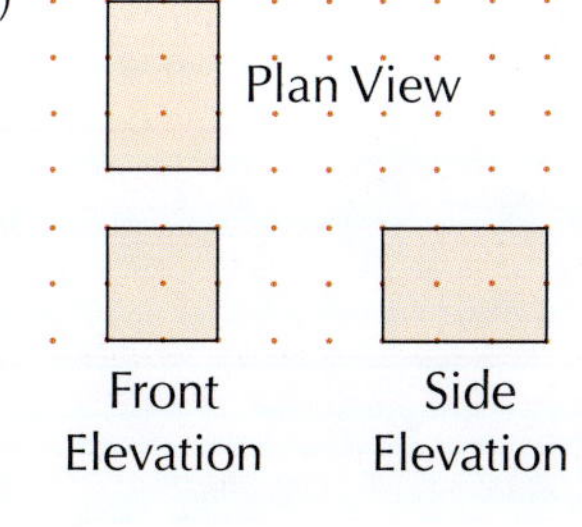

c) 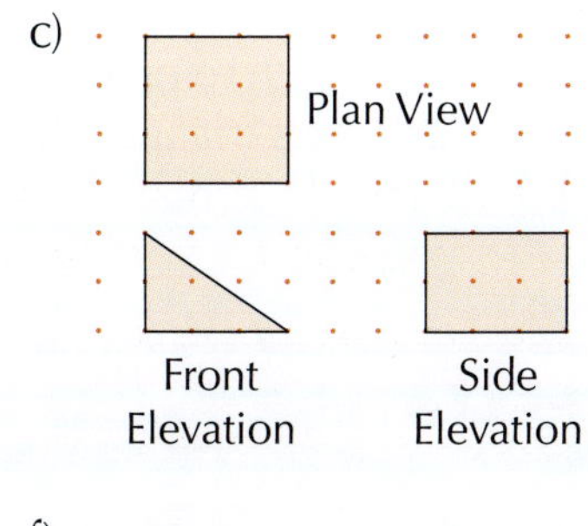

d) 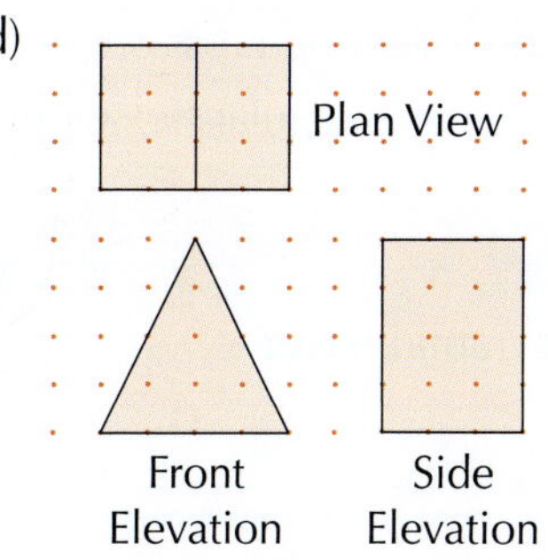

e) 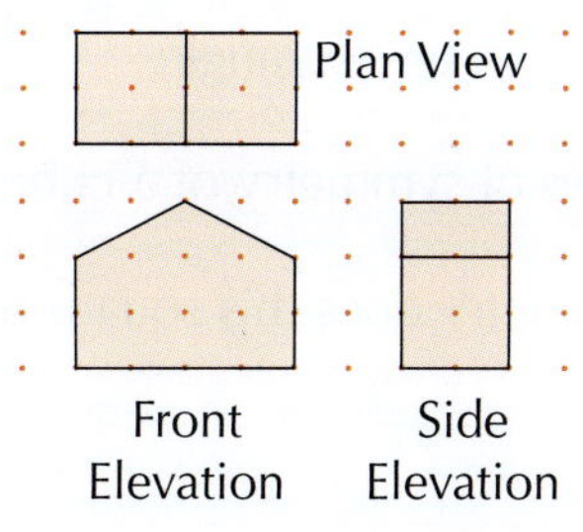

f) 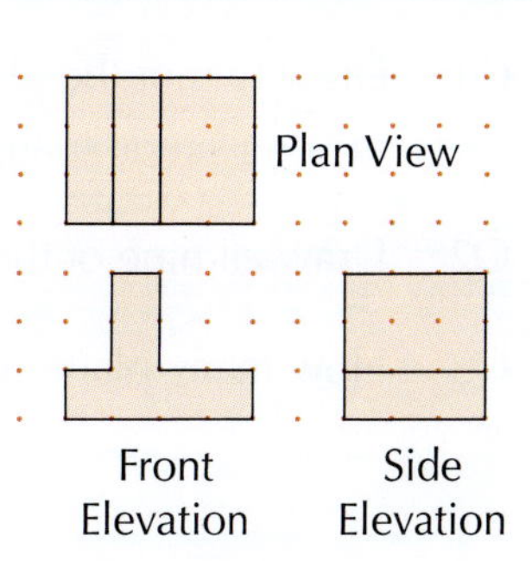

23.4 Symmetry of 3D Shapes

While 2D objects have lines of symmetry, 3D objects have planes of symmetry.

Learning Objective — Spec Ref G12:
Be able to draw the planes of symmetry of a 3D shape.

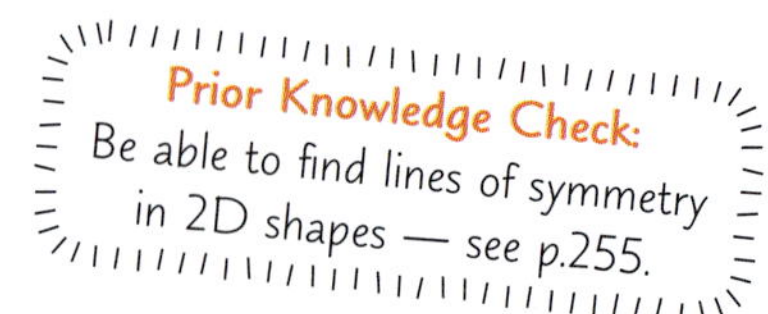

Prior Knowledge Check:
Be able to find lines of symmetry in 2D shapes — see p.255.

A **plane of symmetry** cuts a solid into **two identical halves**. To picture where they are, imagine **slicing** through the solid with a knife. The two pieces that you create should be **exactly the same** and **mirror images** of one another.

To find planes of symmetry, think about the **lines of symmetry** of the faces. You might be able to cut along these to create a plane of symmetry. For **prisms**, you should first look at the face that shows the **cross-section**, while for **pyramids**, you should look at the **base**.

Example 1

Draw the planes of symmetry of this isosceles triangular prism.

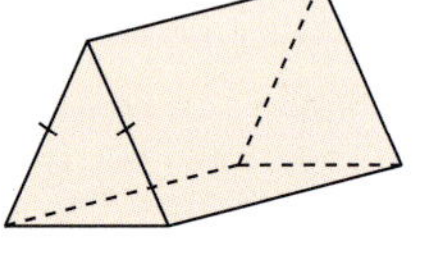

1. Imagine cutting through the solid to produce two halves.
2. First, look at the lines of symmetry of the cross-section. There's only one, and cutting along here splits the prism into two new prisms with right-angled triangles as their cross-section.

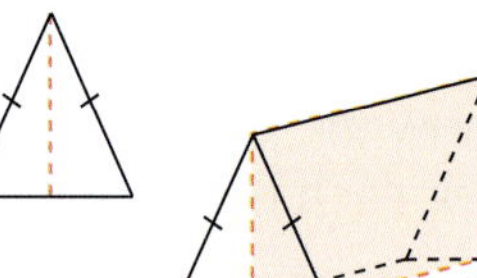

3. You can also cut halfway along the length to produce two smaller isosceles triangular prisms.

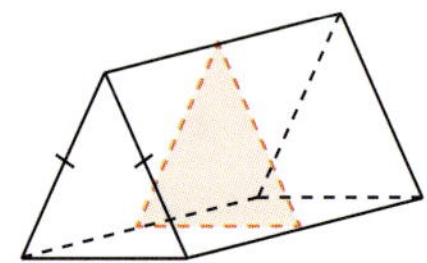

Tip: Prisms usually have one more plane of symmetry than the number of lines of symmetry of the cross-section. The only exception is a cube which has nine planes of symmetry.

Exercise 1

Q1 Draw two of the planes of symmetry of the prisms with the following cross-sections.
a) equilateral triangle b) rectangle c) regular hexagon

Q2 Draw all nine of the planes of symmetry of a cube.

Q3 How many planes of symmetry does this square-based pyramid have?

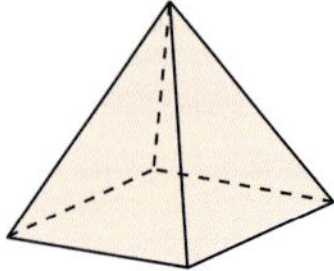

23.5 Volume

The volume of a 3D shape is the amount of space inside the shape — it's measured in cubic units, e.g. cm^3 or m^3.

Cubes and Cuboids

Learning Objective — Spec Ref G16:
Be able to find the volume of cubes and cuboids.

A **cuboid** is a 3D shape with **six rectangular faces** (see p.363).
The **volume** of a cuboid is found using the following formula:

Volume = Length × Width × Height

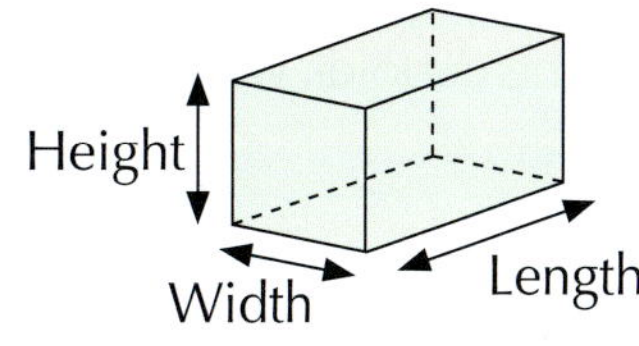

A **cube** is a special type of cuboid — all six of the faces are **squares**.
This means all of the edges have the **same length**, so the volume is given by:

Volume = Length × Length × Length = $(\text{Length})^3$

Tip: The units for volume are cubed because you're multiplying three dimensions — length, width, height. Make sure all three are in the same units.

Example 1

Find the volume of the cuboid shown in the diagram.

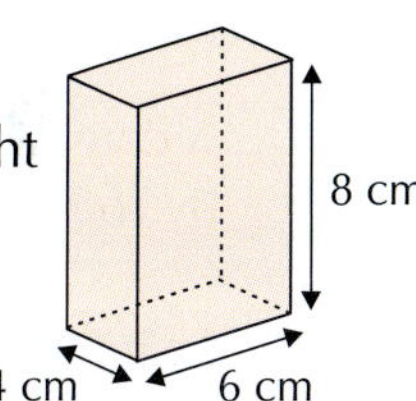

1. Write down the formula for volume. Volume = length × width × height
2. Substitute the values into the formula. Volume = 6 cm × 4 cm × 8 cm
3. Calculate the volume — don't forget the units. = **192 cm^3**

Exercise 1

Q1 The following shapes are made up of cubes with edges of length 1 cm.
Find the volumes of the shapes.

a) 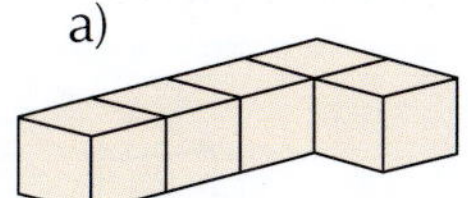

b) 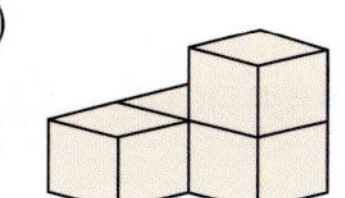

c) 

d) 

Q2 Find the volumes of the following cuboids.

a)

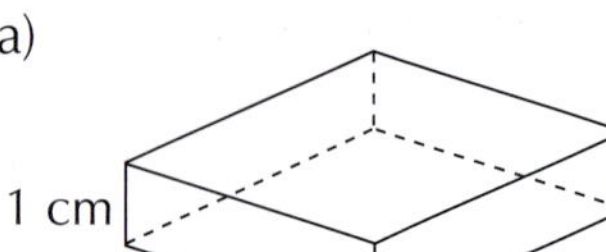

b)

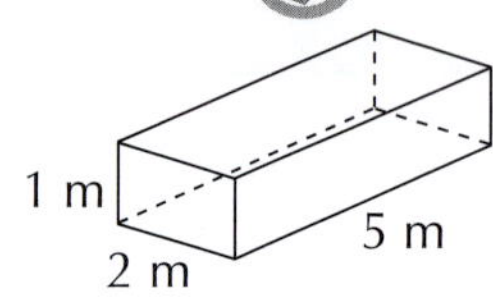

c)

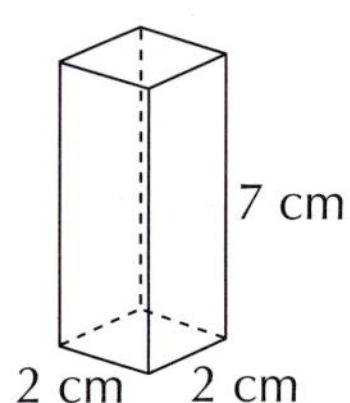

d)

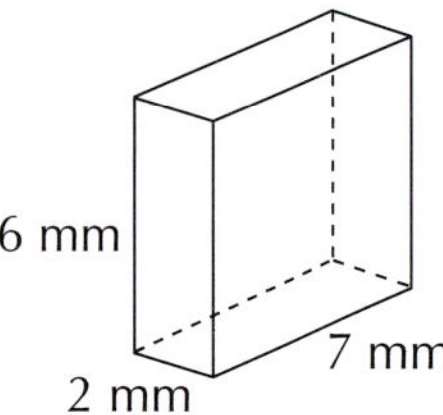

e)

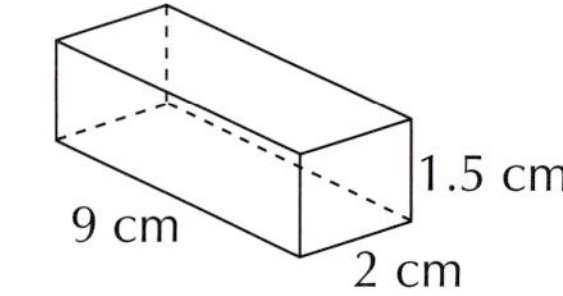

f)

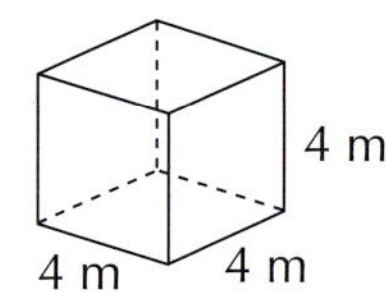

Q3 Find the volumes of the cuboids with the following dimensions.

a) 3 cm × 2 cm × 4 cm

b) 5 m × 2 m × 7 m

c) 20 cm × 10 cm × 8 cm

d) 2.5 cm × 3.0 cm × 4.2 cm

e) 18 m × 14 m × 3 m

f) 1.8 mm × 3.2 mm × 6.1 mm

Q4 a) Estimate the volume of a cube whose edges are 3.2 mm long by rounding the measurements to 1 s.f.

b) Is this an overestimate or an underestimate?

Q5 Will 3.5 m^3 of sand fit in a cuboid-shaped box with dimensions 1.7 m × 1.8 m × 0.9 m?

Q6 A cereal box is 9 cm long, 23 cm wide and 32 cm high. The box is half full of cereal. By rounding measurements to 1 s.f., estimate the volume of cereal in the box.

Q7 Split the following 3D objects into cuboids to find their volumes.

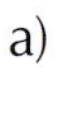

a)

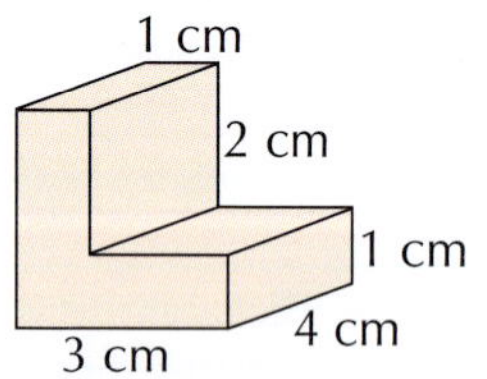

b)

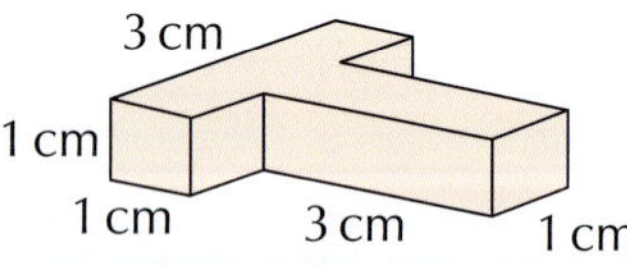

Q8 A matchbox is 5 cm long and 3 cm wide and has a volume of 18 cm^3. What is its height?

Q9 A bath can be modelled as a cuboid with dimensions 1.5 m × 0.5 m × 0.6 m, as shown.

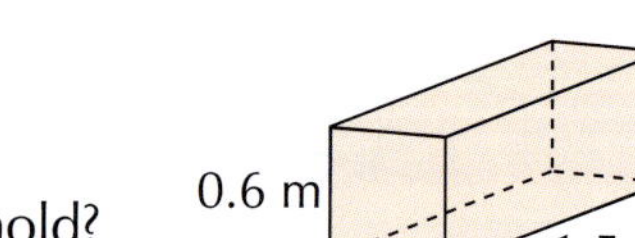

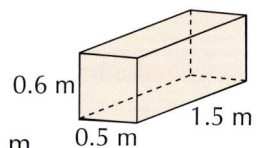

a) What is the maximum volume of water that the bath will hold?

b) Find the volume of water needed to fill the bath to a height of 0.3 m.

c) Find the height of the water if the volume of water in the bath is 0.3 m^3.

Prisms

Learning Objective — Spec Ref G16:
Be able to find the volume of prisms, including cylinders.

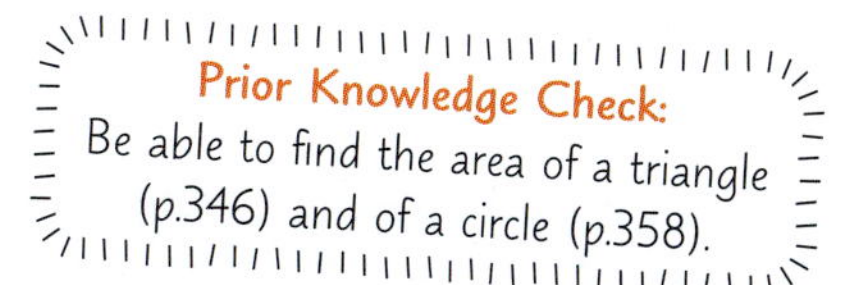

Prior Knowledge Check:
Be able to find the area of a triangle (p.346) and of a circle (p.358).

A **prism** is a 3D shape which has a **constant cross-section** (see p.363).
The **volume** of a prism is given by the following formula:

Volume = Area of Cross-Section × Length

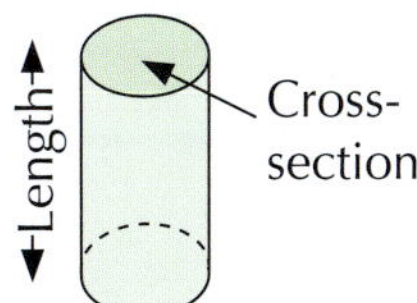

The area of the cross-section for a **triangular prism** is the area of a triangle ($\frac{1}{2}$ **× base × height**), and for a **cylinder** it's the area of a circle (πr^2).

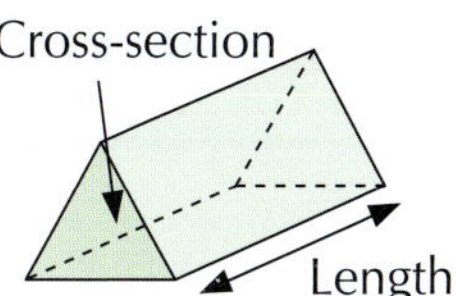

Example 2

Find the volume of each of the shapes shown on the right.

a)

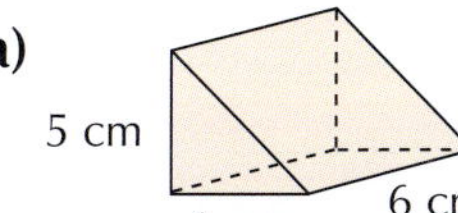

b)

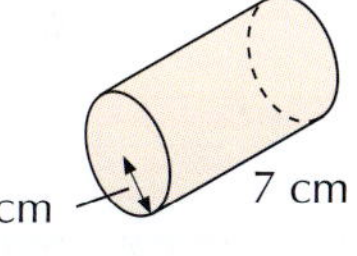

a) 1. Work out the area of the cross-section. Here it's a triangle, so calculate the area of the triangle.

Area of cross-section = area of triangle $= \frac{1}{2} \times \text{base} \times \text{height} = \frac{1}{2} \times 4 \times 5 = 10 \text{ cm}^2$

2. Multiply the cross-sectional area by the length of the prism.

Volume = area of cross-section × length $= 10 \times 6 =$ **60 cm³**

b) 1. Work out the area of the cross-section. Here it's a circle, so use area $= \pi r^2$.

Area of cross-section = area of circle $= \pi r^2 = \pi \times 2^2 = 4\pi \text{ cm}^2$

2. Multiply the cross-sectional area by the length of the prism.

Volume = area of cross-section × length $= 4\pi \times 7 =$ **88.0 cm³** (1 d.p.)

Example 3

Find the volume of the shape shown on the right.

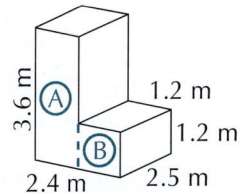

1. To work out the area of the cross-section, split it into 2 separate rectangles, as shown.

Area of rectangle A $= 1.2 \times 3.6 = 4.32 \text{ m}^2$
Area of rectangle B $= 1.2 \times 1.2 = 1.44 \text{ m}^2$

2. Add the two areas together.

Area of cross-section $= 4.32 + 1.44 = 5.76 \text{ m}^2$

3. Multiply the cross-sectional area by the length of the prism.

Volume = area of cross-section × length $= 5.76 \times 2.5 =$ **14.4 m³**

Exercise 2

Q1 Find the volumes of the prisms with the following cross-sectional areas and lengths.

a) area = 2 cm^2, length = 3 cm
b) area = 6 cm^2, length = 9 cm
c) area = 1.5 m^2, length = 6 m
d) area = 3.5 cm^2, length = 3.5 cm
e) area = 9.25 mm^2, length = 1.75 mm
f) area = 11.6 mm^2, length = 9.1 mm

Q2 Find the volumes of the following prisms.

a)
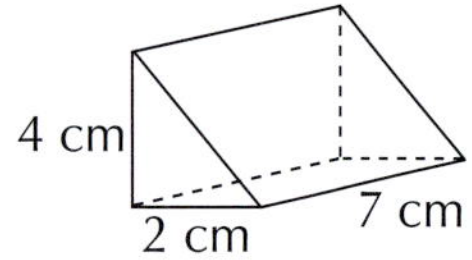

b)
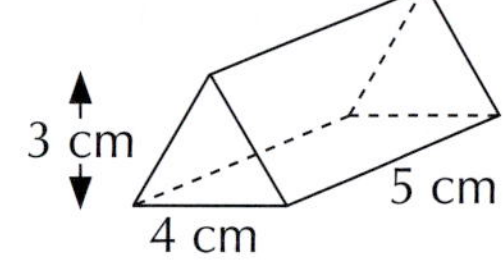

c)
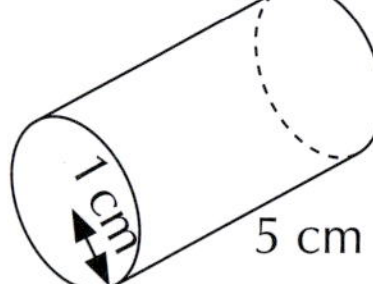

Q3 The following diagrams show the cross-sections of prisms of the length shown. Find the volume of each prism. The grid spacing is 1 cm.

a)
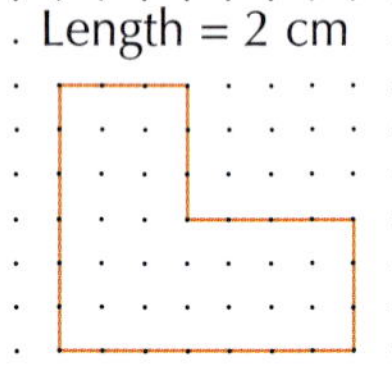

b)
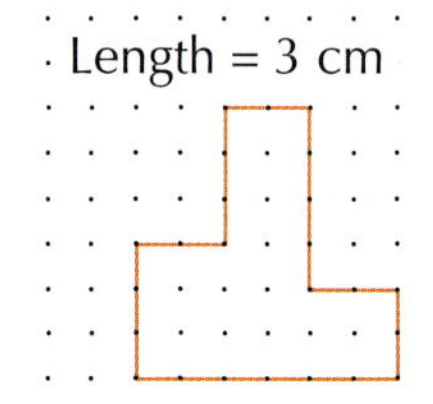

c)
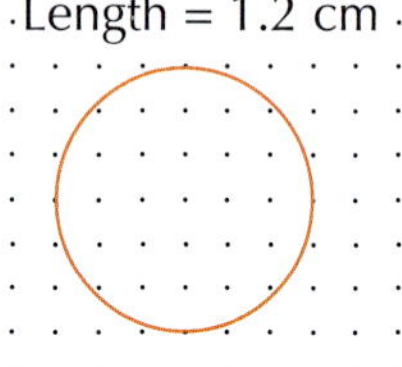

Q4 Find the volumes of the following prisms.

a) a triangular prism of base 13 cm, vertical height 12 cm and length 8 cm
b) a triangular prism of base 4.2 m, vertical height 1.3 m and length 3.1 m
c) a cylinder of radius 4 m and length 18 m
d) a prism with parallelogram cross-section of base 3 m and vertical height 4.2 m, and length 1.5 m

Q5 By first calculating their cross-sectional areas, find the volumes of the following prisms.

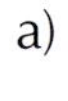

a)
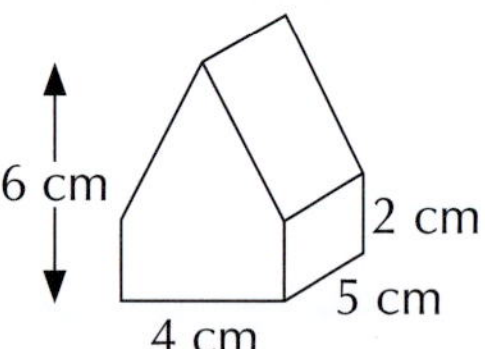

b)
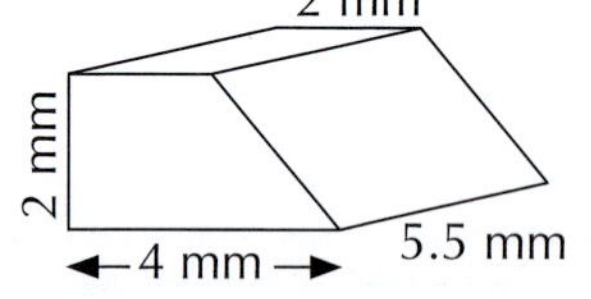

c)
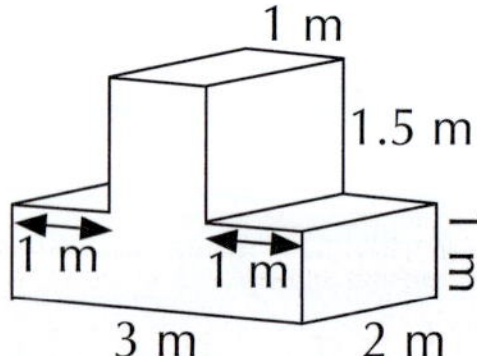

Q6 The following diagrams show prisms drawn on isometric paper with grid spacing 1 cm. Find the volume of each prism.

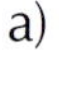

a)
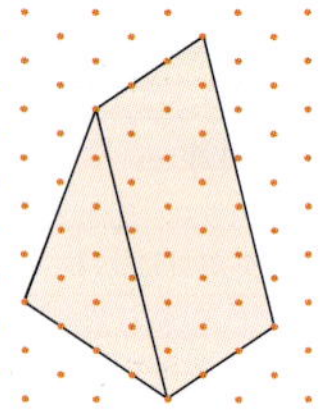

b)
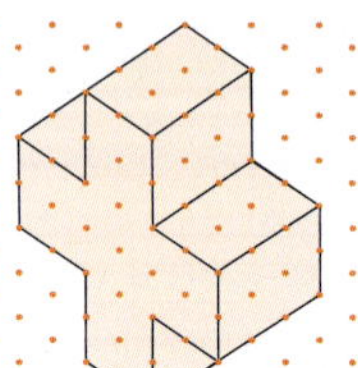

c)
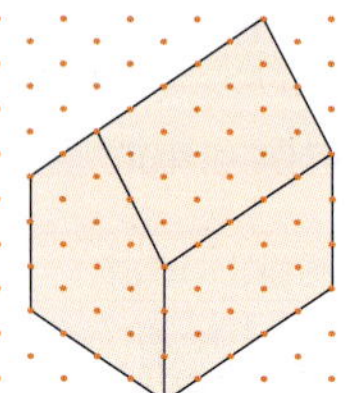

d)
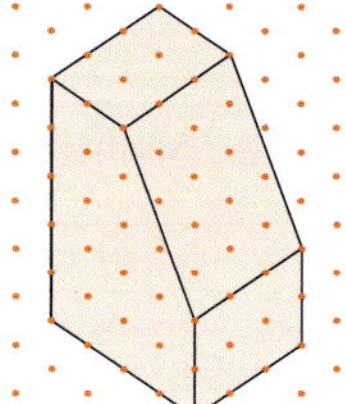

Spheres

Learning Objective — Spec Ref G17:
Be able to find the volume of spheres.

A **sphere** has one curved face, no vertices and no edges.
To find the volume of a sphere, you need to know its **radius** — the distance from the **centre** of the sphere to **any point on its surface**.
For a sphere with radius r, the formula for **volume** is as follows:

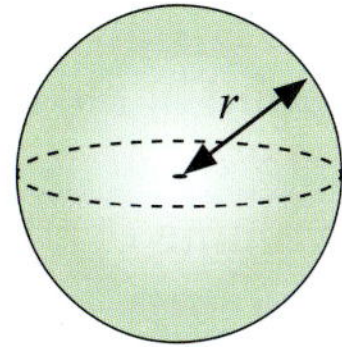

$$\textbf{Volume} = \frac{4}{3}\pi r^3$$

Example 4

Find the exact volume of a sphere with radius 6 cm.

1. Substitute $r = 6$ into the formula for the volume and work it through.
2. 'Exact' means you should leave your answer in terms of π.

$$\text{Volume} = \frac{4}{3}\pi r^3 = \frac{4}{3} \times \pi \times 6^3$$
$$= \mathbf{288\pi\ cm^3}$$

Example 5

A sphere has a volume of 2304π cm^3. What is its radius?

1. Substitute the volume given into the formula for the volume of a sphere. $\quad \text{Volume} = \frac{4}{3}\pi r^3$, so $2304\pi = \frac{4}{3}\pi r^3$
2. Divide by $\frac{4}{3}\pi$ to find r^3. $\quad r^3 = 2304\pi \div \left(\frac{4}{3}\pi\right) = 1728$ cm^3
3. Cube root to find r. $\quad r = \sqrt[3]{1728} = \mathbf{12\ cm}$

Tip: The π's cancel.

Exercise 3

Q1 For each of the following, find the exact volume of the sphere with the given radius, r.

a) $r = 3$ cm b) $r = 2$ m c) $r = 5$ mm

Q2 For each of the following, find the volume of the sphere with the given radius, r. Give your answers to 2 d.p.

a) $r = 4$ cm b) $r = 8$ m c) $r = 9.6$ mm d) $r = 15.7$ m

Q3 Find the radius of the sphere with volume 24 429 cm^3. Give your answer correct to 1 d.p.

Cones and Frustums

Learning Objective — Spec Ref G17:
Be able to find the volume of cones and frustums.

A **cone** is a 3D shape that has a **circular base** and goes up to a **point** at the top. To find the **volume** of a cone, you need to know its base **radius** r and **perpendicular height** h. The **volume** of a cone is given by:

$$\textbf{Volume} = \frac{1}{3}\pi r^2 h$$

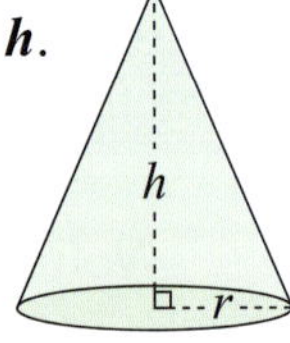

Tip: The perpendicular height goes from the centre of the base to the point.

Example 6

Find the volume of the cone shown on the right. Give your answer to 2 d.p.

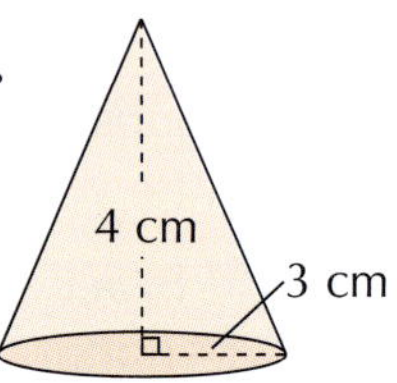

Substitute $r = 3$ and $h = 4$ into the formula for volume.

$$\text{Volume} = \frac{1}{3}\pi r^2 h = \frac{1}{3} \times \pi \times 3^2 \times 4$$
$$= 37.699... = \mathbf{37.70\ cm^3} \text{ (2 d.p.)}$$

Exercise 4

Q1 Find the exact volume of the cones with the given properties.

a) base radius = 5 m, height = 12 m
b) base radius = 7 cm, height = 24 cm
c) base radius = 15 m, height = 8 m
d) base radius = 30 mm, height = 5.5 mm

Q2 Find the volume of the cones with the given properties. Give your answers to 2 d.p.

a) base radius = 4 cm, height = 10 cm
b) base radius = 14 mm, height = 32 mm
c) base radius = 7 m, height = 25 m
d) base radius = 3.6 cm, height = 7.2 cm

Frustums

A **frustum** of a cone is the 3D shape left once you **chop** the top bit off a cone **parallel** to its circular base. The smaller, removed cone is always **similar** to the larger, original cone — see p.414 for more on similarity.

To find the **volume** of a frustum, find the volume of the **original cone** and take away the volume of the **removed cone** (the top bit).

Volume of frustum = Volume of original cone − Volume of removed cone

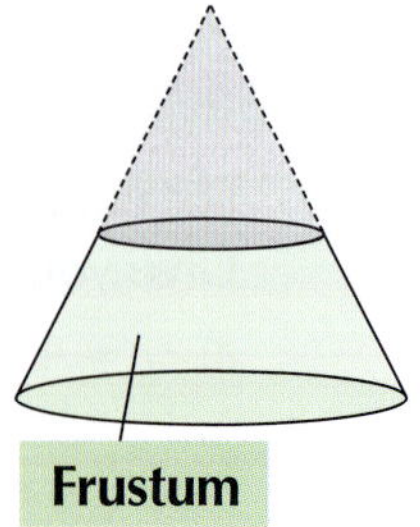

Example 7

Find the exact volume of the frustum shown on the right.

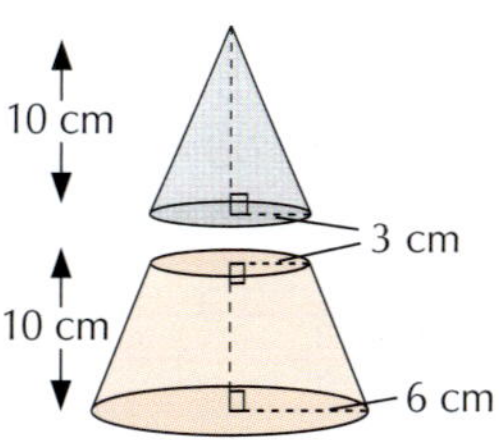

1. Find the volume of the original cone.

   Volume of original cone $= \frac{1}{3}\pi \times 6^2 \times (10 + 10)$

   $= \frac{1}{3}\pi \times 36 \times 20 = 240\pi \text{ cm}^3$

2. Find the volume of the removed cone.

   Volume of removed cone $= \frac{1}{3}\pi \times 3^2 \times 10 = \frac{1}{3}\pi \times 9 \times 10 = 30\pi \text{ cm}^3$

3. Subtract the volume of the removed cone from the volume of the original cone.

   Volume of frustum = vol. of original cone – vol. of removed cone

   $= 240\pi - 30\pi =$ **210π cm³**

Exercise 5

Q1 A cone of height 4 cm and base radius 3 cm is removed from a cone of height 16 cm and base radius 12 cm, as shown in the sketch on the right.

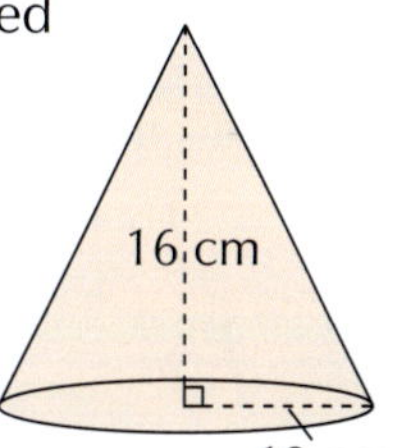

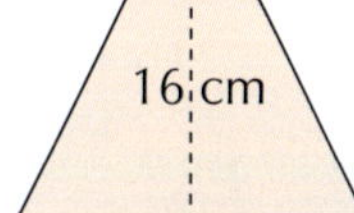

a) Find the exact volume of the original cone.

b) Find the exact volume of the removed cone.

c) Hence find the exact volume of the frustum.

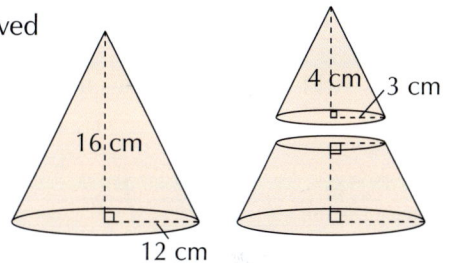

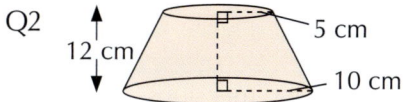

Q2 12 cm, 5 cm, 10 cm

The frustum on the left is what remains after the top 12 cm is removed from a 24 cm tall cone. What is the volume of the frustum? Give your answer to 2 d.p.

Pyramids

Learning Objective — Spec Ref G17:
Be able to find the volume of pyramids.

A **pyramid** is a 3D shape that has a **polygon base** (see page 250) which rises to a **point**.

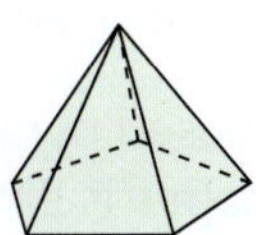

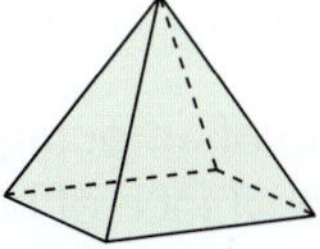

Tip: A cone is a bit like a pyramid with a circular base.

The **volume** of a pyramid can be found by using this formula:

Volume = $\frac{1}{3}$ × base area × height

Example 8

Find the volume of the rectangular-based pyramid shown.

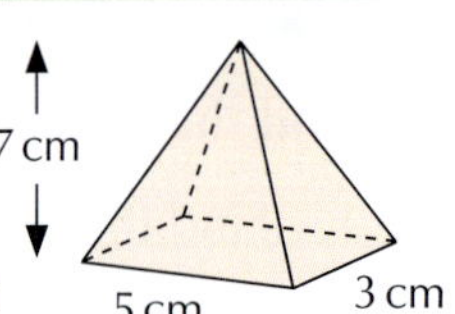

1. Write down the formula for volume of a pyramid. Volume $= \frac{1}{3} \times$ base area $\times$ height
2. Substitute the values into the formula — since the base is a rectangle, base area = length × width. $= \frac{1}{3} \times (5 \times 3) \times 7$

   $=$ **35 cm³**

Example 9

The 3D shape on the right is made up of a square-based pyramid on top of a cube, with dimensions as shown. Find the volume of the shape.

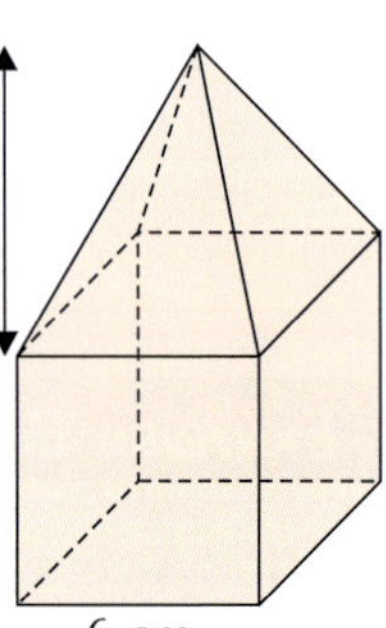

1. Find the volume of the cube (see p.375).

   Volume of cube = $(\text{length})^3 = 6^3 = 216$ cm³
2. Find the volume of the pyramid — the base is a square, so its area is $(\text{side length})^2$.

   Volume of pyramid $= \frac{1}{3} \times$ base area $\times$ height $= \frac{1}{3} \times 6^2 \times 8 = 96$ cm³
3. Add the two volumes together to find the total volume.

   Total volume = 216 + 96 = **312 cm³**

Exercise 6

Q1 Find the volumes of triangular-based pyramids with the following dimensions.

a) base area = 18 cm², height = 10 cm b) base area = 8 m², height = 3 m

Q2 Find the volume of a rectangular-based pyramid of height 10 cm with base dimensions 4 cm × 9 cm.

Q3 A hexagon-based pyramid is 15 cm tall. The area of its base is 18 cm². Calculate its volume.

Q4 Just to be controversial, Pharaoh Tim has decided he wants a pentagon-based pyramid. The area of the pentagon is 27 m² and the height of the pyramid is 12 m. What is the volume of Tim's pyramid?

Q5 A 3D shape is made up of an octagonal-based pyramid on top of an octagonal prism. The area of the octagonal face of both shapes is 24 cm², the height of the prism is 10 cm and the height of the pyramid is also 10 cm. What is the volume of the shape?

Q6 A square-based pyramid has height 13.5 cm and volume 288 cm³. Find the side length of its base.

Rates of Flow

Learning Objective — Spec Ref G17:
Know how to calculate rates of flow into and out of 3D shapes.

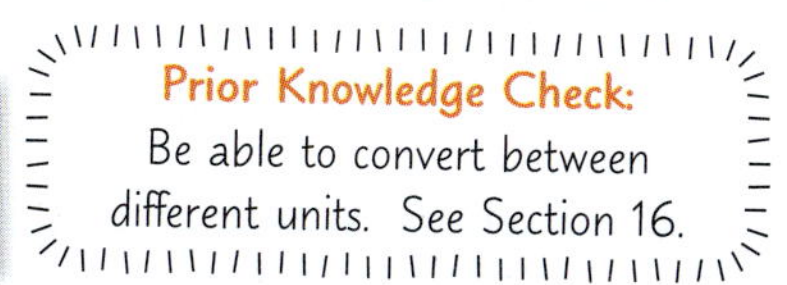

Prior Knowledge Check:
Be able to convert between different units. See Section 16.

The **rate of flow** tells you **how quickly** a liquid is moving **into**, **out of** or **through** a certain **space**. To work out the rate of flow, you need to know the **total volume** of the space and the **time** it would take to **completely fill** (or empty) the space. The volume **divided** by the time gives the rate of flow.

$$\textbf{Rate of Flow} = \frac{\textbf{Volume of container}}{\textbf{Total time taken}}$$

Rates of flow are measured in **volume per unit time**, e.g. litres per second or m^3 per hour (sometimes written as litres/s or m^3/hr).

Example 10

Water flows into this cuboid-shaped tank at a rate of 150 cm^3 per second. How long does it take to fill the tank?

30 cm
50 cm
20 cm

1. Calculate the volume of the cuboid.

   Volume of cuboid = length × width × height
   = 50 × 20 × 30 = 30 000 cm^3

2. Rearrange the formula and divide the volume by the rate of flow to get the time taken.

   $$\text{Time taken to fill tank} = \frac{\text{Volume of container}}{\text{Rate of flow}} = \frac{30\,000}{150} = \textbf{200 seconds}$$

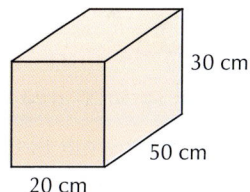

Exercise 7

Q1 Work out the average rates of flow when containers with these volumes are completely filled in the given time:

a) Volume = 600 cm^3, Time = 15 seconds

b) Volume = 7200 litres, Time = 40 minutes

c) Volume = 385 m^3, Time = 5 minutes

d) Volume = 150 litres, Time = 8 hours

Q2 A cube with a side length of 30 cm is filled with sand at a rate of 15 cm^3 per second. How many minutes does it take to fill the cube?

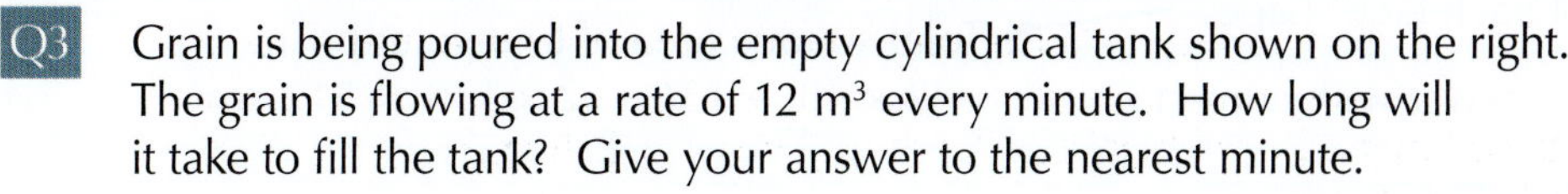

Q3 Grain is being poured into the empty cylindrical tank shown on the right. The grain is flowing at a rate of 12 m^3 every minute. How long will it take to fill the tank? Give your answer to the nearest minute.

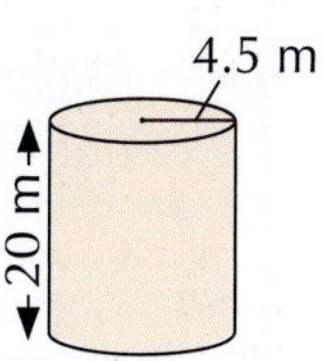

23.6 Surface Area

The surface area of a 3D shape is the sum of the areas of each face — it's measured in square units, e.g. cm² or m².

Cubes, Cuboids, Prisms and Pyramids

Learning Objective — Spec Ref G17:
Be able to find the surface area of cubes, cuboids, prisms and pyramids.

Prior Knowledge Check:
Be able to find the areas of squares, rectangles and triangles (see p.345).

The **surface area** of a 3D shape is the **total area** of all of the **faces** of the shape added together. To find the surface area of a **cube**, **cuboid**, **prism** or **pyramid**, you should sketch the **net** of the shape first to make sure that you include **all** of the faces of the shape.

Tip: See p.365 for more on nets.

Example 1

Find the surface area of the cuboid shown.

5 cm
3 cm
8 cm

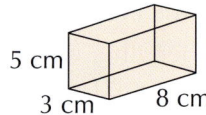

1. Sketch the net of the cuboid.

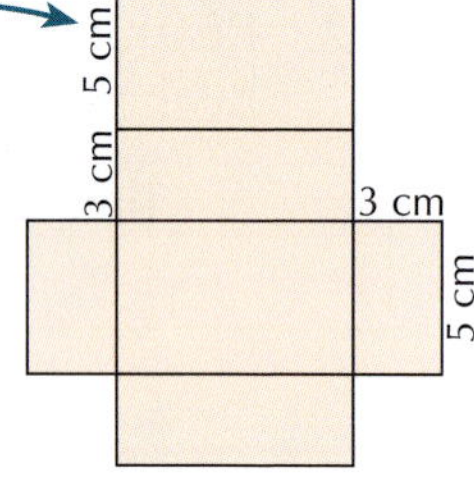

2. Find the area of each face.
   2 faces of area 8 × 5 = 40 cm²
   2 faces of area 8 × 3 = 24 cm²
   2 faces of area 5 × 3 = 15 cm²
3. Add together the areas of the faces.
   So the total surface area is
   (2 × 40) + (2 × 24) + (2 × 15)
4. Give your answer with correct units.
   = 80 + 48 + 30 = **158 cm²**

Example 2

Find this prism's surface area by considering its net.

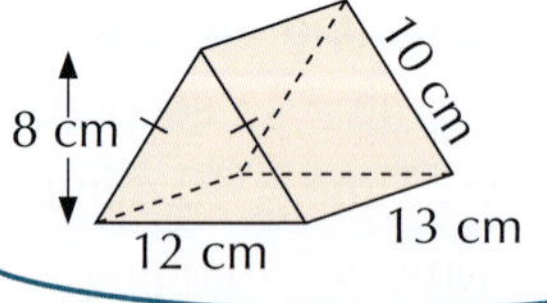

1. Draw the net of the triangular prism.

10 cm
13 cm
10 cm | 12 cm | 10 cm
8 cm

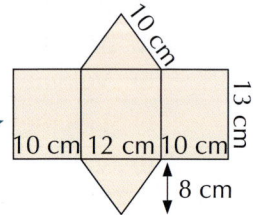

2. Find the area of each face.
   Area of 1 triangular face
   $= \frac{1}{2} \times 12 \times 8 = 48$ cm²
3. Add the different areas to find the total surface area. Make sure you include the correct number of each face shape.

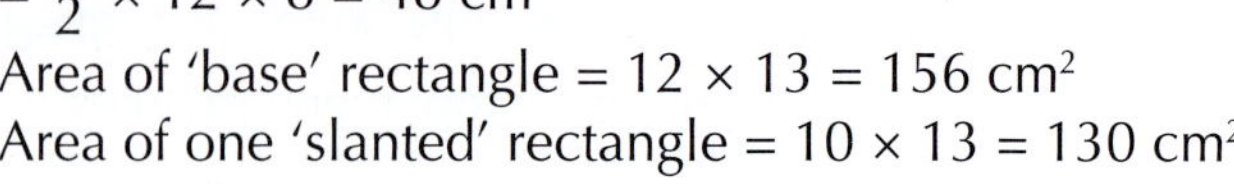

   Area of 'base' rectangle = 12 × 13 = 156 cm²
   Area of one 'slanted' rectangle = 10 × 13 = 130 cm²
   Total surface area of triangular prism
4. Give your answer with correct units.
   = (2 × 48) + 156 + (2 × 130) = **512 cm²**

Exercise 1

Q1 A cube has 6 faces, each of area 2 cm^2. Find the total surface area of the cube. 

Q2 a) Find the area of one face of the cube shown.

b) Find the total surface area of the cube.

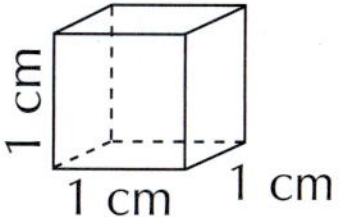

Q3 a) Find the area of one face of a cube with edges of length 2 m.

b) Find the total surface area of the cube.

Q4 a) Find the area of face A of the cuboid shown.

b) Find the area of face B.

c) Find the area of face C.

d) Find the total surface area of the cuboid.

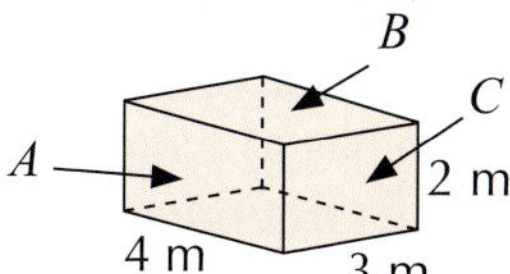

Q5 Find the surface area of the following cubes and cuboids.

a)

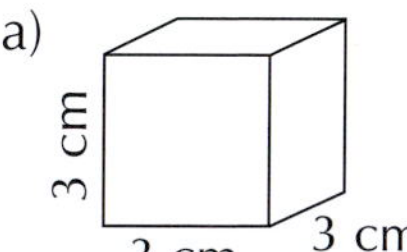

b)

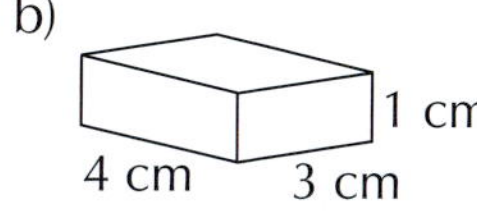

c)

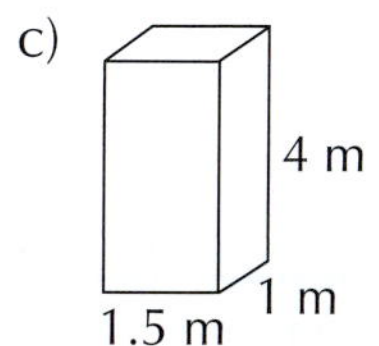

d)

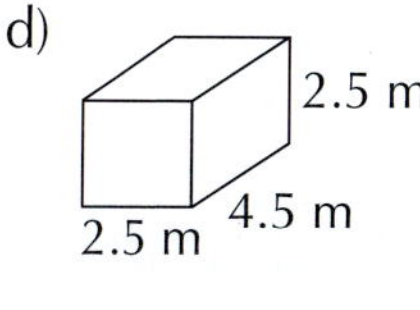

Q6 By considering their nets, find the surface area of these shapes.

a)

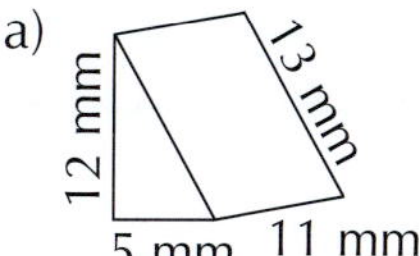

b)

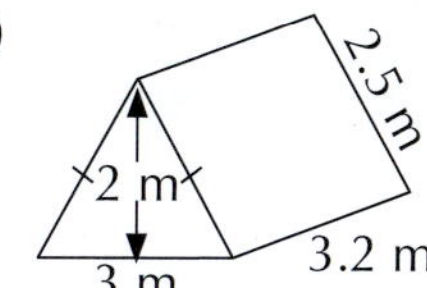

c)

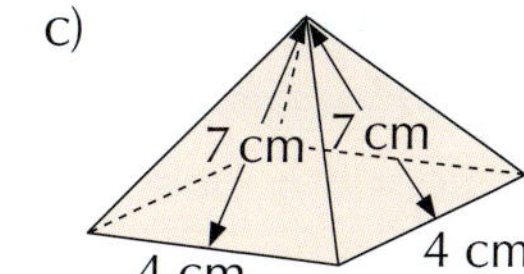

d)

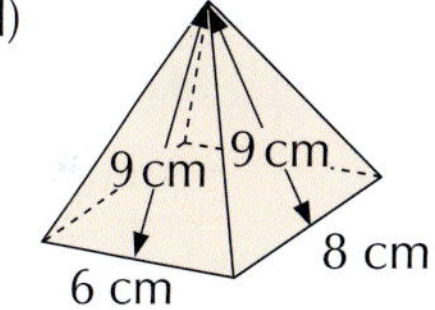

Q7 Find the surface area of the following shapes.

a) a cube with edges of length 5 m

b) a cube with edges of length 6 mm

c) a 1.5 m × 2 m × 6 m cuboid

d) a 7.5 m × 0.5 m × 8 m cuboid

e) a prism of length 2.5 m whose cross-section is an isosceles triangle of height 4 m, slant edge 5 m and base 6 m

Q8 The local scouts are waterproofing their tent, shown on the right.

a) Find the surface area of the outside of the tent.

b) How many tins of waterproofing spray will they need to buy to cover the outside of their tent if each tin covers an area of 4 m^2? PROBLEM SOLVING

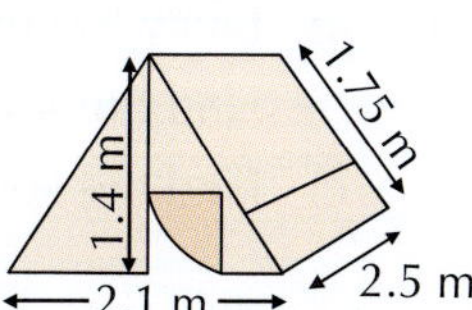

Cylinders

Learning Objective — Spec Ref G17:
Be able to find the surface area of cylinders.

Prior Knowledge Check:
Be able to find the circumference and area of a circle (see p.355 and p.358).

Find the surface area of a **cylinder** using the same method as on p.384 — **sketch its net** and work out the **area** of each **face**. It's just a bit trickier to work out the areas you need.

You saw on p.365 that the **net** of a cylinder has **two circular faces** and one **rectangular face**. The **width** of the rectangle will be the **height** of the cylinder, but you'll have to work out the **length** yourself. The rectangular face has to wrap all around the circular faces, so its length is equal to the **circumference** of the circle — use the formula $C = 2\pi r$.

Tip: You use the formula $A = \pi r^2$ to find the area of the circular faces.

Example 3

Find this cylinder's surface area by considering its net.

8 cm
2 cm

1. Draw the net of the cylinder.
2. Find the missing length, l, of the rectangle — it's equal to the circumference of the circle.

$l = 2\pi r = 2 \times \pi \times 2 = 4\pi$ cm

2 cm
l
8 cm

3. Find the area of each face.

Area of circle $= \pi r^2 = \pi \times 2^2 = 4\pi = 12.566...$ cm^2

Area of rectangle $= 8 \times 4\pi = 100.530...$ cm^2

4. Add together the individual areas.

So total surface area $= (2 \times 12.566...) + 100.530...$
$= \mathbf{125.7\ cm^2}$ (to 1 d.p.)

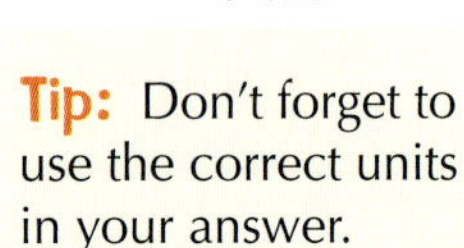

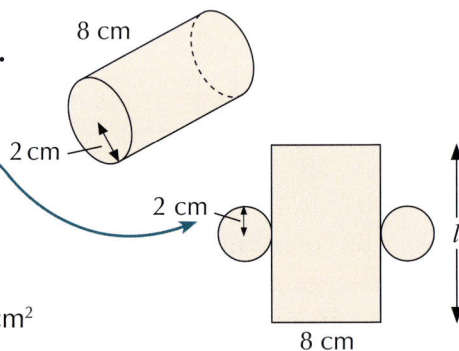

Tip: Don't forget to use the correct units in your answer.

Exercise 2

Round any inexact answers to 2 decimal places unless told otherwise.

Q1 a) Draw the net of the cylinder shown on the right.
b) Find the area of each surface of the cylinder.
c) Find the surface area of the cylinder, correct to 1 decimal place.

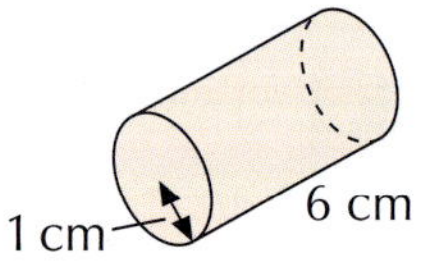

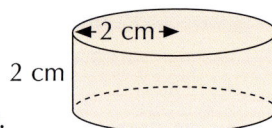

Q2 a) Draw the net of the cylinder shown on the right.
b) Find the area of each surface of the cylinder.
c) Find the surface area of the cylinder, correct to 1 decimal place.

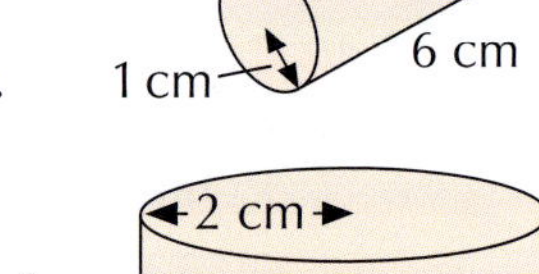

Q3 Find the surface area of the following cylinders.

a) 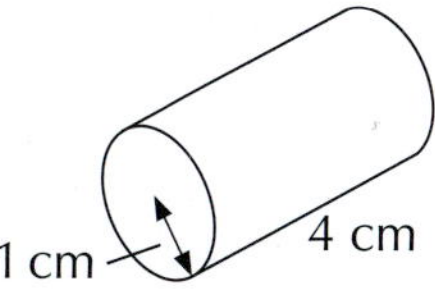

b) 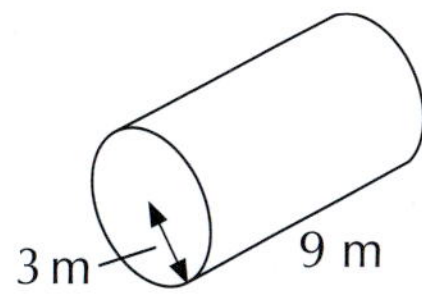

c) 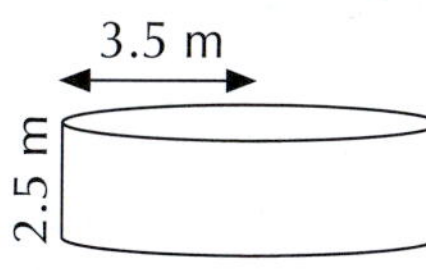

d) 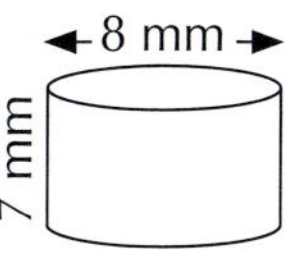

e) 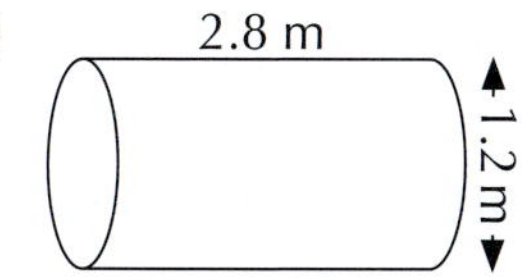

f) 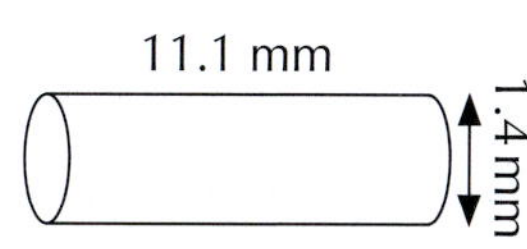

Q4 Find the surface area of the cylinders with the following dimensions.
Give your answers correct to 1 decimal place.

a) radius = 2 m, length = 7 m
b) radius = 7.5 mm, length = 2.5 mm
c) radius = 12.2 cm, length = 9.9 cm
d) diameter = 22.1 m, length = 11.1 m

Q5 Maeve is painting her cylindrical gas tank. The tank has radius 0.8 m and length 3 m. She uses tins of paint which cover an area of 14 m^2.

a) What is the surface area of the tank?
b) How many tins of paint will Maeve need?

Q6 A cylindrical metal pipe has radius 2.2 m and length 7.1 m. The ends of the pipe are open.

a) Find the curved surface area of the outside of the pipe.
b) A system of pipes consists of 9 of the pipes described above. What area of metal is required to build the system of pipes? Give your answer correct to 1 decimal place.

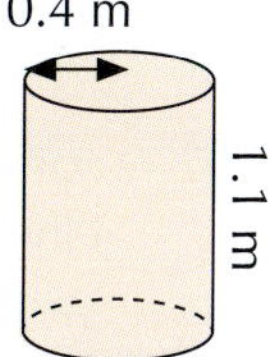

Q7 The diagram shows a cylindrical bin which is closed at one end and open at the other. Find the total surface area of the outside of the bin.

Spheres and Cones

Learning Objective — Spec Ref G17:
Be able to find the surface area of spheres and cones.

For spheres and cones, you **don't** need to sketch the net — just use the **formulas** below.

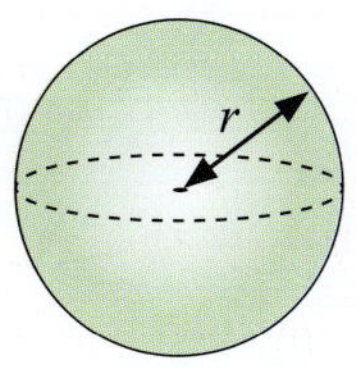

Surface area of a sphere = $4\pi r^2$

Where r is the radius of the sphere.

Surface area of a cone = $\pi rl + \pi r^2$

Where r is the radius at the base of the cone and l is the slant height — the distance from the edge of the base to the point.

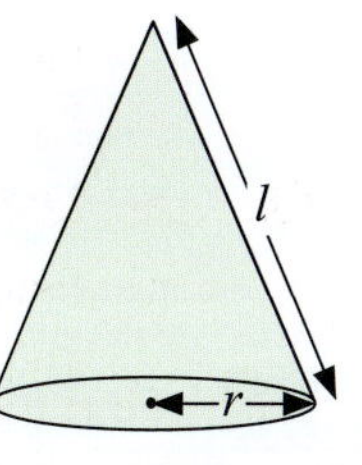

Example 4

Find the exact surface area of:

a) a sphere with radius 3 cm

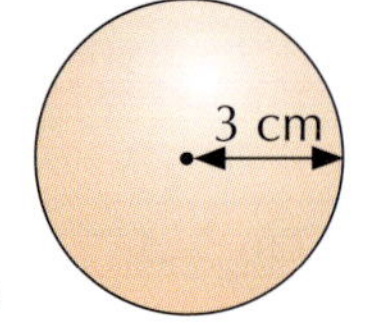

Put $r = 3$ into the formula.
Leave your answer in terms of π (as the question asks for an exact value).

Surface area $= 4\pi r^2$
$= 4 \times \pi \times 3^2 =$ **36π cm²**

b) a cone with base radius 4 cm and a slant height of 10 cm

Put $r = 4$ and $l = 10$ into the formula — leave your answer in terms of π.

Surface area $= \pi rl + \pi r^2$
$= (\pi \times 4 \times 10) + (\pi \times 4^2)$
$= 40\pi + 16\pi =$ **56π cm²**

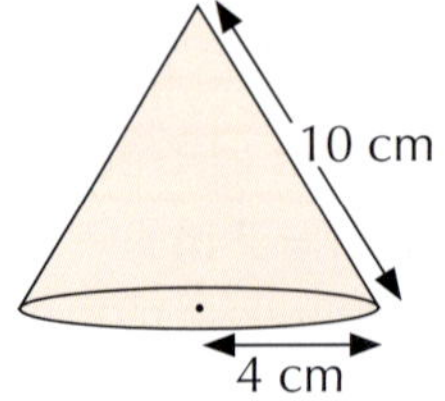

Tip: For the surface area of a cone, make sure you use the slant height (l), not the perpendicular height.

Exercise 3

Q1 For each of the following, find the exact surface area of the sphere with the given radius, r.

a) $r = 2$ cm b) $r = 5$ cm c) $r = 7$ m
d) $r = 9$ mm e) $r = 10.5$ m f) $r = 3.25$ mm

Q2 For each of the following, find the surface area of the sphere with the given radius, r. Give your answers to 2 d.p.

a) $r = 2.5$ cm b) $r = 7.1$ m c) $r = 11.2$ mm
d) $r = 19.3$ m e) $r = 4.88$ cm f) $r = 6.35$ mm

Q3 Find the exact surface area of the cones with the given properties. 

a) $r = 5$ m, $l = 13$ m b) $r = 7$ cm, $l = 25$ cm c) $r = 15$ m, $l = 17$ m

Q4 Find the surface area of the cones with the given properties. Give your answers to 2 d.p.

a) $r = 12$ cm, $l = 30$ cm b) $r = 1.5$ m, $l = 4.5$ m c) $r = 2.8$ mm, $l = 8.2$ mm

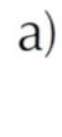

Q5 Find the surface area of each of the following, giving your answers to 2 d.p.

a) 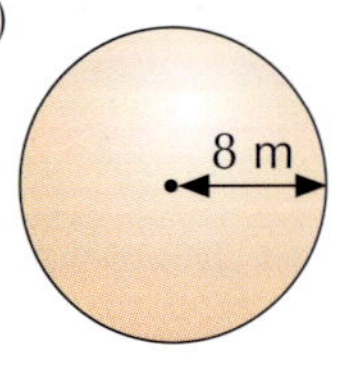

b) 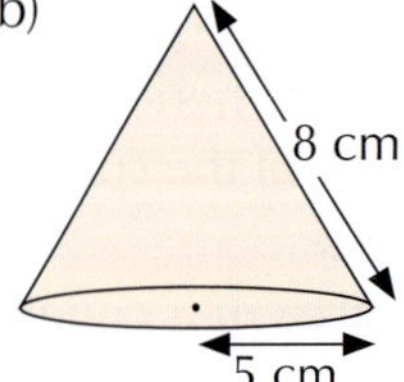

c) 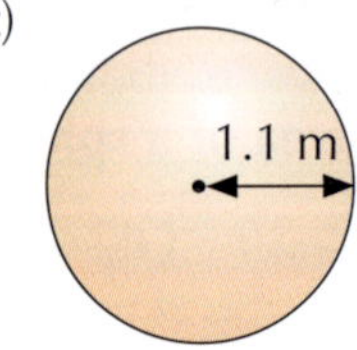

d) 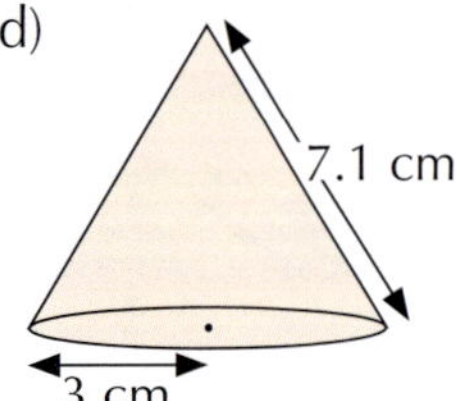

Q6 Find the radius of the sphere with surface area 265.9 cm². Give your answer to 1 d.p.

Review Exercise

Where appropriate, give your answers to these questions to 2 decimal places.

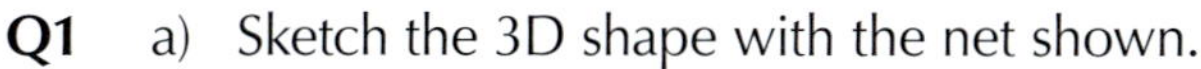

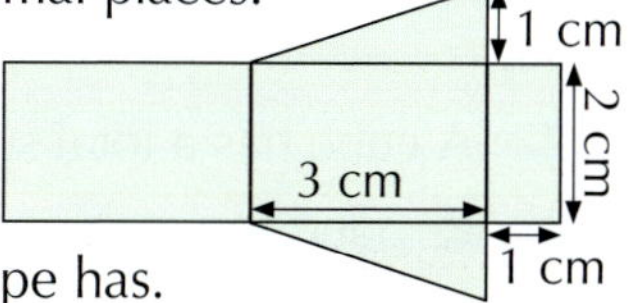

Q1 a) Sketch the 3D shape with the net shown.

b) Use isometric paper to accurately draw the shape.

c) Write down how many faces, vertices and edges the shape has.

Q2 a) Draw an accurate, full-sized net of the triangular prism shown.

b) Measure the appropriate length on your drawing to find the vertical height, h, of the prism.

c) Draw the plan, and the front and side elevations of the prism from the directions shown.

d) How many planes of symmetry does the prism have?

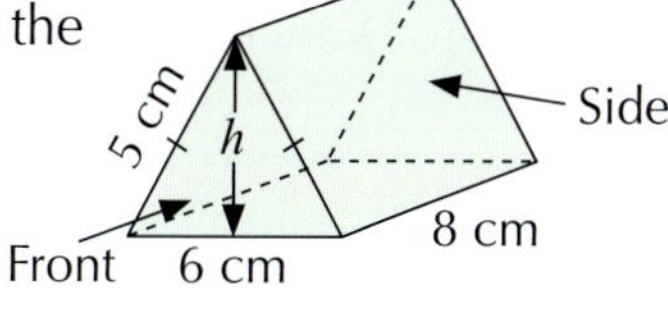

Q3 For each of the shapes P and Q on the right, complete the following.

a) Draw a net of the shape.

b) Draw the plan, and front and side elevations of the shape from the directions indicated.

c) Draw the shape on isometric paper.

d) Calculate the shape's volume.

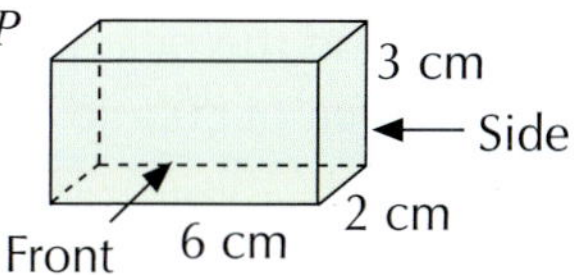

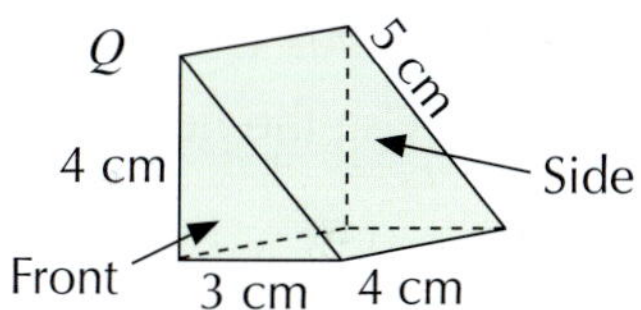

Q4 24 cubes with edges of length 8 cm fit exactly in a tray of depth 8 cm, as shown.

a) Find the volume of one cube.

b) Find the volume of the tray.

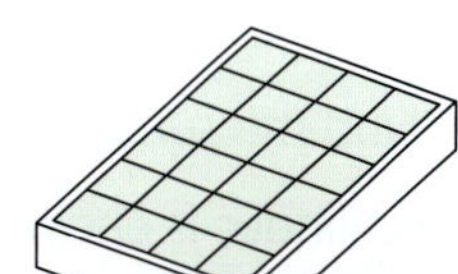

Q5 Beans are sold in cylindrical tins of diameter 7.4 cm and height 11 cm.

a) Find the volume of one tin.

The tins are stored in boxes which hold 12 tins in three rows of 4, as shown.

b) Find the dimensions of the box.

c) Find the volume of the box.

d) Calculate the volume of the box that is not taken up by tins when it is fully packed.
Give your answer correct to 1 decimal place.

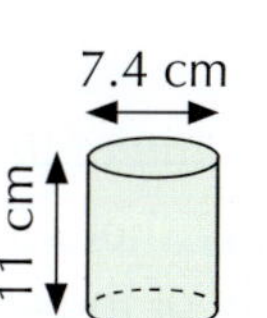

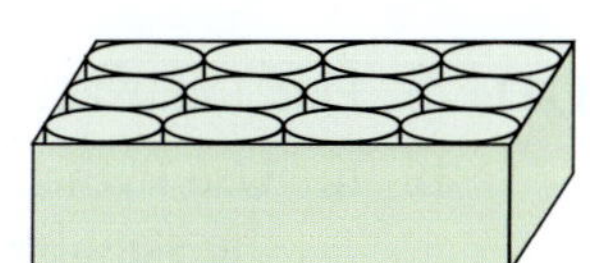

Q6 The shape on the right is made by joining together the bases of two identical square-based pyramids. Each pyramid has height 9 cm and base side length 7 cm. Find the volume of this shape.

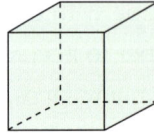

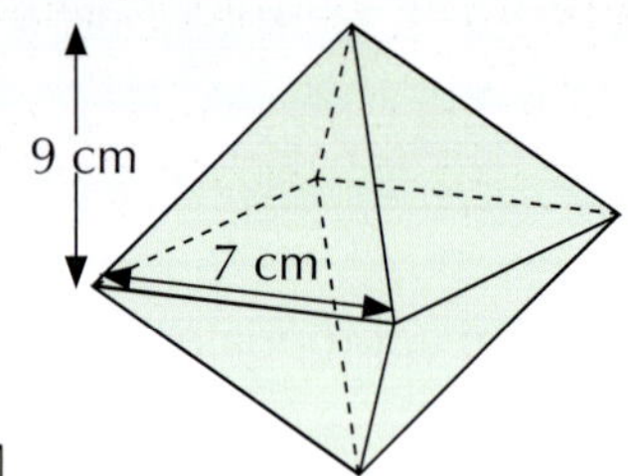

Q7 A cube has a total surface area of 54 cm^2.

a) Find the area of one face of the cube.

b) Find the length of the edges of the cube.

c) Find the cube's volume.

d) How long will it take to fill the cube with water flowing at a rate of 2.5 cm^3/s?

e) Draw the cube on isometric paper.

Q8 Two cuboids, A and B, are shown on the right.

a) Find the ratio of the volume of cuboid A to the volume of cuboid B. Give your answer in its simplest form.

b) Find the ratio of the surface area of cuboid A to the surface area of cuboid B. Give your answer in its simplest form.

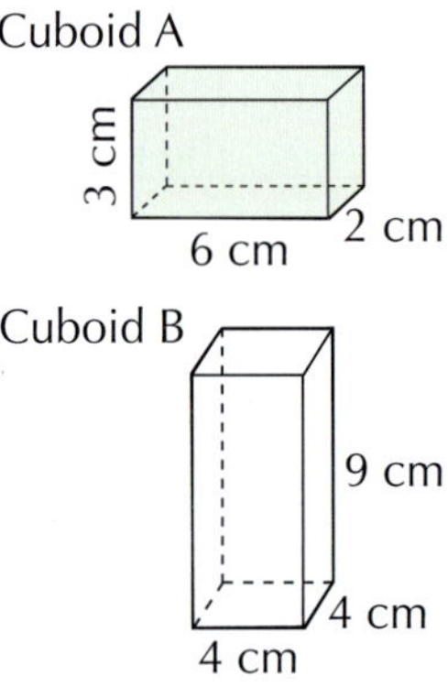

Q9 a) Draw an accurate net of a cylinder of length 3 cm and radius 1.5 cm. Label your diagram with the net's dimensions.

b) Use the net to find the cylinder's surface area.

Q10 A cylinder of diameter 25 mm has volume 7854 mm^3.

a) Find the length of the cylinder.

b) Find the surface area of the cylinder to the nearest mm^2.

The cylinder is enclosed in a cuboid, as shown.

c) Find the volume of the cuboid to the nearest mm^3.

d) Find the volume of the empty space between the cylinder and the cuboid to the nearest mm^3.

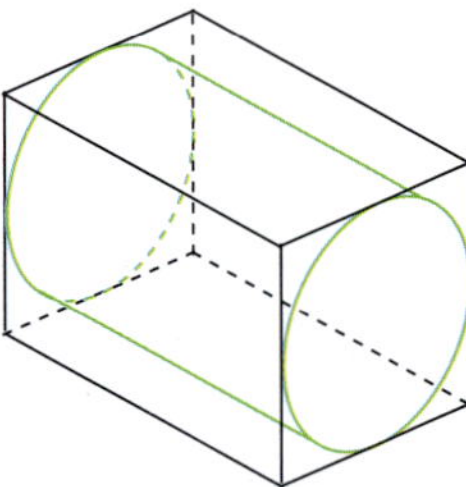

Q11 a) Find the exact volume of the cone shown on the right.

b) (i) Use Pythagoras' theorem $h^2 = a^2 + b^2$ to find h, the slant height of the cone.

(ii) Find the exact surface area of the cone.

The cone is cut parallel to the circular face and a cone of height 8 m and base radius 6 m is removed to leave a frustum.

c) Find the exact volume of the frustum.

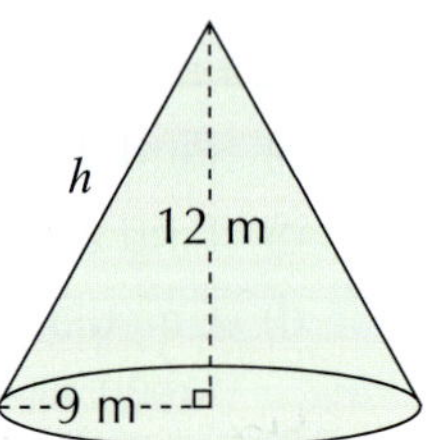

Exam-Style Questions

Q1 The diagram on the right shows three solid shapes, A, B and C.

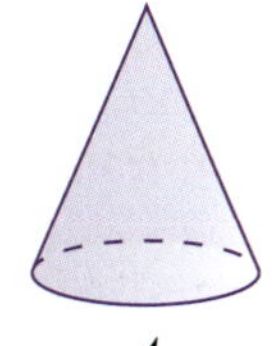

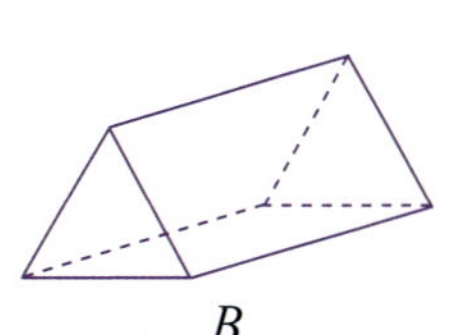

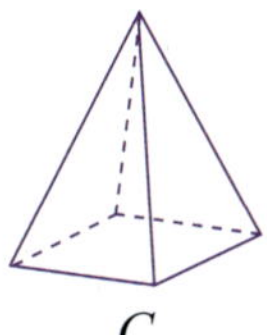

a) Write down the name of each shape.

[2 marks]

b) For shape B, write down:

(i) the number of vertices,

[1 mark]

(ii) the number of faces.

[1 mark]

Q2 The net of a cylinder is drawn on a 1 cm^2 grid, as shown on the right.

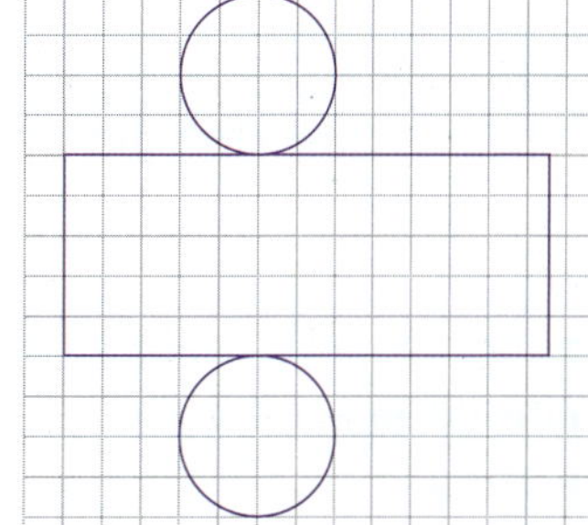

a) Write down the height of the cylinder in cm.

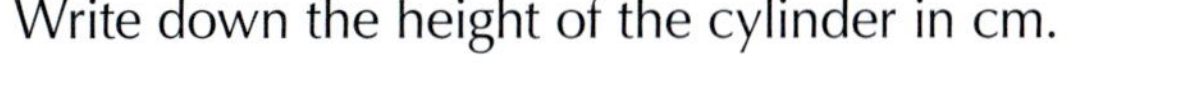

[1 mark]

b) Hence find the exact surface area of the cylinder.

[3 marks]

Q3 The diagram on the right shows a cuboid with a volume of 300 cm^3.
Each edge is a whole number of centimetres long.
The width of the cuboid is double the height.
The area of the shaded face is 30 cm^2.
Find the dimensions of the cuboid.

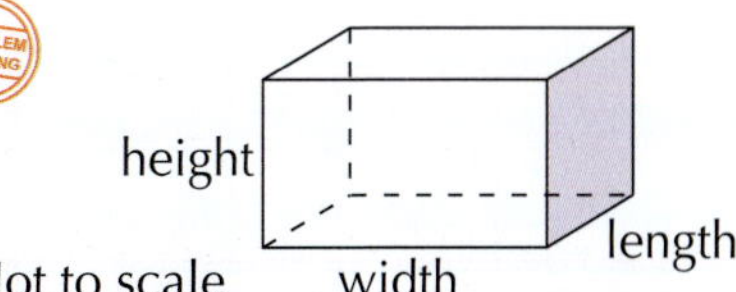

Not to scale

[3 marks]

Q4 Sadiq is making jam for the summer fete. His jam pan is cylindrical with radius 20 cm. The jam in his pan is 18 cm deep. Jam jars are cylindrical with radius 3 cm and can be filled to a depth of 10 cm.
How many jars can Sadiq fill with the amount of jam he has made?

[3 marks]

24.1 Reflections

Transformations can be used to move and resize shapes on a coordinate grid. In this section, you'll meet four different transformations — the first of which is reflection.

Learning Objectives — Spec Ref G7:
- Reflect a shape in a given line.
- Describe the reflection that transforms a shape.

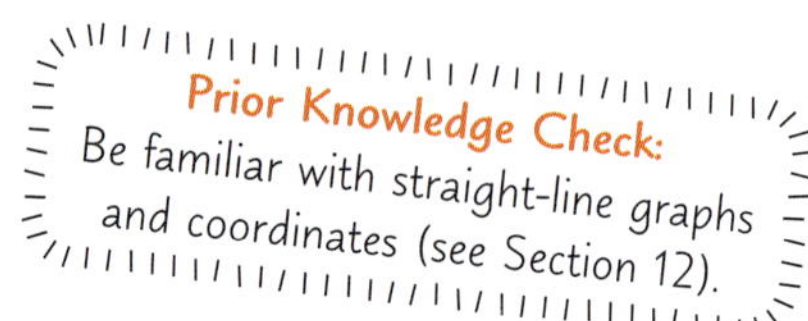

Prior Knowledge Check:
Be familiar with straight-line graphs and coordinates (see Section 12).

To **reflect** a shape, you draw its mirror image.

- First reflect the **vertices** of the shape in the line of symmetry (also known as the **mirror line**). The **reflected points** (called the **image points**) should be the **same distance** from the line as the original points but on the **other side** of it.
- Then **join up** the image points to create the reflected shape. The reflected shape will be the **same size** and **shape** as the original — so the shapes are **congruent** (see p.411).
- A reflection in the **y-axis** will send a point (x, y) to $(-x, y)$.
- A reflection in the **x-axis** will send a point (x, y) to $(x, -y)$.

To **describe** a reflection, you just need to find the **equation** of the mirror line.

Tip: Mirror lines of the form $x = a$ are vertical and mirror lines of the form $y = a$ are horizontal.

Example 1

Reflect the shape below in the mirror line.

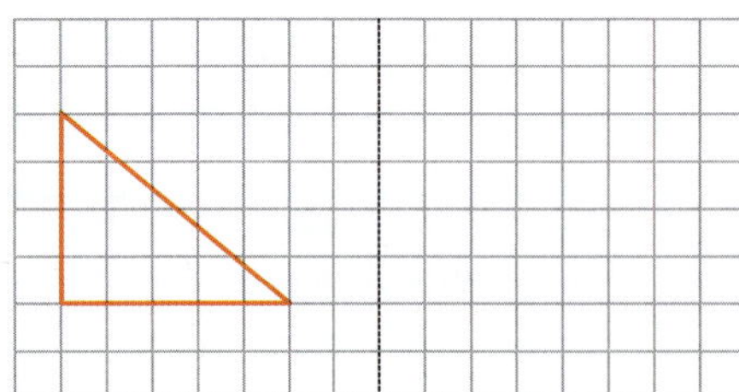

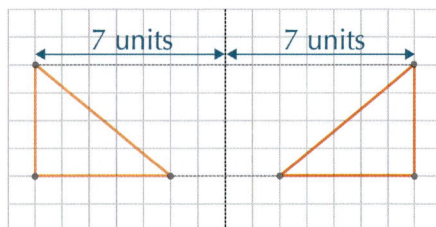

7 units 7 units

1. Reflect one corner at a time.
2. The image of each point is the same distance from the mirror line as the original.
3. Join up the corners to create the image.

Exercise 1

Q1 Copy the diagrams below, and reflect each of the shapes in the mirror line.

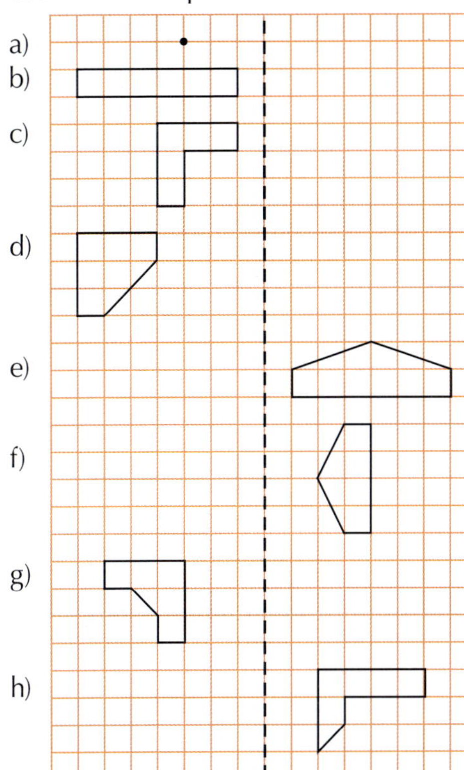

Q2 Copy the diagrams below, and reflect each of the shapes in the mirror line.

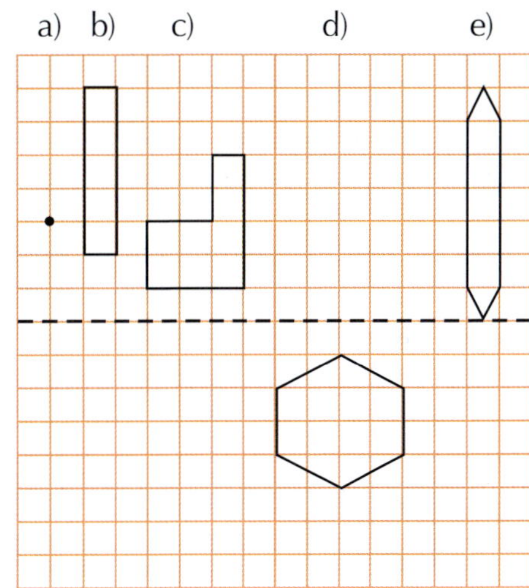

Q3 Copy the diagram.
Reflect the shape in the mirror line.

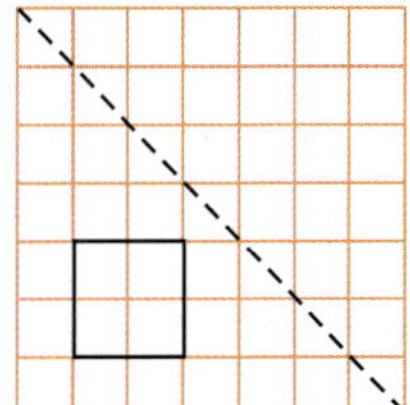

Example 2

a) Reflect the shape *ABCDE* in the *y*-axis.

b) Label the image points A_1, B_1, C_1, D_1 and E_1 with their coordinates.

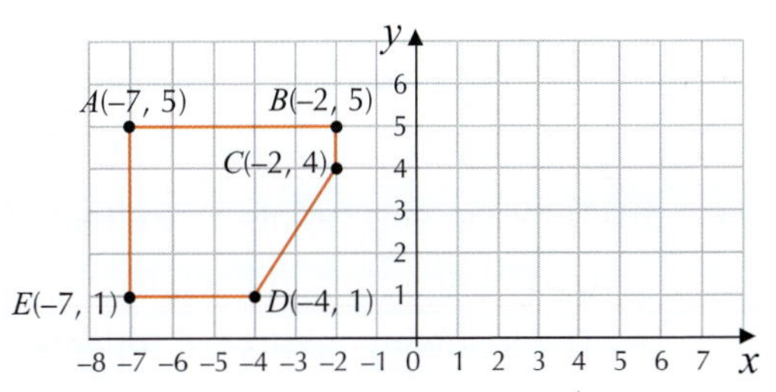

1. Here the *y*-axis is the mirror line.
2. Each image point should be the same distance from the *y*-axis as the original point. E.g. *C* is 2 units to the left of the *y*-axis so its image C_1 should be 2 units to the right of the *y*-axis.
3. Write down the coordinates of each of the image points. Each point (x, y) becomes $(-x, y)$.

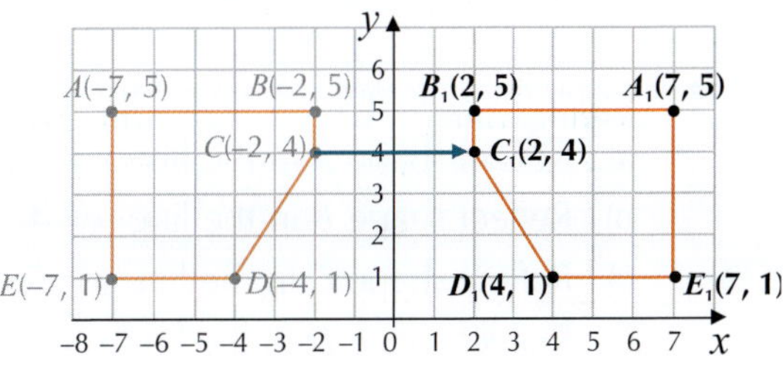

Example 3

Reflect the shape below in the line $x = 5$.

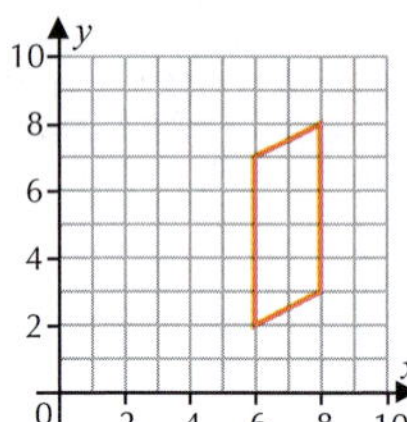

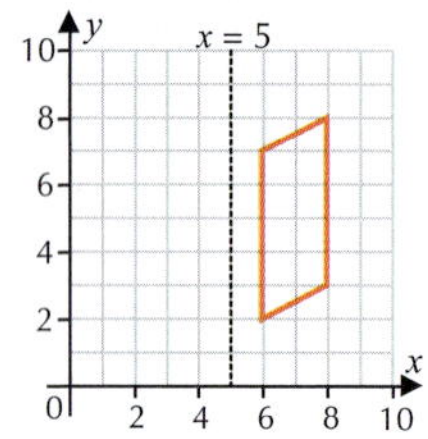

1. Draw in the mirror line, $x = 5$.

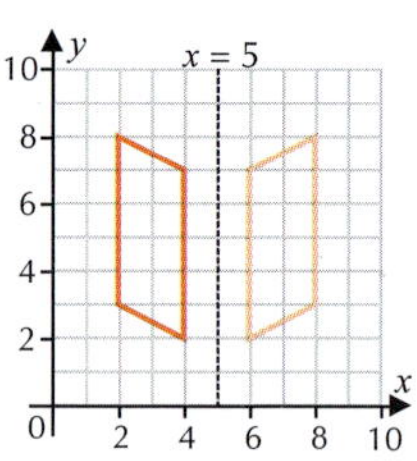

2. Reflect the shape in the line as usual, one point at a time.

Tip: The image of each point should be the same distance from the line $x = 5$ as the original point.

Exercise 2

Q1 a) Copy the diagram on the right, and reflect the shape in the y-axis.

b) Label the image points A_1, B_1, C_1, D_1 and E_1 with their coordinates.

c) Describe a rule connecting the coordinates of A, B, C, D and E and the coordinates of A_1, B_1, C_1, D_1 and E_1.

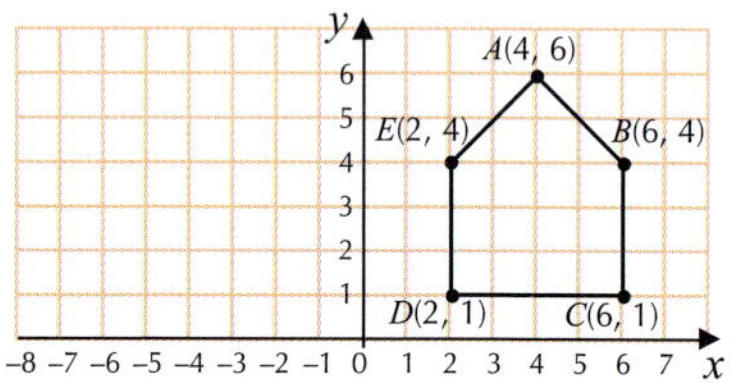

Q2 Copy each of the diagrams below, and reflect the shapes in:

a) the y-axis,

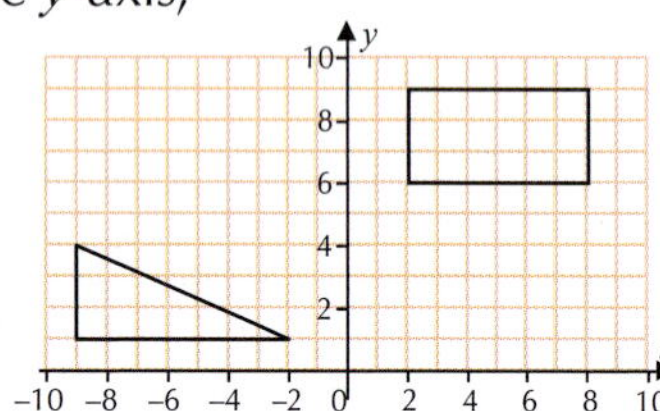

b) the x-axis.

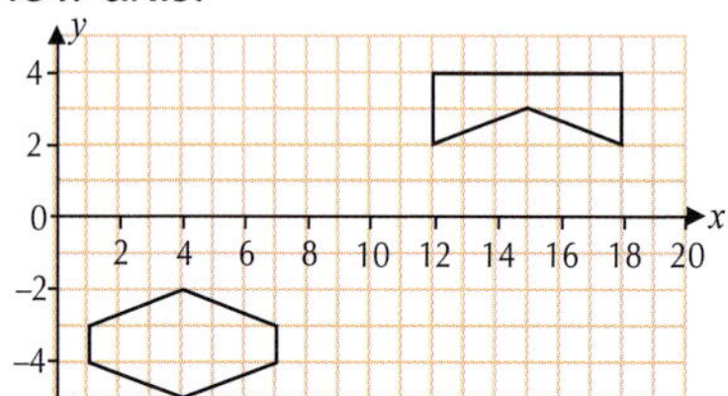

Q3 a) The following points are reflected in the x-axis. Find the coordinates of the image.

(i) (1, 2) (ii) (3, 0) (iii) (–2, 4) (iv) (–1, –3)

b) The following points are reflected in the y-axis. Find the coordinates of the image.

(i) (4, 5) (ii) (7, 2) (iii) (–1, 3) (iv) (–3, –1)

Q4 Copy the diagram shown on the right.

a) Reflect shape A in the line $x = -4$. Label the image A_1.

b) Reflect shape B in the line $y = 4$. Label the image B_1.

c) Reflect shape C in the line $y = 5$. Label the image C_1.

d) Reflect shape D in the line $x = 5$. Label the image D_1.

e) Shape C_1 is the reflection of shape B in which mirror line?

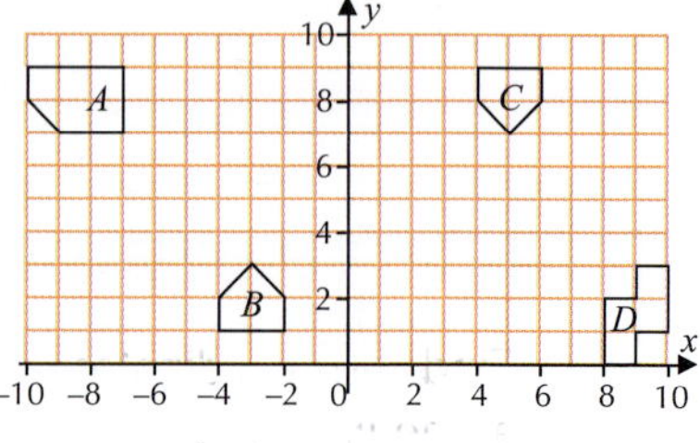

The mirror line isn't always one of the axes or a line parallel to an axis — it could be a **diagonal** line such as $y = x$ or $y = -x$.

(i) A reflection in $y = x$ sends (x, y) to (y, x). (ii) A reflection in $y = -x$ sends (x, y) to $(-y, -x)$.

Follow the same method as before, **reflecting each vertex** and then joining up the **image points**.

Make sure the image points are the **same distance** from the mirror line as the original ones — you measure this distance **perpendicular** to the mirror line.

Example 4

Reflect the shape below in the line $y = x$.

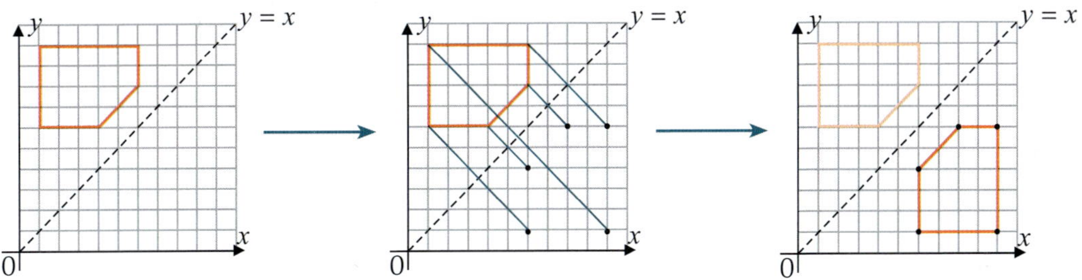

Reflect each corner in the mirror line then join up the vertices. Each image point should be the same perpendicular distance from the line $y = x$ as the original point.

Tip: Perpendicular distance is measured at right angles to the mirror line.

Exercise 3

Q1 a) Copy the diagram below, and reflect the shape $ABCD$ in the line $y = x$.

b) Describe a rule connecting the coordinates of a point and the coordinates of its image after reflection in the line $y = x$.

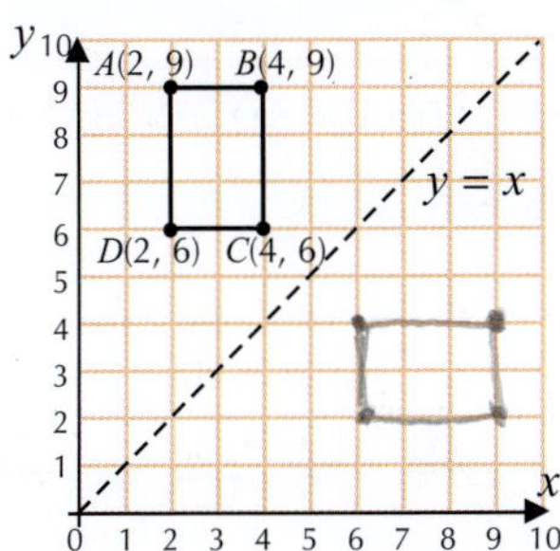

Q2 Copy the diagram below, and reflect the shapes in the line $y = -x$.

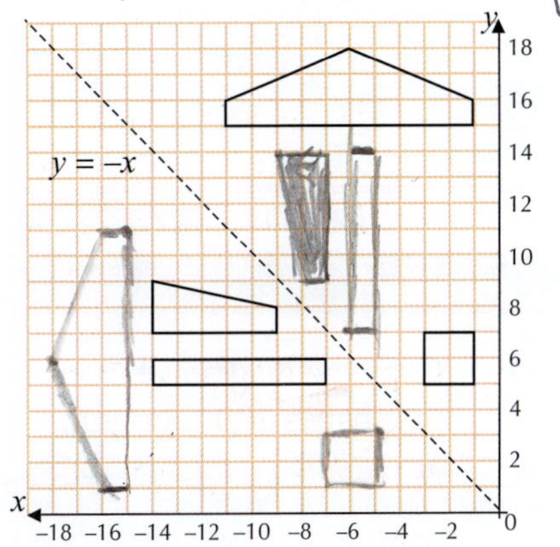

Q3 Find the coordinates of the following points after they have been reflected in:

a) the line $y = x$, b) the line $y = -x$.

(i) (1, 2) (ii) (3, 0) (iii) (–2, 4) (iv) (–1, –3)

24.2 Rotations

The second transformation to learn about is rotation. Rotations spin objects around a fixed point.

Learning Objectives — Spec Ref G7:
- Rotate a shape around a given point.
- Describe the rotation that transforms a shape.

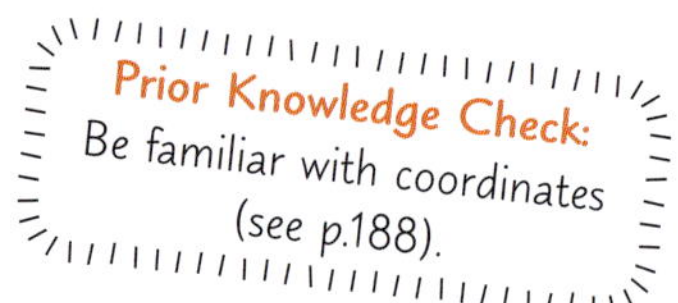

When an object is **rotated** about a point, its size and shape stay the same — so the new shape is **congruent** to the original shape. Also, the **distance** of each vertex from the centre of rotation doesn't change. To describe a rotation, you need to give **three** pieces of information:

(i) the **centre** of rotation (ii) the **direction** of rotation (iii) the **angle** of rotation

The **centre** of rotation can be **any point** — e.g. (5, 1) or the origin (0, 0).
The **direction** of rotation will be either **clockwise** or **anticlockwise** and the **angle** might be given in **degrees** or as a **fraction of a turn** (e.g. 90° or a quarter-turn).

Example 1

Rotate the shape below 180° about point *P*.

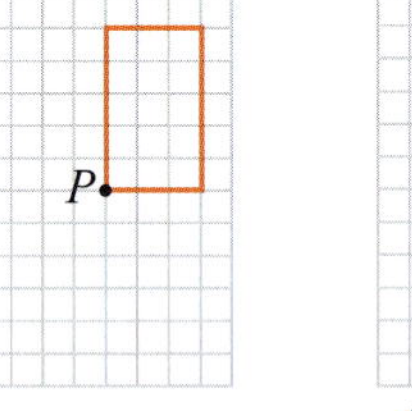

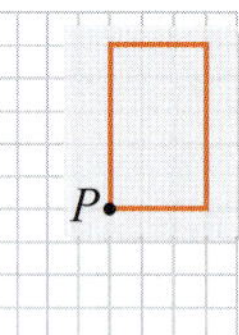

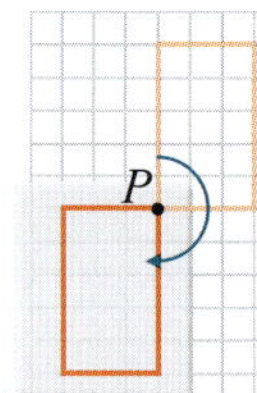

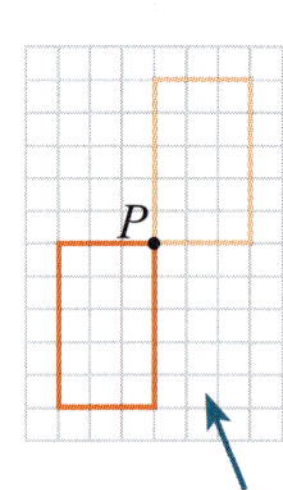

1. Draw the shape on a piece of tracing paper. (Or imagine a drawing of it.)
2. Rotate the tracing paper half a turn about *P*, the centre of rotation. ('About *P*' means *P* doesn't move.)
3. Draw the image in its new position.

Tip: A rotation of 180° gives the same result clockwise or anticlockwise, so you can rotate in either direction.

Exercise 1

Q1 Copy the diagrams below, then rotate the shapes 180° about *P*.

a) 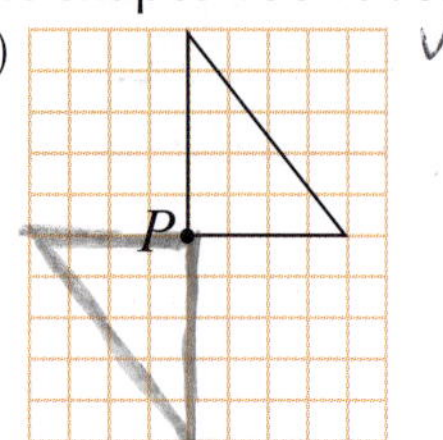

b) 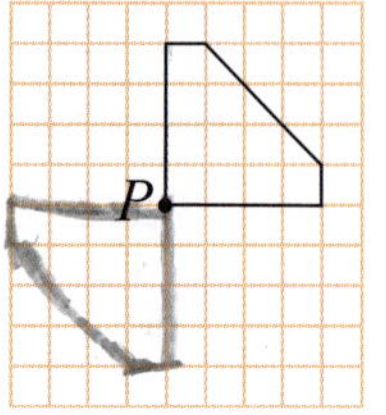

Q2 Copy the diagrams below, then rotate the shapes 90° clockwise about *P*.

a) 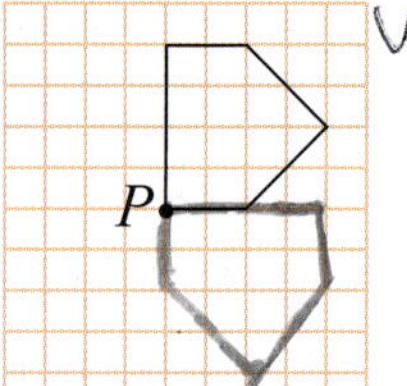

b) 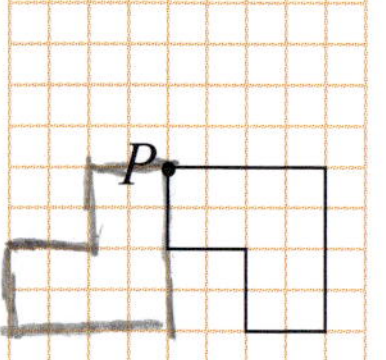

Example 2

Rotate the shape below 90° clockwise about point *P*.

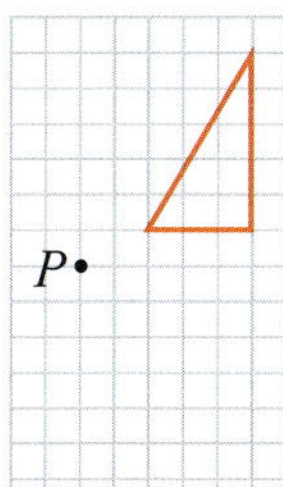

1. Here the centre of rotation is not a point on the shape.

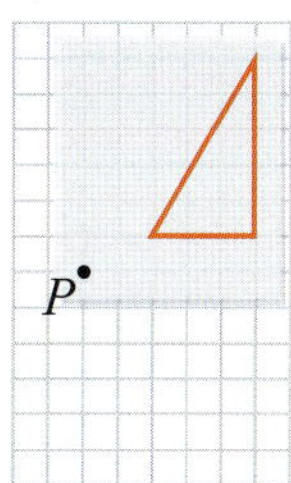

2. Draw the shape on a piece of tracing paper. (Or imagine a drawing of it.)

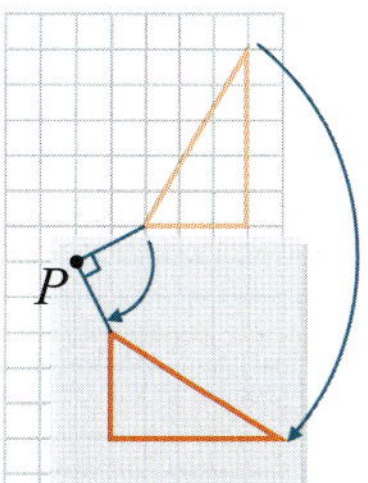

3. Rotate the tracing paper 90° clockwise about *P*.

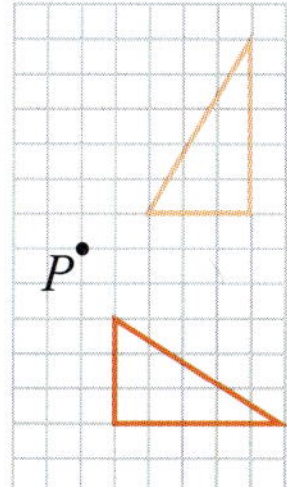

4. Draw the image.

Exercise 2

Q1 Copy the diagrams below, then rotate the shapes 90° anticlockwise about *P*.

a)

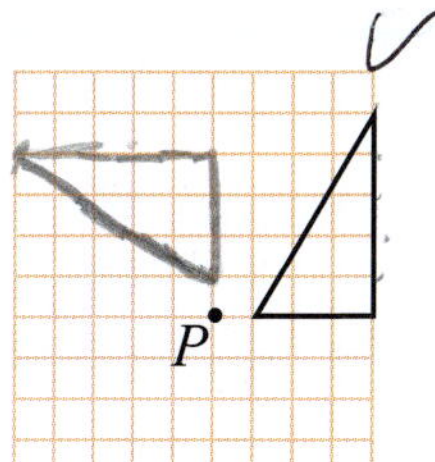

b)

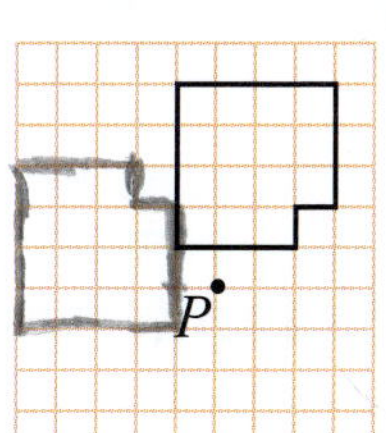

c)

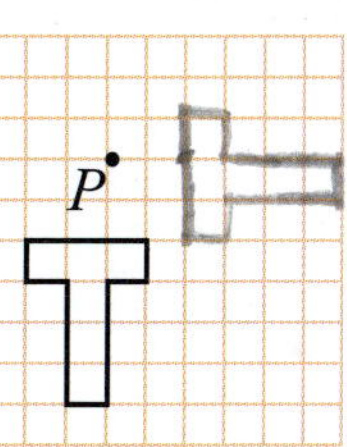

d)

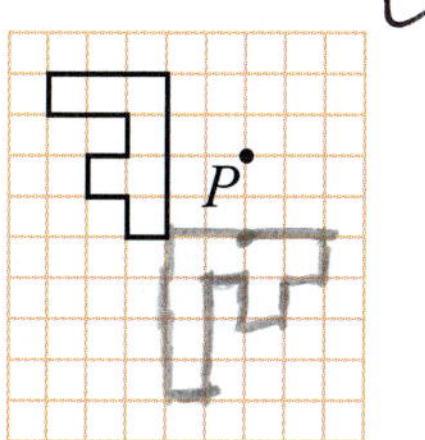

Q2

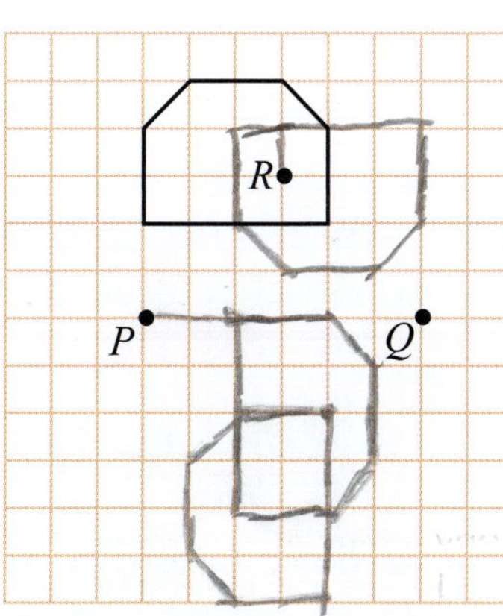

On separate copies of the diagram above, rotate the shape as follows.

a) 90° clockwise about *P*

b) 270° clockwise about *Q*

c) 180° about *R*

Q3

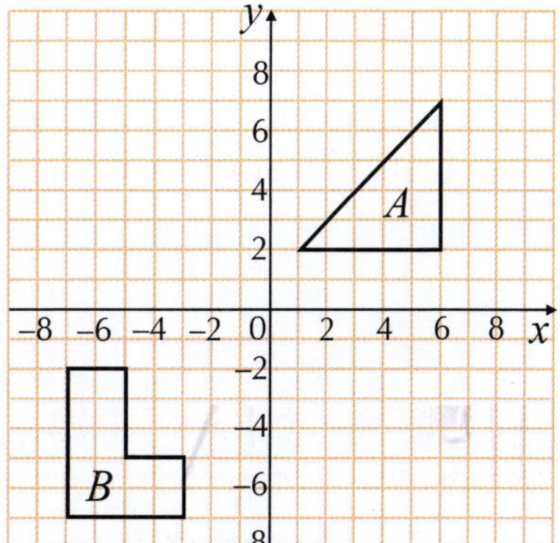

Copy the diagram above, then complete the following.

a) Rotate *A* 90° clockwise about the origin.

b) Rotate *B* 270° anticlockwise about the origin.

Q4 Copy the diagram on the right, then complete the following.

a) Rotate A 90° clockwise about (–8, 5).

b) Rotate B 90° anticlockwise about (6, 4).

c) Rotate C 90° clockwise about (8, –4).

d) Rotate D 180° about (–2, –5).

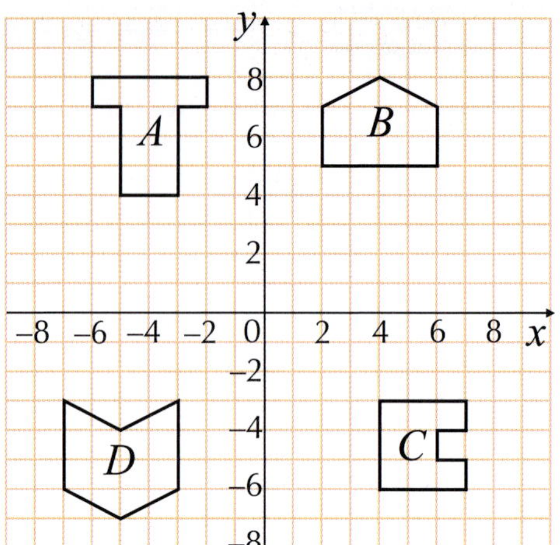

Q5 The triangle ABC has vertices $A(-2, 1)$, $B(-2, 6)$ and $C(4, 1)$.

a) Draw the triangle on a pair of axes.

b) Rotate the triangle 90° anticlockwise about (5, 4). Label the image $A_1B_1C_1$.

c) Write down the coordinates of A_1, B_1 and C_1.

Example 3

Describe fully the rotation that transforms shape A to shape B.

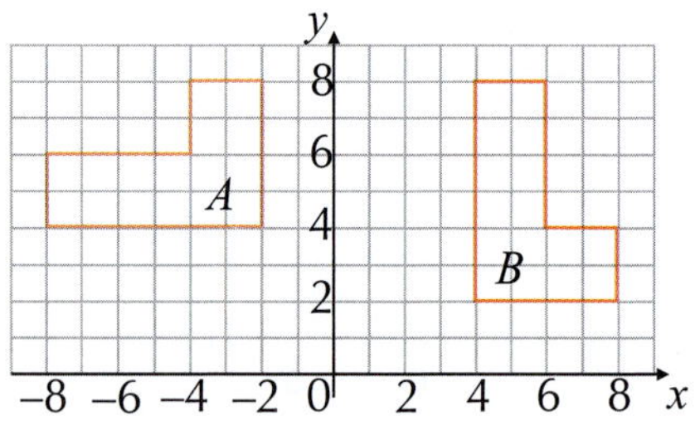

1. The shape looks like it has been rotated clockwise by 90°.
2. Trace shape A using tracing paper. Put your pencil on different possible centres of rotation and turn the tracing paper 90° clockwise until you find a centre that takes shape A onto shape B.

Tip: Remember:
90° = a ¼-turn,
180° = a ½-turn,
270° = a ¾-turn.

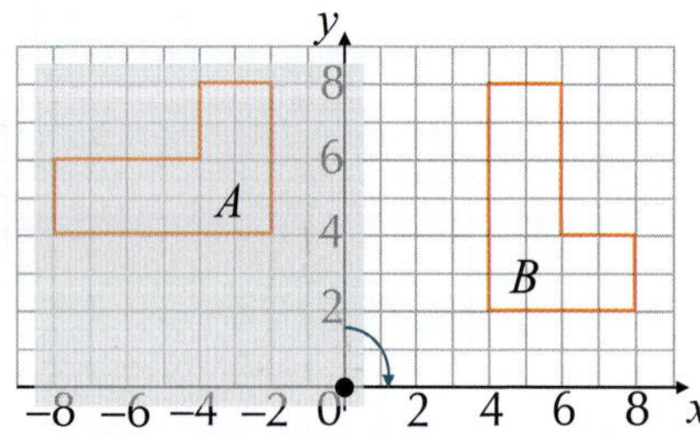

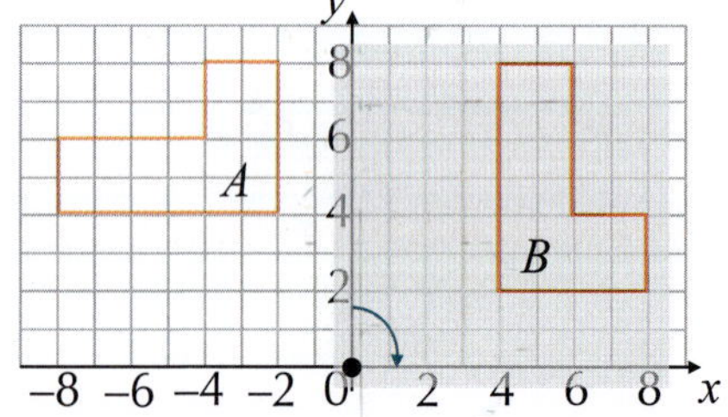

3. To fully describe the rotation, you need to write down the centre, direction and angle of rotation.

So A is transformed to B by a rotation of **90° clockwise** about **the origin (0, 0)**.

Exercise 3

Q1 Shapes *A*, *B*, *C* and *D* are shown on the grid below.

a) Describe fully the rotation that transforms shape *A* to shape *B*.

b) Describe fully the rotation that transforms shape *C* to shape *D*

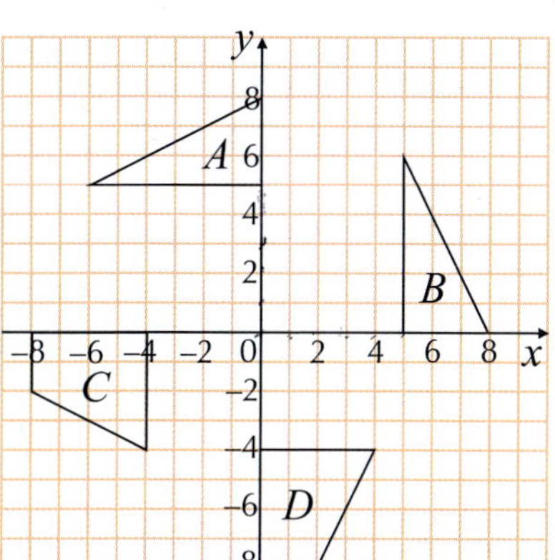

Q2 Shapes *E*, *F*, *G* and *H* are shown on the grid below.

a) Describe fully the rotation that transforms shape *E* to shape *F*.

b) Describe fully the rotation that transforms shape *G* to shape *H*.

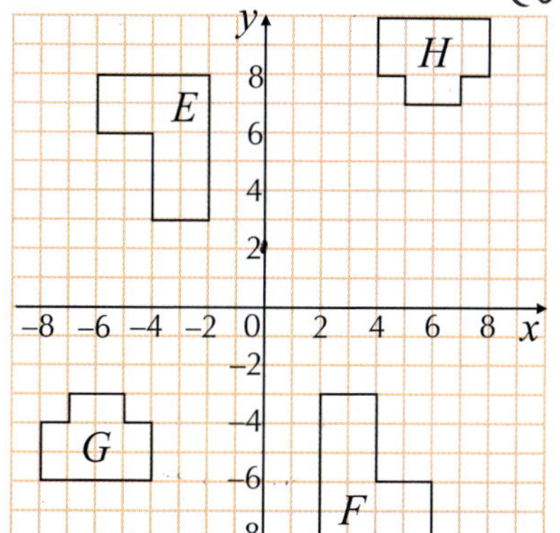

Q3 Shapes *I*, *J*, *K* and *L* are shown on the grid below.

a) Describe fully the rotation that transforms shape *I* to shape *J*.

b) Describe fully the rotation that transforms shape *K* to shape *L*.

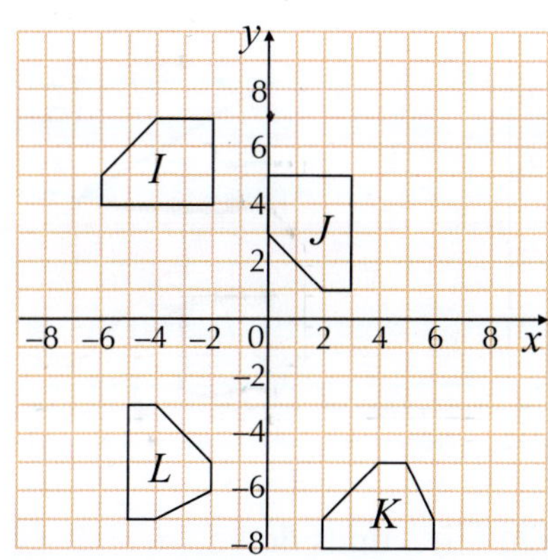

Q4 Shapes *M*, *N* and *P* are shown on the grid below.

a) Describe fully the rotation that transforms shape *M* to shape *N*.

b) Describe fully the rotation that transforms shape *M* to shape *P*.

c) Describe fully the rotation that transforms shape *N* to shape *P*.

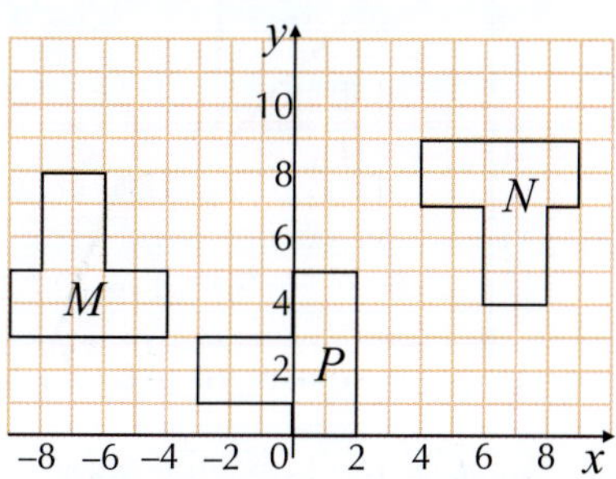

24.3 Translations

Translations are simple — they just slide a shape up/down and left/right.

Learning Objectives — Spec Ref G7/G24:
- Translate a shape on a coordinate grid.
- Find the vector that describes a translation.

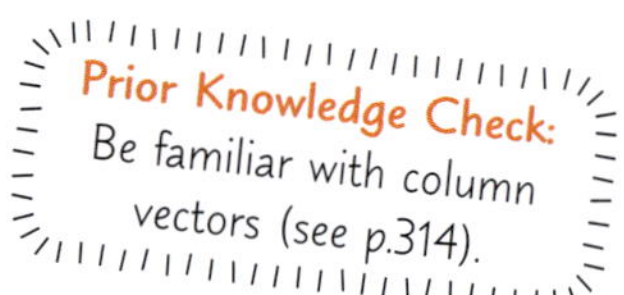

Prior Knowledge Check:
Be familiar with column vectors (see p.314).

To **translate** an object, you need to know the **distance** that it moves and in which **direction** — these are broken down into **horizontal** and **vertical** movements.

- For horizontal movements, **positive** numbers move the shape **right** and **negative** numbers move it **left**.
- For vertical movements, **positive** numbers move the shape **up** and **negative** numbers move it **down**.

Tip: Start by working out where the corners of a shape move to under a translation — then join them to complete the shape.

You can use **column vectors** to represent this information. For example:

$\begin{pmatrix} 3 \\ -2 \end{pmatrix}$

- 3: the object moves 3 units to the right (**positive x-direction**)
- −2: the object moves 2 units down (**negative y-direction**)

When an object is translated, its **size** and **shape** stay the **same**. Only its **position** changes — so the new shape is **congruent** to the original shape.

Example 1

Translate the shape below by the vector $\begin{pmatrix} 5 \\ -3 \end{pmatrix}$.

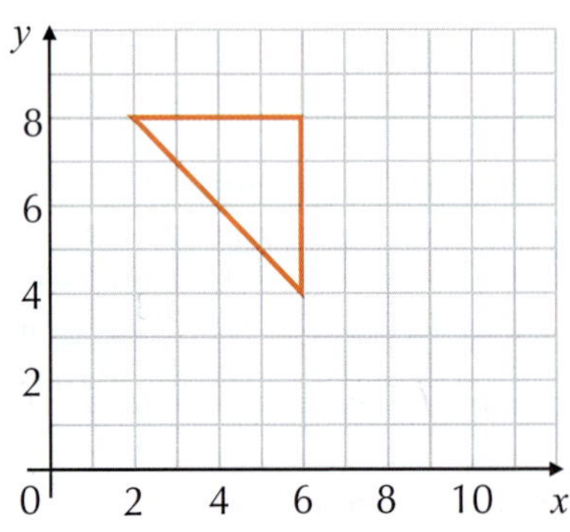

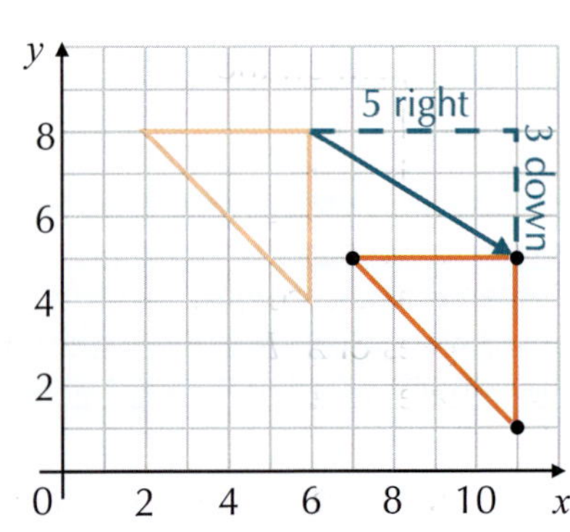

1. $\begin{pmatrix} 5 \\ -3 \end{pmatrix}$ is a translation of: i) 5 units to the right ii) 3 units down.
2. Translate each vertex, then join them up to create the translated shape.

Example 2

Find the coordinates of the point (2, –5) after it has been translated by $\begin{pmatrix} 6 \\ -4 \end{pmatrix}$.

The x-coordinate increases by 6, while the y-coordinate decreases by 4.

$(2 + 6, -5 - 4) = \mathbf{(8, -9)}$

Exercise 1

Q1 Write down in words the translations described by the following vectors.

a) $\begin{pmatrix} 1 \\ 1 \end{pmatrix}$ b) $\begin{pmatrix} 2 \\ 0 \end{pmatrix}$ c) 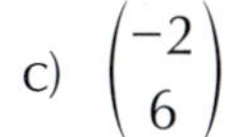 $\begin{pmatrix} -2 \\ 6 \end{pmatrix}$ d) $\begin{pmatrix} -3 \\ -2 \end{pmatrix}$

Q2 Copy the diagram below, then translate each shape by the vector written next to it.

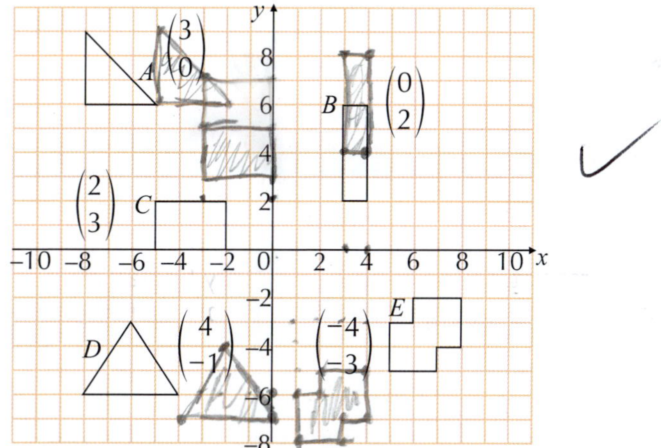

Q3 Copy the diagram on the right, then:

a) Translate the triangle ABC by the vector $\begin{pmatrix} -10 \\ -1 \end{pmatrix}$. Label the image $A_1B_1C_1$.

b) Label A_1, B_1 and C_1 with their coordinates.

c) Describe a rule connecting the coordinates of A, B and C and the coordinates of A_1, B_1 and C_1.

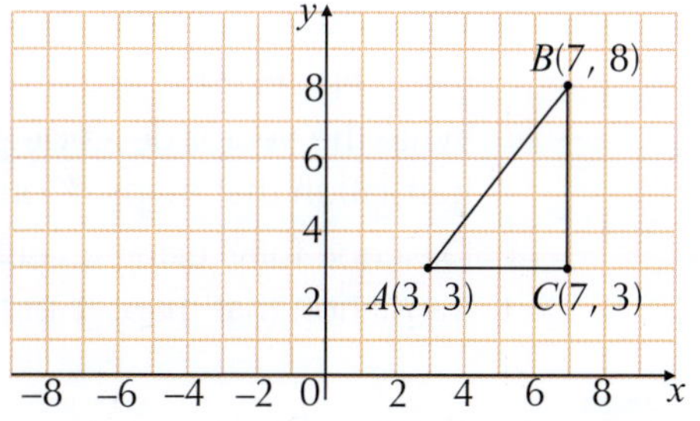

Q4 Find the coordinates of the image of the point (3, –4) after it has been translated by:

a) $\begin{pmatrix} 0 \\ 1 \end{pmatrix}$ b) $\begin{pmatrix} 3 \\ 0 \end{pmatrix}$ c) 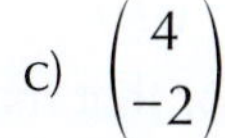 $\begin{pmatrix} 4 \\ -2 \end{pmatrix}$ d) $\begin{pmatrix} -1 \\ -5 \end{pmatrix}$

Q5 The triangle DEF has corners $D(1, 1)$, $E(3, -2)$ and $F(4, 0)$. After the translation $\begin{pmatrix} -2 \\ 2 \end{pmatrix}$, the image of DEF is $D_1E_1F_1$. Find the coordinates of D_1, E_1 and F_1.

Example 3

Describe the transformation that maps shape *A* onto shape *B*.

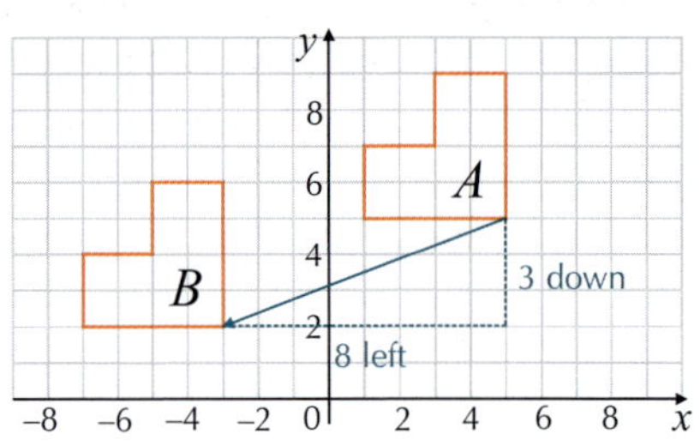

1. The shape hasn't been rotated or reflected and hasn't changed size, so this must be a translation.
2. Choose a pair of corresponding vertices on the two shapes and count how many units horizontally and vertically the point on *A* has moved to become the point on *B*.
3. Write the translation as a vector.

A has moved 8 units to the left and 3 units down so the transformation is a **translation described by the vector** $\begin{pmatrix}-8\\-3\end{pmatrix}$.

Exercise 2

Q1 Write the following translations in vector form.

a) 1 unit to the right, 2 units up
b) 1 unit to the right, 2 units down
c) 3 units down
d) 4 units to the left, 3 units down
e) 6 units to the right, 7 units up
f) 6 units up

Q2

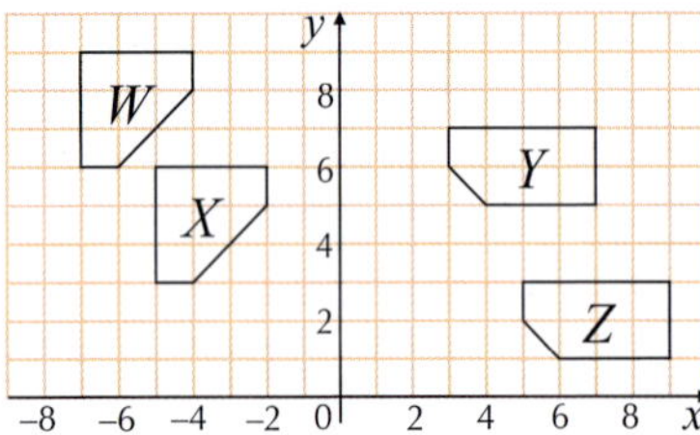

a) Write down in words the translation that maps *W* onto *X*.
b) Write the vector describing the translation that maps *W* onto *X*.
c) Describe fully, using a vector, the translation that maps *Y* onto *Z*.

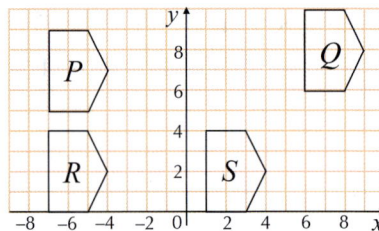

Q3

Give the translation vector that maps:

a) P to R
b) R to S
c) *P* to *Q*
d) S to R
e) Q to R
f) *S* to *P*

Q4 The triangle *DEF* has vertices *D*(–3, –2), *E*(1, –1) and *F*(0, 2). The triangle *GHI* has vertices *G*(0, 2), *H*(4, 3) and *I*(3, 6).

a) Sketch triangles *DEF* and *GHI*.
b) Give the translation vector that maps *DEF* onto *GHI*.

Q5 The triangle *JKL* has vertices *J*(1, 0), *K*(–2, 4) and *L*(–4, 7). The triangle *MNP* has vertices *M*(0, 2), *N*(–3, 6) and *P*(–5, 9). Give the translation vector that maps:

a) *JKL* onto *MNP*,
b) *MNP* onto *JKL*.

Sometimes, you might be told a **translation vector**, and be shown the **image** of a shape after the translation. To find the **original shape** you'll need to work **backwards** and do the opposite translation, represented by the original vector with the **signs** of both components **changed**.

Example 4

Shape B is the image of shape A after the translation $\begin{pmatrix} 7 \\ -3 \end{pmatrix}$. Draw shape A.

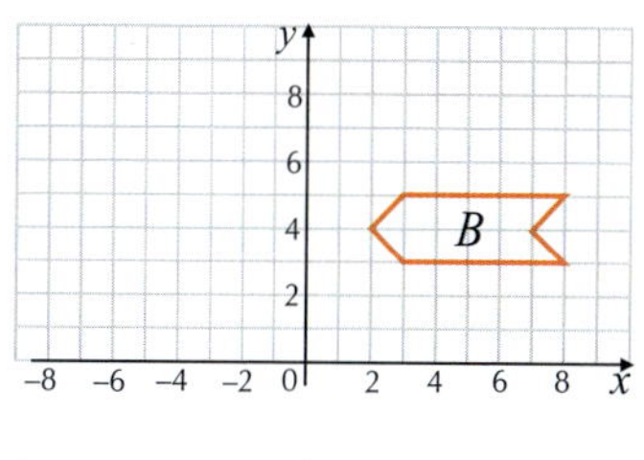

1. Find the vector that maps B onto A — it's the negative of the vector that maps A to B.

   A to B is given by $\begin{pmatrix} 7 \\ -3 \end{pmatrix}$.

   So B to A must be given by $\begin{pmatrix} -7 \\ 3 \end{pmatrix}$.

2. So shape A must be 7 units to the left and 3 units up from shape B.

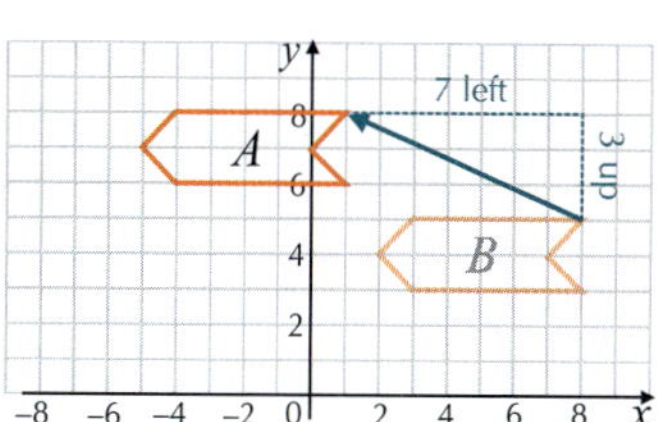

Exercise 3

Q1 This question is about the diagram on the right.

a) Give the translation vector that maps X onto Y.

b) Give the translation vector that maps Y onto X.

c) What do you notice about your answers to a) and b)?

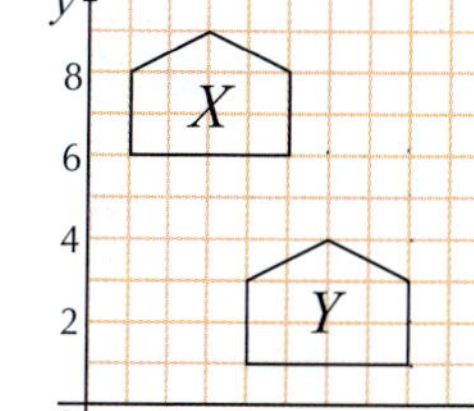

Q2 Shape Z is the image of shape W after the translation $\begin{pmatrix} 1 \\ -4 \end{pmatrix}$. Write down the translation that maps Z onto W.

Q3

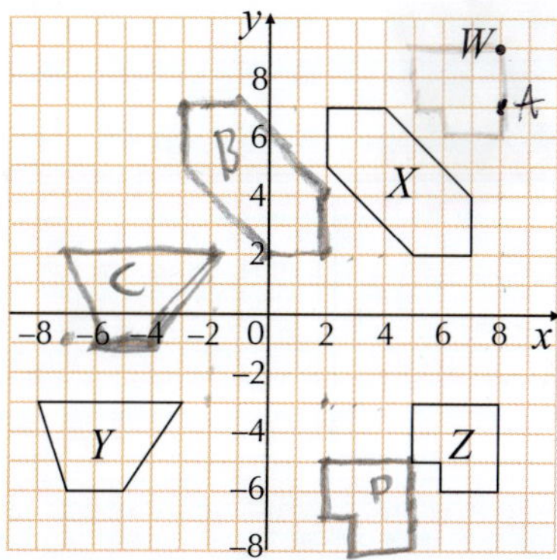

Copy the diagram on the left.

a) W is the image of A after the translation $\begin{pmatrix} 0 \\ 2 \end{pmatrix}$. Draw A.

b) Draw B, given that X is the image of B after the translation $\begin{pmatrix} 5 \\ 0 \end{pmatrix}$.

c) Y is the image of C after the translation $\begin{pmatrix} -1 \\ -5 \end{pmatrix}$. Draw C.

d) Draw D, given that Z is the image of D after the translation $\begin{pmatrix} 3 \\ 2 \end{pmatrix}$.

Q4 The triangle PQR has vertices $P(-1, 0)$, $Q(-4, 4)$ and $R(3, 2)$. PQR is the image of the triangle DEF after the translation $\begin{pmatrix} -1 \\ 4 \end{pmatrix}$. Find the coordinates of D, E and F.

24.4 Enlargements

Enlargements can be a little bit trickier than the other transformations. They are described by two properties — a scale factor (a number) and a centre of enlargement (given using coordinates).

Scale Factors

Learning Objective — Spec Ref G7:
Enlarge a shape using a positive or fractional scale factor.

When an object is **enlarged**, its shape stays the same, but its **size changes**. The image of a shape after an enlargement is **similar** to the original shape (see page 414 for more on similar shapes).

The **scale factor** of an enlargement tells you how many **times longer** the sides of the new shape are **compared** to the old shape. For example, enlarging by a **scale factor of 2** makes each side **twice as long**.

Scale factors can also be **fractions**. If the scale factor is a **fraction** between –1 and 1, then the enlargement will **shrink** the shape. E.g. enlarging by a **scale factor of $\frac{1}{2}$** makes each side **half as long**.

Tip: To draw an enlargement, start by multiplying each side length of the original shape by the scale factor. Then draw the new shape using those lengths.

Example 1

Enlarge the shape on the grid by scale factor 2.

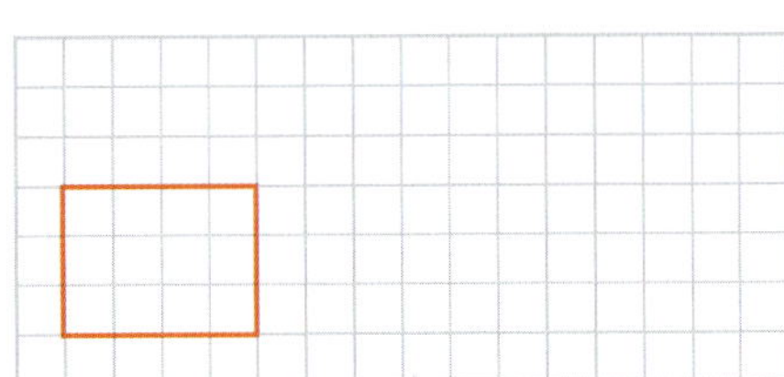

1. Find the dimensions of the shape you're enlarging.

   The original shape is 4 units wide and 3 units tall.

2. Multiply these by the scale factor to find the dimensions of the image.

   The enlargement will be
   $4 \times 2 = 8$ units wide and
   $3 \times 2 = 6$ units tall.

3. Draw the image using the dimensions you've found.

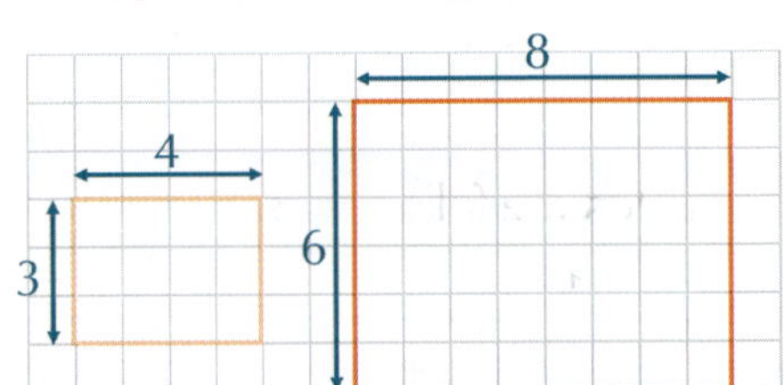

Example 2

Enlarge the shape on the grid by scale factor $\frac{1}{2}$.

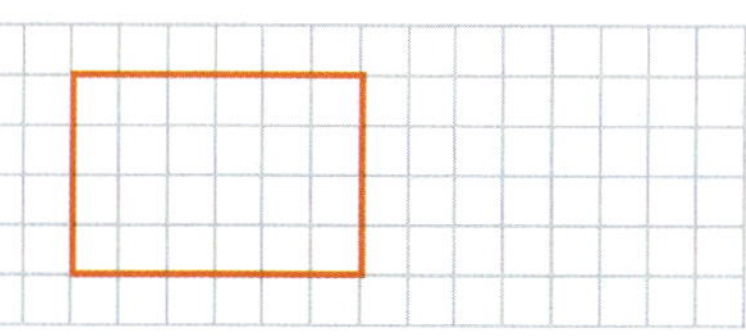

1. Multiply the dimensions of the shape by the scale factor — i.e. multiply by $\frac{1}{2}$ (or divide by 2).

   $6 \times \frac{1}{2} = 3$ and $4 \times \frac{1}{2} = 2$.

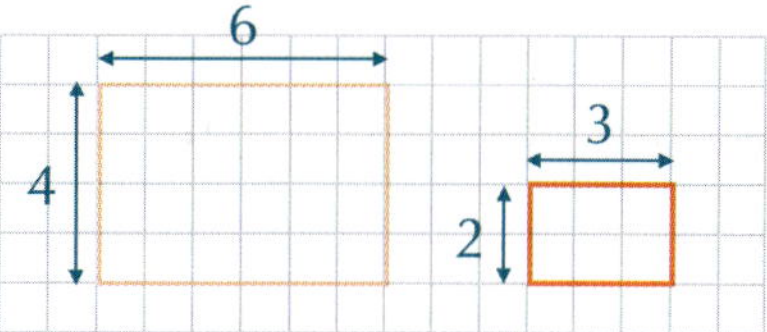

2. Draw the image using the new dimensions — this time, the image will be smaller than the original.

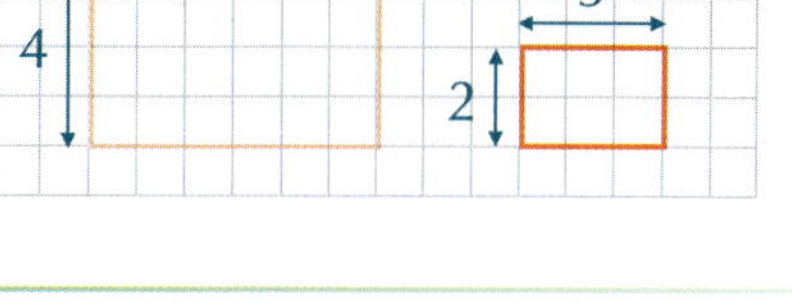

Exercise 1

Q1 Copy the diagram below, then enlarge the shapes by scale factor 2.

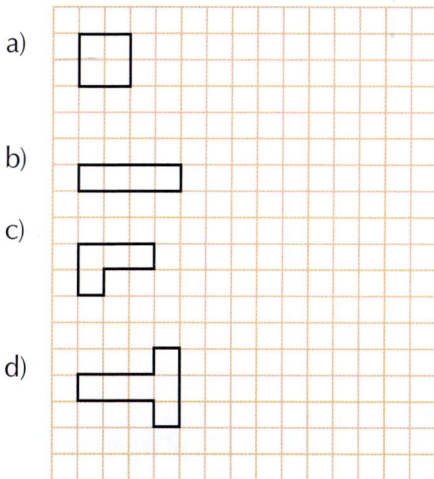

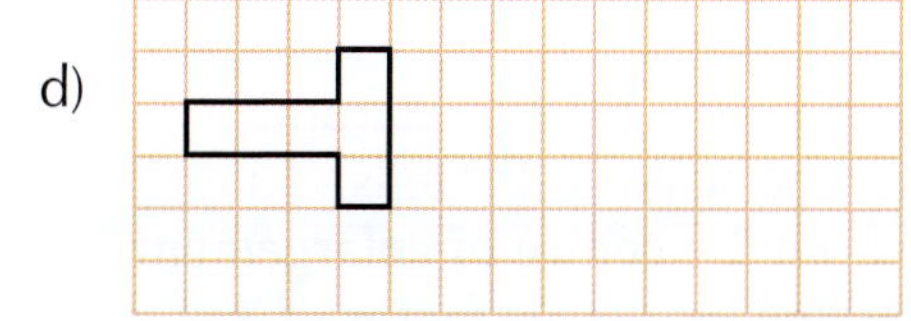

Q2 Copy the diagram below, then enlarge the shapes by scale factor 3.

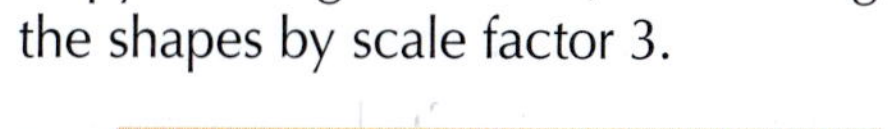

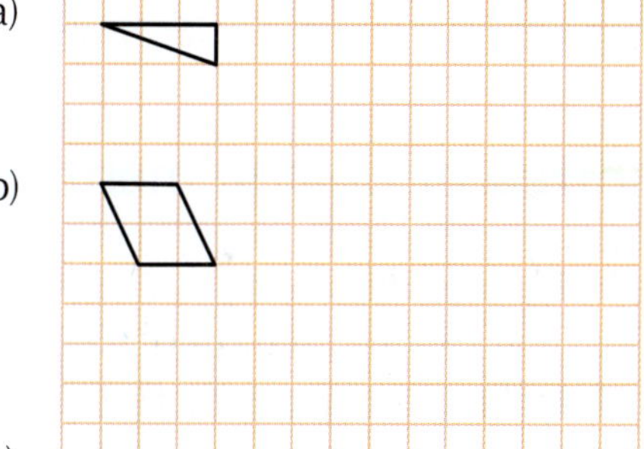

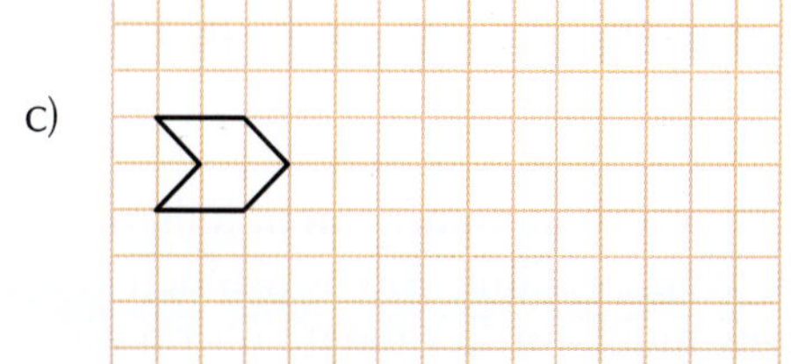

Q3 Sketch the following shapes after they have been enlarged by scale factor 5.

a) 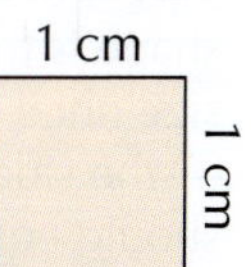

b) 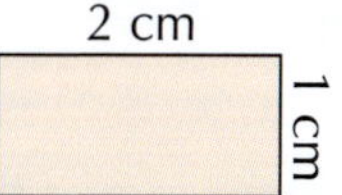

c) 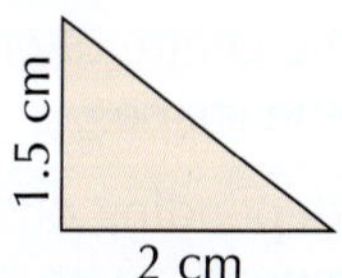

d) 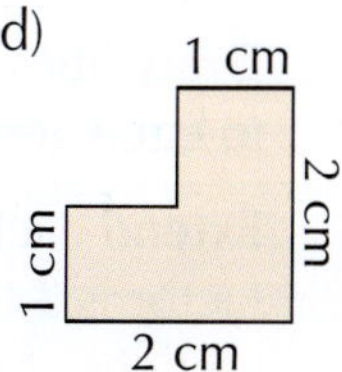

Q4 Copy the diagram below, then enlarge the shapes by scale factor $\frac{1}{2}$.

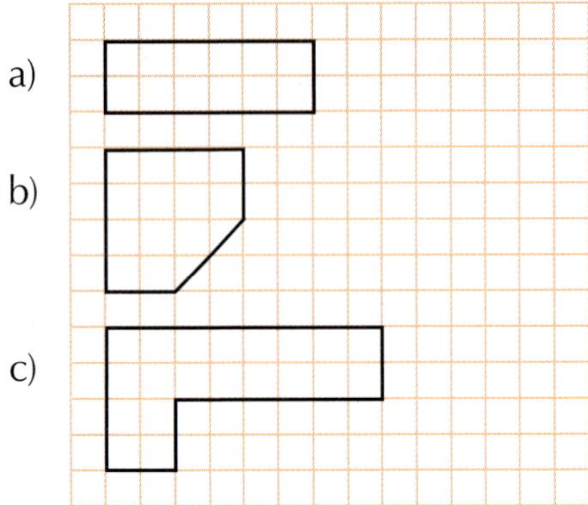

Q5 Copy the diagram below, then enlarge the shapes by scale factor $\frac{1}{3}$.

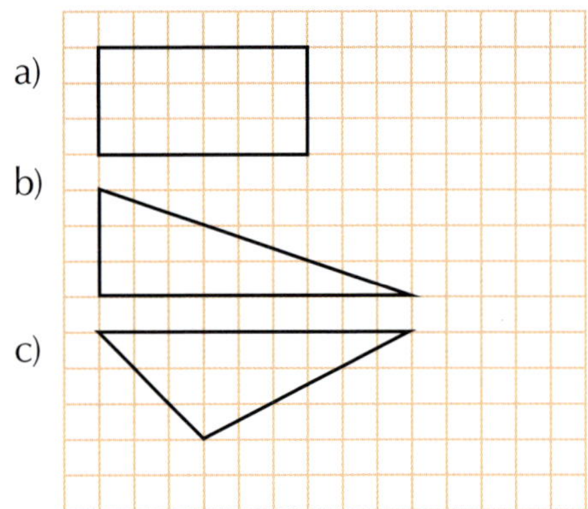

Q6 A square with sides of length 16 cm is enlarged by scale factor $\frac{1}{4}$. How long are the square's sides after the enlargement?

Q7 A 15 cm × 35 cm rectangle is enlarged by scale factor $\frac{1}{5}$. What are the dimensions of the rectangle after the enlargement?

Centres of Enlargement

Learning Objectives — Spec Ref G7:

- Enlarge a shape on a coordinate grid with a given centre of enlargement.
- Describe an enlargement that transforms a shape.

The **centre of enlargement** tells you where the enlargement is measured from. As well as telling you how much bigger the sides are, the **scale factor** tells you **how much further** the points on the new shape are from the **centre of enlargement** than the points on the old shape. For example, enlarging by a **scale factor of 3** makes each point **three times as far** from the centre of enlargement.

To enlarge a shape when you know the centre of enlargement:

- **Draw lines** from the centre of enlargement to **each vertex** of the shape.
- **Extend** each line depending on the scale factor (e.g. if the scale factor is 3 the line needs to be 3 times as long). Mark the vertices of the new shape at the ends of these extended lines.
- **Join up** the new vertices to create the enlarged shape.

Tip: Check your new shape is the correct size once you're done — the side lengths should equal those of the original shape multiplied by the scale factor.

Example 3

Enlarge the shape below by scale factor 2 with centre of enlargement (2, 2).

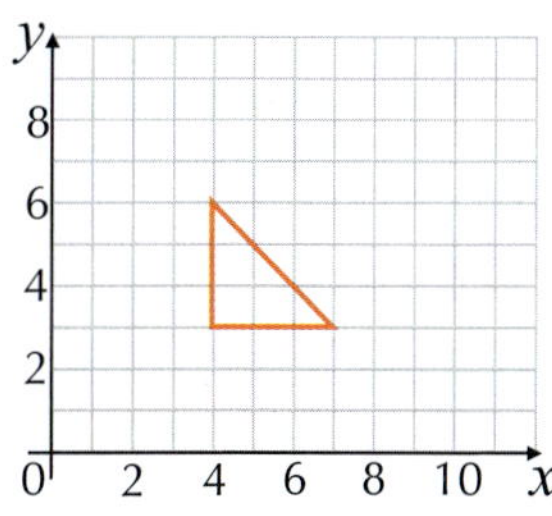

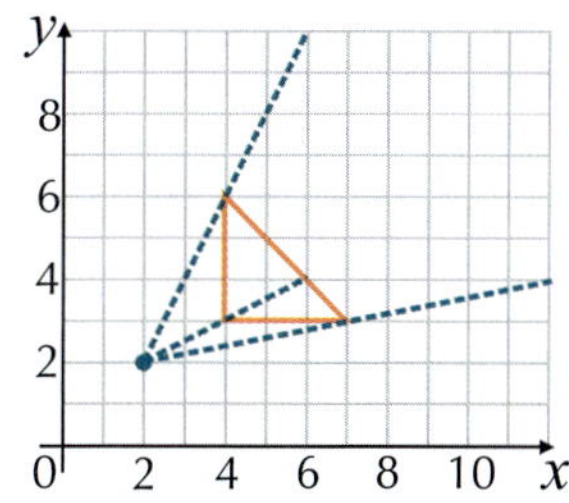

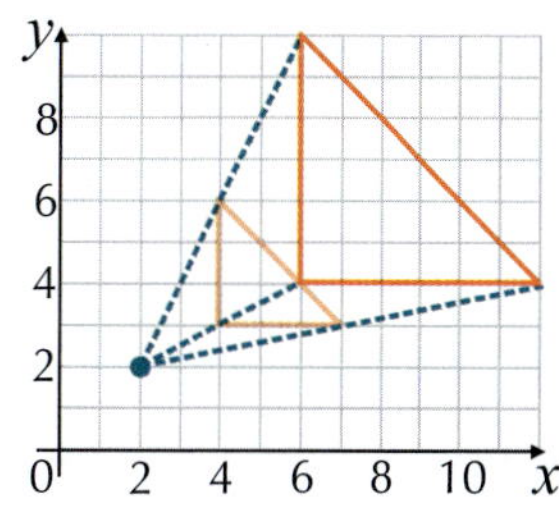

1. Draw a line from (2, 2) through each corner of the shape. Continue each line until it is twice as far away from (2, 2) as the original corner.
2. Join up the ends of the lines to create the image.

Exercise 2

Q1 The triangle PQR is shown on the left. $P_1Q_1R_1$ is the image of PQR after it has been enlarged by scale factor 2 with centre of enlargement (2, 2).

a) Find the distance of each of the following corners from (2, 2).
(i) P (ii) Q (iii) R

b) What will the distance of the following corners be from (2, 2)?
(i) P_1 (ii) Q_1 (iii) R_1

c) Copy the diagram and draw a line from the point (2, 2) through P and Q. Mark the points P_1, Q_1 and R_1 on your diagram. Join up the points P_1, Q_1 and R_1 to draw $P_1Q_1R_1$.

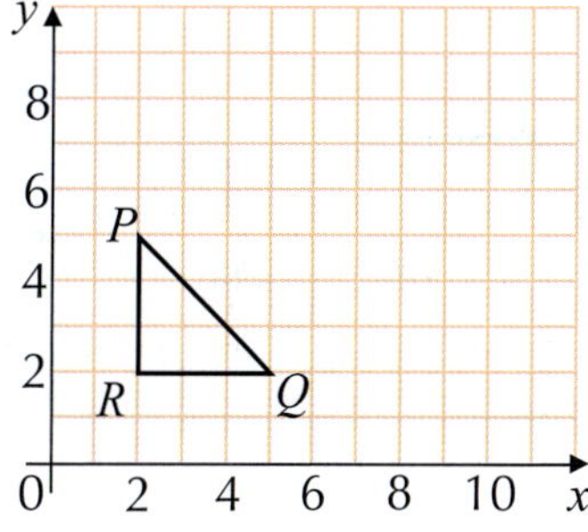

Q2 Copy the diagram on the right.

a) Enlarge A by scale factor 2 with centre of enlargement (–8, 9).

b) Enlarge B by scale factor 2 with centre of enlargement (9, 9).

c) Enlarge C by scale factor 3 with centre of enlargement (9, –8).

d) Enlarge D by scale factor 4 with centre of enlargement (–8, –8).

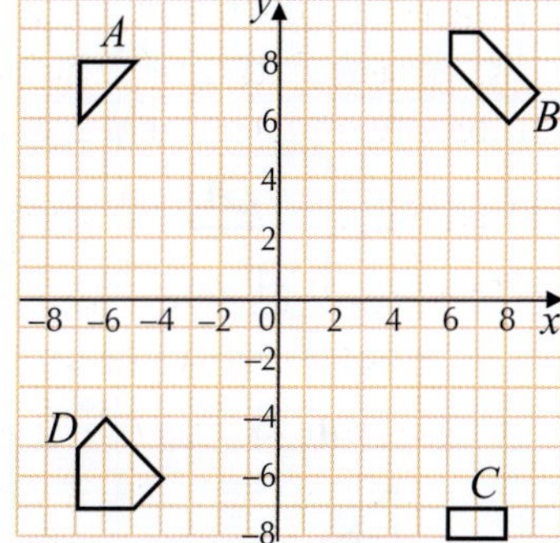

Q3 The triangle PQR has corners at $P(1, 1)$, $Q(1, 4)$ and $R(4, 2)$.

a) Draw PQR on a pair of axes.

b) Enlarge PQR by scale factor 2 with centre of enlargement (–1, 1).

If the **scale factor** is a fraction, each point on the new shape will be **closer** to the **centre of enlargement**.

To enlarge by a fractional scale factor:

- First **draw lines** from the **centre of enlargement** to **each vertex**, just like before.
- Then mark the vertices of the **new shape** a **fraction** of the way along these lines (depending on the **scale factor**). E.g. a scale factor of $\frac{1}{4}$ means the new vertices are a quarter of the way along the lines.
- **Join up** the new vertices to form the new shape.

Tip: When a shape is enlarged, all the angles stay the same — always check your shape looks right.

Example 4

Enlarge the shape below by scale factor $\frac{1}{2}$ with centre of enlargement (2, 7).

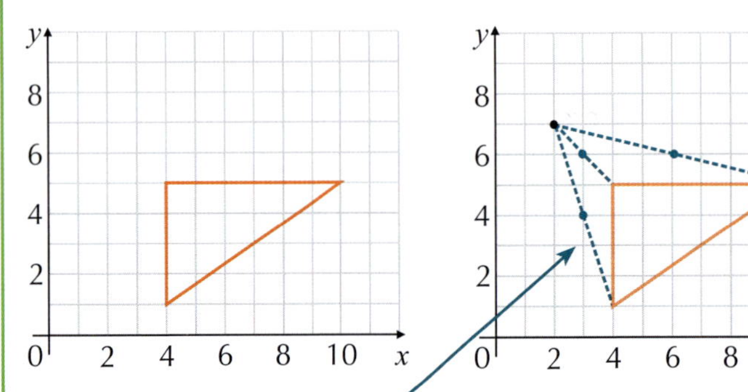

1. Draw lines from (2, 7) to each corner. The image points will lie $\frac{1}{2}$ as far from the centre of enlargement as the original corners.

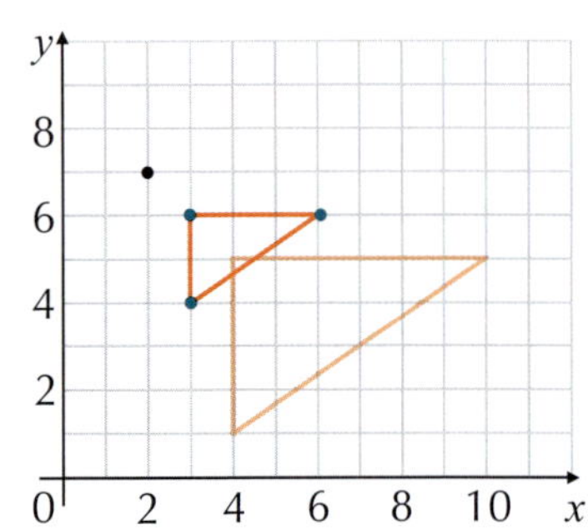

2. Join up the image points.

Exercise 3

Q1

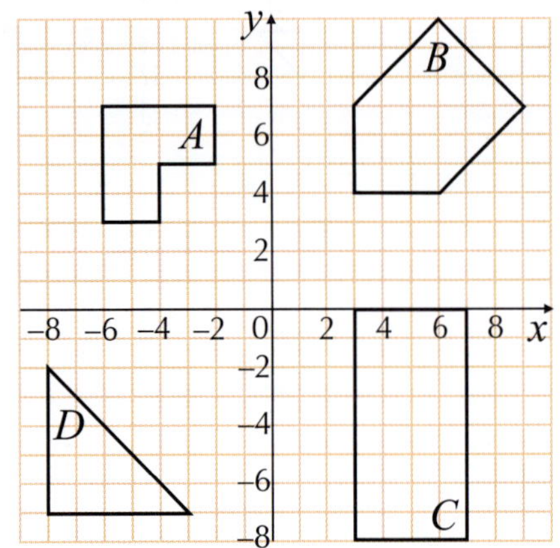

Copy the diagram on the left.

a) Enlarge A by scale factor $\frac{1}{2}$ with centre of enlargement (–8, 9).

b) Enlarge B by scale factor $\frac{1}{3}$ with centre of enlargement (0, 1).

c) Enlarge C by scale factor $\frac{1}{4}$ with centre of enlargement (–1, –8).

d) Enlarge D by scale factor $\frac{1}{5}$ with centre of enlargement (2, 3).

Q2 Copy the diagram on the right.

a) Enlarge A by scale factor $\frac{1}{2}$ with centre of enlargement (–4, 5).

b) Enlarge B by scale factor $\frac{1}{3}$ with centre of enlargement (7, 7).

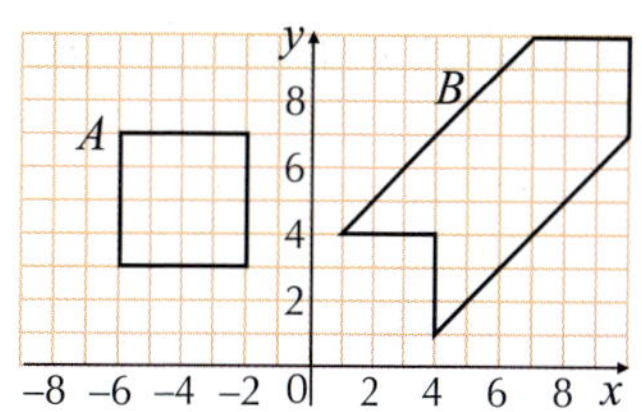

To describe an enlargement, you need to give the **scale factor** and the **centre of enlargement**. To find the **scale factor**, take the length of **any side** on the new shape and the length of its corresponding side on the old shape and use the **formula**:

$$\textbf{scale factor} = \frac{\textbf{new length}}{\textbf{old length}}$$

Tip: You can check the scale factor using a different pair of corresponding sides.

To find the **centre of enlargement**, **draw** and **extend lines** that go through corresponding vertices of both shapes and see where they all **intersect**.

Example 5

Describe the enlargement that maps shape X onto shape Y.

1. Pick any side of the shape, and see how many times bigger this side is on the image than the original. This is the scale factor.
2. Draw a line from each corner on the image through the corresponding corner on the original shape.
3. The point where these lines meet is the centre of enlargement.

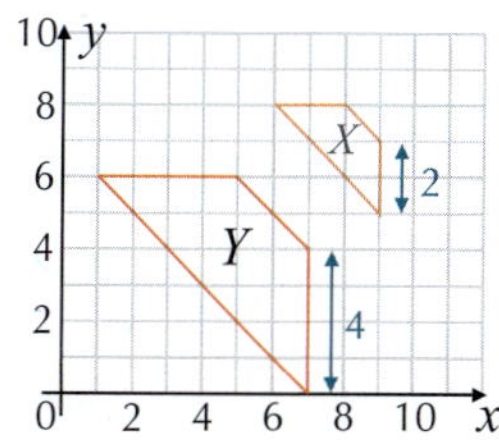

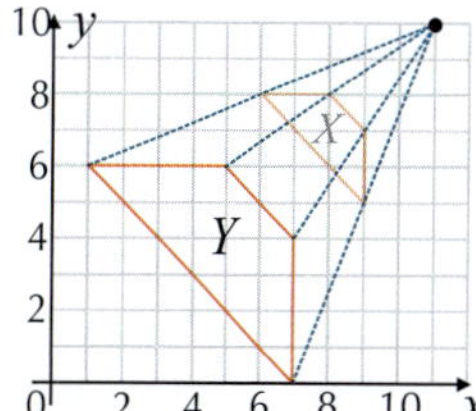

The scale factor = 4 ÷ 2 = 2.
The lines through the vertices intersect at (11, 10).
Enlargement by **scale factor 2**, **centre (11, 10)**.

Exercise 4

Q1 For each of the following, describe the enlargement that maps shape A onto shape B.

a)

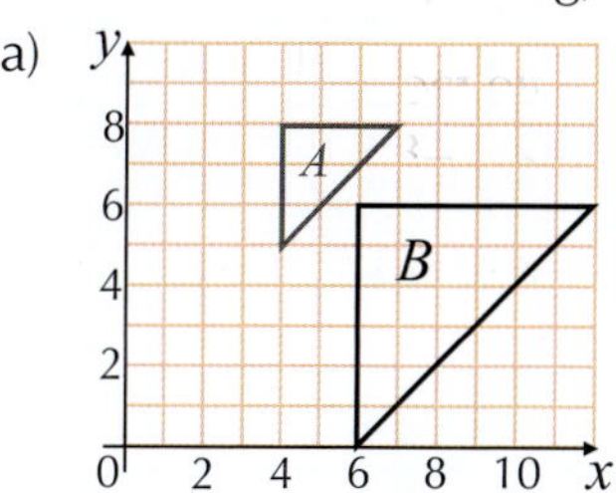

b)

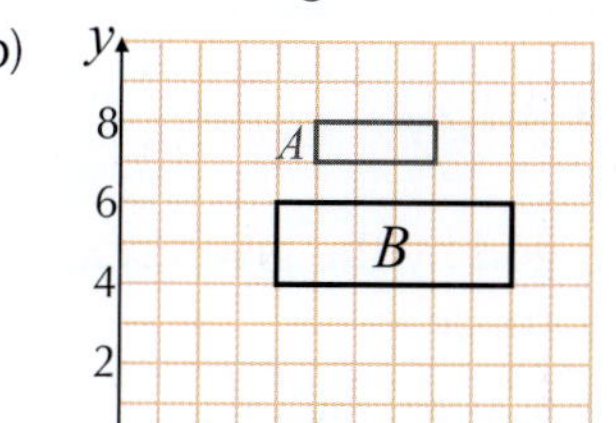

c)

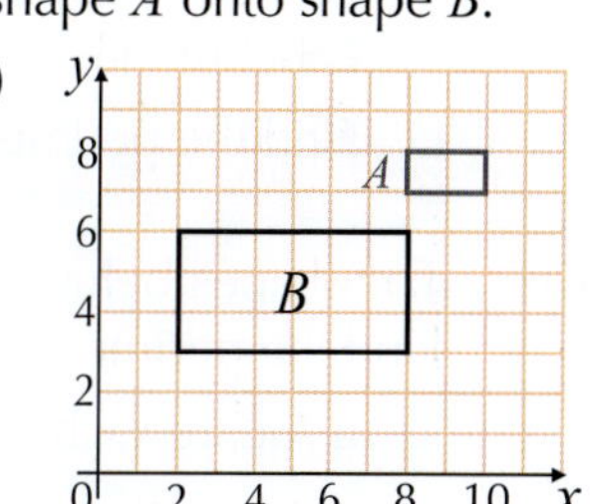

Q2 For each of the following, describe the enlargement that maps shape B onto shape A.

a)

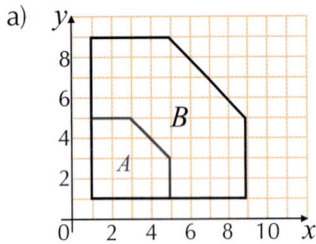

b) 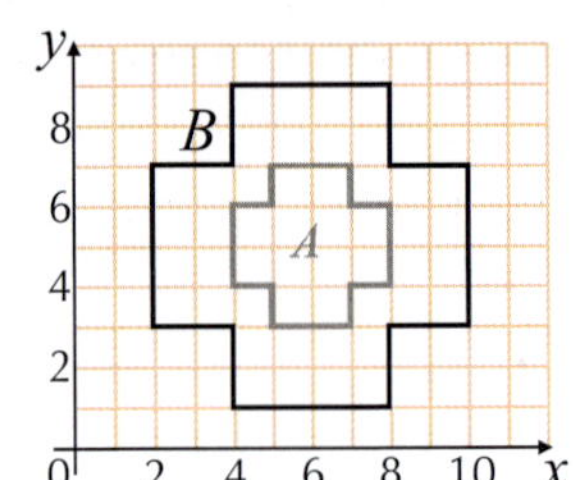

c) 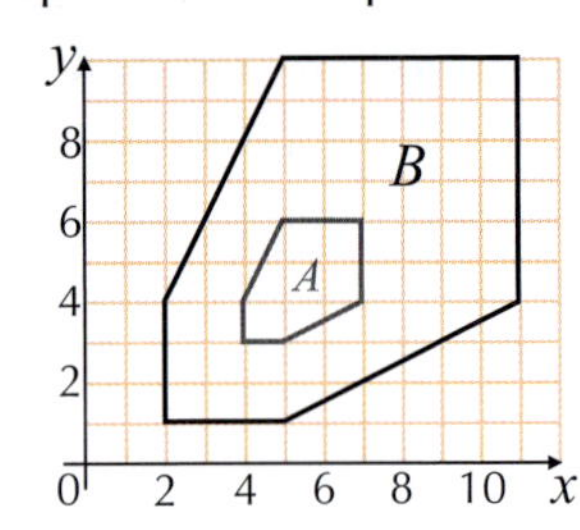

Enlargements and Perimeters

Learning Objective — Spec Ref G19:
Know how an enlargement affects the perimeter of a shape.

You know that in an **enlargement** the side lengths of a shape are multiplied by the scale factor. This means that the **perimeter** is also **multiplied by the scale factor**.

Example 6

Find the perimeter of this triangle after it has been enlarged by scale factor 4.

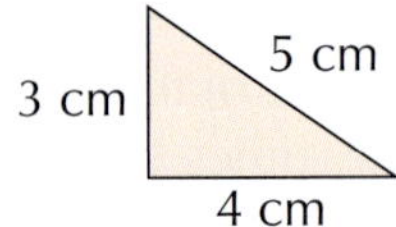

1. Find the perimeter of the original triangle.

Perimeter = 3 + 4 + 5 = 12 cm

2. The perimeter of the enlarged triangle will be 12 + 16 + 20 = 48 cm.
   This is the same as the original perimeter multiplied by the scale factor.

Perimeter after enlargement
= 12 cm × 4 = **48 cm**

Exercise 5

Q1 The rectangle $WXYZ$ has vertices $W(1, 1)$, $X(1, 2)$, $Y(4, 2)$ and $Z(4, 1)$.

a) Draw $WXYZ$ on a pair of axes, and find the perimeter of $WXYZ$.

b) Enlarge $WXYZ$ by scale factor 2 with centre of enlargement (0, 0). Label the image $W_1X_1Y_1Z_1$.

c) Find the perimeter of $W_1X_1Y_1Z_1$.

Q2 The shapes below are enlarged by the given scale factor. Find the perimeter of each image.

a) a square with sides 3 cm; scale factor 3

b) a 2 m × 8 m rectangle; scale factor 5

24.5 Congruence and Similarity

Two shapes are congruent if they are exactly the same shape and size.
Two shapes are similar if they are exactly the same shape but different sizes.

Congruence

Learning Objective — Spec Ref G6:
Be able to identify congruent shapes.

If two shapes are congruent, all the **side lengths** and **angles** on one shape are **identical** to the side lengths and angles on the other shape.

A **translated**, **rotated** or **reflected** shape is always **congruent** to the original shape.

Tip: You can use tracing paper to check whether two shapes are identical.

Example 1

Which two of the shapes A, B and C are congruent?

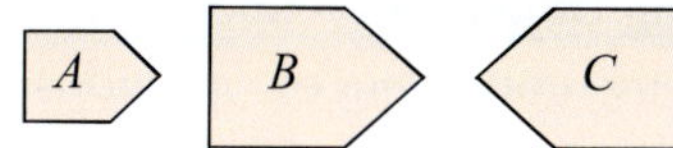

Compare each shape to see if they are the same shape and size. Tracing paper may help with this.

1. A and B are different sizes.
2. A and C are different sizes.
3. B and C are the same size and shape, just in different orientations.

The two congruent shapes are ***B* and *C***.

Exercise 1

Q1 Write down the letters of the congruent pairs of shapes shown in the box below. For example, A is congruent to G.

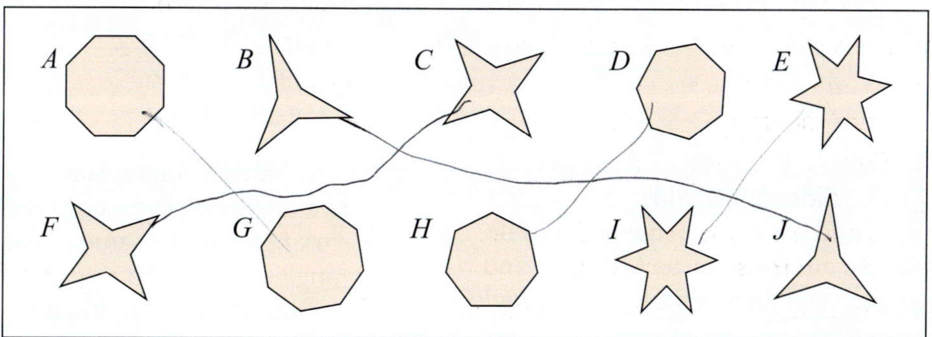

Q2 For each of the following, decide which shape is not congruent to the others.

a) C D E

b) F G H

c) I J K

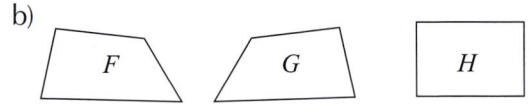

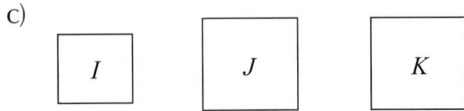

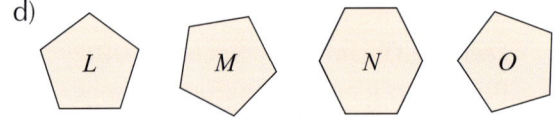

d) L M N O

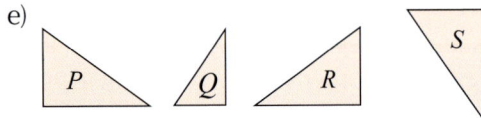

e) P Q R S

f) T U V W

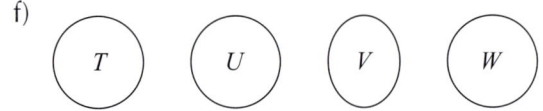

Congruent Triangles

Learning Objective — Spec Ref G5/G6:
Know the congruence conditions for triangles.

To show that two **triangles** are **congruent**, you **don't** need to know all the sides and angles — you just need to show that they satisfy any **one** of the following '**congruence conditions**'. (If any of these conditions are true, trigonometry can be used to show that the other sides and angles in the triangles must also be the same.)

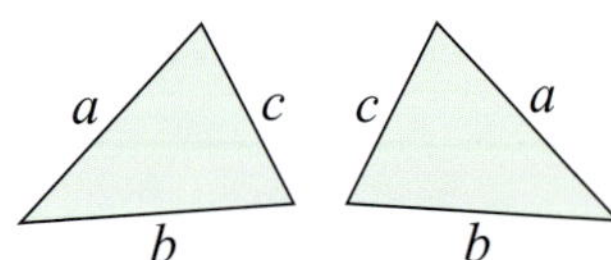

Side, Side, Side:
The three sides on one triangle are the same as the three sides on the other triangle.

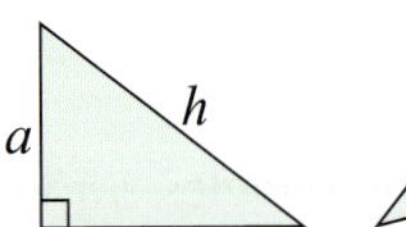

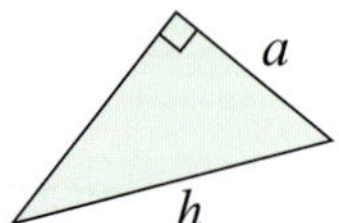

Right angle, Hypotenuse, Side:
Both triangles have a right angle, both triangles have the same hypotenuse and one other side is the same.

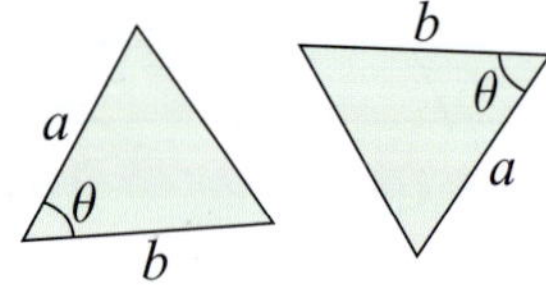

Side, Angle, Side:
Two sides and the angle between them on one triangle are the same as two sides and the angle between them on the other triangle.

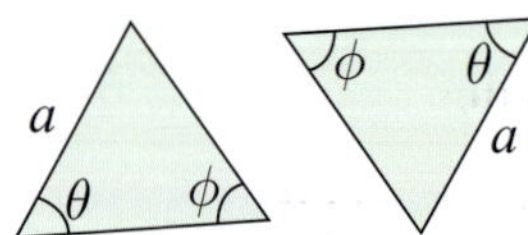

Angle, Angle, Side:
Two angles and any side on one triangle are the same as two angles and the corresponding side on the other triangle.

Be very careful when using 'Side, Angle, Side' and 'Angle, Angle, Side'. For SAS, you have to have the **correct combination** of sides and angles. For AAS, you need to make sure you're comparing **corresponding sides** on the two triangles.

If it isn't obvious which of the conditions apply, you might have to work out some side lengths or angles yourself. **Pythagoras' theorem**, the **properties of isosceles triangles** and the **sum of angles in a triangle** will come in handy — have a look at Sections 15 and 19 for a reminder.

Example 2

Are these two triangles congruent? Give a reason for your answer.

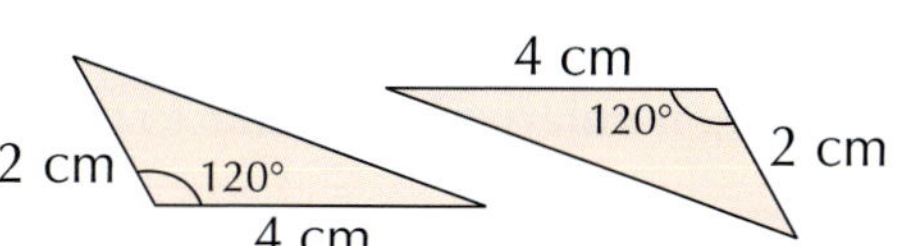

Look to see if the triangles satisfy any of the conditions for congruency. The orientation of the triangles doesn't matter.

Two of the sides and the angle between them are the same on both triangles.

Condition SAS holds, so the triangles **are congruent**.

Tip: The 'congruence conditions' are often abbreviated to SSS, RHS, SAS and AAS.

Exercise 2

Q1 The following pairs of triangles are congruent. Find the values marked with letters.

a)

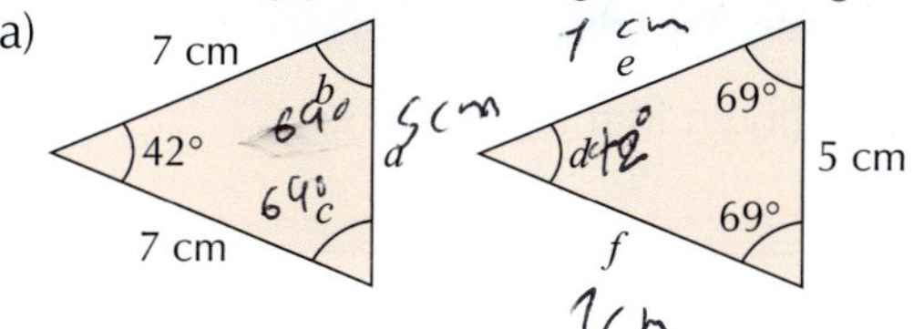

b)

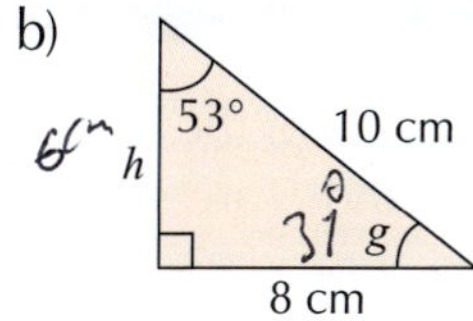

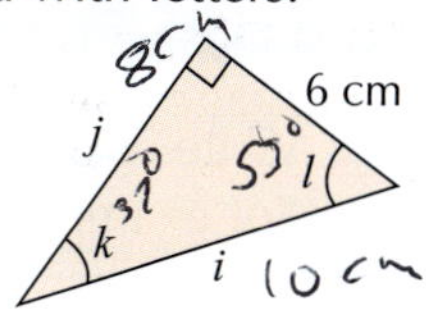

Q2 For each pair of triangles, write down whether the triangles are congruent and explain why.

a)

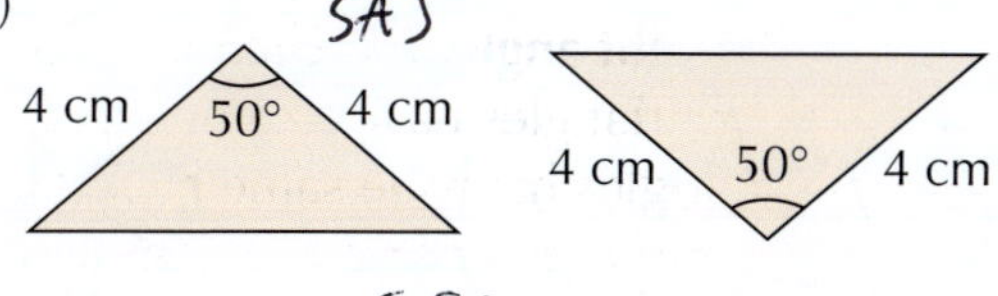

b)

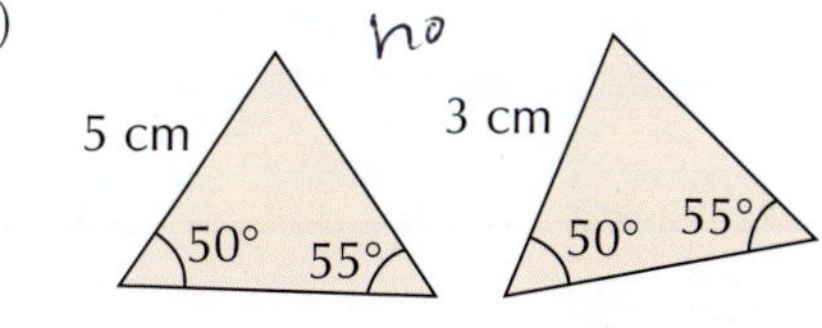

c)

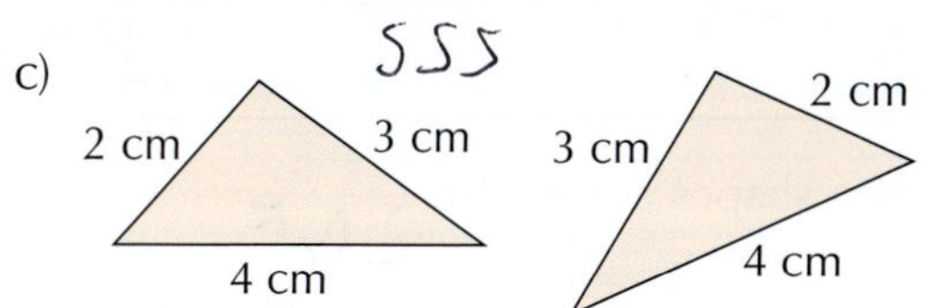

d)

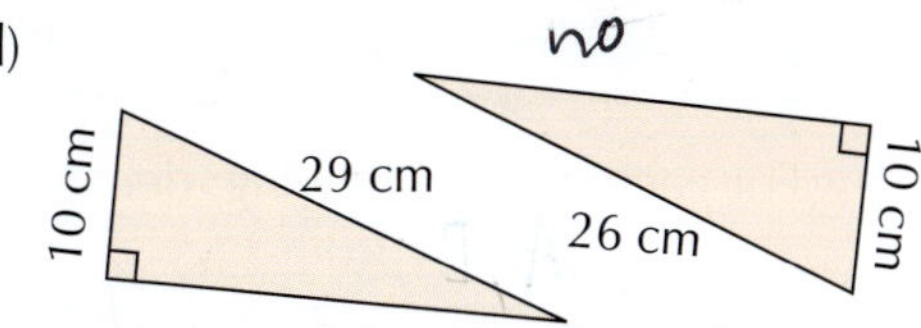

Q3 Show that each pair of triangles below is congruent.

a)

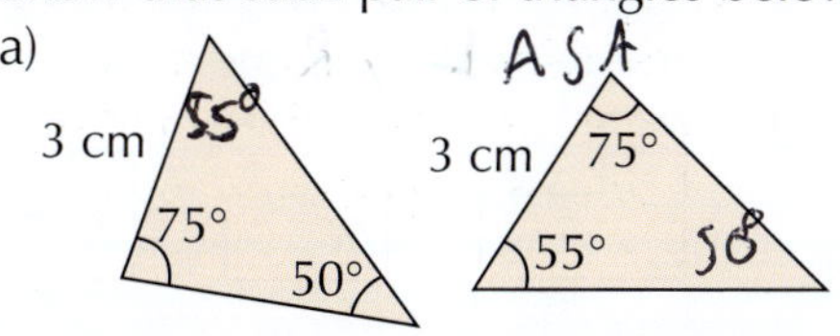

b)

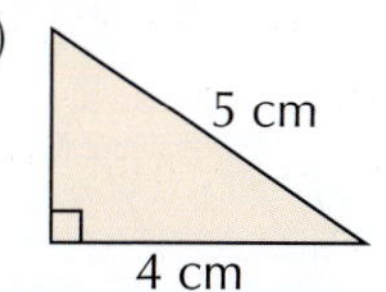

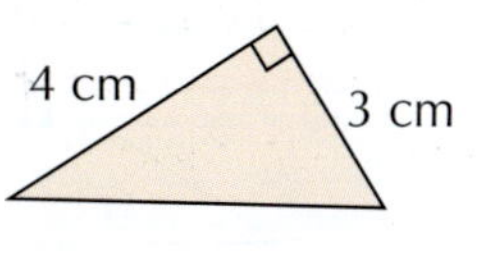

Similarity

Learning Objective — Spec Ref G6:
Be able to identify similar shapes.

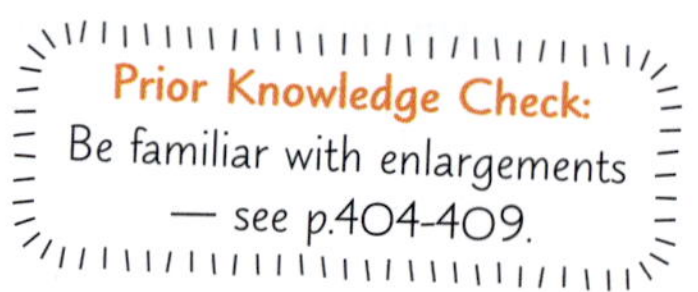
Prior Knowledge Check:
Be familiar with enlargements
— see p.404-409.

Similar shapes are the same shape but can be different sizes. They have the **same angles** as each other, but the **side lengths** can be **different** — they are enlarged by the same **scale factor**. This means that the image of a shape after it has been **enlarged** is **similar** to the original shape.

Tip: Regular polygons with the same number of sides are always similar.

Example 3

Which two of the shapes *P*, *Q* and *R* are similar?

1. Compare *P* and *R* — they are different shapes.
2. Compare *Q* and *R* — they are different shapes.
3. Compare *P* and *Q* — they are the same shape, but different sizes.

The two similar shapes are ***P* and *Q***.

Exercise 3

Q1 Write down the letters of the similar shapes shown in the box below.
For example, *A*, *C* and *F* are similar.

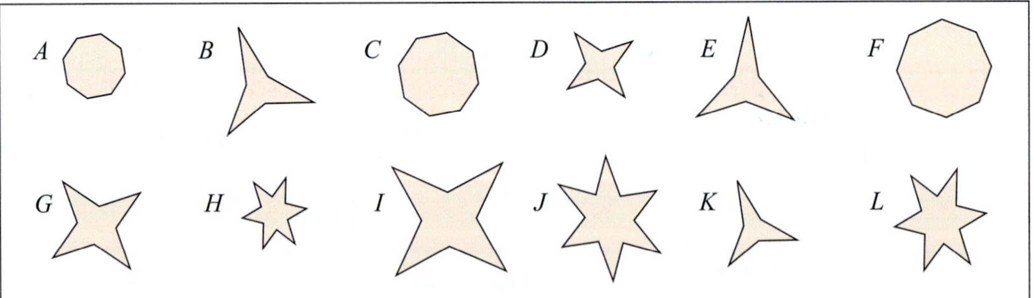

Q2 For each of the following, decide which two shapes are similar.

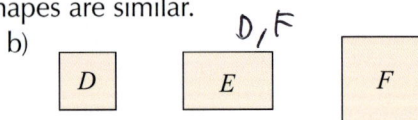

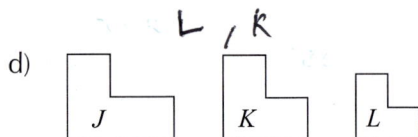

a)

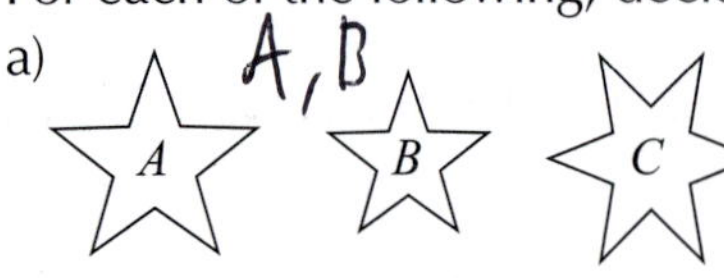

b)

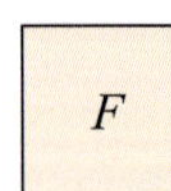

D E F

c)

d)

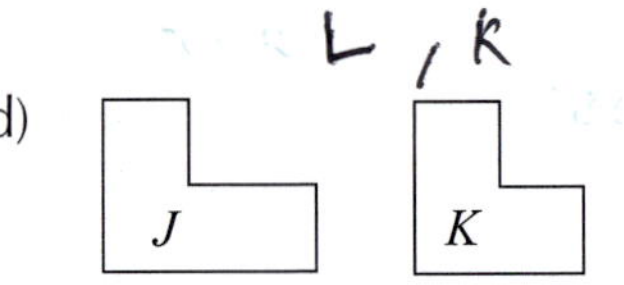

Similar Triangles

Learning Objectives — Spec Ref G6:
- Be able to prove that two triangles are similar.
- Find unknown lengths and angles in similar triangles.

As with congruent triangles, you **don't** need to know **all** the side lengths and angles to show similarity for triangles. Two **triangles** are **similar** if they satisfy any **one** of the following **conditions**:

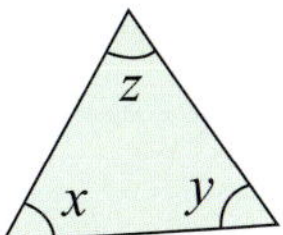

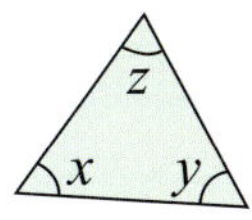

All the **angles** in one triangle are the **same** as the angles in the other triangle.

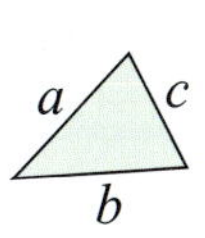

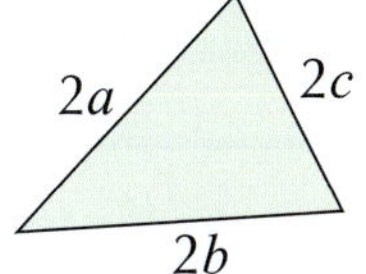

All corresponding **sides** of the two triangles are in the **same ratio**.

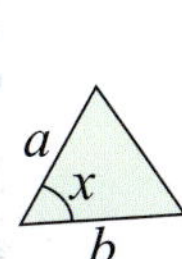

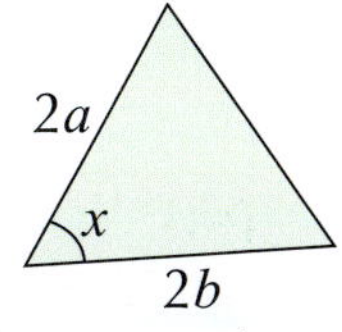

Two sides of the triangles are in the **same ratio** and the **angle between** them is the **same** for both triangles.

Tip: "In the same ratio" means you multiply each side on one shape by the same number to get the other shape.

Example 4

Are these two triangles similar? Give a reason for your answer.

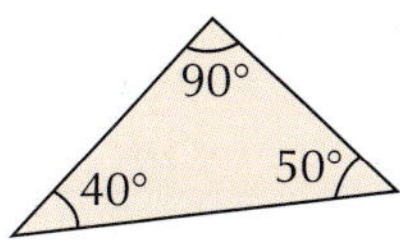

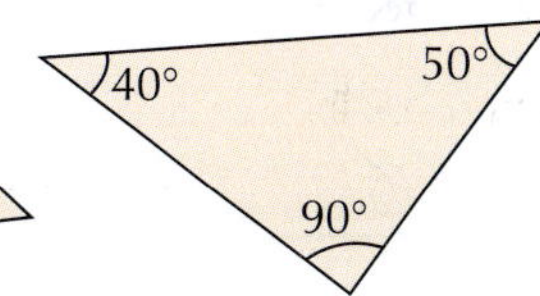

Look to see whether the triangles satisfy any of the conditions for similarity. The orientation of the triangles doesn't matter.

The angles in one triangle are the same as the angles in the other triangle.

So the triangles **are similar**.

Example 5

Explain why these two triangles are similar.

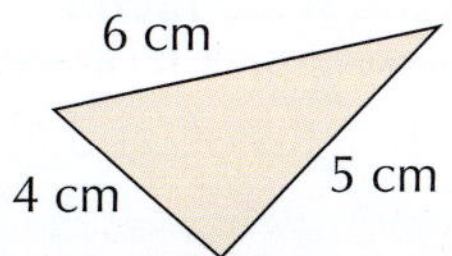

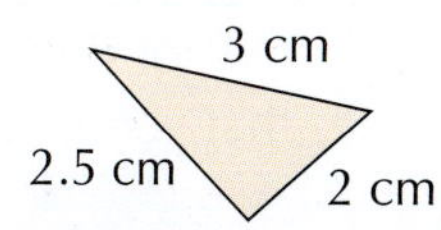

Look to see which condition for similarity the triangles satisfy. Again, the orientation of the triangles doesn't matter.

All the sides in the first triangle are twice the length of those in the second triangle.
So **corresponding sides are in the same ratio**.

Exercise 4

Q1 Explain why each of the following pairs of triangles are similar.

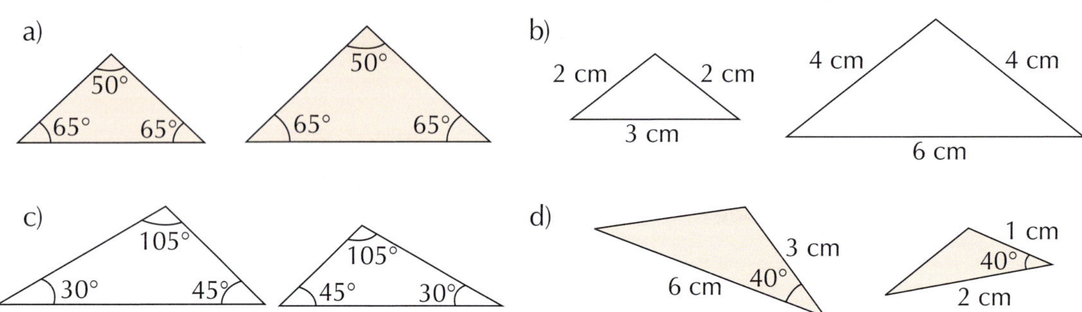

Q2 Decide whether each of the following pairs of triangles are similar.

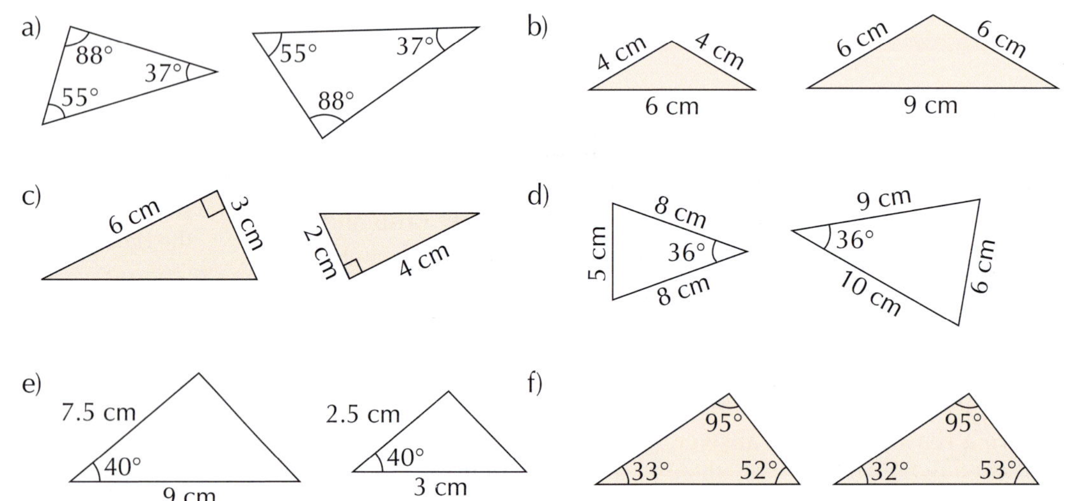

If you **know** that two shapes are **similar**, you can find **missing sides** and **angles** by identifying **corresponding sides and angles** — just remember that similar shapes have **all angles** the **same**, and **all corresponding sides** of the two shapes are in the **same ratio**.

To find a **missing side** using the corresponding side on the other shape, you'll need to work out the **scale factor** that connects the two shapes. If you've got similar shapes A and B, identify a pair of **corresponding** sides that you know the lengths of, and then use the **formula**:

$$\textbf{scale factor} = \frac{\textbf{side length of shape } B}{\textbf{side length of shape } A}$$

Tip: Make sure you use corresponding sides — you can't just pick any two sides.

To find a missing side on shape B, **multiply** the corresponding side on shape A by the **scale factor**.

Example 6

Triangles ABC and DEF are similar. Find the lengths of DE and AC.

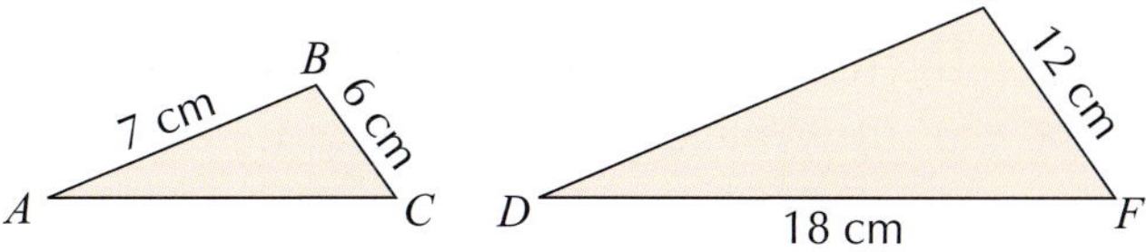

1. Identify a pair of corresponding side lengths.

Side BC corresponds to EF.

2. Use the formula to calculate the scale factor.

Scale factor $= \frac{EF}{BC} = \frac{12}{6} = 2$

3. Use the scale factor to find the missing side lengths.

So $DE = 2 \times AB$
$= 2 \times 7 =$ **14 cm**

$DF = 2 \times AC$ So $AC = DF \div 2$
$= 18 \div 2 =$ **9 cm**

A **question** might not tell you directly the value of the side or angle corresponding to the one you need to find. So you might need to use other rules too, such as the **sum of angles** in a triangle (p.243), the properties of **isosceles triangles** (p.242) and **Pythagoras' theorem** (p.301).

You might also need to use **vertically opposite angles** (p.239), and the angle rules you know for **parallel lines** (p.240-241).

Example 7

Triangles PQR and UVW are similar. Find angle x.

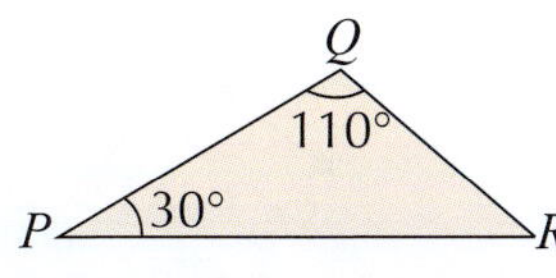

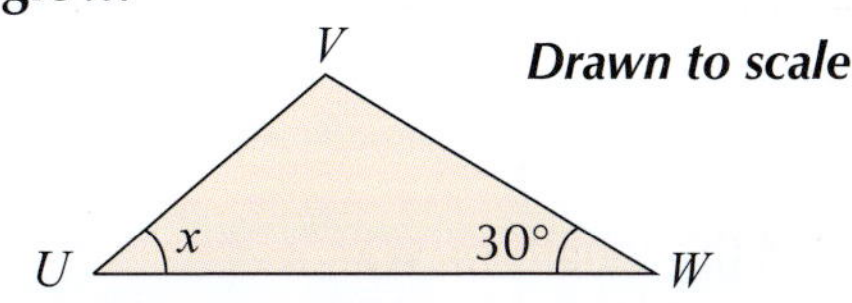

1. Find the missing angle in triangle PQR.

Angle $QRP = 180° - (110° + 30°)$
$= 40°$

2. Work out which angles in the triangles correspond to each other.

The diagrams are drawn to scale, so the obtuse angle PQR corresponds to angle UVW.

Angle QPR corresponds to angle VWU, so angle QRP must correspond to angle VUW.

3. Use the properties of similar triangles to determine the required angle.

This means $\boldsymbol{x = 40°}$.

Exercise 5

Q1 The triangles in each pair below are similar.

a) (i) Write down the value of x.

(ii) Find the value of y.

b) Find the value of z.

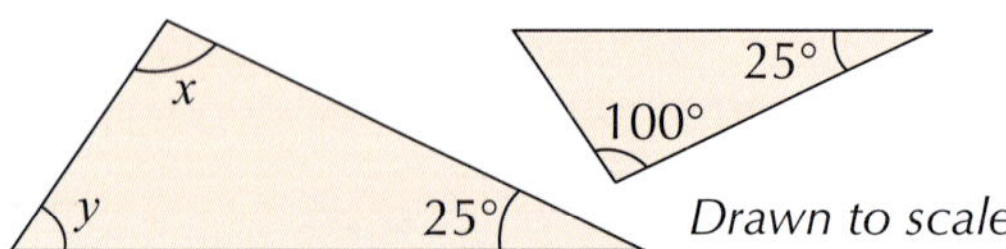

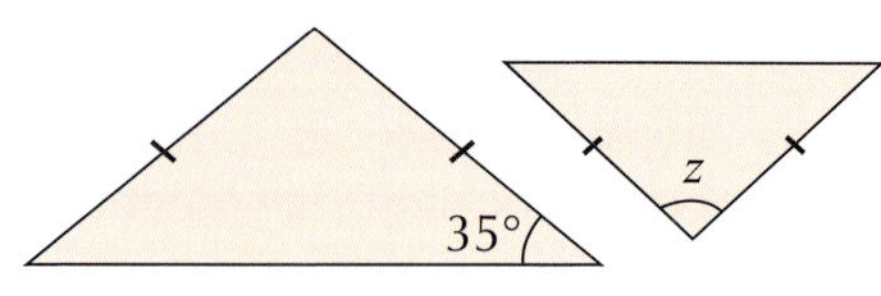

In **Questions 2-5**, the lines marked with arrows are parallel.

Q2 The diagram shows two similar triangles, ABC and ADE.

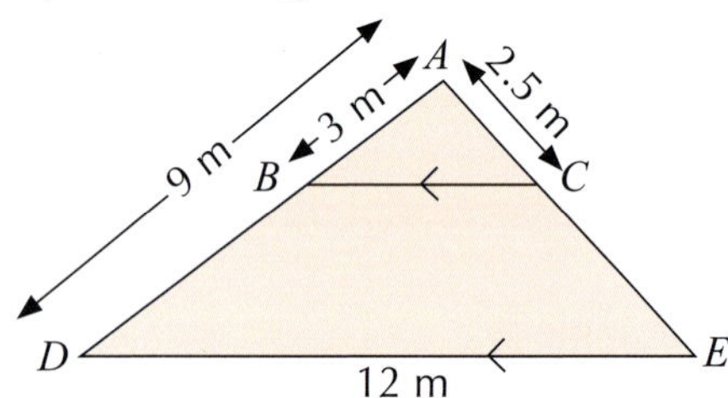

a) State which angle in triangle ABC corresponds to:

(i) angle ADE

(ii) angle AED

(iii) angle DAE

b) Find the scale factor connecting triangles ABC and ADE.

c) Find the length of: (i) AE (ii) BC

Q3 The diagram below shows two similar triangles, QRU and QST.

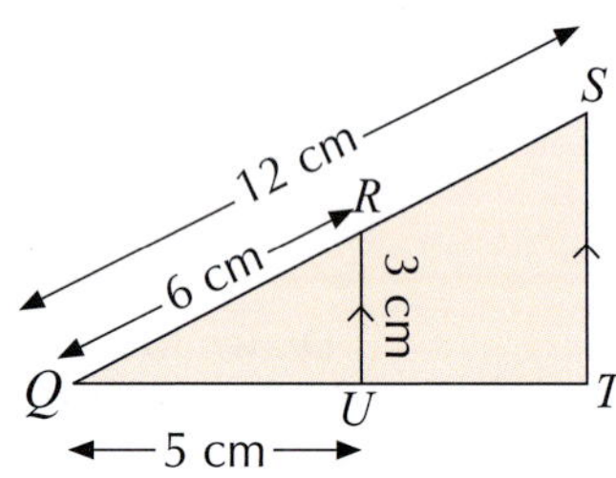

a) Find the length of ST.

b) Find the length of QT.

c) Find the length of UT.

Q4 The diagram below shows two similar triangles, STW and SUV.

a) Find the length of TW.

b) Find the length of SU.

c) Find the length of TU.

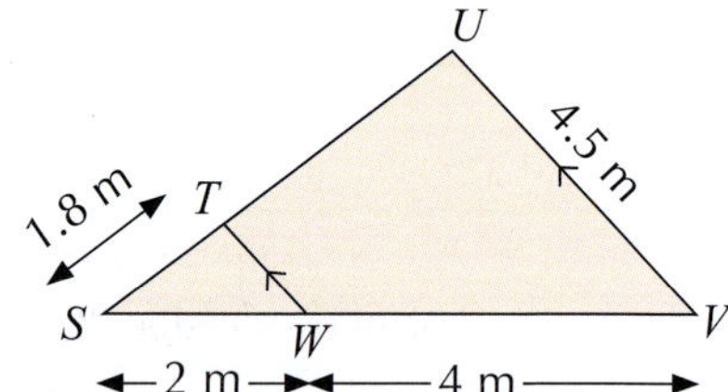

Q5 Triangles XRQ and XYZ are similar. RXY and QXZ are straight lines.

a) State the size of angle QXR.
Explain your answer.

b) Use alternate angles to state which angle in triangle XRQ is equal to angle XYZ.

c) Find the scale factor connecting triangles XRQ and XYZ.

d) Use your answers to find the length of:

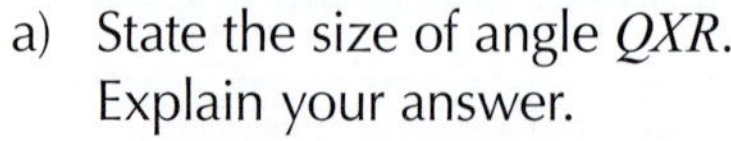

(i) YZ (ii) XQ

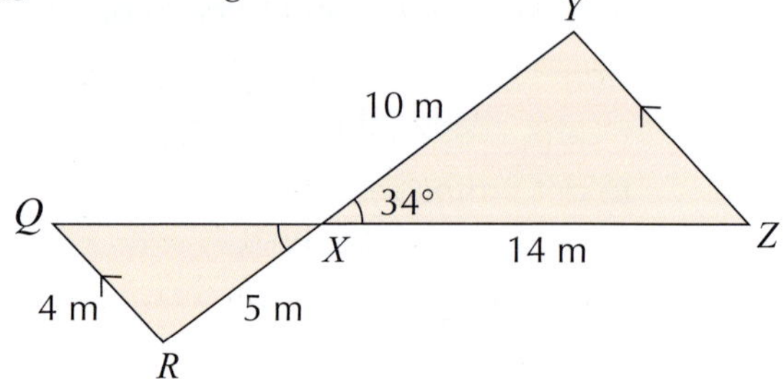

Review Exercise

Q1 a) Copy the diagram on the right.

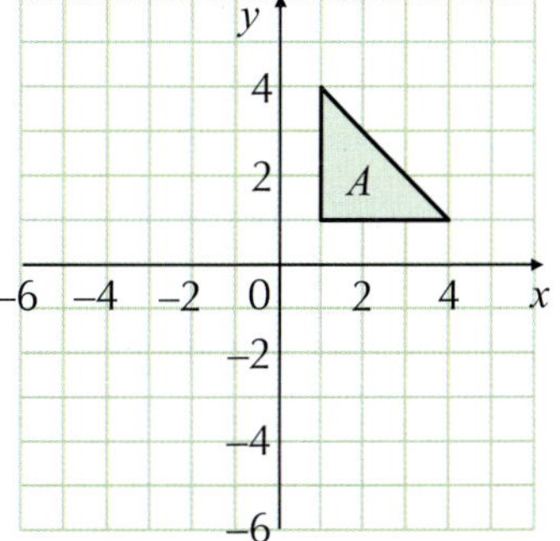

(i) Reflect shape A in the line $y = -1$. Label the new image B.

(ii) Rotate B 90° clockwise about the origin. Label the final image C.

b) Copy the diagram again.

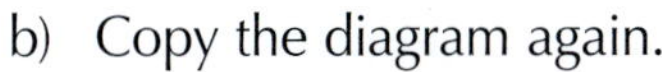

(i) Rotate shape A 90° clockwise about the origin. Label the new image D.

(ii) Reflect this new image in the line $y = -1$. Label the final image E.

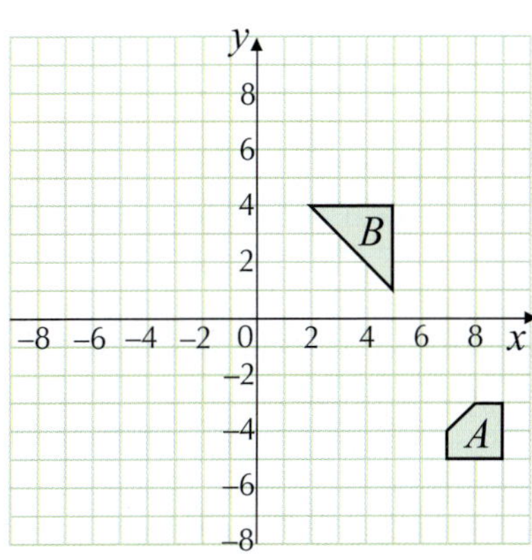

Q2 Copy the diagram on the left.

a) (i) Translate A by $\begin{pmatrix} 0 \\ -2 \end{pmatrix}$. Label the new image A_1.

(ii) Enlarge A_1 by scale factor 3 with centre of enlargement (9, –7). Label the final image A_2.

b) (i) Translate B by $\begin{pmatrix} -2 \\ -1 \end{pmatrix}$. Label the new image B_1.

(ii) Reflect B_1 in the y-axis. Label the final image B_2.

Q3 For each of parts a), b), c) and d), start by making a new copy of the diagram below.

a) (i) Rotate shape P 180° about (4, 5). Label the image P_1.

(ii) Translate the image by $\begin{pmatrix} 2 \\ 2 \end{pmatrix}$. Label the final image P_2.

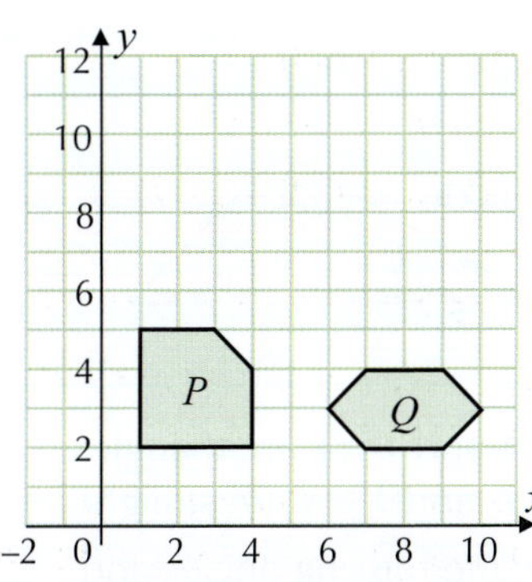

b) Rotate shape P 180° about (5, 6). Label the final image P_3.

c) (i) Rotate shape Q 180° about (4, 5). Label the image Q_1.

(ii) Translate the image by $\begin{pmatrix} 2 \\ 2 \end{pmatrix}$. Label the final image Q_2.

d) Rotate shape Q 180° about (5, 6). Label the final image Q_3.

e) What do you notice about images P_2 and P_3 and about images Q_2 and Q_3?

Q4 Triangle *PQR* has corners at *P*(0, 0), *Q*(4, 2) and *R*(4, 0).

a) Draw *PQR* on a pair of axes.

(i) Rotate *PQR* 90° clockwise about the point (4, 2). Label the image $P_1Q_1R_1$.

(ii) Enlarge $P_1Q_1R_1$ using a scale factor of 1.5 and centre of enlargement (2, 6). Label the image $P_2Q_2R_2$.

b) Draw *PQR* on a new pair of axes.

(i) Enlarge the original shape *PQR* using a scale factor of 1.5 and centre of enlargement (2, 6). Label the image $P_3Q_3R_3$.

(ii) Rotate $P_3Q_3R_3$ 90° clockwise about the point (4, 2). Label the image $P_4Q_4R_4$.

Q5 By considering triangle *STU* with corners at *S*(1, 1), *T*(3, 1) and *U*(1, 2), find the single transformation equivalent to a rotation of 180° about the origin, followed by a translation by $\begin{pmatrix}6\\2\end{pmatrix}$.

Q6 Explain whether each of the following pairs of shapes are congruent, similar or neither.

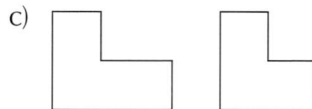

a) 

b) 

c) 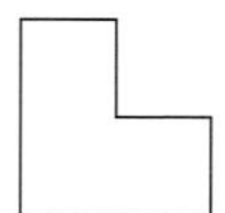

Q7 For each of the following, decide whether the two triangles are congruent, similar or neither. In each case, explain your answer.

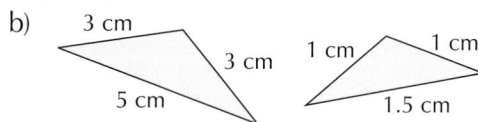

a) 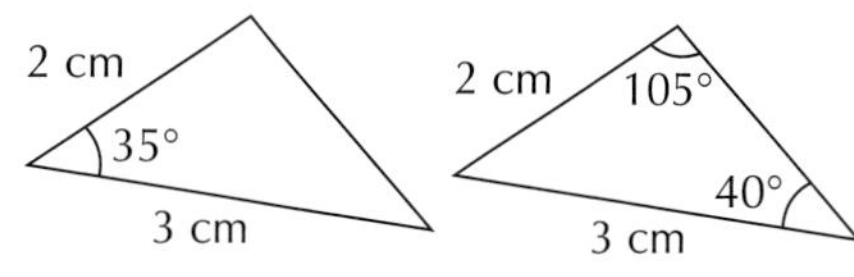

b) 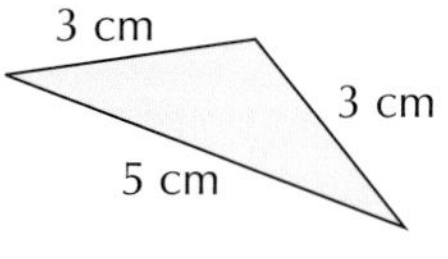

c) 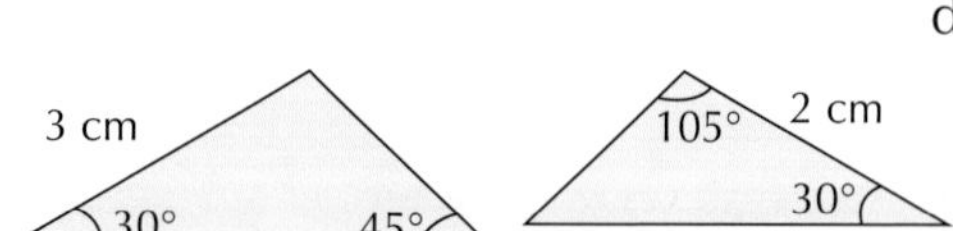

d) 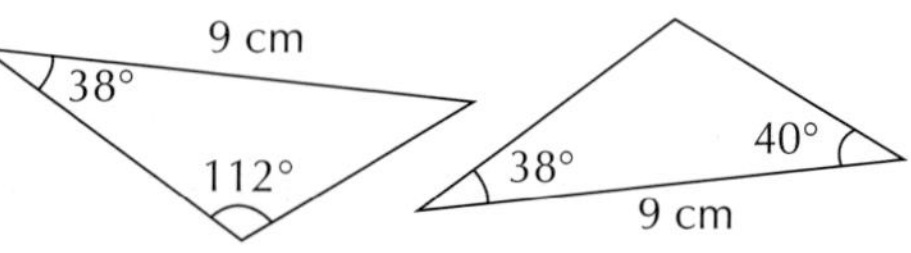

Q8 *UVW* and *WXY* are triangles.
UWY and *VWX* are straight lines.
Find the missing angles and lengths marked *a*-*f* in the diagram.

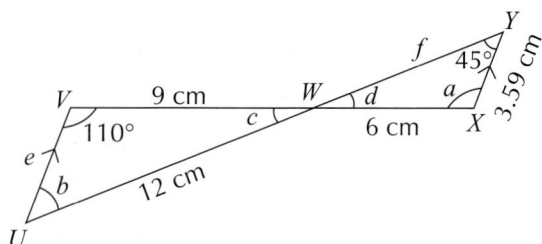

Exam-Style Questions

Q1 In the diagram, shape A was produced by reflecting shape B in the line $y = x$.

a) Draw shape B on the grid.

[2 marks]

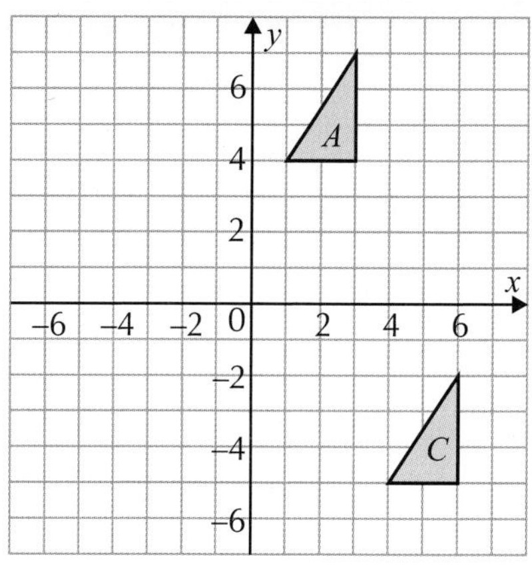

Shape C can be mapped onto shape A by a translation of $\begin{pmatrix} p \\ q \end{pmatrix}$.

b) Write down the values of p and q.

[1 mark]

Q2 Shape P is transformed by a translation of $\begin{pmatrix} 1 \\ -4 \end{pmatrix}$ to produce an image Q.

Shape Q is then transformed by an enlargement of scale factor 2 with centre of enlargement (–2, 3) to give shape R.
Shape P is shown on the diagram below.

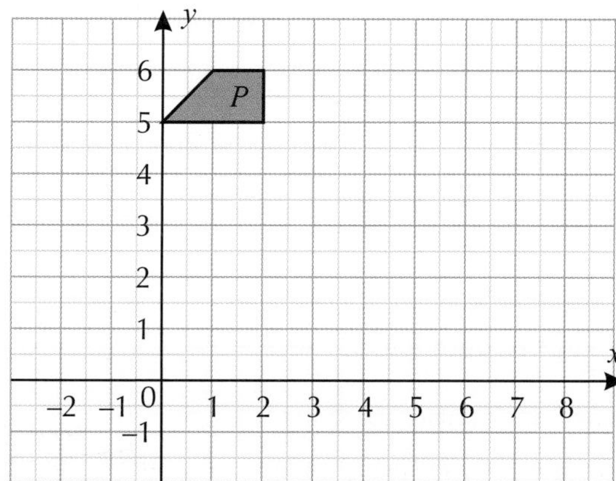

Copy the diagram and draw shape R. Show all your working.

[3 marks]

Q3 The diagram below shows two similar triangles, ABC and ADE.

a) Find length BC.

[2 marks]

b) Find angle ACB.

[1 mark]

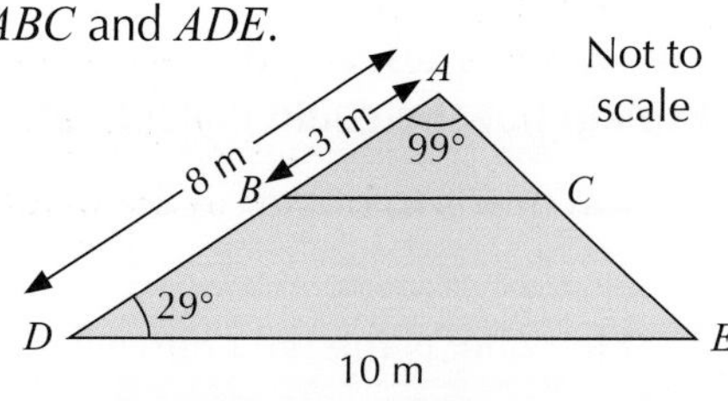

25.1 Using Different Types of Data

To test a hypothesis or conduct an investigation, you first need to plan what data you need, how you're going to collect it and how you're going to analyse it. Data comes in different types depending on who first gathered it and what sort of values/format it takes.

Primary and Secondary Data

Learning Objective — Spec Ref S1:
Know the difference between primary and secondary data.

Primary data is data you **collect yourself**, e.g. by doing a survey or experiment. It's good to use primary data since you can **control** what information is gathered, and how **accurate** it is.

Secondary data is data that has been **collected by someone else**. You can get secondary data from things like newspapers or the internet. You're relying on someone else to collect the data — but secondary data is often **cheap** and **quick** to obtain. This is especially useful if you need a **large** amount of information, or you need data that would be hard for you to **gather** yourself.

Example 1

Marya wants to know if there's a link between area and population in 10 African countries.

a) **What pieces of data does Marya need to find?**
This is the information she needs to answer her question. → The **areas and populations** of the 10 countries she's interested in.

b) **Where could Marya get the data from?** → E.g. she could find it on the **internet**.

c) **Is Marya's data primary or secondary data?**
The data has been collected by someone else, so... → It's **secondary** data.

Example 2

Jon wants to test whether a six-sided dice has an equal chance of landing on any side. Explain how he could collect data for the test. Will his data be primary or secondary data?

1. Jon needs to do an experiment. He could roll the dice lots of times and record how many times it lands on each side using a tally chart.
2. He collects the data himself, so... His data will be **primary** data.

Exercise 1

For **Questions 1-3**, decide if the data is primary or secondary.

Q1 Megan and Jane want to find out the types of music that students like.
   a) Megan plans to send a questionnaire to students from her college.
   b) Jane plans to use the results of an online music survey on the college's website.

Q2 Faheem is going to use the data on election results that appeared in his local newspaper.

Q3 Nancy is going to time how long it takes her friends to run 100 metres.

For **Questions 4-7**: a) Describe what data is needed and give a suitable method for collecting it.
b) Say whether the data will be primary or secondary data.

Q4 Nikita wants to know what the girls in her class think about school dinners.

Q5 Anne wants to compare the daily rainfall in London and Manchester last August.

Q6 Skylar wants to see if the boys in his class can throw a ball further than the girls.

Q7 Jim wants to find out how the temperature in his garden at 10 am each morning compares with the temperature recorded by the Met Office for his local area.

Discrete and Continuous Data

Learning Objectives — Spec Ref S1:

- Know the difference between qualitative and quantitative data.
- Know the difference between discrete and continuous data.

Data can be either **qualitative** or **quantitative**. **Qualitative** data is **descriptive**, meaning it uses **words** instead of numbers — e.g. favourite flavours of ice cream ('vanilla', 'chocolate', 'strawberry', etc.) or opinions ('happy', 'neutral' etc.).

Quantitative data is **numerical** — e.g. the heights of players in a football team or pupils' scores in a Science test. Quantitative data can be split up into two further types:

- **Discrete** data can only take **certain values**. For example, the number of goals scored by a football team — the data must be whole numbers, the team can't score half a goal.
- **Continuous** data can take **any value** in a given **range** — e.g. lengths, heights or weights.

How you **process** and **analyse** your data will depend on the data type. Some of the different types of **graphs** and **diagrams** in Section 26 would be **inappropriate** for showing certain data types — e.g. you shouldn't put qualitative data onto a line graph, but you can make a bar chart or pie chart out of it.

Example 3

Is the following data qualitative, discrete quantitative or continuous quantitative?

a) The hometowns of 100 people.

This data is in the form of words, so... It's **qualitative** data.

b) The weights of the bags of potatoes on sale in a greengrocer's.

This data is numerical and isn't restricted to certain specific values. It's **continuous quantitative** data.

c) The number of students in each class at a school.

This data is numerical and can be counted, so... It's **discrete quantitative** data.

Exercise 2

Q1 Say whether the following data is qualitative, discrete quantitative or continuous quantitative.

a) The number of words in your favourite song.
b) Your favourite food.
c) The numbers of pets in 20 households.
d) The sizes of the crowds at 10 rugby matches.
e) The heights of 100 tomato plants.
f) The time it takes Matt to walk to school.
g) The nationalities of the people in a park.
h) The lengths of 30 worms.
i) The distances of planets from the Sun.
j) The hair colours of 50 people.

Q2 Janka wants to find out if tea or coffee is more popular in a café. She decides to stand outside the café one morning, and ask people as they leave which drink they ordered.

a) Say whether this data is primary data or secondary data.
b) Say whether this data is qualitative, discrete quantitative or continuous quantitative?

Q3 Gemma thinks there is a link between the average number of chocolate bars eaten each week by pupils in her class and how fast they can run 100 metres.

a) Describe two sets of data Gemma should collect to investigate this link.
b) Describe suitable methods for collecting the data.
c) Say whether each set of data is discrete quantitative or continuous quantitative.
d) Say whether each set of data is primary data or secondary data.

25.2 Data Collection

As part of an investigation, you'll probably collect lots of data, so you need a way of recording and organising it. Your collection method should fit the type of data you're trying to collect.

Data Collection Sheets

Learning Objective — Spec Ref S1/S2:
Design and use data collection sheets.

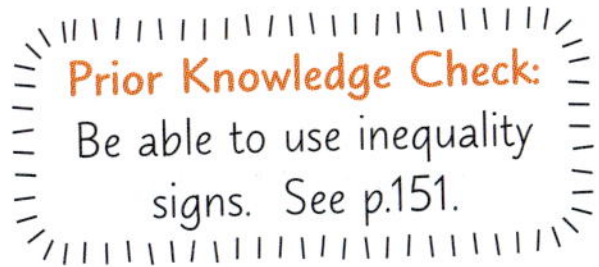

Prior Knowledge Check:
Be able to use inequality signs. See p.151.

Tally charts and **frequency tables** can be used to record qualitative or quantitative data — the only thing that changes is the name of the **categories** or **groups**. There's more about these types of diagrams on p.435.

For **qualitative** data, the **names** of each category are used (e.g. if you're asking about favourite colours, then the categories might be 'red', 'green, 'blue', ...). It's useful to have an '**Other**' category so that all the possible options are included without having to list every category.

Example 1

A restaurant manager asks 50 customers to choose their favourite way to eat potatoes from the following four options: boiled, mashed, baked and roast.

Design a tally chart that could be used to record the data.

Potato type	Tally	Frequency
Boiled		
Mashed		
Baked		
Roast		

Column for data names... (Potato type)

...with a row for every possible answer

Tally column with plenty of space to record the marks

Frequency column for adding up the tally marks

Tip: The tally column lets you record data as you collect it, e.g. as you ask people or count something.

Exercise 1

Q1 Give two things that are wrong with the tally chart on the right for recording the colours of cars in a car park.

Car colour	Frequency
Red	
Black	
Blue	
Silver	

Q2 Design a tally chart that could be used to record the answers to each of the questions below.

a) How many times a week do you go to the supermarket?

b) Where did you go for your last holiday?

For **discrete quantitative** data, you can use **individual** values (e.g. 0, 1, 2) if the range is small or **groups** of values if the range is large (e.g. 0-4, 5-9, 10-14). However, you lose some **accuracy** by grouping the data values as you no longer know the actual data values.

For **continuous quantitative** data, you have to group the data. The groups of values need to cover every possible option, so you write the groups using **inequalities**.

Example 2

A group of students take a test. The tests are marked and given a score out of 50. Design a tally chart to record the students' scores. (Assume that all scores are whole numbers.)

1. This is discrete data, but a large range of scores are possible, so group them into a sensible number of classes.
2. Make sure the classes cover all possible scores between 0 and 50.
3. Make sure the classes don't overlap — each score should only be able to go into one class.

Test Score	Tally	Frequency
0 – 10		
11 – 20		
21 – 30		
31 – 40		
41 – 50		

Example 3

An assault course is designed to take about 10 minutes to complete. Design a tally chart that could be used to record the times taken by a group of people.

1. The data is continuous, so use inequalities for the classes.
2. Make sure there are no gaps between classes and that classes don't overlap. Using '$t \le$' to end a class and '$< t$' to start the next class, means all values can go into exactly one class.
3. Leave the last class open-ended to cover all possible times.

Time (t mins)	Tally	Frequency
$0 < t \le 5$		
$5 < t \le 10$		
$10 < t \le 15$		
$15 < t \le 20$		
$t > 20$		

Exercise 2

Q1 Give two things that are wrong with these tally charts, and design an improved version.

a) Chart for recording the number of people watching a band play at each venue on their tour (max. venue capacity = 20 000).

No. of people	Tally	Frequency
0 – 5000		
6000 – 10 000		
11 000 – 15 000		

b) Chart for recording the weights of pumpkins.

Weight (w kg)	Tally	Frequency
$w \le 3$		
$3 \le w \le 3.5$		
$3.5 \le w \le 4$		

Q2 Write down five classes that could be used in a tally chart to record the sets of data below.

a) The heights of 50 plants, which range from 5 cm to 27 cm.

b) The number of quiz questions, out of 20, answered correctly by some quiz teams.

c) The weights of 30 bags of apples, where each bag should weigh roughly 200 g.

d) The volumes of 50 cups of tea as they're served in a café. Each cup can hold 300 ml.

Q3 Design a tally chart that could be used to record the following data.

a) The average lengths of time 100 people spend watching TV each week.

b) The numbers of pairs of socks owned by 50 students.

c) The lengths of 20 people's feet.

d) The distances that 30 people travel to get to work and back each day.

Two-Way Tables

Learning Objective — Spec Ref S1/S2:
Design two-way tables.

A **two-way table** is a data collection sheet that allows you to record **two** different pieces of information about the **same subject** at once — e.g. for each person, you could collect data on their gender as well as hair colour in one table. One piece of information is covered by the **rows** of the table and the other by the **columns**.

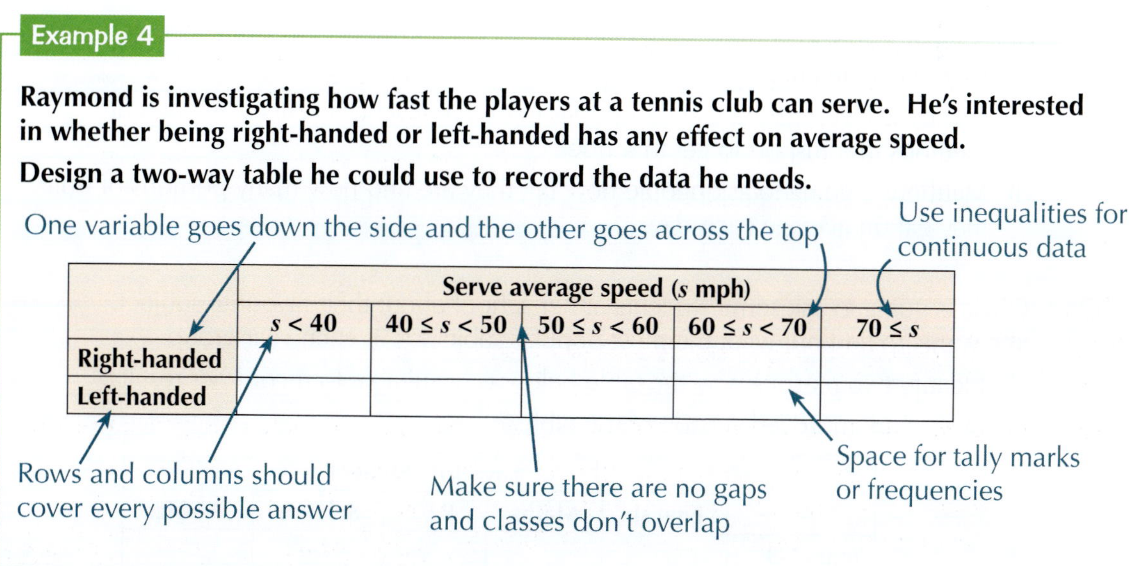

Example 4

Raymond is investigating how fast the players at a tennis club can serve. He's interested in whether being right-handed or left-handed has any effect on average speed.

Design a two-way table he could use to record the data he needs.

One variable goes down the side and the other goes across the top
Use inequalities for continuous data
Rows and columns should cover every possible answer
Make sure there are no gaps and classes don't overlap
Space for tally marks or frequencies

	Serve average speed (s mph)				
	$s < 40$	$40 \le s < 50$	$50 \le s < 60$	$60 \le s < 70$	$70 \le s$
Right-handed					
Left-handed					

Exercise 3

Q1 The table below has been designed to record the hair colour and age (in whole years) of 100 adults.

a) Give three criticisms of the table.

b) Design an improved version of the table.

	Age (in whole years)					
	0 – 15	15 – 30	30 – 45	45 – 60	60 – 75	75 or older
Blonde						
Light brown						
Dark brown						

Q2 Design a two-way table that could be used to record the data for each of the following:

a) The favourite season of the year of 50 men and 50 women.

b) The type of music adults and children prefer listening to out of pop, classical and rock.

c) The average length of time spent doing homework each evening by pupils in each of the school years 7-11. Assume no one spends more than an average of 4 hours an evening on homework.

d) The total number of books people read last year and their favourite genre out of horror, romance, sci-fi and fantasy.

Q3 For each investigation below, design a two-way table for recording the data.

a) Hoi Wan is going to ask 50 adults if they prefer cats or dogs. She wants to find out if it's true that men prefer dogs and women prefer cats.

b) Nathan wants to find out whether children watch more TV on average each day than adults.

c) Felicity is investigating whether pupils in different school years use different methods of transport to get to school.

d) Matthew is going to ask people how tall they are and how many portions of fruit they eat on average each day.

Q4 Olivia is going to ask some students at her school about their favourite subject. She wants to find out what the most popular subject is in each year group.

a) Identify two reasons why the table below is unsuitable to record her results.

b) Design an improved version of the table.

	Favourite Subject				
	English	Maths	P.E.	Science	Music
Years 7-9					
Years 10-11					

25.3 Sampling and Bias

It might not be practical or possible to collect data on every individual that you're interested in. If you wanted to know about the wingspan of all the birds in a forest, you wouldn't be able to find and measure every one. Instead, you'll need to collect data from a smaller group — but you have to pick it carefully.

Populations and Samples

Learning Objectives — Spec Ref S1:
- Know the difference between a population and a sample.
- Understand the reasons for using a population and for using a sample.

When you're collecting data, the **whole group** of people or things you want to find out about is called the **population**. But populations can be very big and so it is often **impractical** to collect data from **every member**. Usually, it's **quicker**, **cheaper** and **easier** to collect data from a **sample** of the population, rather than the whole thing.

A sample is a **smaller group** taken from the population. Different samples will give different results — the **bigger** the sample, the more reliable it should be. It's also important that your sample **fairly represents** the population, so you can apply any **conclusions** to the whole population.

Example 1

Michael and Tina have written a questionnaire to find out what students at their college think about public transport. Michael gives the questionnaire to 10 students and Tina gives the questionnaire to 50 students. Michael concludes that 50% of students are happy with public transport, whereas Tina concludes that only 30% are happy.

a) Why have Michael and Tina only given the questionnaire to some of the students?

Think about the advantages of sampling...

E.g. there are fewer copies to print, so **print costs will be lower**.
Also, it will take them **much less time** to collect and analyse the results.

b) Whose results are likely to be more reliable? Explain your answer.

Think about the size of the sample...

Tina's results are likely to be more reliable because she has used a **bigger sample**.

Exercise 1

Q1 Identify the population and the sample in the following scenario:
A university wants to find out how its students feel about plans to build a new library.
It randomly distributes a survey to 800 of its students.

Q2 Jenny wants to know how long it takes the pupils in Year 7 to type out a poem.
She plans to time a sample of 30 out of the 216 Year 7 pupils.
Give two advantages for Jenny of using a sample.

Q3 Patrick is testing a box of matches to see how long they burn for. He does this by lighting 10 of the matches. Explain why Patrick doesn't test all the matches.

Q4 An audience of 1000 people are watching a musical. Khadija wants to know what they think about it and plans to interview 5 people from the audience afterwards.
What's wrong with Khadija's plan?

Q5 Melissa and Gareth are doing an experiment to see if a coin is fair. They each toss the coin 100 times and record the number of heads. 52% of Melissa's tosses are heads and 47% of Gareth's tosses are heads. Explain why Melissa and Gareth get different results.

Q6 Alfie and Keith want to find out what the most popular flavour of ice cream is.
Alfie asks 30 people and finds that 'chocolate' is the most popular. Keith asks 15 people and finds that it's 'strawberry'. Based on this information, what would you say is the most popular flavour? Explain your answer.

Q7 Jack, Nikhil and Daisy bake a batch of 200 cupcakes to sell on their market stall.
Jack thinks they should taste one cake to check the quality is OK. Nikhil thinks they should taste 10 cakes and Daisy thinks they should taste 50 cakes.
Say who you agree with and explain why.

Bias and Fairness

Learning Objectives — Spec Ref S1:
- Consider the bias or fairness of a sample.
- Know how to take a random sample.

When you're choosing a sample, it's important to make sure that your selection process is **fair** so that results are likely to reflect the **whole population**. A sample is **biased** if some members of the population are **more likely** to be included than others.

Tip: When deciding if a sample is biased, see if you can think of any groups that would be excluded.

To spot bias, think about **when**, **where** and **how** the sample was taken, and **how many** members are in it — a **small** sample is also likely to be biased.

Example 2

Perry plans to sample 50 shoppers at a supermarket to see what they think about the supermarket's decision to close earlier in the evenings. He decides to stand outside the supermarket on a Wednesday morning and ask the first 50 people he sees leaving the shop.

a) Explain why this will give him a biased sample.

Think about when he selects the sample...

E.g. Perry is only asking people who are free to shop on a Wednesday morning, so he's excluding all the shoppers who are at work or school. He's also excluding people who only shop in the evening, who will probably be more affected by the earlier closing.

b) Suggest how Perry could choose a fairer sample.

Think about how he could include more groups of shoppers...

E.g. Perry should ask people on different days of the week and at different times of day.

Exercise 2

Q1 Explain why the following methods of selecting a sample will result in a biased sample.

a) Kelechi wants to know what people at her college think about a particular film, so she asks 10 of her friends for their opinions.

b) A school cook wants to know whether the pupils want all school dinners to be vegetarian. He asks all the members of the school's animal rights group.

c) A library needs to reduce its opening hours. The librarian asks 20 people on a Monday morning whether the library should close on a Monday or a Friday.

d) A market research company wants to find out about people's working hours. They select 100 home telephone numbers and call them at 2 pm one afternoon.

A **fair** way to select a sample is at **random** — every member of the population has an **equal chance** of being selected. To take a random sample:

- Make a **list** of **every member** of the population and assign everyone a **number**.
- Use e.g. a computer or calculator to create a list of **random numbers**.
- **Match** the random numbers to the assigned numbers of the population.

Exercise 3

Q1 A head teacher wants to know what pupils in Year 7 think about after-school clubs. Explain how he could select a random sample of 50 Year 7 pupils.

Q2 The manager of a health club wants to survey a random sample of 40 female members. Explain how she could do this.

Using a Sample to Make Estimates About the Population

Learning Objective — Spec Ref S1:
Know how to infer properties of a population using a sample.

You can use a fair sample to make **estimates** about the **population**.
E.g. if **a third of the people in a sample** have a certain characteristic, you can estimate that **a third of the population** will also have this characteristic.

Example 3

There are 10 000 residents in Sheila's town. She wants to find out how satisfied they are with the street furniture in the town, so she fairly samples 1000 residents. The results are in the table.

Opinion	No. of residents
Very dissatisfied	250
Quite dissatisfied	150
Don't care	216
Quite satisfied	204
Very satisfied	180

a) Estimate how many residents in the town are either quite satisfied or very satisfied with the street furniture.

b) Could you use this sample to estimate how many people in the country are satisfied with the street furniture in their town?

a) 1. Work out the proportion of satisfied residents from the sample.

There are 180 + 204 = 384 residents satisfied in the sample, so the proportion of residents satisfied in the sample is $\frac{384}{1000} = 0.384$.

2. Your estimate is the same proportion in the population.

The number of people satisfied in the town is estimated to be 0.384 × 10 000 = **3840**.

b) Think about whether the sample is still fair or representative.

The sample is **not representative** of the country — it is **biased** in favour of people in one particular town. You **can't use it** to estimate the opinion of the country.

Exercise 4

Q1 A castle has 450 rooms. The king of the castle believes that many of them have damp and so hires a dirty rascal to remove it. The king doesn't have time to inspect all the rooms for damp, so he chooses 20 rooms at random to inspect. Given that seven of these rooms have damp, estimate how many of the rooms in the entire castle have damp.

Q2 A journalist interviews a sample of 50 out of 650 politicians to get their views on three policies X, Y and Z.
The results are in the table on the right.

	X	Y	Z
In Favour	34	4	13
Against	13	45	14
Neutral	3	1	23

a) Use the table to estimate how many of the 650 politicians:
(i) are in favour of policy X, (ii) are neutral about policy Y, (iii) are against policy Z.

b) What assumption has been made in using this data to make these estimations?

Review Exercise

Q1 Steven wants to investigate the most common favourite colour amongst his classmates.

a) Describe the data he needs and suggest a way that he could collect it.

b) Say whether Steven's data is primary or secondary data.

Q2 Is the following data qualitative, continuous quantitative or discrete quantitative?

a) The amount of time it takes people to travel to school.

b) The number of siblings people have.

c) People's favourite film.

d) The prices of different pairs of shoes in a shoe shop.

Q3 Lars wants to know how many days there were in the month that people were born. Design a tally chart that could be used to record his data.

Q4 Pearl makes a tally chart to record how many times people went to the cinema last year. Identify two things that are wrong with her tally chart and design an improved version.

No. of cinema trips	Tally	Frequency
1 – 10		
10 – 20		
20 – 30		
30 – 40		
40 or more		

Q5 Ronaldo wants to do an investigation to test his theory that children spend more time outside each week than adults. Design a data collection sheet for his investigation.

Q6 A supermarket chain wants to know what people in a town think of their plan to build a supermarket there. They hire some researchers to interview a sample of 500 people. Give one reason why they wouldn't want to interview everyone in the town.

Q7 Jasper and Connie want to find out which football team is most popular at their school. Jasper asks a random selection of 30 pupils and Connie asks the first 5 pupils she sees at lunchtime. Give two reasons why Jasper's sample will be more representative of the whole school.

Q8 A factory makes hundreds of the same component each day. PROBLEM SOLVING
Describe how a representative sample of 50 components could be tested each day to make sure the machinery is working properly.

Q9 Sadie is making doughnuts for 50 party guests. She asks 12 party guests at random whether they prefer doughnuts with jam or with sprinkles. Four of them prefer jam. Based on her sample, how many party guests would you expect to prefer jam?

Exam-Style Questions

Q1 Mehran claims:

"Left-handed people can throw farther than right-handed people."

He tests his claim by measuring how far left- and right-handed people throw a ball.

a) Are the distances Mehran measures discrete or continuous data?

[1 mark]

b) Design a suitable data collection sheet for Mehran's investigation.

[2 marks]

Q2 Jill wants to know what the most popular chocolate bar is in her year of 150 students. She decides to select a sample of 10 students from her class to ask about their favourite chocolate bars. The results are shown in the tally chart below.

Chocolate bar	Cocoa Cream	Elephant Bar	Choco Crunch	Martian Milk	Other
Tally	II	IIII	III		I
Frequency	2	4	3	0	1

Jill concludes that the 'Elephant Bar' is the most popular chocolate bar with students in her year. Make two comments on the accuracy of Jill's conclusion.

[2 marks]

Q3 Tahani is investigating how long it takes 200 people to complete a crossword puzzle. She designs a tally chart to record her results:

Time (t minutes)	**Tally**	**Frequency**
$0 < t \leq 10$		
$10 \leq t \leq 20$		
$20 \leq t \leq 30$		

a) Give two problems with her table.

[2 marks]

b) Tahani takes a random sample of 40 of the people and records their times. She finds that 12 people in the sample take between 10 and 20 minutes to complete the crossword. How many of the 200 participants can she expect to complete the crossword puzzle in between 10 and 20 minutes? Write down any assumptions you have made.

[3 marks]

26.1 Tally Charts and Frequency Tables

You saw how to design tables in Section 25 — now you need to use them to analyse data.

Learning Objective — Spec Ref S2:
Complete and interpret tally charts and frequency tables.

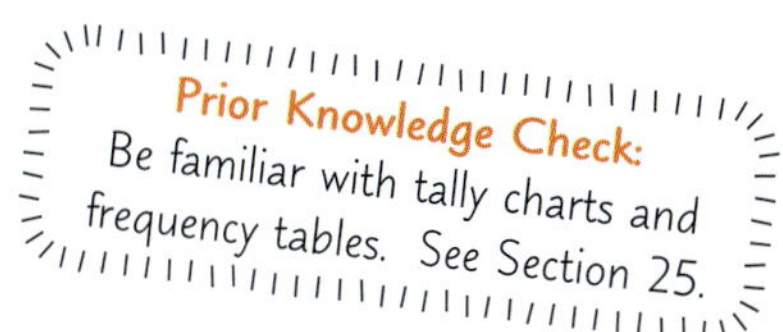

Prior Knowledge Check:
Be familiar with tally charts and frequency tables. See Section 25.

The **frequency** of a data value is the **number of times it occurs** in a data set.

Frequency tables can show frequencies of **individual** data values or of **groups** of values. **Grouping** data makes it **easier to analyse**, but the **exact values** are lost.

Example 1

A mathematics test is marked out of 40. Here are the marks for 20 students.

10	18	28	38	40	40	29	11	13	16
18	20	31	40	27	25	22	40	9	34

a) Complete the grouped frequency table to show the marks.

1. Add a tally mark (|) in the Tally column for every test score. Write the tally marks in groups of 5, with the fifth tally mark across the others to make a '5-bar gate'.
2. Find each frequency by counting the tally marks.

Mark	Tally	Frequency
0-10	||	**2**
11-20	𝍸 |	**6**
21-30	𝍸	**5**
31-40	𝍸 ||	**7**

b) The pass mark for this test was 21 out of 40. How many students passed the test?

Add the frequencies for the bottom two rows. 5 + 7 = **12**

Exercise 1

Q1 Sharla asks a group of people what type of music they like most. Here are their responses.

Pop	R&B	Rock	Indie	Pop	R&B	Indie	Pop	Jazz	Pop
Pop	Rock	Pop	Pop	Jazz	Pop	Pop	Classical	Indie	Rock

a) Copy and complete the frequency table on the right.

b) Use your table to answer the following.

(i) What is the most popular type of music?

(ii) How many more people like pop the most compared to rock?

Type of Music	Tally	Frequency
Classical		
Indie		
Pop		
Rock		
Other		

26.2 Averages and Range

Finding averages and the range is a useful way of summarising a data set — these values give you a good idea of the data set as a whole without needing to see every piece of data within it.

Averages: Mean, Median and Mode

Learning Objective — Spec Ref S4:
Find the mode, median and mean of a set of data.

An **average** is a way of **representing** a whole set of data using a **single value** — it is the **central** or **typical** value within the data set. The **mode**, **median** and **mean** are three common averages that are used. The most **suitable** one to use depends on the data.

The Mode

Mode (or modal value) is the most common value

The mode is the value that appears in the data set **more often** than any other. It's easy to find and **isn't distorted** by **extreme** values (called **outliers**). However, there could be **no mode** (or more than one) and it might **not represent the data well.**

Tip: The mode can be used with qualitative data.

Example 1

Find the mode of these numbers: 3 7 4 8 3

The mode is the most common number. Mode = **3**

Exercise 1

Q1 Find the mode of the following sets of data.

a) 8, 5, 3, 8, 4 b) 6, 9, 2, 7, 7, 6, 5, 9, 6 c) 16, 8, 12, 13, 13, 8, 8, 17

Q2 The test scores of nine students are given below. Find the modal score.

34	67	86	58	51	52	71	65	58

Q3 Find the mode for the following data:

red, yellow, red, black, orange, purple, red, green, black

Q4 The data below shows how long in days it took for 10 tomato seeds to germinate.

3, 6, 17, 4, 3, 6, 6, 5, 4, 3

Is the mode a suitable measure of average for this data?

The Median

Median = middle value once the values have been put in order from smallest to largest

If there is an **even number of values**, there will be **two numbers** in the middle. In this case the median will be **halfway** between the two middle numbers.

The median **isn't distorted** by **outliers**, but it might not be a good representation of the data as it **doesn't take into account the value of every piece of data**.

Example 2

a) Find the median of these numbers: 3 7 4 8 3

1. Put the numbers in order first.
2. There's an odd number of values, so there will be just one value in the middle.

From smallest to largest:
3 3 4 7 8

The median is the 3rd value, so the median = **4**

Tip: There should be an equal number of values either side of the median position, i.e. 3 3 (4) 7 8.

b) The number 5 is added to the list. Find the new median.

1. Write the numbers in order.
2. There's an even number of values so the median will be halfway between the two middle numbers. Find it by adding them together and dividing by 2.

From smallest to largest:
3 3 4 5 7 8

The median is halfway between the 3rd and 4th values, so the median = $\frac{4+5}{2}$ = **4.5**

Exercise 2

Q1 Find the median of the following sets of data.

a) 8, 5, 3, 8, 4 b) 6, 9, 2, 7, 7, 6, 5, 9, 6 c) 16, 18, 12, 13, 17, 8, 8, 17

Q2 Find the median of the following sets of data.

a) 1.5, 2.7, 3.8, 4.8, 5.6 b) 15, 14, 22, 17 c) 3, 3, 3, 3, 3, 3, 3, 4

Q3 The times (to the nearest second) of nine athletes running the 400 m hurdles are:

78	78	84	81	90	79	84	78	95

Find the median time.

Q4 The median of the following data set is 16.7, but one value is missing. What is the smallest that the missing value could be?

16.5	16.9	15.8	14.3	18.9	?

The Mean

Mean = the total of all the values ÷ the number of values

The **mean** is usually the most **representative** average as it **uses all of the data values**. However, it can be **distorted** by **outliers**.

To find the mean, **add up** all the values in the data set and **divide** by the number of values.

Example 3

Find the mean of these numbers: 3 7 4 8 3

1. Find the total of the values. — The total is $3 + 7 + 4 + 8 + 3 = 25$
2. Divide the total by the number of values. — So the mean $= 25 \div 5 =$ **5**

Exercise 3

Q1 Find the mean of the following sets of data.

a) 8, 5, 3, 8, 4 b) 6, 9, 2, 7, 7, 6, 5, 9, 6 c) 16, 18, 12, 13, 13, 8, 8, 17

Q2 Find the mean of the following sets of data.

a) 1.5, 2.7, 3.8, 4.8, 5.6

b) 15.85, 16.96, 22.04, 17.45

c) 3, 3, 3, 3, 3, 3, 3, 4

Q3 The test scores of nine students are given below. Find the mean score.

34	67	86	58	51	52	71	65	58

Q4 The times (to the nearest second) of nine athletes running the 400 m hurdles are:

78	78	84	81	90	79	84	78	95

Find the mean time.

Q5 Find the mean, median and mode for each of the following two sets of data.

a) 2, 3, 2, 1, 3, 2, 8, 5 b) 2, 3, 3, 1, 5, 3, 4, 3

Q6 If the mean of the following data set is 7, find the missing value. PROBLEM SOLVING

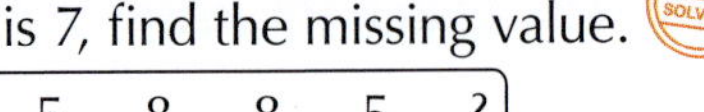

6	5	8	8	5	?

Q7 If the mean of the following data set is 16.3, find the missing value. PROBLEM SOLVING

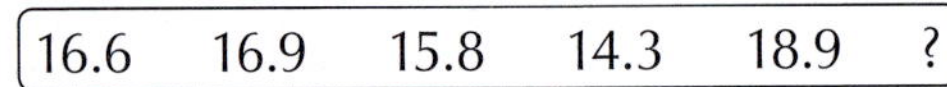

16.6	16.9	15.8	14.3	18.9	?

The Range

Learning Objective — Spec Ref S4:
Find the range of a set of data.

The **range** is the difference between the **largest value** and the **smallest value** in a data set — it tells you how **spread out** the values are.

Range = largest value – smallest value

Data sets with a **small range** are more **consistent** than those with a **large range** — this means there is less variation in the values.

The range can be a **misleading** measure of spread for data sets that contain **outliers** (extreme values). Most of the data could be much **closer together** than the value of the range suggests.

Example 4

Find the range of these numbers: 3 7 4 8 3

Subtract the lowest value from the highest. Range = 8 – 3 = **5**

Exercise 4

Q1 Find the range of the following sets of data.

a) 8, 5, 3, 8, 4 b) 6, 9, 2, 7, 7, 6, 5, 9, 6 c) 16, 8, 12, 13, 13, 8, 8, 17

Q2 Find the range of the following sets of data.

a) 1.5, 2.7, 3.8, 4.8, 5.6 b) 15.85, 16.96, 22.04, 17.45 c) 3, 3, 3, 3, 3, 3, 3, 4

Q3 Hayley takes the temperature (in °C) nine times over the year.
The results are below. Find the range of the temperatures.

15	13	–2	8	3	–1	0	22	10

Q4 The profits made by a number of lemonade stands last Tuesday are given below.
A negative number means the lemonade stand made a loss. Find the range of the data.

£30	£12	£1	–£4	–£40	£8.50

Q5 The range of the following data set is 6: 6, 5, 8, 8, 5, ? PROBLEM SOLVING
What are the two possible values for the missing number?

Q6 The number of skips Simone managed when skimming stones on a lake are given below.

3, 6, 17, 4, 3, 6, 6, 5, 4, 3

a) What is the range of the data?

b) Do you think the range is a good measure of the spread of this data?

Finding Averages and the Range from a Frequency Table

Learning Objective — Spec Ref S2/S4:
Find the mode, median, mean and range for data in a frequency table.

Large data sets are often put into **frequency tables** to make them easier to deal with.

The data looks different, but you can find the averages and range as usual:

- The **mode** is the value that appears the most — the one with the **highest** frequency.
- The **median** is the middle value (or halfway between two middle values).
  Find its position as normal, then count through the table to see which value it takes.
- The **range** is the **difference** between the **largest** and the **smallest** values given in the table.

Example 5

This frequency table shows the number of mobile phones owned by a group of people.

Number of mobile phones	0	1	2	3
Frequency	4	10	4	2

a) Find the modal number of mobile phones owned.

Most people own 1 mobile phone since it has the highest frequency (10). So the mode is 1.

Modal number = **1 mobile phone**

b) What is the median number of mobile phones owned?

1. Find the number of data values and position of the median.

   Total frequency = 4 + 10 + 4 + 2 = 20,
   so the median is halfway between the 10th and 11th values.

2. Count through the 'Frequency' row to find the 10th and 11th values. The raw data is 0, 0, 0, 0, 1, 1, 1, 1, 1, 1, 1, 1, 1, 1...

   10th value = 1 and 11th value = 1,
   so median = $\frac{1+1}{2}$ = **1 mobile phone**

Tip: For larger data sets, it's easier to use $(n + 1) \div 2$ to find the median position, where n is the total frequency.
E.g. if $n = 20$, $(20 + 1) \div 2 = 10.5$

c) Find the range for this data.

Subtract the fewest number of phones from the greatest number of phones: 3 – 0 = **3**

Finding the **mean** from a frequency table is a bit trickier. To work out the total of all the values, it's best to add a third row (or column) to the table. Take a look at the example below...

Example 6

This frequency table shows the number of mobile phones owned by a group of people.

Number of mobile phones	0	1	2	3
Frequency	4	10	4	2

a) How many people were in the group altogether?

This is the total of the frequencies.

Total number of people = 4 + 10 + 4 + 2 = **20**

b) What is the total number of mobile phones owned by this group of people?

1. First multiply each number of mobile phones by its frequency — add a third row to record your values.

Number of mobile phones	0	1	2	3
Frequency	4	10	4	2
Phones × frequency	0	10	8	6

2. Then add the results together. Total number of mobile phones = 0 + 10 + 8 + 6 = **24**

c) Find the mean number of mobile phones owned by each person.

Divide the total number of phones by the number of people in the group.

$$\text{Mean} = \frac{\text{Total number of phones}}{\text{Total number of people}}$$

$$= \frac{24}{20} = \textbf{1.2 mobile phones}$$

Tip: Make sure you remember to divide by the total frequency (i.e. 20) and not the number of groups.

Exercise 5

Q1 This frequency table shows the number of pets the students in a class have.

Number of pets	0	1	2	3	4
Frequency	5	10	5	5	2

a) What is the modal number of pets owned?

b) What is the median number of pets owned?

c) How many students had:
(i) no pets? (ii) 1 pet? (iii) 2 pets? (iv) 3 pets? (v) 4 pets?

d) Use your answer to c) to find the total number of pets owned by the students.

e) How many students are in the class altogether?

f) Use your answers to d) and e) to find the mean number of pets owned by each student.

Q2 The table shows the number of people living in each of 30 houses.

Number of people	1	2	3	4	5
Frequency	7	9	1	10	3

a) Write down the modal number of people living in a house.

b) Find the median number of people living in a house.

c) Calculate the mean number of people living in a house.

d) Work out the range of the data.

Q3 During June, a student wrote down the temperature in his garden in degrees Celsius (°C) every day at noon, as shown in the table.

Temperature (°C)	Frequency
16	4
17	9
18	2
19	5
20	4
21	6

a) Find the median noon temperature.

b) Find the mean noon temperature (correct to 1 decimal place).

c) The average noon temperature in June in the UK is approximately 18.5 °C. What does this suggest about these results?

Finding Averages from a Grouped Frequency Table

Learning Objective — Spec Ref S2/S4:
Find the mode, median, mean and range for data in a grouped frequency table.

If you're given data in the form of a **grouped frequency table**, then you don't know the **exact** data values — so you can't find exact values for the averages or range. You can only **identify** the **modal group** and **group containing the median**, and **estimate** the **mean** and the **range**.

- The **modal group** is the group (sometimes called a **class**) that has the **highest frequency**.
- Find the **group containing the median** by working out the **position** of the median in the usual way. Then use the **group frequencies** to identify which group the median falls into.
- To estimate the mean, you need to find the midpoint of each group — this is used as an **estimate** for all the data values within the group. To find the **midpoint** of a group, add the **lower** and **upper** bounds together and **divide by 2**. The method is then the same as for non-grouped tables.
- The **estimated range** is found by **subtracting** the **lower bound** of the smallest group from the **upper bound** of the largest group — this gives you the **largest possible range** for the data set.

Example 7

This grouped frequency table shows the number of hours that 20 people spent exercising during one week.

Hours, h	$0 \le h < 4$	$4 \le h < 8$	$8 \le h < 12$	$12 \le h < 16$	$16 \le h < 20$	$20 \le h < 24$
Frequency	2	3	6	4	4	1

a) Write down the modal group.

This is the one with the highest frequency.

Modal group is $\mathbf{8 \le h < 12}$

b) Which group contains the median?

Find the position of the median and then count through the groups until you reach this position.

There are 20 values, so $n = 20$.
$(n + 1) \div 2 = (20 + 1) \div 2 = 10.5$
So the median lies halfway between the 10th and 11th values, so it's in the group $\mathbf{8 \le h < 12}$.

c) Find an estimate for the mean.

You don't know how long each person spent exercising, so you assume that each of their times is in the middle of their group. So work out the midpoints:

Hours, h	$0 \le h < 4$	$4 \le h < 8$	$8 \le h < 12$	$12 \le h < 16$	$16 \le h < 20$	$20 \le h < 24$
Frequency	2	3	6	4	4	1
Midpoint of group	$\frac{0+4}{2} = 2$	$\frac{4+8}{2} = 6$	$\frac{8+12}{2} = 10$	$\frac{12+16}{2} = 14$	$\frac{16+20}{2} = 18$	$\frac{20+24}{2} = 22$

Now find the mean as before, using the midpoints instead of the actual data values.

Freq. × midpoint	$2 \times 2 = 4$	$3 \times 6 = 18$	$6 \times 10 = 60$	$4 \times 14 = 56$	$4 \times 18 = 72$	$1 \times 22 = 22$

Add the results together. Total number of hours = $4 + 18 + 60 + 56 + 72 + 22 = 232$

Divide the total number of hours by the total frequency. Mean = $\frac{232}{20}$ = **11.6 hours**

d) Estimate the range.

Subtract the lower bound of the smallest group from the upper bound of the largest group.

Range = $24 - 0$ = **24 hours**

Exercise 6

Q1 The test results of 25 people are shown in this grouped frequency table.

Marks scored	1-5	6-10	11-15	16-20
Frequency	4	5	7	9

a) Write down the modal group.

b) Which group contains the median?

c) Find an estimate for the mean.

d) Estimate the range of marks.

Q2 The table on the right shows some information about the weights of some tangerines in a supermarket.

a) Find an estimate for the mean.

b) Find an estimate for the range of weights.

c) Explain why your answer to part b) might be very different from the actual range.

Weight in grams, w	**Frequency**
$0 \leq w < 20$	1
$20 \leq w < 40$	6
$40 \leq w < 60$	9
$60 \leq w < 80$	24

Q3 Troy collected some information about the number of hours (to the nearest whole hour) students spent watching television over a week.

a) Write down the modal group.

b) Which group contains the median?

c) Find an estimate for the mean to 1 decimal place.

Time in hours	**Frequency**
0-5	3
6-10	8
11-15	11
16-20	4

Q4 This table shows information about the heights of 200 people.

a) Write down the modal group.

b) Which group contains the median?

c) Find an estimate for the mean to 3 significant figures.

d) Find an estimate for the range.

Height (h) in m	**Frequency**
$1.50 \leq h < 1.60$	27
$1.60 \leq h < 1.70$	92
$1.70 \leq h < 1.80$	63
$1.80 \leq h < 1.90$	18

26.3 Two-Way Tables

Two-way tables are really clever, they show two variables (pieces of information) at the same time.

Learning Objective — Spec Ref S2:
Complete and interpret data in two-way tables.

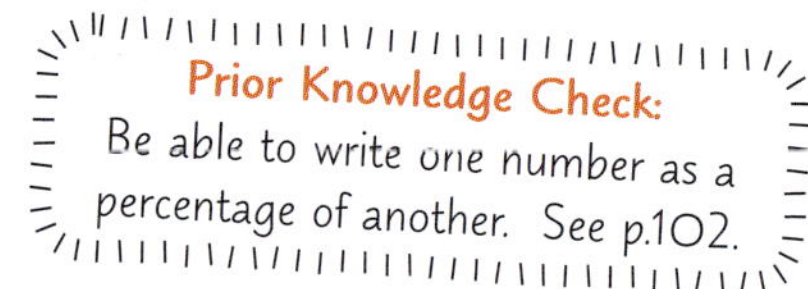

Prior Knowledge Check:
Be able to write one number as a percentage of another. See p.102.

Two-way tables are used to show the frequencies for **two different variables** — e.g. the hair colour and eye colour of school pupils.

- **Rows** represent the **categories** for one variable (e.g. 'brown hair', 'blonde hair', etc.).
- **Columns** represent the **categories** for the other variable (e.g. 'blue eyes', 'brown eyes', etc.).
- Each **cell** then shows the number of items in a particular row AND a particular column — e.g. the number of pupils with brown hair AND blue eyes.
- **Row** and **column totals** show the **total** number of items in each **category** and the bottom-right cell shows the **overall** total.

To interpret two-way tables you may need to find missing values or work out percentages. You can find percentages of the **whole group** or percentages within a **category**.

Tip: Be careful with which totals you use. You need the overall total if you're looking at the whole group, or the row/column totals if you're looking within a category.

Example 1

This table shows how students in a class travel to school.

	Walk	Bus	Car	Total
Boys	8	7		19
Girls	6		2	
Total		12		

a) Complete the table.

Add entries to find row/column totals. Subtract from row/column totals to find other entries.

	Walk	Bus	Car	Total
Boys	8	7	19 – 8 – 7 = **4**	19
Girls	6	12 – 7 = **5**	2	6 + 5 + 2 = **13**
Total	8 + 6 = **14**	12	4 + 2 = **6**	19 + 13 = **32**

b) How many girls take the bus to school?

Find the entry in the Bus column and the Girls row.

5 girls take the bus

c) How many students walk to school?

This is the total of the Walk column.

14 students walk

d) What percentage of students take the bus to school?

Divide the total of the Bus column by the overall total, and multiply by 100 to get the percentage.

12 students take the bus and there are 32 students in total, so:
$12 \div 32 = 0.375$, $0.375 \times 100 =$ **37.5%**

Exercise 1

Q1 Copy and complete these two-way tables, showing how groups of students travel to school.

a)

	Walk	Bus	Car	Total
Boys	9	5	3	
Girls	5	8	6	
Total				

b)

	Walk	Bus	Car	Total
Boys			8	
Girls	11		4	30
Total	21			60

Q2 This two-way table shows how many male and female language students from a university's languages department went to study in Germany, France or Spain.

	Germany	France	Spain	Total
Male	16	7	12	
Female	18	4	16	
Total				

a) Copy the table and fill in the entries in the final row and final column.

b) How many female students went to France?

c) How many male students went to Germany?

d) How many students in total went to Spain?

e) How many female students went to either Germany, France or Spain to study?

f) What was the total number of students from this department that went to either Germany, France or Spain to study?

Q3 This two-way table gives information about some students' favourite type of snack.

	Chocolate	Crisps	Jellies	Total
Male	3			
Female		7	2	
Total	6	12		30

a) Copy and complete the two-way table.

b) How many students preferred crisps?

c) How many females preferred jellies?

d) What percentage of males preferred chocolate?

Q4 This two-way table gives information about the colours of the vehicles in a car park.

	Red	Black	Blue	White	Total
Cars	8	7	4		22
Vans		2	1	10	
Motorbikes	2	1		2	
Total	12		6		

a) Copy and complete the two-way table.

b) How many motorbikes were blue?

c) How many vans were there?

d) What percentage of vehicles were: (i) cars? (ii) vans? (iii) red?

26.4 Bar Charts and Pictograms

Bar charts show how many items fall into different categories.
A pictogram uses symbols to represent a certain number of items.

Bar Charts

Learning Objective — Spec Ref S2:
Display and interpret data in bar charts.

Bar charts show the **number** (or frequency) of items in **different categories**. They're used for **qualitative** or **discrete quantitative data** (see p.423). Each bar represents a different category — the bars **shouldn't touch** because the categories are **distinct**.

Tip: Bars can be replaced by lines, and drawn either vertically or horizontally.

You can easily read the **mode** (see p.436) from a bar chart — it's the category with the highest frequency, so it's shown by the **tallest bar**.

If the data is numerical, you can find (or estimate) the mean, median and range too.

Example 1

The eye colour of 50 students is shown in the frequency table on the right. Draw a bar chart to display this information.

Eye colour	Blue	Brown	Green	Other
Frequency	15	19	10	6

1. Draw a bar of equal width for each eye colour, with height equal to the frequency, and a space between each bar.
2. Label your axes with 'Eye colour' on the horizontal axis and 'Frequency' on the vertical axis.

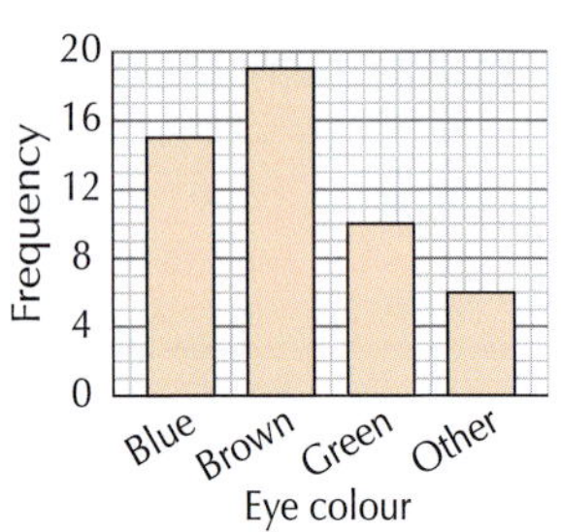

Exercise 1

Q1 Arthur asked some students in the canteen which meal they had bought at lunchtime. His results are in the table below. Draw a bar chart to show this information.

Meal	Pie & Chips	Pasta	Baked potato	Baguette	Salad
Frequency	11	3	7	10	4

Q2 Some people at a bus stop were asked which bus they were waiting for. Their responses are shown in the frequency table below. Draw a bar chart to show this information.

Bus	Number 7	Number 23	Coastlander	X94	12a
Frequency	6	5	2	3	2

Q3 One morning a coffee shop recorded the first 100 drinks that were ordered. Their results are in the frequency table below. Draw a bar chart to show this information

Drink	Espresso	Latte	Cappuccino	Mocha	Tea	Other
Frequency	23	19	12	15	22	9

Multiple sets of data can be displayed on the **same bar chart** — e.g. data for boys and girls or children and adults.

- **Dual bar charts** have two bars per category — one for each data set.
- **Composite bar charts** have single bars split into different sections for each data set.

Example 2

Manpreet and Jack recorded how many TV programmes they watched each day for a week. Their results are shown in the table on the right. Draw a dual bar chart to display this information.

Day	M	T	W	T	F	S	S
No. watched by Manpreet	1	2	4	2	3	7	4
No. watched by Jack	2	1	0	2	3	4	0

1. Each day should have two bars — one for Manpreet and one for Jack.
2. The height of each bar is the frequency.
3. Mark up the bars for Manpreet and Jack in different ways (e.g. shade one and not the other) — and make sure to include a key showing which is which.

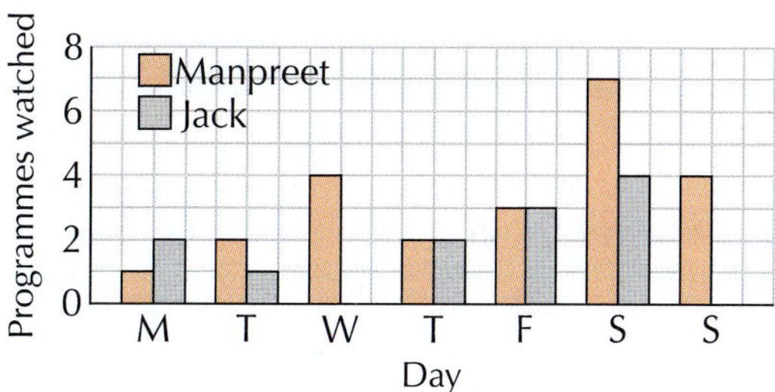

Example 3

The number of cars sold at two car showrooms over a week is shown in the table below. Draw a composite bar chart to display this information.

Day	M	T	W	T	F	S	S
No. sold at Showroom 1	3	1	4	2	2	6	3
No. sold at Showroom 2	2	1	1	0	2	5	1

1. Start with Showroom 1 — the height of the orange bar is the frequency for Showroom 1.
2. Add grey bars onto the top of the orange ones. The height of each grey bar should be the frequency for Showroom 2. Make sure you include a key to show which colour is for which showroom.
3. The total height of the composite bar (the orange and grey bars combined) is the total frequency for both showrooms.

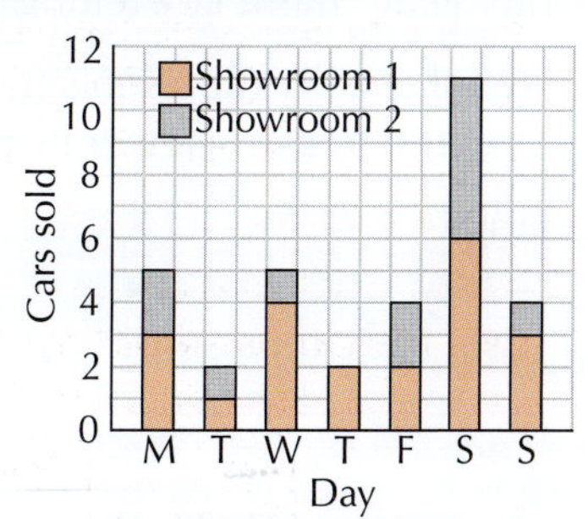

Exercise 2

Q1 The eye colour of 50 students is shown in the table.

Eye colour	Blue	Brown	Green	Other
No. of males	8	7	5	4
No. of females	7	12	5	2

a) Draw a dual bar chart to display the data.

b) Draw a composite bar chart to display the data.

c) Which chart is best for comparing males and females?

d) What is the modal eye colour?

e) Which chart was easier to use to find the mode?

Q2 This composite bar chart shows the ages in whole years of the members of a small gym.

a) How many members are in the age range 26-35 years?

b) How many members does the gym have in total?

c) What is the modal age range for the female members?

d) How many more men aged 26-35 use the gym than women aged 26-35?

e) Which age range has the greatest difference in numbers of men and women?

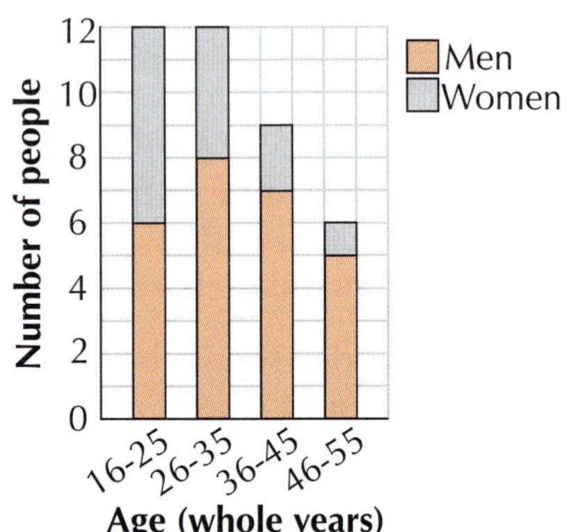

Pictograms

Learning Objective — Spec Ref S2:
Display and interpret data in pictograms.

Pictograms show the number (or frequency) of items using **symbols**. Every pictogram has a key telling you what one symbol represents.

One symbol usually represents more than one item, so a fraction of the symbol is used to show fewer items than the whole symbol represents.

For example:

So, = 3 items

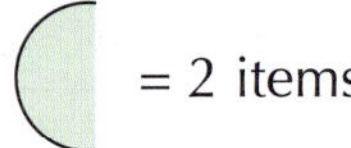
= 2 items

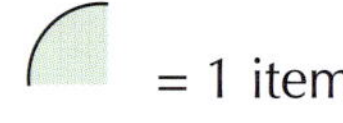
= 1 item

Example 4

This table shows the number of TVs in four secondary schools.

School	Cool School	Great Hall	St. Jimmy's	Parker's Park
TVs	20	10	8	13

Using the symbol ▭ to represent 4 TVs, draw a pictogram to show this information.

1. Work out how many symbols you need to draw for each school. For example, for Great Hall:

× 2.5 4 TVs = ▭ × 2.5
10 TVs = ▭ ▭ ◧

Cool School	▭ ▭ ▭ ▭ ▭
Great Hall	▭ ▭ ◧
St. Jimmy's	▭ ▭
Parker's Park	▭ ▭ ▭ ◸

2. Include a key to show what one symbol represents. ⟶ Key: ▭ represents 4 TVs.

Exercise 3

Q1 Members of a hockey club were asked which activity they would like to do on a team day out. The results are in this frequency table.

Activity	Theme Park	Bowling	Cinema	Boat Trip
Frequency	14	10	5	3

Draw a pictogram to show this information. Show 2 club members using the symbol: ○

Q2 The incomplete pictogram on the right shows the number of chocolate bars a shop sold on Monday, Tuesday and Wednesday.

a) How many chocolate bars were sold on:

(i) Tuesday? (ii) Wednesday?

b) Copy the pictogram, and use the information below to complete it.

- On Thursday the shop sold 20 bars.
- On Friday they sold 50 bars.
- On Saturday they sold 65 bars.
- On Sunday the shop was closed.

Monday	▯▯▯▯ ▯▯▯▯ ▯▯▯▯
Tuesday	▯▯▯▯ ▯▯▯▯
Wednesday	▯▯▯▯ ▯▯
Thursday	
Friday	
Saturday	
Sunday	

Key: ▯▯▯▯ represents 20 packets of sweets

Q3 This pictogram shows the number of letters that were delivered to each of the 6 houses in a street one week.

a) How many letters were delivered to Number 4?

b) Which house received fewest letters during the week?

c) How many letters in total were delivered to the 6 houses?

Number 1	◸
Number 2	⊠ ▽
Number 3	⊠ ⊠ ⊠
Number 4	⊠ ⊠ ◸
Number 5	⊠
Number 6	⊠ ◸

Key: ⊠ represents 4 letters

26.5 Stem and Leaf Diagrams

Stem and leaf diagrams are used to display sets of discrete data. They are useful for showing the spread of data visually, but still showing each data value.

Building Stem and Leaf Diagrams

Learning Objective — Spec Ref S2:
Construct stem and leaf diagrams, including back-to-back diagrams.

In **stem and leaf diagrams**, data values are split up into '**stems**' (their first digit(s)) and '**leaves**' (the remaining digit). So for the value **25**, the stem would be **2** and the leaf would be **5**. The leaves are then **ordered** numerically.

Stem and leaf diagrams always have a **key** — e.g. '2 | 5 means 25'.

Tip: Decimals and three-figure numbers can be shown using different keys, e.g. 0 | 3 = 0.3 or 20 | 4 = 204.

Example 1

Here are the marks scored by pupils in a class test.

56, 52, 82, 65, 76, 82, 57, 63, 69, 73, 58, 81, 73, 52, 73, 71, 67, 59, 63

Use this data to build an ordered stem and leaf diagram.

1. Write down the 'stems' — here use the first digit of the marks. The smallest first digit is 5 and the largest is 8, so use 5, 6, 7 and 8.
2. Next, make a 'leaf' for each data value by adding the second digit to the correct stem.

Stem	Leaves
5	6 2 7 8 2 9
6	5 3 9 7 3
7	6 3 3 3 1
8	2 2 1

3. Put the leaves in each row in order — from lowest to highest.

Stem	Leaves
5	**2 2 6 7 8 9**
6	**3 3 5 7 9**
7	**1 3 3 3 6**
8	**1 2 2**

4. Always include a key. → Key: 5 | 2 means 52

Back-to-back stem and leaf diagrams can be used to display **two sets of data** next to one another — e.g. they might show data for different genders or age groups.

In these diagrams, the stem is in the **centre** and the leaves from the two data sets are placed on **either side** of the stem. This means that one data set has to be read '**backwards**' (the **smaller leaves** are closest to the centre) — so the **key** is really important.

Example 2

The times taken (in minutes) by 14 girls and 14 boys to complete a puzzle were recorded. Using the results below, construct an ordered back-to-back stem and leaf diagram.

Boys: 17, 27, 14, 33, 32, 5, 14, 6, 6, 19, 29, 9, 38, 7

Girls: 32, 31, 2, 25, 23, 28, 38, 29, 37, 34, 2, 4, 25, 28

1. Write down the 'stem' — use the 'tens' digit. For single-digit numbers, this is 0.
2. Make the 'leaves' for one data set by adding the second digit of each value to the correct stem.
3. Repeat step 2 for the other data set, but write the digits on the other side of the stem.
4. Put the leaves in each row in order — from lowest to highest as you read outwards from the stem.
5. Remember to include a key.

Girls		Boys
4 2 2	0	5 6 6 9 7
	1	7 4 4 9
8 5 9 8 3 5	2	7 9
4 7 8 1 2	3	3 2 8

Girls		**Boys**
4 2 2	**0**	**5 6 6 7 9**
	1	**4 4 7 9**
9 8 8 5 5 3	**2**	**7 9**
8 7 4 2 1	**3**	**2 3 8**

Key: 2 | 7 for boys means 27 minutes
3 | 2 for girls means 23 minutes

Exercise 1

Q1 Use the data set below to make an ordered stem and leaf diagram.

41, 48, 51, 54, 59, 65, 65, 69, 74, 80, 86, 89

Q2 Only some of the values from the data sets below have been added to the ordered stem and leaf diagrams. Copy and complete the diagrams by adding the rest of the data values.

a) Key: 3 | 1 means 3.1

3	1
4	0 4
5	1 3 4
6	0
7	1

~~3.1~~	~~4.0~~	~~4.4~~	~~5.3~~
5.7	5.9	~~6.0~~	7.7
3.4	4.9	~~5.4~~	~~5.1~~
6.1	5.7	~~7.1~~	4.4

b) Key: 20 | 1 means 201

20	3 5
30	1
40	2 2
50	0
60	1 6

~~203~~	~~205~~	~~301~~	~~402~~
409	~~500~~	~~606~~	608
304	409	404	501
403	~~601~~	503	~~402~~

Q3 The amount of rainfall (in cm) over Morecambe Bay was recorded every week for 16 weeks. Use the data below to make an ordered stem and leaf diagram.

0.0	3.8	3.6	0.1	2.7	0.6	0.3	1.1
2.0	1.3	0.0	1.6	4.1	0.0	2.5	3.1

Q4 Use these two data sets to draw an ordered back-to-back stem and leaf diagram.

18, 8, 38, 29, 1, 28, 33, 24, 12, 37, 32

27, 25, 19, 15, 22, 18, 13, 23, 22, 32, 13

Using Stem and Leaf Diagrams

Learning Objective — Spec Ref S2/S4:
Interpret data presented in stem and leaf diagrams.

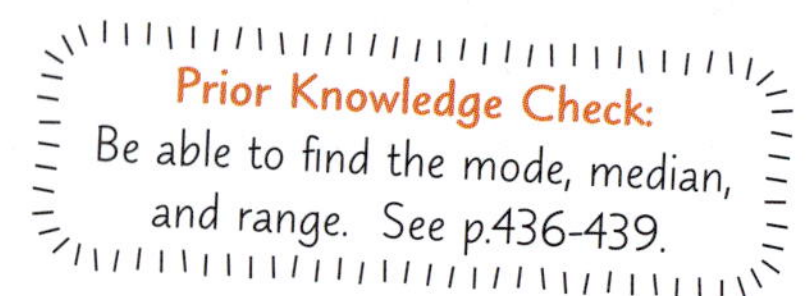

Prior Knowledge Check:
Be able to find the mode, median, and range. See p.436-439.

Once your data is in a **stem and leaf diagram**, you can easily find the **mode**, **median** and **range**, and you can compare two data sets from a back-to-back diagram. You can also quickly see how many values fall between certain limits — e.g. 'between 2 and 8'.

Example 3

The stem and leaf diagram on the right shows the number of seconds 19 children took to open a jar of jam. Use it to find the mode, median and range of the data.

Stem	Leaf
0	6 8 8
1	0 2 4 4 4 5 5 7
2	0 4 5 6 6 7
3	1 3

Key: 2 | 1 means 21 seconds

1. Find the mode by looking for the number that repeats most often in one of the rows — here, there are three 4's in the second row. Use the key to work out what it represents.

   Mode = **14 seconds**

2. There are 19 data values, so the median is the 10th value. Count along the 'leaves' to find it, starting with the first row.

   Median = **15 seconds**

3. Find the range by subtracting the first number from the last.

   Range = 33 – 6
   = **27 seconds**

Exercise 2

Q1 Use the stem and leaf diagram on the right to find:

a) the mode of the data
b) the median of the data
c) the range of the data

Stem	Leaf
0	5 8
1	2 3 7 9
2	0 1 3 9
3	2 2 2

Key: 2 | 1 means 21

Q2 The times in seconds that 16 people took to run a 100 m race are shown in the box.

a) Use these times to create an ordered stem and leaf diagram.
b) Find the mode, median and range of the times.
c) To qualify for the final, a contestant had to finish in under 13 seconds. How many of those who took part qualified?

10.2	13.1	13.9	14.2
17.3	11.7	11.4	12.9
15.4	13.6	13.9	10.6
12.8	13.9	12.4	13.3

Q3 The heart rates in beats per minute (bpm) of 15 people at rest and after exercise are shown on the right.

a) Find the median of each data set.
b) What conclusion can you draw from your answer to part a)?

At rest		After exercise
8 7 6 4 3 2 2	6	5 8 8 9
9 8 6 3 2 2	7	4 5 7 7 8
4 1	8	5 6 7
	9	1 3 7

Key: 6 | 5 after exercise means 65 bpm
2 | 6 at rest means 62 bpm

26.6 Pie Charts

In a pie chart, the size of the angle of each sector represents the frequency of a data value.

Drawing Pie Charts

Learning Objective — Spec Ref S2:
Construct pie charts.

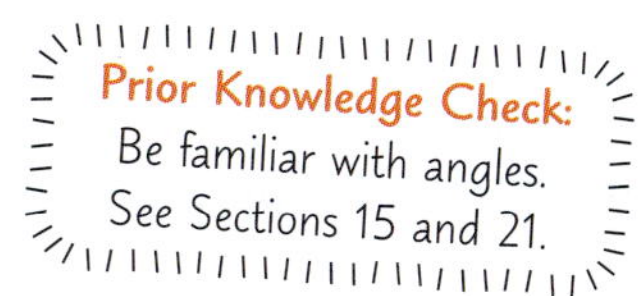
Prior Knowledge Check:
Be familiar with angles.
See Sections 15 and 21.

Pie charts show how data is divided into categories, but they show the **proportion** in each category, rather than the actual frequency. The sizes of the **angles** of the sectors are **proportional** to the **frequencies**.

To **draw** a pie chart:

- Find the **total frequency** by **adding** up the **frequencies** of each category.
- **Divide 360°** (the full circle) by the **total frequency** to find the **angle** which represents a **frequency of 1**.
- **Multiply** this value by the **frequency** of each **category** to find the **angle** of the **sector**.

Tip: The sector angles should add up to 360°.
You can use this to check your working.

Example 1

Kamali asked everyone in her class to name their favourite colour. The frequency table on the right shows her results.

Colour	Red	Green	Blue	Pink
Frequency	12	7	5	6

Draw a pie chart to show her results.

1. Calculate the total frequency — the total number of people in Kamali's class.

Total frequency = 12 + 7 + 5 + 6 = 30

2. Divide 360° by the total frequency to find the number of degrees needed to represent each person.

Each person is represented by 360° ÷ 30 = 12°

3. Multiply each frequency by the number of degrees for one person. This tells you the angle for each colour. (Check the angles add up to 360°. Here: 144° + 84° + 60° + 72° = 360°)

Colour	Red	Green	Blue	Pink
Frequency	12	7	5	6
Angle	144°	84°	60°	72°

4. Draw a pie chart — the sizes of the sectors are the angles you've just calculated.

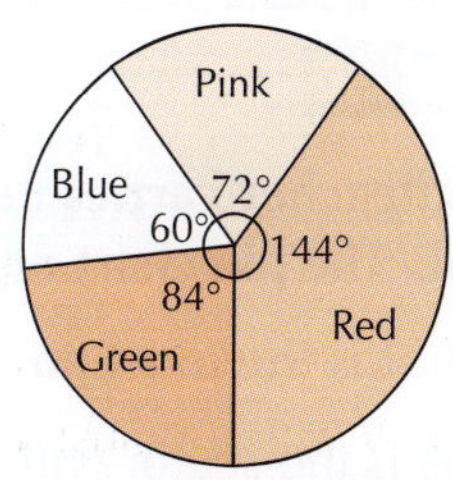
Pink
Blue
72°
60°
144°
84°
Red
Green

Q1 Albert recorded the colours of cars that passed his school. His results are shown in the table on the right.

a) Find the total number of cars Albert recorded.

b) Find how many degrees represent one car.

c) Calculate the angle needed to represent each colour.

d) Draw a pie chart to illustrate this data.

Colour	Frequency
Black	25
Silver	17
Red	8
Other	10

Q2 Becky asked her friends which football team they support. Their answers are shown in the table below.

Team	Carlisle United	Kendal Town	Millom Reds	Bristol
Frequency	13	9	8	6

a) Find the total frequency.

b) Calculate the angle needed to represent each of the four football teams.

c) Draw a pie chart showing Becky's results.

Q3 Vicky asked people entering a sports centre what activity they were going to do.

- 33 were going to play squash
- 21 were going swimming
- 52 were going to use the gym
- 14 had come to play table tennis

Draw a pie chart to show this data.

Interpreting Pie Charts

Learning Objective — Spec Ref S2:
Interpret data presented in pie charts.

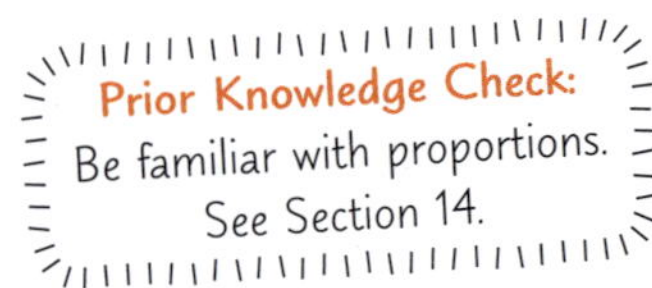
Prior Knowledge Check:
Be familiar with proportions.
See Section 14.

Pie charts let you **compare** the frequencies of different items, and say which ones occurred more often, and which ones occurred less often. However, pie charts **don't show the frequencies** themselves.

To work out the frequencies from a pie chart, you need to know the sizes of the angles of the sectors.

Tip: You can only compare frequencies in two different pie charts if you know the total number of items that each chart represents.

Example 2

A headteacher carries out a survey to find out how pupils travel to school. The pie chart on the right shows the results of the survey.

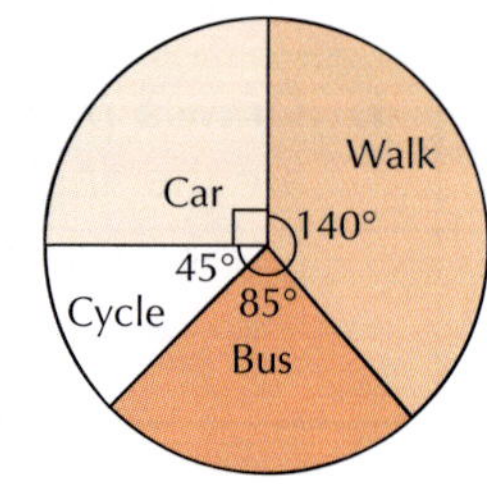
Walk
Car
140°
45°
Cycle
85°
Bus

a) What is the most popular way to travel to school?

This is the sector with the largest angle. **Walking**

b) Which method of transport is twice as common as cycling?

Cycling is represented by a sector with an angle of 45°, so look for a sector with an angle of $45° \times 2 = 90°$.

Travelling by car

c) 280 pupils walk to school. How many pupils took part in the survey altogether?

1. Work out how many pupils are represented by 1°. — 140° represents 280 pupils. So 1° represents $280 \div 140 = 2$ pupils.
2. Use this to work out how many pupils the whole pie chart represents. — This means 360° represents $360 \times 2 =$ **720 pupils.**

d) How many pupils cycle to school?

1. You know what 1° represents. — 1° represents 2 pupils.
2. Multiply this by the 'Cycle' sector angle to find how many pupils cycle to school. — So 45° represents $2 \times 45 =$ **90 pupils.**

Exercise 2

Q1 Match pie charts *P* and *Q* to the correct data set.

P

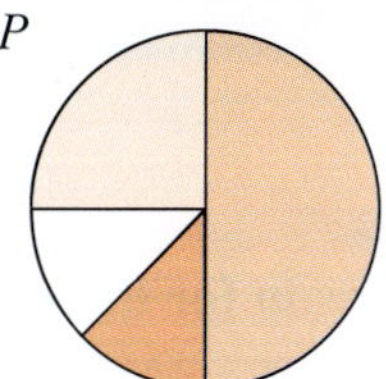

Q

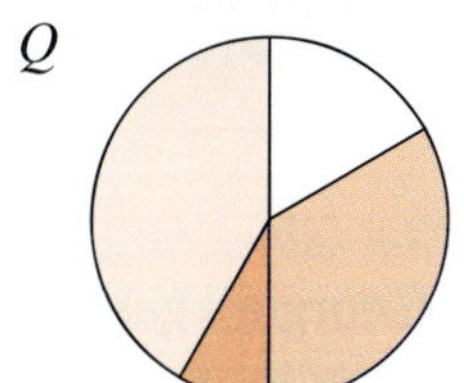

Data Set 1	A	B	C	D
Frequency	24	12	6	6

Data Set 2	A	B	C	D
Frequency	25	20	10	5

Q2 Keemia asked pupils in her school to name their favourite type of pizza. The pie chart on the right shows the results.

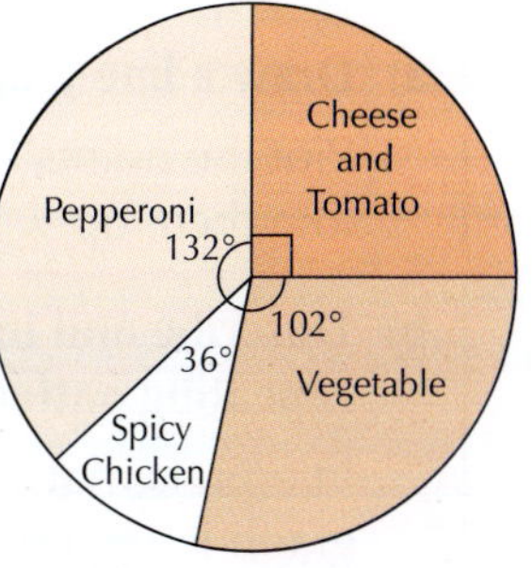

a) Which was the most popular type of pizza?

b) What fraction of the pupils said cheese and tomato was their favourite type of pizza?

c) 17 pupils said that vegetable was their favourite type of pizza. Calculate the total number of pupils that Keemia asked.

d) Use your answer to part c) to calculate the number of pupils that said spicy chicken was their favourite type of pizza.

Q3 Tom and Brooke record the number of homework tasks they are set in their Maths, English and Science lessons during one term.

Their data is displayed in the pie charts on the right.

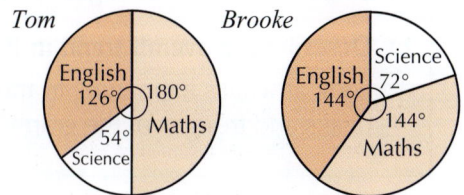

Tom: English 126°, Maths 180°, Science 54°

Brooke: English 144°, Science 72°, Maths 144°

a) Brooke says: "I have a smaller proportion of English homework than Tom." Is she correct?

b) Do the pie charts tell you who spent more time on their English homework? Explain your answer.

26.7 Time Series

Some line graphs can be used to show how things change over time — these are known as time series graphs. They're useful for spotting repeating patterns or trends in data.

Learning Objective — Spec Ref S2:
Display and interpret time series on a line graph.

A **time series** is a set of data collected at **regular intervals** over time — e.g. every day for a week, every month for a year or over several years. Time series graphs are **line graphs**, with 'time' along the bottom and a scale for the data values up the side. You plot the points and **join them with straight lines**.

You can use time series to find **trends** in the data over time. Look for:

- **Seasonality** — a basic pattern that is **repeated** regularly over time. E.g. the average monthly temperatures will follow a similar pattern year on year.
- An **overall trend** — where the data values **generally** get **smaller** or **larger** over time (ignoring seasonal patterns). E.g. the price of a weekly shop may steadily increase or decrease.

Tip: Seasonality doesn't have to match the actual seasons — e.g. tide levels show seasonality over the course of a day.

Example 1

The data below shows the total rainfall in Georgie's garden each season for three years.

Season	Spr	Sum	Aut	Win	Spr	Sum	Aut	Win	Spr	Sum	Aut	Win
Rainfall (mm)	225	200	275	375	250	225	300	425	300	250	325	475

a) **Draw a line graph to display this data.**

Plot the points from the table and join them up with straight lines.

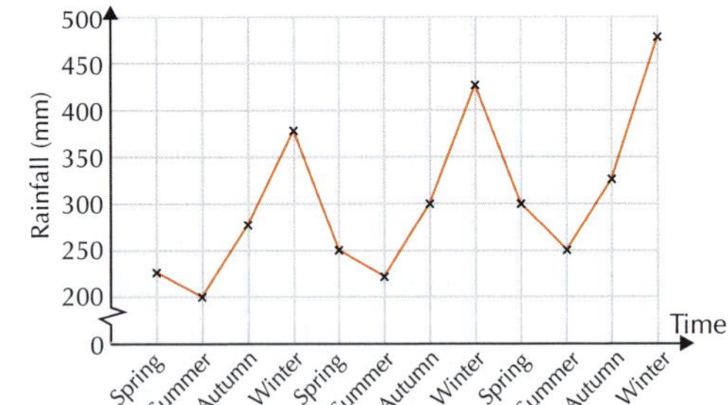

b) **Describe and interpret the repeating pattern in the data.**

Interpret what you see on the graph in the context of the data.

Each year the rainfall is **lower in summer than in spring**. It **increases in the autumn**, and is **even higher in the winter**, then drops again the following spring.

c) **Describe the overall trend in the data.**

Look at what's happening to the peaks and troughs of the graph.

There is an **upward trend** in the amount of rainfall.

Exercise 1

Q1 This table shows the amount of gas used (in m³) by a family over a period of three years.

Season	Spring	Summer	Autumn	Winter
2012	202	80	170	298
2013	196	76	161	283
2014	183	69	149	259

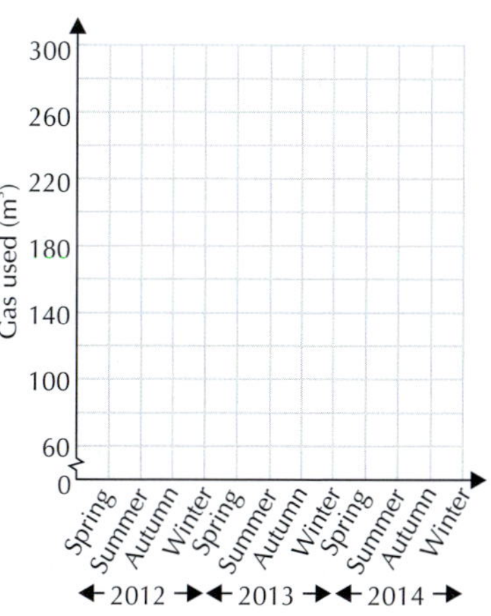

a) Copy the axes on the right, and draw a graph to show how the amount of gas used varied over the three years.

b) Describe and interpret the repeating pattern seen on the graph.

c) Describe the overall trend seen in the data.

Q2 This table shows the highest temperature, in °C, recorded in London and Sydney each month during one year.

Month	Jan	Feb	Mar	Apr	May	Jun	Jul	Aug	Sep	Oct	Nov	Dec
London	7	8	11	13	17	20	23	22	19	15	11	8
Sydney	26	27	25	22	20	17	16	18	19	22	24	25

a) Draw a line graph to show the highest monthly temperature in London during the year.

b) On the same axes, draw a line graph to show the highest monthly temperature in Sydney during the year.

c) Describe the shapes of your two lines. What does this tell you about the way the temperature changes in the two cities during the year?

Q3 The line graph on the right shows the number of pairs of sunglasses sold by a shop over four years.

a) Describe and interpret the repeating pattern seen in the graph.

b) Describe the overall trend shown by the graph.

c) Give a reason why the graph might be misleading.

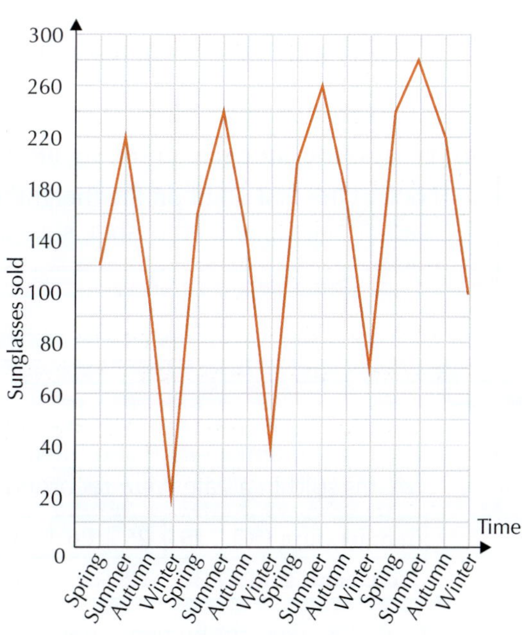

26.8 Scatter Graphs

Scatter graphs show two variables plotted against each other. They are used to show how closely two variables are related to one another — this is known as correlation.

Drawing Scatter Graphs

Learning Objective — Spec Ref S6:
Draw and interpret scatter graphs.

A **scatter graph** shows **two variables** plotted against each other, e.g. height and weight or temperature and BBQ sales. To **draw** a scatter graph:

- Decide **which variable** should go on **which axis** — the one that you think **depends** on the other should go on the **vertical** axis.
- **Plot** your data as points (x, y), where x is the variable on the horizontal axis and y is the variable on the vertical axis.

Example 1

Dougal measured the height and shoe size of 10 people.

Height (cm)	165	159	173	186	176	172	181	169	179	194
Shoe size	6	5	8	9	8.5	7	8	6	8	11

a) **Use his results to plot a scatter graph of shoe size against height in cm.**

1. Draw and label your axes. Here, height has been plotted along the horizontal axis and shoe size up the vertical axis.
2. Plot each point carefully (don't join them up).

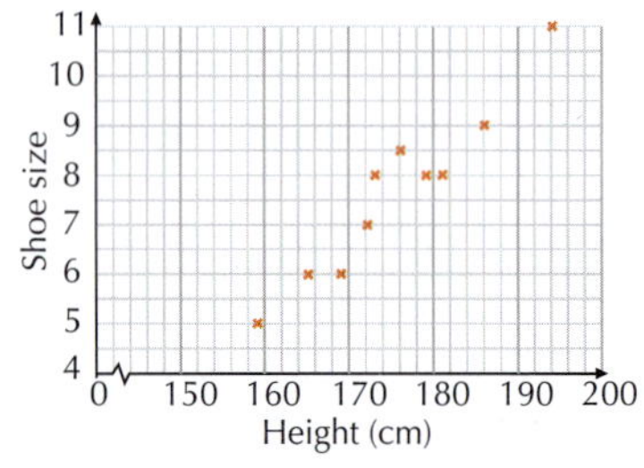

b) **What is the shoe size of the smallest person?**

Look at the first point on the 'height' scale and read off the value on the 'shoe size' scale.

Smallest height is 159 cm, and the corresponding shoe size is **5**

Exercise 1

Q1 The outside temperature and the number of ice creams sold in a cafe were recorded for six days.

Temperature (°C)	28	25	26	21	23	29
Ice creams sold	30	22	27	5	13	33

Copy the axes on the right, then use the data from the table to plot a scatter graph.

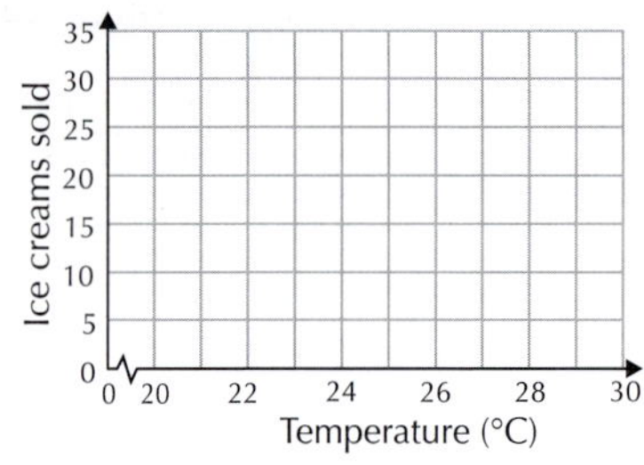

Q2 Ten children of different ages were asked how many baby teeth they still had. Use the results below to plot a scatter graph.

Age (years)	5	6	8	7	9	7	10	6	8	9
Baby teeth	20	17	11	15	7	17	5	19	13	8

Correlation and Lines of Best Fit

Learning Objectives — Spec Ref S6:
- Recognise and describe correlation.
- Draw a line of best fit and use it to estimate and predict data values.
- Be able to recognise outliers.

If two variables are **related** to each other then they are **correlated**.
Variables can be **positively correlated**, **negatively correlated** or **not correlated** at all.

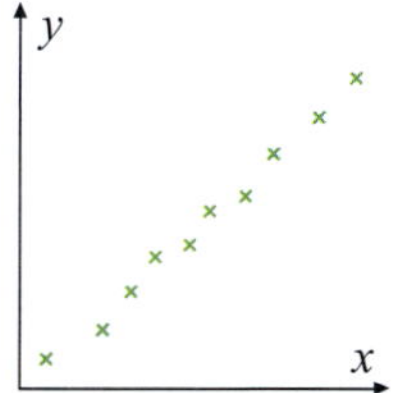

Positive correlation — both variables **increase and decrease together**. The **points** on the scatter graph will look like a line sloping **upward** from left to right.

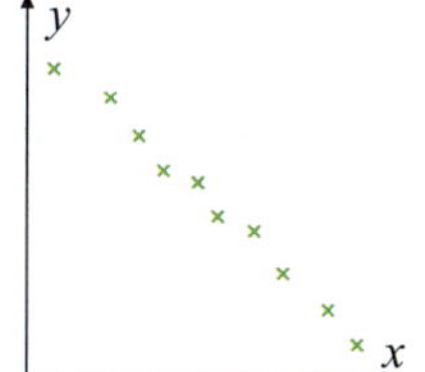

Negative correlation — as one variable **increases**, the other **decreases**. The **points** on the graph will look like a line sloping **downward** from left to right.

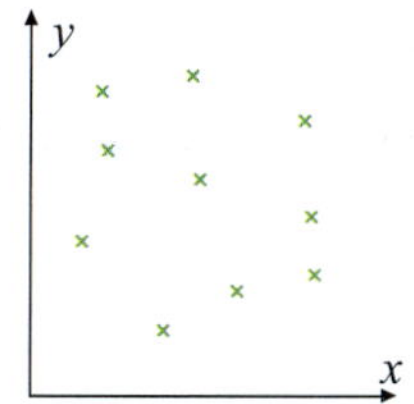

No correlation — there is **no linear relationship** between the variables. The **points** on the graph will look **randomly scattered**.

You can describe the **strength** of the correlation as well. The **closer** the points are to forming a **straight line**, the **stronger** the correlation.

- If most of your points are close to a **straight line**, then you have **strong correlation**.
- If your points are spread **loosely around** a straight line, then you have **moderate correlation**.
- If your points **don't line up** nicely but you can still see that there is a **relationship** between the two variables, then you have **weak correlation**.

Tip: If two variables are correlated it doesn't necessarily mean that one causes the other. There could be a third factor affecting both, or it could just be a coincidence.

Example 2

Describe the strength and type of correlation shown by each of the scatter graphs.

a)

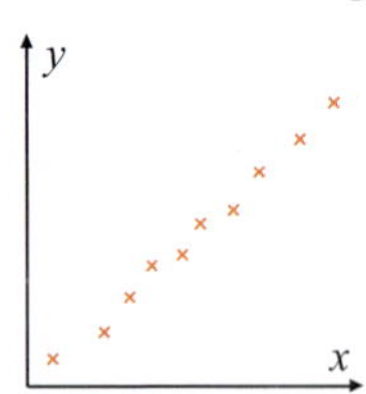

The points form an upward slope fairly close to a straight line, so this is...

Strong positive correlation

b)

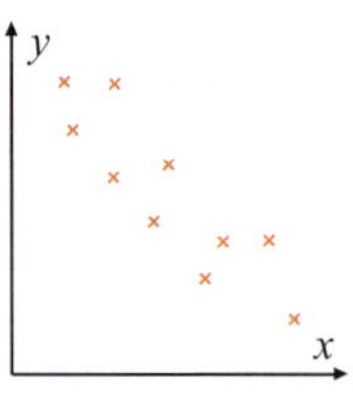

The points form a downward slope loosely around a straight line, so this is...

Moderate negative correlation

c)

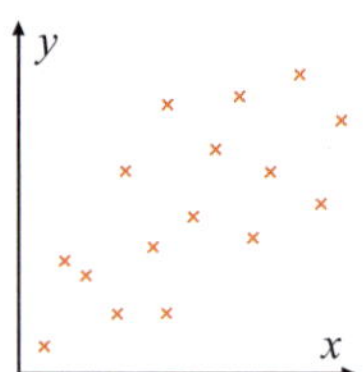

The points form an upward slope, but do not lie close to a straight line, so this is...

Weak positive correlation

Exercise 2

Q1 Describe the strength and type of correlation seen in the scatter graphs below.

a)

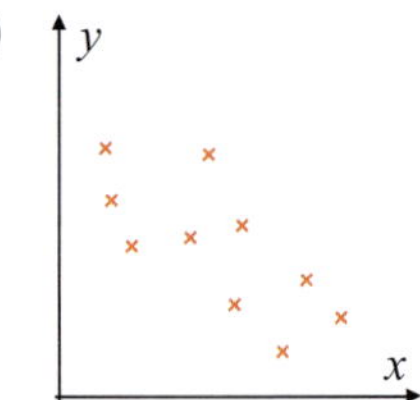

b)

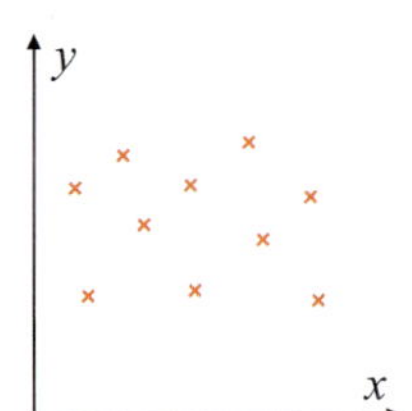

c)

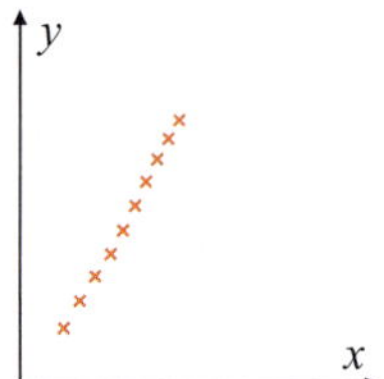

Q2 Are the following pairs of variables likely to show positive correlation, negative correlation or no correlation? Explain your answers.

a) Outside temperature and ice cream sales

b) Outside temperature and hot chocolate sales

c) Outside temperature and bread sales

d) Age of a child and his or her height

e) Speed limit in a street and the average speed of cars as they drive down that street

Q3 Jacob measured the wind speed and boat speed at different times during a sail. The results are shown by the scatter graph to the right.

Describe the relationship between wind speed and boat speed.

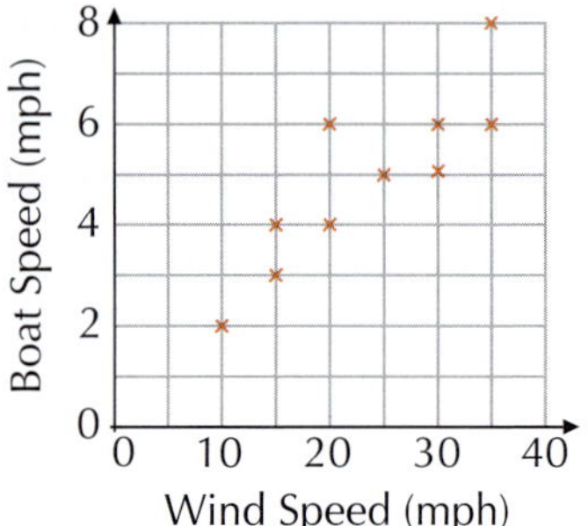

If two variables are correlated, then you can draw a **line of best fit** on their scatter graph. This is a **straight line** that passes through the **middle of the points** with a roughly **equal number** on either side.

Outliers are points that **don't fit** the general pattern of the rest of the data. They can **move** your line of best fit away from other values, so are usually **ignored** when drawing your line. Outliers can sometimes be caused by **errors** in the data, but not always — they can just be **unusually high** or **low values**.

You can use a line of best fit to **predict values** for one variable when you know the value of the other. All you have to do is **draw a line** from the value you're given to the line of best fit, then **read off** the value for the variable on the other axis.

- Predicting values **within** the range of data you have is known as **interpolation**, and should be **fairly reliable**.
- Predicting values **outside** the range of the data is known as **extrapolation**. This can be **unreliable** because you don't know that the pattern continues outside the data range.

Example 3

The scatter graph on the right shows the marks a class of pupils achieved in a Maths test plotted against the marks they achieved in an English test.

a) Draw a line of best fit on the graph.

b) Jimmy was ill on the day of the Maths test. If he scored 75 in his English test, predict what his Maths mark would have been.

c) Elena was ill on the day of the English test. If she scored 35 on her Maths test, predict what her English result would have been.

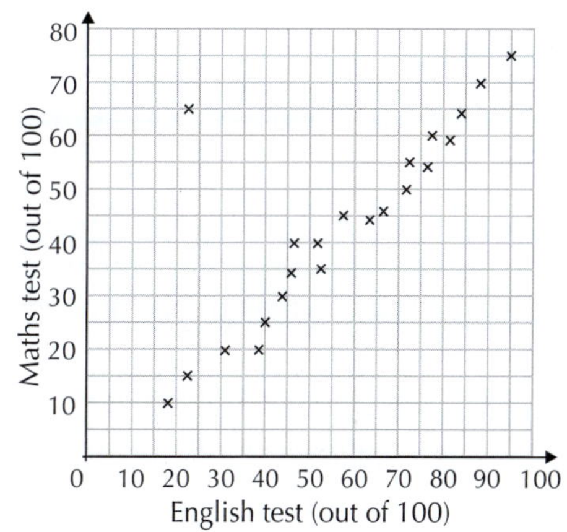

This point is an outlier, so ignore it when you draw your line.

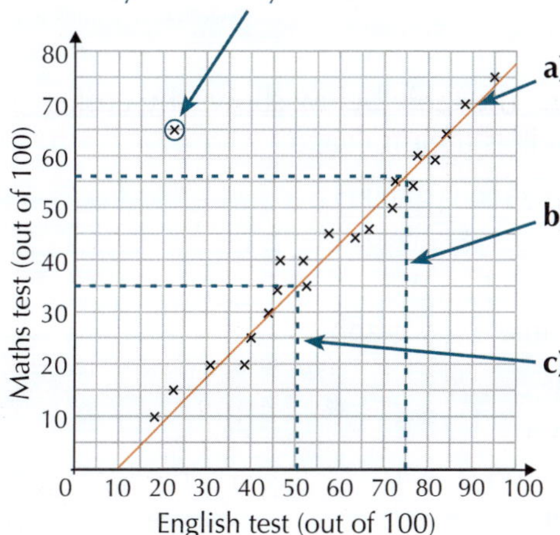

a) Draw a straight line through the middle of the points — have approximately the same number of points on either side of the line.

b) Draw a line up from 75 on the 'English' axis to the line of best fit, then across to the 'Maths' axis.

Predicted Maths mark for Jimmy = **56**

c) Draw a line across from 35 on the 'Maths' axis to the line of best fit, and then down.

Predicted English mark for Elena = **51**

Exercise 3

Q1 Could a line of best fit be drawn on each of these graphs? Explain your answers.

a)

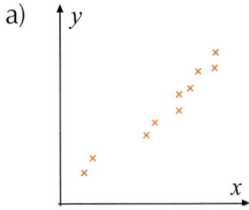

b)

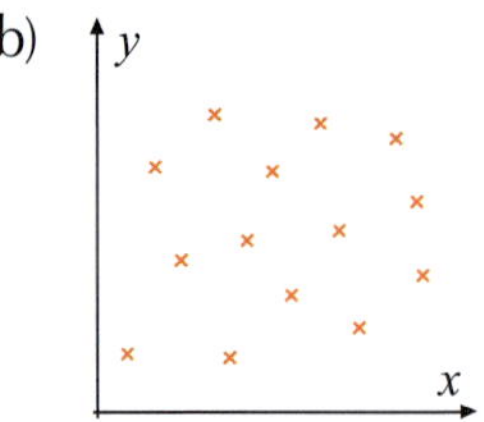

c)

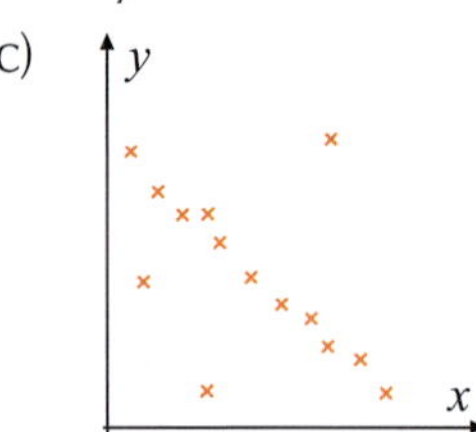

Q2 Pupils in a class were asked how many hours at the weekend they spent doing homework and watching television. The results are shown on this scatter graph.

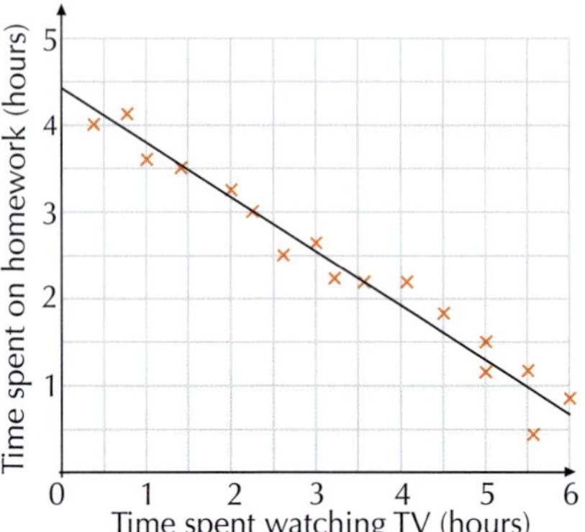

a) Describe the correlation between time spent watching TV and time spent doing homework.

b) Use the line of best fit to predict how long a pupil spends on homework if they watch 5.5 hours of TV at the weekend.

c) Amelia did 3.5 hours of homework at the weekend. Predict how many hours she spent watching TV.

Q3 The graph on the right shows the height of various types of tree plotted against the width of their trunks.

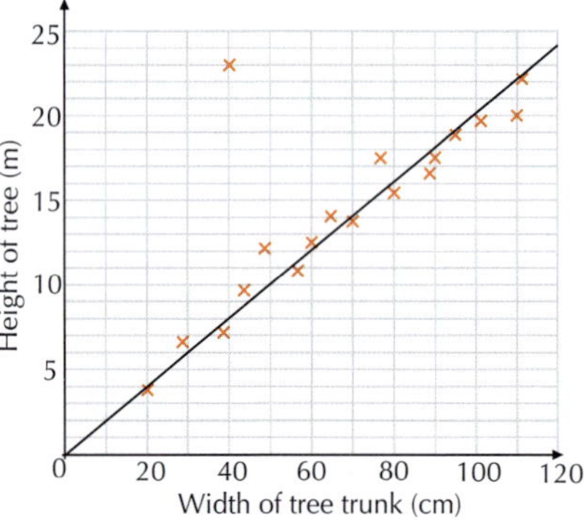

a) Describe the correlation between the width of the trunks and the height of the trees.

b) Give the width and the height of the tree that appears as an outlier on the graph.

c) Use the graph to predict the width of a tree's trunk if it is 13 m tall.

d) Explain whether the prediction that you made in part c) is reliable.

Q4 Anton wants to buy a particular model of car. The table below shows the cost of several of these cars that are for sale, as well as their mileage.

Mileage	5000	20000	10000	12000	5000	25000	27000
Cost (£)	3500	2000	3000	2500	3900	1000	500

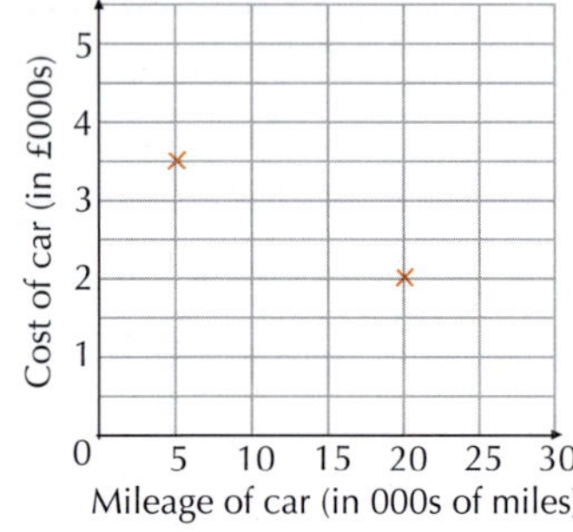

a) The first two points have already been plotted on the scatter graph on the right. Copy and complete the graph.

b) Draw a line of best fit through your points.

c) Thelma has seen a car of this model with a mileage of 50000. She plans to use the trend shown by the graph to predict the cost of this car. Comment on the reliability of this estimate.

Review Exercise

Q1 Eight students sat two maths tests. Their scores out of 20 are shown below.

Test 1: 19, 14, 8, 17, 17, 20, 6, 13

Test 2: 7, 14, 16, 7, 10, 8, 10, 12

a) Calculate the mean score for each test.

b) Find the range for each test.

c) Use your results from parts a) and b) to compare the distributions of the scores in the two tests.

Q2 Susie buys a bag of 5 apples. The weights of the apples are: 

57 g, 60 g, 69 g, 72 g, 75 g

After Susie has eaten two of the apples, the mean weight of the three that remain is 62 g. What were the weights of the two apples that she ate?

Q3 This table shows the number of goals scored one week by 18 teams in the premier division.

Number of goals	0	1	2	3	4	5
Number of teams	1	3	4	5	3	2

a) Find the median number of goals.

b) Find the mean number of goals. Give your answer to 1 decimal place.

c) Write down the mode.

d) The mean, median and modal numbers of goals scored in the same week of the previous year were all 2. How do these results compare?

Q4 This table shows the heights (in metres) of 20 people.

a) Complete the frequency column.

b) Write down the modal group.

c) Which group contains the median?

d) Find an estimate for the mean.

e) Estimate the range.

Height in metres, h	Tally	Frequency
$1.5 < h \leq 1.6$	||	
$1.6 < h \leq 1.7$	~~||||~~ ||||	
$1.7 < h \leq 1.8$	~~||||~~ ||	
$1.8 < h \leq 1.9$	||	

Q5 The vertical line graph shows information on the number of washing machines sold by an electrical shop each day for 40 days.

a) What is the median number of washing machines sold each day?

b) What is the modal number sold each day?

c) Calculate the mean number of machines sold each day.

d) Find the range of the number of machines sold each day.

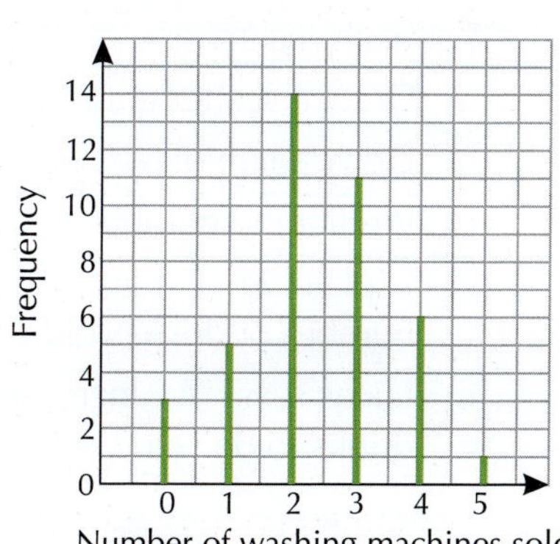

Q6 The children at a youth club were asked to name their favourite flavour of ice cream.
The dual bar chart on the right shows the results.

a) How many girls were asked altogether?

b) How many more boys than girls chose chocolate?

c) What is the modal flavour for the girls?

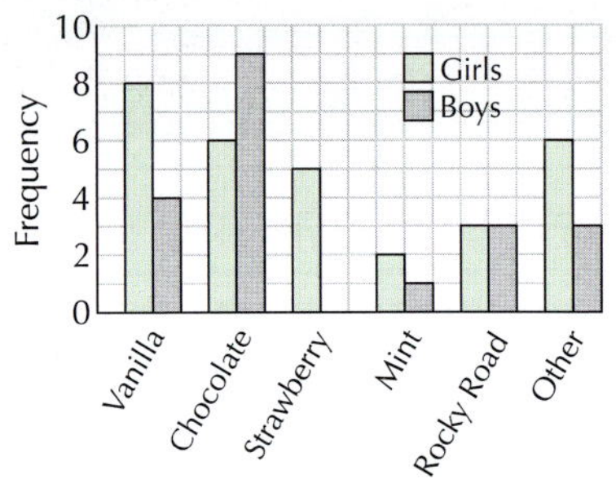

The pie chart on the right shows the same data for the girls.

d) Work out the number of degrees used to represent one girl.

e) Draw a pie chart to show the data for the boys.

f) Rocky road was chosen by the same number of girls and boys. Explain why the sectors representing rocky road in each pie chart are different sizes.

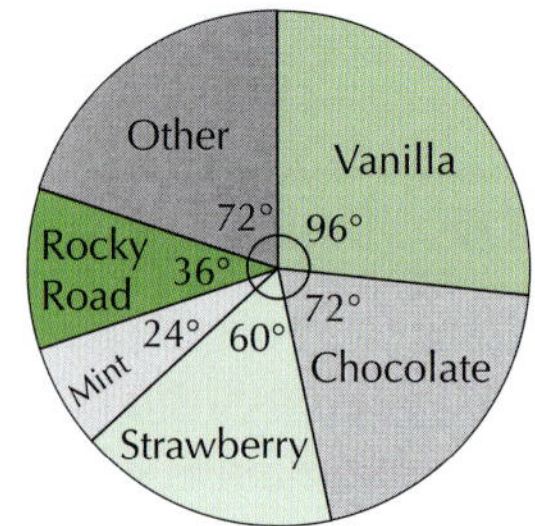

Q7 The data below shows the ages of people queuing in a post office at 10 am and at 3 pm.

10 am:	65	48	51	27	29	35	58	51	54	60	59
3 pm:	15	23	32	31	35	22	24	18	27		

a) Draw a back-to-back stem and leaf diagram to show the data.

b) Find and compare the median age of the people queuing at each time.

Q8 The outside temperature and the number of drinks sold by two vending machines were recorded over a 10-day period. The results are shown in this table.

Temperature (°C)	14	29	23	19	22	31	33	18	27	21
Drinks sold from Machine 1	6	24	16	13	15	28	31	13	22	14
Drinks sold from Machine 2	7	25	18	15	17	32	35	14	24	17

For each machine:

a) Draw a scatter graph of drinks sold against temperature.

b) Draw a line of best fit.

c) Predict the number of drinks that would be sold if the temperature was 25 °C.

d) Explain why it might not be appropriate to use your lines of best fit to estimate the number of drinks sold from each machine if the outside temperature was 3 °C.

e) Lucas says, "An increase in temperature causes more vending machine drinks to be sold." Do you agree with Lucas's statement? Explain your answer.

Exam-Style Questions

Q1 Two groups of students in Mr Green's class took the same test. Both groups contained 5 students who each scored a mark that is a whole number.

Mr Green found the median and range of marks for both groups:

Group	Median	Range
A	50	3
B	48	3

Show that the student who scored the lowest mark could be in group A. 

[2 marks]

Q2 The number of eggs laid by a farmer's hens on each day in one week were:

22 34 6 28 5 31 29

a) Work out the median for this data.

[1 mark]

b) Explain why the mean would not be a good measure of the average number of eggs laid per day.

[1 mark]

Q3 The amount of time (t minutes) spent on a social media website in one day was recorded for some students. The results are shown in the frequency table.

Time (t minutes)	Frequency
$0 \leq t < 40$	3
$40 \leq t < 80$	4
$80 \leq t < 120$	7
$120 \leq t < 160$	15
$160 \leq t < 200$	11

a) Write down the modal class.

[1 mark]

b) Calculate an estimate for the mean time spent.

[3 marks]

c) Explain why your answer to b) is only an estimate.

[1 mark]

Q4 Leah draws a pictogram to show how many books people read in a year. She shows 14 books like this:

Draw how Leah would show 7 books.

[2 marks]

Q5 Over the last year, some students at a school received gold, silver or bronze Duke of Edinburgh awards. Of the awards received, $\frac{1}{3}$ were silver. Five times as many bronze awards were received than gold awards.

PROBLEM SOLVING

a) Show this information as a pie chart.

[3 marks]

18 students received silver awards

b) Work out the number of students who received bronze awards.

[2 marks]

Q6 At the end of each month for a year, Midas recorded the price of gold per gram to the nearest £0.10. He displayed the data he recorded in the time series graph below.

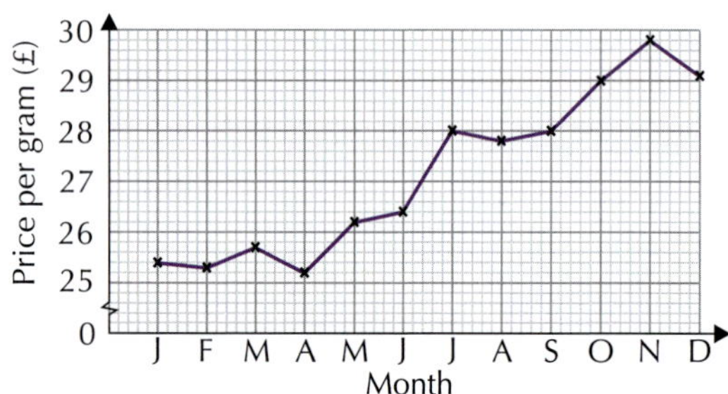

a) Describe the overall trend in gold prices over the course of the year.

[1 mark]

b) Midas owns a 12 kg gold bar. According to the graph, what is the maximum amount of money he could have made from selling the gold bar this year?

[2 marks]

Q7 The scatter diagram shows the percentage obtained in a geography exam and the number of lunchtime revision classes attended by 6 students.

a) Describe the correlation between the percentage obtained and the number of revision classes attended.

[1 mark]

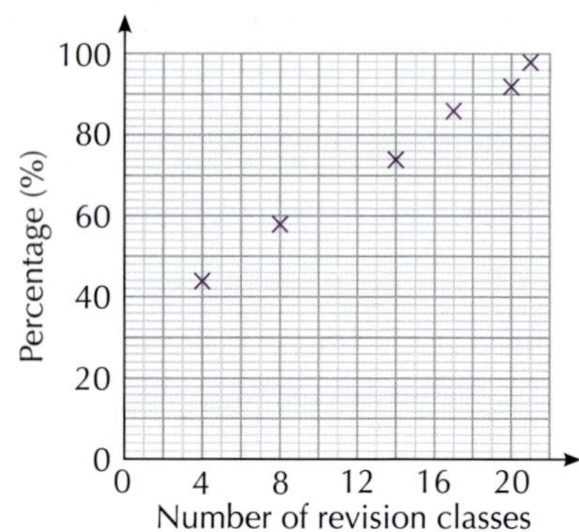

b) Duane was due to sit the exam but was absent. He says:

"I didn't attend any revision classes but I can see from the diagram that I would have got over 20%."

Is Duane correct? Refer to the diagram to explain your answer.

[1 mark]

27.1 Probability — The Basics

Probability is about how likely an event is to happen. For example, if you flip a coin it's just as likely to land on heads as it is tails. You would say the likelihood of each outcome is equal.

Likelihood

Learning Objective — Spec Ref P3:
Understand that probability measures how likely an event is to happen.

The **probability** of any event happening is between **impossible** (definitely won't happen) and **certain** (definitely will happen). Events can be put on a **probability scale** like this:

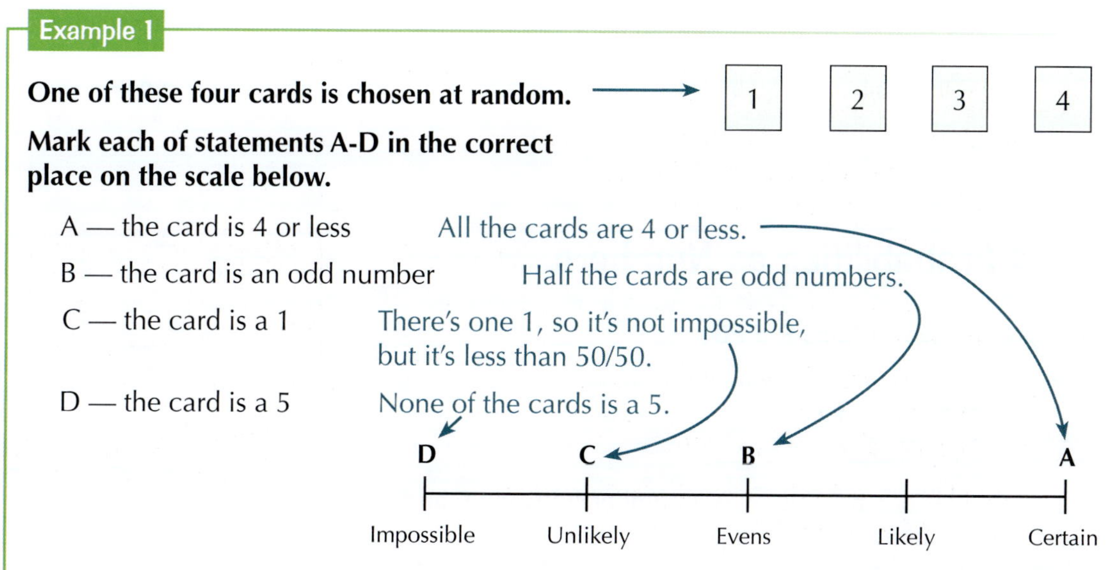

Example 1
One of these four cards is chosen at random.
1
2
3
4
Mark each of statements A-D in the correct place on the scale below.
A — the card is 4 or less
All the cards are 4 or less.
B — the card is an odd number
Half the cards are odd numbers.
C — the card is a 1
There's one 1, so it's not impossible, but it's less than 50/50.
D — the card is a 5
None of the cards is a 5.
D
C
B
A
Impossible
Unlikely
Evens
Likely
Certain
I will travel back in time.
The next baby born will be a girl.
The sun will rise tomorrow.

Exercise 1

Q1 Choose from the words *impossible, unlikely, evens, likely* and *certain* to describe:

a) Tossing a coin and getting tails.
b) A person growing to be 10 metres tall.
c) Rolling an even number on a fair dice.
d) Rolling 1 or more on a fair dice.
e) Picking a red card from a pack of 52.
f) Spinning 2 on a fair spinner labelled 1-4.

Q2 One card is picked at random from eight cards numbered 1 to 8.
Make a copy of this probability scale and add arrows to show the probability of each of the events described below. Each arrow should match one of the words.

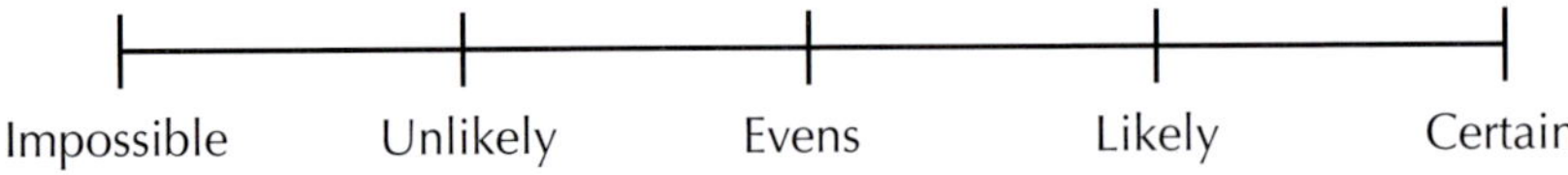

a) The card is less than 9.
b) The card is an odd number.
c) The card is greater than 2.
d) The card is greater than or equal to 7.
e) The card is 6 or less.
f) The card is a zero.

Q3 These eight cards are placed face down on a table and one is selected at random.

P A R A L L E L

a) Which letter is twice as likely to be on the selected card as the letter P?
b) Which letter is three times as likely to be on the selected card as the letter E?
c) The three arrows below show the probability of selecting each of the letters P, A, R, L and E. Match each letter to one of the arrows. (You can use each arrow for more than one letter.)

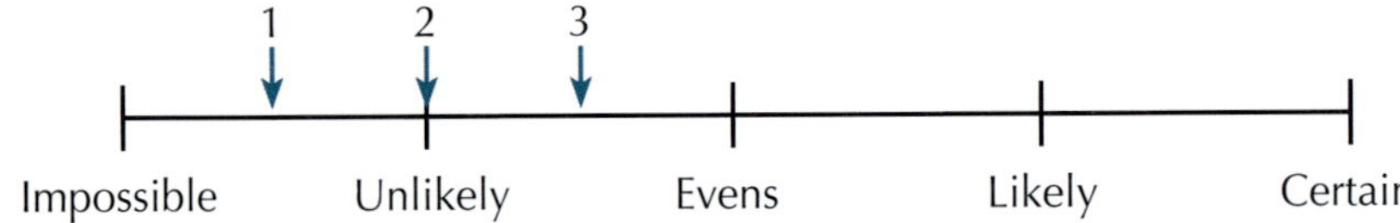

Writing Probabilities as Numbers

Learning Objective — Spec Ref P3:
Be able to write probabilities as fractions, decimals and percentages.

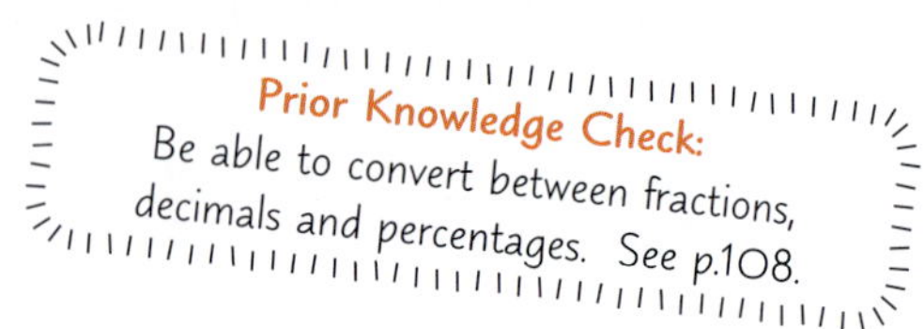

Prior Knowledge Check:
Be able to convert between fractions, decimals and percentages. See p.108.

All probabilities can be written as a **number between 0 and 1**.
An event that's **impossible** has a probability of **0** and an event that's **certain** has a probability of **1**.

So, using **fractions**, the probability scale looks like this.

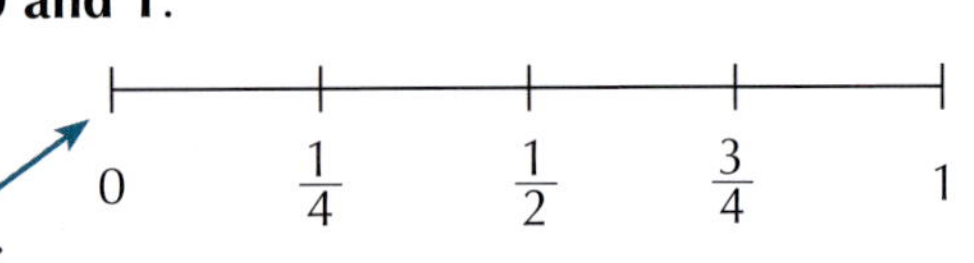

Probabilities can also be written as **decimals** and **percentages**.
For instance, if the probability of something happening is 1 out of 4, it can be written as $\frac{1}{4}$, or as the decimal 0.25, or the percentage 25%.

Example 2

A normal, fair, six-sided dice is rolled. On the scale below, the probabilities of three possible results are labelled by A, B and C.

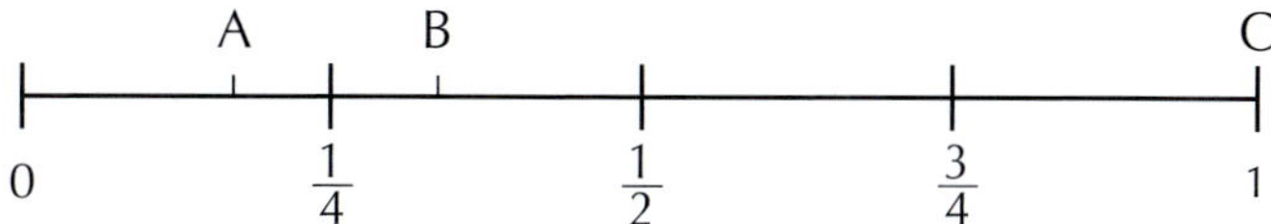

Match each of the results below to the correct letter on the scale.

a) 6 or less is rolled

All possible rolls are 6 or less, so this is certain. **C**

b) 5 is rolled

There's one 5 but six numbers altogether. So the probability of rolling 5 is a sixth of the way along the scale. **A**

c) 1 or 2 is rolled

There are two possibilities for this, meaning it's twice as likely as rolling a 1. This means the probability is twice as big. **B**

Tip: If the dice wasn't fair, the probabilities of rolling each number wouldn't be equal.

Exercise 2

Q1 Match each letter on this scale to the correct probability.

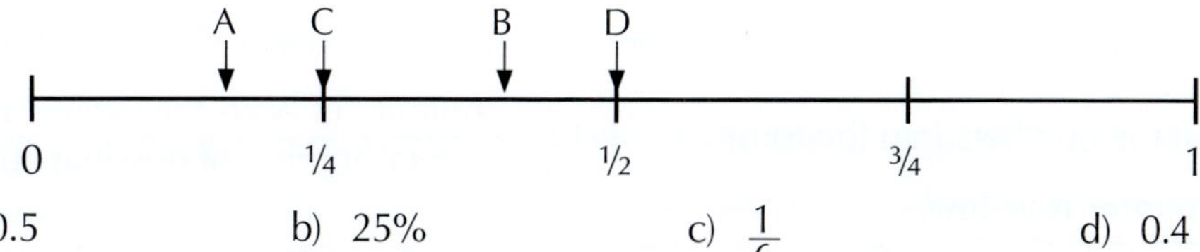

a) 0.5 b) 25% c) $\frac{1}{6}$ d) 0.4

Q2 Match each letter on this probability scale to one of the events below.

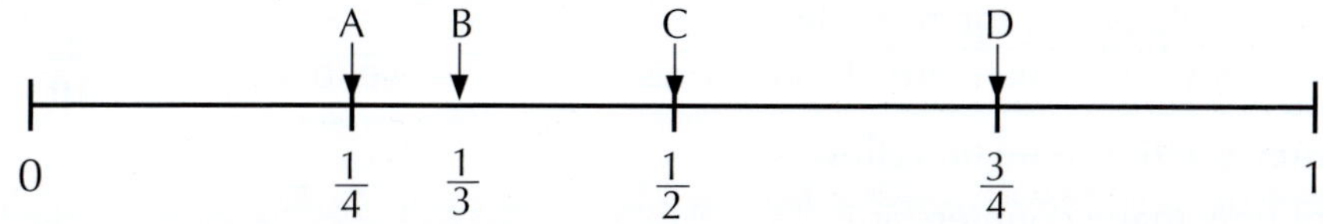

a) Rolling an odd number on a normal fair dice.
b) Selecting a card at random from a standard pack of 52 cards and getting a diamond.
c) Selecting a card at random from a standard pack of 52 cards and not getting a diamond.
d) Spinning blue on a fair, three-sided spinner with 1 blue section and 2 orange sections.

27.2 Calculating Probabilities

If you know (or can work out) the total number of possible outcomes of an activity, you can find the probability of any given event, assuming the outcomes are equally likely.

Learning Objective — Spec Ref P2/P3:
Find the probability of a given event.

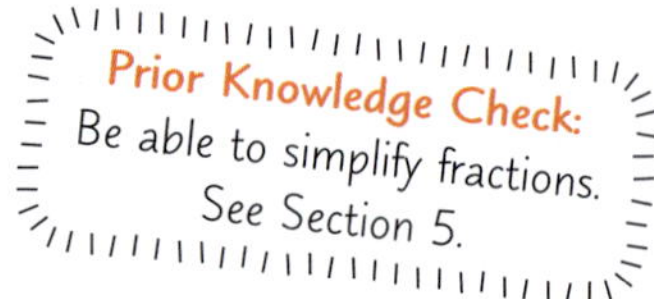

Prior Knowledge Check:
Be able to simplify fractions.
See Section 5.

In **probability**, an **outcome** is the result of an activity (e.g. 'getting tails on a coin flip' or 'rolling 3 on a dice') and an **event** is an outcome or a set of outcomes that you find a **probability** for.

The probability of something happening depends on the **total number of possible outcomes**. When all possible outcomes are **equally likely**, you can find the probabilities using the formula:

$$\textbf{Probability of event} = \frac{\textbf{number of ways the event can happen}}{\textbf{total number of possible outcomes}}$$

Tip: You should always simplify fractions if you can.

The probability of **event A** happening is often written as **P(A)**.

Example 1

A box contains 20 coloured counters numbered 1 to 20.
11 of the counters are blue, 7 of the counters are purple and 2 of the counters are yellow.
If one counter is selected at random, work out the following probabilities:

a) The counter is the number 12.

1. Find the total number of outcomes. There are 20 different counters which can be picked.
   Total outcomes = 20
2. Count the number of ways that you could get a 12. Only one counter has the number 12.
   There's 1 way that the counter is 12.
3. Put the numbers into the formula. $P(12) = \frac{\text{number of ways the event can happen}}{\text{total number of possible outcomes}} = \mathbf{\frac{1}{20}}$

b) The counter is yellow.

1. Count the number of outcomes that are yellow. There are 2 yellow counters.
   There are 2 ways of getting yellow.
2. Put the numbers into the formula. (You already know there are 20 outcomes in total.)
   $P(\text{yellow}) = \frac{2}{20} = \mathbf{\frac{1}{10}}$

c) The counter is either blue or yellow.

1. Count how many counters are either blue or yellow.
   11 blue + 2 yellow = 13 counters
2. Put the numbers into the formula. (You already know there are 20 outcomes in total.)
   $P(\text{blue or yellow}) = \mathbf{\frac{13}{20}}$

Exercise 1

Q1 State the total number of possible outcomes in each of the following situations.

a) A coin is tossed.

b) One card is selected from a pack of 52.

c) A ten-sided dice is rolled.

d) A fair spinner with 8 sections is spun.

e) One day of the week is chosen at random.

f) One day of the year is chosen at random.

Q2 This fair spinner is spun once.

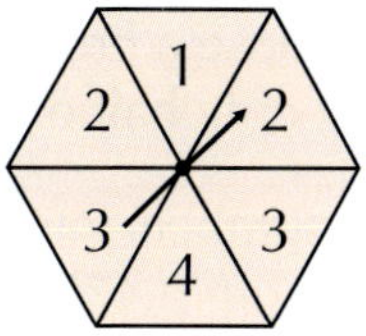

a) What is the total number of possible outcomes?

b) What is the probability of spinning a 1?

c) What is the probability of spinning a 3?

Q3 Calculate the probability of rolling a fair, six-sided dice and getting each of the following:

a) 6 b) 2 c) 7

d) 4 or 5 e) a multiple of 3 f) a factor of 6

Q4 Nine cards numbered 1 to 9 are face down on a table. If one of the cards is selected at random, find the probability of selecting each of the following:

a) card 4 b) an even number c) a number less than 6

Q5 A fair spinner has 12 equal sections. 5 are yellow, 3 are green and the rest are purple. Find the probability that the spinner lands on the following colours:

a) green b) purple c) yellow or green d) not green

Q6 A bag contains some coloured balls — 2 black, 4 blue, 2 green, 3 red, 2 yellow, 1 orange, 1 brown and 1 purple. If a ball is selected at random, find the probabilities that it will be:

a) green b) red c) orange d) black

e) blue or green f) red, green or brown g) not purple h) white

Q7 A standard pack of 52 playing cards is shuffled and one card is selected at random. Find the probability of selecting each of the following:

a) a club b) an ace c) a red card

d) the two of hearts e) not a spade f) a 4 or a 5

Q8 For each of the following, draw a copy of the spinner on the right and number the sections so that the spinner fits the rules.

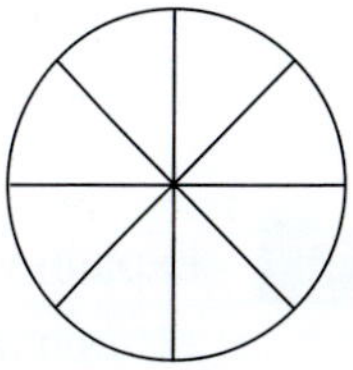

a) The probability of getting 2 is $\frac{3}{8}$.

b) The probability of getting 3 is $\frac{1}{2}$.

c) The probability of getting 5 and the probability of getting 6 are both $\frac{1}{4}$.

Example 2

Maya has 4 cats, 2 dogs and 10 chickens. Half of her cats, dogs and chickens are brown. She decides to give a treat to one animal at random.

Find the probability that she chooses a brown cat.

1. Find the total number of outcomes. — 4 cats + 2 dogs + 10 chickens = 16 outcomes
2. Count the number of ways Maya could choose a brown cat. She has 4 cats, but only half of them are brown. — Number of brown cats = 4 ÷ 2 = 2
3. Put the numbers into the formula from p.470. — P(brown cat) = $\frac{2}{16} = \mathbf{\frac{1}{8}}$

Exercise 2

Q1 Lewis was born in 2004 (a leap year). A friend randomly tries to guess Lewis's exact birthday. What is the probability that he guesses:

a) the correct month? b) the exact date?

Q2 At a summer fair, 100 raffle tickets are sold. Each ticket is bought by a different person. The winning number is drawn at random.

a) What is the probability that the first person to buy a ticket wins the first prize drawn?

b) What is the probability that the last person to buy a ticket wins the first prize drawn?

Q3 Tove has 20 different pairs of socks and has picked 1 sock at random. If she then picks another sock at random from the remaining socks, what is the probability that the 2 socks make a pair?

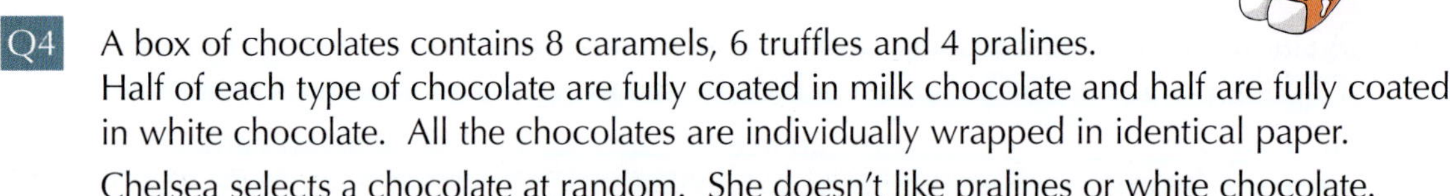

Q4 A box of chocolates contains 8 caramels, 6 truffles and 4 pralines. Half of each type of chocolate are fully coated in milk chocolate and half are fully coated in white chocolate. All the chocolates are individually wrapped in identical paper.

Chelsea selects a chocolate at random. She doesn't like pralines or white chocolate.

a) What is the probability that she gets a white-chocolate-coated praline?

b) (i) How many chocolates are neither praline nor coated in white chocolate?

(ii) What is the probability that Chelsea gets a chocolate she likes?

Q5 Explain why the following statement is false.

"When a football team plays a match there are 3 possible outcomes for the team — win, draw and lose. So the probability that they win the match is always $\frac{1}{3}$."

Mutually Exclusive Events

Learning Objective — Spec Ref P4:
Know that the probabilities of mutually exclusive events add up to 1.

Events that **can't happen at the same time** are called **mutually exclusive**. For example, a coin landing on **heads** and a coin landing on **tails** are **mutually exclusive events** — if the coin lands on heads, it can't also land on tails in the same coin flip.

The probabilities of **mutually exclusive events** covering **all possible outcomes** always **add up to 1**.

Tip: Be careful — this only works for mutually exclusive events.

For any event, there are only **two possibilities** — it either **happens** or it **doesn't happen**. These two facts can be written as the **rule**:

Probability something doesn't happen = 1 – Probability it does happen

Example 3

Jon gets the train to work every day. The probability that his train is late on any day is 0.05.

a) Explain whether the events 'train is late' and 'train is not late' are mutually exclusive.

The train can't be both late and not late, so the events **are mutually exclusive**.

b) Work out the probability that Jon's train is not late.

The train is either late or not late, so you can use the rule above.

P(not late) = 1 – P(late) = 1 – 0.05 = **0.95**

Exercise 3

Q1 A six-sided dice, numbered 1-6, is rolled. Here are three possible events:

A — a 5 is rolled, B — a number less than 3 is rolled, C — an odd number is rolled

Say whether the following pairs of events are mutually exclusive:

a) A and B b) A and C c) B and C

Q2 Charlie chooses one month of the year at random. Here are four possible events:

A — the name begins with J B — the name begins with M
C — the name ends in Y D — it's one of the first four months

Say whether the following pairs of events are mutually exclusive:

a) A and B b) A and C c) A and D d) B and C

Q3 The probability that Aasir's school bus is late is 0.2. What's the probability that it's not late?

Q4 The probability that it will snow in a particular Canadian town on any particular day in February is $\frac{5}{8}$. What is the probability that it won't snow there on 6th February?

Q5 In a class, the probability that a randomly selected pupil is a boy is 0.45, and the probability that a pupil has blond hair is 0.2.
Find the probability that a randomly selected pupil:

a) is not a boy
b) doesn't have blond hair

Activities with mutually exclusive events can have **more than two outcomes**. For example, rolling a dice has six possible outcomes, and each outcome is a **mutually exclusive event** — you can't roll both a 1 and a 3 in the same dice roll.

You can use the fact that the **probabilities** of mutually exclusive events **add up to 1** in problems with more than two outcomes. To find the probability that one thing happens, just **subtract** the probabilities of all the other things happening from **1**.

Example 4

A bag contains red, green, blue and white counters. The table below shows the probabilities of randomly selecting a red, green or white counter.

What is the probability of selecting a blue counter?

Colour	Red	Green	Blue	White
Probability	0.2	0.1		0.5

1. These are mutually exclusive events, so the probabilities must add up to 1.
2. This means the probability of selecting blue is 1 minus the probability of selecting red, green or white.

P(blue) = 1 – (0.2 + 0.1 + 0.5)
= 1 – 0.8 = **0.2**

Exercise 4

Q1 This table shows the probabilities of getting one of the five possible colours on a spinner.

a) Find the missing probability.
b) Find the probability of spinning 'not pink'.

Colour	Red	Blue	Green	Pink	Black
Probability		0.2	0.1	0.1	0.3

Q2 A bag contains some equal-sized discs. The discs are either yellow, orange or red. If Jack takes out one disc without looking, the probability that it's yellow is $\frac{1}{4}$ and the probability that it's orange is $\frac{3}{8}$. Work out the probability that Jack takes a red disc.

Q3 One counter is selected at random from a box containing blue, green and red counters. The probability that it's a blue counter is 0.5 and the probability that it's a green counter is 0.4. If there are 4 red counters in the box, how many counters are there altogether?

27.3 Listing Outcomes

One of the trickiest bits of probability is figuring out what all the possible outcomes are, especially if you've got more than one activity. But don't worry, this topic tells you how to do it all.

Learning Objectives — Spec Ref P6/P7:

- List outcomes of two or more events.
- Use sample space diagrams to list outcomes of more complicated situations.
- Use sample space diagrams to find probabilities.

When **two things** are happening at once, e.g. a coin toss and a dice roll, it's much easier to work out probabilities if you first **list all the possible outcomes** in a systematic way so you don't miss any. For example, a coin toss has two outcomes (heads 'H' and tails 'T'), and a dice roll has 6 outcomes ('1', '2', '3', '4', '5' and '6'), so if both happen together, there will be **12 possible outcomes**.

You can record all the possible outcomes using a **sample space diagram** (also called a **possibility diagram**). A sample space diagram can take the form of a **list** of outcomes — and it can be useful to put those in a **table**. This sets them out in an **ordered** and **logical** way.

Tip: In a simple table, each row is a mutually exclusive outcome.

Example 1

Anna has three tickets for a theme park. She chooses two friends at random to go with her. She chooses one girl from Bea, Claire and Daisy, and one boy from Ethan and Fatik.

a) List all the possible combinations of friends she could choose.

1. Make a sample space diagram — a simple table works here. Have 1 column for the girls and 1 column for the boys.
2. Write in the first girl and then fill in all the possibilities for the boys.
3. Repeat for the other 2 girls.
4. Each row of the table is a possible outcome.

Girls	Boys
Bea	Ethan
Bea	Fatik
Claire	Ethan
Claire	Fatik
Daisy	Ethan
Daisy	Fatik

b) What is the probability that Anna chooses Claire to go with her?

1. Count the number of rows that Claire's name appears in.

   There are 2 rows with outcomes that include Claire.

2. The total number of rows is the total number of outcomes.

   There are 6 rows in total.

3. Divide the two numbers to find the probability.

   P(Claire) = $\frac{2}{6} = \mathbf{\frac{1}{3}}$

Exercise 1

Q1 Use a sample space diagram to list all the possible outcomes when:

a) two coins are tossed

b) a standard six-sided dice is rolled and a coin is tossed

Q2 A bag contains two balls — one green, one blue. A ball is picked at random and replaced. Then a second ball is picked at random. List all the possible combinations of colours.

Q3 A burger bar offers the meal deal shown on the right.

Choose 1 burger and 1 drink	
Burgers	***Drinks***
Hamburger	Cola
Cheeseburger	Lemonade
Veggie burger	Coffee

a) List all the different combinations available.

Jana picks one combination at random.

b) What is the probability she chooses a veggie burger and cola?

c) What is the probability she chooses a cheeseburger?

Q4 The fair spinner on the right is spun twice.

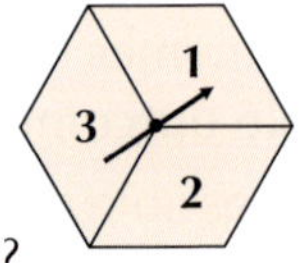

1st spin	2nd spin
1	1
1	2
⋮	⋮

a) Copy and complete the table to list all the possible combinations of scores.

b) What is the probability of spinning 3 on each spin?

c) What is the probability of getting a total of 4 or more over the two spins?

Q5 A fair coin is tossed three times.

a) List all the possible outcomes in a sample space diagram.

b) Work out the probability of getting: (i) three tails (ii) one head and two tails

When two activities have **lots of possible outcomes**, you need more than just a simple table to show all the different possibilities. A table with the outcomes of one activity **along the top** and the outcomes of another activity **down the side** is a good way of doing this.

Example 2

A white four-sided dice and a blue four-sided dice, both numbered 1-4, are rolled together.

a) Draw a sample space diagram to show all the possible total scores.

1. Put the outcomes for one dice across the top and those for the second dice down the side.
2. Fill in each square with the score for the row and the score for the column added together.

		White dice			
		1	**2**	**3**	**4**
Blue dice	**1**	2	3	4	5
	2	3	4	5	6
	3	4	5	6	7
	4	5	6	7	8

b) If both dice are fair, what is the probability of scoring a total of 4?

Count how many times a total of 4 appears in the table and then divide by the total number of outcomes.

4 appears 3 times in the table, and there are 16 outcomes in total, so P(total of 4) = $\frac{\mathbf{3}}{\mathbf{16}}$

Exercise 2

Q1 A coin is tossed and a six-sided dice is rolled.
Copy and complete the sample space diagram below to show all the possible outcomes.

	1	2	3	4	5	6
H	H1	H2				
T						T6

Q2 Two fair, six-sided dice are rolled. A sample space diagram for the results is below.

a) Copy and complete the table to show all the possible total scores.

b) How many possible outcomes are there?

c) Find the probability of each of the following total scores.

(i) 6 (ii) less than 8

(iii) more than 8 (iv) an even number

	1	2	3	4	5	6
1						
2						
3						
4						
5						
6						

Q3 A bag contains 3 balls — 1 blue, 1 green and 1 yellow.
A second bag contains 4 balls — 1 blue, 2 green and 1 yellow.
One ball is taken at random from each bag.

a) Copy and complete this sample space diagram to show all the possible outcomes.

b) Use the table to find the probability of selecting:

(i) 2 blue balls (ii) 2 green balls

(iii) 2 balls the same colour (iv) at least 1 yellow ball

	B	G	G	Y
B				
G				
Y				

Q4 Tom rolls a fair, six-sided dice and spins a fair spinner with four sections — A, B, C and D.

a) Draw a sample space diagram to show all the possible outcomes.

b) Use your diagram to find the probability that Tom gets each of the following.

(i) C and 5 (ii) B and less than 3 (iii) A or B and more than 4

Q5 Hayley and Asha are playing a game.
In each round they both spin a fair spinner with five sections labelled 1 to 5.

a) Copy and complete this sample space diagram to show all the possible outcomes for their spins.

b) What is the probability that Hayley gets a higher score than Asha in a round?

		Asha's score (2nd number)				
		1	2	3	4	5
Hayley's score (1st number)	1	1, 1	1, 2			
	2	2, 1				
	3	3, 1				
	4					
	5					

27.4 Probability from Experiments

So far this section has been about theoretical probabilities, but in reality it's difficult to be sure if outcomes are equally likely. The best way to find out is to run some experiments...

Estimating Probabilities

Learning Objective — Spec Ref P1/P5:
Estimate the probability of an event using relative frequency.

You can **estimate** probabilities using the **results** of an experiment or what you know has already happened. Your estimate is called a **relative frequency** (or an **experimental probability**). You can work out relative frequency using this formula:

$$\text{Relative Frequency} = \frac{\text{number of times the result has happened}}{\text{number of times the experiment has been carried out}}$$

The **more times** you do the experiment, the **more accurate** the estimate should be — i.e. the experimental probability gets **closer** to the theoretical probability. E.g. if you tossed a fair coin **10 times**, you might get 7 heads, so you'd end up with a relative frequency of **0.7**. But if you tossed the coin **100 times**, the relative frequency for heads should end up much **closer to 0.5**.

Example 1

A biased dice is rolled 100 times. Here are the results.

Score	1	2	3	4	5	6
Frequency	11	14	27	15	17	16

a) Estimate the probability of rolling a 1.

1. Look at the table to find the number of times 1 was rolled. — 1 was rolled 11 times.
2. Divide by the total number of rolls. — $P(1) = \frac{11}{100}$

b) Estimate the probability of rolling a 3.

1. Look at the table to find the number of times 3 was rolled. — 3 was rolled 27 times.
2. Divide by the total number of rolls. — $P(3) = \frac{27}{100}$

Exercise 1

Q1 Kano wants to estimate the probability that a drawing pin lands with its point up when dropped. He drops the drawing pin 50 times and finds that it lands point-up 17 times.

a) Use these results to estimate the probability the drawing pin lands with its point up.

b) Estimate the probability that the drawing pin doesn't land with its point up.

Q2 A spinner with four sections is spun 100 times. The results are shown in the table on the right.

Colour	Red	Green	Yellow	Blue
Frequency	49	34	8	9

a) Find the relative frequency of each colour.

b) Sam uses these relative frequencies to estimate the probability of spinning each colour. How could these estimates be made more accurate?

Q3 Stacy rolls a six-sided dice 50 times and 2 comes up 13 times. Jamal rolls the same dice 100 times and 2 comes up 18 times.

a) Use Stacy's results to estimate the probability of rolling a 2 on this dice.

b) Use Jamal's results to estimate the probability of rolling a 2 on this dice.

c) Whose estimate should be more accurate and why?

Q4 Suki wants to know how likely it is that her school bus will arrive on time. She keeps a record for a month and finds that the bus is on time 20 times out of 24 days.

Estimate the probability that the next time Suki gets the bus it will arrive on time.

Q5 George has burnt 12 of the last 20 cakes he's baked. Estimate the probability that the next cake he bakes won't be burnt.

Q6 Lilia wants to estimate the probability that the football team she supports will win a match. Describe how she could do this.

Expected Frequency

Learning Objective — Spec Ref P2/P3:
Find the expected frequency of an event.

If you know (or have an estimate of) the **probability** of an event, you can work out how many times you would **expect** the event to happen in a given number of experiments using the equation:

Expected frequency = number of times the experiment is done × probability of the event happening

Tip: This isn't always going to happen in reality — it's an estimate of how many times you think it will occur.

Example 2

The probability of a biased dice landing on 1 is 0.3.
How many times would you expect to roll a 1 if you rolled the dice 50 times?

Multiply the number of rolls by the probability of rolling a 1.

$50 \times 0.3 =$ **15 times**

Exercise 2

Q1 The probability that a biased dice lands on 4 is 0.75.
How many times would you expect the dice to land on 4 if it's rolled:

a) 20 times? b) 60 times? c) 100 times? d) 1000 times?

Q2 A fair, six-sided dice is rolled 120 times. How many times would you expect to roll:

a) a 5? b) a 6? c) an even number? d) higher than 1?

Q3 The spinner on the right has 3 equal sections.
How many times would you expect to spin 'penguin' in:

a) 60 spins? b) 300 spins? c) 480 spins?

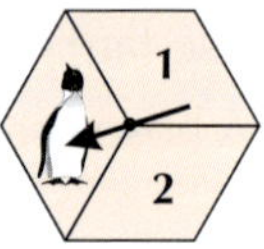

Q4 60% of the people who buy bread from a bakery choose brown bread. If 20 people buy bread there tomorrow, how many of them would you expect to choose brown bread?

Frequency Trees

Learning Objective — Spec Ref P1:
Use frequency trees to display outcomes and find probabilities.

When an experiment has **two or more steps**, you can record the results in a **frequency tree**. The **branches** of a frequency tree show the **different possible outcomes** of each event. The **number** at the end of each branch shows **how many times** that event or **combination** of events happened.

Tip: The numbers at the end of a set of branches should always add up to the number at the start of the branches.

Example 3

James asks 200 people of various ages to roll a dice. There were 120 people under the age of 20 and 16 of them rolled a six. Of the people aged 20 and over, 18 rolled a six.

a) Fill in the frequency tree to show this information.

1. Fill in the bits of the tree given in the question first.
2. Work out the remaining numbers and fill them in.

200 – 120 = 80 people are aged 20 and over
120 – 16 = 104 people under 20 didn't roll a six
80 – 18 = 62 people aged 20 and over didn't roll a six

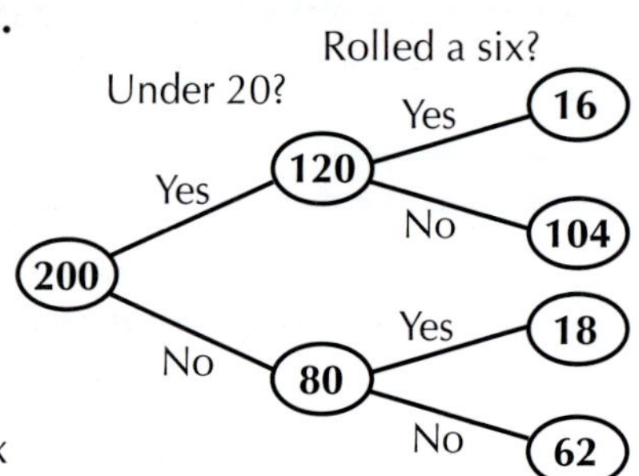

b) What is the probability that a randomly selected roll was a six rolled by someone under 20?

1. Follow the branches of the tree to find the frequency of people under 20 who rolled a six. — 16 people under 20 rolled a six
2. Divide the frequency by the total number of people. — probability = $\frac{16}{200} = \mathbf{\frac{2}{25}}$

Exercise 3

Q1 Copy and complete the frequency trees below:

a)

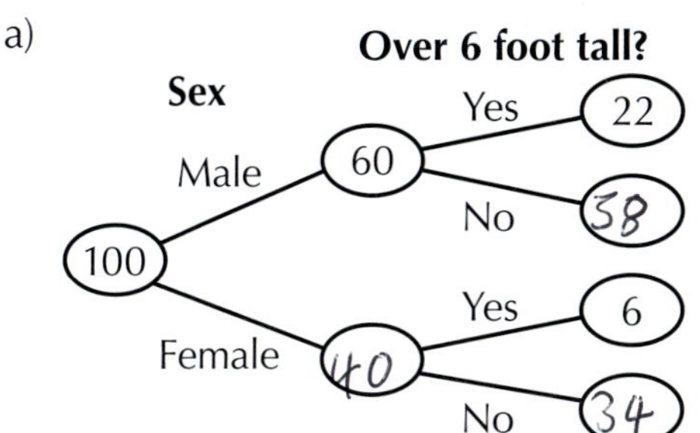

b)

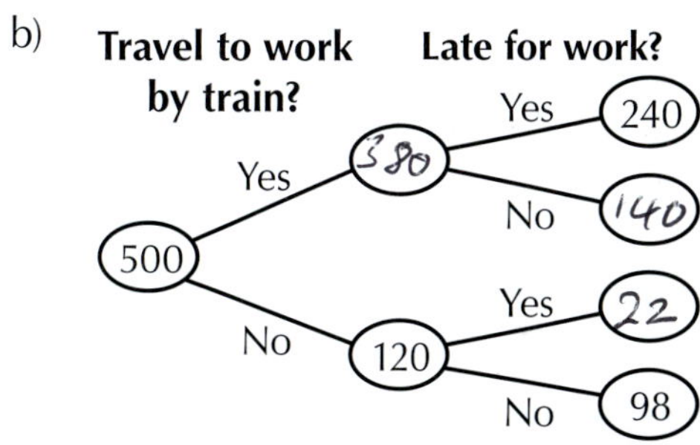

Q2 720 people took an eye test. 640 said their vision was fine.
180 of the people who said their vision was fine failed the eye test.
30 of the people who said their vision wasn't fine passed the eye test.

a) Draw and complete a frequency tree to represent this information.

b) A person who said their vision wasn't fine is selected at random. What is the probability that they failed the eye test?

c) Use your frequency tree to estimate the probability that a randomly selected person says their vision is fine and passes the eye test. Give your answer as a fraction in its simplest form.

Fair or Biased?

Learning Objective — Spec Ref P2:
Use experimental data to decide if outcomes are fair or biased.

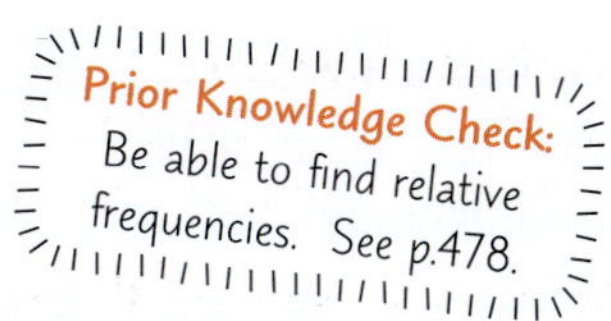

Prior Knowledge Check:
Be able to find relative frequencies. See p.478.

Things like dice and spinners are **fair** if they are **equally likely** to land on any side or section. If they're more likely to give some outcomes than others, they're called **biased**. To decide whether something is fair or biased, you need to do an **experiment**. Then you can **compare** the experimental results with what you would expect in theory (the **theoretical probability**).

For example, if you flip a coin, you expect it to land on heads about half the time — so if you flipped it 100 times, you'd expect **about** 50 heads. If you actually got 80 heads, you could be pretty sure the coin was **biased**.

Example 4

Amir thinks his dice is biased. He rolls it 60 times and records the results shown in the table on the right.

Score	1	2	3	4	5	6
Frequency	12	3	9	10	14	12

a) Work out the relative frequencies of each score.

1. For each, work out frequency ÷ total number of rolls.
2. Write the probabilities as decimals (to 2 d.p. where necessary) so they're easier to compare.

$P(1) = \frac{12}{60} = \mathbf{0.20}$ $P(2) = \frac{3}{60} = \mathbf{0.05}$

$P(3) = \frac{9}{60} = \mathbf{0.15}$ $P(4) = \frac{10}{60} = \mathbf{0.17}$

$P(5) = \frac{14}{60} = \mathbf{0.23}$ $P(6) = \frac{12}{60} = \mathbf{0.20}$

b) Do you think the dice is fair or biased? Explain your answer.

Compare these probabilities to the theoretical probability of $\frac{1}{6} = 0.166...$ for each score.

The relative frequency of a score of 2 is very different from the theoretical probability, so the experiment suggests that the dice is **biased**.

Exercise 4

Q1 A spinner has four sections: blue, green, white and pink. The table shows the results of 100 spins.

Colour	Blue	Green	White	Pink
Frequency	22	21	18	39

a) Work out the relative frequencies of the four colours. Write your answers as decimals.

b) What are the theoretical probabilities of getting each of the colours, assuming the spinner is fair? Write your answers as decimals.

c) Explain whether you think the spinner is fair or biased.

Q2 A six-sided dice is rolled 120 times and 4 comes up 32 times.

a) How many times would you expect 4 to come up on a fair dice in 120 rolls?

b) Use your answer to part a) to explain whether you think the dice is fair or biased.

c) Explain how to find a more accurate estimate for the probability of rolling a 4 on this dice.

Q3 Three friends each toss the same coin and record how many heads they get. The table shows their results.

	Amy	Steve	Hal
Number of tosses	20	60	100
Number of heads	12	33	49
Relative frequency			

a) Copy and complete the table.

b) Explain whose results are likely to be the most accurate.

c) Explain whether you think the coin is fair or biased.

Q4 Information on 800 UK residents' hair and eye colour was collected. The data was recorded in the two-way table shown on the right.

		Has brown hair?	
		Yes	No
Has brown eyes?	Yes	220	105
	No	335	140

a) Show the information from this two-way table on a frequency tree.

b) Find the relative frequency of someone having brown hair and brown eyes.

c) If you collected the same data on another group of 2000 UK residents, how many would you estimate have brown hair and brown eyes?

27.5 The AND / OR Rules

The AND rule lets you work out the probability that one event AND another event will both happen. However, it only works when the events don't affect each other.

The AND Rule

Learning Objective — Spec Ref P8:
Use the AND rule to find the probability of two independent events both occurring.

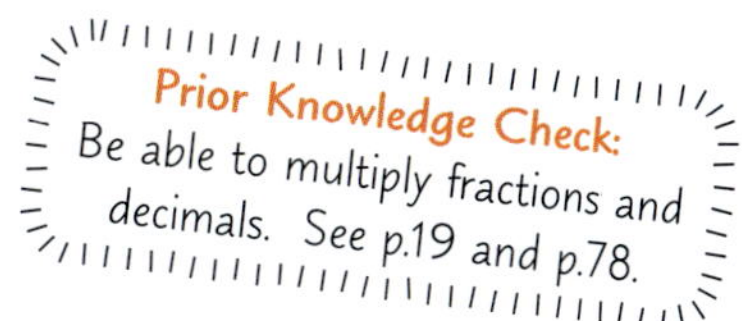

Prior Knowledge Check:
Be able to multiply fractions and decimals. See p.19 and p.78.

Two events are said to be **independent** if one of them happening has **no effect** on the probability of the other happening.

For example, imagine drawing **two cards** at random from a standard deck of playing cards. If you **put the first card back** and shuffle the deck, then it **doesn't affect** the second card drawn, so the events are **independent** (but if you **don't** put the first card back, then the probabilities for the second draw **depend** on the result of the first).

If A and B are **independent** events, you can use the **AND rule**: the probability of **both A and B** happening is equal to the probability of A happening **multiplied** by the probability of B happening. This can be written as:

P(A and B) = P(A) × P(B)

Tip: The AND rule doesn't just apply to two events. If there are more than two independent events you multiply together all of the probabilities.

Example 1

The probability of a biased dice landing on 6 is 0.2. The dice is rolled twice. What is the probability that two sixes are rolled?

The first roll has no effect on the second roll, so the events '6 on first roll' and '6 on second roll' are independent. This means you can use the AND rule.

P(6 on 1st roll and 6 on 2nd roll)
= P(6 on 1st) × P(6 on 2nd)
= 0.2 × 0.2 = **0.04**

Exercise 1

Q1 A fair coin is tossed and a fair, standard dice is rolled. Find the probability the results are:

a) a head and a 6
b) a head and an odd number
c) a tail and a square number
d) a tail and a prime number
e) a head and a multiple of 3
f) a tail and a factor of 5

Q2 10% of the pupils in a school are left-handed and 15% wear glasses.
Assuming that the hand they write with and glasses wearing are independent, find the probability that a pupil picked at random:

a) is right-handed
b) doesn't wear glasses
c) wears glasses and is left-handed
d) doesn't wear glasses and is right-handed

Q3 A bag contains ten coloured balls. Five of them are red and three of them are blue. A ball is taken from the bag at random, then replaced. A second ball is then selected at random. Find the probability that:

a) both balls are red
b) both balls are blue
c) neither ball is blue

The OR Rules

Learning Objective — Spec Ref P8:
Use the OR rules to find the probabilities of mutually exclusive events and non-mutually exclusive events.

Two events are **mutually exclusive** if they **can't both happen** at the same time (see p.473) — for example, rolling a 2 and a 3 on the same dice roll.

The **OR rule** (or **addition rule**) says that if events are **mutually exclusive**, then the probability that one of the events happens is the **sum** of the probabilities of each event happening:

P(A or B) = P(A) + P(B)

Tip: Always check whether the events are mutually exclusive or not before doing your calculations.

Example 2

A bag contains red, yellow and blue counters. The probabilities of randomly selecting each colour are shown in the table opposite.

Red	Yellow	Blue
0.3	0.5	0.2

Find the probability that a randomly selected counter is red or blue.

The counter can't be both red and blue, so the events 'counter is red' and 'counter is blue' are mutually exclusive.

P(red or blue) = P(red) + P(blue)
= 0.3 + 0.2 = **0.5**

When two events are **not mutually exclusive** (e.g. rolling an even number and a number less than 3 on the same dice roll), you need a different version of the **OR rule**. To find the probability of **at least one event happening**, you **add** the probabilities of the **individual events** as before, but then **subtract** the probability that **both events happen**:

P(A or B) = P(A) + P(B) – P(A and B)

Example 3

The fair spinner shown on the right is spun once.
What is the probability that it lands on a 2 or a shaded sector?

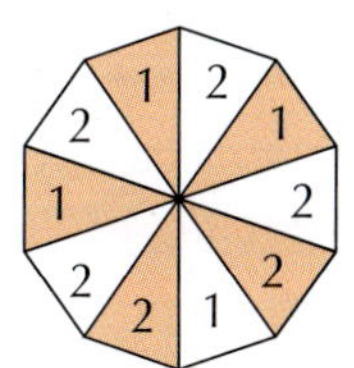

The spinner can land on both 2 and a shaded sector at the same time so they are not mutually exclusive.

This means you use the OR rule
P(A or B) = P(A) + P(B) – P(A and B)

P(2 or shaded) = P(2) + P(shaded) – P(2 and shaded)

$= \frac{6}{10} + \frac{5}{10} - \frac{2}{10} = \frac{9}{10} = \mathbf{0.9}$

Exercise 2

Q1 A bag contains some coloured balls. The probability of randomly selecting a pink ball is 0.5, selecting a red ball is 0.4 and selecting an orange ball is 0.1. Find the probability that a randomly selected ball will be:

a) pink or orange b) pink or red c) red or orange

Q2 Chocolates in a box are wrapped in four different colours of foil — gold, silver, red or blue. The table shows the probabilities of randomly picking a chocolate wrapped in each colour.

Colour	Gold	Silver	Red	Blue
Probability	0.4	0.26	0.14	0.2

Find the probability of picking a chocolate wrapped in:

a) red or gold foil b) silver or red foil

c) gold or blue foil d) silver or gold foil

Q3 On sports day, pupils are split into three equal-sized teams — the Eagles, the Falcons and the Ospreys.
What is the probability that a pupil picked at random belongs to:

a) the Eagles? b) the Eagles or the Falcons? c) the Falcons or the Ospreys?

Q4 A fair 20-sided dice, numbered 1-20, is rolled. What is the probability that it lands on:

a) a multiple of 3 or an odd number? b) a factor of 20 or a multiple of 4?

Q5 A card is randomly chosen from a standard pack of 52 playing cards.

a) What's the probability that it's a red suit or a queen?

b) What's the probability that it's a club or a picture card?

Q6 Jane is told that in a class of 30 pupils, 4 wear glasses and 10 have blond hair.
She says that the probability that a pupil picked at random from the class will have blond hair or wear glasses is $\frac{10}{30} + \frac{4}{30} = \frac{14}{30}$. Do you agree with Jane? Explain your answer.

27.6 Tree Diagrams

Tree diagrams can be used to show all the possible results from an experiment — they're really useful for working out probabilities of combinations of events.

Learning Objective — Spec Ref P6/P8:
Use tree diagrams to represent events and to find probabilities.

Tree diagrams are similar to **frequency trees** (see p.480), except they show the **probabilities** of the events rather than the frequency from an experiment.

The really useful thing about tree diagrams is that you can find the probability of specific **results** (e.g. P(A happens and B doesn't happen)) by **multiplying along the branches** that you follow to get to that result.

Since branches from the same point show all the outcomes of a single activity, their probabilities should **add up to 1**.

Tip: Tree diagrams can get crowded if they show lots of events. Always make sure you leave enough space to draw them.

Example 1

A fair coin is tossed twice.

a) Draw a tree diagram showing all the possible results for the two tosses.

1. Draw a set of branches for the first toss. You need 1 branch for each of the 2 results.
2. Draw a set of branches for the second toss. Again, there are two possible results.
3. Write on the probability for each branch — here it's 0.5 for each possible outcome.

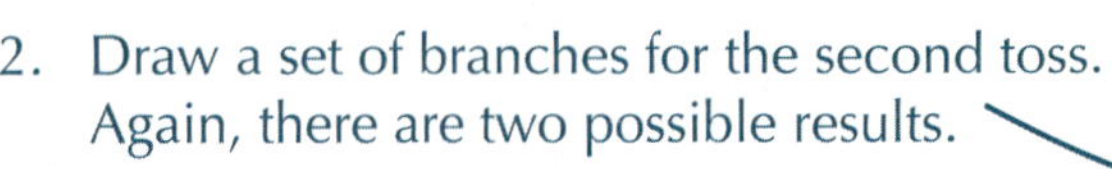

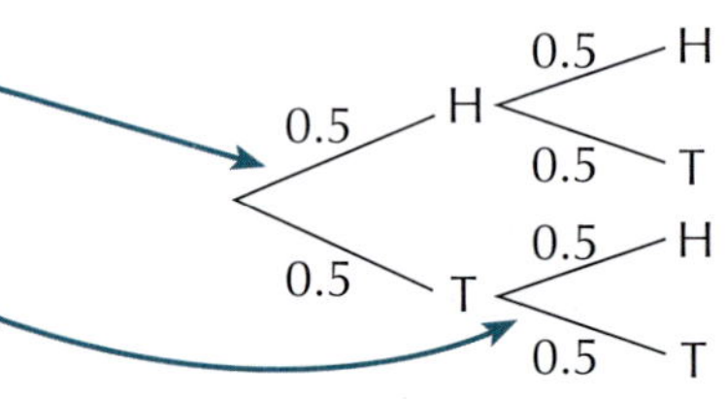

b) Find the probability of getting two heads.

You need to use the AND rule so multiply along the branches for a head AND a head.

P(2H) = 0.5 × 0.5 = **0.25**

c) Find the probability of getting heads and tails in any order.

1. Multiply along the branches for a head AND a tail. P(H then T) = 0.5 × 0.5 = 0.25
2. Multiply along the branches for a tail AND a head. P(T then H) = 0.5 × 0.5 = 0.25
3. Both these results give heads and tails. You need to use the OR rule to find the probability of HT OR TH, so add the probabilities. P(1H and 1T) = 0.25 + 0.25 = **0.5**

Exercise 1

Q1 Copy and complete the following tree diagrams.

a) A fair spinner has five equal sections — three are red and two are blue. The spinner is spun twice.

1st **2nd**

0.6 R — 0.6 R, B

B

b) A bag contains ten coloured balls — five red, three blue and two green. A ball is selected at random and replaced, then a second ball is selected at random.

1st **2nd**

0.5 R

B

G

Q2 For each of these situations, draw a tree diagram showing all the possible results. Write the probability on each branch.

a) A biased coin lands on heads with a probability of 0.65. The coin is tossed twice.

b) The probability a football team wins is 0.7, draws is 0.1 and loses is 0.2. The team plays two matches.

Q3 Freddie and James play two games of pool. The probability that Freddie beats James is 0.8.

a) Draw a tree diagram to show all the possible results for the two games.

b) Find the probability that Freddie wins both games.

Q4 Ifrath owns 12 DVDs, four of which are comedies. Jesse owns 20 DVDs, eight of which are comedies. They each select one of their DVDs at random to watch over the weekend.

a) Draw a tree diagram showing the probabilities of each choice being 'comedy' or 'not a comedy'.

b) Find the probability that neither of them chooses a comedy.

c) Find the probability that at least one of them chooses a comedy.

Q5 On any Saturday, the probability that Alex goes to the cinema is 0.7. The probability that he goes to the cinema on Sunday is 0.2 if he went on Saturday, but 0.6 if he didn't go on Saturday.

a) Draw a tree diagram showing the probabilities of Alex going and not going to the cinema on Saturday and Sunday.

b) What is the probability that Alex goes to the cinema on both days?

c) What is the probability that Alex goes to the cinema on exactly one of the two days?

Q6 In a class there are 16 boys and 14 girls. They all put their names into a box. One name is selected at random and **not** replaced, then another name is selected at random.

a) Draw a tree diagram to show the probabilities of each name selected being a boy or a girl.

b) What is the probability that two boys are picked?

c) What is the probability that exactly one girl is picked?

27.7 Sets and Venn Diagrams

A set is a collection of things — it can be considered as an object in its own right. Venn diagrams can be used to display sets. They're great at showing the overlap between sets.

Sets

Learning Objectives — Spec Ref P6:
- Understand and use set notation.
- Be able to list the elements of a set.

Prior Knowledge Check:
Be familiar with multiples
and factors. See Section 4.

A **set** is a group of items or numbers. Sets are written in pairs of **curly brackets { }**. Each item in a set is called an **element** or **member** of the set. You can describe a set by **listing every element** in that set (e.g. {2, 4, 6}) or by **giving a rule** that all elements follow (e.g. {all red objects}).

Here's the **set notation** you need to become familiar with:

A = {...}	A is the **set** of ...
$x \in$ **A**	x is an **element** of A
n(A)	the **number of elements** in A
ξ	the **universal** set (all the elements that you need to consider)
A $\cup$ B	the **union** of sets A and B (all elements in either set)
A $\cap$ B	the **intersection** of sets A and B (all elements in both sets)
A′	the **complement** of set A (all elements not in set A)

Example 1

Given that ξ = {positive integers less than 20}, list the elements of the following sets:

a) A = {multiples of 2}

A consists of the multiples of 2 in the universal set.

A = {2, 4, 6, 8, 10, 12, 14, 16, 18}

b) B = {x : x is a factor of 40}

B consists of the factors of 40 in the universal set.

B = {1, 2, 4, 5, 8, 10}

Tip: The colon means 'such that'.

c) A $\cup$ B

List all the elements from either set. If a number appears in both sets, it should only be listed once.

A $\cup$ B = {1, 2, 4, 5, 6, 8, 10, 12, 14, 16, 18}

d) A $\cap$ B

List only those elements that appear in both sets.

A $\cap$ B = {2, 4, 8, 10}

Exercise 1

Q1 a) List the elements of the following sets.
(i) A = {even numbers between 11 and 25}
(ii) B = {prime numbers less than 30}
(iii) C = $\{x : x$ is a square number $< 200\}$
(iv) D = {factors of 30}

b) Write down: (i) n(A) (ii) n(B) (iii) n(C) (iv) n(D)

Q2 A = {1, 2, 4, 5, 7, 8}, B = {2, 4, 6, 8}. Find the following: a) $A \cup B$ b) $A \cap B$

Q3 ξ = {positive integers less than 10}, A = {1, 3, 7, 9}, B = {2, 3, 5, 6, 8, 9}. Find the following:
a) n(A) b) n(B) c) A′ d) $A \cup B$
e) B′ f) $A \cap B$ g) $n(A \cup B)$ h) $A' \cup B$

Venn Diagrams

Learning Objective — Spec Ref P6:
Use Venn diagrams to represent sets and to find probabilities.

Venn diagrams use **circles** to represent sets — the **space inside** the circle represents everything in the set. Each **circle** is labelled with a **letter** — this tells you **which set** the circle represents.

The **numbers inside a circle** can tell you either the **number of members** of that set or **actual elements** of the set.

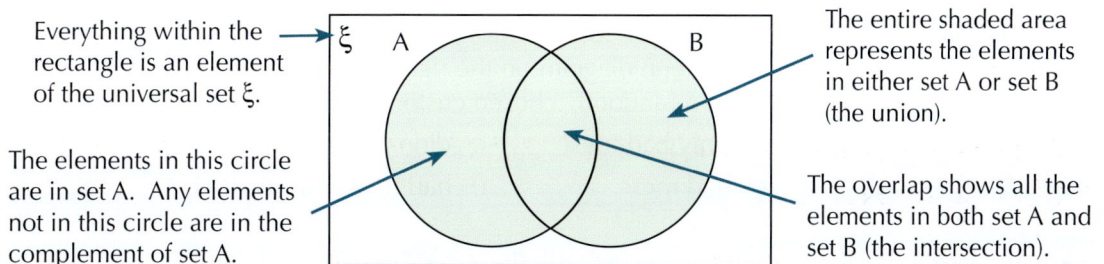

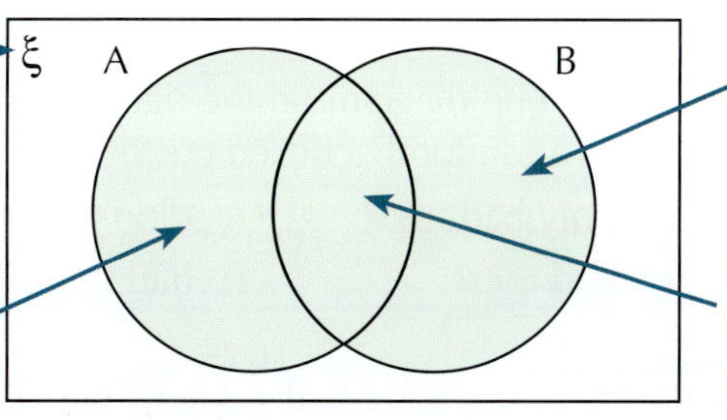

Finding probabilities from Venn diagrams

If you know the **number of elements** in each set in a Venn diagram, you can work out **probabilities** from the Venn diagram. To find the probability of randomly selecting a member of a **particular set** from the **universal set**, you use a similar **formula** to the one for **calculating probabilities** on p.470. The **number of elements** in a set is **divided by the total number of elements** in the universal set:

$$\textbf{Probability of an element being in the set} = \frac{\textbf{number of elements in the set}}{\textbf{total number of elements in the universal set}}$$

Example 2

a) Given that ξ = {positive integers less than or equal to 12}, draw a Venn diagram for the sets A = {x : x is a multiple of 3} and B = {x : x is a factor of 30}.

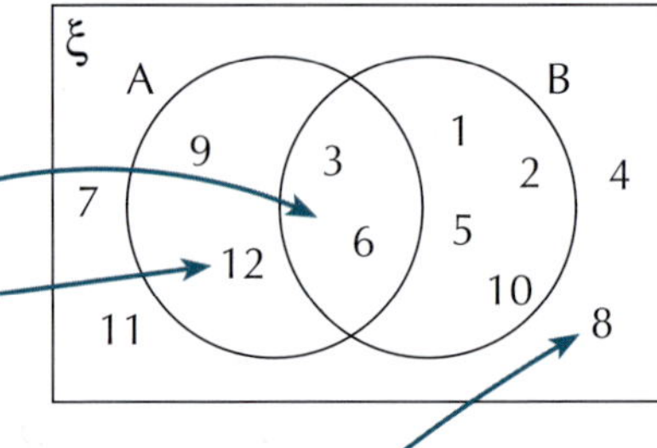

1. Write out sets A and B:
   A = {3, 6, 9, 12}   B = {1, 2, 3, 5, 6, 10}
2. A ∩ B = {3, 6} so these elements go in the overlap (intersection) of the two circles.
3. The elements in the circle for A that aren't in the overlap are the elements of A that aren't in B (and similarly for B).
4. The elements of ξ that aren't in either set go outside the circles.

b) What is the probability that a randomly selected element of ξ is in set A?

Divide the number of elements of set A by the total number of elements in ξ. $\frac{n(A)}{n(\xi)} = \frac{4}{12} = \mathbf{\frac{1}{3}}$

Exercise 2

Q1 Draw Venn diagrams to show the following sets, where ξ = {positive integers ≤ 10}.

a) A = {1, 3, 5}   B = {1, 3, 7}
b) A = {2, 3, 4, 5}   B = {1, 3, 5, 7, 9}
c) A = {2, 6, 10}   B = {1, 3, 6, 9}
d) A = {2, 3, 4, 5, 6}   B = {1, 3, 7}

Q2 At a fast food restaurant there are two options for side dishes — fries or salad. The number of customers (out of a total of 200) who chose each side dish is recorded in the Venn diagram on the right. What is the probability that a randomly chosen customer:

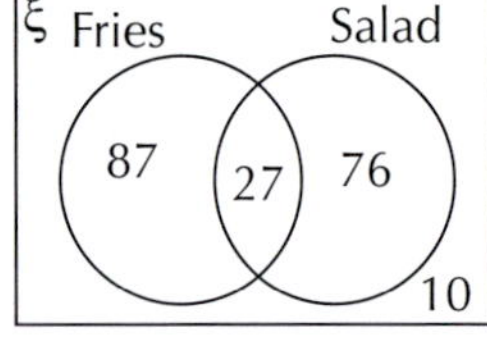

a) only had salad?   b) only had fries?   c) didn't have a side?
d) had salad?   e) had fries?   f) had fries and salad?

Q3 a) Given that ξ = {positive integers ≤ 10}, draw a Venn diagram for the sets A = {x : x is an odd number} and B = {x : x is a prime number}.

b) What is the probability that a randomly chosen element of ξ is:

(i) in B?   (ii) in A ∩ B?   (iii) in A ∩ B′?

Q4 In a class of 30 pupils, 23 like Maths (M), 18 like English (E) and 15 like Maths and English.

a) Draw a Venn diagram to show this information.

b) What is the probability that a randomly selected pupil:

(i) likes Maths and English?   (ii) only likes Maths?
(iii) only likes English?   (iv) doesn't like Maths or English?

Review Exercise

Q1 In a fruit bowl, there are 4 apples, 6 bananas, 5 pears and 5 oranges. Bianca picks out one piece of fruit at random. On the scale, indicate with an arrow:

a) How likely she is to pick an apple or banana.

b) How likely it is that she does not pick an orange.

c) How likely it is that she picks a lemon.

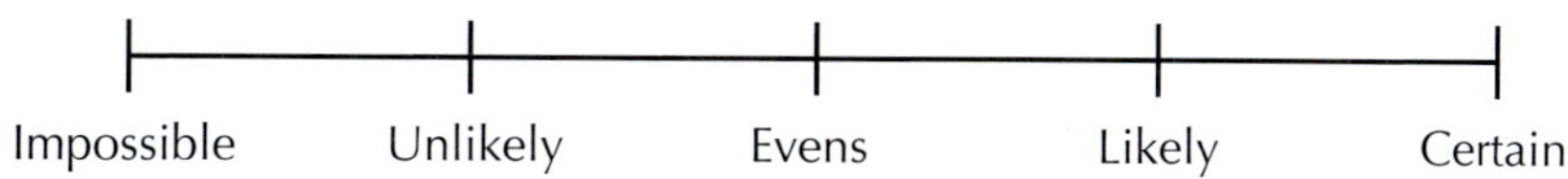

Q2 A fair, standard dice is rolled.

a) What is the probability of rolling an even number?

b) What is the probability of rolling a multiple of 3?

c) Explain why your answers to parts a) and b) don't add up to 1.

Q3 Derek and Eileen have played golf against each other 15 times. Derek has won 8 times, and there have been no draws.

a) Estimate the probability that Derek will win the next time they play.

b) Estimate the probability that Eileen will win the next time they play.

Q4 Miley has a bag of sweets. There are 4 blue sweets, 5 white sweets and 11 red sweets. She selects one at random, puts it back, then selects another at random.

a) Are these events independent?

b) Find the probability that Miley selects:

(i) two blue sweets (ii) a white sweet followed by a red sweet

Q5 A box contains ten coloured marbles — five blue, four white and one red. Two marbles are picked at random and are not replaced.

a) Draw a tree diagram showing all the possible results.

b) Work out the probability that:

(i) both are blue (ii) at least one is blue (iii) they are different

Q6 An ice cream van sells ice creams and ice lollies. The Venn diagram on the right shows the sales for an afternoon.

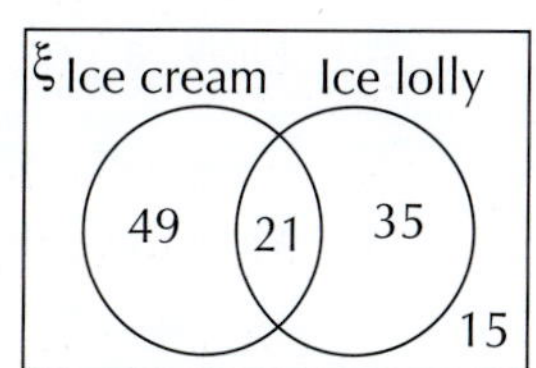

a) How many people bought an ice cream?

b) What is the probability that a randomly selected customer only bought an ice lolly?

Exam-Style Questions

Q1 In Box A are three cards, numbered 1, 2 and 3. In Box B are two cards, numbered 7 and 8. Leila picks one card from each box at random and puts them down in a random order to make a 2-digit number.

Find the probability that she makes an even number.

[3 marks]

Q2 Tania drives to and from work every weekday. There is a set of traffic lights on her route. The probability that she will have to stop at the lights on any given journey is 0.7.

a) Copy and complete the tree diagram below.

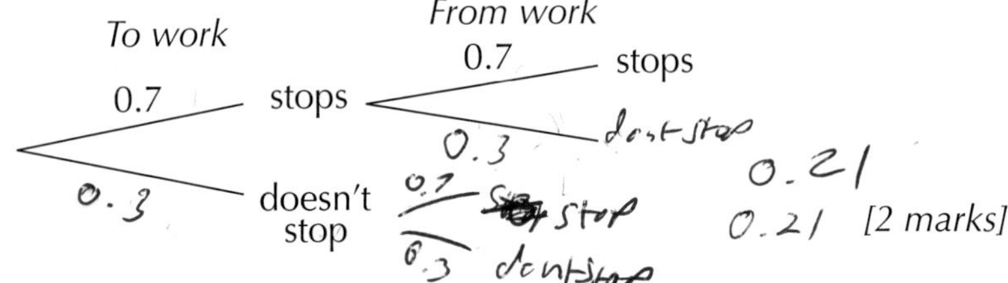

[2 marks]

b) Calculate the probability that on any given day she will stop at the traffic lights exactly once.

[2 marks]

Q3 Ian asked 7 boys and 9 girls in a Year 11 class at his school whether they went to the cinema last week. 5 boys had been to the cinema and 2 boys hadn't. Two thirds of the girls had been to the cinema and the rest of the girls hadn't.

a) What is the probability that a randomly selected pupil from the ones who were asked went to the cinema last week?

[3 marks]

Ian says $\frac{5}{7}$ of Year 11 boys at his school went to the cinema last week.

b) Give one reason why Ian's statement may be unreliable.

[1 mark]

Q4 30 members of a youth club go to an outdoor activity centre to take part in activities. 17 **only** do basketball (B), 10 do archery (A) and 6 do both.

a) Draw a Venn diagram to show the information given.

[2 marks]

b) Find the value of $n(A \cup B)$.

[1 mark]

Mixed Exam-Style Questions

Q1 A cinema is showing a film twice every evening.
The first showing starts at 18:40 and finishes at 20:15.
The second showing starts at 20:30.

a) Work out the time that the second showing finishes.

[2 marks]

Tickets to see the film are the same price for all customers.
Robert buys 5 tickets for him and his family to see the film together.
He pays with one £20 note and three £10 notes. He receives £1.25 change.

b) Work out the cost of a cinema ticket.

[3 marks]

Q2 Here is a list of numbers: 3 5 12 18 25

a) Write down the even number which has 9 as a factor.

[1 mark]

b) Write down the square number.

[1 mark]

c) Write down the two numbers which have a product of 60.

[1 mark]

d) Four of the numbers are added. The total is 58.
Which number was not included in this sum?

[1 mark]

e) The difference between 2 of the numbers is found. The answer is odd.
Work out the largest value that this difference could be.

[1 mark]

Q3 5 shapes are shown on the grid.

a) Write down the letters of the two shapes that are congruent.

[1 mark]

b) Write down the letters of the two shapes which are similar but not congruent.

[1 mark]

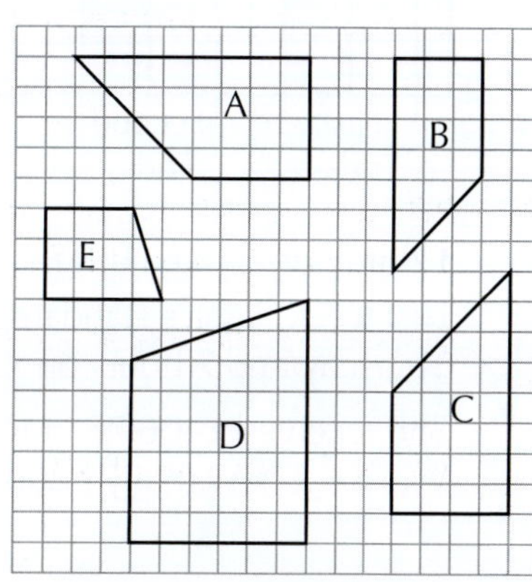

Q4 Ali has some 2p and 5p coins in his pocket.
He buys a fruit bag for 40p and uses all of his coins.
Show that there are five possible way that he could do this.

[2 marks]

Q5 The table shows the populations of China and Italy in 2017, both correct to 4 significant figures.

Country	Population
Italy	5.936×10^7
China	1.410×10^9

Find the ratio of the larger population to the smaller population in the form $n:1$.

[3 marks]

Q6 Every Friday, a school canteen offers a choice of a mini pizza or pasta. The number of Year 11 students who had pizza or pasta over three consecutive Fridays is shown on the dual bar chart below.

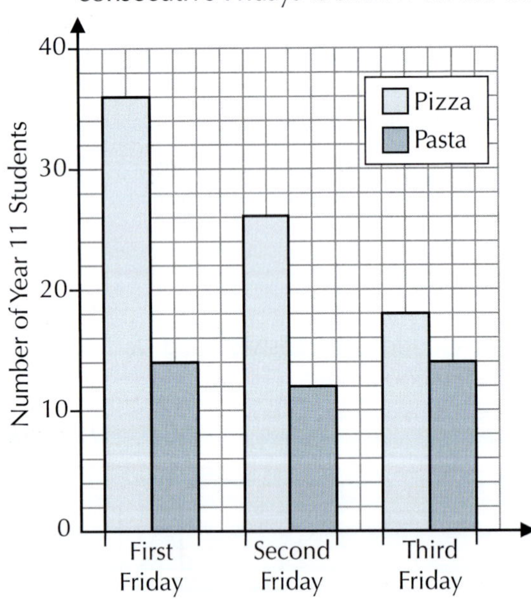

a) What percentage of students who ate in the canteen on the first Friday chose pasta?

[2 marks]

b) What fraction of students who ate in the canteen on the second Friday chose pizza? Give your answer in its simplest form.

[2 marks]

c) Describe a trend in the data over the course of the three Fridays.

[1 mark]

Q7 Uma is paid £9.46 per standard hour of work. She gets double this rate for overtime.

Last week, Uma's standard hours were 7.5 hours on Monday, Tuesday, Wednesday and Thursday and 7 hours on Friday. On Saturday she worked some hours of overtime.

She received £406.78 in total for the hours she worked, including overtime.
Work out how many hours of overtime Uma did last week. Show your working.

[3 marks]

Q8 A motorboat crosses a lake in a straight line from point A to point B, as shown on the map below. The average speed of the boat is 12 km/h. Work out how long it will take for the boat to cross the lake.

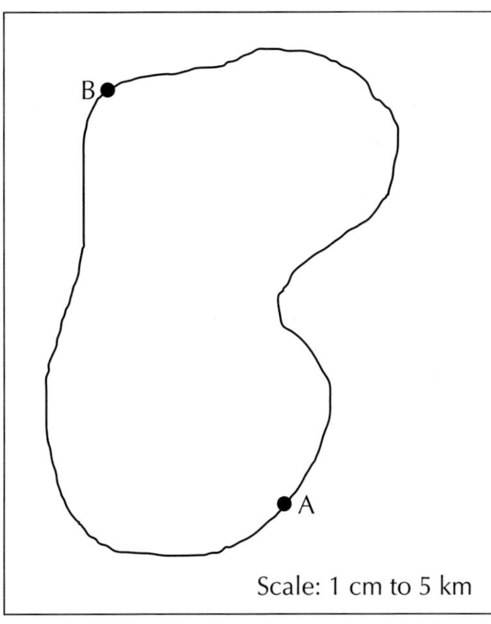

[3 marks]

Q9 For each of the following, work out what single-digit positive integer should go in the box to make the statement true:

a) $\frac{3}{4} = \frac{6}{\square}$

[1 mark]

b) $\frac{3}{4} < \frac{\square}{11}$

[1 mark]

Q10 A brand of breakfast cereal is sold in two different sizes.
The "family" size box contains 750 g.
The "standard" box normally contains 500 g, but as a special offer, these boxes currently contain an extra 25% of cereal.

The "family" box costs £2.25. The special offer "standard" boxes cost £2.
Work out which size of box is the better value for money.
You must show your working.

[4 marks]

Q11 The diagram shows an equilateral triangle.
The length of each side is a whole number of centimetres.

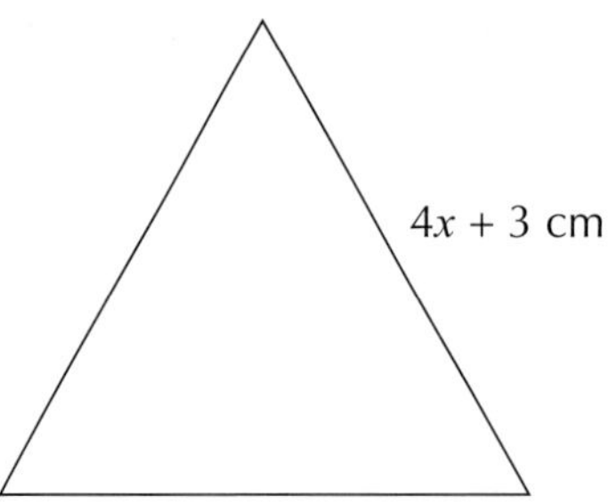

The perimeter of the diagram is greater than 480 cm.
Write an inequality, in terms of x, and solve it to find the lower limit for x.

[4 marks]

Q12 A shape is made when two identical squares overlap at the mid-point of their sides.

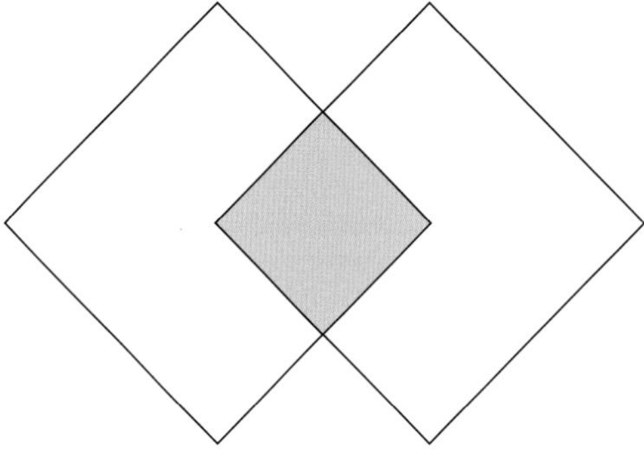

a) What fraction of the shape is shaded?

[1 mark]

b) The area of the shaded shape is 25 cm^2.
What is the length of one side of a large square?

[2 marks]

Q13 Muneera has a bowl of grapes.
8 of the grapes are green, 12 are red and the rest are black.
When Muneera picks a grape from the bowl at random,
the probability that she picks a green grape is $\frac{1}{3}$.
How many black grapes are there in the bowl?

[3 marks]

Q14 Jeremy is looking to buy a new computer on the internet.

A UK seller offers the model he wants with free delivery for £420.

The same model is also available from an American seller priced at 432 US dollars ($). Delivery from America will cost $30 and there will also be a 20% import tax on both the cost of the computer and the delivery charge.

The exchange rate is $1 = £0.75. Work out which is the better deal.

[3 marks]

Q15 The diagram shows a parallelogram with the lengths of three of its sides given in centimetres in terms of x. Show that the perimeter of the parallelogram is 23.2 cm.

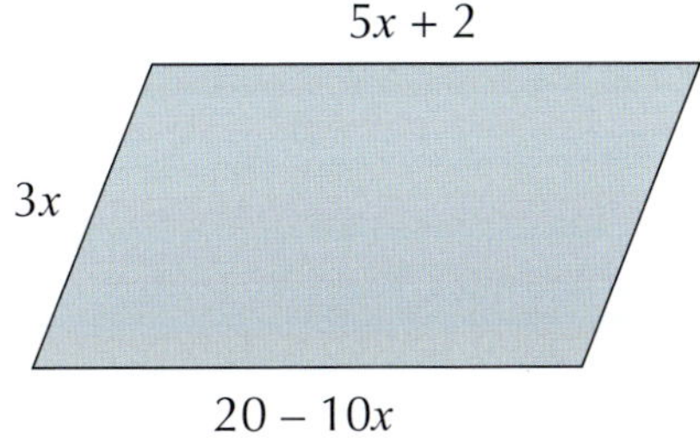

Not drawn accurately

[4 marks]

Q16 The lines $x = -1$, $y = 1$ and $y = 2x + 7$ have been sketched on the axes below. They intersect at points A, B and C.

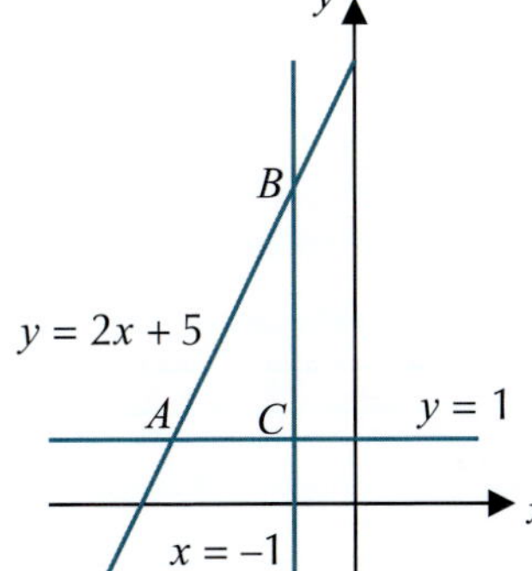

a) Find the coordinates of A, B and C.

[5 marks]

b) Show that the length of AB is $\sqrt{5}$.

[4 marks]

Q17 Three adjacent interior angles of a pentagon are right angles. The other two angles are in the ratio 4 : 11. Work out the size of the largest interior angle in the pentagon.

[4 marks]

Q18 A sealed water tank is partially filled with water.
It is in the shape of a cuboid with dimensions as shown on the diagram.
It stands on one of its smallest faces on level ground and the depth of water is 1.75 m.

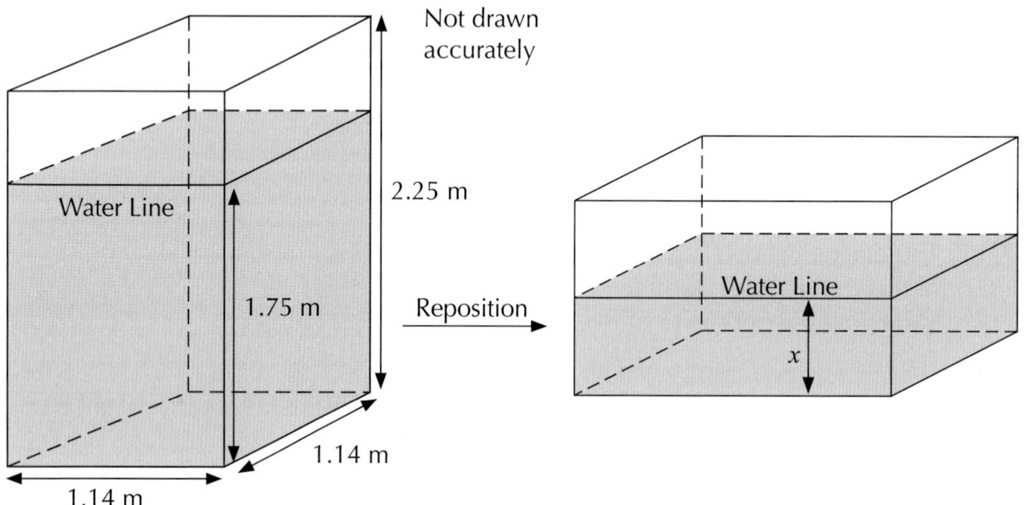

The tank is repositioned on level ground so that it stands on one of its largest faces.
By forming and solving an equation, work out x, the new depth of the water.
Give your answer in metres to an appropriate degree of accuracy.

[3 marks]

Q19 The diagram shows a regular hexagon with a right-angled triangle drawn on one side.
PQ is a diagonal, which divides the hexagon into two identical trapeziums.

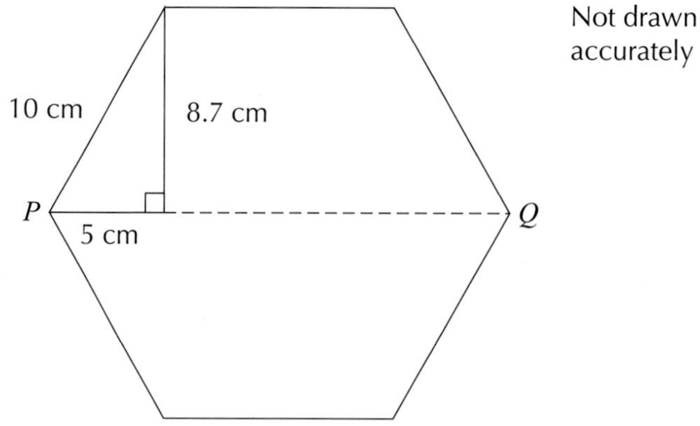

Find the area of the hexagon.

[4 marks]

Section 1 — Non-Calculator Arithmetic

1.1 Order of Operations

Page 2 Exercise 1

1 a) $5 + 1 \times 3 = 5 + 3 = \mathbf{8}$
b) $11 - 2 \times 5 = 11 - 10 = \mathbf{1}$
c) $24 \div 4 + 2 = 6 + 2 = \mathbf{8}$
d) $18 - 10 \div 5 = 18 - 2 = \mathbf{16}$

2 a) $6 \times (4 + 3) = 6 \times 7 = \mathbf{42}$
b) $11 - (2 + 3) = 11 - 5 = \mathbf{6}$
c) $(8 - 7) \times (6 + 5) = 1 \times 11 = \mathbf{11}$
d) $56 \div (2 \times 4) = 56 \div 8 = \mathbf{7}$

3 a) $2 \times (8 + 4) - 7 = 2 \times 12 - 7 = 24 - 7 = \mathbf{17}$
b) $18 \div (9 - 12 \div 4) = 18 \div (9 - 3)$
$= 18 \div 6 = \mathbf{3}$
c) $100 \div (8 + 3 \times 4) = 100 \div (8 + 12)$
$= 100 \div 20 = \mathbf{5}$
d) $20 - (5 \times 3 + 2) = 20 - (15 + 2)$
$= 20 - 17 = \mathbf{3}$
e) $48 \div 3 - 7 \times 2 = 16 - 14 = \mathbf{2}$
f) $36 - (7 + 4 \times 4) = 36 - (7 + 16)$
$= 36 - 23 = \mathbf{13}$

4 a) $9 \times (7 - 5) = 18$
Don't panic if you can't spot the answer to questions like this straight away — try brackets in different positions and see what works.
b) $(18 - 6) \div 3 = 4$
c) $(5 + 2) \times (6 - 2) = 28$
d) $21 \div (4 + 3) = 3$
e) $(13 - 5) \times (13 - 1) = 96$
f) $(6 + 8 - 7) \times 5 = 35$

5 a) $16 - 6 \div 3 = 14$
b) $11 \times 3 + 5 = 38$
c) $3 \times 6 - 9 = 9$
d) $8 \div 2 + 6 = 10$ or $8 \times 2 - 6 = 10$
e) $(3 + 7) \times 4 = 40$
f) $14 \div (6 + 8) = 1$

Page 3 Exercise 2

1 a) Top line: $4 - 1 + 5 = 3 + 5 = 8$
Bottom line: $2 \times 2 = 4$
Top line ÷ bottom line = $8 \div 4 = \mathbf{2}$
b) Top line: $6 + (11 - 8) = 6 + 3 = 9$
Bottom line: $7 - 5 = 2$
Top line ÷ bottom line = $9 \div 2 = \mathbf{\frac{9}{2}}$

Using the same method for c)-h):
c) **2** d) **4** e) $\mathbf{\frac{3}{5}}$
f) $\mathbf{\frac{2}{3}}$ g) **3** h) **1**

1.2 Negative Numbers

Page 4 Exercise 1

1 a) $-4 + 3 = \mathbf{-1}$ b) $-1 + 5 = \mathbf{4}$
c) $-2 + 1 = \mathbf{-1}$ d) $6 - 17 = \mathbf{-11}$
e) $-13 + 18 = \mathbf{5}$ f) $11 - 19 = \mathbf{-8}$

2 a) $-3 + 2 - 1 = \mathbf{-2}$
b) $-2 + 8 - 5 = \mathbf{1}$
c) $8 - 5 - 3 = \mathbf{0}$
d) $-1 - 7 - 4 = \mathbf{-12}$
e) $-9 + 13 + 11 = \mathbf{15}$
f) $7 - 18 + 11 = \mathbf{0}$

3 a) $-3 + \mathbf{2} = -1$ b) $5 - \mathbf{15} = -10$
c) $\mathbf{-3} + 7 = 4$ d) $\mathbf{-4} - 2 = -6$

4 a) Start at –1°C and count 3 places down to get **–4° C.**
b) Start at –5°C and count 8 places up to get to **3° C.**

5 a) Start at 3°C and count how many places down it is to –4° C. The number of places is 7 so the difference is **7° C.**
b) Start at –2°C and count how many places down it is to –5° C. The number of places is 3 so the difference is **3° C.**

6 Start at 6° C and count down 7 places to get to **–1° C.**

7 Start at –5°C and count how many places up it is to –1° C. The number of places is 4 so the difference is **4° C.**

Page 5 Exercise 2

1 a) $4 - (-2) = \mathbf{6}$ b) $-3 - (-5) = \mathbf{2}$
c) $-7 + (-2) = \mathbf{-9}$ d) $-5 + (-5) = \mathbf{-10}$
e) $9 + (-2) = \mathbf{7}$ f) $-13 - (-3) = \mathbf{-10}$
g) $-6 + (-3) = \mathbf{-9}$ h) $1 - (-12) = \mathbf{13}$

2 a) $-1 + (-4) - 1 = \mathbf{-6}$
b) $6 - (-2) + (-3) = \mathbf{5}$
c) $7 + (-6) - (-8) = \mathbf{9}$
d) $-8 + (-8) - (-12) = \mathbf{-4}$
e) $9 - (-13) + (-2) = \mathbf{20}$
f) $-3 + (-11) + (-6) = \mathbf{-20}$

3 a) $6 - (-5) = \mathbf{11}$ b) $-6 - (-10) = \mathbf{4}$
c) $4 - (-8) = \mathbf{12}$ d) $-5 - (-12) = \mathbf{7}$

Page 6 Exercise 3

1 a) $3 \times (-4) = \mathbf{-12}$ b) $2 \times (-8) = \mathbf{-16}$
c) $(-9) \times 6 = \mathbf{-54}$ d) $(-15) \div 3 = \mathbf{-5}$
e) $(-15) \div (-3) = \mathbf{5}$ f) $12 \div (-4) = \mathbf{-3}$

2 a) $-3 \times \mathbf{2} = -6$ b) $-14 \div \mathbf{7} = -2$
c) $\mathbf{-4} \times 4 = -16$ d) $\mathbf{10} \div (-2) = -5$
e) $-8 \times \mathbf{3} = -24$ f) $-18 \div \mathbf{(-6)} = 3$
g) $\mathbf{-12} \times (-3) = 36$ h) $\mathbf{-77} \div 11 = -7$

3 a) $2 \times 4 \div (-2) = 8 \div (-2) = \mathbf{-4}$
b) $(-5) \times (-6) \div 3 = 30 \div 3 = \mathbf{10}$
c) $(-3) \times (-5) \times (-6) = 15 \times (-6) = \mathbf{-90}$
d) $(-63) \times (-2) \div (-9) = 126 \div (-9) = \mathbf{-14}$
e) $[55 \div (-11)] \times (-9) = -5 \times (-9) = \mathbf{45}$
f) $[(-24) \div 8)] \div 3 = -3 \div 3 = \mathbf{-1}$

1.3 Whole Number Arithmetic

Page 8 Exercise 1

1 a) 23 + 56 = **79**
b) 122 + 97 = **219**
c) 243 + 178 = **421**
d) 73 – 27 = **46**
e) 181 – 35 = **146**
f) 233 – 187 = **46**

2 a) 342 + 679 = **1021**
b) 604 + 288 = **892**
c) 506 – 278 = **228**
d) 2513 + 241 = **2754**
e) 2942 – 324 = **2618**
f) 4003 – 1235 = **2768**

3 a) Add the first two numbers: 112 + 41 = **153**
Then add on 213: 153 + 213 = **366**
So 41 + 112 + 213 = **366**
You could do part a) all in one go by writing the three numbers on top of each other and adding. You couldn't do the same for b) though, as that's an addition followed by a subtraction.
b) Add the first two numbers: 764 + 138 = **902**
The subtract 345: 902 – 345 = **557**

Using the same method for c)-f):
c) **816** d) **249**
e) **917** f) **757**

4 38 + 52 + 65 = **155**

5 £1146 – 224 = **£1922**

6 1845 – 1257 = **588**

Page 9 Exercise 2

1 a) 66 × 72: 132 + 4620 = **4752**
b) 79 × 86: 474 + 6320 = **6794**

Using the same method for c)-f):
c) **6723** d) **2600**
e) **3420** f) **11 664**

2 46 × 24: 184 + 920 = **1104**

3 33 × 12: 66 + 330 = **396**

4 a)
1 3 4 7
× 2 0
0 0 0 0
2 6 9 4 0
2 6 9 4 0

b)
3 6 6 9
× 2 1
3 6 6 9
7 3 3 8 0
7 7 0 4 9

c)
2 6 2 3
× 4 2
5 2 4 6
1 0 4 9 2 0
1 1 0 1 6 6

d)
2 5 7 8
× 3 6
1 5 4 6 8
7 7 3 4 0
9 2 8 0 8

Page 10 Exercise 3

1 a)

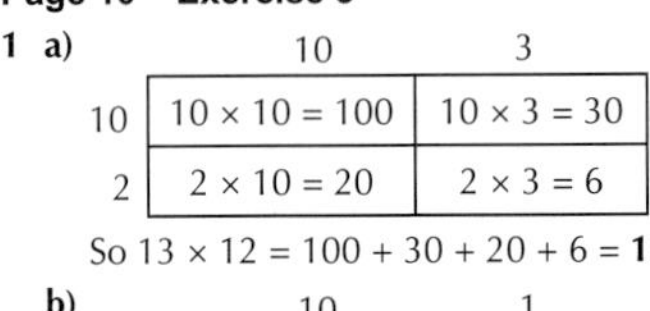

	10	3
10	10 × 10 = 100	10 × 3 = 30
2	2 × 10 = 20	2 × 3 = 6

So 13 × 12 = 100 + 30 + 20 + 6 = **156**

b)

	10	1
10	10 × 10 = 100	10 × 1 = 10
7	7 × 10 = 70	7 × 1 = 7

So 11 × 17 = 100 + 10 + 70 + 7 = **187**

Using the same method for c)-h):

c) 520 **d) 384** **e) 22 754**
f) 34 362 **g) 28 105** **h) 42 032**

2

	200	40	3
50	200 × 50 = 10 000	40 × 50 = 2000	3 × 50 = 150
2	200 × 2 = 400	40 × 2 = 80	3 × 2 = 6

So £243 × 52
= 10 000 + 2000 + 150 + 400 + 80 + 6
= **£12 636**

3

	200	30
10	200 × 10 = 2000	30 × 10 = 300
4	200 × 4 = 800	30 × 4 = 120

So 230 × 14 = 2000 + 300 + 800 + 120
= **3220**

4

	100	60
80	100 × 80 = 8000	60 × 80 = 4800
5	100 × 5 = 500	60 × 5 = 300

So 160 × 85 = 8000 + 4800 + 500 + 300
= **13 600**

5

	20	2
20	20 × 20 = 400	2 × 20 = 40
7	20 × 7 = 140	2 × 7 = 14

27 biscuits requires 22 × 27
= 400 + 40 + 140 + 14 = 594 g of flour,
so **Hamza cannot make 27 biscuits.**

6 a)

	2000	200	70	1
20	2000 × 20 = 40 000	200 × 20 = 4000	70 × 20 = 1400	1 × 20 = 20
5	2000 × 5 = 10 000	200 × 5 = 1000	70 × 5 = 350	1 × 5 = 5

So 2271 × 25
= 40 000 + 4000 + 1400 + 20
+ 10 000 + 1000 + 350 + 5 = **56 775**

Double check you've added all the numbers from the grid — it's easy to miss one when you're dealing with big numbers.

b)

	5000	600	20	4
40	5000 × 40 = 200 000	600 × 40 = 24 000	20 × 40 = 800	4 × 40 = 160
2	5000 × 2 = 10 000	600 × 2 = 1200	20 × 2 = 40	4 × 2 = 8

So 5624 × 42
= 200 000 + 24 000 + 800 + 160
+ 10 000 + 1200 + 40 + 8 = **236 208**

Using the same method for c) and d):

c) 41 174 **d) 85 994**

Page 12 Exercise 4

1 a) 7)357 = 051
So 357 ÷ 7 = **51**

b) 7)238 = 034
So 238 ÷ 7 = **34**

Using the same method for c)-f):

c) 67 **d) 452**
e) 560 **f) 622**

2 a) 5)361 = 072 remainder 1
So 361 ÷ 5 = **$72\frac{1}{5}$**

b) 3)5213 = 1737 remainder 2
So 5213 ÷ 3 = **$1737\frac{2}{3}$**

Using the same method for c)-f):

c) $839\frac{3}{5}$ **d) $74\frac{5}{9}$**
e) $424\frac{1}{6}$ **f) $334\frac{1}{4}$**

3 a)
23)644 = 28
−46
184
−184
0
So 644 ÷ 23 = **28**

b)
19)608 = 32
−57
38
− 38
0
So 608 ÷ 19 = **32**

Using the same method for c)-f):

c) 41 **d) 48**
e) 310 **f) 352**

4 a)
32)846 = 26
− 64
206
− 192
14
So 846 ÷ 32 = **$26\frac{14}{32}$** = **$26\frac{7}{16}$**

b)
45)945 = 21
−90
45
− 45
0
So 945 ÷ 45 = **21**

Using the same method for c)-f):

c) $33\frac{18}{21} = 33\frac{6}{7}$ **d) $268\frac{18}{25}$**
e) $268\frac{15}{31}$ **f) $194\frac{3}{44}$**

5 £5.00 = 500p
41)500 = 12
−41
90
− 82
8
So 500 ÷ 41 = 12 remainder 8
So you can buy **12 stamps** and you would get **8p change.**
Make sure you interpret what the remainder means in the situation in the question.

6
24)672 = 28
−48
192
−192
0
Each group will have **28 people**.

7
6)1350 = 225
You need **225 boxes**.

8
22)7634 = 347
−66
103
− 88
154
− 154
0
Each washing machine costs **£347**.

9 a)
52)22464 = 432
−208
166
−156
104
− 104
0
Mike earns **£432 a week.**

b) 12)24636 = 02053
Andrea earns **£2053 a month.**

1.4 Decimals

Page 13 Exercise 1

1. The 7 is in the hundredths column so has value $\frac{7}{100}$.
2. The 3 is in the tenths column so has value $\frac{3}{10}$.
3. The 8 is in the thousandths column so has value $\frac{8}{1000}$.
4. The 1 is in the ten thousandths column so has value $\frac{1}{10000}$.
5. The 2 is in the units column so has value **2**.
6. **a)** Seven tenths = **0.7**
   b) Two hundredths = **0.02**
   c) Five thousandths = **0.005**
   d) $\frac{7}{100}$ = seven hundredths = **0.07**
   e) $\frac{1}{1000}$ = one thousandth = **0.001**
   f) $\frac{8}{10}$ = eight tenths = **0.8**

Page 14 Exercise 2

1 a) 0.3 and 0.31 can be written as 0.30 and 0.31. Columns are equal until the hundredths column where 1 is bigger than 0, so the larger number is **0.31**

b) 0.09 and 0.009 can be written as 0.090 and 0.009. Columns are equal until the hundredth column where 9 is bigger than 0, so the larger number is **0.09**

c) Compare 0.427 and 0.472. Columns are equal until the hundredth column where 7 is bigger than 2, so the larger number is **0.472**

d) Compare 18.07 and 17.08. Columns are equal until the units column where 8 is bigger than 7, so the larger number is **18.07**

2 a) Write the numbers as 0.02, 0.20 and 0.15. Columns are equal until the tenths column where 2 is the largest, 1 is the next largest and then 0 is the smallest, so the correct order is **0.02, 0.15, 0.2**

b) Positive numbers are always bigger than the negative numbers.
Sorting the positive numbers 0.6 and 6.1: In the units column 6 is bigger than 0, so 6.1 is bigger than 0.6.
Sorting the negative numbers –0.6 and –6: In the units column 6 is bigger than 0, so –6 is lower than –0.6.
Remember — with negative numbers, the number with the larger digit in the column you're comparing is the lower number.
So the correct order is **–6, –0.6, 0.6, 6.1**

Using the same method for c)-f):

c) **4.05, 4.5, 5.04, 5.4**
d) **–1.5, 1.05, 1.5, 1.55**
e) **0.15, 0.16, 0.51, 0.61**
f) **–0.095, –0.09, –0.05, 0.9**

1.5 Adding and Subtracting Decimals

Page 15 Exercise 1

1 a) 5.1 + 1.8 = **6.9**
b) 6.3 + 5.4 = **11.7**
c) 5.7 + 12.6 = **18.3**
d) 4.8 + 5.3 = **10.1**

2 a) 5.6 – 0.3 = **5.3**
b) 9.9 – 4.2 = **5.7**
c) 5.3 – 2.8 = **2.5**
d) 8.5 – 1.9 = **6.6**

3 a) 10.83 + 7.40 = **18.23**
b) 0.029 + 1.800 = **1.829**
c) 91.700 + 0.492 = **92.192**

Make sure you get those decimal points lined up — add zeros after the decimal point if your numbers aren't the same length.

Using the same method for d)-h):

d) **7.394** e) **12.679** f) **1.908**
g) **1.011** h) **25.579**

4 a) 24.63 – 7.50 = **17.13**
b) 6.78 – 5.60 = **1.18**
c) 73.46 – 8.50 = **64.96**

Using the same method for d)-h):

d) **6.215** e) **3.394** f) **2.08**
g) **9.31** h) **0.261**

5 a) 3.81 + 9.54 = **13.35**
b) 2.81 – 0.16 = **2.65**
c) 2.75 + 9.45 = **12.20**

Using the same method for d)-h):

d) **9.62** e) **3.21** f) **15.02**
g) **11.85** h) **23.67**

Page 16 Exercise 2

1 a) 6.0 – 5.1 = **0.9**
b) 23.00 – 18.51 = **4.49**
c) 12.000 – 5.028 = **6.972**
d) 13.000 – 6.453 = **6.547**

2 a) 2.0 + 1.8 = **3.8**
b) 3.7 + 6.0 = **9.7**
c) 12.70 + 7.34 = **20.04**

Using the same method for d)-h):

d) **22.49** e) **44.92** f) **4.2**
g) **4.8** h) **18.3**

3 a) 6.474 + 0.920 = 7.394
So 6.474 + 0.92 + 3 = 7.394 + 3
7.394 + 3.000 = 10.394
So 6.474 + 0.92 + 3 = **10.394**

b) 2.39 + 8.00 = 10.39
So 2.39 + 8 + 0.26 = 10.39 + 0.26
10.39 + 0.26 = 10.65
So 2.39 + 8 + 0.26 =**10.65**

Using the same method for c)-f):

c) **17.44** d) **7.983**
e) **22.97** f) **16.652**

Page 17 Exercise 3

1 2.3 + 4.6 = 6.9
⇒ he travels a distance of **6.9 km**.
Remember to give your answer in the context of the question.

2 18.50 + 31.00 = 49.50 ⇒ she spends a total of **£49.50.**

3 4.00 – 2.75 = 1.25 ⇒ **1.25 m** of wood is left.

4 66.50 – 15.00 = 51.50 ⇒ she has **£51.50** left to pay.

5 71.42 + 11.79 = 83.21 ⇒ he would have spent **£83.21.**

6 15.32 – 0.47 = 14.85 ⇒ his second run took **14.85 seconds**.

1.6 Multiplying and Dividing Decimals

Page 19 Exercise 1

1 a) Multiplying by 10 moves the decimal point one place to the right, so 0.92 × 10 = **9.2**

b) Multiplying by 100 moves the decimal point two places to the right, so 1.41 × 100 = **141**

c) Multiplying by 1000 moves the decimal point three places to the right, so 0.23 × 1000 = **230**

Using the same methods for d)-f):

d) **1460** e) **19** f) **130.4**

2 a) Dividing by 100 moves the decimal point two places to the left, so 861.5 ÷ 100 = **8.615**

b) Dividing by 10 moves the decimal point one place to the left, so 381.7 ÷ 10 = **38.17**

c) Dividing by 1000 moves the decimal point three places to the left, so 549.1 ÷ 1000 = **0.5491**

Using the same methods for d)-f):

d) **0.63** e) **0.0051** f) **0.0094**

Page 19 Exercise 2

1 a) 132 ÷ 10 = 13.2
So 13.2 × 238 = 132 × 238 ÷ 10
= 31 416 ÷ 10 = **3141.6**

b) 132 ÷ 100 = 1.32 and 238 ÷ 10 = 23.8
So 1.32 × 23.8 = 132 × 238 ÷ 100 ÷ 10
= 31 416 ÷ 1000 = **31.416**

c) 132 ÷ 100 = 1.32 and 238 ÷ 1000 = 0.238
So 1.32 × 0.238 = 132 × 238 ÷ 100 ÷ 1000
= 31 416 ÷ 100 000 = **0.31416**

d) 132 ÷ 1000 = 0.132 and 238 ÷ 1000 = 0.238, so
0.132 × 0.238 = 132 × 238 ÷ 1000 ÷ 1000
= 31 416 ÷ 1 000 000 = **0.031416**

2 a) 401 ÷ 10 = 40.1 and 119 ÷ 10 = 11.9
So 40.1 × 11.9 = 401 × 119 ÷ 10 ÷ 10
= 47 719 ÷ 100 = **477.19**

b) 401 ÷ 100 = 4.01 and 119 ÷ 100 = 1.19
So 4.01 × 1.19 = 401 × 119 ÷ 100 ÷ 100
= 47 719 ÷ 10 000
= **4.7719**

c) 401 ÷ 1000 = 0.401 and 119 ÷ 100 = 1.19
So 0.401 × 1.19 = 401 × 119 ÷ 1000 ÷ 100
= 47 719 ÷ 100 000
= **0.47719**

d) 401 ÷ 1000 = 0.401 and
119 ÷ 1000 = 0.119
So 0.401 × 0.119
= 401 × 119 ÷ 1000 ÷ 1000
= 47 719 ÷ 1 000 000 = **0.047719**

Page 20 Exercise 3

1 a)
```
  6 7
×   8
-----
 5 3 6
  5
```
6.7 has one digit after the decimal point and 8 has none, so the answer should have one digit after the decimal point.
6.7 × 8 = **53.6**

b)
```
  6 5
×   9
-----
 5 8 5
  4
```
0.65 has two digits after the decimal point and 9 has none, so the answer should have two digits after the decimal point.
0.65 × 9 = **5.85**

c) 9 × 8 = 72
0.9 and 0.8 both have one digit after the decimal point, so the answer should have two digits after the decimal point.
0.9 × 0.8 = **0.72**

d) 6 × 3 = 18
0.6 and 0.3 both have one digit after the decimal point, so the answer should have two digits after the decimal point.
0.6 × 0.3 = **0.18**

e) 1 × 6 = 6
0.01 has two digits after the decimal point and 0.6 has one digit after the decimal point. So the answer should have three digits after the decimal point.
0.01 × 0.6 = **0.006**
Don't ignore 0's after the decimal point — here 0.01 has two digits after the decimal point, not one. (NB this only applies if the 0's come before other digits — 0.10 only really has one digit after the decimal point, as you can just knock the 0 off the end.)

f)
```
  6 1
×   7
-----
 4 2 7
```
0.61 has two digits after the decimal point and 0.7 has one digit after the decimal point. So the answer should have three digits after the decimal point.
0.61 × 0.7 = **0.427**

g) 33 × 2 = 66
0.33 has two digits after the decimal point and 0.02 has two digits after the decimal point. So the answer should have four digits after the decimal point.
0.33 × 0.02 = **0.0066**

h) 7 × 6 = 42
0.007 and 0.006 both have three digits after the decimal point, so the answer should have six digits after the decimal point.
0.007 × 0.006 = **0.000042**

2 a)
```
    6 3
  × 2 1
  -----
    6 3
  1 2 6 0
  -------
  1 3 2 3
    1
```
6.3 has one digit after the decimal point, and 2.1 has one digit after the decimal point, so the answer should have two digits after the decimal point.
6.3 × 2.1 = **13.23**

b)
```
    1 4
  × 2 3
  -----
    4 2
    1
  2 8 0
  -----
  3 2 2
  1
```
1.4 has one digit after the decimal point, and 2.3 has one digit after the decimal point, so the answer should have two digits after the decimal point.
1.4 × 2.3 = **3.22**

Using the same method for c)-f):
c) 4.32 **d) 59.34**
e) 0.528 **f) 1.173**

Page 21 Exercise 4

1 a) 3.1 × 40 = 3.1 × 4 × 10
```
  3 1
×   4
-----
1 2 4
```
3.1 has one digit after the decimal point and 4 has none, so the answer should have one digit after the decimal point.
3.1 × 4 = 12.4
So 3.1 × 40 = 12.4 × 10 = **124**
If you're doing a multiplication or division, always see if you can split it into a power of 10 and a smaller number.

b) 0.7 × 600 = 0.7 × 6 × 100
7 × 6 = 42
0.7 has one digit after the decimal point and 6 has none, so the answer should have one digit after the decimal point.
0.7 × 6 = 4.2
So 0.7 × 600 = 4.2 × 100 = **420**

c) 0.061 × 2000 = 0.061 × 2 × 1000
```
  6 1
×   2
-----
1 2 2
```
0.061 has three digits after the decimal point and 2 has none, so the answer should have three digits after the decimal point.
So 0.061 × 2 = 0.122
So 0.061 × 2000 = 0.122 × 1000 = **122**

d) 11.06 × 80 = 11.06 × 8 × 10
```
  1 1 0 6
×       8
---------
  8 8 4 8
      4
```
11.06 has two digits after the decimal point and 8 has none, so the answer should have two digits after the decimal point.
11.06 × 8 = 88.48
So 11.06 × 80 = 88.48 × 10 = **884.8**

Using the same method for e)-h):
e) 363 **f) 402.8**
g) 6108 **h) 4515**

Page 22 Exercise 5

1 a) 2)5.^{1}4 = 2.7, so 5.4 ÷ 2 = **2.7**

b) 3)9.6 = 3.2, so 9.6 ÷ 3 = **3.2**

c) 6)9.^{3}2^{2}4 = 1.54, so 9.24 ÷ 6 = **1.54**

d) 5)2.^{2}6^{1}5 = 0.53, so 2.65 ÷ 5 = **0.53**

Using the same method for e)-h):
e) 1.03 **f) 0.45**
g) 14.1 **h) 0.231**

2 a) 4)8.5^{1}2 = 2.13, so 8.52 ÷ 4 = **2.13**

b) 4)1^{1}1^{3}2.8 = 028.2, so 112.8 ÷ 4 = **28.2**

c) 3)1.^{1}0^{1}2 = 0.34, so 1.02 ÷ 3 = **0.34**

d) 8)5.^{5}6 2^{2}0^{4}0 = 0.7025, so 5.62 ÷ 8 = **0.7025**

Using the same method for e)-h):
e) 0.0104 **f) 1.5075**
g) 0.6122 **h) 0.0102**

Page 22 Exercise 6

1 a) 6.4 × 10 = 64 and 0.4 × 10 = 4,
so the calculation becomes **64 ÷ 4**

b) 4)6^{2}4 = 16, so 6.4 ÷ 0.4 = **16**

2 a) 0.384 × 100 = 38.4 and 0.12 × 100 = 12,
so the calculation becomes **38.4 ÷ 12**

b) 12)38.^{2}4 = 03.2, so 0.384 ÷ 0.12 = **3.2**

3 a) 3.8 × 1000 = 3800 and 0.008 × 1000 = 8,
so the calculation becomes **3800 ÷ 8**

b) 8)38^{6}0^{4}0 = 0475, so 3.8 ÷ 0.008 = **475**

4 a) 6.4 × 10 = 64 and 0.2 × 10 = 2,
so the calculation becomes 64 ÷ 2.
2)64 = 32, so 6.4 ÷ 0.2 = **32**
Make sure the number you are dividing by is a whole number.

b) 3.54 × 10 = 35.4 and 0.4 × 10 = 4,
so the calculation becomes 35.4 ÷ 4.
4)3^{3}5.^{3}4^{2}0 = 08.85, so 3.54 ÷ 0.4 = **8.85**

c) 0.624 × 10 = 6.24 and 0.3 × 10 = 3,
so the calculation becomes 6.24 ÷ 3.
3)6.2^{2}4 = 2.08, so 0.624 ÷ 0.3 = **2.08**

5 a) 22.56 × 100 = 2256 and 0.03 × 100 = 3,
so the calculation becomes 2256 ÷ 3.
3)22^{1}56 = 0752, so 22.56 ÷ 0.03 = **752**

b) 0.257 × 100 = 25.7 and 0.05 × 100 = 5,
so the calculation becomes 25.7 ÷ 5.
5)2^{2}5.7^{2}0 = 05.14, so 0.257 ÷ 0.05 = **5.14**

c) 0.039 × 100 = 3.9 and 0.06 × 100 = 6, so the calculation becomes 3.9 ÷ 6.

$$6\overline{)3.{}^{3}9\,{}^{3}0} = 0.65$$ so 0.039 ÷ 0.06 = **0.65**

6 a) 0.081 × 1000 = 81 and 0.009 × 1000 = 9, so the calculation becomes 81 ÷ 9 = **9**

b) 0.008 × 10 = 0.08 and 0.4 × 10 = 4, so the calculation becomes 0.08 ÷ 4

$$4\overline{)0.08} = 0.02$$ so 0.008 ÷ 0.4 = **0.02**

c) 1.44 × 10 = 14.4 and 1.2 × 10 = 12, so the calculation becomes 14.4 ÷ 12

$$12\overline{)14.{}^{2}4} = 01.2$$ so 1.44 ÷ 1.2 = **1.2**

Page 23 Exercise 7

1 a) $5\overline{)7.{}^{2}3{}^{3}0} = 1.46$ so 7.3 ÷ 5 = **1.46**

b) 7.3 ÷ 50 = (7.3 ÷ 5) ÷ 10
= 1.46 ÷ 10 = **0.146**

2 a) $4\overline{)2.41{}^{1}0{}^{2}0} = 0.6025$ so 2.41 ÷ 4 = **0.6025**

b) 2.41 ÷ 400 = (2.41 ÷ 4) ÷ 100
= 0.6025 ÷ 100 = **0.006025**

3 a) 40 = 4 × 10, so first divide by 4 and then divide by 10.

$4\overline{)6.08} = 1.52$ so 6.08 ÷ 4 = 1.52
6.08 ÷ 40 = (6.08 ÷ 4) ÷ 10
= 1.52 ÷ 10 = **0.152**

b) 700 = 7 × 100, so first divide by 7 and then divide by 100.

$7\overline{)5.{}^{5}7\,{}^{1}4} = 0.82$ so 5.74 ÷ 7 = 0.82
5.74 ÷ 700 = (5.74 ÷ 7) ÷ 100
= 0.82 ÷ 100 = **0.0082**

c) 900 = 9 × 100, so first divide by 9 and then divide by 100.

$9\overline{)24.{}^{7}4{}^{2}7} = 02.83$ so 25.47 ÷ 9 = 2.83
25.47 ÷ 900 = (25.47 ÷ 9) ÷ 100
= 2.83 ÷ 100 = **0.0283**

d) 3000 = 3 × 1000, so first divide by 3 and then divide by 1000.

$3\overline{)1{}^{1}3.{}^{1}7{}^{2}2{}^{1}2} = 04.574$ so 13.722 ÷ 3 = 4.574
13.722 ÷ 3000 = (13.722 ÷ 3) ÷ 1000
= 4.574 ÷ 100 = **0.004574**

Page 24 Review Exercise

1 a) 6 + 4 × 2 = 6 + 8 = **14**

b) 48 ÷ (4 + 2) = 48 ÷ 6 = **8**

c) (13 – 5) × 12 = 8 × 12 = **96**

2 a) –5 + 8 = **3** b) 6 – (–2) = 6 + 2 = **8**

c) –8 × – 5 = **40** d) 54 ÷ (–9) = **–6**

3 a) 256 + 312 = **568**

b) $^{7}8{}^{3}4{}^{1}1$ – 346 = **495**

c) 1632 + 421 = **2053** (carry 1)

d) $2\,{}^{7}8{}^{12}3{}^{1}0$ – 394 = **2436**

4 14 × 52:
28
$7_{2}00$
728

so £14 × 52 = **£728**

5 $54\overline{)462} = 008$
–432
30

So 462 ÷ 54 = 8 remainder 30, which means **9 coaches are needed**.

As there is a remainder, 8 coaches wouldn't be enough for everyone on the trip, so you have to round up to 9.

6 The 6 is in the thousands column so it has value $\mathbf{\frac{6}{1000}}$.

7 a) **–0.1, –0.09, –0.01, 0.1**

b) **–5, –0.55, –0.5, –0.45**

c) **–7.1, –7.07, –7, 0.007**

8 a) 6.78 – 5.60 = **1.18**

b) 1.60 + 4.35 = **5.95**

c) 0.78 + 1.30 = **2.08** (carry 1)

d) $4.{}^{2}3{}^{1}2$ – 2.17 = **2.15**

9 a) 7.8 × 1000 = **7800**

b) 0.006 × 100 = **0.6**

c) 25.9 ÷ 10 = **2.59**

d) 901.5 ÷ 100 = **9.015**

10 a) 221 ÷ 100 = 2.21 and 168 ÷ 100 = 1.68
So 2.21 × 1.68 = 221 × 168 ÷ 100 ÷ 100
= 37 128 ÷ 10 000
= **3.7128**

b) 221 ÷ 1000 = 0.221 and 168 ÷ 100 = 1.68,
So 0.221 × 1.68 = 221 × 168 ÷ 1000 ÷ 100
= 37 128 ÷ 100 000
= **0.37128**

c) 168 ÷ 1000 = 0.168,
So 221 × 0.168 = 221 × 168 ÷ 1000
= 37 128 ÷ 1000 = **37.128**

11 176 × 5 = $8_{3}8_{3}0$

there are two digits after the decimal point in 1.76 so 1.76 × 5 = **8.8 pints**

12 2.72 × 100 = 272 and 0.08 × 100 = 8, so the calculation becomes **272 ÷ 8.**

$8\overline{)2{}^{2}7\,{}^{3}2} = 034$ so 2.72 ÷ 0.08 = **34 pieces**

Page 25 Exam-Style Questions

1 –4° – 7° = **–11°** *[1 mark]*

2 12.0 + 1.3 = **13.3**

13.30 + 0.25 = **13.55**

So 12 + 1.3 + 0.25 = **13.55** *[1 mark]*

3 a) 539 × 14 = 539 × 28 ÷ 2
= 15 092 ÷ 2 = **7546** *[1 mark]*

b) 539 × 10 = 5390 and 28 ÷ 100 = 0.28
So 5390 × 0.28 = 539 × 28 × 10 ÷ 100
= 15 092 ÷ 10
= **1509.2** *[1 mark]*

c) Rearrange the equation given:
15 092 ÷ 539 = 28. *[1 mark]*
15 092 × 100 = 1 509 200
and 539 ÷ 10 = 53.9

So 1 509 200 ÷ 53.9
= (15 092 × 100) ÷ (539 ÷ 10)
= 15 092 ÷ 539 × 100 × 10
= 28 × 1000 = **28 000** *[1 mark]*

Careful here — dividing by (539 ÷ 10) is the same as dividing by 539 and then multiplying by 10.

4 E.g. She has performed the addition before the multiplication, to get 5 + 3 × 4 = 8 × 4 = 32, which doesn't follow the rules of BODMAS. *[1 mark]*
She should have done the multiplication first, to get the correct answer of 5 + 3 × 4 = 5 + 12 = **17.** *[1 mark]*

5 $9\overline{)3{}^{3}5.{}^{8}5\,{}^{4}5} = 03.95$ so one book costs £35.55 ÷ 9 = £3.95 *[1 mark]*

395 × 7 = $2\,7_{2}6_{6}5_{3}$ so 7 books cost £3.95 × 7 = **£27.65** *[1 mark]*

6 a) 3 × (2 – 4) ÷ 2 = –3 *[1 mark]*

b) (8 + 6 ÷ 5) × 10 = 92 *[1 mark]*

Section 2 — Approximations

2.1 Rounding — Whole Numbers

Page 27 Exercise 1

1 The last digit is in the units place and the decider is the first number after the decimal point.
For 14.1 the decider is 1 so round down to 14.
For 14.9 the decider is 9 so round up to 15.
For 14.02 the decider is 0 so round down to 14.
Use the same method to round the remaining numbers. So the following numbers from the box all round to 14:
14.1, 14.02, 13.7, 14.09, 14.4999, 13.901

2 The last digit is in the units place and the decider is the first number after the decimal point.

a) The decider is 7 so round up to **10.**

b) The decider is 4 so round down to **8.**

c) The decider is 2 so round down to **12.**

d) The decider is 8 so round up to **40.**

3 The last digit is in the hundreds place and the decider is in the tens place.

a) The decider is 5 so round up to **200.**

b) The decider is 9 so round up to **600.**

c) The decider is 5 so round up to **700.**

d) The decider is 1 so round down to **4700.**

4 The last digit is in the thousands place and the decider is in the hundreds place.

a) The decider is 5 so round up to **3000.**

b) The decider is 5 so round up to **9000.**

c) The decider is 2 so round down to **7000.**

d) The decider is 5 so round up to **10 000.**

5 a) (i) The last digit is 8 and the decider is 2 so round down to **18.**

(ii) The last digit is 1 and the decider is 8 so round up to **20.**

b) (i) The last digit is 6 and the decider is 4 so round down to **16**

(ii) The last digit is 1 and the decider is 6 so round up to **20**

Using the same method for c)-d):

c) (i) **202** (ii) **200**

d) (i) **1** (ii) **0**

6 The last digit is 1 and the decider is 2, so round down to **301 000 km²**.

7 The last (millions) digit is 0 for 39<u>0</u> 682 810. The decider is 6, so round up to **391 000 000 miles**.

2.2 Rounding — Decimal Places

Page 29 Exercise 1

1 The last digit is in the first d.p. and the decider is in the second d.p.
For 0.41, the decider is 1 so round down to 0.4.
For 0.45, the decider is 5 so round up to 0.5.
For 0.347, the decider is 4 so round down to 0.3.
Use the same method to round the remaining numbers. The following numbers from the box all round to 0.4:
0.41, 0.405, 0.35, 0.4295, 0.4124

2 The last digit is in the first d.p. and the decider is in the second d.p.
a) The decider is 3 so round down to **0.2**.
b) The decider is 7 so round up to **0.7**.
c) The decider is 8 so round up to **2.7**.
d) The decider is 3 so round down to **0.9**.

3 The last digit is in the second d.p. and the decider is in the third d.p.
a) The decider is 7 so round up to **4.57**.
b) The decider is 2 so round down to **0.04**.
c) The decider is 7 so round up to **6.30**.
The answer is 6.30 not 6.3 as you're rounding to 2 d.p.
d) The decider is 2 so round down to **0.35**.

4 The last digit is in the third d.p. and the decider is in the fourth d.p.
a) The decider is 3 so round down to **0.967**.
b) The decider is 7 so round up to **0.255**.
c) The decider is 5 so round up to **2.437**.
d) The decider is 5 so round up to **6.533**.

5 a) The last digit is 9 and the decider is 7, so round up to **0.20**.
b) The last digit is 6 and the decider is 8, so round up to **0.7**.
c) The last digit is 1 and the decider is 7, so round up to **5.732**.
d) The last digit is 0 and the decider is 6, so round up to **0.001**.

6 The last digit is 3 and the decider is 8 so round up to **0.04 kg**.
Remember to give the units in your answer — here it's 'kg'.

7 10 cm = 0.1 m so the last digit is in the first d.p. Suppose Usain's exact height was 1.76 m. The last digit is 7 and the decider is 6 so his height would round up to 1.8 m to the nearest 10 cm. So **no**, his exact height could not be 1.76 m.

2.3 Rounding — Significant Figures

Page 31 Exercise 1

1 a) (i) The last digit is the first s.f., which is 7. The decider is 0 so round down to **7000**.
(ii) The last digit is the second s.f., which is 0.
The decider is 3 so round down to **7000**.
(iii) The last digit is the third s.f., which is 3. The decider is 6 so round up to **7040**.
b) (i) The last digit is the first s.f., which is 6. The decider is 5 so round up to **7000**.
(ii) The last digit is the second s.f., which is 5.
The decider is 5 so round up to **6600**.
(iii) The last digit is the third s.f., which is 5. The decider is 1 so round down to **6550**.
Use the same method for c)-d):
c) (i) **7000** (ii) **7100** (iii) **7070**
d) (i) **3000** (ii) **2600** (iii) **2650**

2 a) The last digit is 4 and the decider is 5, so round up to **50**.
b) The last digit is 8 and the decider is 9, so round up to **5690**.
c) The last digit is 9 and the decider is 7, so round up to **6.50**.
Use the same method for d)-i):
d) **360** e) **6500** f) **757 000**
g) **46.7** h) **380** i) **79 000**

3 The last digit is 2 and the decider is 3, so round down to **1200 km/h**.

Page 31 Exercise 2

1 a) (i) The last digit is the first s.f., which is 3. The decider is 7 so round up to **0.004**.
(ii) The last digit is the second s.f., which is 7. The decider is 5 so round up to **0.0038**.
(iii) The last digit is the third s.f., which is 5. The decider is 3 so round down to **0.00375**.
b) (i) The last digit is the first s.f., which is 2. The decider is 6 so round up to **0.03**.
(ii) The last digit is the second s.f., which is 6. The decider is 4 so round down to **0.026**.
(iii) The last digit is the third s.f., which is 4. The decider is 4 so round down to **0.0264**.
Use the same method for c)-f):
c) (i) **0.0002** (ii) **0.00018**
(iii) **0.000179**
d) (i) **0.04** (ii) **0.040**
(iii) **0.0397**
e) (i) **0.6** (ii) **0.56**
(iii) **0.564**
f) (i) **0.0007** (ii) **0.00070**
(iii) **0.000705**

2 a) The decider is 5 so round up to **0.005**.
b) The decider is 6 so round up to **0.20**.
c) The decider is 6 so round up to **0.00439**.
Use the same method for d)-f):
d) **0.006** e) **0.0096** f) **0.000604**

3 The last digit is 8 and the decider is 9, so round up to **0.09 kg/m³**.

2.4 Estimating Answers

Page 33 Exercise 1

1 a) 437 + 175 ≈ 400 + 200 = **600**
b) 310 + 876 ≈ 300 + 900 = **1200**
c) 784 – 279 ≈ 800 – 300 = **500**
Using the same method for d)-f):
d) **0.2** e) **900** f) **700**

2 a) (i) 23 + 43 ≈ 20 + 40 = **60**
(ii) Both numbers were rounded down so it will be an **underestimate**.
b) (i) 59 × 5.7 ≈ 60 × 6 = **360**
(ii) Both numbers were rounded up so it will be an **overestimate**.
Using the same method for c)-f):
c) (i) **45** (ii) **Underestimate**
d) (i) **1600** (ii) **Overestimate**
e) (i) **320** (ii) **Overestimate**
f) (i) **5400** (ii) **Overestimate**

3 a) 1.76 × 6.3 ≈ 2 × 6 = 12.
So correct answer is **C**.
b) 582 × 2.1 ≈ 600 × 2 = 1200.
So correct answer is **B**.
c) $\frac{57.5 \times 3.78}{16.1} \approx \frac{60 \times 4}{20} = \frac{240}{20} = 12.$
So correct answer is **C**.

4 a) (i) $\frac{8.9}{3.1} \approx \frac{9}{3} = \mathbf{3}$
(ii) First number was rounded up and the second number was rounded down so it will be an **overestimate**.
b) (i) 33 – 17 ≈ 30 – 20 = **10**
(ii) First number was rounded down and the second number was rounded up so it will be an **underestimate**.
Using the same method for c)-f):
c) (i) **2** (ii) **Underestimate**
d) (i) **35** (ii) **Overestimate**
e) (i) **30** (ii) **Underestimate**
f) (i) **5** (ii) **Overestimate**

5 a) $\frac{68.8 + 27.3}{23.7} \approx \frac{70 + 30}{20} = \frac{100}{20} = \mathbf{5}$
b) $\frac{5.6 \times 9.68}{5.14} \approx \frac{6 \times 10}{5} = \frac{60}{5} = \mathbf{12}$
c) $\frac{\sqrt{38.6 + 56.3}}{1.678} \approx \frac{\sqrt{40 + 60}}{2} = \frac{\sqrt{100}}{2} = \mathbf{5}$

6 a) 18.5 × 3.2 ≈ 20 × 3 = 60, so actual answer is **59.2**.
b) $\frac{325.26}{5.2} \approx \frac{300}{5} = 60$, so actual answer is **62.55**.
c) $\frac{19.8 \times 27.4}{3.3} \approx \frac{20 \times 30}{3} = 200$, so actual answer is **164.4**.
d) $\frac{\sqrt{48.4 \times 8.1}}{4.8} \approx \frac{\sqrt{50 \times 8}}{5} = \frac{\sqrt{400}}{5} = 4$, so actual answer is **4.125**.

7 £4.70 × 21 ≈ £5 × 20 = **£100**

8 a) 62 × 324 × 14 ≈ 60 × 300 × 10 = **180 000 strawberries**
b) All numbers were rounded down so it will be an **underestimate**.

Page 34 Exercise 2

1 a) (i) **30283.518**
(ii) 112.62 × 268.9 ≈ 100 × 300 = **30 000**
b) (i) **142.12**
(ii) $\frac{52.668 \times \sqrt{104.04}}{3.78} \approx \frac{50 \times \sqrt{100}}{4} = \frac{500}{4}$ = **125**
c) (i) **123.5925705**
(ii) $5.39^2 \times \sqrt[3]{1012} \div 2.36$
$\approx 5^2 \times \sqrt[3]{1000} \div 2$
= 25 × 10 ÷ 2 = **125**

2 a) $56.2 \times 34.7 \approx 60 \times 30 =$ **1800**

b) **Yes**, as Sam's answer is approximately 10 times bigger than the estimate.

3 $987 \times £27.85 \approx 1000 \times £30 = £30\,000$
Both values have been rounded up, so the approximation is an overestimate. So the company must be wrong as their figure is even higher.

4 $£6.85 \times 42 \approx 7 \times 40 = £280$, so it looks like Karen has been paid correctly.

2.5 Rounding Errors

Page 35 Exercise 1

1 a) Rounding unit is 1 and half the rounding unit is 0.5.
Maximum value is 80 + 0.5 = **80.5**
Minimum value is 80 – 0.5 = **79.5**

b) Rounding unit is 100 and half the rounding unit is 50.
Maximum value is 400 + 50 = **450**
Minimum value is 400 – 50 = **350**

2 a) Rounding unit is 10 and half the rounding unit is 5.
Maximum value is 60 + 5 = 65
Minimum value is 60 – 5 = 55
So error interval is $\mathbf{55 \le a < 65}$
Remember: the actual value is greater than or equal to the minimum value, but strictly less than the maximum value.

b) Rounding unit is 1 and half the rounding unit is 0.5.
Maximum value is 9 + 0.5 = 9.5
Minimum value is 9 – 0.5 = 8.5
So error interval is $\mathbf{8.5 \le b < 9.5}$

c) Rounding unit is 100 and half the rounding unit is 50.
Maximum value is 500 + 50 = 550
Minimum value is 500 – 50 = 450
So error interval is $\mathbf{450 \le c < 550}$

d) Rounding unit is 1000 and half the rounding unit is 500.
Maximum value is 15 000 + 500 = 15 500
Minimum value is 15 000 – 500 = 14 500
So error interval is $\mathbf{14\,500 \le d < 15\,500}$

3 a) Rounding unit is 0.1 and half the rounding unit is 0.05.
Maximum value is 7.6 + 0.05 = 7.65
Minimum value is 7.6 – 0.05 = 7.55
So error interval is $\mathbf{7.55 \le a < 7.65}$

b) Rounding unit is 0.1 and half the rounding unit is 0.05.
Maximum value is 0.3 + 0.05 = 0.35
Minimum value is 0.3 – 0.05 = 0.25
So error interval is $\mathbf{0.25 \le b < 0.35}$

c) Rounding unit is 0.01 and half the rounding unit is 0.005.
Maximum value is 2.55 + 0.005 = 2.555
Minimum value is 2.55 – 0.005 = 2.545
So error interval is $\mathbf{2.545 \le c < 2.555}$

Using the same method for d)-f):

d) $\mathbf{45 \le d < 55}$

e) $\mathbf{109.85 \le e < 109.95}$

f) $\mathbf{535 \le f < 545}$

4 The rounding unit is 1 and half the rounding unit is 0.5.
Maximum length is 76 + 0.5 = 76.5
Minimum length is 76 – 0.5 = 75.5.
So the error interval is $\mathbf{75.5\ cm \le l < 76.5\ cm}$.

5 1 km = 1000 m so 100 m = 0.1 km.
The rounding unit is 0.1 and half the rounding unit is 0.05.
Maximum distance is 10 km + 0.05 = 10.05 km
Minimum distance is 10 km – 0.05 = 9.95 km
So the error interval is
$\mathbf{9.95\ km \le d < 10.05\ km}$.

6 The rounding unit is 10 and half the rounding unit is 5.
Maximum number of sweets is 670 + 5 = 675.
But this would round up to 680, so maximum number of sweets is **674**.
The maximum number of sweets in the jar is 674.999999..., but the number of sweets must be a whole number, so the answer is 674.

Page 36 Exercise 2

1 a) To truncate 1.354 to 1 d.p. delete all the digits after the first decimal place.
So it's **1.3**.

Use the same method for b)-c):

b) **19.13** c) **103.671**

2 a) The rounding unit is 0.1.
So the error interval is $\mathbf{1.3 \le x < 1.4}$

b) The rounding unit is 0.01.
So the error interval is $\mathbf{5.13 \le y < 5.14}$

c) The rounding unit is 0.001.
So the error interval is $\mathbf{7.731 \le z < 7.732}$
Remember — the actual value of a truncated number can be up to a whole rounding unit bigger, but no smaller.

Page 37 Review Exercise

1 a) (i) The decider is 4, so round down to **6720**.

(ii) The decider is 2, so round down to **6700**.

(iii) The decider is 7, so round up to **7000**.

b) (i) The decider is 1, so round down to **25 360**.

(ii) The decider is 6, so round up to **25 400**.

(iii) The decider is 3, so round down to **25 000**.

Use the same method for c)-d):

c) (i) **8500** (ii) **8500** (iii) **8000**

d) (i) **3820** (ii) **3800** (iii) **4000**

2 a) (i) The last digit is 6 and the decider is 8 so round up to **2.7**.

(ii) The last digit is 8 and the decider is 9, so round up to **2.69**.

(iii) The last digit is 9 and the decider is 3, so round down to **2.689**.

b) (i) The last digit is 3 and the decider is 2, so round down to **0.3**.

(ii) The last digit is 2 and the decider is 4, so round down to **0.32**.

(iii) The last digit is 4 and the decider is 9, so round up to **0.325**.

Use the same method for c)-d):

c) (i) **5.6** (ii) **5.60** (iii) **5.602**

d) (i) **0.1** (ii) **0.05** (iii) **0.053**

3 a) The decider is 5, so round up to **5000**.

b) The decider is 8, so round up to **57 000**.

c) The decider is 9, so round up to **6.8**.

d) The decider is 6, so round up to **400**.

e) The decider is 2, so round down to **6500**.

f) The decider is 5, so round up to **757 000**.

4 £1.35 + £8.52 + £14.09 + £17.93
≈ £1 + £9 + £14 + £18 = **£42**.

5 a) $\frac{64.4 \times 5.6}{17 \times 9.5} \approx \frac{60 \times 6}{20 \times 10} = \frac{360}{200} = \mathbf{1.8}$

b) $\frac{310.33 \times 2.68}{316.39 \times 0.82} \approx \frac{300 \times 3}{300 \times 1} = \frac{900}{300} = \mathbf{3}$

c) $\frac{13.7 \times 5.2}{12.3 \div 3.9} \approx \frac{10 \times 5}{10 \div 4} = \frac{50}{2.5} = \mathbf{20}$

6 a) Round each number to 1 s.f. to estimate.
32p × 14 ≈ 30p × 10 = 300p = **£3**.

b) Both numbers have been rounded down, so it's an **underestimate**.

7 a) Use a calculator to find $24.37 \div \sqrt{3.9} =$ **12.3402...**

b) $24.37 \div \sqrt{3.9} \approx 20 \div \sqrt{4} = 20 \div 2 = 10$.
Yes, the answer to a) is sensible.

8 a) The rounding unit is 10, so half the rounding unit is 5.
Maximum value is 50 + 5 = 55
Minimum value is 50 – 5 = 45
So the error interval is $\mathbf{45 \le a < 55}$

b) The rounding unit is 10, so half the rounding unit is 5.
Maximum value is 5690 + 5 = 5695
Minimum value is 5690 – 5 = 5685
So the error interval is $\mathbf{5685 \le b < 5695}$

c) The rounding unit is 1, so half the rounding unit is 0.5.
Maximum value is 7 + 0.5 = 7.5
Minimum value is 7 – 0.5 = 6.5
So the error interval is $\mathbf{6.5 \le c < 7.5}$

Use the same method for d)-f):

d) $\mathbf{355 \le d < 365}$

e) $\mathbf{6450 \le e < 6550}$

f) $\mathbf{756\,500 \le f < 757\,500}$

9 For all parts, the rounding unit is 0.01. The actual value can be a whole rounding unit bigger than the truncated number, but no smaller.

a) $\mathbf{6.57 \le s < 6.58}$

b) $\mathbf{25.71 \le t < 25.72}$

c) $\mathbf{13.29 \le w < 13.30}$

Page 38 Exam-Style Questions

1 The last digit is 7 and the decider is 6, so round up to **45.8** *[1 mark]*.

2 a) $\frac{3.5^4}{\sqrt{0.007}} = \frac{150.0625}{0.08366...}$ *[1 mark]*
$=$ **1793.589932** *[1 mark]*
Your answer may be different depending on how many digits your calculator can display.

b) (i) The decider is 9, so round up to **1793.590** *[1 mark]*
The final '0' is required to earn the mark.

(ii) The decider is 3, so round down to **1790** *[1 mark]*

3 a) $\frac{628}{\sqrt{97} + 9.6} \approx \frac{600}{\sqrt{100} + 10} = \frac{600}{10 + 10} = \frac{600}{20}$
$=$ **30**
[2 marks available — 1 mark for correctly rounding all numbers to 1 s.f., 1 mark for correct answer]

b) The calculation is a division where the numerator has been rounded down and the denominator has been rounded up, so it's an **underestimate**. *[1 mark]*
Both numbers in the denominator (97 and 9.6) have been rounded up, so overall their sum has also been rounded up.

4 The rounding unit is 100 and half the rounding unit is 50.
Maximum value is 7300 + 50 = 7350
Minimum value is 7300 – 50 = 7250
So the error interval is **$7250 \le r < 7350$**.
[2 marks available — 1 mark for correct numbers, and 1 mark for correct inequality signs].

5 a) The rounding unit is 1 and half the rounding unit is 0.5.
Maximum value is 8 + 0.5 = 8.5
Minimum value is 8 – 0.5 = 7.5
So the error interval is **7.5 kg $\le r <$ 8.5 kg**
[2 marks available — 1 mark for correct numbers, and 1 mark for correct inequality signs]

b) If the dogs weigh 7.5 kg and 5.5 kg, then their weight would round to 8 kg and 6 kg to the nearest kg.
But the total would be 7.5 kg + 5.5 kg = 13 kg, which is less than 14 kg.
[2 marks available — 1 mark for each weight rounded correctly, 1 mark for showing sum of the weights is less than 14 kg.]

Section 3 — Powers and Roots

3.1 Squares, Cubes and Roots

Page 40 Exercise 1

1 a) $6^2 = 6 \times 6 =$ **36**
Using the same method for b)-d):
b) **144** c) **225** d) **400**
e) $(-4)^2 = -4 \times -4 =$ **16**
Using the same method for f)-h):
f) **0.09** g) **0.36** h) **0.04**

2 a) $3^3 = 3 \times 3 \times 3 =$ **27**
This is one of the standard cubes that is worth remembering.
Using the same method for b)-d):
b) **216** c) **1331** d) **8000**
e) $(-3)^3 = -3 \times -3 \times -3 =$ **–27**
Using the same method for f)-h):
f) **–1000** g) **0.064** h) **–0.125**

Page 40 Exercise 2

1 a) **1, –1** b) **2, –2** c) **3, –3** d) **4, –4**
e) **5, –5** f) **6, –6** g) **8, –8** h) **10, –10**

2 a) **7** b) **–7** c) **9** d) **–9**
e) **11** f) **13** g) **–12** h) **20**

3 a) **8, –8** b) **11, –11** c) **100, –100**
d) **14, –14**

4 a) $\sqrt{9} + \sqrt{16} = 3 + 4 =$ **7**
b) $\sqrt{25} - \sqrt{4} = 5 - 2 =$ **3**
c) $\sqrt{100} - \sqrt{49} = 10 - 7 =$ **3**

Page 41 Exercise 3

1

x	1	8	27	1000	–1	–8	–27	–1000
$\sqrt[3]{x}$	**1**	**2**	**3**	**10**	**–1**	**–2**	**–3**	**–10**

2 a) **4** b) **5** c) **11** d) **–4**
e) **–5** f) **8** g) **6** h) **–9**

3 a) $\sqrt[3]{15-7} = \sqrt[3]{8} =$ **2**
b) $\sqrt[3]{(39+5^2)} = \sqrt[3]{39+25} = \sqrt[3]{64} =$ **4**
c) $\sqrt[3]{4^2-43} = \sqrt[3]{16-43} = \sqrt[3]{-27} =$ **–3**

3.2 Indices

Page 42 Exercise 1

1 a) $\mathbf{3^2}$ b) $\mathbf{2^3}$ c) $\mathbf{7^5}$
d) $\mathbf{9^6}$ e) $\mathbf{12^4}$ f) $\mathbf{17^3}$

2 a) (i) **100 000** (ii) **10 000 000**
(iii) **100 000 000** (iv) **1 000 000 000**
b) (i) 10^{15} can be written as a '1' followed by **15** zeros.
(ii) 10^n can be written as a '1' followed by n zeros.
The rule in part (ii) is a key one to remember — it makes it really easy to work out powers of 10.

3 a) $\mathbf{10^2}$ b) $\mathbf{10^3}$ c) $\mathbf{10^4}$ d) $\mathbf{10^6}$

4 a) **16** b) **32** c) **81** d) **4096**
e) **1296** f) **4913** g) **3125** h) **243**

5 a) $3^4 + 2^3 = 81 + 8 =$ **89**
b) $2^6 + 3^5 = 64 + 243 =$ **307**
c) $3^7 - 4^2 = 2187 - 16 =$ **2171**
d) $10^3 - 6^4 = 1000 - 1296 =$ **–296**

6 a) $8^7 \div 4^6 = 2\,097\,152 \div 4096 =$ **512**
b) $10^4 \times 10^3 = 10\,000 \times 1000 =$ **10 000 000**
c) $2^4 \times 2^2 = 16 \times 4 =$ **64**
d) $3^4 \div 5^4 = 81 \div 625 =$ **0.1296**

7 a) $(5-2)^3 = 3^3 =$ **27**
b) $(2^2)^2 = 4^2 =$ **16**
c) $(3^2)^2 = 9^2 =$ **81**
d) $(8-5)^4 = 3^4 =$ **81**
e) $(7+3)^5 = 10^5 =$ **100 000**
f) $6^4 - 7^2 = 1296 - 49 =$ **1247**
g) $2 + 10^4 = 2 + 10\,000 =$ **10 002**
h) $(150-50)^6 = 100^6 =$ **1 000 000 000 000**

Page 43 Exercise 2

1 a) $\mathbf{h^4}$ b) $\mathbf{t^5}$ c) $\mathbf{s^7}$

2 a) $\mathbf{a^2b^3}$ b) $\mathbf{k^4f^3}$ c) $\mathbf{m^4n^2}$
d) $\mathbf{s^4t}$ e) $\mathbf{w^3v^3}$ f) $\mathbf{p^2q^5}$

3 a) $2^2 \times 5^2 = 4 \times 25 =$ **100**
b) $2^3 \times 5^2 = 8 \times 25 =$ **200**
c) $2^2 \times 5^3 = 4 \times 125 =$ **500**
d) $2^5 \times 5^2 = 32 \times 25 =$ **800**
e) $2^4 \times 5^3 = 16 \times 125 =$ **2000**
f) $2^4 \times 5^4 = 16 \times 625 =$ **10 000**

3.3 Laws of Indices

Page 44 Exercise 1

1 a) $3^2 \times 3^6 = 3^{2+6} = \mathbf{3^8}$
b) $10^7 \times 10^3 = 10^{7+3} = \mathbf{10^{10}}$
c) $4^7 \times 4^4 = 4^{7+4} = \mathbf{4^{11}}$
d) $7 \times 7^6 = 7^{1+6} = \mathbf{7^7}$

2 a) $6^7 \div 6^4 = 6^{7-4} = \mathbf{6^3}$
b) $8^6 \div 8^3 = 8^{6-3} = \mathbf{8^3}$
c) $5^7 \div 5^2 = 5^{7-2} = \mathbf{5^5}$
d) $6^8 \div 6^6 = 6^{8-6} = \mathbf{6^2}$

3 a) $(4^3)^3 = 4^{3\times3} = \mathbf{4^9}$
b) $(11^2)^5 = 11^{2\times5} = \mathbf{11^{10}}$
c) $(100^3)^{23} = 100^{3\times23} = \mathbf{100^{69}}$
d) $\frac{2^8}{2^5} = 2^8 \div 2^5 = \mathbf{2^3}$
e) $\left(\frac{2^7}{5}\right)^3 = \mathbf{\frac{2^{21}}{5^3}}$
f) $\left(\frac{4^6}{4^3}\right)^2 = (4^{6-3})^2 = (4^3)^2 = \mathbf{4^6}$

4 a) $4^5 \times 4^{11} = 4^{5+11} = \mathbf{4^{16}}$
b) $12^7 \div 12^3 = 12^{7-3} = \mathbf{12^4}$
c) $8^2 \times 8^9 = 8^{2+9} = \mathbf{8^{11}}$
d) $(6^8)^4 = 6^{8\times4} = \mathbf{6^{32}}$
e) $(3^{12})^4 = 3^{12\times4} = \mathbf{3^{48}}$
f) $7^{11} \div 7^6 = 7^{11-6} = \mathbf{7^5}$
g) $4^{15} \div 4^7 = 4^{15-7} = \mathbf{4^8}$
h) $(11^0)^9 = 11^{0\times9} = 11^0 =$ **1**
For this final part you could also write $(11^0)^9 = (1)^9 = 1$.

5 a) 9 + ■ = 14 ⇒ ■ = **5**
b) 5 – ■ = 3 ⇒ ■ = **2**
c) 7 + ■ = 13 ⇒ ■ = **6**
d) 7 × ■ = 49 ⇒ ■ = **7**
e) ■ – 5 = 0 ⇒ ■ = **5**
f) ■ + 7 = 15 ⇒ ■ = **8**
g) 5 – (–4) = 9 ⇒ ■ = **9**
h) 5 × ■ = 25 ⇒ ■ = **5**

Page 45 Exercise 2

1 a) $8^{-2} = \frac{1}{8^2} = \mathbf{\frac{1}{64}}$
b) $2^{-3} = \frac{1}{2^3} = \mathbf{\frac{1}{8}}$
c) $5^{-2} = \frac{1}{5^2} = \mathbf{\frac{1}{25}}$
d) $3^{-3} = \frac{1}{3^3} = \mathbf{\frac{1}{27}}$
e) $2^{-4} = \frac{1}{2^4} = \mathbf{\frac{1}{16}}$
f) $\left(\frac{1}{9}\right)^{-2} = \left(\frac{9}{1}\right)^2 = 9^2 =$ **81**
g) $\left(\frac{4}{5}\right)^{-2} = \left(\frac{5}{4}\right)^2 = \frac{5^2}{4^2} = \mathbf{\frac{25}{16}}$
h) $\left(\frac{2}{6}\right)^{-3} = \left(\frac{6}{2}\right)^3 = 3^3 =$ **27**

2 a) $j^{-13} \div j^7 = j^{-13-7} = \mathbf{j^{-20}}$
b) $(n^7)^{-3} = n^{7\times-3} = \mathbf{n^{-21}}$
c) $p^{-8} \times p^{-6} = p^{-8+(-6)} = \mathbf{p^{-14}}$
d) $y^8 \div y^{-2} = y^{8-(-2)} = \mathbf{y^{10}}$
e) $(k^{-3})^6 = k^{-3\times6} = \mathbf{k^{-18}}$
f) $\frac{b^5}{b^9} = b^{5-9} = \mathbf{b^{-4}}$
g) $d^{-7} \times d^2 = d^{-7+2} = \mathbf{d^{-5}}$
h) $\frac{x^{60}}{x^{-8}} = x^{60} \div x^{-8} = x^{60-(-8)} = \mathbf{x^{68}}$

3 a) ■ + (–8) = 3 ⇒ ■ = **11**
b) ■ – 7 = –10 ⇒ ■ = **–3**
c) –15 + ■ = 8 ⇒ ■ = **23**
d) –4 × ■ = 16 ⇒ ■ = **–4**

Page 46 Exercise 3

1 a) $3^2 \times 3^5 \times 3^7 = 3^{2+5+7} = \mathbf{3^{14}}$
b) $(8^6)^2 \times 8^5 = 8^{6\times2+5} = 8^{12+5} = \mathbf{8^{17}}$
c) $(12^8 \div 12^4)^3 = 12^{(8-4)\times3} = 12^{4\times3} = \mathbf{12^{12}}$
d) $(4^3)^6 \div 4^{16} = 4^{3\times6-16} = 4^{18-16} = \mathbf{4^2}$
Remember to read the question carefully to see if it wants the answers in index form.

2 a) $\frac{3^4 \times 3^5}{3^6} = \frac{3^9}{3^6} = 3^{9-6} = \mathbf{3^3}$
b) $\frac{8^{25} \div 8^2}{8^6 \times 8^{10}} = \frac{8^{25-2}}{8^{6+10}} = \frac{8^{23}}{8^{16}} = 8^{23-16} = \mathbf{8^{17}}$
c) $\frac{(7^5)^7 \div 7^{12}}{7^5 \times 7^9} = \frac{7^{5\times7} \div 7^{12}}{7^{5+9}} = \frac{7^{35-12}}{7^{14}} = \frac{7^{23}}{7^{14}}$
$= 7^{23-14} = \mathbf{7^9}$
d) $\frac{(5^{10} \div 5^8)^4}{5^4 \div 5^2} = \frac{(5^{10-8})^4}{5^{4-2}} = \frac{5^{2\times4}}{5^2} = 5^{8-2} = \mathbf{5^6}$

3 $\frac{4^4 \div 4^3}{4} = \frac{4^{4-3}}{4} = \frac{4}{4} = \mathbf{1}$

$\frac{7^{16}}{7^8 \times 7^2} = \frac{7^{16}}{7^{8+2}} = \frac{7^{16}}{7^{10}} = 7^6 \neq 1$

$\frac{3^8 - 3^7}{3} = 3^7 - 3^6 \neq 1$

$\frac{5^5 \times 5^9}{(5^2)^7} = \frac{5^{5+9}}{5^{2\times7}} = \frac{5^{14}}{5^{14}} = \mathbf{1}$

$\frac{(9^2)^2 - 9^0}{9^3} = \frac{(9^2)^2 - 9^0}{9^3} = \frac{9^4 - 1}{9^3} = 9 - 9^{-3} \neq 1$

So $\mathbf{\frac{4^4 \div 4^3}{4}}$ and $\mathbf{\frac{5^5 \times 5^9}{(5^2)^7}}$ are equal to 1.

4 a) $\left(\frac{2^{-5} \times 2^7}{2^3}\right)^5 = \left(\frac{2^{-5+7}}{2^3}\right)^5 = \left(\frac{2^2}{2^3}\right)^5 = (2^{-1})^5$
$= 2^{-1\times5} = \mathbf{2^{-5}}$

b) $\left(\frac{7^3}{7}\right)^3 \times 7^{-2} = (7^2)^3 \times 7^{-2} = 7^6 \times 7^{-2} = \mathbf{7^4}$

c) $\frac{9^{-3} \times 9^{15}}{(9^{-3})^{-2}} = \frac{9^{12}}{9^6} = \mathbf{9^6}$

d) $\left(\frac{3^{-8} \times 3^{12}}{3^2}\right)^{-6} = \left(\frac{3^4}{3^2}\right)^{-6} = (3^2)^{-6} = \mathbf{3^{-12}}$

5 a) $a^6 \times a^5 \div a^4 = a^{6+5-4} = \mathbf{a^7}$

b) $(p^5 \div p^3)^6 = (p^{5-3})^6 = (p^2)^6 = \mathbf{p^{12}}$

c) $\frac{(t^6 \div t^3)^4}{t^9 \div t^4} = \frac{(t^{6-3})^4}{t^{9-4}} = \frac{(t^3)^4}{t^5} = \frac{t^{12}}{t^5} = \mathbf{t^7}$

d) $\frac{(c^{-4})^3}{c^{-8} \div c^4} = \frac{c^{-12}}{c^{-8-4}} = \frac{c^{-12}}{c^{-12}} = c^0 = \mathbf{1}$

3.4 Standard Form

Page 47 Exercise 1

1 a) $\mathbf{2.5 \times 10^2}$ b) $\mathbf{7.34 \times 10^3}$
c) $\mathbf{4.8 \times 10^4}$ d) $\mathbf{5.9 \times 10^6}$

2 a) $\mathbf{3.75 \times 10^{-1}}$ b) $\mathbf{6.7 \times 10^{-3}}$
c) $\mathbf{7.8 \times 10^{-5}}$ d) $\mathbf{7.07 \times 10^{-2}}$

Page 48 Exercise 2

1 a) **3 000 000** b) **94 000**
c) **198 900 000** d) **7.2**
e) **0.00000356** f) **0.0423**
g) **0.0000888** h) **0.000000019**

Page 49 Exercise 3

1 a) $(3 \times 10^7) \times (2 \times 10^4)$
$= (3 \times 2) \times (10^7 \times 10^4)$
$= 6 \times 10^{7+4} = \mathbf{6 \times 10^{11}}$

b) $(4 \times 10^9) \times (2 \times 10^{-4})$
$= (4 \times 2) \times (10^9 \times 10^{-4})$
$= 8 \times 10^{9-4} = \mathbf{8 \times 10^5}$

c) $(6 \times 10^5) \times (1.4 \times 10^2)$
$= (6 \times 1.4) \times (10^5 \times 10^2)$
$= 8.4 \times 10^{5+2} = \mathbf{8.4 \times 10^7}$

2 a) $(9 \times 10^6) \div (3 \times 10^4)$
$= \frac{9 \times 10^6}{3 \times 10^4} = \frac{9}{3} \times \frac{10^6}{10^4} = 3 \times 10^{6-4} = \mathbf{3 \times 10^2}$

b) $(1.8 \times 10^{-4}) \div (0.9 \times 10^8)$
$= \frac{1.8 \times 10^{-4}}{0.9 \times 10^8} = \frac{1.8}{0.9} \times \frac{10^{-4}}{10^8} = 2 \times 10^{-4-8}$
$= \mathbf{2 \times 10^{-12}}$

c) $(8.1 \times 10^{-1}) \div (9 \times 10^{-3})$
$= \frac{8.1 \times 10^{-1}}{9 \times 10^{-3}} = \frac{8.1}{9} \times \frac{10^{-1}}{10^{-3}} = 0.9 \times 10^{-1-(-3)}$
$= 0.9 \times 10^2$
$= 9 \times 10^{-1} \times 10^2 = \mathbf{9 \times 10^1}$

Make sure your final answer is actually in standard form, with the front number between 1 and 10, otherwise you will lose marks.

Page 49 Exercise 4

1 a) $(5 \times 10^3) + (3 \times 10^3)$
$= (5 + 3) \times 10^3 = \mathbf{8 \times 10^3}$

b) $(6.4 \times 10^2) + (3.2 \times 10^2)$
$= (6.4 + 3.2) \times 10^2 = \mathbf{9.6 \times 10^2}$

c) $(6.9 \times 10^{-4}) + (3.8 \times 10^{-4})$
$= (6.9 + 3.8) \times 10^{-4}$
$= 10.7 \times 10^{-4}$
$= 1.7 \times 10 \times 10^{-4} = \mathbf{1.7 \times 10^{-3}}$

2 a) $(4.5 \times 10^{-2}) - (3.3 \times 10^{-2})$
$= (4.5 - 3.3) \times 10^{-2} = \mathbf{1.2 \times 10^{-2}}$

b) $(1.8 \times 10^4) - (1.2 \times 10^4)$
$= (1.8 - 1.2) \times 10^4$
$= 0.6 \times 10^4$
$= 6 \times 10^{-1} \times 10^4 = \mathbf{6 \times 10^3}$

c) $(6.4 \times 10^2) - (6.3 \times 10^2)$
$= (6.4 - 6.3) \times 10^2$
$= 0.1 \times 10^2$
$= 1 \times 10^{-1} \times 10^2 = \mathbf{1 \times 10^1}$

Page 50 Review Exercise

1 a) $(-5)^3 = (-5 \times -5 \times -5) = \mathbf{-125}$
b) $(0.5)^3 = (0.5 \times 0.5 \times 0.5) = \mathbf{0.125}$
c) $(-0.3)^3 = (-0.3 \times -0.3 \times -0.3) = \mathbf{-0.027}$
d) $(-12)^3 = (-12 \times -12 \times -12) = \mathbf{-1728}$
e) $0.1^2 = 0.1 \times 0.1 = \mathbf{0.01}$
f) $(-0.4)^2 = -0.4 \times -0.4 = \mathbf{0.16}$
g) $((-2)^2)^3 = (-2 \times -2)^3 = 4^3 = \mathbf{64}$
h) $((-2)^3)^2 = (-2 \times -2 \times -2)^2 = (-8)^2 = \mathbf{64}$

2 a) $3^2 - 2^3 = 9 - 8 = \mathbf{1}$
b) $5^2 - 6^2 = 25 - 36 = \mathbf{-11}$
c) $3 \times 2^8 = 3 \times 256 = \mathbf{768}$
d) $8 \times 5^4 = 8 \times 625 = \mathbf{5000}$

3 a) **–6** b) **19** c) **–7**
d) $-\sqrt{10^2 - 19} = -\sqrt{100 - 19} = -\sqrt{81} = \mathbf{-9}$

4 a) $\mathbf{k^4 l^2}$ b) $\mathbf{zy^3}$ c) $\mathbf{m^3 n^2}$

5 a) $a^6 \times a^4 = a^{6+4} = \mathbf{a^{10}}$
b) $15^{12} \div 15^{-14} = 15^{12-(-14)} = \mathbf{15^{26}}$
c) $(45^2)^{-9} = 45^{2\times(-9)} = \mathbf{45^{-18}}$
d) $\frac{20^{222}}{20^{210}} = 20^{222-210} = \mathbf{20^{12}}$

6 a) $8^{-1} = \mathbf{\frac{1}{8}}$
b) $4^{-2} = \left(\frac{1}{4}\right)^2 = \frac{1}{4^2} = \mathbf{\frac{1}{16}}$
c) $\left(\frac{1}{3}\right)^{-3} = \left(\frac{3}{1}\right)^3 = 3^3 = \mathbf{27}$
d) $\left(\frac{4}{6}\right)^{-2} = \left(\frac{6}{4}\right)^2 = \left(\frac{3}{2}\right)^2 = \frac{3^2}{2^2} = \mathbf{\frac{9}{4}}$

When you're evaluating quantities with negative indices, it's often helpful to rewrite them using positive indices.

7 a) $\frac{4^4 \times 4^6}{4^8 \times 4} = \frac{4^{10}}{4^9} = \mathbf{4}$
b) $\frac{(5^5 \times 5^5)^2}{5^8 \div 5^3} = \frac{(5^{10})^2}{5^5} = \frac{5^{20}}{5^5} = \mathbf{5^{15}}$
c) $\left(\frac{2^5 \times 2^5}{2^3}\right)^4 = \left(\frac{2^{10}}{2^3}\right)^4 = (2^7)^4 = \mathbf{2^{28}}$

8 a) $\mathbf{3.3 \times 10^2}$ b) $\mathbf{2.75 \times 10^6}$
c) $\mathbf{2.5 \times 10^{-3}}$ d) $\mathbf{5.002 \times 10^{-4}}$

9 a) **400** b) **880 000**
c) **0.669** d) **0.00000705**

10 a) $(7 \times 10^5) \times (1.3 \times 10^2)$
$= (7 \times 1.3) \times (10^5 \times 10^2)$
$= (9.1) \times 10^{5+2} = \mathbf{9.1 \times 10^7}$

b) $(8.8 \times 10^3) \div (4 \times 10^8)$
$= \frac{8.8 \times 10^3}{4 \times 10^8} = \frac{8.8}{4} \times \frac{10^3}{10^8} = \mathbf{2.2 \times 10^{-5}}$

c) $(1.9 \times 10^6) + (9.1 \times 10^6)$
$= (1.9 + 9.1) \times 10^6$
$= 11 \times 10^6$
$= 1.1 \times 10 \times 10^6 = \mathbf{1.1 \times 10^7}$

d) $(5.9 \times 10^{-8}) - (3.4 \times 10^{-8})$
$= (5.9 - 3.4) \times 10^{-8} = \mathbf{2.5 \times 10^{-8}}$

Page 51 Exam-Style Questions

1 $(4.2 - 0.81)^2 + \sqrt{289} = 3.39^2 + 17 = \mathbf{28.4921}$
[1 mark]

2 a) $2x^3 \times 4x^4 = (2 \times 4) \times (x^3 \times x^4) = 8x^{3+4} = \mathbf{8x^7}$
[1 mark]
b) $(3y^2)^4 = 3^4 \times (y^2)^4 = 81y^{2\times4} = \mathbf{81y^8}$
[2 marks available – 1 mark for the 81 and one mark for the y^8]
c) $5z^0 = 5 \times 1 = \mathbf{5}$ *[1 mark]*

3 a) $4^3 = 64$ so $\mathbf{n = 3}$ *[1 mark]*
It's important to be able to recognise the first few cube numbers.
b) $2^2 \times 3^k \times 5 = 540$
$4 \times 3^k \times 5 = 540$
$20 \times 3^k = 540$ *[1 mark]*
$3^k = 27$ *[1 mark]*
Therefore $\mathbf{k = 3}$ *[1 mark]*

4 a) **0.65 is not between 1 and 10, so the number is not in correct standard form.** *[1 mark]*
b) $0.000234 = 2.34 \times 10^{-4}$, so the **power of 10 should be –4 rather than 4.** *[1 mark]*

5 In one Earth day, Mercury travels:
3.6×10^8 km $\div 88 = 3.6 \div 88 \times 10^8$ km
$= 0.040909 \times 10^8$ km (to 5 s.f) *[1 mark]*
$= 4.0909 \times 10^6$ km (to 5 s.f)
In one Earth day, Venus travels:
6.8×10^8 km $\div 225 = 6.8 \div 225 \times 10^8$ km
$= 0.030222 \times 10^8$ km (to 5 s.f) *[1 mark]*
$= 3.0222 \times 10^6$ km (to 5 s.f)
So Mercury travels further than Venus in one Earth day. *[1 mark]*
The difference is
4.0909×10^6 km $- 3.0222 \times 10^6$ km
$= \mathbf{1.07 \times 10^6}$ **km (to 3 s.f.)**
[1 mark for subtracting the two distances, 1 mark for correct answer in standard form]
You could leave the distances per day as multiples of 10^8, and just convert to correct standard form at the end.

Section 4 — Multiples and Factors

4.1 Finding Multiples and Factors

Page 53 Exercise 1

1 a) **4, 8, 12, 16, 20**
b) **10, 20, 30, 40, 50**
c) **3, 6, 9, 12, 15**
d) **6, 12, 18, 24, 30**
e) **7, 14, 21, 28, 35**

2 a) **16** b) **27, 36, 45**

3 a) **10, 20, 30, 40, 50, 60, 70, 80, 90, 100**
b) **15, 30, 45, 60, 75, 90, 105**
c) **30, 60, 90**

4 Multiples of 5: 5, 10, 15, 20, 25, 30, 35
Multiples of 6: 6, 12, 18, 24, 30, 36
Common multiple: **30**

5 Multiples of 3: 21, 24, 27, 30, 33
Multiples of 4: 20, 24, 28, 32
Common multiple: **24**

Page 54 Exercise 2

1 a) 2 × 3 = 6 so both 2 and 3 are factors.
5 × – = 6 so 5 is not a factor.
6 × 1 = 6 so 6 is a factor.
The other numbers cannot be factors as they are greater than 6.
Factors are **2, 3, 6**

b) 2 × 12 = 24 so both 2 and 12 are factors.
3 × 8 = 24 so 3 is factor.
5 × – = 24 so 5 is not a factor.
6 × 4 = 24 so 6 is a factor.
15 × – = 24 so 15 is not a factor.
Factors are **2, 3, 6, 12**

Using the same method for c)-f):

c) 2, 3, 5, 6, 15 **d) 2, 3, 6, 12**
e) 2, 5 **f) 3, 5, 15**

2 a) 1 × 10 = 10 so both 1 and 10 are factors.
2 × 5 = 10 so both 2 and 5 are factors.
3 × – = 10 so 3 is not a factor.
4 × – = 10 so 4 is not a factor.
Stop as 5 has already been used.
So factors are **1, 2, 5, 10**

b) 1 × 4 = 4 so both 1 and 4 are factors.
2 × 2 = 4 so 2 is a factor.
3 × – = 4 so 3 is not a factor.
Stop as 4 has already been used.
So factors are **1, 2, 4**

Using the same method for c)-f):

c) 1, 13 **d) 1, 5, 25**
e) 1, 2, 3, 4, 6, 8, 12, 24 **f) 1, 5, 7, 35**

3 a) 1 × 15 = 15
2 × – = 15
3 × 5 = 15
4 × – = 15
So the factors of 15 are **1, 3, 5, 15**

b) 1 × 21 = 21
2 × – = 21
3 × 7 = 21
4 × – = 21
5 × – = 21
6 × – = 21
So the factors of 21 are **1, 3, 7, 21**

c) Common factors appear on both lists, so the common factors of 15 and 21 are **1 and 3**.

4 a) Factors of 15: 1, 3, 5, 15
Factors of 20: 1, 2, 4, 5, 10, 20
Common factors: **1, 5**

b) Factors of 12: 1, 2, 3, 4, 6, 12
Factors of 15: 1, 3, 5, 15
Common factors: **1, 3**

Using the same method for c)-f):

c) 1, 3, 5, 15 **d) 1, 2, 5, 10**
e) 1, 5, 25 **f) 1**

5 **a) 1** **b) 1, 2** **c) 1, 5**

6 a) Factors of 15: 1, 3, 5, 15
Factors of 20: 1, 2, 4, 5, 10, 20
Factors of 25: 1, 5, 25
Common factors: **1, 5**
Using the same method for b)-d):

b) 1, 2 **c) 1, 5** **d) 1**

4.2 Prime Numbers

Page 55 Exercise 1

1 a) 33 = 11 × 3 so 33 is not prime.
35 = 5 × 7 so 35 is not prime.
39 = 3 × 13 so 39 is not prime.
So the numbers that are not prime are **33, 35, 39**

b) Using part a)
Two factors of 33 are **3 and 11**
Two factors of 35 are **5 and 7**
Two factors of 39 are **3 and 13**

2 15 = 3 × 5 so 15 is not prime.
22 = 2 × 11 so 22 is not prime.
34 = 2 × 17 so 34 is not prime.
51 = 3 × 17 so 51 is not prime.
So primes are **5, 47, 59**

3 **23, 29**

4 a) (i) 4 = 2 × 2 so a factor of 4 is **2**.
(ii) 14 = 2 × 7 so a factor of 14 is **2**.
7 is also a factor.
(iii) 34 = 2 × 17 so a factor of 34 is **2**.
17 is also a factor.
(iv) 74 = 2 × 37 so a factor of 74 is **2**.
37 is also a factor.

b) Because 2 will always be a factor.

5 E.g. Because they all end in zero so 10 will always be a factor.
You could also have said that all the numbers in the list are even, so they must have 2 as a factor.

Page 57 Exercise 2

1 a) (i)

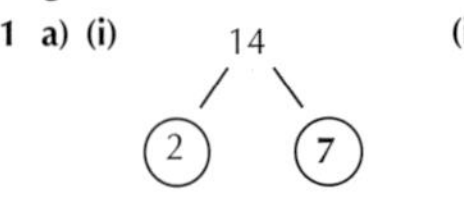

(ii)

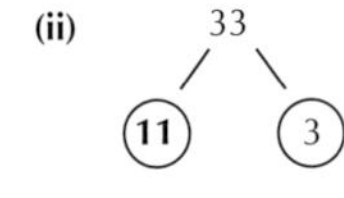

(iii)

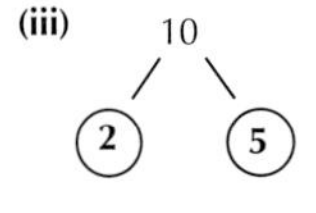

(iv)

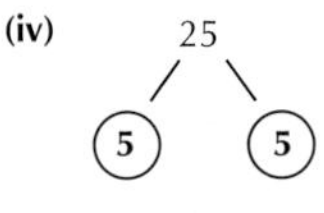

b) (i) 14 = **2 × 7** (ii) 33 = **3 × 11**
(iii) 10 = **2 × 5** (iv) 26 = **2 × 13**

2 a) 15 = **3 × 5** b) 21 = **3 × 7**
c) 22 = **2 × 11** d) 6 = **2 × 3**
e) 14 = **2 × 7** f) 26 = **2 × 13**

3 a) (i)

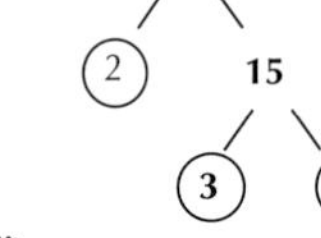

(ii)

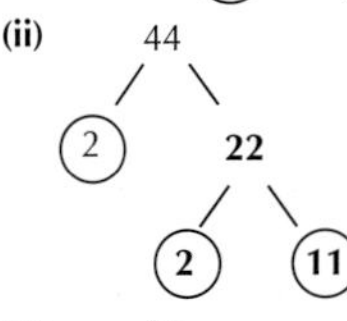

(iii)

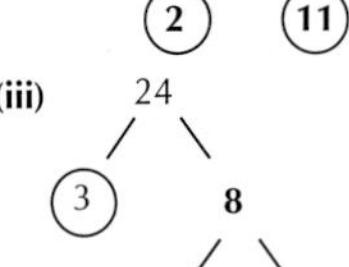

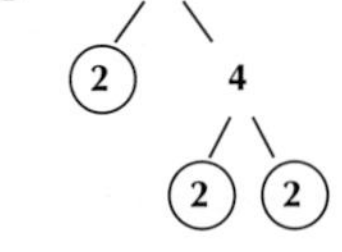

(iv)

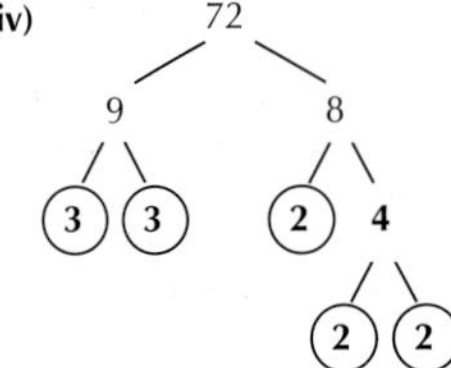

b) (i) 30 = **2 × 3 × 5** (ii) 44 = $\mathbf{2^2 \times 11}$
(iii) 24 = $\mathbf{2^3 \times 3}$ (iv) 72 = $\mathbf{2^3 \times 3^2}$

4 E.g.

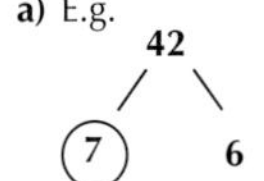

70 = **2 × 5 × 7**
You might have a different looking factor tree (e.g. you might have split 70 into 2 × 35). But your final prime factorisation of 70 should always turn out to be 2 × 5 × 7.

5 a) E.g.

42
7 **6**
2 3

42 = **2 × 3 × 7**

Using the same method for b)-d):

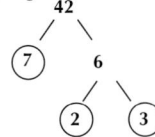

b) 84 = $\mathbf{2^2 \times 3 \times 7}$
c) 190 = **2 × 5 × 19**
d) 210 = **2 × 3 × 5 × 7**

6 a) 128 = $\mathbf{2^7}$ b) 168 = $\mathbf{2^3 \times 3 \times 7}$
c) 325 = $\mathbf{5^2 \times 13}$ d) 98 = $\mathbf{2 \times 7^2}$
e) 225 = $\mathbf{3^2 \times 5^2}$ f) 1000 = $\mathbf{2^3 \times 5^3}$

7 a) 75 = 3 × 5 × 5 = $\mathbf{3 \times 5^2}$
b) **3** — this is the smallest number you can multiply by that gives even powers of all the prime factors, giving $3^2 \times 5^2 = 15^2$.

4.3 LCM and HCF

Page 58 Exercise 1

1 a) First five multiples of 9: **9, 18, 27, 36, 45**
First five multiples of 12: **12, 24, 36, 48, 60**
b) The LCM is the smallest number in both lists: **36**

2 a) First ten multiples of 5: **5, 10, 15, 20, 25, 30, 35, 40, 45, 50**
First ten multiples of 7: **7, 14, 21, 28, 35, 42, 49, 56, 63, 70**
b) The LCM is the smallest number in both lists: **35**

3 a) Multiples of 3: 3, 6, 9, 12, 15...
Multiples of 4: 4, 8, 12, 16...
LCM = smallest number in both lists = **12**
b) Multiples of 6: 6, 12, 18, 24, 30...
Multiples of 8: 8, 16, 24, 32...
LCM = smallest number in both lists = **24**

Using the same method for c)-f):

c) 10 **d) 42** **e) 30** **f) 60**

4 a) Multiples of 3: 3, 6, 9, 12, 15, 18, 21, 24, 27...
Multiples of 6: 6, 12, 18, 24, 30...
Multiples of 8: 8, 16, 24, 32...
LCM = smallest number in all lists = **24**

Using the same method for b) and c):

b) 30 **c) 36**

Page 59 Exercise 2

1 **a) 8, 16, 24, 32, 40, 48, 56, 64, 72, 80**
b) 12, 24, 36, 48, 60, 72, 84, 96, 108, 120
c) After 24 minutes

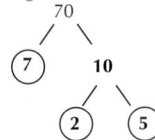

2 Mike visits Oscar on day: 4, 8, 12, 16, 20...
Narinda visits Oscar on day: 5, 10, 15, 20...
So they will both visit Oscar on the same day after **20 days**.

3 Number of sweets must be a multiple of 5. Number of sweets must also be a multiple of 7.
Multiples of 5: 5, 10, 15, 20, 25, 30, 35, 40...
Multiples of 7: 7, 14, 21, 28, 35...
The smallest possible number of sweets is the LCM of 5 and 7, which is **35**.

4 Number of plants must be a multiple of 25. Number of plants must also be a multiple of 30. So you need to find a common multiple of 25 and 30. Between 95 and 205, the multiples of 25 are: 100, 125, 150, 175, 200 and the multiples of 30 are: 120, 150, 180. So there must be **150 plants**.

Page 60 Exercise 3

1 a) Factors of 12: 1, 2, 3, 4, 6, 12
Factors of 20: 1, 2, 4, 5, 10, 20
Common factors of 12 and 20: **1, 2, 4**

b) **4**

2 a) Factors of 20: 1, 2, 4, 5, 10, 20
Factors of 30: 1, 2, 3, 5, 6, 10, 15, 30
Common factors of 20 and 30: **1, 2, 5, 10**

b) **10**

3 a) Factors of 8: 1, 2, 4, 8
Factors of 12: 1, 2, 3, 4, 6, 12
The HCF is the biggest number in both lists: **4**.

b) Factors of 24: 1, 2, 3, 4, 6, 8, 12, 24
Factors of 32: 1, 2, 4, 8, 16, 32
The HCF is the biggest number in both lists: **8**.

Using the same method for c)-f):

c) **6** d) **12**
e) **1** f) **12**

4 a) Factors of 11: 1, 11
Factors of 12: 1, 2, 3, 4, 6, 12
HCF is the biggest number in both lists: **1**

b) Factors of 21: 1, 3, 7, 21
Factors of 22: 1, 2, 11, 22
HCF is the biggest number in both lists: **1**

5 a) Factors of 6: 1, 2, 3, 6
Factors of 8: 1, 2, 4, 8
Factors of 12: 1, 2, 3, 4, 6, 12
HCF is the biggest number in all three lists: **2**

b) Factors of 12: 1, 2, 3, 4, 6, 12
Factors of 15: 1, 3, 5, 15
Factors of 18: 1, 2, 3, 6, 9, 18
HCF is the biggest number in all three lists: **3**

Using the same method for c) and d):

c) **6** d) **18**

Page 61 Review Exercise

1 a) Multiples of 3: **9, 12, 15, 18, 21**

b) Multiples of 4: **8, 12, 16, 20**

c) Multiples of 5: **5, 15, 20**

2 Multiples of 8: 8, 16, 24, 32, 40, 48, 56, 64, 72, 80, 88, 96
Multiples of 10: 10, 20, 30, 40, 50, 60, 70, 80, 90, 100
Common multiples of 8 and 10: **40, 80**

3 a) Multiples of 20 between 95 and 155: **100, 120, 140**

b) Multiples of 30 between 95 and 155: **120, 150**

c) Number of animals is the only common multiple of 20 and 30 between 95 and 155: **120**

4 a) Factors of 10: 1, 2, 5, 10
Factors of 42: 1, 2, 3, 6, 7, 21, 28, 42
Common factors: **1, 2**

b) Factors of 14: 1, 2, 7, 14
Factors of 27: 1, 3, 9, 27
Common factors: **1**

c) Factors of 12: 1, 2, 3, 4, 6, 12
Factors of 24: 1, 2, 3, 4, 6, 8, 12, 24
Common factors: **1, 2, 3, 4, 6, 12**

5 The baker could have:
1 packet of 12 cakes, 2 packets of 6 cakes
3 packets of 4 cakes, 4 packets of 3 cakes
6 packets of 2 cakes, 12 packets of 1 cake
So there are **6 ways** the baker could divide up the cakes.

6 a) 51 = 3 × 17 so 51 is not prime.
55 = 5 × 11 so 55 is not prime.
57 = 3 × 19 so 57 is not prime.
So numbers which are not prime are **51, 55, 57**.

b) From a):
Two factors of 51 are **3 and 17**.
Two factors of 55 are **5 and 11**.
Two factors of 57 are **3 and 19**.

7 18 = 3 × 6 so 18 is not prime.
33 = 3 × 11 so 33 is not prime.
51 = 3 × 17 so 51 is not prime.
54 = 6 × 9 so 54 is not prime.
So prime numbers are **7, 17, 31**.

8 a)

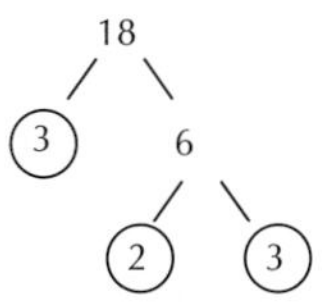

18 = $\mathbf{2 \times 3^2}$

Using the same method for b)-d):

b) 50 = $\mathbf{2 \times 5^2}$

c) 36 = $\mathbf{2^2 \times 3^2}$

d) 150 = $\mathbf{2 \times 3 \times 5^2}$

9 a) (i) Factors of 5: 1, 5
Factors of 9: 1, 3, 9
HCF is the biggest number in both lists: **1**.

Using the same method for (ii)-(iv):

(ii) **3** (iii) **5** (iv) **4**

b) (i) Multiples of 5: 5, 10, 15, 20, 25, 30, 35, 40, 45, 50...
Multiples of 9: 9, 18, 27, 36, 45...
LCM is the smallest number in both lists: **45**.

Using the same method for (ii)-(iv):

(ii) **30** (iii) **36** (iv) **60**

Page 62 Exam-Style Questions

1 a) 2 × 14 = 28 and 4 × 7 = 28, so **28** is a multiple of 4 and 7 *[1 mark]*.

b) 8 × 4 = 32, so **8** is a factor of 32 *[1 mark]*.

c) **8** is 1 more than 7, which is a prime number *[1 mark]*.

2 a) Factors of 50: **1, 2, 5, 10, 25, 50** *[1 mark]*

b) 51 is divisible by 3 so not prime.
52 is divisible by 2 so not prime.
53 is the smallest prime number that is bigger than 50 *[1 mark]*.

3 Factors of 48: 1, 2, 3, 4, 6, 8, 12, 16, 24, 48
Factors of 60: 1, 2, 3, 4, 5, 6, 10, 12, 15, 20, 30, 60
HCF is biggest number in both lists: **12**
[2 marks available — 1 mark for correctly listing factors of 48 and 60, 1 mark for HCF]

4

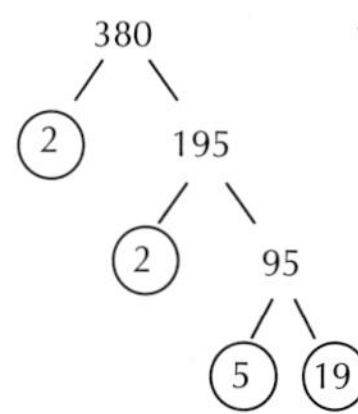

380 = $\mathbf{2^2 \times 5 \times 19}$
[2 marks available — 1 mark for at least two correct divisions by a prime number, 1 mark for correct prime factorisation]
You don't have to use a factor tree to find the prime factorisation, but you do need to write down some working showing how you got your final answer.

5 As the LCM is 60, the two numbers must be factors of 60: 1, 2, 3, 4, 5, 6, 10, 12, 15, 20, 30, 60. But as the HCF is 4, both numbers must also be multiples of 4, which leaves 4, 12, 20 and 60 *[1 mark for correct reasoning]*. Since the numbers are not 4 and 60, they must be **12** *[1 mark]* and **20** *[1 mark]*.

6 a)

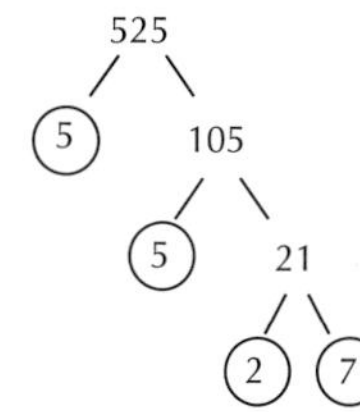

525 = $\mathbf{3 \times 5^2 \times 7}$
[2 marks available — 1 mark for at least two correct divisions by a prime number, 1 mark for correct prime factorisation]

b) 275 625 = $525^2 = (3 \times 5^2 \times 7)^2$
= $\mathbf{3^2 \times 5^4 \times 7^2}$ *[1 mark]*

Section 5 — Fractions

5.1 Equivalent Fractions

Page 64 Exercise 1

1 a) $\frac{1}{3} = \frac{\star}{6}$, $\frac{1}{3} = \frac{1 \times 2}{3 \times 2} = \frac{2}{6}$, so $\star$ = **2**

b) $\frac{1}{3} = \frac{\star}{9}$, $\frac{1}{3} = \frac{1 \times 3}{3 \times 3} = \frac{3}{9}$, so $\star$ = **3**

c) $\frac{1}{3} = \frac{\star}{12}$, $\frac{1}{3} = \frac{1 \times 4}{3 \times 4} = \frac{4}{12}$, so $\star$ = **4**

2 a) $\frac{1}{5} = \frac{1 \times 2}{5 \times 2} = \frac{2}{10}$, so $\boldsymbol{a = 2}$

b) $\frac{1}{4} = \frac{1 \times 3}{4 \times 3} = \frac{3}{12}$, so $\boldsymbol{b = 3}$

Using the same method for d)-h):

c) $\boldsymbol{c = 25}$ d) $\boldsymbol{d = 18}$ e) $\boldsymbol{e = 5}$
f) $\boldsymbol{f = 27}$ g) $\boldsymbol{g = 16}$ h) $\boldsymbol{h = 11}$

Page 65 Exercise 2

1 a) $\frac{3}{9} = \frac{3 \div 3}{9 \div 3} = \mathbf{\frac{1}{3}}$ b) $\frac{5}{20} = \frac{5 \div 5}{20 \div 5} = \mathbf{\frac{1}{4}}$

Using the same method for c)-h):

c) $\mathbf{\frac{1}{2}}$ d) $\mathbf{\frac{1}{8}}$ e) $\mathbf{\frac{1}{5}}$
f) $\mathbf{\frac{5}{12}}$ g) $\mathbf{\frac{3}{8}}$ h) $\mathbf{\frac{3}{4}}$

2 a) $\frac{6}{18}=\frac{6\div 6}{18\div 6}=\frac{1}{3}$, $\frac{4}{20}=\frac{4\div 4}{20\div 4}=\frac{1}{5}$,
$\frac{9}{27}=\frac{9\div 9}{27\div 9}=\frac{1}{3}$

So the fraction that is not equivalent to the other two is $\mathbf{\frac{4}{20}}$.

b) $\frac{6}{8}=\frac{6\div 2}{8\div 2}=\frac{3}{4}$, $\frac{9}{15}=\frac{9\div 3}{15\div 3}=\frac{3}{5}$,
$\frac{15}{25}=\frac{15\div 5}{25\div 5}=\frac{3}{5}$

So the fraction that is not equivalent to the other two is $\mathbf{\frac{6}{8}}$.

c) $\frac{4}{18}=\frac{4\div 2}{18\div 2}=\frac{2}{9}$, $\frac{6}{33}=\frac{6\div 3}{33\div 3}=\frac{2}{11}$,
$\frac{10}{45}=\frac{10\div 5}{45\div 5}=\frac{2}{9}$

So the fraction that is not equivalent to the other two is $\mathbf{\frac{6}{33}}$.

The answers for Q2 always simplify by dividing by the highest common factor. You might have simplified some of the fractions using more than one step — that's fine as long as you got to the correct final answer.

3 cows: $\frac{\text{cows}}{\text{animals}}=\frac{50}{300}=\frac{50\div 50}{300\div 50}=\mathbf{\frac{1}{6}}$

pigs: $\frac{\text{pigs}}{\text{animals}}=\frac{70}{300}=\frac{70\div 10}{300\div 10}=\mathbf{\frac{7}{30}}$

300 – 50 – 70 = 180 sheep, so:

sheep: $\frac{\text{sheep}}{\text{animals}}=\frac{180}{300}=\frac{180\div 60}{300\div 60}=\mathbf{\frac{3}{5}}$

5.2 Mixed Numbers

Page 66 Exercise 1

1 a) $2=\frac{2}{1}=\frac{2\times 3}{1\times 3}=\frac{6}{3}$, so ☆ **= 6**

b) $3=\frac{3}{1}=\frac{3\times 4}{1\times 4}=\frac{12}{4}$, so ☆ **= 12**

2 a) $4=\frac{a}{3}$, $4=\frac{4}{1}=\frac{4\times 3}{1\times 3}=\frac{12}{3}$, so $\mathbf{a = 12}$

b) $4\frac{1}{3}=4+\frac{1}{3}=\frac{12}{3}+\frac{1}{3}=\frac{12+1}{3}=\mathbf{\frac{13}{3}}$

3 a) $1\frac{1}{3}=\frac{3}{3}+\frac{1}{3}=\frac{4}{3}$, so $\mathbf{a = 4}$

b) $1\frac{2}{7}=\frac{7}{7}+\frac{2}{7}=\frac{9}{7}$, so $\mathbf{b = 9}$

c) $2\frac{1}{2}=\frac{4}{2}+\frac{1}{2}=\frac{5}{2}$, so $\mathbf{c = 5}$

4 a) $1\frac{4}{5}=\frac{5}{5}+\frac{4}{5}=\mathbf{\frac{9}{5}}$

b) $1\frac{5}{12}=\frac{12}{12}+\frac{5}{12}=\mathbf{\frac{17}{12}}$

Using the same method for c)-f):

c) $\mathbf{\frac{29}{10}}$ d) $\mathbf{\frac{53}{10}}$

e) $\mathbf{\frac{19}{4}}$ f) $\mathbf{\frac{59}{6}}$

Page 67 Exercise 2

1 a) 11 ÷ 7 = **1 remainder 4**

b) $\frac{11}{7}=\mathbf{1\frac{4}{7}}$

2 a) 5 ÷ 3 = 1 remainder 2, so $\frac{5}{3}=\mathbf{1\frac{2}{3}}$

b) 9 ÷ 5 = 1 remainder 4, so $\frac{9}{5}=\mathbf{1\frac{4}{5}}$

Using the same method for c)-f):

c) $\mathbf{1\frac{2}{11}}$ d) $\mathbf{2\frac{1}{4}}$ e) $\mathbf{2\frac{2}{9}}$ f) $\mathbf{3\frac{2}{3}}$

3 a) $\mathbf{\frac{12}{5}}$

b) 12 ÷ 5 = 2 remainder 2, so $\frac{12}{5}=\mathbf{2\frac{2}{5}}$

5.3 Ordering Fractions

Page 68 Exercise 1

1 a) E.g. $\frac{1}{3}=\frac{1\times 2}{3\times 2}=\mathbf{\frac{2}{6}}$, $\frac{1}{6}=\mathbf{\frac{1}{6}}$

b) E.g. $\frac{1}{5}=\frac{1\times 2}{5\times 2}=\mathbf{\frac{2}{10}}$, $\frac{3}{10}=\mathbf{\frac{3}{10}}$

Using the same method for c)-h):

c) $\mathbf{\frac{4}{16}, \frac{5}{16}}$ d) $\mathbf{\frac{8}{20}, \frac{7}{20}}$ e) $\mathbf{\frac{2}{9}, \frac{3}{9}}$

f) $\mathbf{\frac{8}{12}, \frac{9}{12}}$ g) $\mathbf{\frac{35}{42}, \frac{6}{42}}$ h) $\mathbf{\frac{4}{18}, \frac{9}{18}}$

2 a) The lowest common multiple of 4, 8 and 12 is 24.

$\frac{3}{4}=\frac{3\times 6}{4\times 6}=\mathbf{\frac{18}{24}}$, $\frac{5}{8}=\frac{5\times 3}{8\times 3}=\mathbf{\frac{15}{24}}$,
$\frac{7}{12}=\frac{7\times 2}{12\times 2}=\mathbf{\frac{14}{24}}$

b) The lowest common multiple of 5, 10 and 20 is 20.

$\frac{1}{5}=\frac{1\times 4}{5\times 4}=\mathbf{\frac{4}{20}}$, $\frac{7}{10}=\frac{7\times 2}{10\times 2}=\mathbf{\frac{14}{20}}$,
$\frac{9}{20}=\mathbf{\frac{9}{20}}$

Using the same method for c)-f):

c) $\mathbf{\frac{6}{42}, \frac{8}{42}, \frac{15}{42}}$ d) $\mathbf{\frac{12}{24}, \frac{9}{24}, \frac{16}{24}}$

e) $\mathbf{\frac{24}{60}, \frac{25}{60}, \frac{22}{60}}$ f) $\mathbf{\frac{5}{40}, \frac{14}{40}, \frac{24}{40}}$

Page 70 Exercise 2

1 a) $\frac{1}{4}=\frac{1\times 2}{4\times 2}=\frac{2}{8}$, $\frac{2}{8}<\frac{5}{8}$, so $\mathbf{\frac{5}{8}}$ **is larger.**

b) $\frac{3}{5}=\frac{3\times 2}{5\times 2}=\frac{6}{10}$, $\frac{6}{10}<\frac{7}{10}$, so $\mathbf{\frac{7}{10}}$ **is larger.**

Using the same method for c)-h):

c) $\mathbf{\frac{9}{14}}$ d) $\mathbf{\frac{2}{3}}$ e) $\mathbf{\frac{5}{6}}$

f) $\mathbf{\frac{2}{3}}$ g) $\mathbf{\frac{3}{4}}$ h) $\mathbf{\frac{3}{4}}$

2 a) E.g. $\frac{1}{2}=\frac{1\times 8}{2\times 8}=\frac{8}{16}$, $\frac{5}{8}=\frac{5\times 2}{8\times 2}=\frac{10}{16}$, $\frac{7}{16}$

$\frac{7}{16}<\frac{8}{16}<\frac{10}{16}$,

so order from smallest to largest is

$\mathbf{\frac{7}{16}, \frac{1}{2}, \frac{5}{8}}$.

b) E.g. $\frac{2}{5}=\frac{2\times 4}{5\times 4}=\frac{8}{20}$,

$\frac{3}{10}=\frac{3\times 2}{10\times 2}=\frac{6}{20}$, $\frac{7}{20}$

$\frac{6}{20}<\frac{7}{20}<\frac{8}{20}$,

so order from smallest to largest is

$\mathbf{\frac{3}{10}, \frac{7}{20}, \frac{2}{5}}$.

c) E.g. $\frac{3}{4}=\frac{3\times 6}{4\times 6}=\frac{18}{24}$, $\frac{7}{12}=\frac{7\times 2}{12\times 2}=\frac{14}{24}$,

$\frac{5}{8}=\frac{5\times 3}{8\times 3}=\frac{15}{24}$

$\frac{14}{24}<\frac{15}{24}<\frac{18}{24}$,

so order from smallest to largest is

$\mathbf{\frac{7}{12}, \frac{5}{8}, \frac{3}{4}}$.

You could have used different common denominators for any of the parts in Q2 — the ones used here are the lowest common denominators.

3 a) E.g. $\frac{7}{8}=\frac{7\times 6}{8\times 6}=\frac{42}{48}$, $\frac{5}{6}=\frac{5\times 8}{6\times 8}=\frac{40}{48}$,

$\frac{13}{16}=\frac{13\times 3}{16\times 3}=\frac{39}{48}$

$\frac{39}{48}<\frac{40}{48}<\frac{42}{48}$,

so order from smallest to largest is

$\mathbf{\frac{13}{16}, \frac{5}{6}, \frac{7}{8}}$.

b) E.g. $\frac{4}{15}=\frac{4\times 9}{15\times 9}=\frac{36}{135}$,

$\frac{7}{27}=\frac{7\times 5}{27\times 5}=\frac{35}{135}$, $\frac{13}{45}=\frac{13\times 3}{45\times 3}=\frac{39}{135}$.

$\frac{35}{135}<\frac{36}{135}<\frac{39}{135}$,

so order from smallest to largest is

$\mathbf{\frac{7}{27}, \frac{4}{15}, \frac{13}{45}}$.

c) E.g. $\frac{5}{16}=\frac{5\times 25}{16\times 25}=\frac{125}{400}$,

$\frac{7}{20}=\frac{7\times 20}{20\times 20}=\frac{140}{400}$, $\frac{9}{25}=\frac{9\times 16}{25\times 16}=\frac{144}{400}$

$\frac{125}{400}<\frac{140}{400}<\frac{144}{400}$,

so order from smallest to largest is

$\mathbf{\frac{5}{16}, \frac{7}{20}, \frac{9}{25}}$.

Page 70 Exercise 3

1 a) E.g. $-\frac{4}{15}=-\frac{4\times 3}{15\times 3}=\mathbf{-\frac{12}{45}}$,

$\frac{2}{9}=\frac{2\times 5}{9\times 5}=\mathbf{\frac{10}{45}}$, $-\frac{1}{3}=-\frac{1\times 15}{3\times 15}=\mathbf{-\frac{15}{45}}$

b) $-\frac{15}{45}<-\frac{12}{45}<\frac{10}{45}$

so $\mathbf{-\frac{1}{3}<-\frac{4}{15}<\frac{2}{9}}$

2 a) E.g. $-\frac{4}{9}=-\frac{4\times 4}{9\times 4}=-\frac{16}{36}$,

$-\frac{5}{12}=-\frac{5\times 3}{12\times 3}=-\frac{15}{36}$

$-\frac{16}{36}<-\frac{15}{36}$, so $\mathbf{-\frac{4}{9}}$ **is smaller.**

b) E.g. $\frac{4}{5}=\frac{4\times 2}{5\times 2}=\frac{8}{10}$

$-\frac{9}{10}<\frac{8}{10}$, so $\mathbf{-\frac{9}{10}}$ **is smaller.**

c) E.g. $-\frac{1}{4}=-\frac{1\times 11}{4\times 11}=-\frac{11}{44}$,

$\frac{5}{2}=\frac{5\times 22}{2\times 22}=\frac{110}{44}$,

$-\frac{3}{11}=-\frac{3\times 4}{11\times 4}=-\frac{12}{44}$

$-\frac{12}{44}<-\frac{11}{44}<\frac{110}{44}$, so $\mathbf{-\frac{3}{11}}$ **is smaller.**

5.4 Adding and Subtracting Fractions

Page 71 Exercise 1

1 a) $\frac{1}{3}+\frac{1}{3}=\frac{1+1}{3}=\mathbf{\frac{2}{3}}$

b) $\frac{4}{5}-\frac{2}{5}=\frac{4-2}{5}=\mathbf{\frac{2}{5}}$

c) $\frac{5}{11}-\frac{3}{11}=\frac{5-3}{11}=\mathbf{\frac{2}{11}}$

d) $\frac{1}{10}+\frac{3}{10}=\frac{1+3}{10}=\frac{4}{10}=\mathbf{\frac{2}{5}}$

Don't forget to simplify your answer in part d).

2 a) $\frac{5}{8}+\frac{7}{8}=\frac{5+7}{8}=\frac{12}{8}=1\frac{4}{8}=\mathbf{1\frac{1}{2}}$

b) $\frac{3}{4}+\frac{3}{4}=\frac{3+3}{4}=\frac{6}{4}=1\frac{2}{4}=\mathbf{1\frac{1}{2}}$

c) $\frac{8}{15}+\frac{13}{15}-\frac{2}{15}=\frac{8+13-2}{15}=\frac{19}{15}=\mathbf{1\frac{4}{15}}$

d) $\frac{17}{20}+\frac{19}{20}-\frac{7}{20}=\frac{17+19-7}{20}=\frac{29}{20}=\mathbf{1\frac{9}{20}}$

3 a) $\frac{1}{2}=\frac{1\times 2}{2\times 2}=\mathbf{\frac{2}{4}}$ and $\mathbf{\frac{1}{4}}$

b) $\frac{1}{2}+\frac{1}{4}=\frac{2}{4}+\frac{1}{4}=\frac{2+1}{4}=\mathbf{\frac{3}{4}}$

4 a) $\frac{3}{5}+\frac{1}{10}=\frac{6}{10}+\frac{1}{10}=\frac{6+1}{10}=\mathbf{\frac{7}{10}}$

b) $\frac{1}{4}+\frac{3}{8}=\frac{2}{8}+\frac{3}{8}=\frac{2+3}{8}=\mathbf{\frac{5}{8}}$

c) $\frac{4}{9}-\frac{1}{3}=\frac{4}{9}-\frac{3}{9}=\frac{4-3}{9}=\mathbf{\frac{1}{9}}$

d) $\frac{3}{4}-\frac{3}{8}=\frac{6}{8}-\frac{3}{8}=\frac{6-3}{8}=\mathbf{\frac{3}{8}}$

5 a) $\frac{1}{9}+\frac{5}{9}+\frac{11}{18}=\frac{2}{18}+\frac{10}{18}+\frac{11}{18}$
$=\frac{2+10+11}{18}=\frac{23}{18}=\mathbf{1\frac{5}{18}}$

b) $\frac{3}{4}+\frac{1}{8}-\frac{7}{16}=\frac{12}{16}+\frac{2}{16}-\frac{7}{16}$
$=\frac{12+2-7}{16}=\mathbf{\frac{7}{16}}$

Using the same method for c) and d):

c) $\mathbf{\frac{3}{7}}$ **d)** $\mathbf{1\frac{3}{4}}$

Page 72 Exercise 2

1 The fraction of boys and fraction of girls must add up to 1.
So the fraction of girls is
$1-\frac{4}{9}=\frac{9}{9}-\frac{4}{9}=\frac{9-4}{9}=\mathbf{\frac{5}{9}}$.

2 The fractions of cake must add up to 1.
So Olga eats $1-\frac{2}{7}-\frac{3}{7}=\frac{7}{7}-\frac{2}{7}-\frac{3}{7}$
$=\frac{7-2-3}{7}=\mathbf{\frac{2}{7}}$ of the cake.

3 The fractions of flowers must add up to 1.
So the fraction that is neither a rose nor a tulip is $1-\frac{1}{5}-\frac{3}{10}=\frac{10}{10}-\frac{2}{10}-\frac{3}{10}$
$=\frac{10-2-3}{10}=\frac{5}{10}=\mathbf{\frac{1}{2}}$.

4 The fractions of sweets must add up to 1.
So the fraction of sweets that are mints is
$1-\frac{2}{5}-\frac{1}{4}=\frac{20}{20}-\frac{8}{20}-\frac{5}{20}=\frac{20-8-5}{20}=\mathbf{\frac{7}{20}}$.

5 The fractions of pupils must add up to 1.
So the fraction of pupils that come to school by car is
$1-\frac{1}{2}-\frac{1}{5}=\frac{10}{10}-\frac{5}{10}-\frac{2}{10}=\frac{10-5-2}{10}=\mathbf{\frac{3}{10}}$.

Page 73 Exercise 3

1 a) $1\frac{4}{5}=\frac{5}{5}+\frac{4}{5}=\frac{5+4}{5}=\mathbf{\frac{9}{5}}$

b) $1\frac{4}{5}+\frac{3}{5}=\frac{9}{5}+\frac{3}{5}=\frac{12}{5}$
$12 \div 5 = 2$ remainder 2, so $\frac{12}{5}=\mathbf{2\frac{2}{5}}$

2 a) (i) $2\frac{1}{5}=\frac{10}{5}+\frac{1}{5}=\mathbf{\frac{11}{5}}$

(ii) $1\frac{3}{5}=\frac{5}{5}+\frac{3}{5}=\mathbf{\frac{8}{5}}$

b) $2\frac{1}{5}-1\frac{3}{5}=\frac{11}{5}-\frac{8}{5}=\frac{11-8}{5}=\mathbf{\frac{3}{5}}$

3 a) $1\frac{2}{3}=\frac{3}{3}+\frac{2}{3}=\frac{5}{3}$,
so $1\frac{2}{3}+\frac{1}{3}=\frac{5}{3}+\frac{1}{3}=\frac{6}{3}=\mathbf{2}$

b) $2\frac{3}{8}=\frac{16}{8}+\frac{3}{8}=\frac{19}{8}$,
so $2\frac{3}{8}+\frac{7}{8}=\frac{19}{8}+\frac{7}{8}=\frac{26}{8}$
$26 \div 8 = 3$ remainder 2, so $\frac{26}{8}=3\frac{2}{8}=\mathbf{3\frac{1}{4}}$

Using the same method for c)-f):

c) 3 **d)** $\mathbf{1\frac{1}{2}}$

e) $\mathbf{6\frac{1}{11}}$ **f)** $\mathbf{2\frac{3}{5}}$

Page 74 Exercise 4

1 a) $4 + 3 = 7$ and $\frac{1}{9}+\frac{4}{9}=\frac{5}{9}$,
so $4\frac{1}{9}+3\frac{4}{9}=\mathbf{7\frac{5}{9}}$

b) $3 + 2 = 5$ and $\frac{1}{5}+\frac{3}{7}=\frac{7}{35}+\frac{15}{35}=\frac{22}{35}$,
so $3\frac{1}{5}+2\frac{3}{7}=5+\frac{22}{35}=\mathbf{5\frac{22}{35}}$

c) $2 + 6 = 8$ and
$\frac{5}{8}+\frac{2}{3}=\frac{15}{24}+\frac{16}{24}=\frac{31}{24}=1\frac{7}{24}$,
so $2\frac{5}{8}+6\frac{2}{3}=8+1\frac{7}{24}=\mathbf{9\frac{7}{24}}$

2 a) $\frac{2}{5}-\frac{4}{5}=\frac{2-4}{5}=\mathbf{-\frac{2}{5}}$

b) $2\frac{2}{5}-1\frac{4}{5}=(2-1)+(\frac{2}{5}-\frac{4}{5})$
$=1-\frac{2}{5}=\frac{5}{5}-\frac{2}{5}=\mathbf{\frac{3}{5}}$

3 a) $3 - 0 = 3$ and $\frac{3}{4}-\frac{5}{7}=\frac{21}{28}-\frac{20}{28}=\frac{1}{28}$,
so $3\frac{3}{4}-\frac{5}{7}=3+\frac{1}{28}=\mathbf{3\frac{1}{28}}$

b) $2 - 1 = 1$ and $\frac{1}{4}-\frac{6}{7}=\frac{7}{28}-\frac{24}{28}=-\frac{17}{28}$,
so $2\frac{1}{4}-1\frac{6}{7}=1-\frac{17}{28}=\frac{28}{28}-\frac{17}{28}=\mathbf{\frac{11}{28}}$

c) $5 - 3 = 2$ and $\frac{2}{5}-\frac{7}{9}=\frac{18}{45}-\frac{35}{45}=-\frac{17}{45}$,
so $5\frac{2}{5}-3\frac{7}{9}=2-\frac{17}{45}=\frac{90}{45}-\frac{17}{45}$
$=\frac{73}{45}=\mathbf{1\frac{28}{45}}$

Watch your signs in b) and c) — subtracting the fraction parts gives you a negative fraction, so you end up subtracting a fraction from the whole number when you combine the parts.

5.5 Multiplying and Dividing Fractions

Page 75 Exercise 1

1 a) $8\times\frac{1}{4}=\frac{8}{4}=\mathbf{2}$ **b)** $10\times\frac{1}{5}=\frac{10}{5}=\mathbf{2}$

c) $15\times\frac{1}{5}=\frac{15}{5}=\mathbf{3}$ **d)** $45\times\frac{1}{3}=\frac{45}{3}=\mathbf{15}$

2 a) $18\times\frac{1}{4}=\frac{18}{4}=4\frac{2}{4}=\mathbf{4\frac{1}{2}}$

b) $15\times\frac{1}{6}=\frac{15}{6}=2\frac{3}{6}=\mathbf{2\frac{1}{2}}$

Using the same method for c) and d):

c) $\mathbf{8\frac{1}{2}}$ **d)** $\mathbf{2\frac{1}{2}}$

3 a) $48\times-\frac{1}{6}=-\frac{48}{6}=\mathbf{-8}$

b) $80\times-\frac{1}{10}=-\frac{80}{10}=\mathbf{-8}$

c) $25\times-\frac{1}{6}=-\frac{25}{6}=\mathbf{-4\frac{1}{6}}$

d) $40\times-\frac{1}{3}=-\frac{40}{3}=\mathbf{-13\frac{1}{3}}$

Page 77 Exercise 2

1 a) E.g. multiply by the numerator, $12 \times 2 = 24$, then divide by the denominator, $24 \div 3 =$ **8**.

b) E.g. divide by the denominator, $28 \div 4 = 7$, then multiply by the numerator, $7 \times 3 =$ **21**.
Remember you can multiply and divide in either order — just do whatever works best for the numbers you have.

Using the same method for c)-h):

c) 12 **d) 18** **e) 25**

f) 14 **g) –28** **h) 56**

2 a) $15\times\frac{3}{4}=\frac{15\times3}{4}=\frac{45}{4}=\mathbf{11\frac{1}{4}}$

b) $22\times\frac{2}{5}=\frac{22\times2}{5}=\frac{44}{5}=\mathbf{8\frac{4}{5}}$

c) $7\times-\frac{3}{11}=-\frac{7\times3}{11}=-\frac{21}{11}=\mathbf{-1\frac{10}{11}}$

d) $6\times-\frac{5}{8}=-\frac{6\times5}{8}=-\frac{30}{8}=-3\frac{6}{8}=\mathbf{-3\frac{3}{4}}$

3 $45\times\frac{5}{18}=\frac{45\times5}{18}=\frac{5\times\cancel{9}\times5}{2\times\cancel{9}}=\frac{25}{2}=\mathbf{12\frac{1}{2}}$

Page 77 Exercise 3

1 a) $\frac{3}{4}$ of $36=\frac{3}{4}\times36=3\times\frac{36}{4}=3\times9=\mathbf{27}$

b) $\frac{2}{3}$ of $33=\frac{2}{3}\times33=2\times\frac{33}{3}=2\times11=\mathbf{22}$

Using the same method for c)-h):

c) 24 **d) 30** **e) 15**

f) 9 **g)** $\mathbf{27\frac{1}{2}}$ **h)** $\mathbf{26\frac{1}{4}}$

2 a) $\frac{3}{2}$ of $18=\frac{3}{2}\times18=3\times\frac{18}{2}=3\times9=\mathbf{27}$

b) $\frac{5}{3}$ of $21=\frac{5}{3}\times21=5\times\frac{21}{3}=5\times7=\mathbf{35}$

c) $\frac{11}{9}$ of $72=11\times\frac{72}{9}=11\times8=\mathbf{88}$

3 $\frac{2}{3}$ of $27=\frac{2}{3}\times27=2\times\frac{27}{3}=2\times9$
= **18** students prefer rounders

Page 78 Exercise 4

1 a) $\frac{1}{6}\times\frac{1}{3}=\frac{1\times1}{6\times3}=\mathbf{\frac{1}{18}}$

b) $\frac{2}{5}\times\frac{1}{3}=\frac{2\times1}{5\times3}=\mathbf{\frac{2}{15}}$

Using the same method for c)-h):

c) $\mathbf{\frac{3}{28}}$ **d)** $\mathbf{\frac{3}{25}}$ **e)** $\mathbf{\frac{5}{24}}$

f) $\mathbf{\frac{8}{35}}$ **g)** $\mathbf{-\frac{10}{49}}$ **h)** $\mathbf{\frac{21}{80}}$

In h) the two minus signs cancel out (negative × negative = positive).

2 a) $\frac{1}{4}\times\frac{2}{3}=\frac{1\times2}{4\times3}=\frac{2}{12}=\mathbf{\frac{1}{6}}$

b) $\frac{3}{5}\times\frac{1}{6}=\frac{3\times1}{5\times6}=\frac{3}{30}=\mathbf{\frac{1}{10}}$

c) $\frac{5}{6}\times\frac{2}{15}=\frac{\cancel{5}}{\cancel{2}\times3}\times\frac{\cancel{2}}{3\times\cancel{5}}=\frac{1}{3}\times\frac{1}{3}=\frac{1\times1}{3\times3}$
$=\mathbf{\frac{1}{9}}$

d) $\frac{5}{12}\times\frac{3}{4}=\frac{5}{\cancel{3}\times4}\times\frac{\cancel{3}}{4}=\frac{5}{4\times4}=\mathbf{\frac{5}{16}}$

Using the same method for e)-h):

e) $\mathbf{\frac{3}{14}}$ **f)** $\mathbf{\frac{6}{7}}$

g) $\mathbf{-\frac{3}{4}}$ **h)** $\mathbf{-\frac{1}{4}}$

3 $\frac{3}{5}$ of $\frac{15}{8}=\frac{3}{5}\times\frac{15}{8}=\frac{3}{\cancel{5}}\times\frac{3\times\cancel{5}}{8}=\frac{3\times3}{8}$
$=\frac{9}{8}=\mathbf{1\frac{1}{8}}$

Page 79 Exercise 5

1 a) $1\frac{1}{2}=\frac{2}{2}+\frac{1}{2}=\frac{3}{2}$,
so $1\frac{1}{2}\times\frac{1}{3}=\frac{\cancel{3}}{2}\times\frac{1}{\cancel{3}}=\mathbf{\frac{1}{2}}$

b) $2\frac{1}{5}=\frac{10}{5}+\frac{1}{5}=\frac{11}{5}$,
so $2\frac{1}{5}\times\frac{3}{4}=\frac{11}{5}\times\frac{3}{4}=\frac{11\times3}{5\times4}=\frac{33}{20}=\mathbf{1\frac{13}{20}}$

Using the same method for c)-f):

c) $\mathbf{1\frac{2}{9}}$ **d)** $\mathbf{1\frac{1}{2}}$

e) $\mathbf{\frac{10}{21}}$ **f)** $\mathbf{\frac{11}{12}}$

2 a) $3\frac{2}{5}=\frac{15}{5}+\frac{2}{5}=\mathbf{\frac{17}{5}}$

b) $1\frac{1}{2}=\frac{2}{2}+\frac{1}{2}=\mathbf{\frac{3}{2}}$

c) $3\frac{2}{5}\times1\frac{1}{2}=\frac{17}{5}\times\frac{3}{2}=\frac{51}{10}=\mathbf{5\frac{1}{10}}$

3 a) $1\frac{1}{5}=\frac{5}{5}+\frac{1}{5}=\frac{6}{5}$ and $1\frac{1}{4}=\frac{4}{4}+\frac{1}{4}=\frac{5}{4}$,
so $1\frac{1}{5}\times1\frac{1}{4}=\frac{6}{\cancel{5}}\times\frac{\cancel{5}}{4}=\frac{6}{4}=1\frac{2}{4}=\mathbf{1\frac{1}{2}}$

b) $2\frac{2}{5}=\frac{10}{5}+\frac{2}{5}=\frac{12}{5}$ and $1\frac{2}{3}=\frac{3}{3}+\frac{2}{3}=\frac{5}{3}$,
so $2\frac{2}{5}\times1\frac{2}{3}=\frac{12}{\cancel{5}}\times\frac{\cancel{5}}{3}=\frac{12}{3}=\mathbf{4}$

Using the same method for c)-f):

c) $\mathbf{2\frac{4}{5}}$ **d)** $\mathbf{7\frac{29}{42}}$

e) $\mathbf{6\frac{11}{24}}$ **f)** $\mathbf{6\frac{2}{63}}$

Page 80 Exercise 6

1 a) Reciprocal of 5 is $1 \div 5 = \mathbf{\frac{1}{5}}$.

b) Reciprocal of 12 is $1 \div 12 = \mathbf{\frac{1}{12}}$.

c) Reciprocal of 9 is $1 \div 9 = \mathbf{\frac{1}{9}}$.

d) Reciprocal of 27 is $1 \div 27 = \mathbf{\frac{1}{27}}$.

2 a) Reciprocal of $\frac{1}{3} = \frac{3}{1} = \mathbf{3}$.

b) Reciprocal of $-\frac{1}{7} = -\frac{7}{1} = \mathbf{-7}$.

c) Reciprocal of $\frac{4}{5}$ is $\mathbf{\frac{5}{4}}$.

d) Reciprocal of $-\frac{5}{8}$ is $\mathbf{-\frac{8}{5}}$.

Don't forget to keep the minus sign when you find the reciprocal of a negative number.

3 a) $1\frac{3}{5} = \frac{5}{5} + \frac{3}{5} = \frac{8}{5}$, so reciprocal of $1\frac{3}{5}$ is $\mathbf{\frac{5}{8}}$.

b) $2\frac{1}{7} = \frac{14}{7} + \frac{1}{7} = \frac{15}{7}$,
so reciprocal of $2\frac{1}{7}$ is $\mathbf{\frac{7}{15}}$.

c) $1\frac{4}{9} = \frac{9}{9} + \frac{4}{9} = \frac{13}{9}$,
so reciprocal of $1\frac{4}{9}$ is $\mathbf{\frac{9}{13}}$.

d) $-2\frac{3}{4} = -\left(\frac{8}{4} + \frac{3}{4}\right) = -\frac{11}{4}$,
so reciprocal of $-2\frac{3}{4}$ is $\mathbf{-\frac{4}{11}}$.

Page 81 Exercise 7

1 a) $\frac{1}{5} \div \frac{2}{3} = \frac{1}{5} \times \frac{3}{2} = \frac{1 \times 3}{5 \times 2} = \mathbf{\frac{3}{10}}$

b) $\frac{1}{6} \div \frac{2}{5} = \frac{1}{6} \times \frac{5}{2} = \frac{1 \times 5}{6 \times 2} = \mathbf{\frac{5}{12}}$

Using the same method for c)-h):

c) **3** d) $\mathbf{\frac{1}{6}}$ e) $\mathbf{\frac{25}{48}}$

f) $\mathbf{\frac{5}{14}}$ g) $\mathbf{-\frac{15}{16}}$ h) $\mathbf{-\frac{49}{50}}$

2 a) $1\frac{1}{2} = \frac{2}{2} + \frac{1}{2} = \frac{3}{2}$,
so $1\frac{1}{2} \div 4 = \frac{3}{2} \div 4 = \frac{3}{2} \times \frac{1}{4} = \frac{3 \times 1}{2 \times 4} = \mathbf{\frac{3}{8}}$

b) $3\frac{1}{3} = \frac{9}{3} + \frac{1}{3} = \frac{10}{3}$,
so $3\frac{1}{3} \div 6 = \frac{10}{3} \times \frac{1}{6} = \frac{10 \times 1}{3 \times 6} = \frac{10}{18} = \mathbf{\frac{5}{9}}$

c) $1\frac{3}{5} = \frac{5}{5} + \frac{3}{5} = \frac{8}{5}$,
so $5 \div 1\frac{3}{5} = 5 \div \frac{8}{5} = 5 \times \frac{5}{8} = \frac{25}{8} = \mathbf{3\frac{1}{8}}$

d) $1\frac{7}{8} = \frac{8}{8} + \frac{7}{8} = \frac{15}{8}$,
so $2 \div 1\frac{7}{8} = 2 \div \frac{15}{8} = 2 \times \frac{8}{15}$
$= \frac{2 \times 8}{15} = \frac{16}{15} = \mathbf{1\frac{1}{15}}$

3 a) $1\frac{1}{3} = \frac{3}{3} + \frac{1}{3} = \frac{4}{3}$,
so $1\frac{1}{3} \div \frac{2}{5} = \frac{4}{3} \times \frac{5}{2} = \frac{4 \times 5}{3 \times 2}$
$= \frac{20}{6} = 3\frac{2}{6} = \mathbf{3\frac{1}{3}}$

b) $2\frac{1}{2} = \frac{4}{2} + \frac{1}{2} = \frac{5}{2}$,
so $2\frac{1}{2} \div \frac{1}{3} = \frac{5}{2} \times \frac{3}{1} = \frac{15}{2} = \mathbf{7\frac{1}{2}}$

c) $2\frac{1}{3} = \frac{6}{3} + \frac{1}{3} = \frac{7}{3}$,
so $\frac{3}{4} \div 2\frac{1}{3} = \frac{3}{4} \times \frac{3}{7} = \mathbf{\frac{9}{28}}$

d) $3\frac{1}{2} = \frac{6}{2} + \frac{1}{2} = \frac{7}{2}$,
so $\frac{4}{7} \div 3\frac{1}{2} = \frac{4}{7} \times \frac{2}{7} = \mathbf{\frac{8}{49}}$

e) $1\frac{1}{4} = \frac{4}{4} + \frac{1}{4} = \frac{5}{4}$ and $1\frac{1}{5} = \frac{5}{5} + \frac{1}{5} = \frac{6}{5}$,
so $1\frac{1}{4} \div 1\frac{1}{5} = \frac{5}{4} \times \frac{5}{6} = \frac{25}{24} = \mathbf{1\frac{1}{24}}$

f) $2\frac{2}{3} = \frac{6}{3} + \frac{2}{3} = \frac{8}{3}$ and $1\frac{1}{4} = \frac{4}{4} + \frac{1}{4} = \frac{5}{4}$,
so $2\frac{2}{3} \div 1\frac{1}{4} = \frac{8}{3} \times \frac{4}{5} = \frac{32}{15} = \mathbf{2\frac{2}{15}}$

g) $4\frac{5}{6} = \frac{24}{6} + \frac{5}{6} = \frac{29}{6}$ and $2\frac{1}{3} = \frac{6}{3} + \frac{1}{3} = \frac{7}{3}$,
so $4\frac{5}{6} \div 2\frac{1}{3} = \frac{29}{6} \times \frac{3}{7} = \frac{29}{\cancel{3} \times 2} \times \frac{\cancel{3}}{7} = \frac{29}{14}$
$= \mathbf{2\frac{1}{14}}$

h) $3\frac{2}{3} = \frac{9}{3} + \frac{2}{3} = \frac{11}{3}$ and
$-2\frac{1}{10} = -\left(\frac{20}{10} + \frac{1}{10}\right) = -\frac{21}{10}$,
so $3\frac{2}{3} \div \left(-2\frac{1}{10}\right) = \frac{11}{3} \times \left(-\frac{10}{21}\right) = -\frac{110}{63}$
$= \mathbf{-1\frac{47}{63}}$

5.6 Fractions and Decimals

Page 82 Exercise 1

1 a) $\frac{5}{8} = 5 \div 8 = \mathbf{0.625}$

b) $\frac{7}{20} = 7 \div 20 = \mathbf{0.35}$

No trick questions here — just pop the numbers into your calculator.

Using the same method for c)-h):

c) **0.4375** d) **0.15625** e) **0.175**

f) **0.46** g) **0.88** h) **0.658**

2 a) $\frac{3}{8} = 3 \div 8 = 0.375$,
so $1\frac{3}{8} = 1 + 0.375 = \mathbf{1.375}$
(or $1\frac{3}{8} = \frac{8}{8} + \frac{3}{8} = \frac{11}{8} = 11 \div 8 = \mathbf{1.375}$)

b) $\frac{1}{8} = 1 \div 8 = 0.125$, so $2\frac{1}{8} = 2 + 0.125 = \mathbf{2.125}$
(or $2\frac{1}{8} = \frac{16}{8} + \frac{1}{8} = \frac{17}{8} = 17 \div 8 = \mathbf{2.125}$)

Using the same method for c)-h):

c) **6.35** d) **2.37** e) **4.719**

f) **5.76** g) **7.34375** h) **8.4375**

Page 84 Exercise 2

1 a) $\frac{9}{10} = 9 \times \frac{1}{10} = 9 \times 0.1 = \mathbf{0.9}$

Using the same method for b)-d):

b) **0.2** c) **0.3** d) **0.8**

e) $\frac{91}{100} = 91 \times \frac{1}{100} = 91 \times 0.01 = \mathbf{0.91}$

Using the same method for f)-h):

f) **0.42** g) **0.99** h) **0.08**

i) $\frac{7}{1000} = 7 \times \frac{1}{1000} = 7 \times 0.001 = \mathbf{0.007}$

Using the same method for j)-l):

j) **0.201** k) **0.041** l) **0.027**

2 a) $\frac{8}{25} = \frac{8 \times 4}{25 \times 4} = \mathbf{\frac{32}{100}}$

b) $\frac{32}{100} = 32 \times \frac{1}{100} = 32 \times 0.01 = \mathbf{0.32}$

3 a) $\frac{3}{5} = \frac{3 \times 2}{5 \times 2} = \frac{6}{10} = 6 \times \frac{1}{10} = 6 \times 0.1 = \mathbf{0.6}$

b) $\frac{9}{30} = \frac{9 \div 3}{30 \div 3} = \frac{3}{10} = 3 \times \frac{1}{10} = 3 \times 0.1$
$= \mathbf{0.3}$

c) $\frac{45}{50} = \frac{45 \times 2}{50 \times 2} = \frac{90}{100} = 90 \times \frac{1}{100}$
$= 90 \times 0.01 = \mathbf{0.9}$

d) $\frac{22}{25} = \frac{22 \times 4}{25 \times 4} = \frac{88}{100} = 88 \times \frac{1}{100}$
$= 88 \times 0.01 = \mathbf{0.88}$

e) $\frac{96}{300} = \frac{96 \div 3}{300 \div 3} = \frac{32}{100} = 32 \times \frac{1}{100}$
$= 32 \times 0.01 = \mathbf{0.32}$

f) $\frac{33}{250} = \frac{33 \times 4}{250 \times 4} = \frac{132}{1000} = 132 \times \frac{1}{1000}$
$= 132 \times 0.001 = \mathbf{0.132}$

g) $\frac{103}{200} = \frac{103 \times 5}{200 \times 5} = \frac{515}{1000} = 515 \times \frac{1}{1000}$
$= 515 \times 0.001 = \mathbf{0.515}$

h) $\frac{306}{3000} = \frac{306 \div 3}{3000 \div 3} = \frac{102}{1000} = 102 \times \frac{1}{1000}$
$= 102 \times 0.001 = \mathbf{0.102}$

4 a) E.g. $\frac{11}{10} = 11 \times 0.1 = \mathbf{1.1}$

b) E.g. $\frac{14}{5} = \frac{14 \times 2}{5 \times 2} = \frac{28}{10} = 28 \times 0.1 = \mathbf{2.8}$

c) E.g. $5\frac{7}{25} = 5 + \frac{7}{25} = 5 + \frac{7 \times 4}{25 \times 4} = 5 + \frac{28}{100}$
$= 5 + 28 \times 0.01 = 5 + 0.28 = \mathbf{5.28}$

d) E.g. $3\frac{11}{200}$
$= 3 + \frac{11}{200} = 3 + \frac{11 \times 5}{200 \times 5} = 3 + \frac{55}{1000}$
$= 3 + 55 \times 0.001 = 3 + 0.055 = \mathbf{3.055}$

To convert mixed numbers to decimals you can either separate the whole and fraction parts, as in parts c) and d) above, or you can convert them to improper fractions.

Page 85 Exercise 3

1 a) $8\overline{)3.{}^{3}0{}^{6}0{}^{4}0}$ with quotient 0.375, so $\frac{3}{8} = 3 \div 8 = \mathbf{0.375}$

b) $16\overline{)5.{}^{5}0{}^{2}0{}^{4}0{}^{8}0}$ with quotient 0.3125, so $\frac{5}{16} = 5 \div 16 = \mathbf{0.3125}$

2 a) $4\overline{)1.{}^{1}0{}^{2}0}$ with quotient 0.25, so $\frac{1}{4} = 1 \div 4 = \mathbf{0.25}$

b) $4\overline{)3.{}^{3}0{}^{2}0}$ with quotient 0.75, so $\frac{3}{4} = 3 \div 4 = \mathbf{0.75}$

c) $20\overline{)1.{}^{1}0{}^{10}0}$ with quotient 0.05, so $\frac{1}{20} = 1 \div 20 = \mathbf{0.05}$

Using the same method for d)-h):

d) **0.025** e) **0.0625** f) **0.875**

g) **0.175** h) **0.1625**

Page 86 Exercise 4

1 a) 0.7 has one decimal place, so the denominator is 10.
$0.7 = \mathbf{\frac{7}{10}}$

b) 0.9 has one decimal place, so the denominator is 10.
$0.9 = \mathbf{\frac{9}{10}}$

Using the same method for c) and d):

c) $\mathbf{\frac{1}{10}}$ d) $\mathbf{\frac{2}{5}}$

2 a) 0.93 has two decimal places, so the denominator is 100.
$0.93 = \mathbf{\frac{93}{100}}$

b) 0.07 has two decimal places, so the denominator is 100.
$0.07 = \mathbf{\frac{7}{100}}$

Using the same method for c) and d):

c) $\mathbf{\frac{23}{100}}$ d) $\mathbf{\frac{47}{100}}$

3 a) 0.004 has 3 decimal places, so the denominator is 1000.
$0.004 = \frac{4}{1000} = \mathbf{\frac{1}{250}}$

b) 0.801 has 3 decimal places, so the denominator is 1000.
$0.801 = \mathbf{\frac{801}{1000}}$

Using the same method for c) and d):

c) $\mathbf{\frac{983}{1000}}$ d) $\mathbf{\frac{49}{500}}$

4 0.1002 has 4 decimal places, so the denominator is 10 000.
$0.1002 = \frac{1002}{10\,000} = \mathbf{\frac{501}{5000}}$

Page 86 Exercise 5

1 a) 1.2 has one decimal place, so the denominator is 10.
$1.2 = \frac{12}{10} = \frac{12 \div 2}{10 \div 2} = \mathbf{\frac{6}{5}}$

b) 3.4 has one decimal place, so the denominator is 10.
$3.4 = \frac{34}{10} = \frac{34 \div 2}{10 \div 2} = \mathbf{\frac{17}{5}}$

Using the same method for c) and d):
c) $\mathbf{\frac{47}{10}}$ d) $\mathbf{\frac{42}{5}}$

2 a) 3.02 has two decimal places, so the denominator is 100.
So $3.02 = \frac{302}{100} = \frac{302 \div 2}{100 \div 2} = \mathbf{\frac{151}{50}}$

b) 1.55 has two decimal places, so the denominator is 100.
So $1.55 = \frac{155}{100} = \frac{155 \div 5}{100 \div 5} = \mathbf{\frac{31}{20}}$

c) 2.05 has two decimal places, so the denominator is 100.
So $2.05 = \frac{205}{100} = \frac{205 \div 5}{100 \div 5} = \mathbf{\frac{41}{20}}$

d) 18.2 has one decimal place, so the denominator is 10.
So $18.2 = = \frac{182}{10} = \frac{182 \div 2}{10 \div 2} = \mathbf{\frac{91}{5}}$

Careful with d) — although there are 3 digits, there's only one number after the decimal point, so the denominator's 10.

Page 87 Review Exercise

1 a) $\frac{3}{4} = \frac{3 \times 4}{4 \times 4} = \frac{12}{16}$, so $\mathbf{a = 12}$.

b) $\frac{7}{12} = \frac{7 \times 5}{12 \times 5} = \frac{35}{60}$, so $\mathbf{b = 60}$.

c) $\frac{10}{15} = \frac{10 \div 5}{15 \div 5} = \frac{2}{3}$, so $\mathbf{c = 2}$.

2 a) 45 = 9 × 5 and 75 = 15 × 5, so **5 is the common factor**.

b) E.g. $\frac{45}{75} = \frac{45 \div 5}{75 \div 5} = \frac{9}{15} = \frac{9 \div 3}{15 \div 3} = \mathbf{\frac{3}{5}}$.

3 a) 4 out of 24 = $\frac{4}{24} = \frac{4 \div 4}{24 \div 4} = \mathbf{\frac{1}{6}}$.

b) 12 out of 66 = $\frac{12}{66} = \frac{12 \div 6}{66 \div 6} = \mathbf{\frac{2}{11}}$.

4 a) $7\frac{2}{3} = \frac{21}{3} + \frac{2}{3} = \mathbf{\frac{23}{3}}$

b) 26 ÷ 4 = 6 remainder 2,
so $\frac{26}{4} = 6\frac{2}{4} = \mathbf{6\frac{1}{2}}$

5 a) $\frac{2}{7} = \frac{2 \times 4}{7 \times 4} = \mathbf{\frac{8}{28}}$, $\frac{5}{28} = \mathbf{\frac{5}{28}}$,
so $\mathbf{\frac{5}{28}}$ is the smaller fraction.

b) $\frac{1}{8} = \frac{1 \times 3}{8 \times 3} = \mathbf{\frac{3}{24}}$, $\frac{1}{6} = \frac{1 \times 4}{6 \times 4} = \mathbf{\frac{4}{24}}$,
so $\mathbf{\frac{1}{8}}$ is the smaller fraction.

c) $\frac{2}{5} = \frac{2 \times 9}{5 \times 9} = \mathbf{\frac{18}{45}}$, $\frac{4}{9} = \frac{4 \times 5}{9 \times 5} = \mathbf{\frac{20}{45}}$,
so $\mathbf{\frac{2}{5}}$ is the smaller fraction.

6 a) $\frac{1}{5} + \frac{1}{3} = \frac{3}{15} + \frac{5}{15} = \frac{3+5}{15} = \mathbf{\frac{8}{15}}$

b) $\frac{9}{10} - \frac{5}{6} = \frac{27}{30} - \frac{25}{30} = \frac{27-25}{30} = \frac{2}{30} = \mathbf{\frac{1}{15}}$

c) $6\frac{3}{8} = \frac{48}{8} + \frac{3}{8} = \frac{51}{8}$,
so $6\frac{3}{8} - \frac{7}{8} = \frac{51}{8} - \frac{7}{8} = \frac{44}{8} = \frac{(5 \times 8) + 4}{8}$
$= 5\frac{4}{8} = \mathbf{5\frac{1}{2}}$

7 a) $1\frac{3}{7} = \frac{7}{7} + \frac{3}{7} = \mathbf{\frac{10}{7}}$

b) $1\frac{3}{7} \times \frac{2}{3} = \frac{10}{7} \times \frac{2}{3} = \frac{10 \times 2}{7 \times 3} = \mathbf{\frac{20}{21}}$

8 a) $\mathbf{\frac{8}{3}}$

b) $\frac{1}{6} \div \frac{3}{8} = \frac{1}{6} \times \frac{8}{3} = \frac{1 \times 8}{6 \times 3} = \frac{8}{18} = \mathbf{\frac{4}{9}}$

9 23 ÷ 40 = **0.575**

10 a) $\frac{12}{25} = \frac{12 \times 4}{25 \times 4} = \frac{48}{100} = 48 \times \frac{1}{100}$
$= 48 \times 0.01 = \mathbf{0.48}$

b) 0.35 has two decimal places, so the denominator is 100.
$0.35 = \frac{35}{100} = \frac{35 \div 5}{100 \div 5} = \mathbf{\frac{7}{20}}$

Page 88 Exam-Style Questions

1 a) $\frac{5}{12}$ of $78 = \frac{5}{12} \times 78 = \frac{5 \times 78}{12}$ *[1 mark]*
$= \frac{5 \times \cancel{2} \times \cancel{3} \times 13}{2 \times \cancel{2} \times \cancel{3}} = \frac{65}{2} = \mathbf{32\frac{1}{2}}$ **cm**
(or **32.5 cm**) *[1 mark]*

b) $2\frac{1}{2} = \frac{4}{2} + \frac{1}{2} = \frac{5}{2}$ *[1 mark]*
$15 \div 2\frac{1}{2} = 15 \div \frac{5}{2}$
$= 15 \times \frac{2}{5} = \frac{15 \times 2}{5} = \frac{30}{5} = \mathbf{6}$ *[1 mark]*

2 $3.125 = 3 + 0.125 = 3 + \frac{125}{1000}$ *[1 mark]*
$= 3 + \frac{125 \div 25}{1000 \div 25} = 3 + \frac{5}{40} = 3 + \frac{1}{8} = \mathbf{3\frac{1}{8}}$
[1 mark]

3 $\frac{3}{4}$ is used, so $1 - \frac{3}{4} = \frac{1}{4}$ is left over.
$\frac{3}{5}$ is then used, so $1 - \frac{3}{5} = \frac{2}{5}$ of $\frac{1}{4}$ is left over *[1 mark]*.
$\frac{2}{5}$ of $\frac{1}{4} = \frac{2}{5} \times \frac{1}{4} = \frac{2 \times 1}{5 \times 4} = \frac{2}{20}$ *[1 mark]*
$= \mathbf{\frac{1}{10}}$ *[1 mark]*

4 Divide the total butter by the butter per dumpling:
$120 \div 5\frac{1}{3} = 120 \div \frac{16}{3} = 120 \times \frac{3}{16}$ *[1 mark]*
$= \frac{120 \times 3}{16} = \frac{30 \times 3}{4} = \frac{15 \times 3}{2} = \frac{45}{2}$ *[1 mark]*
= 22.5
So Sam can make **22 dumplings** *[1 mark]*.

5 a) $\frac{2}{5}$ of the box are green, so $1 - \frac{2}{5} = \frac{3}{5}$ of the box are red or yellow *[1 mark]*.
There are 24 red and $\frac{24}{4} = 6$ yellow,
so 24 + 6 = 30 peppers equal $\frac{3}{5}$ of the box *[1 mark]*.
So $\frac{1}{5}$ of the box is 30 ÷ 3 = 10 peppers, which means the box has 5 × 10
= **50 peppers** *[1 mark]*.
Part a) might look tricky — but once you've found number of peppers in a fifth of the box, you can just scale up to find the number in the full box.

b) $\frac{24}{50} = \frac{24 \times 2}{50 \times 2} = \frac{48}{100}$ *[1 mark]*
$= 48 \times \frac{1}{100} = 48 \times 0.01 = \mathbf{0.48}$ *[1 mark]*

Section 6 — Ratios

6.1 Ratios

Page 90 Exercise 1

1 There are 4 stars and 3 triangles.
So the ratio of stars to triangles is **4:3**.

2 The ratio cows:pigs is **23:15**.
Make sure you write the ratio in the correct order. The question asks for the ratio of cows to pigs, so write down the 23 cows first.

3 a) The highest common factor of 2 and 8 is 2. 2 ÷ 2 = 1 and 8 ÷ 2 = 4, so the simplest form of 2:8 is **1:4**.

b) The highest common factor of 5 and 15 is 5. 5 ÷ 5 = 1 and 15 ÷ 5 = 3, so the simplest form of 5:15 is **1:3**.

Use the same method for c) and d):
c) (÷ 10) **4:1** d) (÷ 2) **2:3**

4 a) The highest common factor of 6, 2 and 4 is 2. 6 ÷ 2 = 3, 2 ÷ 2 = 1 and 4 ÷ 2 = 2. So the simplest form is **3:1:2**.

b) The highest common factor of 15, 12 and 3 is 3. 15 ÷ 3 = 5, 12 ÷ 3 = 4 and 3 ÷ 3 is 1. So the simplest form is **5:4:1**.

Use the same method for c) and d):
c) (÷ 2) **7:5:1** d) (÷ 4) **6:3:5**

5 black tiles:white tiles = 24:8. 8 is highest common factor of 24 and 8. 24 ÷ 8 = 3 and 8 ÷ 8 = 1, so the simplest form is **3:1**.

6 girls:boys = 36:27. 9 is the highest common factor of 36 and 27. 36 ÷ 9 = 4 and 27 ÷ 9 = 3, so the simplest form is **4:3.**

7 computers:pupils = 170 :595
Divide both sides by 5:
170 ÷ 5:595 ÷ 5 = 34:119
Then divide both sides by 17:
34 ÷ 17:119 ÷ 17 = **2:7**
You could get straight to the final answer by dividing by the highest common factor, which is 85.

8 Soraya has 42 – 16 = 26 sweets.
The ratio of Soraya's sweets:Paul's sweets is 26:16. Divide both sides by 2 to get **13:8**.

Page 91 Exercise 2

1 a) £1 = 100p, so 10p:£1 = 10p:100p.
The highest common factor of 10 and 100 is 10. Divide both sides by 10 to get **1:10**.

b) 1 cm = 10 mm, so 20 mm:4 cm = 20 mm:40 mm.
The highest common factor of 20 and 40 is 20. Divide both sides by 20 to get **1:2**.

c) 1 kg = 1000 g, so 10 g:1 kg = 10 g:1000 g.
The highest common factor of 10 and 1000 is 10. Divide both sides by 10 to get **1:100**.

d) 1 week = 7 days,
so 2 weeks:7 days = 14 days:7 days.
The highest common factor of 14 and 7 is 7. Divide both sides by 7 to get **2:1**.

e) £1 = 100p, so 40p:£1 = 40p:100p.
The highest common factor of 40 and 100 is 20. Divide both sides by 20 to get **2:5**.

f) 1 m = 100 cm,
so 30 cm:2 m = 30 cm:200 cm.
The highest common factor of 30 and 200 is 10. Divide both sides by 10 to get **3:20**.

2 a) 1 m = 1000 mm,
so 1 m : 150 mm = 1000 mm : 150 mm.
The highest common factor of 1000 and 150 is 50. Divide both sides by 50 to get the ratio **20:3**.

b) 1 m = 100 cm, so
8 cm : 1.1 m = 8 cm : 110 cm.
The highest common factor of 8 and 110 is 2. Divide both sides by 2 to get **4:55**.

c) 1 kg = 1000 g, so 9 g : 0.3 kg = 9 g : 300 g.
The highest common factor of 9 and 300 is 3. Divide both sides by 3 to get **3:100**.

d) 1 hr = 60 mins,
so 2.5 hrs : 20 mins = 150 mins : 20 mins.
The highest common factor of 150 and 20 is 10. Divide both sides by 10 to get **15:2**.

e) £1 = 100p, so £1.25 : 75p = 125p : 75p.
The highest common factor of 125 and 75 is 25. Divide both sides by 25 to get **5:3**.

f) 1 km = 1000 m,
so 65 m : 1.3 km = 65 m : 1300 km.
The highest common factor of 65 and 1300 is 65. Divide both sides by 65 to get **1:20**.

3 1 litre = 1000 ml,
so 50 ml : 1 litre = 50 ml : 1000 ml.
The highest common factor of 50 and 1000 is 50. 50 ÷ 50 = 1 and 1000 ÷ 50 = 20, so the ratio in its simplest form is **1:20**.

4 1 hour = 60 minutes, so 45 minutes : 3.5 hours = 45 minutes : 210 minutes. The highest common factor of 45 and 210 is 15.
45 ÷ 15 = 3 and 210 ÷ 15 = 14,
so the ratio in its simplest form is **3:14**.

5 1 kg = 1000 g. The ratio of butter : icing sugar is 640 g : 1.6 kg = 640 g : 1600 g.
640 : 1600 = 640 ÷ 10 : 1600 ÷ 10 = 64 : 160
64 : 160 = 64 ÷ 16 : 160 ÷ 16 = 4 : 10 = **2:5**.

Page 92 Exercise 3

1 a) $2:6 = 1:\frac{6}{2} = \mathbf{1:3}$

b) $7:35 = 1:\frac{35}{7} = \mathbf{1:5}$

Use the same method for c)-h):

c) (÷ 6) **1:4** **d)** (÷ 30) **1:4**
e) (÷ 2) **1:3.5** **f)** (÷ 4) **1:6.5**
g) (÷ 8) **1:3.25** **h)** (÷ 2) **1:0.5**

2 a) 1 cm = 10 mm,
so 10 mm : 5 cm = 10 mm : 50 mm.
Divide both sides by 10 to get **1:5**.

b) £1 = 100p, so 12p : £6 = 12p : 600p.
Divide both sides by 12 to get **1:50**.

c) 1 hour = 60 mins,
so 30 mins : 2 hours = 30 mins : 120 mins.
Divide both sides by 30 to get **1:4**.

d) 1 kg = 1000 g,
so 500 g : 20 kg = 500 g : 20 000 g.
Divide both sides by 500 to get **1:40**.

3 The ratio of frogs to fish is
$7:56 = 1:\frac{56}{7} = \mathbf{1:8}$.

4 The ratio of red to silver cars is
$15:45 = 1:\frac{45}{15} = \mathbf{1:3}$.

5 1 litre = 1000 ml,
so 125 ml : 2.5 litres = 125 ml : 2500 ml.
The ratio of syrup to milk is
$125:2500 = 1:\frac{2500}{125} = \mathbf{1:20}$.

6 1 km = 1000 m and 1 m = 100 cm,
so 4.8 km = 4800 m = 480 000 cm.
So 12 cm : 4.8 km = 12 cm : 480 000 cm.
The ratio of map distance to true distance is $12:480\,000 = 1:\frac{480\,000}{12} = \mathbf{1:40\,000}$.
The question asks for the ratio of map distance to true distance, so remember to give your answer in the correct order.

Page 93 Exercise 4

1 The ratio blue : white = 1 : 3 has 1 + 3 = 4 parts, with 1 part blue. So the fraction of blue tiles is $\mathbf{\frac{1}{4}}$.

2 The ratio yellow : red = 3 : 2 has 3 + 2 = 5 parts, with 2 parts red. So the fraction of red beads is $\mathbf{\frac{2}{5}}$.

3 a) True. The total number of parts is 1 + 2 + 4 = 7. The blue part of the ratio is 1, so $\frac{1}{7}$ of the balls are blue.

b) True. As a) is true, you know the bag contains $\frac{1}{7} \times 21 = 3$ blue balls.

c) False. From a) $\frac{1}{7}$ balls are blue, so $1 - \frac{1}{7} = \frac{6}{7}$ are red or green.

d) True. The ratio blue : red = 1 : 4 is contained in the given ratio — it's found by ignoring the green part.

e) True. The ratio says there are 4 red balls for every 2 green, so there must be more red balls than green balls.

Page 93 Exercise 5

1 If $\frac{1}{3}$ of the Jelly Babies are red,
then $1 - \frac{1}{3} = \frac{2}{3}$ are green.
The two fractions have a common denominator (3), so the ratio of red to green is **1:2**.

2 If $\frac{3}{19}$ members are left-handed, then $1 - \frac{3}{19} = \frac{16}{19}$ are right-handed. The two fractions have a common denominator (19), so the ratio of right-handed to left-handed members is **16:3**.

3 The fraction of pepperoni pizzas is $\frac{3}{8}$.
The fraction of goat's cheese pizzas is $\frac{1}{2} = \frac{1 \times 4}{2 \times 4} = \frac{4}{8}$.
So the fraction of spicy chicken pizzas is $1 - \frac{3}{8} - \frac{4}{8} = \frac{1}{8}$.
These fractions have a common denominator (8), so the ratio is **3:4:1**.

6.2 Using Ratios

Page 94 Exercise 1

1 blue eyes : brown eyes = 2 : 3 = 8 : ?
Multiply both sides by 8 ÷ 2 = 4, so the ratio becomes 8 : 12.
So there are **12 brown eyed pupils**.

2 father's age : son's age = 8 : 3 = 48 : ?
Multiply both sides by 48 ÷ 8 = 6, so the ratio becomes 48 : 18. So the son's age is **18**.

3 red : yellow = 3 : 4 = ? : 12.
Multiply both sides by 12 ÷ 4 = 3, so the ratio becomes 9 : 12. So there are **9 red sweets** in the bag.

4 oak : beech = 2 : 9 = 42 : ?
Multiply both sides by 42 ÷ 2 = 21, so the ratio becomes 42 : 189. So there are **189 beech trees**.

5 apples : bananas = 5 : 3 = ? : 450
Multiply both sides by 450 ÷ 3 = 150, so the ratio becomes 750 : 450.
So there are **750 apples**.

6 sugar : butter = 2 : 1 = 100 : ?
Multiply both sides by 100 ÷ 2 = 50, so the ratio becomes 100 : 50. So **50 g** of butter is needed.
If there are units in this type of question, don't forget to include them in your answer.

7 small photo : large photo = 2 : 7 = 10 : ?
Multiply both sides by 10 ÷ 2 = 5, so the ratio becomes 2 : 35.
So the enlarged photo **35 cm** wide.

8 The ratio children : adults is 5 : 1, so there must be at least 1 adult for every 5 children.
If there are 32 children, then there must be at least $\frac{32}{5} = 6.4$ adults — you need a whole number, so the answer is **7 adults** (round up, as 6 adults is too few).

9 The ratio 'under 30s' : '30 or over' is at least 8 : 1, so there must be at least 8 'under 30s' for every '30 or over'. If there are 100 'under 30s', at most $\frac{100}{8} = 12.5$ can be '30 or over' — you need a whole number, so the answer is **12** (round down, as 13 is too many).

Page 95 Exercise 2

1 pineapple juice : orange juice = 1 : 3 = 500 : ?
Multiply both sides by 500, so the ratio becomes 500 : 1500. So **1500 ml** of orange juice are needed.

2 Mai : Lizzy : Dave = 31 : 33 : 37 = 155 : ? : ?
Multiply all parts by 155 ÷ 31 = 5, so the ratio becomes 155 : 165 : 185. So Lizzy is **165 cm** tall and Dave is **185 cm** tall.

3 1 hour and 10 minutes = 60 + 10 minutes = 70 minutes.
Max : Molly : Hasan = 3 : 7 : 2 = ? : 70 : ?
Multiply all parts by 70 ÷ 7 = 10, so the ratio becomes 30 : 70 : 20. So Max has been waiting **30 minutes** and Hasan has been waiting **20 minutes**.

Page 96 Exercise 3

1 7 – 4 = 3 parts are bourbons, so the ratio of digestives : bourbons = **4:3**.

2 There are 15 + 2 = 17 liquid parts in total, of which 15 parts are water. So the ratio water : total is **15:17**.

3 There are 99 parts in total, of which 53 parts are digital downloads. So 99 – 53 = 46 parts are CDs. So the ratio digital downloads : CDs sold is **53:46**.

4 There are 3 + 5 + 9 = 17 parts in total, of which 3 are roses. So the ratio roses : total is **3:17**.

6.3 Dividing in a Given Ratio

Page 98 Exercise 1

1 a) There are 2 + 1 = 3 parts in total.
3 parts = £48, so 1 part = 48 ÷ 3 = £16.
The shares are 2 × 16 = **£32** and **£16**.
Check your answer makes sense by seeing if the shares add up to the total. £32 + £16 = £48, so the answer looks good.

b) There are 1 + 3 = 4 parts in total.
4 parts = £48, so 1 part = 48 ÷ 4 = £12.
The shares are **£12** and 3 × 12 = **£36**.

Use the same method for c) and d):

c) **£40** and **£8** **d)** **£28** and **£20**

2 a) There are 4 + 1 = 5 parts in total.
5 parts = 90 kg, so 1 part = 18 kg.
The shares are 4 × 18 = **72 kg** and **18 kg**.

b) There are 7 + 2 = 9 parts in total.
9 parts = 90 kg, so 1 part = 10 kg.
The shares are 7 × 10 = **70 kg** and 2 × 10 = **20 kg**.

Use the same method for c) and d):

c) 48 kg and **42 kg** **d) 36 kg** and **54 kg**

3 a) There are 2 + 3 + 1 = 6 parts in total.
6 parts = 72 cm, so 1 part = 12 cm. The shares are 2 × 12 = **24 cm**, 3 × 12 = **36 cm** and **12 cm**.

b) There are 2 + 2 + 5 = 9 parts in total.
9 parts = 72 cm, so 1 part = 8 cm.
The shares are 2 × 8 = **16 cm**, **16 cm** and 5 × 8 = **40 cm**.

Use the same method for c) and d):

c) 30 cm, **18 cm** and **24 cm**

d) 28 cm, **24 cm** and **20 cm**

4 The total number of parts is 3 + 2 = 5.
5 parts = 30 cupcakes, so 1 part = 6 cupcakes.
The shares are 3 × 6 = **18** for Kat and 2 × 6 = **12** for Lincoln.

5 The total number of parts is 3 + 5 + 4 = 12.
12 parts = £6000, so 1 part = £500.
The shares are 3 × £500 = **£1500**, 5 × £500 = **£2500** and 4 × 500 = **£2000**.

6 The perimeter is 72 cm, so the length + width is half of this: 72 ÷ 2 = 36 cm. You need to share 36 cm in the ratio 5:1.
Number of parts = 5 + 1 = 6.
1 part = 36 ÷ 6 = 6 cm.
So length = 5 × 6 = **30 cm** and width = **6 cm**.

Page 98 Exercise 2

1 a) The first share is 1 part, the second share is 2 – 1 = 1 part.
2 parts = 60 sheep, so
1 part = 60 ÷ 2 = 30 sheep.
The flock is divided into **30 sheep** and **30 sheep**.

b) The first share is 2 parts, the second share is 3 – 2 = 1 part.
3 parts = 60 sheep, so
1 part = 60 ÷ 3 = 20 sheep.
The flock is divided into 2 × 20 = **40 sheep** and **20 sheep**.

Use the same method for c) and d):

c) 48 sheep and **12 sheep**

d) 35 sheep and **25 sheep**

2 The ratio yellow paint:total is 4:7, so the red part is 7 – 4 = 3.
7 parts = 42 litres, so 1 part = 6 litres.
The shares are 4 × 6 = **24 litres of yellow** and 3 × 6 = **18 litres of red**.

3 The ratio right-handed:total is 7:8, so the left-handed part is 8 – 7 = 1.
8 parts = 600 pupils, so 1 part = 75 pupils.
The left-handed share is **75 pupils**.

Page 99 Exercise 3

1 The ratio of 5p coins to 20p coins is 3:1.
The total number of parts is 3 + 1 = 4.
4 parts = 32 coins, so
1 part = 32 ÷ 4 = 8 coins. 20p coins make up 1 part, so there are **8** of them.

2 The ratio of passengers not on the phone to on the phone is 4:1. The total number of parts is 4 + 1 = 5. 5 parts = 30 passengers, so 1 part = 6 passengers. So there are 4 × 6 = **24 passengers not on their phone**.

3 The ratio Elsa:Daniel is 1:1.5. The total number of parts is 1 + 1.5 = 2.5.
2.5 parts = £5700, so 1 part = £2280.
So the profit that goes to Daniel is 1.5 × 2280 = **£3420**.

4 The ratio grapes:raspberries:strawberries is 1:2:3. The total number of parts is 1 + 2 + 3 = 6. 6 parts = 450 g, so 1 part = 75 g.
The shares are grapes: 1 × 75 = **75 g**, raspberries: 2 × 75 = **150 g** and strawberries: 3 × 75 = **225 g**.

5 The ratio Jacinta:Nicky:Samir is $1:\frac{1}{2}:\frac{1}{4}$ = 4:2:1. The total number of parts is 4 + 2 + 1= 7. 7 parts = 35 sweets, so 1 part = 5 sweets.
The shares are Jacinta: 4 × 5 = **20 sweets**, Nicky: 2 × 5 = **10 sweets** and Samir: **5 sweets**.

Page 100 Review Exercise

1 It's girls:boys so 14 comes first, the ratio is **14:17**.

2 a) The highest common factor of 24 and 6 is 6. Divide both sides by 6, so the ratio becomes **4:1**.

b) 1 cm = 10 mm, so 2 cm:8 mm = 20 mm:8 mm.
The highest common factor of 20 and 8 is 4. Divide both sides by 4, so the ratio becomes **5:2**.

c) The highest common factor of 6, 3 and 15 is 3. Divide all parts by 3, so the ratio becomes **2:1:5**.

d) 1 kg = 1000 g, so 0.03 kg = 30 g, so the ratio is 30 g:10 g:25 g.
The highest common factor of 30, 10 and 25 is 5. Divide all parts by 5, so the ratio becomes **6:2:5**.

3 There are 120 – 40 = 80 other animals.
So the ratio of donkeys:other animals = 40:80. Divide both sides by 40 to get the answer **1:2**.

4 The total number of parts is 5 + 1 + 4 = 10.
The stripy part is 1. So as a fraction it's $\mathbf{\frac{1}{10}}$.

5 As $\frac{5}{12}$ students eat school dinners,
$1-\frac{5}{12}=\frac{7}{12}$ students have a packed lunch.
The fractions already have a common denominator (12), so put the numerators into a ratio. It's packed lunch:school diners, so the answer is **7:5**.

6 green:red = 2:5 = ?:20.
As 20 = 5 × 4, the multiplier is 4, so there are 2 × 4 = **8 green peppers**.

7 Meera:Sabrina = 7:6 = ?:48. As 48 = 8 × 6 the multiplier is 8, so Meera gets 8 × 7 = **£56**.

8 a) The total number of parts is 1 + 7 = 8.
8 parts = 56 m, so 1 part = 7 m.
The shares are **7 m** and 7 × 7 = **49 m**.

b) The total number of parts is 4 + 4 = 8.
8 parts = 56 m, so 1 part = 7 m.
The shares are both 4 × 7 = **28 m**.

Use the same methods for c) and d):

c) 40 m and **16 m** **d) 44 m** and **12 m**

9 The total is 19 + 20 + 23 = 62.
62 parts = 496, so 1 part = 496 ÷ 62 = 8.
The shares are: **Gemma**: 19 × 8 = **152 cm**, **Alisha**: 20 × 8 = **160 cm** and **Omar**: 23 × 8 = **184 cm**.

10 Cara gets 3 – 2 = 1 part.
3 parts = £1200 so 1 part = 1200 ÷ 3 = £400.
So Cara gets **£400**.

11 a) daisies:dandelions = 1:2 and dandelions:thistles = 1:3 = 2:6, so daisies:dandelions:thistles = **1:2:6**

b) The total number of parts is 1 + 2 + 6 = 9.
9 parts = 54 plants, so
1 part = 54 ÷ 9 = 6 plants
Number of thistles = 6 × 6 = **36**

Page 101 Exam-Style Questions

1 a) 30:48 = 5:8 by dividing both sides by 6 *[1 mark]*

b) 30:48 = 5:8 = $1:\frac{8}{5}$ *[1 mark]*
= $1:1\frac{3}{5}$ = **1:1.6** *[1 mark]*

2 a) For every left-footed player there are 3 right-footed players, so the ratio right-footed:left-footed is **3:1** *[1 mark]*

b) The total number of parts is 3 + 1 = 4.
4 parts = 24 players, so 1 part = 6 players *[1 mark]*.
The number of right-footed players is 6 × 3 = **18** *[1 mark]*.

c) E.g. there are 4 parts in total and left-footed players make up 1 part *[1 mark]*, so $\mathbf{\frac{1}{4}}$ of the players are left-footed *[1 mark]*.

3 a) adults:children is 240:90 *[1 mark]*
so adults:boys:girls is 240:60:30 = **8:2:1** *[1 mark — show all working]*
You could simplify the adult:children ratio to 8:3 first and then split up the 3 to give 8:2:1.

b) 8 parts = 200, so 1 part = 200 ÷ 8 *[1 mark]* = 25, so the number of boys = 2 × 25 = 50 *[1 mark]*.
Or you could do 200 ÷ 240 × 60 = 50.

4 a) Divide both sides by 4 to get the ratio 1:1.25 *[1 mark]*.

b) E.g. if the two bags contained 400 g and 500 g of flour, then their weights would be in the ratio 400:500 = 4:5 = 1:1.25.
If 100 g is added to each bag, the ratio becomes 500:600 = 1:600 ÷ 500 = 1:1.2.
So the ratio is different from 1:1.25.
[2 marks — 1 mark for example weight in correct ratio, 1 mark for calculating correct ratio after adding same weight to each bag]

c) Alan could multiply or divide the weight in each bag by the same amount. *[1 mark]*

Section 7 — Percentages

7.1 Percentages

Page 103 Exercise 1

1 a) 40 squares out of 100 are shaded, which is **40%**.

b) 47 squares out of 100 are shaded, which is **47%**.

c) 89 squares out of 100 are shaded, which is **89%**.

2 a) 13% **b) 27%** **c) 76%** **d) 243%**

3 13 out of 100 goals were penalties, so 100 – 13 = 87 goals were not penalties.
87 out of 100 goals is **87%**.
If something is out of 100, you can write down the percentage straight away.

4 a) $\mathbf{\frac{45}{300}}$

b) Divide the numerator and denominator by 3.
$\frac{45}{300} = \mathbf{\frac{15}{100}}$

c) **15%**

5 a) $\frac{11}{25} = \frac{44}{100} = \mathbf{44\%}$

b) $\frac{33}{50} = \frac{66}{100} = \mathbf{66\%}$

c) $\frac{3}{20} = \frac{15}{100} = \mathbf{15\%}$

d) $\frac{21}{10} = \frac{210}{100} = \mathbf{210\%}$

e) $\frac{12}{200} = \frac{6}{100} = \mathbf{6\%}$

f) $\frac{99}{300} = \frac{33}{100} = \mathbf{33\%}$

g) $\frac{600}{400} = \frac{150}{100} = \mathbf{150\%}$

h) $\frac{890}{1000} = \frac{89}{100} = \mathbf{89\%}$

Page 104 Exercise 2

1 a) $\frac{8}{32} = \frac{1}{4} = \frac{25}{100} = \mathbf{25\%}$

b) $\frac{36}{60} = \frac{6}{10} = \frac{60}{100} = \mathbf{60\%}$

c) $\frac{24}{40} = \frac{6}{10} = \frac{60}{100} = \mathbf{60\%}$

d) $\frac{48}{120} = \frac{4}{10} = \frac{40}{100} = \mathbf{40\%}$

e) $\frac{34}{170} = \frac{2}{10} = \frac{20}{100} = \mathbf{20\%}$

f) $\frac{42}{35} = \frac{6}{5} = \frac{120}{100} = \mathbf{120\%}$

2 a) $\frac{18}{24} = \frac{3}{4} = \frac{75}{100} = \mathbf{75\%}$

b) 100% – 75% = **25%**

3 55 – 33 = 22
$\frac{22}{55} = \frac{2}{5} = \frac{40}{100} = \mathbf{40\%}$

4 65 – 39 = 26
$\frac{26}{65} = \frac{2}{5} = \frac{40}{100} = \mathbf{40\%}$

Page 105 Exercise 3

1 a) (15 ÷ 24) × 100% = **62.5%**

b) (77 ÷ 275) × 100% = **28%**

c) (61 ÷ 500) × 100% = **12.2%**

d) (1512 ÷ 375) × 100% = **403.2%**

2 (525 ÷ 875) × 100% = **60%**

3 (£252 ÷ £560) × 100% = **45%**

4 (171 ÷ 180) × 100% = **95%**

5 a) (31.36 ÷ 32) × 100% = **98%**

b) (£117.30 ÷ £782) × 100% = **15%**

6 (£1896.25 ÷ £10 250) × 100% = **18.5%**

7 Total pocket money = £5.60 + £2.40 = £8
(£2.40 ÷ £8) × 100% = **30%**

Page 106 Exercise 4

1 a) 50% of 24 = 24 ÷ 2 = **12**

b) 50% of 15 = 15 ÷ 2 = **7.5**

c) 25% of 36 = 36 ÷ 4 = **9**

d) 25% of 120 = 120 ÷ 4 = **30**

e) 10% of 90 = 90 ÷ 10 = **9**

f) 10% of 270 = 270 ÷ 10 = **27**

2 a) 25% of 48 = 48 ÷ 4 = **12**

b) 75% = 25% × 3 = 12 × 3 = **36**

3 a) 10% of 120 = 120 ÷ 10 = **12**

b) (i) 5% = 10% ÷ 2 = 12 ÷ 2 = **6**

(ii) 20% = 10% × 2 = 12 × 2 = **24**

(iii) 25% = 20% + 5% = 24 + 6 = **30**

4 a) 25% of 12 = 12 ÷ 4 = 3
75% = 25% × 3 = 3 × 3 = **9**

b) 25% of 20 = 20 ÷ 4 = 5
125% = 25% × 5 = 5 × 5 = **25**

c) 10% of 260 = 260 ÷ 10 = 26
5% = 10% ÷ 2 = 26 ÷ 2 = **13**

d) 10% of 200 = 200 ÷ 10 = 20
1% = 10% ÷ 10 = 20 ÷ 10 = 2
30% = 10% × 3 = 20 × 3 = 60
31% = 30% + 1% = 60 + 2 = **62**

e) 10% of 70 = 70 ÷ 10 = 7
110% = 100% + 10% = 70 + 7 = **77**

f) 10% of 500 = 500 ÷ 10 = 50
40% = 10% × 4 = 50 × 4 = 200
1% = 10% ÷ 10 = 50 ÷ 10 = 5
6% = 1% × 6 = 5 × 6 = 30
46% = 40% + 6% = 200 + 30 = **230**

5 10% of £30 = £30 ÷ 10 = £3
80% of £30 = 10% × 8 = £3 × 8 = £24
1% of £30 = 10% ÷ 10 = £3 ÷ 10 = £0.30
3% of £30 = 1% × 3 = £0.30 × 3 = £0.90
83% of £30 = 80% + 3%
= £24 + £0.90 = **£24.90**

6 50% of 9 m = 9 m ÷ 2 = 4.5 m
10% of 9 m = 9 m ÷ 10 = 0.9 m
5% of 9 m = 10% ÷ 2 = 0.9 m ÷ 2 = 0.45 m
55% of 9 m = 50% + 5%
= 4.5 m + 0.45 m = **4.95 m**

7 10% of £1400 = £1400 ÷ 10 = £140
5% of £1400 = 10% ÷ 2 = £140 ÷ 2 = £70
90% of £1400 = 10% × 9 = £140 × 9
= £1260
95% of £1400 = 90% + 5% = £1260 + £70
= **£1330**
You could also subtract 5% from 100%.

Page 107 Exercise 5

1 a) 17% ÷ 100% = 0.17
0.17 × 200 = **34**

b) 9% ÷ 100% = 0.09
0.09 × 11 = **0.99**

Using the same method for c)-f)

c) **6.3** d) **971.7**

e) **420.67** f) **2320.86**

2 12% ÷ 100% = 0.12
0.12 × 68 = **8.16 kg**

3 31% ÷ 100% = 0.31
0.31 × 385 = **119.35 km**

4 52% ÷ 100% = 0.52
0.52 × 125 = **65 men**

5 68% ÷ 100% = 0.68
0.68 × £42 = **£28.56**

6 22% of £57: 22% ÷ 100% = 0.22
0.22 × £57 = £12.54

46% of £28: 46% ÷ 100% = 0.46
0.46 × £28 = £12.88

£12.88 > £12.54, so **46% of £28 is larger** than 22% of £57.
The difference is £12.88 – £12.54 = **£0.34**

7 34% ÷ 100% = 0.34
0.34 × 2.4 = 0.816 litres
It can hold another 2.4 – 0.816 = **1.584 litres.**

7.2 Percentages, Fractions and Decimals

Page 109 Exercise 1

1 a) 50 out of 100 squares are shaded.
(i) **50%** (ii) **0.5** (iii) $\mathbf{\frac{1}{2}}$

b) 25 out of 100 squares are shaded.
(i) **25%** (ii) **0.25** (iii) $\mathbf{\frac{1}{4}}$

c) 10 out of 100 squares are shaded.
(i) **10%** (ii) **0.1** (iii) $\mathbf{\frac{1}{10}}$

2 a) $\frac{3}{20} = \frac{3 \times 5}{20 \times 5} = \mathbf{\frac{15}{100}}$

b) (i) **15%** (ii) 15% ÷ 100% = **0.15**

3 a) (i) 30% ÷ 100% = **0.3**

(ii) $0.3 = \mathbf{\frac{3}{10}}$

b) (i) 5% ÷ 100% = **0.05**

(ii) $0.05 = \frac{5}{100} = \mathbf{\frac{1}{20}}$

Using the same method for c) and d):

c) (i) **0.13** (ii) $\mathbf{\frac{13}{100}}$

d) (i) **0.96** (ii) $\mathbf{\frac{24}{25}}$

4 a) (i) 79 ÷ 100 = **0.79**

(ii) 0.79 × 100% = **79%**

b) (i) $\frac{2}{5} = \frac{4}{10} = \mathbf{0.4}$

(ii) 0.4 × 100% = **40%**

c) (i) $\frac{4}{25} = \frac{16}{100} = \mathbf{0.16}$

(ii) 0.16 × 100% = **16%**

d) (i) $7 \div 8 = \begin{array}{r} 0.875 \\ 8\overline{)7.{}^{7}0{}^{6}0{}^{4}0} \end{array} = \mathbf{0.875}$

(ii) 0.875 × 100% = **87.5%**

5 a) (i) 0.35 × 100% = **35%**

(ii) $0.35 = \frac{35}{100} = \mathbf{\frac{7}{20}}$

b) (i) 0.86 × 100% = **86%**

(ii) $0.86 = \frac{86}{100} = \mathbf{\frac{43}{50}}$

c) (i) 1.2 × 100% = **120%**

(ii) $1.2 = \frac{12}{10} = \mathbf{\frac{6}{5}}$

d) (i) 0.125 × 100% = **12.5%**

(ii) $0.125 = \frac{125}{1000} = \mathbf{\frac{1}{8}}$

6 76% ÷ 100% = **0.76**

7 $\frac{3}{5} = \frac{60}{100} = \mathbf{60\%}$

Page 110 Exercise 2

1 a) 0.35 × 100% = 35%
35% > 32% so **0.35** is larger.
You could have changed 32% into a decimal instead.

b) 0.4 × 100% = 40%
40% > 4% so **0.4** is larger.

c) 0.09 × 100% = 9%
90% > 9% so **90%** is larger.

d) $0.2 = \frac{20}{100}$
$\frac{21}{100} > \frac{20}{100}$ so $\mathbf{\frac{21}{100}}$ is larger.

e) $0.6 = \frac{6}{10}$
$\frac{7}{10} > \frac{6}{10}$ so $\mathbf{\frac{7}{10}}$ is larger.

f) $0.55 = \frac{55}{100}$
$\frac{3}{5} = \frac{60}{100}$
$\frac{60}{100} > \frac{55}{100}$ so $\mathbf{\frac{3}{5}}$ is larger.

2 a) 25% ÷ 100% = 0.25
$\frac{2}{5} = \frac{4}{10} = 0.4$
0.25 < 0.4 < 0.42, so ordered list is
25%, $\frac{2}{5}$, 0.42

b) 45% ÷ 100% = 0.45
$\frac{1}{2} = 0.5$
0.45 < 0.5 < 0.505, so ordered list is
45%, $\frac{1}{2}$, 0.505

Using the same method for c)-f):

c) 0.37, 38%, $\frac{4}{10}$

d) 0.2, 22%, $\frac{6}{25}$

e) 12.5%, 0.13, $\frac{3}{20}$

f) $\frac{9}{40}$, 23%, 0.25

3 $\frac{1}{25} = \frac{4}{100} = 4\%$
5% > 4% so **Shop B** is reducing their prices by the greater percentage.

4 $\frac{2}{5} = \frac{40}{100} = 40\%$
40% > 35%, so 35% is **not enough** to pay the deposit.

5 $\frac{14}{20} = \frac{7}{10} = \frac{70}{100} = 70\%$
70% > 60%, so **Team X** had a higher proportion of wins.

6 $\frac{11}{20} = \frac{55}{100} = 55\%$
55% < 65%, so **Oliver** got more counters into the box.

Page 111 Exercise 3

1 $\frac{3}{4} = \frac{75}{100}$ = 75% arrived by train.
0.05 × 100% = 5% walked.
People that came by car = 100% – 75% – 5% = **20%**

2 $\frac{3}{5} = \frac{60}{100}$ = 60% are white footballs.
20% are black footballs.
Blue footballs = 100% – 60% – 20% = **20%**

3 Beverley eats 0.3 × 100% = 30% of the pie.
Victoria eats = $\frac{1}{10} = \frac{10}{100}$ = 10%.
Patrick eats 20%.
So Gus eats 100% – 30% – 10% – 20% = **40%**.

4 $\frac{3}{8} = 3 \div 8 = 8\overline{)3.{}^{3}0{}^{6}0{}^{4}0}$ = 0.375 (quotient 0.375)
0.375 × 100% = 37.5% were sparrows and 41.5% were blackbirds, so
100% – 37.5% – 41.5% = **21%** were robins.
Look back at section 1 for help with dividing without a calculator.

7.3 Percentage Increase and Decrease

Page 112 Exercise 1

1 a) 50% of 360 = 360 ÷ 2 = **180**
b) 360 + 180 = **540**

2 a) 10% of 120 = 120 ÷ 10 = 12
30% of 120 = 10% × 3 = 12 × 3 = **36**
b) 120 + 36 = **156**

3 a) 10% of 160 = 160 ÷ 10 = **16**
b) 160 – 16 = **144**

4 a) 10% of 84 = 84 ÷ 10 = 8.4
20% of 84 = 10% × 2 = 8.4 × 2 = **16.8**
b) 84 – 16.8 = **67.2**

5 a) 10% of 90 = 90 ÷ 10 = 9
90 + 9 = **99**
b) 10% of 11 = 11 ÷ 10 = 1.1
80% of 11 = 10% × 8 = 1.1 × 8 = 8.8
11 + 8.8 = **19.8**
c) 10% of 140 = 140 ÷ 10 = 14
5% of 140 = 10% ÷ 2 = 14 ÷ 2 = 7
40% of 140 = 10% × 4 = 14 × 4 = 56
45% of 140 = 40% + 5% = 56 + 7 = 63
140 + 63 = **203**

6 a) 25% of 24 = 24 ÷ 4 = 6
24 – 6 = **18**
b) 10% of 55 = 55 ÷ 10 = 5.5
70% of 55 = 10% × 7 = 5.5 × 7 = 38.5
55 – 38.5 = **16.5**
c) 10% of 150 = 150 ÷ 10 = 15
5% of 150 = 10% ÷ 2 = 15 ÷ 2 = 7.5
50% of 150 = 150 ÷ 2 = 75
55% of 150 = 50% + 5% = 75 + 7.5 = 82.5
150 – 82.5 = **67.5**

Page 113 Exercise 2

1 a) 11% ÷ 100% = 0.11
Multiplier = 0.11 + 1 = 1.11
490 × 1.11 = **543.9**
b) 16% ÷ 100% = 0.16
Multiplier = 0.16 + 1 = 1.16
101 × 1.16 = **117.16**
Using the same method for c)-f):
c) 75.35 **d) 4213.41**
e) 1274.28 **f) 48 180**

2 a) 8% ÷ 100% = 0.08
Multiplier = 1 – 0.08 = 0.92
77 × 0.92 = **70.84**
b) 21% ÷ 100% = 0.21
Multiplier = 1 – 0.21 = 0.79
36 × 0.79 = **28.44**
Using the same method for c)-f):
c) 57.57 **d) 5253.32**
e) 72 240 **f) 95 120**

3 a) 62% ÷ 100% = 0.62
Multiplier = 1 + 0.62 = 1.62
£89.50 × 1.62 = **£144.99**
Remember to include the units given in the question.
b) 19% ÷ 100% = 0.19
Multiplier = 1 – 0.19 = 0.81
58 kg × 0.81 = **46.98 kg**

Page 114 Exercise 3

1 10% of £230 = £230 ÷ 10 = £23
5% of £230 = £23 ÷ 2 = £11.50
Total after 1 year = £230 + £11.50 = **£241.50**

2 1% of £890 = £890 ÷ 100 = £8.90
3% of £890 = 1% × 3 = £8.90 × 3 = £26.70
After three years Kimberley has
£890 + 3 × £26.70 = **£970.10**

Page 115 Exercise 4

1 10% of £24 500 = £24 500 ÷ 10 = £2450
5% of £24 500 = £2450 ÷ 2 = £1225
15% of £24 500 = £2450 + £1225 = £3675
New salary = £24 500 + £3675 = **£28 175**

2 25% of £42 = £42 ÷ 4 = £10.50
75% of £42 = £10.50 × 3 = £31.50
Sale price = £42 – £31.50 = **£10.50**

3 10% of £485 = £485 ÷ 10 = £48.50
20% of £485 = £48.50 × 2 = £97
Selling price = £485 + £97 = **£582**

4 13% ÷ 100% = 0.13
Multiplier = 1 – 0.13 = 0.87
Total = £63 × 0.87 = **£54.81**

5 20% ÷ 100% = 0.2
Multiplier = 1 + 0.2 = 1.2
Height at 10 years old = 50 × 1.2 = **60 inches**

6 25% of 8 = 8 ÷ 4 = 2
Natalie's remaining fuel = 8 – 2 = 6 gallons
10% of 12 = 12 ÷ 10 = 1.2
40% of 12 = 1.2 × 4 = 4.8
Jason's remaining fuel = 12 – 4.8 = 7.2 gallons
7.2 > 6 and 7.2 – 6 = 1.2
So **Jason had 1.2 gallons more fuel** than Natalie at the end of the journey.

7 2% ÷ 100% = 0.02
Multiplier = 1 + 0.02 = 1.02
Gas bill = £480 × 1.02 = £489.60
4% ÷ 100% = 0.04
Multiplier = 1 – 0.04 = 0.96
Electricity bill = £612 × 0.96 = £587.52
£587.52 > £489.60 and £587.52 – £489.60 = £97.92, so **electricity bill** is still more expensive, by **£97.92**.
In questions 7 and 8, one step of the question is a % increase and the other is a % decrease, so you need to be really careful with your multipliers.

8 3% ÷ 100% = 0.03
Multiplier = 1 + 0.03 = 1.03
Salary after 3% increase = £31 000 × 1.03 = £31 930
2% ÷ 100% = 0.02
Multiplier = 1 – 0.02 = 0.98
New salary after 2% decrease = £31 930 × 0.98 = **£31 291.40**

Page 116 Exercise 5

1 a) £12 – £10 = £2
$\frac{2}{10} = \frac{20}{100}$ = 20% ⇒ **20% increase**
b) £22 – £20 = £2
$\frac{2}{20} = \frac{10}{100}$ = 10% ⇒ **10% increase**
c) £161 – £140 = £21
$\frac{21}{140} = \frac{3}{20} = \frac{15}{100}$ = 15%
⇒ **15% increase**
d) £174 – £120 = £54
$\frac{54}{120} = \frac{9}{20} = \frac{45}{100}$ = 45%
⇒ **45% increase**

2 a) £10 – £8 = £2
$\frac{2}{10} = \frac{20}{100}$ = 20% ⇒ **20% decrease**
b) £25 – £22 = £3
$\frac{3}{25} = \frac{12}{100}$ = 12% ⇒ **12% decrease**
c) £80 – £64 = £16
$\frac{16}{80} = \frac{2}{10} = \frac{20}{100}$ = 20% ⇒ **20% decrease**
d) £150 – £138 = £12
$\frac{12}{150} = \frac{4}{50} = \frac{8}{100}$ = 8% ⇒ **8% decrease**

3 a) 72 – 50 = **22**
b) $\frac{22}{50}$
c) $\frac{22}{50} = \frac{44}{100}$ = 44% ⇒ **44% increase**

4 100p – 80p = 20p
$\frac{20}{80} = \frac{1}{4} = \frac{25}{100}$ = 25% ⇒ **25% increase**

5 £50 – £30 = £20
$\frac{20}{50} = \frac{40}{100}$ = 40% ⇒ **40% reduction**

6 a) 90 kg – 72 kg = **18 kg**
b) $\frac{18}{90} = \frac{2}{10} = \frac{20}{100}$ = 20% ⇒ **20% decrease**

Page 117 Exercise 6

1 £70.20 – £52 = £18.20
(18.20 ÷ 52) × 100% = 35% ⇒ **35% profit**

2 2.08 m – 1.3 m = 0.78 m
(0.78 ÷ 1.3) × 100% = 60% ⇒ **60% increase**

3 11 350 – 11 123 = 227
(227 ÷ 11 350) × 100% = 2%
⇒ **2% decrease**

4 a) £12 950 – £8806 = £4144
(4144 ÷ 12 950) × 100% = 32%
⇒ **32% decrease** in first 3 years.

b) £8806 – £4403 = £4403
(4403 ÷ 8806) × 100% = 50%
⇒ **50% decrease** in the next 3 years.

c) £12 950 – £4403 = £8547
(8547 ÷ 12 950) × 100% = 66%
⇒ **66% decrease** over 6 years.

Page 118 Exercise 7

1 50% of original price = £200
100% of original price = £200 × 2 = **£400**

2 100% – 35% = 65%,
so 65% of original price = £13.00
1% of original price = £13.00 ÷ 65 = £0.20
Original price = £0.20 × 100 = **£20**

3 100% + 26% = 126%,
so 126% of original price = £819
1% of original price = £819 ÷ 126 = £6.50
Original price = £6.50 × 100 = **£650**

4 100% – 4% = 96%,
so 96% of original price = £192 000
1% of original price = £192 000 ÷ 96
= £2000
Original price = £2000 × 100 = **£200 000**

5 100% + 10% = 110%
110% of number of frogs last year = 528
Number of frogs last year = (528 ÷ 110) × 100
= **480**
100% + 15% = 115%
115% of number of newts last year = 621
Number of newts last year
= (621 ÷ 115) × 100 = **540**

7.4 Compound Growth and Decay

Page 119 Exercise 1

1 3% ÷ 100% = 0.03
Multiplier = 1 + 0.03 = 1.03

a) £250 × 1.03 = £257.50
Interest earned = £257.50 – £250 = **£7.50**
You need to subtract the original amount to find the interest earned.

b) First year: £45 × 1.03 = £46.35
Second year: £46.35 × 1.03 = £47.7405
Third year: £47.7405 × 1.03 = £49.172715
Interest earned = £49.172715 – £45
= £4.172715 = **£4.17** (nearest penny)

c) First year: £1500 × 1.03 = £1545
Second year: £1545 × 1.03 = £1591.35
Interest earned = £1591.35 – £1500
= **£91.35**

2 a) 4.5% ÷ 100% = 0.045
Multiplier = 1 + 0.045 = 1.045
First year: £3500 × 1.045 = £3657.50
Second year: £3657.50 × 1.045
= £3822.0875 = **£3822.09** (nearest penny)

b) Third year: £3822.0875 × 1.045
= £3994.081438
= **£3994.08** (nearest penny)

Page 120 Exercise 2

1 a) 15% ÷ 100% = 0.15
Multiplier = 1 – 0.15 = 0.85
First year: £320 × 0.85 = £272
Second year: £272 × 0.85 = **£231.20**

b) Third year: £231.20 × 0.85 = **£196.52**

2 5% ÷ 100% = 0.05
Multiplier = 1 – 0.05 = 0.95
Day 1: $1000 × 0.95 = $950
Day 2: $950 × 0.95 = **$902.50**

3 6% ÷ 100% = 0.06
Multiplier for first two years = 1 – 0.06 = 0.94
First year: £12 000 × 0.94 = £11 280
Second year: £11 280 × 0.94 = £10 603.20
17% ÷ 100% = 0.17
Multiplier for third year = 1 – 0.17 = 0.83
Third year: £10 603.20 × 0.83 = £8800.656
= **£8800.66** (nearest penny)

Page 121 Exercise 3

1 a) 4% ÷ 100% = 0.04
Multiplier = 1 + 0.04 = 1.04
Final amount = £1000 × $(1.04)^8$
= £1368.56905
= **£1368.57** (nearest penny)

b) 5.2% ÷ 100% = 0.052
Multiplier = 1 + 0.052 = 1.052
Final amount = £600 × $(1.052)^7$
= £855.5815862
= **£855.58** (nearest penny)

2 2% ÷ 100% = 0.02
Multiplier = 1 – 0.02 = 0.98
Final value = £650 000 × $(0.98)^6$
= £575 797.5476 = **£575 800** (nearest £100)

3 6% ÷ 100% = 0.06
Multiplier = 1 + 0.06 = 1.06
n = number of days = 5
Number of ants = 250 × $(1.06)^5$
= 334.556... = **334 ants**
Check to see if you should round your final answer based on the context. Here, you can't have '0.55...' of an ant, so you need to round down.

4 2% ÷ 100% = 0.02
Multiplier = 1 – 0.02 = 0.98
Final body weight = 110 kg × $(0.98)^8$
= 93.583... kg = **93.6 kg** (1 d.p.)

Page 122 Review Exercise

1 $\frac{12}{25} = \frac{48}{100}$ = **48%**

2 10% of £160 = £160 ÷ 10 = £16
5% of £160 = £16 ÷ 2 = £8
30% of £160 = 10% × 3 = £16 × 3 = £48
35% of £160 = 30% + 5% = £48 + £8 = **£56**

3 a) There are 5 shaded squares.
(i) $\frac{5}{25} = \mathbf{\frac{1}{5}}$
(ii) $\frac{5}{25} = \frac{20}{100}$ = **20%**
(iii) 20% ÷ 100% = **0.2**

b) There are 17 shaded squares.
(i) $\mathbf{\frac{17}{25}}$
(ii) $\frac{17}{25} = \frac{68}{100}$ = **68%**
(iii) 68% ÷ 100% = **0.68**

4 $\frac{31}{500}$ = 0.062, 6% ÷ 100% = 0.06,
so ordered list from smallest to largest is
6%, 0.061, $\mathbf{\frac{31}{500}}$

5 50% of 450 g = 450 g ÷ 2 = 225 g
10% of 450 g = 450 g ÷ 10 = 45 g
5% of 450 g = 45 g ÷ 2 = 22.5 g
55% of 450 g = 225 g + 22.5 g = 247.5 g
450 g + 247.5 g = **697.5 g**

6 Shop A: 70% ÷ 100% = 0.7
Multiplier = 1 – 0.7 = 0.3
Sale price = £92 × 0.3 = £27.60
Shop B: $\frac{7}{8}$ = 0.875
Multiplier = 1 – 0.875 = 0.125
Sale price = £92 × 0.125 = £11.50
£27.60 – £11.50 = £16.10
So **Shop B** had the lower price by **£16.10**
You could also have found the price in Shop B by calculating $\frac{7}{8}$ using fraction methods (see page 105).

7 8.5% ÷ 100% = 0.085
Multiplier = 1 + 0.085 = 1.085
Amount at end of the year
= £3250 × 1.085 = **£3526.25**

8 75 g – 69 g = 6 g
$\frac{6}{75} = \frac{2}{25} = \frac{8}{100}$ = **8%**

9 100% – 70% = 30%
So 30% of original price = £2.85
1% of original price = £2.85 ÷ 30 = £0.095
Original price = 100 × £0.095 = **£9.50**

10 8% ÷ 100% = 0.08
Multiplier = 1 + 0.08 = 1.08
Using the formula, the population after 5 years is given by: 12 500 × $(1.08)^5$ = 18 366.600...
So population will be **18 366**.

Page 123 Exam-Style Questions

1 10% of 750 MB = 750 MB ÷ 10 = 75 MB
5% of 750 MB = 10% ÷ 2 = 75 MB ÷ 2
= 37.5 MB
15% = 75 MB + 37.5 MB = 112.5 MB
[1 mark]
750MB + 112.5 MB = **862.5 MB** *[1 mark]*

2 24% ÷ 100% = 0.24
Multiplier = 1 + 0.24 = 1.24 *[1 mark]*
3.7 m × 1.24 = 4.588 m *[1 mark]*
= **4.59 m** (nearest centimetre)
[1 mark]

3 £450 million – £375 million
= £75 million *[1 mark]*
$\frac{75}{375}$ × 100% = **20%** *[1 mark]*

4 Total number of balls in the box
= 20 + 12 + 8 = 40
Total number of basketballs = 20 + 8 = 28
Percentage of balls that are basketballs
= $\frac{28}{40} = \frac{7}{10} = \frac{70}{100}$ = **70%**
[2 marks available — 1 mark for calculating both totals, 1 mark for correct percentage]

5 20% ÷ 100% = 0.2
Multiplier for first two years = 1 – 0.2 = 0.8
First year: £68 000 × 0.8 = £54 400
Second year: £54 400 × 0.8 = £43 520
15% ÷ 100% = 0.15
Multiplier for following three years = 1 – 0.15
= 0.85
Third year: £43 520 × 0.85 = £36 992
Fourth year: £36 992 × 0.85 = £31 443.20
Fifth year: £31 443.20 × 0.85 = **£26 726.72**
[4 marks available — 1 mark for each correct multiplier, 1 mark for correct answer after two years, 1 mark for correct final answer]

6 If 30% are lemurs and 40% of lemurs are ring-tailed lemurs then you need to find 40% of 30%.
10% of 30% = 3%
40% of 30% = 4 × 3% = **12%**
[2 marks available — 1 mark for correct method of finding 40% of 30%, 1 mark for the correct answer]
There's more than one correct method — you could work out $\frac{40}{100} \times \frac{30}{100}$, then simplify and read off the numerator.

Section 8 — Algebraic Expressions

8.1 Simplifying Expression

Page 125 Exercise 1

1 a) $2x + 3x + x = \mathbf{6x}$
b) $7p - 2p + 3p - 4p = \mathbf{4p}$
c) $c + c + c + d + d = \mathbf{3c + 2d}$
d) $a + b + a - a + b = (a + a - a) + (b + b) = \mathbf{a + 2b}$
e) $5a - 2a + 5b + 2b = (5a - 2a) + (5b + 2b) = \mathbf{3a + 7b}$
f) $4b + 8c - b - 5c = (4b - b) + (8c - 5c) = \mathbf{3b + 3c}$

2 a) $2c + 4 + c + 7 = (2c + c) + (4 + 7) = \mathbf{3c + 11}$
b) $3x + 6 - 6x - 4 = (3x - 6x) + (6 - 4) = \mathbf{-3x + 2}$
Using the same method for c)-f):
c) $\mathbf{-4y + 5}$ d) $\mathbf{-9m + 21}$
e) $\mathbf{3x + 10}$ f) $\mathbf{21a + 10}$

3 a) $x + 7 + 4x + y + 5 = (x + 4x) + y + (7 + 5) = \mathbf{5x + y + 12}$
Using the same method for b)-d):
b) $\mathbf{-4a + 3b - 8}$ c) $\mathbf{21a + 7b + 7}$
d) $\mathbf{4p + 4q - 20r - 9}$

Page 125 Exercise 2

1 a) $x^2 + 3x + 2 + 2x + 3 = \mathbf{x^2 + 5x + 5}$
b) $x^2 + 4x + 1 + 3x - 3 = \mathbf{x^2 + 7x - 2}$
Using the same method for c)-f):
c) $\mathbf{2x^2 + 6x + 4}$ d) $\mathbf{3x^2 + x}$
e) $\mathbf{3p^2 - 2p}$ f) $\mathbf{7p^2 + 2q}$
g) $8 + 6p^2 - 5 + pq + p^2$
$= (6p^2 + p^2) + pq + (8 - 5)$
$= \mathbf{7p^2 + pq + 3}$
The extra step of grouping 'like terms' makes it less likely you'll make an error.
h) $4p + 5q - pq + p^2 - 7q$
$= p^2 + 4p - pq + (5q - 7q)$
$= \mathbf{p^2 + 4p - 2q - pq}$
i) $a^2 + 7b + 2a^2 + 5ab - 3b$
$= (a^2 + 2a^2) + (7b - 3b) + 5ab$
$= \mathbf{3a^2 + 4b + 5ab}$

2 a) $ab + cd - xy + 3ab - 2cd + 3yx + 2x^2$
$= (ab + 3ab) + (cd - 2cd) + (3xy - xy) + 2x^2$
$= \mathbf{4ab - cd + 2xy + 2x^2}$
b) $pq + 3pq + p^2 - 2qp + q^2$
$= p^2 + (pq + 3pq - 2pq) + q^2$
$= \mathbf{p^2 + 2pq + q^2}$

3 a) $7 + 3\sqrt{3} + 6 - 2\sqrt{3}$
$= (7 + 6) + (3\sqrt{3} - 2\sqrt{3})$
$= \mathbf{13 + \sqrt{3}}$
b) $-2 - 13\sqrt{7} - 7 + 3\sqrt{7}$
$= (-2 - 7) + (3\sqrt{7} - 13\sqrt{7})$
$= \mathbf{-9 - 10\sqrt{7}}$
c) $11 - 7\sqrt{5} - 11 - 8\sqrt{5}$
$= (11 - 11) + (-7\sqrt{5} - 8\sqrt{5})$
$= \mathbf{-15\sqrt{5}}$

Page 126 Exercise 3

1 a) $a \times a \times a = \mathbf{a^3}$
b) $2a \times 3a = 2 \times 3 \times a \times a = \mathbf{6a^2}$
c) $-8p \times 2q = -8 \times 2 \times p \times q = \mathbf{-16pq}$
Using the same method for d)-h):
d) $\mathbf{21a^2}$ e) $\mathbf{15xy}$ f) $\mathbf{-m^4}$
g) $\mathbf{48ab}$ h) $\mathbf{48p^2}$

2 a) $a \times ab = a \times a \times b = \mathbf{a^2b}$
b) $4m^3 \div m = (4 \div 1) \times (m^3 \div m) = \mathbf{4m^2}$
c) $(r^2)^3 = r^{2 \times 3} = \mathbf{r^6}$
Using the same method for d)-h):
d) $\mathbf{3s^2t^2}$ e) $\mathbf{20a^3}$ f) $\mathbf{3s}$
g) $\mathbf{8a^5b^5}$ h) $\mathbf{2y}$

8.2 Expanding Brackets

Page 127 Exercise 1

1 a) $2(a + 5) = (2 \times a) + (2 \times 5) = \mathbf{2a + 10}$
b) $4(b + 3) = (4 \times b) + (4 \times 3) = \mathbf{4b + 12}$
c) $5(d + 7) = (5 \times d) + (5 \times 7) = \mathbf{5d + 35}$
Using the same method for d)-h):
d) $\mathbf{3p + 12}$ e) $\mathbf{15 + 3p}$ f) $\mathbf{42 + 7g}$
g) $\mathbf{15 - 5y}$ h) $\mathbf{8a - 8b}$

2 a) $x(y + 5) = (x \times y) + (x \times 5) = \mathbf{xy + 5x}$
b) $p(q + 2) = (p \times q) + (p \times 2) = \mathbf{pq + 2p}$
c) $x(8 - x) = (x \times 8) + (x \times -x) = \mathbf{8x - x^2}$
Be careful when expanding a bracket with a negative term inside it.
d) $a(b - 12) = (a \times b) + (a \times -12) = \mathbf{ab - 12a}$
e) $3(2p + 4) = (3 \times 2p) + (3 \times 4) = \mathbf{6p + 12}$
f) $5(4t - 8) = (5 \times 4t) + (5 \times -8) = \mathbf{20t - 40}$
g) $3(u + 8v) = (3 \times u) + (3 \times 8v) = \mathbf{3u + 24v}$
h) $7(5n - 6m) = (7 \times 5n) + (7 \times -6m) = \mathbf{35n - 42m}$

Page 128 Exercise 2

1 a) $-(q + 2) = (-1 \times q) + (-1 \times 2) = \mathbf{-q - 2}$
b) $-(x + 7) = (-1 \times x) + (-1 \times 7) = \mathbf{-x - 7}$
Using the same method for c)-h):
c) $\mathbf{-56 + 8w}$ d) $\mathbf{-25 + 5x}$ e) $\mathbf{-v^2 - 4v}$
f) $\mathbf{-v^2 + 5v}$ g) $\mathbf{-12x + x^2}$ h) $\mathbf{-4y - y^2}$

2 a) $-6(5g - 3) = (-6 \times 5g) - (-6 \times 3)$
$= -30g - (-18)$
$= \mathbf{-30g + 18}$
b) $-7(4v + 8) = (-7 \times 4v) + (-7 \times 8)$
$= -28v + (-56)$
$= \mathbf{-28v - 56}$
Using the same method for c)-h):
c) $\mathbf{-10 - 8m}$ d) $\mathbf{-50 + 40v}$
e) $\mathbf{-10 - 15n}$ f) $\mathbf{-32z + 8z^2}$
g) $\mathbf{-12b + 6}$ h) $\mathbf{-8y^2 - 24y}$

Page 128 Exercise 3

1 a) $2(z + 3) + 4(z + 2) = 2z + 6 + 4z + 8 = \mathbf{6z + 14}$
b) $3(c + 1) + 5(c + 7) = 3c + 3 + 5c + 35 = \mathbf{8c + 38}$
c) $4(u + 6) + 8(u + 5) = 4u + 24 + 8u + 40 = \mathbf{12u + 64}$
Using the same method for d)-i):
d) $\mathbf{9t + 3}$ e) $\mathbf{17m + 29}$ f) $\mathbf{4p - 21}$
g) $\mathbf{j - 7}$ h) $\mathbf{4y - 18}$ i) $\mathbf{14c - 27}$

2 a) $5(2q + 5) - 2(q - 2) = 10q + 25 - (2q - 4)$
$= 10q - 2q + 25 + 4$
$= \mathbf{8q + 29}$
b) $2(3c - 8) - 8(c + 4) = 6c - 16 - (8c + 32)$
$= 6c - 8c - 16 - 32$
$= \mathbf{-2c - 48}$
c) $5(q - 2) - 3(q - 4) = 5q - 10 - (3q - 12)$
$= 5q - 3q - 10 + 12$
$= \mathbf{2q + 2}$

3 a) $2(-z + 2) + 3z(3z + 6) = -2z + 4 + 9z^2 + 18z$
$= \mathbf{9z^2 + 16z + 4}$
b) $4p(3p + 5) - 3(p + 1)$
$= 12p^2 + 20p - (3p + 3)$
$= 12p^2 + 20p - 3p - 3$
$= \mathbf{12p^2 + 17p - 3}$
c) $9b(2b + 5) + 4b(6b + 6)$
$= 18b^2 + 45b + 24b^2 + 24b$
$= \mathbf{42b^2 + 69b}$

Page 130 Exercise 4

1 a) $(a + 2)(b + 3) = \mathbf{ab + 3a + 2b + 6}$
b) $(j + 4)(k - 5) = \mathbf{jk - 5j + 4k - 20}$
Using the same method for c)-h):
c) $\mathbf{xy - x - 4y + 4}$ d) $\mathbf{xy + 2x + 6y + 12}$
e) $\mathbf{9b - 27 - ab + 3a}$ f) $\mathbf{st + 3t - 5s - 15}$
g) $\mathbf{15x - 5xy + 12 - 4y}$
h) $\mathbf{6ab + 6a - 2b - 2}$

2 a) $(x + 8)(x + 3) = x^2 + 3x + 8x + 24$
$= \mathbf{x^2 + 11x + 24}$
b) $(b + 2)(b - 4) = b^2 - 4b + 2b - 8$
$= \mathbf{b^2 - 2b - 8}$
c) $(a - 1)(a + 2) = a^2 + 2a - a - 2$
$= \mathbf{a^2 + a - 2}$
Using the same method for d)-f):
d) $\mathbf{d^2 + 13d + 42}$ e) $\mathbf{z^2 - 3z - 108}$
f) $\mathbf{-c^2 - 2c + 15}$
g) $(3y - 8)(6 - y) = 18y - 3y^2 - 48 + 8y$
$= \mathbf{-3y^2 + 26y - 48}$
h) $(2x + 2)(2x + 3) = 4x^2 + 6x + 4x + 6$
$= \mathbf{4x^2 + 10x + 6}$

Page 130 Exercise 5

1 a) $(x + 1)^2 = (x + 1)(x + 1) = x^2 + x + x + 1$
$= \mathbf{x^2 + 2x + 1}$
b) $(x + 4)^2 = (x + 4)(x + 4) = x^2 + 4x + 4x + 16$
$= \mathbf{x^2 + 8x + 16}$
Using the same method for c)-f):
c) $\mathbf{x^2 + 10x + 25}$ d) $\mathbf{x^2 - 4x + 4}$
e) $\mathbf{x^2 - 6x + 9}$ f) $\mathbf{x^2 - 14x + 49}$
g) $3(x + 3)^2 = 3 \times (x + 3)(x + 3)$
$= 3 \times (x^2 + 3x + 3x + 9)$
$= 3 \times (x^2 + 6x + 9)$
$= \mathbf{3x^2 + 18x + 27}$
h) $2(x - 6)^2 = 2 \times (x - 6)(x - 6)$
$= 2 \times (x^2 - 6x - 6x + 36)$
$= 2 \times (x^2 - 12x + 36)$
$= \mathbf{2x^2 - 24x + 72}$

2 a) $(5x + 2)^2 = (5x + 2)(5x + 2)$
$= (25x^2 + 10x + 10x + 4)$
$= \mathbf{25x^2 + 20x + 4}$
b) $(2x + 6)^2 = (2x + 6)(2x + 6)$
$= (4x^2 + 12x + 12x + 36)$
$= 4x^2 + 24x + 36$
c) $(3x - 1)^2 = (3x - 1)(3x - 1)$
$= (9x^2 - 3x - 3x + 1)$
$= \mathbf{9x^2 - 6x + 1}$

8.3 Factorising

Page 132 Exercise 1

1 a) $2a + 10 = (2 \times a) + (2 \times 5) = \mathbf{2(a + 5)}$
Remember to check your factorisation by expanding afterwards.
b) $3b + 12 = (3 \times b) + (3 \times 4) = \mathbf{3(b + 4)}$
Using the same method for c)-h):
c) $\mathbf{5(4c + 3)}$ d) $\mathbf{6(3 + 2x)}$
e) $\mathbf{4(2c + 3f)}$ f) $\mathbf{5(5d + 7e)}$
g) $\mathbf{4(3x + 4y)}$ h) $\mathbf{3(x + 3y)}$

2 a) $3a^2 + 7a = (a \times 3a) + (a \times 7) = \mathbf{a(3a + 7)}$
b) $4b^2 + 19b = (b \times 4b) + (b \times 19) = \mathbf{b(4b + 19)}$
Using the same method for c)-h):
c) $\mathbf{x(2x + 9)}$ d) $\mathbf{y(7 + 15y)}$
e) $\mathbf{x(4x - 9)}$ f) $\mathbf{q(21q - 16)}$
g) $\mathbf{y(15 - 7y)}$ h) $\mathbf{z(27z + 11)}$

Page 132 Exercise 2

1 a) **4** b) $\mathbf{x}$ c) $\mathbf{y}$
d) The HCF of $4xy^2$ and $8x^2y$ is $4xy$.
$4xy^2 + 8x^2y = (y \times 4xy) + (2x \times 4xy)$
$= \mathbf{4xy(y + 2x)}$

2 a) The HCF of 5 and 5 is 5.
The HCF of a^2 and a is a.
So the HCF of $5a^2$ and $5a$ is $5a$.
$5a^2 + 5a = (5a \times a) + (5a \times 1)$
$= \mathbf{5a(a + 1)}$
Using the same method for b)-d):
b) $\mathbf{4b(1 + 2b)}$ c) $\mathbf{3c(2c - 3)}$
d) $\mathbf{4d(3 - 4d)}$

3 a) The HCF of 10 and 5 is 5.
The HCF of c^2 and c is c.
There is no d in $10c^2$ so d won't come outside the brackets.
So the HCF of $10c^2$ and $5cd$ is $5c$.
$10c^2 - 5cd = (5c \times 2c) - (5c \times d)$
$= \mathbf{5c(2c - d)}$
b) The HCF of 20 and 10 is 10.
The HCF of x^2 and x is x.
There is no y in $20x^2$ so y won't come outside the brackets.
So the HCF of $20x^2$ and $10xy$ is $10x$.
$20x^2 - 10xy = (10x \times 2x) - (10x \times y)$
$= \mathbf{10x(2x - y)}$
Using the same method for c)-h):
c) $\mathbf{3x(3x + 2y)}$ d) $\mathbf{4x(3x + 2y)}$
e) $\mathbf{3a(2a + 3b)}$ f) $\mathbf{4p(3q - 2p)}$
g) $\mathbf{2a(4a + 3b^2)}$ h) $\mathbf{8xy(3x - 2y)}$

Page 134 Exercise 3

In this exercise the order of the brackets in the factorisations does not matter.

1 a) Find pairs of numbers that multiply to give 6: 1×6, 2×3
To make +7, you need to do +1 + 6, so:
$x^2 + 7x + 6 = \mathbf{(x + 1)(x + 6)}$
If you can spot the 2 numbers you need, you can write down the answer straight away.
b) Find pairs of numbers that multiply to give 12: 1×12, 2×6, 3×4
To make +7, you need to do +3 + 4, so:
$x^2 + 7x + 12 = \mathbf{(x + 3)(x + 4)}$
Using the same method for c)-h):
c) $\mathbf{(x + 1)(x + 7)}$ d) $\mathbf{(x + 3)^2}$
$(x + 3)(x + 3) = (x + 3)^2$
e) $\mathbf{(x + 2)(x + 4)}$ f) $\mathbf{(y + 3)(y + 5)}$
g) $\mathbf{(z + 2)(z + 7)}$ h) $\mathbf{(v + 3)(v + 8)}$

2 a) Find pairs of numbers that multiply to give 3: 1×3
To make +2, you need to do –1 + 3, so:
$x^2 + 2x - 3 = \mathbf{(x - 1)(x + 3)}$
b) Find pairs of numbers that multiply to give 8: 1×8, 2×4
To make –6, you need to do –2 – 4, so:
$x^2 - 6x + 8 = \mathbf{(x - 2)(x - 4)}$
Using the same method for c)-h):
c) $\mathbf{(x - 4)(x + 2)}$ d) $\mathbf{(x - 4)(x - 1)}$
e) $\mathbf{(x - 5)(x + 2)}$ f) $\mathbf{(x + 4)(x - 2)}$
g) $\mathbf{(r - 3)(r + 9)}$ h) $\mathbf{(u - 6)(u - 9)}$

Page 134 Exercise 4

1 a) $25 = 5^2$, so:
$x^2 - 25 = x^2 - 5^2 = \mathbf{(x + 5)(x - 5)}$
b) $9 = 3^2$, so:
$x^2 - 9 = x^2 - 3^2 = \mathbf{(x + 3)(x - 3)}$
Using the same method for c)-h):
c) $\mathbf{(x + 2)(x - 2)}$ d) $\mathbf{(x + 6)(x - 6)}$
e) $\mathbf{(x + 9)(x - 9)}$ f) $\mathbf{(x + 8)(x - 8)}$
g) $\mathbf{(b + 11)(b - 11)}$ h) $\mathbf{(t + 12)(t - 12)}$

2 a) $x^2 - 5 = x^2 - \sqrt{5}^2$
$= \mathbf{(x + \sqrt{5})(x - \sqrt{5})}$
Using the same method for b)-c):
b) $\mathbf{(x + \sqrt{3})(x - \sqrt{3})}$
c) $\mathbf{(x + \sqrt{11})(x - \sqrt{11})}$
d) $\mathbf{(x + y)(x - y)}$

Page 135 Review Exercise

1 a) $\mathbf{14s}$ b) $\mathbf{5m}$
c) $x + y + x + y + x - y = (x + x + x) + (y + y - y)$
$= \mathbf{3x + y}$
d) $16p + 4q + 4 - 2p + 3q - 8$
$= (16p - 2p) + (4q + 3q) + (4 - 8)$
$= \mathbf{14p + 7q - 4}$
Using the same method for e)-f):
e) $\mathbf{6s + 9t^2 - 3s^2}$ f) $\mathbf{2b^2 + 12b + 7}$

2 a) $a \times ab = a \times a \times b = \mathbf{a^2b}$
b) $4a^2 \div 2a = (4 \div 2) \times (a^2 \div a) = \mathbf{2a}$
Using the same method for c)-f):
c) $\mathbf{14pq^2}$ d) $\mathbf{3e^2}$ e) $\mathbf{-24i^5}$ f) $\mathbf{3d^2}$

3 a) $4(x + 8) = (4 \times x) + (4 \times 8) = \mathbf{4x + 32}$
b) $6(5 - r) = (6 \times 5) + (6 \times r) = \mathbf{30 - 6r}$
c) $-2(7 + y) = (-2 \times 7) + (-2 \times y) = \mathbf{-14 - 2y}$
d) $8(h - 2) = (8 \times h) - (8 \times 2) = \mathbf{8h - 16}$
e) $h(h + 3) = (h \times h) + (h \times 3) = \mathbf{h^2 + 3h}$
f) $-4n(n + 2) = (-4n \times n) + (-4n \times 2)$
$= \mathbf{-4n^2 - 8n}$
g) $4w(u - 7) = (4w \times u) - (4w \times 7) = \mathbf{4uw - 28w}$
h) $-2x(12 - v) = (-2x \times 12) - (-2x \times v)$
$= \mathbf{-24x + 2xv}$

4 a) $4(c + 3) + 6(c + 2) = 4c + 12 + 6c + 12$
$= (4c + 6c) + (12 + 12) = \mathbf{10c + 24}$
b) $5(u + 4) + 3(u + 8) = 5u + 20 + 3u + 24$
$= (5u + 3u) + (20 + 24) = \mathbf{8u + 44}$
Using the same method for c)-f):
c) $\mathbf{12b - 2}$ d) $\mathbf{c - 17}$
e) $\mathbf{4q - 16}$ f) $\mathbf{j - 7}$

5 a) $(2 + x)(8 + y) = \mathbf{16 + 2y + 8x + xy}$
b) $(x - 3)(x - 5) = x^2 - 5x - 3x + 15$
$= \mathbf{x^2 - 8x + 15}$
c) $3(j - 2)(k + 4) = 3 \times (jk + 4j - 2k - 8)$
$= \mathbf{3jk + 12j - 6k - 24}$
d) $(n + 5)(m - 4) = \mathbf{nm + 5m - 4n - 20}$
e) $(3 + r)(s + 4) = \mathbf{3s + 12 + rs + 4r}$
f) $(z - 8)^2 = (z - 8)(z - 8)$
$= z^2 - 8z - 8z + 64$
$= \mathbf{z^2 - 16z + 64}$

6 a) The HCF of $2x$ and $4y$ is 2.
$2x + 4y = (2 \times x) + (2 \times 2y) = \mathbf{2(x + 2y)}$
b) The HCF of $8x$ and 24 is 8.
$8x + 24 = (8 \times x) + (8 \times 3) = \mathbf{8(x + 3)}$
c) The HCF of $4y$ and $6y^2$ is $2y$.
$4y - 6y^2 = (2y \times 2) - (2y \times 3y) = \mathbf{2y(2 - 3y)}$
Using the same method for d)-i):
d) $\mathbf{4y(5 + 3x)}$ e) $\mathbf{5a(3b - 2a)}$
f) $\mathbf{12(5x + 12y)}$ g) $\mathbf{4r(7 + 10rs)}$
h) $\mathbf{4ab(1 - 2a)}$ i) $\mathbf{7mn(2m - 5n)}$

7 a) Find pairs of numbers that multiply to give 21: 3×7
To make +10, you need to do 3 + 7, so:
$y^2 + 10y + 21 = \mathbf{(y + 3)(y + 7)}$
b) Find pairs of numbers that multiply to give 5: 1×5
To make –4, you need to do –5 + 1, so:
$x^2 - 4x - 5 = \mathbf{(x - 5)(x + 1)}$
Using the same method for c)-f):
c) $\mathbf{(t - 4)^2}$ d) $\mathbf{(x - 4)(x + 3)}$
e) $\mathbf{(x + 6)(x - 1)}$ f) $\mathbf{(x - 9)(x + 5)}$

8 a) $100 = 10^2$, so:
$x^2 - 100 = x^2 - 10^2 = \mathbf{(x + 10)(x - 10)}$
b) $36 = 6^2$, so:
$y^2 - 36 = y^2 - 6^2 = \mathbf{(y - 6)(y + 6)}$
c) $y^2 - 121 = y^2 - 11^2$
$= \mathbf{(y + 11)(y - 11)}$

Page 136 Exam-Style Questions

1

Expression	Simplified expression
$a + a + a$	$\mathbf{3a}$
$3a^2 + 2a^2$	$\mathbf{5a^2}$
$4a^2 + 6a - a^2$	$\mathbf{3a^2 + 6a}$

[3 marks available — 1 mark for each correct answer in the table]

2 a) $v + v + w - w - w - w - w = 2v + w - 4w$
$= \mathbf{2v - 3w}$ *[1 mark]*
b) $5 \times 7 \times x \times x = \mathbf{35x^2}$ *[1 mark]*
c) $6y - 3yz - 8y + 10yz = 6y - 8y + 10yz - 3yz$
$= \mathbf{-2y + 7yz}$ *[1 mark]*

3 a) $x(x^2 - 4y) + 9xy = x^3 - 4xy + 9xy$ *[1 mark]*
$= \mathbf{x^3 + 5xy}$ *[1 mark]*
b) $(2x - 7)^2 = (2x - 7)(2x - 7)$
$= 4x^2 - 14x - 14x + 49$ *[1 mark]*
$= \mathbf{4x^2 - 28x + 49}$ *[1 mark]*

4 a) $7c + 56 = (7 \times c) + (7 \times 8)$
$= \mathbf{7(c + 8)}$ *[1 mark]*
b) $d^2 + 5d - 2de = (d \times d) + (d \times 5) - (d \times 2e)$
$= \mathbf{d(d + 5 - 2e)}$
[2 marks available – 1 mark for taking out a common factor of d, 1 mark for a fully correct expression]

5 a) Find pairs of numbers that multiply to give 32: 1×32, 2×16, 4×8
To make 12, you need to do +4 + 8.
So $y^2 + 12y + 32 = \mathbf{(y + 4)(y + 8)}$
[2 marks available — 1 mark for the correct numbers in the brackets, 1 mark for the correct signs]
b) $169 = 13^2$ so you can use difference of two squares.
$x^2 - 169 = \mathbf{(x + 13)(x - 13)}$
[2 marks available — 1 mark for using the fact that 13 is the square root of 169, 1 mark for fully correct factorisation]

Section 9 — Equations, Identities and Inequalities

9.1 Solving Equations

Page 138 Exercise 1

1 a) $x + 9 = 12$
$x = 12 - 9 \Rightarrow \mathbf{x = 3}$
b) $x + 5 = 16$
$x = 16 - 5 \Rightarrow \mathbf{x = 11}$
c) $x - 2 = 14$
$x = 14 + 2 \Rightarrow \mathbf{x = 16}$
d) $x - 7 = -19$
$x = -19 + 7 \Rightarrow \mathbf{x = -12}$
e) $-2 = 7 + x$
$-2 - 7 = x \Rightarrow \mathbf{x = -9}$
f) $32 = x - 17$
$32 + 17 = x \Rightarrow \mathbf{x = 49}$

2 a) $12 - x = 9$
$12 = 9 + x$
$12 - 9 = x \Rightarrow \mathbf{x = 3}$
b) $4 - x = 2$
$4 = 2 + x$
$4 - 2 = x \Rightarrow \mathbf{x = 2}$
c) $2 - x = 7$
$2 = 7 + x$
$2 - 7 = x \Rightarrow \mathbf{x = -5}$
d) $19 = 14 - x$
$19 + x = 14$
$x = 14 - 19 \Rightarrow \mathbf{x = -5}$
e) $14 = 8 - x$
$14 + x = 8$
$x = 8 - 14 \Rightarrow \mathbf{x = -6}$
f) $7 = 5 - x$
$7 + x = 5$
$x = 5 - 7 \Rightarrow \mathbf{x = -2}$

3 a) $x + 7 = 12$
$x = 12 - 7 \Rightarrow \mathbf{x = 5}$
b) $5 - x = 21$
$5 = 21 + x$
$5 - 21 = x \Rightarrow \mathbf{x = -16}$
c) $16 = x + 10$
$16 - 10 = x \Rightarrow \mathbf{x = 6}$
d) $x - 8 = 14$
$x = 14 + 8 \Rightarrow \mathbf{x = 22}$
e) $12 - x = 23$
$12 = 23 + x$
$12 - 23 = x \Rightarrow \mathbf{x = -11}$
f) $35 = 31 - x$
$35 + x = 31$
$x = 31 - 35 \Rightarrow \mathbf{x = -4}$

4 a) $x - 7.3 = 1.6$
$x = 1.6 + 7.3 \Rightarrow \mathbf{x = 8.9}$
b) $6.03 - x = 0.58$
$6.03 = 0.58 + x$
$6.03 - 0.58 = x \Rightarrow \mathbf{x = 5.45}$
c) $3.47 = 7.18 + x$
$3.47 - 7.18 = x \Rightarrow \mathbf{x = -3.71}$
d) $5.2 = 2.8 - x$
$5.2 + x = 2.8$
$x = 2.8 - 5.2 \Rightarrow \mathbf{x = -2.4}$

Page 139 Exercise 2

1 a) $\frac{x}{3} = 2 \Rightarrow \frac{x}{3} \times 3 = 2 \times 3 \Rightarrow \mathbf{x = 6}$
b) $\frac{x}{6} = -3 \Rightarrow \frac{x}{6} \times 6 = -3 \times 6 \Rightarrow \mathbf{x = -18}$
c) $\frac{x}{3} = 0.4 \Rightarrow \frac{x}{3} \times 3 = 0.4 \times 3 \Rightarrow \mathbf{x = 1.2}$
d) $\frac{x}{11} = -0.5 \Rightarrow \frac{x}{11} \times 11 = -0.5 \times 11$
$\Rightarrow \mathbf{x = -5.5}$
e) $8x = 24 \Rightarrow 8x \div 8 = 24 \div 8 \Rightarrow \mathbf{x = 3}$
f) $4.5x = 81 \Rightarrow 4.5x \div 4.5 = 81 \div 4.5$
$\Rightarrow \mathbf{x = 18}$
g) $5x = -20 \Rightarrow 5x \div 5 = -20 \div 5 \Rightarrow \mathbf{x = -4}$
h) $3.5x = -7 \Rightarrow 3.5x \div 3.5 = -7 \div 3.5$
$\Rightarrow \mathbf{x = -2}$

2 a) $-7x = -56 \Rightarrow -7x \div -7 = -56 \div -7$
$\Rightarrow \mathbf{x = 8}$
You could add 7x to both sides and then rearrange, but it would take more steps.
b) $-9x = 108 \Rightarrow -9x \div -9 = 108 \div -9$
$\Rightarrow \mathbf{x = -12}$
c) $-4.5x = -2.7 \Rightarrow -4.5x \div -4.5$
$= -2.7 \div -4.5 \Rightarrow \mathbf{x = 0.6}$
d) $-\frac{x}{4} = 3 \Rightarrow -\frac{x}{4} \times -4 = 3 \times -4 \Rightarrow \mathbf{x = -12}$
e) $-\frac{x}{5} = 6 \Rightarrow -\frac{x}{5} \times -5 = 6 \times -5 \Rightarrow \mathbf{x = -30}$
f) $-\frac{x}{10} = 1.1 \Rightarrow -\frac{x}{10} \times -10 = 1.1 \times -10$
$\Rightarrow \mathbf{x = -11}$

Page 139 Exercise 3

1 a) $\frac{4x}{3} = 12 \Rightarrow 4x = 12 \times 3 = 36$
$\Rightarrow x = 36 \div 4 \Rightarrow \mathbf{x = 9}$
b) $\frac{2x}{5} = 6 \Rightarrow 2x = 6 \times 5 = 30 \Rightarrow x = 30 \div 2$
$\Rightarrow \mathbf{x = 15}$
Using the same method for c)-h):
c) $\mathbf{x = 14}$ d) $\mathbf{x = 3.6}$ e) $\mathbf{x = 1}$
f) $\mathbf{x = -0.15}$ g) $\mathbf{x = -0.02}$ h) $\mathbf{x = 1.26}$

Page 140 Exercise 4

1 a) $8x + 10 = 66$
$8x = 66 - 10 = 56$
$x = 56 \div 8 \Rightarrow \mathbf{x = 7}$
b) $10x + 15 = 115$
$10x = 115 - 15 = 100$
$x = 100 \div 10 \Rightarrow \mathbf{x = 10}$
Using the same method for c)-f):
c) $\mathbf{x = 8}$ d) $\mathbf{x = 60}$
e) $\mathbf{x = -5}$ f) $\mathbf{x = -5.5}$

2 a) $16x - 6 = 10$
$16x = 10 + 6 = 16$
$x = 16 \div 16 \Rightarrow \mathbf{x = 1}$
b) $15x - 8 = 22$
$15x = 22 + 8 = 30$
$x = 30 \div 15 = 2 \Rightarrow \mathbf{x = 2}$
Using the same method for c)-f):
c) $\mathbf{x = 3}$ d) $\mathbf{x = -20}$
e) $\mathbf{x = -3}$ f) $\mathbf{x = -6}$

3 $\frac{x}{2} - 1 = 3$
$\frac{x}{2} - 1 + 1 = 3 + 1 \Rightarrow \frac{x}{2} = 4$
$\frac{x}{2} \times 2 = 4 \times 2 \Rightarrow \mathbf{x = 8}$ is the solution.
'Undo' means doing the opposite. Adding 1 is the opposite of subtracting 1, and multiplying by 2 is the opposite of dividing by 2.

4 a) $\frac{x}{2} + 1 = 7$
$\frac{x}{2} = 7 - 1 = 6$
$x = 6 \times 2 \Rightarrow \mathbf{x = 12}$
b) $\frac{x}{6} + 4 = 16$
$\frac{x}{6} = 16 - 4 = 12$
$x = 12 \times 6 \Rightarrow \mathbf{x = 72}$
Using the same method for c)-f):
c) $\mathbf{x = 20}$ d) $\mathbf{x = -16}$
e) $\mathbf{x = 9}$ f) $\mathbf{x = -21}$

5 a) $20 - 5x = 10$
$20 - 5x + 5x = 10 + 5x$
$\mathbf{20 = 10 + 5x}$
b) $20 = 10 + 5x$
$20 - 10 = 5x \Rightarrow 5x = 10$
$x = 10 \div 5 \Rightarrow \mathbf{x = 2}$

6 a) $12 - 4x = 8$
$12 = 8 + 4x$
$12 - 8 = 4x \Rightarrow 4x = 4$
$x = 4 \div 4 \Rightarrow \mathbf{x = 1}$
b) $47 - 9x = 11$
$47 = 11 + 9x$
$47 - 11 = 9x \Rightarrow 9x = 36$
$x = 36 \div 9 \Rightarrow \mathbf{x = 4}$
Using the same method for c) and d):
c) $\mathbf{x = -2}$ d) $\mathbf{x = -9}$

Page 142 Exercise 5

1 a) $7(x + 4) = 63$
$7x + 28 = 63$
$7x = 63 - 28 = 35$
$x = 35 \div 7 \Rightarrow \mathbf{x = 5}$
Alternatively, you could start by dividing both sides by 7, and then rearrange.
b) $8(x + 4) = 88$
$8x + 32 = 88$
$8x = 88 - 32 = 56$
$x = 56 \div 8 \Rightarrow \mathbf{x = 7}$
Using the same method for c)-f):
c) $\mathbf{x = 9}$ d) $\mathbf{x = -2}$
e) $\mathbf{x = -3}$ f) $\mathbf{x = -5}$

2 a) $315 = 21(6 - x)$
$315 \div 21 = 6 - x \Rightarrow 15 = 6 - x$
$\Rightarrow x = 6 - 15 \Rightarrow \mathbf{x = -9}$
Dividing first keeps the numbers small, but you could start by expanding the brackets if you wanted to.
b) $12.5(x - 4) = 75$
$x - 4 = 75 \div 12.5 \Rightarrow x - 4 = 6$
$\Rightarrow x = 6 + 4 \Rightarrow \mathbf{x = 10}$
c) $36 = 7.2(2 - x)$
$36 \div 7.2 = 2 - x \Rightarrow 5 = 2 - x$
$\Rightarrow x = 2 - 5 \Rightarrow \mathbf{x = -3}$

Page 142 Exercise 6

1 a) $6x - 4 = 2x + 16$
$6x - 2x - 4 = 16 \Rightarrow 4x - 4 = 16$
$4x = 16 + 4 = 20$
$x = 20 \div 4 \Rightarrow \mathbf{x = 5}$
b) $17x + 2 = 7x - 8$
$17x - 7x + 2 = -8 \Rightarrow 10x + 2 = -8$
$10x = -8 - 2 = -10$
$x = -10 \div 10 \Rightarrow \mathbf{x = -1}$
Using the same method for c)-f):
c) $\mathbf{x = 3}$ d) $\mathbf{x = 6}$
e) $\mathbf{x = 5}$ f) $\mathbf{x = 1}$

2 a) $13x - 35 = 45 - 3x$
$13x + 3x - 35 = 45 \Rightarrow 16x - 35 = 45$
$16x = 45 + 35 = 80$
$x = 80 \div 16 = 5 \Rightarrow \mathbf{x = 5}$
b) $20x + 18 = 54 - 16x$
$20x + 16x + 18 = 54 \Rightarrow 36x + 18 = 54$
$36x = 54 - 18 = 36$
$x = 36 \div 36 \Rightarrow \mathbf{x = 1}$
Using the same method for c)-f):
c) $\mathbf{x = 3}$ d) $\mathbf{x = 36}$
e) $\mathbf{x = 9}$ f) $\mathbf{x = 9}$

3 a) $4x - 3 = 0.5 - 3x$
$4x + 3x - 3 = 0.5 \Rightarrow 7x - 3 = 0.5$
$7x = 0.5 + 3 = 3.5$
$x = 3.5 \div 7 \Rightarrow \mathbf{x = \frac{1}{2}}$

b) $10x - 18 = 10.2 + 4x$
$10x - 4x - 18 = 10.2 \Rightarrow 6x - 18 = 10.2$
$6x = 10.2 + 18 = 28.2$
$x = 28.2 \div 6 \Rightarrow \mathbf{x = 4.7}$

c) $4x - 8.6 = 48.1 - 5x$
$4x + 5x - 8.6 = 48.1 \Rightarrow 9x - 8.6 = 48.1$
$9x = 48.1 + 8.6 = 56.7$
$x = 56.7 \div 9 \Rightarrow \mathbf{x = 6.3}$

d) $-x + 1 = 28 + 2x$
$1 = 28 + 2x + x \Rightarrow 1 = 28 + 3x$
$1 - 28 = 3x \Rightarrow 3x = -27$
$x = -27 \div 3 \Rightarrow \mathbf{x = -9}$

Page 143 Exercise 7

1 a) $3(x + 2) = x + 14$
$3x + 6 = x + 14$
$3x - x + 6 = 14 \Rightarrow 2x + 6 = 14$
$2x = 14 - 6 = 8$
$x = 8 \div 2 \Rightarrow \mathbf{x = 4}$

b) $9(x - 1) = x + 15$
$9x - 9 = x + 15$
$9x - x - 9 = 15 \Rightarrow 8x - 9 = 15$
$8x = 15 + 9 = 24$
$x = 24 \div 8 \Rightarrow \mathbf{x = 3}$

c) $6(x + 2) = 3x + 48$
$6x + 12 = 3x + 48$
$6x - 3x + 12 = 48 \Rightarrow 3x + 12 = 48$
$3x = 48 - 12 = 36$
$x = 36 \div 3 \Rightarrow \mathbf{x = 12}$

d) $8(x - 8) = 2(x - 2)$
$8x - 64 = 2x - 4$
$8x - 2x - 64 = -4 \Rightarrow 6x - 64 = -4$
$6x = -4 + 64 = 60$
$x = 60 \div 6 \Rightarrow \mathbf{x = 10}$

e) $4(4 - x) = 2(x - 1)$
$16 - 4x = 2x - 2$
$16 - 4x - 2x = -2 \Rightarrow -6x + 16 = -2$
$-6x = -2 - 16 = -18$
$x = -18 \div -6 \Rightarrow \mathbf{x = 3}$

f) $20(x - 2) = 5(x + 1)$
$20x - 40 = 5x + 5$
$20x - 5x - 40 = 5 \Rightarrow 15x - 40 = 5$
$15x = 5 + 40 = 45$
$x = 45 \div 15 \Rightarrow \mathbf{x = 3}$

2 a) $5(x - 5) = 2(x - 14)$
$5x - 25 = 2x - 28$
$5x - 2x - 25 = -28 \Rightarrow 3x - 25 = -28$
$3x = -28 + 25 = -3$
$x = -3 \div 3 \Rightarrow \mathbf{x = -1}$

b) $2(x - 2) = 5(x - 8)$
$2x - 4 = 5x - 40$
$-4 = 5x - 2x - 40 \Rightarrow -4 = 3x - 40$
$\Rightarrow -4 + 40 = 3x \Rightarrow 36 = 3x$
$x = 36 \div 3 \Rightarrow \mathbf{x = 12}$
You could have done 2x − 5x but you would have a negative multiple of x, which would make rearranging things slightly trickier.

c) $4(x - 2) = 6(x + 3)$
$4x - 8 = 6x + 18$
$-8 = 6x - 4x + 18 \Rightarrow -8 = 2x + 18$
$\Rightarrow -8 - 18 = 2x \Rightarrow -26 = 2x$
$x = -26 \div 2 \Rightarrow \mathbf{x = -13}$

d) $6(x - 1.5) = 2(x - 3.5)$
$6x - 9 = 2x - 7$
$6x - 2x - 9 = -7 \Rightarrow 4x - 9 = -7$
$4x = -7 + 9 = 2$
$x = 2 \div 4 \Rightarrow \mathbf{x = 0.5}$

e) $9(x - 3.3) = -6(x + 1.7)$
$9x - 29.7 = -6x - 10.2$
$9x + 6x - 29.7 = -10.2$
$\Rightarrow 15x - 29.7 = -10.2$
$15x = -10.2 + 29.7 = 19.5$
$x = 19.5 \div 15 \Rightarrow \mathbf{x = 1.3}$

f) $-4(x - 3) = 8(0.7 - x)$
$-4x + 12 = 5.6 - 8x$
$-4x + 8x + 12 = 5.6 \Rightarrow 4x + 12 = 5.6$
$4x = 5.6 - 12 = -6.4$
$x = -6.4 \div 4 \Rightarrow \mathbf{x = -1.6}$

3 a) $7(3x + 2) = 5(9x - 0.08)$
$21x + 14 = 45x - 0.4$
$45x - 21x - 0.4 = 14 \Rightarrow 24x - 0.4 = 14$
$24x = 14 + 0.4 = 14.4$
$x = 14.4 \div 24 \Rightarrow \mathbf{x = 0.6}$

b) $7(2x + \frac{1}{7}) = 14(3x - 0.5)$
$14x + 1 = 42x - 7$
$1 = 42x - 14x - 7 \Rightarrow 1 = 28x - 7$
$\Rightarrow 28x = 1 + 7 = 8$
$x = 8 \div 28 \Rightarrow \mathbf{x = \frac{2}{7}}$

c) $10(x - 2) = -2(\frac{4}{3} + 7x)$
$10x - 20 = -\frac{8}{3} - 14x$
$10x = -14x + 20 - \frac{8}{3} \Rightarrow 10x = -14x + \frac{52}{3}$
$24x = \frac{52}{3}$
$x = \frac{52}{72} = \mathbf{\frac{13}{18}}$

d) $4(3x - 3) = -2(\frac{76}{9} + 5x)$
$12x - 12 = -\frac{152}{9} - 10x$
$12x + 10x - 12 = -\frac{152}{9}$
$22x - 12 = -\frac{152}{9}$
$22x = -\frac{152}{9} + 12 = -\frac{44}{9}$
$x = -\frac{44}{9} \div 22 \Rightarrow \mathbf{x = -\frac{2}{9}}$

Page 144 Exercise 8

1 a) $\frac{x}{4} = 1 - x$
$x = 4(1 - x) = 4 - 4x$
$x + 4x = 4 \Rightarrow 5x = 4 \Rightarrow x = \mathbf{\frac{4}{5}}$ or **0.8**

b) $\frac{x}{3} = 8 - x$
$x = 3(8 - x) = 24 - 3x$
$x + 3x = 24 \Rightarrow 4x = 24$
$x = 24 \div 4 \Rightarrow \mathbf{x = 6}$

Using the same method for c)-f):

c) $\mathbf{x = 5}$ **d)** $\mathbf{x = 8}$
e) $\mathbf{x = -5}$ **f)** $\mathbf{x = -10}$

2 a) $\frac{x}{3} = 2(x - 5)$
$x = 3 \times 2(x - 5) = 6(x - 5) = 6x - 30$
$x + 30 = 6x$
$30 = 6x - x \Rightarrow 5x = 30$
$x = 30 \div 5 \Rightarrow \mathbf{x = 6}$

b) $\frac{x}{2} = 4(x - 7)$
$x = 2 \times 4(x - 7) = 8(x - 7) = 8x - 56$
$x + 56 = 8x$
$56 = 8x - x \Rightarrow 56 = 7x$
$x = 56 \div 7 \Rightarrow \mathbf{x = 8}$

Using the same method for c)-f):

c) $\mathbf{x = -10}$ **d)** $\mathbf{x = -\frac{20}{3}}$
e) $\mathbf{x = -16}$ **f)** $\mathbf{x = 60}$

Page 144 Exercise 9

1 a) $\frac{x+4}{2} = \frac{x+10}{3}$
$3(x + 4) = 2(x + 10)$
$3x + 12 = 2x + 20$
$3x - 2x + 12 = 20$
$x + 12 = 20$
$x = 20 - 12 \Rightarrow \mathbf{x = 8}$

b) $\frac{x+2}{2} = \frac{x+4}{6}$
$6(x + 2) = 2(x + 4)$
$6x + 12 = 2x + 8$
$6x - 2x + 12 = 8$
$4x + 12 = 8$
$4x = 8 - 12 = -4$
$x = -4 \div 4 \Rightarrow \mathbf{x = -1}$

Using the same method for c)-f):

c) $\mathbf{x = 5}$ **d)** $\mathbf{x = 11}$
e) $\mathbf{x = 8}$ **f)** $\mathbf{x = 21}$

2 a) $\frac{x-6}{2} = \frac{8-2x}{4}$
$4(x - 6) = 2(8 - 2x)$
$4x - 24 = 16 - 4x$
$4x + 4x - 24 = 16 \Rightarrow 8x - 24 = 16$
$8x = 16 + 24 = 40$
$x = 40 \div 8 \Rightarrow \mathbf{x = 5}$

b) $\frac{x-9}{2} = \frac{2-3x}{4}$
$4(x - 9) = 2(2 - 3x)$
$4x - 36 = 4 - 6x$
$4x + 6x - 36 = 4 \Rightarrow 10x - 36 = 4$
$10x = 4 + 36 = 40$
$x = 40 \div 10 \Rightarrow \mathbf{x = 4}$

c) $\frac{x-12}{6} = \frac{4-2x}{3}$
$3(x - 12) = 6(4 - 2x)$
$3x - 36 = 24 - 12x$
$3x + 12x - 36 = 24 \Rightarrow 15x - 36 = 24$
$15x = 24 + 36 = 60$
$x = 60 \div 15 \Rightarrow \mathbf{x = 4}$

9.2 Forming Your Own Equations

Page 145 Exercise 1

1 a) Call the number x.
Add 5 $\Rightarrow x + 5$
Result equals 12, so:
$x + 5 = 12 \Rightarrow x = 12 - 5 = 7$
The number they were thinking of was **7**.

b) Call the number x.
Multiply by 2 $\Rightarrow 2x$
Subtract 5 $\Rightarrow 2x - 5$
Result equals 15, so:
$2x - 5 = 15$
$2x = 15 + 5 = 20$
$x = 20 \div 2 = 10$
The number they were thinking of was **10**.

c) Call the number x.
Divide by 4 $\Rightarrow \frac{x}{4}$
Add 10 $\Rightarrow \frac{x}{4} + 10$
Result equals 14, so:
$\frac{x}{4} + 10 = 14$
$\frac{x}{4} = 14 - 10 = 4$
$x = 4 \times 4 = 16$
The number they were thinking of was **16**.

Page 146 Exercise 2

1 Call the number of people that the bride and the groom each invited x.
The total number of people invited was $2x$.
8 people couldn't come so $2x - 8$ could attend.
So $2x - 8 = 60$
$2x = 60 + 8 = 68$
$x = 68 \div 2 = 34$
So the groom invited **34 guests**.

2 Call the number of single beds x.
Number of king-size beds = $x - 10$
Number of double beds = $x + 16$.
So $x + (x - 10) + (x + 16) = x + x + x + 16 - 10$
$= 3x + 6 = 54$
$3x = 54 - 6 = 48$
$x = 48 \div 3 = 16$
So **16 single beds** were sold that day.

3 a) A fruit scone sells for £x and a cheese scone sells for £x + 0.1, so the total amount in £ that she sells the scones for is:
$20x + 10(x + 0.1) = 20x + 10x + 1$
$= 30x + 1$
Subtract the cost of the ingredients to find the profit in £:
profit = $\mathbf{30x + 1 - y}$.

b) Substitute profit = 10 and $y = 6$ into the expression from a):
$10 = 30x + 1 - 6 \Rightarrow 10 = 30x - 5$
$10 + 5 = 30x \Rightarrow 15 = 30x$
$x = 30 \div 15 = 0.5$
So a fruit scone costs **50p**.

Page 147 Exercise 3

1 a) Sum of angles in a triangle = 180°.
This is a rule for all triangles that you need to know.
So $110° + 3x + 4x = 180°$
$\Rightarrow \mathbf{110° + 7x = 180°}$

b) $110° + 7x = 180°$
$7x = 180° - 110° = 70°$
$x = 70° \div 7 \Rightarrow \mathbf{x = 10°}$

2 a) (i) $4x + (x + 8) + 4x + (x + 8) = 146$
$4x + x + 8 + 4x + x + 8 = 146$
So $\mathbf{10x + 16 = 146}$

(ii) $10x + 16 = 146$
$10x = 146 - 16 = 130$
$x = 130 \div 10 \Rightarrow \mathbf{x = 13\ cm}$

b) (i) The hexagon is regular, so all sides are the same length:
$(x + 2) + (x + 2) + (x + 2) + (x + 2) + (x + 2) + (x + 2) = 102$
$6(x + 2) = 102$
$\mathbf{6x + 12 = 102}$

(ii) $6x + 12 = 102$
$6x = 102 - 12 = 90$
$x = 90 \div 6 \Rightarrow \mathbf{x = 15\ cm}$

9.3 Identities

Page 148 Exercise 1

1 a) $4x = 10$ only when $x = 2.5$.
So **no** the '≡' symbol can't be used.

b) When $x = 1$,
$x^2 + 2x + 1 = 1 + 2 + 1 = 4 \neq 0$.
So **no**, the '≡' symbol can't be used.
If you can find one value of x that makes the identity false, then it isn't an identity.

c) Rearranging the order of $-x^2 + 3$ gives $3 - x^2$, which is the same as the right-hand side. So **yes**, the '≡' symbol can be used.

d) $2(x + 1) = 2x + 2$ which is different to the right-hand side.
So **no**, the '≡' symbol can't be used.

e) Expanding the left-hand side gives
$3(x + 2) - x = 3x + 6 - x = 2x + 6$
Expanding the right-hand side gives
$2(x + 3) = 2x + 6$, which is the same as the left-hand side.
So **yes**, the '≡' symbol can be used.

f) Expanding the left-hand side gives
$3(2 - 3x) + 2 = 6 - 9x + 2 = 4 - 9x$
$4 - 9x$ is different to $8x$ so **no**, the '≡' symbol can't be used.

2 a) Expanding the left-hand side gives
$(x + 4)^2 - 4 = (x + 4)(x + 4) - 4$
$= x^2 + 4x + 4x + 16 - 4$
$= \mathbf{x^2 + 8x + 12}$
Expanding the right-hand side gives
$(x + 6)(x + 2) = x^2 + 2x + 6x + 12$
$= \mathbf{x^2 + 8x + 12}$
The two sides are the same so the identity is true.

b) Expanding the left-hand side gives
$5(x + 2) + (x^2 - 4) = 5x + 10 + x^2 - 4$
$= \mathbf{x^2 + 5x + 6}$
Expanding the right-hand side gives
$(x + 4)(x + 1) + 2 = x^2 + x + 4x + 4 + 2$
$= \mathbf{x^2 + 5x + 6}$
The two sides are the same so the identity is true.

9.4 Proof

Page 149 Exercise 1

1 Take an even number and an odd number — $2a$ and $(2b + 1)$. Their product is
$2a(2b + 1) = 4ab + 2a$
$= 2(2ab + a)$
$= \mathbf{2n}$, where $n = 2ab + a$
So the product of an even number and an odd number is **even**.

2 Take two consecutive square numbers — a^2 and $(a + 1)^2$.
Their sum is $a^2 + (a + 1)^2 = a^2 + (a + 1)(a + 1)$
$= a^2 + a^2 + a + a + 1$
$= 2a^2 + 2a + 1$
$= 2(a^2 + a) + 1$
$= \mathbf{2n + 1}$,
where $n = a^2 + a$.
So the sum of two consecutive square numbers is **odd**.

Page 150 Exercise 2

1 E.g. $(-3) + (-2) + (-1) = -6$ which is **less** than each individual number.

2 E.g. 2 and 3 are both prime, but $3 - 2 = 1$ which is **odd**.

Page 150 Exercise 3

1 Take $2n + 1$ and $2n + 3$ as consecutive odd integers.
Then $(2n + 1) + (2n + 3) = 4n + 4 = \mathbf{4(n + 1)}$
where $n + 1$ is an integer.
So the sum of two consecutive odd integers is a **multiple of 4**.

2 Expanding gives: $x = 2(y + 5) + 4(y + 1) - 2$
$= 2y + 10 + 4y + 4 - 2$
$= 6y + 12$
$= 6(y + 2)$
$= \mathbf{6n}$, where $n = y + 2$.
As n is an integer, x is a **multiple of 6**.

9.5 Inequalities

Page 151 Exercise 1

1 a) **6 > 1** b) **2 < 8** c) **–1 > –3** d) **–7 < 1**

2 a) **x is greater than or equal to 1.**
b) **x is less than 7.**
c) **x is greater than –4.**
d) **x is less than or equal to 9.**

3 a) $\mathbf{x > 4}$ b) $\mathbf{x \leq 12}$ c) $\mathbf{x < 3}$

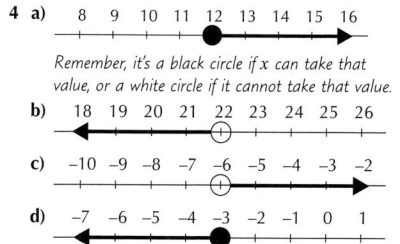

4 a) 8 9 10 11 12 13 14 15 16

Remember, it's a black circle if x can take that value, or a white circle if it cannot take that value.

b) 18 19 20 21 22 23 24 25 26

c) –10 –9 –8 –7 –6 –5 –4 –3 –2

d) –7 –6 –5 –4 –3 –2 –1 0 1

Page 152 Exercise 2

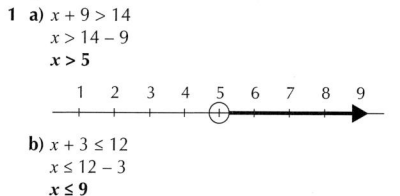

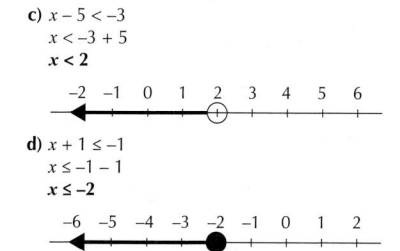

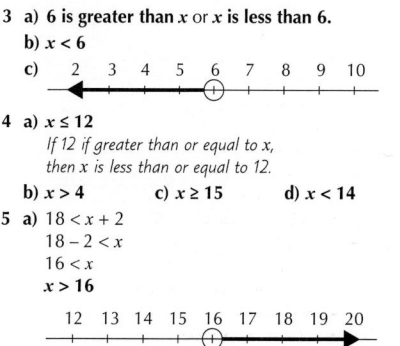

1 a) $x + 9 > 14$
$x > 14 - 9$
$\mathbf{x > 5}$

1 2 3 4 5 6 7 8 9

b) $x + 3 \leq 12$
$x \leq 12 - 3$
$\mathbf{x \leq 9}$

5 6 7 8 9 10 11 12 13

c) $x - 5 < -3$
$x < -3 + 5$
$\mathbf{x < 2}$

–2 –1 0 1 2 3 4 5 6

d) $x + 1 \leq -1$
$x \leq -1 - 1$
$\mathbf{x \leq -2}$

–6 –5 –4 –3 –2 –1 0 1 2

2 a) $x - 9 > 8$
$x > 8 + 9$
$\mathbf{x > 17}$

b) $x + 7 < 17$
$x < 17 - 7$
$\mathbf{x < 10}$

c) $x + 12 < -18$
$x < -18 - 12$
$\mathbf{x < -30}$

d) $x - 8 \leq -3$
$x \leq -3 + 8$
$\mathbf{x \leq 5}$

3 a) **6 is greater than x or x is less than 6.**
b) $\mathbf{x < 6}$
c) 2 3 4 5 6 7 8 9 10

4 a) $\mathbf{x \leq 12}$
If 12 if greater than or equal to x, then x is less than or equal to 12.
b) $\mathbf{x > 4}$ c) $\mathbf{x \geq 15}$ d) $\mathbf{x < 14}$

5 a) $18 < x + 2$
$18 - 2 < x$
$16 < x$
$\mathbf{x > 16}$

12 13 14 15 16 17 18 19 20

b) $12 \le x - 4$
$12 + 4 \le x$
$16 \le x$
$\mathbf{x \ge 16}$

12 13 14 15 16 17 18 19 20

c) $1 > x - 17$
$1 + 17 > x$
$18 > x$
$\mathbf{x < 18}$

14 15 16 17 18 19 20 21 22

d) $31 \ge x + 30$
$31 - 30 \ge x$
$1 \ge x$
$\mathbf{x \le 1}$

–3 –2 –1 0 1 2 3 4 5

Page 153 Exercise 3

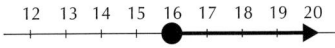

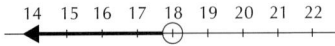

1 a) $3x \ge 9 \Rightarrow x \ge 9 \div 3 \Rightarrow \mathbf{x \ge 3}$
b) $5x < -25 \Rightarrow x < -25 \div 5 \Rightarrow \mathbf{x < -5}$
c) $2x > 8 \Rightarrow x > 8 \div 2 \Rightarrow \mathbf{x > 4}$
d) $7x \le 21 \Rightarrow x \le 21 \div 7 \Rightarrow \mathbf{x \le 3}$

2 a) $\frac{x}{2} \ge 3 \Rightarrow x \ge 3 \times 2 \Rightarrow \mathbf{x \ge 6}$
b) $\frac{x}{5} < 2 \Rightarrow x < 2 \times 5 \Rightarrow \mathbf{x < 10}$
c) $\frac{x}{5.5} < 1.2 \Rightarrow x < 1.2 \times 5.5 \Rightarrow \mathbf{x < 6.6}$
d) $\frac{x}{2.5} > -3.2 \Rightarrow x > -3.2 \times 2.5 \Rightarrow \mathbf{x > -8}$

3 a) $-4x < -16 \Rightarrow x > -16 \div (-4) \Rightarrow \mathbf{x > 4}$
Remember to swap the inequality sign when dividing or multiplying by a negative number.
b) $-9x > -72 \Rightarrow x < -72 \div (-9) \Rightarrow \mathbf{x < 8}$
c) $-11x \le 33 \Rightarrow x \ge 33 \div (-11) \Rightarrow \mathbf{x \ge -3}$
d) $-2x < 45 \Rightarrow x > 45 \div (-2) \Rightarrow \mathbf{x > -22.5}$

4 a) $-\frac{x}{3} < 8 \Rightarrow x > 8 \times (-3) \Rightarrow \mathbf{x > -24}$
b) $-\frac{x}{5} \le -4 \Rightarrow x \ge -4 \times (-5) \Rightarrow \mathbf{x \ge 20}$
c) $-\frac{x}{1.1} \ge 10 \Rightarrow x \le 10 \times (-1.1) \Rightarrow \mathbf{x \le -11}$
d) $-\frac{x}{0.2} > -2.1 \Rightarrow x < (-2.1) \times (-0.2)$
$\Rightarrow \mathbf{x < 0.42}$

Page 154 Exercise 4

1 a) $7x - 12 > 65$
$7x > 65 + 12 \Rightarrow 7x > 77$
$x > 77 \div 7 \Rightarrow \mathbf{x > 11}$
b) $2x + 16 \ge -8$
$2x \ge -8 - 16 \Rightarrow 2x \ge -24$
$x \ge -24 \div 2 \Rightarrow \mathbf{x \ge -12}$
c) $-8x - 4.2 < 12.6$
$-8x < 12.6 + 4.2 \Rightarrow -8x < 16.8$
$x > 16.8 \div (-8) \Rightarrow \mathbf{x > -2.1}$
d) $4x + 2.6 \le 28.6$
$4x \le 28.6 - 2.6 \Rightarrow 4x \le 26$
$x \le 26 \div 4 \Rightarrow \mathbf{x \le 6.5}$

2 a) $\frac{x+2}{3} < 1$
$x + 2 < 1 \times 3 \Rightarrow x + 2 < 3$
$x < 3 - 2 \Rightarrow \mathbf{x < 1}$
b) $\frac{x-8}{2} > 7$
$x - 8 > 7 \times 2 \Rightarrow x - 8 > 14$
$x > 14 + 8 \Rightarrow \mathbf{x > 22}$
c) $\frac{x+4}{5} \ge 2$
$x + 4 \ge 2 \times 5 \Rightarrow x + 4 \ge 10$
$x \ge 10 - 4 \Rightarrow \mathbf{x \ge 6}$
d) $-\frac{x-6}{4} \le 0.5$
$x - 6 \ge 0.5 \times -4 \Rightarrow x - 6 \ge -2$
$x \ge -2 + 6 \Rightarrow \mathbf{x \ge 4}$

3 a) $\frac{x}{4} - 2.5 \ge 1$
$\frac{x}{4} \ge 1 + 2.5 \Rightarrow \frac{x}{4} \ge 3.5$
$x \ge 3.5 \times 4 \Rightarrow \mathbf{x \ge 14}$
b) $\frac{x}{2} + 5.5 > 7$
$\frac{x}{2} > 7 - 5.5 \Rightarrow \frac{x}{2} > 1.5$
$x > 1.5 \times 2 \Rightarrow \mathbf{x > 3}$
c) $-\frac{x}{8} - 3.1 < -1$
$-\frac{x}{8} < -1 + 3.1 \Rightarrow -\frac{x}{8} < 2.1$
$x > 2.1 \times -8 \Rightarrow \mathbf{x > -16.8}$
d) $\frac{x}{3.2} + 1.3 \le 5$
$\frac{x}{3.2} \le 5 - 1.3 \Rightarrow \frac{x}{3.2} \le 3.7$
$x \le 3.7 \times 3.2 \Rightarrow \mathbf{x \le 11.84}$

Page 155 Exercise 5

1 a) 3, 4
Each number must satisfy both parts of the inequality.
b) –5, –4, –3, –2, –1, 0
c) 6, 7, 8, 9, 10, 11, 12, 13

2 a)
0 1 2 3 4 5 6 7 8

b)
–1 0 1 2 3 4 5 6 7 8

c)
–3 –2 –1 0 1

3 a) $7 < x + 3 \le 15$
1st inequality: $7 < x + 3$
$7 - 3 < x \Rightarrow 4 < x$
2nd inequality: $x + 3 \le 15$
$x \le 15 - 3 \Rightarrow x \le 12$
So combining the two solved inequalities gives $\mathbf{4 < x \le 12}$.

4 5 6 7 8 9 10 11 12

b) $2 \le x - 4 \le 12$
1st inequality: $2 \le x - 4$
$2 + 4 \le x \Rightarrow 6 \le x$
2nd inequality: $x - 4 \le 12$
$x \le 12 + 4 \Rightarrow x \le 16$
So combining the two solved inequalities gives $\mathbf{6 \le x \le 16}$.

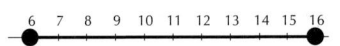

6 7 8 9 10 11 12 13 14 15 16

c) $-5.6 < x - 6.8 < 12.9$
1st inequality: $-5.6 < x - 6.8$
$-5.6 + 6.8 < x \Rightarrow 1.2 < x$
2nd inequality: $x - 6.8 < 12.9$
$x < 12.9 + 6.8 \Rightarrow x < 19.7$
So combining the two solved inequalities gives $\mathbf{1.2 < x < 19.7}$.

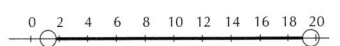

0 2 4 6 8 10 12 14 16 18 20

4 a) $32 < 2x \le 42$
1st inequality: $32 < 2x$
$32 \div 2 < x \Rightarrow 16 < x$
2nd inequality: $2x \le 42$
$x \le 42 \div 2 \Rightarrow x \le 21$
So combining the two solved inequalities gives $\mathbf{16 < x \le 21}$.
b) $-24 < 8x \le 40$
1st inequality: $-24 < 8x$
$-24 \div 8 < x \Rightarrow -3 < x$
2nd inequality: $8x \le 40$
$x \le 40 \div 8 \Rightarrow x \le 5$
So combining the two solved inequalities gives $\mathbf{-3 < x \le 5}$
c) $27 < 4.5x \le 72$
1st inequality: $27 < 4.5x$
$27 \div 4.5 < x \Rightarrow 6 < x$
2nd inequality: $4.5x \le 72$
$x \le 72 \div 4.5 \Rightarrow x \le 16$
So combining the two solved inequalities gives $\mathbf{6 < x \le 16}$

5 a) $17 < 6x + 5 < 29$
1st inequality: $17 < 6x + 5$
$17 - 5 < 6x \Rightarrow 12 < 6x$
$12 \div 6 < x \Rightarrow 2 < x$
2nd inequality: $6x + 5 < 29$
$6x < 29 - 5 \Rightarrow 6x < 24$
$x < 24 \div 6 \Rightarrow x < 4$
So combining the two solved inequalities gives $\mathbf{2 < x < 4}$.
b) $8 < 3x - 4 \le 26$
1st inequality: $8 < 3x - 4$
$8 + 4 < 3x \Rightarrow 12 < 3x$
$12 \div 3 < x \Rightarrow 4 < x$
2nd inequality: $3x - 4 \le 26$
$3x \le 26 + 4 \Rightarrow 3x \le 30$
$x \le 30 \div 3 \Rightarrow x \le 10$
So combining the two solved inequalities gives $\mathbf{4 < x \le 10}$
c) $-42 \le 7x + 7 < 91$
1st inequality: $-42 \le 7x + 7$
$-42 - 7 \le 7x \Rightarrow -49 \le 7x$
$-49 \div 7 \le x \Rightarrow -7 \le x$
2nd inequality: $7x + 7 < 91$
$7x < 91 - 7 \Rightarrow 7x < 84$
$x < 84 \div 7 \Rightarrow x < 12$
So combining the two solved inequalities gives $\mathbf{-7 \le x < 12}$
d) $9 \le 1.5x + 3 \le 9.9$
1st inequality: $9 \le 1.5x + 3$
$9 - 3 \le 1.5x \Rightarrow 6 \le 1.5x$
$6 \div 1.5 \le x \Rightarrow 4 \le x$
2nd inequality: $1.5x + 3 \le 9.9$
$1.5x \le 9.9 - 3$
$\Rightarrow 1.5x \le 6.9$
$x \le 6.9 \div 1.5 \Rightarrow x \le 4.6$
So combining the two solved inequalities gives $\mathbf{4 \le x \le 4.6}$

9.6 Simultaneous Equations

Page 156 Exercise 1

1 a) $x + 3y = 10$
$\underline{-(x + y = 6)}$
$2y = 4$
$\mathbf{y = 2}$
$x + 3 \times 2 = 10 \Rightarrow x = 10 - 6 \Rightarrow \mathbf{x = 4}$
Don't forget to put your values into the other equation to check them.

b) $x + 3y = 13$
$\underline{-(x - \ \ y = \ \ 5)}$
$4y = 8$
$\mathbf{y = 2}$
$x + 3 \times 2 = 13 \Rightarrow x = 13 - 6 \Rightarrow \mathbf{x = 7}$

c) $x + 2y = 6$
$\underline{-(x + \ \ y = 2)}$
$\mathbf{y = 4}$
$x + 2 \times 4 = 6 \Rightarrow x = 6 - 8 \Rightarrow \mathbf{x = -2}$

d) $2x - y = 7$
$\underline{+(4x + y = 23)}$
$6x = 30$
$\mathbf{x = 5}$
$2 \times 5 - y = 7 \Rightarrow 10 - 7 = y \Rightarrow \mathbf{y = 3}$

e) $3x - 2y = 16$
$\underline{+(2x + 2y = 14)}$
$5x = 30$
$\mathbf{x = 6}$
$3 \times 6 - 2y = 16 \Rightarrow 18 - 16 = 2y$
$\Rightarrow 2y = 2 \Rightarrow \mathbf{y = 1}$

f) $2x + 4y = 16$
$\underline{-(3x + 4y = 24)}$
$-x = -8$
$\mathbf{x = 8}$
$2 \times 8 + 4y = 16 \Rightarrow 4y = 16 - 16 = 0$
$\Rightarrow \mathbf{y = 0}$

Page 157 Exercise 2

1 a) (1) $3x + 2y = 16$,
(2) $2x + y = 9$
(1) $3x + 2y = 16$
(2) × 2: $\underline{-(4x + 2y = 18)}$
$-x = -2$
$\mathbf{x = 2}$
$2 \times 2 + y = 9 \Rightarrow 4 + y = 9 \Rightarrow y = 9 - 4$
$\Rightarrow \mathbf{y = 5}$

b) (1) $4x + 3y = 16$,
(2) $5x - y = 1$
(1) $4x + 3y = 16$
(2) × 3: $\underline{+(15x - 3y = 3)}$
$19x = 19$
$\mathbf{x = 1}$
$5 \times 1 - y = 1 \Rightarrow 5 - 1 = y \Rightarrow \mathbf{y = 4}$

c) (1) $5x - 3y = 12$,
(2) $2x - y = 5$
(2) × 3: $6x - 3y = 15$
(1) $\underline{-(5x - 3y = 12)}$
$\mathbf{x = 3}$
$2 \times 3 - y = 5 \Rightarrow 6 - 5 = y \Rightarrow \mathbf{y = 1}$

d) (1) $2e + 5f = 16$
(2) $3e - 2f = 5$
(1) × 2: $4e + 10f = 32$
(2) × 5: $\underline{+(15e - 10f = 25)}$
$19e = 57$
$\mathbf{e = 3}$
$3 \times 3 - 2f = 5 \Rightarrow 9 - 5 = 2f \Rightarrow 4 = 2f$
$\Rightarrow \mathbf{f = 2}$
There's more than one way to solve equations like this — here you could have started by multiplying (1) by 3 and (2) by 2 instead, and then subtracting the equations.

e) (1) $3d - 2e = 8$,
(2) $5d - 3e = 14$
(1) × 3: $(9d - 6e = 24)$
(2) × 2: $\underline{-(10d - 6e = 28)}$
$-d = -4$
$\mathbf{d = 4}$
$12 - 2e = 8 \Rightarrow 12 - 8 = 2e \Rightarrow 4 = 2e$
$\Rightarrow \mathbf{e = 2}$

f) (1) $5k + 3l = 4$,
(2) $3k + 2l = 3$
(2) × 3: $9k + 6l = 9$
(1) × 2: $\underline{-(10k + 6l = 8)}$
$-k = 1$
$\mathbf{k = -1}$
$3 \times (-1) + 2l = 3 \Rightarrow 2l = 3 + 3 = 6$
$\Rightarrow \mathbf{l = 3}$

Page 158 Exercise 3

1 If the sum of x and y is 58, then $x + y = 58$.
If the difference between x and y is 22, then $x - y = 22$.
Solving the two simultaneous equations gives:
$x + y = 58$
$\underline{+(x - y = 22)}$
$2x = 80$
$\mathbf{x = 40}$
$40 + y = 58 \Rightarrow \mathbf{y = 18}$

2 Let M be the price of a mountain bike and R be the cost of a road bike.
Then considering the total price of the bikes sold gives:
$M + 2R = 350$
Considering the difference in price gives:
$M = R + 50 \Rightarrow M - R = 50$.
Solve this pair of simultaneous equations:
$M + 2R = 350$
$\underline{-(M - R = 50)}$
$3R = 300$
$R = 100$
$M - 100 = 50 \Rightarrow M = 150$
So the price of a road bike is **£100** and the price of a mountain bike is **£150**.

3 Let d = price of sherbet dip, c = price of chocolate bar
Considering the total price last week gives:
$6d + c = 1.7$
Considering the total price the week before gives: $3d + 4c = 2.6$
(1) $6d + c = 1.7$
(2) $3d + 4c = 2.6$
(1) × 4: $24d + 4c = 6.8$
(2): $\underline{-(3d + 4c = 2.6)}$
$21d = 4.2$
$d = 0.2$
$6 \times 0.2 + c = 1.7$
$1.2 + c = 1.7 \Rightarrow c = 1.7 - 1.2 = 0.5$
So a sherbet dip costs **20p** and a chocolate bar costs **50p**.

9.7 Solving Quadratic Equations

Page 159 Exercise 1

1 a) $x^2 - 4 = 0 \Rightarrow x^2 = 4$
$\mathbf{x = -2, x = 2}$
There are always two solutions when taking the square root.

b) $x^2 - 1 = 0 \Rightarrow x^2 = 1$
$\mathbf{x = -1, x = 1}$
Using the same method for c)-h):
c) $\mathbf{x = -5, x = 5}$ **d)** $\mathbf{x = -8, x = 8}$
e) $\mathbf{x = -11, x = 11}$ **f)** $\mathbf{x = -10, x = 10}$
g) $\mathbf{x = -\sqrt{2}, x = \sqrt{2}}$ **h)** $\mathbf{x = -\sqrt{7}, x = \sqrt{7}}$

Page 160 Exercise 2

1 a) $x(x + 8) = 0 \Rightarrow x = 0$ or $x + 8 = 0$
So $\mathbf{x = 0}$ or $\mathbf{x = -8}$

b) $x(x - 5) = 0 \Rightarrow x = 0$ or $x - 5 = 0$
So $\mathbf{x = 0}$ or $\mathbf{x = 5}$
Using the same method for c)-f):
c) $\mathbf{x = 0}$ or $\mathbf{x = -6}$ **d)** $\mathbf{x = 0}$ or $\mathbf{x = 3}$
e) $\mathbf{x = 0}$ or $\mathbf{x = 4}$ **f)** $\mathbf{x = 0}$ or $\mathbf{x = -2}$

2 a) $x^2 + 6x = 0$
$x(x + 6) = 0 \Rightarrow x = 0$ or $x + 6 = 0$
So $\mathbf{x = 0}$ or $\mathbf{x = -6}$

b) $x^2 - 6x = 0$
$x(x - 6) = 0 \Rightarrow x = 0$ or $x - 6 = 0$
So $\mathbf{x = 0}$ or $\mathbf{x = 6}$

c) $x^2 - 24x = 0$
$x(x - 24) = 0 \Rightarrow x = 0$ or $x - 24 = 0$
So $\mathbf{x = 0}$ or $\mathbf{x = 24}$

d) $x^2 + 5x = 0$
$x(x + 5) = 0 \Rightarrow x = 0$ or $x + 5 = 0$
So $\mathbf{x = 0}$ or $\mathbf{x = -5}$

e) $x - x^2 = 0$
$x(1 - x) = 0 \Rightarrow x = 0$ or $1 - x = 0$
So $\mathbf{x = 0}$ or $\mathbf{x = 1}$

f) $12x - x^2 = 0$
$x(12 - x) = 0 \Rightarrow x = 0$ or $12 - x = 0$
So $\mathbf{x = 0}$ or $\mathbf{x = 12}$

Page 160 Exercise 3

1 a) $(x - 5)(x - 1) = 0 \Rightarrow x - 5 = 0$ or $x - 1 = 0$
So $\mathbf{x = 5}$ or $\mathbf{x = 1}$

b) $(x + 2)(x + 6) = 0 \Rightarrow x + 2 = 0$ or $x + 6 = 0$
So $\mathbf{x = -2}$ or $\mathbf{x = -6}$

c) $(x - 9)(x + 7) = 0 \Rightarrow x - 9 = 0$ or $x + 7 = 0$
So $\mathbf{x = 9}$ or $\mathbf{x = -7}$

2 a) **(i)** $\mathbf{(x + 2)(x + 5)}$ **(ii)** $\mathbf{(x + 4)(x + 5)}$
(iii) $\mathbf{(x + 4)(x + 9)}$ **(iv)** $\mathbf{(x + 6)(x - 4)}$

b) **(i)** $x^2 + 7x + 10 = 0 \Rightarrow (x + 2)(x + 5) = 0$
$\Rightarrow x + 2 = 0$
or $x + 5 = 0$
So $\mathbf{x = -2}$ or $\mathbf{x = -5}$

(ii) $x^2 + 9x + 20 = 0 \Rightarrow (x + 4)(x + 5) = 0$
$\Rightarrow x + 4 = 0$
or $x + 5 = 0$
So $\mathbf{x = -4}$ or $\mathbf{x = -5}$
Using the same method for (iii) and (iv):
(iii) $\mathbf{x = -4}$ or $\mathbf{x = -9}$
(iv) $\mathbf{x = -6}$ or $\mathbf{x = 4}$

3 a) $x^2 + 2x + 1 = 0 \Rightarrow (x + 1)(x + 1) = 0$
$\Rightarrow (x + 1)^2 = 0$
$\Rightarrow x + 1 = 0$
So $\mathbf{x = -1}$

b) $x^2 - 7x + 12 = 0 \Rightarrow (x - 3)(x - 4) = 0$
$\Rightarrow x - 3 = 0$ or $x - 4 = 0$
So $\mathbf{x = 3}$ or $\mathbf{x = 4}$

c) $x^2 + 4x + 4 = 0 \Rightarrow (x + 2)(x + 2) = 0$
$\Rightarrow (x + 2)^2 = 0$
$\Rightarrow x + 2 = 0$
So $\mathbf{x = -2}$
Using the same method for d)-f):
d) $\mathbf{x = 2}$ **e)** $\mathbf{x = -5}$ or $\mathbf{x = 3}$
f) $\mathbf{x = 7}$ or $\mathbf{x = -3}$

Page 161 Review Exercise

1 a) $\frac{x + 8}{3} = 4$
$x + 8 = 4 \times 3 \Rightarrow x + 8 = 12$
$x = 12 - 8 \Rightarrow \mathbf{x = 4}$

b) $9 + 5x = 54$
$5x = 54 - 9 \Rightarrow 5x = 45$
$x = 45 \div 5 \Rightarrow \mathbf{x = 9}$

c) $72 = 4.5(8 + 2x)$
$72 \div 4.5 = 8 + 2x \Rightarrow 16 = 8 + 2x$
$16 - 8 = 2x \Rightarrow 8 = 2x$
$x = 8 \div 2 \Rightarrow \mathbf{x = 4}$

d) $7(x - 3) = 3(x - 6)$
$7x - 21 = 3x - 18$
$7x - 3x - 21 = -18 \Rightarrow 4x - 21 = -18$
$4x = -18 + 21 \Rightarrow 4x = 3$
$\mathbf{x = \frac{3}{4}}$ or **0.75**

2 Four hours at £x an hour cost £$4x$.
Adding the call-out charge gives £$4x + 35$.
So $4x + 35 = 170$.
$4x = 170 - 35 \Rightarrow 4x = 135$
$x = 135 \div 4 \Rightarrow x = 33.75$
So the electrician charges **£33.75** per hour.

3 a) Sum of angles in a triangle = 180°, so:
$(3x + 10°) + (x + 10°) + (x + 10°) = 180°$
$3x + x + x + 10° + 10° + 10° = 180°$
$\Rightarrow \mathbf{5x + 30° = 180°}$

b) $5x + 30° = 180°$
$5x = 180° - 30° = 150°$
$x = 150° \div 5 \Rightarrow x = 30°$
Bottom left angle = 30° + 10° = **40°**
Bottom right angle = 30° + 10° = **40°**
Top angle = 3 × 30° + 10° = **100°**
Check these angles work for a triangle: 40° + 40° + 100° = 180°.

4 Expanding the left-hand side gives
$x(x - 1) + 2(x - 3) = x^2 - x + 2x - 6 = \mathbf{x^2 + x - 6}$
Expanding the right-hand side gives
$(x + 3)(x - 2) = x^2 - 2x + 3x - 6 = \mathbf{x^2 + x - 6}$
The two sides are the same so the identity is **true.**

5 E.g. $3^2 + 4^2 = 9 + 16 = 25 = 5^2$
so the statement is **false**.

6 Take an even number and an odd number — $2a$ and $(2b + 1)$. Their sum is
$2a + 2b + 1 = 2(a + b) + 1$
$= \mathbf{2n + 1}$, where $n = a + b$
So the sum of an even number and an odd number is **odd**.

7 a) $x + 2.7 \geq 6.2$
$x \geq 6.2 - 2.7$
$\mathbf{x \geq 3.5}$

b) $-\frac{x}{9} < 7$
$x > 7 \times -9$
$\mathbf{x > -63}$

c) $-5 \leq 12x + 7 < 43$
1st inequality: $-5 \leq 12x + 7$
$-5 - 7 \leq 12x \Rightarrow -12 \leq 12x$
$-12 \div 12 \leq x \Rightarrow -1 \leq x$
2nd inequality: $12x + 7 < 43$
$12x < 43 - 7 \Rightarrow 12x < 36$
$x < 36 \div 12 \Rightarrow x < 3$
So combining the two solved inequalities gives $\mathbf{-1 \leq x < 3}$.

8 a) (1) $m - 3n = 7$,
(2) $5m + 4n = -3$
(1) × 5: $5m - 15n = 35$
(2) : $-(5m + 4n = -3)$
$-19n = 38$
$n = (38 \div -19)$
$\mathbf{n = -2}$
$m - 3 \times (-2) = 7 \Rightarrow m + 6 = 7 \Rightarrow \mathbf{m = 1}$

b) (1) $4u + 7v = 15$,
(2) $5u - 2v = 8$
(1) × 2: $8u + 14v = 30$
(2) × 7: $+(35u - 14v = 56)$
$43u = 86$
$\mathbf{u = 2}$
$5 \times 2 - 2v = 8 \Rightarrow 10 - 8 = 2v \Rightarrow 2 = 2v$
$\Rightarrow \mathbf{v = 1}$
You could also have started by multiplying (1) by 5 and (2) by 4.

9 a) $x^2 - 36 = 0$
$x^2 = 36$
$\mathbf{x = -6, x = 6}$

b) $x^2 - 81 = 0$
$x^2 = 81$
$\mathbf{x = -9, x = 9}$

c) $x^2 - 3 = 0$
$x^2 = 3$
$\mathbf{x = -\sqrt{3}, x = \sqrt{3}}$

10 a) $x^2 - 4x = 0 \Rightarrow x(x - 4) = 0$
$\Rightarrow x = 0$ or $x - 4 = 0$
So $\mathbf{x = 0}$ or $\mathbf{x = 4}$

b) $x^2 + 9x + 18 = 0 \Rightarrow (x + 3)(x + 6) = 0$
$\Rightarrow x + 3 = 0$ or $x + 6 = 0$
So $\mathbf{x = -3}$ or $\mathbf{x = -6}$

c) $x^2 + 9x - 22 = 0 \Rightarrow (x + 11)(x - 2) = 0$
$\Rightarrow x + 11 = 0$ or $x - 2 = 0$
So $\mathbf{x = -11}$ or $\mathbf{x = 2}$

Page 162 Exam-Style Questions

1 a) $2x + 5 = 19$
$2x = 19 - 5 \Rightarrow 2x = 14$
$x = 14 \div 2 \Rightarrow \mathbf{x = 7}$ *[1 mark]*

b) $3(2x - 1) = 2(x + 4)$
$6x - 3 = 2x + 8$ *[1 mark]*
$6x - 2x - 3 = 8 \Rightarrow 4x - 3 = 8$
$4x = 8 + 3 \Rightarrow 4x = 11$ *[1 mark]*
$x = 11 \div 4 \Rightarrow \mathbf{x = 2.75}$ *[1 mark]*

2 a) **14** *[1 mark]*

b) Minimum value of $x = 7$, so minimum value of x^2 is $7^2 = \mathbf{49}$ *[1 mark]*

3 Bethany is 3 times as old as Anish, so Bethany's age = $3x$.
Cate is two years younger than Anish, so Cate's age = $x - 2$.
[1 mark for both expressions]
The sum of their ages is $x + 3x + (x - 2)$
$= 5x - 2$.
So $5x - 2 = 58$ *[1 mark]*
$\Rightarrow 5x = 58 + 2 = 60 \Rightarrow \mathbf{x = 12}$ *[1 mark]*

4 Let x be the cost of a chew and let y be the cost of a lolly.
Bill buys 2 chews ($2x$) and 3 lollies ($3y$) and pays 84p.
So $2x + 3y = 84$
Aisha buys 3 chews ($3x$) and 1 lolly (y) and pays 63p.
So $3x + y = 63$
Solving:
(1) $2x + 3y = 84$
(2) $3x + y = 63$
(2) × 3: $9x + 3y = 189$
(1) $-(2x + 3y = 84)$
$7x = 105$
$x = 105 \div 7 \Rightarrow x = 15$
$3 \times 15 + y = 63$
$45 + y = 63$
$y = 63 - 45 \Rightarrow y = 18$
For 7 chews and 5 lollies:
$7 \times (15) + 5 \times (18) = 195$p or £1.95
[4 marks available — 1 mark for forming both equations, 1 mark for combining the two equations to eliminate a variable, 1 mark for correctly finding both variables, 1 mark for the correct answer]

5 a) The area of the rectangle is given by
$x(x + 3) = x^2 + 3x$ *[1 mark]*
From the question the area of the rectangle is 10 cm², so $x^2 + 3x = 10$.
Rearranging gives $\mathbf{x^2 + 3x - 10 = 0}$ *[1 mark]*

b) $x^2 + 3x - 10 = 0 \Rightarrow (x + 5)(x - 2) = 0$
[1 mark]
So $x = -5$ or $x = 2$ *[1 mark]*
A distance can't be negative, so $x = 2$.
Length = $x + 3 = 2 + 3 =$ **5 cm** *[1 mark]*
Width = x = **2 cm** *[1 mark]*

Section 10 — Formulas and Functions

10.1 Formulas

Page 164 Exercise 1

1 a) "I have c carrots" — start with the letter c. "Su has 6 more carrots than me" — so add 6. The expression is $\mathbf{c + 6}$.

b) "Daisy has p plants" — start with the letter p. "Iris has 8 fewer plants" — so subtract 8. The expression is $\mathbf{p - 8}$

2 a) "Claudia has f films" — start with the letter f. "Barry owns twice as many..." — so multiply by 2. $2 \times f = \mathbf{2f}$ **films.**

b) The total is $f + 2f = \mathbf{3f}$ **films.**

c) Subtract 3 for both Claudia and Barry from $3f$. $3f - 3 - 3 = \mathbf{3f - 6}$ **films.**

3 Start with b bulbs. Multiply by 3 to get $3b$. Then add 5 to get: $\mathbf{3b + 5}$ **flowers.**

4 Alf earns £8 per hour, so multiply h (number of hours) by 8 to get $8h$. Then add the £18 that Alf started with to get: $\mathbf{8h + 18}$.

5 a) Square the smaller number, y, to get y^2. Cube the larger number, x, to get x^3. Now subtract x^3 from y^2 to get the expression: $\mathbf{y^2 - x^3}$.

b) Add the numbers to get $x + y$, then take the square root to get the expression: $\mathbf{\sqrt{x + y}}$.
Make sure you put the square root sign over all of 'x + y'.

Page 165 Exercise 2

1 The subject is cost, C, so the formula begins 'C = '. It costs £3 per hour, so multiply h (number of hours) by 3 to get the formula $\mathbf{C = 3h}$.

2 The subject is time, T, so the formula begins 'T = '. It takes 2 minutes per km, so multiply k (number of km) by 2 to get the formula $\mathbf{T = 2k}$.

3 The subject is amount paid, P, so the formula begins 'P = '. Tom is paid w pounds per hour and works for 8 hours, so multiply w by 8 to get the formula $\mathbf{P = 8w}$.

4 The subject is Ellie's distance, d, so the formula begins 'd = '. Kojo runs r km and Ellie runs 5 km less, so subtract 5 from r to get the formula $\mathbf{d = r - 5}$.

5 The subject is total cost, C, so the formula begins 'C = '. It's £5.50 per hour so multiply n (number of hours) by 5.5 to get $5.5n$. Add on the fixed cost, £F, to get the formula $\mathbf{C = F + 5.5n}$.

6 The subject is time, t, so the formula begins 't = '. It takes 50 minutes per kg and the goose weighs n kg, so multiply 50 by n to get $50n$. Add on the fixed time of 25 minutes to get the formula $\mathbf{t = 50n + 25}$.

7 The subject is total cost, C, so the formula begins 'C = '. It costs £p per tree and t trees are cut down, so multiply p by t to get pt. Add on the fixed cost of £25 to get the formula $\mathbf{C = pt + 25}$.

8 The subject is cost, C, so the formula begins 'C = '. It costs 22p = £0.22 per mile and m miles are covered, so multiply 0.22 by m to get $0.22m$. Add on the fixed cost of £10 to get the formula $\mathbf{C = 0.22m + 10}$.
Watch out for where the units need converting. The question asks for the answer in pounds, so convert pence to pounds here.

9 The subject is cost, C, so the formula begins '$C =$'. It costs 80p per minute, but C is a cost in pounds and h is a number of hours, so work out the cost in pounds per hour. 80p = £0.80 and 1 hour = 60 minutes, so it costs £0.80 × 60 = £48 per hour. So the cost of h hours is $48 \times h = 48h$. Add on the fixed cost of £125 to get the formula $\mathbf{C = 48h + 125}$.

Page 167 Exercise 3

1 a) $x = 7$, so $y = x + 4 = 7 + 4 = \mathbf{11}$
b) $x = 7$, so $y = x - 3 = 7 - 3 = \mathbf{4}$
Using the same method for c)-d):
c) 5 **d) 42**

2 a) $m = -3$, so $y = m - 8 = -3 - 8 = \mathbf{-11}$
b) $m = -3$, so $y = 3m^2 = 3 \times (-3)^2 = 3 \times 9 = \mathbf{27}$
Using the same method for c)-d):
c) –7 **d) –4**

3 a) $m = 4$ and $n = 3$, so $p = mn = 4 \times 3 = \mathbf{12}$
b) $m = 4$, so $p = m^2 = 4^2 = \mathbf{16}$
c) $m = 4$ and $n = 3$, so $p = m - n^2 = 4 - 3^2 = 4 - 9 = \mathbf{-5}$
d) $m = 4$ and $n = 3$, so $p = \frac{3m}{n} = \frac{\cancel{3} \times 4}{\cancel{3}} = \mathbf{4}$

4 a) $x = -4$, so $z = x + 2 = -4 + 2 = \mathbf{-2}$
b) $y = -3$, so $z = y - 1 = -3 - 1 = \mathbf{-4}$
c) $x = -4$ and $y = -3$, so $z = -x + 2y = -(-4) + 2 \times (-3) = 4 - 6 = \mathbf{-2}$
d) $x = -4$ and $y = -3$, so $z = 6x - y = 6 \times (-4) + 3 = -24 + 3 = \mathbf{-21}$

5 a) $n = 10$, so $S = \frac{1}{2}n(n + 1)$
$= \frac{1}{2} \times 10 \times (10 + 1) = 5 \times 11 = \mathbf{55}$
b) $n = 100$, so $S = \frac{1}{2}n(n + 1)$
$= \frac{1}{2} \times 100 \times (100 + 1)$
$= 50 \times 101 = \mathbf{5050}$
Using the same method for c)-d):
c) 500 500 **d) 12 502 500**

6 a) $u = 7$, $a = 2$ and $t = 4$, so:
$s = ut + \frac{1}{2}at^2 = 7 \times 4 + \frac{1}{2} \times 2 \times 4^2$
$= 28 + 16 = \mathbf{44}$
b) $u = 24$, $a = 11$ and $t = 13$, so:
$s = ut + \frac{1}{2}at^2 = 24 \times 13 + \frac{1}{2} \times 11 \times 13^2$
$= 312 + 929.5 = \mathbf{1241.5}$
Using the same method for c)-d):
c) –864.2602 **d) 780.3752**

Page 168 Exercise 4

1 a) $b = 4$ and $h = 6$, so $A = \frac{1}{2}bh$
$= \frac{1}{2} \times 4 \times 6 = \mathbf{12\ m^2}$
Remember to give your answer with units — here it's m².
b) $b = 2$ and $h = 3$, so $A = \frac{1}{2}bh$
$= \frac{1}{2} \times 2 \times 3 = \mathbf{3\ m^2}$
c) $b = 0.4$ and $h = 1.8$, so $A = \frac{1}{2}bh$
$= \frac{1}{2} \times 0.4 \times 1.8 = \mathbf{0.36\ m^2}$

2 a) The runner travels 800 metres, so $d = 800$, and the time taken is 110 seconds, so $t = 110$.
$s = \frac{d}{t} = \frac{800}{110} = \mathbf{7.27\ m/s\ (to\ 3\ s.f.)}$
b) The cheetah travels 400 metres, so $d = 400$, and the time taken is 14 seconds, so $t = 14$.
$s = \frac{d}{t} = \frac{400}{14} = \mathbf{28.6\ m/s\ (to\ 3\ s.f.)}$

3 $a = 3$ and $b = 4$, so:
$c = \sqrt{a^2 + b^2} = \sqrt{3^2 + 4^2} = \sqrt{9 + 16} = \sqrt{25} = \mathbf{5\ cm}$
You could have used a = 4 and b = 3 instead.

4 a) $r = 5$ cm, so:
$A = \pi r^2 = \pi \times 5^2 = \pi \times 25 = 78.539...$
$= \mathbf{78.5\ cm^2\ (to\ 1\ d.p.)}$
b) $r = 3.5$ cm, so:
$A = \pi \times 3.5^2 = \pi \times 12.25 = 38.484...$
$= \mathbf{38.5\ cm^2\ (to\ 1\ d.p.)}$
Using the same method for c)-d):
c) 387.1 cm² (to 1 d.p.)
d) 128.7 cm² (to 1 d.p.)

5 a) $l = 1$, so:
$T = 2\pi\sqrt{\frac{l}{10}} = 2 \times \pi \times \sqrt{\frac{1}{10}} = 1.986...$
$= \mathbf{2.0\ s\ (to\ 1\ d.p.)}$
b) $l = 0.5$, so:
$T = 2\pi\sqrt{\frac{l}{10}} = 2 \times \pi \times \sqrt{\frac{0.5}{10}} = 1.404...$
$= \mathbf{1.4\ s\ (to\ 1\ d.p.)}$
c) $l = 16$, so:
$T = 2\pi\sqrt{\frac{l}{10}} = 2 \times \pi \times \sqrt{\frac{16}{10}} = 7.947...$
$= \mathbf{7.9\ s\ (to\ 1\ d.p.)}$

Page 170 Exercise 5

1 a) The opposite of + 2 is – 2, so subtract 2 from both sides:
$y = x + 2$, so $y - 2 = x$. Rewrite as $\mathbf{x = y - 2}$.
b) The opposite of – 5 is + 5, so add 5 to both sides: $b = x - 5$, so $b + 5 = x$.
Rewrite as $\mathbf{x = b + 5}$.
Using the same method for c):
c) $\mathbf{x = z - 7}$

2 a) The opposite of × 4 is ÷ 4, so divide both sides by 4:
$z = 4x$, so $\frac{z}{4} = x$. Rewrite as $\mathbf{x = \frac{z}{4}}$.
b) The opposite of × 17 is ÷ 17, so divide both sides by 17:
$p = 17x$, so $\frac{p}{17} = x$. Rewrite as $\mathbf{x = \frac{p}{17}}$.
Using the same method for c):
c) $\mathbf{x = \frac{r}{4.2}}$

3 a) The opposite of ÷ 8 is × 8, so multiply both sides by 8:
$y = \frac{x}{8}$, so $8y = x$. Rewrite as $\mathbf{x = 8y}$.
b) The opposite of ÷ 17 is × 17, so multiply both sides by 17:
$z = \frac{x}{17}$, so $17z = x$. Rewrite as $\mathbf{x = 17z}$.
Using the same method for c):
c) $\mathbf{x = 8.6t}$

4 a) The opposite of × 2 is ÷ 2, so divide both sides by 2:
$abc = 2x$, so $\frac{abc}{2} = x$. Rewrite as $\mathbf{x = \frac{abc}{2}}$.
b) The opposite of × y is ÷ y, so divide both sides by y:
$t = xy$, so $\frac{t}{y} = x$. Rewrite as $\mathbf{x = \frac{t}{y}}$.
Using the same method for c):
c) $\mathbf{x = \frac{uv + y}{4.2}}$

5 a) The opposite of $\times \frac{4}{5}$ is $\div \frac{4}{5}$.
$\div \frac{4}{5}$ is the same as $\times \frac{5}{4}$.
So multiply both sides by $\frac{5}{4}$:
$m = \frac{4}{5}s$, so $\frac{5}{4}m = s$. Rewrite as $\mathbf{s = \frac{5}{4}m}$.
b) The opposite of ×(–16) is ÷(–16), so divide both sides by –16:
$r = -16s$, so $\frac{r}{-16} = s$. Rewrite as $\mathbf{s = -\frac{r}{16}}$.
c) The opposite of ×(–14.2) is ÷(–14.2), so divide both sides by –14.2:
$p = -14.2s$, so $\frac{p}{-14.2} = s$.
Rewrite as $\mathbf{s = -\frac{p}{14.2}}$.
d) The opposite of $\times \frac{5}{4}$ is $\div \frac{5}{4}$. $\div \frac{5}{4}$ is the same as $\times \frac{4}{5}$.
So multiply both sides by $\frac{4}{5}$:
$a = \frac{5}{4}s$, so $\frac{4}{5}a = s$. Rewrite as $\mathbf{s = \frac{4}{5}a}$.
e) s is under a square root, so square both sides:
$b = \sqrt{s}$, so $b^2 = s$. Rewrite as $\mathbf{s = b^2}$.
f) s is squared, so take square roots:
$c = s^2$, so $\pm\sqrt{c} = s$. Rewrite as $\mathbf{s = \pm\sqrt{c}}$.

Page 171 Exercise 6

1 a) $y = 5x + 3$
Subtract 3 from both sides: $y - 3 = 5x$
Divide both sides by 5: $\frac{y - 3}{5} = x$,
so $\mathbf{x = \frac{y - 3}{5}}$
b) $z = 8x - 2$
Add 2 to both sides: $z + 2 = 8x$
Divide both sides by 8: $\frac{z + 2}{8} = x$,
so $\mathbf{x = \frac{z + 2}{8}}$
c) $p = 15x + 18$
Subtract 18 from both sides: $p - 18 = 15x$
Divide both sides by 15: $\frac{p - 18}{15} = x$,
so $\mathbf{x = \frac{p - 18}{15}}$

2 a) $z = \frac{y + 4}{3}$
Multiply both sides by 3: $3z = y + 4$
Subtract 4 from both sides: $3z - 4 = y$,
so $\mathbf{y = 3z - 4}$
b) $x = \frac{7 + y}{4}$
Multiply both sides by 4: $4x = 7 + y$
Subtract 7 from both sides: $4x - 7 = y$,
so $\mathbf{y = 4x - 7}$
c) $s = \frac{y - 2}{9}$
Multiply both sides by 9: $9s = y - 2$
Add 2 to both sides: $9s + 2 = y$,
so $\mathbf{y = 9s + 2}$

3 a) $u = 4(x - 2)$
Divide both sides by 4: $\frac{u}{4} = x - 2$
Add 2 to both sides: $\frac{u}{4} + 2 = x$,
so $\mathbf{x = \frac{u}{4} + 2}$ or $\mathbf{x = \frac{u + 8}{4}}$
b) $v = 8(x + 4)$
Divide both sides by 8: $\frac{v}{8} = x + 4$
Subtract 4 from both sides: $\frac{v}{8} - 4 = x$,
so $\mathbf{x = \frac{v}{8} - 4}$ or $\mathbf{x = \frac{v - 32}{8}}$

c) $w = 3(x - 4)$
Divide both sides by 3: $\frac{w}{3} = x - 4$
Add 4 to both sides: $\frac{w}{3} + 4 = x$,
so $\mathbf{x = \frac{w}{3} + 4}$ or $\mathbf{x = \frac{w + 12}{3}}$

4 a) $p + 3 = 4y - 2$
Add 2 to both sides: $p + 3 + 2 = 4y$,
so $p + 5 = 4y$
Divide both sides by 4: $\frac{p + 5}{4} = y$,
so $\mathbf{y = \frac{p + 5}{4}}$

b) $q + 7 = 9y + 11$
Subtract 11 from both sides:
$q + 7 - 11 = 9y$, so $q - 4 = 9y$
Divide both sides by 9: $\frac{q - 4}{9} = y$,
so $\mathbf{y = \frac{q - 4}{9}}$

c) $r - 5 = 21y - 9$
Add 9 to both sides: $r - 5 + 9 = 21y$,
so $r + 4 = 21y$
Divide both sides by 21: $\frac{r + 4}{21} = y$,
so $\mathbf{y = \frac{r + 4}{21}}$

5 a) $A = 21.5d^2$
Divide both sides by 21.5: $\frac{A}{21.5} = d^2$
d is squared, so take the square root of each side:
$\sqrt{\frac{A}{21.5}} = d$, so $\mathbf{d = \sqrt{\frac{A}{21.5}}}$
The positive square root is used because d is a length.

b) (i) $A = 344$, so $d = \sqrt{\frac{344}{21.5}} = \sqrt{16}$ **= 4 cm**

(ii) $A = 134.375$, so
$d = \sqrt{\frac{134.375}{21.5}} = \sqrt{6.25}$ **= 2.5 cm**

6 a) $P = 2(2x + y)$
Divide both sides by 2: $\frac{P}{2} = 2x + y$
Subtract y from both sides: $\frac{P}{2} - y = 2x$
Divide both sides by 2: $\frac{P}{4} - \frac{y}{2} = x$,
so $\mathbf{x = \frac{P}{4} - \frac{y}{2}}$ or $\mathbf{x = \frac{P - 2y}{4}}$

b) (i) $P = 14$ and $y = 3$,
so $x = \frac{P}{4} - \frac{y}{2} = \frac{14}{4} - \frac{3}{2} = \mathbf{2}$

(ii) $P = 32$ and $y = 4$,
so $x = \frac{P}{4} - \frac{y}{2} = \frac{32}{4} - \frac{4}{2} = \mathbf{6}$

7 a) $x + y = 6x$
Subtract x from both sides: $y = 5x$
Divide both sides by 5: $\frac{y}{5} = x$, so $\mathbf{x = \frac{y}{5}}$

b) $y = \sqrt{x} + 2$
Subtract 2 from both sides: $y - 2 = \sqrt{x}$
x is under a square root, so square both sides:
$(y - 2)^2 = x$, so $\mathbf{x = (y - 2)^2}$

c) $\frac{3 + xy + x}{x + 1} = y$
Multiply both sides by $(x + 1)$:
$3 + xy + x = y(x + 1)$
Multiply out the brackets: $3 + xy + x = xy + y$
Subtract xy from both sides: $3 + x = y$
Subtract 3 from both sides: $\mathbf{x = y - 3}$

10.2 Functions

Page 173 Exercise 1

1 a) $x = 20$, divide by 5 to get $20 \div 5 = 4$.
Add 7 to get $4 + 7 = 11$. So $\mathbf{y = 11}$.
Using the same method for b)-d):
b) $\mathbf{y = 14}$ c) $\mathbf{y = 16}$ d) $\mathbf{y = 5}$

2 a) $x = 11$, subtract 3 to get $11 - 3 = 8$.
Multiply by 6 to get $8 \times 6 = 48$. So $\mathbf{y = 48}$.
b) Work backwards using opposite operations.
$y = 72$, divide by 6 to get $72 \div 6 = 12$.
Add 3 to get $12 + 3 = 15$. So $\mathbf{x = 15}$.

3 a) $x = -1$, multiply by 7 to get $-1 \times 7 = -7$.
Subtract 2 to get $-7 - 2 = -9$. So $\mathbf{y = -9}$.
b) Work backwards using opposite operations.
$y = 19$, add 2 to get $19 + 2 = 21$.
Divide by 7 to get $21 \div 7 = 3$. So $\mathbf{x = 3}$.

4 a) x is multiplied by 4, then 1 is added to get y. So the function machine is:
$x \longrightarrow$ [× 4] $\longrightarrow$ [+ 1] $\longrightarrow y$
b) Work backwards using opposite operations.
$y = 17$, subtract 1 to get $17 - 1 = 16$.
Divide by 4 to get $16 \div 4 = 4$. So $\mathbf{x = 4}$.

5 The output is equal to the input when $\mathbf{x = 2}$, as $2 \times 6 = 12$ and $12 - 10 = 2 = x$

Page 174 Review Exercise

1 a) The subject is c, the number of free minutes Chloe gets, so the formula begins '$c =$ '. Wassim gets w free minutes and Chloe gets 45 fewer minutes, so subtract 45 from w. The formula is $\mathbf{c = w - 45}$.
b) Substitute $w = 125$ into $c = w - 45$ to find $c = 125 - 45 = \mathbf{80}$.

2 a) $m = 5h + 1$
Subtract 1 from both sides: $m - 1 = 5h$
Divide both sides by 5: $\frac{m - 1}{5} = h$,
so $\mathbf{h = \frac{m - 1}{5}}$
b) Substitute $m = 36$ into $h = \frac{m - 1}{5}$ to find $h = \frac{36 - 1}{5} = \mathbf{7}$.

3 a) Substitute $x = 30°$ into $y = \frac{180° - x}{2}$ to find
$y = \frac{180° - 30°}{2} = \mathbf{75°}$.
b) $y = \frac{180° - x}{2}$
Multiply both sides by 2: $2y = 180° - x$
Add x to both sides: $2y + x = 180°$
Subtract $2y$ from both sides: $\mathbf{x = 180° - 2y}$

4 a) $n = 275$ units, multiply by 0.06 to get $275 \times 0.06 = 16.5$.
Next add 7.5 to get $16.5 + 7.5 = 24$.
So $C =$ **£24**.
b) Work backwards using opposite operations.
$C =$ £40.50, subtract 7.5 to get $40.5 - 7.5 = 33$.
Next divide by 0.06 to get $33 \div 0.06 = 550$.
So **550 units** were used.

5 a) Use the letter b for the number of black tiles. '3 white tiles for every black tile' — so multiply b by 3.
'plus an extra 50 white tiles' — so add 50 to get w.
So the completed function machine is:
$b \longrightarrow$ [× 3] $\longrightarrow$ [+ 50] $\longrightarrow w$
b) Put $b = 200$ into the machine.
Multiply by 3 to get $200 \times 3 = 600$,
add 50 to get $600 + 50 = 650$.
So **650 white tiles** are used.
c) Work backwards using opposite operations.
$t = 530$ total tiles, subtract 50 to get $530 - 50 = 480$.
Next divide by 4 to get $b = 480 \div 4 = 120$.
So **120 black tiles** are used.

Page 175 Exam-Style Questions

1 $y = a + \frac{b}{x}$
Subtract a from both sides: $y - a = \frac{b}{x}$ *[1 mark]*
Multiply both sides by x: $xy - xa = b$,
so $\mathbf{b = xy - xa}$ *[1 mark]*

2 a) $17 - 4 = 13$, $13 \div 25 = \mathbf{0.52}$ *[1 mark]*
b) $5 \times 25 = 125$ *[1 mark]*,
$125 + 4 = \mathbf{129}$ *[1 mark]*
c) $3x \times 25 + 4 = \mathbf{75x + 4}$ *[1 mark]*

3 a) Multiply n (number of people) by £1.25 (cost per person), then add on the fixed fee of £30. $\mathbf{C = 1.25n + 30}$ *[1 mark]*
b) Substitute $n = 32$ into $C = 1.25n + 30$.
$C = 1.25 \times 32 + 30 =$ **£70** *[1 mark]*
c) $C = 1.25n + 30$, so $C - 30 = 1.25n$ *[1 mark]*
and $\frac{C - 30}{1.25} = n$, so $\mathbf{n = \frac{C - 30}{1.25}}$ *[1 mark]*
d) Substitute $C =$ £80 into $n = \frac{C - 30}{1.25}$ to get
$n = \frac{80 - 30}{1.25} =$ **40 people** *[1 mark]*

4 Work backwards using opposite operations: $10 + 4 = 14$ *[1 mark]*, so the first step needs to turn 7 into 14. $14 = 7 \times 2$, so the missing operation is **× 2** *[1 mark]*.
You could also do ÷ 0.5 or + 7.

Section 11 — Sequences

11.1 Term to Term Rules

Page 177 Exercise 1

1 1st term: **5**
2nd term: $5 + 4 = \mathbf{9}$
3rd term: $9 + 4 = \mathbf{13}$
4th term: $13 + 4 = \mathbf{17}$
5th term: $17 + 4 = \mathbf{21}$

2 1st term: **2**
2nd term: $2 \times 2 = \mathbf{4}$
3rd term: $4 \times 2 = \mathbf{8}$
4th term: $8 \times 2 = \mathbf{16}$
5th term: $16 \times 2 = \mathbf{32}$

3 a) 1st term: **100**
2nd term: $100 - 6 = \mathbf{94}$
3rd term: $94 - 6 = \mathbf{88}$
4th term: $88 - 6 = \mathbf{82}$
5th term: $82 - 6 = \mathbf{76}$
b) 1st term: **40**
2nd term: $40 \div 2 = \mathbf{20}$
3rd term: $20 \div 2 = \mathbf{10}$
4th term: $10 \div 2 = \mathbf{5}$
5th term: $5 \div 2 = \mathbf{2.5}$
c) 1st term: **11**
2nd term: $11 \times -2 = \mathbf{-22}$
3rd term: $-22 \times -2 = \mathbf{44}$
4th term: $44 \times -2 = \mathbf{-88}$
5th term: $-88 \times -2 = \mathbf{176}$

4 a) The difference between the terms is:
$6 - 3 = 3$, $9 - 6 = 3$,
so the rule is '**add 3 to the previous term**'.
b) 5th term: $12 + 3 = \mathbf{15}$
6th term: $15 + 3 = \mathbf{18}$
7th term: $18 + 3 = \mathbf{21}$

5 a) (i) The difference between the terms is $5 - 3 = 2$, $7 - 5 = 2$, so the rule is '**add 2 to the previous term**'

(ii) 5th term: $9 + 2 =$ **11**
6th term: $11 + 2 =$ **13**
7th term: $13 + 2 =$ **15**

b) (i) The ratio between the terms is $12 \div 4 = 3$, $36 \div 12 = 3$, so the rule is '**multiply the previous term by 3**'

(ii) 5th term: $108 \times 3 =$ **324**
6th term: $324 \times 3 =$ **972**
7th term: $972 \times 3 =$ **2916**

Using the same method for c)-h):

c) (i) The rule is '**divide the previous term by 2**'.

(ii) The next three terms are **1**, **0.5**, **0.25**.

d) (i) The rule is '**subtract 2 from the previous term**'.

(ii) The next three terms are **–3**, **–5**, **–7**.

e) (i) The rule is '**add 0.5 to the previous term**'.

(ii) The next three terms are **3**, **3.5**, **4**.

f) (i) The rule is '**multiply the previous term by 3**'.

(ii) The next three terms are **–81**, **–243**, **–729**.

g) (i) The rule is '**divide the previous term by 10**'.

(ii) The next three terms are **0.1**, **0.01**, **0.001**.

h) (i) The rule is '**multiply the previous term by –2**'.

(ii) The next three terms are **16**, **–32**, **64**.

6 a) The difference between the terms is $10 - 4 = 6$, $16 - 10 = 6$, so the rule is '**add 6 to the previous term**'.

b) (i) The 5th term is $22 + 6 =$ **28**

(ii) The 6th term is $28 + 6 =$ **34**

(iii) The 8th term is $34 + 6 + 6$
$= 40 + 6 =$ **46**

7 a) The terms are decreasing by 4 each time ($5 - 9 = 4$, $-7 - (-3) = -4$) so the missing number is $5 - 4 =$ **1**.

b) The terms are being divided by 2 each time ($-18 \div -9 = 2$), so the missing terms are $-72 \div 2 =$ **–36** and $-9 \div 2 =$ **–4.5**.

c) The terms are being multiplied by 4 each time ($3.2 \div 0.8 = 4$), so the missing terms are $0.8 \div 4 =$ **0.2** and $204.8 \div 4 =$ **51.2**.

d) The terms are increasing by 8 each time ($-55 - (-63) = 8$), so the missing terms are $-55 + 8 =$ **–47**, $-47 + 8 =$ **–39** and $-39 + 8 =$ **–31**.

Page 179 Exercise 2

1 a) $8 - 7 = 1$ $\quad 10 - 8 = 2$
$13 - 10 = 3$ $\quad 17 - 13 = 4$
So the differences are **+1**, **+2**, **+3**, **+4**.

b) The rule is 'increase the amount added each time by 1':
6th term: $17 + 5 =$ **22**
7th term: $22 + 6 =$ **28**
8th term: $28 + 7 =$ **35**

2 a) (i) $7 - 5 = 2$ $\quad 11 - 7 = 4$
$17 - 11 = 6$ $\quad 25 - 17 = 8$
So the differences are **+2**, **+4**, **+6**, **+8**.

(ii) The rule is 'increase the amount added each time by 2':
6th term: $25 + 10 =$ **35**
7th term: $35 + 12 =$ **47**
8th term: $47 + 14 =$ **61**

b) (i) $18 - 20 = -2$ $\quad 15 - 18 = -3$
$11 - 15 = -4$ $\quad 6 - 11 = -5$
So the differences are **–2**, **–3**, **–4**, **–5**.

(ii) The rule is 'increase the amount subtracted each time by 1':
6th term: $6 - 6 =$ **0**
7th term: $0 - 7 =$ **–7**
8th term: $-7 - 8 =$ **–15**

c) (i) $4 - 3 = 1$ $\quad 6 - 4 = 2$
$9 - 6 = 3$ $\quad 13 - 9 = 4$
So the differences are **+1**, **+2**, **+3**, **+4**.

(ii) The rule is 'increase the amount added each time by 1':
6th term: $13 + 5 =$ **18**
7th term: $18 + 6 =$ **24**
8th term: $24 + 7 =$ **31**

d) (i) $2 - 1 = 1$ $\quad 0 - 2 = -2$
$3 - 0 = 3$ $\quad -1 - 3 = -4$
So the differences are **1**, **–2**, **3**, **–4**.

(ii) The rule is 'alternate between adding and subtracting and increase the amount each time by 1':
6th term: $-1 + 5 =$ **4**
7th term: $4 - 6 =$ **–2**
8th term: $-2 + 7 =$ **5**

3 Add together the two previous terms to get the next one:
6th term: 4th term + 5th term $= 3 + 5 =$ **8**
7th term: 5th term + 6th term $= 5 + 8 =$ **13**
8th term: 6th term + 7th term $= 8 + 13 =$ **21**

Page 180 Exercise 3

1 a) (i) E.g. **Add 2 matches** to the right hand side to form another equilateral triangle.

(ii)

(iii) There are 11 matches in the 5th pattern (from part (ii)) and 2 matches added each time, so the 6th pattern has $11 + 2 =$ **13 matches**.

b) (i) E.g. **Add 3 matches** to form another square to the right of the top right square **and 3 matches** to form another square below the bottom left square.

(ii)

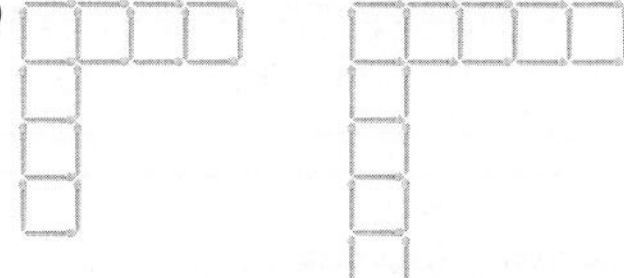

(iii) There are 28 matches in the 5th pattern (from part (ii)) and 3 + 3 matches added each time, so the 6th pattern has $28 + 3 + 3 =$ **34 matches**

c) (i) E.g. **Add 3 matches** to the left hand side to form a new square.

(ii)

(iii) There are 15 matches in the 5th pattern (from part (ii)) and 3 matches added each time, so the 6th pattern has $15 + 3 =$ **18 matches**.

2 a)

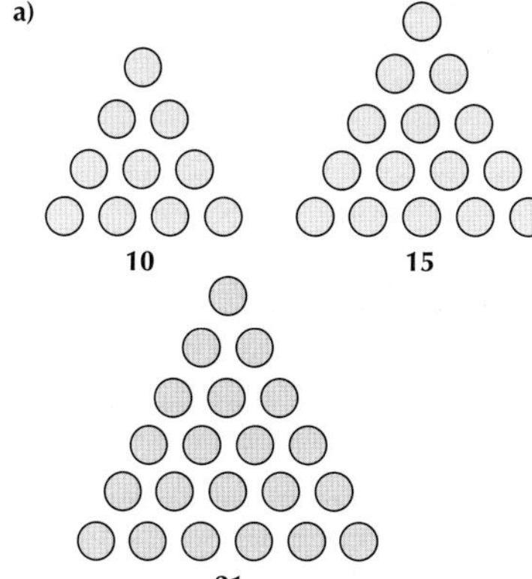

b) E.g. **Add a row of circles** to the bottom of the triangle, **with one more circle** in the new row than in the bottom row of the previous shape in the pattern.

c) The sequence of the number of dots is 1, 3, 6, 10, 15, 21...
The rule is 'increase the amount added each time by 1' and the difference between the 5th and 6th terms is $21 - 15 = 6$, so the 7th term is $21 + 7 =$ **28**.

3 a) (i)

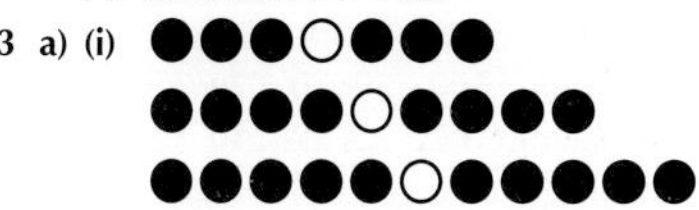

(ii) The number of white circles in each pattern is **always 1**.
The number of black circles in each pattern **increases by 2** each time.

(iii) There is always 1 white circle, so there will be **1 white circle** in the 7th pattern.

(iv) There are 10 black circles in the 6th pattern (from part (i)) and 2 added each time, so add on 4 lots of 2 to get the 10th pattern:
$10 + (4 \times 2) =$ **18 black circles**.

b) (i)

(ii) The number of white circles **increases by 1** each time.
The number of black circles **increases by 1** each time.

(iii) There are 6 white circles in the 6th pattern (from part (i)) and 1 added each time, so in the 7th pattern there are: $6 + 1 =$ **7 white circles**.

(iv) There are 7 black circles in the 6th pattern (from part (i)) and 1 added each time, so add on 4 lots of 1 to get the 10th pattern:
$7 + (4 \times 1) =$ **11 black circles**.

11.2 Position to Term Rules

Page 181 Exercise 1

1 a) Substitute $n = 1$ into $20 - 2n$ to find the first term: $20 - 2 \times 1 =$ **18**

b) Substitute $n = 2$ into $20 - 2n$ to find the second term: $20 - 2 \times 2 =$ **16**

c) Substitute $n = 3$ into $20 - 2n$ to find the third term: $20 - 2 \times 2 =$ **14**

d) Substitute $n = 4$ into $20 - 2n$ to find the fourth term: $20 - 2 \times 2 =$ **12**

2 a) 1st term ($n = 1$): $1 + 5 =$ **6**
2nd term ($n = 2$): $2 + 5 =$ **7**
3rd term ($n = 3$): $3 + 5 =$ **8**
4th term ($n = 4$): $4 + 5 =$ **9**

b) 1st term ($n = 1$): $3 \times 1 + 2 =$ **5**
2nd term ($n = 2$): $3 \times 2 + 2 =$ **8**
3rd term ($n = 3$): $3 \times 3 + 2 =$ **11**
4th term ($n = 4$): $3 \times 4 + 2 =$ **14**

Using the same method for c)-h):

c) **2, 12, 22, 32**

d) **11, 10, 9, 8**

e) **–10, –13, –16, –19**

f) **–1, –5, –9, –13**

g) **2, 8, 18, 32**

h) **5, 11, 21, 35**

3 a) 5th term: $2 \times 5 + 20 =$ **30**

b) 10th term: $2 \times 10 + 20 =$ **40**

c) 20th term: $2 \times 20 + 20 =$ **60**

d) 100th term: $2 \times 100 + 20 =$ **220**

4 a) 5th term: $100 - 3 \times 3 =$ **91**

b) 10th term: $100 - 3 \times 10 =$ **70**

c) 20th term: $100 - 3 \times 30 =$ **10**

d) 100th term: $100 - 3 \times 40 =$ **–20**

Page 182 Exercise 2

1 Solve the equation $2n + 6 = 20 \Rightarrow 2n = 14$
$\Rightarrow$ $\boldsymbol{n = 7}$

2 a) Solve the equation $17 - 2n = 3 \Rightarrow 2n = 14$
$\Rightarrow$ $\boldsymbol{n = 7}$

b) Solve the equation $17 - 2n = 9 \Rightarrow 2n = 8$
$\Rightarrow$ $\boldsymbol{n = 4}$

c) Solve the equation $17 - 2n = -7$
$\Rightarrow 2n = 24 \Rightarrow$ $\boldsymbol{n = 12}$

3 a) Solve the equation $n^2 + 1 = 5 \Rightarrow n^2 = 4$
$\Rightarrow$ $\boldsymbol{n = 2}$

b) Solve the equation $n^2 + 1 = 50 \Rightarrow n^2 = 49$
$\Rightarrow$ $\boldsymbol{n = 7}$

c) Solve the equation $n^2 + 1 = 82 \Rightarrow n^2 = 81$
$\Rightarrow$ $\boldsymbol{n = 9}$
You can discount the negative solution to $n^2 = a$ here as n can only be positive.

4 Solve the equation $4n - 10 = 75 \Rightarrow 4n = 85$
$\Rightarrow n = 21.25$
Since $4n - 10$ is increasing, the last term with a value less than 75 will be the last whole number before 21.25, so $\boldsymbol{n = 21}$.

5 Solve the equation $6n + 2 = 40 \Rightarrow 6n = 38$
$\Rightarrow n = 6.333...$
Since $6n + 2$ is increasing, the first term with a value greater than 40 will be the next whole number after 6.333, so $\boldsymbol{n = 7}$.

6 a) (i) Substitute $n = 6$ into $2n + 1$:
$2 \times 6 + 1 =$ **13 matches**

(ii) Solve the equation $2n + 1 = 100$
$\Rightarrow 2n = 99 \Rightarrow n = 49.5$
You need to find the last pattern that uses fewer than 100 matches, so $\boldsymbol{n = 49}$.

b) (i) Substitute $n = 6$ into $4n - 1$:
$4 \times 6 - 1 =$ **23 matches**

(ii) Solve the equation $4n - 1 = 100$
$\Rightarrow 4n = 101 \Rightarrow n = 25.25$
You need to find the last pattern that uses fewer than 100 matches, so $\boldsymbol{n = 25}$.

Page 183 Exercise 3

1 Solve the equation $2n + 1 = 54 \Rightarrow 2n = 53$
$\Rightarrow n = 26.5$
n is not a whole number so **54 is not a term in the sequence**.

2 Solve the equation $3n - 1 = 80 \Rightarrow 3n = 81$
$\Rightarrow n = 27$
n is a whole number so **80 is a term in the sequence**.

3 Solve the equation $21 - 2n = -1 \Rightarrow 2n = 22$
$\Rightarrow n = 11$
n is a whole number so **–1 is in the sequence and has position $\boldsymbol{n = 11}$**.

4 a) Solve the equation $17 + 3n = 52$
$\Rightarrow 3n = 35 \Rightarrow n = 11.66...$
n is not a whole number so **52 is not a term in the sequence**.

b) Solve the equation $17 + 3n = 98$
$\Rightarrow 3n = 81 \Rightarrow n = 27$
n is a whole number so **98 is a term in the sequence**.

c) Solve the equation $17 + 3n = 248$
$\Rightarrow 3n = 231 \Rightarrow n = 77$
n is a whole number so **248 is a term in the sequence**.

d) Solve the equation $17 + 3n = 996$
$\Rightarrow 3n = 979 \Rightarrow n = 326.33...$
n is not a whole number so **996 is not a term in the sequence**.

5 a) Solve the equation $4n - 9 = 43 \Rightarrow 4n = 52$
$\Rightarrow n = 13$
n is a whole number so **52 is a term in the sequence with position $\boldsymbol{n = 13}$**.

b) Solve the equation $4n - 9 = 71 \Rightarrow 4n = 80$
$\Rightarrow n = 20$
n is a whole number so **71 is a term in the sequence with position $\boldsymbol{n = 20}$**.

c) Solve the equation $4n - 9 = 138$
$\Rightarrow 4n = 147 \Rightarrow n = 36.75$
n is not a whole number so **138 is not a term in the sequence**.

d) Solve the equation $4n - 9 = 879$
$\Rightarrow 4n = 888 \Rightarrow n = 222$
n is a whole number so **879 is a term in the sequence with position $\boldsymbol{n = 222}$**.

11.3 Finding a Position to Term Rule

Page 185 Exercise 1

1 a) $13 - 9 = 4$ $17 - 13 = 4$ $21 - 17 = 4$
The difference between each term and the next is **+4**.

b) Common difference is +4, so compare the sequence with $4n$:
$4n$: 4 8 12 16
↓+5 ↓+5 ↓+5 ↓+5
Term: 9 13 17 21
You need to add 5, so the nth term is $\boldsymbol{4n + 5}$.
Check your rule using e.g. $n = 2$:
$(4 \times 2) + 5 = 8 + 5 =$ **13** ✔

2 a) $13 - 7 = 6$ $19 - 13 = 6$ $25 - 19 = 6$
The difference between each term and the next is +6, so compare the sequence with $6n$:
$6n$: 6 12 18 24
↓+1 ↓+1 ↓+1 ↓+1
Term: 7 13 19 25
You need to add 1, so the nth term is $\boldsymbol{6n + 1}$.

b) $16 - 6 = 10$ $26 - 16 = 10$
$36 - 26 = 10$
The difference between each term and the next is +10, so compare the sequence with $10n$:
$10n$: 10 20 30 40
↓–4 ↓–4 ↓–4 ↓–4
Term: 6 16 26 36
You need to subtract 4, so the nth term is $\boldsymbol{10n - 4}$.

Using the same method for c)-f):

c) $\boldsymbol{40n + 1}$ d) $\boldsymbol{2n - 3}$

e) $\boldsymbol{4n - 13}$ f) $\boldsymbol{19n - 64}$

3 a) $8 - 10 = -2$ $6 - 8 = -2$ $4 - 6 = -2$
The difference between each term and the next is –2, so compare the sequence with $-2n$:
$-2n$: –2 –4 –6 –8
↓+12 ↓+12 ↓+12 ↓+12
Term: 10 8 6 4
You need to add 12, so the nth term is $\boldsymbol{-2n + 12}$.

b) $37 - 40 = -3$ $34 - 37 = -3$
$31 - 34 = -3$
The difference between each term and the next is –3, so compare the sequence with $-3n$:
$-3n$: –3 –6 –9 –12
↓+43 ↓+43 ↓+43 ↓+43
Term: 40 37 34 31
You need to add 43, so the nth term is $\boldsymbol{-3n + 43}$.

Using the same method for c)-f):

c) $\boldsymbol{-9n + 87}$

d) $\boldsymbol{-5n + 9}$

e) $\boldsymbol{-15n + 5}$

f) $\boldsymbol{-12n - 27}$

4 a) The sequence of the number of matchsticks is 4, 10, 16...
$10 - 4 = 6$ $16 - 10 = 6$
The difference between each term and the next is +6, so compare the sequence with $6n$:
$6n$: 6 12 18
↓–2 ↓–2 ↓–2
Term: 4 10 16
You need to subtract 2, so the nth term is $\boldsymbol{6n - 2}$.

b) The sequence of the number of matchsticks is 7, 12, 17...
$12 - 7 = 5$ $17 - 12 = 5$
The difference between each term and the next is +5, so compare the sequence with $5n$:
$5n$: 5 10 15
↓+2 ↓+2 ↓+2
Term: 7 12 17
You need to add 2, so the nth term is $\boldsymbol{5n + 2}$.

5 a) $11 - 8 = 3$ $14 - 11 = 3$
$17 - 14 = 3$
The difference between each term and the next is +3, so compare the sequence with $3n$:

$3n$:	3	6	9	12
	$\downarrow$+5	$\downarrow$+5	$\downarrow$+5	$\downarrow$+5
Term:	8	11	14	17

You need to add 5, so the nth term is $\mathbf{3n + 5}$.

b) Each term in the sequence is 1 greater than the corresponding term in the sequence from part a), so these terms can be found using the formula $(3n + 5) + 1 = \mathbf{3n + 6}$.

Page 186 Review Exercise

1 a) (i) The rule is '**add 3 to the previous term**'
(ii) 5th term: $13 + 3 = \mathbf{16}$
6th term: $16 + 3 = \mathbf{19}$
7th term: $19 + 3 = \mathbf{22}$

b) (i) The rule is '**divide the previous term by 2**'
(ii) 5th term: $24 \div 2 = \mathbf{12}$
6th term: $12 \div 2 = \mathbf{6}$
7th term: $6 \div 2 = \mathbf{3}$

c) (i) The rule is '**subtract 4 from the previous term**'
(ii) 5th term: $-12 - 4 = \mathbf{-16}$
6th term: $-16 - 4 = \mathbf{-20}$
7th term: $-20 - 4 = \mathbf{-24}$

d) (i) The rule is '**add 2 to the previous term**'
(ii) 5th term: $2 + 2 = \mathbf{4}$
6th term: $4 + 2 = \mathbf{6}$
7th term: $6 + 2 = \mathbf{8}$

e) (i) The rule is '**subtract 3 from the previous term**'
(ii) 5th term: $2 - 3 = \mathbf{-1}$
6th term: $-1 - 3 = \mathbf{-4}$
7th term: $-4 - 3 = \mathbf{-7}$

f) (i) The rule is '**multiply the previous term by –3**'
(ii) 5th term: $-54 \times -3 = \mathbf{162}$
6th term: $162 \times -3 = \mathbf{-486}$
7th term: $-486 \times -3 = \mathbf{1458}$

2 a) $9 - 7 = 2$ $13 - 9 = 4$
$19 - 13 = 6$ $27 - 19 = 8$
The differences between terms are **+2, +4, +6, +8**

b) The rule is 'increase the amount added each time by 2':
6th term: $27 + 10 = \mathbf{37}$
7th term: $37 + 12 = \mathbf{49}$
8th term: $49 + 14 = \mathbf{63}$

3 a)

b) Add two more circles on the right of the previous pattern.

c) There are 12 circles in the 6th pattern (from part a)), so in the 7th pattern there will be $12 + 2 = 14$ circles and in the 8th pattern there will be $14 + 2 = $ **16 circles**.

4 1st term ($n = 1$): $-3 - 2 \times 1 = \mathbf{-5}$
2nd term ($n = 2$): $-3 - 2 \times 2 = \mathbf{-7}$
3rd term ($n = 3$): $-3 - 2 \times 3 = \mathbf{-9}$
4th term ($n = 4$): $-3 - 2 \times 4 = \mathbf{-11}$

5 a) (i) 5th term: $4 \times 5 + 12 = \mathbf{32}$
(ii) 10th term: $4 \times 10 + 12 = \mathbf{52}$
(iii) 100th term: $4 \times 100 + 12 = \mathbf{412}$

b) (i) 5th term: $30 - 3 \times 5 = \mathbf{15}$
(ii) 10th term: $30 - 3 \times 10 = \mathbf{0}$
(iii) 100th term: $30 - 3 \times 100 = \mathbf{-270}$

Using the method for c)-d):
c) (i) 492 **(ii) 992** **(iii) 9992**
d) (i) 20 **(ii) 90** **(iii) 9900**

6 a) Solve the equation $50 - 6n = 2 \Rightarrow 6n = 48$
$\Rightarrow \mathbf{n = 8}$.

b) Solve the equation $50 - 6n = 8 \Rightarrow 6n = 42$
$\Rightarrow \mathbf{n = 7}$.

c) Solve the equation $50 - 6n = 14$
$\Rightarrow 6n = 36 \Rightarrow \mathbf{n = 6}$.

d) Solve the equation $50 - 6n = 26$
$\Rightarrow 6n = 24 \Rightarrow \mathbf{n = 4}$.

7 a) Solve the equation $7n - 3 = 100$
$\Rightarrow 7n = 103 \Rightarrow n = 14.714...$
You want the last whole number smaller than 14.714...
so the last term with value smaller than 100 is the **14th term**.

b) Solve the equation $7n - 3 = 205$
$\Rightarrow 7n = 208 \Rightarrow n = 29.714...$
You want the next whole number greater than 29.714...
so the first term with value greater than 205 is the **30th term**.

8 a) $18 - 12 = 6$ $24 - 18 = 6$
$30 - 24 = 6$
The difference between each term and the next is +6, so compare the sequence with $6n$:

$6n$:	6	12	18	24
	$\downarrow$+6	$\downarrow$+6	$\downarrow$+6	$\downarrow$+6
Term:	12	18	24	30

You need to add 6, so the nth term is $\mathbf{6n + 6}$.

b) Solve the equation $6n + 6 = 86 \Rightarrow 6n = 80$
$\Rightarrow n = 13.33...$
n is not a whole number, so **86 is not a term in the sequence.**

9 The sequence of the number of dots is 5, 7, 9...
$7 - 5 = 2$ $9 - 7 = 2$
The difference between each term and the next is +2, so compare the sequence with $2n$:

$2n$:	2	4	6
	$\downarrow$+3	$\downarrow$+3	$\downarrow$+3
Term:	5	7	9

You need to add 3, so the nth term is $\mathbf{2n + 3}$.

Page 187 Exam-Style Questions

1 $5 - 3 = 2$ $9 - 5 = 4$ $15 - 9 = 6$
The rule is 'increase the amount added each time by 2'. *[1 mark]*
so the 5th term is $15 + 8 = \mathbf{23}$ *[1 mark]*

2 a)

Design 4 *[1 mark]*

b) The number of rods forms the sequence 4, 7, 10, 13...
To get the next term of the sequence, you add 3 to the previous term *[1 mark]*.
So the 5th term is 16, 6th term is 19, 7th term is 22, and the **8th term is 25**. *[1 mark]*

c) The number of rods is one less than the number of balls, so the expression for the number of rods is:
$(3n + 2) - 1 = 3n + 1$ *[1 mark]*

3 a) $6 - 2 = 4$ $10 - 6 = 4$ $14 - 10 = 4$
The rule is 'add 4 to the previous term', so the next term is $14 + 4 = \mathbf{18}$ *[1 mark]*

b) Substitute $n = 210$ into $4n - 2$:
$4 \times 210 - 2 = \mathbf{838}$
[2 marks available — 1 mark for the expression $4 \times 210 - 2$, 1 mark for the correct answer]

c) $4n - 2 = 74 \Rightarrow 4n = 76 \Rightarrow n = 19$.
Yes, Jane is correct, because n is a whole number.
[2 marks available — 1 mark for the expression $4n - 2 = 74$, 1 mark for correct answer]

4 $-2 - (-11) = 9$ $7 - (-2) = 9$ $16 - 7 = 9$
Common difference is +9, so compare the sequence with $9n$: *[1 mark]*

$9n$:	9	18	27	36
	$\downarrow$–20	$\downarrow$–20	$\downarrow$–20	$\downarrow$–20
Term:	–11	–2	7	16

You need to subtract 20, so the nth term is $\mathbf{9n - 20}$. *[1 mark]*

Section 12 — Graphs and Equations

12.1 Coordinates

Page 189 Exercise 1

1

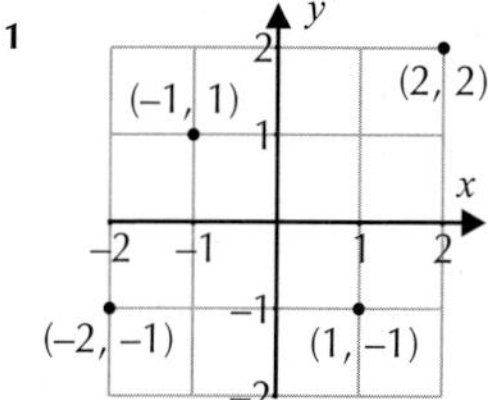

a) (2, 2) lies in quadrant **I**.
b) (1, –1) lies in quadrant **IV**.
c) (–2, –1) lies in quadrant **III**.
d) (–1, 1) lies in quadrant **II**.

2 a) (i) (0, 0) **(ii) (2, 2)**
(iii) (1, 3) **(iv) (0, 4)**
(v) (4, 4)
b) X-COORDINATE COMES FIRST

3 a) (i) SQUARE **(ii) CIRCLE**
(iii) CUBOID
b) (i) (2, 1) (–4, 1) (4, –4) (–5, 3)
(ii) (2, –4) (5, –2) (5, 3) (–5, 3) (–2, –4) (–5, 3)
(iii) (4, –4) (–2, –4) (–4, 1) (–4, 5) (–3, –2) (3, 3) (4, 1) (–5, 3)

Page 190 Exercise 2

1 a)

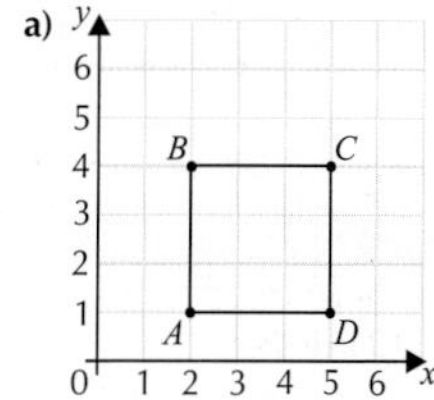

b) 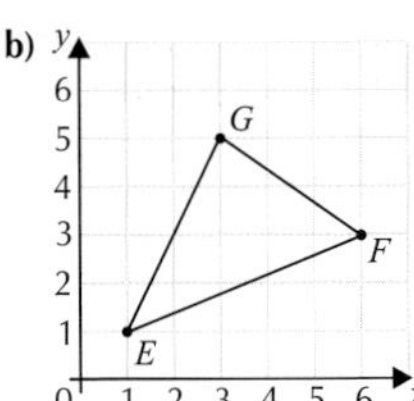

c) 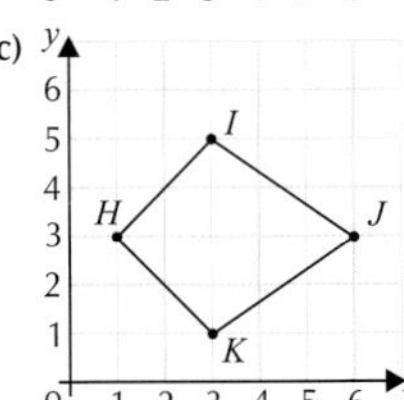

d) 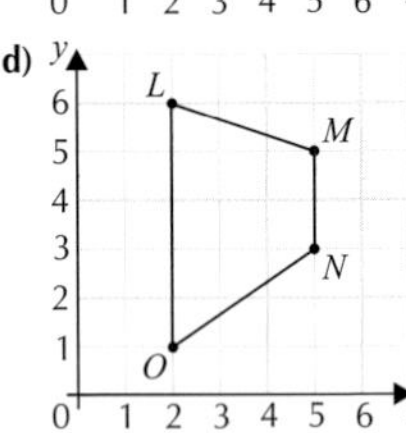

When joining points to make shapes, connect A to B, B to C, etc.

2

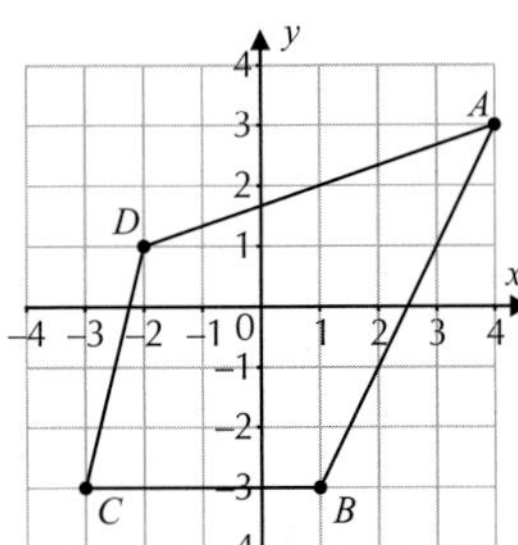

3

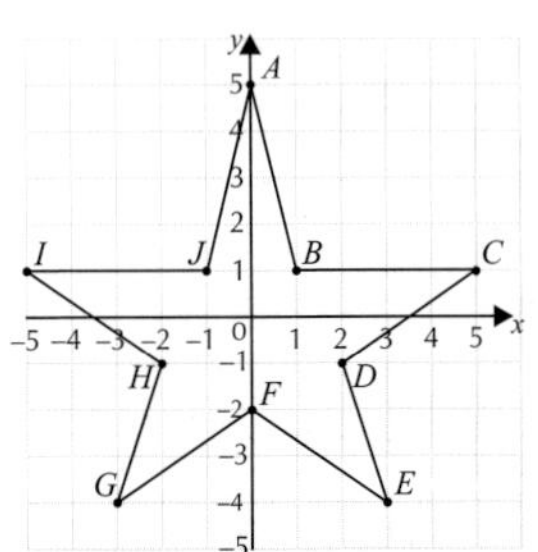

Page 191 Exercise 3

1 a) X: **(–5, 1)**, Y: **(3, 5)**

b) M: $\left(\frac{-5+3}{2}, \frac{1+5}{2}\right) = \left(\frac{-2}{2}, \frac{6}{2}\right) = $ **(–1, 3)**

c)

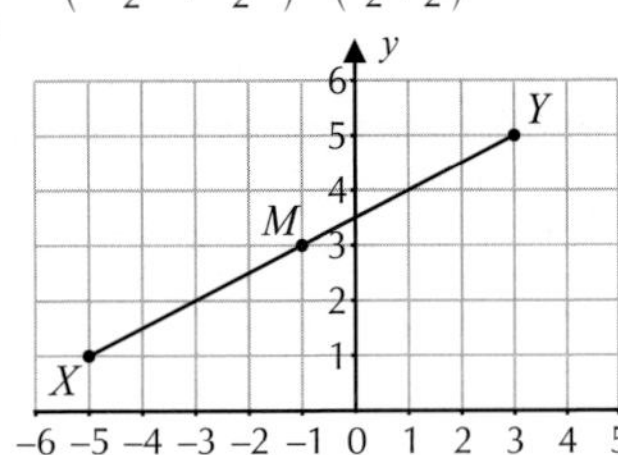

Check to see if the midpoint you have calculated looks about right. It should be halfway along the line segment from X to Y.

2 a) M: $\left(\frac{1+3}{2}, \frac{0+5}{2}\right) = \left(\frac{4}{2}, \frac{5}{2}\right) = $ **(2, 2.5)**

b) **(i), (ii)**

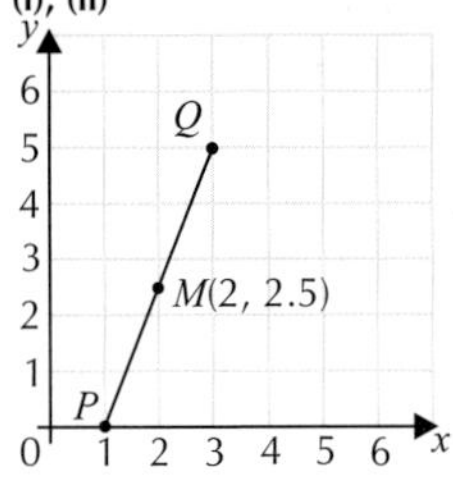

3 a) $\left(\frac{1+3}{2}, \frac{1+5}{2}\right) = \left(\frac{4}{2}, \frac{6}{2}\right) = $ **(2, 3)**

b) $\left(\frac{0+6}{2}, \frac{1+3}{2}\right) = \left(\frac{6}{2}, \frac{4}{2}\right) = $ **(3, 2)**

c) $\left(\frac{0+(-5)}{2}, \frac{-4+1}{2}\right) = \left(\frac{-5}{2}, \frac{-3}{2}\right)$

= **(–2.5, –1.5)**

d) $\left(\frac{-2+1}{2}, \frac{0+(-8)}{2}\right) = \left(\frac{-1}{2}, \frac{-8}{2}\right) = $ **(–0.5, –4)**

4 a) A is (–5, 5) and F is (5, 5),
so midpoint of AF
$= \left(\frac{-5+5}{2}, \frac{5+5}{2}\right) = \left(\frac{0}{2}, \frac{10}{2}\right) = $ **(0, 5)**

b) A is (–5, 5) and C is (–2, 3),
so midpoint of AC
$= \left(\frac{-5+-2}{2}, \frac{5+3}{2}\right) = \left(\frac{-7}{2}, \frac{8}{2}\right) = $ **(– 3.5, 4)**

Using the same method for c)-f):

c) **(3.5, 3)** d) **(–0.5, –2.5)**

e) **(0.5, 1)** f) **(0.5, 0.5)**

12.2 Horizontal and Vertical Graphs

Page 193 Exercise 1

1 Every point on A has x-coordinate = –5, so it has equation $\boldsymbol{x = -5}$.
Every point on B has x-coordinate = –2, so it has equation $\boldsymbol{x = -2}$.
Every point on C has y-coordinate = 3, so it has equation $\boldsymbol{y = 3}$.
Every point on D has x-coordinate = 5, so it has equation $\boldsymbol{x = 5}$.
Every point on E has y-coordinate = –2, so it has equation $\boldsymbol{y = -2}$.

2

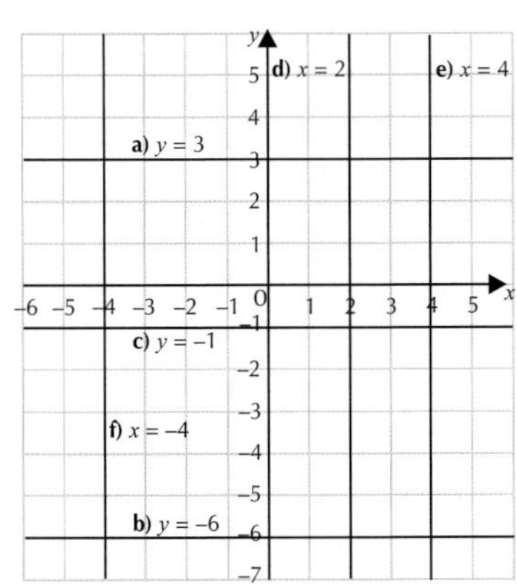

3 a) Every point on the x-axis has y-coordinate = **0**.

b) So the x-axis has equation $\boldsymbol{y = 0}$.

Don't get mixed up — y = 0 on the x-axis, and x = 0 on the y-axis.

4 a)

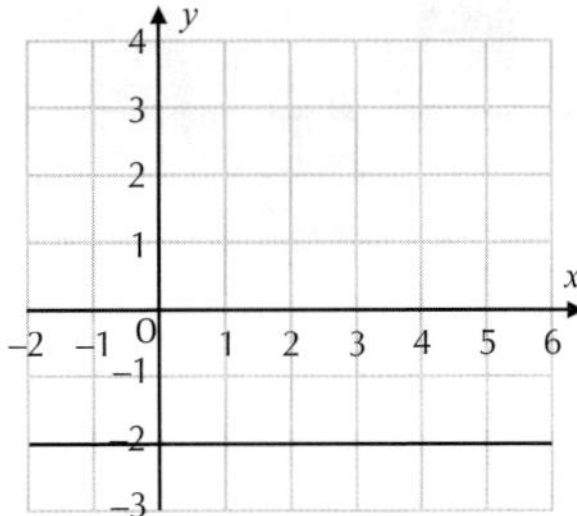

b) $\boldsymbol{y = -2}$

5 a)

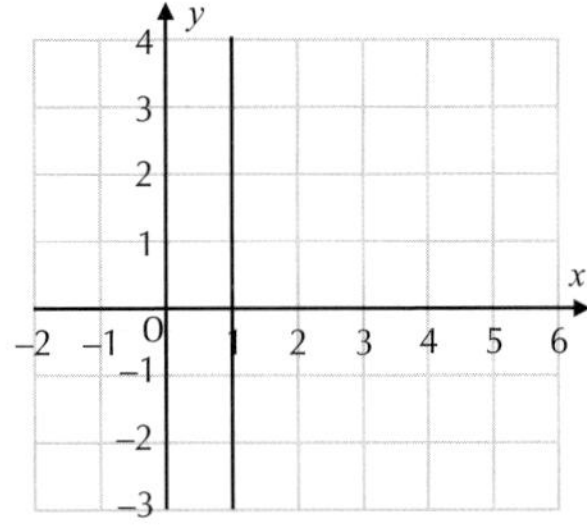

b) $\boldsymbol{x = 1}$

6 'Parallel to the x-axis' means the line is horizontal.
The point (4, 8) has y-coordinate = 8, so the line has equation $\boldsymbol{y = 8}$.

7 'Parallel to the y-axis' means the line is vertical.
The point (–2, –6) has x-coordinate = –2, so the line has equation $\boldsymbol{x = -2}$.

8 a)

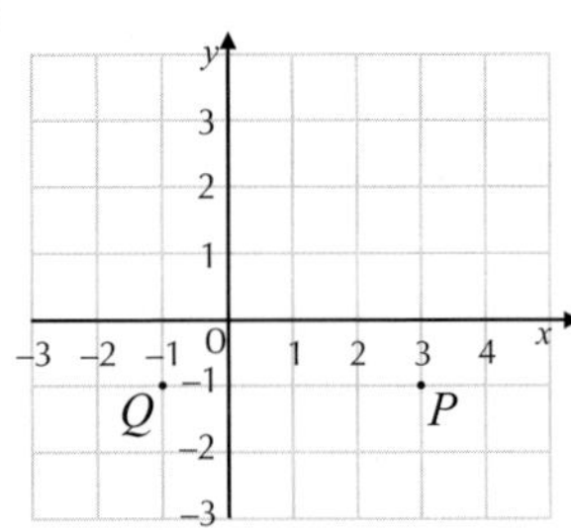

b) The line through Q and P is horizontal, so it has equation $\boldsymbol{y = -1}$.

12.3 Other Straight-Line Graphs

Page 195 Exercise 1

1 a) When x = 2, y = 2 + 2 = 4.
When x = 3, y = 3 + 2 = 5.
When x = 4, y = 4 + 2 = 6.
When x = 5, y = 5 + 2 = 7.

x	0	1	2	3	4	5
y	2	3	**4**	**5**	**6**	**7**
Coords	(0, 2)	**(1, 3)**	**(2, 4)**	**(3, 5)**	**(4, 6)**	**(5, 7)**

b), c)

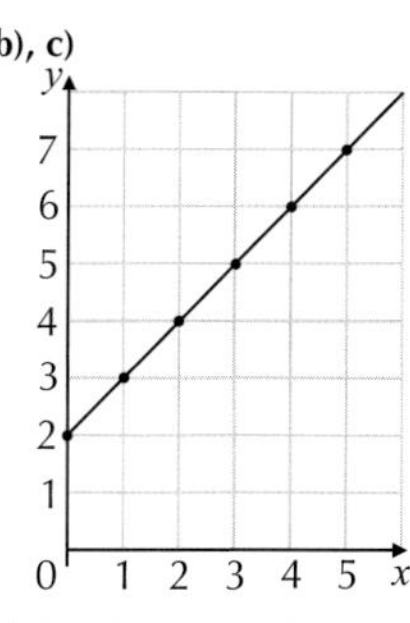

2 a) $2y - 2x = -8 \Rightarrow 2y = 2x - 8 \Rightarrow \mathbf{y = x - 4}$.

b) When $x = 1$, $y = 1 - 4 = -3$.
When $x = 2$, $y = 2 - 4 = -2$.
When $x = 3$, $y = 3 - 4 = -1$.
When $x = 4$, $y = 4 - 4 = 0$.
When $x = 5$, $y = 5 - 4 = 1$.

x	0	1	2	3	4	5
y	–4	**–3**	**–2**	**–1**	**0**	**1**
Coords	**(0, –4)**	**(1, –3)**	**(2, –2)**	**(3, –1)**	**(4, 0)**	**(5, 1)**

c), d)

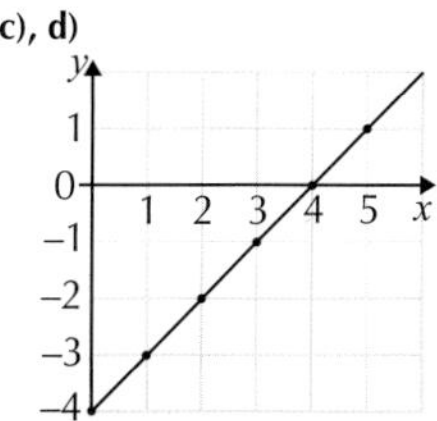

3 a) When $x = 0$, $y = 0 + 7 = 7$.
When $y = 0$, $0 = x + 7 \Rightarrow x = -7$.
You can check you have calculated the x- and y-intercepts correctly by putting the x- and y-values back into the equation.
Plot the points (0, 7) and (–7, 0) and draw a straight line between them.

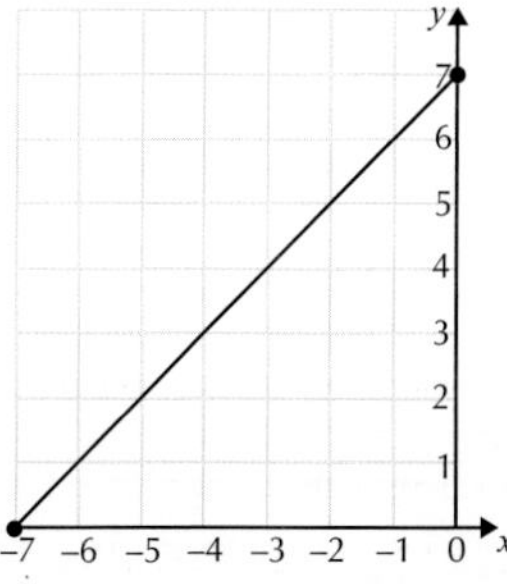

b) When $x = 0$, $y = 3 \times 0 - 6 = -6$.
When $y = 0$, $0 = 3x - 6 \Rightarrow x = 6 \div 3 = 2$.
Plot the points (0, –6) and (2, 0) and draw a straight line passing through them. Extend the line to cover the range of x from 0 to 4.

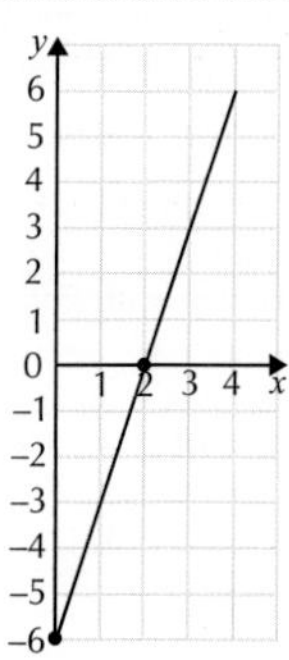

c) When $x = 0$, $y + 2 \times 0 = 8$.
When $y = 0$, $0 + 2x = 8 \Rightarrow x = 8 \div 2 = 4$.
Plot the points (0, 8) and (4, 0) and draw a straight line passing through them. Extend the line to cover the range of x from 0 to 5.

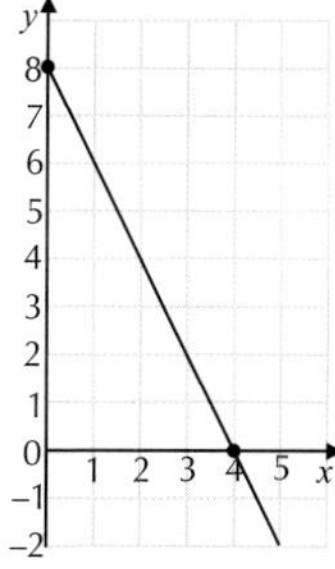

d) When $x = 0$, $y + 5 \times 0 = 7.5$.
When $y = 0$, $0 + 5x = 7.5$
$\Rightarrow x = 7.5 \div 5 = 1.5$.
Plot the points (0, 7.5) and (1.5, 0) and draw a straight line passing through them. Extend the line to cover the range of x from 0 to 2.

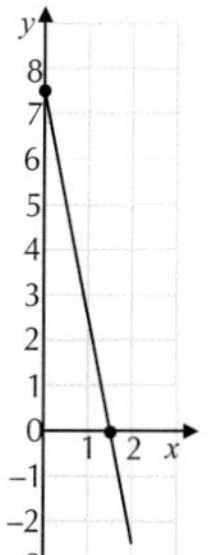

Page 196 Exercise 2

1 a) **(2, 0)**

b) Read off the x-coordinate: $\mathbf{x = 2}$

2 a) The graph of $y = 0.5x - 2$ crosses the x-axis at (4, 0). So the solution to the equation $0.5x - 2 = 0$ is $\mathbf{x = 4}$.

b) The graph of $y = -2x + 1$ crosses the x-axis at (0.5, 0). So the solution to the equation $-2x + 1 = 0$ is $\mathbf{x = 0.5}$.

Page 197 Exercise 3

1 a) Draw the line $y = 1$ and find the intersection point with the graph of $y = -2x - 3$.

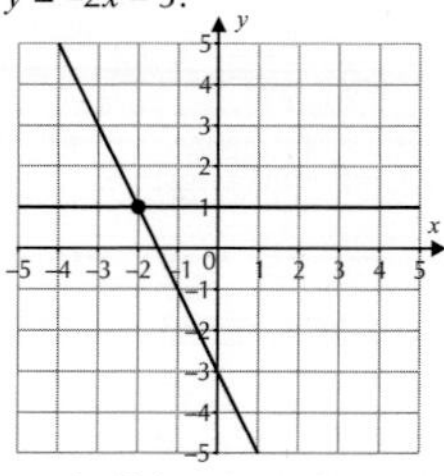

Read off the x-coordinate: $\mathbf{x = -2}$.
Check your answer by putting the x-value back into the equation.

b) Draw the line $y = -4$ and find the intersection point with the graph of $y = x - 2$.

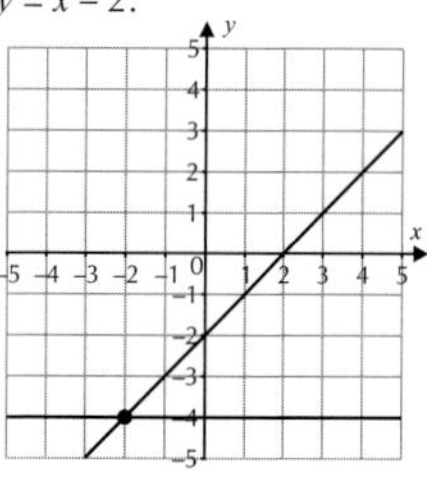

Read off the x-coordinate: $\mathbf{x = -2}$.

c) Draw the line $y = -5$ and find the intersection point with the graph of $y = -2x - 3$.

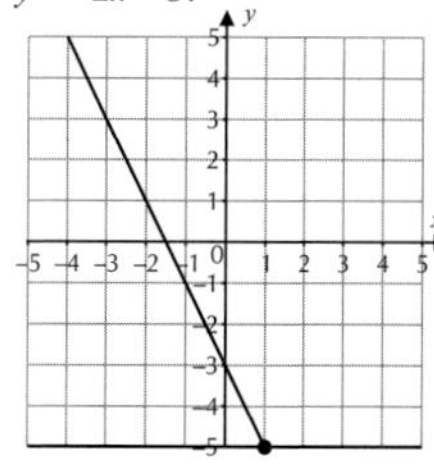

Read off the x-coordinate: $\mathbf{x = 1}$.

d) Draw the line $y = 2\frac{1}{2}$ and find the intersection point with the graph of $y = -\frac{1}{2}x + 4$.

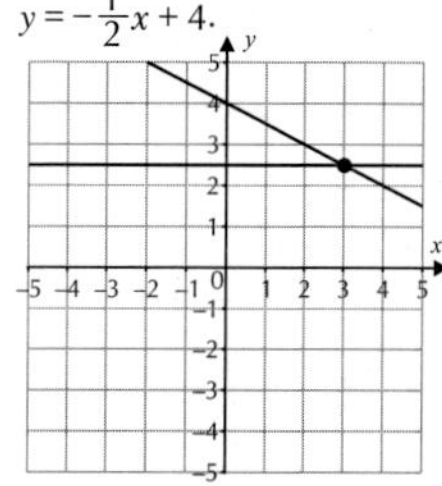

Read off the x-coordinate: $\mathbf{x = 3}$.

2 a) $-2x + 2 = 1 \Rightarrow -2x + 2 - 5 = 1 - 5$
$\Rightarrow \mathbf{-2x - 3 = -4}$

b) Draw the line $y = -4$ and find the intersection point with the graph of $y = -2x - 3$.

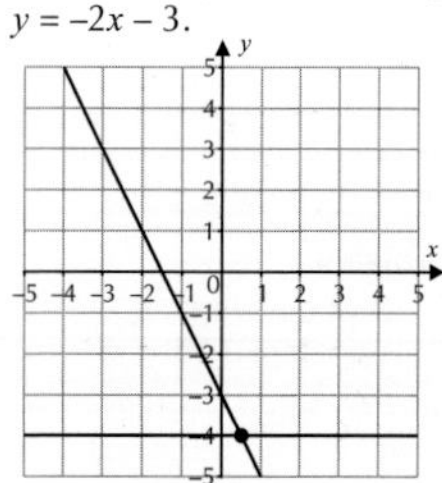

Read off the x-coordinate: $\mathbf{x = 0.5}$.

3 a) $x - 1 = 2 \Rightarrow x - 1 - 1 = 2 - 1 \Rightarrow x - 2 = 1$.
The step above transforms the equation so its left-hand side matches the right-hand side of the one the graph equations, y = x – 2.
Draw the line $y = 1$ and find the intersection point with the graph of $y = x - 2$.

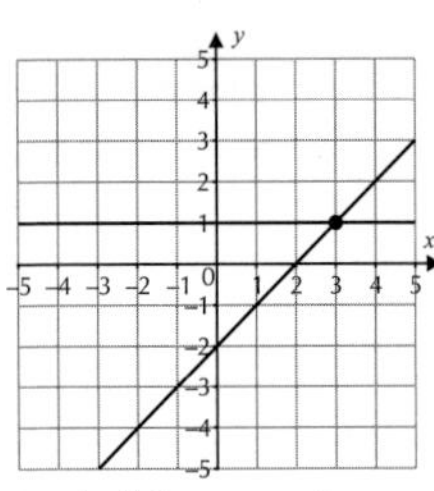

Read off the x-coordinate: $\boldsymbol{x = 3}$.

b) $-2x - 5 = 0 \Rightarrow -2x - 5 + 2 = 0 + 2$
$\Rightarrow -2x - 3 = 2$.

The step above transforms the equation so its left-hand side matches the right-hand side of the graph equation $y = -2x - 3$.

Draw the line $y = 2$ and find the intersection point with the graph of $y = -2x - 3$.

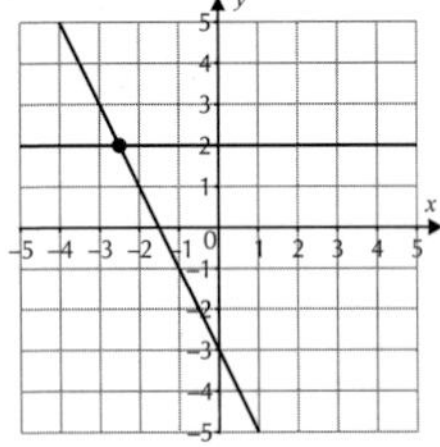

Read off the x-coordinate: $\boldsymbol{x = -2.5}$.

c) $-\frac{1}{2}x - 1 = -2 \Rightarrow -\frac{1}{2}x - 1 + 5 = -2 + 5$
$\Rightarrow -\frac{1}{2}x + 4 = 3$.

The step above transforms the equation so its left-hand side matches the right-hand side of the graph equation $y = -\frac{1}{2}x + 4$.

Draw the line $y = 3$ and find the intersection point with the graph of $y = -\frac{1}{2}x + 4$.

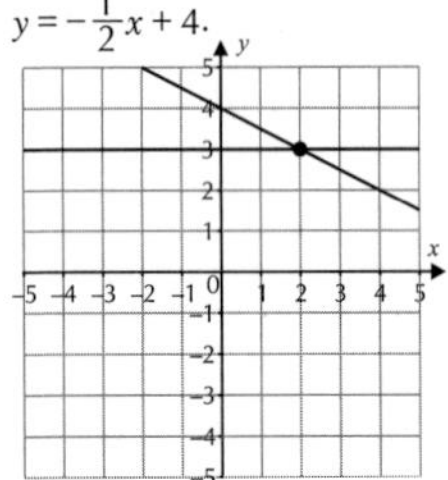

Read off the x-coordinate: $\boldsymbol{x = 2}$.

Page 198 Exercise 4

1 The lines intersect at the point (2, 5).
So the solution is $\boldsymbol{x = 2}$ and $\boldsymbol{y = 5}$.
Check your answer by putting the x- and y-values into both equations.

2 **a), b)** Draw the graphs of $y = 5 - x$ and $y = x - 3$ using the methods on p.194.

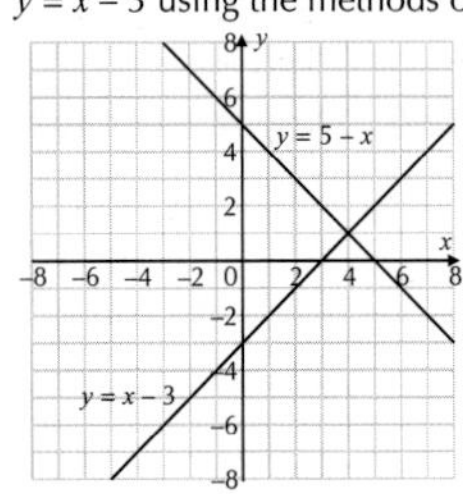

c) The lines intersect at the point (4, 1).
So the solution is $\boldsymbol{x = 4}$ and $\boldsymbol{y = 1}$.

3 **a)** Draw the graphs of $y = 2 - 2x$ and $y = x + 5$ using the methods on p.194.

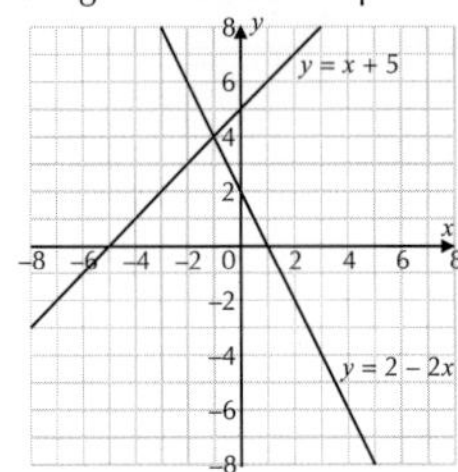

b) At the point where the lines cross, the values of y are the same, and hence the values of the right-hand side of the two equations are also the same.
So the solution to $2 - 2x = x + 5$ is at the point (–1, 4): $\boldsymbol{x = -1}$ and $\boldsymbol{y = 4}$.

4 **a)** Draw the graphs of $y = x + 3$ and $y = x - 2$ using the methods on p.194.

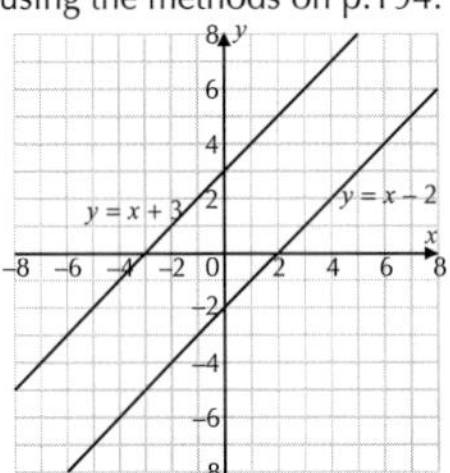

b) E.g. The lines are **parallel** and so **do not intersect**. This means there are **no points** where **both** the **x-** and the **y-values** are the **same** for **both lines**, and so there are **no solutions** to the corresponding simultaneous equations.

12.4 Gradients

Page 200 Exercise 1

1 **a)** **4** **b)** **3**

c) The line slopes upwards from left to right, so the gradient is **positive.**

d) gradient $= \frac{\text{change in } y}{\text{change in } x} = \boldsymbol{\frac{4}{3}}$

2 **a)** The line slopes upwards from left to right, so the gradient is positive.
gradient $= \frac{\text{change in } y}{\text{change in } x} = \frac{3}{3} = \boldsymbol{1}$

b) The line slopes upwards from left to right, so the gradient is positive.
gradient $= \frac{\text{change in } y}{\text{change in } x} = \frac{4}{1} = \boldsymbol{4}$

c) The line slopes downwards from left to right, so the gradient is negative.
gradient $= \frac{\text{change in } y}{\text{change in } x} = -\frac{2}{2} = \boldsymbol{-1}$

d) The line slopes downwards from left to right, so the gradient is negative.
gradient $= \frac{\text{change in } y}{\text{change in } x} = \boldsymbol{-\frac{5}{3}}$

3 **a)** gradient $= \frac{\text{change in } y}{\text{change in } x} = \frac{3-5}{6-1} = \frac{-2}{5} = \boldsymbol{-\frac{2}{5}}$

b) gradient $= \frac{\text{change in } y}{\text{change in } x} = \frac{1-6}{6-(-4)} = \frac{-5}{10}$
$= \boldsymbol{-\frac{1}{2}}$

c) gradient $= \frac{\text{change in } y}{\text{change in } x} = \frac{6-0}{4-(-5)} = \frac{6}{9}$
$= \boldsymbol{\frac{2}{3}}$

As a quick check of your answer, look at the direction of the line to see if the gradient should be positive or negative.

4 **a) (i)** $\boldsymbol{G}$**: (2, –5),** $\boldsymbol{H}$**: (6, 6)**
(ii) $\frac{6-(-5)}{6-2} = \boldsymbol{\frac{11}{4}}$

b) (i) $\boldsymbol{I}$**: (–10, 5),** $\boldsymbol{J}$**: (30, –25)**
(ii) $\frac{-25-5}{30-(-10)} = \frac{-30}{40} = \boldsymbol{-\frac{3}{4}}$

c) (i) Line 1: $\boldsymbol{K}$**: (–8, –25),** $\boldsymbol{L}$**: (8, 35)**
Line 2: $\boldsymbol{M}$**: (–4, 30),** $\boldsymbol{N}$**: (6, –15)**
(ii) Line 1: $\frac{35-(-25)}{8-(-8)} = \frac{60}{16} = \boldsymbol{\frac{15}{4}}$
Line 2: $\frac{-15-30}{6-(-4)} = \frac{-45}{10} = \boldsymbol{-\frac{9}{2}}$

5 **a)** gradient $= \frac{\text{change in } y}{\text{change in } x} \Rightarrow 1 = \frac{a-5}{7-3} = \frac{a-5}{4}$
$\Rightarrow 4 = a - 5$
$\Rightarrow \boldsymbol{a = 9}$

b) gradient $= \frac{\text{change in } y}{\text{change in } x} \Rightarrow 2 = \frac{5-1}{b-1} = \frac{4}{b-1}$
$\Rightarrow b - 1 = \frac{4}{2}$
$\Rightarrow \boldsymbol{b = 3}$

c) gradient $= \frac{\text{change in } y}{\text{change in } x} \Rightarrow \frac{1}{2} = \frac{c-0}{8-0} = \frac{c}{8}$
$\Rightarrow c = \frac{8}{2} \Rightarrow \boldsymbol{c = 4}$

12.5 Equations of Straight-Line Graphs

Page 201 Exercise 1

1 $m = 2$ and $c = 3$, so the equation is $\boldsymbol{y = 2x + 3}$.

2 For a line of the form $y = mx + c$, the gradient is m and the y-intercept has coordinates $(0, c)$.
a) gradient = **3**, y-intercept = **(0, 2)**
b) gradient = **2**, y-intercept = **(0, –4)**
c) gradient = **5**, y-intercept = **(0, –11)**
d) gradient = **–3**, y-intercept = **(0, 7)**
e) gradient = **4**, y-intercept = **(0, 0)**
f) gradient = $\boldsymbol{\frac{1}{2}}$, y-intercept = **(0, –1)**
g) gradient = **1**, y-intercept = **(0, –6)**
h) gradient = **–1**, y-intercept = **(0, 5)**
i) gradient = **–6**, y-intercept = **(0, 3)**

3 Start by looking at the y-intercept of the graphs and equations. If the two lines have the same y-intercept, look at the gradient.

$\boldsymbol{A}$**:** $\boldsymbol{y = -\frac{1}{3}x + 4}$ $\boldsymbol{B}$**:** $\boldsymbol{y = 3x}$
$\boldsymbol{C}$**:** $\boldsymbol{y = \frac{1}{3}x + 2}$ $\boldsymbol{D}$**:** $\boldsymbol{y = \frac{7}{3}x - 1}$
$\boldsymbol{E}$**:** $\boldsymbol{y = x + 2}$ $\boldsymbol{F}$**:** $\boldsymbol{y = -x + 6}$

Page 202 Exercise 2

1 Rearrange each equation into the form $y = mx + c$, then m is the gradient and $(0, c)$ is the y-intercept.

a) $3y = 9 - 3x \Rightarrow y = -x + 3$
gradient = **–1**, y-intercept = **(0, 3)**

b) $y - 5 = 7x \Rightarrow y = 7x + 5$
gradient = **7**, y-intercept = **(0, 5)**

c) $3x + y = 1 \Rightarrow y = -3x + 1$
gradient = **–3**, y-intercept = **(0, 1)**

d) $3y - 6x = 15 \Rightarrow 3y = 6x + 15$
$\Rightarrow y = 2x + 5$
gradient = **2**, y-intercept = **(0, 5)**

e) $4y - 6x + 8 = 0 \Rightarrow 4y = 6x - 8$
$\Rightarrow y = \frac{3}{2}x - 2$
gradient = $\mathbf{\frac{3}{2}}$, y-intercept = **(0, –2)**

f) $6x - 3y + 1 = 0 \Rightarrow 6x + 1 = 3y$
$\Rightarrow y = 2x + \frac{1}{3}$
gradient = **2**, y-intercept = $\mathbf{(0, \frac{1}{3})}$

Page 203 Exercise 3

1 a) Lines parallel to $y = 5x - 1$ have a gradient of 5, e.g. $\mathbf{y = 5x + 1, y = 5x + 2, y = 5x + 3}$
You can have $y = 5x + c$ for any value of c except –1 here.

b) $x + y = 7$, so $y = -x + 7$ and parallel lines have a gradient of –1,
e.g. $\mathbf{y = -x + 6, y = -x + 5, y = -x + 3}$
You can have $y = -x + c$ for any value of c except 7 here.

2 Rearrange the lines A-F into $y = mx + c$ form:
A: $y = 2x + 4$ $\quad B$: $y = x + 2.5$
C: $y = 2x - 2$ $\quad D$: $y = -2x - 7$
E: $y = -\frac{2}{3}x + \frac{2}{3}$ $\quad F$: $y = \frac{2}{3}x + \frac{2}{9}$

a) $y = 2x - 1$ has a gradient of 2, so lines $\mathbf{A}$ and $\mathbf{C}$ are parallel to it.

b) $2x - 3y = 0 \Rightarrow y = \frac{2}{3}x$. This line has a gradient of $\frac{2}{3}$, so line $\mathbf{F}$ is parallel to it.

3 (3, 1) and (–3, 3) are two points on the line, so the line has gradient $\frac{3-1}{(-3)-3} = \frac{2}{-6} = -\frac{1}{3}$.
You can pick any two points on the line to work out the gradient, but it's best to pick whole numbers that are nice and easy to work with.
Rearrange the lines A-F into $y = mx + c$ form:
A: $y = -3x + 2$ $\quad B$: $y = -\frac{1}{3}x + \frac{7}{3}$
C: $y = -3x + 4$ $\quad D$: $y = \frac{1}{3}x - \frac{8}{3}$
E: $y = -\frac{1}{3}x + 3$ $\quad F$: $y = -\frac{1}{3}x$
So the lines $\mathbf{B}$, $\mathbf{E}$ and $\mathbf{F}$ are parallel to the line on the diagram.

Page 204 Exercise 4

1 For parts a) and b) you're given the gradient (m) and the y-intercept in the form $(0, c)$, so put these values into $y = mx + c$.

a) $\mathbf{y = 8x + 2}$ $\quad$ **b)** $\mathbf{y = -x + 7}$

For the rest of the question, use the gradient and the given point to find the value of c.

c) Gradient = 3, so $10 = 3 \times 1 + c$, so $c = 7$.
So the equation of the line is $\mathbf{y = 3x + 7}$.

d) Gradient = $\frac{1}{2}$, so $-5 = \frac{1}{2} \times 4 + c$, so $c = -7$.
So the equation of the line is $\mathbf{y = \frac{1}{2}x - 7}$.

e) Gradient = –7, so $-4 = -7 \times 2 + c$, so $c = 10$.
So the equation of the line is $\mathbf{y = -7x + 10}$.

f) Gradient = 5, so $-7 = 5 \times (-3) + c$, so $c = 8$.
So the equation of the line is $\mathbf{y = 5x + 8}$.

2 For each part, find the gradient m from the original equation. Then use that and the given point to find the value of c in the equation $y = mx + c$ of the parallel line.

a) Gradient = 3, so $5 = 3 \times 0 + c \Rightarrow c = 5$
So the line has equation $\mathbf{y = 3x + 5}$.

b) Gradient = 5, so $-4 = 5 \times 1 + c \Rightarrow c = -9$
So the line has equation $\mathbf{y = 5x - 9}$.

c) Gradient = 2, so $6 = 2 \times 1 + c \Rightarrow c = 4$
So the line has equation $\mathbf{y = 2x + 4}$

d) Gradient = $\frac{1}{2}$, so $-7 = \frac{1}{2} \times 6 + c \Rightarrow c = -10$
So the line has equation $\mathbf{y = \frac{1}{2}x - 10}$

e) $2y = 6x + 3 \Rightarrow y = 3x + \frac{3}{2}$
Gradient = 3, so for the parallel line:
$4 = 3 \times (-3) + c \Rightarrow c = 13$
So the parallel line has equation
$\mathbf{y = 3x + 13}$

f) $x + y = 4 \Rightarrow y = -x + 4$
Gradient = –1, so for the parallel line:
$8 = -1 \times 8 + c \Rightarrow c = 16$
So the parallel line has equation
$\mathbf{y = -x + 16}$

Page 205 Exercise 5

1 a) Gradient = $\frac{11-7}{5-3} = \frac{4}{2} = 2$,
so $7 = 2(3) + c$ and $c = 1$.
So the equation of the line is $\mathbf{y = 2x + 1}$.

b) Gradient = $\frac{(-5)-1}{2-5} = \frac{-6}{-3} = 2$,
so $1 = 2(5) + c$ and $c = -9$.
So the equation of the line is $\mathbf{y = 2x - 9}$.

Using the same method for c)-f):

c) $\mathbf{y = x - 3}$ $\quad$ **d)** $\mathbf{y = 2x + 5}$
e) $\mathbf{y = 3x + 2}$ $\quad$ **f)** $\mathbf{y = 3x + 11}$

2 (–2, 4) and (2, 0) are two points on line A.
Gradient of line $A = \frac{4-0}{(-2)-2} = \frac{4}{-4} = -1$,
y-intercept = 2, so its equation is $\mathbf{y = -x + 2}$.
Gradient of line $B = \frac{5-0}{1-0} = \frac{5}{1} = 5$.
It goes through the origin so y-intercept = 0, so its equation is $\mathbf{y = 5x}$.
Using the same method for lines C-H:
line C: $\mathbf{y = x - 1}$ $\quad$ line D: $\mathbf{y = -3}$
line E: $\mathbf{y = -\frac{1}{2}x + 2}$ $\quad$ line F: $\mathbf{y = \frac{2}{5}x + 1}$
line G: $\mathbf{y = \frac{2}{5}x - 4}$ $\quad$ line H: $\mathbf{y = \frac{3}{2}x - \frac{5}{2}}$

3 For Q3, you need to pick your own two points on the line to find the gradient — choose points that lie on the grid lines so they're accurate.
E.g. the line passes through (–2.5, –1.5) and (1.5, 0.5),
so gradient = $\frac{0.5-(-1.5)}{1.5-(-2.5)} = \frac{2}{4} = \frac{1}{2} = 0.5$
so $0.5 = 0.5 \times 1.5 + c$ and $c = -0.25$.
The equation of the line is $\mathbf{y = 0.5x - 0.25}$.

12.6 Quadratic Graphs

Page 207 Exercise 1

1 a)

x	–3	–2	–1	0	1	2	3
x^2	9	4	1	0	1	4	9
2	2	2	2	2	2	2	2
$x^2 + 2$	11	6	3	2	3	6	11

Don't get put off by the constant row (the 2 row here) — just fill in every entry in that row with the value given in the first column.

b), c)

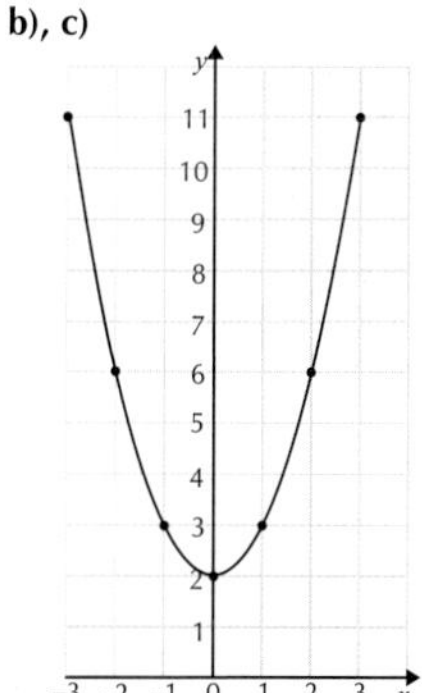

2 a)

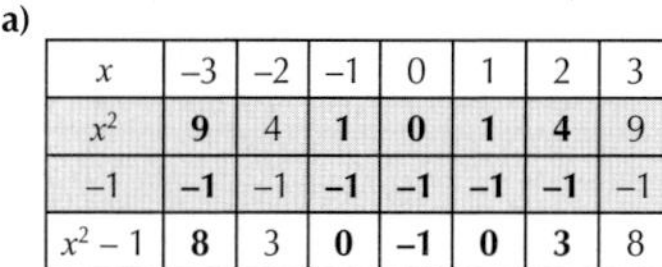

x	–3	–2	–1	0	1	2	3
x^2	9	4	1	0	1	4	9
–1	–1	–1	–1	–1	–1	–1	–1
$x^2 - 1$	8	3	0	–1	0	3	8

b)

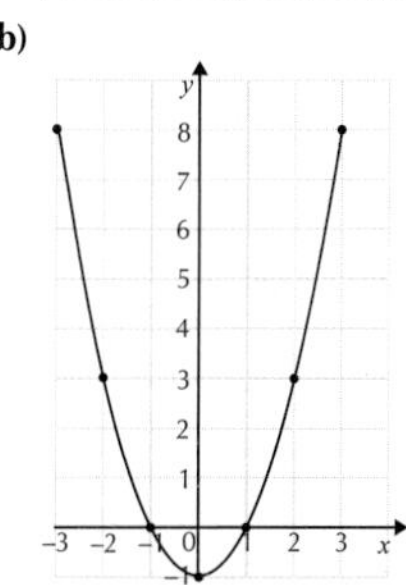

3 a) (i) E.g.

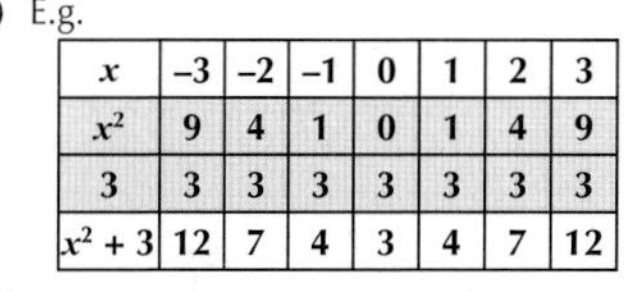

x	–3	–2	–1	0	1	2	3
x^2	9	4	1	0	1	4	9
3	3	3	3	3	3	3	3
$x^2 + 3$	12	7	4	3	4	7	12

(ii)

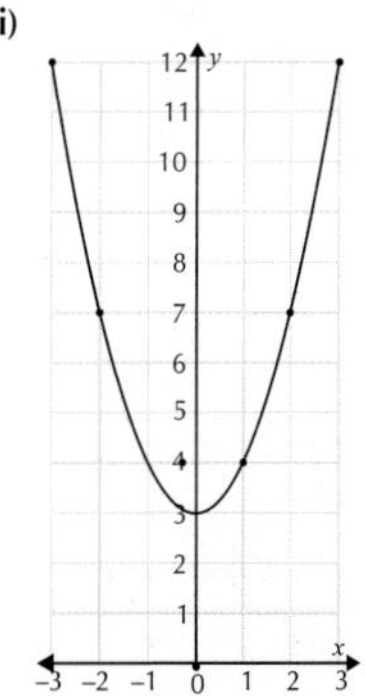

b) (i) E.g.

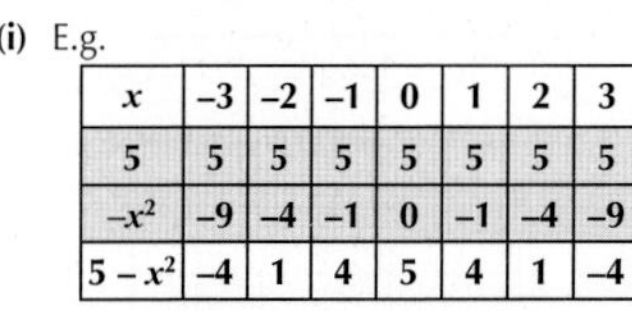

x	–3	–2	–1	0	1	2	3
5	5	5	5	5	5	5	5
$-x^2$	–9	–4	–1	0	–1	–4	–9
$5 - x^2$	–4	1	4	5	4	1	–4

(ii)

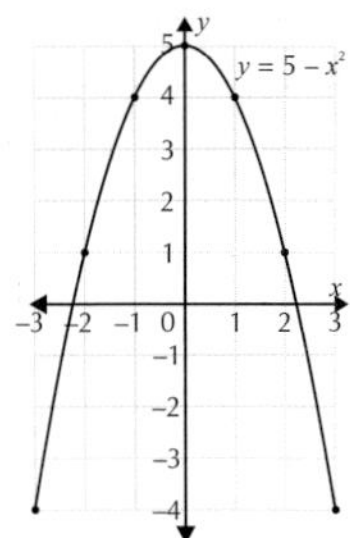

Remember, if the coefficient of x^2 is negative (–1 here), you get a n-shaped graph.

Page 208 Exercise 2

1 a)

x	–3	–2	–1	0	1	2	3
x^2	9	4	1	0	1	4	9
$-2x$	6	4	2	0	–2	–4	–6
$x^2 - 2x$	15	8	3	0	–1	0	3

b)

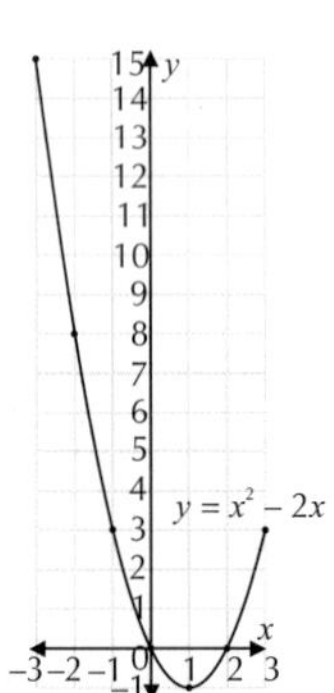

2 a) (i)

x	–3	–2	–1	0	1	2	3
x^2	9	4	1	0	1	4	9
$3x$	–9	–6	–3	0	3	6	9
$x^2 + 3x$	0	–2	–2	0	4	10	18

(ii)

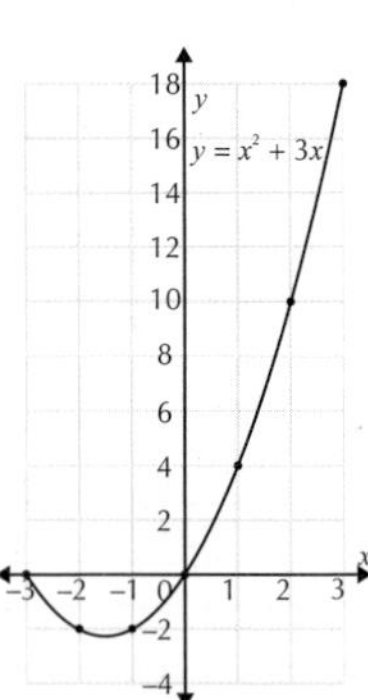

b) (i)

x	–3	–2	–1	0	1	2	3
x^2	9	4	1	0	1	4	9
$-4x$	12	8	4	0	–4	–8	–12
$x^2 - 4x$	21	12	5	0	–3	–4	–3

(ii)

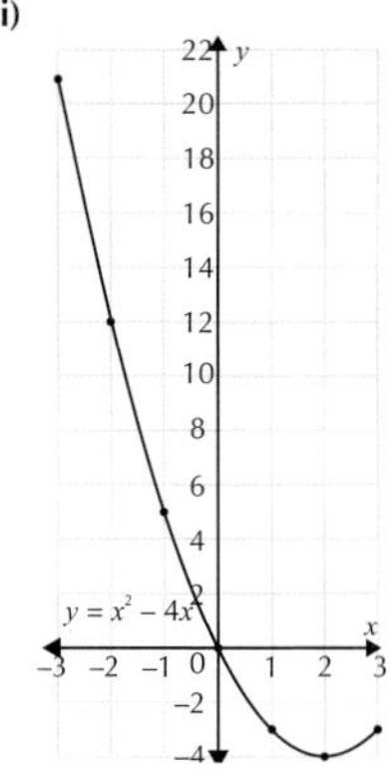

Page 208 Exercise 3

1 a) (i)

x	–3	–2	–1	0	1	2	3
x^2	9	4	1	0	1	4	9
$2x$	–6	–4	–2	0	2	4	6
5	5	5	5	5	5	5	5
$x^2 + 2x + 5$	8	5	4	5	8	13	20

(ii)

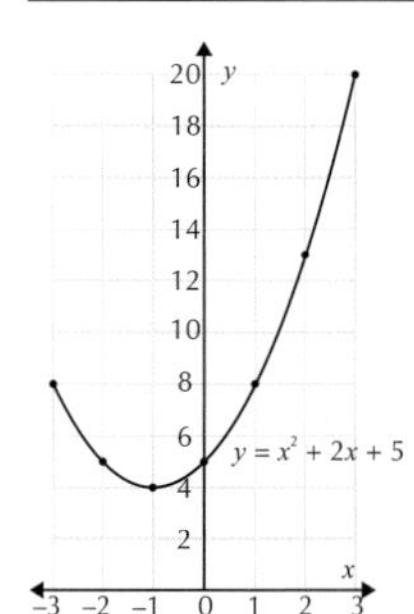

b) (i)

x	–3	–2	–1	0	1	2	3
$-x^2$	–9	–4	–1	0	–1	–4	–9
$-x$	3	2	1	0	–1	–2	–3
–1	–1	–1	–1	–1	–1	–1	–1
$-x^2 - x - 1$	–7	–3	–1	–1	–3	–7	–13

(ii)

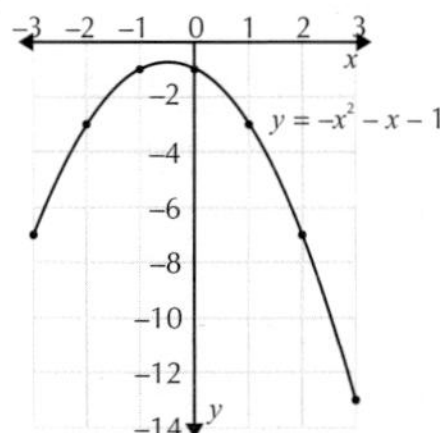

2 a)

x	–4	–3	–2	–1	0	1	2	3	4
$2x^2$	32	18	8	2	0	2	8	18	32
$3x$	–12	–9	–6	–3	0	3	6	9	12
–7	–7	–7	–7	–7	–7	–7	–7	–7	–7
$2x^2 + 3x - 7$	13	2	–5	–8	–7	–2	7	20	37

b)

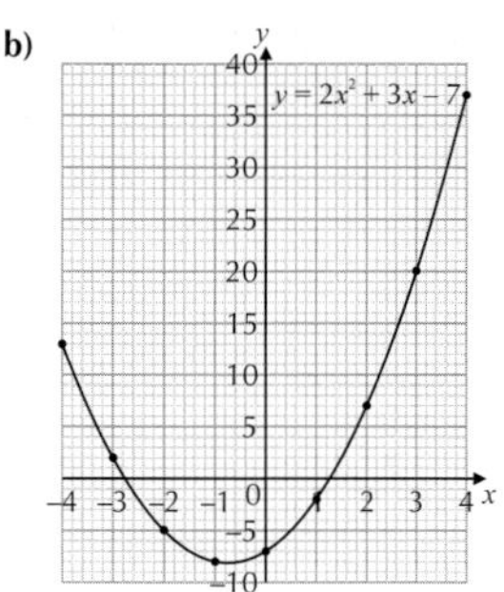

Page 209 Exercise 4

1 a) $x = -4$ and $x = 0$

The solutions are the points where the graph crosses the x-axis.

b) $x = -1$ and **$x = 3$** **c) $x = -2$** and **$x = 2$**

2 a)

x	0	1	2	3	4	5
x^2	0	1	4	9	16	25
$-5x$	0	–5	–10	–15	–20	–25
3	3	3	3	3	3	3
$x^2 - 5x + 3$	3	–1	–3	–3	–1	3

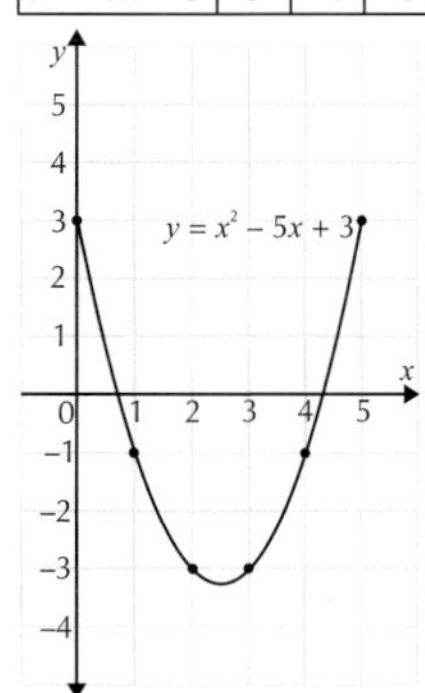

b) $x = 0.7$ and $x = 4.3$
(accept 0.6 to 0.8 and 4.2 to 4.4)

Page 210 Exercise 5

1 a) minimum

The turning point is a minimum if the x^2 term is positive.

b) maximum

The turning point is a maximum if the x^2 term is negative.

c) minimum **d) minimum**

e) maximum **f) maximum**

2 a) E.g. $y = 0$ at $x_1 = -4$ and $x_2 = -1$,
so turning point is at $x = \frac{-4 + (-1)}{2} = -2.5$.
When $x = -2.5$,
$y = (-2.5)^2 + (5 \times -2.5) + 4 = -2.25$.
The turning point is **(–2.5, –2.25)**.

b) E.g. $y = 0$ at $x_1 = -4$ and $x_2 = 1$, so turning point is at $x = \frac{-4 + 1}{2} = -1.5$.
When $x = -1.5$,
$y = -(-1.5)^2 - (3 \times -1.5) + 4 = 6.25$.
The turning point is **(–1.5, 6.25)**.

3 For Q3 you don't know the points where the curve intersects the x-axis — but it doesn't matter, because you're given two other points with the same y-value. So just use those to find the x-value of the turning point.

a) $y = 7$ at $x_1 = -1$ and $x_2 = 7$, so turning point is at $x = \frac{-1+7}{2} = 3$.
When $x = 3$, $y = (3)^2 - (6 \times 3) = -9$.
The turning point is **(3, –9)**.

b) $y = 3$ at $x_1 = 0$ and $x_2 = 2$, so turning point is at $x = \frac{0+2}{2} = 1$.
When $x = 1$, $y = (1)^2 - (2 \times 1) + 3 = 2$.
The turning point is **(1, 2)**.

c) $y = 12$ at $x_1 = 2$ and $x_2 = 6$, so turning point is at $x = \frac{2+6}{2} = 4$.
When $x = 4$, $y = (8 \times 4) - (4)^2 = 16$.
The turning point is **(4, 16)**.

Page 211 Exercise 6

1 For each part a)-f), make a table of values and look for two x-values that give the same y-value. The average of these gives the x-coordinate of the turning point, and the y-coordinate can be found using either the table or the equation.

a)

x	–3	–2	–1	0	1	2	3
$x^2 - 2x$	15	8	3	0	–1	0	3

$x = 0$ and $x = 2$ have the same y-value of $y = 0$, so the x-coordinate of the turning point is $x = \frac{0+2}{2} = 1$. So using the table, the turning point is **(1, –1)**.

b)

x	–3	–2	–1	0	1	2	3
$x^2 + 3x + 11$	11	9	9	11	15	21	29

$x = -2$ and $x = -1$ have the same y-value of $y = 9$, so the x-coordinate of the turning point is $x = \frac{-2+(-1)}{2} = -1.5$.
The y-coordinate of the turning point is $y = (-1.5)^2 + (3 \times -1.5) + 11 = 8.75$ so the turning point is **(–1.5, 8.75)**

Using the same method for c)-f):

c) (–2.5, –15.25) **d) (–2, –20)**

e) (–0.5, 9.5) **f) (1.5, 10.5)**

12.7 Harder Graphs

Page 213 Exercise 1

1 **a)**

x	–3	–2	–1	0	1	2	3
x^3	–27	–8	–1	0	1	8	27
$x^3 + 5$	–22	–3	4	5	6	13	32

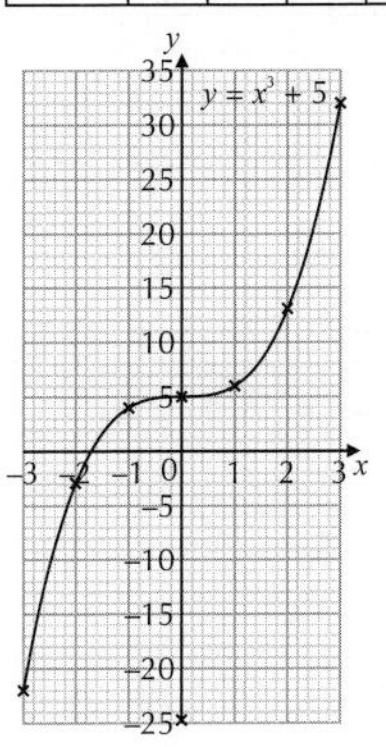

b)

x	–3	–2	–1	0	1	2	3
5	5	5	5	5	5	5	5
$-x^3$	27	8	1	0	–1	–8	–27
$5 - x^3$	32	13	6	5	4	–3	–22

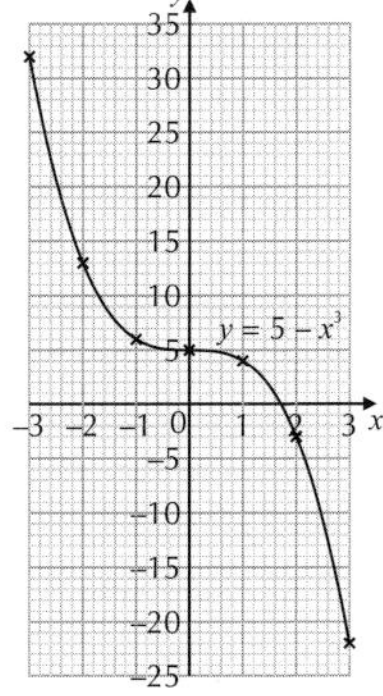

Remember, when the coefficient of x^3 is negative, it goes downwards from left to right — by looking at the coefficient you can do a quick check that your curve is the right shape.

c)

x	–3	–2	–1	0	1	2	3
–4	–4	–4	–4	–4	–4	–4	–4
$-x^3$	27	8	1	0	–1	–8	–27
$-4 - x^3$	23	4	–3	–4	–5	–12	–31

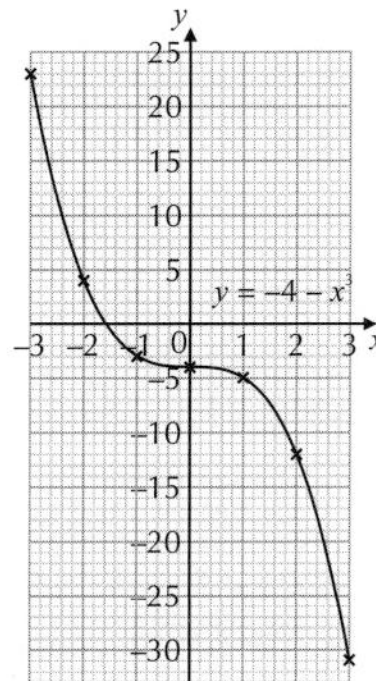

2

x	–3	–2	–1	0	1	2	3
x^3	–27	–8	–1	0	1	8	27
3	3	3	3	3	3	3	3
$x^3 + 3$	–24	–5	2	3	4	11	30

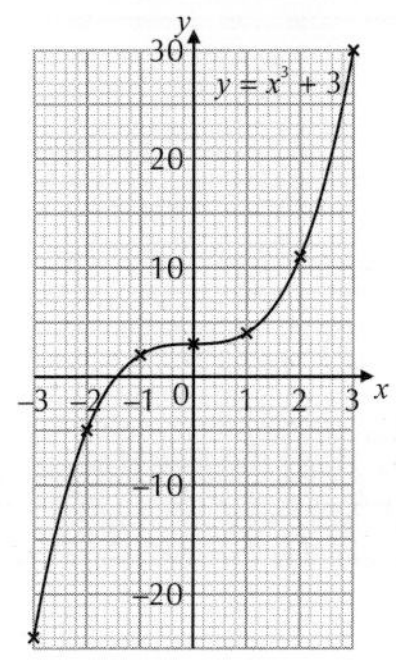

3

x	–4	–3	–2	–1	0	1	2	3	4
x^3	–64	–27	–8	–1	0	1	8	27	64
$-3x$	12	9	6	3	0	–3	–6	–9	–12
7	7	7	7	7	7	7	7	7	7
$x^3 + 3$	–45	–11	5	9	7	5	9	25	59

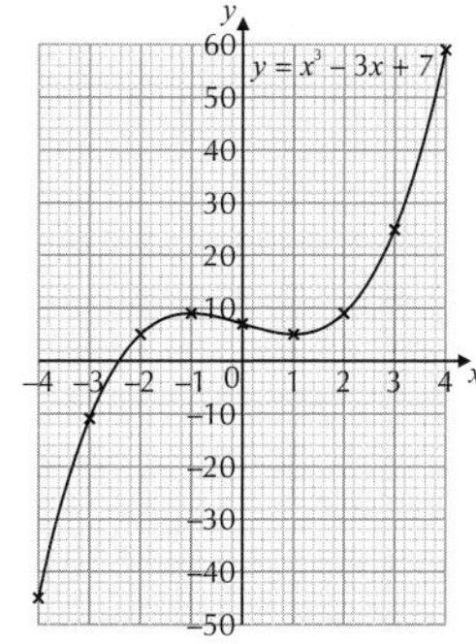

Page 214 Exercise 2

1 A basic reciprocal equation has the form $y = \frac{A}{x}$. The following equations are either in or can be rearranged into this form:
B*, *C*, *E* and *G

2 **a)**

x	–5	–4	–2	–1	–0.5	–0.1
$\frac{2}{x}$	–0.4	–0.5	–1	–2	–4	–20

x	0.1	0.5	1	2	4	5
$\frac{2}{x}$	20	4	2	1	0.5	0.4

Lots goes on between $x = -1$ and $x = 1$ in a reciprocal graph, so decimal values are included in the table to make sure nothing's missed.

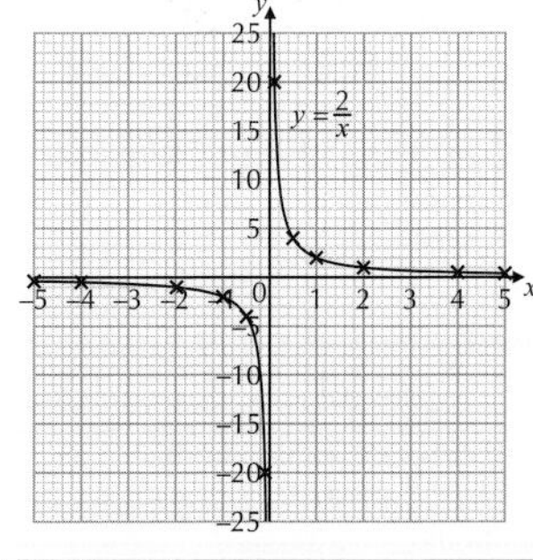

b)

x	–5	–4	–2	–1	–0.5	–0.1
$-\frac{1}{x}$	0.2	0.25	0.5	1	2	10

x	0.1	0.5	1	2	4	5
$-\frac{1}{x}$	–10	–2	–1	–0.5	–0.25	–0.2

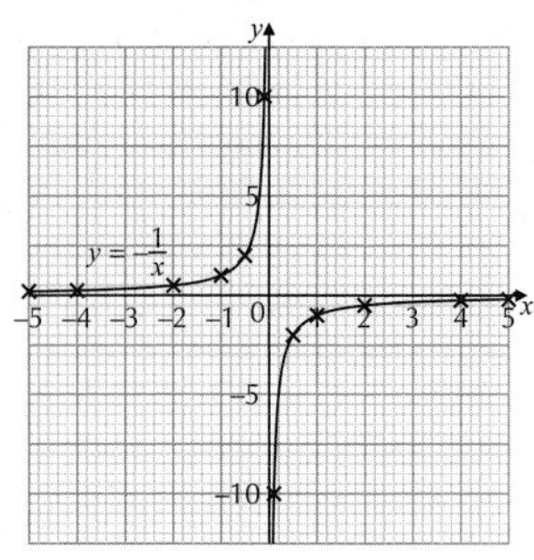

c)

x	–5	–4	–2	–1	–0.5	–0.1
$\frac{3}{x}$	**–0.6**	–0.75	**–1.5**	–3	**–6**	**–30**

x	0.1	0.5	1	2	4	5
$\frac{3}{x}$	**30**	**6**	**3**	**1.5**	**0.75**	**0.6**

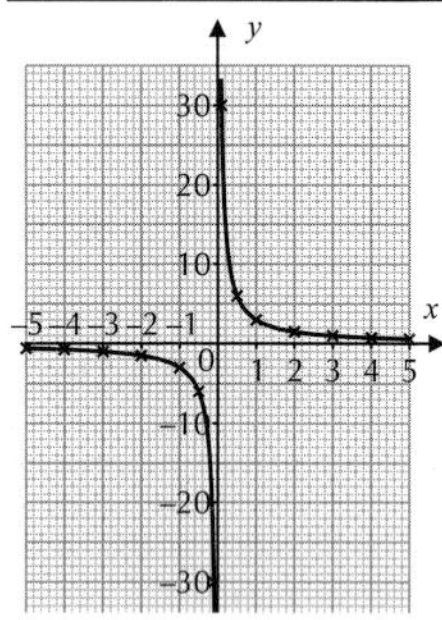

Page 215 Review Exercise

1 a), b)

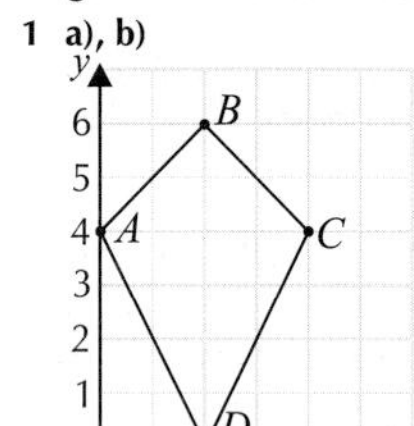

this is a kite.

2 Midpoint $= \left(\frac{2+(-4)}{2}, \frac{5+1}{2}\right) = \left(\frac{-2}{2}, \frac{6}{2}\right) =$ **(–1, 3)**

3 a) ***A*: (1, 5)** ***B*: (4, 5)** ***C*: (6, 3)** ***D*: (4, 1)** ***E*: (1, 1)**

b) Midpoint $= \left(\frac{1+4}{2}, \frac{5+5}{2}\right) = \left(\frac{5}{2}, \frac{10}{2}\right) =$ **(2.5, 5)**

c) Midpoint $= \left(\frac{4+6}{2}, \frac{5+3}{2}\right) = \left(\frac{10}{2}, \frac{8}{2}\right) =$ **(5, 4)**

d) $\boldsymbol{x = 1}$

Remember, vertical lines have an equation of the form x = a.

e) gradient $= \frac{3-5}{6-4} = \frac{-2}{2} = \mathbf{-1}$.

4 a)

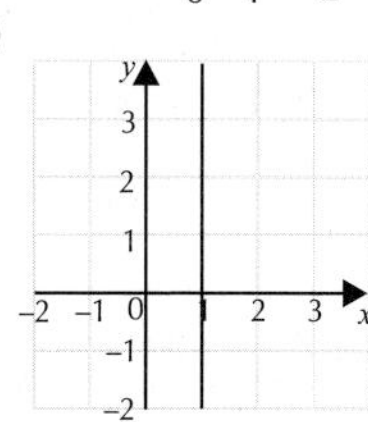

b)

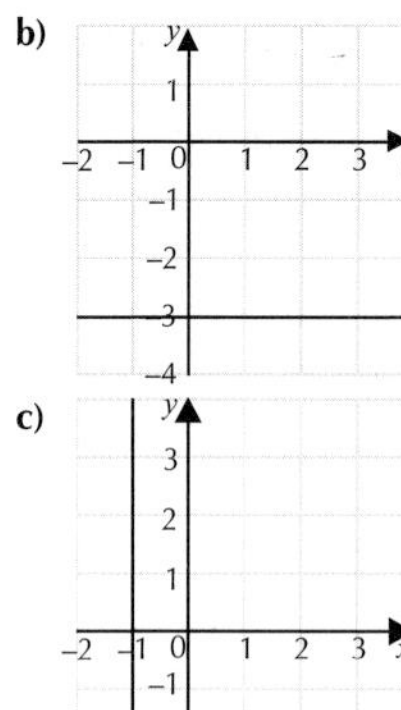

c)

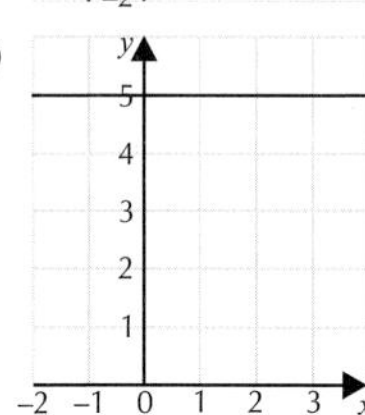

d)

5 ***AB***: gradient $= \frac{4-1}{-5-(-2)} = \frac{3}{-3} = \mathbf{-1}$

CD: gradient $= \frac{5-1}{3-5} = \frac{4}{-2} = \mathbf{-2}$

EF: gradient $= \frac{-3-(-5)}{2-(-5)} = \mathbf{\frac{2}{7}}$

6 ***A*: $x = -5$** — it's a vertical line through (–5, 0).

***B*: $y = x^2$** — it's a u-shaped parabola.

***C*: $y = x$** — it's a straight line through (0, 0) with a gradient of 1.

***D*: $y = -4$** — it's a horizontal line through (0, –4).

Look for the main features of each graph — e.g. is it straight or curved? What are the x- and y-intercepts?

7 a)

x	–3	–2	–1	0	1	2	3
y	–4	–2	0	2	4	6	8
	(–3, –4)	**(–2, –2)**	**(–1, 0)**	**(0, 2)**	**(1, 4)**	**(2, 6)**	**(3, 8)**

b)

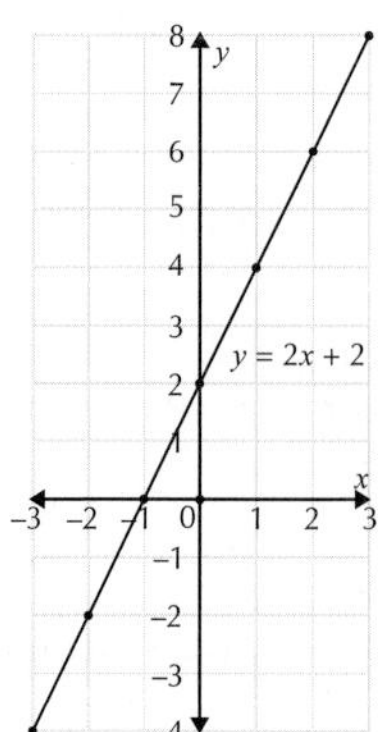

c) On the same axes, draw the line $y = 5$. Find its intersection with the graph of $y = 2x + 2$ and read off the x-coordinate to get the solution $\boldsymbol{x = 1.5}$.

8 a) Draw the graphs of $y = 2x + 3$ and $y = 4x + 2$ using the methods on p.194.

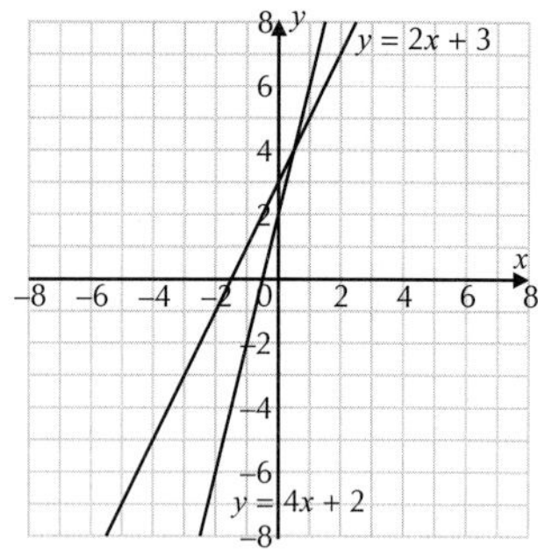

b) The lines intersect at the point $(\frac{1}{2}, 4)$. So the solution is $\boldsymbol{x = \frac{1}{2}}$ and $\boldsymbol{y = 4}$.

9 a) gradient $= \frac{15-0}{3-0} = \frac{15}{3} = \mathbf{5}$

b) gradient $= \frac{4-(-5)}{-1-(-4)} = \frac{9}{3} = \mathbf{3}$

c) gradient $= \frac{-1-2}{-4-(-7)} = \frac{-3}{3} = \mathbf{-1}$

d) gradient $= \frac{10-(-2)}{2-5} = \frac{12}{-3} = \mathbf{-4}$

10 Compare each equation with $y = mx + c$. m is the gradient and $(0, c)$ is the y-intercept.

a) (i) 2 **(ii) (0, 3)**

b) (i) –1 **(ii) (0, 3)**

c) (i) $-\frac{2}{3}$ **(ii) (0, –1)**

11 a) Draw the graph of $y = 6 - 3x$ using the methods on p.194.

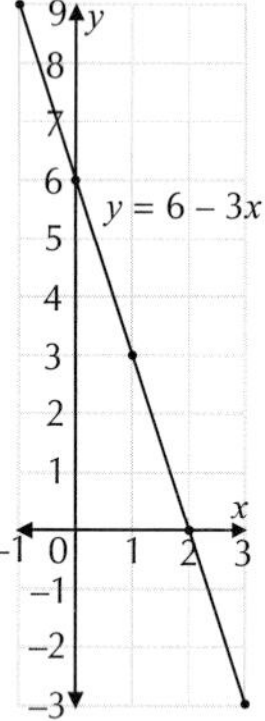

b) gradient = –3, so plugging this and the point (2, –4) into $y = mx + c$ gives $-4 = -3 \times 2 + c \Rightarrow c = 2$.
So the equation of the line is $\boldsymbol{y = 2 - 3x}$.

12 a) E.g.

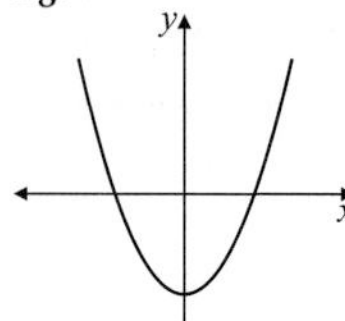

b) E.g.

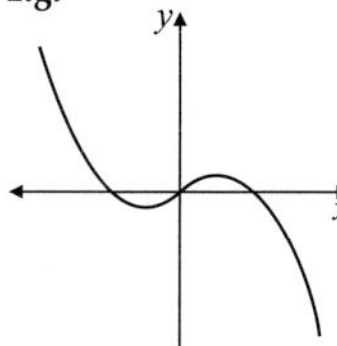

c)

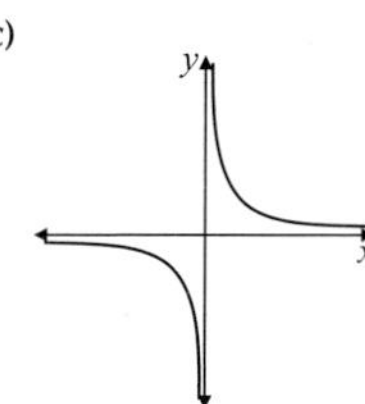

13 Find where the curve intersects the x-axis, and read off the x-coordinates to get the solutions $\mathbf{x = -2.3, x = 1.3}$

14 a)

x	−4	−3	−2	−1	0	1	2
x^2	**16**	**9**	4	**1**	**0**	**1**	**4**
$5x$	**−20**	**−15**	−10	**−5**	**0**	**5**	**10**
$x^2 + 5x$	**−4**	**−6**	−6	**−4**	**0**	**6**	**14**

b)

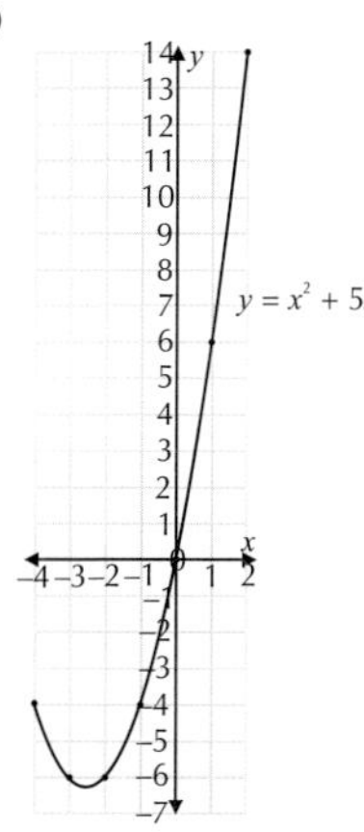

c) E.g. $y = -6$ at $x_1 = -3$ and $x_2 = -2$, so the turning point is at

$$x = \frac{-3+(-2)}{2} = \frac{-5}{2} = -2.5.$$

When $x = -2.5$, $y = (-2.5)^2 + (5 \times -2.5)$ $= -6.25$.

The turning point is $\mathbf{(-2.5, -6.25)}$.

You could also have used $x = -4$ and $x = -1$ as your two values, since $y = -4$ at both of those points — you'd still have come out with the same answer at the end.

Page 217 Exam-Style Questions

1

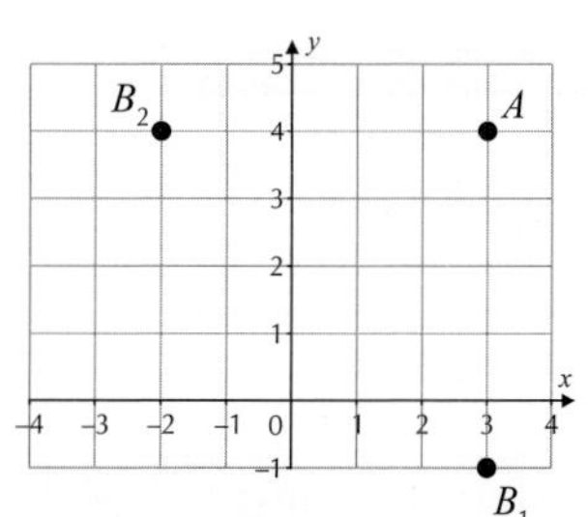

The two possible locations are shown on the grid by $\mathbf{B_1}$ and $\mathbf{B_2}$.

[2 marks available — 1 mark for each correct location]

2 Difference in x-values between A and B is $3 - (-2) = 5$.

Difference in y-values between A and B is $k - 1$.

Gradient $= \frac{k-1}{5}$ *[1 mark]*

So $\frac{k-1}{5} = -1.5$ *[1 mark]*

$k - 1 = -1.5 \times 5 \Rightarrow k - 1 = -7.5$

$k = -7.5 + 1 \Rightarrow \mathbf{k = -6.5}$ *[1 mark]*

3 a) $\mathbf{A = (4, 3)}$ *[1 mark]*

$\mathbf{B = (8, 1)}$ *[1 mark]*

b) Difference in x values between A and B is $8 - 4 = 4$.

Difference in y values between A and B is $1 - 3 = -2$

So gradient $= \frac{-2}{4} = -\frac{1}{2}$ *[1 mark]*

Equation of line is $\mathbf{y = 5 - \frac{1}{2}x}$ *[1 mark]*

The right-hand side of the equation begins with 5 because that's the value of the y-intercept on the graph.

4 a) **(0, 1.5)** *[1 mark]*

b) Midpoint $= \left(\frac{-3+5}{2}, \frac{3+(-1)}{2}\right) = \left(\frac{2}{2}, \frac{2}{2}\right)$

$= \mathbf{(1, 1)}$ *[1 mark]*

5 a) **(1, 2)** *[1 mark]*

b) Go up from 3 on the x-axis until you reach the curve, then go across to the y-axis. This gives $\mathbf{y = 6}$ *[1 mark]*.

c) Go left from 6 on the y-axis until you reach the curve, then go down to the x-axis. This gives $\mathbf{x = -1}$ *[1 mark]*.

6 a) $\mathbf{x = 1}$ *[1 mark]*

b) Find where the curve intersects the x-axis and read off the x-coordinates to get $\mathbf{x = -0.9}$ and $\mathbf{x = 2.9}$.

[2 marks available — 1 mark for each correct x-coordinate. Accept $x = -0.8$ and $x = 2.8$ as alternative answers.]

7 The curve has not been drawn smoothly *[1 mark]*.

The point (2, 2) should not lie on this graph of $y = \frac{1}{x}$ *[1 mark]*.

Section 13 — Real-Life Graphs

13.1 Interpreting Real-Life Graphs

Page 220 Exercise 1

1 a) Read up from £50 on the horizontal axis and then across to the vertical axis to get an answer of **€60**.

b) Read up from £250 on the horizontal axis and then across to the vertical axis to get an answer of **€290**.

c) Read up from £110 on the horizontal axis and then across to the vertical axis to get an answer of **€130**.

2 a) Read across from €50 on the vertical axis and then down to the horizontal axis to get an answer of **£40**.

b) Read across from €200 on the vertical axis and then down to the horizontal axis to get an answer of **£170**.

c) Read across from €360 on the vertical axis and then down to the horizontal axis to get an answer of **£310**.

3 Read across from €130 on the vertical axis and then down to the horizontal axis to get an answer of **£110**.

4 a) Read up from £420 on the horizontal axis and then across to the vertical axis to get an answer of **€490**.

b) Read across from €470 on the vertical axis and then down to the horizontal axis to get an answer of **£400**.

c) €470 = £400 is less than £420, so it's cheaper in **France**.

Make sure you're comparing numbers that have the same units.

Page 221 Exercise 2

1 a) The basic fine is shown by the horizontal line on the graph. This intersects the vertical axis at 5, so the basic fine is **£5**.

b) Read down from the right-hand end of the horizontal line.

The longest time that receives the basic fine is **20 days**.

2 Go up from 50 days until you reach the graph, then go across to the horizontal axis.

The fine for 50 days overdue is **£27.50**.

Any answer between £27 and £28 is OK.

3 Go across from £38 on the vertical axis until you reach the graph, then go down to the horizontal axis.

This shows the book was overdue by **64** days.

4 a) Look at whether the graphs for each climber reach 1 km:

Katherine reached a **height of 1 km** after **4 hours** and **Lemar** reached **1 km** after **3 hours**. **Morag's greatest height** was **0.75 km**, so she **didn't** reach the summit.

So the climbers that **reached the summit** were **Katherine and Lemar**.

b) **Lemar** reached the summit in less time than Katherine, so he was first.

Page 222 Exercise 3

1 a) Look for a graph that increases with a steep gradient and then decreases gently. This matches graph **L**.

b) Look for a graph that neither rises nor falls (i.e. is horizontal). This matches graph **N**.

c) Look for a graph that increases and has a gradient which gets more and more steep. This matches graph **M**.

d) Look for a graph that decreases initially but then rises steeply. This matches graph **K**.

2

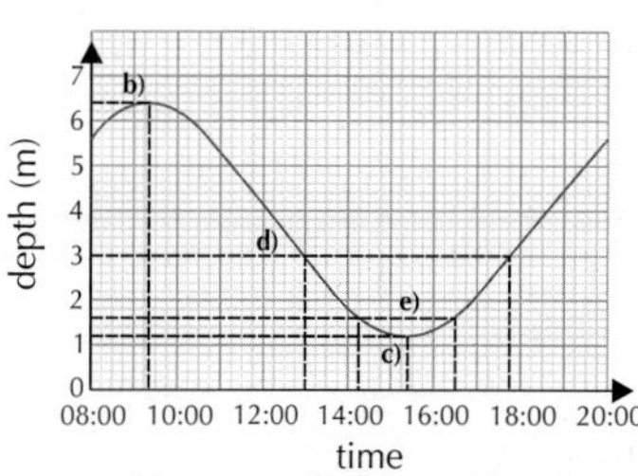

a) E.g. The water got **deeper** for about **an hour** (since the graph **increases**), then **shallower** for about **6 hours** (since the graph **decreases**). Finally it got **deeper** for about **5 hours** (since the graph **increases** again).

Make sure you describe each feature of the graph in the context of the question.

b) The greatest depth corresponds to the highest point on the graph. This occurs at about **09:20** (accept 09:15-09:30).

c) The minimum depth corresponds to the lowest point on the graph. At this point, the depth is **1.2 m**.

d) Read across from 3 m. The graph is at this depth twice, once at approx. **13:00** and again at approx. **17:45**.

e) The depth of the water is below 1.6 m between about 14:15 and 16:30. So his boat is not floating for **2h 15m** (135 mins). (Accept answers between 2 hours 10 minutes and 2 hours 20 minutes.)

3

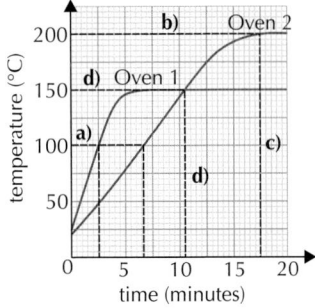

a) Reading across from 100 °C on the vertical axis, the graph for Oven 1 shows it's at this temperature after about 2.5 minutes, while the graph for Oven 2 shows it's at this temperature after about 6.5 minutes. So **Oven 1** reaches 100 °C more quickly.

b) The maximum point on the graph for Oven 1 is at 150 °C, while the maximum point on the graph for Oven 2 is at about 200 °C. So **Oven 2** reaches a higher maximum temperature.

c) Reading down from the highest point on the Oven 2 graph gives a time of about **18 minutes** (accept 17.5-18.5 minutes).

d) The ovens are the same temperature where the lines intersect. This point occurs at:

(i) **10.5 minutes**

(ii) **150 °C**

e) E.g. The gradients show the change in the temperature of each oven per unit of time — this is the rate at which the temperature of each oven changes.

4 a) (i) At 0 s the depth is 0 cm, at 5 s the depth is 5 cm. The increase in depth is 5 cm – 0 cm = **5 cm**.

(ii) At 10 s the depth is 10 cm, at 15 s the depth is 15 cm. The increase in depth is 15 cm – 10 cm = **5 cm**.

(iii) At 25 s the depth is 25 cm, at 30 s the depth is 30 cm. The increase in depth is 30 cm – 25 cm = **5 cm**.

b) (i) At 0 s the depth is 0 cm, at 5 s the depth is 10 cm. The increase in depth is 10 cm – 0 cm = **10 cm**.

(ii) At 10 s the depth is 17 cm, at 15 s the depth is 21.5 cm. The increase in depth is 21.5 cm – 17 cm = **4.5 cm**.

(iii) At 25 s the depth is 27.5 cm, at 30 s the depth is 30 cm. The increase in depth is 30 cm – 27.5 cm = **2.5 cm**.

c) The depth of water in Vase P increases steadily while the depth of water in Vase Q increases quickly at first, and then more slowly as the vase fills up. When the vases are nearly empty, the depth of water in Vase Q increases more quickly than the depth of water in Vase P, but as the vases fill up the depth of water in Vase Q increases at a slower rate than the depth of water in vase P.

13.2 Drawing Real-Life Graphs

Page 225 Exercise 1

1 a) You would cook a chicken weighing 1 kg for (35 × 1) + 25 = 60 minutes.
You would cook a chicken weighing 2 kg for (35 × 2) + 25 = 95 minutes.
Using the same method for the remaining weights, the table can be completed as follows.

Weight (kg)	1	2	3	4	5
Time (minutes)	**60**	**95**	**130**	**165**	**200**

b) Plot each pair of values on suitable axes and join with a straight line:

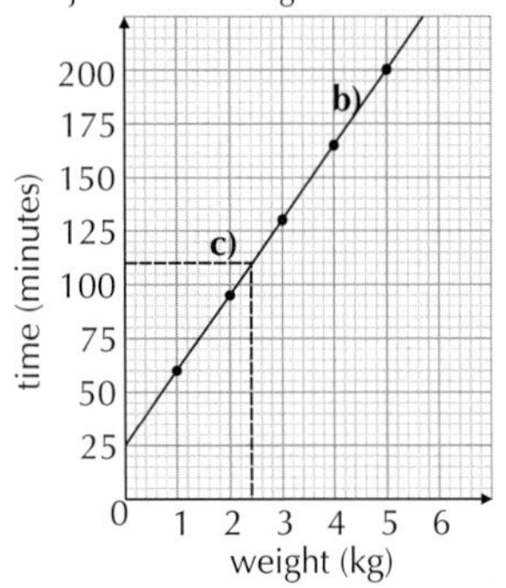

c) Reading across from 110 minutes on the vertical axis and then down to the horizontal axis, the weight is **2.4 kg**. (Accept 2.3-2.5 kg)

2 a) Fuel efficiency depends on speed, so fuel efficiency should go on the vertical axis and speed on the horizontal axis.
Plot each pair of values from the table and join them with a smooth curve:

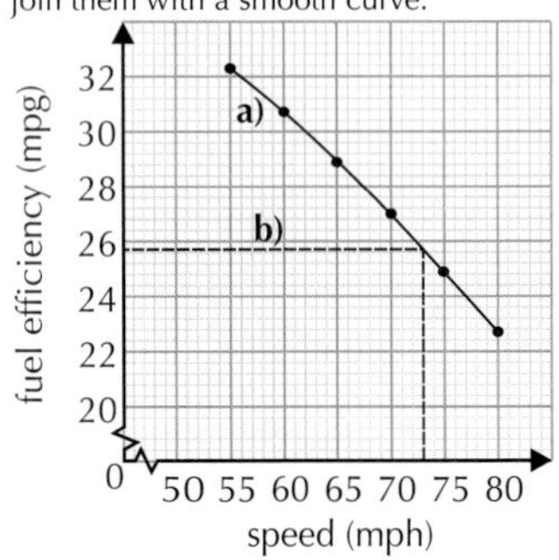

You don't need speeds lower than 55 mph or fuel efficiencies lower than 22.7 mpg so you can remove parts of both axes (shown by the squiggles).

b) Reading up from 73 mph on the horizontal axis and then across to the vertical axis, the fuel efficiency is about **25.7 mpg**. (Accept 25.5-25.9 mpg)

Page 226 Review Exercise

1 a) Read up from 38 km/h on the horizontal axis and then across to the vertical axis to get an answer of **23.5 mph**. (Accept 23-24 mph)

b) Read across from 27 mph on the vertical axis and then down to the horizontal axis to get an answer of **43 km/h**. (Accept 42-44 km/h)

c) Read up from 52 km/h on the horizontal axis and then across to the vertical axis to find that 52 km/h ≈ 32.5 mph. So the driver is about 32.5 – 30 = **2.5 mph** over the speed limit. (Accept 2-3 mph)

d) Read up from 60 km/h on the horizontal axis and then across to the vertical axis to find 60 km/h ≈ 37.5 mph. Double this to find that 120 km/h ≈ 75 mph, which is greater than 70 mph. So the speed limit is greater in **Spain** by about 75 – 70 = **5 mph**. (Accept 4-6 mph)
Alternatively, you could convert the UK speed limit into km/h. Using the graph, 35 mph ≈ 56 km/h. Double that to find that 70 mph ≈ 112 km/h. So the speed limit is greater in Spain by about 8 km/h.

2 a) The graph initially increases and then decreases so the temperature **rises for the first 3 seconds** and then **decreases for the remaining 5 seconds**. Over the first 3 seconds, the gradient of the graph decreases to zero, so the temperature **rises at a slower rate over time** until it **stops rising**. In the final 5 seconds, the gradient gets steeper and steeper so the temperature **falls at a more rapid rate** as time goes on.

b) The graph is at its highest when $t = 3$. Reading across to the vertical axis, this is at a temperature of **9 °C**.

c) Reading across from 8 °C on the vertical axis and down to the horizontal axis, the times are **t = 2 seconds** and **t = 4 seconds**.

3 a) Plot each pair of values from the table on suitable axes and join them with a smooth curve:

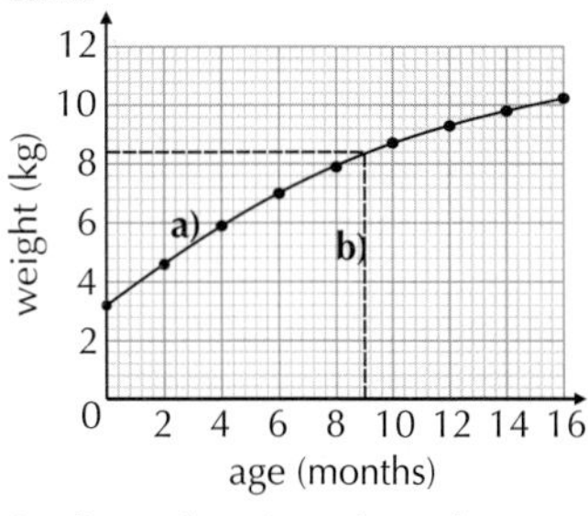

b) Reading up from 9 months on the horizontal axis and across to the vertical axis, the weight is about 8.4 kg.
So Keira is about 9.1 – 8.4 = **0.7 kg** heavier. (Accept 0.5-0.9 kg)

Page 227 Exam-Style Questions

1 a) **60 m** *[1 mark]*
Find the highest point on the graph and read across to the vertical axis.

b) **Beach B** *[1 mark]*
E.g. the graph **flattens out** towards Beach B so the **depth** of the water is **lower** there than near Beach A *[1 mark]*.

2 a)

Weight (kg)	10	20	30	40	50
Cost (£) of Kenyan coffee	25	50	**75**	**100**	**125**
Cost (£) of Peruvian coffee	35	**45**	**55**	**65**	**75**

[2 marks available — 1 mark for each correct row of the table]

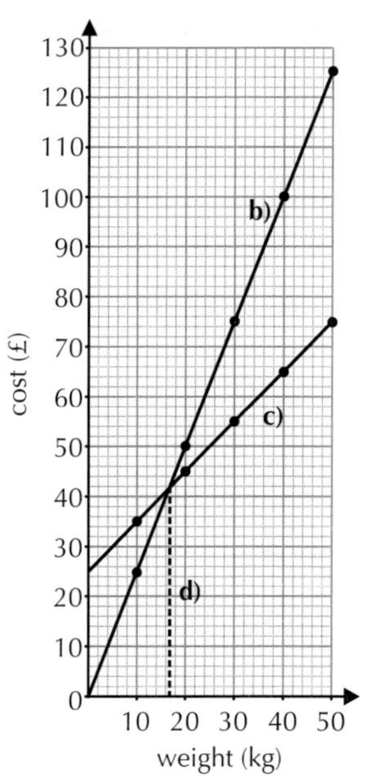

b) Plot each pair of values on suitable axes and join with a straight line (see above).
[2 marks available — 1 mark for plotting points, 1 mark for joining with a straight line]

c) Plot each pair of values and join with a straight line (see above).
[2 marks available — 1 mark for plotting points, 1 mark for joining with a straight line]

d) Find the intersection point of the two lines, then draw a line down to the vertical axis to get an estimate of **16.5 kg**.
[1 mark available — answers in the range 16.0-17.0 kg are acceptable]

Section 14 — Proportion

14.1 Direct Proportion

Page 229 Exercise 1

1 a) 1 pair of jeans costs £35, so 2 pairs cost £35 × 2 = **£70**

b) 5 pairs of jeans cost £35 × 5 = **£175**

c) 20 pairs of jeans cost £35 × 20 = **£700**

2 8 books cost £36, so 1 book costs £36 ÷ 8 = £4.50.
12 books cost £4.50 × 12 = **£54.**

3 a) Each DVD costs £7.50, so with £22.50 you can buy £22.50 ÷ £7.50 = **3 DVDs.**

b) With £60, you can buy £60 ÷ £7.50 = **8 DVDs.**
You could also divide 1 DVD by 7.50 to find the number of DVDs per pound, then multiply by 22.5 and 60.

4 a) On 1 litre of petrol, the car travels 250 ÷ 35 = 7.142... km
On 50 litres of petrol, the car travels 50 × 7.142... = 357.142... km
= **357 km (to the nearest km)**

b) Travelling 1 km uses 35 ÷ 250 = 0.14 litres of petrol. So travelling 400 km uses 400 × 0.14 = **56 litres**
Don't round any numbers while you're doing your working or you might get the wrong answer.

5 11 pens cost £12.32 ⇒ 1 pen costs £12.32 ÷ 11 = £1.12.
8 pens cost 8 × £1.12 = £8.96.
6 note pads cost £5.88
⇒ 1 note pad costs £5.88 ÷ 6 = £0.98.
Then 5 note pads cost 5 × £0.98 = £4.90.
In total 8 pens and 5 note pads cost £8.96 + £4.90 = **£13.86**

Page 229 Exercise 2

1 Pack of 6: £1.50 ÷ 6 = £0.25 or 25p per apple
Bag of 10: £2.40 ÷ 10 = £0.24 or 24p per apple
Individually: 30p
So the **bag of 10 apples** represents the best value for money.

2 Find how many ml you get per £1 for each size of coffee cup:
Small cup: 240 ÷ 2 = 120 ml per £1
Medium cup: 350 ÷ 3 = 116.666... ml per £1
Large cup: 470 ÷ 4 = 117.5 ml per £1
So the **small cup** represents the best value for money.
You could also find the price per ml and see which is cheapest.

3 6 pack: £2.18 = 218p ÷ 6
= 36.333...p per sausage
8 pack: £2.80 = 280p ÷ 8 = 35p per sausage
10 pack: £3.46 = 346p ÷ 10
= 34.6p per sausage
So the **pack of 10 sausages** represents the best value for money.

Page 231 Exercise 3

1 **Graph C — it is a straight line through the origin.**
Graph A does not go through the origin and Graph B isn't a straight line, so neither of them can be directly proportional to x.

2 a)

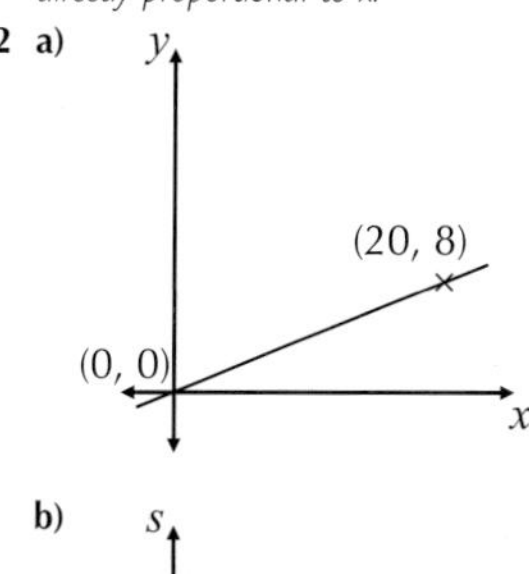

b)

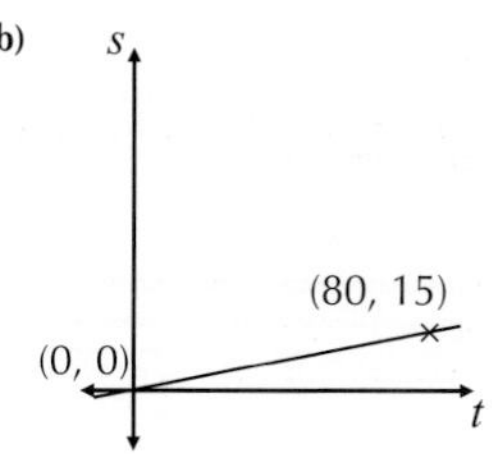

3 a) (i) Use the 'divide for one, multiply for all' method:
When $x = 1$, $y = 2 \div 8 = 0.25$,
so when $x = 12$, $y = 12 \times 0.25 = 3$.

x	8	12
y	2	**3**

(ii) x and y are directly proportional, so the graph is a straight line through the origin. Plot the points from your table and draw a line through them:

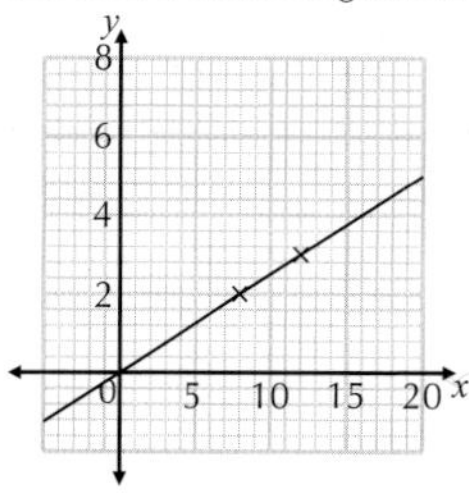

b) (i) When $x = 1$, $y = 21 \div 7 = 3$,
so when $x = 2$, $y = 2 \times 3 = 6$,
when $y = 30$, $x = 30 \div 3 = 10$.

x	2	7	**10**
y	**6**	21	30

(ii) Plot your points and draw a straight line through them:

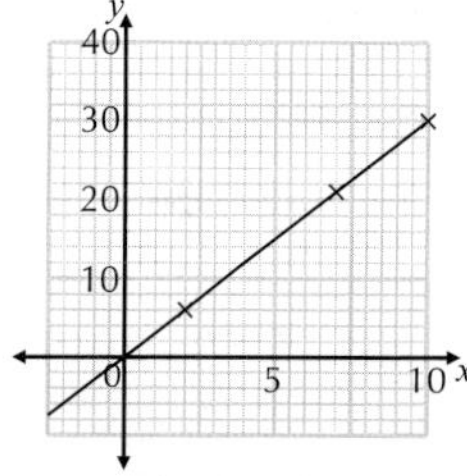

c) (i) When $x = 1$, $y = -10 \div -2 = 5$,
so when $x = 0$, $y = 0 \times 5 = 0$,
when $x = 3$, $y = 3 \times 5 = 15$,
when $y = 30$, $x = 30 \div 5 = 6$.

x	−2	**0**	3	**6**
y	−10	**0**	**15**	30

(ii) Plot your points and draw a straight line through them:

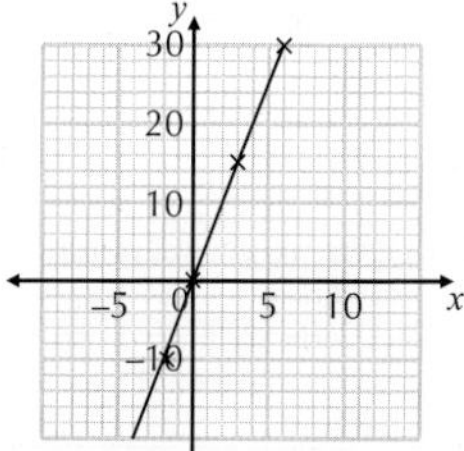

Page 231 Exercise 4

1 a) $j = Ah$
$15 = A \times 5$, so $A = 15 \div 5 = 3 \Rightarrow$ $\boldsymbol{j = 3h}$

b) When $h = 40$, $j = 3 \times 40 =$ **120**

c)

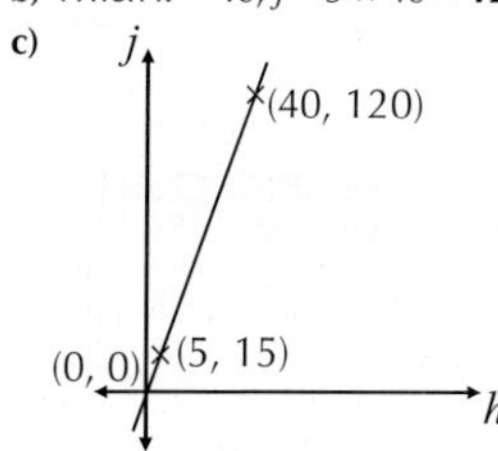

2 a) p and q are directly proportional, so the graph is a straight line through the origin. It also goes through the point (4, 14).

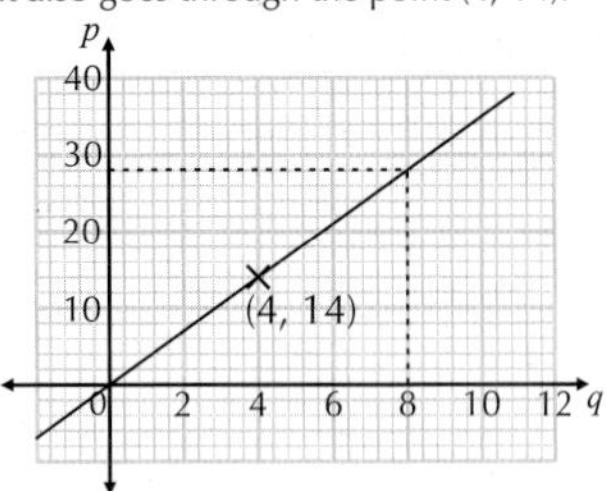

b) Read off the graph — go up from $q = 8$ to the line, then across to the axis for p (see dashed lines on graph above).
When $q = 8$, $\boldsymbol{p = 28}$.

14.2 Inverse Proportion

Page 232 Exercise 1

1 3 people take 2 hours to paint the wall
1 person would take 3 × 2 = 6 hours
6 people would take 6 ÷ 6 = **1 hour**

2 At 30 mph, the journey takes 2 hours
At 1 mph, it would take 2 × 30 = 60 hours
At 45 mph, it would take
60 ÷ 45 = **1.333... hours**
= **1 hour and 20 minutes**

3 4 chefs take 20 minutes
1 chef would take 4 × 20 = 80 minutes
5 chefs would take 80 ÷ 5 = **16 minutes**

4 a) 5 builders take 62 days
1 builder would take 5 × 62 = 310 days
2 builders would take 310 ÷ 2 = **155 days**

b) 1 builder would take 310 days
To do it in 1 day, you would need
310 × 1 = 310 builders
To do it in 40 days, you would need
310 ÷ 40 = 7.75 builders
So **8 builders** would be needed.

Page 233 Exercise 2

1 2 people take 3 hours to clean 6 rooms
First change the number of people:
1 person would take
3 × 2 = 6 hours to clean 6 rooms
5 people would take
6 ÷ 5 = 1.2 hours to clean 6 rooms
Then change the number of rooms:
5 people would take
1.2 ÷ 6 = 0.2 hours to clean 1 room,
so cleaning 20 rooms would take 5 people
0.2 × 20 = **4 hours**

2 2 bakers take 144 minutes to bake 72 buns
First change the number of bakers:
1 baker would take
144 × 2 = 288 minutes to bake 72 buns
5 bakers would take
288 ÷ 5 = 57.6 minutes to bake 72 buns
Then change the number of buns:
5 bakers would take
57.6 ÷ 72 = 0.8 minutes to bake 1 bun,
so baking 90 buns would take 5 bakers
0.8 × 90 = **72 minutes**

3 14 people take 2 hours to paint 35 plates
First change the number of people:
1 person would take
2 × 14 = 28 hours to paint 35 plates
20 people would take
28 ÷ 20 = 1.4 hours to paint 35 plates
Then change the number of plates:
20 people would take
1.4 ÷ 35 = 0.04 hours to paint 1 plate,
so painting 60 plates would take
0.04 × 60 = **2.4 hours** = **2 hours 24 minutes**

Page 234 Exercise 3

1 Graph A — y decreases as x increases

2 Look for equations in the form $y = \frac{A}{x}$ or $xy = A$
— $\boldsymbol{y = \frac{4}{x}}$ and $\boldsymbol{yx = 9}$ show inverse proportion.

3 a) When $x = 12$, and $y = 15$,
$A = xy = 12 \times 15 = 180$.
When $x = 6$, $y = 180 \div 6 = 30$.

x	12	6
y	15	**30**

b) When $x = 8$ and, $y = 20$,
$A = xy = 8 \times 20 = 160$,
so when $x = 2$, $y = 160 \div 2 = 80$,
when $x = 4$, $y = 160 \div 4 = 40$,
when $x = 10$, $y = 160 \div 10 = 16$.

x	2	4	8	10
y	**80**	**40**	20	**16**

c) When $x = 20$, and $y = 4$,
$A = xy = 20 \times 4 = 80$,
so when $x = 4$, $y = 80 \div 4 = 20$,
when $x = 100$, $y = 80 \div 100 = 0.8$,
when $y = 320$, $x = 80 \div 320 = 0.25$.

x	**0.25**	4	20	100
y	320	**20**	4	**0.8**

4 a) When $q = 2$, and $p = 1$, $A = pq = 2 \times 1 = 2$,
so when $q = 0.2$, $p = 2 \div 0.2 = 10$,
when $q = 0.4$, $p = 2 \div 0.4 = 5$.
Continue for each value of q to get:

q	0.2	0.4	0.5	1	2	4	5	10
p	**10**	**5**	**4**	**2**	1	**0.5**	**0.4**	**0.2**

b) Plot each point from the table in part a). p and q are inversely proportional so you will get a reciprocal graph.

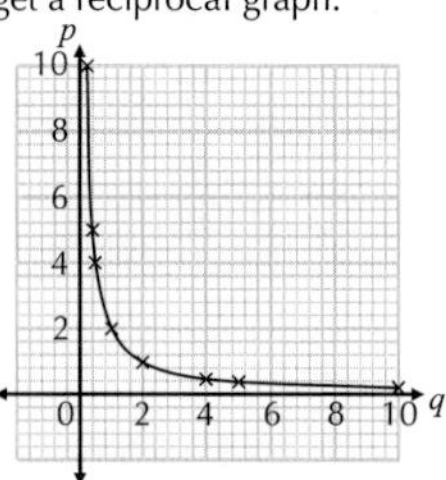

Page 235 Review Exercise

1 12.5 litres cost £20
1 litre costs 20 ÷ 12.5 = £1.60.
60 litres cost 60 × £1.60 = **£96**

2 a) £1 = R17.5 ⇒ £500 = 500 × 17.5
= **R8750**

b) Emma has 8750 – 6200 = R2550 left over from her holiday. The exchange rate is now £1 = R16.9, so
R1 = £1 ÷ 16.9 = £0.0591...
⇒ R2550 = 2550 × £0.0591... =
£150.887...
= **£150.89** (to the nearest penny)

3 5 laps of a 400 m track takes 8 minutes.
First change the length of the track:
1 lap of the 400 m track takes
8 ÷ 5 = 1.6 minutes
1 lap of a 200 m track would take
1.6 ÷ 2 = 0.8 minutes.
Then change the number of laps:
9 laps of the 200 m track would take
9 × 0.8 = **7.2 minutes**
= **7 mins, 12 secs**
(Alternative method:
5 × 400 m = 2000 m takes 8 minutes, so
1 m takes 8 ÷ 2000 = 0.004 minutes
9 × 200 m = 1800 m takes
0.004 × 1800 = **7.2 minutes**)

4 Box of 8: £3.50 ÷ 8 = 43.75p per chocolate
Box of 12: £4.70 ÷ 12
= 39.166...p per chocolate
Box of 20: £8.15 ÷ 20 = 40.75p per chocolate
So the best value for money is **the box of 12 chocolates**.

5 a) When $a = 1$, $b = 6 \div 2 = 3$,
so when $a = 4$, $b = 4 \times 3 = 12$,
when $a = 7$, $b = 7 \times 3 = 21$,
when $a = 10$, $b = 10 \times 3 = 30$.

a	2	4	7	10
b	6	**12**	**21**	**30**

b) Plot your points and draw a straight line through them and the origin:

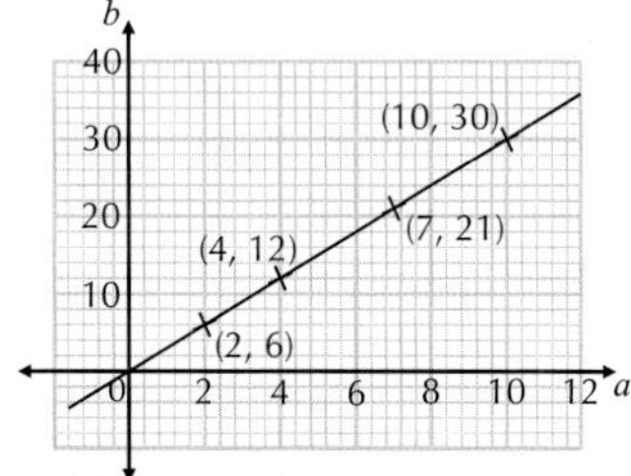

6 a) When $x = 4 \div 4 = 1$, $y = 32 \div 4 = 8$,
so when $x = 1 \times 8 = 8$, $y = 8 \times 8 = \mathbf{64}$

b) When $x = 1$, $y = 8$,
so when $y = 2$, $x = 2 \div 8 = \mathbf{2.5}$

c) $y = Ax$.
$A = 32 \div 4 = 8$, so $\boldsymbol{y = 8x}$

7 a) 8 chickens lay 20 eggs in 3 days
1 chicken lays 20 eggs in 8 × 3 = 24 days
12 chickens lay 20 eggs in 24 ÷ 12
= **2 days**

b) 12 chickens lay 20 eggs in 2 days, so they lay 10 eggs in 1 day, and 10 × 3 = 30 eggs in 3 days.
So to get 30 eggs in 1 day, you would need
3 × 12 = **36 chickens**

8 a) When $x = 7$, and $y = 9$, $A = xy = 7 \times 9 = 63$, so when $y = 25.2$, $x = 63 \div 25.2 = 2.5$.

x	**2.5**	7
y	25.2	9

b) When $x = 6$, and $y = 15$,
$A = xy = 6 \times 15 = 90$,
so when $x = 3$, $y = 90 \div 3 = 30$,
when $x = 30$, $y = 90 \div 30 = 3$,
when $y = 180$, $x = 90 \div 180 = 0.5$.

x	**0.5**	3	6	30
y	180	**30**	15	**3**

Page 236 Exam-Style Questions

1 Original roll: 1 sheet costs £1.20 ÷ 100 = £0.012
New roll: 1 sheet costs £1.10 ÷ 90 = £0.01222...
The new roll **is not** better value for money.
[2 marks for finding both costs per sheet and correct answer, or 1 mark for finding one correct cost per sheet]
You could also find the number of sheets bought per £1 spent.

2 a) 12 muffins: 360 g
1 muffin: 360 ÷ 12 = 30 g *[1 mark]*
20 muffins: 20 × 30 g = **600 g** *[1 mark]*

b)
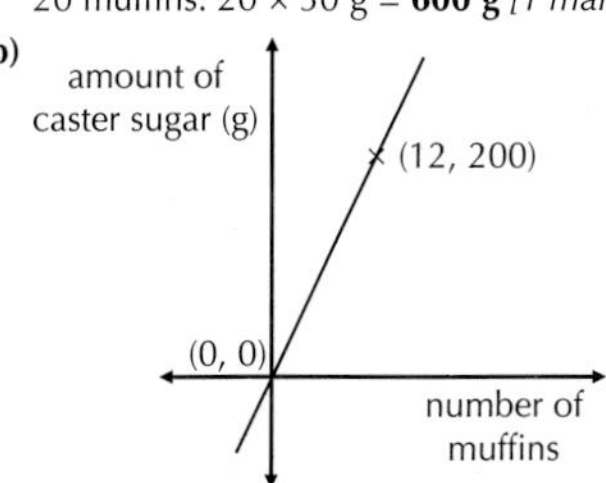

[2 marks available — 1 mark for drawing correctly labelled axes and a straight line through the origin, 1 mark for showing the point (12, 200)]

3 Cleaning 1 m² takes Niall 24 ÷ 258 = 0.093... minutes *[1 mark]*
⇒ 68.8 m² will take 68.8 × 0.093... = 6.4 minutes *[1 mark]*
Convert 0.4 minutes into seconds:
0.4 × 60 = 24 seconds,
so it will take Niall **6 minutes 24 seconds** *[1 mark]*.
Alternatively, Niall cleans 258 ÷ 24 = 10.75 m² in one minute, so cleaning 68.8 m² would take 68.8 ÷ 10.75 = 6.4 minutes = 6 minutes 24 seconds.

4 a) It takes 96 minutes for 840 people to count 45 802 votes. Changing the number of votes:
840 people would take 96 ÷ 2 = 48 minutes to count half as many votes *[1 mark]*.
Changing the number of people:
1 person would take
840 × 48 = 40 320 minutes *[1 mark]*
560 people would take
40 320 ÷ 560 = **72 minutes** *[1 mark]*

b) The assumption is that the staff of the second council count votes at the **same rate** as the staff of the first council *[1 mark]*.

Section 15 — Angles and 2D Shapes

15.1 Basic Angle Properties

Page 237 Exercise 1

1 a) $34° + b + 90° = 180°$
$b = 180° - 90° - 34° \Rightarrow \mathbf{b = 56°}$

b) $d + 30° + 20° = 90°$
$d = 90° - 30° - 20° \Rightarrow \mathbf{d = 40°}$

c) $28° + 55° + d + 35° = 180°$
$d = 180° - 28° - 55° - 35° \Rightarrow \mathbf{d = 62°}$

2 a) $d + 3d = 180° \Rightarrow 4d = 180°$
$\Rightarrow d = 180° \div 4 \Rightarrow \mathbf{d = 45°}$

b) $a + 110° + a = 180° \Rightarrow 2a + 110° = 180°$
$\Rightarrow 2a = 180° - 110° \Rightarrow 2a = 70°$
$\Rightarrow a = 70° \div 2 \Rightarrow \mathbf{a = 35°}$

c) $57° + 57° + c + c = 180°$
$\Rightarrow 114° + 2c = 180°$
$\Rightarrow 2c = 180° - 114° \Rightarrow 2c = 66°$
$\Rightarrow c = 66° \div 2 \Rightarrow \mathbf{c = 33°}$

Page 238 Exercise 2

1 a) $100° + c + 120° = 360°$
$c = 360° - 120° - 100° \Rightarrow \mathbf{c = 140°}$

b) $41° + 161° + d + 45° = 360°$
$d = 360° - 41° - 161° - 45° \Rightarrow \mathbf{d = 113°}$

c) $99° + a + 44° + 90° = 360°$
$a = 360° - 99° - 44° - 90° \Rightarrow \mathbf{a = 127°}$

2 a) $e + e + e + e + e + e = 360° \Rightarrow 6e = 360°$
$\Rightarrow e = 360° \div 6 \Rightarrow \mathbf{e = 60°}$

b) $50° + 98° + g + 3g = 360°$
$\Rightarrow 148° + 4g = 360°$
$\Rightarrow 4g = 360° - 148° \Rightarrow 4g = 212°$
$\Rightarrow g = 212° \div 4 \Rightarrow \mathbf{g = 53°}$

c) $160° + 90° + h + h + 50° = 360°$
$\Rightarrow 300° + 2h = 360°$
$2h = 360° - 300° \Rightarrow 2h = 60°$
$\Rightarrow h = 60° \div 2 \Rightarrow \mathbf{h = 30°}$

15.2 Parallel and Intersecting Lines

Page 239 Exercise 1

1 a) 160° and b and vertically opposite so **b = 160°**

b) 75° and c are vertically opposite so **c = 75°**
75° and d are on a straight line so
$75° + d = 180° \Rightarrow d = 180° - 75°$
$\Rightarrow \mathbf{d = 105°}$

c) e and the right angle are vertically opposite so **e = 90°**
f and the right angle are on a straight line so $f + 90° = 180° \Rightarrow f = 180° - 90°$
$\Rightarrow \mathbf{f = 90°}$
f and g are vertically opposite so **g = 90°**
You could also have used the fact that g and the right angle are on a straight line so $g + 90° = 180° \Rightarrow g = 90°$

2 The 40° angle and the angle labelled $3a - 5°$ are vertically opposite, so
$40° = 3a - 5°$
$40° + 5° = 3a \Rightarrow 45° = 3a$
$\Rightarrow a = 45° \div 3 \Rightarrow \mathbf{a = 15°}$

Page 240 Exercise 2

1 a) 72° and b are alternate angles so **b = 72°**

b) 135° and g are on a straight line so
$135° + g = 180°$
$g = 180° - 135° \Rightarrow \mathbf{g = 45°}$
g and h are alternate angles so **h = g = 45°**.

c) 48° and i are alternate angles so **i = 48°**
i and j are on a straight line so
$i + j = 180° \Rightarrow 48° + j = 180°$
$\Rightarrow j = 180° - 48° \Rightarrow \mathbf{j = 132°}$

2 a) **42°**

b) x and the angle of 42° are **alternate angles** as the floors are **parallel** and the stairs are a **straight line** crossing them.
Try not to let the context of the question put you off — you just need to use the same rules as in question 1.

Page 241 Exercise 3

1 a) 52° and f are allied angles so
$52° + f = 180° \Rightarrow f = 180° - 52°$
$\Rightarrow \mathbf{f = 128°}$
f and g are alternate angles so **g = 128°**
52° and h are alternate angles so **h = 52°**
There are often a few different methods you can use for questions like this — for example, you could use the fact that g and 52° lie on a straight line to work out g, and the fact that g and h are allied to work out h.

b) 141° and h are corresponding angles so **h = 141°**
141° and i are allied angles so
$i + 141° = 180° \Rightarrow i = 180° - 141°$
$\Rightarrow \mathbf{i = 39°}$
i and j are corresponding angles so **j = 39°**

c) 78° and v are on a straight line so
$78° + v = 180° \Rightarrow v = 180° - 78°$
$\Rightarrow \mathbf{v = 102°}$
78° and w are vertically opposite angles so **w = 78°**
x and v are vertically opposite so **x = 102°**
78° and r are corresponding angles so **r = 78°**
x and s are corresponding angles so **s = 102°**
v and t are corresponding angles so **t = 102°**
w and u are corresponding angles so **u = 78°**

2 The angle made by the second post and the downward slope is 99°, since this and the 99° angle shown in the diagram are corresponding angles. Then y and 99° lie on a straight line so $y + 99° = 180° \Rightarrow y = 180° - 99° \Rightarrow \mathbf{y = 81°}$

15.3 Triangles

Page 242 Exercise 1

1 a) **Equilateral triangle; acute-angled**

b) **Right-angled triangle**
This triangle is also a scalene triangle as all sides are different lengths.

c) **Isosceles triangle; acute-angled**

d) **Isosceles triangle; right-angled**
Make sure you look at every part of the triangle — in d) you need to spot the tick marks as well as the right angle.

Page 243 Exercise 2

1 a) $68° + 90° + b = 180° \Rightarrow 158° + b = 180°$
$\Rightarrow b = 180° - 158° \Rightarrow \mathbf{b = 22°}$

b) $d + 90° + 74° = 180° \Rightarrow d + 164° = 180°$
$\Rightarrow d = 180° - 164° \Rightarrow \mathbf{d = 16°}$

c) Call the unlabelled angle in the triangle h.
h and the right angle lie on a straight line, so $h + 90° = 180° \Rightarrow h = 180° - 90°$
$\Rightarrow h = 90°$
So as the angles in a triangle add up to 180°,
$90° + g + 38° = 180° \Rightarrow g + 128° = 180°$
$\Rightarrow g = 180° - 128° \Rightarrow \mathbf{g = 52°}$

2 The angles in a triangle must add up to **180°**, but the angles in this triangle add up to **$74° + 26° + 90° = 190°$**, so such a triangle **can't exist**.

3 a) $a + 55° + 72° = 180° \Rightarrow a + 127° = 180°$
$\Rightarrow a = 180° - 127° \Rightarrow \boldsymbol{a = 53°}$

b) $21° + c + 144° = 180° \Rightarrow c + 165° = 180°$
$\Rightarrow c = 180° - 165° \Rightarrow \boldsymbol{c = 15°}$

c) $57° + 74° + h = 180° \Rightarrow h + 131° = 180°$
$h = 180° - 131° \Rightarrow \boldsymbol{h = 49°}$
i and h lie on a straight line so $i + h = 180°$
$i + 49° = 180° \Rightarrow i = 180° - 49°$
$\Rightarrow \boldsymbol{i = 131°}$

Page 244 Exercise 3

1 a) $2a + a + 120° = 180° \Rightarrow 3a + 120° = 180°$
$\Rightarrow 3a = 180° - 120° \Rightarrow 3a = 60°$
$\Rightarrow a = 60° \div 3 \Rightarrow \boldsymbol{a = 20°}$

b) $2b + (2b + 50°) + 90° = 180°$
$\Rightarrow 4b + 140° = 180°$
$\Rightarrow 4b = 180° - 140° \Rightarrow 4b = 40°$
$\Rightarrow b = 40° \div 4 \Rightarrow \boldsymbol{b = 10°}$

c) $60° + (c - 16°) + (c + 16°) = 180°$
$\Rightarrow 2c + 60° + 16° - 16° = 180°$
$\Rightarrow 2c + 60° = 180°$
$\Rightarrow 2c = 180° - 60° \Rightarrow 2c = 120°$
$\Rightarrow c = 120° \div 2 \Rightarrow \boldsymbol{c = 60°}$

2 a) The triangle is isosceles, so $\boldsymbol{a = 30°}$.
As all the angles in a triangle add up to $180°$, $30° + b + 30° = 180°$
$\Rightarrow b + 60° = 180° \Rightarrow b = 180° - 60°$
$\Rightarrow \boldsymbol{b = 120°}$

b) As the triangle is isosceles, the non-labelled angle and angle e are equal.
As all the angles in a triangle add up to $180°$,
$e + 3e + e = 180° \Rightarrow 5e = 180°$
$\Rightarrow e = 180° \div 5 \Rightarrow \boldsymbol{e = 36°}$

c) Call the unlabelled angle in the triangle h.
The triangle is isosceles, so h and angle f are equal.
As all the angles in a triangle add up to $180°$, $48° + f + f = 180° \Rightarrow 2f = 180° - 48°$
$\Rightarrow 2f = 132° \Rightarrow f = 132° \div 2 \Rightarrow \boldsymbol{f = 66°}$
and $h = 66°$
Since h and g lie on a straight line:
$66° + g = 180° \Rightarrow g = 180° - 66°$
$\Rightarrow \boldsymbol{g = 114°}$

3 a) The triangle is an equilateral triangle, so all the angles are $60° \Rightarrow \boldsymbol{x = 60°}$
You could also work this out by calling each angle x. Then the sum of angles in a triangle gives 3x = 180° and so x = 60°.

b) y lies on a straight line with one of the angles in the triangle: $60° + y = 180°$
$\Rightarrow y = 180° - 60° \Rightarrow \boldsymbol{y = 120°}$

4 a) Call the bottom left angle in the triangle l.
The triangle is isosceles, so $l = 55°$.
As l lies on a straight line with p, then
$p + 55° = 180° \Rightarrow p = 180° - 55°$
$\Rightarrow \boldsymbol{p = 125°}$

b) Call the top angle in the triangle t.
$t = 180° - (55° + 55°)$
$\Rightarrow t = 180° - 110° \Rightarrow t = 70°$
t and q lie on a straight line so
$70° + q = 180° \Rightarrow q = 180° - 70°$
$\Rightarrow \boldsymbol{q = 110°}$

15.4 Quadrilaterals

Page 245 Exercise 1

1 a) $a + 93° + 86° + 69° = 360°$
$a = 360° - 93° - 86° - 69° \Rightarrow \boldsymbol{a = 112°}$

b) $129° + c + 74° + 67° = 360°$
$c = 360° - 129° - 74° - 67° \Rightarrow \boldsymbol{c = 90°}$

c) $72° + 112° + d + 106° = 360°$
$d = 360° - 72° - 112° - 106° \Rightarrow \boldsymbol{d = 70°}$

2 a) The missing angle in the quadrilateral is $360° - 90° - 108° - 85° = 77°$.
Then this angle and r lie on a straight line so $r + 77° = 180° \Rightarrow \boldsymbol{r = 103°}$

b) w and $71°$ are vertically opposite angles so $\boldsymbol{w = 71°}$.
x and $95°$ are vertically opposite angles so $\boldsymbol{x = 95°}$.
$71° + 95° + 102° + y = 360° \Rightarrow \boldsymbol{y = 92°}$

Page 246 Exercise 2

1

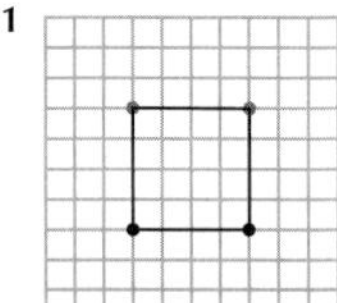

2 **E.g.**

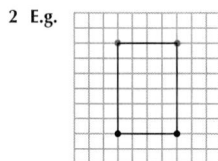

There are lots of different rectangles you could have drawn — make sure it has 4 right angles and 2 pairs of equal sides.

3 a) **They are the same length.**

b) **90°**

c) The only shape with diagonals of equal length is shape **iii)**, so that is the only square.
All squares have diagonals of equal length that meet at 90°.

4 In a rectangle, opposite side lengths are equal.
$2^2 + 5 = 4 + 5 = 9$ so the top and bottom sides are equal.
$\frac{4+20}{4} + 2 = \frac{24}{4} + 2 = 6 + 2 = 8 \neq 6$
so the left and right sides are not equal.
Therefore, either 6 cm or $\frac{4+20}{4} + 2$ cm must be **incorrect**.

Page 247 Exercise 3

1 a)

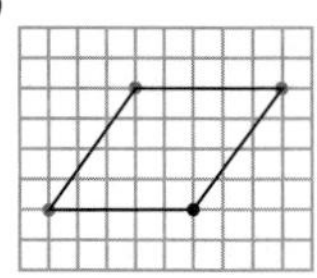

b) **E.g.**

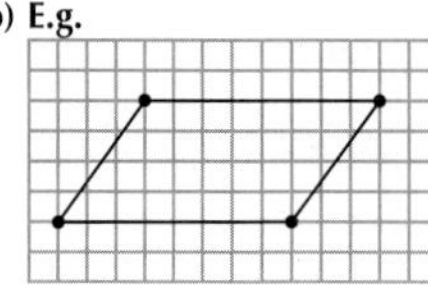

2 a) d and $118°$ are opposite angles so $d = 118°$
$118°$ and e are neighbouring angles so $118° + e = 180° \Rightarrow e = 180° - 118°$
$\Rightarrow \boldsymbol{e = 62°}$

b) f and $51°$ are opposite angles so $\boldsymbol{f = 51°}$
$51°$ and g are neighbouring angles so $51° + g = 180° \Rightarrow g = 180° - 51°$
$\Rightarrow \boldsymbol{g = 129°}$

c) $108°$ and a are neighbouring angles so $108° + a = 180° \Rightarrow a = 180° - 108°$
$\Rightarrow \boldsymbol{a = 72°}$
b and a are opposite angles so $\boldsymbol{b = 72°}$
c and $108°$ are opposite angles so $\boldsymbol{c = 108°}$

Page 248 Exercise 4

1 a) d b) Q c) S

2 a) $111°$ and b are equal angles so $\boldsymbol{b = 111°}$
$c + 111° + 48° + 111° = 360$
$\Rightarrow c + 270° = 360°$
$\Rightarrow c = 360° - 270° \Rightarrow \boldsymbol{c = 90°}$

b) The missing angle inside the kite and the angle marked $124°$ are equal angles, so the missing angle is also $124°$.
Angles in a quadrilateral add up to $360°$ so $42° + 124° + d + 124° = 360°$
$\Rightarrow 290° + d = 360°$
$\Rightarrow d = 360° - 290° \Rightarrow \boldsymbol{d = 70°}$

c) The missing angle inside the kite and the angle e are equal angles, so the missing angle equals e.
Angles in a quadrilateral add up to $360°$ so $e + 101° + e + 61° = 360°$
$\Rightarrow 2e + 162° = 360°$
$2e = 360° - 162° \Rightarrow 2e = 198°$
$\Rightarrow e = 198° \div 2 \Rightarrow \boldsymbol{e = 99°}$

Page 249 Exercise 5

1 a) **parallel** b) **two pairs** c) **one pair** d) **one pair** e) **360°**

2 a) This is an isosceles trapezium so both the base angles equal f.
$f + 124° = 180° \Rightarrow f = 180° - 124°$
$\Rightarrow \boldsymbol{f = 56°}$

b) $d + 106° = 180° \Rightarrow d = 180° - 106°$
$\Rightarrow \boldsymbol{d = 74°}$
$e + 64° = 180° \Rightarrow e = 180° - 64°$
$\Rightarrow \boldsymbol{e = 116°}$

c) This is an isosceles trapezium so $\boldsymbol{b = 120°}$
$c + 120° = 180° \Rightarrow c = 180° - 120°$
$\Rightarrow \boldsymbol{c = 60°}$

15.5 Interior and Exterior Angles

Page 251 Exercise 1

1 a) E.g.

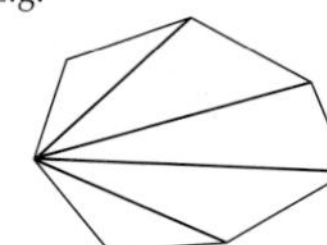

The shape can be divided into 5 triangles and each triangle's angles add up to $180°$. So the sum of the interior angles is $5 \times 180° = \mathbf{900°}$.

b) E.g.

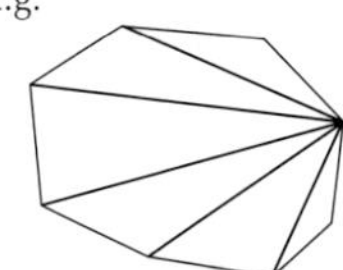

The shape can be divided into 6 triangles and each triangle's angles add up to 180°. So the sum of the interior angles is $6 \times 180° = \mathbf{1080°}$.

2 a) One triangle is partly outside the original shape.

b)

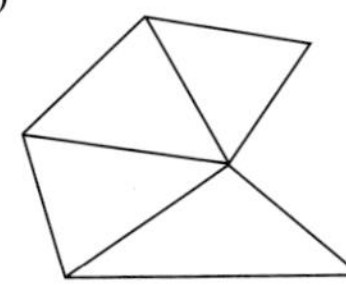

c) The shape can be divided into 4 triangles and each triangle's angles add up to 180°. So the sum of the interior angles is $4 \times 180° = \mathbf{720°}$.

d) The sum of all the interior angles is 720° from part c).
$116° + 128° + 65° + x + 39° + 107° = 720°$
$x + 455° = 720° \Rightarrow \mathbf{x = 265°}$

Page 252 Exercise 2

1 a) No — as it has 1 curved edge and all polygons only have straight edges.

b) Yes — it's a triangle.

c) No — as it's a 3D shape and all polygons are 2D.

2 Using the formula for the sum of a polygon's interior angles:

a) $n = 10$ so $S = (10 - 2) \times 180° = 8 \times 180° = \mathbf{1440°}$

b) $n = 12$ so $S = (12 - 2) \times 180° = 10 \times 180° = \mathbf{1800°}$

c) $n = 20$ so $S = (20 - 2) \times 180° = 18 \times 180° = \mathbf{3240°}$

3 a) Using the formula for the sum of a polygon's interior angles with $n = 7$, $S = (7 - 2) \times 180° = 5 \times 180° = \mathbf{900°}$

b) There are seven interior angles which are all equal due to the shape being regular. So one interior angle $= \frac{900°}{7} = 128.571...°$
$= \mathbf{128.57°}$ (2 d.p.)

4 a) Using the formula for the sum of a polygon's interior angles with $n = 8$, $S = (8 - 2) \times 180° = 6 \times 180° = 1080°$
There are eight interior angles which are all equal due to the shape being regular. So one interior angle $= \frac{1080°}{8} = \mathbf{135°}$

b) Using the formula for the sum of a polygon's interior angles with $n = 9$, $S = (9 - 2) \times 180° = 7 \times 180° = 1260°$
There are nine interior angles which are all equal due to the shape being regular. So one interior angle $= \frac{1260°}{9} = \mathbf{140°}$

5 a) (i) Using the formula for the sum of a polygon's interior angles with $n = 4$, $S = (4 - 2) \times 180° = \mathbf{360°}$
This is a quadrilateral so you already know that the angles have to sum to 360°.

(ii) $41° + 112° + 89° + a = 360°$
$a = 360° - 41° - 112° - 89°$
$\Rightarrow \mathbf{a = 118°}$

b) (i) Using the formula for the sum of a polygon's interior angles with $n = 6$, $S = (6 - 2) \times 180° = \mathbf{720°}$

(ii) $107° + 101° + b + 90° + 90° + 85° = 720°$
$b = 720° - 107° - 101° - 90° - 90° - 85° \Rightarrow \mathbf{b = 247°}$

c) (i) Using the formula for the sum of a polygon's interior angles with $n = 9$, $S = (9 - 2) \times 180° = \mathbf{1260°}$

(ii) $93° + c + 104° + 121° + 91° + 230° + 150° + 102° + 159° = 1260°$
$\Rightarrow c = 1260° - 93° - 104° - 121° - 91° - 230° - 150° - 102° - 159°$
$\Rightarrow \mathbf{c = 210°}$
Don't let the large number of angles put you off — the method is exactly the same as in parts a) and b).

Page 254 Exercise 3

1 a) $a = \frac{360°}{5} \Rightarrow \mathbf{a = 72°}$

b) $b + a = 180° \Rightarrow b + 72° = 180°$
$\Rightarrow b = 180° - 72° \Rightarrow \mathbf{b = 108°}$

2 a) (i) Exterior angle $= \frac{360°}{7} = 51.428...$
$= \mathbf{51.43°}$ (2 d.p.)

(ii) Exterior angle $= \frac{360°}{8} = \mathbf{45°}$

(iii) Exterior angle $= \frac{360°}{9} = \mathbf{40°}$

b) (i) Interior angle + 51.43° = 180°
Interior angle = 180° – 51.43°
= **128.57°** (2 d.p)

(ii) Interior angle + 45° = 180°
Interior angle = 180° – 45° = **135°**

(iii) Interior angle + 40° = 180°
Interior angle = 180° – 40° = **140°**

3 a) The exterior angles add up to 360°, so
$90° + 31° + 83° + 72° + 30° + a = 360°$
$a = 360° - 90° - 31° - 83° - 72° - 30°$
$\Rightarrow \mathbf{a = 54°}$

b) c and the angle marked 106° are on a straight line, so $c = 180° - 106° \Rightarrow \mathbf{c = 74°}$
The exterior angles add up to 360°, so
$151° + 74° + d = 360°$
$d = 360° - 151° - 74° \Rightarrow \mathbf{d = 135°}$

4 a) Call the unknown exterior angle x.
The exterior angles add up to 360°, so
$100° + 68° + 84° + 55° + x = 360°$
$x = 360° - 100° - 68° - 84° - 55° = \mathbf{53°}$

b) Call the unknown exterior angle x.
The exterior angles add up to 360°, so
$30° + 68° + 45° + 52° + 75° + 50° + x = 360°$
$x = 360° - 30° - 68° - 45° - 52° - 75° - 50° = \mathbf{40°}$

Page 254 Exercise 4

1 a) (i) $360° \div n = 90° \Rightarrow n = 360° \div 90° = \mathbf{4}$

(ii) $180° - 90° = \mathbf{90°}$

(iii) $4 \times 90° = \mathbf{360°}$

b) (i) $360° \div n = 40° \Rightarrow n = 360° \div 40° = \mathbf{9}$

(ii) $180° - 40° = \mathbf{140°}$

(iii) $9 \times 140° = \mathbf{1260°}$

c) (i) $360° \div n = 6° \Rightarrow n = 360° \div 6° = \mathbf{60}$

(ii) $180° - 6° = \mathbf{174°}$

(iii) $60 \times 174° = \mathbf{10\,440°}$

d) (i) $360° \div n = 4° \Rightarrow n = 360° \div 4° = \mathbf{90}$

(ii) $180° - 4° = \mathbf{176°}$

(iii) $90 \times 176° = \mathbf{15\,840°}$

15.6 Symmetry

Page 255 Exercise 1

1 a)

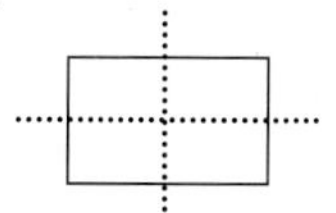

2 lines of symmetry

b)

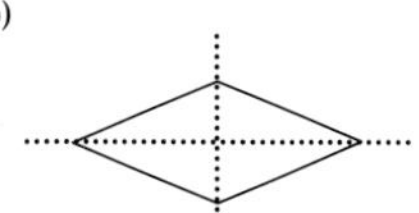

2 lines of symmetry

c)

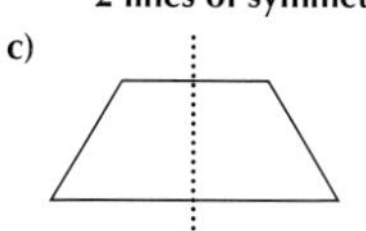

1 line of symmetry

d)

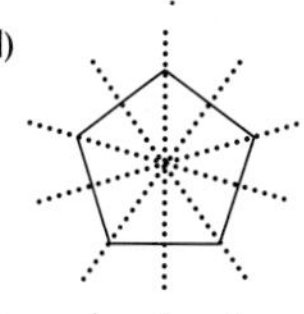

5 lines of symmetry

e)

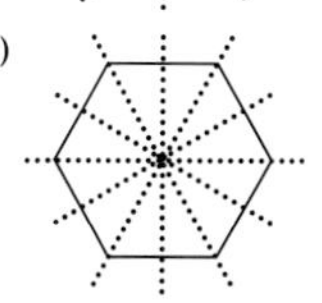

6 lines of symmetry

f)

7 lines of symmetry

2 a) 2 b) 6 c) 1 d) 3

Page 256 Review Exercise

1 a) $f + f + f + f = 180° \Rightarrow 4f = 180°$
$f = 180° \div 4 \Rightarrow \mathbf{f = 45°}$

b) $j + 31° = 90°$
$j = 90° - 31° \Rightarrow \mathbf{j = 59°}$

c) $h + 41° + 90° + 135° = 360°$
$\Rightarrow h + 266° = 360° \Rightarrow h = 360° - 266°$
$\Rightarrow \mathbf{h = 94°}$

2 If the lines AB and CD were parallel then the angles BAC and DCA would be allied. Allied angles add up to 180°, but 52° + 126° = 178°, so the lines are **not parallel**.
For this type of question, assume that the answer is yes and then see if the rules hold.

3 a) The angle that is vertically opposite to the angle labelled 58° is also corresponding with angle m, so $\mathbf{m = 58°}$

b) The top angle in the triangle is vertically opposite to 94° so it equals 94°.
Similarly the bottom-left angle is vertically opposite to 52° so it equals 52°.
Angles in a triangle sum to 180° so
$94° + p + 52° = 180° \Rightarrow p + 146° = 180°$
$\Rightarrow p = 180° - 146° \Rightarrow \mathbf{p = 34°}$

c) The triangle is an isosceles triangle so the bottom-right angle is equal to 62°.
Angles in a triangle sum to 180° so
$62° + p + 62° = 180° \Rightarrow p + 124° = 180°$
$\Rightarrow p = 180° - 124° \Rightarrow \mathbf{p = 56°}$
The bottom-right angle and q lie on a straight line so they must add up to 180°.
$62° + q = 180° \Rightarrow q = 180° - 62°$
$\Rightarrow \mathbf{q = 118°}$

d) Call the top-left angle in the triangle l.
The 90° angle, 35° angle and l lie on a straight line, so they must add up to 180°.
$90° + 35° + l = 180° \Rightarrow 125° + l = 180°$
$\Rightarrow l = 180° - 125° \Rightarrow l = 55°$
Angles in a triangle add up to 180°, so
$55° + b + 55° = 180° \Rightarrow b + 110° = 180°$
$\Rightarrow b = 180° - 110° \Rightarrow \mathbf{b = 70°}$

e) The triangle is an isosceles triangle, so the top-right angle is equal to c.
Angles in a triangle add up to 180°, so
$48° + c + c = 180° \Rightarrow 48° + 2c = 180°$
$\Rightarrow 2c = 180° - 48° = 132°$
$\Rightarrow c = 132° \div 2 \Rightarrow \mathbf{c = 66°}$
As the top-right angle is equal to c, it must equal 66°.
Angles around a point add up to 360°, so
$66° + d = 360° \Rightarrow d = 360° - 66°$
$\Rightarrow \mathbf{d = 294°}$

4 a) **Parallelogram** **b)** **Rectangle**
c) **Kite** **d)** **Trapezium**

5 Angles in a quadrilateral add up to 360°, so
40° + 83° + 99° + (fourth angle) = 360°
222° + (fourth angle) = 360°
fourth angle = 360° – 222°
fourth angle = **138°**

6 a) a and the angle labelled 122° add up to 180°.
$a + 122° = 180° \Rightarrow a = 180° - 122°$
$\Rightarrow \mathbf{a = 58°}$
As this is an isosceles trapezium,
$\mathbf{b = a = 58°}$

b) Using the symmetry of the kite, $\mathbf{s = 103°}$.
Angles in a quadrilateral add up to 360°, so
$103° + 95° + 103° + t = 360°$
$\Rightarrow 301° + t = 360°$
$\Rightarrow t = 360° - 301° \Rightarrow \mathbf{t = 59°}$

c) The angles 74°, e and 40° lie on a straight line, so $74° + e + 40° = 180°$
$\Rightarrow e + 114° = 180°$
$\Rightarrow e = 180° - 114° \Rightarrow \mathbf{e = 66°}$
Opposite angles in a parallelogram are equal, so $\mathbf{f = 66°}$
Neighbouring angles always add up to 180°, so $66° + g = 180° \Rightarrow g = 180° - 66°$
$\Rightarrow \mathbf{g = 114°}$
As g and h are opposite, $\mathbf{h = 114°}$ as well.

7 a) Using the symmetry of the kite, $\mathbf{a = 105°}$.

b) Angles around a point add up to 360°, so
$105° + b + 90° = 360° \Rightarrow b + 195° = 360°$
$\Rightarrow b = 360° - 195° \Rightarrow \mathbf{b = 165°}$
Call the bottom angle in the kite m.
c is made up of a right angle and m.
As angles in a quadrilateral add up to 360°,
$94° + 105° + m + 105° = 360°$
$\Rightarrow m + 304° = 360°$
$\Rightarrow m = 360° - 304° \Rightarrow m = 56°$
So $c = 56° + 90° \Rightarrow \mathbf{c = 146°}$

8 a) Using the formula,
$S = (6 - 2) \times 180° = 4 \times 180° = \mathbf{720°}$

b) So summing up the internal angles must give 720°.
$x + 130° + 130° + 130° + 130° + 130° = 720°$
$x + 650° = 720° \Rightarrow x = 720° - 650°$
$\Rightarrow \mathbf{x = 70°}$

9 a) Since the polygon is regular you can use the formula, $360° \div n = 45°$
$\Rightarrow n = 360° \div 45° = \mathbf{8}$
This is an **octagon**.

b)

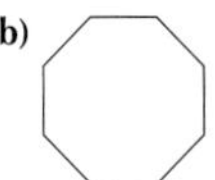

c) Interior angle = 180° – 45° = **135°**

d) 8 × 135° = **1080°**
You could also use the formula to get (8 – 2) × 180° = 1080°.

10 a) B **b)** A **c)** D **d)** C

Page 258 Exam-Style Questions

1 Angles on a straight line add up to 180°, so
$3h + h = 180°$ *[1 mark]*
$4h = 180° \Rightarrow h = 180° \div 4 \Rightarrow \mathbf{h = 45°}$
[1 mark]

2 g and the angle labelled 134° lie on a straight line, so $g + 134° = 180°$
$\Rightarrow \mathbf{g} = 180° - 134° = \mathbf{46°}$ *[1 mark]*
Angles in a quadrilateral add up to 360°, so
$55° + 46° + 29° + h = 360°$
$\Rightarrow 130° + h = 360°$
$\Rightarrow \mathbf{h} = 360° - 130° = \mathbf{230°}$ *[1 mark]*
Angles around a point add up to 360°, so
$230° + i = 360°$
$\Rightarrow \mathbf{i} = 360° - 230° = \mathbf{130°}$ *[1 mark]*

3 a) **56°** *[1 mark]*
This is because angle EBC and angle BFG are corresponding.

b) E.g. As angle EBC and angle FBC lie on a straight line, they must add up to 180°, so 56° + (angle FBC) = 180°
angle FBC = 180° – 56° = 124° *[1 mark]*
Angle FBC and angle DCG are corresponding, so **angle DCG = 124°** *[1 mark]*.
You'll still get the marks if you used a different method, as long as you explain each step and get the correct answer. For example, you could have used the fact that angles BFG and FGC are allied, so FGC = 180° – 56° = 124°. Then FGC and DCG are alternate angles, meaning DCG is also 124°.

4 Angles around a point add up to 360°, so
$w + 90° = 360°$
$w = 360° - 90° \Rightarrow \mathbf{w = 270°}$ *[1 mark]*
Using the formula for interior angles,
$S = (7 - 2) \times 180° = 5 \times 180° = 900°$ *[1 mark]*
So $90° + 90° + 270° + 90° + 97° + z + 146° = 900°$
$z + 783° = 900°$
$z = 900° - 783° \Rightarrow \mathbf{z = 117°}$ *[1 mark]*

5 Exterior angles always add up to 360°, so
$6u + 4u + 5u + 3u = 360° \Rightarrow 18u = 360°$
[1 mark]
$\Rightarrow u = 360° \div 18 \Rightarrow \mathbf{u = 20°}$ *[1 mark]*

6 As triangle ABC is equilateral, angle BCA is 60° and so angle ACE = 60° – 38° = 22° *[1 mark]*.
Triangle ACE is an isosceles so angle EAC = angle AEC
Angles in a triangle add up to 180°, so
2 × angle EAC + 22° = 180°
2 × angle EAC = 180° – 22° = 158°
angle EAC = 158° ÷ 2 = 79° *[1 mark]*.
Angle EAC and angle DAC lie on a straight line so they must add up to 180°.
79° + (angle DAC) = 180°
angle DAC = 180° – 79°, so **angle DAC = 101°**
[1 mark for a fully correct proof with all reasons included]

Section 16 — Units, Measuring and Estimating

16.1 Reading Scales

Page 260 Exercise 1

1 a) There are four divisions between the labelled marks, and the pairs of labelled marks have a difference of 4 – 2 = 2, so each division is worth 2 ÷ 4 = 0.5 cm.
A is two divisions along from 2, so 2 + (2 × 0.5) = **3 cm**.
B is two divisions along from 6, so 6 + (2 × 0.5) = **7 cm**.
C is three divisions along from 8, so 8 + (3 × 0.5) = **9.5 cm**.

b) There are ten divisions between the labelled marks, and the pairs of labelled marks have a difference of 40 – 20 = 20, so each division is worth 20 ÷ 10 = 2 cm.
A is four divisions along from 20, so 20 + (4 × 2) = **28 cm**.
B is three divisions along from 40, so 40 + (3 × 2) = **46 cm**.
C is six divisions along from 40, so 40 + (6 × 2) = **52 cm**.

2 Each division is one tenth of a centimetre, i.e. 1 millimetre, so:

a) The bug is 7 divisions long.
7 × 1 mm = **7 mm**

b) The bug is 4 divisions long.
4 × 1 mm = **4 mm**

c) The bug is 10 – 2 = 8 divisions long.
8 × 1 mm = **8 mm**
You can't see the divisions to count them because the bug is in the way, but there are two divisions left before it reaches the 1 cm mark.

3 a) There are four divisions between the labelled marks, and the pairs of labelled marks have a difference of 12 – 8 = 4, so each division is worth 4 ÷ 4 = 1 g.
The arrow is pointing at the mark one division more than 8, so the mass shown is 8 + 1 = **9 g**.

b) There are ten divisions between the labelled marks, and the pairs of labelled marks have a difference of 6 – 5 = 1, so each division is worth 1 ÷ 10 = 0.1 kg.
The arrow is pointing at the mark three divisions more than 5, so the mass shown is 5 + (3 × 0.1) = **5.3 kg**.

c) There are two divisions between the labelled marks, and the pairs of labelled marks have a difference of 4.4 – 4.3 = 0.1, so each division is worth 0.1 ÷ 2 = 0.05 kg. The arrow is pointing at the mark one division more than 4.3, so the mass shown is 4.3 + 0.05 = **4.35 kg**.

4 There are five divisions between the labelled marks, and the pairs of labelled marks have a difference of 200 – 100 = 100, so each division is worth 100 ÷ 5 = 20 g.
The arrow is pointing at the mark three divisions more than 100, so the mass shown is 100 + (3 × 20) = **160 g**.

5 There are five divisions between the labelled marks, and the pairs of labelled marks have a difference of 75 – 50 = 25, so each division is worth 25 ÷ 5 = 5 ml.
The liquid reaches the mark that is three divisions more than 50, so the volume shown is 50 + (3 × 5) = **65 ml**.

Page 262 Exercise 2

1 The general maximum and minimum values are '+ half a unit' and '– half a unit'.

a) This is measured to the nearest cm, so the maximum value is 10 + 0.5 = **10.5 cm**, and the minimum value is 10 – 0.5 = **9.5 cm**.
Remember — the 'real' maximum value is 10.499999.... cm, but we use 10.5 to make it easier to write down.

b) This is measured to the nearest litre, so the maximum value is 18 + 0.5 = **18.5 litres**, and the minimum value is 18 – 0.5 = **17.5 litres**.

c) This is measured to the nearest 5 litres, so the maximum value is 65 + 2.5 = **67.5 litres**, and the minimum value is 65 – 2.5 = **62.5 litres**.

d) This is measured to the nearest 2 m, so the maximum value is 20 + 1 = **21 m**, and the minimum value is 20 – 1 = **19 m**.

2 The volume is measured to the nearest 0.1 cm^3, so the maximum value is 0.1 ÷ 2 = 0.05 cm^3 more: 5.7 + 0.05 = **5.75 cm^3**

3 To be sure that the table will fit through the door, Elliot needs to check that the maximum possible width of the table is smaller than the width of the door frame. The table is measured to the nearest 2 cm, so the maximum width of the table is 95 + 1 = 96 cm.
96 cm < 96.5 cm, so **yes, Elliot can be sure that the table will fit.**

4 The scales are correct to 10 g, so the maximum and minimum values are 100 + (10 ÷ 2) = **105 g** and 100 – (10 ÷ 2) = **95 g**.

5 The maximum possible difference happens when one of their heights is the maximum value and the other is the minimum value. The maximum value is 170 + (10 ÷ 2) = 175 cm and the minimum value is 170 – (10 ÷ 2) = 165 cm, so the greatest possible difference is 175 cm – 165 cm = **10 cm**.

16.2 Converting Units — Length, Mass and Volume

Page 264 Exercise 1

1 a) The conversion factor for cm to mm is 10, and mm are smaller than cm so you need to multiply.
2 cm = 2 × 10 = **20 mm**.

b) The conversion factor for ml to cm^3 is 1, so 15 ml = **15 cm^3**.

c) The conversion factor for tonnes to kg is 1000, and kg are smaller than tonnes so you need to multiply.
2.3 tonnes = 2.3 × 1000 = **2300 kg**

2 a) The conversion factor for m to km is 1000, and km are bigger than m so you need to divide.
3400 m = 3400 ÷ 1000 = **3.4 km**.

b) The conversion factor for cm to m is 100, and m are bigger than cm so you need to divide.
50 cm = 50 ÷ 100 = **0.5 m**.

c) The conversion factor for kg to tonnes is 1000, and tonnes are bigger than kg so you need to divide.
246 kg = 246 ÷ 1000 = **0.246 tonnes**.

3 a) The conversion factor for kg to g is 1000, and g are smaller than kg so you need to multiply.
3 kg = 3 × 1000 = **3000 g**.

b) The conversion factor for mm to cm is 10, and cm are bigger than mm so you need to divide.
379 mm = 379 ÷ 10 = **37.9 cm**.

c) The conversion factor for mg into g is 1000, and g are bigger than mg so you need to divide.
22.3 mg = 22.3 ÷ 1000 = **0.0223 g**.

4 a) The conversion factor for kg into g is 1000, and grams are smaller than kg so you need to multiply.
1.2 kg = 1.2 × 1000 = **1200 g**.

b) Part a) gives the weight in g, so 1200 ÷ 30 = **40 servings**

5 a) Do the conversion for tonnes into g in two parts. The conversion factor for tonnes into kg is 1000:
0.6 tonnes = 0.6 × 1000 = 600 kg.
The conversion factor for kg into g is 1000:
600 kg = 600 × 1000 = 600 000 g.
So 0.6 tonnes = **600 000 g**.

b) Do the conversion for m into mm in two parts. The conversion factor for m into cm is 100: 62 m = 62 × 100 = 6200 cm.
The conversion factor for cm into mm is 10:
6200 cm = 6200 × 10 = 62 000 mm.
So 62 m = **62 000 mm**.

c) Do the conversion for mg into kg in two parts. The conversion factor for mg into g is 1000:
302 300 mg = 302 300 ÷ 1000 = 302.3 g.
The conversion factor for g into kg is 1000:
302.3 g = 302.3 ÷ 1000 = 0.3023 kg.
So 302 300 mg = **0.3023 kg**.

Page 264 Exercise 2

1 a) Convert 3200 ml into litres:
3200 ÷ 1000 = 3.2 litres.
Then 3.2 + 75.3 = **78.5 litres**

b) Convert 51.2 m into cm:
51.2 × 100 = 5120 cm
Then 681 + 5120 = **5801 cm**

Using the same method for c)-f):

c) **3.575 kg** d) **1395 cm**
e) **1204 kg** f) **1250 ml**

2 Convert km into m:
3.4 km = 3.4 × 1000 = 3400 m.
Then the difference is 3400 – 1800 = **1600 m**

3 Convert all of the masses into kg:
3200 g = 3200 ÷ 1000 = 3.2 kg
0.72 tonnes = 0.72 × 1000 = 720 kg
Then add the masses together:
3.2 kg + 15 kg + 720 kg + 3.2 kg = **741.4 kg**

4 Convert the weight of one person's equipment into kg:
9000 g = 9000 ÷ 1000 = 9 kg.
There are 3 people so the three lots of equipment weigh 9 × 3 = 27 kg.
1 tonne = 1 × 1000 = 1000 kg, so a quarter of a tonne is 250 kg.
The combined mass of Amirah, Trevor, Elsie and their equipment is
55.2 + 78.1 + 65.9 + 27 = 226.2 kg,
so **they will be safe**.

Page 265 Exercise 3

1 Convert 2 tonnes into kg:
2 tonnes = 2 × 1000 = 2000 kg
He uses 250 kg each day, so it will last 2000 ÷ 250 = **8 days**

2 Convert the distances in m into km:
1500 m = 1500 ÷ 1000 = 1.5 km
100 m = 100 ÷ 1000 = 0.1 km
So the total of the runs is 1.5 + 0.1 + 13.2 = **14.8 km**

3 The cafe uses two slices of ham per sandwich, so they use 2 × 10 g = 20 g per sandwich.
The total weight of the ham they need is 20 g × 500 = 10 000 g.
Convert this into kg: 10 000 ÷ 1000 = 10 kg.
So the café needs 10 ÷ 1.5 = 6.666... = **7 packs of ham**

4 a) Convert 750 000 ml into litres:
750 000 ÷ 1000 = **750 litres**

b) The reservoir will overflow when 800 000 – 600 000 = 200 000 litres of water has been added.
750 litres are added each day, so it will take 200 000 ÷ 750 = 266.66... = **267 days** (to the nearest day)

5 a) Convert all of the weights in kg:
400 g = 400 ÷ 1000 = 0.4 kg
300 g = 300 ÷ 1000 = 0.3 kg
2500 mg = 2500 ÷ 1000 = 2.5 g, and
2.5 g = 2.5 ÷ 1000 = 0.0025 kg
Adding all of the weights in kg together:
0.7 + 0.4 + 0.3 + 0.2 + 0.0025 = **1.6025 kg**

b) 1.6025 ÷ 0.2 = 8.0125, so the recipe will feed **8 people**.

16.3 Converting Units — Area and Volume

Page 267 Exercise 1

1 a) 2 km = 2 × 1000 = 2000 m and
3 km = 3 × 1000 = 3000 m
So area = 2000 × 3000 = **6 000 000 m²**

b) Area in km² = 2 × 3 = 6 km².
The conversion factor for km² to m² is 1000² = 1 000 000, and m are smaller than km so you need to multiply.
6 km² = 6 × 1 000 000 = **6 000 000 m²**

2 a) The conversion factor for cm² to mm² is 10² = 100, and mm are smaller than cm so you need to multiply.
26 cm² = 26 × 100 = **2600 mm²**.

Using the same method for b) and c):

b) 10 500 cm² **c) 12 000 cm²**

d) The conversion factor for cm² to m² is 100² = 10 000, and m are bigger than cm so you need to divide.
1750 cm² = 1750 ÷ 10 000 = **0.175 m²**.

Using the same method for e) and f):

e) 85 cm² **f) 0.0027 m²**

3 Find the area of the lawn in cm²:
990 × 430 = 425 700 cm²
Convert this into m²:
425 700 cm² = 425 700 ÷ 100²
= 425 700 ÷ 10 000 = 42.57 m²
So Ali needs 42.57 ÷ 16 = 2.660... bottles, so she should buy **3 bottles of weedkiller**.

4 Convert the measurements from cm to m:
670 cm = 670 ÷ 100 = 6.7 m, and
420 cm = 420 ÷ 100 = 4.2 m
The area of the rooms are 1.7 × 3 = 5.1 m² and 6.7 × 4.2 = 28.14 m². The total area is 5.1 + 28.14 = **33.24 m²**

Page 268 Exercise 2

1 a) 1000 cm = 1000 ÷ 100 = 10 m,
400 cm = 400 ÷ 100 = 4 m and
150 cm = 150 ÷ 100 = 1.5 m, so the volume in m³ is: 10 × 4 × 1.5 = **60 m³**

b) The volume in cm³ is 1000 × 400 × 150
= 60 000 000 cm³
The conversion factor from cm³ to m³ is 100³ = 1 000 000, and m are bigger than cm so you need to divide.
60 000 000 cm³ = 60 000 000 ÷ 1 000 000
= **60 m³**

2 a) The conversion factor for km³ to m³ is 1000³, and m are smaller than km so you need to multiply.
0.001 km³ = 0.001 × 1000³
= **1 000 000 m³**.

Using the same method for b) and c):

b) 17 600 000 cm³

c) 1 200 000 000 m³

d) The conversion factor for mm³ to cm³ is 10³ and cm are bigger than mm so you need to divide.
16 000 mm³ = 16 000 ÷ 10³
= 16 000 ÷ 1000 = **16 cm³**

Using the same method for e) and f):

e) 0.00000015 km³ **f) 0.0000359 m³**

3 Volume in cm³ is: 20 × 25 × 10 = 5000 cm³.
The conversion factor for cm³ to m³ is 100³
5000 cm³ = 5000 ÷ 100³ = 0.005 m³.
So the volume of coffee powder left over is 0.005 – 0.003 = **0.002 m³**
You could also have converted the dimensions of the packet into m first.

4 The volume in cm³ is: 10.5 × 5.3 × 8.67
= 482.4855 cm³
The conversion factor for cm³ to mm³ is 10³
482.4855 cm³ = 482.4855 × 10³
= **482 485.5 mm³**

5 Volume of one brick in cm³ is: 3.2 × 3.12 × 2.8 = 27.9552 cm³.
1 m³ = 100³ cm³. 100³ ÷ 27.9552
= 35 771.5..., so
35 771 complete bricks can be made out of 1 m³ of plastic.
There's not enough plastic to make 35 772 bricks, so you have to round your answer down to 35 771.

6 a) The volume is 3 × 375 = **1125 m³**

b) Convert m³ to cm³:
The conversion factor for cm³ to m³ is 100³
1125 m³ = 1125 × 100³
= **1 125 000 000 cm³**

c) 1 125 000 000 cm³ = 1 125 000 000 ml
1 125 000 000 ml = 1 125 000 000 ÷ 1000
= **1 125 000 litres**

7 a) The conversion factor for cm³ to m³ is 100³
0.56 m³ = 0.56 × 100³ = **560 000 cm³**

b) The conversion factor for cm³ to mm³ is 10³
560 000 cm³ = 560 000 × 10³
= **560 000 000 mm³**

16.4 Metric and Imperial Units

Page 270 Exercise 1

1 a) The conversion factor for feet to inches is 12, and inches are smaller than feet so you need to multiply.
2 feet = 2 × 12 = **24 inches**

Using the same method for b) and c):

b) 4 pints **c) 72 pints**

d) The conversion factor for pounds to stone is 14, and stone are bigger than pounds so you need to divide.
56 pounds = 56 ÷ 14 = **4 stone**

Using the same method for e) and f):

e) 5 feet **f) 4 gallons**

2 a) The conversion factor for inches to cm is 2.5, and cm are smaller than inches so you need to multiply.
4 inches ≈ 4 × 2.5 = **10 cm**

b) The conversion factor for ounces to g is 28, and g are smaller than ounces so you need to multiply.
3 ounces ≈ 3 × 28 = **84 g**

c) The conversion factor for stone to g is 6400, and g are smaller than stone so you need to multiply.
10 stone ≈ 10 × 6400 = **64 000 g**

d) The conversion factor for cm to yards is 90 and cm are smaller than yards so you need to multiply.
5 yards ≈ 5 × 90 = **450 cm**

e) The conversion factor for miles to km is 1.6, and km are smaller than miles so you need to multiply.
25 miles ≈ 25 × 1.6 = **40 km**

f) The conversion factor for feet to cm is 30, and cm are smaller than feet so you need to multiply.
6 feet ≈ 6 × 30 = **180 cm**

3 a) The conversion factor for km to miles is 1.6, and miles are bigger than km so you need to divide.
8 km ≈ 8 ÷ 1.6 = **5 miles**

b) The conversion factor for pints to litres is 1.76 and litres are larger than pints so you need to divide.
100 pints ≈ 100 ÷ 1.76 = 56.818...
= **57 litres** (to the nearest litre)

c) The conversion factor for g to stones is 6400, and stones are bigger than g so you need to divide.
12 800 g ≈ 12 800 ÷ 6400 = **2 stones**

d) The conversion factor for cm to inches is 2.5 and inches are larger than cm so you need to divide.
25 cm ≈ 25 ÷ 2.5 = **10 inches**

e) The conversion factor for g to ounces is 28, and ounces are bigger than g so you need to divide.
56 g ≈ 56 ÷ 28 = **2 ounces**

f) The conversion factor for pounds to kg is 2.2 and kg are bigger than pounds so you need to divide.
16.5 pounds ≈ 16.5 ÷ 2.2 = **7.5 kg**

4 1 mile ≈ 1.6 km = 1600 m, so 1 mile is 1600 ÷ 400 = **4 laps**

5 a) The conversion factor for yards to cm is 90, and cm are smaller than yards, so you need to multiply.
18 yards ≈ 18 × 90 = **1620 cm**

b) The conversion factor for cm to m is 100, and m are bigger than cm so you need to divide.
1620 cm = 1620 ÷ 100 = **16.2 m**

6 a) The conversion factor for feet to cm is 30, and cm are smaller than feet so you need to multiply.
11 feet = 11 × 30 = 330 cm
330 cm = 330 ÷ 100 = **3.3 m**

b) The conversion factor for stones to g is 6400 and g are smaller than stones so you need to multiply.
1 stone ≈ 1 × 6400 = 6400 g
6400 g = 6400 ÷1000 = **6.4 kg**

c) The conversion factor for pints to litres is 1.76 and litres are bigger than pints so you need to divide.
16 pints ≈ 16 ÷ 1.76 = 9.090... litres
9.090... litres = 9.090... × 1000
= **9091 ml** (to the nearest ml)

Page 271 Exercise 2

1 a) 3 ft 7 in = (3 × 12) + 7 = **43 inches**

b) 12 ft 5 in = (12 × 12) + 5 = **149 inches**

c) 5 lb 2 oz = (5 × 16) + 2 = **82 ounces**

d) 280 in = 280 ÷ 12 = 23 remainder 4
= **23 feet 4 inches**

e) 72 oz = 72 ÷ 16 = 4 remainder 8
= **4 pounds 8 ounces**

f) 200 oz = 200 ÷ 16 = 12 remainder 8
= **12 pounds 8 ounces**

2 a) (i) 1904 g ≈ 1904 ÷ 28 = **68 ounces**

(ii) There are 16 ounces in 1 pound.
68 ÷ 16 = 4 remainder 4,
so 1904 g ≈ **4 pounds 4 ounces**

b) (i) 840 g = 840 ÷ 28 = **30 ounces**

(ii) There are 16 ounces in 1 pound.
30 ÷ 16 = 1 remainder 14,
so 840 g ≈ **1 pound 14 ounces**

Using the same method for c) and d):

c) (i) **175 ounces**

(ii) **10 pounds 15 ounces**

d) (i) **35 ounces**

(ii) **2 pounds 3 ounces**

For c) and d), you have to convert kg to g first.

3 a) The conversion factor for cm to inches is 2.5. 50 cm ≈ 50 ÷ 2.5 = 20 inches.
1 foot = 12 inches, and
20 ÷ 12 = 1 remainder 8,
so 50 cm ≈ **1 foot 8 inches**

Using the same method for b)-d):

b) 3 feet 6 inches **c) 6 feet 8 inches**

d) 11 feet 4 inches

In parts c) and d) you need to convert from metres to cm first.

4 Maddie: 4 foot 5 inches = (4 × 12) + 5 = 53 inches
53 inches ≈ 53 × 2.5 = 132.5 cm
Lily: 4 foot 9 inches = (4 × 12) + 9 = 57 inches
57 inches ≈ 57 × 2.5 = 142.5 cm
No, only Lily is tall enough to go on the ride.

5 1 pound 12 oz = (1 × 16) + 12 = 28 oz.
28 oz ≈ 28 × 28 = 784 g,
so **no, it will not be enough.**

6 7 stone 2 pounds = (7 × 14) + 2 = 100 pounds
11 stone 4 pounds = (11 × 14) + 4
= 158 pounds
16 stone = 16 × 14 = 224 pounds
15 stone 4 pounds = (15 × 14) + 4
= 214 pounds
10 stone 3 pounds = (10 × 14) + 3
= 143 pounds
12 stone = 12 × 14 = 168 pounds
8 stone 9 pounds = (8 × 14) + 9
= 121 pounds
13 stone 1 pounds = (13 × 14) + 1
= 183 pounds
The total sum of the weights is 1311 pounds.
The conversion factor for pounds to grams is 450, so 1311 pounds ≈ 1311 × 450
= 589 950 g
589 950 g = 589 950 ÷ 1000 = 589.95 kg
589.95 kg = 589.95 ÷ 1000 = 0.58995 tonnes
No, the total weight will not exceed the limit.

16.5 Estimating in Real Life

Page 273 Exercise 1

1 a) (i) **centimetres (or millimetres)**

(ii) **inches**

b) (i) **grams** (ii) **ounces**

c) (i) **metres** (ii) **yards (or feet)**

d) (i) **millimetres**

(ii) **inches (as a fraction)**

e) (i) **tonnes** (ii) **stone**

f) (i) **kg** (ii) **pounds**

g) (i) **km** (ii) **miles**

2 a) E.g **2.5 m** b) E.g. **2.5 m**

c) Between **1.5 and 2 m** d) E.g. **350 ml**

3 a) The height of the house is roughly 4 times the height of the man. Average height of man ≈ 1.8 m,
so height of house ≈ 1.8 × 4 = 7.2 m.
So the height of the house is between
6 m and 8 m

b) Average height of a woman is 1.6 m, so the elephant is between **2 m and 2.5 m.**

4 Estimating the man's height to be 1.8 metres, the length of the bus is between **10 m and 12 m**, and the height of bus is between **3 m and 4 m**.

5 The dinosaur is about 3 times as tall as the chicken and 7 times as long. Estimating the height and length of a chicken at around 30 cm, the dinosaur will be **about 0.9 m tall and 2.1 m long.**

6 The rhino is about 6 times as tall as the cat. Estimating the height of an average cat at around 25 cm, the rhino will be **around 1.5 m tall.**

Page 274 Review Exercise

1 a) **400 ml**

b) There are 8 divisions between the labelled marks, and the difference between the labelled marks is 50 – 10 = 40 cm^3.
So each division represents
40 ÷ 8 = 5 cm^3.
The liquid is at the level three divisions above 10, so 10 + (3 × 5) = **25 cm^3**

c) There are 4 divisions between the labelled marks, and the difference between the labelled marks is 4 – 3 = 1.
So each division represents
1 ÷ 4 = 0.25 litres
The liquid is at the level three divisions above 3, so 3 + (3 × 0.25) = **3.75 litres**

d) There are 10 divisions between the labelled marks, and the difference between the labelled marks is 100 – 50 = 50.
So each division represents
50 ÷ 10 = 5 cm^3
The liquid is at the level five divisions above 50, so 50 + (5 × 5) = **75 cm^3**

2 Maximum value is 10.6 + (0.2 ÷ 2)
= 10.6 + 0.1 = **10.7 m**
Minimum value is 10.6 – (0.2 ÷ 2)
= 10.6 – 0.1 = **10.5 m**

3 30 × 400 ml = 12 000 ml.
Conversion factor for ml to litres is 1000, and litres are bigger than ml so divide:
12 000 ml = 12 000 ÷ 1000 = 12 litres
12 ÷ 2 = 6, so she needs **6 bottles of juice.**

4 Convert all weights to kg. Conversion factor for g to kg is 1000.
450 g = 450 ÷ 1000 = 0.45 kg,
300 g = 300 ÷ 1000 = 0.3 kg
The sum of the weights of all the ingredients is: 0.45 + 0.2 + 0.3 + 0.1 = 1.05 kg,
so the mass is **0.05 kg more.**

5 a) 20 × 40 = **800 mm^2**

b) The conversion factor from mm^2 to cm^2 is 10^2 = 100, so 800 mm^2 = 800 ÷ 100
= **8 cm^2**

6 a) Convert all measurements to cm:
50 mm = 50 ÷ 10 = 5 cm,
0.17 m = 0.17 × 100 = 17 cm
Volume = 7 × 5 × 17 = **595 cm^3**

b) 7 × 20 = **140 cm^3**

c) 595 – 140 = 455 cm^3
455 cm^3 = 455 × 10^3 = **455 000 mm^3**

7 a) 3 ounces ≈ 3 × 28 = **84 g**

b) 2 gallons ≈ 2 × 4.5 = **9 litres**

Using the same method for c)-f):

c) 64 000 g **d) 450 cm**

e) 6.75 cm **f) 2.565 litres**

8 a) E.g. **4.5 m**

b) E.g. **22 cm**

c) E.g. **2 m**

d) E.g **150 ml**

Page 275 Exam-Style Questions

1 a) 625 cm = 625 ÷ 100 = **6.25 m** *[1 mark]*

b) 3.94 kg = 3.94 × 1000 = **3940 g** *[1 mark]*

2 The average height for a woman is around 1.5 m to 1.7 m. The bus is about 2.5 times the height of the woman, so an approximate height for the bus would be **3.75 m – 4.25 m.**
[2 marks available — 1 mark for an appropriate estimate for the average height of a woman, 1 mark for using this to estimate the height of the bus]

3 1.2 kg = 1.2 × 1000 = 1200 g
1200 ÷ 300 = **4 pizzas** *[1 mark]*

4 a) 7.35 litres = 7.35 × 1000 = 7350 ml
[1 mark]
7350 ÷ 250 = 29.4, so she will be able to serve **29 glasses** *[1 mark]*

b) 250 ml × 29 = 7250 ml = 7.25 litres
So there is 7.35 – 7.25 = **0.1 litres left**
[1 mark]

5 10 pounds ≈ 10 × 450 = 4500 g and
2 ounces ≈ 2 × 28 = 56 g,
so the first bag weighs 4500 + 56 = 4556 g.
2 stone ≈ 2 × 6400 = 12 800 g
The total weight of her bags is 4556 + 12 800
= 17 356 g = 17.356 kg
17.356 kg < 18 kg, so **she can take both bags on her flight.**
[3 marks available — 1 mark for converting the first bag's weight units, 1 mark for converting the second bag's weight units, 1 mark for finding their total and stating the conclusion]

6 a) 45 litres ≈ 45 ÷ 4.5 = 10 gallons
10 gallons × 55 miles/gallon = **550 miles**
[2 marks available — 1 mark for conversion between litres and gallons, 1 mark for correct answer]

b) 45 litres ≈ 10 gallons (from a))
10 gallons × £5 = **£50** *[1 mark]*

Section 17 – Speed, Density and Pressure

17.1 Speed, Distance and Time

Page 277 Exercise 1

1 a) speed = $\frac{\text{distance}}{\text{time}} = \frac{30}{2}$ = **15 km/h**

Using the same method for b)-d):

b) 20 km/h **c) 30 mph** **d) 35 mph**

2 a) speed = $\frac{\text{distance}}{\text{time}} = \frac{80}{2}$ = **40 km/h**

b) speed = $\frac{\text{distance}}{\text{time}} = \frac{50}{500}$ = **0.1 cm/s**

Using the same method for c) and d):

c) 600 mph **d) 1.25 m/s**

3 a) 1 hour = 60 minutes
30 min = 0.5 hours
speed = $\frac{10}{0.5}$ = **20 km/h**

b) 1 km = 1000 m
30 000 m = $\frac{30\,000}{1000}$ = 30 km
speed = $\frac{30}{2.5}$ = **12 km/h**

Using the same method for c) and d):

c) 3 km/h **d) 14 km/h**

Page 278 Exercise 2

1 a) distance = speed × time = 20 × 2 = **40 km**
Using the same method for b)-d):
b) 500 m c) 72 km d) 175 miles

2 a) time = $\frac{\text{distance}}{\text{speed}} = \frac{4}{2}$ = **2 hours**
Using the same method for b)-d):
b) 3 s c) 2.5 hours
d) 0.25 hours (or 15 minutes)

3 distance = speed × time = 30 × 4 = **120 miles**

4 time = $\frac{\text{distance}}{\text{speed}} = \frac{2.4}{15}$ = **0.16 s**

5 distance = 490 × 2 = **980 miles**

6 time = $\frac{\text{distance}}{\text{speed}} = \frac{5.6}{56}$ = 0.1 h
0.1 × 60 = **6 minutes**

7 15 min = $\frac{15}{60}$ = 0.25 h
distance = speed × time = 7.5 × 0.25
= **1.875 miles**

Page 279 Exercise 3

1 a) 1 km = 1000 m
50 m/s = $\frac{50}{1000}$ = 0.05 km/s
1 h = (60 × 60) s = 3600 s
0.05 × 3600 = **180 km/h**

b) 1 km = 1000 m
72 km/h = 72 × 1000 = 72 000 m/h
1 h = (60 × 60) s = 3600 s
72 000 m/h = $\frac{72\,000}{3600}$ = **20 m/s**
Using the same method for c):
c) 95.4 km/h

2 1 km = 1000 m
18 km/h = 18 × 1000 = 18 000 m/h
1 h = (60 × 60) s = 3600 s
18 000 m/h = $\frac{18\,000}{3600}$ = **5 m/s**

3 a) 1 mile ≈ 1.6 km
54 km/h ≈ $\frac{54}{1.6}$ = **33.75 mph**
Remember — ≈ means 'is approximately equal to'.

b) 1 mile ≈ 1.6 km
25 mph ≈ 25 × 1.6 = **40 km/h**

c) 1 mile ≈ 1.6 km
94.4 km/h ≈ $\frac{94.4}{1.6}$ = **59 mph**

4 100 cm = 1 m
0.5 cm/s = $\frac{0.5}{100}$ = 0.005 m/s
60 seconds = 1 minute
0.005 m/s = 0.005 × 60 = **0.3 m/min**

5 1000 m = 1 km
40 m/s = $\frac{40}{1000}$ = 0.04 km/s
1 h = 60 × 60 = 3600 s
0.04 km/s = 0.04 × 3600 = 144 km/h
1 mile ≈ 1.6 km
144 km/h ≈ $\frac{144}{1.6}$ = **90 mph**

17.2 Density, Mass and Volume

Page 281 Exercise 1

1 a) density = $\frac{\text{mass}}{\text{volume}} = \frac{20}{5}$ = **4 kg/m³**
Using the same method for b)-d):
b) 60 kg/m³ c) 250 kg/m³ d) 90 kg/m³

2 density = $\frac{\text{mass}}{\text{volume}} = \frac{1840}{0.8}$ = **2300 kg/m³**

3 **a) volume = $\frac{\text{mass}}{\text{density}}$**

b) (i) volume = $\frac{40}{8}$ = **5 m³**
(ii) volume = $\frac{750}{15}$ = **50 m³**
(iii) volume = $\frac{4\,800}{240}$ = **20 m³**

4 **a) mass = density × volume**
b) mass = 2600 × 0.4 = **1040 kg**

5 1 m³ = (100 × 100 × 100) cm³
= 1 000 000 cm³
200 cm³ = $\frac{200}{1\,000\,000}$ = 0.0002 m³
density = $\frac{\text{mass}}{\text{volume}} = \frac{0.15}{0.0002}$ = **750 kg/m³**

6 1 m³ = 1 000 000 cm³
11 500 kg/m³ = $\frac{11500}{1\,000\,000}$ = 0.0115 kg/cm³
mass = density × volume
= 0.0115 × 8 = **0.092 kg or 92 g**
You could also do this by converting the volume of the paperweight to m³ and finding the density.

7 1 m³ = 1 000 000 cm³
2.7 g/cm³ = 2.7 × 1 000 000 = 2 700 000 g/m³
1 kg = 1000 g
2 700 000 g/m³ = $\frac{2\,700\,000}{1000}$ = **2700 kg/m³**

17.3 Pressure, Force and Area

Page 283 Exercise 1

1 a) pressure = $\frac{\text{force}}{\text{area}} = \frac{27}{3}$ = **9** N/cm²
Using the same method for b)-d):
b) 25 N/m² c) 1200 N/m² d) 8 N/cm²

2 a) area = $\frac{\text{force}}{\text{pressure}} = \frac{36}{6}$ = **6 cm²**
Using the same method for b)-d):
b) 7 m² c) 4 cm² d) 3 m²

3 a) force = pressure × area = 300 × 5 = **1500 N**
b) force = pressure × area = 36 × 30 = **1080 N**

4 Area of cube face = 10 × 10 = 100 cm²
Force = pressure × area = 0.02 × 100 = **2 N**

5 a) Cube side length = $\sqrt[3]{512}$ = 8 cm
Area of cube face = 8 × 8 = **64 cm²**
b) pressure = $\frac{\text{force}}{\text{area}} = \frac{1792}{64}$ = **28 N/cm²**

6 a) Area of square face = 3 × 3 = 9 cm²
pressure = $\frac{\text{force}}{\text{area}} = \frac{45}{9}$ = **5 N/cm²**
b) E.g. 1 m² = (100 × 100) cm² = 10 000 cm²
5 N/m² = 5 × 10 000 = **50 000 N/m²**
You could also have found the area of the square face in m² (9 cm = 0.09 m) and used the formula for pressure again.

17.4 Distance-Time Graphs

Page 285 Exercise 1

1 a)

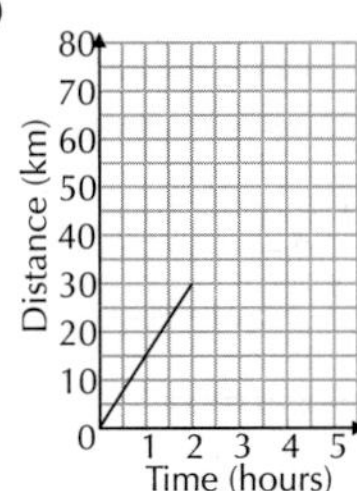

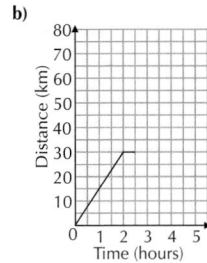

b)

c) (i) 30 + 40 = **70 km**
(ii)

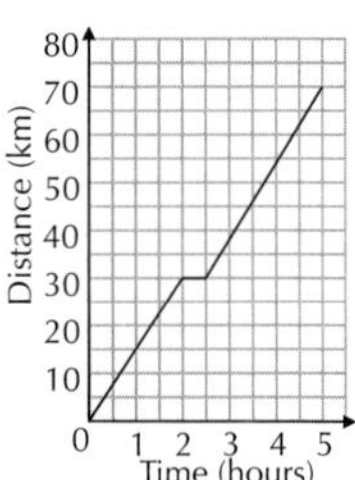

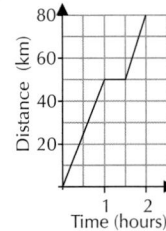

2

3

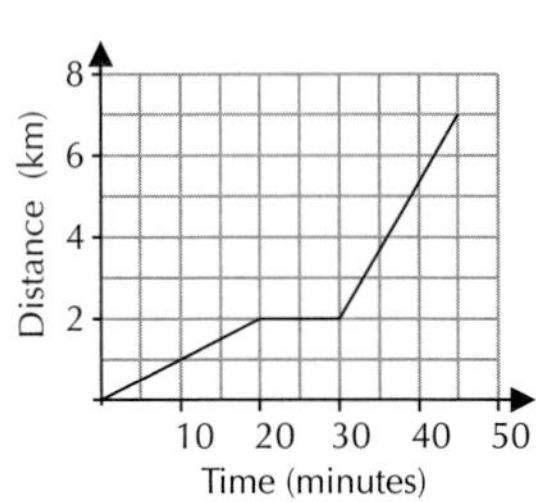

4 a) They stopped at the horizontal part of the graph, so, reading the y-axis at the point where they stopped, they travelled for **50 miles.**

b) The graph is horizontal between 1 hour and 2 hours, so they stayed at their destination for 2 – 1 = **1 hour.**

c) (i) The graph starts to decline at 2 hours, which shows they started the journey back at 8:00 am + 2 hours = **10:00 am.**
(ii) They set off after 2 hours and got back after 4 hours, so the journey home took 4 – 2 = **2 hours.**

5 a) The object travels 5 km in 2 hours. It stops for 1 hour. It then continues its journey for another hour, during which it travels a further 3 km. It then stops for 30 minutes. Finally, it travels back to its starting point in 1.5 hours.

b) The object travels 1 km in 1 hour. It then stops for 30 minutes. It then travels 0.5 km in 30 minutes before stopping again for 15 minutes. It then travels 2 km in 30 minutes and then stops for 15 minutes.

c) The object travels 35 miles in 45 minutes. It then stops for 45 minutes before it travels back towards its starting point, for 15 miles in 30 minutes. It stops for 30 minutes, and then travels away from its starting point again for 30 minutes, in which it travels for 20 miles.

Page 287 Exercise 2

1 a) distance travelled = 22.5 – 0 = 22.5 miles
time taken = 2 – 0 = 2 hours

speed = $\frac{\text{distance}}{\text{time}} = \frac{22.5}{2}$ = **11.25 mph**

b) distance travelled = 3.75 – 0 = 3.75 km
time taken = 3 – 0 = 3 hours

speed = $\frac{\text{distance}}{\text{time}} = \frac{3.75}{3}$ = **1.25 km/h**

c) distance travelled = 0 – 1 = –1 m
time taken = 5 – 0 = 5 s

speed = $\frac{\text{distance}}{\text{time}} = \frac{-1}{5}$ = –0.2, so the speed is **0.2 m/s**

The gradient is negative, which means the object is moving back towards you — but an object can't have a negative speed so you take the positive value.

2 a) **The second stage** of the journey was at a higher speed since the gradient is steeper for that part of the graph.

b) (i) Reading off the y-axis, he travelled **2 km**.

(ii) Time taken = 30 min = 0.5 hours

speed = $\frac{\text{distance}}{\text{time}} = \frac{2}{0.5}$ = **4 km/h**

c) distance travelled = 5 – 2 = 3 km
time taken = 15 min = 0.25 hours

speed = $\frac{\text{distance}}{\text{time}} = \frac{3}{0.25}$ = **12 km/h**

3 a) She was walking fastest **between 13:30 and 14:30** since between these times the gradient is steepest.

b) (i) 12:00 – 11:00 = **1 hour**

(ii) Reading from the y-axis on the graph she had travelled **3 km** before she stopped for a rest.

(iii) speed = $\frac{\text{distance}}{\text{time}} = \frac{3}{1}$ = **3 km/h**

c) Time taken = 13:00 – 12:15 = 45 min
= 0.75 hours.
Distance travelled = 4.5 – 3 = 1.5 km.

Speed = $\frac{\text{distance}}{\text{time}} = \frac{1.5}{0.75}$ = **2 km/h**

d) Time taken = 14:30 – 13:30 = 1 hour
Distance travelled = 4.5 – 0 = 4.5 km

Speed = $\frac{\text{distance}}{\text{time}} = \frac{4.5}{1}$ = **4.5 km/h**

4 a) Time = $\frac{\text{distance}}{\text{speed}} = \frac{200}{100}$ = 2 hours.
Ashna starts travelling at 10:00 so she will stop at 12:00 having travelled 200 miles. This gives the graph:

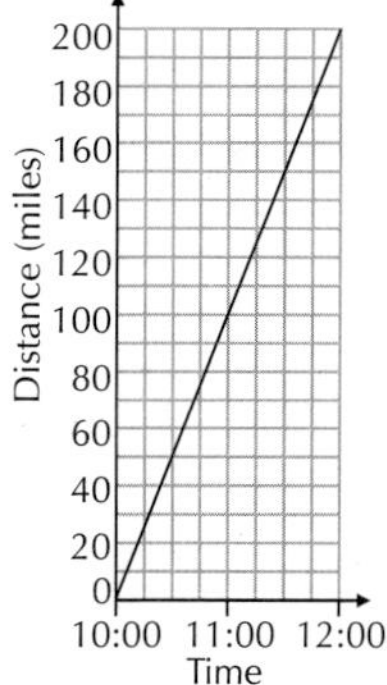

b) For the first leg of Jasper's journey,
time = $\frac{\text{distance}}{\text{speed}} = \frac{120}{40}$ = 3 hours. He sets of 9:00 so he will reach his destination at 12:00. After 1 hour, it will be 13:00 when he sets of back and it will take $\frac{120}{60}$ = 2 hours, so he will arrive back at 15:00. This gives the graph:

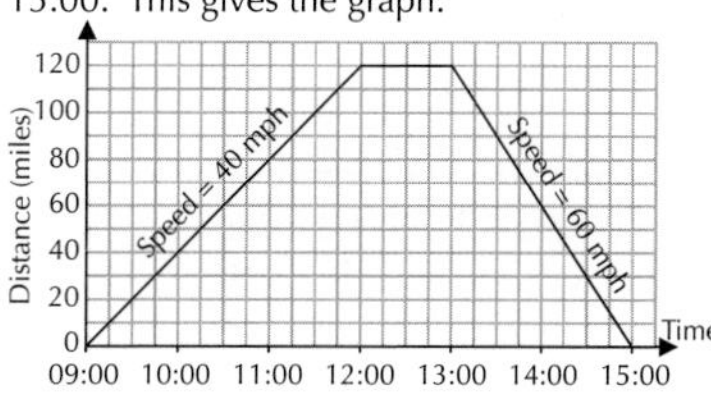

Page 288 Review Exercise

1 speed = $\frac{\text{distance}}{\text{time}} = \frac{10}{2.5}$ = **4 m/s**

2 a) 15 minutes = 0.25 hours

$\frac{13.5}{0.25}$ = **54 km/h**

b) 1 km = 1000 m
54 km/h = 54 × 1000 = 54 000 m/h
1 hour = (60 × 60) s = 3600 s
54 000 m/h = $\frac{54\,000}{3\,600}$ = **15 m/s**

3 a) density = $\frac{\text{mass}}{\text{volume}} = \frac{2500}{50}$ = **50 kg/m³**

b) 1 kg = 1000 g
50 kg/m³ = 50 000 g/m³
1 m³ = (100 × 100 × 100) cm³
= 1 000 000 cm³

50 000 g/m³ = $\frac{50\,000}{1\,000\,000}$ = **0.05 g/cm³**

4 a) pressure = $\frac{\text{force}}{\text{area}} = \frac{4800}{4}$ = **1200 N/m²**

b) area = $\frac{\text{force}}{\text{pressure}} = \frac{540}{180}$ = **3 m²**

c) force = pressure × area
= 28 × 14 = **392 N**

5 a) i) Helena was on the bus between 8:00 and 9:00 so time = 1 hour, distance = 40 km

speed = $\frac{\text{distance}}{\text{time}} = \frac{40}{1}$ = **40 km/h**

ii) Helena was on the train for 1.5 hours, distance = 90 – 40 = 50 km

speed = $\frac{\text{distance}}{\text{time}} = \frac{50}{1.5}$ = **33.3 km/h** (to 1 d.p.)

b)

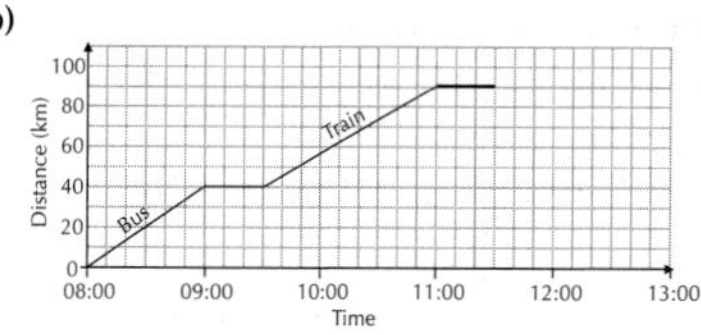

c) Helena is 90 km from home and she travels at 60 km/h

time = $\frac{\text{distance}}{\text{speed}} = \frac{90}{60}$ = **1.5 hours**

d)

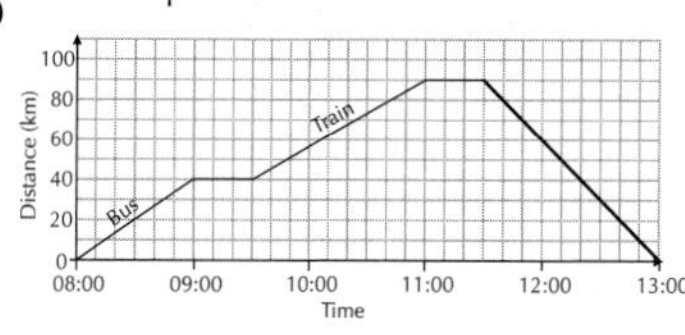

Page 289 Exam-Style Questions

1 a) Tash runs 10 km in 2.5 hours. *[1 mark]*
She stops to rest for 1.5 hours. *[1 mark]*
She then returns to her starting point in 2 hours. *[1 mark]*

b) The gradient of the graph represents Tash's speed *[1 mark]*

c) Find the total distance and time and then use the formula speed = $\frac{\text{distance}}{\text{time}}$ to calculate the speed.
distance = 0 – 10 = –10 km
time = 6 – 4 = 2 hours
speed = $\frac{-10}{2}$ = **5 km/h**
[2 marks available — 1 mark for finding the distance travelled and time taken and 1 mark for finding the speed in km/h]
The gradient is negative so the object is moving back towards you — but an object can't have a negative speed so you take the positive value.

2 time = $\frac{\text{distance}}{\text{speed}} = \frac{60}{24}$
= 2.5 hours (2 hours 30 minutes) *[1 mark]*
11:10 – 2.5 hours = **8:40 am** *[1 mark]*

3 Volume of cube = 5 × 5 × 5 = 125 cm³ *[1 mark]*
mass = density × volume = 8 × 125
= 1000 g = **1 kg** *[1 mark]*

4 1 m² = (100 × 100) cm² = 10 000 cm² *[1 mark]*
40 000 cm² = $\frac{40\,000}{10\,000}$ = 4 m² *[1 mark]*
force = pressure × area = 625 × 4 = **2500 N** *[1 mark]*

5 1 km = 1000 m
4 min 45 s = (4 × 60) + 45 = 285 s,
speed = $\frac{\text{distance}}{\text{time}} = \frac{1000}{285}$
= 3.508... m/s *[1 mark]*

time = $\frac{\text{distance}}{\text{speed}}$

$\frac{800}{3.508...}$ = 228 s *[1 marks]*
= **3 minutes 48 seconds** *[1 mark]*

6 density = $\frac{\text{mass}}{\text{volume}}$
⇒ mass = density × volume
Mass of copper = 9 × 36 = 324 g
Mass of tin = 4 × 7 = 28 g *[1 mark for both]*
Total mass = 324 + 28 = **352 g** *[1 mark]*

Section 18 – Scale Drawings and Bearings

18.1 Scale Drawings

Page 291 Exercise 1

1 a) The scale is 1 cm:2 km, so to convert from cm on the map to km in real life, multiply by 2.
(i) 4 × 2 = **8 km**
(ii) 22 × 2 = **44 km**
(iii) 0.5 × 2 = **1 km**
(iv) 0.25 × 2 = **0.5 km**

b) The scale is 1 cm:2 km, so to convert from km in real life to cm on the map, divide by 2.
(i) 10 ÷ 2 = **5 cm**
(ii) 14 ÷ 2 = **7 cm**
(iii) 7 ÷ 2 = **3.5 cm**
(iv) 1.4 ÷ 2 = **0.7 cm**

2 The scale is 1 cm:100 km, so to convert from cm on the map to km in real life, multiply by 100.
a) 7 × 100 = **700 km**
b) 1.5 × 100 = **150 km**
c) 6.22 × 100 = **622 km**
d) 1 cm = 10 mm, so 43 mm
= 43 ÷ 10 = 4.3 cm
4.3 × 100 = **430 km**

3 The scale is 1 cm:50 km, so to convert from the real distance in km to cm on the map, divide by 50.
a) 150 ÷ 50 = **3 cm**
b) 600 ÷ 50 = **12 cm**
c) 1000 ÷ 50 = **20 cm**
d) 1 km = 1000 m, so 15 000 m
= 15 000 ÷ 1000 = 15 km
15 ÷ 50 = **0.3 cm**

4 The distances give a scale of 11 cm:440 km. Divide both sides by 11 to get 1 cm on the LHS: **1 cm:40 km**

5 a) The measurements give a scale of 4 cm:12 km.
Divide both sides by 4 to get 1 cm on the LHS: **1 cm:3 km**

b) The scale is 1 cm:3 km, so to convert from cm on the map to km in real life, multiply by 3.
7 × 3 = **21 km**

6 The scale is 1 cm:0.5 m, so to convert from m in real life to cm on the diagram, divide by 0.5.
Dividing by 0.5 is the same as multiplying by 2.
a) 4 ÷ 0.5 = **8 cm**
b) 18 ÷ 0.5 = **36 cm**
c) 21 ÷ 0.5 = **42 cm**
d) 1 m = 100 cm, so
1180 cm = 1180 ÷ 100 = 11.8 m
11.8 ÷ 0.5 = **23.6 cm**

7 The scale is 1 mm:3 cm. The left-hand side is in mm, so the measurements you make should be in mm too. Multiply by 3 to find the real-life measurements in cm.

a) The measurements from the diagram for the sink are:
Width = 19 mm, Height = 10 mm, so multiplying by 3 gives:
Width = 19 × 3 = **57 cm**,
Height = 10 × 3 = **30 cm**

b) The measurements from the diagram for the hob are:
Width = 22 mm, Height = 15 mm, so multiplying by 3 gives:
Width = 22 × 3 = **66 cm**,
Height = 115 × 3 = **45 cm**

Page 292 Exercise 2

1 a) The map distances are in cm, so write the scale as 1 cm:350 cm. To convert from distances on the map to real life, multiply by 350. Then convert to m.
(i) 2 × 350 = 700 cm
100 cm = 1 m, so 700 cm = **7 m**
(ii) 7 × 350 = 2450 cm
2450 ÷ 100 = **24.5 m**
Using the same method for (iii)-(iv):
(iii) 34.65 m **(iv) 89.95 m**

b) To convert from distances in real life to distances on the map, divide by 350.
(i) 700 ÷ 350 = **2 cm**
(ii) 875 ÷ 350 = **2.5 cm**
(iii) 945 ÷ 350 = **2.7 cm**
(iv) 1.47 m = 1.47 × 100 = 147 cm
147 ÷ 350 = **0.42 cm**

2 The map distances are in cm, so write the scale as 1 cm:75 cm. To convert from distances on the plan to real life, multiply by 75. Then convert to m.
a) 4 × 75 = 300 cm = **3 m**
b) 11 × 75 = 825 cm = **8.25 m**
c) 7.9 × 75 = 592.5 cm = **5.925 m**
d) 17.2 × 75 = 1290 cm = **12.9 m**

3 The actual distances are in m, so write the scale as 1:1000 = 1 m:1000 m. To convert from distances in real life to distances on the map, divide by 1000. Then convert to cm.
a) 300 ÷ 1000 = 0.3 m = **30 cm**
b) 1400 ÷ 1000 = 1.4 m = **140 cm**
c) 120 ÷ 1000 = 0.12 m = **12 cm**
d) 1 km = 1000 m, so 0.43 km
= 0.43 × 1000 = 430 m
430 ÷ 1000 = 0.43 m = **43 cm**
You could write the scale as 1 cm:1000 cm = 1 cm:10 m. Then divide by 10 to convert the real-life distances in m directly to cm.

4 The toy measurements are in cm, so write the scale as 1 cm:40 cm. To convert from the toy measurements to actual furniture measurements, multiply by 40. Then convert to m.
a) 3.5 × 40 = 140 cm = **1.4 m**
b) 3.2 × 40 = 128 cm = **1.28 m**
c) 2.4 × 40 = 96 cm = **0.96 m**

5 You've got a big number on the RHS of the scale, so write the scale in cm, and then convert the units on the RHS.
1:250 000 = 1 cm:250 000 cm
= 1 cm:2500 m
= 1 cm:2.5 km
To convert from distances in real life to distances on the map, divide by 2.5:
6.7 ÷ 2.5 = **2.68 cm**
Starting with cm on both sides of the scale and then converting the units on the RHS makes the calculation a lot nicer — if you used 1 km:250 000 km you'd get the map distance as 0.0000268 km, which you'd then need to convert to cm.

6 The actual distances are in m, so write the scale as 1 m:500 m.
To convert from actual measurements to model measurements, divide by 500. Then convert to cm.
a) 20 ÷ 500 = 0.04 m = **4 cm**
b) 30 ÷ 500 = 0.06 m = **6 cm**
c) 100 ÷ 500 = 0.2 m = **20 cm**
d) 6 ÷ 500 = 0.012 m = **1.2 cm**
You could write the scale as 1 cm:500 cm = 1 cm:5 m and then divide by 5 to convert the actual measurements directly into model measurements in cm.

7 a) The measurements give a scale of 3 cm:18 m.
Divide both sides by 3 to get 1 cm on the LHS: **1 cm:6 m**
b) Using the scale from a),
actual width = 1.2 × 6 = **7.2 m**
c) Using the scale from a),
plan length = 4.5 ÷ 6 = **0.75 cm**

8 a) The measurements give a scale of 3 cm:4.5 km.
Divide both sides by 3 to get 1 cm on the LHS: **1 cm:1.5 km**
b) Convert the RHS of the ratio to cm so both sides have the same units, and then remove the units:
1 km = 1000 m = (100 × 1000) cm
= 100 000 cm
1.5 km = 1.5 × 100 000 = 150 000 cm
So the scale is 1 cm:150 000 cm
= **1:150 000**

9 1:120 000 = 1 cm:120 000 cm
= 1 cm:1200 m
= 1 cm:1.2 km
To convert cm on the map to km in real life, multiply by 1.2.
a) The museum to the cathedral measures 1 cm
1 × 1.2 = **1.2 km**
You may have a slightly different measurement — any answer between 1.08 km and 1.32 km is fine.
b) Art gallery to theatre measures 2.5 cm
2.5 × 1.2 = **3 km**
Any answer between 2.88 km and 3.12 km is fine.
c) Cathedral to park measures 2.2 cm
2.2 × 1.2 = **2.64 km**
Any answer between 2.52 km and 2.76 km is fine.

Page 294 Exercise 3

For this exercise, use a ruler to make sure that your drawings have the correct measurements.

1 1 : 50 = 1 cm : 50 cm = 1 cm : 0.5 m
So to convert from metres in real life to cm on the plan, divide by 0.5:
1.5 ÷ 0.5 = 3 cm   6.5 ÷ 0.5 = 13 cm
9.5 ÷ 0.5 = 19 cm   2.5 ÷ 0.5 = 5 cm

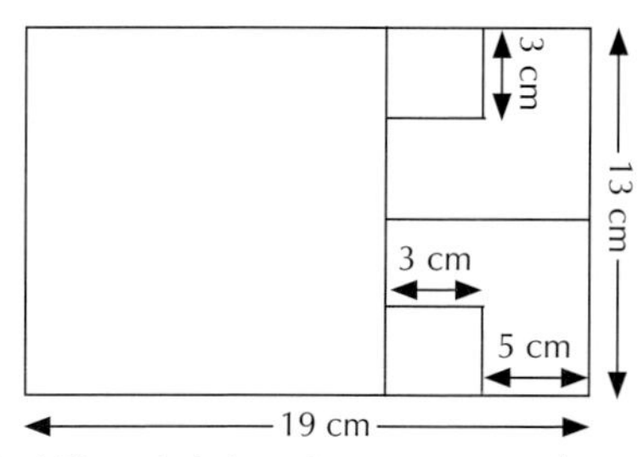

2 a) The scale is 1 cm : 3 m, so to convert from metres in real life to cm on the plan, divide by 3:
33 ÷ 3 = 11 cm, 24 ÷ 3 = 8 cm
42 ÷ 3 = 14 cm, 7.5 ÷ 3 = 2.5 cm

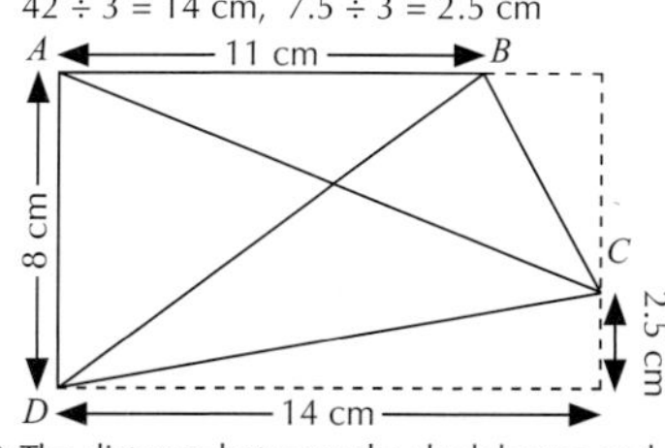

b) The distance between the duck house and *B* measures about 48 mm = 4.8 cm. To convert from cm on the plan to metres in real life, multiply by 3:
4.8 × 3 = **14.4 m**
You might have a slightly different measurement for the distance between the duck house and B — any answer between 13.8 m and 14.7 m is fine.

18.2 Bearings

Page 295 Exercise 1

1 a) East is 90° clockwise from North so the bearing is **090°**.
b) Northeast is 45° clockwise from North so the bearing is **045°**.
c) South is 180° clockwise from North so the bearing is **180°**.
d) Northwest is 45° anti-clockwise from North so the bearing is 360°– 45° = **315°**.
Remember — the bearing is always the clockwise angle.

2 a) **062°**   b) 47° + 180° = **227°**
c) 31° + 270° = **301°**   d) 180° – 67° = **113°**

3 East is 90° clockwise from North, so the bearing is 90° – 25° = **065°**

4 a) 111° – 90° = **21°**   b) 203° – 180° = **23°**
c) 243° – 180° = **63°**   d) 270° – 222° = **48°**

5

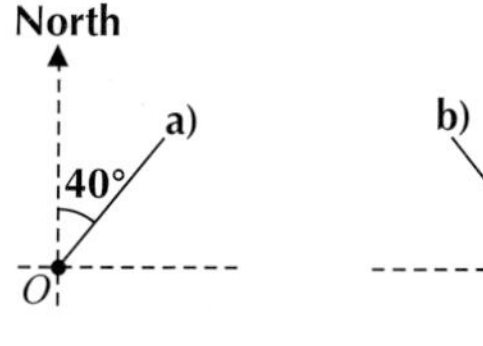

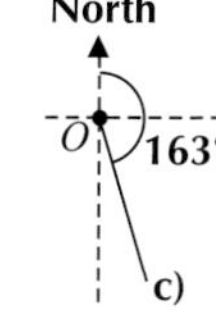

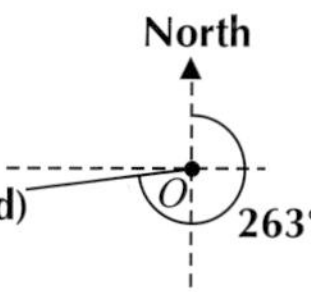

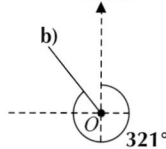

Page 297 Exercise 2

1 a) The angle you need to find is labelled z in the diagram below.

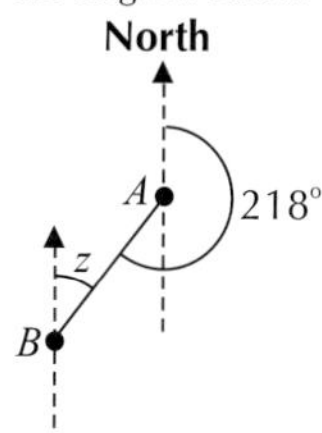

Using alternate angles, z is equal to 218° – 180° = 38°.
So the bearing is **038°**.

b) The angle you need to find is labelled z in the diagram below.

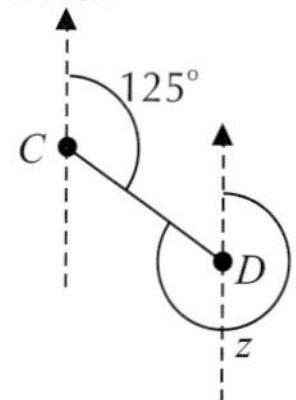

Using alternate angles, z is equal to 125° + 180° = 305°.
So the bearing is **305°**.

c) The angle you need to find is labelled z in the diagram below.

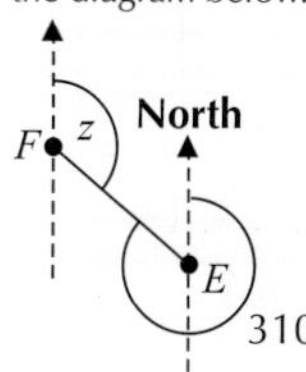

Using alternate angles, z is equal to 310° – 180° = 130°.
So the bearing is **130°**.

2 a) 200° – 180° = **020°**
b) 330° – 180° = **150°**
c) 117° + 180° = **297°**
d) 15° + 180° = **195°**
If you're unsure if you should add or subtract 180°, draw a diagram to check.

3 a) **32°**
An answer between 31° and 33° is okay.
b) Using alternate angles, the angle clockwise from a north line at *S* to the line *RS* is also 32°. So the bearing is **032°**.

4 a) Bearing of *Z* from *Y* = 90° + 45° = **135°**
b) The bearing of *Z* from *Y* is less than 180°, so add 180° to it to find the bearing of *Y* from *Z*:
135° + 180° = **315°**

5 a) **055°**
b) 55° + 88° = **143°**
c) 360° – 34° = **326°**
d) 55° + 180° = **235°**
The bearing of B from A is 055°, as you found in part a). This is less than 180°, so you add it to 180° to find the bearing of A from B.
e) 143° + 180° = **323°**
143° is the bearing of C from A, which you worked out in part b) — this is less than 180°, so you add it to 180° to find the bearing of A from C.
f) Bearing of *D* from *A*
= 55° + 88° + 101° = 244°
So bearing of *A* from *D* is
244° – 180° = **064°**.
Since the bearing of D from A is greater than 180°, you subtract 180° from it to find the bearing of A from D.

Page 298 Exercise 3

1 a) The scale is 1 cm : 100 km, so to convert from distances on the map to real life, multiply by 100.
(i) Bern and Stuttgart are 2.5 cm apart on the diagram.
2.5 × 100 = **250 km**
You may have a slightly different measurement — any answer between 240 km and 260 km is fine.
The angle from Bern to Stuttgart, measured clockwise from North, is 50°. So the bearing is **050°**.
Any answer between 049° and 051° is fine.
(ii) Stuttgart and Munich are 1.9 cm apart on the diagram.
1.9 × 100 = **190 km**
Any answer between 180 km and 200 km is fine.
The angle from Stuttgart to Munich, measured clockwise from North, measures 125° so the bearing is **125°**.
Any answer between 124° and 126° is fine.
b) Bern and Munich are 3.5 cm apart on the diagram.
3.5 × 100 = **350 km**
You may have a slightly different measurement — any answer between 340 km and 360 km is fine.

2 The scale is 1 cm : 30 km so to convert from real-life distance in km to cm on the diagram, divide by 30.
150 ÷ 30 = 5, so the distance should be 5 cm on the diagram.

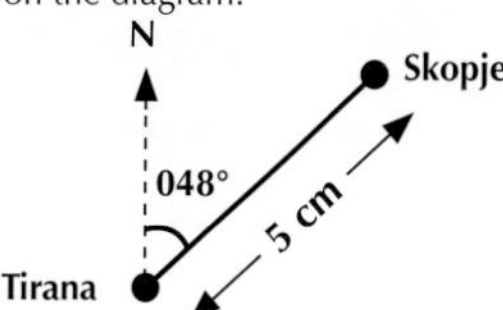

3 The scale is 1 cm : 90 km so to convert from real-life distance in km to cm on the diagram, divide by 90.
540 ÷ 90 = 6, so the distance should be 6 cm on the diagram.

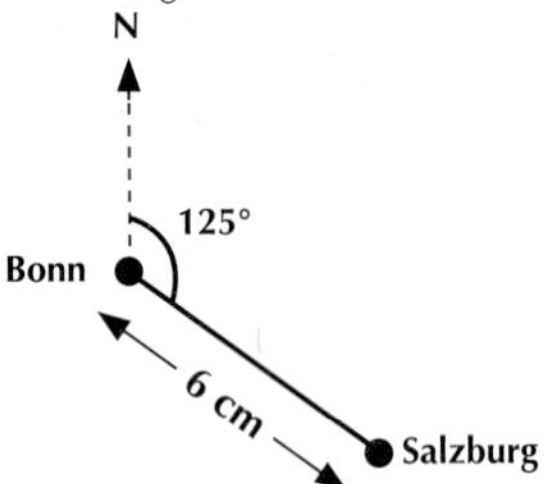

4 1 : 100 000 000 = 1 cm : 100 000 000 cm
= 1 cm : 1 000 000 m
= 1 cm : 1000 km

So to convert from distances in real life to distances on the map, divide by 1000.
2000 ÷ 1000 = 2, so the distance should be 2 cm on the diagram.

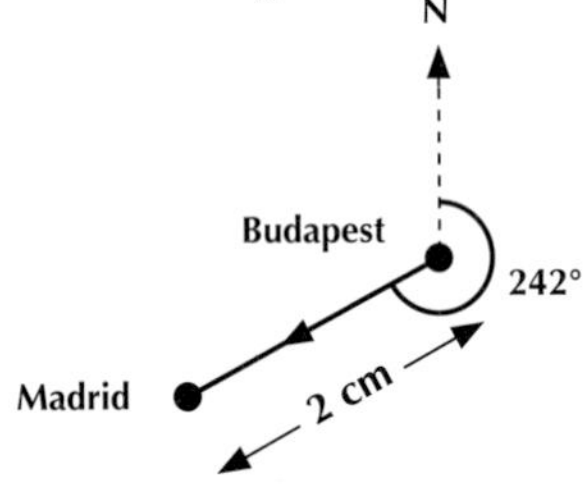

5 1 : 22 000 000 = 1 cm : 22 000 000 cm
= 1 cm : 220 000 m
= 1 cm : 220 km

So to convert from distances in real life to distances on the map, divide by 220.
880 ÷ 220 = 4, so the distance should be 4 cm on the diagram.

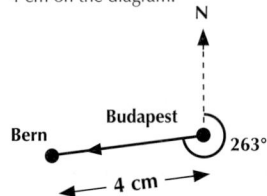

N
Budapest
Bern
263°
4 cm

6 a) 1 : 10 000 000 = 1 cm : 10 000 000 cm
= 1 cm : 100 000 m
= 1 cm : 100 km

(i) Distance PQ on the diagram measures 3 cm. The scale is 1 cm : 100 km so to convert from distances on the plan to real life, multiply by 100.
3 × 100 = **300 km**
You may have a slightly different measurement — any answer between 290 km and 310 km is fine

Using the same method for (ii) and (iii):

(ii) 450 km
Any answer between 440 km and 460 km is fine.

(iii) 580 km
Any answer between 570 km and 590 km is fine.

b) (i) 060°
You may have a slightly different measurement — any answer between 059° and 061° is fine.

(ii) 140°
Any answer between 139° and 141° is fine.

(iii) 290°
Any answer between 289° and 291° is fine.

Page 299 Review Exercise

1 The scale is 1 cm : 2 m, so to convert from cm on the map to m in real life, multiply by 2.

a) 2.7 × 2 = **5.4 m** by 1.5 × 2 = **3 m**

b) 3.2 × 2 = **6.4 m** by 2.2 × 2 = **4.4 m**

c) 1.85 × 2 = **3.7 m** by 1.4 × 2 = **2.8 m**

d) 0.9 × 2 = **1.8 m** by 1.35 × 2 = **2.7 m**

2 a) The distance AB measures 3 cm, so the scale is 3 cm : 150 m.
Divide by 3 to get 1 cm on the left-hand side: **1 cm : 50 m.**

b) (i) The distance AC measures 1.5 cm. Multiply by 50 to find the real-life distance:
1.5 × 50 = **75 m**

(ii) The distance BC measures 2.5 cm. Multiply by 50 to get the real-life distance:
2.5 × 50 = **125 m**

3 The scale is 1 : 20, so to convert measurements in real life to measurements on the plan, divide by 20.
3000 mm ÷ 20 = 150 mm = 15 cm
900 mm ÷ 20 = 45 mm = 4.5 cm
600 mm ÷ 20 = 30 mm = 3 cm
1000 mm ÷ 20 = 50 mm = 5 cm
750 mm ÷ 20 = 37.5 mm = 3.75 cm

These lengths produce the plan below. Use a ruler to check your drawing has the correct measurements.

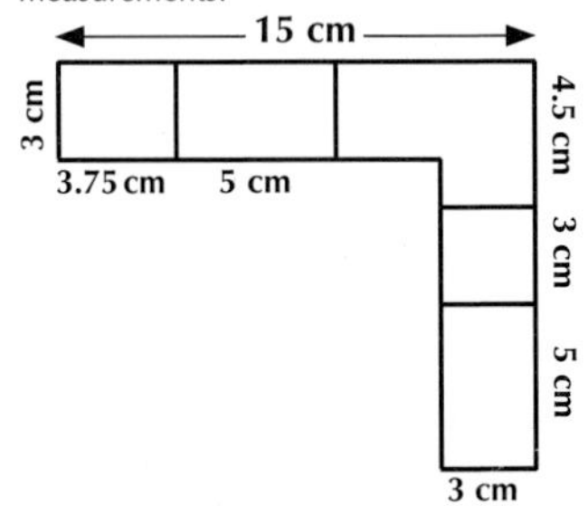

4 a) The scale is 1 cm : 100 m so to convert from the real-life distances to the scale diagram distances, divide by 100.
230 ÷ 100 = 2.3 cm
390 ÷ 100 = 3.9 cm
This will give the diagram:

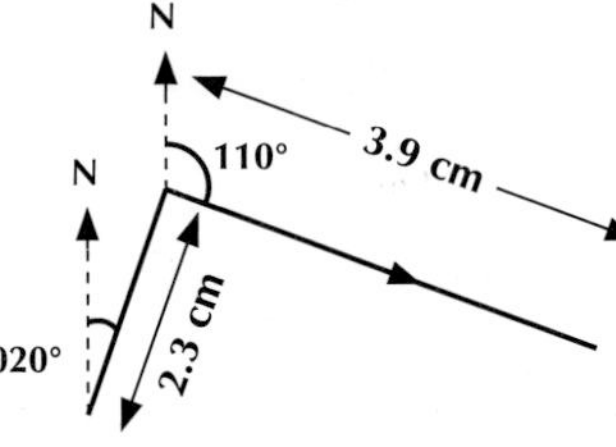

b) 110° – 20° = **90°**

5 a) Town B is south of town A so the bearing = **180°**

b) Town C is west of town B so the bearing = **270°**

c) Town C is southwest of town A so the bearing = **225°**
Draw a sketch if you're struggling to picture the towns.

6 a)

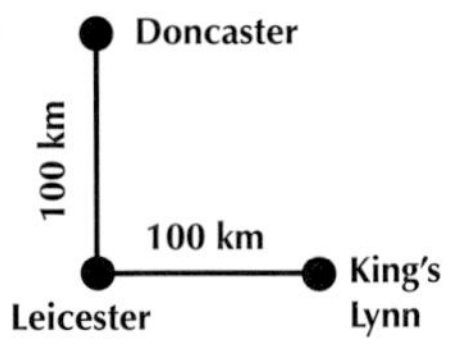

b) King's Lynn is due east of Leicester so the bearing is **090°**

c) (i) Leicester is due south of Doncaster so the bearing is **180°**

(ii) King's Lynn is due south east of Doncaster so, 90° + 45° = **135°**

d) (i) 90° + 180° = **270°**

(ii) 135° + 180° = **315°**

Page 300 Exam-Style Questions

1 1 : 25 000 = 1 cm : 25 000 cm = 1 cm : 250 m *[1 mark]*
So multiply by 250 to convert to the real-life distance: 3.8 × 250 = **950 m** *[1 mark]*

2 a) The distance from The Knott to Hartsop Village on the map is 3 cm, so the scale is 3 cm : 12 km *[1 mark]*.
Dividing both sides by 3 gives **1 cm : 4 km** *[1 mark]*.

b) The angle between North and the line between X and The Knott is 50°, measured anticlockwise.
So the bearing is 360° – 50° = **310°** *[1 mark]*.

3 a) The clockwise angle between a north line at A and the line AB is 45°, since the grid is made of squares.
So the bearing is **045°** *[1 mark]*.

b) The clockwise angle between a north line at C and the line CA is 360° – 45° (or 270° + 45°) = **315°** *[1 mark]*.

4 a) The scale is 1 cm : 500 m so to convert from real-life distances to distances on the diagram, divide by 500.
2000 ÷ 500 = 4 cm, 1500 ÷ 500 = 3 cm *[1 mark]*
This will give the diagram:

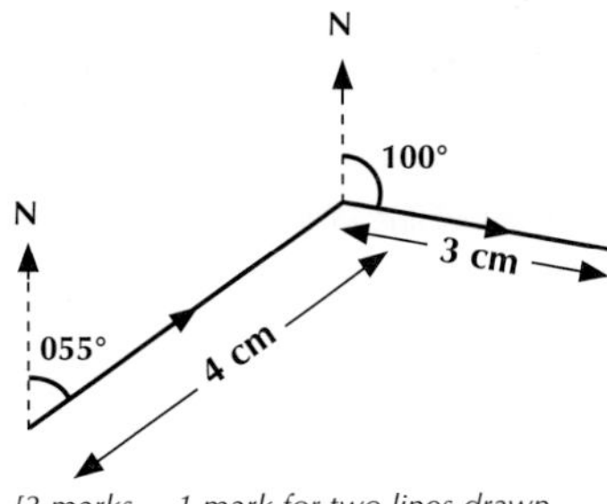

[2 marks — 1 mark for two lines drawn to the correct lengths, 1 mark for the lines drawn at the correct angles and with the bearings labelled.]

b) The distance measures 6.5 cm.
To convert cm on the map to m in real life, multiply by 500.
$6.5 \times 500 =$ **3250 m (or 3.25 km)** *[1 mark]*
You may have a slightly different measurement — any answer between 3200 m and 3300 m is okay.

c) **255°** *[1 mark]*
Any answer between 253° and 257° is fine.

Section 19 — Pythagoras and Trigonometry

19.1 Pythagoras' Theorem

Page 302 Exercise 1

1 a) $x^2 = 3^2 + 4^2 = 9 + 16 = 25$
$x = \sqrt{25} = \mathbf{5\ cm}$

b) $z^2 = 12^2 + 5^2 = 144 + 25 = 169$
$z = \sqrt{169} = \mathbf{13\ mm}$

c) $q^2 = 24^2 + 18^2 = 576 + 324 = 900$
$q = \sqrt{900} = \mathbf{30\ cm}$

Using the same method for Q2-Q6:

2 a) **22.83 m** (2 d.p.) b) **7.75 cm** (2 d.p.)
c) **1.39 m** (2 d.p.)

3 a) $\sqrt{41}$ **m** b) $\sqrt{58}$ **cm**
c) $\sqrt{29}$ **m**
Remember to leave the square roots in your answers as the question asks for the exact length.

4 **10.63 cm** (2 d.p.)

5 a) **8.60 cm** (2 d.p.) b) **11.70 cm** (2 d.p.)
c) **6.58 mm** (2 d.p.)

6 $\sqrt{1465}$ **cm**
Sketch the triangle if you're struggling to figure out which side goes where. You'll find that XZ is opposite the right angle, so it's the hypotenuse.

Page 303 Exercise 2

1 a) $13^2 = l^2 + 12^2$
$l^2 = 13^2 - 12^2$
$l^2 = 169 - 144 = 25$
$l = \sqrt{25} = \mathbf{5\ cm}$

b) $41^2 = t^2 + 9^2$
$t^2 = 41^2 - 9^2$
$t^2 = 1681 - 81 = 1600$
$t = \sqrt{1600} = \mathbf{40\ cm}$

c) $26^2 = p^2 + 10^2$
$p^2 = 26^2 - 10^2$
$p^2 = 676 - 100 = 576$
$p = \sqrt{576} = \mathbf{24\ cm}$

Using the same method for Q2-Q5:

2 a) **25.61 mm** (2 d.p.) b) **8.49 mm** (2 d.p.)
c) **14.77 km** (2 d.p.)

3 a) $\sqrt{19}$ **mm** b) $\sqrt{33}$ **cm**
c) $\sqrt{77}$ **m**

4 a) **7.94 cm** (2 d.p.) b) **11.53 m** (2 d.p.)
c) **10.53 mm** (2 d.p.) d) **14.53 cm** (2 d.p.)

5 **15.99 cm** (2 d.p.)

Page 304 Exercise 3

1 a) $9^2 + 12^2 = 81 + 144 = 225$
$15^2 = 225 = 9^2 + 12^2$ so the triangle **is right-angled**.

b) $8^2 + 7^2 = 64 + 49 = 113$
$11^2 = 121 \neq 8^2 + 7^2$ so the triangle **is not right-angled**.

2 $PS^2 = PR^2 + RS^2 = 120^2 + 180^2 = 46\,800$
$PS = \sqrt{46\,800} = \mathbf{216.33\ m}$

3 $\text{distance}^2 = 540^2 + 970^2 = 1\,232\,500$
$\text{distance} = \sqrt{1232\,500} = 1110.180... = \mathbf{1110\ m}$ (to the nearest m)
The distances run south and east form the two shorter sides of a right-angled triangle — so the final distance from the starting point is the hypotenuse of that triangle.

4 XYM is a right-angled triangle with hypotenuse XY.
Length $YM = YZ \div 2 = 9.4 \div 2 = 4.7$ cm
So $XY^2 = XM^2 + YM^2 = 3.7^2 + 4.7^2$
$= 13.69 + 22.09 = 35.78$
$XY = \sqrt{35.78} = 5.981... = \mathbf{5.98\ cm}$ (2 d.p.)

5 The ladder is the hypotenuse of a right-angled triangle, so $3.3^2 = 0.8^2 + (\text{height})^2$
$(\text{height})^2 = 3.3^2 - 0.8^2$
$(\text{height})^2 = 10.89 - 0.64 = 10.25$
$\text{height} = \sqrt{10.25} = 3.201... = \mathbf{3.20\ m}$ (2 d.p.)

6 Call the missing side of the piece of toast t.
$14^2 = 11^2 + t^2$
$t^2 = 14^2 - 11^2$
$t^2 = 196 - 121 = 75$
$t = \sqrt{75} = 8.660... = \mathbf{8.66\ cm}$ (2 d.p.)

7 a) $JL^2 = JK^2 + KL^2 = 4.9^2 + 6.8^2$
$= 24.01 + 46.24 = 70.25$
$JL = \sqrt{70.25} = 8.381... = \mathbf{8.38\ cm}$ (2 d.p.)

b) JL is the diameter of the circle, so radius $= JL \div 2 = 8.381... \div 2 = 4.190...$
$= \mathbf{4.19\ cm}$ (2 d.p.)

8 a) Difference in x-coordinates $= 6 - 2 = 4$
Difference in y-coordinates $= 10 - 3 = 7$
$AB^2 = 4^2 + 7^2 = 16 + 49 = 65$
$AB = \sqrt{65}$ **units**

b) Difference in x-coordinates $= 4 - 1 = 3$
Difference in y-coordinates $= 7 - 2 = 5$
$AB^2 = 3^2 + 5^2 = 9 + 25 = 34$
$AB = \sqrt{34}$ **units**

9 $29.2^2 = 22.4^2 + (\text{radius})^2$
$(\text{radius})^2 = 29.2^2 - 22.4^2$
$(\text{radius})^2 = 852.64 - 501.76 = 350.88$
$\text{radius} = \sqrt{350.88} = 18.731...$
$= \mathbf{18.73\ cm}$ (2 d.p.)

10 The kite's string forms the hypotenuse of a right-angled triangle with base length equal to the distance between the end of the string and the tree.
$15^2 = 8.5^2 + (\text{height})^2$
$(\text{height})^2 = 15^2 - 8.5^2$
$(\text{height})^2 = 225 - 72.25 = 152.75$
$\text{height} = \sqrt{152.75} = 12.359...$
$= \mathbf{12.36\ m}$ (2 d.p.)

11 The lines NW and NE from the same point form a right angle. Use this to sketch a diagram:

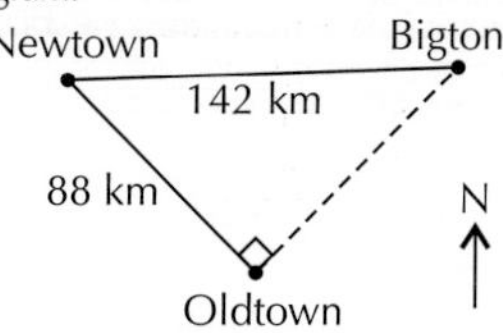

$NB^2 = ON^2 + OB^2$
$142^2 = 88^2 + OB^2$
$OB^2 = 142^2 - 88^2$
$OB^2 = 20\,164 - 7744 = 12\,420$
$OB = \sqrt{12\,420} = 111.445... =$ **111 km** (to the nearest km)
It really helps to draw a diagram for this one — it's a bit tricky to get your head around which town is where.

12 The longest stick of spaghetti that will fit in the jar will be the hypotenuse of a right-angled triangle with sides that are the height (28 cm) and full width ($6 \times 2 = 12$ cm) of the jar.
$h^2 = 28^2 + 12^2 = 784 + 144 = 928$
$h = \sqrt{928} = 30.463... = \mathbf{30.46\ cm}$ (2 d.p.)
Careful here — you need to double the radius of the jar to get the side of the right-angled triangle you need.

13 The height of the kite is the sum of the missing sides of the two right-angled triangles. One triangle has hypotenuse 0.3 m and one side measuring 0.2 m, so the missing side of that triangle (call it A) is:
$0.3^2 = 0.2^2 + A^2$
$A^2 = 0.3^2 - 0.2^2$
$A^2 = 0.09 - 0.04 = 0.05$
$A = \sqrt{0.05} = 0.223...$
The other triangle has hypotenuse 0.4 m and one side measuring 0.2 m, so the missing side of that triangle (call it B) is:
$0.4^2 = 0.2^2 + B^2$
$B^2 = 0.4^2 - 0.2^2$
$B^2 = 0.16 - 0.04 = 0.12$
$B = \sqrt{0.12} = 0.346...$
So the height of the kite is:
$0.223... + 0.346... = 0.570... = \mathbf{0.57\ m}$ (2 d.p.)

19.2 Trigonometry — Sin, Cos and Tan

Page 307 Exercise 1

1 a)

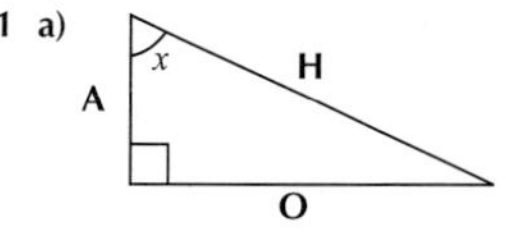

b)

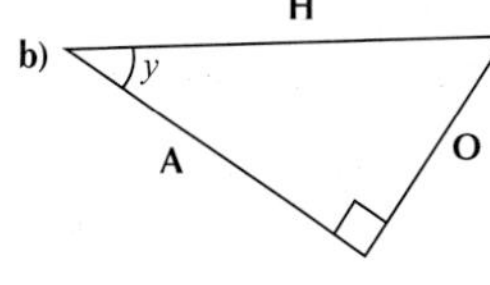

c)

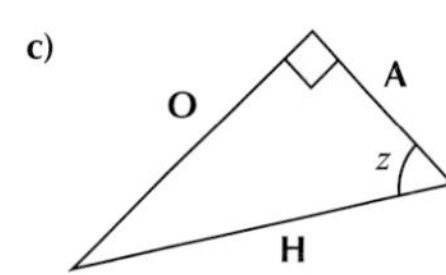

For all the trigonometry questions in this section, make sure you label the triangle first (draw your own sketch if you need to).

2 a) You know the hypotenuse and want to find the adjacent, so use the formula for cos x:
$\cos 43° = \frac{a}{6}$, so $a = 6 \cos 43° = 4.388...$
$= \mathbf{4.39\ cm}$ (3 s.f.)

b) You know the hypotenuse and want to find the opposite, so use the formula for sin x:
$\sin 58° = \frac{b}{11}$, so $b = 11 \sin 58° = 9.328...$
$= \mathbf{9.33\ cm}$ (3 s.f.)

c) You know the adjacent and want to find the opposite, so use the formula for tan x:
$\tan 12° = \frac{c}{5}$, so $c = 5 \tan 12° = 1.062...$
$= \mathbf{1.06\ cm}$ (3 s.f.)

d) You know the hypotenuse and want to find the opposite, so use the formula for sin x:
$\sin 63° = \frac{d}{9}$, so $d = 9 \sin 63° = 8.019...$
$= \mathbf{8.02\ cm}$ (3 s.f.)

3 a) You know the opposite and want to find the adjacent, so use the formula for tan x:

$\tan 37° = \frac{6}{p}$, so $p = \frac{6}{\tan 37°} = 7.962...$
$= \mathbf{7.96\ cm}$ (3 s.f.)

b) You know the opposite and want to find the hypotenuse, so use the formula for sin x:

$\sin 34° = \frac{20}{q}$, so $q = \frac{20}{\sin 34°} = 35.765...$
$= \mathbf{35.8\ cm}$ (3 s.f.)

c) You know the opposite and want to find the adjacent, so use the formula for tan x:

$\tan 48° = \frac{7}{r}$, so $r = \frac{7}{\tan 48°} = 6.302...$
$= \mathbf{6.30\ cm}$ (3 s.f.)

d) You know the adjacent and want to find the hypotenuse, so use the formula for cos x:

$\cos 11° = \frac{4.5}{s}$, so $s = \frac{4.5}{\cos 11°} = 4.584...$
$= \mathbf{4.58\ cm}$ (3 s.f.)

Page 308 Exercise 2

1 a) To find m, consider the right-angled triangle with angle $66° \div 2 = 33°$, and adjacent 10 cm. m is the hypotenuse, so use the formula for cos x:

$\cos 33° = \frac{10}{m}$, so $m = \frac{10}{\cos 33°} = 11.923...$
$= \mathbf{11.9\ cm}$ (3 s.f.)

b) To find n, consider the right-angled triangle with angle $84° \div 2 = 42°$, and opposite $14 \div 2 = 7$ cm. n is the hypotenuse, so use the formula for sin x:

$\sin 42° = \frac{7}{n}$, so $n = \frac{7}{\sin 42°} = 10.461...$
$= \mathbf{10.5\ cm}$ (3 s.f.)

2 a) p is double the length of the adjacent side of the right-angled triangle with angle 43° and hypotenuse 6 cm.
Use the formula for cos x:

$\cos 43° = \frac{\text{adj}}{6}$, so adj $= 6 \cos 43°$
$= 4.388...$

So $p = 4.388... \times 2 = 8.776...$
$= \mathbf{8.78\ cm}$ (3 s.f.)

b) q is double the length of the opposite side of the right-angled triangle with angle 51° and hypotenuse 12 cm.
Use the formula for sin x:

$\sin 51° = \frac{\text{opp}}{12}$, so opp $= 12 \sin 51°$
$= 9.325...$

So $q = 9.325... \times 2 = 18.651...$
$= \mathbf{18.7\ cm}$ (3 s.f.)

3 The third side is double the length of the opposite side of the right-angled triangle with angle $98° \div 2 = 49°$ and hypotenuse 22 cm.
Use the formula for sin x:

$\sin 49° = \frac{\text{opp}}{22}$, so opp $= 22 \sin 49°$
$= 16.603...$

So the length of the third side is
$16.603... \times 2 = 33.207... = \mathbf{33.2\ cm}$ (3 s.f.)
Sketch a diagram for this question if you're struggling to figure out which side goes where.

Page 310 Exercise 3

1 a) You know the adj and hyp, so use the formula for cos x:

$\cos a = \frac{3}{8}$, so $a = \cos^{-1}\left(\frac{3}{8}\right) = 67.975...$
$= \mathbf{68.0°}$ (1 d.p.)

b) You know the opp and hyp, so use the formula for sin x:

$\sin b = \frac{10}{14}$, so $b = \sin^{-1}\left(\frac{10}{14}\right) = 45.584...$
$= \mathbf{45.6°}$ (1 d.p.)

c) You know the opp and adj, so use the formula for tan x:

$\tan c = \frac{12}{11}$, so $c = \tan^{-1}\left(\frac{12}{11}\right) = 47.489...$
$= \mathbf{47.5°}$ (1 d.p.)

2 a) You know the adj and hyp, so use the formula for cos x:

$\cos d = \frac{2}{12}$, so $d = \cos^{-1}\left(\frac{2}{12}\right) = 80.405...$
$= \mathbf{80.4°}$ (1 d.p.)

b) You know the opp and adj so use the formula for tan x:

$\tan e = \frac{5}{7.5}$, so $e = \tan^{-1}\left(\frac{5}{7.5}\right) = 33.690...$
$= \mathbf{33.7°}$ (1 d.p.)

c) You know the opp and hyp so use the formula for sin x:

$\sin f = \frac{13}{15}$, so $f = \sin^{-1}\left(\frac{13}{15}\right) = 60.073...$
$= \mathbf{60.1°}$ (1 d.p.)

3 a) You know the opp and hyp, so use the formula for sin x:

$\sin m = \frac{8}{24}$, so $m = \sin^{-1}\left(\frac{8}{24}\right) = 19.471...$

So the angle of elevation of the slide is **19.5°** (1 d.p.).

b) Using alternate angles, q is the same as the angle opposite the ladder. You know the opp and adj so use the formula for tan x:

$\tan q = \frac{4}{5.5}$, so $q = \tan^{-1}\left(\frac{4}{5.5}\right) = 36.027...$

So the angle of depression from the top of the slide is **36.0°** (1 d.p.).

Page 311 Exercise 4

Use the exact values from the green box on p.311 to find the values of sin, cos and tan of 30°, 45°, 60° and 90° in this exercise.

1 a) The sides given are the opposite and hypotenuse,

so $\sin a = \frac{\sqrt{3}}{2}$, which means $\boldsymbol{a = 60°}$.

b) The sides given are the adjacent and hypotenuse,

so $\cos b = \frac{\sqrt{2}}{2}$, which means $\boldsymbol{b = 45°}$.

c) The sides given are the opposite and adjacent,

so $\tan c = \frac{\sqrt{3}}{1} = \sqrt{3}$, which means $\boldsymbol{c = 60°}$.

2 a) You know the opposite and want to find the adjacent, so use the formula for tan x:

$\tan 30° = \frac{1}{e}$, which means $\frac{1}{\sqrt{3}} = \frac{1}{e}$ so

$\boldsymbol{e = \sqrt{3}}$ **m**

b) You know the hypotenuse and want to find the adjacent, so use the formula for cos x:

$\cos 60° = \frac{f}{2}$, which means $\frac{1}{2} = \frac{f}{2}$ so

$\boldsymbol{f = 1}$ **cm**

c) You know the opposite and want to find the adjacent, so use the formula for tan x:

$\tan 45° = \frac{8}{g}$, which means $1 = \frac{8}{g}$ so

$\boldsymbol{g = 8}$ **mm**

3 $\tan 45° + \sin 60° =$
$1 + \frac{\sqrt{3}}{2} = \frac{2}{2} + \frac{\sqrt{3}}{2} = \boldsymbol{\frac{2 + \sqrt{3}}{2}}$

4 DEF is isosceles, and as angle DEF is 90°, the other two angles must both be 45°. DF is opposite the right angle, so is the hypotenuse. DE is opposite one of the 45° angles, so use the formula for sin x:

$\sin 45° = \frac{DE}{7\sqrt{2}}$, so $\frac{1}{\sqrt{2}} = \frac{DE}{7\sqrt{2}}$, which means

$\boldsymbol{DE = 7}$ **cm**

You could have used the cos formula here — since both the other angles are 45°, DE is also adjacent to a 45° angle. cos 45° and sin 45° are the same, so you'd have ended up with the same answer. You might want to draw a sketch for this question.

Page 312 Review Exercise

1 Difference in x-coordinates $= 7 - 1 = 6$
Difference in y-coordinates $= 8 - 3 = 5$
$PR^2 = 6^2 + 5^2 = 36 + 25 = 61$
$PR = \sqrt{61} = 7.810... = \mathbf{7.8\ units}$

2 Draw a sketch:

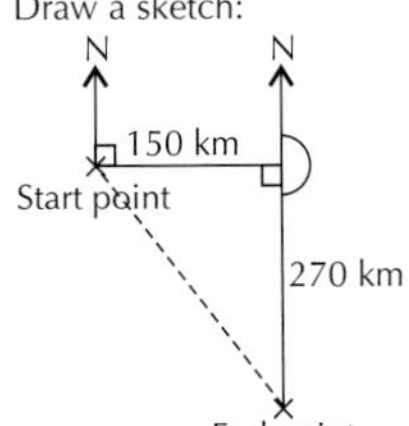

So the direct distance is the hypotenuse of the triangle with shorter sides measuring 150 km and 270 km.
$(\text{distance})^2 = 150^2 + 270^2$
$= 22\,500 + 72\,900 = 95\,400$
distance $= \sqrt{95\,400} = 308.868...$
$= \mathbf{309\ km}$ (to the nearest km)
See p295 for more on bearings.

3 a) $a^2 = 3^2 + 5^2 = 9 + 25 = 34$
$a = \sqrt{34} = 5.830... = \mathbf{5.83\ cm}$ (3 s.f.)

b) b is the opposite and you know the adjacent, so use the formula for tan x:

$\tan 32° = \frac{b}{28}$, so $b = 28 \tan 32° = 17.496...$
$= \mathbf{17.5\ cm}$ (3 s.f.)

c) c is the opposite and you know the hypotenuse, so use the formula for sin x:

$\sin 62° = \frac{c}{17}$, so $c = 17 \sin 62° = 15.010...$
$= \mathbf{15.0\ cm}$ (3 s.f.)

d) d is the hypotenuse and you know the adjacent, so use the formula for cos x:

$\cos 29° = \frac{2.1}{d}$, so $d = \frac{2.1}{\cos 29°} = 2.401...$
$= \mathbf{2.40\ m}$ (3 s.f.)

4 The ladder forms the hypotenuse of a right-angled triangle.
The 8 m side is the adjacent, and the height is the opposite, so use the formula for tan x:

$\tan 68° = \frac{h}{8}$, so $h = 8 \tan 68° = 19.800...$
$= \mathbf{19.8\ m}$ (3 s.f.)

5 The string forms the hypotenuse, and you also know the opposite, so use the formula for sin x:

$\sin x = \frac{4.1}{5.8}$, so $x = \sin^{-1}\left(\frac{4.1}{5.8}\right) = 44.982...$
$= \mathbf{45.0°}$ (1 d.p.)

Draw a sketch here if you need to.

6 Call the side common to both triangles p. Use Pythagoras' theorem to find p:
$7^2 = 1^2 + p^2$, so $p^2 = 7^2 - 1^2 = 48$, so $p = \sqrt{48}$.
You now have the hypotenuse and opposite of the left-hand triangle, so use the formula for sin x:

$\sin x = \frac{\sqrt{48}}{10}$, so $x = \sin^{-1}\left(\frac{\sqrt{48}}{10}\right) = 43.853...$
$= \mathbf{43.9°}$ (1 d.p.)

7 Draw a sketch:

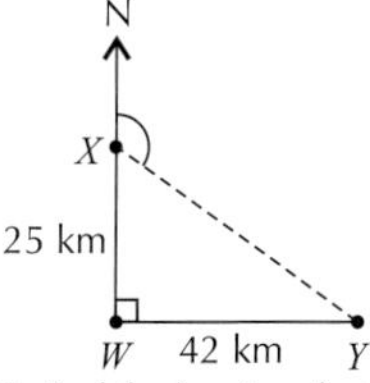

To find the bearing, first find angle WXY. You know the opposite and the adjacent, so use the formula for tan x:

$\tan WXY = \frac{42}{25}$, so

$WXY = \tan^{-1}\left(\frac{42}{25}\right) = 59.237...$

So the bearing of Y from X is:
$180° - 59.237...° = 120.762...°$
$= \mathbf{120.8°}$ (1 d.p.)

8 a) To find a, first find the base of the right-angled triangle formed by splitting the isosceles triangle in two. This creates a right-angled triangle with angle 60° and hypotenuse 12 cm. You want to find the opposite, so use the formula for sin x:

$\sin 60° = \frac{\text{opp}}{12}$, so $\frac{\sqrt{3}}{2} = \frac{\text{opp}}{12}$,

which means $\text{opp} = \frac{12\sqrt{3}}{2} = 6\sqrt{3}$.

$a = 2 \times \text{opp} = 2 \times 6\sqrt{3} = \mathbf{12\sqrt{3}\ cm}$

b) Split length b into two different bits, b_1 and b_2, where b_1 is the base of the left-hand triangle and b_2 is the base of the right-hand triangle.
The left-hand triangle has angles of 45° and 90°, so the missing angle must also be 45°, which means the triangle is isosceles. b_1 is the same as the 3 cm side, so $b_1 = 3$ cm.
b_2 is the adjacent in the right-hand triangle, and the opposite is 3 cm, so use the formula for tan x:

$\tan 30° = \frac{3}{b_2}$, which means $\frac{1}{\sqrt{3}} = \frac{3}{b_2}$,

so $b_2 = 3\sqrt{3}$ cm

$b = b_1 + b_2 = \mathbf{3 + 3\sqrt{3}\ cm}$

You could have also used the value of tan 45° to find the value of b_1.

Page 313 Exam-Style Questions

1 $860^2 = 426^2 + (\text{distance})^2$
$(\text{distance})^2 = 860^2 - 426^2$
$(\text{distance})^2 = 739\,600 - 181\,476 = 558\,124$
$\text{distance} = \sqrt{558\,124} = 747.076... = \mathbf{747\ km}$
(to the nearest km)
[2 marks available — 1 mark for using Pythagoras' theorem, 1 mark for the correct answer]

2 You know the hypotenuse and want to find the opposite, so use the formula for sin x:
$\sin 38° = \frac{\text{opp}}{5.4}$, so $\text{opp} = 5.4 \sin 38° = 3.324...$
$= \mathbf{3.32\ cm}$ (2 d.p.)
[2 marks available — 1 mark for using the correct trigonometric formula, 1 mark for the correct answer]

3 To use the formula for sin ACB, you need to find the hypotenuse AC. Find the length of side AC using Pythagoras' theorem:
$AC^2 = AB^2 + BC^2 = 5^2 + 12^2 = 25 + 144 = 169$
$AC = \sqrt{169} = 13$ cm
AB is the opposite and AC is the hypotenuse, so $\sin ACB = \mathbf{\frac{5}{13}}$.
[3 marks available — 1 mark for using Pythagoras' theorem to find AC, 1 mark for the correct value of AC, 1 mark for the correct value of sin ACB]

4 Find length QC using Pythagoras' theorem:
$QR^2 = RC^2 + QC^2$
$8^2 = 3^2 + QC^2$
$QC^2 = 8^2 - 3^2$
$QC^2 = 64 - 9 = 55$, so $QC = \sqrt{55}$ cm
$BC = BQ + QC = 3 + \sqrt{55} = 10.416...$
$= \mathbf{10.4\ cm}$ (1 d.p.)
[3 marks available — 1 mark for using Pythagoras' theorem, 1 mark for the correct length of QC (or equivalent side), 1 mark for the correct answer]

5 Half of diagonal AC is the adjacent side of a right-angled triangle with opposite $12 \div 2 = 6$ cm and angle $60° \div 2 = 30°$, so use the formula for tan x:
$\tan 30° = \frac{6}{\text{adj}}$, which means $\frac{1}{\sqrt{3}} = \frac{6}{\text{adj}}$,
so $\text{adj} = 6\sqrt{3}$ cm
AC is double this length, so
$AC = 6\sqrt{3} \times 2 = \mathbf{12\sqrt{3}\ cm}$
[3 marks available — 1 mark for creating a right-angled triangle, 1 mark for using trigonometry to find a side, 1 mark for the correct answer]

Section 20 — Vectors

20.1 Column Vectors

Page 315 Exercise 1

1

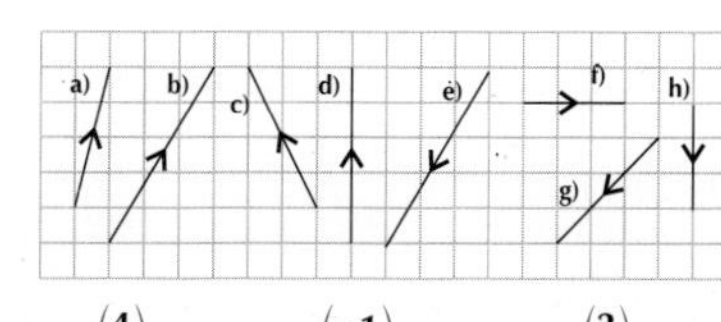

2 $\mathbf{a} = \begin{pmatrix} 4 \\ 0 \end{pmatrix}$ $\mathbf{b} = \begin{pmatrix} -1 \\ -1 \end{pmatrix}$ $\mathbf{c} = \begin{pmatrix} 2 \\ 6 \end{pmatrix}$

$\mathbf{d} = \begin{pmatrix} -3 \\ 0 \end{pmatrix}$ $\mathbf{e} = \begin{pmatrix} -4 \\ -1 \end{pmatrix}$ $\mathbf{f} = \begin{pmatrix} 2 \\ 3.5 \end{pmatrix}$

$\mathbf{g} = \begin{pmatrix} -4 \\ -3 \end{pmatrix}$ $\mathbf{h} = \begin{pmatrix} -2 \\ 2 \end{pmatrix}$

Page 316 Exercise 2

1 a) $3\mathbf{q} = 3\begin{pmatrix} -1 \\ 3 \end{pmatrix} = \begin{pmatrix} 3 \times (-1) \\ 3 \times 3 \end{pmatrix} = \begin{pmatrix} \mathbf{-3} \\ \mathbf{9} \end{pmatrix}$

b) $5\mathbf{q} = 5\begin{pmatrix} -1 \\ 3 \end{pmatrix} = \begin{pmatrix} 5 \times (-1) \\ 5 \times 3 \end{pmatrix} = \begin{pmatrix} \mathbf{-5} \\ \mathbf{15} \end{pmatrix}$

c) $\frac{3}{2}\mathbf{q} = \frac{3}{2}\begin{pmatrix} -1 \\ 3 \end{pmatrix} = \begin{pmatrix} \frac{3}{2} \times (-1) \\ \frac{3}{2} \times 3 \end{pmatrix} = \begin{pmatrix} \mathbf{-1.5} \\ \mathbf{4.5} \end{pmatrix}$

d) $-2\mathbf{q} = -2\begin{pmatrix} -1 \\ 3 \end{pmatrix} = \begin{pmatrix} -2 \times (-1) \\ -2 \times 3 \end{pmatrix} = \begin{pmatrix} \mathbf{2} \\ \mathbf{-6} \end{pmatrix}$

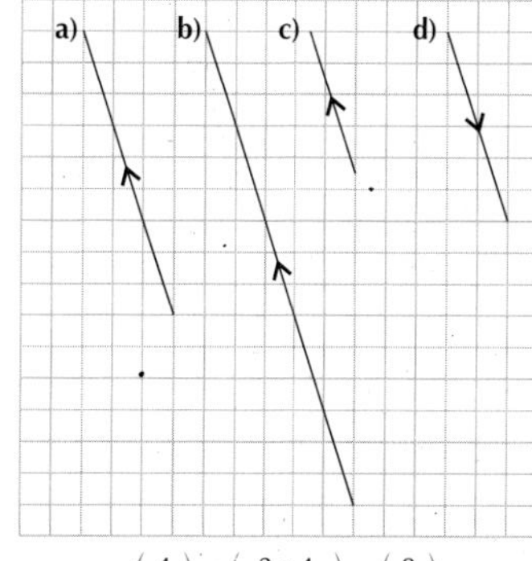

2 a) $2\mathbf{a} = 2\begin{pmatrix} 4 \\ -2 \end{pmatrix} = \begin{pmatrix} 2 \times 4 \\ 2 \times (-2) \end{pmatrix} = \begin{pmatrix} 8 \\ -4 \end{pmatrix} = \mathbf{d}$

b) $-3\mathbf{b} = -3\begin{pmatrix} -1 \\ 4 \end{pmatrix} = \begin{pmatrix} -3 \times (-1) \\ -3 \times 4 \end{pmatrix} = \begin{pmatrix} 3 \\ -12 \end{pmatrix} = \mathbf{g}$

c) Look at the x- and y-components of **e** — the x-component represents a distance of 1 horizontal unit and the y-component represents a distance of 4 vertical units. The same is true in the vector **b**. So **b** is the same length as **e**.

d) Parallel vectors are multiples of one another.

$\mathbf{c} = \begin{pmatrix} 3 \\ 12 \end{pmatrix} = \begin{pmatrix} 3 \times 1 \\ 3 \times 4 \end{pmatrix} = 3\begin{pmatrix} 1 \\ 4 \end{pmatrix} = 3\mathbf{e}$.

So **e** is parallel to **c**.

Page 317 Exercise 3

1 a) $\begin{pmatrix} 5 \\ 2 \end{pmatrix} + \begin{pmatrix} 3 \\ 4 \end{pmatrix} = \begin{pmatrix} 5+3 \\ 2+4 \end{pmatrix} = \begin{pmatrix} \mathbf{8} \\ \mathbf{6} \end{pmatrix}$

b) $\begin{pmatrix} 4 \\ -1 \end{pmatrix} + \begin{pmatrix} 1 \\ 6 \end{pmatrix} = \begin{pmatrix} 4+1 \\ -1+6 \end{pmatrix} = \begin{pmatrix} \mathbf{5} \\ \mathbf{5} \end{pmatrix}$

c) $\begin{pmatrix} 2 \\ -1 \end{pmatrix} - \begin{pmatrix} -2 \\ 2 \end{pmatrix} = \begin{pmatrix} 2-(-2) \\ -1-2 \end{pmatrix} = \begin{pmatrix} \mathbf{4} \\ \mathbf{-3} \end{pmatrix}$

d) $\begin{pmatrix} -3 \\ 0 \end{pmatrix} - \begin{pmatrix} 6 \\ 2 \end{pmatrix} = \begin{pmatrix} -3-6 \\ 0-2 \end{pmatrix} = \begin{pmatrix} \mathbf{-9} \\ \mathbf{-2} \end{pmatrix}$

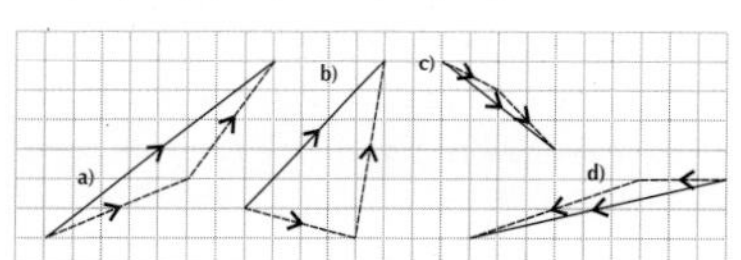

2 a) $\mathbf{b}+\mathbf{c}=\begin{pmatrix}0\\-2\end{pmatrix}+\begin{pmatrix}-1\\4\end{pmatrix}=\begin{pmatrix}0+(-1)\\-2+4\end{pmatrix}=\begin{pmatrix}\mathbf{-1}\\\mathbf{2}\end{pmatrix}$

b) $\mathbf{c}-\mathbf{a}=\begin{pmatrix}-1\\4\end{pmatrix}-\begin{pmatrix}2\\3\end{pmatrix}=\begin{pmatrix}-1-2\\4-3\end{pmatrix}=\begin{pmatrix}\mathbf{-3}\\\mathbf{1}\end{pmatrix}$

c) $2\mathbf{c}+\mathbf{a}=2\begin{pmatrix}-1\\4\end{pmatrix}+\begin{pmatrix}2\\3\end{pmatrix}=\begin{pmatrix}2\times(-1)+2\\2\times4+3\end{pmatrix}$

$=\begin{pmatrix}\mathbf{0}\\\mathbf{11}\end{pmatrix}$

Using the same method for d)-h):

d) $\begin{pmatrix}\mathbf{6}\\\mathbf{7}\end{pmatrix}$ **e)** $\begin{pmatrix}\mathbf{4}\\\mathbf{-5}\end{pmatrix}$ **f)** $\begin{pmatrix}\mathbf{3}\\\mathbf{-3}\end{pmatrix}$ **g)** $\begin{pmatrix}\mathbf{-4}\\\mathbf{6}\end{pmatrix}$

h) $\begin{pmatrix}\mathbf{5}\\\mathbf{26}\end{pmatrix}$

Don't be put off by there being three vectors in parts f), g) and h). You still answer them in the same way by adding all the x-components and all the y-components separately.

3 a) $\mathbf{u}+2\mathbf{v}=\begin{pmatrix}6\\-2\end{pmatrix}+2\begin{pmatrix}-2\\3\end{pmatrix}=\begin{pmatrix}6+2\times(-2)\\-2+2\times3\end{pmatrix}$

$=\begin{pmatrix}\mathbf{2}\\\mathbf{4}\end{pmatrix}$

b)

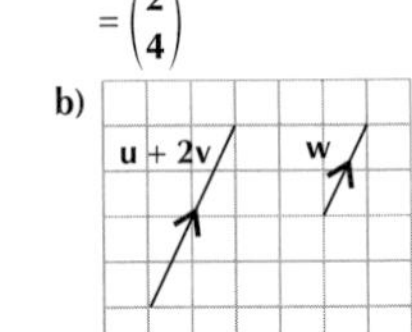

c) The two vectors are **parallel** because $\mathbf{u}+2\mathbf{v}=2\mathbf{w}$.

Page 318 Exercise 4

1 a)

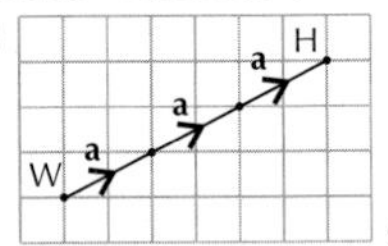

so $\overrightarrow{WH}=\mathbf{3a}$

b)

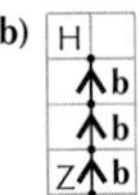

so $\overrightarrow{ZH}=\mathbf{3b}$

c)

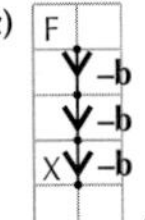

so $\overrightarrow{FX}=\mathbf{-3b}$

d)

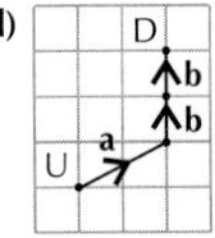

so $\overrightarrow{UD}=\mathbf{a+2b}$

Using the same method for e)-h):

e) –a – 2b **f) 2a – 5b**

g) 5a – 8b **h) a – 4b**

*Be careful with the direction of the vectors. For instance, the vector **b** is pointing up but in part c) you're asked for the vector from F to X — this is going downwards. So you have to use the reverse of **b**, which is –**b**.*

20.2 Vector Geometry

Page 320 Exercise 1

1 a) $\overrightarrow{BA}=-\overrightarrow{AB}=\mathbf{-4p}$

b) $\overrightarrow{CD}=-\overrightarrow{DC}=\mathbf{-p}$

c) $\overrightarrow{AC}=\overrightarrow{AD}+\overrightarrow{DC}=\mathbf{q+p}$

d) $\overrightarrow{CA}=-\overrightarrow{AC}=-(\mathbf{q}+\mathbf{p})=\mathbf{-q-p}$

e) $\overrightarrow{CB}=\overrightarrow{CD}+\overrightarrow{DA}+\overrightarrow{AB}=\overrightarrow{CD}-\overrightarrow{AD}+\overrightarrow{AB}$
$=-\mathbf{p}-\mathbf{q}+4\mathbf{p}=\mathbf{3p-q}$

f) $\overrightarrow{BD}=\overrightarrow{BA}+\overrightarrow{AD}=\mathbf{-4p+q}$

2 Add point C onto the diagram.

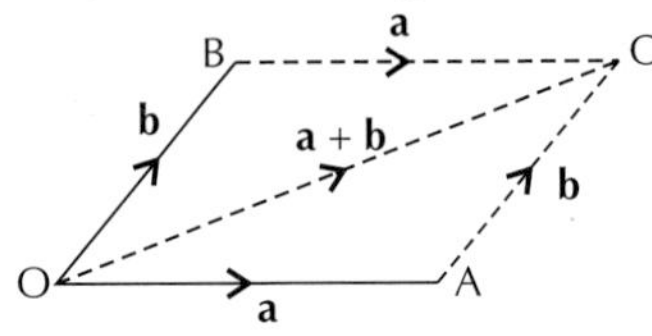

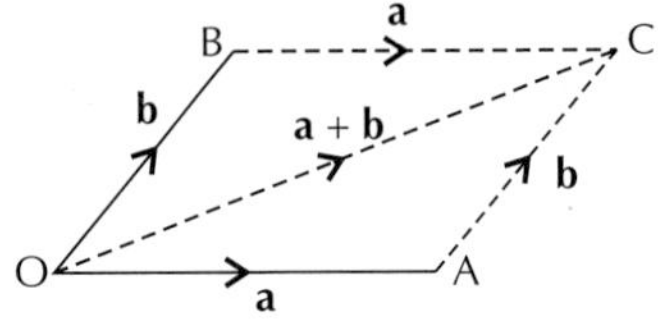

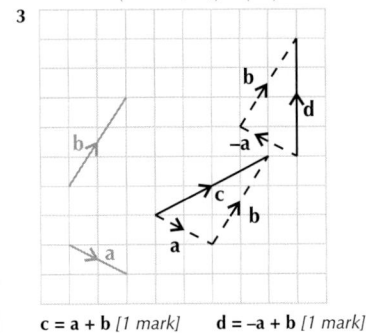

a) (i) $\overrightarrow{CO}=-\overrightarrow{OC}=-(\mathbf{a}+\mathbf{b})=\mathbf{-a-b}$

(ii) $\overrightarrow{AB}=\overrightarrow{AO}+\overrightarrow{OB}=-\overrightarrow{OA}+\overrightarrow{OB}=\mathbf{-a+b}$

b) The sides OA and BC are both represented by vector **a**, so they're parallel, and the sides OB and AC are both represented by the vector **b**, so they're parallel. So the shape is a **parallelogram**.

3 a) $\overrightarrow{OB}$ is in the same direction as $\overrightarrow{OA}$ and it is 4 times as long, so $\overrightarrow{OB}=4\overrightarrow{OA}=\mathbf{4a}$.

b) $\overrightarrow{OD}$ is in the same direction as $\overrightarrow{OC}$ and it is 3 times as long, so $\overrightarrow{OD}=3\overrightarrow{OC}=\mathbf{3c}$.

c) $\overrightarrow{AB}=-\overrightarrow{OA}+\overrightarrow{OB}=-\mathbf{a}+4\mathbf{a}=\mathbf{3a}$

d) $\overrightarrow{CD}=-\overrightarrow{OC}+\overrightarrow{OD}=-\mathbf{c}+3\mathbf{c}=\mathbf{2c}$

e) $\overrightarrow{DB}=\overrightarrow{DO}+\overrightarrow{OB}=-\overrightarrow{OD}+\overrightarrow{OB}=\mathbf{-3c+4a}$

f) $\overrightarrow{BD}=-\overrightarrow{DB}=-(-3\mathbf{c}+4\mathbf{a})=\mathbf{3c-4a}$

4 a) E.g. $\overrightarrow{ED}=\mathbf{p}$ since ED and AB are parallel and the same length.
$\overrightarrow{ED}=\overrightarrow{EM}+\overrightarrow{MD}=\mathbf{-r+q}$ since EM and DC are parallel and the same length, and MD and BC are parallel and the same length.

Using the same method for b)-f):

b) E.g. **q** and **p + r** **c)** E.g. **r** and **q – p**

d) E.g. **–q** and **–r – p** **e)** E.g. **–p** and **r – q**

f) E.g. **–r** and **p – q**

Page 321 Review Exercise

1 a) $\mathbf{a}=\begin{pmatrix}3\\4\end{pmatrix}$ $\mathbf{b}=\begin{pmatrix}4\\-2\end{pmatrix}$ $\mathbf{c}=\begin{pmatrix}-2\\-4\end{pmatrix}$

$\mathbf{d}=\begin{pmatrix}-4\\-1\end{pmatrix}$ $\mathbf{e}=\begin{pmatrix}4\\-1\end{pmatrix}$ $\mathbf{f}=\begin{pmatrix}1\\4\end{pmatrix}$

$\mathbf{g}=\begin{pmatrix}0\\-5\end{pmatrix}$ $\mathbf{h}=\begin{pmatrix}1\\-4\end{pmatrix}$

b) b **c) d, e, f, h**

2 a) $3\mathbf{p}=3\begin{pmatrix}4\\-3\end{pmatrix}=\begin{pmatrix}3\times4\\3\times(-3)\end{pmatrix}=\begin{pmatrix}\mathbf{12}\\\mathbf{-9}\end{pmatrix}$

b) $2\mathbf{q}+\mathbf{r}=2\begin{pmatrix}0\\2\end{pmatrix}+\begin{pmatrix}-1\\5\end{pmatrix}=\begin{pmatrix}2\times0+(-1)\\2\times2+5\end{pmatrix}$

$=\begin{pmatrix}\mathbf{-1}\\\mathbf{9}\end{pmatrix}$

c) $\mathbf{r}-2\mathbf{p}=\begin{pmatrix}-1\\5\end{pmatrix}-2\begin{pmatrix}4\\-3\end{pmatrix}=\begin{pmatrix}-1-2\times4\\5-2\times(-3)\end{pmatrix}$

$=\begin{pmatrix}\mathbf{-9}\\\mathbf{11}\end{pmatrix}$

d) $\mathbf{p}+5\mathbf{r}-3\mathbf{q}=\begin{pmatrix}4\\-3\end{pmatrix}+5\begin{pmatrix}-1\\5\end{pmatrix}-3\begin{pmatrix}0\\2\end{pmatrix}$

$=\begin{pmatrix}4+5\times(-1)-3\times0\\-3+5\times5-3\times2\end{pmatrix}=\begin{pmatrix}\mathbf{-1}\\\mathbf{16}\end{pmatrix}$

3 a)

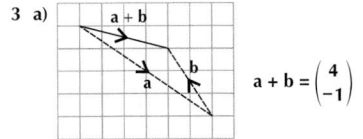

$\mathbf{a}+\mathbf{b}=\begin{pmatrix}\mathbf{4}\\\mathbf{-1}\end{pmatrix}$

b)

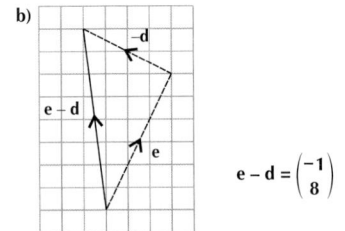

$\mathbf{e}-\mathbf{d}=\begin{pmatrix}\mathbf{-1}\\\mathbf{8}\end{pmatrix}$

c) a and f **d) b and e**

Look at the x- and y-components separately. E.g. in part c), you need the x-components to add to 10 and the y-components to add to –10.

e) $\mathbf{e}=\begin{pmatrix}3\\6\end{pmatrix}=\begin{pmatrix}3\times1\\3\times2\end{pmatrix}=3\begin{pmatrix}1\\2\end{pmatrix}=\mathbf{3c}$, so **e** is parallel to **c**.

f) $\mathbf{f}=\begin{pmatrix}4\\-6\end{pmatrix}=\begin{pmatrix}-2\times(-2)\\-2\times3\end{pmatrix}=-2\begin{pmatrix}-2\\3\end{pmatrix}=\mathbf{-2b}$, so **f** is parallel to **b**.

4 a) $\overrightarrow{SR}=5\times\overrightarrow{PQ}=\mathbf{5m}$

b) $\overrightarrow{QR}=\overrightarrow{QP}+\overrightarrow{PS}+\overrightarrow{SR}=-\overrightarrow{PQ}-\overrightarrow{SP}+\overrightarrow{SR}$
$=-\mathbf{m}-\mathbf{n}+5\mathbf{m}$
$=\mathbf{4m-n}$

Page 322 Exam-Style Questions

1 $\overrightarrow{AC}=\overrightarrow{AB}+\overrightarrow{BC}=\overrightarrow{AB}-\overrightarrow{CB}$ *[1 mark]*
$=\mathbf{u-v}$ *[1 mark]*

2 $\mathbf{m}+4\mathbf{n}=\begin{pmatrix}5\\0\end{pmatrix}+4\begin{pmatrix}-3\\-1\end{pmatrix}$ *[1 mark]*

$=\begin{pmatrix}5+4\times(-3)\\0+4\times(-1)\end{pmatrix}=\begin{pmatrix}\mathbf{-7}\\\mathbf{-4}\end{pmatrix}$ *[1 mark]*

3

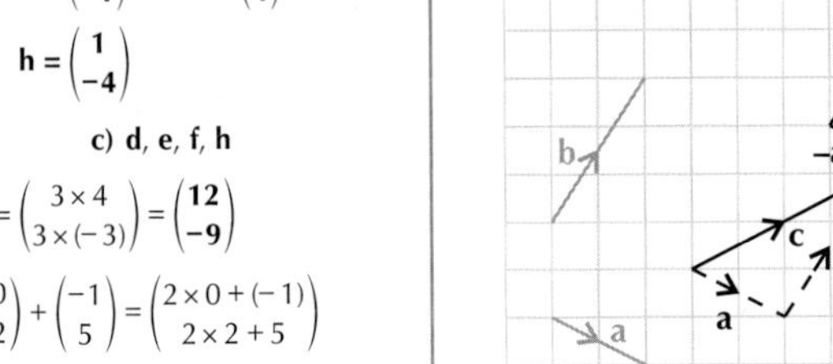

c = a + b *[1 mark]* **d = –a + b** *[1 mark]*

4 $2\mathbf{a} - 3\mathbf{b} = 2\begin{pmatrix}5p\\4q\end{pmatrix} - 3\begin{pmatrix}4\\0\end{pmatrix}$

$= \begin{pmatrix}(2\times 5p)-(3\times 4)\\(2\times 4q)-(3\times 0)\end{pmatrix}$ *[1 mark]*

$= \begin{pmatrix}10p-12\\8q\end{pmatrix}$ *[1 mark]*

$2\mathbf{a} - 3\mathbf{b} = \begin{pmatrix}10p-12\\8q\end{pmatrix} = \begin{pmatrix}18\\-32\end{pmatrix}$, so:

$10p - 12 = 18 \Rightarrow 10p = 30$
$\Rightarrow \mathbf{p = 3}$ *[1 mark]*

$8q = -32 \Rightarrow q = -32 \div 8 \Rightarrow \mathbf{q = -4}$ *[1 mark]*

Section 21 — Constructions

21.1 Circles

Page 323 Exercise 1

1 a) $d = 2r = 2 \times 4$ cm = **8 cm**
b) $d = 2r = 2 \times 6$ cm = **12 cm**
c) $d = 2r = 2 \times 30$ mm = **60 mm**
d) $d = 2r = 2 \times 4.2$ mm = **8.4 mm**

2 a) $d = 2r \Rightarrow r = \frac{d}{2} = \frac{2\text{ cm}}{2} = $ **1 cm**
b) $d = 2r \Rightarrow r = \frac{d}{2} = \frac{12\text{ cm}}{2} = $ **6 cm**
c) $d = 2r \Rightarrow r = \frac{d}{2} = \frac{13\text{ m}}{2} = $ **6.5 m**
d) $d = 2r \Rightarrow r = \frac{d}{2} = \frac{0.02\text{ cm}}{2} = $ **0.01 cm**

3 a)

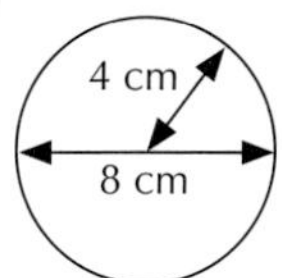

b)

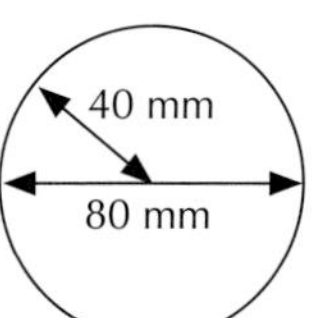

Remember that 80 mm is 8 cm.

c)

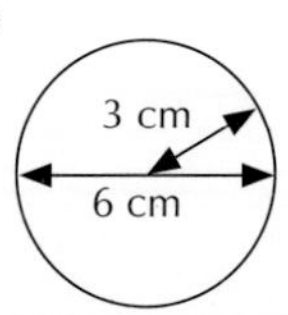

Page 324 Exercise 2

1 a) chord **b) segment**
c) tangent **d) sector**
e) circumference **f) arc**

2 E.g.

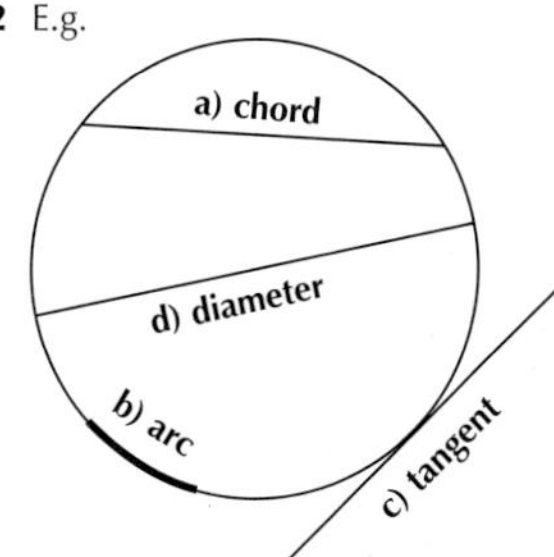

For Q2 & Q3, there are lots of possible correct diagrams — make sure each feature you've drawn has the properties described on p.323 & 324.

3 E.g.

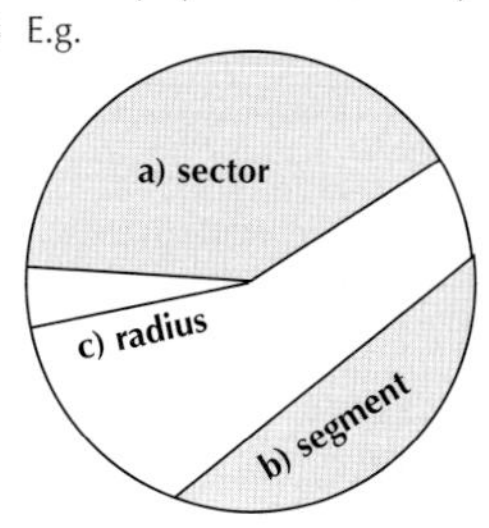

21.2 Lines, Angles and Triangles

Page 326 Exercise 1

1 a) $\mathbf{a = 40°}$ $\mathbf{b}$ **= 3.9 cm - 4 cm**
$\mathbf{c}$ **= 4.9 cm - 5 cm**
b) $\mathbf{d = 65°}$ $\mathbf{e}$ **= 4.4 cm - 4.5 cm**
$\mathbf{f}$ **= 2.9 cm - 3 cm**

2 a) and b)

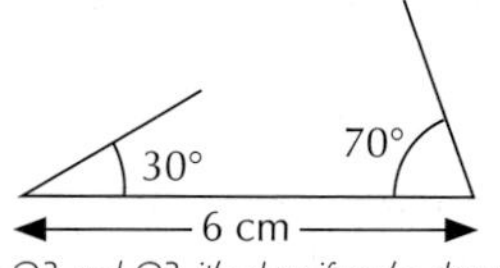

In Q2 and Q3, it's okay if you've drawn the angles at the other ends of the line.

3 a) and b)

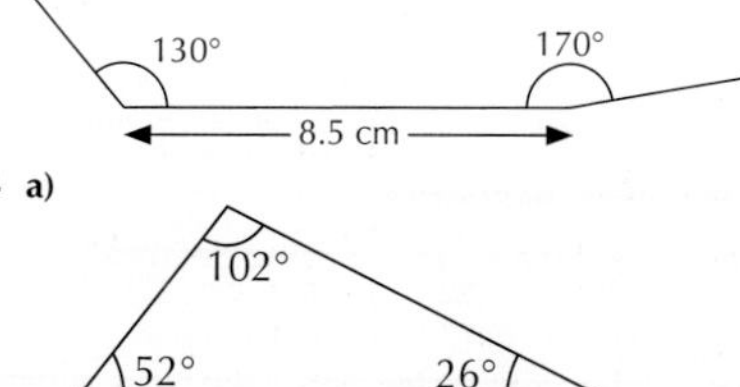

4 a)

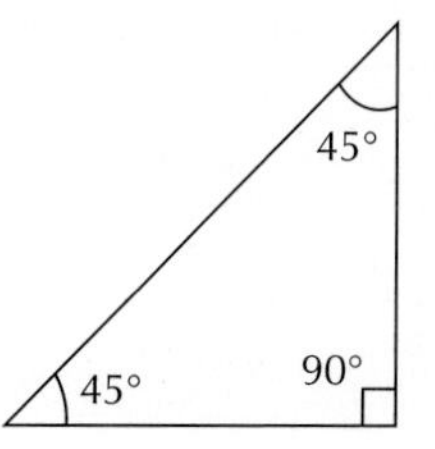

b)

Page 327 Exercise 2

In this exercise, use a ruler and a protractor to make sure that your diagrams have the measurements shown (given rounded to the nearest mm or degree). Allow 1 mm or 1° either side for all answers — including written answers.

1 a) Draw a 4 cm line, using a ruler to measure the correct length. Measure an angle of 90° at the end using a protractor, mark it with a dot and draw a line from the end of the first line through the dot. Repeat at the other end of the line with an angle of 37°. Mark the point where these two lines intersect and join it to each end of the 4 cm line. Measuring side $l \Rightarrow$ $\mathbf{l}$ **= 5.0 cm**
Draw the triangles in parts b)-c) using the same method as part a).
b) $\mathbf{l}$ **= 6.1 cm** **c)** $\mathbf{l}$ **= 8.9 cm**

Using the same method as Q1:

2 a) (i)

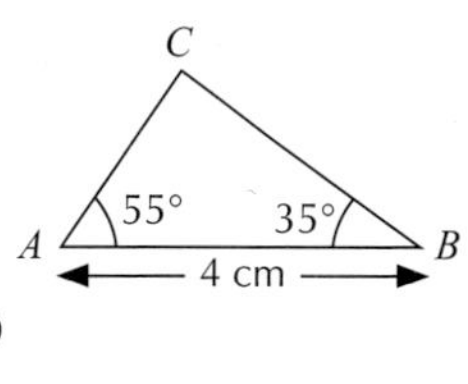

(ii)

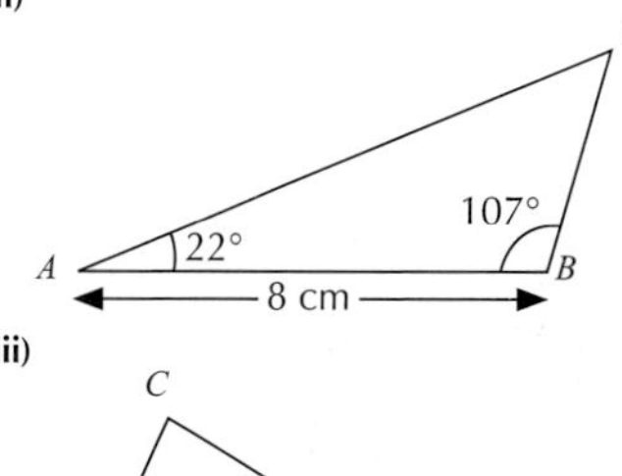

(iii)

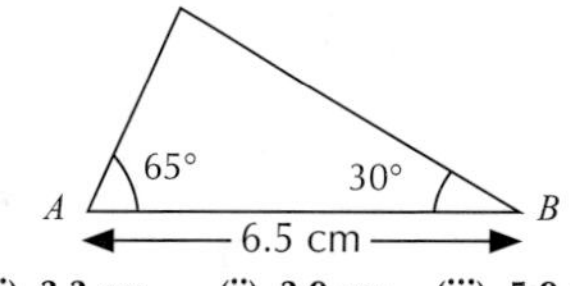

b) (i) 3.3 cm **(ii) 3.9 cm** **(iii) 5.9 cm**

3 Using a protractor, draw a line with a 45° angle (measured anticlockwise from the 5 cm line) at Alec and another line with an angle of 45° (measured clockwise from the 5 cm line) at Brenda. Mark the intersection of these two lines.

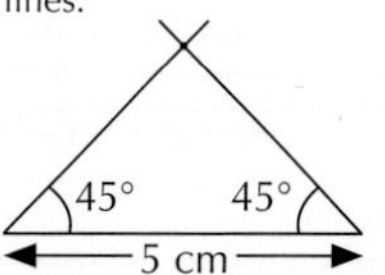

Length of each new side is 3.5 cm.
So they will meet after **3.5 km**.

Page 328 Exercise 3

In this exercise, use a ruler and a protractor to make sure that your diagrams have the measurements shown (given rounded to the nearest mm or degree). Allow 1 mm or 1° either side for all answers — including written answers.

1 a) Draw a 12 cm line, using a ruler to measure the correct length. Measure an angle of 90° at the end using a protractor and mark it with a dot. Draw a line from the end of the 12 cm line through the dot. Measure 5 cm along, mark this point, and join it to the other end of the 12 cm line. Measuring side $l \Rightarrow$ **l = 13 cm**

Draw the triangles in parts b)-c) using the same method as part a).

b) **l = 5.6 cm** **c)** **l = 4.9 cm**

2 a) (i) Draw a 6 cm line, using a ruler to measure the correct length. Measure an angle of 40° at the end using a protractor and mark it with a dot. Draw a line from the end of the 6 cm line through the dot. Measure 7 cm along, mark this point, and join it to the other end of the 6 cm line.

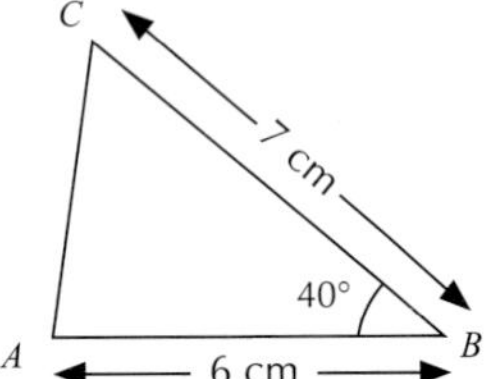

Draw the triangles in parts (ii)-(iv) using the same method as part a).

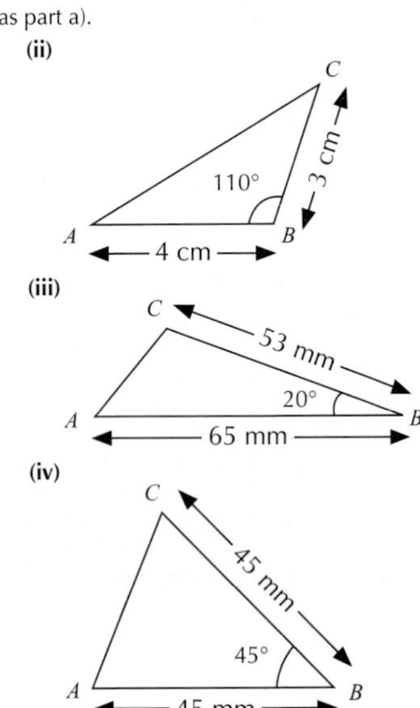

b) (i) **4.5 cm** **(ii)** **5.8 cm**
(iii) **24 mm** **(iv)** **34 mm**

3 Draw a 5 cm line, using a ruler to measure the correct length. Measure an angle of 50° at the end of the line using a protractor and mark it with a dot. Draw a line from the end of the 5 cm line through the dot. Then measure 5 cm along, mark this point, and join it to the other end of the original 5 cm line.

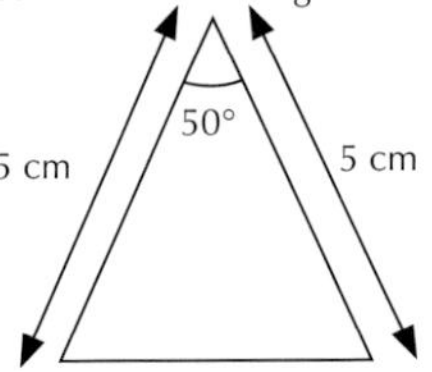

4 a) Angles in a quadrilateral add up to 360° and opposite angles in a rhombus are equal, so find the missing angle (x):
$40° + x + 40° + x = 360°$
$\Rightarrow 2x + 80° = 360°$
$2x = 280° \Rightarrow x = 140°$
Draw a 6 cm line, using a ruler to measure the correct length. Measure an angle of 40° at the end of the line using a protractor and mark it with a dot. Draw a line from the end of the 6 cm line through the dot. Then measure 6 cm along and mark this point. Measure an angle of 140° at this point and mark it with a dot.
Draw a line from the end of the line through the dot. Then measure 6 cm along and mark this point. Connect this point to the end of the original 6 cm line to complete the rhombus.

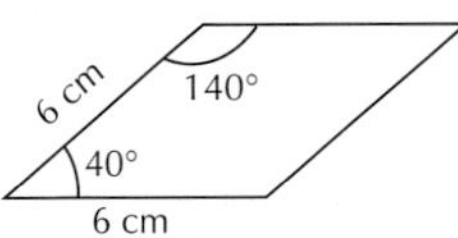

Using the same method for b):

b)

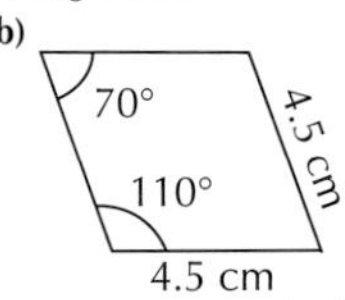

You could have also drawn the rhombus so that the 70° angle was in the bottom left corner.

Page 329 Exercise 4

In this exercise, use a ruler and a protractor to make sure that your diagrams have the measurements shown (given rounded to the nearest mm or degree). Allow 1 mm or 1° either side for all answers — including written answers.

1 a) E.g. Draw the 8 cm line, using a ruler to measure the correct length. Then, set your compasses to 10 cm, and draw an arc from the right-hand end. Next, set your compasses to 6 cm, and draw an arc from the left-hand end. Mark the point where these arcs cross and join it to the ends of the 8 cm line.

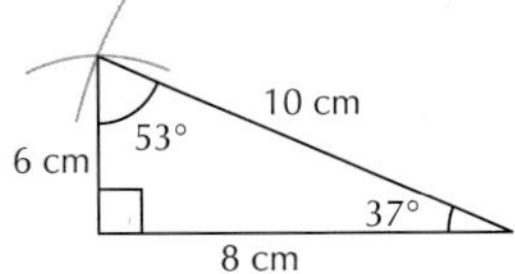

b) E.g. First, draw the 5 cm side. Next, set your compasses to 4.5 cm and draw an arc from the left-hand end of the 5 cm line. Then, set your compasses to 3 cm and draw an arc from the other end. Mark the point where these arcs cross and join it to the ends of the 5 cm line.

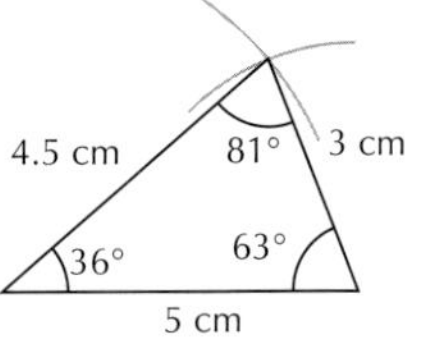

c) E.g. First, draw the 72 mm (= 7.2 cm) side. Next, set your compasses to 40 mm (= 4 cm) and draw an arc from the left-hand end of the 72 mm line. Then, set your compasses to 88 mm (= 8.8 cm) and draw an arc from the other end. Mark the point where these arcs cross and join it to the ends of the 72 mm line.

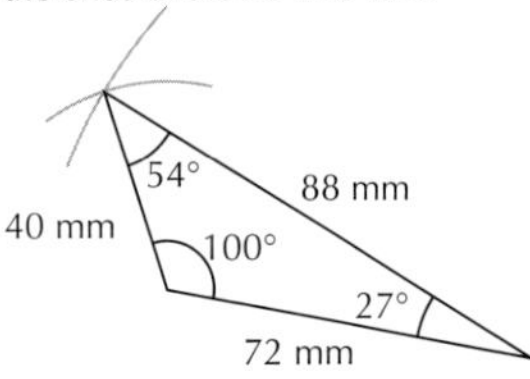

The angles don't appear to add up to 180° as they have been rounded to the nearest degree.

Using the same method for Q2:

2 a) E.g.

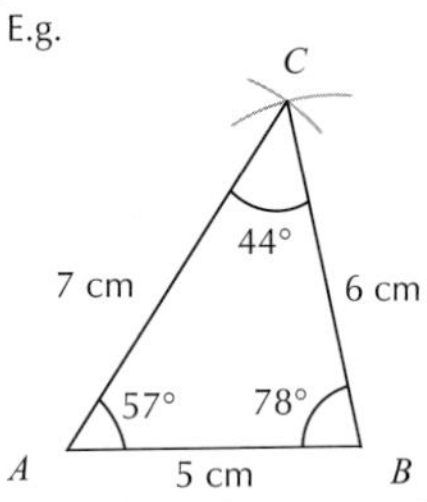

The angles don't appear to add up to 180° as they have been rounded to the nearest degree.

b) E.g.

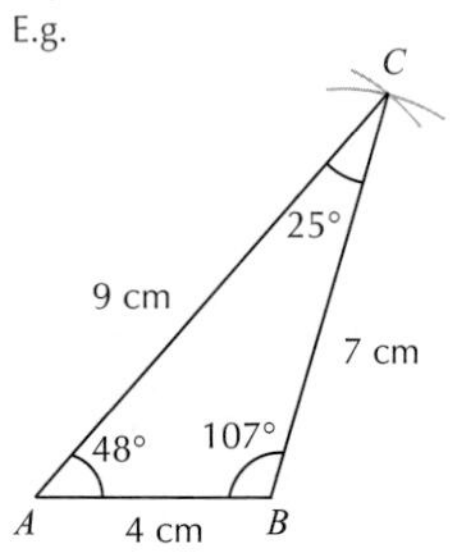

c) E.g.

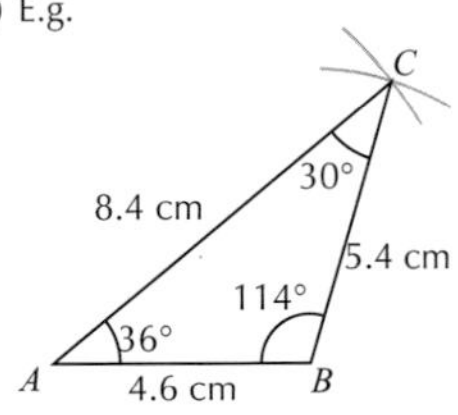

21.3 More Constructions

Page 331 Exercise 1

1 First, draw a horizontal line that is 5 cm long. Next, set your compasses so that they are more than 2.5 cm apart, and draw two arcs from P (one above PQ and one below) and two arcs from Q. Then, draw the line that passes through the points where the arcs cross.

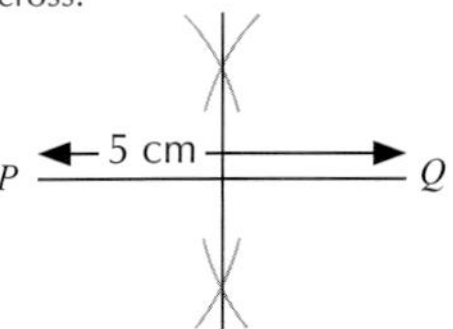

Leave the construction marks on the diagram to show your method.

Using the same method for Q2-4:

2

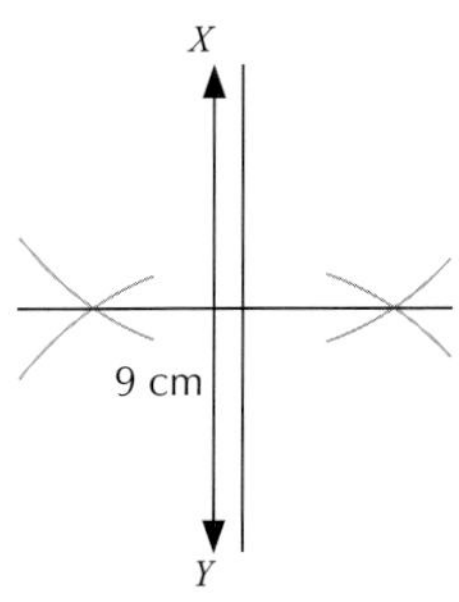

3

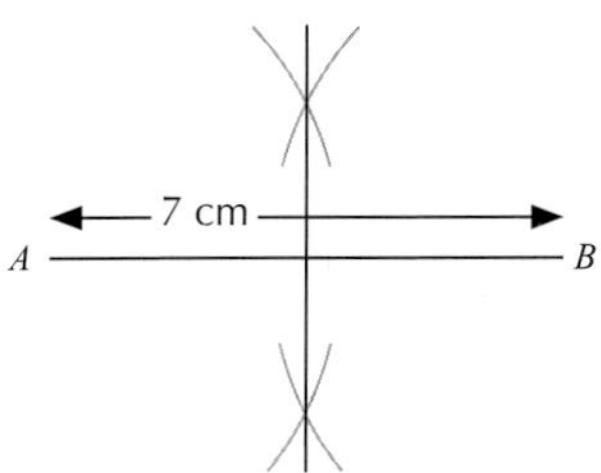

4 a)

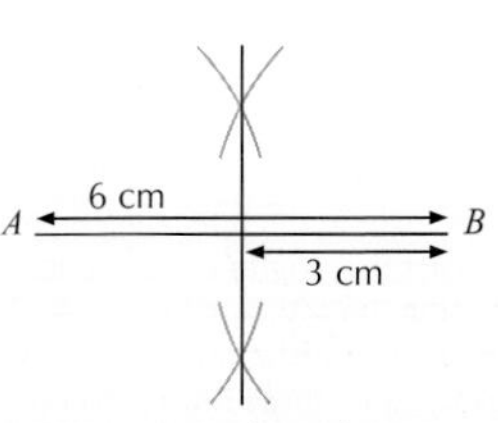

b) Measure 4 cm along the perpendicular bisector each way from the 6 cm line, and mark these points C and D. Since they lie the same distance along the bisector, AC, BC, AD and BD will all be the same length, so you can form a rhombus by joining the points $ACBD$.

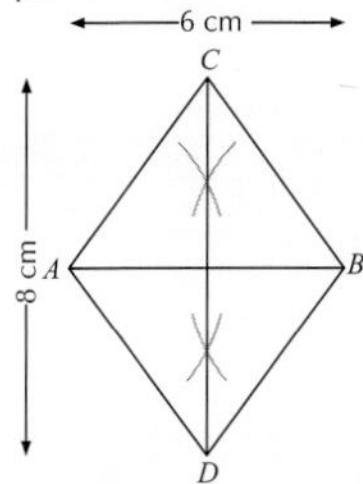

Remember, the diagonals of a rhombus cross at right angles — see page 247.

5 a) Set your compasses to 5 cm to draw a circle with radius 5 cm. Then draw your chords. E.g.

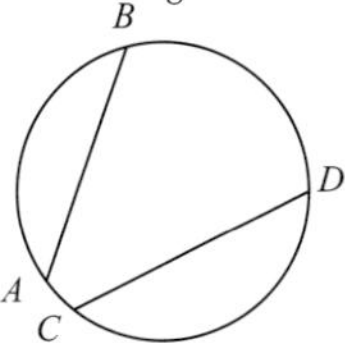

b) E.g.

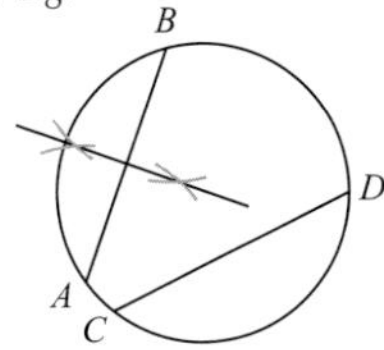

Construct the perpendicular bisectors using the same method used in question 1.

c) E.g.

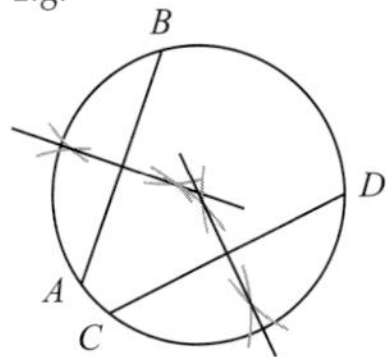

d) **They meet at the circle's centre.**

Page 332 Exercise 2

In this exercise, mark your answers by using a protractor to measure the angles and checking that they match the diagrams given. Allow 1° either side.

1 a) Draw the 100° angle using your protractor. Next, place the point of your compasses on the angle and draw arcs crossing both lines. Then, put the point of your compasses on the points where these arcs cross the lines and draw two more arcs using the same radius. Finally, draw a line through the point where these arcs cross.

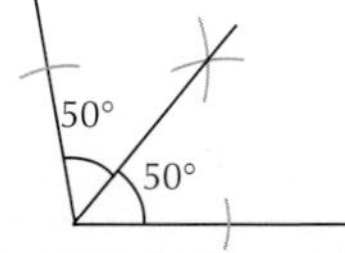

Using the same method for b)-d) and Q2-3:

b)

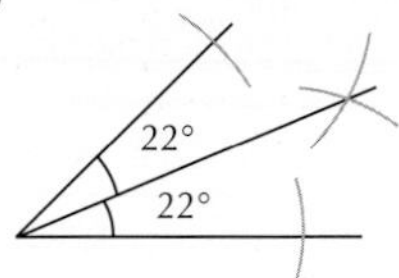

c)

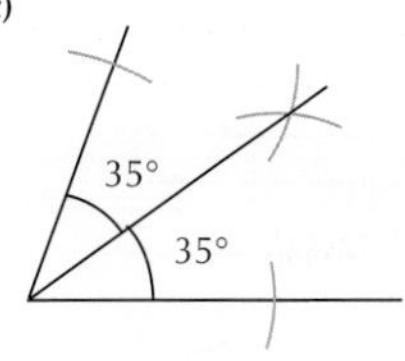

d)

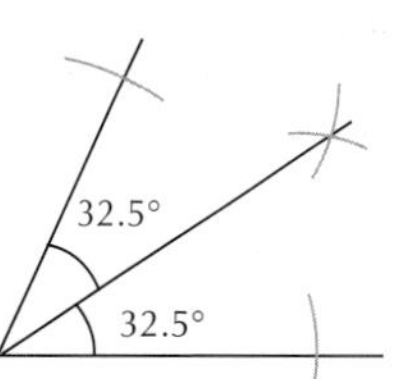

2 a), b) E.g.

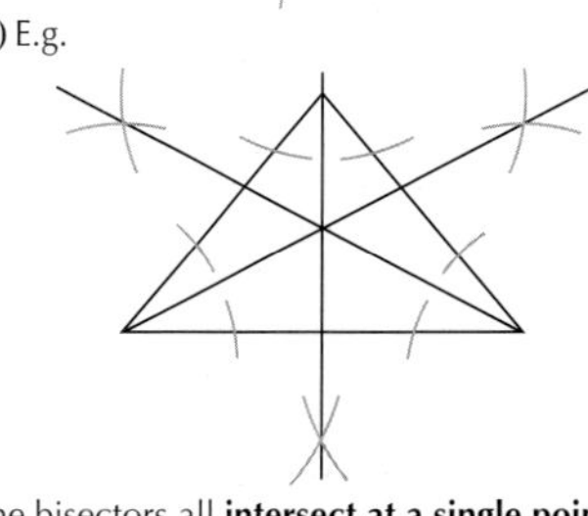

The bisectors all **intersect at a single point**.
This is true for all triangles.

3 a)

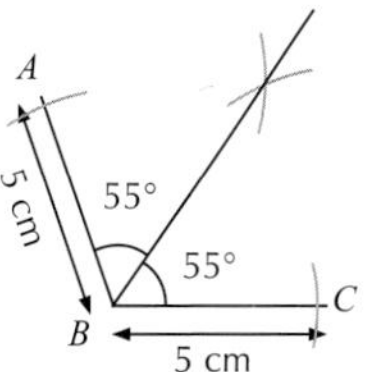

b) Use your ruler to measure 8 cm along the angle bisector:

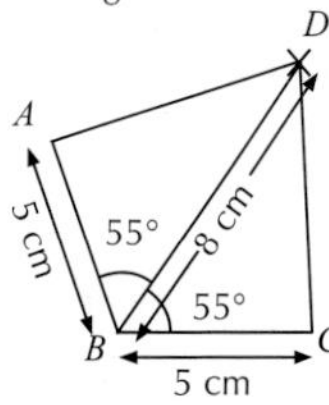

The shape is symmetrical along the line BD, so AD and CD are the same length, meaning $ABCD$ is a **kite**.

Page 333 Exercise 3

In this exercise, mark your answers by using a protractor to check that all perpendiculars make an angle of 90° with the line.

1 Draw the triangle, then draw an arc centred on X that crosses the line YZ twice (you may need to extend the line so that you get two crossing points). Then, draw two arcs of the same radius centred on each of these crossing points. Finally, draw a line from X through the point where these two arcs intersect.

E.g.

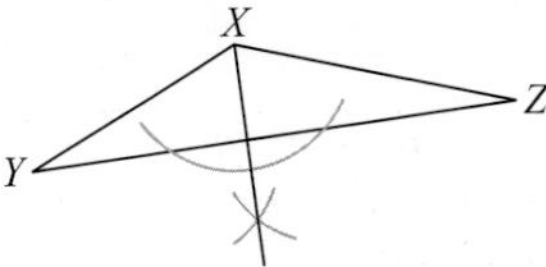

Using the same method for Q2-3:

2 a)-c)

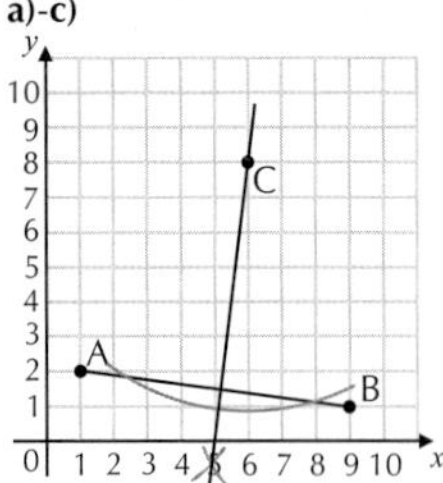

3 E.g.

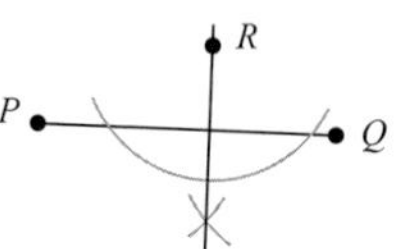

or

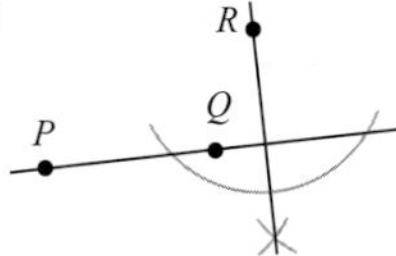

Your diagram might look different depending on where you placed P, Q and R.

4 a), b) E.g.

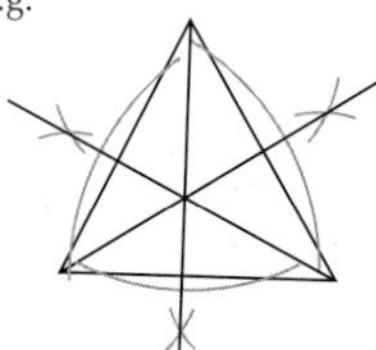

The perpendiculars **intersect at a single point**.

This is true for any triangle.

5 a) E.g. Draw DE by using your ruler to measure 5 cm.
Next, measure an angle of 55° at D, marking it with a dot.
Draw a line from D through this dot.
Finally, measure 6 cm from D with your ruler and mark F, joining it to E to complete the triangle.

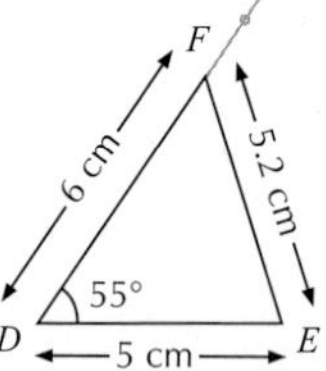

b) Using the same method as in Q1:

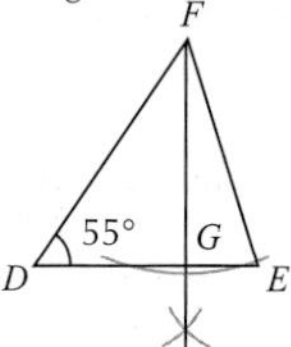

c) Using your ruler, FG = **4.9 cm**.
Accept 4.8-5.0 cm.

Area of a triangle = $\frac{1}{2}$ × base × height
= $\frac{1}{2}$ × 5 × 4.9 = **12.3 cm²** (1 d.p.)

Page 335 Exercise 4

In this exercise, mark your answers by using a ruler and protractor to measure the lengths and angles and checking that they match the diagrams given.

1 Use your ruler to measure a 5 cm line and label it AB. Then, place your compass point at A and draw a long arc that crosses AB. Next, draw an arc of the same radius centred on the point where the first arc crosses AB. Finally, draw a line from A through the point where these arcs cross.

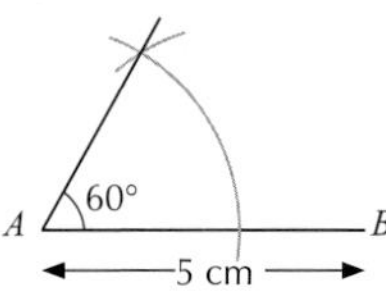

2 a), b) Use the same method as in Q1 to construct the 60° angle(s).

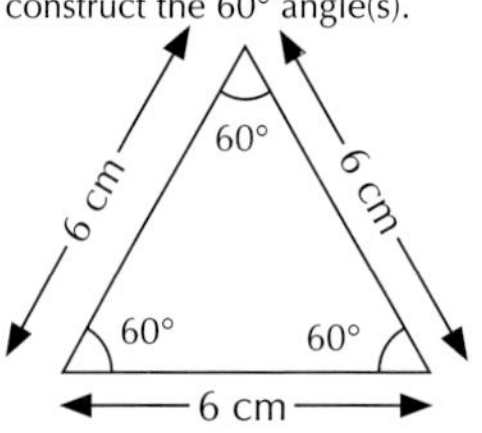

Page 335 Exercise 5

1 Use your ruler to measure a line 6 cm long, and construct a 60° angle at A (see p.334). Then, use your compasses to draw two arcs of the same radius about the points where the long arc from the 60° construction crosses each line. Finally, draw a line from A through the point where these arcs cross.

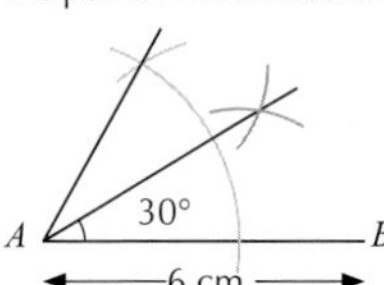

2 a) E.g. Use your ruler to measure a line 7 cm long and label it AB. Next, set your compasses to 7 cm and draw arcs from both ends of the line. Join A and B to the point where these lines cross to form an equilateral triangle. Then, bisect the 60° angle at B using the method from p.331. Mark the point where the angle bisector crosses the 60° line from A as point C, then join C to A and B to complete the triangle.

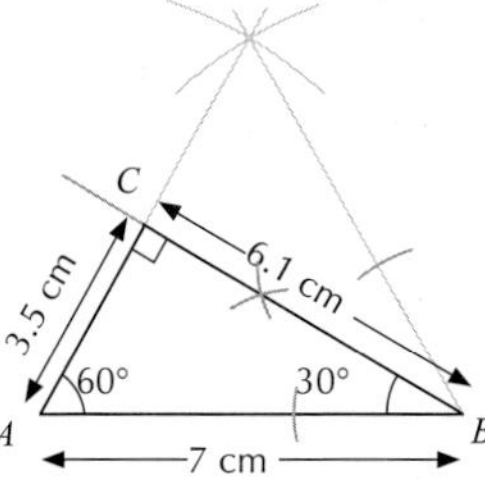

b) Check with protractor.

Using the same method for Q3:

3 Bisect both base angles.

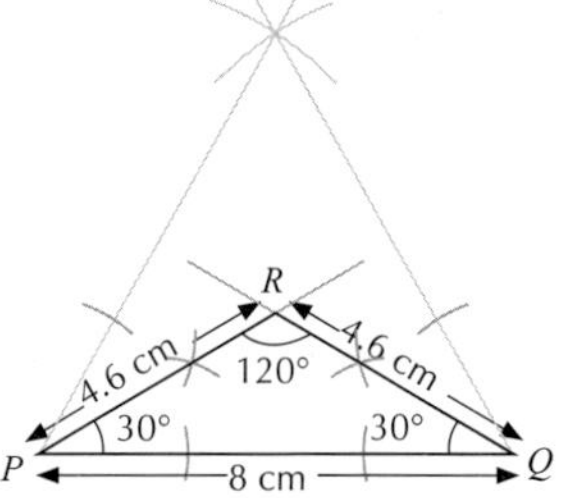

Page 336 Exercise 6

In this exercise, mark your answers by using a ruler and protractor to measure the lengths and angles and checking that they match the diagrams given.

1 a)

b) Place your compass point at X and draw two arcs that cross the line either side of X. Then, increase the radius of your compasses and draw an arc from each intersection. Finally, draw a line through X and the point where these arcs cross.

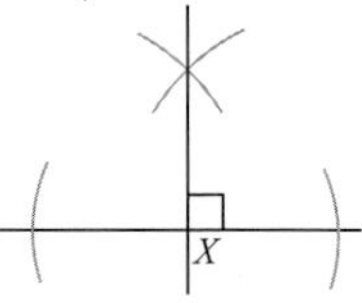

2 E.g. Draw the 7 cm line, mark each end of the line, then extend the line at each end. Next, construct 90° angles at each end of the 7 cm line using the same method as in Q1. Measure 5 cm along each line and mark these points. Finally, join these points to complete the rectangle.

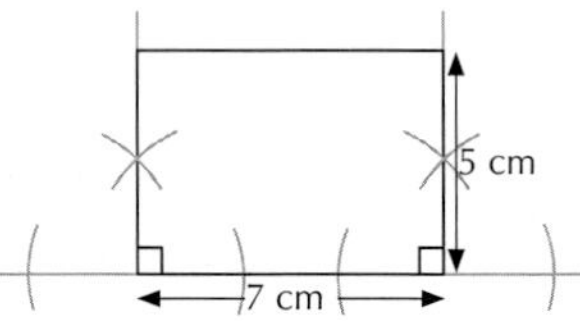

3 E.g. Draw the 6 cm line, mark each end of the line, then extend the line at each end. Next, construct 90° angles at each end of the 6 cm line using the same method as in Q1. Measure 6 cm along each line and mark these points. Finally, join these points to complete the square.

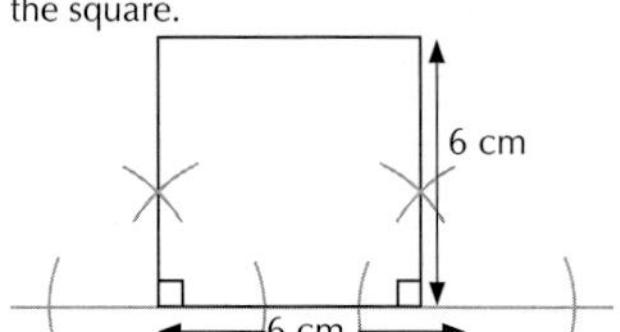

Page 337 Exercise 7

1 a) 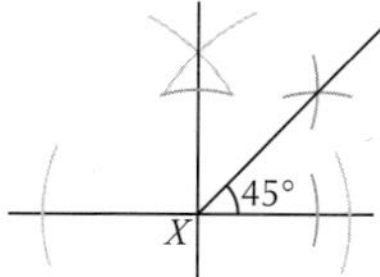

b) First construct a 90° angle (see page 336) and then place your compass point at X and draw two arcs — one through the original line and one through the perpendicular line.
Then, use your compasses to draw two arcs of the same radius about the intersections. Finally, draw a line from X through the point where these arcs cross.

2 Draw a line 8 cm long, label the ends A and B, and extend it at each end. Then, construct 45° angles at A and B using the same method as in Q1. Label the point where the 45° lines intersect as C, then join it to A and B to complete the triangle.

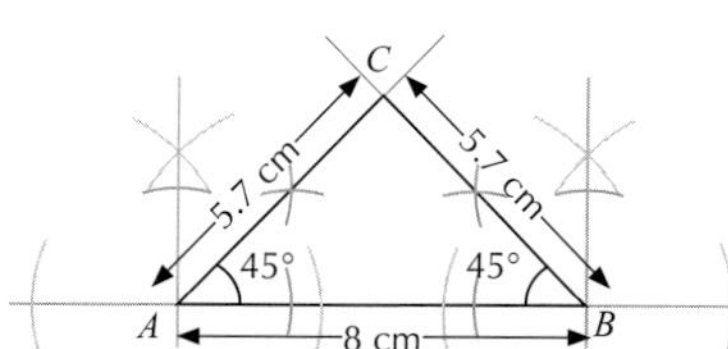

Check your measurements are within 0.1 cm or 1°.

Page 338 Exercise 8

In this exercise, mark your answers by using a protractor to measure any right angles and checking that they are all 90°.

1 Place your compass point at P and draw an arc that crosses AB twice, then draw an arc from each intersection.
Draw a line through P from the point where these arcs cross.
Next, draw two arcs of the same radius from P that cross this new line, and draw an arc from each intersection. Finally, draw another line through P and the point where these arcs cross.
E.g.

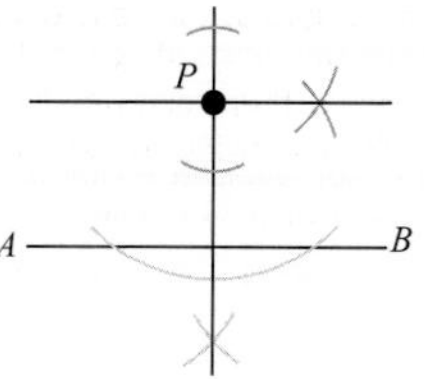

2 a)-c) Using the same method as in Q1.

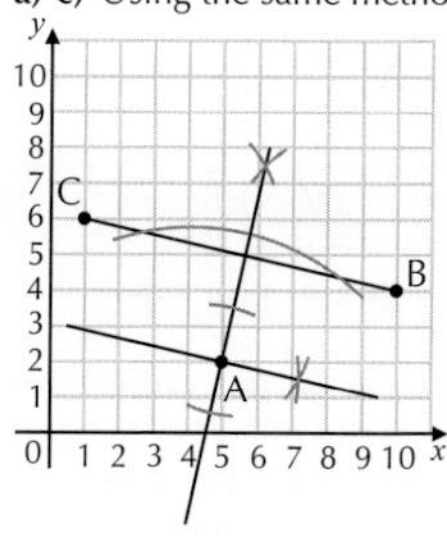

3 First, draw the two lines and draw a point not on the lines. Using the same method as for Q1, construct a line parallel to one of the original lines through this point. Then, draw a new point (or use the same one) and construct a line parallel to the other original line through this point. The shape enclosed by these four lines will be a parallelogram.
E.g.

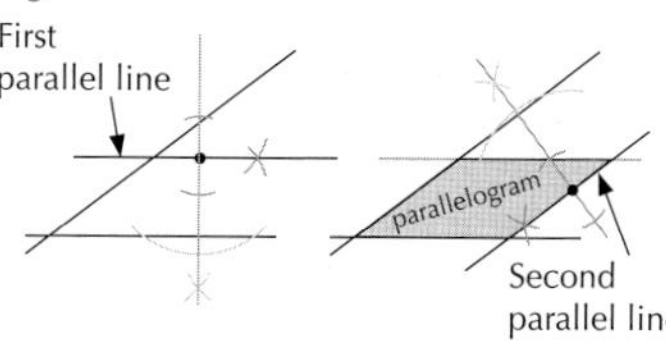

4 a) E.g. First, draw line AB by measuring 10 cm with your ruler. Next, construct a 60° angle at A and B using the method from page 334.

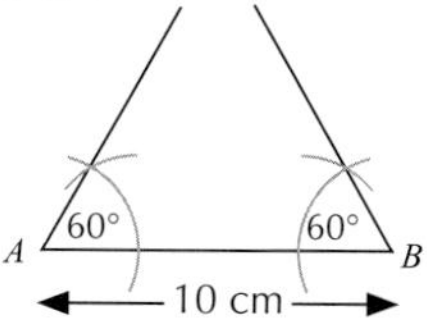

b) Draw a line 3 cm along the 60° line from B, marking C at the end.

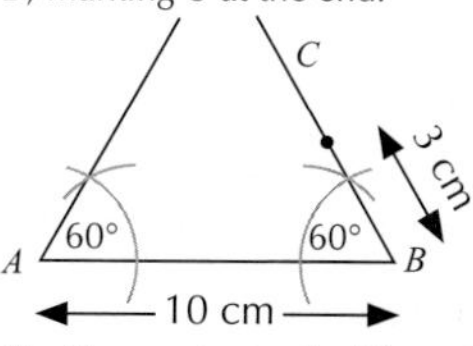

c) Finally, use the method from Q1 to construct a line parallel to AB that passes through C — the point where this line and the 60° line from A intersect is point D.

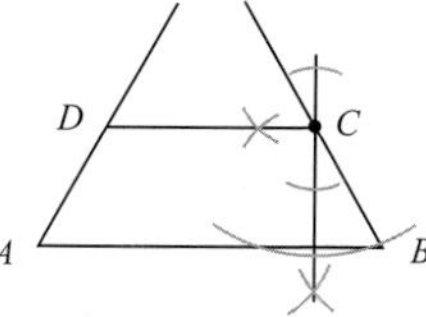

21.4 Loci

Page 340 Exercise 1

For this exercise, use a ruler to check that your drawings have the measurements shown.

1 Use your ruler to draw a 7 cm line. Next, set your compasses to 2 cm and draw a long arc around each end of the line. Finally, use your ruler to join the tops and the bottoms of each arc.

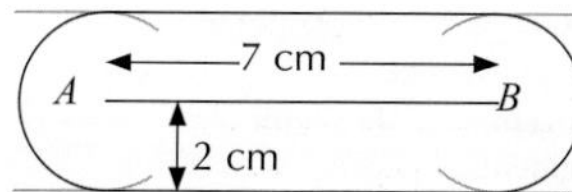

2 a) Set your compasses to 3 cm, place the point on X and draw a **circle**.

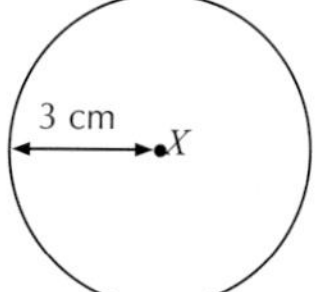

b) Shade the **inside** of the circle.

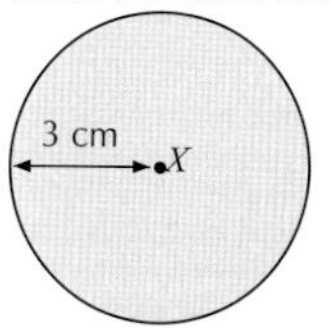

3 Use your ruler to draw two points 6 cm apart, then construct the **perpendicular bisector** of these points using the method from page 330.

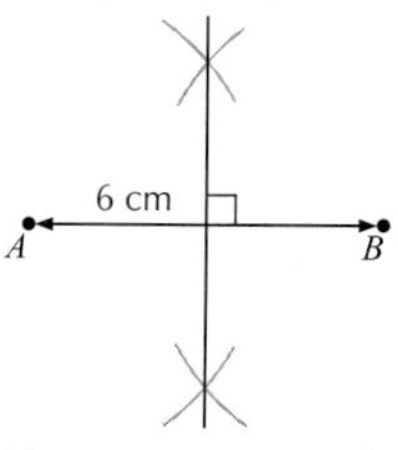

4 Use your protractor to draw two lines that meet at an angle of 50°, then construct the **angle bisector** of these lines using the method from page 331.

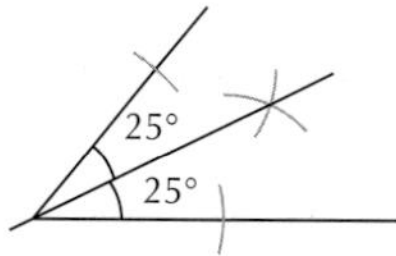

5 Using the same method as Q1:

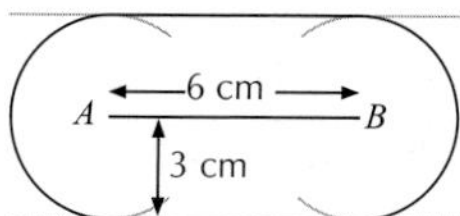

6 a), b) Using the same method as Q3:

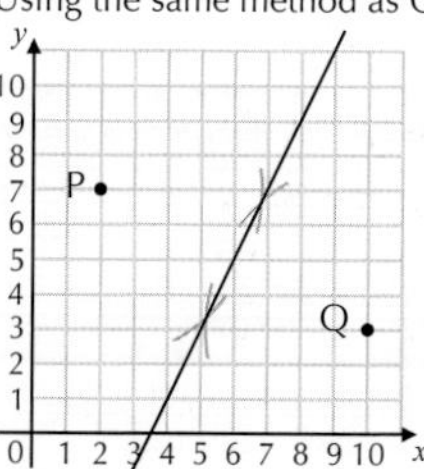

Page 341 Exercise 2

1 a)-d) Draw two points P and Q that are 5 cm apart. Draw a circle of radius 3 cm around P, and a circle of radius 4 cm around Q:

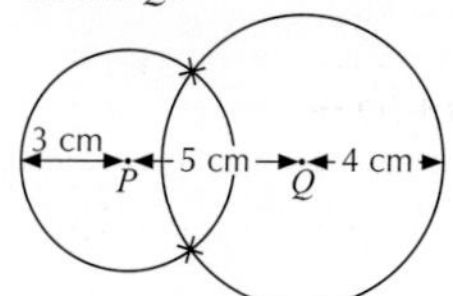

The points marked with crosses are both 3 cm from P and 4 cm from Q.

2 Set your compasses to 3 cm, place them at point B and draw an arc that is 3 cm from point B. Then using a ruler draw a line which is 4 cm from AD. Finally shade the required locus as showed below.

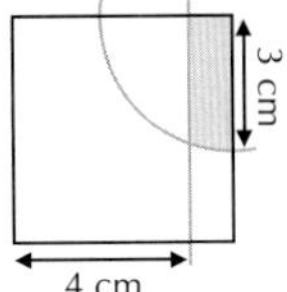

3 a) Using the method from page 329:

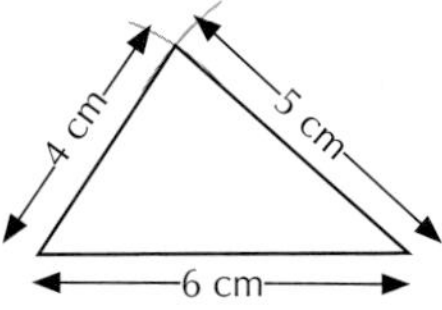

b) Set your compasses to 1 cm, and draw circles around each corner of the triangle. Then, draw two lines from each circle to each of the others, as shown in grey below. Finally, mark the required locus as shown below (it has two parts — one inside the original triangle and one outside).

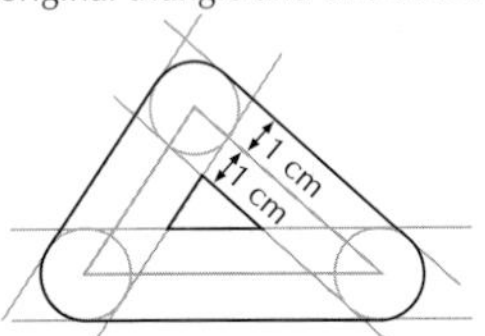

4 a) Using the method from page 329:

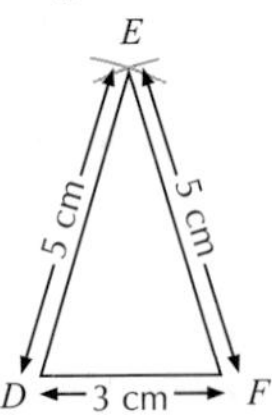

b) E.g. First, use your compasses to draw a circle of radius 2 cm around E. Next, construct the perpendicular bisector of DF using the method from page 330. The required locus is the set of points that are both on this line and inside the circle:

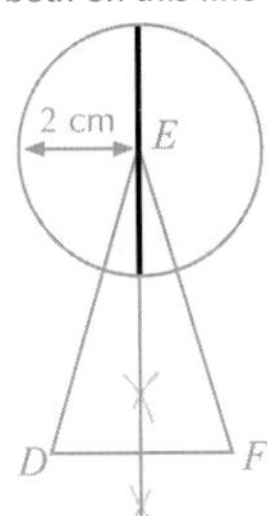

Page 342 Exercise 3

1 a)-b) The scale is 1 cm:1 km, so 3 km in real life will be 3 cm on the diagram. Draw P and L 3 cm apart, then construct the perpendicular bisector using the method from page 330.

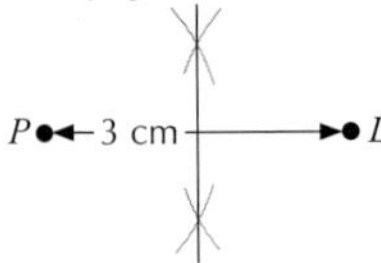

Remember to make all your measurements in relation to the scale given in the question.

2 a), b) The scale is 1 cm:10 miles, so 50 miles will be 50 ÷ 10 = 5 cm on the diagram. Draw A and B 5 cm apart.
40 miles will be 40 ÷ 10 = 4 cm on the diagram, so draw circles of radius 4 cm around each point.
The area where these circles overlap is the region where the camels could possibly meet.

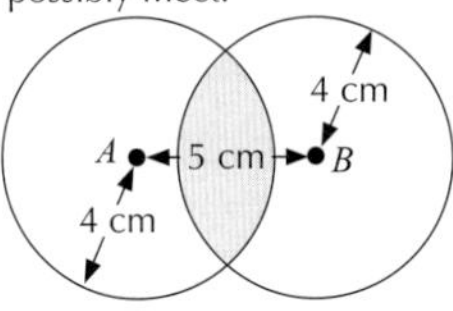

3 a) The scale is 1 cm:1 m so the length of the yard on the diagram is 4 cm, the width is 2 cm and the dog's lead is 1 cm. Use your ruler to draw a 2 cm by 4 cm rectangle. Then, set your compasses to 1 cm and draw an arc from one of the corners.
The required area is the inside of this quarter-circle:

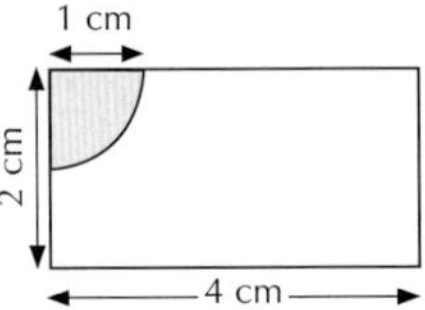

b) The rail will be 3 cm on the diagram. Use your ruler to measure 3 cm from the corner, then use your compasses to draw an arc of radius 1 cm around this point. Then, draw a horizontal line 1 cm from the top of the rectangle. Finally, shade the required area as shown below:

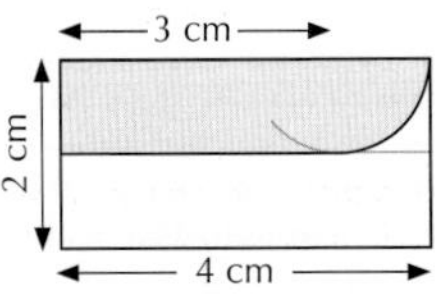

Page 343 Review Exercise

1 a) A: **radius** B: **diameter**
C: **circumference**

b) D: **tangent** E: **sector**
F: **segment**

2 a = **4.8 cm**
You may have a slightly different measurement — any answer between 4.7 cm and 4.9 cm is okay.
b = **120°**
Any answer between 118° and 122° is okay.
c = **1.8 cm**
Any answer between 1.7 cm and 1.9 cm is okay.

3 a) E.g. Draw the 11 cm line, using a ruler to measure the correct length. Then, set your compasses to 6.5 cm, and draw an arc from the right-hand end. Next set your compasses to 7 cm, and draw an arc from the left-hand end. Mark the point where these arcs cross and join it to the ends of the 11 cm line. If drawn correctly, the angles inside the triangle will be:

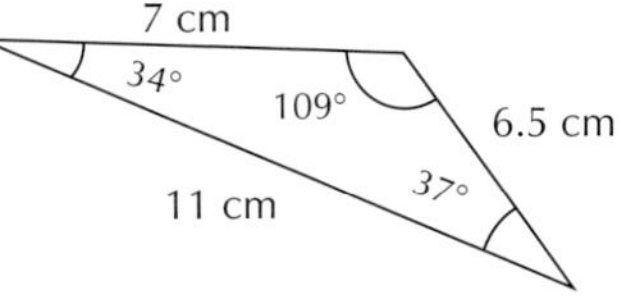

Using the same method for part b), the angles inside the triangle will be:

b)

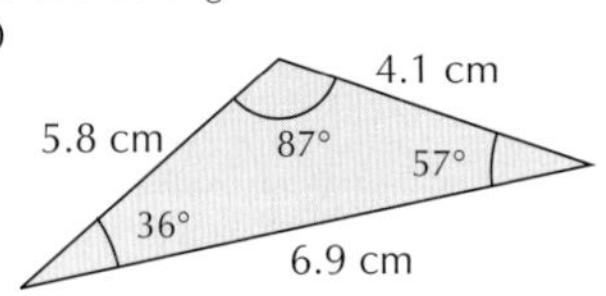

4 a) E.g. Use your ruler to draw line DE 5.8 cm long. Then, set your compasses to 5.8 cm and draw arcs from D and E. Mark point F where these arcs intersect. Then connect F to D and E using a ruler.

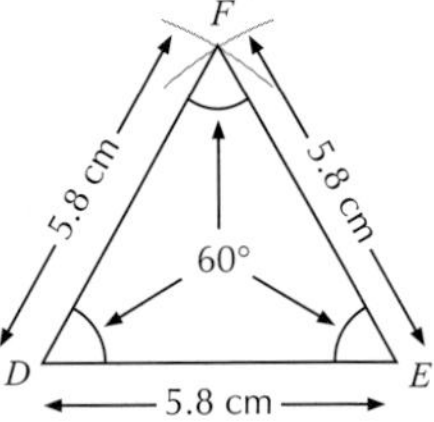

b) Using the method from page 337:

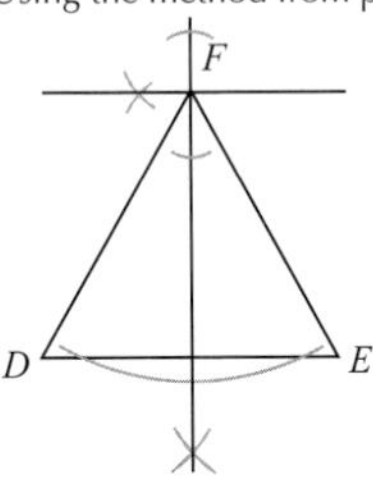

5 a) E.g. Use your ruler to draw line AB 7.4 cm long. Then, construct a 60° angle at A using the method from page 334.
Next, construct a 90° angle at B and bisect it, as shown on page 331. Mark the point where these two lines cross as C and join it to A and B.

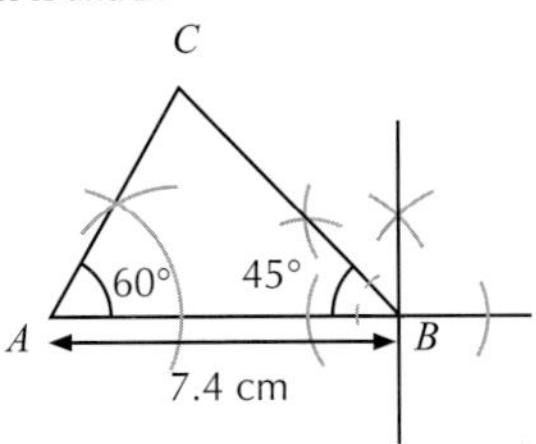

b) Angles in a triangle add up to 180°, so angle ACB + 45° + 60° = 180°
angle ACB = 180° – 45° – 60° = **75°**
Triangle rules are covered on page 242.

6 Copy the diagram, then construct the angle bisector using the method from page 331. The scale is 1 cm:0.5 m, so 3 m in real life will be 6 cm on the diagram. Use your ruler to measure 6 cm along the angle bisector and mark the position of the bonfire.

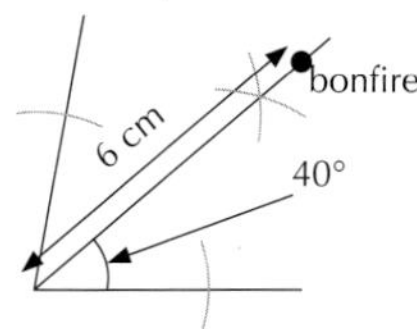

Page 344 Exam-Style Questions

1 Draw a 7.1 cm line, using a ruler to measure the correct length. Measure an angle of 22° at the end of the line using a protractor and mark it with a dot. Draw a line from the end of the 7.1 cm line through the dot. Then measure 7.1 cm along, mark this point, and join it to the other end of the original line.

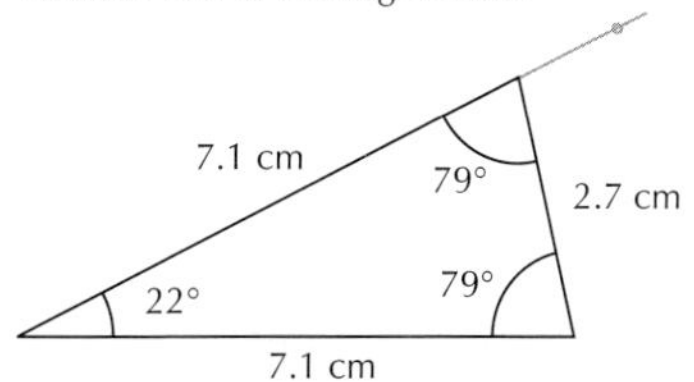

[3 marks available — 1 mark for accurately drawing one line, 1 mark for a correctly drawn angle of 22°, 1 mark for a fully correct triangle]

You can check you have the right triangle by measuring the other angles and making sure they are they same as those in the diagram above.

2 Construct a perpendicular line from S to the beach.

The shortest distance from a point to a line is always the perpendicular distance.

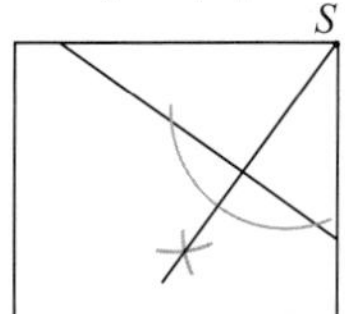

[3 marks available – 1 mark for the 2 arcs on the beach line (or a single arc crossing the line twice), 1 mark for the pair of intersecting arcs and 1 mark for the line from point S to the beach (or beyond) – the drawn line and the beach line must meet at angles between 89° and 91° inclusive]

3 a) Use your ruler to draw line AB 8 cm long. Set your compasses to 8 cm and draw arcs from A and B. Draw a line from A to where these arcs cross.

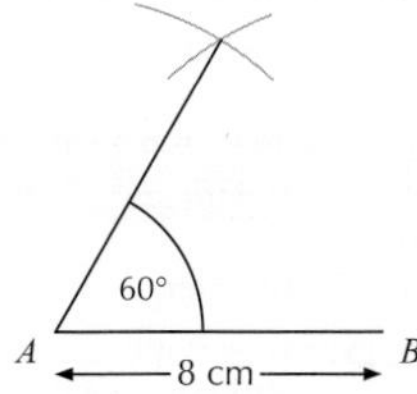

[2 marks available — 1 mark for two intersecting construction arcs and 1 mark for a fully correct construction of 60° angle]

b) E.g. Measure 8 cm along the 60° line and mark this point D.

This will be the point where the arcs crossed if you used the same method as above.

Set your compasses to 8 cm and draw arcs from B and D. Mark the point where these cross as point C and join it to B and D to complete the rhombus.

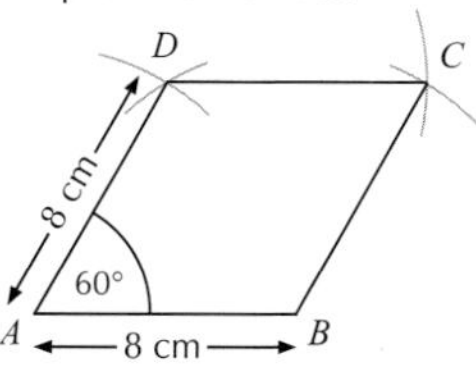

[3 marks available — 1 mark for accurately drawing one 8 cm line, 1 mark for two intersecting construction arcs and 1 mark for a fully correct rhombus]

4 The scale is 1 cm:100 m so on the diagram the road is 4 cm above the motorway. First, construct a perpendicular line to the motorway using your compasses using the method shown on page 333. Measure 4 cm from the motorway along this line using a ruler, and mark this point with a dot. Construct a parallel line to the motorway at this dot using the method shown on page 337.

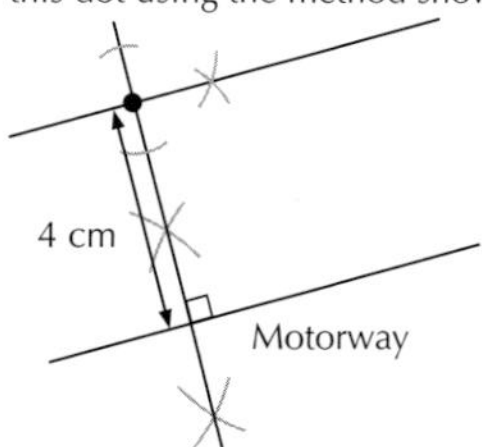

[3 marks available — 1 mark for at least one pair of two intersecting construction arcs, 1 mark for a correct perpendicular constructed to the motorway, 1 mark for a parallel line constructed 4 cm from the motorway]

5 The scale is 1 cm:1 m so on the diagram, region $ABCD$ is 10 cm × 10 cm and the treasure is 7 cm from corner C.

E.g. First, use your ruler to draw a 10 cm by 10 cm square using a ruler and a protractor. Since the treasure is the same distance from AB and AD, the treasure must lie on the angle bisector of the angle between these two lines. Since this is a square, the angle bisector is AC, so join A and C with a straight line. Next, set your compasses to 7 cm and draw an arc around C. The treasure is at the point where the arc and angle bisector intersect.

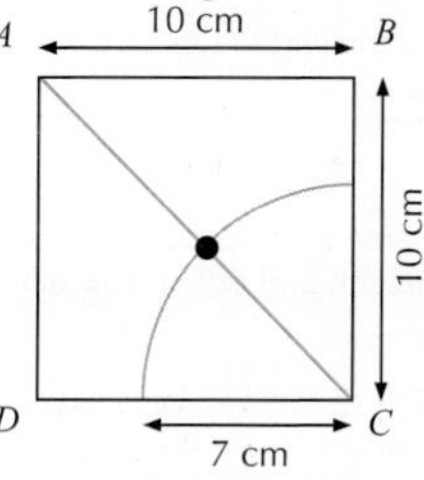

(location of treasure shown by the dot)

[4 marks available — 1 mark for correctly drawing a 10 cm × 10 cm square, 1 mark for finding the angle bisector of the angle between AB and AD, 1 mark for an arc of radius 7 cm from C and 1 mark for a fully correct answer with position of treasure clearly indicated]

Section 22 — Area and Perimeter

22.1 Rectangles and Triangles

Page 346 Exercise 1

1 a) $P = a + b + c = 3 + 4 + 5 =$ **12 cm**

b) $P = 2l + 2w = (2 \times 3) + (2 \times 11)$
$= 6 + 22 =$ **28 m**

c) $P = 4l = 4 \times 5 =$ **20 cm**

d) $P = 2l + 2w = (2 \times 4) + (2 \times 6)$
$= 8 + 12 =$ **20 cm**

e) $P = a + b + c = 14 + 11 + 18 =$ **43 m**

f) $P = 2l + 2w = (2 \times 15) + (2 \times 30)$
$= 30 + 60 =$ **90 mm**

2 a) $P = 4l = 4 \times 4 =$ **16 cm**

b) $P = a + b + c = 5 + 5 + 7 =$ **17 cm**

c) $P = 2l + 2w = (2 \times 8) + (2 \times 6)$
$= 16 + 12 =$ **28 m**

3 $P = (2 \times 2.1) + (2 \times 2.8) = 4.2 + 5.6 =$ **9.8 m**

Page 347 Exercise 2

1 a) $A = lw = 5 \times 10 =$ **50 cm²**

b) $A = \frac{1}{2}bh = \frac{1}{2} \times 9 \times 4 =$ **18 m²**

c) $A = l^2 = 4^2 =$ **16 mm²**

d) $A = l^2 = 11^2 =$ **121 cm²**

e) $A = lw = 3 \times 11 =$ **33 m²**

f) $A = \frac{1}{2}bh = \frac{1}{2} \times 10 \times 2 =$ **10 mm²**

2 a) $A = lw = 23 \times 15 =$ **345 mm²**

b) $A = l^2 = 17^2 =$ **289 m²**

c) $A = \frac{1}{2}bh = \frac{1}{2} \times 4 \times 12.5 =$ **25 cm²**

3 The lawn is a rectangle, so its area is:
$A = 23.5 \times 17.3 = 406.55$ m² = **407 m²** (to the nearest m²)

4 a) $A_{floor} = 9 \times 7.5 =$ **67.5 m²**

b) $A_{tile} = 0.5^2 =$ **0.25 m²**

c) $67.5 \div 0.25 =$ **270 tiles**

5 Area of the garden = 24 × 5.4 = 129.6 m²
60 cm = 60 ÷ 100 = 0.6 m, so the area covered by one roll of turf is 8 × 0.6 = 4.8 m².
So 129.6 ÷ 4.8 = **27 rolls** are needed.

6 The area of icing is made up from rectangles.

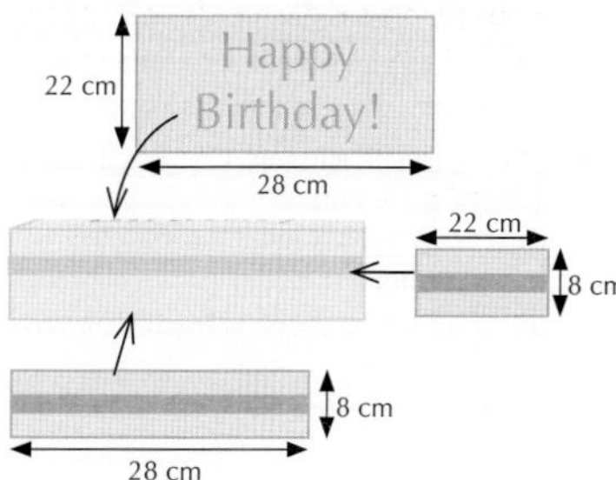

Area of top = 22 × 28 = 616 cm²
Area of front / back = 8 × 28 = 224 cm²
Area of sides = 8 × 22 = 176 cm²
So area of icing needed
= 616 + (2 × 224) + (2 × 176)
= **1416 cm²**

Page 349 Exercise 3

1 a) Split the shape into two rectangles along the dashed line.

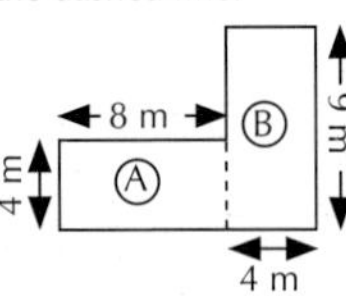

Area of A = 4 × 8 = 32 m²
Area of B = 9 × 4 = 36 m²
So total area = 32 + 36 = **68 m²**

b)

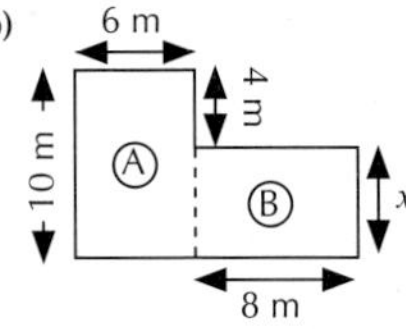

Missing side length x = 10 – 4 = 6 m
Area of A = 10 × 6 = 60 m²
Area of B = 6 × 8 = 48 m²
So total area = 60 + 48 = **108 m²**

c)

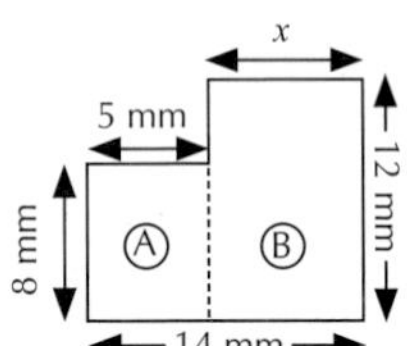

Missing side length x = 14 – 5 = 9 mm
Area of A = 8 × 5 = 40 mm²
Area of B = 12 × 9 = 108 mm²
So total area = 40 + 108 = **148 mm²**
Alternatively, you could have split the shape horizontally to make one rectangle with dimensions 8 × 14 and one with dimensions 4 × 9.

2 a) Missing side lengths are 12 – 8 = 4 cm and 13 – 5 = 8 cm.
(i) P = 8 + 5 + 4 + 8 + 12 + 13 = **50 cm**
(ii) Splitting the shape vertically into two rectangles:
A = (13 × 8) + (8 × 4) = **136 cm²**

b) Missing side lengths are 7 – 4 = 3 cm and 5 + 3 = 8 cm.
(i) P = 5 + 3 + 3 + 4 + 8 + 7 = **30 cm**
(ii) Splitting the shape vertically into two rectangles:
A = (7 × 5) + (4 × 3) = **47 cm²**

c) Missing side lengths are 15 + 8 = 23 mm and 23 – 10 = 13 mm.
(i) P = 23 + 23 + 8 + 13 + 15 + 10 = **92 mm**
(ii) Splitting the shape vertically into two rectangles:
A = (10 × 15) + (23 × 8) = **334 mm²**

3 a) Area of rectangle = 4 × 8 = 32 m²
Base of triangle = 20 – 8 = 12 m,
so area of triangle = $\frac{1}{2}$ × 12 × 4 = 24 m²
Total area = 32 + 24 = **56 m²**

b) Area of rectangle = 5 × 9 = 45 cm²
Base of triangle = 21 – 9 = 12 cm,
so area of triangle = $\frac{1}{2}$ × 12 × 5 = 30 cm²
Total area = 45 + 30 = **75 cm²**
The shapes in this question are trapeziums, so you could also have used the formula from page 351 to find their areas.

22.2 Other Quadrilaterals

Page 350 Exercise 1

1 a) $A = bh$ = 7 × 4 = **28 cm²**
b) $A = bh$ = 4 × 2 = **8 m²**
c) $A = bh$ = 6 × 8 = **48 mm²**

2 a) (i) A = 9 × 6 = **54 mm²**
(ii) P = (2 × 8) + (2 × 9) = **34 mm**
The lengths of opposite sides in a parallelogram are equal.
b) (i) A = 18 × 35 = **630 m²**
(ii) P = (2 × 50) + (2 × 18) = **136 m**
c) (i) A = 5.8 × 8.2 = **47.56 mm²**
(ii) P = (2 × 5.8) + (2 × 10) = **31.6 mm**

3 Area of one parallelogram = 8.2 × 3.1
= 25.42 cm²
So area of logo = 2 × 25.42 = **50.84 cm²**

4 Area of the part of the wall = 66 × 44
= 2904 cm²
There are 25 tiles on the wall, so the area of one tile is 2904 ÷ 25 = **116.16 cm²**.

5 **The square has the larger area.** The vertical height of the rhombus (a special type of parallelogram) is less than 6 cm, so its area will be less than the area of the square.

Page 352 Exercise 2

1 a) $A = \frac{1}{2}(a + b) \times h = \frac{1}{2}(4 + 10) \times 4$
$= \frac{1}{2} \times 14 \times 4$ = **28 m²**
b) $A = \frac{1}{2}(a + b) \times h = \frac{1}{2}(12 + 8) \times 9$
$= \frac{1}{2} \times 20 \times 9$ = **90 mm²**
c) $A = \frac{1}{2}(a + b) \times h = \frac{1}{2}(3 + 13) \times 5$
$= \frac{1}{2} \times 16 \times 5$ = **40 mm²**

2 a) Find the area of the two trapeziums separately.
Area of left trapezium = $\frac{1}{2}(7 + 4) \times 10$
= 55 m²
Area of right trapezium = $\frac{1}{2}(4 + 3) \times 10$
= 35 m²
So the area of the end of the barn is 55 + 35 = **90 m²**.
b) P = 10 + 10 + 7 + 10.44 + 10.05 + 3
= **50.49 m**

3 **They have the same area, since they have the same vertical height, and ½(9 + 3) = 6.**

Page 354 Exercise 3

1 a) Area of parallelogram = 10 × 6 = 60 cm²
Area of trapezium = $\frac{1}{2}(5 + 10) \times 3$
= 22.5 cm²
So the total area of the shaded region is 60 + 22.5 = **82.5 cm²**.
b) Area of large parallelogram = 16 × 10
= 160 mm²
Area of small parallelogram = 7 × 3
= 21 mm²
So the total area of the shaded region is 160 – 21 = **139 mm²**.

2 a) Split the shape along the dashed line to create two identical parallelograms.
(i) Area of one parallelogram = 8 × 6
= 48 mm²
Area of shape = 2 × 48 = **96 mm²**
(ii) P = 7 + 8 + 8 + 7+ 8 + 8 = **46 mm**
b) Split the shape along the dashed line to create two identical trapeziums.
(i) Height of one trapezium = 8.5 ÷ 2
= 4.25 m
Area of one trapezium
= $\frac{1}{2}(5 + 16) \times 4.25$ = 44.625 m²
Area of shape = 2 × 44.625 = **89.25 m²**
(ii) P = 6 + 5 + 6 + 6 + 5 + 6 = **34 m**
c) The shape is already split into two identical parallelograms and a square.
(i) Area of one parallelogram = 12 × 8
= 96 m²
Area of square = 12² = 144 m²
Area of shape = (2 × 96) + 144
= **336 m²**
(ii) P = 12 + 10 + 12 + 10 + 12
+ 10 + 12 + 10 = **88 m**
d) The shape is already split into a trapezium and a triangle.
(i) Area of trapezium = $\frac{1}{2}(14 + 26) \times 30$
= 600 m²
Area of triangle = $\frac{1}{2}$ × 14 × 30
= 210 m²
Area of shape = 600 + 210 = **810 m²**
(ii) P = 26 + 31 + 31 + 31 + 31 = **150 m**

3 a) $A = \frac{1}{2}(20 + 40) \times 60$ = **1800 cm²**
b) Base of one parallelogram = 20 ÷ 2 = 10 cm
Area of one parallelogram = 10 × 60
= 600 cm²
Total area of coloured strips = 2 × 600
= **1200 cm²**

22.3 Circumference of a Circle

Page 356 Exercise 1

1 a) $C = \pi d = \pi \times 5$ = 15.707......
= **15.7 cm** (1 d.p.)
b) $C = \pi d = \pi \times 12$ = 37.699...
= **37.7 cm** (1 d.p.)
c) $C = \pi d = \pi \times 2$ = 6.283... = **6.3 cm** (1 d.p.)
d) $C = \pi d = \pi \times 10$ = 31.415...
= **31.4 cm** (1 d.p.)

2 a) $C = \pi d = \pi \times 30$ = **30π mm**
Using the same method for b)-d):
b) **5π mm** c) **7π m**
d) **9π cm**

3 a) (i) $d = 2r = \mathbf{4\ cm}$

(ii) $C = \pi d = \pi \times 4 = 12.566...$
$= \mathbf{12.6\ cm}$ (1 d.p.)

b) (i) $d = 2r = \mathbf{5\ cm}$

(ii) $C = \pi d = \pi \times 5 = 15.707...$
$= \mathbf{15.7\ cm}$ (1 d.p.)

c) (i) $d = 2r = \mathbf{1\ m}$

(ii) $C = \pi d = \pi \times 1 = 3.141...$
$= \mathbf{3.1\ m}$ (1 d.p.)

d) (i) $d = 2r = \mathbf{3\ mm}$

(ii) $C = \pi d = \pi \times 3 = 9.424...$
$= \mathbf{9.4\ mm}$ (1 d.p.)

4 a) $C = \pi d = \mathbf{4\pi\ cm}$

b) $C = \pi d = \mathbf{8\pi\ mm}$

c) $C = 2\pi r = 2 \times \pi \times 14 = \mathbf{28\pi\ km}$

d) $C = 2\pi r = 2 \times \pi \times 0.1 = \mathbf{0.2\pi\ km}$ or $\mathbf{\frac{\pi}{5}\ km}$

Page 357 Exercise 2

1 a) Circumference of full circle $= \pi d = \pi \times 4$
$= 12.566...$ cm
Curved part of semicircle $= 12.566... \div 2$
$= 6.283...$ cm
Perimeter $= 6.283... + 4 = 10.283...$
$= \mathbf{10.3\ cm}$ (1 d.p.)

b) Circumference of full circle $= \pi d = \pi \times 26$
$= 81.681...$ mm
Curved part of semicircle $= 81.681... \div 2$
$= 40.840...$ mm
Perimeter $= 40.840... + 26 = 66.840...$
$= \mathbf{66.8\ mm}$ (1 d.p.)

c) Circumference of full circle $= 2\pi r$
$= 2 \times \pi \times 2 = 12.566...$ m
Curved part of semicircle $= 12.566... \div 2$
$= 6.283...$ m
Perimeter $= 6.283... + 4 = 10.283...$
$= \mathbf{10.3\ m}$ (1 d.p.)
The straight edge of the semicircle is the diameter of the circle, which is twice the radius (i.e. 2 × 2 = 4 m).

d) Circumference of full circle $= 2\pi r$
$= 2 \times \pi \times 7 = 43.982...$ cm
Curved part of semicircle $= 43.982... \div 2$
$= 21.991...$ cm
Perimeter $= 21.991... + 14 = 35.991...$
$= \mathbf{36.0\ cm}$ (1 d.p.)

2 a) Curved side $= (\pi \times 4) \div 2$
$= 6.283...$ cm
Perimeter $= 3 + 4 + 3 + 6.283... = 16.283...$
$= \mathbf{16.3\ cm}$ (1 d.p.)

b) Curved side $= (2 \times \pi \times 8) \div 2$
$= 25.132...$ mm
Perimeter $= 10 + 16 + 10 + 25.132...$
$= 61.132... = \mathbf{61.1\ mm}$ (1 d.p.)
The vertical straight edge of the shape has the same length as the diameter of the full circle: 2 × 8 = 16 mm.

c) Curved side $= (\pi \times 5) \div 2 = 7.853...$ cm
Perimeter $= 4 + 4 + 7.853... = 15.853...$
$= \mathbf{15.9\ cm}$ (1 d.p.)

d) Curved side $= (2 \times \pi \times 9) \div 4$
$= 14.137...$ mm
Perimeter $= 9 + 9 + 14.137... = 32.137...$
$= \mathbf{32.1\ mm}$ (1 d.p.)
The shape is a quarter-circle, so you have to divide the circumference of the full circle by 4 to find the length of the curved side.

e) Curved side $= (2 \times \pi \times 9) \div 4$
$= 14.137...$ mm
Perimeter $= 9 + 9 + 9 + 9 + 14.137...$
$= 50.137... = \mathbf{50.1\ mm}$ (1 d.p.)

f) One curved side $= (\pi \times 3) \div 2$
$= 4.712...$ cm
Perimeter $= 2 + 4.712... + 2 + 4.712...$
$= 13.424... = \mathbf{13.4\ cm}$ (1 d.p.)

3 Circumference of full circle $= 2 \times \pi \times 16$
$= 100.530...$ m
So amount of fencing needed is
$100.530... \div 2 = 50.265... = \mathbf{50.3\ m}$ (1 d.p.)

4 Length of one curved section
$= (2 \times \pi \times 80) \div 2 = 251.327...$ m
Total length
$= 251.327... + 100 + 251.327... + 100$
$= 702.654... = \mathbf{703\ m}$ (to the nearest metre)

22.4 Area of a Circle

Page 358 Exercise 1

1 a) $A = \pi r^2 = \pi \times 2^2 = 12.566...$
$= \mathbf{12.6\ cm^2}$ (1 d.p.)

b) $A = \pi r^2 = \pi \times 10^2 = 314.159...$
$= \mathbf{314.2\ mm^2}$ (1 d.p.)

c) $d = 7$ m, so $r = 7 \div 2 = 3.5$ m
$A = \pi r^2 = \pi \times 3.5^2 = 38.484...$
$= \mathbf{38.5\ m^2}$ (1 d.p.)

d) $d = 12$ mm, so $r = 12 \div 2 = 6$ mm
$A = \pi r^2 = \pi \times 6^2 = 113.097...$
$= \mathbf{113.1\ mm^2}$ (1 d.p.)

2 a) $A = \pi r^2 = \pi \times 7^2 = \mathbf{49\pi\ mm^2}$

b) $A = \pi r^2 = \pi \times 5^2 = \mathbf{25\pi\ cm^2}$

c) $d = 18$ km, so $r = 18 \div 2 = 9$ km
$A = \pi r^2 = \pi \times 9^2 = \mathbf{81\pi\ km^2}$

d) $d = 3$ m, so $r = 3 \div 2 = 1.5$ m
$A = \pi r^2 = \pi \times 1.5^2 = \mathbf{2.25\pi\ m^2}$ or $\mathbf{\frac{9\pi}{4}\ m^2}$

3 Area of reservoir $= \pi r^2 = \pi \times 0.82^2 = 2.112...$
$= \mathbf{2.11\ km^2}$ (2 d.p.)

4 Area of rectangle $= 20 \times 22 = 440\ \text{mm}^2$
Area of circle $= \pi \times 12^2 = 452.389...\ \text{mm}^2$
So the **circle** has the greater area.
Remember to use the radius of the circle to find the area. The diameter of this circle is 24 mm, so the radius is 24 ÷ 2 = 12 mm.

Page 359 Exercise 2

1 a) Area of full circle $= \pi r^2 = \pi \times 7^2$
$= 153.938...\ \text{cm}^2$
Area of semicircle $= 153.938... \div 2$
$= 76.969... = \mathbf{77.0\ cm^2}$ (1 d.p.)

b) Split the shape into a semicircle and a square.
Area of semicircle $= (\pi \times 5^2) \div 2$
$= 39.269...\ \text{mm}^2$
Area of square $= 10^2 = 100\ \text{mm}^2$
Total area of shape $= 39.269... + 100$
$= 139.269...\ \text{mm}^2 = \mathbf{139.3\ mm^2}$ (1 d.p.)
The radius of the semicircle is 5 mm, so the diameter is 2 × 5 = 10 mm. This diameter is also the top side of the quadrilateral, so the width of the quadrilateral is 10 mm, making it a square.

c) Split the shape into a semicircle and a rectangle.
Area of semicircle $= (\pi \times 3^2) \div 2$
$= 14.137...\ \text{cm}^2$
Area of rectangle $= 2 \times 6 = 12\ \text{cm}^2$
Total area of shape $= 14.137... + 12$
$= 26.137... = \mathbf{26.1\ cm^2}$ (1 d.p.)

d) Split the shape into two identical semicircles and a rectangle.
Area of one semicircle $= (\pi \times 4^2) \div 2$
$= 25.132...\ \text{mm}^2$
Length of rectangle $= 20 - 4 - 4 = 12$ mm
Area of rectangle $= 12 \times 8 = 96\ \text{mm}^2$
Total area of shape $= (2 \times 25.132...) + 96$
$= 146.265... = \mathbf{146.3\ mm^2}$ (1 d.p.)
You might have noticed that if you put the two semicircles together, then you get the full circle with radius 4 mm. So you could have just used the area of the circle and the rectangle, instead of using the area of two semicircles.

e) Split the shape into a quarter-circle and a square.
Area of quarter-circle $= (\pi \times 10^2) \div 4$
$= 78.539...\ \text{mm}^2$
Area of square $= 10^2 = 100\ \text{mm}^2$
Total area of shape $= 78.539... + 100$
$= 178.539... = \mathbf{178.5\ mm^2}$ (1 d.p.)
The area of a quarter-circle is one quarter of the area of the full circle, so you divide by 4 to find it.

f) Split the shape into two quarter-circles and a square.
Area of one quarter-circle $= (\pi \times 2^2) \div 4$
$= 3.141...\ \text{cm}^2$
Area of square $= 2^2 = 4\ \text{cm}^2$
Total area of shape $= (2 \times 3.141...) + 4$
$= 10.283... = \mathbf{10.3\ cm^2}$ (1 d.p.)

2 Label the diagram with the length and width of the rectangle, and the radius of the semicircle.

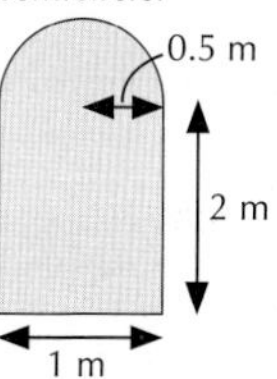

Area of semicircle $= (\pi \times 0.5^2) \div 2$
$= 0.392...\ \text{m}^2$
Area of rectangle $= 2 \times 1 = 2\ \text{m}^2$
Total area of church window
$= 0.392... + 2$
$= 2.392... = \mathbf{2.39\ m^2}$ (2 d.p.)

3 The pond is a circle of radius 2 m. Including the path creates a circle with radius 3 m. To find the area of the path, subtract the area of the pond from the total area.
Area including path $= \pi \times 3^2 = 28.274...\ \text{m}^2$
Area of pond $= \pi \times 2^2 = 12.566...\ \text{m}^2$
So area of path $= 28.274... - 12.566...$
$= 15.707... = \mathbf{16\ m^2}$ (to the nearest m²)

22.5 Arcs and Sectors of Circles

Page 360 Exercise 1

1 a) Arc length $= \frac{\theta}{360°} \times 2\pi r$
$= \frac{15°}{360°} \times 2 \times \pi \times 3 = \frac{1}{24} \times 6\pi = \mathbf{\frac{\pi}{4}\ cm}$
Sector area $= \frac{\theta}{360°} \times \pi r^2$
$= \frac{15°}{360°} \times \pi \times 3^2 = \frac{1}{24} \times \pi \times 9 = \mathbf{\frac{3\pi}{8}\ cm^2}$

b) Arc length $= \frac{100°}{360°} \times 2 \times \pi \times 4 = \mathbf{\frac{20\pi}{9}\ cm}$
Sector area $= \frac{100°}{360°} \times \pi \times 4^2 = \mathbf{\frac{40\pi}{9}\ cm^2}$

c) Arc length = $\frac{45°}{360°} \times 2 \times \pi \times 10 = \mathbf{\frac{5\pi}{2}}$ **cm**

Sector area = $\frac{45°}{360°} \times \pi \times 10^2 = \mathbf{\frac{25\pi}{2}}$ **cm²**

d) Diameter = 10 cm, so radius = 10 ÷ 2 = 5 cm

Arc length = $\frac{120°}{360°} \times 2 \times \pi \times 5 = \mathbf{\frac{10\pi}{3}}$ **cm**

Sector area = $\frac{120°}{360°} \times \pi \times 5^2 = \mathbf{\frac{25\pi}{3}}$ **cm²**

2 a) Sector area = $\frac{311°}{360°} \times \pi \times 5.5^2$
= 82.098... cm²
= **82.10 cm²** (2 d.p.)

Arc length = $\frac{311°}{360°} \times 2 \times \pi \times 5.5$
= 29.853... = **29.85 cm** (2 d.p.)

b) Sector area = $\frac{206°}{360°} \times \pi \times 10.5^2$
= 198.195... = **198.20 in²** (2 d.p.)

Arc length = $\frac{206°}{360°} \times 2 \times \pi \times 10.5$
= 37.751... = **37.75 in** (2 d.p.)

c) 39° < 180°, so 39° is the angle of the minor sector. The angle of the major sector is 360° – 39° = 321°.

Sector area = $\frac{321°}{360°} \times \pi \times 12^2$
= 403.380... = **403.38 in²** (2 d.p.)

Arc length = $\frac{321°}{360°} \times 2 \times \pi \times 12$
= 67.230... = **67.23 in** (2 d.p.)

d) The angle of the major sector is 360° – 172° = 188°.

Sector area = $\frac{188°}{360°} \times \pi \times 6.5^2$
= 69.315... = **69.32 m²** (2 d.p.)

Arc length = $\frac{188°}{360°} \times 2 \times \pi \times 6.5$
= 21.327... = **21.33 m** (2 d.p.)

Page 361 Review Exercise

1 a) (i) $P = (2 \times 1.4) + (2 \times 3.1) =$ **9 cm**

(ii) $A = 1.4 \times 3.1 =$ **4.34 cm²**

b) (i) $P = (2 \times 1.1) + (2 \times 3.1) =$ **8.4 mm**

(ii) $A = 1.1 \times 3.1 =$ **3.41 mm²**

c) (i) $P = 4 \times 1.8 =$ **7.2 cm**

(ii) $A = 1.8^2 =$ **3.24 cm²**

2 a) (i) $P = 7 + 8 + 9 =$ **24 cm**

(ii) $A = \frac{1}{2} \times 8 \times 6.7 =$ **26.8 cm²**

b) (i) $P = 4 + 13 + 13 =$ **30 mm**

The tick marks on the triangle show that two of the sides are equal — so the triangle is isosceles (see p.242).

(ii) $A = \frac{1}{2} \times 4 \times 12.8 =$ **25.6 mm²**

c) (i) $P = 8.9 + 15.1 + 18.8 =$ **42.8 mm**

(ii) $A = \frac{1}{2} \times 18.8 \times 7 =$ **65.8 mm²**

3 a) $A = \frac{1}{2}(3 + 8) \times 4 =$ **22 cm²**

b) $A = 21 \times 10 =$ **210 m²**

c) $A = \frac{1}{2}(20 + 55) \times 25 =$ **937.5 mm²**

4 a) Split the shape into two trapeziums.

$A_1 = \frac{1}{2}(1 + 4) \times 1.5 = 3.75$ m²

$A_2 = \frac{1}{2}(4 + 6) \times 1.5 = 7.5$ m²

So total shaded area = 3.75 + 7.5 = 11.25
= **11.3 m²** (1 d.p.)

b) Split the shape into a trapezium and a semicircle.

Area of trapezium = $\frac{1}{2}(20 + 40) \times 50$
= 1500 mm²

Area of semicircle = $(\pi \times 20^2) \div 2$
= 628.318... mm²

So total shaded area = 1500 + 628.318...
= 2128.318... =
2128.3 mm² (1 d.p.)

c) Area of one parallelogram = 9 × 6
= 54 mm²

So total area of shaded region = 4 × 54
= **216.0 mm²**

5 a) Circumference = 2 × π × 1.3 = 8.168...
= **8.17 cm** (2 d.p.)

b) Area of 2p coin = π × 1.3² = 5.309... cm²

Radius of 5p coin = 1.8 ÷ 2 = 0.9 cm

Area of 5p coin = π × 0.9² = 2.544... cm²

So area of two 5p coins = 2 × 2.544...
= 5.089... cm²

So the **2p coin** has the greater area.

6 The angle of the major sector is 320°, so the angle of the minor sector is 360° – 320° = 40°. The radius is 10 ÷ 2 = 5 m.

Arc length = $\frac{40°}{360°} \times 2 \times \pi \times 5 = \frac{1}{9} \times 10 \times \pi$
$= \mathbf{\frac{10\pi}{9}}$ **m**

Sector area = $\frac{40°}{360°} \times \pi \times 5^2 = \frac{1}{9} \times \pi \times 25$
$= \mathbf{\frac{25\pi}{9}}$ **m²**

Page 362 Exam-Style Questions

1 Circumference = $2\pi r = \pi^2$ *[1 mark]*

So $r = \frac{\pi^2}{2\pi} = \mathbf{\frac{\pi}{2}}$ **cm** *[1 mark]*

2 Let the top and bottom pieces of the frame have area A_1 and the two sides have area A_2:

$A_1 = \frac{1}{2}(14 + 22) \times 2 = 36$ cm²

$A_2 = \frac{1}{2}(8 + 16) \times 2 = 24$ cm²

[1 mark for a correct method to find the area of one of the trapeziums]

So total area = (2 × 36) + (2 × 24) *[1 mark]*
= **120 cm²** *[1 mark]*

3 Diameter of a circle = 12 ÷ 2 = 6 cm

Radius of a circle = 6 ÷ 2 = 3 cm

Area of one circle = π × 3² = 28.274... cm² *[1 mark]*

Area of all four circles = 4 × 28.274...
= 113.097... cm²

Area of square = 12² = 144 cm² *[1 mark]*

So area of unshaded region = 144 – 113.097... *[1 mark]* = 30.902... = **31 cm²** (2 s.f.) *[1 mark]*

4 Perimeter = 16 + 16 + Arc length = 41 cm
⇒ Arc length = 41 – 16 – 16 = 9 cm

Arc length = $\frac{\theta}{360°} \times 2 \times \pi \times 16 = 9$

$\Rightarrow \frac{\theta}{360°} \times 32\pi = 9 \Rightarrow \frac{\theta}{360°} = 9 \div 32\pi$
= 0.0895...

So θ = 0.0895... × 360° = 32.228... = **32°** (to the nearest degree)

[4 marks available — 1 mark for the correct arc length, 1 mark for using the formula for the arc length, 1 mark for attempting to rearrange to find θ, 1 mark for the correct final answer]

Section 23 — 3D Shapes

23.1 Properties of 3D Shapes

Page 364 Exercise 1

1 The faces are the flat surfaces, the vertices are the corners and the edges are the places where the faces meet.

a) (i) **Cuboid**

(ii) Faces:

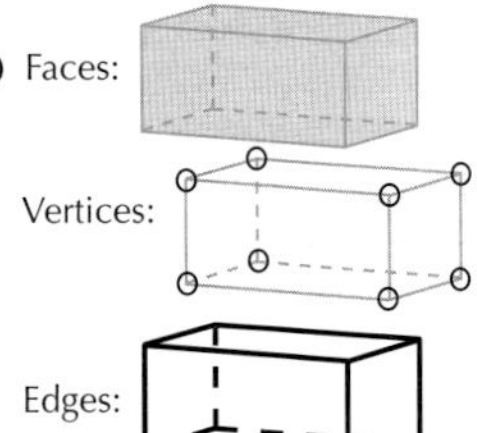

Vertices:

Edges:

So there are **6 faces, 8 vertices, 12 edges.**

b) (i) **Triangular prism**

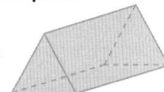

(ii) Faces:

Vertices:

Edges:

So there are **5 faces, 6 vertices, 9 edges.**

Using the same method for c)-d):

c) (i) **Tetrahedron (or triangular based pyramid)**

(ii) **4 faces, 4 vertices, 6 edges**

d) (i) **Square-based pyramid**

(ii) **5 faces, 5 vertices, 8 edges**

2 a) **Cube** b) **Triangular prism**

c) **Tetrahedron (or triangular-based pyramid)**

d) **Square-based pyramid** e) **Cylinder**

3 Prisms have a constant cross-section. Imagine slicing each of the shapes along its length — if it's a prism, the new face will be the same as the face parallel to your slice: ***A***, ***B*** and ***C*** are prisms.

A cube is a special type of prism — the cross-sections along its length, width and height are all the same.

Page 365 Exercise 2

1 a)

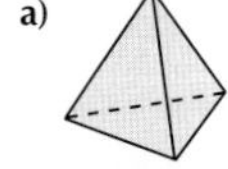

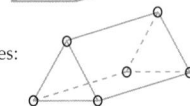

(i) **0 squares** (ii) **4 triangles**

b)

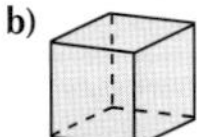

(i) **6 squares** (ii) **0 triangles**

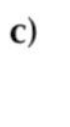

c)

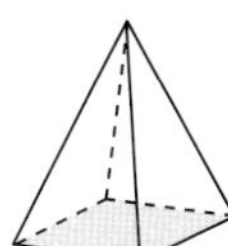

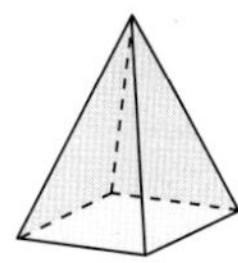

(i) 1 square (ii) 4 triangles

2 The 3D shape will have the same number of faces as the number of shapes that make up the net. There are 8 triangles in the net, so there will be **8 faces**.

3 Imagine folding up the nets to make them into solids.

a) **Square-based Pyramid**

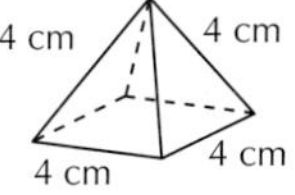

b) **Triangular Prism**

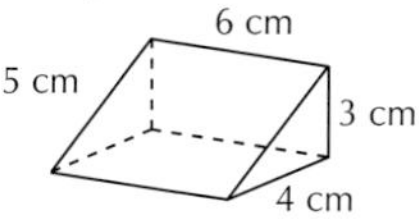

c) **Cuboid**

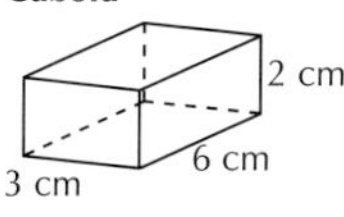

4 The base and top rectangles are 3 cm × 4 cm. The two smaller vertical rectangles are 2 cm × 3 cm. The two larger vertical rectangles are 2 cm × 4 cm. This gives:

a) 2 b) 2 c) 2 d) 0

5 The base of the prism is 4 cm × 6 cm. The vertical rectangle at the back is 3 cm × 6 cm. The sloping rectangle is 5 cm × 6 cm. This gives:

a) 1 b) 1 c) 1 d) 0

6 **Net *C*** because it's the only net where the edges match correctly when it's folded.

Page 367 Exercise 3

1 a) You need to add two 5 cm × 3 cm rectangles.

E.g.

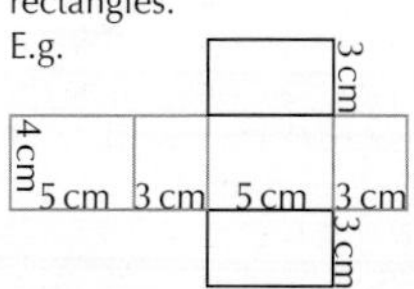

There's more than one possible net for any 3D shape, so your answers to this exercise might look different from the diagrams given. If your net could be folded up to make the given 3D shape then it's correct.

b) You need to add two 1 cm × 3 cm rectangles and one triangle with sides of length 1 cm.

E.g.

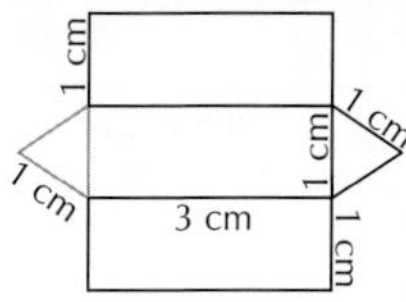

2 a) There should be six faces, each with 1 cm sides.

E.g.

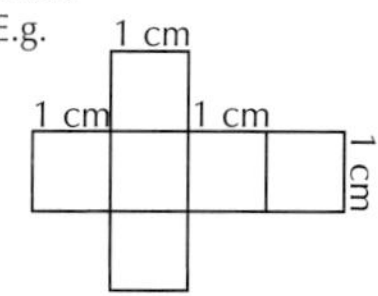

b) There should be two 3 cm × 1 cm rectangles, two 1 cm × 1.5 cm rectangles and two 3 cm × 1.5 cm rectangles. E.g.

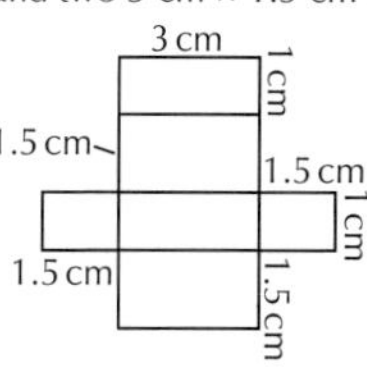

c) There should be two triangles and three rectangles with dimensions as shown. E.g.

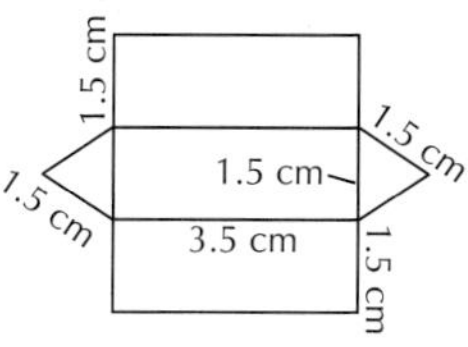

d) There should be three rectangles and two triangles, with dimensions as shown. E.g.

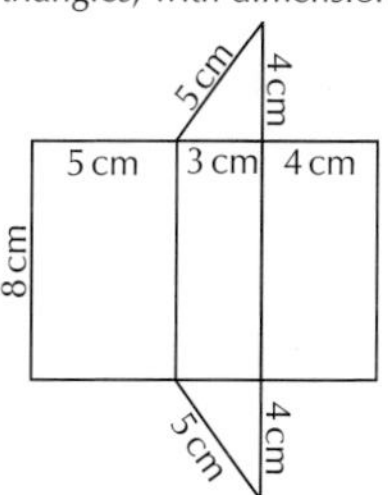

e) There should be a 2 cm × 2 cm square and four triangles with dimensions as shown. E.g.

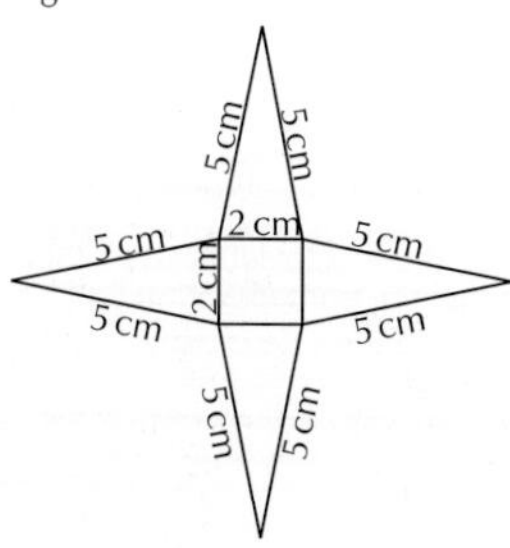

f) There should be four triangles with sides of 5 cm. E.g.

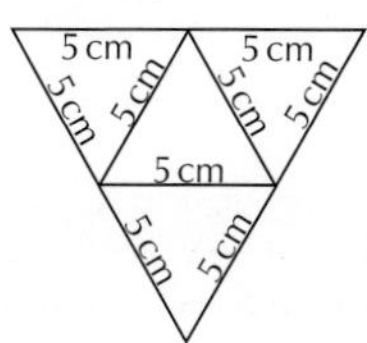

g) There should be one rectangular face of width 7 cm and length $2\pi r = 2 \times \pi \times 2$ = 12.57 cm (2 d.p.), and two circular faces with radius 2 cm attached to either side of the rectangle as shown. E.g.

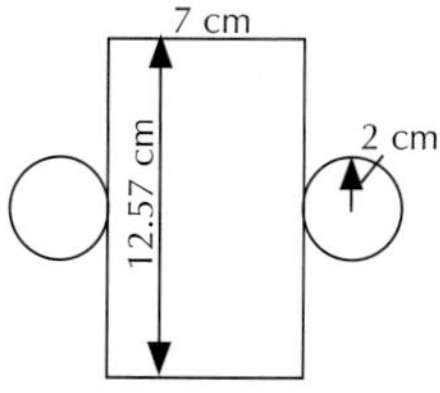

h) There should be one rectangular face of width 3 cm and length $\pi d = \pi \times 6$ = 18.85 cm (2 d.p.), and two circular faces with diameter 6 cm attached to either side of the rectangle as shown. E.g.

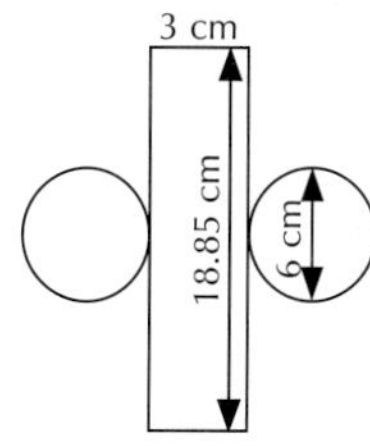

Using the same methods for Q3:

3 a) E.g.

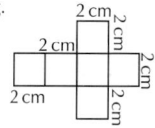

2 cm, 2 cm, 2 cm, 2 cm, 2 cm, 2 cm

b) E.g.

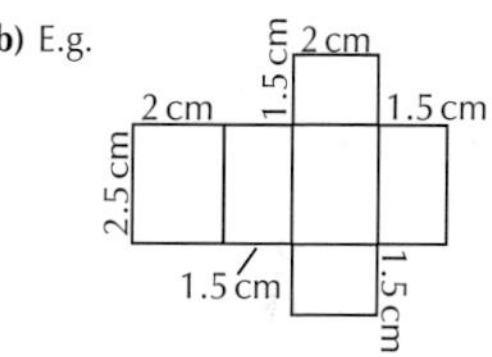

c) E.g.

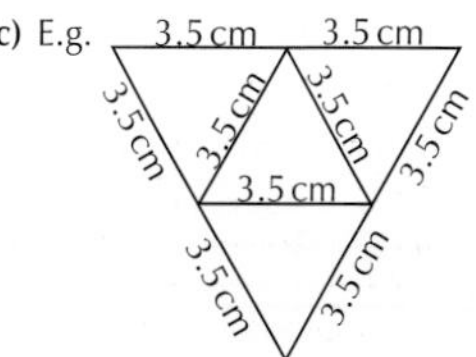

d) E.g.

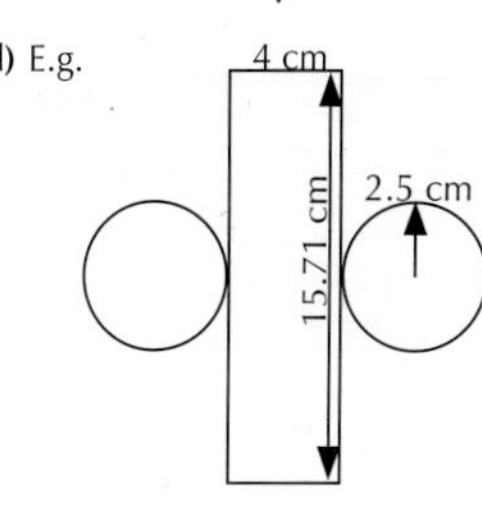

23.2 Plans and Elevations

Page 369 Exercise 1

1 The plan is the view of the shape from above.

a) From above, the shape looks like a 2 × 2 square:

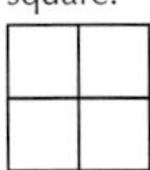

To picture the plan for a 3D shape, imagine you're hovering directly above the shape, looking down on it.

b) From above, the shape looks like an upside down L-shape 3 high and 2 across:

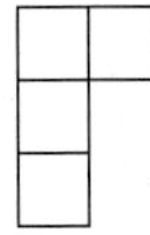

2 The side elevation is the view of the shape from the direction indicated 'Side'.

a) From the side, the shape looks like a 2 × 1 rectangle:

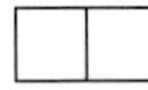

b) From the side, the shape looks like a backwards L-shape 2 high and 2 across:

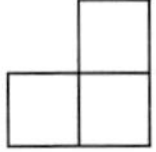

3 a) (i) The plan view is the view from above, so only one square is seen:

Plan

(ii) The front elevation and side elevation both show three squares on top of each other:

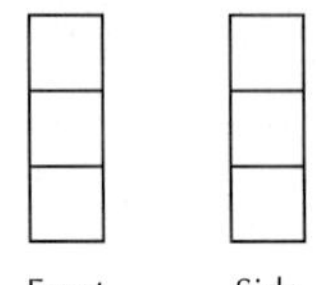

b) (i) Looking vertically from above, you can see an upside down L-shape:

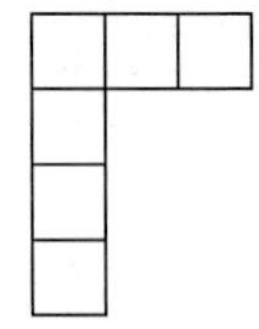

Plan

(ii) The views from the front and the side are also L-shapes:

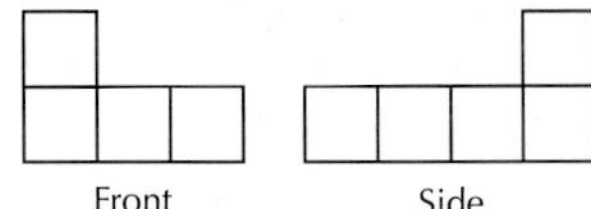

Check the "front" and "side" directions on the 3D diagram, to make sure you're labelling your elevations correctly.

Using the same method for c)-d):

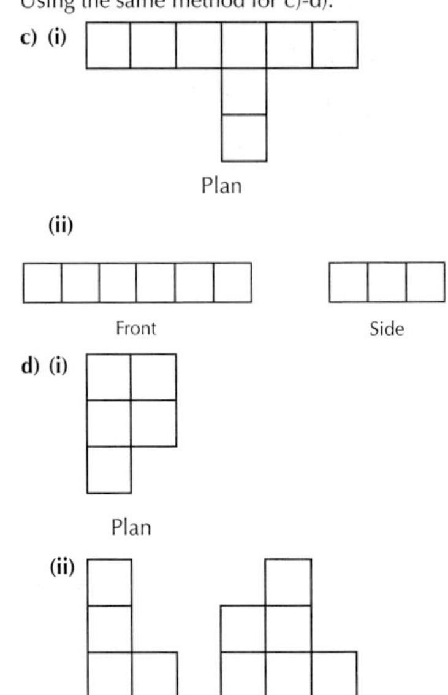

4 *B* — the side elevation is a sideways T-shape, which only matches shape *B*. The plan view matches *B* because the vertical line down the centre indicates the step on the top of the shape. The front elevation matches *B* because the two horizontal lines indicate where the piece sticks out at the front of the shape.

Page 370 Exercise 2

1 a) As the shape is a cube, all elevations will be the same:

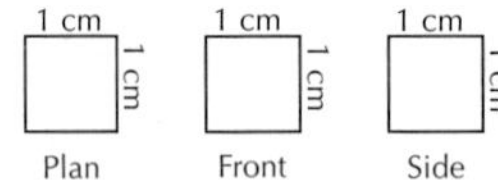

b) The plan and front elevation will be rectangles. The side elevation will be a square:

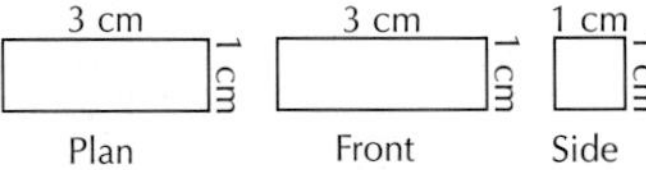

c) The plan will be a rectangle divided down the middle, the front elevation will be a triangle and the side elevation will be a rectangle.

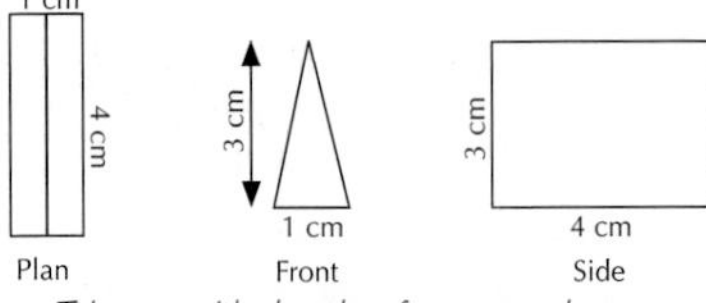

Take care with sloped surfaces — make sure you have chosen the correct dimensions from the diagram. The line down the centre of the plan indicates where the two sloping sides of the 3D shape meet.

d) The plan will be a square split into four triangles. The front and side elevations will be triangles.

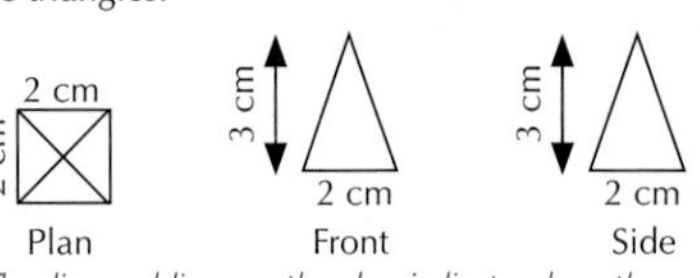

The diagonal lines on the plan indicate where the four sloping sides of the pyramid meet.

e) The plan will be a circle, radius 2 cm. The front and side elevations will be rectangles with width equal to the diameter of the circular face.

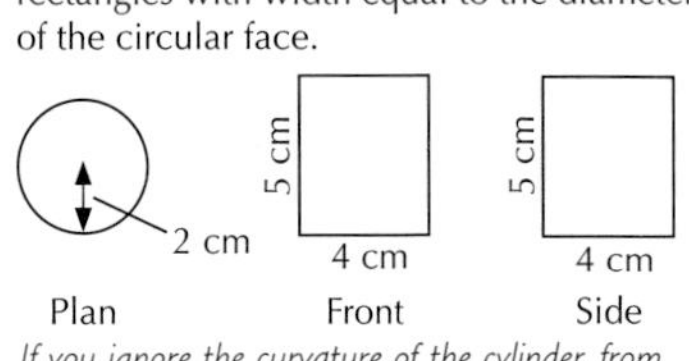

If you ignore the curvature of the cylinder, from the front or side it looks like a rectangle whose width is the diameter of the cylinder's base (2 × 2 cm = 4 cm) — that gives you the front and side elevations.

f) The plan will be a circle, radius 3 cm. The front and side elevations will be triangles.

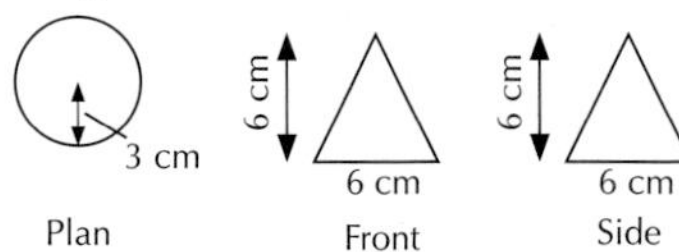

This time when you ignore the curvature, you get a triangle who's base length is the diameter of the base of the cone.

23.3 Isometric Drawings

Page 372 Exercise 1

1 Each space between the dots in the vertical and diagonal directions is equal to 1 cm.

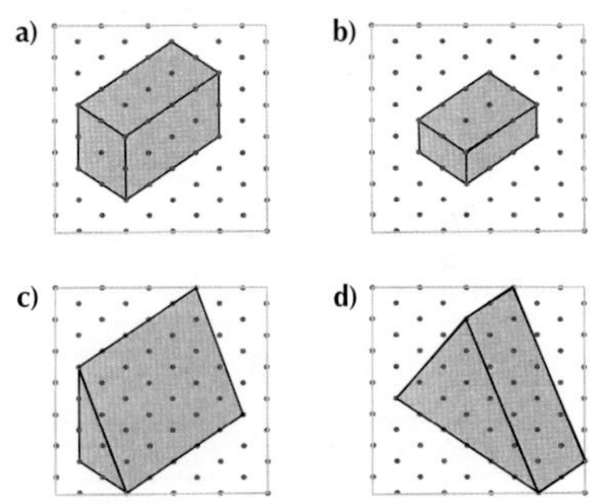

Draw the 3D shape's horizontal and vertical edges first, and then connect them up to form the sloped edges.

2 Each space between the dots in the vertical and diagonal directions is equal to 1 cm.

a)

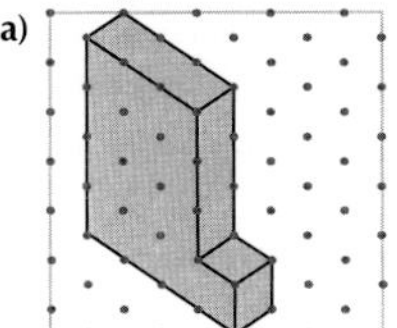

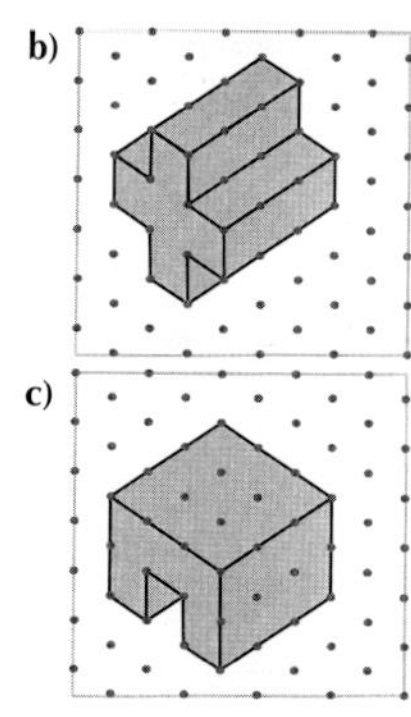

Page 373 Exercise 2

1 Draw the cross-sections given, then extend them by 3 dots diagonally to create the prisms.

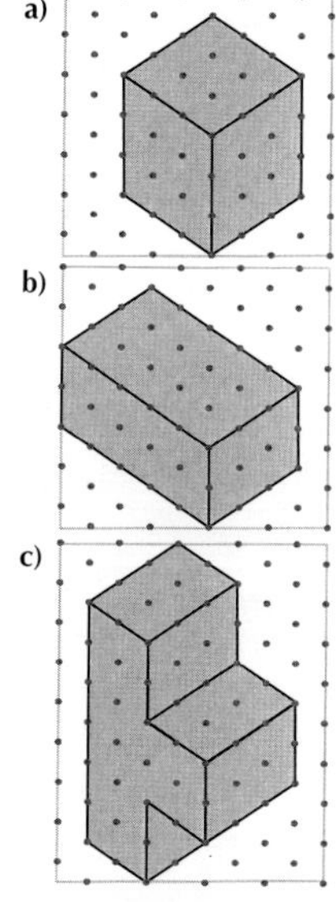

2 Draw the cross-sections given, then extend them by 2 dots diagonally to create the prisms.

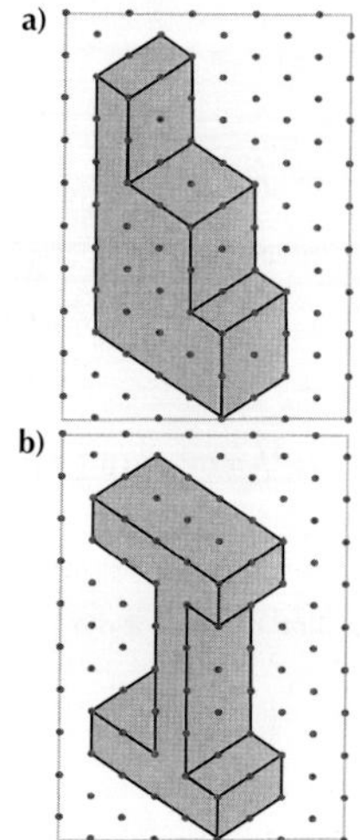

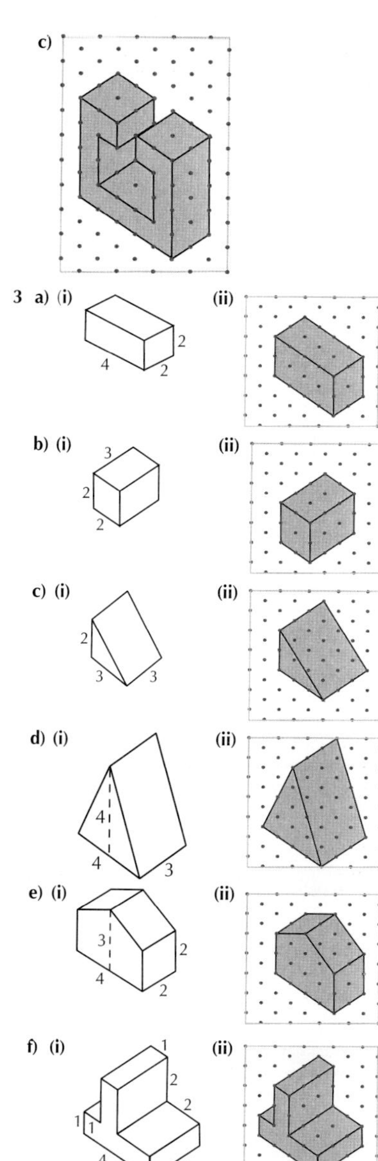

23.4 Symmetry of 3D Shapes

Page 374 Exercise 1

1 a) Any two from:

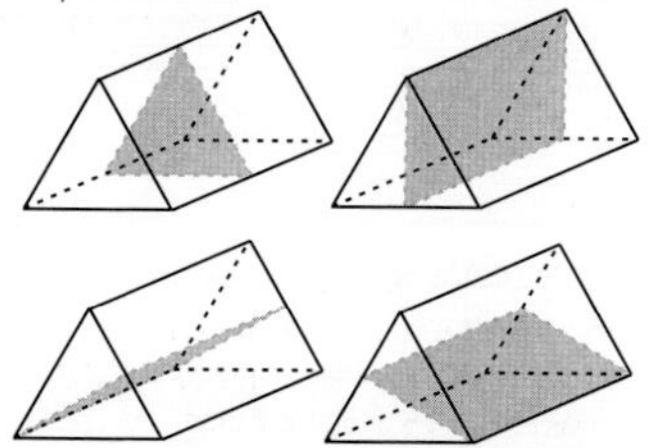

Remember, the number of planes of symmetry in a prism is usually one more than the number of lines of symmetry in the cross-section.

b) Any two from:

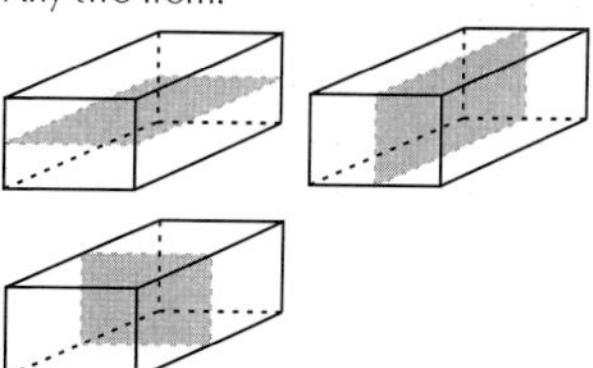

c) Any two from:

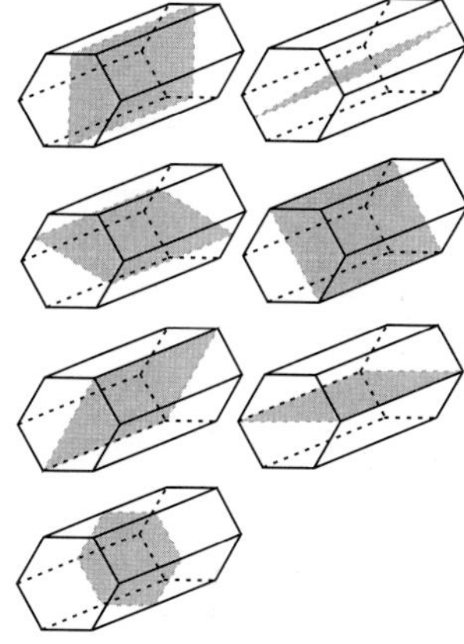

2 The planes of symmetry correspond to the lines of symmetry of the faces of the cube:

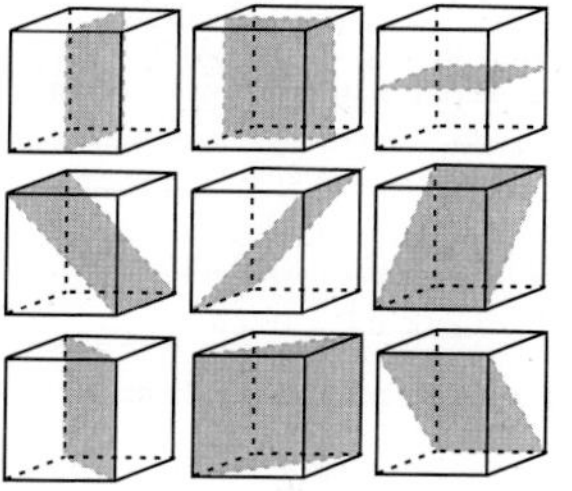

3 The base of the pyramid has 4 lines of symmetry, which correspond to **4 planes of symmetry** in the 3D shape.

23.5 Volume

Page 375 Exercise 1

1 Each cube has a length of 1 cm, so a volume of $1 \times 1 \times 1 = 1$ cm^3. To find the volume of the solids, count the number of cubes.

a) **5 cm^3** b) **4 cm^3**

c) **8 cm^3** d) **7 cm^3**

Don't forget the hidden cubes you can't see.

2 a) Volume = length × width × height
= 6 × 5 × 1 = **30 cm^3**

b) Volume = length × width × height
= 5 × 2 × 1 = **10 m^3**

Using the same method for c)-f):

c) **28 cm^3** d) **84 mm^3**

e) **27 cm^3** f) **64 m^3**

3 a) Volume = 3 × 2 × 4 = **24 cm^3**

b) Volume = 5 × 2 × 7 = **70 m^3**

Using the same method for c)-f):

c) **1600 cm^3** d) **31.5 cm^3**

e) **756 m^3** f) **35.136 mm^3**

4 a) Length = 3 mm to 1 s.f.
So volume ≈ $3 \times 3 \times 3 = 27$ mm^3

b) The lengths were rounded down from 3.2, so this is an underestimate.
Actual volume = $3.2^3 = 32.768$ mm^3

5 Volume of box = $1.7 \times 1.8 \times 0.9 = 2.754$ m^3
2.754 m^3 < 3.5 m^3, so **the sand will not fit**.

6 The dimensions of the box are 9 cm, 20 cm and 30 cm to 1 s.f.
Volume of box ≈ $9 \times 20 \times 30 = 5400$ cm^3
Box is half full, so volume of cereal ≈ $5400 \div 2 =$ **2700 cm^3**.

7 a) Split the solid into two cuboids, e.g.

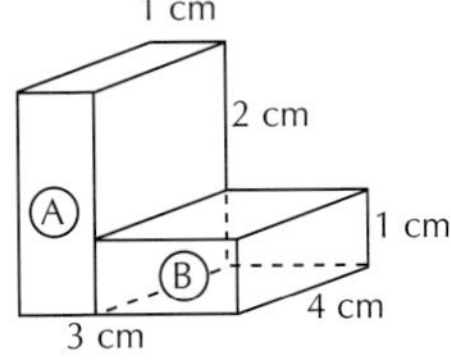

Volume of A = $4 \times 3 \times 1 = 12$ cm^3
Volume of B = $4 \times 2 \times 1 = 8$ cm^3
So volume of the solid = $12 + 8 =$ **20 cm^3**

b)

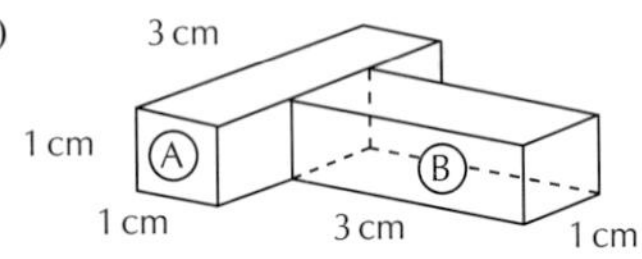

Volume of A = $3 \times 1 \times 1 = 3$ cm^3
Volume of B = $1 \times 3 \times 1 = 3$ cm^3
So volume of the solid = $3 + 3 =$ **6 cm^3**
Always try to split the shapes into as few pieces as possible, so you don't have loads of calculations to do.

8 Volume = 5 cm × 3 cm × height
= 15 × height = 18 cm^3
So height = $\frac{18}{15} = \frac{6}{5} = 1\frac{1}{5} =$ **1.2 cm**

9 a) Volume of bath = $1.5 \times 0.5 \times 0.6 =$ **0.45 m^3**

b) $1.5 \times 0.5 \times 0.3 =$ **0.225 m^3**

c) Volume = 1.5 × 0.5 × height
= 0.75 × height = 0.3 m^3
So height = $0.3 \div 0.75 =$ **0.4 m**

Page 378 Exercise 2

1 a) Volume = cross-sectional area × length
$= 2 \times 3 =$ **6 cm^3**

b) Volume = cross-sectional area × length
$= 6 \times 9 =$ **54 cm^3**

c) Volume = cross-sectional area × length
$= 1.5 \times 6 =$ **9 m^3**

Using the same method for d)-f):
d) 12.25 cm^3 **e) 16.1875 mm^3**
f) 105.56 mm^3

2 a) Cross-sectional area = $\frac{1}{2} \times 2 \times 4 = 4$ cm^2
So volume = $4 \times 7 =$ **28 cm^3**

b) Cross-sectional area = $\frac{1}{2} \times 4 \times 3 = 6$ cm^2
So volume = $6 \times 5 =$ **30 cm^3**

c) Cross-sectional area = $\pi r^2 = \pi \times 1^2$
= 3.141... cm^2
So volume = 3.141... × 5
= 15.707... = **15.71 cm^3** (2 d.p.)

3 a) Split the cross-section into two rectangles to find its area.

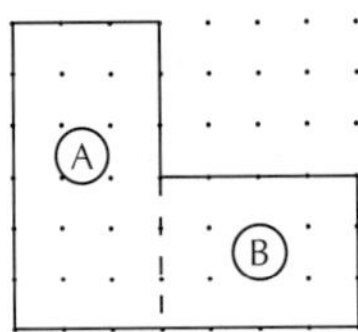

Area of A = $3 \times 6 = 18$ cm^2
Area of B = $4 \times 3 = 12$ cm^2
So area of cross-section = $18 + 12$
= 30 cm^2
Volume = $30 \times 2 =$ **60 cm^3**

b) Split the cross-section into three rectangles to find its area.

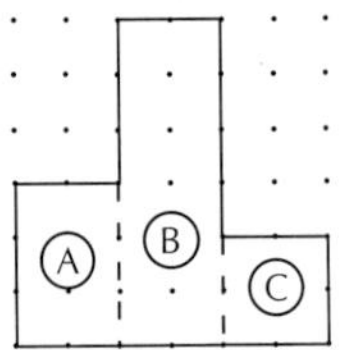

Area of A = $2 \times 3 = 6$ cm^2
Area of B = $2 \times 6 = 12$ cm^2
Area of C = $2 \times 2 = 4$ cm^2
So area of cross-section = $6 + 12 + 4$
= 22 cm^2
Volume = $22 \times 3 =$ **66 cm^3**

c) Diameter = 6 cm, so radius = $6 \div 2 = 3$ cm
Cross-sectional area = $\pi r^2 = \pi \times 3^2$
= 28.274... cm^2
Volume = 28.274... × 1.2
= **33.93 cm^3** (2 d.p.)

4 a) Area of cross-section = $\frac{1}{2} \times 13 \times 12$
= 78 cm^2
Volume = $78 \times 8 =$ **624 cm^3**

b) Area of cross-section = $\frac{1}{2} \times 4.2 \times 1.3$
= 2.73 m^2
Volume = $2.73 \times 3.1 =$ **8.463 m^3**

c) Area of cross-section = $\pi \times 4^2$
= 50.265... m^2
Volume = 50.265... × 18
= **904.78 m^3** (2 d.p.)

d) Area of cross-section = $3 \times 4.2 = 12.6$ m^2
Volume = $12.6 \times 1.5 =$ **18.9 m^3**

5 a) The cross-section can be split into a rectangle and a triangle.

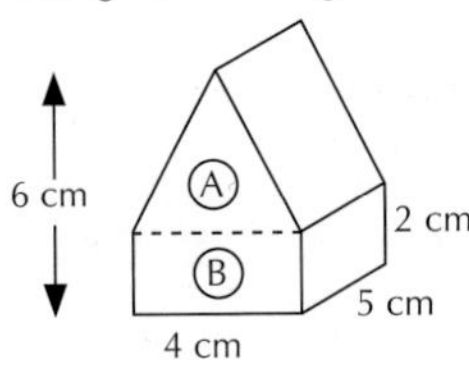

Area of A = $\frac{1}{2} \times 4 \times 4 = 8$ cm^2
Area of B = $4 \times 2 = 8$ cm^2
So area of cross-section = $8 + 8 = 16$ cm^2
Volume = $16 \times 5 =$ **80 cm^3**

b) The cross-section is a trapezium.

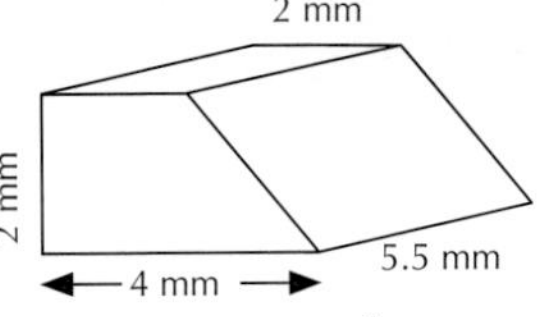

Area of cross-section = $\frac{1}{2} \times (2 + 4) \times 2$
$= \frac{1}{2} \times 6 \times 2 = 6$ mm^2
Volume = $6 \times 5.5 =$ **33 mm^3**
You could also work out the cross-sectional area by splitting the shape into a triangle and a square.

c) The cross-section can be split into two squares and a rectangle.

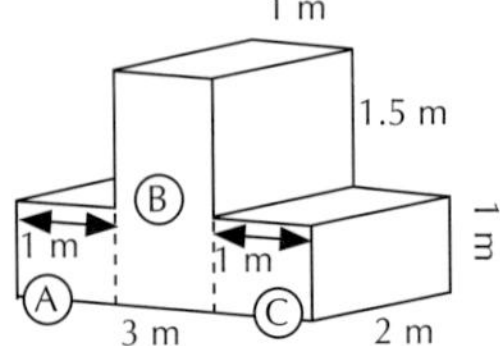

Area of A = $1^2 = 1$ m^2
Area of B = $1 \times 2.5 = 2.5$ m^2
Area of C = $1^2 = 1$ m^2
So area of cross-section = $1 + 2.5 + 1$
= 4.5 m^2
Volume = $4.5 \times 2 =$ **9 m^3**
A and C are identical so have the same area — always look out for symmetry in your shapes to reduce the number of calculations you need to do.

6 a) Area of cross-section = $\frac{1}{2} \times 4 \times 5 = 10$ cm^2
Volume = $10 \times 3 =$ **30 cm^3**

b) Area of cross-section = $2 \times 2^2 + (6 \times 2)$
= $8 + 12 = 20$ cm^2
Volume = $20 \times 3 =$ **60 cm^3**

c) Area of cross-section
$= (4 \times 3) + (\frac{1}{2} \times 4 \times 2)$
= $12 + 4 = 16$ cm^2
Volume = $16 \times 5 =$ **80 cm^3**

d) Area of cross-section
$= (4 \times 2) + (2 \times 3) + (\frac{1}{2} \times 2 \times 3)$
= $8 + 6 + 3 = 17$ cm^2
Volume = $17 \times 3 =$ **51 cm^3**

Page 379 Exercise 3

1 a) Volume = $\frac{4}{3}\pi r^3 = \frac{4}{3}\pi \times 3^3 = 4\pi \times 9$
= **36π cm^3**
'Exact' means leave your answer in terms of π, and use fractions rather than decimals where needed.

b) Volume = $\frac{4}{3}\pi r^3 = \frac{4}{3}\pi \times 2^3$
$= \frac{4}{3}\pi \times 8 = \mathbf{\frac{32}{3}\pi}$ **m^3** or $\mathbf{10\frac{2}{3}\pi}$ **m^3**

c) Volume = $\frac{4}{3}\pi r^3 = \frac{4}{3}\pi \times 5^3 = \frac{4}{3}\pi \times 125$
$= \mathbf{\frac{500}{3}\pi}$ **mm^3** or $\mathbf{166\frac{2}{3}\pi}$ **mm^3**

2 a) Volume = $\frac{4}{3} \times \pi \times 4^3 = 268.082...$
$= \mathbf{268.08\ cm^3}$ (2 d.p.)

b) Volume = $\frac{4}{3} \times \pi \times 8^3 = 2144.660...$
$= \mathbf{2144.66\ m^3}$ (2 d.p.)

c) Volume = $\frac{4}{3} \times \pi \times 9.6^3 = 3705.973...$
$= \mathbf{3705.97\ mm^3}$ (2 d.p.)

d) Volume = $\frac{4}{3} \times \pi \times 15.7^3 = 16\,210.169...$
$= \mathbf{16\,210.17\ m^3}$ (2 d.p.)

3 Volume = $\frac{4}{3}\pi r^3 = 24\,429$
So $r^3 = 24\,429 \div \frac{4}{3}\pi = 5831.9941...$
$\Rightarrow r = \sqrt[3]{5831.9941...} = 17.999...$
$= \mathbf{18.0\ cm}$ (1 d.p.)

Page 380 Exercise 4

1 a) Volume = $\frac{1}{3}\pi r^2 h = \frac{1}{3}\pi \times 5^2 \times 12$
$= \pi \times 25 \times 4 = \mathbf{100\pi\ m^3}$

b) Volume = $\frac{1}{3}\pi r^2 h = \frac{1}{3}\pi \times 7^2 \times 24$
$= \pi \times 49 \times 8 = \mathbf{392\pi\ cm^3}$

c) Volume = $\frac{1}{3}\pi r^2 h = \frac{1}{3}\pi \times 15^2 \times 8$
$= \frac{1}{3}\pi \times 225 \times 8 = \pi \times 75 \times 8 = \mathbf{600\pi\ m^3}$

d) Volume = $\frac{1}{3}\pi r^2 h = \frac{1}{3}\pi \times 30^2 \times 5.5$
$= \frac{1}{3}\pi \times 900 \times 5.5$
$= \pi \times 300 \times 5.5 = \mathbf{1650\pi\ mm^3}$

2 a) Volume = $\frac{1}{3} \times \pi \times 4^2 \times 10$
$= 167.551... = \mathbf{167.55\ cm^3}$ (2 d.p.)

b) Volume = $\frac{1}{3} \times \pi \times 14^2 \times 32$
$= 6568.023... = \mathbf{6568.02\ mm^3}$ (2 d.p.)

c) Volume = $\frac{1}{3} \times \pi \times 7^2 \times 25$
$= 1282.817... = \mathbf{1282.82\ m^3}$ (2 d.p.)

d) Volume = $\frac{1}{3} \times \pi \times 3.6^2 \times 7.2$
$= 97.716... = \mathbf{97.72\ cm^3}$ (2 d.p.)

Page 381 Exercise 5

1 a) Volume of original cone
$= \frac{1}{3}\pi \times 12^2 \times 16 = \mathbf{768\pi\ cm^3}$

b) Volume of removed cone = $\frac{1}{3}\pi \times 3^2 \times 4$
$= \mathbf{12\pi\ cm^3}$

c) Volume of frustum = $768\pi - 12\pi$
$= \mathbf{756\pi\ cm^3}$

2 Volume of original cone = $\frac{1}{3}\pi \times 10^2 \times 24$
$= 2513.274...\ cm^3$
Volume of removed cone = $\frac{1}{3}\pi \times 5^2 \times 12$
$= 314.159...\ cm^3$
Volume of frustum = $2513.274... - 314.159...$
$= \mathbf{2199.11\ cm^3}$

Page 382 Exercise 6

1 a) Volume = $\frac{1}{3}$ × base area × height
$= \frac{1}{3} \times 18 \times 10 = \mathbf{60\ cm^3}$

b) Volume = $\frac{1}{3}$ × base area × height
$= \frac{1}{3} \times 8 \times 3 = \mathbf{8\ m^3}$

2 Area of base = $4 \times 9 = 36\ cm^2$
Volume = $\frac{1}{3} \times 36 \times 10 = \mathbf{120\ cm^3}$

3 Volume = $\frac{1}{3} \times 18 \times 15 = \mathbf{90\ cm^3}$

4 Volume = $\frac{1}{3} \times 27 \times 12 = \mathbf{108\ m^3}$

5 Find the volume of the pyramid and the prism separately.
Volume of pyramid = $\frac{1}{3} \times 24 \times 10 = 80\ cm^3$
Volume of prism = $24 \times 10 = 240\ cm^3$
So area of solid = $80 + 240 = \mathbf{320\ cm^3}$

6 Volume = $\frac{1}{3}$ × base area × 13.5
= base area × 4.5 = $288\ cm^3$
So base area = $288 \div 4.5 = 64\ cm^2$
Area of square = $(\text{length})^2 = 64\ cm^2$
So side length = $\sqrt{64} = \mathbf{8\ cm}$

Page 383 Exercise 7

1 a) Rate of flow = volume ÷ time
$= 600 \div 15 =$ **40 cm³ per second**

b) Rate of flow = volume ÷ time
$= 7200 \div 40 =$ **180 litres per minute**

c) Rate of flow = volume ÷ time
$= 385 \div 5 =$ **77 m³ per minute**

d) Rate of flow = volume ÷ time
$= 150 \div 8 =$ **18.75 litres per hour**

2 Volume of cube = $30^3 = 27\,000\ cm^3$
Time = volume ÷ rate of flow
$= 27\,000 \div 15 = 1800$ seconds
Convert to minutes: $1800 \div 60 =$ **30 minutes**

3 Area of cross-section = $\pi \times 4.5^2$
$= 63.617...\ m^2$
Volume of tank = $63.617... \times 20$
$= 1272.345...\ m^3$
Time = volume ÷ rate of flow
$= 1272.345... \div 12 = 106.028...$
= **106 minutes** (to the nearest minute)

23.6 Surface Area

Page 385 Exercise 1

For all the questions in this exercise, sketch the net of the shape to help you find its surface area.

1 The cube has 6 faces with area 2 cm², so its surface area is $6 \times 2 = \mathbf{12\ cm^2}$

2 a) Area of 1 face = $1 \times 1 = \mathbf{1\ cm^2}$

b) Surface area of cube = $6 \times 1 = \mathbf{6\ cm^2}$

3 a) Area of 1 face = $2 \times 2 = \mathbf{4\ m^2}$

b) Surface area of cube = $6 \times 4 = \mathbf{24\ m^2}$

4 a) Area of face $A = 4 \times 2 = \mathbf{8\ m^2}$

b) Area of face $B = 4 \times 3 = \mathbf{12\ m^2}$

c) Area of face $C = 3 \times 2 = \mathbf{6\ m^2}$

d) Surface area of cuboid
$= (2 \times 8) + (2 \times 12) + (2 \times 6) = \mathbf{52\ m^2}$
There are two of each size of rectangle in the net.

5 a) Area of 1 face = $3 \times 3 = 9\ cm^2$
Surface area of cube = $6 \times 9 = \mathbf{54\ cm^2}$

b) Surface area
$= 2(3 \times 1) + 2(4 \times 1) + 2(4 \times 3) = \mathbf{38\ cm^2}$

c) Surface area
$= 2(1.5 \times 4) + 2(1 \times 4) + 2(1.5 \times 1) = \mathbf{23\ m^2}$

d) Surface area
$= 4(2.5 \times 4.5) + 2(2.5 \times 2.5) = \mathbf{57.5\ m^2}$

6 a) Area of triangular face = $\frac{1}{2} \times 5 \times 12$
$= 30\ mm^2$
Area of rectangular base = 5×11
$= 55\ mm^2$
Area of vertical rectangular face
$= 12 \times 11 = 132\ mm^2$
Area of sloping rectangular face
$= 13 \times 11 = 143\ mm^2$
Surface area = $(2 \times 30) + 55 + 132 + 143$
$= \mathbf{390\ mm^2}$
Remember, there are two triangular faces in a triangular prism.

b) Area of triangular face = $\frac{1}{2} \times 3 \times 2 = 3\ m^2$
Area of rectangular base = $3 \times 3.2 = 9.6\ m^2$
Area of sloping rectangular face
$= 2.5 \times 3.2 = 8\ m^2$
Surface area = $(2 \times 3) + 9.6 + (2 \times 8)$
$= \mathbf{31.6\ m^2}$

c) Area of square base = $4 \times 4 = 16\ cm^2$
Area of each triangular face
$= \frac{1}{2} \times 4 \times 7 = 14\ cm^2$
Surface area = $16 + (4 \times 14) = \mathbf{72\ cm^2}$

d) Area of rectangular base = $6 \times 8 = 48\ cm^2$
Area of smaller triangular face
$= \frac{1}{2} \times 6 \times 9 = 27\ cm^2$
Area of larger triangular face
$= \frac{1}{2} \times 8 \times 9 = 36\ cm^2$
Surface area = $48 + (2 \times 27) + (2 \times 36)$
$= \mathbf{174\ cm^2}$

7 a) Surface area = $6(5 \times 5) = \mathbf{150\ m^2}$

b) Surface area = $6(6 \times 6) = \mathbf{216\ mm^2}$

c) Surface area
$= 2(1.5 \times 2) + 2(1.5 \times 6) + 2(2 \times 6) = \mathbf{48\ m^2}$

d) Surface area
$= 2(7.5 \times 0.5) + 2(7.5 \times 8) + 2(0.5 \times 8)$
$= \mathbf{135.5\ m^2}$

e) Area of triangular face = $\frac{1}{2} \times 6 \times 4 = 12\ m^2$
Area of rectangular base = $6 \times 2.5 = 15\ m^2$
Area of sloping rectangular face
$= 5 \times 2.5 = 12.5\ m^2$
Surface area = $(2 \times 12) + 15 + (2 \times 12.5)$
$= \mathbf{64\ m^2}$

8 a) Area of triangular face = $\frac{1}{2} \times 2.1 \times 1.4$
$= 1.47\ m^2$
Area of sloping rectangular face
$= 2.5 \times 1.75 = 4.375\ m^2$
Surface area = $(2 \times 1.47) + (2 \times 4.375)$
$= \mathbf{11.69\ m^2}$
You don't need to include the base here, as you're only interested in the outside of the tent.

b) $11.69 \div 4 = 2.9225$, so they will need to buy **3 tins** to cover the outside of the tent.
2 tins isn't enough, so you need to round up.

Page 386 Exercise 2

1 a)

6 cm
1 cm
2π cm

b) Area of each circular face = $\pi \times 1^2$
$= 3.141... = \mathbf{3.14\ cm^2}$
Area of rectangular face = $6 \times 2\pi$
$= 37.699... = \mathbf{37.70\ cm^2}$ (both to 2 d.p.)

c) Surface area = $(2 \times 3.141...) + 37.699...$
$= 43.982... = \mathbf{44.0\ cm^2}$ (1 d.p.)

2 a)

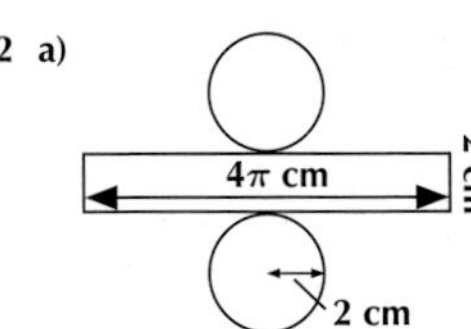

b) Area of each circular face = $\pi \times 2^2$
= 12.566... = **12.57 cm²**
Area of rectangular face = $2 \times 4\pi$
= 25.132... = **25.13 cm²** (both to 2 d.p.)

c) Surface area = (2 × 12.566...) + 25.132...
= 50.265... = **50.3 cm²** (1 d.p.)

For the remaining questions in this exercise, sketch the net first to help you find the areas.

3 a) Area of each circular face = $\pi \times 1^2$
= 3.141... cm²
Area of rectangular face = $4 \times 2\pi \times 1$
= 25.132... cm²
Surface area = (2 × 3.141...) + 25.132...
= 31.415... = **31.42 cm²** (2 d.p.)

b) Area of each circular face = $\pi \times 3^2$
= 28.274... m²
Area of rectangular face = $9 \times 2\pi \times 3$
= 169.646... m²
Surface area = (2 × 28.274...) + 169.646...
= ... 226.194...
= **226.19 m²** (2 d.p.)

Using the same method for c):

c) 131.95 m² (2 d.p.)

d) Radius = diameter ÷ 2 = 8 ÷ 2 = 4 mm
Area of each circular face = $\pi \times 4^2$
= 50.265... mm²
Area of rectangular face = $7 \times 8\pi$
= 175.929... mm²
Surface area = (2 × 50.265...) + 175.929...
= 276.459... = **276.46 mm²** (2 d.p.)

Using the same method for e) and f):

e) 12.82 m² **f) 51.90 mm²**

4 a) Area of each circular face = $\pi \times 2^2$
= 12.566... m²
Area of rectangular face = $7 \times 4\pi$
= 87.964... m²
Surface area = (2 × 12.566...) + 87.964...
= 113.097... = **113.1 m²** (1 d.p.)

Using the same method for b)-c):

b) 471.2 mm² (1 d.p.)

c) 1694.1 cm² (1 d.p.)

d) Radius = diameter ÷ 2 = 22.1 ÷ 2
= 11.05 m
Area of each circular face = $\pi \times 11.05^2$
= 383.596... m²
Area of rectangular face = $11.1 \times 22.1\pi$
= 770.664... m²
Surface area = (2 × 383.596...) + 770.664...
= 1537.856... = **1537.9 m²** (1 d.p.)

5 a) Area of each circular face = $\pi \times 0.8^2$
= 2.010... m²
Area of rectangular face = $3 \times 1.6\pi$
= 15.079... m²
Surface area = (2 × 2.010...) + 15.079...
= 19.100... = **19.10 m²** (2 d.p.)

b) 1 tin covers 14 m² and 2 tins cover 28 m², so Maeve will need **2 tins** of paint.
You could do 19.100... ÷ 14 = 1.364... and round up to 2, but it's much easier to just use common sense here.

6 a) Curved surface area = $7.1 \times 4.4\pi$
= 98.143... = **98.14 m²** (2 d.p.)

b) Area of metal = 98.143... × 9
= 883.290... = **883.3 m²** (1 d.p.)

7 Area of circular face = $\pi \times 0.4^2$ = 0.502... m²
Area of rectangular face = $1.1 \times 0.8\pi$
= 2.764... m²
Surface area = 0.502... + 2.764... = 3.267...
= **3.27 m²** (2 d.p.)

Page 388 Exercise 3

1 a) Surface area = $4 \times \pi \times 2^2$ = **16π cm²**

b) Surface area = $4 \times \pi \times 5^2$ = **100π cm²**

Using the same method for c)-f):

c) 196π m² **d) 324π mm²**

e) 441π m² **f) 42.25π mm²**

2 a) Surface area = $4 \times \pi \times 2.5^2$ = 78.539...
= **78.54 cm²** (2 d.p.)

b) Surface area = $4 \times \pi \times 7.1^2$ = 633.470...
= **633.47 m²** (2 d.p.)

Using the same method for c)-f):

c) 1576.33 mm² (2 d.p.)

d) 4680.85 m² (2 d.p.)

e) 299.26 cm² (2 d.p.)

f) 506.71 mm² (2 d.p.)

3 a) Surface area = $(\pi \times 5 \times 13) + (\pi \times 5^2)$
= $65\pi + 25\pi$ = **90π m²**

b) Surface area = $(\pi \times 7 \times 25) + (\pi \times 7^2)$
= $175\pi + 49\pi$ = **224π cm²**

c) Surface area = $(\pi \times 15 \times 17) + (\pi \times 15^2)$
= $255\pi + 225\pi$ = **480π m²**

4 a) Surface area = $(\pi \times 12 \times 30) + (\pi \times 12^2)$
= 1583.362... = **1583.36 cm²** (2 d.p.)

b) Surface area = $(\pi \times 1.5 \times 4.5) + (\pi \times 1.5^2)$
= 28.274... = **28.27 m²** (2 d.p.)

c) Surface area = $(\pi \times 2.8 \times 8.2) + (\pi \times 2.8^2)$
= 96.761... = **96.76 mm²** (2 d.p.)

5 a) Surface area = $4 \times \pi \times 8^2$ = 804.247...
= **804.25 m²** (2 d.p.)

b) Surface area = $(\pi \times 5 \times 8) + (\pi \times 5^2)$
= 204.203... = **204.20 cm²** (2 d.p.)

c) Surface area = $4 \times \pi \times 1.1^2$ = 15.205...
= **15.21 m²** (2 d.p.)

d) Surface area = $(\pi \times 3 \times 7.1) + (\pi \times 3^2)$
= 95.190... = **95.19 cm²** (2 d.p.)

6 Surface area = $4\pi r^2$, so $265.9 = 4\pi r^2$
$r^2 = 265.9 \div 4\pi = 21.159...$
$r = \sqrt{21.159...} = 4.599... =$ **4.6 cm** (1 d.p.)

Page 389 Review Exercise

1 a)

b)

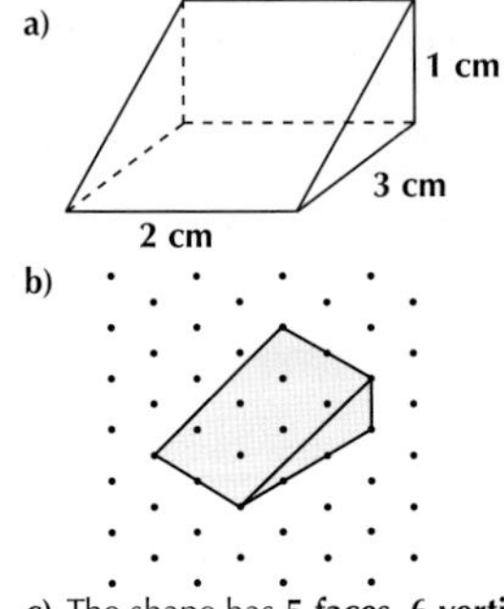

c) The shape has **5 faces**, **6 vertices** and **9 edges**.

2 a) E.g.

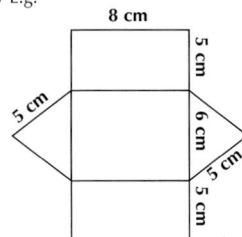

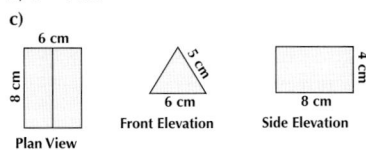

8 cm
5 cm
5 cm
6 cm
5 cm
5 cm

b) h = **4 cm**

c)

6 cm
8 cm
Plan View

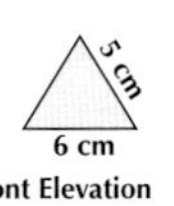

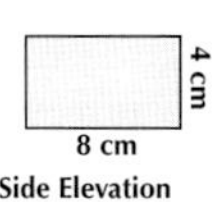

d) The prism has **2** planes of symmetry.
The cross-section is an isosceles triangle so it has one line of symmetry — that gives the prism one plane of symmetry. The other plane of symmetry cuts the prism in two halfway along its length.

3 a) E.g.

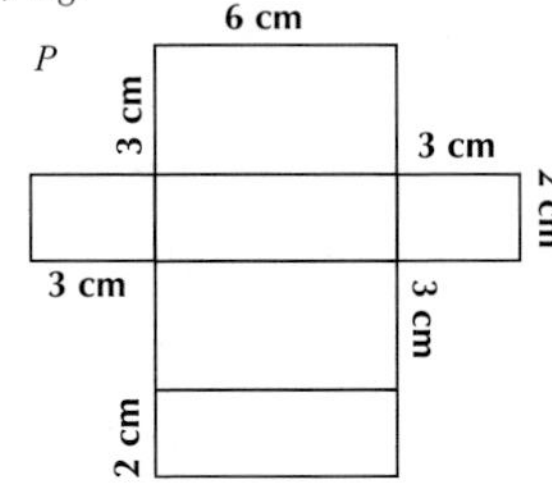

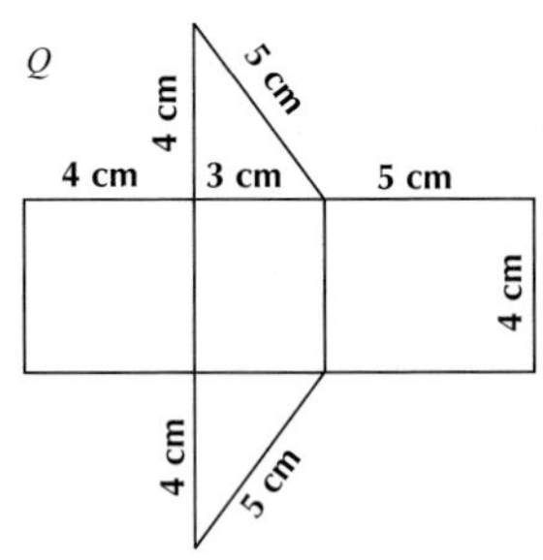

b) P

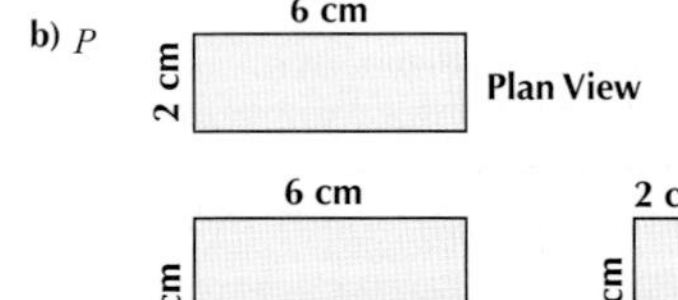

Q

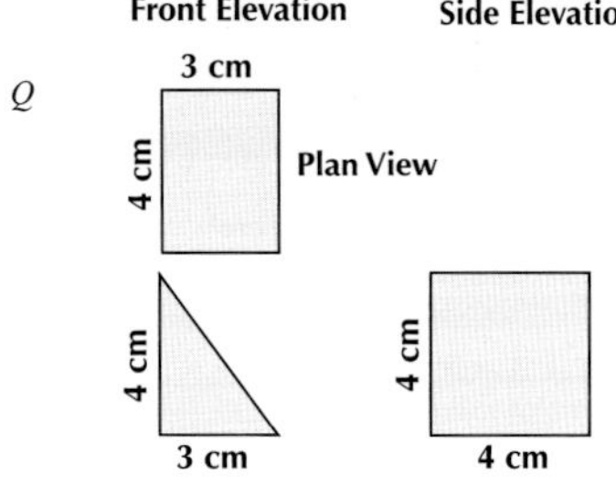

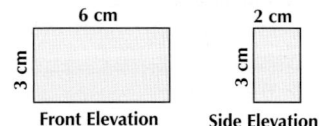

c) P

Q

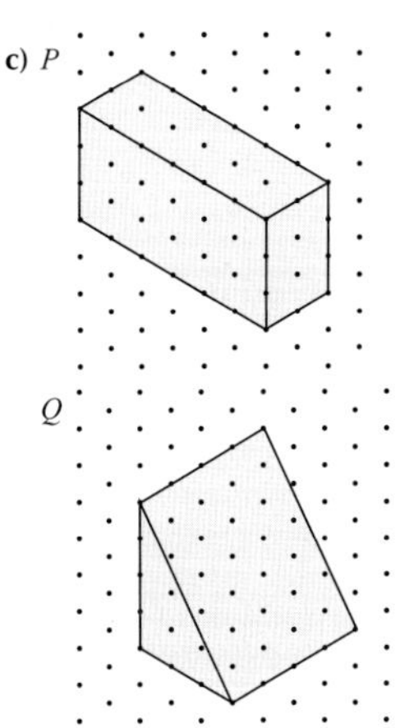

d) P: Volume = $6 \times 2 \times 3$ = **36 cm³**

Q: Volume = $(\frac{1}{2} \times 3 \times 4) \times 4$ = **24 cm³**

4 a) Volume of one cube = (length)³ = 8^3
= **512 cm³**

b) Volume of tray = 24×512 = **12 288 cm³**

5 a) Radius = diameter ÷ 2 = 7.4 ÷ 2 = 3.7 cm
Cross-sectional area = $\pi r^2 = \pi \times 3.7^2$
= 43.008... cm²
So volume = 43.008... × 11 = 473.092...
= **473.09 cm³** (2 d.p.)

b) 4 tins fit into the width of the box,
so w = 7.4 × 4 = 29.6 cm
3 tins fit into the length of the box,
so l = 7.4 × 3 = 22.2 cm
The height of the box is the height of 1 tin,
so h = 11 cm
So the box has dimensions
29.6 cm × 22.2 cm × 11 cm

c) Volume = 29.6 × 22.2 × 11
= **7228.32 cm³**

d) Volume not taken up by tins
= 7228.32 – (473.092... × 12)
= 1551.210... = **1551.2 cm³** (1 d.p.)

6 Volume of 1 pyramid:
area of base = 7^2 = 49 cm²
Volume = $\frac{1}{3} \times 49 \times 9$ = 147 cm³
So volume of whole shape = 147 × 2
= **294 cm³**

7 a) Area of one face = 54 ÷ 6 = **9 cm²**

b) Length of edge = $\sqrt{9}$ = **3 cm**

c) Volume = (length)³ = 3^3 = **27 cm³**

d) Time = volume ÷ rate of flow
= 27 ÷ 2.5 = **10.8 seconds**

e)

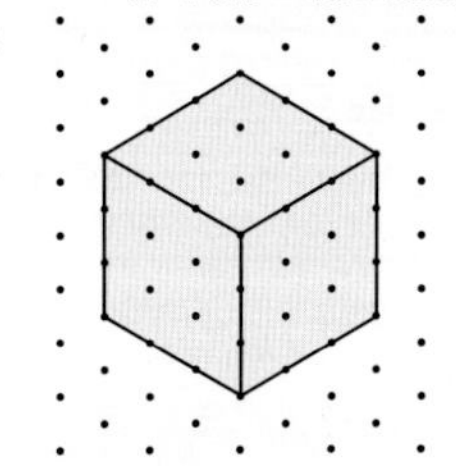

8 a) Volume of cuboid A = 6 × 2 × 3 = 36 cm³
Volume of cuboid B = 4 × 4 × 9 = 144 cm³
So ratio of volumes A : B = 36 : 144 = **1 : 4**
Have a look at Section 6 if you need a reminder about ratios.

b) Surface area of cuboid A
= 2(3 × 6) + 2(2 × 3) + 2(2 × 6) = 72 cm²
Surface area of cuboid B
= 2(4 × 4) + 4(4 × 9) = 176 cm²
So ratio of surface areas A : B = 72 : 176
= **9 : 22**

9 a)

3 cm

3π cm

1.5 cm

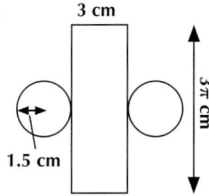

b) Area of each circular face = $\pi \times 1.5^2$
= 7.068... cm²
Area of rectangular face = $3 \times 3\pi$
= 28.274... cm²
Surface area = (2 × 7.068...) + 28.274...
= 42.411... = **42.41 cm²** (2 d.p.)

10 a) Radius = diameter ÷ 2 = 25 ÷ 2 = 12.5 mm
Volume = πr^2 × length,
so 7854 = $\pi \times 12.5^2$ × length
7854 = 156.25π × length
length = 7854 ÷ 156.25π
= 16.000... = **16.00 mm**

b) Area of each circular face = $\pi \times 12.5^2$
= 490.873... cm²
Area of rectangular face = 16.000... × 25π
= 1256.637... cm²
Surface area
= (2 × 490.873...) + 1256.637...
= 2238.384...
= **2238 mm²** (nearest mm²)

c) Length of cuboid = length of cylinder
= 16.000...
Width of cuboid = height of cuboid
= diameter of cylinder = 25 mm
So volume of cuboid = 16.000... × 25 × 25
= 10 000.023...
= **10 000 mm³** (nearest mm³)

d) Volume of empty space
= 10 000.023... – 7854
= 2146.023... = **2146 mm³** (nearest mm³)

11 a) Volume = $\frac{1}{3} \times \pi \times 9^2 \times 12$ = **324π m³**

b) (i) $h^2 = 9^2 + 12^2 = 81 + 144 = 225$
$h = \sqrt{225}$ = **15 m**

(ii) Surface area = $(\pi \times 9 \times 15) + (\pi \times 9^2)$
= **216π m²**

c) Volume of removed cone = $\frac{1}{3} \times \pi \times 6^2 \times 8$
= 96π m³
Volume of frustum = $324\pi - 96\pi$
= **228π m³**

Page 391 Exam-Style Questions

1 a) **Cone**
Triangular prism
Square-based pyramid
[2 marks if all three shapes are named correctly, otherwise 1 mark if one or two shapes are named correctly]

b) (i) Number of vertices = **6** *[1 mark]*

(ii) Number of faces = **5** *[1 mark]*

2 a) Height = **5 cm** *[1 mark]*
Count the number of squares up one side of the rectangle that isn't attached to the circular faces.

b) Radius = 2 cm
Area of each circular face = $\pi \times 2^2$
= 4π cm² *[1 mark]*
Area of rectangular face = $5 \times 4\pi$
= 20π cm² *[1 mark]*
Surface area = $(2 \times 4\pi) + 20\pi$
= **28π cm²** *[1 mark]*

3 Volume of cuboid
= area of shaded face × width, so
width = volume ÷ area of shaded face
= 300 ÷ 30 = **10 cm** *[1 mark]*.
Width = 2 × height, so height = width ÷ 2
= 10 ÷ 2 = **5 cm** *[1 mark]*.
Area of the shaded face = length × height, so
length = area of shaded face ÷ height
= 30 ÷ 5 = **6 cm** *[1 mark]*.

4 Volume of jam made: $(\pi \times 20^2) \times 18$
= 7200π cm³ *[1 mark]*
Volume of one jar: $(\pi \times 3^2) \times 10 = 90\pi$ cm³ *[1 mark]*
So Sadiq can fill $7200\pi \div 90\pi$ = **80 jars** with jam *[1 mark]*.
Leaving the volumes in terms of π makes the numbers easier to deal with — but you'll still get the marks if you wrote them as decimals.

Section 24 — Transformations

24.1 Reflections

Page 393 Exercise 1

For each question in this exercise, reflect the vertices of the shape in the line of symmetry, and then join them up to form the shape. For each vertex, count how many squares it is from the mirror line. The image point is the same number of squares to the opposite side of the mirror line.

1

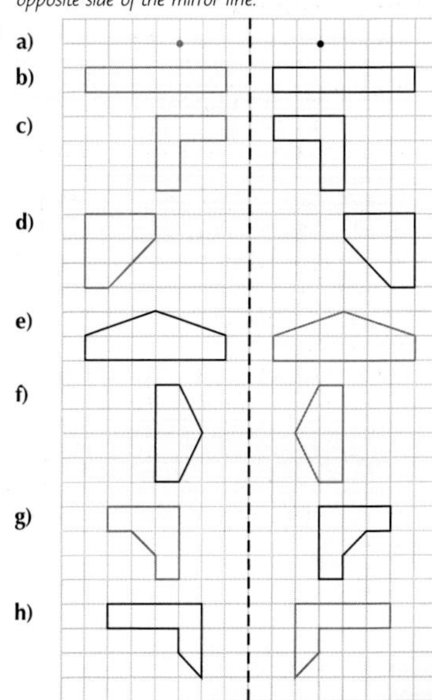

2 a) b) c) d) e)

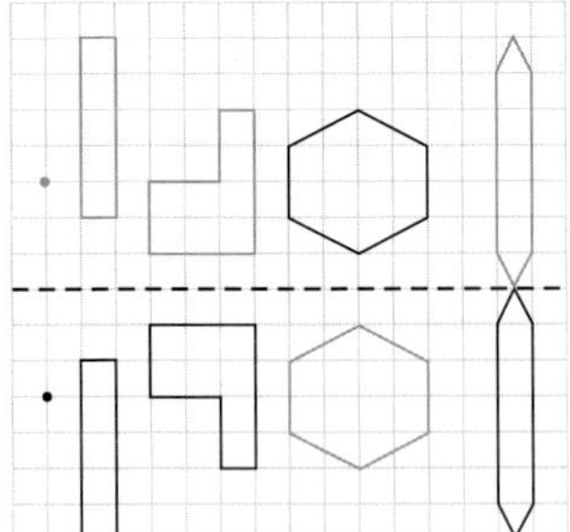

3

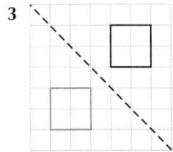

Page 394 Exercise 2

For Qs 1, 2 and 4, reflect the vertices of the shape in the line of symmetry, and then join them up to form the shape. For each vertex, count how many squares it is from the mirror line. The image point is the same number of squares to the opposite side of the mirror line.

1 a)

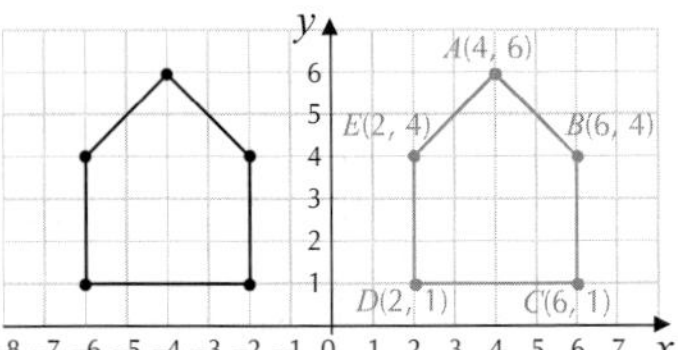

b)

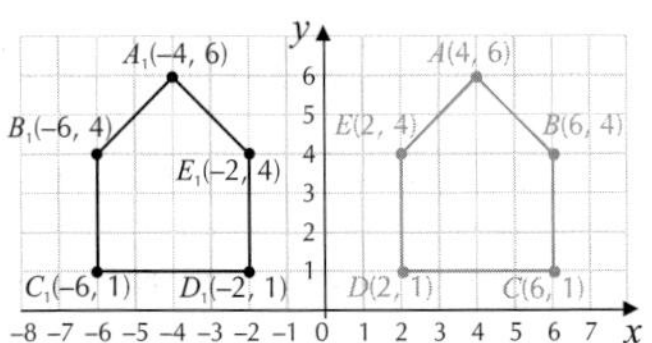

c) The x-coordinates become negative in the reflected shape, and the y-coordinates stay the same.

2 a)

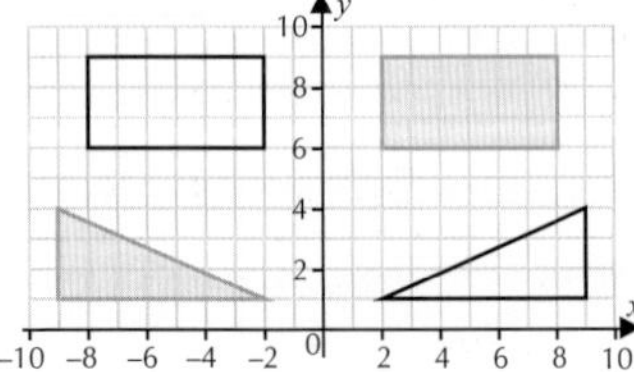

b)

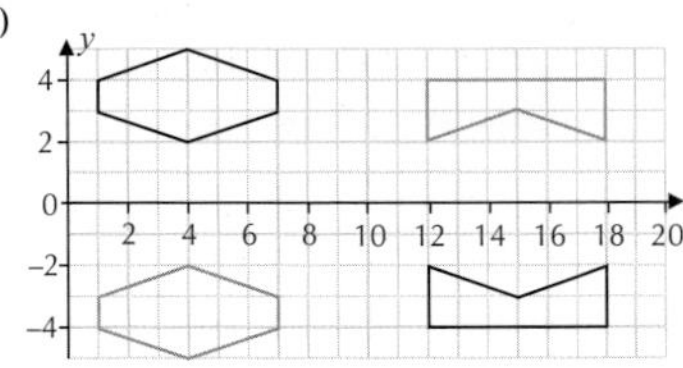

3 a) The point (x, y) is sent to $(x, -y)$ under a reflection in the x-axis, so the new coordinates are:

(i) (1, –2) **(ii) (3, 0)**
(iii) (–2, –4) **(iv) (–1, 3)**

b) The point (x, y) is sent to $(-x, y)$ under a reflection in the y-axis, so the new coordinates are:

(i) (–4, 5) **(ii) (–7, 2)**
(iii) (1, 3) **(iv) (3, –1)**

4 a)-d) Start by drawing the mirror line. Then reflect the vertices and join up the image points — see below.

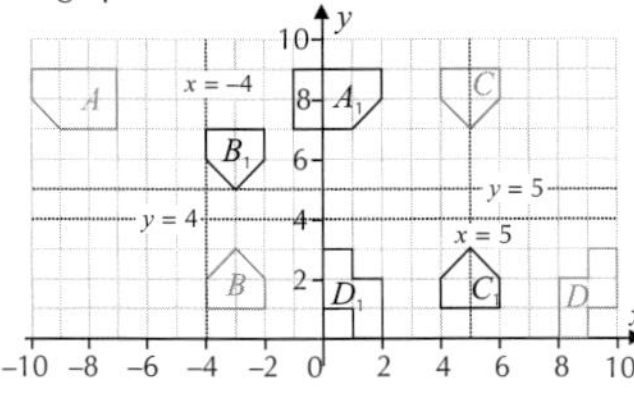

e) Pick a pair of corresponding vertices on shapes B and C_1, e.g. (–3, 3) on B and (5, 3) on C_1. They are 8 horizontal units apart and the mirror line must be the same distance from each (8 ÷ 2 = 4 units). So the mirror line is $\boldsymbol{x = 1}$.

Page 395 Exercise 3

1 a) Each image point is the same perpendicular distance from the mirror line as the vertex but on the other side of it.

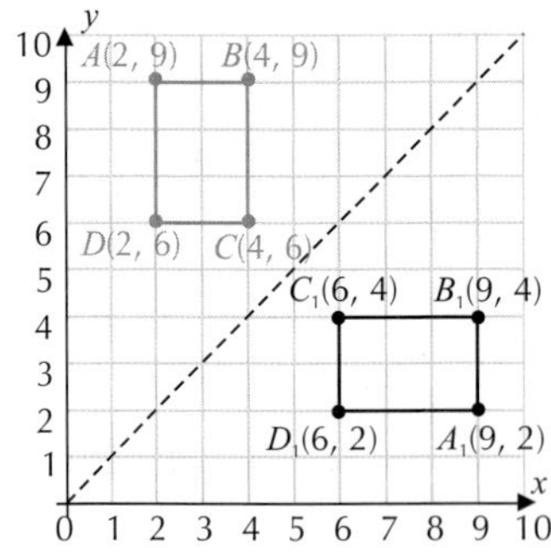

b) E.g. **The x-coordinate becomes the y-coordinate, and the y-coordinate becomes the x-coordinate.**

2 Each image point is the same perpendicular distance from the mirror line as the vertex but on the other side of it.

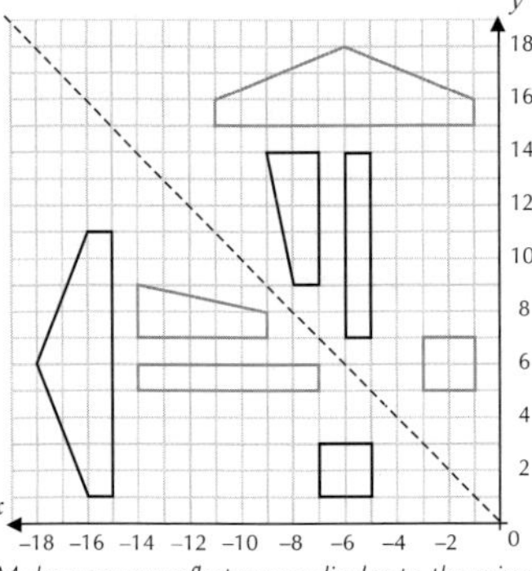

Make sure you reflect perpendicular to the mirror line. Turn your book so that the mirror line is horizontal or vertical if it helps.

3 a) The point (x, y) is sent to (y, x) under a reflection in $y = x$.

(i) (2, 1) **(ii) (0, 3)**
(iii) (4, –2) **(iv) (–3, –1)**

b) The point (x, y) is sent to $(-y, -x)$ under a reflection in $y = -x$.

(i) (–2, –1) **(ii) (0, –3)**
(iii) (–4, 2) **(iv) (3, 1)**

24.2 Rotations

Page 396 Exercise 1

For the rotations in this exercise, use tracing paper to draw the shapes then put your pencil on the centre of rotation and rotate the tracing paper by the required angle in the direction given. Draw the rotated shape in its new position.

1 a)

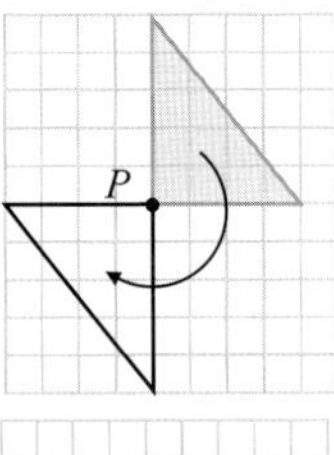

b)

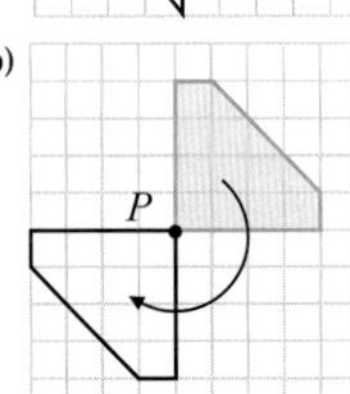

Since these rotations are by an angle of 180°, you could go clockwise or anticlockwise.

2 a)

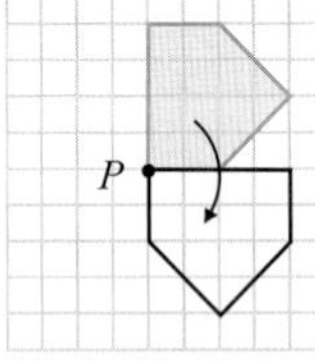

b)

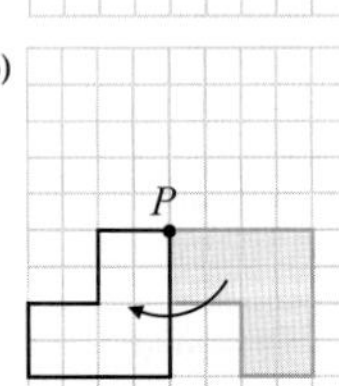

Page 397 Exercise 2

For the rotations in this exercise, use tracing paper to draw the shapes then put your pencil on the centre of rotation and rotate the tracing paper by the required angle in the direction given. Draw the rotated shape in its new position.

1 a)

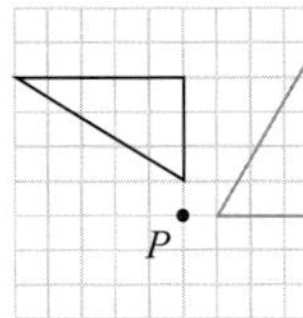

b)

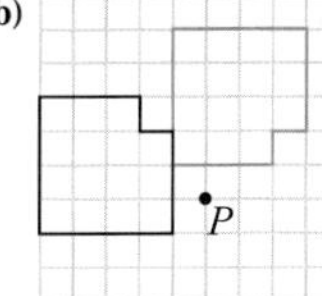

c)

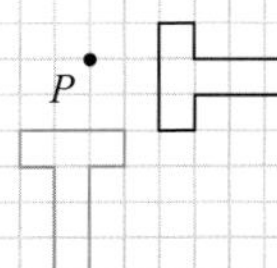

d)

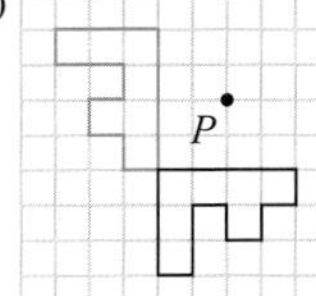

2 a)

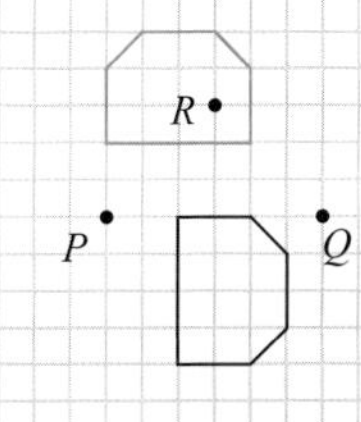

b)

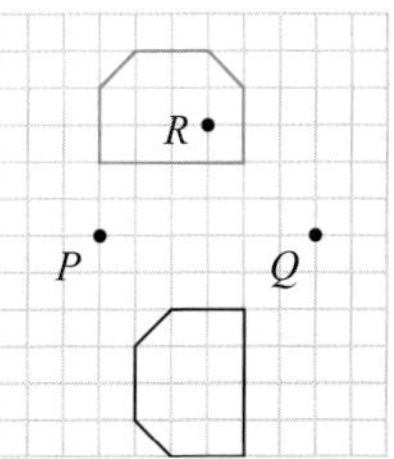

A 270° clockwise rotation is the same as a 90° anticlockwise rotation.

c)

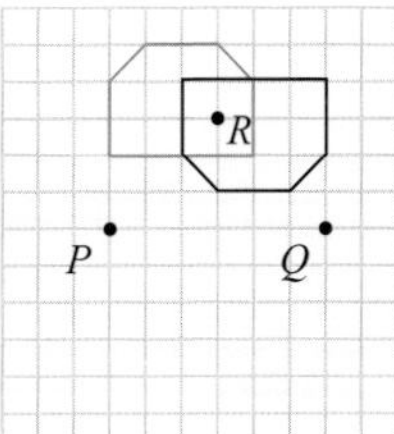

3 a), b)

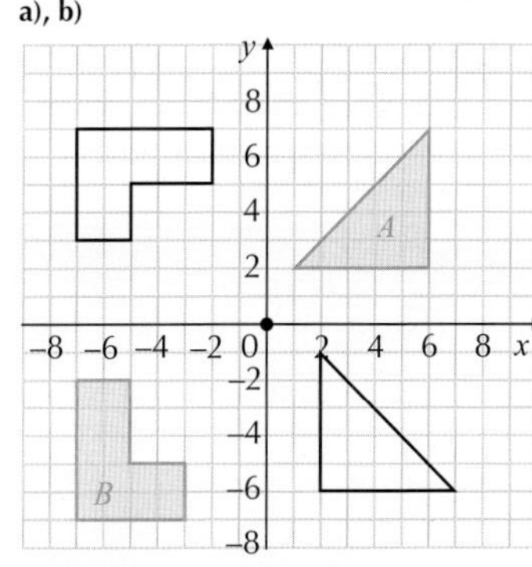

4 a), b), c), d)

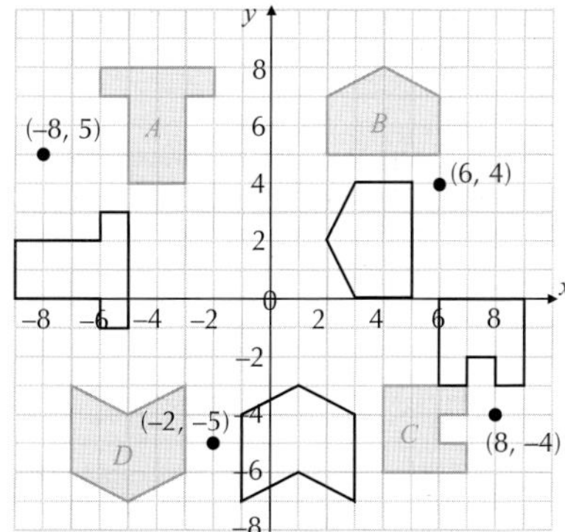

5 a), b)

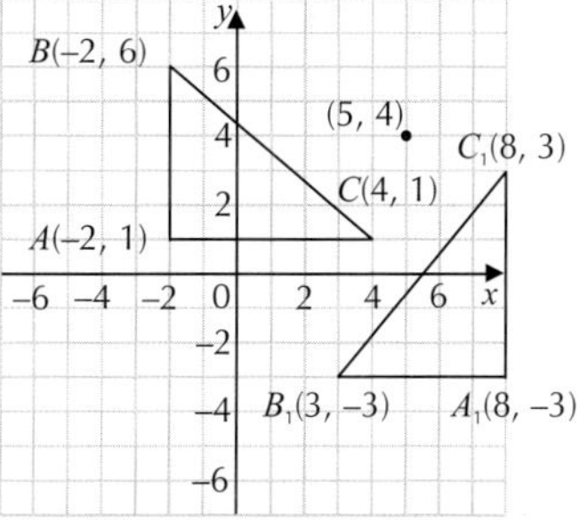

c) A_1**(8, –3),** B_1**(3, –3),** C_1**(8, 3).**

Page 399 Exercise 3

To describe the transformations, draw the shape being rotated on tracing paper. Then place your pencil at different centres of rotation and rotate the tracing paper until you find a point and rotation that takes it on top of the new shape.

1 a) **Rotation of 90° clockwise about the origin.**
Alternatively, this is a rotation 270° anticlockwise about (O, O).

b) **Rotation of 90° anticlockwise about the origin.**
Alternatively, this is a rotation 270° clockwise about (O, O).

2 a) **Rotation of 180° about the origin.**

b) **Rotation of 180° about (0, 2).**

3 a) **Rotation of 90° anticlockwise about (0, 7).**

b) **Rotation of 90° clockwise about (1, –2).**

4 a) **Rotation of 180° about (0, 6).**

b) **Rotation of 90° anticlockwise about (–2, 7).**

c) **Rotation of 90° clockwise about (1, 8).**

24.3 Translations

Page 401 Exercise 1

1 a) **1 to the right, 1 up**

b) **2 to the right**

c) **2 to the left, 6 up**

d) **3 to the left, 2 down**

2 Shape *A* moves 3 units to the right.
Shape *B* moves 2 units up.
Shape *C* moves 2 units to the right and 3 units up.
Shape *D* moves 4 units to the right and 1 unit down.
Shape *E* moves 4 units to the left and 3 units down.

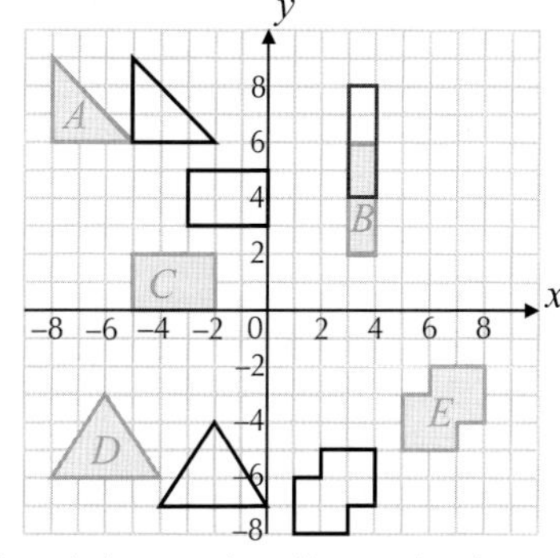

For each shape, start by working out where the corners of the shape move to and then join them to form the shape.

3 a), b) Translate each of *A*, *B* and *C* 10 units to the left and 1 unit down.
Then join them up to create $A_1B_1C_1$.

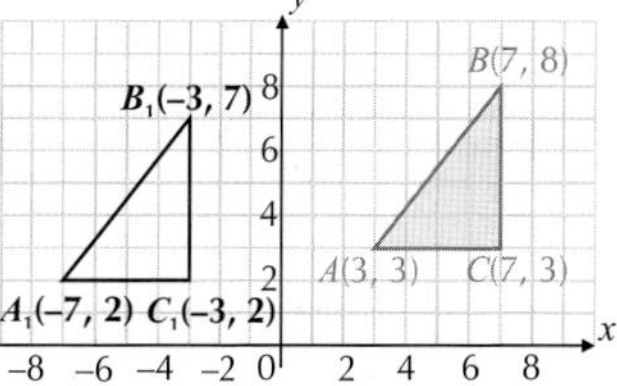

c) To get from the original point to its image, **subtract 10** from the ***x*-coordinate**, and **subtract 1** from the ***y*-coordinate**.
You could also write this as (x – 10, y – 1).

4 a) 3 + 0 = 3, –4 + 1 = –3, so the coordinates are **(3, –3)**

b) 3 + 3 = 6, –4 + 0 = –4, so the coordinates are **(6, –4)**

c) 3 + 4 = 7, –4 – 2 = –6, so the coordinates are **(7, –6)**

d) 3 – 1 = 2, –4 – 5 = –9, so the coordinates are **(2, –9)**

5 D: 1 + (–2) = –1, 1 + 2 = 3,
so the new coordinates are D_1**(–1, 3)**
E: 3 + (–2) = 1, –2 + 2 = 0,
so the new coordinates are E_1**(1, 0)**
F: 4 + (–2) = 2, 0 + 2 = 2,
so the new coordinates are F_1**(2, 2)**

Page 402 Exercise 2

1 a) The translation is 1 unit in the positive *x* direction and 2 units in the positive *y* direction, so the vector is $\begin{pmatrix} \mathbf{1} \\ \mathbf{2} \end{pmatrix}$.

b) The translation is 1 unit in the positive *x* direction and 2 units in the negative *y* direction, so the vector is $\begin{pmatrix} \mathbf{1} \\ \mathbf{-2} \end{pmatrix}$.

c) The translation is 3 units in the negative *y* direction only, so the vector is $\begin{pmatrix} \mathbf{0} \\ \mathbf{-3} \end{pmatrix}$.

d) The translation is 4 units in the negative *x* direction and 3 units in the negative *y* direction, so the vector is $\begin{pmatrix} \mathbf{-4} \\ \mathbf{-3} \end{pmatrix}$.

e) The translation is 6 units in the positive x direction and 7 units in the positive y direction, so the vector is $\begin{pmatrix}6\\7\end{pmatrix}$.

f) The translation is 6 units in the positive y direction only, so the vector is $\begin{pmatrix}0\\6\end{pmatrix}$.

2 a) **2 units to the right, 3 units down**

b) The translation is 2 units in the positive x direction and 3 units in the negative y direction, so the vector is $\begin{pmatrix}2\\-3\end{pmatrix}$.

c) Z is 2 units in the positive x direction from Y and 4 units in the negative y direction, so the translation is $\begin{pmatrix}2\\-4\end{pmatrix}$.

3 a) The image R is 5 units in the negative y direction from P so the translation is described by the vector $\begin{pmatrix}0\\-5\end{pmatrix}$.

b) The image S is 8 units in the positive x direction from R so the translation is described by the vector $\begin{pmatrix}8\\0\end{pmatrix}$.

Using the same method for c)-f):

c) $\begin{pmatrix}13\\1\end{pmatrix}$ d) $\begin{pmatrix}-8\\0\end{pmatrix}$

e) $\begin{pmatrix}-13\\-6\end{pmatrix}$ f) $\begin{pmatrix}-8\\5\end{pmatrix}$

4 a) Drawing the points and connecting them up gives:

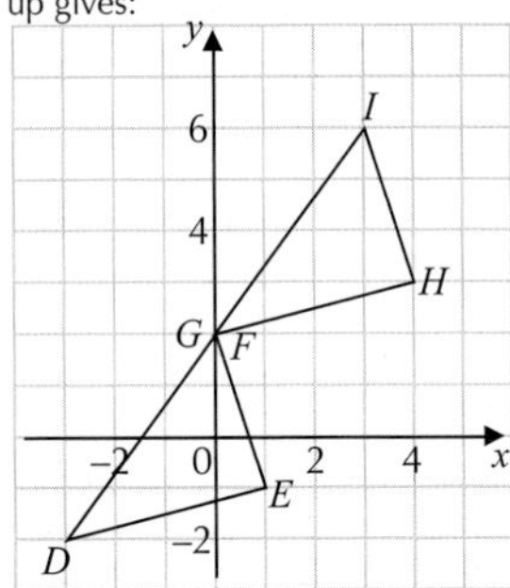

b) GHI is 3 units to the right fom DEF and 4 units up, so the vector is $\begin{pmatrix}3\\4\end{pmatrix}$.

5 a) To get from J to M, K to N and L to P, you subtract 1 from the x-coordinate and add 2 to the y-coordinate. So the vector describing the translation is $\begin{pmatrix}-1\\2\end{pmatrix}$.

b) MNP to JKL is opposite to the translation in a), so the vector is $\begin{pmatrix}1\\-2\end{pmatrix}$.

Page 403 Exercise 3

1 a) Y is 3 units to the right and 5 units down from X so the vector describing the translation is $\begin{pmatrix}3\\-5\end{pmatrix}$.

b) X is 3 units to the left and 5 units up from Y so the vector describing the translation is $\begin{pmatrix}-3\\5\end{pmatrix}$.

c) **The x and y components have changed signs.**

2 The vector describing the translation from Z onto W is the negative of the vector $\begin{pmatrix}1\\-4\end{pmatrix}$, i.e. $\begin{pmatrix}-1\\4\end{pmatrix}$.

3 The negatives of the vectors given in each part are:

a) $\begin{pmatrix}0\\-2\end{pmatrix}$ b) $\begin{pmatrix}-5\\0\end{pmatrix}$ c) $\begin{pmatrix}1\\5\end{pmatrix}$ d) $\begin{pmatrix}-3\\-2\end{pmatrix}$

Translate the each shape by the relevant vector above:

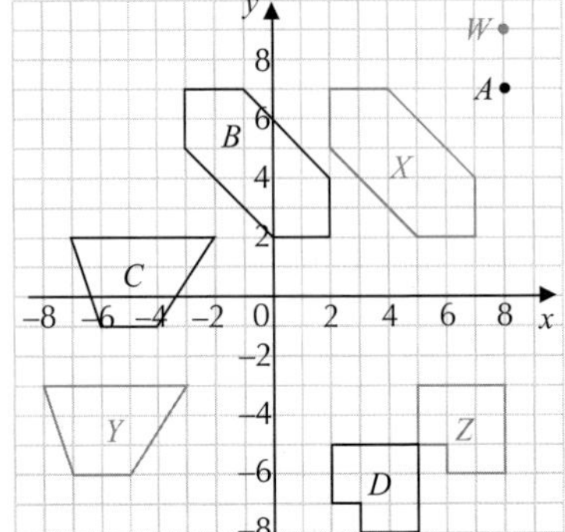

4 The vector describing the translation from PQR onto DEF is the negative of the vector $\begin{pmatrix}-1\\4\end{pmatrix}$, i.e. $\begin{pmatrix}1\\-4\end{pmatrix}$. Applying this vector to the coordinates of PQR gives:

D: $-1 + 1 = 0$, $0 - 4 = -4$, so $\boldsymbol{D = (0, -4)}$,
E: $-4 + 1 = -3$, $4 - 4 = 0$, so $\boldsymbol{E = (-3, 0)}$,
F: $3 + 1 = 4$, $2 - 4 = -2$, so $\boldsymbol{F = (4, -2)}$.

24.4 Enlargements

Page 405 Exercise 1

1 The scale factor is 2, so multiply each of the side lengths by 2.

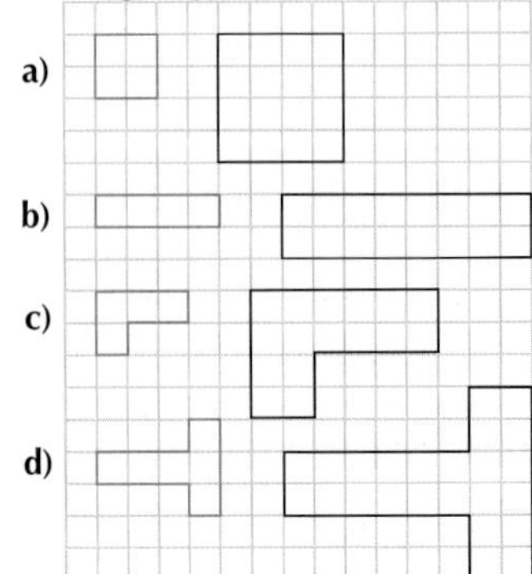

2 The scale factor is 3, so multiply each of the side lengths by 3.

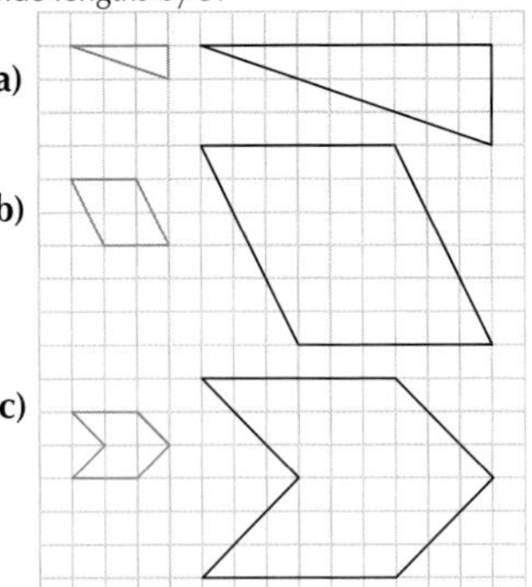

3 The scale factor is 5, so multiply each of the side lengths by 5.

a)

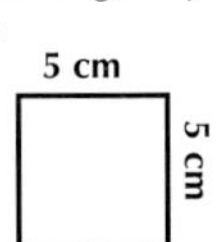

Your diagrams don't have to be full size, but they do need to be labelled correctly.

b)

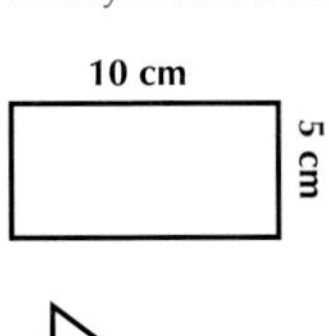

c)

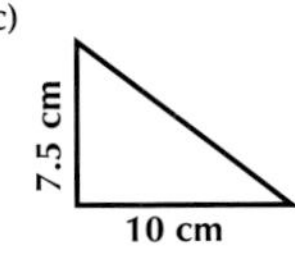

d)

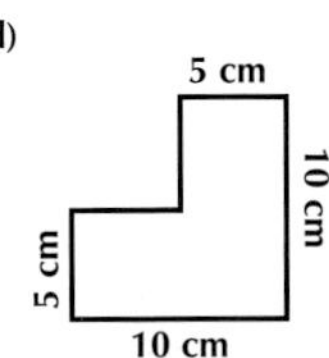

4 The scale factor is $\frac{1}{2}$, so multiply each of the side lengths by $\frac{1}{2}$.

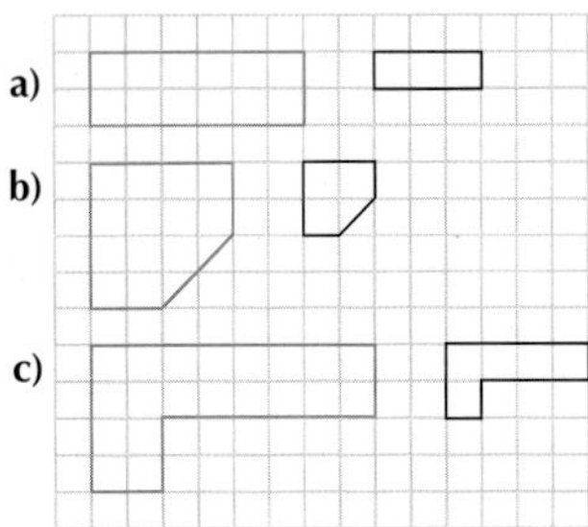

5 The scale factor is $\frac{1}{3}$, so multiply each of the side lengths by $\frac{1}{3}$.

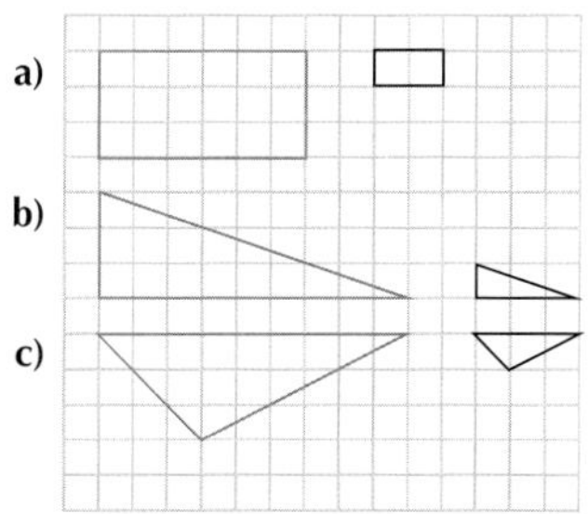

6 The shape is a square so all the sides will be the same length. The scale factor is $\frac{1}{4}$ so the new sides will be:

$16 \times \frac{1}{4}$ = **4 cm**

7 The scale factor is $\frac{1}{5}$ so the new side lengths will be:

$15 \times \frac{1}{5}$ = **3 cm** and $35 \times \frac{1}{5}$ = **7 cm**

Page 407 Exercise 2

1 a) (i) **3 units** (ii) **3 units** (iii) **0 units**

b) (i) 3×2 = **6 units**

(ii) 3×2 = **6 units**

(iii) 0×2 = **0 units**

c)

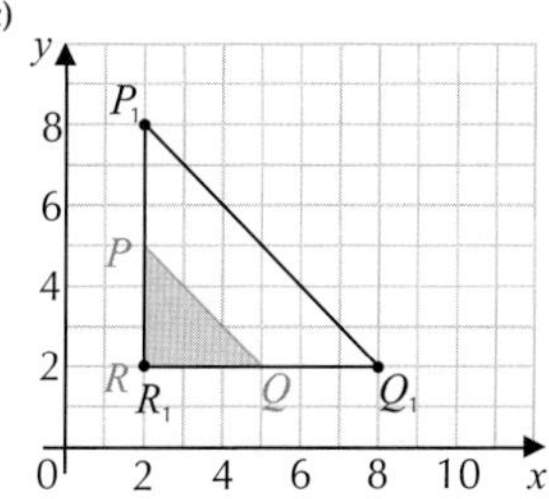

For the enlargements in Q2 and Q3, draw lines from the centre of enlargement to each vertex of the shape. Extend these lines depending on the scale factor (e.g. for a scale factor of 3 the lines should be 3 times as long). Mark the new vertices at the end of these lines and join them up to create the new shape.

2 a), b), c), d)

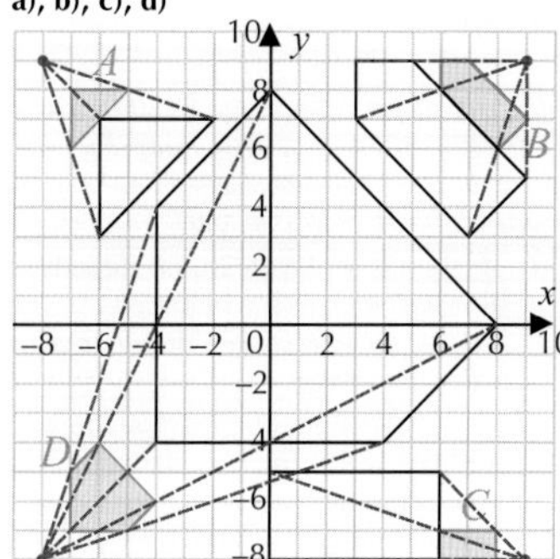

3 a), b)

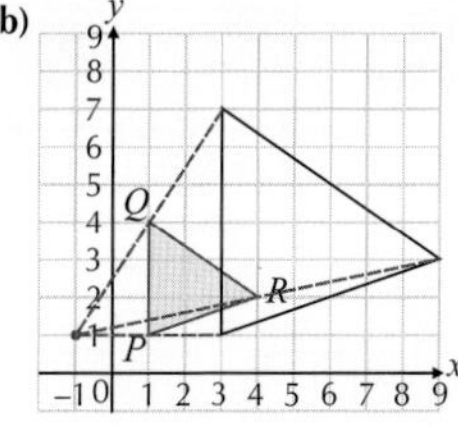

Page 408 Exercise 3

For each enlargement in this exercise, draw lines from the centre of enlargement to each vertex of the shape. Mark the new vertices a fraction of the way along these lines (e.g. for a scale factor of $\frac{1}{4}$ the vertices should be a quarter of the way along the lines from the centre of enlargement). Join the vertices up to create the new shape.

1 a), b)

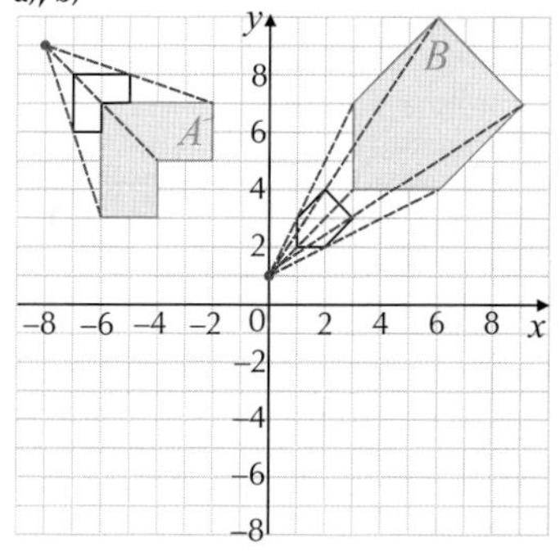

c), d)

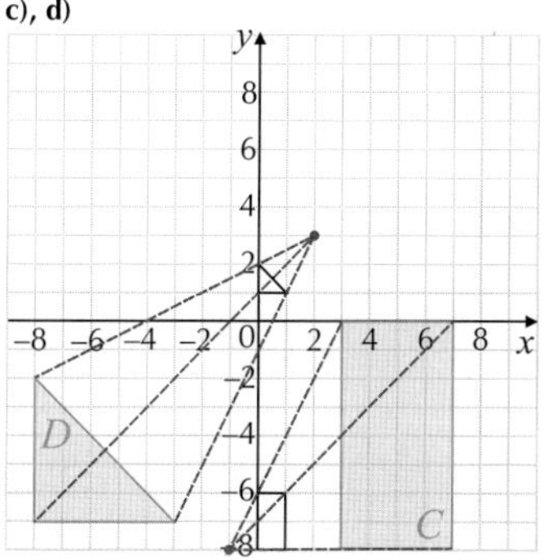

It's fine if you've drawn all the Q1 enlargements on the same grid.

2 a), b)

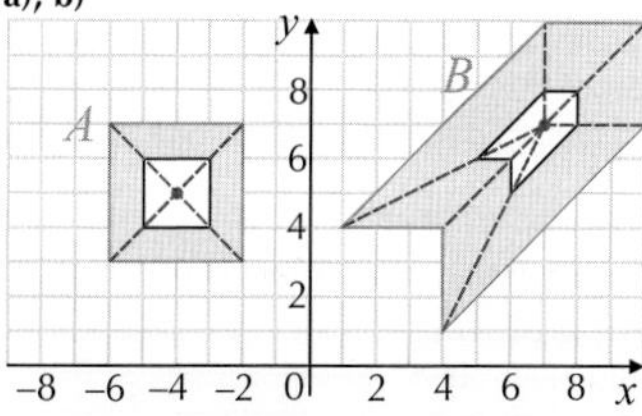

Page 409 Exercise 4

1 a) Measure corresponding sides of shapes A and B — e.g. the vertical side of A is 3 units and of B is 6 units. So the scale factor is $6 \div 3 = 2$. Draw lines through corresponding vertices of shapes A and B. These intersect at the point (2, 10). So the transformation is an enlargement, **scale factor 2, centre (2, 10)**.

b) E.g. vertical side of A is 1 unit and of B is 2 units. So the scale factor is $2 \div 1 = 2$. Draw lines through corresponding vertices of shapes A and B. These intersect at the point (6, 10). So the transformation is an enlargement, **scale factor 2, centre (6, 10)**.

c) E.g. vertical side of A is 1 unit and of B is 3 units. So the scale factor is $3 \div 1 = 3$. Draw lines through corresponding vertices of shapes A and B. These intersect at the point (11, 9). So the transformation is an enlargement, **scale factor 3, centre (11, 9)**.

2 a) Measure corresponding sides of shapes A and B — e.g. the bottom horizontal side of shape A is 4 units and of B is 8 units. The new shape is A, so the scale factor is $\frac{4}{8} = \frac{1}{2}$. Draw lines through corresponding vertices of shapes A and B. These intersect at the point (1, 1). So the transformation is an enlargement, **scale factor $\frac{1}{2}$, centre (1, 1)**.

b) E.g. the bottom horizontal side of shape A is 2 units and of B is 4 units. The new shape is A, so the scale factor is $\frac{2}{4} = \frac{1}{2}$. Draw lines through corresponding vertices of shapes A and B. These intersect at the point (6, 5). So the transformation is an enlargement, **scale factor $\frac{1}{2}$, centre (6, 5)**.

c) E.g. the bottom horizontal side of shape A is 1 unit and of B is 3 units. The new shape is A, so the scale factor is $\frac{1}{3}$. Draw lines through corresponding vertices of shapes A and B. These intersect at the point (5, 4). So the transformation is an enlargement, **scale factor $\frac{1}{3}$, centre (5, 4)**.

Page 410 Exercise 5

1 a)

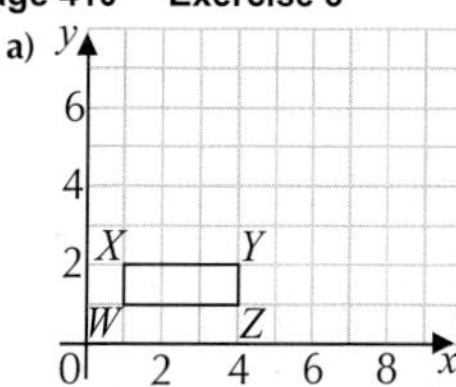

Perimeter = 3 + 1 + 3 + 1 = **8 units**

b) Draw lines from the origin to each vertex of the shape. The scale factor is 2 so extend these lines so they are twice as long. Mark the new vertices at the ends of these lines and join them up to create the new shape:

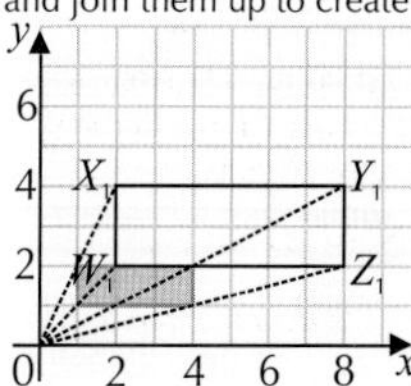

c) Perimeter of $W_1X_1Y_1Z_1$ is the old perimeter multiplied by the scale factor:

8×2 = **16 units**

You can check your answer by working out the perimeter from your diagram.

2 a) A square with sides 3 cm has a perimeter of $3 \times 4 = 12$ cm. Enlarging by scale factor 3 gives a perimeter of 12×3 = **36 cm**

b) The rectangle has a perimeter of:

$(2 \times 2) + (2 \times 8) = 20$ m.

Enlarging by a scale factor of 5 gives a perimeter of 20×5 = **100 m**

24.5 Congruence and Similarity

Page 411 Exercise 1

1 Shapes are congruent if they are the same size and shape, so:
A is congruent to G, B is congruent to J,
C is congruent to F, D is congruent to H,
E is congruent to I.

2 Shapes are congruent if they are the same size and shape, so the odd ones out are:
a) **D** b) **H** c) **I**
d) **N** e) **Q** f) **V**

Page 413 Exercise 2

1 a) The triangles are congruent, so match the sides and angles:
a = 5 cm, b = 69°, c = 69°,
d = 42°, e = 7 cm, f = 7 cm

b) g = 180° – 90° – 53° = **37°**
The triangles are congruent, so match the remaining sides and angles:
h = 6 cm, i = 10 cm, j = 8 cm,
k = 37°, l = 53°

2 You need to show whether or not one of the 'congruence conditions' holds:
a) **Yes.** Two sides and the angle between on one triangle are the same as two sides and the angle between on the other triangle, so condition **SAS** holds.
b) **No.** The two angles shown are the same, but the corresponding sides are not equal, so **AAS** doesn't hold.
c) **Yes,** all the sides are the same in both triangles so **SSS** holds.
d) **No.** Their hypotenuses are different, so **RHS** doesn't hold.

3 You need to show whether or not one of the 'congruence conditions' holds:
a) E.g. Missing angle in first triangle: 180° – 75° – 50° = 55°. Two angles and one corresponding side are the same in both triangles so condition **AAS** holds and **the triangles are congruent**.
b) Using Pythagoras' theorem the hypotenuse of the triangle on the right is 5 cm. Both triangles have a right angle, the same hypotenuse and another side the same, so condition **RHS holds** and **the triangles are congruent**.

Page 414 Exercise 3

1 Shapes are similar if they have the same shape, but they can be different sizes so:
A, C and F are similar
B, E and K are similar
D, G and I are similar
H, J and L are similar

2 Shapes are similar if they have the same shape, but they can be different sizes, so the pairs of similar shapes are:
a) **A and B** b) **D and F**
c) **H and I** d) **K and L**

Page 416 Exercise 4

1 For each part of the question find the condition for similarity which applies:
a) **All the angles in one triangle are the same as the angles in the other triangle.**
b) **All corresponding sides of the two triangles are in the same ratio,** since each side in the 2nd triangle is twice as long as the corresponding side in the 1st.
c) **All the angles in one triangle are the same as the angles in the other triangle.**
The triangles are in a different orientation but they are still similar — one is an enlarged reflection of the other.
d) **Two sides of the triangles are in the same ratio** (the sides in the second triangle are a third of the length of those in the first) **and the angle between them is the same in both triangles.**

2 To prove if triangles are similar, you need to show whether or not one of the 'similarity conditions' holds:
a) **Similar** — all of the angles are the same in the two triangles.
b) **Similar** — all corresponding sides are in the same ratio, since each side in the second triangle is 1.5 times as long as the corresponding side in the first.
c) **Similar** — two sides are in the same ratio (the sides in the second triangle are two thirds of the length of those in the first) and there's a right angle between them in both triangles.
d) **Not similar** — the sides either side of the given angle are the same in one triangle and different in the other.
e) **Similar** — two sides are in the same ratio (the sides in the second triangle are a third of the length of those in the first) and there's a 40° angle between them in both triangles.
f) **Not similar** — only one angle matches.

Page 418 Exercise 5

1 a) (i) The angle is the same as the corresponding angle in the other triangle, so x = **100°**.
The diagrams are drawn to scale, and there's only one obtuse angle, so x must be 100°.
(ii) All angles in a triangle add up to 180° so y = 180° – 100° – 25° = **55°**

b) The triangles are isosceles, so both base angles in the first triangle must be 35°. Since the triangles are similar, both angles at the top of the second triangle must also be 35°. So z = 180° – 35° – 35° = **110°**.

2 a) The triangles are similar so the corresponding angles are:
(i) **angle ABC**
(ii) **angle ACB**
(iii) **angle BAC**
b) Scale factor = $AD \div AB$ = 9 ÷ 3 = **3**
c) (i) $AE = AC \times 3$ = 2.5 m × 3 = **7.5 m**
(ii) $DE = BC \times 3$ so $BC = DE \div 3$ = 12 m ÷ 3 = **4 m**

3 Scale factor = $QS \div QR$ = 12 cm ÷ 6 cm = **2**
a) $ST = RU \times 2$ = 3 cm × 2 = **6 cm**
b) $QT = QU \times 2$ = 5 cm × 2 = **10 cm**
c) $UT = QT - QU$ = 10 cm – 5 cm = **5 cm**

4 Use lengths SW and SV to find the scale factor.
$SV = SW + WV$ = 2 + 4 = 6 m,
so the scale factor = $SV \div SW$ = 6 ÷ 2 = 3
a) $TW = UV \div 3$ = 4.5 ÷ 3 = **1.5 m**
b) $SU = ST \times 3$ = 1.8 × 3 = **5.4 m**
c) $TU = SU - ST$ = 5.4 – 1.8 = **3.6 m**

5 a) Angle QXR = **34°**
Angle QXR is vertically opposite angle ZXY so they are equal.
b) angle XYZ is alternate to **angle XRQ**
c) Scale factor = $XY \div RX$ = 10 ÷ 5 = **2**
d) (i) $YZ = QR \times 2$ = 4 × 2 = **8 m**
(ii) $XQ = XZ \div 2$ = 14 ÷ 2 = **7 m**

Page 419 Review Exercise

1 a) (i) Start by drawing the mirror line at y = –1. Then reflect the vertices and join up the image points to form image B — see below.
Remember, the vertices should be the same perpendicular distance from the mirror line.
(ii) Use tracing paper to draw the shape, then put your pencil on the origin and rotate the tracing paper by 90° clockwise. Draw the rotated shape C in its new position — see below.

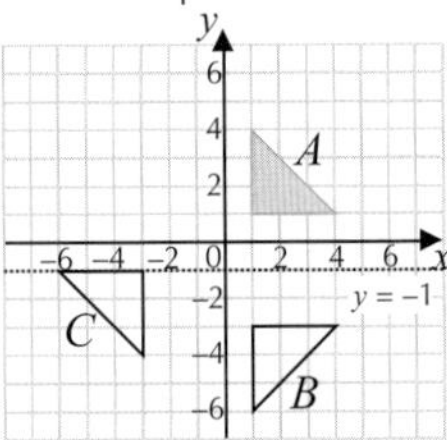

b) (i) Use tracing paper to draw the shape, then put your pencil on the origin and rotate the tracing paper by 90° clockwise. Draw the rotated shape D in its new position — see below.
(ii) Draw the mirror line at y = –1. Then reflect the vertices and join up the image points to form image E — see below.

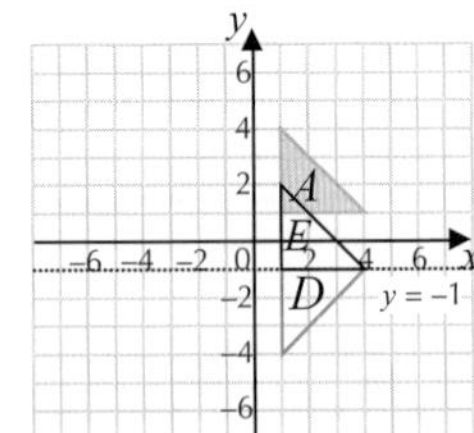

Notice that shapes C and E aren't in the same place even though you started with the same shape (A) and did the same transformations. This shows that it matters in which order you do the transformations.

2 a) (i) A_1 should be drawn 2 units directly down from A — see below.
Translate the vertices and then join them up to form the image.
(ii) Draw lines from (9, –7) through the vertices of A_1. The scale factor is 3, so extend the lines so that they are 3 times as long. Mark the new vertices at the ends of these lines and then join them up to make the new shape A_2 — see below.
You can check your answer by checking the sides of A_2 are 3 times as long as those of A and A_1.

b) (i) B_1 should be 2 units to the left of B and 1 unit down — see below.

(ii) Reflect the vertices and join up the image points to form image B_2 — see below.

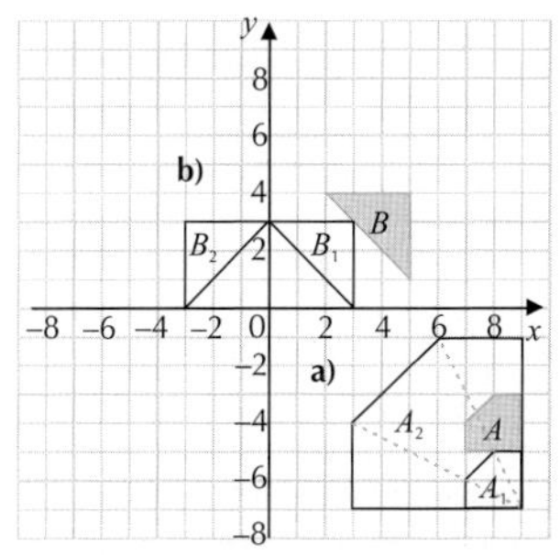

3 a) (i) Use tracing paper to draw shape P, then put your pencil on the point (4, 5) and rotate the tracing paper by 180°. Draw the rotated shape P_1 in its new position — see below.

(ii) P_2 should be 2 units to the right and 2 units up from P_1 — see below.

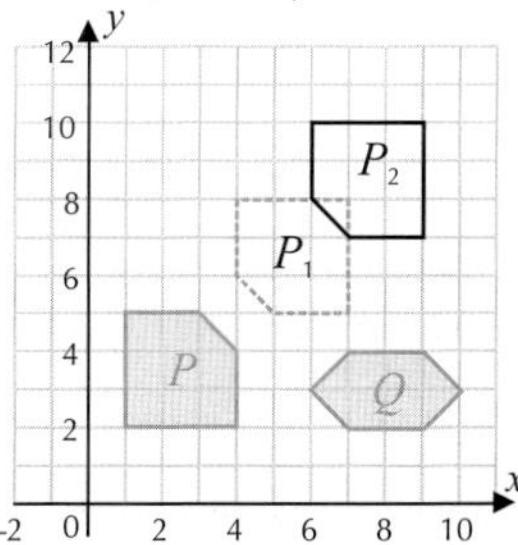

b) Place the tracing paper drawing from part a) back over P. Put your pencil on the point (5, 6) and rotate the tracing paper by 180°. Draw the rotated shape P_3 in its new position.

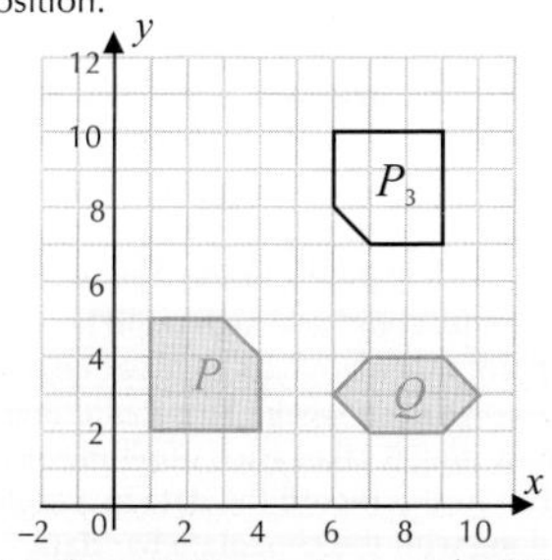

Since these rotations are by an angle of 180°, you could go clockwise or anticlockwise.

c) (i) Use tracing paper to draw shape Q, then put your pencil on the point (4, 5) and rotate the tracing paper by 180°. Draw the rotated shape Q_1 in its new position — see below.

(ii) Q_2 should be 2 units to the right and 2 units up from Q_1 — see below.

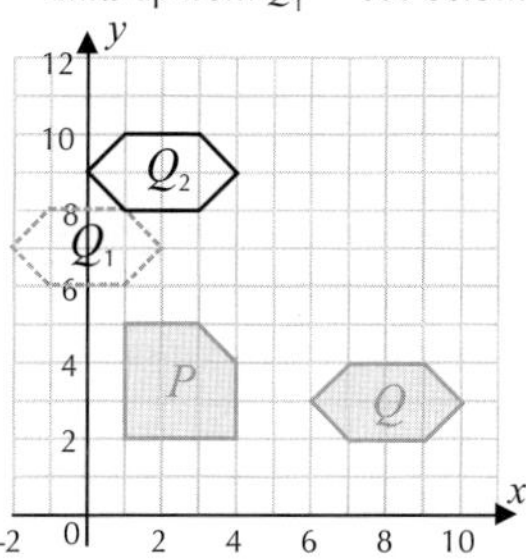

d) Place the tracing paper drawing from part c) back over Q. Put your pencil on the point (5, 6) and rotate the tracing paper by 180°. Draw the rotated shape Q_3 in its new position.

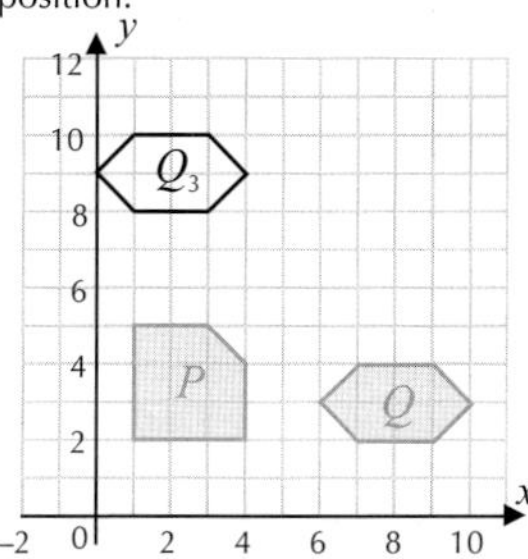

e) P_2 and P_3 are identical and in exactly the same position, and Q_2 and Q_3 are identical and in exactly the same position.

4 a) (i) Use tracing paper to draw the shape, then put your pencil on the point (4, 2) and rotate the tracing paper by 90° clockwise. Draw the rotated shape in its new position.

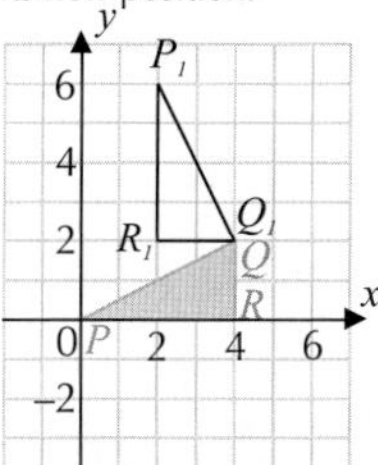

(ii) Draw lines from (2, 6) through the vertices of $P_1Q_1R_1$. The scale factor is 1.5, so extend the lines so that they are one and a half times as long. Mark the new vertices at the ends of these lines and then join them up to make the new shape $P_2Q_2R_2$.

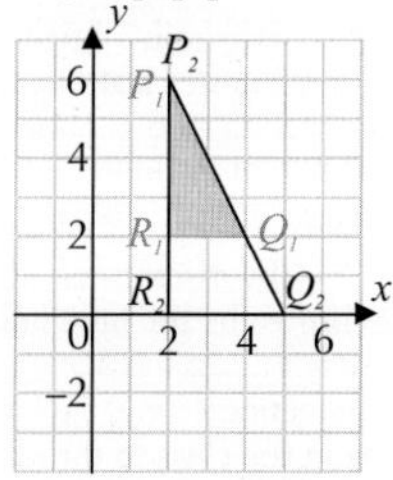

You can check your answer for the enlargement by dividing the side lengths of the image by the corresponding side lengths of the original shape, which should be equal to the scale factor.

b) (i) Draw lines from (2, 6) through the vertices of PQR. The scale factor is 1.5, so extend the lines so that they are one and a half times as long. Mark the new vertices at the ends of these lines and then join them up to make the new shape $P_3Q_3R_3$.

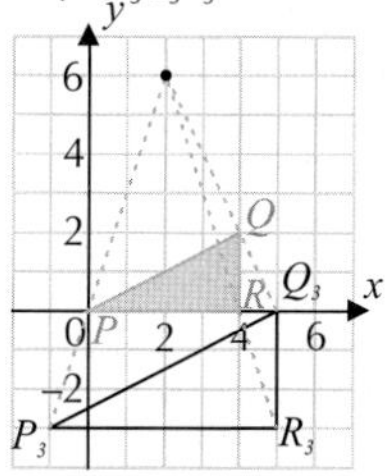

(ii) Use tracing paper to draw the shape, then put your pencil on the point (4, 2) and rotate the tracing paper by 90° clockwise. Draw the rotated shape in its new position.

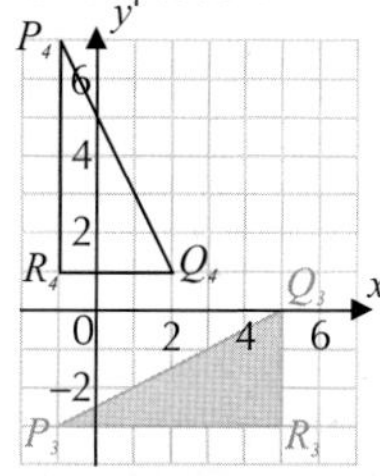

5 First draw the triangle onto a coordinate grid. Then find the image of the 180° rotation about the origin using tracing paper. Find the second image after the translation by moving the first image 6 units to the right and 2 units up. Then by comparing STU with the final image, you can see the final image is equivalent to a **rotation of 180° about (3, 1)**.

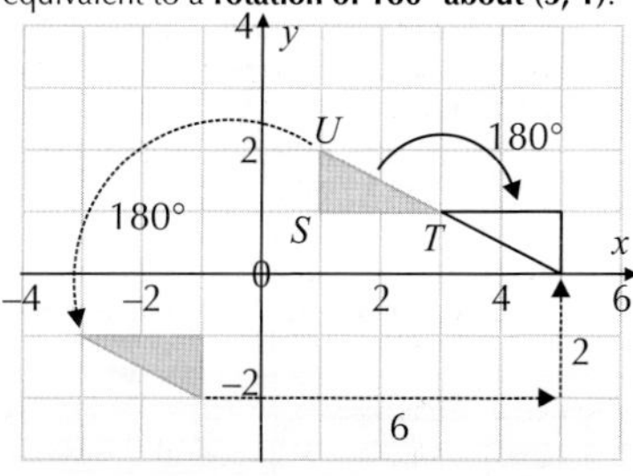

The rotations are 180° so you can rotate clockwise or anticlockwise.

6 a) The shapes are the same shape but different sizes so they are **similar**.

b) The shapes are the same shape and size so they are **congruent**.

Remember that orientation does not affect whether a shape is congruent or similar.

c) The shapes are different so are **neither congruent nor similar**.

7 a) The missing angle on right-hand triangle is $180° - 105° - 40° = 35°$, so two sides and the angle between on one triangle are the same as two sides and the angle between on the other triangle. Condition **SAS** holds so the triangles are **congruent**.

b) The 3 cm sides on the first triangle are 3 times the length of the 1 cm sides on the second. But the 5 cm side is not 3 times as long as the corresponding side on the second triangle ($1.5 \times 3 = 4.5$ cm $\neq 5$ cm). The lengths are not in the same ratio, so the triangles are **neither** similar nor congruent.

c) The missing angle on the left-hand triangle is $180° - 30° - 45° = 105°$.
The missing angle on the right-hand triangle is $180° - 105° - 30° = 45°$.
All the angles on one triangle are the same as the angles on the other triangle but corresponding sides are not the same length so the triangles are **similar**.

d) The missing angle on the left-hand triangle is $180° - 38° - 112° = 30°$, so there's no 40° angle in this triangle. The angles in one triangle are not all the same as the angles in the other triangle, so the triangles are **neither** similar nor congruent.

8 Using alternate angles $\boldsymbol{a = 110°}$ and $\boldsymbol{b = 45°}$,
All angles in a triangle sum to 180° so
$c = 180° - 45° - 110° = \mathbf{25°}$.
Using vertically opposite angles $\boldsymbol{d = 25°}$.
All of the angles in the two triangles are the same, so they are similar. The 9 cm and 6 cm sides are corresponding sides, so the scale factor is given by $9 \div 6 = 1.5$.
$e = 3.59 \times 1.5 = \mathbf{5.385}$ **cm,**
$f = 12 \div 1.5 = \mathbf{8}$ **cm**

Page 421 Exam-Style Questions

1 a) Draw in the mirror line $y = x$, reflect each point of A and then join them up to form the image B.

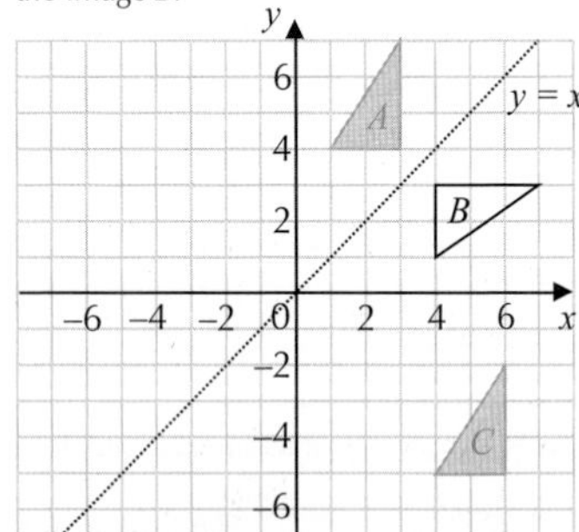

[2 marks available – 1 mark for the correct line $y = x$ used, 1 mark for shape B in the correct position.]
The vertices of the image should be the same perpendicular distance from the mirror line, but on the opposite side to the original shape.

b) Shape C needs to move 3 units left and 9 up so the translation vector would be $\begin{pmatrix} -3 \\ 9 \end{pmatrix}$.
So $\boldsymbol{p = -3}$ and $\boldsymbol{q = 9}$. *[1 mark]*

2 First, translate shape P by $\begin{pmatrix} 1 \\ -4 \end{pmatrix}$, so P moves 1 unit to the right and 4 units down to produce shape Q. Then enlarge shape Q by scale factor 2 with centre of enlargement (–2, 3) to produce shape R. Draw lines from (–2, 3) to each vertex of the shape. Extend these lines to twice as long. Mark the new vertices at the end of these lines and join them up to create the new shape R.

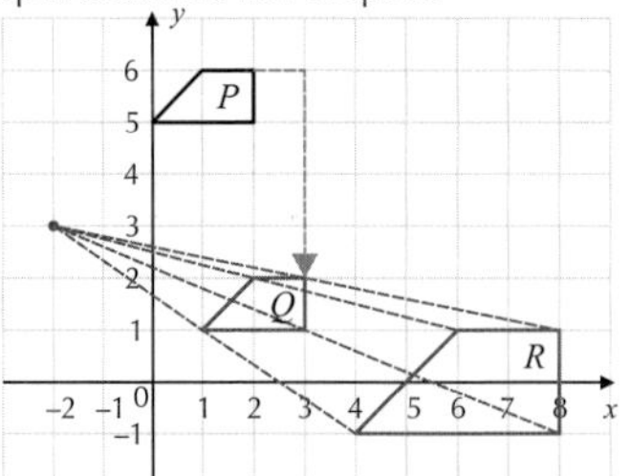

[3 marks available — 1 mark for translating P to the correct position to get Q, 1 mark for attempting to enlarge Q by scale factor 2 centred on (–2, 3), 1 mark for R drawn in the correct position]
You can check your answer for the enlargement by dividing the side lengths of the image by the corresponding side lengths of the original shape, which should be equal to the scale factor.

3 a) Scale factor $= 8 \div 3 = \frac{8}{3}$ *[1 mark]*
$BC = 10 \div \frac{8}{3} = \mathbf{3.75}$ **m** *[1 mark]*

b) The triangles are similar, so
angle ACB = angle $AED = 180° - 29° - 99°$
$= \mathbf{52°}$ *[1 mark]*

Section 25 — Collecting Data

25.1 Using Different Types of Data

Page 423 Exercise 1

1 a) Megan collects the data herself, so it is **primary**.

b) Jane gets her data from the internet, so it is **secondary**.

2 Faheem gets his data from a newspaper, so it is **secondary**.

3 Nancy collects her data herself, so it is **primary**.

4 a) Data needed — **girls' answers to some questions about school dinners.**
Method of collecting — e.g. **Nikita could ask all the girls in her class to fill in a questionnaire.**

b) Primary data

5 a) Data needed — **daily rainfall figures for London and Manchester last August.**
Method of collecting — e.g. **Anne could look for rainfall figures on the internet.**

b) Secondary data

6 a) Data needed — **the distance an identical ball can be thrown by the boys and girls in his class.**
Method of collecting — e.g. **Skylar could ask everyone in the class to throw the same ball as far as they can.**
He could measure the distances and record them in a table, along with whether each thrower was male or female.

b) Primary data

7 a) Data needed — **one set of data consists of the temperature readings in Jim's garden taken at 10 am each day.**
The other set consists of the Met Office's temperatures recorded for Jim's area at the same time.
Method of collecting — e.g. **Jim could collect the data from his garden by taking readings from a thermometer.**
He can get the Met Office temperatures from their website. He should record both temperatures for each day in a table.

b) Data collected in Jim's garden is **primary** data. The Met Office data is **secondary** data.

Page 424 Exercise 2

1 a) The number of words is numerical and it can only be whole values so this is **discrete quantitative**.

b) Foods are descriptive so this is **qualitative**.

c) The number of pets is numerical and it can only take whole values so this is **discrete quantitative**.

d) The size of a crowd is numerical and it can only take whole values so this is **discrete quantitative**.

e) Heights are numerical and they can take any value greater than zero so this is **continuous quantitative**.

f) Times are numerical and they can take any value greater than zero so this is **continuous quantitative**.

g) Nationalities are descriptive so this is **qualitative**.

h) Lengths are numerical and they can take any value greater than zero so this is **continuous quantitative**.

i) Distances are numerical and they can take any value greater than zero so this is **continuous quantitative**.

j) Colours are descriptive so this is **qualitative**.

2 a) Janka collects the data herself, so it is **primary data**.

b) Drinks are descriptive, so this is **qualitative**.

3 a) One set of data is the **average number of chocolate bars eaten each week by each pupil**. The other set of data is the **time it takes these pupils to run 100 metres**.

b) Gemma could **ask each pupil how many chocolate bars they eat on average each week.** She could **time how long it takes each pupil to run 100 m** and **record the data in a table, along with the chocolate bar data.**

c) The number of chocolate bars is numerical and can only take whole values so it is **discrete quantitative data**.
The running time is numerical and can take any value greater than zero so it is **continuous quantitative data**.

d) Both sets of data are **primary data**.

25.2 Data Collection

Page 425 Exercise 1

1 There is **no 'tally' column**.
There could be a car in the car park that isn't one of the colours listed — **the rows do not cover every possibility**.

2 a) E.g.

Visits	Tally	Frequency
0		
1		
2		
3		
More than 3		

b) E.g.

Destination	Tally	Frequency
UK		
Spain		
USA		
Asia		
Other		

Make sure your groups cover all possible options, e.g. by having an 'other' or 'more than...' row. Also, none of your groups should overlap — e.g. if you had a row for New York and for USA, then these would overlap (if you went to New York, then you also went to the USA).

Page 426 Exercise 2

1 a) **There are gaps between the data classes. The rows do not cover every possibility.**
E.g.

No. of people	Tally	Frequency
0 - 5000		
5001 - 10 000		
10 001 - 15 000		
15 001 - 20 000		

b) **The data classes overlap. The rows do not cover every possibility.**
E.g.

Weight (w kg)	Tally	Frequency
$w \le 3$		
$3 < w \le 3.5$		
$3.5 < w \le 4$		
$w > 4$		

2 a) The heights are continuous so you need classes with inequalities to cover values ranging between 5 and 27.
E.g. $5 \le h < 10$ $10 \le h < 15$ $15 \le h < 20$ $20 \le h < 25$ $25 \le h \le 27$

b) The number of quiz questions answered correctly is discrete. All whole numbers between 0 and 20 are possible so you need classes with grouped values.
E.g. **0-4 5-8 9-12 13-16 17-20**

c) The weights are continuous so you need classes with inequalities covering a sensible range around 200 g.
E.g. $w \le 180$ $180 < w \le 190$ $190 < w \le 200$ $200 < w \le 210$ $w > 210$

d) The volumes are continuous so you need classes with inequalities covering a sensible range up to 300 ml.
E.g. $v \le 260$ $260 < v \le 270$ $270 < v \le 280$ $280 < v \le 290$ $290 < v \le 300$

3 a) E.g.

Time (t hrs)	Tally	Frequency
$t \le 5$		
$5 < t \le 10$		
$10 < t \le 20$		
$20 < t \le 40$		
$t > 40$		

b) E.g.

No. of pairs	Tally	Frequency
0 - 4		
5 - 8		
9 - 12		
13 - 16		
17 or more		

c) E.g.

Length (s cm)	Tally	Frequency
$s \le 15$		
$15 < s \le 20$		
$20 < s \le 25$		
$25 < s \le 30$		
$s > 30$		

d) E.g.

Distance (d km)	Tally	Frequency
$d \le 5$		
$5 < d \le 10$		
$10 < d \le 20$		
$20 < d \le 40$		
$d > 40$		

Page 428 Exercise 3

1 a) **There are not enough hair colour data classes. The age data classes overlap. The data is for adults so doesn't need a 0-15 data class.**

b) E.g.

Hair Colour	Age (in whole years)				
	18-30	31-45	46-60	61-75	76 or more
Blonde					
Light brown					
Dark brown					
Ginger					
Grey					
Other					

2 a) E.g.

Season	Gender	
	Male	Female
Spring		
Summer		
Autumn		
Winter		

b) E.g.

Music	Age Group	
	Adult	Child
Pop		
Classical		
Rock		

c) E.g.

Time spent (t hours)	School Year				
	7	8	9	10	11
$t \le 1$					
$1 < t \le 2$					
$2 < t \le 3$					
$3 < t \le 4$					

d) E.g.

Total books read last year	Favourite Genre			
	Horror	Romance	Sci-Fi	Fantasy
0-10				
11-20				
21-30				
More than 30				

3 a) E.g.

Cats or dogs	Gender	
	Male	Female
Cats		
Dogs		

b) E.g.

TV time (t hours)	Age Group	
	Adult	Child
$t \le 1$		
$1 < t \le 2$		
$2 < t \le 3$		
$3 < t \le 4$		
$t > 4$		

c) E.g.

Transport	School Year				
	7	8	9	10	11
Walking					
Bus					
Car					
Bicycle					
Train					
Other					

d) E.g.

Height (h cm)	No. of fruit portions eaten			
	0-1	2-3	4-5	6 or more
$h \le 120$				
$120 < h \le 140$				
$140 < h \le 160$				
$160 < h \le 180$				
$h > 180$				

4 a) **The favourite subject data classes don't cover every option.**
Olivia wants to know the most popular subject in each year group so the year group data classes shouldn't be grouped.

b) E.g.

Year	Favourite Subject					
	English	Maths	P.E.	Science	Music	Other
Year 7						
Year 8						
Year 9						
Year 10						
Year 11						

25.3 Sampling and Bias

Page 430 Exercise 1

1 The population is all the students of that university, and the sample is the students who complete the survey.

2 E.g. It would take too long to time all 216 pupils and a smaller sample would create less disruption in the school routine.

3 E.g. It would take a long time to test all the matches, and Patrick wouldn't have any matches left to use at the end of it.

4 E.g. Khadija's sample is too small so her results could be very unrepresentative of the whole audience.

5 E.g. There is a random element to the results of tossing a coin, so different samples will usually give different results.

6 Alfie's sample was bigger than Keith's and would be expected to be more accurate, so 'chocolate' is more likely to be the most popular flavour.

7 E.g. Nikhil's idea is best, as only tasting one cake would not be reliable, and tasting 50 out of the 200 would take too long and use up a quarter of their cakes.

Page 431 Exercise 2

1 a) Kelechi's friends could have similar opinions about the film.

b) Animal rights activists are more likely to want vegetarian food, so the sample will be biased towards vegetarian food.

c) People using the library on a Monday are unlikely to want it to close on a Monday, so the sample will be biased away from a Monday closure.

d) People at work probably won't be able to answer the phone in the afternoon, so the only replies they will get will be from people who don't work, home workers, and people with the day off.

Page 431 Exercise 3

1 E.g. The teacher could make a list of all the Year 7 pupils and assign each pupil a number. He could then generate 50 random numbers with a computer or calculator, and match the numbers to the pupils to create the sample.

2 E.g. The manager could assign each of the female members on her database a number, generate 40 random numbers with a computer or calculator, and match the numbers to the members to create the sample.

Page 432 Exercise 4

1 $7 \div 20 = 0.35$ of the sampled rooms have damp, so you could expect $0.35 \times 450 = 157.5$ $\approx$ **158 rooms** in the castle to have damp.
The calculated answer is a decimal, so you need to round your answer to the nearest whole number.

2 a) (i) $34 \div 50 = 0.68$ so you could expect $0.68 \times 650 =$ **442 politicians** to be in favour of policy X.

(ii) $1 \div 50 = 0.02$ so you could expect $0.02 \times 650 =$ **13 politicians** to be neutral about policy Y.

(iii) $14 \div 50 = 0.28$ so you could expect $0.28 \times 650 =$ **182 politicians** to be against policy Z.

b) This assumes that the sample of 50 politicians is **representative of the population of 650 politicians**.

Page 433 Review Exercise

1 a) E.g. The data he needs is his classmates' favourite colours. He could use a tally chart to record his classmates' answers.

b) He collects the data himself so it is primary data.

2 a) The time taken to travel to school is numerical and can take any value greater than zero so it is continuous quantitative.

b) The number of siblings is numerical and can only take certain values so it is discrete quantitative.

c) Films are descriptive so it is qualitative.

d) Shoe prices are numerical and only take certain values so it is discrete quantitative.

3 E.g.

Days in birth month	Tally	Frequency
28		
29		
30		
31		

4 **There is no row for someone who went to the cinema 0 times.**
The data classes overlap.
E.g.

No. of trips	Tally	Frequency
0 - 10		
11 - 20		
21 - 30		
31 - 40		
41 or more		

5 E.g.

Average time spent outside per week (t hours)	Age Group	
	Adult	Child
$t \le 3$		
$3 < t \le 6$		
$6 < t \le 9$		
$9 < t \le 12$		
$t > 12$		

6 E.g. It would be **expensive/time-consuming/impractical** to interview everyone in the town.

7 Jasper's sample will be a much higher percentage of the total number of pupils, and Connie's sample is not random.
For example, it could be a group of friends who may all support the same football team.

8 E.g. If the factory runs for 24 hours a day, test one freshly made component roughly every 30 minutes (or at 50 random times throughout the day).

9 $4 \div 12 = 0.333...$ of the sample prefer jam, so you could expect that $0.333... \times 50 = 16.666... \approx$ **17 party guests** would prefer jam doughnuts.

Page 434 Exam-Style Questions

1 a) Distances can take any value greater than zero so the data is **continuous data** *[1 mark]*.

b) E.g.

Distance (s metres)	Left- or Right-handed	
	Left-handed	Right-handed
$s \le 5$		
$5 < s \le 10$		
$10 < s \le 15$		
$15 < s \le 20$		
$t > 20$		

[2 marks available — 1 mark for using a two-way table, 1 mark for choosing appropriate data classes]

2 E.g. Jill wants to find out about her entire year but the students in the sample are all from the same class so their views might not accurately represent the whole year *[1 mark]*.
Jill's sample is quite small — there are only 10 students in the sample to represent the views of 150 students, so the results could be unreliable *[1 mark]*.

3 a) The data classes don't cover every possibility — there's no row for taking longer than 30 minutes *[1 mark]*.
The data classes overlap *[1 mark]*.

b) $12 \div 40 = 0.3$ of the sample take between 10 and 20 minutes *[1 mark]*, so Tahani can expect $0.3 \times 200 = 60$ participants to take between 10 and 20 minutes to complete the puzzle *[1 mark]*. It is assumed that the sample is representative of the whole population of 200 participants *[1 mark]*.

Section 26 — Analysing Data

26.1 Tally Charts and Frequency Tables

Page 435 Exercise 1

1 a) Write a tally mark for every response and then count the marks to find the frequency:

Type of Music	Tally	Frequency
Classical	|	1
Indie	|||	3
Pop	𝍸 ||||	9
Rock	|||	3
Other	||||	4

b) (i) **Pop** music is the type with the highest frequency.

(ii) The frequency for pop is 9 and for rock is 3. So the difference is $9 - 3 =$ **6**.

26.2 Averages and Range

Page 436 Exercise 1

In questions 1-3, you need to count up how many times the different data values appear. The mode (or modal value) is the value that appears most.

1 a) 8 **b) 6** **c) 8**

2 58

3 red

4 E.g. There are two modes for this data, 3 and 6, so the mode does not give a good indication of the average value of the data.

Page 437 Exercise 2

1 a) The numbers in order are: 3, 4, 5, 8, 8. The middle value is the 3rd value, so the median is **5**.

b) The numbers in order are: 2, 5, 6, 6, 6, 7, 7, 9, 9. The middle value is the 5th value, so the median is **6**.

c) The numbers in order are: 8, 8, 12, 13, 16, 17, 17, 18. The middle values are the 4th and 5th values, so the median is halfway between 13 and 16: (13 + 16) ÷ 2 = **14.5**.
You might find it easier to find the position of the median using the formula (n + 1) ÷ 2, where n is the number of values.

Using the same method for Q2-3:

2 a) 3.8 **b) 16** **c) 3**

3 81 seconds

4 The known data values in order are 14.3, 15.8, 16.5, 16.9, 18.9. There are six values in total, so 16.7 (the median) must be between the third and fourth values. So the missing value must be greater than 16.5, i.e. 16.5 is the third value. 16.7 is halfway between 16.5 and 16.9, so the missing value must be at least **16.9**.

Page 438 Exercise 3

1 a) Total = 8 + 5 + 3 + 8 + 4 = 28
Mean = 28 ÷ 5 = **5.6**

b) Total = 6 + 9 + 2 + 7 + 7 + 6 + 5 + 9 + 6 = 57
Mean = 57 ÷ 9 = 6.333...
= **6.33** (2 d.p.)

c) Total = 16 + 18 + 12 + 13 + 13 + 8 + 8 + 17 = 105
Mean = 105 ÷ 8 = **13.125**

Using the same method for Q2-4:

2 a) 3.68 **b) 18.075** **c) 3.125**

3 60.222... = **60.2 marks** (1 d.p.)

4 83 seconds

5 a) Put the data in order: 1, 2, 2, 2, 3, 3, 5, 8
Total = 1 + 2 + 2 + 2 + 3 + 3 + 5 + 8 = 26
Mean = 26 ÷ 8 = **3.25**
The middle values are the 4th and 5th values, so the **median** is halfway between 2 and 3: (2 + 3) ÷ 2 = **2.5**
2 appears more than any other number so the **mode** = **2**

b) Put the data in order: 1, 2, 3, 3, 3, 3, 4, 5
Total = 1 + 2 + 3 + 3 + 3 + 3 + 4 + 5 = 24
Mean = 24 ÷ 8 = **3**
The middle values are the 4th and 5th values, so the **median** is halfway between 3 and 3, so **3**.
3 appears more than any other number so the **mode** = **3**

6 Including the missing value there are 6 values, so the total of the values
= the mean × number of values = 7 × 6
= 42. To find the missing value, subtract the known values from the total:
42 – (6 + 5 + 8 + 8 + 5) = 42 – 32 = **10**

7 Including the missing value there are 6 values, so the total of the values
= the mean × number of values = 16.3 × 6
= 97.8. To find the missing value, subtract the known values from the total:
97.8 – (16.6 + 16.9 +15.8 + 14.3 + 18.9)
= 97.8 – 82.5 = **15.3**

Page 439 Exercise 4

1 a) Highest value = 8, lowest value = 3, so the range = 8 – 3 = **5**

b) Highest value = 9, lowest value = 2, so the range = 9 – 2 = **7**

c) Highest value = 17, lowest value = 8, so the range = 17 – 8 = **9**

Using the same method for Q2:

2 a) 4.1 **b) 6.19** **c) 1**

3 22 – (–2) = 22 + 2 = **24 °C**

4 £30 – (–£40) = £30 + £40 = **£70**

5 The range is 6, so the two possible values are the highest known number minus 6, or the lowest known number plus 6.
Missing number = 8 – 6 = **2**, or 5 + 6 = **11**

6 a) Highest value = 17, lowest value = 3, so the range = 17 – 3 = **14 skips**

b) E.g. Most of the data is much closer together than the range suggests, so the range is not a good measure of spread. The range is affected by the data value 17, which is an outlier.

Page 441 Exercise 5

1 a) The frequency is highest for 1 pet, so mode = **1 pet.**

b) The total frequency is 5 + 10 + 5 + 5 + 2 = 27, so the median position is (27 + 1) ÷ 2 = 14. The 14th value is 1, so the median = **1 pet.**

c) Find the frequency for each group:
(i) 5 **(ii) 10** **(iii) 5**
(iv) 5 **(v) 2**

d) The total number of pets
= (0 × 5) + (1 × 10) + (2 × 5) + (3 × 5) + (4 × 2)
= 0 + 10 + 10 + 15 + 8 = **43**

e) The total number of students
= 5 + 10 + 5 + 5 + 2 = **27**

f) Mean = 43 ÷ 27 = 1.592...
= **1.6 pets** (1 d.p.)

2 a) The frequency is highest for 4 people, so mode = **4 people.**

b) There are 30 data values, so the position of the median is (30 + 1) ÷ 2 = 15.5.
The median is halfway between the 15th value = 2 and 16th value = 2, so median = **2 people.**

c) Total number of people
= (1 × 7) + (2 × 9) + (3 × 1) + (4 × 10) + (5 × 3) = 83
Mean = 83 ÷ 30 = 2.766...
= **2.8 people** (1 d.p.)

d) Smallest value = 1, largest value = 5, so the range is 5 – 1 = **4.**

3 a) Total frequency = 4 + 9 + 2 + 5 + 4 + 6 = 30
There are 30 data values, so the median position is (30 + 1) ÷ 2 = 15.5. The median is halfway between the 15th value = 18 and 16th value = 19,
so median = (18 + 19) ÷ 2 = **18.5 °C.**

b) Total of temperatures
= (16 × 4) + (17 × 9) + (18 × 2) + (19 × 5) + (20 × 4) + (21 × 6)
= 64 + 153 + 36 + 95 + 80 + 126
= 554
Mean = 554 ÷ 30 = 18.466...
= **18.5 °C** (1 d.p.)

c) E.g. The student's garden has experienced some fairly typical June temperatures for the UK.

Page 443 Exercise 6

1 a) The group with the highest frequency is 16-20 so the modal group is **16-20.**

b) The total frequency = 4 + 5 + 7 + 9 = 25, so the position of the median is (25 + 1) ÷ 2 = 13. The 13th value is in the 11-15 group so the group containing the median = **11-15.**

c)

Marks scored	1-5	6-10	11-15	16-20
Frequency	4	5	7	9
Midpoint	$\frac{1+5}{2}$ = 3	$\frac{6+10}{2}$ = 8	$\frac{11+15}{2}$ = 13	$\frac{16+20}{2}$ = 18
Freq. × Midpoint	4 × 3 = 12	5 × 8 = 40	7 × 13 = 91	9 × 18 = 162

Total frequency = 4 + 5 + 7 + 9 = 25
Total no. of marks = 12 + 40 + 91 + 162 = 305
Mean = 305 ÷ 25 = **12.2**

d) Lower bound of smallest group = 1
Upper bound of largest group = 20
Range = 20 – 1 = **19**

2 a)

Weight (w)	Freq.	Midpoint	Freq. × Midpoint
$0 \le w < 20$	1	(0 + 20) ÷ 2 = 10	1 × 10 = 10
$20 \le w < 40$	6	(20 + 40) ÷ 2 = 30	6 × 30 = 180
$40 \le w < 60$	9	(40 + 60) ÷ 2 = 50	9 × 50 = 450
$60 \le w < 80$	24	(60 + 80) ÷ 2 = 70	24 × 70 = 1680

Total frequency = 1 + 6 + 9 + 24 = 40
Total weight = 10 + 180 + 450 + 1680
= 2320 grams
Mean = 2320 ÷ 40 = **58 grams**

b) Lower bound of smallest group = 0
Upper bound of largest group = 80
Range = 80 – 0 = **80 grams**

c) E.g. You don't know where the data values lie within the groups. The one tangerine in the $0 \le w < 20$ g group could weigh 19 g, in which case the actual range would be no greater than 61 g.

3 a) The group 11-15 has the highest frequency, so the modal group is **11-15**.

b) There are 3 + 8 + 11 + 4 = 26 data values, so the position of the median is (26 + 1) ÷ 2 = 13.5. The median is halfway between the 13th and 14th values. Both values are in the group 11-15, so the median is in **11-15**.

c)

Time (hours)	Freq.	Midpoint	Freq. × Midpoint
0-5	3	(0 + 5) ÷ 2 = 2.5	3 × 2.5 = 7.5
6-10	8	(6 + 10) ÷ 2 = 8	8 × 8 = 64
11-15	11	(11 + 15) ÷ 2 = 13	11 × 13 = 143
16-20	4	(16 + 20) ÷ 2 = 18	4 × 18 = 72

Total frequency = 3 + 8 + 11 + 4 = 26
Total time = 7.5 + 64 + 143 + 72
= 286.5 hours
Mean = 286.5 ÷ 26 = **11.0 hours** (1 d.p.)

4 a) The group $1.60 \le h < 1.70$ has the highest frequency, so the modal group is $\mathbf{1.60 \le h < 1.70}$.

b) There are 200 data values, so the position of the median is (200 + 1) ÷ 2 = 100.5. The median is halfway between the 100th and 101st values. Both values are in the group $1.60 \le h < 1.70$, so the median is in $\mathbf{1.60 \le h < 1.70}$.

c)

Height (h) in m	Freq.	Midpoint	Freq. × Midpoint
$1.50 \le h < 1.60$	27	(1.5 + 1.6) ÷ 2 = 1.55	27 × 1.55 = 41.85
$1.60 \le h < 1.70$	92	(1.6 + 1.7) ÷ 2 = 1.65	92 × 1.65 = 151.8
$1.70 \le h < 1.80$	63	(1.7 + 1.8) ÷ 2 = 1.75	63 × 1.75 = 110.25
$1.80 \le h < 1.90$	18	(1.8 + 1.9) ÷ 2 = 1.85	18 × 1.85 = 33.3

Total frequency = 27 + 92 + 63 + 18
= 200
Total height = 41.85 + 151.8
+ 110.25 + 33.3 = 337.2 m
Mean = 337.2 ÷ 200 = **1.69 m** (3 s.f.)

d) Lower bound of smallest group = 1.50 m
Upper bound of largest group = 1.90 m
Range = 1.90 – 1.50 = **0.4 m**

26.3 Two-Way Tables

Page 445 Exercise 1

1 a)

	Walk	Bus	Car	Total
Boys	9	5	3	9 + 5 + 3 = **17**
Girls	5	8	6	5 + 8 + 6 = **19**
Total	9 + 5 = **14**	5 + 8 = **13**	3 + 6 = **9**	17 + 19 = **36**

b)

	Walk	Bus	Car	Total
Boys	21 – 11 = **10**	27 – 15 = **12**	8	60 – 30 = **30**
Girls	11	30 – 11 – 4 = **15**	4	30
Total	21	60 – 21 – 12 = **27**	8 + 4 = **12**	60

It's okay if you've used different calculations to work out the correct missing values.

2 a) Adding the entries for each column and row gives:

	Germany	France	Spain	Total
Male	16	7	12	**35**
Female	18	4	16	**38**
Total	**34**	**11**	**28**	**73**

b) The entry in the female row and France column is **4**.

c) The entry in the male row and Germany column is **16**.

d) The total of the Spain column is **28**.

e) The total of the female row is **38**.

f) The total number of students (in the bottom right cell) is **73**.

3 a)

	Choc.	Crisps	Jellies	Total
Male	3	12 – 7 = **5**	12 – 2 = **10**	3 + 5 + 10 = **18**
Female	6 – 3 = **3**	7	2	30 – 18 = **12**
Total	6	12	30 – 6 – 12 = **12**	30

b) The total of the crisps column is **12.**

c) The entry in the female row and jelly column is **2**.

d) Number of males who prefer chocolate = 3
Total number of males = 18
Percentage = (3 ÷ 18) × 100 = 16.666...
= **16.7%** (1 d.p.)

4 a) Using the same method for completing the table as in Q1-3:

	Red	Black	Blue	White	Total
Cars	8	7	4	**3**	22
Vans	**2**	2	1	10	**15**
Motorbikes	2	1	**1**	2	**6**
Total	12	**10**	6	**15**	**43**

b) The entry in the motorbikes row and blue column is **1**.

c) The total of the vans row is **15**.

d) (i) Total number of cars = 22
Total number of vehicles = 43
(22 ÷ 43) × 100 = 51.162...
= **51.2%** (3 s.f.)

(ii) Total number of vans = 15
Total number of vehicles = 43
(15 ÷ 43) × 100 = 34.883...
= **34.9%** (3 s.f.)

(iii) Total number of red vehicles = 12
Total number of vehicles = 43
(12 ÷ 43) × 100 = 27.906...
= **27.9%** (3 s.f.)

26.4 Bar Charts and Pictograms

Page 446 Exercise 1

1

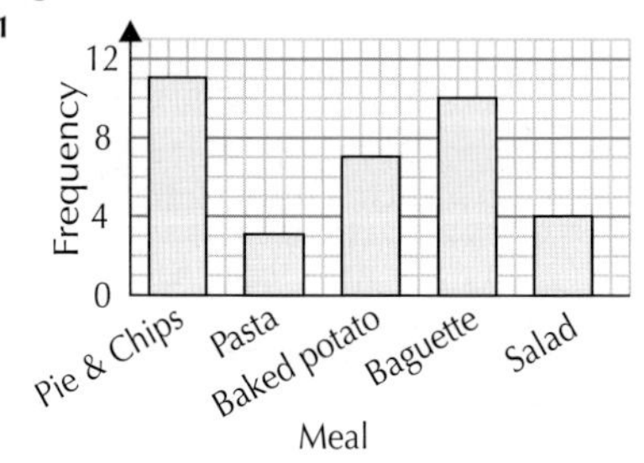

Remember to label your axes and to leave gaps between the bars.

2

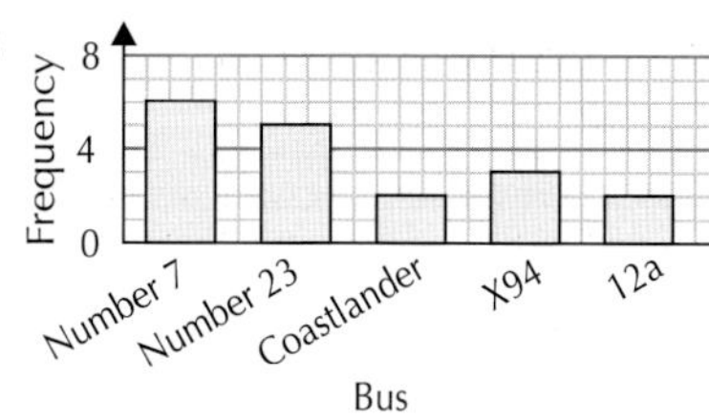

3

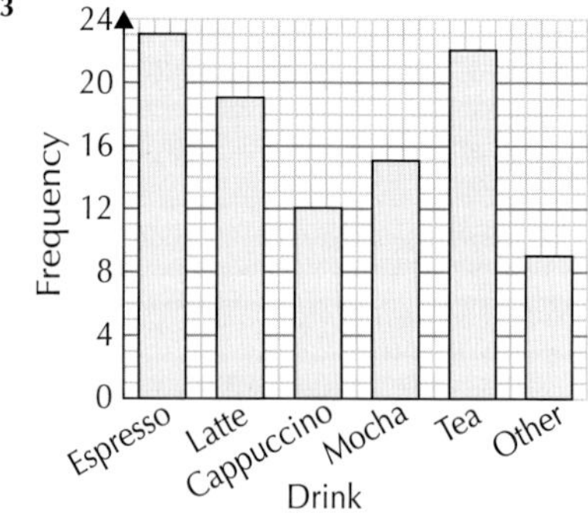

Page 448 Exercise 2

1 a)

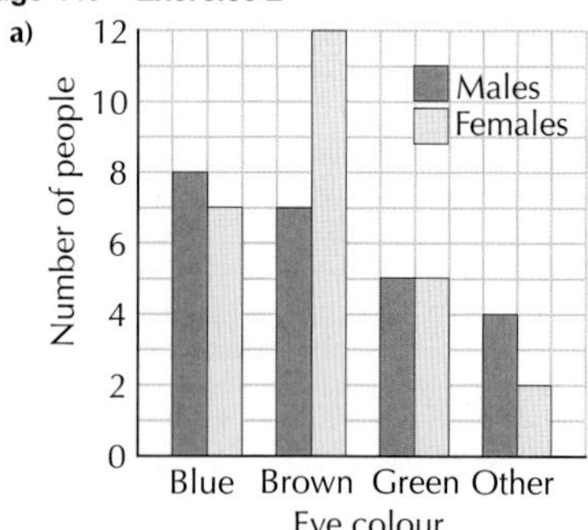

b)

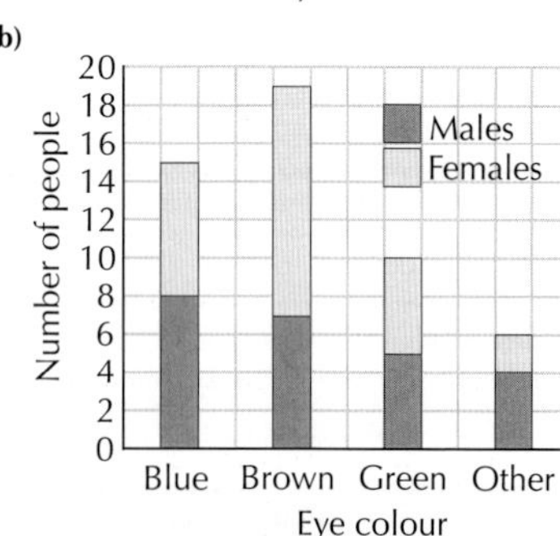

c) The **dual bar chart** is the best for comparing male and female eye colours — it is easy to see the difference in the heights of the pair of bars for each eye colour.

d) The most common eye colour is **brown.**

e) The **composite bar chart** is easier to use to find the modal eye colour, as you can just look for the tallest bar.

2 a) The height of the composite bar for the 26-35 age group is **12**.
  b) 12 + 12 + 9 + 6 = **39**
  c) The mode is the most common, so look for the tallest bar for women: **16-25 yrs**.
  d) 8 men aged 26-35 use the gym.
  4 women aged 26-35 use the gym.
  So 8 – 4 = **4** more men aged 26-35 use the gym than women aged 26-35.
  e) 16-25: Difference = 6 – 6 = 0
  26-35: Difference = 4 (from part d) above)
  36-45: Difference = 7 – 2 = 5
  46-55: Difference = 5 – 1 = 4
  So the age group with the greatest difference is **36-45 yrs**.

Page 449 Exercise 3

1

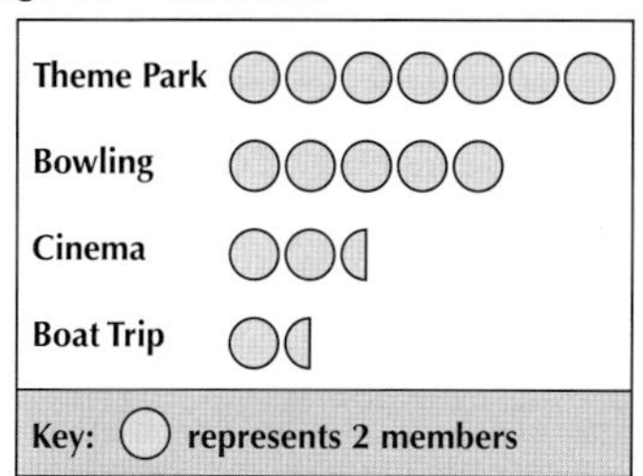

Use half a symbol to represent 1 member.

2 a) (i) In the Tuesday row there are 2 complete symbols, so there were 20 × 2 = **40** packets of sweets sold.
  (ii) In the Wednesday row there are one and a half symbols, so there were 20 × 1.5 = **30** packets of sweets sold.
  b)

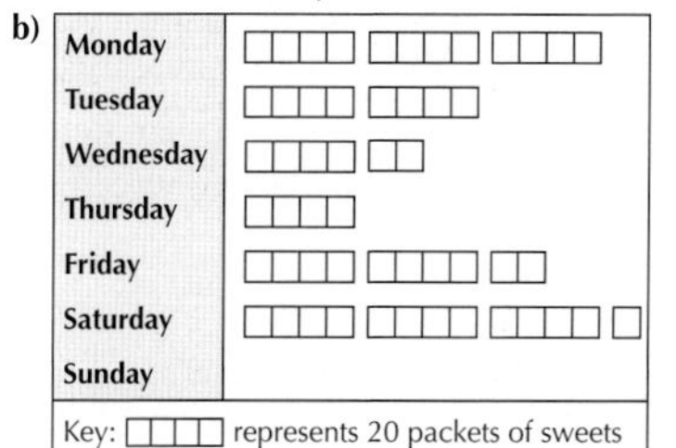

3 a) In the number 4 row there are 2 and a half symbols, so there were 4 × 2.5 = **10** letters delivered.
  b) **Number 1** has the fewest symbols in its row.
  c) In the whole pictogram there are 8 whole symbols, 3 half symbols and one quarter symbol, so total letters
  $= (8 \times 4) + (3 \times \frac{4}{2}) + (1 \times \frac{4}{4}) = 32 + 6 + 1$
  $= \mathbf{39}$

26.5 Stem and Leaf Diagrams

Page 451 Exercise 1

1

Stem	Leaves
4	1 8
5	1 4 9
6	5 5 9
7	4
8	0 6 9

Key: 4 | 1 means 41

Don't forget to order the leaves.

2 a)

Stem	Leaves
3	1 4
4	0 4 4 9
5	1 3 4 7 7 9
6	0 1
7	1 7

Key: 3 | 1 means 3.1

  b)

Stem	Leaves
20	3 5
30	1 4
40	2 2 3 4 9 9
50	0 1 3
60	1 6 8

Key: 20 | 1 means 201

3

Stem	Leaves
0	0 0 0 1 3 6
1	1 3 6
2	0 5 7
3	1 6 8
4	1

Key: 0 | 1 means 0.1 cm

4 E.g.

Set 2		Set 1
	0	1 8
9 8 5 3 3	1	2 8
7 5 3 2 2	2	4 8 9
2	3	2 3 7 8

Key: 1 | 2 for Set 1 means 12
3 | 1 for Set 2 means 13

You might have put Set 1 on the left and Set 2 on the right.

Page 452 Exercise 2

1 a) Mode = most common value = **32**
  b) There are 13 values so the median is the 7th value. Median = **20**
  Remember, the median position for n values is (n + 1) ÷ 2.
  c) Range = 32 – 5 = **27**

2 a)

Stem	Leaves
10	2 6
11	4 7
12	4 8 9
13	1 3 6 9 9 9
14	2
15	4
16	
17	3

  b) **Mode** = most common value
  = **13.9 seconds**
  There are 16 values so the median lies halfway between the 8th value = 13.1 and the 9th value = 13.3.
  Median = (13.1 + 13.3) ÷ 2
  = **13.2 seconds**.
  Range = 17.3 – 10.2 = **7.1 seconds**.
  c) **7** contestants finished in under 13 seconds.

3 a) There are 15 data values, so the median is the 8th value.
  Median for 'at rest' = **72 bpm**
  Median for 'after exercise' = **77 bpm**
  b) The higher median for the 'after exercise' data suggests that, on average, **people's heart rate was faster after they'd exercised.**

26.6 Pie Charts

Page 454 Exercise 1

1 a) 25 + 17 + 8 + 10 = **60**
  b) 360° ÷ 60 = **6°**
  c) **Black** = 25 × 6° = **150°**,
  Silver = 17 × 6° = **102°**,
  Red = 8 × 6° = **48°**,
  Other = 10 × 6° = **60°**
  d) Use the angles from part c) to draw and label the pie chart:

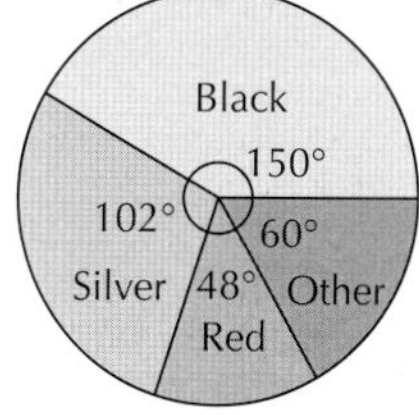

2 a) 13 + 9 + 8 + 6 = **36**
  b) Degrees for 1 friend = 360° ÷ 36 = 10°, so:
  Carlisle = 13 × 10° = **130°**,
  Kendal = 9 × 10° = **90°**,
  Millom = 8 × 10 = **80°**,
  Bristol = 6 × 10° = **60°**
  c) Use the angles from part b) to draw and label the pie chart:

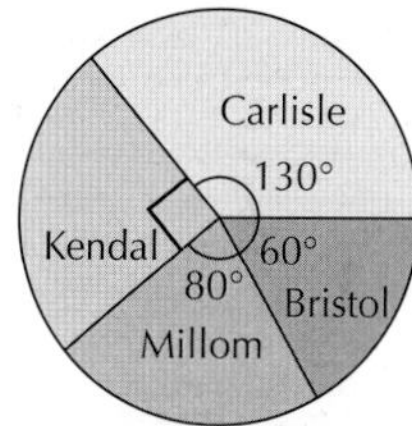

3 Total frequency = 33 + 52 + 21 + 14 = 120
Angle for one person = 360° ÷ 120 = 3°
Squash = 33 × 3° = 99°
Gym = 52 × 3° = 156°
Swimming = 21 × 3° = 63°
Table Tennis = 14 × 3° = 42°

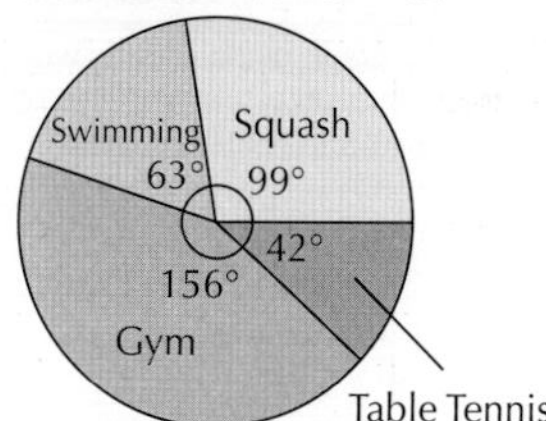

Page 455 Exercise 2

1 By comparing the proportions in the pie charts with the proportions of the frequency in the tables: **Set 1 = *P*** and **Set 2 = *Q***

2 a) The sector with the largest angle is **pepperoni**.

b) The angle for cheese and tomato is a right angle so is 90°. $\frac{90°}{360°} = \mathbf{\frac{1}{4}}$

c) 102° represents 17 pupils:
Degrees for one pupil = 102° ÷ 17 = 6°
Total pupils = 360° ÷ 6° = **60 pupils**

d) Fraction of pupils who like spicy chicken $= \frac{36°}{360°} = \frac{1}{10}$, then $60 \times \frac{1}{10}$ = **6 pupils**.

3 a) **No** — The **angle** for English for Brooke is 144° which is **larger** than Tom's which is 126°.

b) **No** — The pie charts **do not show times**, just the **proportion** of homework tasks set for each subject.

26.7 Time Series

Page 457 Exercise 1

1 a)

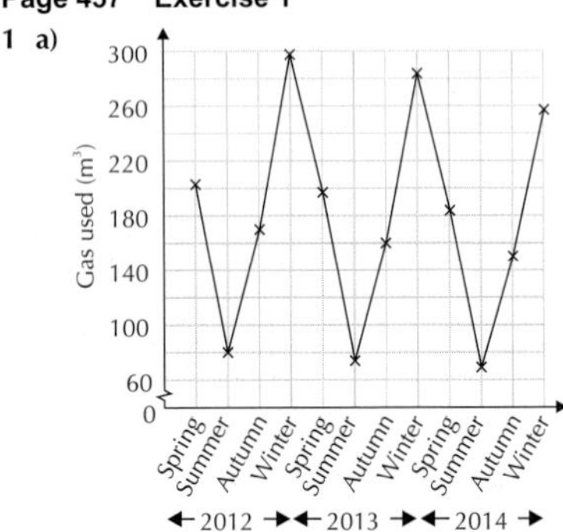

b) E.g. The amount of gas they use rises through autumn and winter. It then decreases in spring and drops further in summer, before rising again in autumn.

c) E.g. Overall there is a slight downward trend in the amount of gas they use.

2

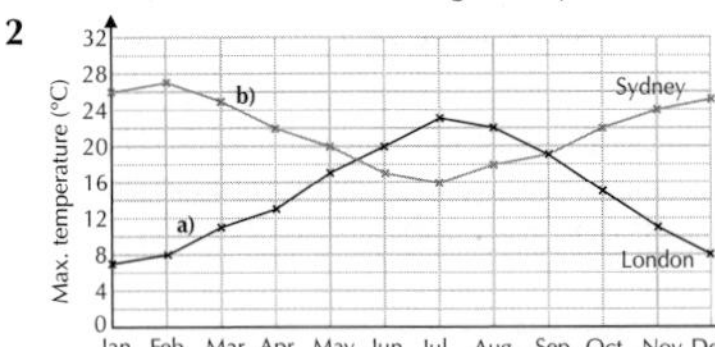

c) E.g. The London graph peaks in July, when the Sydney graph is at its lowest. The Sydney graph peaks in February, when the London graph is very low. Warmer temperatures in one city correspond to lower temperatures in the other city.

3 a) E.g. The number of sunglasses sold increases from spring to summer, then falls in autumn and again in winter, before rising again the next spring.

b) E.g. There is an overall upward trend in the number of sunglasses sold.

c) E.g. The scale on the vertical axis is inconsistent. At the lower end of the axis, the numbers on the scale increase in increments of 20 and each grid square represents 10 pairs of sunglasses. But after 100 it increases in increments of 40 and each square represents 20 pairs of sunglasses. This makes it hard to interpret the graph.

26.8 Scatter Graphs

Page 458 Exercise 1

1 Carefully plot the data points — the first point is (28, 30), the second is (25, 22), etc.

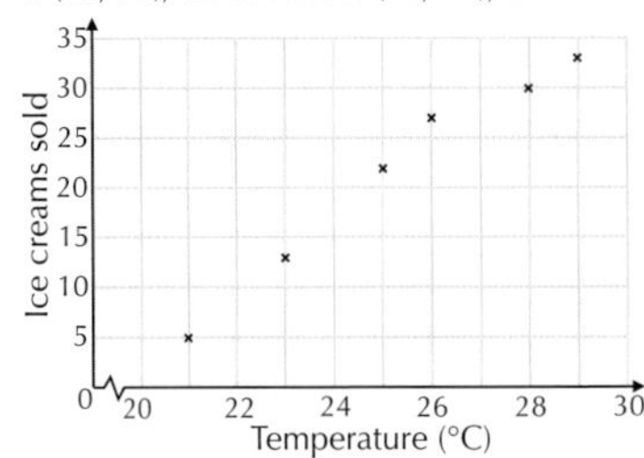

You can use the 'zig zag' on the 'Temperature' axis to miss out the numbers between 0 and 20.

2 The number of baby teeth will depend on age, so plot the number of baby teeth on the vertical axis. Then plot the data points: (5, 20), (6, 17), etc.

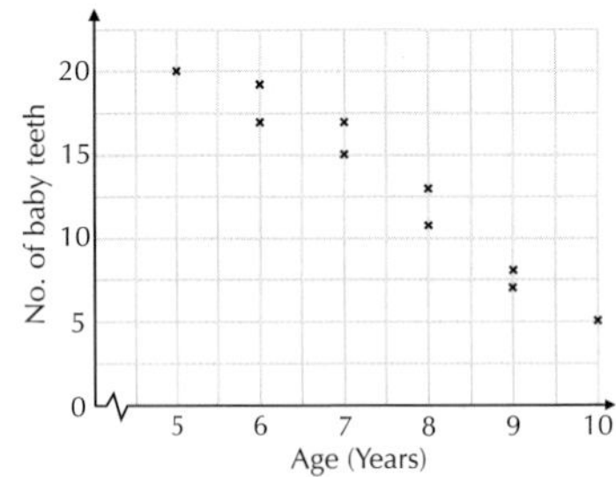

Page 460 Exercise 2

1 a) **Weak negative correlation** — the points form a downward slope but do not lie close to a straight line.

b) **No correlation** — the points don't seem to form a line in any direction.

c) **Strong positive correlation** — the points form an upward slope fairly close to a straight line.

2 a) **Positive correlation** — as it gets warmer, people will probably be more likely to buy ice cream.

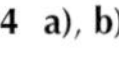

b) **Negative correlation** — as it gets warmer, people will probably be less likely to buy hot chocolate.

c) **No correlation** — there probably isn't any connection between how hot it is and how much bread people buy.

d) **Positive correlation** — as a child grows, he or she gets taller.

e) **Positive correlation** — most people will probably drive more slowly in an area with a low speed limit.

3 There is **moderate positive correlation** between the wind speed and boat speed OR **the boat speed increased as the wind speed increased**.

Page 462 Exercise 3

1 a) **Yes**, the points will lie close to a straight line.

b) **No**, the points are randomly scattered.

c) **Yes**, most of the points will lie close to a straight line. There are 3 outliers which don't match the general pattern and so can be ignored.

2 a) The points form a downward slope fairly close to a straight line so there is **strong negative correlation** OR **the more time spent watching TV, the less time was spent on homework.**

b) Find 5.5 hours on the 'Time spent watching TV' axis. Draw a vertical line up to the line of best fit and then read off the value on the 'Time spent on homework' axis, which is **1 hour**.

c) Find 3.5 hours on the 'Time spent on homework' axis and draw a horizontal line across to the line of best fit. Then read off the value on the 'Time spent watching TV' axis, which is **1.5 hours**.

3 a) The points form an upward slope fairly close to a straight line so there is **strong positive correlation** OR **the wider the trunk the taller the tree.**

b) Width = **40 cm**, height = **23 m**

c) Draw a line from 13 m on the vertical axis to the line of best fit and read off the value on the horizontal axis, which is **65 cm** (allow 64-66 cm).

d) 13 m lies within the data range for the height of the tree, which means the prediction is from interpolation, so it should be **reliable**.

4 a), b)

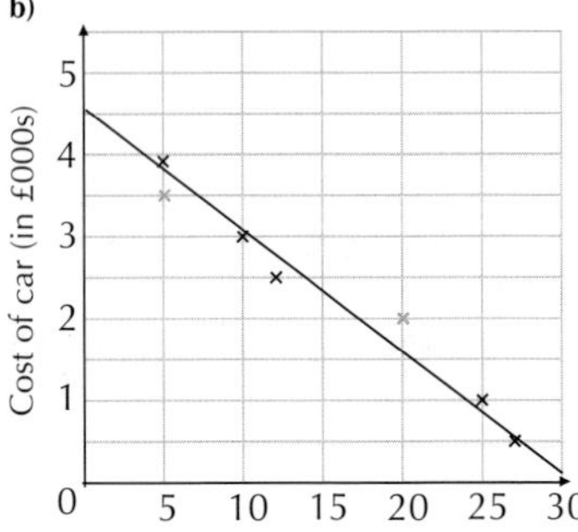

c) E.g. 50 000 miles lies outside the range of the data so the data would need to be extrapolated and her estimate would be **unreliable**. If the line of best fit was continued to 50 000 miles, you would get a negative cost.

Page 463 Review Exercise

1 a) Test 1: Total frequency
= 19 + 14 + 8 + 17 + 17 + 20 + 6 + 13
= 114

Mean = 114 ÷ 8 = **14.25**

Test 2: Total frequency
= 7 + 14 + 16 + 7 + 10 + 8 + 10 + 12
= 84

Mean = 84 ÷ 8 = **10.5**

b) Test 1: Range = 20 – 6 = **14**
Test 2: Range = 16 – 7 = **9**

c) E.g. The mean score was higher in Test 1, so the score achieved was generally higher in that test. The range of scores was lower in Test 2, so there was less variation in the scores in Test 2.

2 Total weight of original 5 apples
= 57 + 60 + 69 + 72 + 75 = 333 g
Total weight of remaining three = 62 × 3
= 186 g
Weight of two apples eaten = 333 – 186
= 147 g, so the apples eaten must be the ones which weigh **72 g** and **75 g**.

3 a) Total frequency = 1 + 3 + 4 + 5 + 3 + 2
= 18
Median will be the (18 + 1) ÷ 2
= 9.5th value, so the median lies halfway between the 9th value = 3 and 10th value = 3. So the median is **3 goals**.

b) Total goals = (0 × 1) + (1 × 3) + (2 × 4)
+ (3 × 5) + (4 × 3) + (5 × 2) = 48
Mean = 48 ÷ 18 = 2.66... = **2.7 goals** (1 d.p.)

c) Mode = most common value = **3 goals**

d) The values of all three averages were lower in the previous year, so **more goals were scored on average than in the previous year**.

4 a)

Height in metres, h	Tally	Frequency
$1.5 < h \le 1.6$	||	**2**
$1.6 < h \le 1.7$	~~||||~~ ||||	**9**
$1.7 < h \le 1.8$	~~||||~~ ||	**7**
$1.8 < h \le 1.9$	||	**2**

b) Modal group has the highest frequency so is $\mathbf{1.6 < h \le 1.7}$.

c) Total frequency is 20, so the position of the median is (20 + 1) ÷ 2 = 10.5, so the median lies between the 10th and 11th values. Both are in the $1.6 < h \le 1.7$ group, so median group = $\mathbf{1.6 < h \le 1.7}$.

d) Total frequency = 20

Height in metres, h	Tally	Freq.	Freq. × Midpoint
$1.5 < h \le 1.6$	||	2	2 × 1.55 = 3.1
$1.6 < h \le 1.7$	~~||||~~ ||||	9	9 × 1.65 = 14.85
$1.7 < h \le 1.8$	~~||||~~ ||	7	7 × 1.75 = 12.25
$1.8 < h \le 1.9$	||	2	2 × 1.85 = 3.7

Estimate of total height
= 3.1 + 14.85 + 12.25 + 3.7 = 33.9
Mean = 33.9 ÷ 20 = **1.695 m**

e) Range = upper bound of largest group
– lower bound of smallest group
= 1.9 – 1.5 = **0.4 m**

5 a) There are 40 values so the median position is (40 + 1) ÷ 2 = 20.5.
The median lies between the 20th and 21st values. Both values are in the 2 washing machines group so the median = **2 washing machines**.

b) Mode = most common value
= **2 washing machines**

c) Total machines sold
= (0 × 3) + (1 × 5) + (2 × 14) + (3 × 11)
+ (4 × 6) + (5 × 1) = 95
Mean = 95 ÷ 40 = **2.375 washing machines**

d) Range = highest value – lowest value
= 5 – 0 = **5**

6 a) Total frequency of girls:
8 + 6 + 5 + 2 + 3 + 6 = **30**

b) 9 boys chose chocolate and 6 girls chose chocolate, so 9 – 6 = **3** more boys than girls chose chocolate.

c) The highest bar for girls is vanilla, so **vanilla** is the modal flavour for girls.

d) E.g. 360° ÷ 30 girls = **12° per girl**
Alternatively, you could have used any of the categories. E.g., using vanilla: 96° ÷ 8 = 12°.

e) Total frequency of boys:
4 + 9 + 1 + 3 + 3 = 20
360° ÷ 20 = 18° per boy
Vanilla: 4 × 18° = 72°
Chocolate: 9 × 18° = 162°
Strawberry: 0 × 18° = 0°
Mint: 1 × 18° = 18°
Rocky road: 3 × 18 = 54°
Other = 3 × 18° = 54°

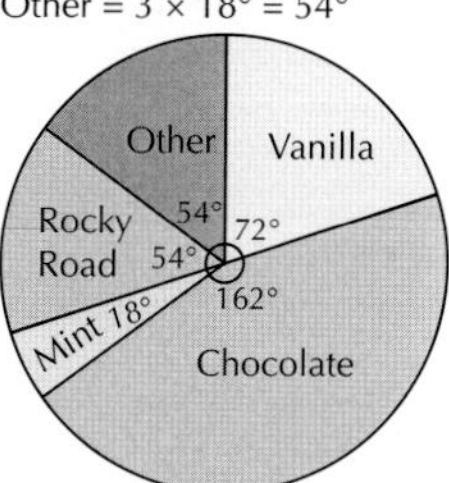

f) There are **fewer boys than girls** — so even though the number who chose rocky road is the same, the proportion of boys is larger, so the sector on the pie chart is larger.

7 a) E.g.

10 am		3 pm
	1	5 8
9 7	2	2 3 4 7
5	3	1 2 5
8	4	
9 8 4 1 1	5	
5 0	6	

Key: 7 | 2 for 10 am means 27
1 | 5 for 3 pm means 15

b) There are 11 people queuing at 10 am so the median is in the (11 + 1) ÷ 2 = 6th position. That person has an age of **51**.
There are 9 people queueing at 3 pm so the median is in the (9 + 1) ÷ 2 = 5th position. That person has an age of **24**.
So the median is **much lower for people queuing at 3 pm**.

8 a), b) The number of drinks sold is dependent on the temperature, so the number of drinks sold should go on the vertical axis.

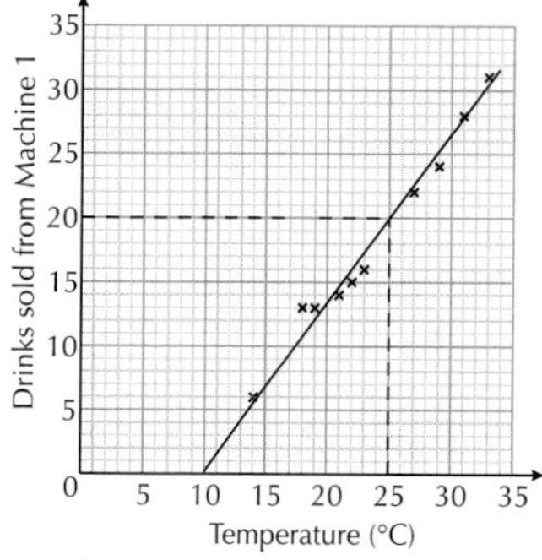

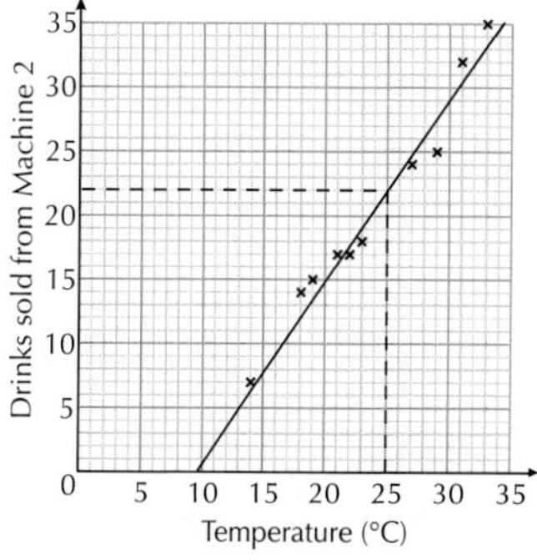

c) Draw a line from 25°C to the line of best fit on both graphs (see graphs above) and read off the number of drinks sold. The predicted number of drinks sold from Machine 1 is **20**. The predicted number of drinks sold from Machine 2 is **22**.
Your readings might be slightly different, depending on how you've drawn your line of best fit. We'll allow answers within 21 - 23 drinks.

d) 3 °C is well below the temperature range for this data — you'd need to **extrapolate** to find your answer, which is **unreliable**. In this case, it would give you a negative number of drinks sold which is impossible.

e) **No** — just because the two things are correlated does not mean that one thing causes the other. They both could be influenced by a third variable.

Page 465 Exam-Style Questions

1 The middle number must be 50 for A, but 50 could also be the highest number if there are 3 marks of 50. Similarly for group B, the lowest mark could be 48 if there are three marks of 48. So the lowest mark in group A could be 50 – 3 = 47 *[1 mark]* and the lowest mark in group B could be 48 *[1 mark]*, so the student who scored the lowest mark could be in group A.
You'd also pick up the marks if you wrote out a list of data values that work — e.g. A: 47, 48, 50, 50, 50 and B: 48, 48, 48, 50, 51.

2 a) There are 7 values so the median is the 4th value. The values in order are:
5, 6, 22, 28, 29, 31, 34, so the median is **28 eggs**. *[1 mark]*

b) E.g. There are two extreme values (5 and 6), which distort the value of the mean OR the data is not evenly spread out so the mean will not be a good measure of the centre of the data *[1 mark]*.

3 a) The group with the highest frequency is $120 \leq t < 160$, so the modal class is $\mathbf{120 \leq t < 160}$. *[1 mark]*

b) Use the midpoints of the groups to estimate the mean:

Time (t minutes)	Freq.	Midpoint	Freq. × Midpoint
$0 \leq t < 40$	3	$(0 + 40) \div 2 = 20$	$3 \times 20 = 60$
$40 \leq t < 80$	4	$(40 + 80) \div 2 = 60$	$4 \times 60 = 240$
$80 \leq t < 120$	7	$(80 + 120) \div 2 = 100$	$7 \times 100 = 700$
$120 \leq t < 160$	15	$(120 + 160) \div 2 = 140$	$15 \times 140 = 2100$
$160 \leq t < 200$	11	$(160 + 200) \div 2 = 180$	$11 \times 180 = 1980$

Total Frequency = 3 + 4 + 7 + 15 + 11 = 40
Total Time = 60 + 240 + 700 + 2100 + 1980 = 5080 *[1 mark]*
Mean = 5080 ÷ 40 *[1 mark]*
= **127 minutes** *[1 mark]*

c) E.g. The method assumes that all the values in a group are equal to the midpoint of the group (or are evenly spread across the group) OR you do not know the exact times/original values since the data is grouped *[1 mark]*.

4 14 books is shown by 3.5 shapes, so one shape represents 14 ÷ 3.5 = 4 books and $\frac{1}{4}$ of a shape represents 1 book.
7 books = 4 books + 3 books, so that's 1 full shape and $\frac{3}{4}$ of a shape.

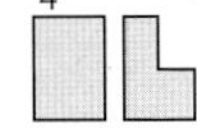

[2 marks available — 1 mark for finding that one shape represents 4 books, 1 mark for a correct diagram]

5 a) Silver requires a sector with angle = 360° ÷ 3 = 120°.
The remaining 360° – 120° = 240° needs to be split in the ratio 5 : 1. 6 parts = 240°, so 1 part = 240° ÷ 6 = 40°.
Bronze needs an angle of 5 × 40° = 200° and gold needs an angle of 40°.

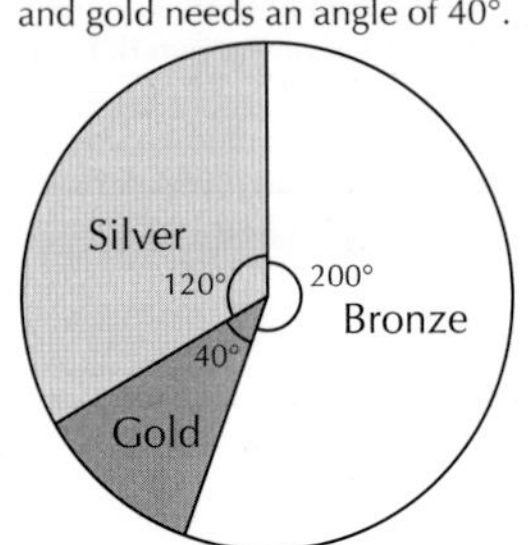

[3 marks for a fully correct and labelled pie chart, otherwise 2 marks for all three angles calculated correctly, or one mark for finding the angle for silver]

b) Silver = 120° so 120° represents 18 students.
1° represents 18 ÷ 120 = 0.15 students *[1 mark]*, so Bronze awards were received by 200 × 0.15 = **30 students** *[1 mark]*.

6 a) The price of gold per gram showed an **upward trend** — there was a general **increase over time**.
[1 mark for the correct observation]

b) The highest price per gram was £29.80 in November. 12 kg = 12 × 1000 = 12 000 g. So Midas could have sold his gold bar for 29.8 × 12 000 = **£357 600**
[2 marks available — 1 mark for finding the highest price per gram, 1 mark for the correct answer]

7 a) The marks show a **strong positive correlation** with the number of revision classes. *[1 mark for the correct observation]*

b) No — to predict what a student would get if they didn't attend any revision classes requires extrapolation and this is unreliable.
[1 mark for a correct explanation of why Duane is incorrect]

Section 27 — Probability

27.1 Probability — The Basics

Page 468 Exercise 1

1 a) There are 2 possible outcomes that are equally likely — heads or tails.
So tossing a coin and getting tails is **evens**.

b) No person can grow to 10 metres tall, so it's **impossible**.

c) Half of the numbers on a dice are even, so it's **evens**.

d) All numbers on a normal dice are 1 or more, so it's **certain**.

e) Half of the cards in a pack of 52 are red, so it's **evens**.

f) There are 4 possible outcomes — 1, 2, 3 and 4.
1 out of the 4 outcomes is 2, so it's **unlikely**.

2

f) d) b) c) e) a)
Impossible Unlikely Evens Likely Certain

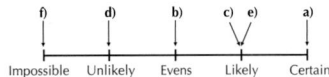

a) All the cards are less than 9, so this is **certain**.

b) Half of the numbers are odd, so this is **evens**.

c) All but two of the cards are greater than 2, so this is **likely**.

d) All but two of the cards are not greater than or equal to 7, so this is **unlikely**.

e) All but two of the cards are 6 or less, so this is **likely**.

f) None of the cards are zero, so this is **impossible**.

3 a) There's one P and two A's, so **A** is twice as likely to be selected as P.

b) There's one E and three L's, so **L** is three times as likely to be selected as E.

c) Count the number of times the letter appears. The more times a letter appears, the more likely it is to be chosen, so it will correspond to a higher-numbered arrow (as the arrows show an increase in likelihood as the numbers increase).
P: **1**   A: **2**   R: **1**   L: **3**   E: **1**
All of the probabilities are less likely than 'evens' — there are 8 letters in total and the maximum times one letter appears is 3 (for an even chance, there'd have to be 4 out of the 8 cards the same).

Page 469 Exercise 2

1 a) $0.5 = \frac{1}{2}$ so the correct probability is **D**.

b) $25\% = \frac{1}{4}$ so the correct probability is **C**.

c) $\frac{1}{6}$ is less than $\frac{1}{4}$ so the correct probability is **A**.

d) $0.4 = \frac{2}{5}$, which is less than $\frac{1}{2}$ but greater than $\frac{1}{4}$, so the correct probability is **B**.

2 a) Half of the numbers on a dice are odd, which means the probability is $\frac{1}{2}$, so the letter is **C**.

b) A quarter of the cards in a pack are diamonds, which means the probability is $\frac{1}{4}$, so the letter is **A**.

c) One quarter of the cards are diamonds, which means three-quarters of the cards are not diamonds, so the probability of not getting a diamond is $\frac{3}{4}$, so the letter is **D**.

d) 1 of the 3 sections is blue, which means the probability of spinning blue is $\frac{1}{3}$, so the letter is **B**.

27.2 Calculating Probabilities

Page 471 Exercise 1

1 a) You can either get heads or tails, so there are **2 outcomes**.

b) There are 52 cards, so there are **52 outcomes**.

Using the same method for c)-f):
c) 10   **d) 8**   **e) 7**
f) 365 (or 366 for a leap year)

2 a) There are 6 sections, so there are **6 outcomes**.

b) There's 1 section with a 1, so P(1) = $\mathbf{\frac{1}{6}}$.

c) There are 2 sections with a 3, so P(3) = $\frac{2}{6} = \mathbf{\frac{1}{3}}$.

3 There are 6 possible outcomes: 1, 2, 3, 4, 5 and 6. So:

a) There's one 6, so P(6) = $\mathbf{\frac{1}{6}}$.

b) There's one 2, so P(2) = $\mathbf{\frac{1}{6}}$.

c) There is no 7, so P(7) = **0**.

d) Two outcomes will give a 4 or 5, so P(4 or 5) = $\frac{2}{6} = \mathbf{\frac{1}{3}}$.

e) 3 and 6 are multiples of 3,
so P(multiple of 3) = $\frac{2}{6} = \mathbf{\frac{1}{3}}$.

f) 1, 2, 3 and 6 are factors of 6,
so P(factor of 6) = $\frac{4}{6} = \mathbf{\frac{2}{3}}$.

Remember to always simplify your fractions if possible.

4 a) One card is a 4, so P(4) = $\mathbf{\frac{1}{9}}$.

b) 4 of the 9 cards (2, 4, 6, and 8) are even, so P(even) = $\mathbf{\frac{4}{9}}$.

c) 5 of the cards are less than 6,
so P(less than 6) = $\mathbf{\frac{5}{9}}$.

5 a) 3 of the 12 sections are green,
so P(green) = $\frac{3}{12} = \mathbf{\frac{1}{4}}$.

b) 12 – 5 – 3 = 4, so there are 4 purple sections. So P(purple) = $\frac{4}{12} = \mathbf{\frac{1}{3}}$.

c) 5 + 3 = 8, so P(yellow or green) = $\frac{8}{12} = \mathbf{\frac{2}{3}}$.

d) 3 sections are green, so 12 – 3 = 9 sections are not green.
P(not green) = $\frac{9}{12} = \mathbf{\frac{3}{4}}$.

6 First, find the total number of balls in the bag:
2 + 4 + 2 + 3 + 2 + 1 + 1 + 1 = 16 balls.

a) There are 2 green balls,
so P(green) = $\frac{2}{16} = \mathbf{\frac{1}{8}}$.

b) There are 3 red balls, so P(red) = $\mathbf{\frac{3}{16}}$.

c) There is 1 orange ball, so P(orange) = $\mathbf{\frac{1}{16}}$.

d) There are 2 black balls, so
P(black) = $\frac{2}{16} = \mathbf{\frac{1}{8}}$.

e) There are 4 blue balls and 2 green balls, so the number of outcomes = 4 + 2 = 6, and
P(blue or green) = $\frac{6}{16} = \mathbf{\frac{3}{8}}$.

f) There are 3 red balls, 2 green balls and 1 brown ball, so the number of outcomes = 3 + 2 + 1 = 6,
and P(red, green or brown) = $\frac{6}{16} = \mathbf{\frac{3}{8}}$.

g) There is only 1 purple ball, so there are 16 – 1 = 15 balls which are not purple.
P(not purple) = $\mathbf{\frac{15}{16}}$.

h) There are no white balls so P(white) = **0**.

7 a) 13 cards are clubs, so P(clubs) = $\frac{13}{52} = \mathbf{\frac{1}{4}}$.

b) There are 4 aces in a pack,
so P(ace) = $\frac{4}{52} = \mathbf{\frac{1}{13}}$.

c) 26 cards are red, so P(red) = $\frac{26}{52} = \mathbf{\frac{1}{2}}$.

d) Only one card is the 2 of hearts,
so P(2 of hearts) = $\mathbf{\frac{1}{52}}$.

e) 13 cards are spades, so 52 – 13 = 39 cards are not spades. P(not spades) = $\frac{39}{52} = \mathbf{\frac{3}{4}}$.

f) There are four 4s and four 5s in the pack.
4 + 4 = 8, so P(4 or 5) = $\frac{8}{52} = \mathbf{\frac{2}{13}}$.

8 a) 3 of the 8 sections need to be a 2:
E.g.

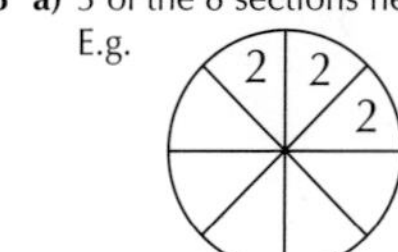

b) Half of 8 is 4, so 4 of the 8 sections need to be a 3:
E.g.

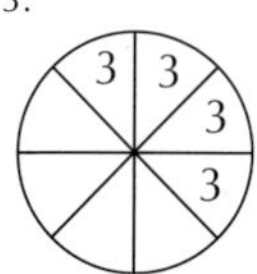

c) $\frac{1}{4}$ of 8 is 2, so there needs to be a 5 in two sections and a 6 in two sections:
E.g.

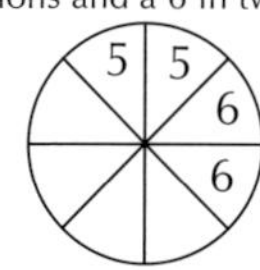

Page 472 Exercise 2

1 a) There are 12 months in a year, so P(correct month) = $\mathbf{\frac{1}{12}}$

b) There are 366 days in a leap year, so P(correct date) = $\mathbf{\frac{1}{366}}$

2 Each ticket is equally likely to be chosen, so:

a) P(first person wins) = $\mathbf{\frac{1}{100}}$

b) P(last person wins) = $\mathbf{\frac{1}{100}}$

3 20 pairs of socks = 40 socks. Tove picks 1 sock, so there are now 40 – 1 = 39 socks to pick from. So the probability of picking a second sock that makes a pair is $\mathbf{\frac{1}{39}}$.

4 a) There are 8 + 6 + 4 = 18 chocolates in the box. There are 4 pralines, half of which are white chocolate. This means there are 2 white-chocolate-coated pralines.
So P(white-chocolate-coated praline) = $\frac{2}{18} = \mathbf{\frac{1}{9}}$.

b) (i) 4 chocolates are praline, so 18 – 4 = 14 chocolates are not praline. Of these 14, you know half of them are white chocolate and half are milk chocolate. 14 ÷ 2 = 7, so there are **7 chocolates** that are neither praline nor white chocolate.

(ii) Chelsea will like 7 chocolates, so the probability that Chelsea gets a chocolate she likes is $\mathbf{\frac{7}{18}}$.

5 It doesn't take into account how good the team is or how good their opponents are. This means the **three outcomes are not equally likely**.

Page 473 Exercise 3

1 a) A 5 and a number less than 3 can't be rolled at the same time, so these events **are mutually exclusive**.

b) 5 is an odd number, so if a 5 was rolled, an odd number would also be rolled. This means these two events are **not mutually exclusive**.

c) If a number less than 3 is rolled it will be a 1 or a 2. 1 is an odd number, so these events are **not mutually exclusive**.

2 a) If the name of a month begins with J, it can't also begin with M, so these events **are mutually exclusive**.

b) January and July both begin with J and end in Y, so these events are **not mutually exclusive**.

c) The first four months are January, February, March and April. January begins with J, so these events are **not mutually exclusive**.

d) The month of May begins with M and ends with Y, so these events are **not mutually exclusive**.

It's a good idea to write out all the months of the year so you don't miss any.

3 Use the rule P(event happening)
= 1 – P(event not happening).
So, P(not late) = 1 – P(late) = 1 – 0.2 = **0.8**

An event happening and the event not happening are always mutually exclusive events — things can't both happen and not happen.

4 P(no snow) = 1 – P(snow) = 1 – $\frac{5}{8} = \mathbf{\frac{3}{8}}$

5 a) P(not boy) = 1 – P(boy) = 1 – 0.45 = **0.55**

b) P(not blond) = 1 – P(blond) = 1 – 0.2 = **0.8**

Page 474 Exercise 4

1 a) P(red) = 1 – (0.2 + 0.1 + 0.1 + 0.3)
= 1 – 0.7 = **0.3**

b) P(not pink) = 1 – P(pink) = 1 – 0.1 = **0.9**

2 P(red) = 1 – ($\frac{1}{4} + \frac{3}{8}$) = 1 – $\frac{5}{8} = \mathbf{\frac{3}{8}}$

3 P(red) = 1 – (0.5 + 0.4) = 1 – 0.9 = 0.1
There are 4 red counters, so P(red) = $\frac{4}{\text{total}}$ = 0.1,
so total = 4 ÷ 0.1 = **40 counters**.

27.3 Listing Outcomes

Page 475 Exercise 1

1 a)

1st coin	2nd coin
Heads	Heads
Heads	Tails
Tails	Heads
Tails	Tails

b)

Dice	Coin
1	Heads
1	Tails
2	Heads
2	Tails
3	Heads
3	Tails
4	Heads
4	Tails
5	Heads
5	Tails
6	Heads
6	Tails

Writing your table in order makes it much easier to spot if you miss out an outcome.

2

1st ball	2nd ball
Green	Green
Green	Blue
Blue	Green
Blue	Blue

3 a)

Burger	Drink
Hamburger	Cola
Hamburger	Lemonade
Hamburger	Coffee
Cheeseburger	Cola
Cheeseburger	Lemonade
Cheeseburger	Coffee
Veggie burger	Cola
Veggie burger	Lemonade
Veggie burger	Coffee

b) There are 9 possible combinations, and only 1 way to choose a veggie burger and cola, so P(veggie burger and cola) = $\mathbf{\frac{1}{9}}$.

c) There are 3 ways she could choose a cheeseburger, so P(cheeseburger) = $\frac{3}{9} = \mathbf{\frac{1}{3}}$.

4 a)

1st spin	2nd spin
1	1
1	2
1	3
2	1
2	2
2	3
3	1
3	2
3	3

b) There are 9 possible outcomes but only 1 way to spin a 3 for both spins, so the probability is $\mathbf{\frac{1}{9}}$.

c) There are 6 ways of getting a total of 4 or more:
1 and 3, 2 and 2, 2 and 3, 3 and 1, 3 and 2, 3 and 3.
So the probability is $\frac{6}{9} = \mathbf{\frac{2}{3}}$.

5 a)

1st toss	2nd toss	3rd toss
Heads	Heads	Heads
Heads	Heads	Tails
Heads	Tails	Heads
Heads	Tails	Tails
Tails	Heads	Heads
Tails	Heads	Tails
Tails	Tails	Heads
Tails	Tails	Tails

b) (i) There are 8 possible outcomes and 1 way of getting three tails, so the probability is $\mathbf{\frac{1}{8}}$.

(ii) There are three ways of getting one head and two tails:
Heads, Tails, Tails; Tails, Heads, Tails; Tails, Tails, Heads
So the probability is $\mathbf{\frac{3}{8}}$.

Page 477 Exercise 2

1

	1	2	3	4	5	6
H	H1	H2	H3	H4	H5	H6
T	T1	T2	T3	T4	T5	T6

2 a)

	1	2	3	4	5	6
1	2	3	4	5	6	7
2	3	4	5	6	7	8
3	4	5	6	7	8	9
4	5	6	7	8	9	10
5	6	7	8	9	10	11
6	7	8	9	10	11	12

b) 6 × 6 = **36 outcomes**

c) (i) There are 5 ways to score 6:
1 and 5, 2 and 4, 3 and 3, 4 and 2, 5 and 1.
So P(6) = $\mathbf{\frac{5}{36}}$.

(ii) P(less than 8) = probability of scoring 2, 3, 4, 5, 6 or 7. There are 6 ways to score 7, 5 ways to score 6, 4 ways to score 5, 3 ways to score 4, 2 ways to score 3 and 1 way to score 2. So there are 6 + 5 + 4 + 3 + 2 + 1 = 21 ways to score less than 8.
P(less than 8) = $\frac{21}{36} = \mathbf{\frac{7}{12}}$.

(iii) P(more than 8) = probability of scoring 9, 10 , 11 or 12. There are 4 ways to score 9, 3 ways to score 10, 2 ways to score 11 and 1 way to score 12. So there are 4 + 3 + 2 + 1 = 10 ways to score more than 8.
P(more than 8) = $\frac{10}{36} = \mathbf{\frac{5}{18}}$.

(iv) 18 of the 36 options are even, so P(even) = $\frac{18}{36} = \mathbf{\frac{1}{2}}$.

3 a)

	B	G	G	Y
B	BB	BG	BG	BY
G	GB	GG	GG	GY
Y	YB	YG	YG	YY

b) There are 3 × 4 = 12 possible outcomes.

(i) There's only 1 way to get 2 blue balls, so P(2 blue balls) = $\mathbf{\frac{1}{12}}$.

(ii) There are 2 ways to get 2 green balls, so P(2 green balls) = $\frac{2}{12} = \mathbf{\frac{1}{6}}$.

(iii) There are 4 ways to get 2 balls of the same colour (BB, GG, GG, YY), so P(2 balls same colour) = $\frac{4}{12} = \mathbf{\frac{1}{3}}$.

(iv) There are 6 ways to get at least 1 yellow ball (YB, YG, YG, YY, BY, GY), so P(at least 1 yellow) = $\frac{6}{12} = \mathbf{\frac{1}{2}}$.

4 a)

	1	2	3	4	5	6
A	A1	A2	A3	A4	A5	A6
B	B1	B2	B3	B4	B5	B6
C	C1	C2	C3	C4	C5	C6
D	D1	D2	D3	D4	D5	D6

b) There are 4 × 6 = 24 possible outcomes.

(i) There's only 1 way to get C and 5, so P(C and 5) = $\mathbf{\frac{1}{24}}$.

(ii) There are 2 ways to get B and less than 3: B1 and B2,
so P(B and less than 3) = $\frac{2}{24} = \mathbf{\frac{1}{12}}$.

(iii) There are 4 ways to get A or B and more than 4:
A5, A6, B5, B6. So P(A or B and more than 4) = $\frac{4}{24} = \mathbf{\frac{1}{6}}$.

5 a)

		Asha's score (2nd number)				
		1	2	3	4	5
Hayley's score (1st number)	1	1, 1	1, 2	1, 3	1, 4	1, 5
	2	2, 1	2, 2	2, 3	2, 4	2, 5
	3	3, 1	3, 2	3, 3	3, 4	3, 5
	4	4, 1	4, 2	4, 3	4, 4	4, 5
	5	5, 1	5, 2	5, 3	5, 4	5, 5

b) There are 5 × 5 = 25 possible outcomes. If Hayley spins a 5, there are four outcomes where she beats Asha (if Asha rolls a 4, 3, 2 or 1). If she spins a 4, there are three outcomes where she beats Asha. If she spins a 3, there are two outcomes and if she spins a 2 then there is one outcome. If Hayley spins a 1 there are no outcomes where she beats Asha. So there are 4 + 3 + 2 + 1 = 10 outcomes where Hayley can get a higher score than Asha.
So P(Hayley wins) = $\frac{10}{25} = \mathbf{\frac{2}{5}}$.

The outcomes where Hayley wins are found in the bottom-left corner of the table — you can just count them directly from there.

27.4 Probability from Experiments

Page 478 Exercise 1

1 a) The experiment was carried out 50 times, and the pin landed point up 17 times. So the probability is $\mathbf{\frac{17}{50}}$.

b) P(not point up) = 1 – P(point up)
$= 1 - \frac{17}{50} = \mathbf{\frac{33}{50}}$.

2 a) Red came up 49 times out of 100, so its relative frequency is $\mathbf{\frac{49}{100}}$.
Green came up 34 times, so its relative frequency is $\frac{34}{100} = \mathbf{\frac{17}{50}}$.
Yellow came up 8 times, so its relative frequency is $\frac{8}{100} = \mathbf{\frac{2}{25}}$.
Blue came up 9 times, so its relative frequency is $\mathbf{\frac{9}{100}}$.

b) The more times an experiment is done, the more accurate the estimates should be. So Sam could perform the experiment more times.

3 a) Stacy rolled a two 13 times out of 50, so the estimated probability is $\mathbf{\frac{13}{50}}$.

b) Jamal rolled a two 18 times out of 100, so the estimated probability is $\frac{18}{100} = \mathbf{\frac{9}{50}}$.

c) **Jamal's estimate** should be more accurate as he has performed the experiment more times.

4 The bus is on time 20 out of 24 days, so the estimated probability that the bus is on time is $\frac{20}{24} = \mathbf{\frac{5}{6}}$.

5 The estimated probability that George will burn the next cake he bakes is $\frac{12}{20}$, so the estimated probability that he won't burn it is $1 - \frac{12}{20} = \frac{8}{20} = \mathbf{\frac{2}{5}}$.

6 E.g. Lilia could look at recent results of her team's matches against a similar level of opposition to find the estimated probability that her team will win. To do this, she could count the number of wins and divide it by the total number of matches in those records.

Page 480 Exercise 2

1 a) 20 × 0.75 = **15 times**

b) 60 × 0.75 = **45 times**

c) 100 × 0.75 = **75 times**

d) 1000 × 0.75 = **750 times**

2 a) P(5) = $\frac{1}{6}$, 120 × $\frac{1}{6}$ = **20 times**

b) P(6) = $\frac{1}{6}$, 120 × $\frac{1}{6}$ = **20 times**

c) P(even) = $\frac{3}{6} = \frac{1}{2}$, 120 × $\frac{1}{2}$ = **60 times**

d) P(higher than 1) = $\frac{5}{6}$, 120 × $\frac{5}{6}$ = **100 times**

3 There are 3 sections so the probability of spinning a penguin is $\frac{1}{3}$:

a) 60 × $\frac{1}{3}$ = **20 times**

b) 300 × $\frac{1}{3}$ = **100 times**

c) 480 × $\frac{1}{3}$ = **160 times**

4 60% = 0.6 and 0.6 × 20 = 12, so you would expect **12 people** to buy brown bread.

You could also have converted 60% to a fraction instead of a decimal and used that to find the number.

Page 481 Exercise 3

1 a)

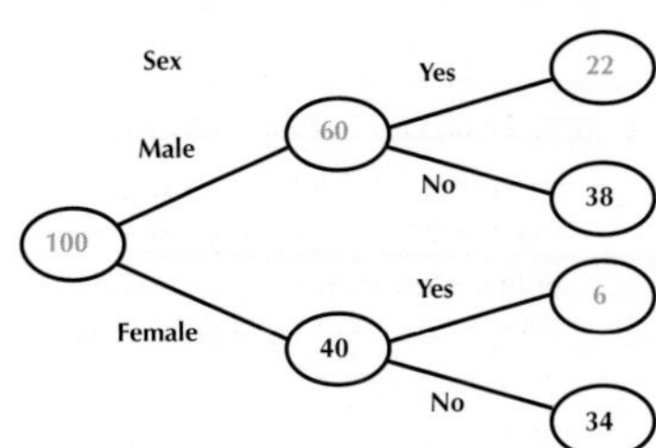

Add up all the numbers at the end to make sure they equal the number at the start. 22 + 38 + 6 + 34 = 100.

b)

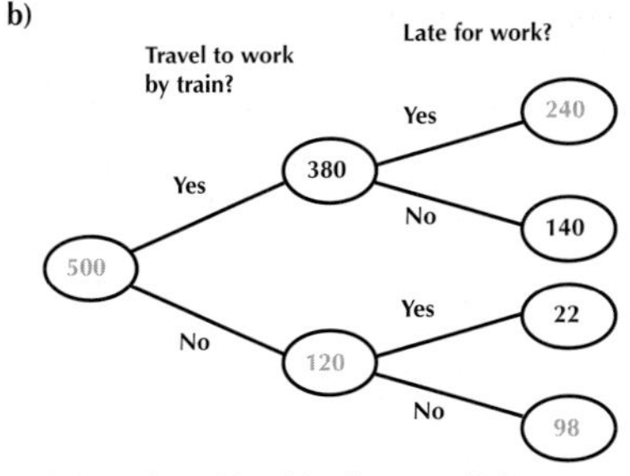

240 + 140 + 22 + 98 = 500, so this is correct.

2 a) E.g.

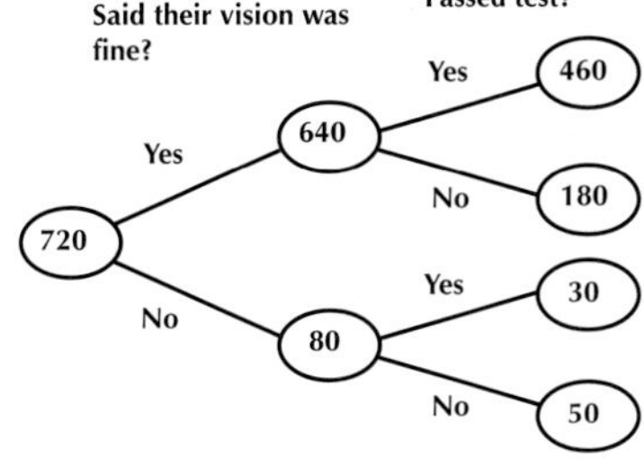

b) From the tree in part a) you know 80 drivers said their vision wasn't fine. Of these 80 drivers, 50 failed the test. So the probability is $\frac{50}{80} = \mathbf{\frac{5}{8}}$.

c) 460 drivers said that their vision was fine and passed the eye test. So the probability is $\frac{460}{720} = \mathbf{\frac{23}{36}}$.

Page 482 Exercise 4

1 a) Blue is $\frac{22}{100}$ = **0.22**, green is $\frac{21}{100}$ = **0.21**, white is $\frac{18}{100}$ = **0.18**, pink is $\frac{39}{100}$ = **0.39**.

b) There are 4 possible outcomes of equal probability, so blue is **0.25**, green is **0.25**, white is **0.25**, and pink is **0.25**.

c) The spinner seems to be biased as the relative frequency for pink (0.39) is a long way off the theoretical probability.

2 a) P(4) = $\frac{1}{6}$, so expected frequency of rolling a 4 is 120 × $\frac{1}{6}$ = **20 times**.

b) The dice may be biased as the number 4 comes up much more than expected — 32 times rather than 20 times.

c) Roll the dice more times.

3 a)

	Amy	Steve	Hal
No. of tosses	20	60	100
No. of heads	12	33	49
Relative frequency	**0.6**	**0.55**	**0.49**

b) **Hal's results** should be the most accurate because he performed the experiment the greatest number of times.

c) The coin seems fair as the theoretical probability of heads for a fair coin is 0.5 and Hal's result is very close to that (0.49).

You could also show that, as the same coin is used, the three friends's results can be combined to give a relative frequency of $\frac{94}{180}$ *= 0.522...*

4 a) E.g.

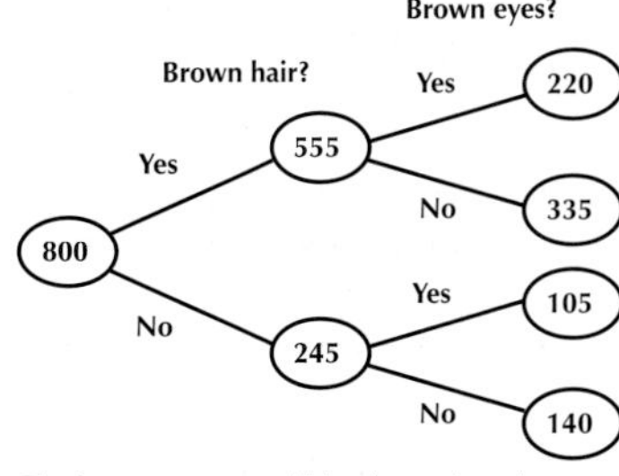

The frequency tree could be drawn the other way round, with eyes first and then hair.

b) 220 residents have brown hair and brown eyes, so the relative frequency is $\frac{220}{800} = \frac{11}{40}$ = **0.275**.

c) Estimated frequency = 2000 × 0.275 = **550 residents**

27.5 The AND / OR Rules

Page 483 Exercise 1

1 a) P(a head and a 6) = P(head) × P(6)
$= \frac{1}{2} \times \frac{1}{6} = \mathbf{\frac{1}{12}}$

b) P(a head and an odd number)
= P(head) × P(odd number)
$= \frac{1}{2} \times \frac{3}{6} = \frac{1}{2} \times \frac{1}{2} = \mathbf{\frac{1}{4}}$

c) There are 2 square numbers on a dice (1 and 4), so P(a tail and a square number)
= P(tail) × P(square number)
$= \frac{1}{2} \times \frac{2}{6} = \frac{1}{2} \times \frac{1}{3} = \mathbf{\frac{1}{6}}$

d) There are 3 prime numbers on a dice (2, 3 and 5), so P(a tail and a prime number)
= P(tail) × P(prime number)
$= \frac{1}{2} \times \frac{3}{6} = \frac{1}{2} \times \frac{1}{2} = \mathbf{\frac{1}{4}}$

e) There are 2 multiples of 3 on a dice (3 and 6), so P(a head and a multiple of 3)
= P(head) × P(multiple of 3)
$= \frac{1}{2} \times \frac{2}{6} = \frac{1}{2} \times \frac{1}{3} = \mathbf{\frac{1}{6}}$

f) There are 2 factors of 5 on a dice (1 and 5), so P(a tail and a factor of 5)
= P(tail) × P(factor of 5)
$= \frac{1}{2} \times \frac{2}{6} = \frac{1}{2} \times \frac{1}{3} = \mathbf{\frac{1}{6}}$

2 a) 10% = 0.1, so P(right-handed)
= 1 – P(left-handed) = 1 – 0.1 = **0.9**

b) 15% = 0.15, so P(no glasses)
= 1 – P(glasses) = 1 – 0.15 = **0.85**

c) P(left-handed) = 0.1, P(glasses) = 0.15
P(glasses and left-handed)
= P(glasses) × P(left-handed)
= 0.15 × 0.1 = **0.015**

Be careful with the decimal places here.

d) P(no glasses) = 0.85,
P(right-handed) = 0.9
P(no glasses and right-handed)
= P(no glasses) × P(right-handed)
= 0.85 × 0.9 = **0.765**

3 a) 5 out of the 10 balls are red, so P(red) $= \frac{5}{10} = \frac{1}{2}$, so

P(red and red) = P(red) × P(red)

$= \frac{1}{2} \times \frac{1}{2} = \mathbf{\frac{1}{4}}$ or **0.25**

b) P(blue) $= \frac{3}{10}$, so P(blue and blue)

= P(blue) × P(blue)

$= \frac{3}{10} \times \frac{3}{10} = \mathbf{\frac{9}{100}} = \mathbf{0.09}$

c) P(not blue) = 1 – P(blue) $= 1 - \frac{3}{10} = \frac{7}{10}$

P(neither ball is blue)

= P(not blue) × P(not blue)

$= \frac{7}{10} \times \frac{7}{10} = \mathbf{\frac{49}{100}} = 0.49$

Page 485 Exercise 2

1 The events in this question are mutually exclusive — balls can't be two different colours.

a) P(pink or orange) = 0.5 + 0.1 = **0.6**

b) P(pink or red) = 0.5 + 0.4 = **0.9**

c) P(red or orange) = 0.4 + 0.1 = **0.5**

2 The events in this question are mutually exclusive — chocolate cannot be wrapped in two colours of foil.

a) P(red or gold) = 0.14 + 0.4 = **0.54**

b) P(silver or red) = 0.26 + 0.14 = **0.4**

c) P(gold or blue) = 0.4 + 0.2 = **0.6**

d) P(silver or gold) = 0.26 + 0.4 = **0.66**

3 The events in this question are mutually exclusive — a student can't be in two different teams.

a) P(Eagle) $= \mathbf{\frac{1}{3}}$

b) P(Eagle or Falcon) $= \frac{1}{3} + \frac{1}{3} = \mathbf{\frac{2}{3}}$

c) P(Falcon or Osprey) $= \frac{1}{3} + \frac{1}{3} = \mathbf{\frac{2}{3}}$

4 a) The events are not mutually exclusive — the dice can land on both an odd number and a multiple of 3.

P(multiple of 3) = P(3, 6, 9, 12, 15 or 18) $= \frac{6}{20}$

P(odd) = P(1, 3, 5, 7, 9, 11, 13, 15, 17 or 19) $= \frac{10}{20}$

P(multiple of 3 and odd)

= P(3, 9 or 15) $= \frac{3}{20}$

So P(multiple of 3 or odd) $= \frac{6}{20} + \frac{10}{20} - \frac{3}{20} = \mathbf{\frac{13}{20}}$

b) The events are not mutually exclusive — the dice can land on a factor of 20 which is also a multiple of 4.

P(factor of 20) = P(1, 2, 4, 5, 10 or 20) $= \frac{6}{20}$

P(multiple of 4) = P(4, 8, 12, 16 or 20) $= \frac{5}{20}$

P(factor of 20 and multiple of 4)

= P(4 or 20) $= \frac{2}{20}$

So P(factor of 20 or multiple of 4)

$= \frac{6}{20} + \frac{5}{20} - \frac{2}{20} = \mathbf{\frac{9}{20}}$

5 a) The events are not mutually exclusive — a card can be both a red suit and a queen.

P(red suit) = P(heart or diamond) $= \frac{26}{52}$

P(queen) = P(Q♠, Q♥, Q♣ or Q♦) $= \frac{4}{52}$

P(red suit and queen) = P(Q♥ or Q♦) $= \frac{2}{52}$

So P(red suit or queen) $= \frac{26}{52} + \frac{4}{52} - \frac{2}{52} = \frac{28}{52} = \mathbf{\frac{7}{13}}$

b) The events are not mutually exclusive — a card can be both a club and a picture card.

P(club) $= \frac{13}{52}$

P(picture card) = P(Jack, Queen or King) $= \frac{12}{52}$

P(club and picture card) = P(J♣, Q♣ or K♣) $= \frac{3}{52}$

So P(club or picture card) $= \frac{13}{52} + \frac{12}{52} - \frac{3}{52} = \frac{22}{52} = \mathbf{\frac{11}{26}}$

A pack of cards is a popular context in Maths questions — so it's a good idea to familiarise yourself with the different suits, colours, picture cards etc. (and how many there are of each).

6 No, having glasses and having blond hair are not mutually exclusive (some people could have both). This means that the probability of picking a pupil with blond hair or glasses isn't just the sum of the separate probabilities (unless you know that none of the pupils both wear glasses and have blond hair).

27.6 Tree Diagrams

Page 487 Exercise 1

1 a) P(R) $= \frac{3}{5} = 0.6$, P(B) $= \frac{2}{5} = 0.4$

1st: 0.6 R, 0.4 B
2nd: after R: 0.6 R, 0.4 B; after B: 0.6 R, 0.4 B

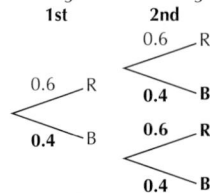

b) P(R) $= \frac{5}{10} = 0.5$, P(B) $= \frac{3}{10} = 0.3$, P(G) $= \frac{2}{10} = 0.2$

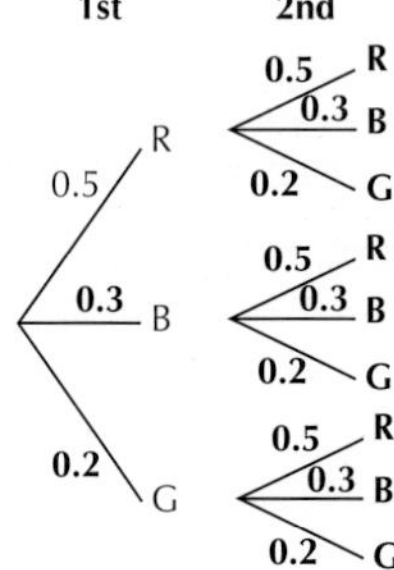

2 a) P(H) = 0.65, P(T) = 1 – 0.65 = 0.35

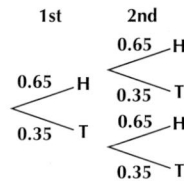

1st: 0.65 H, 0.35 T
2nd: after H: 0.65 H, 0.35 T; after T: 0.65 H, 0.35 T

b)

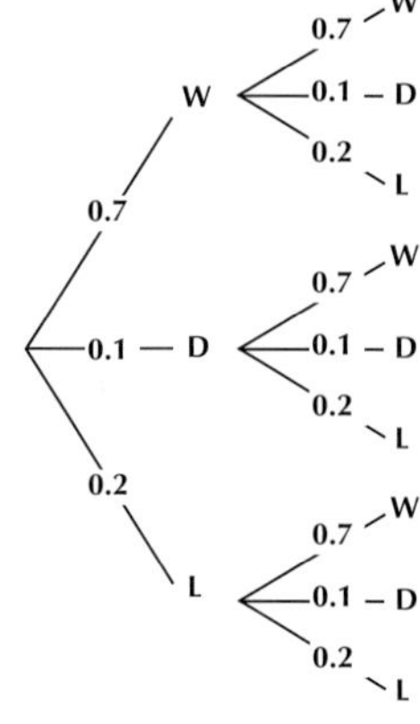

3 a) P(Freddie wins) = 0.8,
P(James wins) = 1 – 0.8 = 0.2

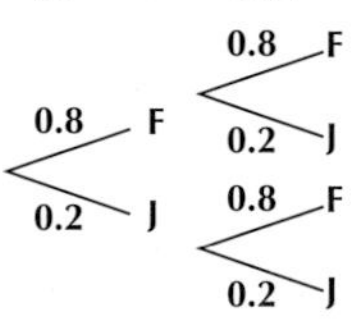

b) P(F, F) = 0.8 × 0.8 = **0.64**

4 a) P(Ifrath chooses a comedy) $= \frac{4}{12} = \frac{1}{3}$

P(Ifrath doesn't choose a comedy) $= 1 - \frac{1}{3} = \frac{2}{3}$

P(Jesse chooses a comedy) $= \frac{8}{20} = \frac{2}{5}$

P(Jesse doesn't choose a comedy) $= 1 - \frac{2}{5} = \frac{3}{5}$

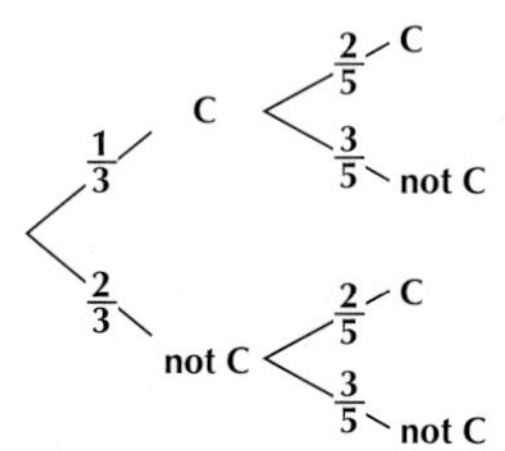

b) P(not C, not C) $= \frac{2}{3} \times \frac{3}{5} = \frac{6}{15} = \mathbf{\frac{2}{5}}$

c) P(at least one comedy) = 1 – P(not C, not C)

$= 1 - \frac{2}{5} = \mathbf{\frac{3}{5}}$

5 a)

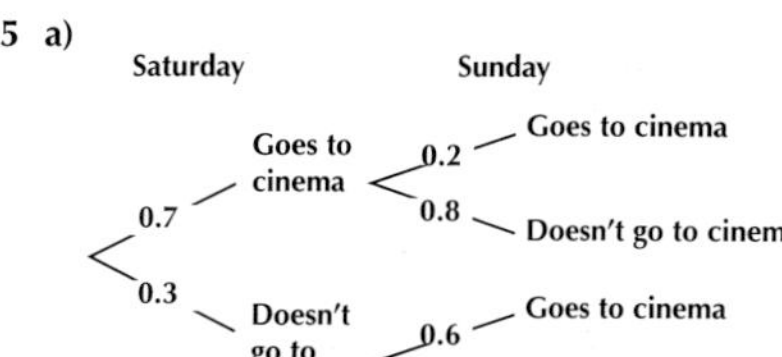

b) P(cinema, cinema) = 0.7 × 0.2 = **0.14**

c) P(cinema, not cinema)
+ P(not cinema, cinema)
= (0.7 × 0.8) + (0.3 × 0.6) = 0.56 + 0.18
= **0.74**

6 a)

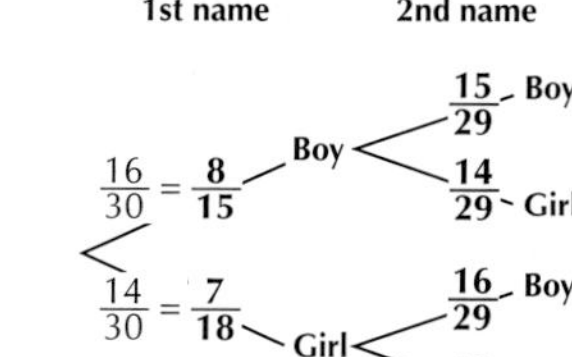

The probabilities change for the 2nd name because one name has been removed and not replaced.

b) P(boy, boy) = $\frac{8}{15} \times \frac{15}{29} = \mathbf{\frac{8}{29}}$

c) P(one girl) = P(boy, girl) + P(girl, boy)

$= \left(\frac{8}{15} \times \frac{14}{29}\right) + \left(\frac{7}{15} \times \frac{16}{29}\right)$

$= \frac{112}{435} + \frac{112}{435} = \mathbf{\frac{224}{435}}$

27.7 Sets and Venn Diagrams

Page 489 Exercise 1

1 a) (i) A = **{12, 14, 16, 18, 20, 22, 24}**

(ii) B = **{2, 3, 5, 7, 11, 13, 17, 19, 23, 29}**

(iii) C = **{1, 4, 9, 16, 25, 36, 49, 64, 81, 100, 121, 144, 169, 196}**

(iv) D = **{1, 2, 3, 5, 6, 10, 15, 30}**

b) n(A) means the number of elements in set A, so:

(i) 7 **(ii) 10**

(iii) 14 **(iv) 8**

2 a) A ∪ B is the union of set A and set B. All the elements in either set A or set B are **{1, 2, 4, 5, 6, 7, 8}**.

b) A ∩ B is the intersection of set A and set B. The elements that are in both sets are **{2, 4, 8}**.

Make sure you're happy with all the bits of set notation — the questions aren't too tricky as long as you know what each symbol means.

3 a) n(A) = **4** **b)** n(B) = **6**

c) A′ is the complement of set A, i.e. all the elements of the universal set that are not in set A. So A′ = **{2, 4, 5, 6, 8}**

d) A ∪ B = **{1, 2, 3, 5, 6, 7, 8, 9}**

e) B′ = **{1, 4, 7}**

f) A ∩ B = **{3, 9}**

g) n(A ∪ B) = **8**

h) A′ ∪ B is the union of the complement of set A and set B. This is all the elements in either the complement of set A or set B.
A′ ∪ B = **{2, 3, 4, 5, 6, 8, 9}**

Page 490 Exercise 2

1 a) A = {1, 3, 5}, B = {1, 3, 7}. 1 and 3 are in both sets, so these go in the overlap between the circles. 5 goes only in set A, 7 goes only in set B, and the rest of the positive integers ≤ 10 go around the outside of the circles.

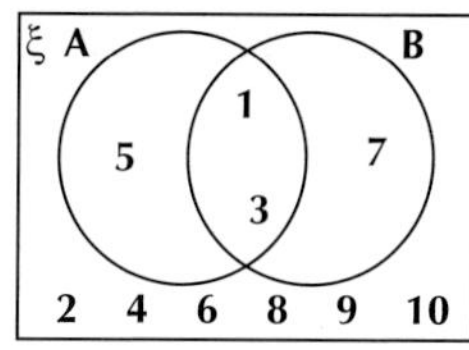

b) A = {2, 3, 4, 5}, B = {1, 3, 5, 7, 9}. 3 and 5 are in both sets, so these go in the overlap between the circles. 2 and 4 only go in set A, 1, 7 and 9 only go in set B, and the rest of the positive integers ≤ 10 go around the outside of the circles.

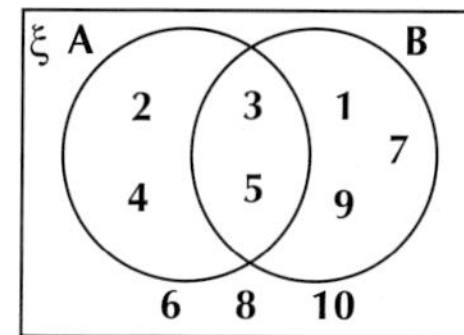

Using the same method for c)-d):

c)

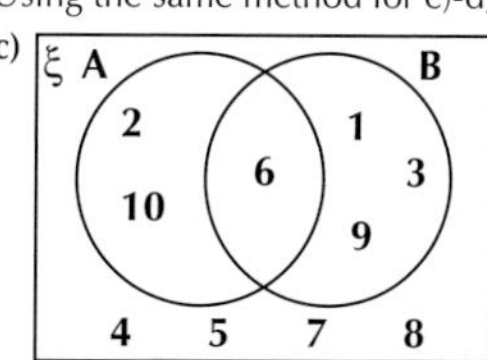

d)

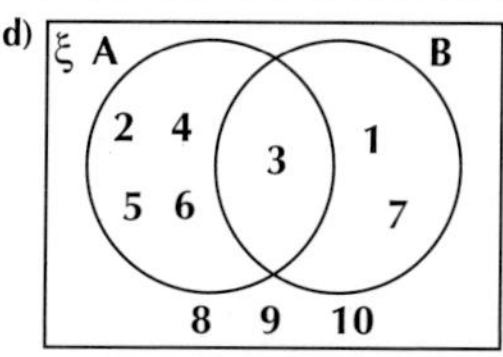

2 a) People who only had salad are in the part of the salad circle that's not overlapping the fries circle.
So P(only salad) = $\frac{76}{200} = \mathbf{\frac{19}{50}} = \mathbf{0.38}$.

b) People who only had fries are in the part of the fries circle that's not overlapping the salad circle.
So P(only fries) = $\mathbf{\frac{87}{200}} = \mathbf{0.435}$.

c) People who had no side are not part of any circle so are outside both circles.
So P(no side) = $\frac{10}{200} = \mathbf{\frac{1}{20}} = \mathbf{0.05}$.

d) All the customers in the salad circle: 76 + 27 = 103, so P(salad) = $\mathbf{\frac{103}{200}} = \mathbf{0.515}$.

e) All the customers in the fries circle:
87 + 27 = 114, so
P(fries) = $\frac{114}{200} = \mathbf{\frac{57}{100}} = \mathbf{0.57}$.

f) People who had fries and salad are in the intersection of the two circles,
so P(fries and salad) = $\mathbf{\frac{27}{200}} = \mathbf{0.135}$.

3 a) A = {1, 3, 5, 7, 9}, B = {2, 3, 5, 7}. 3, 5 and 7 are in both sets, so these go in the overlap. The positive integers ≤ 10 that aren't in A or B go outside the circles.

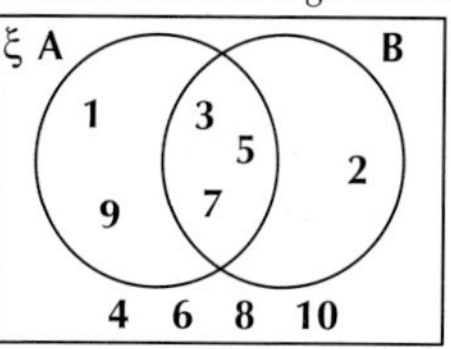

b) (i) n(B) = 4, so P(B) = $\frac{4}{10} = \mathbf{\frac{2}{5}} = \mathbf{0.4}$

(ii) A ∩ B = {3, 5, 7}, so n(A ∩ B) = 3 and P(A ∩ B) = $\mathbf{\frac{3}{10}} = \mathbf{0.3}$

(iii) A ∩ B′ means the numbers which are in A and not in B so are the numbers ≤ 10 which are odd and not prime (the ones in the part of circle A that's not overlapping circle B).
A ∩ B′ = {1, 9}, so n(A ∩ B′) = 2 and P(A ∩ B′) = $\frac{2}{10} = \mathbf{\frac{1}{5}} = \mathbf{0.2}$

4 a) 15 pupils like Maths and English, so 15 goes in the intersection. 23 – 15 = 8 pupils just like Maths and 18 – 15 = 3 pupils just like English, so 8 and 3 go in the other parts of the M and E circles respectively. That leaves 30 – 8 – 15 – 3 = 4 pupils who like neither Maths nor English, so 4 goes outside the circles.

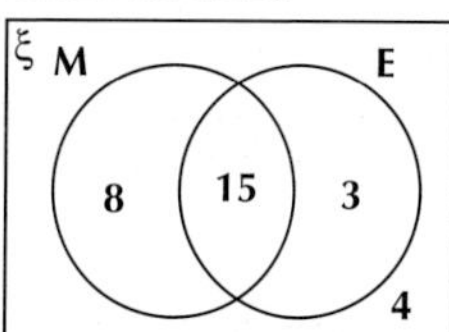

Always check that the numbers in your Venn diagram add up to the total from the question — here 8 + 15 + 3 + 4 = 30, which is the total number of pupils in the class.

b) (i) P(M and E) = $\frac{15}{30} = \mathbf{\frac{1}{2}}$

(ii) P(M only) = $\frac{8}{30} = \mathbf{\frac{4}{15}}$

(iii) P(E only) = $\frac{3}{30} = \mathbf{\frac{1}{10}}$

(iv) P(not M and not E) = $\frac{4}{30} = \mathbf{\frac{2}{15}}$

Page 491 Review Exercise

1 There are 4 + 6 + 5 + 5 = 20 pieces of fruit in total.

a) There are 4 apples and 6 bananas, so 4 + 6 = 10 pieces in total.
So the likelihood is **evens**.

b) There are 5 oranges, so there are 20 – 5 = 15 pieces of fruit which are not oranges. So Bianca is **likely** to pick a piece of fruit which isn't an orange.

c) There are no lemons so it is **impossible** to pick one.

On the scale the arrows should be:

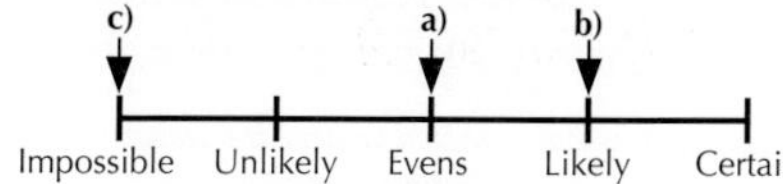

2 There are 6 possible outcomes — 1, 2, 3, 4, 5 and 6.

a) P(even) = P(2, 4 or 6) = $\frac{3}{6} = \mathbf{\frac{1}{2}}$

b) P(multiple of 3) = P(3 or 6) = $\frac{2}{6} = \mathbf{\frac{1}{3}}$

c) The answers to part a) and b) don't add up to 1 because these are not mutually exclusive outcomes that cover all the possibilities. (The two events aren't mutually exclusive because both events happen if a 6 is rolled, and the outcomes 1 and 5 are not included in either event.)

3 a) P(Derek wins) = $\mathbf{\frac{8}{15}}$

b) P(Eileen wins) = 1 – P(Derek wins) $= 1 - \frac{8}{15} = \mathbf{\frac{7}{15}}$

4 a) **Yes**, these events are independent because the outcome of one does not affect the other.

b) 4 + 5 + 11 = 20 sweets in total.

(i) P(blue, blue) = P(blue) × P(blue) $= \frac{4}{20} \times \frac{4}{20} = \frac{16}{400} = \mathbf{\frac{1}{25}}$

(ii) P(white then red)

= P(white) × P(red)

$= \frac{5}{20} \times \frac{11}{20} = \frac{55}{400} = \mathbf{\frac{11}{80}}$

5 a) After the first pick, there are only 9 marbles left, and 1 fewer of the colour that was picked, so:

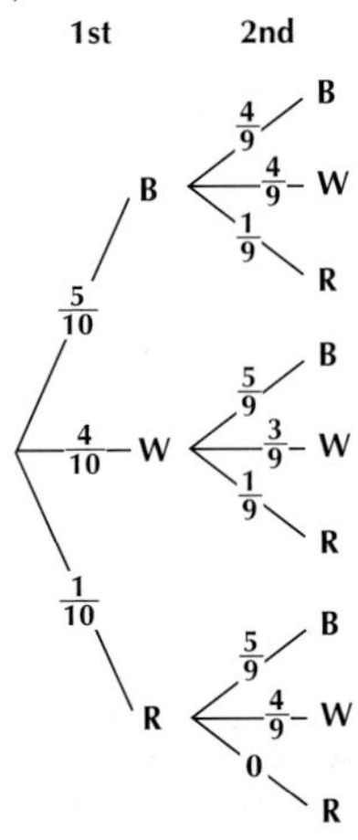

The probabilities on the second set of branches are different because the marbles are not replaced

b) (i) P(B, B) = $\frac{5}{10} \times \frac{4}{9} = \frac{20}{90} = \mathbf{\frac{2}{9}}$

(ii) P(at least one blue)
= 1 – P(not blue, not blue)
$= 1 - \left(\frac{5}{10} \times \frac{4}{9}\right) = 1 - \frac{2}{9} = \mathbf{\frac{7}{9}}$

You could also add up all of the probabilities that there is at least one blue marble.

(iii) P(different colours)
= 1 – P(same colours)
= 1 – P((B, B) or (W, W) or (R, R))
$= 1 - \left(\left(\frac{5}{10} \times \frac{4}{9}\right) + \left(\frac{4}{10} \times \frac{3}{9}\right) + \left(\frac{1}{10} \times 0\right)\right)$
$= 1 - \left(\frac{10}{45} + \frac{6}{45} + 0\right) = 1 - \frac{16}{45} = \mathbf{\frac{29}{45}}$

You could also add up all of the probabilities that the marbles are different colours.

6 a) 49 + 21 = **70 people**

b) 49 + 35 + 21 + 15 = 120 possible outcomes.
35 people bought only an ice lolly, so
P(only ice lolly) = $\frac{35}{120} = \mathbf{\frac{7}{24}}$

Page 492 Exam-Style Questions

1 The possible numbers she can make are 17, 18, 27, 28, 37, 38, 71, 72, 73, 81, 82, 83. So there are 12 possible outcomes in total *[1 mark]*. Five of these are even *[1 mark]*, so P(even) = $\mathbf{\frac{5}{12}}$ *[1 mark]*.

The question didn't ask you to list the outcomes, but it's a good idea to write them all down to make sure you don't miss any.

2 a)

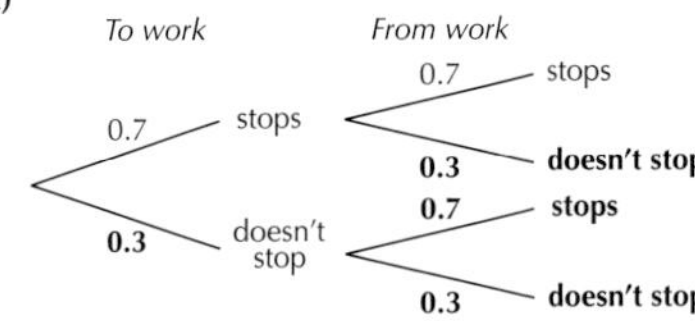

[2 marks available — 1 mark for calculating the probability that she doesn't have to stop, 1 mark for correctly completing the rest of the tree diagram]

b) P(stop only once) = P(stop, doesn't stop) + P(doesn't stop, stop)
= (0.7 × 0.3) + (0.3 × 0.7) *[1 mark]*
= 0.21 + 0.21 = **0.42** *[1 mark]*

3 a) Number of pupils asked = 7 + 9 = 16 *[1 mark]*.
Number of girls who went to the cinema last week = $\frac{2}{3} \times 9 = 6$ *[1 mark]*. 5 boys also went to the cinema, so probability $= \frac{(6+5)}{16} = \mathbf{\frac{11}{16}}$ or **0.6875** *[1 mark]*.

b) E.g. His sample of Year 11 boys may not be representative of all Year 11 boys. *[1 mark]* OR The sample size (of 7 boys) is too small to give a reliable answer *[1 mark]*.

4 a) 10 members do archery, and 6 members do both activities, so the number doing only archery is 10 – 6 = 4. 17 members do only basketball. That leaves 30 – (4 + 6 + 17) = 3 that do neither activity.
So the Venn diagram looks like this:

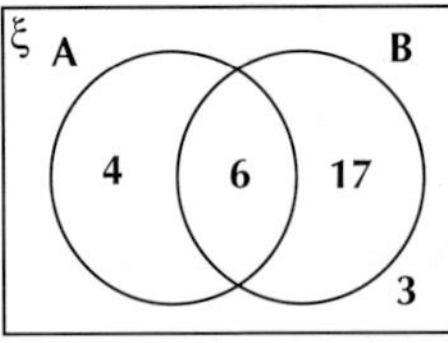

[2 marks available — 2 marks for a fully correct diagram, otherwise 1 mark for 2 correct numbers in the Venn diagram]

b) n(A ∪ B) is the number in the union of the sets = 4 + 6 + 17 = **27** *[1 mark]*

Mixed Exam-Style Questions

Page 493

1 a) Find the duration of the film using the start and finish times of the first showing:

18:40 —(+ 20 mins)→ 19:00 —(+ 1 hour)→ 20:00 —(+ 15 mins)→ 20:15

So the film lasts 1 hour 35 minutes. *[1 mark]*
Add 1 hour 35 minutes to 20:30:

20:30 —(+ 1 hour)→ 21:30 —(+ 30 mins)→ 22:00 —(+ 5 mins)→ 22:05

So the second showing will finish at **22:05** (or **10:05 pm**) *[1 mark]*.

b) The total cost was
£20 + (3 × £10) – £1.25 *[1 mark]* = £48.75
So one ticket costs £48.75 ÷ 5 *[1 mark]*
= **£9.75** *[1 mark]*.

2 a) **18** (2 × 9 = 18) *[1 mark]*

b) **25** (5^2 = 25) *[1 mark]*

c) **5** and **12** (5 × 12 = 60) *[1 mark]*

d) 3 + 12 + 18 + 25 = 58, so **5** was not included in the sum *[1 mark]*

e) For the difference between two numbers to be odd, one number must be even and one must be odd. You're looking for the biggest difference, so the two numbers must be either 18 and 3 or 25 and 12.
18 – 3 = 15 and 25 – 12 = 13. So the largest odd difference is **15** *[1 mark]*.

3 a) **A** and **C** are the same shape and size, so they are congruent *[1 mark]*.

b) E is the same shape as D, but half the size. So **D** and **E** are similar *[1 mark]*.

4 You can make 40p from 2p and 5p coins as follows:
8 × 5p = 40p
6 × 5p + 5 × 2p = 40p
4 × 5p + 10 × 2p = 40p
2 × 5p + 15 × 2p = 40p
20 × 2p = 40p
[2 marks available — 2 marks if all five correct ways have been found, otherwise 1 mark if three or four correct ways have been found]
The number of 5p's has to be even — the difference between 40p and an odd multiple of 5p would be odd, and so couldn't be a multiple of 2p.

5 The population of China is bigger, as it has the higher power of 10, so
larger population : smaller population
= $1.410 \times 10^9 : 5.936 \times 10^7$
To get this in the form n : 1, divide both sides by 5.936×10^7, to get 1 on the RHS.
On the LHS this gives
$\frac{1.410 \times 10^9}{5.936 \times 10^7} = 23.753... = 23.75$ (to 4 s.f.)
So the ratio is **23.75 : 1**
[3 marks available — 1 mark for identifying China as having the larger population, 1 mark for attempting to divide by Italy's population, 1 mark for the correct final ratio]

6 a) On the first Friday, 36 students ate pizza and 14 ate pasta *[1 mark]*.
$\frac{14}{36+14} = \frac{14}{50} = \frac{28}{100} = \mathbf{28\%}$ chose pasta
[1 mark]

b) On the second Friday, 26 students chose pizza and 12 chose pasta *[1 mark]*.
$\frac{26}{26+12} = \frac{26}{38} = \mathbf{\frac{13}{19}}$ chose pizza *[1 mark]*

c) E.g. The number of students having pizza has decreased each week.
or The number of students eating pasta has stayed roughly the same.
or The number of students eating in the canteen has decreased.
[1 mark for any suitable trend]

7 Uma worked for 4 × 7.5 + 7 = 37 hours from Monday to Friday.
Her pay for this work is 37 × £9.46 = £350.02 *[1 mark]*.
So for the Saturday overtime she was paid £406.78 – £350.02 = £56.76 *[1 mark]*
The hourly rate for overtime is £9.46 × 2 = £18.92, so she worked £56.76 ÷ £18.92 = **3 hours** overtime *[1 mark]*.

8 On the map, AB = 6 cm
1 cm = 5 km, so multiply by 5 to find the real-life distance: 6 × 5 = 30 km *[1 mark]*.
Time taken = distance ÷ speed
= 30 ÷ 12 *[1 mark]*
= **2.5 hours** or **2 hours 30 minutes** *[1 mark]*

9 a) $\frac{3}{4} = \frac{3 \times 2}{4 \times 2} = \mathbf{\frac{6}{8}}$ *[1 mark]*

b) $\frac{3}{4} = \frac{3 \times 11}{4 \times 11} = \frac{33}{44}$, $\frac{8}{11} = \frac{4 \times 8}{44} = \frac{32}{44}$ and $\frac{9}{11} = \frac{4 \times 9}{44} = \frac{36}{44}$, so $\frac{3}{4} < \mathbf{\frac{9}{11}}$ *[1 mark]*

10 Find how much the special offer standard box contains: 25% = 25 ÷ 100 = 0.25,
so multiplier = 1 + 0.25 = 1.25
500 g × 1.25 = 625 g *[1 mark]*
Now find the cost per gram for each box.
Family box:
225p ÷ 750 g = 0.3 pence per gram *[1 mark]*
Special offer standard box:
200p ÷ 625 g = 0.32 pence per gram *[1 mark]*
The cost per gram for the family box is less than that for the standard box, so the **family box** is better value *[1 mark]*.
You'd also get the marks if you divided the weight of each box by its cost to find the weight per penny. The more grams you get per penny, the better value.

11 Perimeter = $4x + 3 + 4x + 3 + 4x + 3$
$= 12x + 9$ *[1 mark]*
So $12x + 9 > 480$ *[1 mark]*
$\Rightarrow 12x > 480 - 9 \Rightarrow 12x > 471$ *[1 mark]*
$\Rightarrow x > 471 \div 12 \Rightarrow \mathbf{x > 39.25}$ *[1 mark]*

12 a) The shape can be divided into 7 small squares the same size as the shaded area:

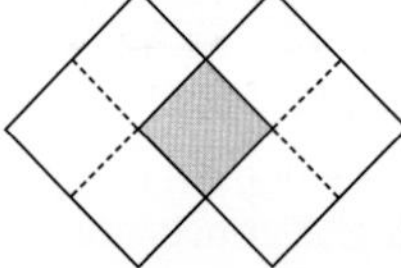

So $\mathbf{\frac{1}{7}}$ of the shape is shaded *[1 mark]*

b) The shaded shape is a square, so it has side length $\sqrt{25}$ = **5 cm** *[1 mark]*.
Since the large squares overlap at the mid-point of their sides, side length of large square = 2 × 5 cm = 10 cm *[1 mark]*.

13 P(green grape) = $\frac{1}{3}$ and there are 8 green grapes, so 8 = $\frac{1}{3}$ of the total number of grapes. That means there are 8 × 3 = 24 grapes in the bowl *[1 mark]*. Let x be the number of black grapes in the bowl,
then $24 = 8 + 12 + x$ *[1 mark]* $\Rightarrow 24 = 20 + x$
$\Rightarrow x = 24 - 20 = 4$
So there are **4** black grapes in the bowl *[1 mark]*.

14 Price of computer from US plus delivery
= \$432 + \$30 = \$462
20% = 20 ÷ 100 = 0.2, so multiplier for import tax is 1 + 0.2 = 1.2.
Cost of US computer including import tax:
\$462 × 1.2 = \$554.40 *[1 mark]*
Exchange rate is \$1 = £0.75, so multiply by 0.75 to find cost in £:
\$554.40 × 0.75 = £415.80 *[1 mark]*. So the **American seller** offers the better deal *[1 mark]*.
Alternatively, you could convert the UK price into US dollars and compare that to \$544.40.

15 Opposite sides of a parallelogram are equal:
$5x + 2 = 20 - 10x$ *[1 mark]*
$\Rightarrow 5x + 10x = 20 - 2$
$\Rightarrow 15x = 18 \Rightarrow x = 1.2$ *[1 mark]*
So the shorter side of the parallelogram has length $3x = 3 \times 1.2 = 3.6$ cm and the longer side has length $5x + 2 = 5 \times 1.2 + 2 = 8$ cm *[1 mark]*.
So perimeter = 2 × 3.6 + 2 × 8 = **23.2 cm** *[1 mark]*
You could also find an expression for the perimeter in terms of x, and plug in your value of x. You'll get marks for any sensible method.

16 a) At A, $y = 2x + 5$ and $y = 1$ intersect,
so $2x + 5 = 1$ *[1 mark]*
$\Rightarrow 2x = -4 \Rightarrow x = -2$
So $A = (-2, 1)$ *[1 mark]*.
At B, $y = 2x + 5$ and $x = -1$ intersect,
so $y = 2 \times (-1) + 5$ *[1 mark]* $= 3$
So $B = (-1, 3)$ *[1 mark]*.
At C, $x = -1$ and $y = 1$, so $C = (-1, 1)$ *[1 mark]*.

b) ABC is a right-angled triangle with hypotenuse AB, so use Pythagoras.

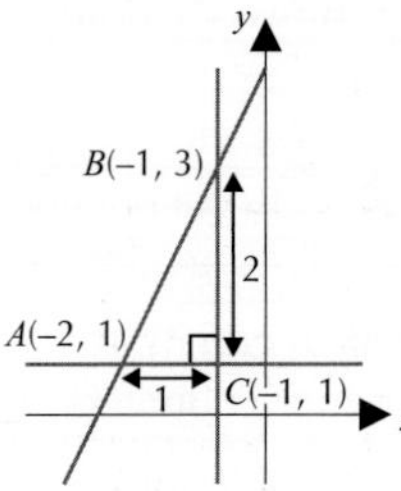

From a), $A = (-2, 1)$ and $C = (-1, 1)$,
so length of AC is $-1 - (-2) = 1$ *[1 mark]*.
$B = (-1, 3)$ so length of BC is $3 - 1 = 2$ *[1 mark]*.
Length of $AB = \sqrt{(AC)^2 + (BC)^2}$ *[1 mark]*
$= \sqrt{1^2 + 2^2} = \sqrt{1 + 4}$
$= \mathbf{\sqrt{5}}$ *[1 mark]*
You don't need to have drawn the diagram in order to get all of the marks.

17 The sum of the interior angles in a polygon with n sides equals $(n - 2) \times 180°$.
So the sum of the interior angles of a pentagon is (5 – 2) × 180° = 540° *[1 mark]*.
There are three right angles in the pentagon, so the sum of the other two angles is 540° – 3 × 90° = 270° *[1 mark]*.
These angles are in the ratio 4 : 11.
1 part = 270° ÷ (4 + 11) *[1 mark]* = 18°
So the largest angle is 11 × 18° = **198°** *[1 mark]*.

18 Volume of water = 1.14 × 1.14 × 1.75
= 2.2743 m^3 *[1 mark]*
When the tank is repositioned, the volume is the same so $1.14 \times 2.25 \times x = 2.2743$ *[1 mark]*
$\Rightarrow x = 2.2743 \div (1.14 \times 2.25) = 0.88666...$,
so the depth is **0.887 m** (3 s.f.) *[1 mark]*.

19 Use the properties of the hexagon to work out the other lengths you need. The hexagon is regular, so all sides have length 10 cm. This also means the hexagon has a vertical line of symmetry, so an identical right-angled triangle can be drawn on the RHS.

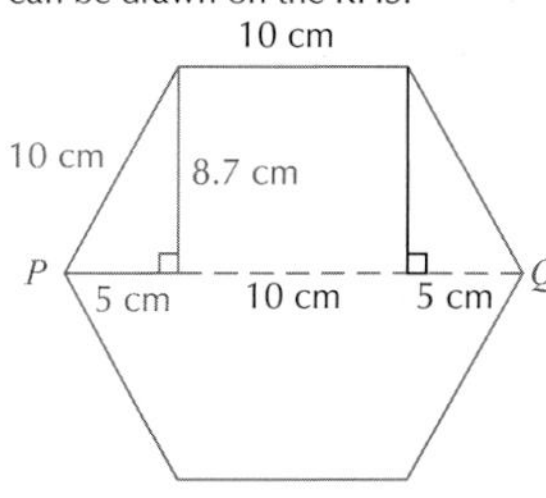

The area of a trapezium is given by
$A = \frac{1}{2}(a + b) \times h$
Considering the trapezium that makes up the top half of the hexagon: a = 10 cm, b = 5 + 10 + 5 = 20 cm and h = 8.7 cm.
So $A = \frac{1}{2}(10 + 20) \times 8.7 = 15 \times 8.7$
= 130.5 cm^2
So area of full hexagon = 2 × 130.5
= **261 cm^2**
[4 marks available — 1 mark for working out the missing lengths, 1 mark for attempting to use the formula for area, 1 mark for doubling to find the area of the hexagon, 1 mark for the correct final answer]
If you weren't sure about the formula for the area of a trapezium, you could instead work out the areas of the right-angled triangles and the rectangle, then add them together to get 130.5 cm^2.

Glossary

A

Acute-angled triangle A triangle where all angles are less than 90°.

Adjacent In a **right-angled triangle**, it's the side between the angle under consideration and the right angle.

Allied angles The pair of angles in a C- or U-shape formed when a straight line crosses two **parallel lines**. The angles add up to 180°.

Alternate angles The pair of equal angles in a Z-shape formed when a straight line crosses two **parallel lines**.

AND rule (for independent events) The **probability** of both A and B happening is equal to the probability of A happening multiplied by the probability of B happening.

Angle bisector The line that cuts an angle into two equal smaller angles.

Angle of depression/elevation The angle between a horizontal line and the line of sight of an observer at the same level looking down or up, respectively.

Arc A part of the **circumference** of a circle.

Area The space inside a 2D shape. It's measured in units squared.

Arithmetic sequence A **sequence** where the **terms** increase or decrease by the same amount each time (the **common difference**).

Average A way of representing a set of data with a central or typical value of the set. The three common averages used are the **mode**, **median** and **mean**.

B

Bar chart A chart to display **discrete** or categorical data. The height of bars shows the number (or frequency) of items in different categories.

Bearing A three-figure angle measured clockwise from the **north line** to tell you the position of one object in relation to another.

Bias (in outcomes) Applies to e.g. rolling dice, where the **outcomes** are not equally likely.

Biased sample One in which some members of a **population** are more likely to be included than others.

Bisect Split a line or angle exactly in half.

BODMAS The correct order to carry out mathematical operations — it stands for Brackets, Other, Division, Multiplication, Addition, Subtraction.

C

Centre of enlargement The point where an **enlargement** is measured from.

Chord A line between two points on the edge of a circle.

Circumference The distance around the outside of a circle.

Coefficient The number in front of a **variable**. E.g. in the term $2x$, 2 is the coefficient.

Common denominator The same bottom number in two or more **fractions**.

Common difference The number you add or subtract to get between **terms** in an **arithmetic sequence**.

Common factor A common **factor** of two or more numbers is a factor of both or all of those numbers.

Common multiple A common **multiple** of two or more numbers is a multiple of both or all of those numbers.

Common ratio The number you multiply by to get between **terms** in a **geometric sequence**.

Complement of a set All **elements** of the **universal set** that aren't in the set. The complement of a set A is written A′.

Composite bar chart A **bar chart** which has single bars split into different sections for each set of data displayed.

Composite shape A shape made up of two or more basic shapes.

Compound decay When a quantity gets smaller over time due to successive **percentage** decreases based on the decreasing value itself.

Compound growth When a quantity gets larger over time due to successive **percentage** increases based on the increasing value itself.

Compound inequality A combination of multiple **inequalities**, e.g. $a < x < b$.

Compound interest **Compound growth** applied to money.

Compound measure A measurement made up of two or more other measurements, e.g. speed = distance ÷ time.

Cone A 3D shape with a circular base and a curved sloping face that goes up to a point at the top.

Congruent Shapes which are exactly the same shape and size as each other.

Construction An accurate drawing made using a pair of compasses, a protractor and a ruler.

Continuous data Numerical data which can take any value in a given range.

Conversion factor The number you multiply or divide by to convert a measurement from one unit to another. E.g. A conversion factor of 100 is used to convert between centimetres and metres.

Coordinates Two numbers in a pair of brackets which describe the position of a point on a grid.

Correlation How two variables are related to each other. Positive correlation means the variables increase and decrease together. Negative correlation mean that as one variable increases, the other decreases.

Corresponding angles The pair of equal angles in an F-shape formed when a straight line crosses two parallel lines.

Cosine The cosine of an angle x in a right-angled triangle is the length of the adjacent side divided by the length of the hypotenuse side, i.e. $\cos x = \frac{\text{adjacent}}{\text{hypotenuse}}$.

Counter example An example which doesn't work, used to show that a statement is false.

Cross-section The face exposed when cutting through a 3D shape.

Cube A cuboid where all six faces are squares.

Cube (power) A number multiplied by itself twice — written as the power of 3, x^3.

Cubic graph The graph of a cubic function, which has x^3 as its highest power. Cubic graphs all have the same basic shape — a curve with a 'wiggle' in the middle.

Cuboid A 3D shape with six rectangular or square faces.

Cylinder A 3D shape with a constant circular cross-section.

Decimal place (d.p.) The position of a digit that comes after the decimal point.

Denominator The bottom number of a fraction.

Density The mass per unit volume of a substance.

Depreciation The loss of value over time due to compound decay.

Diameter The line from one side of a circle to the other through its centre. The diameter is twice the length of the radius.

Difference of two squares A quadratic expression with just two square terms separated by a minus sign, $a^2 - b^2$, which can be factorised as $(a + b)(a - b)$.

Direct proportion Two variables are in direct proportion when the ratio between them is always the same, i.e. $y = Ax$.

Discrete data Numerical data which can only take certain values.

Distance-time graph A graph with distance travelled on the vertical axis and time taken on the horizontal axis.

Dual bar chart A bar chart which shows two sets of data by having two bars per category.

Element An item contained in a set, also called a member of the set. $x \in A$ means 'x is an element of set A'.

Elevation The 2D view of a 3D object looking at it either from the front or side horizontally.

Enlargement A transformation where a shape is enlarged by a particular scale factor, sometimes in relation to a centre of enlargement.

Equation A way of showing that two expressions are equal to each other for a particular value or values of an unknown.

Equidistant When a set of points are the same distance from two points or a line.

Equilateral triangle A triangle with 3 equal sides and equal angles (of 60°).

Equivalent fraction A fraction that shows the same proportion as another fraction using a different numerator and denominator.

Error interval The range of values that a rounded number could actually be.

Estimate An approximation to the answer to a calculation or the size of an amount.

Event A set of one or more outcomes to which a probability is assigned.

Exact A value which is precise and completely accurate. Exact answers may include square roots or π, and are often given as fractions rather than decimals.

Exchange rate The conversion factor between two currencies.

Expanding brackets Removing brackets by multiplying everything inside the brackets by everything in front of the brackets.

Expected frequency The number of times an event is expected to happen — the probability of the event multiplied by the number of times an experiment is done.

Experimental probability The number of times a result has occurred divided by the number of times an experiment has been done. It's used to estimate probabilities. Also known as relative frequency.

Expression An algebraic expression is a combination of terms separated by + and – signs.

Exterior angles The angle between a side of a polygon and a line that extends out from a neighbouring side.

Extrapolation Using e.g. a line of best fit to predict values outside the range of data you have.

Factor The factors of a number are the numbers that divide into it exactly.

Factorising Finding a common factor in the terms of an expression and taking it outside a pair of brackets.

Fair (in probability) A situation where all outcomes are equally likely to happen.

Fair sample A **sample** selected at random so that every member in the **population** has an equal chance of being selected.

Fibonacci-type sequence A **sequence** where each **term** is found by adding together the two previous terms.

Formula The mathematical relationship between different quantities.

Fraction A value written as one number divided by another.

Frequency The number of times that a data value occurs.

Frequency table A table to record the **frequency** of a response or **event**.

Frequency tree A diagram made up of branches to show the different possible **outcomes** of multiple **events**. The number at the end of each branch shows how many times that event or combination of events happened.

Frustum The 3D shape left once you chop off the top bit of a **cone** parallel to its circular base.

Function A rule that turns one number (the input) into another number (the output).

Geometric sequence A **sequence** where the **terms** are found by multiplying by the same value each time (the **common ratio**).

Gradient The slope or steepness of a graph, which can be found by dividing the change in y by the change in x.

Highest common factor (HCF) The largest number that will divide exactly into both (or all) of a given pair (or set) of numbers.

Hypotenuse The longest side in a **right-angled triangle**, opposite the right angle.

Identity A way of showing that two **expressions** are always equal to each other, not just for a particular value or values. Identities use the sign '≡'.

Image The shape formed by carrying out a **transformation**.

Imperial units A set of non-metric units for measuring, e.g. inches, ounces, miles.

Improper fraction A **fraction** where the **numerator** (the top number) is bigger than the **denominator** (the bottom number).

Independent events Two (or more) **events** are independent if one of them happening has no effect on the **probability** of the other(s) happening.

Index (or power) A repeated multiplication of a number or **variable**. a^x means 'a to the power of x' or 'x lots of a multiplied together'.

Inequality A pair of **expressions** separated by one of the symbols $<$, $>$, $\leq$, $\geq$. Like an **equation**, but with a range of solutions.

Intercept The point where a graph crosses an axis.

Interior angles The angles inside each **vertex** (corner) of a **polygon**.

Interpolation Using e.g. a **line of best fit** to predict values within the range of data you have.

Intersection (of sets) The intersection of two **sets** ($A \cap B$) contains only the **elements** that are in both sets.

Inverse proportion Two **variables** are inversely proportional when one variable increases as the other decreases, i.e. $y = \frac{A}{x}$. The product of the two variables is constant.

Isometric drawing A 2D drawing of a 3D object on an isometric grid of dots or lines in a pattern of **equilateral triangles**.

Isosceles triangle A triangle with 2 equal sides and 2 equal angles.

Kite A **quadrilateral** with two pairs of equal sides and one pair of equal angles in opposite corners.

Like terms Algebraic **terms** that contain exactly the same combination of letters (in any order).

Line of best fit A straight line on a **scatter graph** to show the general **trend** of the data.

Line of symmetry A **mirror line** on a graph or 2D shape which divides it so that each half is a **reflection** of the other.

Locus A set of points which satisfy a particular condition, e.g. points that are a fixed distance away from a point or line. The plural of locus is loci.

Lowest common multiple (LCM) The smallest number that is a **multiple** of both (or all) of a given pair (or group) of numbers.

Magnitude (vectors) The size or length of a **vector**.

Mean The total of all the values in a set of data divided by the number of values.

Median The middle value in a set of data written in size order.

Member See **element**.

Metric units Units for measuring using a decimal-based system (so units are based on **powers** of 10), e.g. metres, kilograms.

Midpoint A point which is halfway between two other points.

Mirror line The line in which an object is reflected. **Image** points will be the same perpendicular distance from the mirror line as the corresponding points on the object, but on the opposite side.

Mixed number A number that has a whole number part and a **fraction** part.

Modal group/class The group with the highest **frequency** in a set of grouped data.

Mode The most common value in a set of data.

Multiple The multiples of a number are the numbers in its times table.

Mutually exclusive events **Events** that cannot happen at the same time. E.g. choosing a club and choosing a red card from a pack of cards are mutually exclusive events.

N

Net The 2D representation of a 3D object that can be folded up to make the object.

North line The line vertically upwards from a point, used as the start point for **bearings**.

***n*th term** A general **term** in a **sequence** in the position *n*, which can be used to find any term in the sequence.

Numerator The top number of a **fraction**.

Obtuse-angled triangle A triangle with one angle greater than 90°.

Opposite In a **right-angled triangle**, it's the side opposite the angle under consideration.

Order of rotational symmetry The number of positions you can **rotate** a shape into so that it still looks exactly the same.

Origin The point (0, 0) on a **coordinate** grid. This is where the *x*- and *y*-axis intersect.

OR rule (for mutually exclusive events) The **probability** of at least one of the **events** happening is the sum of the probabilities of each event happening. It's also called the addition rule.

OR rule (general) If two **events** are not **mutually exclusive**, the **probability** that at least one event happens is equal to the sum of the probabilities of each event happening, minus the probability that both events happen.

Outcome The result of an activity in **probability**. E.g. flipping a coin and getting tails.

Outlier An extreme value in a data set.

Overestimate An **estimated** value that's greater than the actual value.

P

Parabola The shape of a graph of a **quadratic** function.

Parallel Two lines are parallel if they have the same **gradient**. They are always at the same distance apart and never meet.

Parallelogram A **quadrilateral** with two pairs of equal, **parallel** sides.

Percentage A **proportion** of something compared to the whole, where the whole is taken to be 100.

Perimeter The distance around the outside of a shape. It's found by adding up the lengths of the edges.

Perpendicular bisector The perpendicular bisector of a line is at right angles to the line and cuts it in half.

Perpendicular height The height of a shape measured at a right angle to the base.

Perpendicular lines Two lines that cross at a right angle.

Pictogram A diagram which uses a symbol to represent a certain number of items.

Pie chart A circular chart showing the **proportion** of the data set in each category rather than the actual frequency.

Plan The 2D view of a 3D object looking vertically downwards on it.

Plane of symmetry A 2D shape that cuts a 3D solid into two identical halves.

Polygon A 2D shape with straight sides.

Population The whole group of people or things you want to find out about when collecting data.

Position to term rule The rule relating a number in a sequence to its position in the sequence. Often referred to as the ***n*th term**.

Power See **index**.

Pressure A force per unit area.

Primary data Data you have collected yourself.

Prime factorisation Breaking a number down into a unique string of **prime numbers** (its prime factors) multiplied together.

Prime number A number that has no **factors** except itself and 1.

Prism A 3D shape with a constant **cross-section**.

Probability How likely an **event** is to happen.

Projections **Plans** and **elevations** — 2D representations of a 3D object.

Proof A mathematical explanation to show that something is true.

Proportion How the size of one quantity relates to the size of another, or to the total.

Pyramid A 3D shape which has a **polygon** base and which rises to a point.

Pythagoras' theorem The rule connecting lengths of sides in **right-angled triangles**: $h^2 = a^2 + b^2$, where h is the **hypotenuse** of the triangle and a and b are the shorter sides.

Q

Quadrant One of the four sections of a **coordinate** grid separated by the x-axis and y-axis.

Quadratic An **expression**, **equation** or **function** where the highest **power** of the **variable** is 2. They take the form $ax^2 + bx + c$, where a, b and c are constants and x is a variable.

Quadratic graph The graph of a quadratic **function** — a u- or n-shaped symmetrical curve.

Quadratic sequence A **sequence** where the difference between terms changes by the same amount each time.

Quadrilateral A shape that has 4 sides.

Qualitative data Data which is descriptive, so it records words instead of numbers.

Quantitative data Data which is numerical. It can be **discrete** or **continuous**.

R

Radius The line from the centre to the edge of a circle.

Range The difference between the largest and smallest value in a set of data — a measure of spread.

Rate of flow How quickly a liquid is moving into, out of, or through a certain space.

Ratio A way of showing **proportion** between quantities in the form $a : b$.

Reciprocal The reciprocal of a number is 1 ÷ that number.

Reciprocal graph The graph of a **reciprocal** function, i.e. $y = \frac{A}{x}$.

Reflection A **transformation** where a shape is mirrored in a straight line.

Regular polygon A **polygon** where all its sides and angles are equal.

Relative frequency See **experimental probability**.

Remainder The amount left over after carrying out a division.

Resultant vector The sum of two or more **vectors**.

Rhombus A **parallelogram** where all sides are the same length.

Right-angled triangle A triangle with a right-angle (90°).

Root (of an equation) Another word for the solution of an **equation**, usually used when solving an equation that has zero on one side of the equals sign.

Root The inverse operation of **squaring** and **cubing** (and raising to other **powers**). Square roots are written as $\pm\sqrt{x}$, cube roots as $\sqrt[3]{x}$.

Rotation A **transformation** where a shape is turned about a particular point — the centre of rotation.

Rotational symmetry Where a shape looks exactly the same after it has been **rotated** by a certain number of degrees.

Rounding Where numbers are approximated to make them easier to work with, e.g. to• a certain number of **decimal places** or **significant figures**.

S

Sample A smaller group of the **population** used to represent the population and to collect data from.

Sample space diagram A list, grid or **two-way table** to show all the possible **outcomes** of an **event** in a systematic way. Also known as a possibility diagram.

Scalar A quantity with magnitude (size) but no direction.

Scale drawing A diagram where all lengths are related to their real-life lengths by a constant **scale factor**.

Scale factor The number that tells you how many times longer the sides of an **enlarged** shape are compared to the original shape. Or how many times bigger one quantity is in relation to another proportional quantity.

Scalene triangle A triangle whose sides and angles are all different.

Scatter graph A graph of two variables plotted against each other, which can show if these variables are related or not.

Seasonality A basic pattern in data that is repeated regularly over time.

Secondary data Data collected by someone else. You can get secondary data from.
E.g. newspapers or the internet.

Sector An area of a circle from the centre to the edge, like a "slice of pie".

Segment An area of a circle between an **arc** and a **chord**.

Semicircle Half of a circle.

Sequence A list of numbers or shapes which follows a particular rule. Each number or shape is called a **term**.

Set A set is a group of items or numbers, written in a pair of curly brackets { }.

Set notation A collection of symbols used to help define the **elements** of (objects within) a **set**.

Significant figures (s.f.) The digits in a number after and including the first digit that is not a 0.

Similar Shapes that have the same size angles (and so are the same shape) but the lengths of corresponding sides are different, related by a **scale factor**.

Simple interest A **percentage** of an initial amount of money added on at regular intervals. The amount of interest added each time doesn't change.

Simplify Reduce an **expression**, **equation**, **fraction** or **ratio** to the form which is easiest to use.

Simultaneous equations A pair of **equations** which are both true for particular values of the unknowns.

Sine The sine of an angle x in a **right-angled triangle** is the length of the **opposite** side divided by the length of the **hypotenuse**, i.e. $\sin x = \frac{\text{opposite}}{\text{hypotenuse}}$.

Solid A 3D shape.

Speed The distance travelled per unit of time.

Sphere A 3D shape with one curved surface, no vertices (corners) and no edges.

Square (power) A number multiplied by itself — written as the **power** of 2, x^2.

Standard form A way to write very big or small numbers as $A \times 10^n$, where $1 \leq A < 10$ and n is an integer.

Stem and leaf diagram A diagram that displays data values. They consist of 'stems' (the first digit(s)) and 'leaves' (the remaining digit) of the data values arranged in numerical order.

Subject The letter before the equals sign in a formula. E.g. in $s = \frac{d}{t}$, s is the subject.

Substituting Replacing the letters in a **formula**, **expression** or **equation** with actual values.

Surface area The total area of all the faces of a 3D shape.

T

Tally chart A way to record **qualitative** or **quantitative** data, where the number of marks (tallies) for each category gives the **frequency**.

Tangent (to a circle) A straight line that just touches the circle at a point.

Tangent The tangent of an angle x in a **right-angled triangle** is the length of the **opposite** side divided by the length of the **adjacent** side, i.e. $\tan x = \frac{\text{opposite}}{\text{adjacent}}$.

Term (algebra) An individual part of an **expression**, e.g. 3, $2x$, a^2b.

Term (sequence) A number in a **sequence**.

Term to term rule The rule which determines how to get from one number in a **sequence** to the next.

Tetrahedron A **pyramid** with a triangular base.

Theoretical probability **Probability** calculated without performing an experiment. It can be found when all possible **outcomes** are equally likely, by dividing the number of ways an **event** can occur by the total number of outcomes.

Time series graph A line graph that shows data collected at regular intervals over time.

Transformation The changing of the size and/or position of a shape.

Translation A **transformation** where a shape is moved horizontally and/or vertically but keeps its original shape and size.

Trapezium A **quadrilateral** with one pair of **parallel** sides.

Tree diagram A diagram made up of branches to show the **probabilities** of different possible **outcomes** of multiple **events**.

Trend A pattern in data.

Truncating Chopping off the digits of a decimal number after a certain number of **decimal places** without rounding.

Turning point The point on a curve where the **gradient** is zero, e.g. a maximum or minimum point.

Two-way table A data collection sheet which records two pieces of information about the same subject at once. It shows the **frequency** for two different variables.

U

Underestimate An **estimated** value which is less than the actual value.

Union The union of two **sets** ($A \cup B$) contains all the **elements** that are in either set.

Unique factorisation theorem This states that the **prime factorisation** of every number is unique to that number.

Unit fraction A **fraction** where the **numerator** is one.

Universal set The **set** of all things under consideration for a particular situation, denoted by ξ.

V

Variable Letters in **expressions**, **formulas** or **equations** which can take different numerical values.

Vector A quantity or straight line with **magnitude** (size) and direction.

Venn diagram A diagram with two or more circles used to represent **sets**, which may overlap.

Vertex A corner of a 2D or 3D shape (the plural is vertices).

Vertically opposite angles The pair of equal angles opposite each other when two lines intersect.

Volume The amount of space a 3D shape takes up.

Y

$y = mx + c$ The **equation** for a straight line where m is the **gradient** and c is the **y-intercept** (the point where the line crosses the y-axis).

Index

F

G

H

I

K

L

M

N

O

P

Q

R

S

T

U

V

W